BRITISH MILITARY HISTORY

MILITARY HISTORY BIBLIOGRAPHIES
(General Editors: Robin Higham, Jacob Kipp)
Vol. 10

GARLAND REFERENCE LIBRARY
OF THE HUMANITIES
Vol. 715

MILITARY HISTORY BIBLIOGRAPHIES

Advisory Editors:
Robin Higham
Jacob W. Kipp

1. *Israeli Military History: A Guide to the Sources*
   by Jehuda L. Wallach
2. *German Military Aviation: A Guide to the Literature*
   by Edward H. Homze
3. *German Military History: 1648–1982: A Critical Bibliography*
   by Dennis E. Showalter
4. *The Military in Imperial History: The French Connection*
   by Alf Andrew Heggoy and John M. Haar
5. *Japanese Military History: A Guide to the Literature*
   by Shinji Kondo
6. *French Military History, 1661–1799: A Guide to the Literature*
   by Steven T. Ross
7. *German Naval History: A Guide to the Literature*
   by Keith W. Bird
8. *Balkan Military History: A Bibliography*
   by John E. Jessup
9. *Napoleonic Military History: A Bibliography*
   edited by Donald D. Horward
10. *British Military History: A Supplement to Robin Higham's Guide to the Sources*
    by Gerald Jordan

BRITISH MILITARY HISTORY

A Supplement to Robin Higham's

Guide to the Sources

Gerald Jordan, Ed.

GARLAND PUBLISHING, INC. • NEW YORK & LONDON
1988

© 1988 Gerald Jordan
All rights reserved

Library of Congress Cataloging-in-Publication Data

British military history : a supplement to Robin Higham's Guide to the sources / [edited by] Gerald Jordan.
    p. cm.—(Military history bibliographies : vol. 10)
(Garland reference library of humanities : vol. 715)
    Includes bibliographies.
    ISBN 0-8240-8450-0 (alk. paper)
    1. Great Britain—History, Military—Bibliography. I. Jordan, Gerald, 1933– . II. Higham, Robin D. S. Guide to the sources of British military history. III. Series. IV. Series: Garland reference library of humanities ; vol. 715.
Z2021.M5H54 Suppl.
[DA50]
016.355'00941—dc19

Printed on acid-free, 250-year-life paper
Manufactured in the United States of America

CONTENTS

Foreword		Robin Higham	vii
Acknowledgements			ix
Authors			xi
I	Introduction	Gerald Jordan	1
II	The Economic, Scientific and Technological Background: From the beginnings to 1914	W.H.G. Armytage	31
III	Military Developments to 1485	John Marshall Carter	101
IV	The Army, 1485-1689	John Childs	117
V	The Navy to 1714	Daniel A. Baugh & Geoffrey Scammell	135
VI	The 18th-Century Army, 1702-1815	John Houlding	161
VII	The Royal Navy, 1714-1860	Roger Knight & Alan Pearsall	195
VIII	The Royal Navy, 1860-1919	Jon Tetsuro Sumida	213
IX	The Army in the Nineteenth Century	Albert Tucker	231
X	Politics and the High Command, 1899-1965	David French	243
XI	The First World War on Land	Dominick Graham	273
XII	The Home Front in the First World War	David R. Woodward	289
XIII	The Royal Navy since 1919	Barry D. Hunt	317
XIV	The Development of the Royal Air Force, 1909-1945	Stephen Harris & Norman Hillmer	345
XV	The British Army 1919-1945	Keith Neilson	367
XVI	The Home Front in the Second World War	Harold L. Smith	385
XVII	The Dominion Services: Australia and New Zealand	Ronald Haycock	401
XVIII	The Dominion Services: Canada	Ronald Haycock	419
XIX	The Dominion Services: South Africa	Ronald Haycock	445
XX	British Arms in India	Ronald Haycock	457
XXI	Science, Technology and Economics in the Twentiethth Century	David Edgerton & Philip Gummett	477
XXII	Intelligence since 1900	Wesley K. Wark	501
XXIII	Medicine in the Services	Rosalie Stott	525

XXIV	Military and Martial Law	F.H. Dean	553
XXV	The History of British Defence Policy and Practice, 1945-85	Martin Edmonds & David Weston	561

FOREWORD

This volume picks up where the original contributors left off in 1967/68. A few stalwarts are still from that first crew, but most of the chapters in this supplement have been supplied by new authors. Yet a great continuity remains not merely in the topics and the numbering, but also in the format and the approach. The latter seems to have stood the test well in a family of volumes of which *A Guide to the Sources of British Military History* was the first.

I had known Gerry Jordan professionally for a good many years through the Marder connection before we met face to face. A desire to see the *Guide* up-dated, our meeting at the annual Royal Military College of Canada symposium in March 1982, and above all trust in his professional drive and judgment led to our agreement then and there that he would undertake the task of seeing the new volume to print.

The authors, old and new, are all persons whose work is respected in their fields and whose knowledge of the subject comes through well in their essays and suggestions for further research. From what I have seen, they well uphold the standards of the original contributors. Theirs has been a labor of academic and scholarly love, for no one gets rich except professionally, doing bibliographical spadework to enable others to get ahead in the field. So to them we must all say thanks.

We must be grateful as well to such publishers as Garland who have been willing to take the risks over the years of supporting bibliographical series. Garland have in full measure for they do those by librarians and now these by historians, two groups which have different approaches to the concepts of scholarship in terms of what is useful and worthwhile.

                                    Robin Higham
                                    Manhattan, Kansas

ACKNOWLEDGEMENTS

Without Robin Higham's drive and enthusiasm this project would never have got under way or reached completion. Despite the demands of his own work, Professor Higham made the initial contacts with several of the authors and throughout the enterprise was a freely available source of help and wise counsel. My debt to him is enormous. I hope that I have taken sufficient advantage of his generosity.

Ultimately, of course, it is the contributors who make the compilation of a volume such as this possible. I must acknowledge a debt to them all for their co-operation and diligence, which helped to make the editorial job pleasant as well as possible. Many waited patiently, their finished essays dormant on the disk, while others suffered through tiresome revisions, some of which were not completed until seventeen months after the March 1986 deadline. They will be as relieved as the editor to see the book in print.

Several people at York University smoothed the way to the project's conclusion. In particular, I must thank Susan Rainey, who waved her magic wand over a jungle of manuscripts to produce the camera-ready copy. Pat Cates, the head of Secretarial Services, was co-operative far beyond the call of duty. The indefatigable Frances Trozzolo, always cheerful and efficient, found countless hours in which to assist with the tedious job of proof-reading and other editorial duties.

My thanks go also to Julia Johnson and Pamela Chergotis of Garland Publishers. Well aware of the trials and tribulations of an editor, they guided me with great forbearance around many obstacles. My wife, Gail Jordan, lived with the book from the beginning, gave constant encouragement and patiently endured its production.

NOTES ON CONTRIBUTORS

W.H.G. ARMYTAGE has been Professor of Education in the University of Sheffield since 1954 and was Pro-Vice Chancellor 1964-68 and served on the planning board for the New University of Ulster. He is the author of many scholarly books and articles on such diverse subjects as the history of science and predictive fantasies.

DANIEL BAUGH is Professor of History at Cornell University. He is a Fellow of the Royal Historical Society and author of *British Naval Administration in the Age of Walpole* (1965) and *Naval Administration, 1715-1750* (1977).

JOHN MARSHALL CARTER teaches at East Carolina University. He is the author of *Sports and Pastimes of the Middle Ages* (1984) and *The Bayeux Tapestry as a Social Document* (1985) and several articles on medieval history.

JOHN CHILDS is Lecturer in Modern History at the University of Leeds. His publications include: *The Army of Charles II* (1976); *The Army, James II and the Glorious Revolution* (1980); *Armies and Warfare in Europe, 1648-1789* (1982). His *Army of William III* is in press as is a biographical dictionary of British army officers, 1660-88. He is now writing a biography of the Duke of Marlborough.

HAROLD DEAN was born in 1908. He practiced at the bar on the Northern Circuit for eleven years before joining the Office of the Judge Advocate General. After service around the world, he became in 1968 Vice Judge Advocate General; in 1972 the Queen appointed him to be Judge Advocate General. He retired in 1979. He was principal author of the *Royal Forces* in the new edition of *Halsbury's Laws of England*.

DAVID EDGERTON is a Lecturer in the University of Manchester. He has written articles on the military aircraft industry and is writing a work on the British aircraft industry, c. 1930-1950s.

MARTIN EDMONDS' latest books include *International Arms Procurement: New Directions* (1981), *Peace Movements in Contemporary Europe: Britain* (1984) and *The Defence Equation* (1986). Since 1972 he has been a member of the department of politics in the University of Lancaster.

DAVID FRENCH teaches at University College, London. Among his recently published works are books on *British Economic and Strategic*

xi

Planning, 1905-1915 (1982) and *British Strategy and War Aims, 1914-1916* (1986).

DOMINICK GRAHAM was a founder in 1980 of the Centre for Conflict Studies at the University of New Brunswick. He retired as Professor of Modern Military History in 1987 but continues to teach post-graduate students. Among his most recent published works are (with Shelford Bidwell) *Fire-Power: British Army Weapons and Theories of War, 1904-45* (1982) and *Tug of War: The Campaign in Italy, 1943-45* (1986); a third joint venture on commanders and staffs in the twentieth century is underway.

PHILIP GUMMETT is acting head of the department of science and technology policy in the University of Manchester. His published work includes *Scientists in Whitehall* (1980) and a number of essays on economic defence and research policy.

STEPHEN HARRIS is a historian with the Directorate of History, Department of National Defence, Ottawa. He is the author of a forthcoming study of officer professional development in the Canadian Army and conducted research for volumes II and III of the official history of the Royal Canadian Air Force.

RONALD HAYCOCK teaches military history at the Royal Military College of Canada and has been a visiting professor at the Royal Military College, Duntroon, Australia. His most recent work is a biography of Sam Hughes.

NORMAN HILLMER is Senior Historian in the Department of National Defence, Ottawa, and Visiting Professor at Carleton University. His specialty is Canadian foreign and defence policy, an area in which he has published widely. He is editor-in-chief of volume II of the official history of the Royal Canadian Air Force, *The Creation of a National Air Force*.

JOHN A. HOULDING lives in Brantford, Ontario. His first book, *Fit for Service*, won the Templer Medal awarded by the Society for Army Historical Research. He is currently preparing studies of the British army in the Boston garrison, 1774-75, and of the career attitudes of eighteenth century officers.

BARRY HUNT teaches naval history at the Royal Military College of Canada. He was a visiting professor at the U.S. Naval Post-Graduate School in Monterey, California, 1980-81. His most recent book is a biography of Admiral Sir Herbert Richmond.

GERALD JORDAN is an associate professor of history at York University, Toronto. He has written several articles on British radicalism and naval history and is completing a study of the Nelson tradition in Britain.

R.J.B. KNIGHT is head of the Documentation and Research Division at the National Maritime Museum, Greenwich, and a Councillor of the Navy Records Society. The author of several books and articles on the

18th century Royal Navy, he has also produced the two-volume guide to the museum's manuscripts collection.

KEITH NEILSON has taught since 1979 at the Royal Military College of Canada, where he is an associate professor. He is the author of *Strategy and Supply: The Anglo-Russian Alliance, 1914-1917* (1984) and a number of articles on Anglo-Russian relations and British military history.

ALAN W.H. PEARSALL is the Historian of the National Maritime Museum, Greenwich, and a Vice-President of the Navy Records Society. He has written many works on 18th and 19th century naval history.

GEOFFREY SCAMMELL is a Fellow of Pembroke College, Cambridge. Among his recent books are *The World Encompassed: The First European Maritime Empires, c. 800-1650* (1981) and *The English Chartered Trading Companies and the Sea* (1983).

HAROLD L. SMITH is professor of history at the University of Houston, Victoria, Texas. He has written a number of articles on British women in the Second World War and edited *War and Social Change: British Society in the Second World War* (1986), to which he contributed a chapter on women.

ROSALIE STOTT is Hannah Institute Fellow in the history of medicine at McMaster University in Hamilton, Ontario. She is the author of several articles on medical history and is writing a monograph on military medical practice in British North America, 1783-1854.

JON SUMIDA teaches at the University of Maryland. For the Navy Records Society, he edited *The Pollen Papers* (1984) and is now compiling a volume of *Papers on Naval Gunnery and Tactics, 1899-1925*. His book *In Defence of Naval Supremacy* will be published by Allen & Unwin in 1988.

ALBERT V. TUCKER is Professor of History at Glendon College, York University, Toronto. He has written several books and articles on nineteenth century army reform and on business history.

WESLEY K. WARK is an assistant professor of history at the University of Calgary. He is the author of *The Ultimate Enemy: British Intelligence and Nazi Germany, 1933-1939* (1985) and several articles on aspects of the history of British intelligence in the twentieth century.

DAVID WESTON teaches at the University of Manchester. His recent publications include "Mother, Sister, Mistress?: The British Regiment" in Martin Edmonds' *The Defence Equation* (1986).

DAVID R. WOODWARD is professor of history and chairperson of the department of history at Marshall University in West Virginia. He has published *Lloyd George and the Generals* (1983) and co-compiled (with R.F. Maddox) *America and World War I: An Annotated Bibliography of English Language Sources* (1985) and is the author of several scholarly articles.

I

INTRODUCTION

Gerald Jordan

When Robin Higham's *Guide to the Sources of British Military History* was published in 1971 there were, as Higham noted, signs that military history had begun to move out of the academic doldrums in which, but for a few notable squalls, it had lain becalmed since the nineteenth century and was gaining momentum on its passage towards scholarly respectability. Military history had been written mainly by enthusiastic amateurs whose often romantic narrative prose took little notice of the society as a whole or by official historians whose narrow and detached technical descriptions of campaigns and battles seemed to deny that there was anything dirty about warfare. The essays in the present volume demonstrate how, over the last decade and a half, military history has become assimilated into the mainstream of British historical scholarship. No longer is it possible to write a satisfactory essay on the sources of British military history without straying into several other fields. At the same time, the knowledge and opinions of historians of war have begun to exert influence in other areas of British history. This two-way process has been attended by a still unresolved debate about the scope and nature of military history.

The difficulties of arriving at a definition of military history today are exemplified in a recent article which contains statements from seven scholars who are generally regarded as military historians (23). For Michael Howard, the Regius Professor of History at Oxford, military history deals with armed forces and the conduct of war. The nature of warfare, he says, however, cannot be understood without taking into account social, economic, technological, logistical and moral factors. Brian Bond and J.C.A. Stagg view the subject in its broadest "war and society" sense. John Terraine, perhaps surprisingly, takes a similarly broad view. "Military history," he writes, " ... cannot be separated from the large, increasingly urban populations, from their means of production and their productivity, from their technology and the techniques which it imposed. Nor can it be separated from their social systems, their physical condition and their ideologies. Armies, in the age of masses, are peoples in arms, putting their survival to the most critical test." Turning that view upside-down, John Childs believes that although social, economic and political historians have now come to acknowledge the importance of a military dimension in their own brands of history, military history remains the study of armed forces, their institutions, methods and operations in time of war." Geoffrey Best agrees. Military history, Best says, is the study of "Battles and how to fight them, Campaigns and how to conduct them, and the ways armed forces gear themselves up for these special tasks. All the rest of the war-related work that has been going on since the 1960s ... is not military history proper." By the definition, Dr. Best's own learned and broad-based writings cannot be considered military history proper. In a distinctly utilitarian fashion, David Chandler, who teaches at Sandhurst, sees military history as "important to inculcate *esprit d'armée* in the aspiring officer ... [and] also an ideal source of pleasure for the layman with a genuine interest in the 'passionate dramas' of the past." All of the commentators in the article agree, however, that the scholarly study of the military has broadened in scope during the last twenty years and that this expansion has accompanied the changes taking place in the more traditionally academic areas.

The change in the nature of military historiography since the late 1960s created some difficulties for the organization of a book the purpose of which is to provide an "up-date" to Higham's *Guide*. Initially, authors were asked to confine their essays to material published, or which became available, since the appearance of Higham's volume. For some authors it was clear that the subject had broadened so much that areas not, previously thought of as military history had now entered the picture and that earlier works had to be mentioned. Others, like David French and Wesley Wark, were writing essays on topics not in the earlier volume; for them, of course, free rein was essential. Following from the Higham volume, the editor had expected that Dominion and Indian forces would be covered adequately in one chapter. Ronald Haycock's early reservations about that piece of wisdom were borne out when he produced four chapters covering those services. Within general stylistic guidelines, authors were free to adopt their own approach to the subject; hence, some essays are more highly detailed than others. Several of them complement each other and are best used together. Some duplication was unavoidable, especially for topics dealing with the twentieth century.

As a prelude to the more narrowly defined chapters which follow, the wide range of subjects pertaining to military historical studies up to the twentieth century is shown in the long chapter and massive bibliography drawn up by W.H.G. Armytage of Sheffield University. The object of his expose is to sketch for the reader the ways in which military and naval affairs have been intertwined with the fabric of the economic, social, medical and other developments--including the scientific and technological progress--of Great Britain over the last 2,500 years; a tall order indeed. The essay and bibliography provide hints as to the sort of sources which exist and, it is hoped, will suggest ramifications and interesting leads for the specialist.

That these connections are still too often disregarded is demonstrated in the collection of historiographical essays, *Recent Views on British History* (228), published for the Conference on British Studies in the United States. The editor's prefatory remark that the "traditional fields such as political, diplomatic, religious, and military history ... continue to lose ground, comparatively, to the newer fields [like social history]" and the fleeting references to military affairs in the essays do not reflect the degree to which the fields interact with each other. A number of recent works demonstrate more clearly the growing interest in questions of war and society. William McNeill's broad and masterful treatment, *The Pursuit of Power* (180) is essential reading. The relationships between warfare, the military and other areas are dealt with more succinctly by Michael Howard in *War in European History* (146), an elegantly-written piece of impressive scholarship. Geoffrey Best, Brian Bond and V.G. Kiernan have written sound volumes covering 1770-1970 in the Fontana History of European War and Society (21, 28, 162). In similar vein are works by Larry Addington (1) and Hew Strachan (241). A fourth edition of Preston and Wise's *Men in Arms* (216) was published in 1979. Some fine essays are to be found in the two volumes of the *War and Society Yearbook* (29) edited by Brian Bond and Ian Roy; unfortunately, the series has been discontinued. A new Australian journal, *War and Society* (263), started in May 1983 and published every May and September, deals with all aspects of warfare and is unrestricted by geographical area or historical period. All of these works contain material and ideas of value to historians of the British military experience. Howard's *War and the Liberal Conscience* (145) and Best's *Humanity in Warfare* (20) are valuable explorations of the idea of the "just war," international law and other moral questions in the nineteenth and twentieth centuries. The relationships between warfare, the economy and military institutions in Europe between 1815 and 1918 are explored in a book edited by Best and Andrew Wheatcroft (22). The essays in Weigley's anthology (265) investigate the possibilities of "a practical approach to the study of [military] history." Norman Dixon's idiosyncratic book *On the Psychology of Military Incompetence* (84) is suggestive of a potentially valuable inter-disciplinary approach to military leadership. A novel and challenging, if relatively narrow, view of military history can be found in John Keegan's aptly titled book *The Face of Battle* (156). Farther afield, two volumes on Indian historiography recognize the importance of the military dimension to historians in post-independence India (176, 230).

An idea of the growth of interest in studies with a military dimension can be gleaned from the bibliographies, archival lists and finding aids which have been issued in the last fifteen or twenty years. Some of the major guides which pertain in general to more than one chapter are mentioned here and are supplementary to those discussed in the following chapters and by Robin Higham in his Introduction to the 1971 *Guide* (141).

General Bibliographical Material. The basic serial reference works continue to be issued. The Historical Association's *Annual Bulletin of Historical Literature* (7) remains the starting point for any bibliographical search in British history. From 1975 to 1984, G.R. Elton edited the useful but not annotated Royal Historical Society's annual bibliography (89); the task was taken over by D.M. Palliser in 1985. It is now produced jointly with the Institute of Historical Research in the University of London. The IHR has also published two volumes covering historical works issued in Britain between 1966 and 1975 (159, 244) and has recently concluded a twelve-volume series on *Writings on British History* which lists books and articles wherever published and covers the years 1946 to 1974 (154). These can be supplemented by the American Historical Association's comprehensive *Recently Published Articles* (220), issued three times a year, and by the quarterly *Historical Abstracts* (142), a two-part reference guide to scholarly articles in some forty English and foreign language journals; both parts have sections on military history. Further leads to finding journal articles are suggested in the section on periodicals and newspapers (below). Several nonperiodic bibliographies should be noted. The Conference on British Studies has sponsored an admirable series of annotated guides which contain sections on military and naval history (4, 5, 134, 168, 227). Elton has produced *A Critical Bibliography* (91) which examines the work of historians writing between 1945 and 1969. The various sections of Roach's bibliography (222), compiled by the authors of *The New Cambridge Modern History*, are highly selective and have a cut-off date of about 1961. A guide to medieval studies written between 1930 and 1975 has been compiled by G.C. Boyce (32) as a supplement to Paetow's massive work. Graves' bibliography (119) is based on the original by Charles Gross and covers England to 1485; Elton's *England, 1200-1640*, as would be expected, is particularly strong on the sixteenth century (90); Godfrey Davies' bibliography of the Stuart period has been up-dated in a second edition by Mary Keeler (158). An up-dated version of Pargellis and Medley's bibliography of the eighteenth century has been published by Harvester Press (205). The Historical Association's bibliography of British history since 1760 (55) is brief and highly selective. The period from 1789 to 1851 is well-covered in a work edited by Lucy Brown and Ian Christie and issued in 1977 under the auspices of the American Historical Association and the Royal Historical Society (39). A year earlier, the Clarendon Press also published H.J. Hanham's comprehensive bibliography for the last half of the nineteenth century to 1914 (130). In the series published for the Conference on British Studies, the bibliography of the Victorian era by Altholz (4) is well worth attention. Perhaps because of the vast mass of material available, the twentieth century is less well-served by general bibliographies other than those already mentioned. However, Havighurst's *Modern England, 1901-1970* (134), in the CBS series, provides fairly good coverage. Peter Lowe's revision of C.L. Mowat's *British History since 1926* (186), like Mowat's earlier work (187), is less detailed. Some topical bibliographies deserve mention. Chaloner and Richardson's *Bibliography of British Economic and Social History* (50) provides an excellent introduction to the varieties of material available. The *Economic History Review* prints annual lists of works on economic and social history. There is a bibliography of the labour movement to 1970 (233) and a two volume work which covers industrial relations to 1979 (11, 12). Lloyd De Mause has edited a bibliographical guide to psychohistory (77).

A number of bibliographies of particular interest to the military historian have appeared recently. Anthony Bruce has produced basic bibliographies of British military history to 1660 and from 1660 to 1914 (42, 43). A.S. White's 1965 bibliography of regimental histories (266) unfortunately excludes articles and memoirs. For the military involvement in the Chartist movement, the bibliography by J.F.C. Harrison and Dorothy Thompson (132) is an essential guide. Manwaring's venerable bibliography of British naval history has been re-printed by Conway Maritime Press (177). A fourth edition, revised and expanded, of Albion's annotated bibliography of

Introduction

naval and maritime history was published in 1973 (2). The library catalogue of the National Maritime Museum in Greenwich is a particularly valuable bibliographical and reference tool for naval historians (195). A hundred years of writing on capital ships has been listed by Myron Smith (234). Bayliss' annotated survey of reference materials (18) and Enser's subject bibliographies (94, 95, 96) on both world wars handle only English language works. There is a subject list of books on the First World War acquired by the British Museum between 1914 and 1920 (36). The European and Mediterranean theatres in World War II are covered in Myron Smith's annotated bibliography (235). The same author has compiled a bibliography of English language works on the war at sea (236). For Britain's role in NATO, see Augustus Norton's excellent bibliography and resource guide (197). Kurt Lang's guide to the sociology of war (166) provides a suggestive introduction to that subject. Recent articles are listed in the quarterly *Military Affairs*.

A few general bibliographies of works pertaining to imperial questions have appeared in recent years. William Olson (201) and Vincent Ponko (214) cover British involvement in the Middle East in the first half of the twentieth century. Thomas Ofcansky's guide to British East Africa, 1856-1963 (199) and Naomi Musiker's guide to South African history (192) are thorough bibliographies of those areas and Robert Heussler has performed the same service for British Malaya (139). The fifth volume of Gann and Duignan's history of colonialism in Africa (111) provides a complete bibliographical guide for the period 1870 to 1960. For a guide to Irish materials, Eager's *Bibliography of Irish Bibliographies* (87) is the best starting point. The RHS *Annual Bibliography* (89) contains a section on Ireland.

Theses and Current Research. Unpublished theses are an indispensable source of bibliographical information, as well as of research results. The best finding aids for British research degrees are issued by the Institute of Historical Research in the University of London. Lists of theses in progress and completed from 1911/18 to 1927/28 were published in *History* from 1920 to 1929; those for 1928/29 to 1930/31 appeared in the *Bulletin of the Institute of Historical Research* from 1930 to 1932; between 1933 and 1966 the lists were published in annual *Theses Supplements* to the *Bulletin* together with a second part, *Theses in Progress*; from 1967 to 1984 they appeared in two parts as *Historical Research for University Degrees in the United Kingdom*; since 1985 the title has been *Historical Research for Higher Degrees in the United Kingdom* (150). For the modern period, the *Theses in Progress* contain sections on "Administrative, military and naval history." The Institute has also published two cumulative volumes, covering the years from 1901 to 1980 (151, 152). Abstracts of doctoral theses in the humanities and social sciences accepted by North American and some other universities appear annually in *Dissertation Abstracts International* (83). The American publication *Doctoral Dissertations in Military Affairs* (183), together with the annual supplements in the journal *Military Affairs*, and Warren Kuehl's *Dissertations in History, 1970-June 1980* (165) contain enough British material to be of interest. Lists of theses dealing with the army appear periodically in the *Journal of the Society for Army Historical Research*. Among other guides to theses likely to be useful to military historians are those on subjects relating to Ireland (250), Islam, the Middle East and Northwest Africa (251), the Indian sub-continent (249), the Caribbean (247, 248), Latin America (252), Asia (245) and Canada (246). The Human Sciences Research Council in Pretoria maintains a list of theses submitted to South African universities. Research in progress by British scholars is listed in volumes published by the British Library (71, 72). *Current Research in British Studies* (86) lists research being conducted by North American scholars.

General Reference Works. Historical listings, biographical dictionaries and other reference materials have multiplied in the last decade and a half. Chris Cook's four volumes of historical facts contain separate chapters on holders of public office, parliament, local government, the church, the armed forces, trade, education and population (59, 60, 61, 62). These volumes may be supplemented with the *Annual Register*. Issued yearly since 1758, it remains the most valuable contemporary compendium of events (8). The Royal Historical Society's *Handbook of Dates* was reprinted in 1982 (54). The Institute of Historical Research has published nine volumes in its extremely valuable series "Office-Holders in Modern Britain." Each volume includes a short essay discussing the institutional development of the department concerned and notes explaining the various offices and grades within it, with lists of appointments and periods of service (153). For the twentieth century, David Butler and Anne Sloman, *British Political Facts, 1900-1979* (45), provides in compact form listings by religion, pressure groups, armed forces, the press, royalty, social conditions and trade unions as well as the more conventional civil service, elections, parliament, parties and ministries. Wider afield, Bidwell's *Guide to Government Ministers* (26) covers the period from 1900 to 1972 and is in three volumes: volume one, the major powers and Western Europe; volume two, the Arab world; and volume three, the British Empire and successor states. British parliamentary election results, 1885-1918, can be found in Craig (67). The *Cambridge Historical Encyclopedia of Great Britain and Ireland* (128) consists of seven chronological sections from pre-history to the 1980s and a biographical addendum which briefly identifies over eight hundred figures. Ten of the projected thirteen volumes of Strayer's comprehensive *Dictionary of the Middle Ages* (242) have been published and contain some material of interest to British military historians. There are good dictionaries for British social and political history (66, 161, 237), the history of science (46), for Ireland since 1800 (140), India (24), Australia (191), Scotland (85) and Afro-Latin America (198). Alan Palmer's compact and popular *Dictionary of Twentieth Century History* (204) contains much on Britain. Two dictionaries cover the European Community in the late twentieth century (206, 209). The *Macmillan Dictionary of Historical Terms* (64) concentrates on Britain, the USA and Europe and explains such terms as "praemunire" and "sans culottes." There are nearly 50,000 instructive and often amusing entries in Eric Partridge's *Dictionary of Historical Slang* (208), first published in 1937 as the *Dictionary of Slang and Unconventional English*.

On the more distinctly military side of things, G.C. Stone's, *A Glossary of the Construction, Decoration and Use of Arms and Armour in All Countries and in All Times* (239) and John Quick's *Dictionary*

Introduction 7

of *Weapons and Military Terms* (218) cover much more than merely British arms and armour but contain enough on the British Isles to make them of some importance. They can be supplemented by Blackmore's guide to the armouries of the Tower of London (27), Bowen's *Encyclopedia of War Machines* (31), and the more detailed *English Weapons for Warfare, 449-1660* (196) by Norman and Pottinger. The complexities of heraldry are explained in two recent books (217, 256). Chandler's *Dictionary of the Napoleonic Wars* (51) and Keegan's *Encyclopedia of World War II* (157) are reliable reference works. The *The Dictionary of Modern War* (171) leans towards American subject matter but does contain some material of interest to the British historian. Frederick's *Lineage Book of the British Army* (107) sets out in great detail the dates of raising and disbandment, amalgamation and name changes of the regiments from the Restoration to 1968. Also useful for the modern period are David Ascoli's *Companion to the British Army, 1660-1983* (9) and Arthur Swinson's *Register of the Regiments* (243). *Jane's Dictionary of Military Terms* is a valuable reference work (135). Brassey's annual review of defense and strategic matters (226) provides an authoritative survey of international strategic affairs, contemporary weapons and developments. Max Hastings' *Encyclopedia of Military Anecdotes* (133) is of only passing interest to the serious historian.

Biographical dictionaries continue to proliferate to supplement the standard British *Dictionary of National Biography* (82), itself still an on-going project. For general guidance, two supplements, 1972 and 1978, to Slocum's *Biographical Dictionaries and Related Works* have been published (232) and the British Library has issued a *Bibliography of Biography* (25). National biographical dictionaries have appeared for Australia (80), Canada (81), India (44, 229), Ireland (33), South Africa (76) and the United States (79). Some brief biographies are in Heussler's bibliographical guide to British Malaya (139) and in the *Dictionary of African Historical Biography* (169). For Great Britain, *The Dictionary of Labour Biography*, edited by Joyce Bellamy and John Saville, in 8 volumes, (19) is intended to include any important person who was active in the labour movement from the late eighteenth century to the present. Covering some of the same territory and figures, the first two volumes of Baylen and Gossman's *Biographical Dictionary of Modern British Radicals* (17) take a broad view of the term radicalism. The first volume of the *Biographical Dictionary of British Radicals in the Seventeenth Century* (120) appeared in 1982 and contains much of value to the military historian of the period. The entries in these publications are lengthy, interpretative and contain brief bibliographical information. For what is usually the other end of the political and economic spectrum *The Dictionary of Business Biography* (155), is beginning to appear. The first four volumes of the Harvester press *Who's Who of British Members of Parliament* have been published (238). Brian Harrison's *Dictionary of British Temperance Biography* (131) is particularly valuable for the historian of the nineteenth century. Herwig and Heyman's *Biographical Dictionary of World War I* (138) provides a guide to the major military leaders, politicians, diplomats and statesmen and revolutionaries, together with an historical introduction, maps, chronology and bibliography. The second world war is covered in a similar volume by Christopher Tunney (255).

General reference works on the Royal Navy are in rather short supply. An enormous amount of valuable information, biographical and other, can be found, however, in Peter Kemp's *Oxford Companion to Ships and the Sea* (160), which leans heavily towards things British. There is a valuable list of *Ships of the Royal Navy* by J.J. Colledge (57). Myron Smith's bibliography of battleships and battlecrusiers includes a chronology (234). Lists of *Admiralty Officials, 1660-1870* and of *Navy Board officials, 1660-1832* are volumes IV and VII of *Office-Holders in Modern Britain* (153). The first volume of Roger Knight's guide to the National Maritime Museum's manuscript holdings (164) contains brief biographical details of naval figures. Another major work published recently, W.P. Gosset's *The Lost Ships of the Royal Navy, 1793-1900* (117), is a guide to RN ships lost by enemy action, mutiny, shipwreck or fire. It is arranged in four indexes. A chronological index gives the ship's name(s), description, measurements, dates, name of commander, personnel aboard and lost, circumstances of the loss and the date of any ensuing court martial. This is supplemented by a ship's name index, a geographical index and an index of courts martial reports which gives the ADM 1 references under which the reports are indexed at the Public Record Office in London.

Historical atlases are of little value to the advanced researcher. They are useful, however, to the student who is unfamiliar with the general outline of British historical geography. With so many atlases on the market, a few of the best should be mentioned. Although S.R. Gardiner's atlas of English history (112) has still to be bettered for straightforward political and military campaign maps, the *Historical Atlas of Britain* by Falkus and Gillingham (97) more accurately illustrates current historical scholarship in chronological and thematic maps, diagrams, text and pictures. The *Longman Atlas of Modern British History* (63) contains black and white maps and diagrams of the economic, social and political history of the British Isles from 1700 to 1970. There is an up-to-date *Atlas of the Industrial Revolution* (167). Chris Cook's *Atlas of Modern Warfare* (58) and Arthur Banks's World War I atlas (14) have more in them for the British military historian than do the broader efforts by Banks and Martin Gilbert (15, 114, 115, 116). Catchpole and Freeman-Grenville (49, 108) appear to be aimed at high school audiences. Christopher Lloyd's *Atlas of Maritime History* (170) leans towards the British side of naval history. Irish history is covered in an atlas compiled by Ruth Edwards (88). Unique in its presentation, *The Times Atlas of World History* is concerned with broad movements rather than particular events in particular countries (16).

Newspapers, Periodicals and Society Publications. The most ambitious attempt to catalogue British newspapers for all periods is being conducted by Charles Toase, whose *Bibliography of British Newspapers* (254) now runs to five volumes. Organized by county (vol. I, Wiltshire; II, Durham and Northumberland; III, Kent; IV, Derbyshire; V, Nottinghamshire), they are comprehensive and easy to use. There is still no general systematic finding aid for the seventeenth and eighteenth centuries. Dahl's brief bibliography (73) is cumbersome and covers only 1620-1642. The listing by Crane and Kaye (68), a reprint of the original 1927 publication, is useful but patchy in its coverage. It can be supplemented by the works of Geoffrey Cranfield (69, 70) on the provincial press during the first half of the century. The British Library's *Short Title Catalogue* (3) also provides a great deal of information on the newspaper and periodical press. Valuable leads can be gleaned by working backwards from the subject and persons indexes to *The Gentleman's Magazine* (113) but it is a tedious task. The *Catalogue of English Broadsides, 1505-1897* (48), originally published in 1898, remains a good introduction to the subject. The situation for the nineteenth century is much brighter. A veritable industry dedicated to the location and indexing of Victorian periodicals has developed since Higham wrote the introduction to the previous volume. The most convenient reference tool is *The Wellesley Index* (144) which identifies, with biographical and bibliographical data, about 12,000 editors and authors in forty-three major British monthlies and quarterlies, together with an index of the journals' contents and an essay on publishing history. The *Waterloo Directory* (264) is basically a finding list of some 29,000 different titles between 1824 and 1900; for North American libraries, it can be used in conjunction with the *Union List of Victorian Periodicals* (109) whose 1,847 titles include the serials listed in the *New Cambridge Bibliography of English Literature*, augmented by about 100 science and engineering titles. For research into newspapers, Lucy Brown's *Victorian News and Newspapers* (40) provides a good introduction. Lionel Madden and Diana Dixon have produced a bibliography of modern studies of the nineteenth century periodical press (174). The British Library's *London Publishers and Printers* (41) may be of peripheral interest. A bibliographical treatment of imperial matters as they appeared in the early Victorian press is in preparation (203). Mullins's *Texts and Calendars* lists publications by official bodies and private societies devoted to the printing of sources for English and Welsh history (189, 190). The first volume covers the period 1802-March 1957 with a few entries from the 18th century; the second volume continues to October 1982. Included are such official bodies as the Record Commissioners, the Public Record Office, the Royal Commission on Historical Manuscripts and county record offices and private organizations like the British Academy, the Hakluyt Society and the Navy Records Society. Mullins has also produced a valuable list of titles and authors of books and articles issued between 1901 and 1933 by more than 400 local and national societies including such organizations as the Aldershot Military Society, the Institute of Marine Engineers, the Naval Society (*Naval Review*), the Royal Artillery Association, the Society for Army Historical Research and the Society for Nautical Research (188). To mark the centenary of the Royal Historical Society a guide to their publications and those of the Camden Society was published in 1968 (182). Guides to current British periodicals are issued by the Library Association and the British Library (261, 268). The Newspaper Library at Colindale prints a list of microfilms of newspapers and journals for sale (181). A valuable guide to new periodical titles can be found in the *British Union Catalogue* (38). The British Museum has issued a check list of official serials (37). Janet Fyfe's *History Journals and Serials* (110) is divided by topic and geographical area but leans heavily towards North American subjects and has no section on military history. The Historical Association's *Guide to Historical*

Periodicals (163) provides a brief selective list of "all the more important journals" published in Britain and some from overseas. Robin Higham's introduction to the 1971 *Guide* has a comprehensive list of professional journals.

Statistics. Statistical evidence holds many pitfalls and must be used with great care. A good introduction is Halsey's *Trends in British Society* (129) which covers such areas as the economic environment, population and family, social mobility, and health. Although it contains little reference to the military, the book is a sound guide to the use of statistical sources and points out the dangers in interpreting statistics which are gathered for administrative purposes rather than for the use of historians. A *Guide to Official Statistics* (127) has been published by the Central Statistical Office in London. Since 1853 with the exception of the war years, 1914-18, the CSO has issued an *Annual Abstract of Statistics* (6) and, for more recent years, a *Monthly Digest of Statistics*. Various government departments issue their own statistical reports. For example, there are Home Office statistics relating to immigration, criminal activities, prisons and other areas; judicial statistics for England and Wales are issued by the Lord Chancellor's department; the Ministry of Defence issues annual statements on the defense estimates and on defence. A wide range of these publications, 1801-1977, have been reproduced on microform by Chadwyck-Healey (a catalogue can be obtained from Chadwyck-Healey Ltd., Cambridge Place, Cambridge CB2 1NR). Economic tables are in Mitchell and Deane's *Abstract of British Historical Statistics* (184) and its successor by Mitchell and Jones, *Second Abstract of British Historical Statistics* (185). Deane and Cole's *British Economic Growth, 1688-1959* (75) contains some of the same data and is easier to use. Figures related to the national income during the century since 1855 are listed in Feinstein's book (99). Key statistics for the twentieth century have been compiled by Times Newspapers on the economy (35) and by A. Sillitoe on social trends (231); since 1949 a wide-ranging handbook containing official statistics has been published annually by the Central Office of Information (34). Two works provide an introduction to the whole range of British government publications (200, 212).

Archival Sources. The recent publication of several guides to the location and use of archival materials has made the researcher's task a lot easier than it was when Higham wrote the introduction to his volume. Listed below are some of the best general guides to archival sources. The various chapters in the Higham *Guide* and in the present volume give more detailed coverage of their particular subjects.

The guide by Foster and Sheppard (106) provides a solid but somewhat complicated introduction to the great mass of archival resources in Britain. There is also a brief pamphlet guide to *Record Repositories in the United Kingdom* (221). More immediately useful to the experienced researcher are the volumes in the on-going series *Guides to Sources for British History* (225). Compiled by the Royal Commission on Historical Manuscripts, this series records information from the Commission's National Register of Archives and gives clear and concise details about the nature and location of the records. At the time of writing (1986) four volumes have been issued:

Introduction   11

1. *Papers of British Cabinet Ministers, 1782-1900.* Identifies and locates almost 500 collections of papers of over 200 statesmen and politicians.
2. *The Manuscript Papers of British Scientists, 1600-1942.* Deals with the manuscript papers of 635 British scientists, including mathematicians, astronomers, physicists, botanists, medical people and engineers.
3. *Guide to the Location of Collections Described in the Reports and Calendars Series, 1870-1980.* The Royal Commission on Historical Manuscripts has published 236 volumes of Reports and Calendars, describing 620 collections of papers. This volume locates all the major groups of papers. It is essential to a full use of the Reports and Calendars series, and is a sound guide to the location of private collections in British archives.
4. *Private Papers of British Diplomats, 1782-1900.* Describes 728 groups of the private papers of 382 diplomats, consuls and Foreign Office officials. They are a major source of information on foreign policy at a time when Britain's influence was at its height, and also on the external relations and internal affairs of Europe, Asia and the Americas.

The *Guides* should be supplemented by the Commission's periodic Accession Lists. Between 1923 and 1953 the Institute of Historical Research published in its *Bulletin* lists of accessions to national and local repositories. In 1954 the Historical Manuscripts Commission assumed responsibility for the annual lists of accessions, which appeared for 1954, 1955 and 1956 as special numbers of the *Bulletin* of the National Register of Archives. Since 1957 the *List of Accessions to Repositories* has been published by HMSO as one of the publications of the Historical Manuscripts Commission. In 1972 the title changed to *Accessions to Repositories and Reports added to the National Register of Archives* (224). Indexes have been published at intervals since 1959. Routine accessions of local government and parish records in local record offices, which researchers might expect to find in the *Accessions* lists, are usually excluded. They can be found, however, among the research facilities in local history which are detailed below. For manuscript materials which cannot be located elsewhere, the Commission's National Register of Archives possesses lists, often with tables of contents, of private papers.

Recently issued on microfiche, *The National Inventory of Documentary Sources* (194) gives a detailed listing of collections in libraries and record offices, museums and private collections in the UK, including the Imperial War Museum and the National Army Museum, and reproduces the finding aids produced for use with those collections. The work includes a names and subject index and a list of finding aids by repository. *The National Inventory* is produced by Chadwyck-Healey who also publish an 11 volume *Index of Manuscripts in the British Library* covering over a million items in the Department of Manuscripts to 1950 (148).

For the first half of the twentieth century, Chris Cook's six volumes of guides to the *Sources in British Political History* (65), provide a quick and easy-to-use guide to modern archival sources and major libraries. The series takes a broad view of politics. Volume one deals with the records of political parties, organizations, pressure groups and institutions; volume two locates the papers of some 1500 senior public servants including members of the armed forces, the civil service, the colonial civil administrations and the diplomatic corps; volumes three and four provide an exhaustive guide to the papers of Members of Parliament; volume five includes the papers of selected trade union leaders, publicists and writers etc.; volume six is a supplement to the previous volumes. The entry for each individual concerned contains a biographical note and a brief list of unpublished papers and their location. Cameron Hazlehurst's listing of the papers of Cabinet Ministers (136) for the same period is an essential supplement to the Cook volumes.

Since the Higham volume was published the Public Record Office has been completely re-organized. Almost all of the modern records, including those of the Air Ministry, Admiralty, War Office and Committee of Imperial Defence, are located at the new PRO in Kew. Most of the early materials remain at Chancery Lane. An introduction to the holdings can be found in the *Guide to the Contents of the Public Record Office* (123). In addition, the PRO has issued a number of handbooks relating to various collections of papers; several of these are mentioned in the chapters which follow and in the bibliography to Higham's Introduction (141).

Many museums and universities have archival collections. For the former, T. Wise's *Guide to Military Museums* (267) is a good starting point. The broader treatment by Hudson and Nicholls (147) is useful for quick reference. HMSO has issued a general *Guide to London Museums and Galleries* (125). The *Guide to Research Facilities in History in the Universities of Great Britain and Ireland* by Kitson Clark and Elton (56) may be of value to the uninitiated student. Some of the more important repositories should be mentioned here (addresses are appended to the bibliography of this chapter). The National Army Museum in Chelsea has archives relating to the British Army before 1914; it has a particularly good collection of material on the army in India. The Liddell Hart Centre for Military Archives at King's College, London, is a major repository for materials relating to the armed forces and defence matters in the twentieth century. For both world wars, a large collection of the private papers of military personnel of all ranks and of some civilians is housed at the Imperial War Museum in London. The Museum also has lists of records on the two wars held by private individuals and in foreign archives. Other important collections are held at the Churchill College Archives Centre, Cambridge, at the University of London and at the Modern Records Centre in the University of Warwick (122, 213, 240). The Aviation Records Department of the Royal Air Force Museum at Hendon, Middlesex, has an important and growing collection of manuscripts, books, photographs, sound recordings and films dealing with all aspects of air force history. The Museum has not issued, as yet, a printed catalogue. The Air Library, Ministry of Defence, has a collection of material relating to the Royal Air Force. A number of private papers are housed in various regimental museums (267). The House of Lords Record Office has a large collection of manuscripts, including those of the former Beaverbrook Library. There are collections relating to the history of science, technology and engineering at the Science Museum in South Kensington. In the United States, collections of some value to British military historians are at the Huntington Library and at the Hoover Institution on War, Revolution and Peace (121, 202).

Introduction 13

For naval historians the collections of the National Maritime Museum at Greenwich are essential. R.J.B. Knight has edited a two volume *Guide to the Manuscripts* (164). Volume 1 covers the personal papers, together with short biographies, of some 300 naval and maritime figures of the last 325 years. Volume 2 covers public records, including Admiralty and Board of Trade archives from the seventeenth to the twentieth century and records relating to the Royal Naval dockyards; business records, including records of Lloyds Register of Shipping, shipbuilders, shipping lines, marine insurance companies and other commercial concerns. The Museum's extensive printed holdings are listed in their library catalogue (195). The Naval Library, housed in the Ministry of Defence, Empress State Building, London, has a large collection of books, pamphlets, broadsheets and other printed material, together with some personal papers.

A few other specialized guides should be mentioned. A second edition of Upton's guide to the early reports of the Historical Manuscripts Commission for 1603-1660 was published in 1964 (257). Madden and Storey have produced a brief finding aid for unpublished materials relating to Victorian studies (175). Madden has also written a general introduction to research into the Victorian era (173). Mayer and Koenig's *The Two World Wars: A Guide to Manuscript Collections in the United Kingdom* (179) provides an alphabetical listing by town or city where the archive is held (for example, the Devon Record Office will be found under Exeter; the Essex Record Office under Chelmsford). There is a guide to resources for the study of British foreign policy from 1918 to 1945 (10). *Britain and Europe since 1945* (137) is an author, title and chronological index to British primary source material on European integration from 1945 to about 1972 contained in the Harvester/Primary Social Sources microfiche collection of the same title. Even without the collection, it is a useful bibliographical tool.

The records of Parliament are voluminous. There is a general guide by Maurice Bond (30). The debates of the Houses of Lords and Commons are readily available, both bound and in microform, and well indexed. Parliamentary Papers include sessional and command papers which cover almost every conceivable subject and vary in size from a single sheet to large tomes. Ford's brief guide is an excellent introduction (103). Since the publication in 1968 of the Irish University Press Indexes (149) to their one-thousand volume set of nineteenth century British Parliamentary Papers, the finding of materials for that period has been greatly simplified. The first of the twelve volumes issued to date contains Hansard's Catalogue and Breviate of Parliamentary Papers, 1696-1834. There are seven volumes of general subject series which includes four volumes of indexes of papers relating to China, Japan, the East Indies, and the United States. Even without the massive documentary collection published by IUP to which they are specific, the indexes are an invaluable finding aid which can be used in conjunction with the standard (and much cheaper) microform editions of parliamentary papers possessed by many libraries. The IUP have also issued a checklist of parliamentary papers and a large (293p.) catalogue to the indexes (53). Ford's select lists cover the period from 1688 to 1974 with a gap between 1800 and 1832 (100, 101, 102, 104, 105, 178). There is also a breviate of diplomatic blue books for the inter-war years (259). The

Numerical Finding List of British Command Papers published 1833-1961/62 (78) can be extremely useful when only the number of a paper is known. Local sources are important for historians interested in military organization and in the use of the military in times of civil war, riots, strikes and other civil disturbances. Former Essex County Archivist, F.G. Emmison has written an introduction to the sources and methods of research in local history aimed primarily at the amateur historian (92). W.G. Hoskins' treatment is much more detailed (143). Alan Rogers' *Approaches to Local History* (223) is a scholarly work which deals more with the recent past than do Emmison or Hoskins. A collection of essays by Antonia Gransden provides a stimulating introduction to the English chroniclers from the sixth to the early sixteenth centuries; the second volume contains two chapters on the Wars of the Roses (118). Most county record offices have issued guides to their collections; Emmison's *Guide to the Essex Record Office* is a model of its kind (93). Alan Macfarlane's brief *Guide to English Historical Records* (172) is based upon the author's research on the village of Earl's Colne in Essex and is a useful supplement to Geoffrey Elton's 1969 survey of the fundamental sources for the study of early modern England (90) and an indispensable aid to the use of local archival material. Graves' *Bibliography of English History to 1485* contains much information on local material for the medieval period (119). The Royal Historical Society's *Guide to the Local Administrative Units of England* tells in what parish, county, etc., a place was and is (124). Since 1966 the Society of Genealogists in London has published eight of a projected twelve volume *National Index of Parish Registers* (193) which is an invaluable guide to Anglican, Roman Catholic and Nonconformist registers before 1837, together with information on marriage licenses, bishop's transcripts and modern copies. The first volume contains a brief section on army and navy records. The 192 volumes of the on-going *Victoria History of the Counties of England* contain an enormous amount of bibliographical information and are an essential reference work (258). The *General Introduction* to the V.C.H. lists the contents of volumes and indexes the titles and authors of chapters. A pamphlet by W.R. Powell (215) provides a list of parliamentary papers likely to be of use to local historians. Mullins' guides to publications of societies (188, 189, 190) contain some items of interest to scholars of local military history.

Over the last two decades, the collection and use of oral evidence has become increasingly important to historians. The best introduction is Paul Thompson's *The Voice of the Past* (253). In addition to providing sound advice on interview techniques, the book has an informative bibliographical discussion. Many archives now possess special research collections of tapes and transcribed interviews with men and women from all walks of life. For the military historian, the most important collections are at the Imperial War Museum, the National Maritime Museum, the Sunderland Polytechnic and, particularly for the memories of other ranks, the University of Essex.

In addition to those discussed in the chapters which follow, a few general works relating to foreign and imperial affairs are worth noting. A three-volume index of treaties from 1101 to 1968 is useful for quick reference (207). Two guides to materials concerning

American history in British and Irish archives contain leads of value to military historians (126, 219). For the Royal Navy in the West Indies, the guides to archival holdings in the Caribbean islands and in British repositories are essential (13, 52, 262). Scholars conducting research on the Indian Army, the British Army in India or the Indian Marine, should consult the guide to the papers of the India Office Military Department (98). The Bombay archives' massive and mostly uncatalogued collection of East India Company records is introduced in a handbook by Kanjiv Desai (74). There are sound guides to manuscripts relating to Africa and the Far East held in British repositories (210, 211, 260). An introduction to research in British foreign policy from the end of the First World War to the end of the Second can be found in the guide by Sidney Aster (10).

Two new projects which may be important for military historians should be mentioned. The Institute of Historical Research in London is planning a new Centre for Metropolitan History to be established in 1988 under the directorship of Derek Keene. It will focus on the history of London up to the present. The Wellcome Institute has recently launched a nationwide survey of sources relating to the history of medicine in the British Isles. It will cover all aspects of health and disease from 1600 to 1945. Local and central government records relating to public health as well as the papers of individuals will be included. The results of the survey are scheduled for publication in 1990 and should be invaluable to historians interested in military medicine and questions of health as they related to recruiting and training at both the local and national levels.

BIBLIOGRAPHY

1. Addington, Larry H. *The Patterns of War since the Eighteenth Century.* Bloomington, Ind.: Indiana University Press, 1984.
2. Albion, Robert Greenhalgh. *Naval and Maritime History: An Annotated Bibliography.* 4th edn. Newton Abbot: David and Charles, 1973.
3. Alston, R.C. (ed.). *The Eighteenth Century Short Title Catalogue: The British Library Collections.* London: British Library, 1983.
4. Altholz, J.L. *Victorian England, 1837-1901.* Cambridge: Cambridge University Press, 1970.
5. Altschul, Michael. *Anglo-Norman England, 1066-1154.* Cambridge: Cambridge University Press, 1969.
6. *Annual Abstract of Statistics.* London: Central Statistical Office, annual publication.
7. *Annual Bulletin of Historical Literature.* London: Historical Association, 1911-present.
8. *Annual Register: A Review of Public Events at Home and Abroad.* London, 1758-present; pub. Longmans since 1890; since 1954 entitled *Annual Register of World Events.*
9. Ascoli, David. *A Companion to the British Army, 1660-1983.* London, 1983.
10. Aster, Sidney. *British Foreign Policy, 1918-1945: A Guide to*

Research and Research Materials. Wilmington, Del.: Scholarly Resources Inc., 1984.
11. Bain, G.S. and J.D. Bennett. A Bibliography of British Industrial Relations, 1971-1979. Cambridge: Cambridge University Press, 1985.
12. ———— and G.B. Woolven. A Bibliography of British Industrial Relations. Cambridge: Cambridge University Press, 1978.
13. Baker, E. A Guide to Records in the Windward Islands. Oxford: Basil Blackwell, 1968.
14. Banks, Arthur. A Military Atlas of the First World War, with commentary by Alan Palmer. London: Heinemann Educational Books, 1975.
15. ————. A World Atlas of Military History, with introduction by Lord Chalfont. London: Seeley Service, 1973.
16. Barraclough, Geoffrey (ed.). The Times Atlas of World History, rev. edn. London: Times Books, 1984.
17. Baylen, J.O. and Norbert J. Gossman (eds.). Biographical Dictionary of Modern British Radicals. vols. 1 & 2. Hassocks, Sussex: Harvester Press, 1979, 1984.
18. Bayliss, Gwyn M. Bibliographic Guide to the Two World Wars: An Annotated Survey of English-Language Reference Materials. London: Bowker, 1977.
19. Bellamy, Joyce and John Saville (eds.). Dictionary of Labour Biography. 8 vols. London: Macmillan, 1972-1986.
20. Best, Geoffrey. Humanity in Warfare: The Modern History of the International Law of Armed Conflicts. London: Weidenfeld and Nicolson, 1980.
21. ————. War and Society in Revolutionary Europe, 1770-1870. Fontana History of European War and Society. London: Fontana.
22. ———— and Andrew Wheatcroft (eds.). War, Economy and the Military Mind, London: Croom Helm, 1976.
23. ———— et al. "What is Military History?" History Today, vol. 34 (December, 1984), pp. 5-13.
24. Bhattacharya, Sachchidananda. A Dictionary of Indian History. New York: Braziller, 1967.
25. Bibliography of Biography, 1970-1984. London: British Library, Bibliographic Services Division, 1985.
26. Bidwell, Robin Leonard (ed.). Guide to Government Ministers. 3 vols. London: Frank Cass, 1973.
27. Blackmore, H.L. The Armouries of the Tower of London. London: Ordnance, 1976.
28. Bond, Brian. War and Society in Europe, 1870-1970. Fontana History of European War and Society. London: Fontana, 1984.
29. ———— and Ian Roy (eds.). War and Society: A Yearbook of Military History. 2 vols. London: Croom Helm, 1975, 1977.
30. Bond, Maurice F. Guide to the Records of Parliament. London: HMSO, 1971.
31. Bowen, Daniel. An Encyclopedia of War Machines. London: Octopus Books, 1984.
32. Boyce, G.C. (ed.). Literature of Medieval History, 1930-1975: A Supplement to Louis J. Paetow's "A Guide to the Study of Medieval History". 5 vols. New York: Kraus, 1981.

33. Boylan, Henry. *A Dictionary of Irish Biography*. New York: Barnes and Noble, 1978.
34. *Britain: An Official Handbook*. London: Central Office of Information, annually since 1949/50.
35. *The British Economy: Key Statistics, 1900-1970*. London: Times Newspapers for the London and Cambridge Economic Service, [1973?].
36. British Library, Department of Printed Books. *Subject Index of the Books relating to the European War, 1914-1918, acquired by the British Museum, 1914-1920*. London: H. Pordes, 1970.
37. British Museum, State Papers Room. *Check List of British Official Serial Publications*. London: British Museum, 1972.
38. *British Union Catalogue of Periodicals: New Periodical Titles*. London: Butterworths, 1960-
39. Brown, Lucy M. & Ian R. Christie (eds.). *Bibliography of British History: 1789-1851*. Oxford: Clarendon Press, 1977.
40. ———. *Victorian News and Newspapers*. London: Oxford University Press, 1985.
41. Brown, Philip A.H. *London Publishers and Printers, c. 1800-1870*. London: British Library, 1982.
42. Bruce, Anthony P.C. *An Annotated Bibliography of the British Army, 1660-1914*. New York: Garland, 1975. 2nd. edn. Munich: K.G. Saur, 1985.
43. ———. *Bibliography of British Military History: From the Roman Invasions to the Restoration, 1660*. Munich: K.G. Saur, 1981.
44. Buckland, Charles E. *Dictionary of Indian Biography*. New York: Greenwood Press, 1969.
45. Butler, David and Anne Sloman. *British Political Facts, 1900-1979*. 5th edn. London: Macmillan, 1980.
46. Bynum, W.F. et al. *Dictionary of the History of Science*. Princeton, N.J.: Princeton University Press and London: Macmillan, 1981.
47. *Catalogue of British Parliamentary Papers in the Irish University Press 1000-volume series and Area Studies series, 1801-1900*. Dublin: Irish University Press, 1977.
48. *Catalogue of English Broadsides, 1505-1897*. New York: Burt Franklin, 1968.
49. Catchpole, Brian. *A Map History of the British People, 1700-1970*. London: Heinemann Educational Books, 1971.
50. Chaloner, W.H. and R.C. Richardson (eds.). *A Bibliography of British Economic and Social History*. Manchester: Manchester University Press, 1984.
51. Chandler, David G. *Dictionary of the Napoleonic Wars*. London: Arms and Armour Press, 1979.
52. Chandler, M.J. *Guide to Records in Barbados*. Oxford: Basil Blackwell, 1965.
53. *Checklist of British Parliamentary Papers in the Irish University Press 1000-volume series, 1801-1899*. Dublin: Irish University Press, 1972.
54. Cheney, C.R. *Handbook of Dates for Students of English History*. London: Royal Historical Society, 1945, reprinted with corrections 1978.

55. Christie, Ian. *British History since 1760: A Select Bibliography*. London: Historical Association, 1970.
56. Clark, G. Kitson and G.R. Elton. *Guide to Research Facilities in History in the Universities of Great Britain and Ireland*. Cambridge, Eng.: Cambridge University Press, 1965.
57. Colledge, J.J. *Ships of the Royal Navy: An Historical Index*. 2 vols. Newton Abbot: David and Charles, 1969-70.
58. Cook, Chris and John Stevenson. *The Atlas of Modern Warfare*. London: Weidenfeld and Nicolson, 1978.
59. ———— (eds.). *British Historical Facts, 1760-1830*. London: Macmillan, 1980.
60. ———— and Brendan Keith (eds.). *British Historical Facts, 1830-1900*. London: Macmillan, 1975, paperback 1984.
61. ———— and Ken Powell (eds.). *English Historical Facts, 1485-1603*. London: Macmillan, 1977.
62. ———— and John Wroughton (eds.). *English Historical Facts, 1603-1688*. London: Macmillan, 1980.
63. ———— and John Stevenson. *Longman Atlas of Modern British History*. London: Longman, 1978.
64. ———— (ed.). *Macmillan Dictionary of Historical Terms*. London: Macmillan, 1983.
65. ———— (ed.). *Sources in British Political History, 1900-1951*. vol. 1: *A Guide to the Archives of Selected Organisations and Societies*; vol. 2: *A Guide to the Private Papers of Selected Public Servants*; vol. 3: *A Guide to the Private Papers of Members of Parliament, A-K*; vol. 4: *A Guide to the Private Papers of Members of Parliament, L-Z*; vol. 5: *A Guide to the Private Papers of Selected Writers, Intellectual Publicists*, vol. 6: *First Consolidated Supplement*. London: Macmillan, 1975-1985.
66. Cowie, L.W. (ed.). *A Dictionary of British Social History*. London: Bell, 1973.
67. Craig, F.W.S. (ed.). *British Parliamentary Election Results, 1885-1918*. London: Macmillan, 1974.
68. Crane, R.S. and F.B. Kaye. *A Census of British Newspapers and Periodicals, 1620-1800*. London: Holland, 1966, reprint of 1927 edn.
69. Cranfield, Geoffrey Alan. *The Development of the Provincial Newspaper, 1700-1760*. Oxford: Clarendon, 1962.
70. ————. *A Handlist of English Provincial Newspapers and Periodicals, 1700-1760*. London: Bowes and Bowes, 1961.
71. *Current Research in Britain. The Humanities*. Boston Spa, W. Yorkshire: British Library, Lending Division, 1985.
72. *Current Research in Britain. Social Sciences*. Boston Spa, W. Yorkshire: British Library, Lending Division, 1985; formerly *Research in British Universities, Polytechnics and Colleges*. vol. III, *Social Sciences*. Boston Spa, W. Yorkshire: British Library, 1979-84.
73. Dahl, Folke. *A Bibliography of English Corantos and Periodical Newsbooks, 1620-1642*. London: The Bibliographical Society, 1952.
74. Dasai, Sanjiv P. *The Handbook of the Bombay Archives*. Bombay: Archives, 1978.

75. Deane, P. and W.A. Cole. *British Economic Growth, 1688-1959*. 2nd edn. Cambridge: Cambridge University Press, 1976.
76. de Kock, W.J. (ed.). *Dictionary of South African Biography*. vol. 1. Pretoria: Nasional Boekhandel Bpk. for National Council for Social Research, 1968-
77. De Mause, Lloyd et al. (eds.). *A Bibliography of Psychohistory*. New York: Garland, 1977.
78. Di Roma, Edward and Joseph A. Rosenthal. *A Numerical Finding List of British Command Papers published 1833-1961/62*. New York: New York Public Library, 1967.
79. *Dictionary of American Biography*. 11 vols. + supplements. New York: Scribner, 1946-58; 1973-
80. *Dictionary of Australian Biography*. 2 vols. Sydney: Angus & Robertson, 1949-
81. *Dictionary of Canadian Biography*. 11 vols. Toronto: University of Toronto Press, 1966-
82. *Dictionary of National Biography, 1961-1970*, with an index covering the years 1901-1970 in one alphabetical series. Oxford: Oxford University Press, 1981.
83. *Dissertation Abstracts International*. Ann Arbor, Michigan: University Microfilms, annually, 1938-present.
84. Dixon, Norman F. *On the Psychology of Military Incompetence*. London: Jonathan Cape, 1976.
85. Donaldson, Gordon and R.S. Morpeth. *A Dictionary of Scottish History*. Edinburgh: Donald, 1977.
86. Donovan, Robert K. (ed.). *Current Research on British Studies*. 9th edn. Manhattan, Kansas: MA-AH Publishers, 1986.
87. Eager, Alan R. *A Guide to Irish Bibliographical Material: A Bibliography of Irish Bibliographies and Sources of Information*. 2nd rev. and enl. edn. Westport, Conn.: Greenwood Press, 1980.
88. Edwards, Ruth Dudley. *An Atlas of Irish History*. 2nd. edn. London: Methuen, 1981.
89. Elton, G.R. (ed.). *Annual Bibliography of British and Irish History*. London: Royal Historical Society, 1975-84 and ed. D.M. Palliser, 1985-. Brighton: Harvester Press, 1986-
90. ─────. *England, 1200-1640*. London: Hodder and Stoughton, 1969.
91. ─────. *Modern Historians on British History, 1485-1945: A Critical Bibliography, 1945-1969*. London: Methuen, 1970.
92. Emmison, F.G. *Archives and Local History*. 2nd. edn. Chichester: Phillimore, 1974.
93. ─────. *Guide to the Essex Record Office*. 2nd edn. revised. Chelmsford: Essex County Council, 1969.
94. Enser, A.G.S. *A Subject Bibliography of the First World War: Books in English, 1914-1978*. London: Andre Deutsch, 1979.
95. ─────. *A Subject Bibliography of the Second World War: Books in English, 1939-1974*. London: Deutsch, 1977.
96. ─────. *A Subject Bibliography of the Second World War: Books in English, 1975-1983*. Aldershot: Gower, 1985.
97. Falkus, Malcolm and John Gillingham. *Historical Atlas of Britain*. London: Granada, 1981.
98. Farrington, Anthony. *Guide to the Records of the India Office Military Department*. London: Foreign and Commonwealth Office, 1982.

99. Feinstein, C.H. *National Income, Expenditure and Output of the United Kingdom, 1855-1965*. 2nd edn. Cambridge: Cambridge University Press, 1977.
100. Ford, Grace. *A Select List of Reports and other Papers in Journals of the House of Commons, 1688-1800*. Nendeln, Liechtenstein: KTO Press, 1976.
101. Ford, P. and G. Ford. *A Breviate of Parliamentary Papers, 1900-1916*. Oxford: Blackwell, 1957.
102. ─────. *A Breviate of Parliamentary Papers, 1917-1939*. Oxford: Blackwell, 1951.
103. ─────. *A Guide to Parliamentary Papers: What they are, how to find them, how to use them*. 3rd edn. Shannon: Irish University Press, 1972.
104. ─────. *Select List of British Parliamentary Papers, 1833-1899*. rev. edn. Shannon: Irish University Press, 1969.
105. ───── and Diana Marshallsay. *Select List of British Parliamentary Papers, 1955-1964*. Shannon: Irish University Press, 1970.
106. Foster, Janet and Julia Sheppard (eds.). *British Archives: A Guide to Archival Resources in the United Kingdom*. Detroit, Michigan: Gale Research Company, 1982.
107. Frederick, J.B.M. *Lineage Book of the British Army. Mounted Corps and Infantry, 1660-1968*. Cornwallville, N.Y., 1969.
108. Freeman-Grenville, G.S.P. *Atlas of British History*. London: Rex Collings, 1979.
109. Fulton, Richard D. and Charles M. Colee. *Union List of Victorian Serials: A Union List of Selected Nineteenth-Century British Serials available in United States and Canadian Libraries*. New York: Garland, 1984.
110. Fyfe, Janet. *History Journals and Serials: An Analytical Guide*. New York: Greenwood Press, 1986.
111. Gann, L.H. and Peter Duignan (eds.). *Colonialism in Africa, 1870-1960*. vol. 5: *Bibliographical Guide to Colonialism in Sub-Saharan Africa*. Cambridge: Cambridge University Press, 1974.
112. Gardiner, Samuel Rawson (ed.). *A School Atlas of English History*. New impression. London: Longmans, 1914.
113. *Gentleman's Magazine*. London: W.H. Allen, etc. Title varies: 1731-35, *The Gentleman's Magazine: or, Monthly Intelligencer*; 1736-1833, *The Gentleman's Magazine and Historical Chronicle*; 1856-68, *The Gentleman's Magazine and Historical Review*. -1907.
114. Gilbert, Martin. *British History Atlas*. London: Weidenfeld & Nicolson, 1968.
115. ─────. *First World War Atlas*. rev. edn. London: Weidenfeld & Nicolson, 1985.
116. ─────. *Recent History Atlas: 1860-1960*. 3rd edn. London: Weidenfeld and Nicolson, 1977.
117. Gosset, W.P. *The Lost Ships of the Royal Navy, 1793-1900*. London: Mansell, 1986.
118. Gransden, Antonia. *Historical Writing in England*, vol. I, c. 550 to 1307, vol. II, c. 1307 to the Early Sixteenth Century. London: Routledge & Kegan Paul, 1974, 1982.
119. Graves, Edgar (ed.). *A Bibliography of English History to 1485*. Oxford: Clarendon Press, 1975.

Introduction   21

120. Greaves, Richard L. and Robert Zaller (eds.). *Biographical Dictionary of British Radicals in the Seventeenth Century.* vol. 1. Hassocks, Sussex: Harvester Press, 1982.
121. *Guide to British Historical Manuscripts in the Huntington Library.* San Marino, Calif.: Huntington Library, 1982.
122. *Guide to the Holdings of the Churchill College Archives Centre.* Cambridge: Churchill College, 1980.
123. *Guide to the Contents of the Public Record Office.* 2 vols. London: HMSO, 1968.
124. *Guide to the Local Administrative Units of England.* London: Royal Historical Society, 1979.
125. *Guide to London Museums and Galleries.* London: HMSO, 1974.
126. *A Guide to Manuscripts relating to American History in British Depositories.* Washington: Library of Congress, 1946.
127. *Guide to Official Statistics.* London: Central Statistical Office, 1976.
128. Haigh, Christopher (ed.). *The Cambridge Historical Encyclopedia of Great Britain and Ireland.* Cambridge, Eng.: Cambridge University Press, 1985.
129. Halsey, A.H. (ed.). *Trends in British Society since 1900: A Guide to the changing social structure of Britain.* London: Macmillan, 1972.
130. Hanham, H.J. (ed.). *Bibliography of British History, 1851-1914.* Oxford: Clarendon Press, 1976.
131. Harrison, Brian. *Dictionary of British Temperance Biography.* Coventry: Society for the Study of Labour History, 1973.
132. Harrison, J.F.C. and Dorothy Thompson. *Bibliography of the Chartist Movement, 1837-1976.* Hassocks, Sussex: Harvester Press, 1978.
133. Hastings, Max (ed.). *Encyclopedia of Military Anecdotes.* London: Oxford University Press, 1985.
134. Havighurst, Alfred F. *Modern England, 1901-1970.* London: Cambridge University Press, 1976.
135. Hayward, P.H.C. (ed.). *Jane's Dictionary of Military Terms.* London: Macdonald & Jane's, 1975.
136. Hazlehurst, Cameron and Christine Woodland. *A Guide to the Papers of British Cabinet Ministers, 1900-1951.* London: Royal Historical Society, 1974.
137. Hennessy, James (ed.). *Britain and Europe since 1945: A Bibliographical Guide.* Brighton: Harvester Press, 1973.
138. Herwig, Holger H. and Neil Heyman (eds.). *Biographical Dictionary of World War I.* Westport, Conn.: Greenwood Press, 1982.
139. Heussler, Robert (ed.). *British Malaya: A Bibliographical and Biographical Compendium.* New York: Garland, 1980.
140. Hickey, D.J. and J. Doherty. *A Dictionary of Irish History since 1800.* Dublin: Gill & Macmillan, 1980.
141. Higham, Robin (ed.). *A Guide to the Sources of British Military History.* Berkeley: University of California Press, 1971.
142. *Historical Abstracts.* Santa Barbara, California: American Bibliographical Center - Clio Press, 1955-present. Part A: *Modern History Abstracts, 1775-1914* (vols. 1-16) and *1450-1914* (vols. 17-). Part B: *Twentieth Century Abstracts, 1914-present.*

143. Hoskins, W.G. *Local History in England*. 3rd edn. London: Longman, 1984.
144. Houghton, Walter E. (ed.). *The Wellesley Index to Victorian Periodicals, 1824-1900*. London: Routledge & Kegan Paul; Toronto: University of Toronto Press, 1966-
145. Howard, Michael. *War and the Liberal Conscience*. London: Maurice Temple, 1978; Oxford University Press paperback, 1981.
146. ————. *War in European History*. Oxford: Oxford University Press, 1976.
147. Hudson, Kenneth and Ann Nicholls (eds.). *The Directory of Museums and Living Displays*. 3rd edn. London: Macmillan, 1985.
148. *Index of Manuscripts in the British Library*. 11 vols. Cambridge, Eng.: Chadwyck-Healey, 1984.
149. *Indexes to the Irish University Press Series of British Parliamentary Papers*. Subject set. 8 vols. plus special area studies series 4 vols. Dublin: Irish University Press, 1968.
150. Institute of Historical Research. *Historical Research for Higher Degrees in the United Kingdom*. London: Institute of Historical Research, 1985-present. Lists were printed in *History* from 1920 to 1929; from 1930 to 1932 in *Bulletin of the Institute of Historical Research*; from 1933 to 1966 in annual *Theses Supplements* to the *B.I.H.R.*; between 1967 and 1984 as *Historical Research for University Degrees in the United Kingdom* issued in two parts, *Theses Completed* and *Theses in Progress*.
151. ————. *History Theses, 1901-70: Historical Research for Higher Degrees in the Universities of the United Kingdom*. Compiled by Phyllis Jacobs. London: Institute of Historical Research, 1976.
152. ————. *History Theses, 1971-80: Historical Research for Higher Degrees in the Universities of the United Kingdom*. Compiled by J.M. Horn. London: Institute of Historical Research, 1984.
153. ————. *Office-Holders in Modern Britain*. London: Institute of Historical Research, 1972-84:
    Vol. I: J.C. Sainty. *Treasury Officials, 1660-1870*.
    II: ————. *Officials of the Secretary of State, 1660-1782*.
    III: ————. *Officials of the Boards of Trade, 1660-1870*.
    IV: ————. *Admiralty Officials, 1660-1870*.
    V: ————. *Home Office Officials, 1782-1870*.
    VI: ————. *Colonial Office Officials, 1794-1870*.
    VII: J.M. Collinge, *Navy Board Officials, 1660-1832*.
    VIII: ————. *Foreign Office Officials, 1782-1870*.
    IX: ————. *Officials of Royal Commissions of Inquiry, 1815-70*.
154. ————. *Writings on British History*. 12 vols. covering 1946-1974. London: Institute of Historical Research, 1973-86.

155. Jeremy, D.J. (ed.). *The Dictionary of Business Biography*. London: Butterworths, 1984-
156. Keegan, John. *The Face of Battle*. London: Jonathan Cape, 1976 (Penguin, 1978).
157. ————. *Rand McNally Encyclopedia of World War II*. Chicago: Rand McNally, 1977.
158. Keeler, Mary Frear. *Bibliography of British History: Stuart Period, 1603-1714*. 2nd rev. edn. London: Oxford University Press, 1976.
159. Kellaway, W. *Bibliography of Historical Works issued in the United Kingdom, 1966-70*. London: Institute of Historical Research, 1972.
160. Kemp, Peter (ed.). *The Oxford Companion to Ships and the Sea*. London: Oxford University Press, 1976.
161. Kenyon, J.P. (ed.). *A Dictionary of British History*. London: Secker and Warburg, 1981.
162. Kiernan, V.G. *European Empires from Conquest to Collapse, 1815-1960*. Fontana History of European War and Society. London: Fontana, 1982.
163. Kirby, J.L. *Guide to Historical Periodicals in the English Language*. Helps for Students of History series. London: Historical Association, 1970.
164. Knight, R.J.B. (ed.). *Guide to the Manuscripts in the National Maritime Museum*. 2 vols. London: Mansell, 1977, 1980.
165. Kuehl, Warren F. *Dissertations in History, 1970-June 1980*. Santa Barbara, Calif.: American Bibliographical Center, Clio Press, 1986.
166. Lang, Kurt (ed.). *Military Institutions and the Sociology of War: A Review of the Literature with Annotated Bibliography*. London: Sage Publications, 1972.
167. Langton, John and R.J. Morris. *Atlas of the Industrial Revolution*. London: Methuen, 1985.
168. Levine, Mortimer. *Tudor England, 1485-1603*. Cambridge: Cambridge University Press, 1968.
169. Lipschutz, Mark R. and R. Kent Rasmussen. *Dictionary of African Historical Biography*. Chicago: Aldine Publishing, 1978.
170. Lloyd, Christopher. *Atlas of Maritime History*. London: Hamlyn Group, 1975.
171. Luttwak, Edward. *A Dictionary of Modern War*. New York: Harper and Row, 1971.
172. Macfarlane, Alan. *A Guide to English Historical Records*. Cambridge: Cambridge University Press, 1983.
173. Madden, Lionel. *How to Find Out about the Victorian Period*. Oxford: Pergamon Press, 1970.
174. ———— and Diana Dixon. *The Nineteenth Century Periodical Press in Britain: A Bibliography of Modern Studies, 1901-1971*. New York: Garland, 1976.
175. ———— and Richard Storey. *Primary Sources for Victorian Studies: A Guide to the Location and Use of Unpublished Materials*. London: Phillimore, 1977.
176. Majumdar, R.C. *Historiography in Modern India*. New York: Asia Publishing House, 1971.
177. Manwaring, G. *A Bibliography of British Naval History: A Bibliographical and Historical Guide to Printed and Manuscript Sources*. London: Conway Maritime Press, 1970.

178. Marshallsay, Diana and J.H. Smith. *Ford List of British Parliamentary Papers, 1965-1974*. Nendeln, Liechtenstein: KTP Press, 1979.
179. Mayer, S.L. and W.J. Koenig (eds.). *The Two World Wars: A Guide to Manuscript Collections in the United Kingdom*. London: Bowker, 1976.
180. McNeill, William H. *The Pursuit of Power: Technology, Armed Force and Society since A.D. 1000*. Chicago: University of Chicago Press, 1982.
181. *Microfilms of Newspapers and Journals for Sale*. Colindale: British Library, Newspaper Library, 1979.
182. Milne, Alexander T. *A Centenary Guide to the Publications of the Royal Historical Society, 1868-1968, and of the former Camden Society, 1838-1897*. London: Royal Historical Society, 1968.
183. Mitchell, A.R. and B.R. Cooling (eds.). *Doctoral Dissertations in Military Affairs*. Manhattan: Kansas State University, 1972, and annual supplements in *Military Affairs*.
184. Mitchell, B.R. and P. Deane. *Abstract of British Historical Statistics*. Cambridge: Cambridge University Press, 1962.
185. ———— and H.G. Jones. *Second Abstract of British Historical Statistics*. Cambridge: Cambridge University Press, 1971.
186. Mowat, Charles L. *British History since 1926*. Revised by Peter Lowe. London: The Historical Association, 1977.
187. ————. *Great Britain since 1914*. London: Hodder and Stoughton, 1971.
188. Mullins, E.L.C. *A Guide to the Historical and Archaeological Publications of Societies in England and Wales, 1901-33*. London: Athlone Press for the Institute of Historical Research, 1968.
189. ————. *Texts and Calendars: An Analytical Guide to Serial Publications*. London: Royal Historical Society, 1978.
190. ————. *Texts and Calendars II: An Analytical Guide to Serial Publications, 1957-1982*. London: Royal Historical Society, 1983.
191. Murphy, Brian. *Dictionary of Australian History*. Sydney & New York: McGraw-Hill, 1982.
192. Musiker, Naomi. *South African History: A Bibliographical Guide with Special Reference to Territorial Expansion and Colonization*. New York: Garland, 1982.
193. *National Index of Parish Registers*. vol. 1. *Sources of Births, Marriages and Deaths before 1837*, by D.J. Steel with additional articles by E. Gillett, M. Macguinness and E.A. Wrigley. London: Society of Genealogists, 1968; vol. 2. *Sources for Nonconformist Genealogy and Family History*, by D.J. Steel, 1973; vol. 3. *Sources for Roman Catholic and Jewish Genealogy and Family History*, by D.J. Steel and E.R. Samuel, 1974; vol. 4. *South East England: Kent, Surrey and Sussex*, by Patrick Palgrave-Moore, 1980; vol. 5. *South Midlands and Welsh Border: Gloucestershire, Herefordshire, Oxfordshire, Shropshire, Warwickshire and Worcestershire*, by D.J. Steel and C.W. Field, second edn., 1971 (first edn. 1966); vol. 6. *The North Midlands, part 1, Staffordshire*, by P.D. Bloore and P. Palgrave-Moore, 1982; vol. 11. *Durham and*

Northumberland, by C.P. Neat, 1979; vol. 12. *Sources for Scottish Genealogy and Family History*, by D.J. Steel, 1970. vols. 7-10 to come.
194. *National Inventory of Documentary Sources in the United Kingdom.* Microfiche. Cambridge, Eng.: Chadwyck-Healey, 1984-
195. National Maritime Museum, Greenwich. *Catalogue of the Library.* 5 vols. London: Her Majesty's Stationary Office, 1968-76.
196. Norman, A.V.B. and Don Pottinger. *English Weapons for Warfare, 449-1660.* London: Arms and Armour Press, 1979.
197. Norton, Augustus R. et al. (eds.). *NATO: A Bibliography and Resource Guide.* New York: Garland, 1980.
198. Nunez, Benjamin. *Dictionary of Afro-Latin American Civilization.* African Bibliographic Center. Westport, Conn.: Greenwood Press, 1980.
199. Ofcansky, Thomas P. *British East Africa, 1856-1963: An Annotated Bibliography.* New York: Garland, 1982.
200. Olle, James G. *An Introduction to British Government Publications.* London: Association of Assistant Librarians, 1965.
201. Olson, William J. (ed.). *Britain's Elusive Empire in the Middle East, 1900-1921: An Annotated Bibliography.* New York: Garland, 1981.
202. Palm, Charles G. and Dale Reed. *Guide to the Hoover Institution Archives.* Hoover Institution on War, Revolution and Peace. Stanford, Calif.: Hoover Institution Press, 1980.
203. Palmegiano, Eugenia. *The British Empire in the Victorian Press, 1832-1867: A Bibliography.* New York: Garland, forthcoming.
204. Palmer, Alan. *Dictionary of Twentieth Century History.* London: A. Lane, 1979.
205. Pargellis, Stanley M. and D.J. Medley. *Bibliography of British History: The Eighteenth Century, 1714-1789.* Hassocks, Sussex: Harvester Press, 1977.
206. Parker, Geoffrey and Brenda. *A Dictionary of the European Communities.* London: Butterworths, 1981.
207. Parry, Clive and Charity Hopkins. *An Index of British Treaties, 1101-1968.* 3 vols. London: HMSO, 1970.
208. Partridge, Eric. *The Routledge Dictionary of Historical Slang.* London: Routledge & Kegan Paul, 1973; abridged edition published as *The Penguin Dictionary of Historical Slang,* 1972 & 1980.
209. Paxton, John. *A Dictionary of the European Economic Community.* London: Macmillan, 1978.
210. Pearson, J.D. (ed.). *A Guide to Manuscripts and Documents in the British Isles relating to Africa.* London: Oxford University Press, 1971.
211. ———— (ed.). *A Guide to Manuscripts and Documents in the British Isles relating to the Far East.* London: Oxford University Press, 1977.
212. Pemberton, John E. *British Official Publications.* Oxford: Pergamon, 1971.
213. Percival, Janet (ed.). *A Guide to Archives and Manuscripts in the University of London.* 2 vols. London: University of London, 1983-84.
214. Ponko, Vincent Jr. (ed.). *Britain in the Middle East, 1921-1956.* New York: Garland, forthcoming.

215. Powell, W.R. *Local History from Blue Books: A Select List of Sessional Papers of the House of Commons.* London: Historical Association, 1962.
216. Preston, Richard A. and Sydney F. Wise. *Men in Arms: A History of Warfare and its Interrelationships with Western Society.* 4th edition. New York: Holt, Rinehart and Winston, 1979; first edn. published by Frederick Praeger, New York, 1956.
217. Puttock, A.G. *A Dictionary of Heraldry and Related Subjects.* London: Gifford, 1970.
218. Quick, John. *Dictionary of Weapons and Military Terms.* New York: McGraw-Hill, 1973.
219. Raimo, John W. *A Guide to Manuscripts relating to America in Great Britain and Ireland: A Revision of the Guide edited in 1961 by B.R. Crick and Miriam Alman.* Westport, Conn.: Meckler Books, 1979. The 1961 edition was published for the British Association for American Studies by Oxford University Press.
220. *Recently Published Articles.* (formerly a section of the *American Historical Review*) Washington, D.C.: American Historical Association, February, June & October each year since 1976.
221. *Record Repositories in the United Kingdom.* 4th edn. London: HMSO, 1971.
222. Roach, John (ed.). *A Bibliography of Modern History.* Cambridge: Cambridge University Press, 1968.
223. Rogers, Alan. *Approaches to Local History.* 2nd edn. London: Longman, 1977; first published 1972 as *This Was Their World.*
224. Royal Commission on Historical Manuscripts, *Accessions to Repositories and Reports added to the National Register of Archives.* London: HMSO, annually since 1972. Up to and including 1971 entitled *List of Accessions to Repositories.*
225. ————. *Guides to Sources for British History.* 4 vols.: 1. *Papers of British Cabinet Ministers, 1782-1900.* London: HMSO, 1982; 2. *The Manuscript Papers of British Scientists, 1600-1942.* London: HMSO, 1982; 3. *Guide to the Location of Collections Described in the Reports and Calendars Series, 1870-1980.* London: HMSO, 1982; 4. *Private Papers of British Diplomats, 1782-1900.* London: HMSO, 1985.
226. *RUSI/Brassey's Defence Yearbook, 1987.* 97th edn., London: RUSI, Whitehall, 1987.
227. Sachse, William L. *Restoration England, 1660-1689.* Cambridge: Cambridge University Press, 1971.
228. Schlatter, Richard (ed.). *Recent Views on British History: Essays on Historical Writing since 1966.* New Brunswick, N.J.: Rutgers University Press, 1984.
229. Sen, S.P. (ed.). *Dictionary of National Biography.* 4 vols. Calcutta: Institute of Historical Studies, 1972.
230. ————. *Historians and Historiography in Modern India.* Calcutta: Institute of Historical Studies, 1973.
231. Sillitoe, A. *Britain in Figures: A Handbook of Social Statistics.* 2nd. edn. London: Penguin, 1973.
232. Slocum, Robert B. *Biographical Dictionaries and Related Works,*

supplement and second supplement. Detroit: Gale Research Company, 1972, 1978.
233. Smith, Harold. *The British Labour Movement to 1970: A Bibliography*. London: Mansell, 1981.
234. Smith, Myron J. *Battleships and Battlecruisers, 1884-1984: A Bibliography and Chronology*. New York: Garland, 1984.
235. ―――――. *World War II: The European and Mediterranean Theatres, An Annotated Bibliography*. New York: Garland, 1984.
236. ―――――. *World War II at Sea: A Bibliography of Sources in English*. Metuchen, N.J.: Scarecrow Press, 1976.
237. Steinberg, S.H. and H.I. Evans (eds.). *Steinberg's Dictionary of British History*. 2nd edn. New York: St. Martins Press, 1971.
238. Stenton, Michael. *Who's Who of British Members of Parliament: A Biographical Dictionary of the House of Commons based on annual volumes of Dod's Parliamentary Companion and other sources*. 4 vols. Brighton: Harvester Press, 1976-
239. Stone, G.C. *A Glossary of the Construction, Decoration and Use of Arms and Armour in All Countries and in All Times*. New York: Jack Brussel, 1984.
240. Storey, Richard and Janet Drucker (eds.). *Guide to the Modern Records Centre, University of Warwick Library*. Warwick: University of Warwick, 1977.
241. Strachan, Hew. *European Armies and the Conduct of War*. London: George Allen & Unwin, 1983.
242. Strayer, Joseph R. *Dictionary of the Middle Ages*. New York: Scribner, 1982.
243. Swinson, Arthur. *A Register of the Regiments and Corps of the British Army*. London, 1972.
244. Taylor, R. *Bibliography of Historical Works issued in the United Kingdom, 1971-75*. London: Institute of Historical Research, 1977.
245. *Theses on Asia accepted by Universities in the United Kingdom and Ireland*. Compiled by B.C. Bloomfield. London: Cass, 1967.
246. *Theses in Canada: A Bibliographic Guide*. Compiled by Denis Robitaille and Joan Waiser. Ottawa: National Library of Canada, 1986.
247. *Theses on Caribbean Topics, 1778-1968*. Compiled by Enid Baa. San Juan: Institute of Caribbean Studies, University of Puerto Rico, 1970.
248. *Theses on the Commonwealth Caribbean, 1891-1973*. Commonwealth Caribbean Resource Centre. London, Ontario: Office of International Education, University of Western Ontario, 1974.
249. *Theses on Indian Sub-continent (1877-1971)*. Compiled by K. Gopal. Delhi: Hindustan Publishing Corp., 1977.
250. *Theses on Subjects relating to Ireland presented for Higher Degrees, 1950-1967*. Belfast: Queen's University, Institute of Irish Studies, 1968.
251. *Theses on Islam, the Middle East and North-west Africa, 1880-1978, accepted by Universities in the United Kingdom and Ireland*. Compiled by Peter Sluglett. London: Mansell, 1983.

252. *Theses on Latin American Studies at British Universities in Progress or Recently Completed.* London: University of London, Institute of Latin American Studies, annually 1966-present.
253. Thompson, Paul. *The Voice of the Past: Oral History.* Oxford: Oxford University Press, 1978.
254. Toase, Charles (ed.). *Bibliography of British Newspapers.* 5 vols. London: Library Association, 1975-87.
255. Tunney, Christopher. *A Biographical Dictionary of World War II.* New York: St. Martin's Press, 1972.
256. Uden, Grant (ed.). *A Dictionary of Chivalry.* London: Longman, 1968.
257. Upton, Eleanor Stuart. *Guide to the Sources of English History from 1603 to 1660 in the Early Reports of the Royal Commission on Historical Manuscripts.* 2nd edn. New York and London: Scarecrow Press, 1964.
258. *The Victoria History of the Counties of England.* 192 vols. London: Institute of Historical Research, 1899-
259. Vogel, Robert. *A Breviate of British Diplomatic Blue Books, 1919-1939.* Montreal: McGill University Press, 1963.
260. Wainwright, M.D. (ed.). *A Guide to Western Manuscripts and Documents in the British Isles relating to South and South East Asia.* London: Oxford University Press, 1965.
261. Walford, A.J. and Joan Harvey. *Guide to Current British Periodicals in the Humanities and Social Sciences.* London: Library Association, 1985.
262. Walne, Peter. *A Guide to Manuscript Sources for the History of Latin America and the Caribbean in the British Isles.* London: Oxford University Press, 1973.
263. *War and Society,* Duntroon, ACT 2600, Australia: Department of History, University of New South Wales, May 1983-
264. *The Waterloo Directory of Victorian Periodicals, 1824-1900.* Waterloo, Ontario: Wilfred Laurier University Press, 1970-
265. Weigley, Russell F. (ed.). *New Dimensions in Military History.* San Rafael: Presidio Press, 1975.
266. White, A.S. *Bibliography of Regimental Histories of the British Army.* London, 1965.
267. Wise, T. *A Guide to Military Museums.* 2nd edn. Hemel Hempstead, 1971.
268. Woodworth, David (ed.). *Current British Journals: A Subject Guide to Periodicals/Editors.* 4th edn. Boston Spa, W. Yorkshire: British Library Lending Division in association with U.K. Serials Group, 1986; formerly *Guide to Current British Journals.* Wetherby: British Library for U.K. Serials Group, 1982 (and in two vols., 1973 London: Library Association).

Libraries and Repositories Mentioned in the Text

Air Library, Ministry of Defence, Adastral House, Theobalds Road, London WC1X 8RU

British Library, Department of Manuscripts, Great Russell Street, London WC 1B 3DG

Churchill College Archives Centre, Churchill College, Cambridge CB 3 ODS

Introduction

University of Essex, Oral History Project, Department of Sociology, Wivenhoe Park, Colchester CO4 3SQ
House of Lords Record Office, House of Lords, London SW 1A 0PW
Imperial War Museum, Department of Documents, Lambeth Road, London SE 1 6HZ
India Office Library, Foreign and Commonwealth Office, Blackfriars Road, London SE 1 8NG
Institute of Historical Research, University of London, Senate House, Malet Street, London WC 1E 7HU
Liddell Hart Centre for Military Archives, King's College, Strand, London WC2R 2LS
National Army Museum, Royal Hospital Road, London SW3 4HT
National Maritime Museum Library, Greenwich, London SE 10 9NF
National Register of Archives, Historical Manuscripts Commission, Quality House, Quality Court, Chancery Lane, London WC2A 1HP
Naval Library, Ministry of Defence, Empress State Building, Fulham, London SW6 1TR
Public Record Office, Ruskin Avenue, Kew, Richmond, Surrey TW9 4DU
Royal Air Force Museum, Aviation Records Department, The Hyde, Hendon, London NW9 5LL
Science Museum, South Kensington, London SW7 2DD
Sunderland Polytechnic, Langham Tower, Ryhope Road, Sunderland SR2 7EE
University of Warwick, Modern Records Centre, Coventry CV4 7AL
Wellcome Institute of the History of Medicine, 183 Euston Road, London NW1 2BP

II

THE ECONOMIC, SCIENTIFIC AND TECHNOLOGICAL BACKGROUND:
FROM THE BEGINNINGS TO 1914

W.H.G. Armytage

"A man will turn over half a library to make one book," observed Dr. Johnson on 6 April 1775. Today, in addition to computer searches like KWIC, he (or she) has recourse to overviews of the literature that has exfoliated round the subject and explanatory and interpretative bibliographies are issued for afficionados of a special field.
Since the Higham volume was published in 1971, the structural revolution has been taking place which posits the mind as a set of structural transforms of primary data taken from the world and, by the selective destruction of information, "stronger structures are formed from weaker ones."[1]
Such a structure seems to be emerging from the vast output of writing on the intertwining of the scientific and technological progress of the United Kingdom with naval and military affairs.[2] Indeed, the link between them was symbolised by T.H. Huxley--a former naval doctor--when he described science as "nothing but trained and organized common sense, differing from the latter only as a veteran may differ from a raw recruit; and its methods differ from those of common sense only as far as the guardsman's cut and thrust differ from the manner in which a savage wields his club."[3]
That "cut and thrust" is visible in some of the articles and books listed in this bibliography, and has been an essential part of bringing down pretentious theory--as when the professor of modern history at Cambridge was accused by Cardinal Newman of trying to "poison the wells" in his review of J.A. Froude's *History of England*. He also went to the armed forces for his argument, saying "there is such a thing as legitimate warfare: war has its laws ... there are things which may fairly be done, and things which may not be done." Similar criticisms, if not quite so categorical, have been made by

---

[1] Gunther Stent, "Prematurity and Uniqueness in Scientific Discovery", *Scientific American*, vol. 227 (1972), pp. 84-93.

[2] R. Johnston, "Contextual knowledge: A model for the overthrow of the internal-external dichotomy in science", *The Australian and New Zealand Journal of Sociology*, vol. 12 (1976), pp. 196-203.

[3] T.H. Huxley, *Collected Essays*, London: Macmillan, 1893-4, vol. IV, The Method of Zadig.

some authors listed in this bibliography of others who are also listed. So, happily for the progress of knowledge, the conflict model in scholarship continues.

The incarnation of this model was the famous Dr. Johnson, who was reported as saying, "I dogmatise and am contradicted, and in this conflict of opinions and sentiments I find delight."[4]

Readers of this bibliography will appreciate that such cut and thrust is necessary in academic circles, and those so criticised may comfort themselves with another observation of Dr. Johnson--that "whatever makes the past, the distant or the future predominate over the present, advances us in the dignity of human beings."[5]

Prehistoric revolution. Proclaimed at the very time the previous volume of this bibliography was being published, the "revolution in pre-history" (869, 870, 871) necessitates a more substantial treatment of "The Beginnings."

For human families lived at Swanscombe near the Thames Estuary between the great Ice Ages, more than 150,000 years ago. Armed with general purpose flint axes, flint tools and fire, they seem to have lived off the woods.

So the first "mines" and "factories" appear to have existed to provide axes. 400 pits at Grime's Graves in Norfolk covered 34 acres, some up to 40 feet deep. There were others in the same county at Lynford and Massingham and in other counties like Sussex and Wiltshire and in North Wales. Such was the demand to clear the wild wood that these products were diffused throughout the British Isles.

Radio carbon dating, pollen analysis and dendrochronology, to say nothing of aerial photography (itself a technique evolved in wartime) have pushed back this bibliography 60,000 or 70,000 years, which barely extends to the last glaciation. And these glaciations, thanks to oxygen isotope analysis of deep sea cores, may have numbered seventeen instead of the traditional three or four.

Britain itself seems to have been really colonised when agriculturalists began--c. 4,500 B.C.--to clear the forests to cultivate barley. They used ploughs, hoes and spades and kept sheep and goats, building causewayed camps near circular "henges" and stone circles. Of the 960 stone circles in Britain, 243 were in England, 49 in Wales, 128 in Ulster, 133 in Eire and 407 in Scotland. A superb gazetteer is now available (155, 156).

Should some of these henges be seen as "standing stone observatories," "temples and training schools of the learned orders" which undertook work in them--or indeed as "the world's oldest computers"? Such claims by Thom (1039, 1040) and Euan Mackie (682) have been contested by Heggie (493), Chippendale (196) and others.

From the hill forts (constructed in the thousand years before the Romans by a warrior class (376)) emerged the first recorded British military leader, Cassivellaunus. His resources and organization enabled him to out-general and out-manoeuvre the greatest Roman general, Julius Caesar, in 55 and 54 B.C. These resources have

---

[4] Sir John Hawkins, *The Life of Johnson*, 1797, p. 92.

[5] S. Johnson, *Journey to the Western Islands of Scotland*, 1775 (Inch Kenneth).

recently been the subject of the Butser Experiment on a reconstructed ancient farm on the South Downs of Hampshire. This was followed in 1976 by an unusual drought which enabled an aerial survey of parch and crop marks to be made which indicated that there could well have been "virtually total domination of the landscape and a proportionately large population" (872). Reynolds calls attention to the export of grain, leather, hunting dogs and slaves to the Continent and the reverse passage of Celtic scholars from Europe to Britain for "the finest training available" (872).

Debts to Rome. To lure the Britons from warlike barbarism, the Romans--especially Agricola--encouraged them "to build temples, markets and houses" in their tribal capitals. The Romans also stimulated a woollen and cloth industry as well as mining, tile making and various other industries made possible by their introduction of new materials and their needs.

Pollen analysis and the electron microscope have enabled Sir Harry Godwin to include five times as many Roman contributions to British Flora in the second edition of his phytogeographical study as in the first. These included building materials, clothing, dyes (woad), fruits (apple, cherry, damson, fig, grape vine, medlar, mulberry and plum), hedging materials (bay), medicines (deadly nightshade, dill, hemlock--for euthanasia--hemp--a hallucinogen--henbane, opium and poppy), oil seed (flax), pot herbs (Alexander, coriander, mustard) and vegetables (broad bean, Buckwater nuts for flour, celery, crab-apples, fennel, lentil, pea and radish). And, zoologically, the pea fowl and the edible snail (419).

The Romans also introduced the rotary quern--necessary for feeding a population of four million--and oil lamps of scallop shells filled with imported olive oil. Coal from the North Somerset coalfield was used in the Temple of Minerva at Bath, c. 230, as well as in the villas of Somerset, Gloucestershire and Wiltshire (114).

Such has been the explosion of evidence that the famous Volume I of the *Oxford History of England* (second edition 1937) has now become IB and a new Volume IA by Peter Salway was published in 1981 (915), whilst a new journal, *Britannia*, was launched in 1970 by the Society for the Promotion of Roman Studies.

Civil amphitheaters existed at Dorchester, Silchester, Cirencester and Carmarthen and military amphitheaters at Caerleon, Chester and Tornen-y-Mur.

Agricola seems to have built over 1,300 miles of roads and at least 60 forts, to say nothing of temples, fora and houses, and cultivating the wearing of the toga. Thus, as his shrewd son-in-law, Tacitus, observed, the Britons were seduced into alluring vices: arcades, baths and sumptuous banquets. "In their simplicity they called such novelties 'civilization', when in reality they were part of their enslavement" (937).

Since the very words in the title of this book are Latin--and the term "miles literatus" survived to define a certain type of Englishman over a thousand years later--the Roman occupation of Britain has evoked a continuous stream of commentary, ever since Tacitus recorded the British adopting the Latin language, the toga, hot baths and elaborate dinner parties.

The "enslavement" of the British was security from tribal assaults. Of these tribes, Caesar considered those in Kent--the

Cantiaci--to be the most civilized ("humanissimi"). Those in East Anglia, the Iceni, revolted early, joined by the Trinobantes. There were also the Atrebates in Southampton, the Durotriges and the Dumnonii in the South West, the Catervalloni, spanning modern Britain's Silicon Valley, the seven tribes in Wales (Dubuni, Silures, Demetae, Cornovii, Ofdovias, Gangani and Deceangli) and the Brigantes and Parisi in the North of England. Against those in Scotland, Hadrian later built a wall to keep them out of England.

With a gene-pool enriched by soldiers from Italy, Southern France and Southern Spain in the first century and from North Africa and the Danubean provinces in the second, generations of native British craftsmen supplied the Roman army with help in building the stone barracks, the walls, the statues, and even making beer (twice the cost of that produced in Egypt), duffle coats and woollen rugs. They also mined and made jewels, fabric and pots.

An early schoolmaster--brought from Greece by Agricola to help his policy of Romanization--was Demetrius, whom Plutarch later met at Delphi. Demetrius went to the remoter parts of the British Isles, where he learned of the meteorological and mythological ideas of a community of holy men he found there (937).

Wooden writing tablets, tiles made by the legions and graffiti all indicate the impact of Latin on native speech. H.H. Scullard estimates that some 600 words were absorbed by the Celts to cope with new ideas and concepts. Thus the English "school" and the Welsh "ysgol" was the Roman "schola" (937).

Educationally and culturally, Latin remained the official language of the country until 1650, when it was first abolished, only to be restored in 1660 and then finally abolished in 1733. But its influence on English has been profound (468, 704). Probably the greatest reason for literacy in Latin (evidenced by the graffiti on tiles) was the army, where recruits served for at least twenty years of practical experience in using it and, on discharge, after another five years, received a "diploma" which could be used to obtain a civilian post in the Roman service.

Deciphered by infra-red photography, 200 writing tablets, dating between A.D. 90 and A.D. 125, reveal cursive writing and phonetic spelling unique in the Roman Empire outside Egypt.

Urbanization was one of the greatest contributions of Rome to Britain. The Romans selected sites with such skill that though the original Roman towns disappeared, the sites later nourished other cities and towns, in the building of which discoveries like Roman wooden water pipes have been made. A civic culture nurtured in public buildings constructed between A.D. 70 and A.D. 125 seems to have flourished in London, Lincoln, Gloucester, Cirencester and Verulamium (later St. Albans). Forts, once of wood, were now constructed in stone. Writing tablets housed wax, connected by string or leather, on which writing was scored by a stylus--one end sharp for that purpose, the other flat to erase mistakes--or on thinner wooden tablets by metal pens with split nibs dipped in ink (109).

Anglo-Saxon Mexico. A particularly thick overlay, not of earth and stones, but of earnest tomes of historiographical propaganda, depicted the "Anglo-Saxons" as the real racial stock from which the "true-born Englishman" has sprung. Building their houses of timber

Economic, Scientific and Technological Background 35

on sites not settled by the Romans, these "Anglo-Saxons" became, in the minds of nineteenth century scholars, an entity--which we now know they were not. There were Angles, Saxons, Jutes, Frisians and former Roman mercenaries.

Aptly named from the knife (seax) found in their burial places until the Christians took control of the burial ceremonies, the impact of the Saxons and that of their contemporary invaders of Britain, the Angles, survives in the racist term WASP: a cohesive term arising from the work of nineteenth century historians who canonised the medley of Angles, Saxons, Jutes and Frisians who originally tumbled into Britain as mercenaries for King Vortigern of the Britons as pioneers of "democracy."

Anglo-Saxon as a language still survives in the universities of the United Kingdom--and occupants of chairs are active in justifying their appointments (1129, 794). But it is the 'P' in the modern term WASP that is historically important, since the spread of Christianity from A.D.597 onwards had profound effects, not only in removing instruments of war from the graves but in building churches--some of which are still in use.

Their parish registers have provided the first reliable demographic information on the country, warranting the later appointment of parish clerks, whose "chests" have become the archival treasure houses. Cathedrals and monasteries have also incubated schools and colleges in a civilization as discrete as that of the Aztecs.

The threat posed to this Anglo-Saxon Mexico by the Vikings is revealed by the fivefold increase in the hoards of Anglo-Saxon coins from 870-880.

For these Vikings, driven by polyphiloprogenitivity and land hunger, had been raiding and plundering the Saxons even before the century began (657, 658). Now raids were developing into full scale settlement east of the Roman road known as Watling Street. Thus Lincolnshire, Norfolk and Suffolk have some 303 towns and villages ending in "by" and 106 ending in "thorpe": as authentic a mark of their Danish origins as those ending in "cester," "chester" or "caster" are of their Roman. Their mastering of the "haven finding arts" (possibly exploiting the light-polarising qualities of Iceland Spar) and their manoeuvrable oak ships were economic assets to Eastern England.

Was the Scandinavian settlement as dense as Stenton originally portrayed in his *Anglo-Saxon England* (1943)? Thirty years of research since that time has been reviewed by Gillian Fellows Jensen (570).

Inventories. The first detailed inventory of what were then regarded as the national resources of England made in 1086, twenty years after its conquest by William the Norman, was a tribute to the "shire" system of Anglo-Saxon administration that effected it. 6,000 mills are recorded, 45 vineyards, innumerable sheep and horses--wild and forest mares as well as packhorses--bees and inland and coastal fisheries, and industries like salt-making, the extracting and forging of iron, lead working, quarrying, pottery-making, forestry, game parks and hawking. Most remarkable is that 80 per cent of the land cultivated in 1914 was already under the plough (511). Only 15 per cent of England was woodland (511). But the population-- seemingly of from one and a quarter to two million--had decreased markedly since the Roman times when the figure of four million had been reached. This was not to be reached again until 1300.

Introduced by William the Conqueror, some 322 castles rose in the subsequent centuries, which have recently been identified, located, illustrated and described by Stuart Barton (49). These were inevitable in a society where most of the land had been granted to his supporters in order to defend the borders against the Welsh and the Scots and the rebellious natives, many of whom were now their under-tenants or had been deprived of their land altogether. For even the manors had courts where justice was dispensed for fees.

Names still seem to have been descriptive, occupational or from places of origin: Harvey the Commissioner, Richard the Artificer, Fulchere the Bowman, Fin the Dane, Alfred of Spain or even Ralph the Haunted or Alwyn the Rat (a complete text for a county is obtainable from Phillimore & Co. Ltd., Shopwyke Hall, Chichester, West Sussex).

Following this first detailed inventory, historians living after it was taken seem to regard society as an evolving system for producing and using military power (803). And following the Norman hegemony, French was the only vernacular language permitted in the schools up to 1380.

Latin could have been a bridge between French and English, as the *Dialogue de Scacarrio* (a dialogue between teacher and pupil on the Royal Exchequer), together with the *Tractatus de Legibus et Consuetudinibus* (the first great treatise on the laws of England) were, like the satirical writings of Walter Map or the *Topographica Hibernica* (read aloud to the assembled masters at the emerging University of Oxford in 1184-5), targeted to a new reading public represented by the *Miles Literatus* in the twelfth century (1079) and offered many more examples of work produced for such a public.

M.B. Parkes (801) has warned us that "the extent of literacy among the laity in the middle ages must always be a matter for debate" however. Clanchy has even suggested that members of the peasant class may, by the fourteenth century, have acquired some knowledge of Latin (199). Certainly Lollardy seems to have been not uninfluenced by a literate laity (24).

Population had increased in the years 1086-1193 to 3.4 million and by 1230 to 5.1 million. During the thirteenth century it continued to increase to 6.3 million by 1265 and 7.2 million by 1294, leading to the establishment of some 400 new towns in England and Wales and to the "colonisation of the uplands" and, possibly, Ireland (662).

Crusades. Pressure of population on food supplies necessitated ploughing with "oat-burning engines"--horses, which work twice as fast as oxen and eat twice as much--and hence to further advances in field system crop rotation and crop nutrition.

Feuding over land prompted expeditions to the East, as the notion of "crusade" was an eighteenth century concept. Prompted by the popes to recover the Holy Sepulchre, some nine "crusades" took place between 1097 and 1272. In one of these King Richard I participated. By using mercenaries, Richard I (like King Stephen and Henry II before him) did not call on the knights to do their normal military service but to pay scutage. As a result, King John, Richard's successor, was forced to sign Magna Carta in 1215, which obliged him to send away "all foreign knights and crossbowmen and mercenaries who had crossed over with their arms and horses to harm the land."

Marching eastwards with "the best military equipment in the world at that time" (1128), the crusaders acquired one new weapon: Greek fire, which Lynn White saw as accelerating "chemical artillery," i.e. harnessing expanding pages in a metal tube to create the cannon, which first appeared at Florence in 1326. But it was the longbow--discovered by the English kings in their struggle to subdue the Welsh--which won the Battle of Falkirk against the Scots in 1298 (1093).

One side effect of the crusades was to lead to direct contact with China, for in the year Magna Carta was signed Genghis Khan seized Pekin and eight years later his Mongolians reached the Caspian to pillage a Genoese warehouse. But pillaging was not unique to the Mongols, for the cities of Hamburg and Lubeck formed the Hanseatic League to defend themselves against English pirates. Following their example, the ports of Hastings, Romney, Hythe, Dover and Sandwich called themselves the Cinque Ports and acquired the right to plunder all non-English shipping passing through the English Channel.

Warfare in Normandy also helped disintegrate the barriers between local markets in that cheese, bacon, beans and horseshoes were dispatched by local sheriffs for the Normandy campaign. Entries in the pipe rolls of the central exchequers dealing with local sheriffs contain "dozens of such payments" which represent "a whole series of local economies harnessed to the needs of empire" (612).

Medieval Women. As the result of the Black Death, an English bishop gave permission to laymen to make confession to each other and "if no man is present then even to a woman." This reflects the great surge of research into (and criticism of) the stereotypes of women provided by medieval writers (225, 285, 353, 600, 762, 1120), together with a fresh edition of Eileen Power's classic text (838). This has led to a study of the first English Gynaecological Handbook (904), to semantic revaluations of "woman" and "wife" (812), nuns (542), virginity (148), marriage litigation (494) and even a working bibliography of studies (333).

New perspectives have also emerged on women's role other than as "dependants" of Britain's fighting army (995). Some, once dismissed as witches, are now seen as "women healers" (428, 590, 838, 839). Male hostility to such "healers" as "witches" may have been due to their skills in abortion (617), helping their less knowledgeable "sisters" to avoid annual pregnancies: an economic threat to peasant farmers who needed family, not hired, help on the land, especially after the Black Death (1185). Their emergence as a "fourth estate" (950) can be followed as nuns (162, 542) and other medieval women (29, 179, 225, 353, 333, 409, 600, 615, 848) are seen in the context of chivalry (36, 37, 302, 303), and the accent on virginity (148).

These more realistic assessments of medieval women in religion, marriage and letters (659) have been accompanied by a revaluation of the idea of the "decadence" or "fading" of late medieval culture" (11, 595) (which, however, still lives on, e.g. (44)) by M.H. Keen and C.T. Allmand.

Toe-hold in France. When the Black Death struck England, King Edward III established the Order of the Garter to firm up knightly spirit for the war against France, which had begun twelve years earlier and so far had resulted in the capture of Calais. Though he may have bankrupted the Italian bankers, the Bardi and Peruzzi, his demands catalyzed the formation of syndicates by English merchants to help him by guaranteeing them customs revenues.

One especially wealthy country in such transactions was the great wine country of Guinne (Gascony) and especially the port of Bordeaux (which gave the Crown a rich customs income as well as loaning money). This accounted for the persistency of the English in France--and indeed for the length of the war. As seventy-five per cent of all ships paying customs there were British, this helped the war to continue. Even the Archbishop of York had a house there (1086).

Was this "Hundred Years' War" a "mainspring" (673, 674, 675, 1087, 1088) or a "makeweight" (835, 836) of social change? The debate continues, as it did when Postan and McFarlane were active.

Even as a makeweight it was heavy in its demands on shipping to transport armies to France, on farming for crops to feed and barley to provide beer, on clothing industries for uniforms, on the metallurgical industry for weapons, and even on those who gathered feathers for tufting the arrows--"names such as Bowyer, Arrowsmith and Fletcher symbolised the civilian population's real involvement in war, which was now including all branches of society in its manifold activities (10, 500).

Before the war the King's smith, the King's armourer and the makers of the King's crossbows and crossbow bolts were being paid and housed in the Tower of London. By 1346 gunpowder was being manufactured there and Master Walter the Smith was making "engines of war" for Crecy. By 1370 a sub-department of gunnery was in existence, the distributor (*clericus pro officio gunnorum regis*) seemingly going on to make some in the smithy. Cannon were also being repaired there. A London gunfounder, William Woodward, was making them in numbers between 1382 and 1396. Breastplates were also made--Richard Davy being ordered in 1382 to instruct others in the mystery of making them.

Victorious vernacular. As the first king of England who preferred to conduct business in the vernacular and encourage its use by others, Henry V nevertheless assumed his succession to the French crown. His example was followed by the London brewers deciding to keep their records in English. His son (who lost both Gascony and his own wits) founded Eton College before his death, to prevent the decay of Latin in the kingdom (441, 1158).

Henry VI's death inaugurated the longest period of civil war in English history, resulting in Edward IV obtaining, through the great series of attainder in 1461, involving 113 of his enemies, "the most magnificent accretion of landed revenue in the entire Middle Ages" (197). Edward IV encouraged Caxton to start work as a printer in England (599). Now "every gentleman born to arms and all manner of war captains, soldiers, victuallers and all other" could "have knowledge how they ought to behave them in feats of war and of battles." This was Henry VII's command to William Caxton on 28 January 1489 at Westminster (424) when ordering him to translate Christian de Pisan's *Le Livre des Faits d'Armes et de la Chevalerie*. 300 of Caxton's 800 books between 1491 and 1535 were for grammar

Economic, Scientific and Technological Background

school use. That the second printer in England was a schoolmaster of St. Albans (413) shows that education was growing in importance (787, 788, 789, 790).

Another new activity was foreshadowed before the fifteenth century was out when the first English blast furnace was established in Sussex by a London businessman. For this new method of making iron was spread throughout the Weald and elsewhere by gentry and other entrepreneurs. Over the next century and a half two out of every five such blast furnaces were on the estates of titled peers (206).

It is interesting to note that one of the two recent synoptic histories of the British armies begins in 1485 (51), the other in 1507 (42). The former begins with Henry VII's founding of the Yeomen of the Guard, the latter with Henry VIII's raising of 24,000 shire levies for the invasion of France.

Warfare, demographic decline and the disruption of the European economy by plague in the late Middle Ages and the controversies surrounding them have been well synthesised by John H. Munro (760). The startling fall in the population of England (which seems to have virtually halved between 1300 and 1500 (223)) may not be unrelated to Henry VIII's employment of mercenaries. For Henry VIII "lamented oft that he was constrained to hire foreign aid for want of a competent store of soldiers here at home" (527).

Domestic gunpowder. Since heavy guns began to be cast in England in 1535 by John Owen and experts hired from Europe as "overseers of the science of artillerie ... long bowes, cross bowes and hand gonnes," the Guild of St. George (now the Honourable Artillery Company) was formed in 1537. Two years later the king reviewed 15,000 trained bands-- or London militiamen--led by the artillery. To provide ammunition and further guns in 1543 he established a new post of Lieutenant of the Ordnance. These guns and others were deployed in a line of forts from the Medway to Cornwall (527).

The domestication of gunpowder manufacture by importing Honrick from Germany in 1561 enabled gunpowder mills to be erected, for which the necessary saltpetre was obtained by compulsory searches of farmyards for it and, after 1625, by its importation from India by the East India Company. The Crown bought all the saltpetre it imported after 1664 (190).

The increasing size of the army--48,000 men were sent to Northern France with 20,000 horse--"created a class of large purveyors and victuallers and an officer class to oversee them which presented many opportunities for corruption and quiet plunder" (527). So too the private moneyers profited by the depreciation of the coinage (183). Fears that Catholic Ireland with its great harbour at Cork and its potential as an anchored market garden might be utilised by Catholic Spain and France to encircle Britain led to its destruction. Even contact with Europe by students was also hopefully cut off by the establishment of a third university in the British Isles--Trinity College, Dublin (306, 492).

As an expression of the idea that "Irish" culture needed supplanting, Trinity College, Dublin should be seen in the context of the "plantations" essayed by Henry VIII's two daughters, Queens Mary and Elizabeth, especially the latter, who, from the 1570's onwards, made grants of whatever they could conquer in the two Ulster counties

of Antrim and Down. Soldiers were loaned by the Crown on promise of a share in the land.
   Despite the collapse of this attempt, further ferocious attempts were made in Munster which, by 1598, had attracted some 12,000 men, women and children. Ireland was in fact Britain's first "colony," with the ethnic Irish suffering in the same way as, forty years later, the inhabitants of the North American littoral were to suffer (175). Further "settlements" (by Scotsmen) in the reign of James I (815) and by Cromwell (105) were followed by the frustration of King James II unsuccessfully besieging Londonderry with only one gun--a 24 pounder--capable of breaching the walls.

Plantation problems. Well might Francis Bacon compare "a forraine war" to "the heat of *Exercise*" which "serveth to keep the Body in Health," for he grew to maturity when much was going forward.
   Such was the fear of Spanish reprisals for privateering (of which the Crown took its share) that arms, powder, bullets and matches were ordered in 1570 to be kept in churches. This lasted for at least a century. After 1570 too there was a considerable growth of English inland trade (340, 967). Wood for houses, ashes for soap, together with gunpowder, sabre blades, iron balls, pikehooks, armour and saltpetre, were imported from the Baltic via the Eastland Company chartered in 1579 (349), which had become the largest importer of military hardware by the seventeenth century. An early energy crisis necessitated by the conservation of timber for ships and housing resulted in the increasing use of coal to replace it as a fuel. York Corporation even considered emulating Worcester (313) and managing their own coal mine--but they drew back (797).
   Training--as opposed to mustering--was "virtually unknown before 1573" according to Boynton (111). But the fear of the French prompted the Privy Council to propose it and the arrival of Alva's army in the Low Countries in 1567 accelerated it. Shooting practice was held twice a month. Sir John Norris took a poor view of their readiness twenty years later, but himself failed to co-operate with Drake in the Great Expedition to Portugal in 1589 which followed the defeat of the Armada.
   Evidenced after 1600, not only by the exfoliation of books in English on natural science but by the drive for natural products from the "plantations" by the botanists (132), the interest in science intensified (714). Whether Royalists or Puritans were responsible (759, 1113, 1114, 1115) has been debated since the last bibliography. A pioneer essay in chemical warfare occurred when John Dalbey failed to asphyxiate the garrison of Basinghouse by setting fire to heaps of straw, sulphur and arsenic (1074). For not only was chemistry (562) developing as a independent science but so were marine science (269) and mathematics (563, 444), especially after the establishment of the Royal Society in 1662.

Metallurgy and maps. If the earliest blast furnaces and cannon foundries depended on French technical skill (426), the earliest steel was imported from Germany. Even when German workmen were imported to make steel at Robertsbridge in Sussex, imports were preferred until the cementation process in the seventeenth century was established in the Forest of Dean and later in Birmingham, Sheffield and Newcastle. Shot and ball competed with pewter and guttering, water pipes and glazed windows and paint-making for the products of the English lead mines which, by the time of the wars against Louis XIV, were producing 28,000 tons a year, of which half was exported (94).

From 1683 the War Office emerged under William Blaythwayt (194) and Charles II's army (not the new model) became the real forerunner of the British regular army. Moreover, Tangier and Bombay (which Charles II acquired by marriage) became, with Dunkirk, "the Military School or Seminary to breed up soldiers" (195).

The Board of Ordnance became even more associated with the scientific life of Britain, as growing awareness of the physical environment and the invention of engraving fostered the emergence of scientific and thematic cartography. Maps of ocean currents, magnetic variations and trade winds had all been published by 1686. Early printed world maps from 1472 to 1700 have recently (1983) been published as Volume 9 in the Holland Press Cartographical Series. So has a sixth edition of R.V. Tooley's *Maps and Mapmakers* (1978).

If invasion scares prompted military mapping, private gain had prompted surveys like that of Saxton (966). But the real custodian of the lands, depots and forts required for the defence of the realm and its overseas possessions, was the Board of Ordnance, suppliers of munitions and equipment to both the Army and the Navy. Now it had begun to pay, maintain, educate and organize a corps of its own. Comprised of Artillery and Engineers (whose officers wore Blue Coats) this was independent of the Army (whose officers wore Red Coats) and its administrators who, in the late eighteenth century, had begun a cartographic service of their own.

Victuals and empire. A major victualling contractor for Cromwell's army became, in 1673, the largest shareholder in the East India Company. This became one of the legs of the economic tripod--the other two being the Royal African Company and the Hudson's Bay Company--on which the English thalassocracy of the next century and a half was based (394).

The future founder of Calcutta, Job Charnock, indicated its military importance by building the first of the East India Company's saltpetre warehouses at Patna in 1665. If saltpetre was the homeward ballast of the Company's ships--300 tons a month before 1650--lead came by return from English mines. The King's lease of Bombay--with Tangier part of his Queen's marriage dowry--to the Company in 1668, proved a more satisfactory headquarters than Surat.

As readers of Wilkie Collins' *The Moonstone* and R.F. Delderfield's *God is an Englishman* will know, loot and prize money were the attractions to Englishmen and foreigners to join one of the East India Company's great armies; The Bengal, Madras and Bombay, whose growth from 6,680, 9,000 and 2,500 in 1763 to 64,000, 64,000 and 26,000 in forty-two years reflected the continuous warfare in India. Provisioned by bazaars--a system of mobile markets--and transported by bullocks, the careful administration needed for continuous movement schooled Wellington for his Peninsular campaigns in the early nineteenth century.

So shrewd and powerful did the British officers of these three armies become that they successfully defied the British government's attempt to control them, later becoming a strategic reserve in the establishment of British hegemony in South East Asia. These officers included two of Benedict Arnold's sons (169).

Stimulus or strain? Peter Mathias has recently maintained that economic and social historians "have not given the army and navy ... the attention which their importance deserves" (713, 714, 715). Certainly, as McNeill has argued, the boom in war orders between 1756 and 1815 seemed to stimulate rapid technological change in some industries (692). "Spin-off," suggested Trebilcock (1069, 1066). Negative effects were even noticed in the iron industry by Hyde (551).

Since contemporary economists like Adam Smith, Ricardo and Malthus did not even mention "the industrial revolution"--a retrospectively applied term to the period from 1760 to 1815--McCloskey and North conclude that nothing unusual was going forward (1045) that could not be explained by the efficient specification of property rights secured by the shift in power from Crown to Parliament (777).

Indeed, the verb "contaminate" has been invoked by Mokyr (739, 740) and Savin to describe the economic effects of the French and Napoleonic wars on economic life and development at the time, whilst Williamson asks, "Why was British Growth so slow during the Industrial Revolution?" (1142). And was it worth it anyway (1141)? The debate has been highlighted most recently by Mokyr (740) in a book which will surely become a classic.

Contemporary illumination was forthcoming at this time with the invention of gas light, enabling work by night to take place (341) and signalling the first useful by-product of coal that was to culminate in the unlocking of the hydrocarbon storehouse of dyes, explosives and medicaments in the nineteenth century (448, 449).

Certainly the provision of arms, money and clothing to British allies was both a "stimulus and strain" to the British economy (476) since some £32 millions of British money was spent by some thirty European powers (956). The giving of some £65,830,228 boosted Baring Brothers, Rothschilds and other financiers.

Catalysis of conflict? Further updraught for the furnaces and crucibles of war material was provided by some nine wars up to 1854 in the Far East and the Antipodes, waged with no thought of any embarrassments in the Atlantic. Thus it was that the third Maratha War of 1817-18, the first Burmese War of 1824-6, the Wars with China 1804-42 and Afghanistan 1839-42, the Conquest of Sind in 1843, the Maori War of 1843-8 and the Sikh Wars of 1845-6 and 1848-9 could be waged with confidence.

These factors, coupled with Britain's commanding lead in steam powered technology, enabled ship-building contracts to be obtained from abroad. There was even a trade in wood pre-fabricated houses which emigrants could take to the colonies, iron churches and prefabricated hospitals which Brunel erected in the Crimea (532) where yet another war began in 1854.

The Crimean War produced "many real and lasting results" (1107), like the creation of the War Office (from the old War Department, the Artillery, Engineers and Ordnance, together with the old Treasury responsibility for Supplies and Commissariat). An Army Clothing Factory replaced the colonel's responsibility for organising the supply of clothing for their troops. Small arms were to come from

Enfield. Training camps were established at the Curragh, Colchester and Aldershot. For other economic effects see Anderson (16).

The Crimean War so increased the price of tallow that recourse to African palm oil products (1145) and incidentally cocoa, butter, cotton and rubber (72) was made. The relaxation of the newspaper tax in that war stimulated the exfoliation of newspapers, which depended increasingly on wood-pulp products and paper (860). Officers who managed this overseas trade needed duplicating facilities (849) and typewriters (62, 4).

Perhaps the most drastic case for revising the view that the Crimean War was the catalyst of change has been put forward by Hew Strachan, who has effectively charted the diffusion of the scientific spirit in the army. Accelerated by the efforts of Major T.H. Shadwell Clerke, F.R.S., editor of the *United Service Journal* from 1829 to 1842, and thereafter chairman of the United Service Institution (the latter attended not only by the most distinguished officers of the day but by Henry Wilkinson the gunsmith and N.C.O.'s), it marked the exfoliation of a military press. A former War Office employee started *The Naval and Military Gazette*. A third journal, originally opposed to these two, joined their reforming lobby in 1846 by attacking Wellington as "the greatest enemy perhaps to innovation," advocating the universal adoption of the percussion musket and far more solicitude for the other ranks. Needless to say, Wellington refused to read the *United Service Journal*.

The American Civil War stimulated cotton growing in Egypt whose foreign trade with Britain increased by a factor of 12 between 1860 and 1913.

Irish problems. Having provided Britain with 35 per cent of the total amount of grains, meals and flour consumed between 1810 and 1814 and, sixteen years later, provided 42.2 per cent of the British infantry (1019), Irish folk memories, which had not forgotten the Elizabethan and Cromwellian "settlements," were intensified in the 1840's by the Great Famine and its attendant horrors. The startling decline in the recruitment of the Irish had been noticed by the Commander-in-Chief in 1854. For the availability of the Irish had hitherto obscured the difficulty of raising soldiers from England. Added to emigration and the deterrent effects of press coverage of the Crimea, coupled with the economic boom, one can see why Sir Charles Napier (who had commanded the Northern district when the Chartists had to be contained) should have advocated the Defence of England by Volunteer Corps and Militia.

This volunteer movement began to surge in England from 1859, prompting Friedrich Engels (nicknamed "The General" by his political associates) to write some 39 articles for the *Volunteer Journal for Lancashire and Cheshire* between September 1860 and March 1862. These cast light on the history of the rifle that won praise from the *United Services Gazette* of 23 March 1861 for "its accuracy." Engels' views were endorsed by Sir William Napier, who saw in the volunteers ideal handlers of the rifle. A seven year-old at the time Engels was writing, Henry Spencer Wilkinson became such an enthusiast for military studies that after six years at Owens College, Manchester (later the University), he went on to join the Manchester Volunteers and at Oxford founded a Kriegspiel Club. On returning to Manchester, he founded the Manchester Tactical Society and in the spare time from his practice at the Manchester Bar, translated French and German military texts--one of them being adopted by the War Office.

Jewel in the Crown. But the next development in the "utilization of volunteers" and "militia" was taking place in Canada which, unbelievably, the sugar interests in the 1760s had wanted to barter for Guadaloupe. Happily, shrewder politicians saw Canada as the only countervailing power to the turbulent thirteen American colonies to the South. The third leg in the English thallassocratic tripod--the Hudson's Bay Company--had its profile deliberately kept low by its chairman from 1712 to 1743. Then it rose steadily, with the prestige of the beaver hat. For a century and a quarter the appeal of the beaver bonnets of the successful Swedish cavalrymen of the Thirty Years' War was supplemented by an appreciation of the analgesic properties of the beaver's scent glands, which contain acetylsalicylic acid (now taken in aspirin).

Vaulting still further after the American War of Independence and the Anglo-American War of 1812, Canada's future potential prompted British engineer officers like Major R.C. Smyth and Lieutenant Millington Henry Synge to propose an Atlantic Pacific Railway. Ten year's service in Canada also qualified Lt. Col. MacDougall (Canadian Rifles) to become the first principal of the new Staff College in Britain. Returning to Canada again after service in the Crimea, he was again recalled from being adjutant general of the Canadian Militia to become Chief of the newly established Intelligence Branch of the War Office. To him is credited the idea of linking British regiments of the line with those of the Militia to secure reserves for the regular army. He returned to Canada for the third time in 1878 as Commander-in-Chief of the forces in British North America (841). Experience in training the Canadian Militia in 1865 and 1866 also influenced Wolseley who, twenty years later, used Canadian Militia officers on contract to ferry his forces down the Nile to rescue Gordon at Khartoum.

Economically, the first paper from Canadian wood was made in 1864 and nineteen years later, in the construction of the Canadian Pacific Railway, the fabulous nickel deposits of Sudbury were discovered (318).

So Canada became the destination of the largest number of emigrants (410,000) from Britain between 1843 and 1913 (as opposed to the 301,000 going to Australia and New Zealand or the 90,000 going to South Africa). It also became the repository of the largest percentage of British Overseas Investment in publicly issued securities (13.7) as opposed to 10 per cent in India and Ceylon and 9.8 per cent in South Africa (1161).

Yet another Canadian influence was seen in the concept of a Union of South Africa, which was effected in 1910 (709).

Touring Canada in 1907, Rudyard Kipling remarked that Medicine Hat had "all hell for a basement." He was paying tribute to the gas serendipitously discovered by the Canadian Geological Survey when it was looking for coal and water to power the steam locomotives of the C.P.R. The use of this gas to burn lime to make plaster was the first industrial application of natural gas in Alberta (976). Alberta's deep, rich soil that covered much of its quarter of a million square miles was a real magnet for immigrants, since it could be shipped to sell at Liverpool for 21 cents a bushel.

Burma to World War I. A year after the Canadians inaugurated their first transcontinental railroad, the Manchester Chamber of Commerce, in 1886, advocated the quick establishment of a railway link between China and Burma, indicating that they regarded the third (and successful) 'bite' at occupying Burma in 1885 as affording a commanding back door to that market (50) in which Britain by 1864 enjoyed seven eighths of all trade.

Attempts to market by the front door had led to the first Opium War. The second had raised income tax to the unheard-of level of 10d. in the £. (61). So, since the export of cotton piece goods to China had quadrupled between 1856 and 1880, the Manchester merchants were hoping that it would increase still further, since railways, as Macaulay had said, were the most important achievement since the alphabet and printing. The Germans were already envisaging a large Empire along the line between Berlin and Baghdad, just as Cecil Rhodes was envisaging a British Africa with a Cape to Cairo Railway as its vertebrae. A railway helped Kitchener to capture Khartoum. It was built for him by the French Canadian military engineer, Percy Girouard, who later became Director of Railways for the South African Field Force in the Boer War and a director of the British armaments firm of Armstrong Whitworth (687).

The Boer War was the climax of a century-long British involvement in Africa. From 60 to 80 per cent of capital in the Rand was British and from providing 0.16 per cent of the world's gold in 1886, it was providing 27.55 per cent twelve years later (623). Only the United States attracted more emigrants. British race pride rose to such heights that Lady Randolph Churchill, mother of a young war correspondent who went out to cover the Anglo-Boer War that broke out, founded the *Anglo-Saxon Review* with the motto, "Blood is thicker than Water." Another war correspondent--a former medical orderly in the British Army in South Africa--scooped the peace treaty terms for Reuters and returned to make a second reputation as a writer of mystery stories--Edgar Wallace (1109). The two richest men whose wills had, up to 1912, been proved at Somerset House--Otto Beit (d.1906) and Sir Julius Wernher (d.1912)--had exerted a great influence on the South African War. The former endowed the teaching of imperial history at Oxford and helped found the Imperial College of Science and Technology.

In the war itself, wireless sets were used by Methuen--to supplement the heliograph--and steam traction engines by Buller to pull ox-wagons out of the river. It was a tribute to the effectiveness of state education that many soldiers wrote home. Indeed, troops were billeted in schools. Perhaps this was one reason why the 400,000 troops used there were a vindication of the short-service system, for only three fifths were regulars.

That a Ministry of Science for Britain should have been proposed in 1867 by an Indian army veteran--Colonel Alexander Strange--can now be seen as a response to the long cultivation of science in India (87, 104, 564), a cultivation which even indicated why the Tatars endowed the engineering department at Cambridge University. Moreover, when the Secretary of War complained in the House of Commons on 25 March 1905 that he was "dealing with at least six armies ... the army in India, the Indian Army, the Army at Home, the Militia, the Volunteers, and the great army of those who have left the colours and are now entrenched in the clubs of this city," he was exposing the dilemma facing all ministers of war in the early twentieth century before Haldane's reforms.

For the Commander-in-Chief of the first two armies he mentioned, Lord Kitchener, had, less than a year before, not only forced Lord Curzon, one of the most dazzling Viceroys, to resign, but had elicited from the Cabinet the crushing rebuke that they were "more interested in the economics than the ethics of the situation." Certainly his successor, Lord Minto, who had begun his career as an ensign in the Scots Guards and who had just left the Governor-Generalship of Canada, appointed an Indian to his executive council and two others to his Executive Council and enlarged the provincial legislatures giving Indians majorities so that the moderates were pacified and India gave widespread support when the First World War broke out in 1914 (38, 57, 97, 289).

Grasping the six nettles firmly, R.B. Haldane appointed a General Staff of seventy-two officers to study strategy, which included the first ranker to become a Field Marshal--Sir William Robertson. Disbanding some units, reviving Edward Cardwell's system of linked battalions, organising the territorials and creating officers' training corps, he proved himself, in the words of Earl Haig, "the greatest Secretary for War England has ever had" (294, 421, 464).

Women and Eugenics. As the twentieth century dawned, the campaign for the political emancipation of women bloomed, but its roots had been growing for a long time (367, 685, 686, 904, 907, 929) as women took up activities outside the home.

As operants in the burgeoning communications industry (165, 358, 828), welfare workers (741) and clerical workers (849), they wanted to vote too (850). With new and easier methods of birth control (685, 686, 904) their freedom to work was enhanced and, as life expectancy increased, their potential expanded. Semantics changed (812).

Detailed studies of family structure for the nineteenth century (15) now exist. Is all this to be interpreted as a "revolt" (894)? Perhaps their increasing activity as trade unionists (983) may well justify such a term. Nor have sexual aberrations remained unchronicled (408). More girls and women were rendering their most unobtrusive service as operants of that invaluable instrument of bureaucracy: the typewriter (62). Further bibliographies of their emergence can be consulted (588).

The initiative of a young naval officer's widow led to the formation of a Eugenics Education Society, inspired by Francis Galton (grandson of a Birmingham gun founder and a cousin of Charles Darwin) who, twenty years earlier had employed an army sergeant at the International Health Exhibition of 1885 to measure the height, weight, arm span and breathing power of some nine thousand people-- many of whom were parents--and their grown children (601).

Twenty-seven years later his cousin's son, Major Leonard Darwin of the Royal Engineers (son of the author of the *Origin of Species* (1859)) began in 1911 a seventeen years presidency of the Eugenics Education Society. A year later, 750 people from Britain, Europe and the United States attended the First International Eugenics Conference in London to hear Arthur Balfour deliver the opening address. Among the sponsoring vice-presidents were Winston Churchill, the Bishop of Ripon and the former President of Harvard, C.W. Eliot. "The organic betterment of the race through wise application of the laws of heredity," as the new eleventh edition of the *Encyclopedia Britannica* put it in 1911, seemed feasible.

Though there was no article on "Militarism" in the 1911 edition of the *Encyclopedia Britannica*, there was one on "Arbitration, International" by Montague Crackenthorpe of the Eugenics Society. He concluded that there was only faint hope of such arbitration whilst "commercial jealousy" and "imperialist ambitions" were supported by the doctrine of the survival of the fittest. And that doctrine was firmed up by the biosocialism of the Eugenics Society.

What went wrong? So what Spengler called a *Buch-und-Lesen Kultur* emerged as enterprising merchants emancipated themselves from clerical scribes. This was personified in the *miles literatus* or latinate knight (1079). Nor did peasants necessarily lack Latin (199). Literacy (and learning) in York was early (792) and in the west of England.

Indeed, schools (788) and schoolmasters (790) in the Middle Ages seem to have flourished side by side with universities (180) with the example of the aristocracy and the kings before them (339, 789). So much so, in fact, that the so-called Reformation and the Henrican and Elizabeth grammar schools are now seen as a "tardy response" to losses sustained by these medieval foundations. Such has been the unearthing of evidence for the growth of schools in the Middle Ages that one historian has posed the question, "Did the growth in education prepare the way for the Reformation?" (745). But not all research conducted between 1970 and 1985 warrants such a question being put, as it has also been argued that 90 per cent of Englishmen and 99 per cent of Englishwomen were illiterate at the beginning of the sixteenth century (235, 236). For the varieties and consequences of medieval literacy see (51) and (274).

A similar debate has flourished between 1970 and 1985 over the interaction between education and industry during the Industrial Revolution. That industry would be the prime expansive force seems obvious (1123, 1124, 1125) but evidence of initial decline or nongrowth has also been discerned (337, 631, 632). But there is little doubt that the twin commercial and industrial reagents of literacy and education were active in promoting institutional growth of schools and colleges (198) and other institutions (74, 184, 202), some of which have disappeared (401).

Though latent and specific social Darwinism was by some recognised as inevitable (33, 238, 579), nevertheless its manifestation in riots and unrest (15, 53, 125, 137, 208, 296, 413, 415, 490, 540, 541, 568, 575, 606, 638, 722, 854, 1038, 1050, 1083) necessitated agencies of social control (251) other than the army, the Church and the schools, like purity movements (131, 148), local administration (571) and sports and recreation (556, 559, 698, 531, 1104), the press (321) propaganda (695) and welfare.

But perhaps the most unusual explanation of the familiar social Darwinist thesis to emerge since the last bibliography is that propounded by the psychohistorians: i.e., that groups attached to one another and their leaders by umbilical cords fight for life against "poisoning placentas" by cutting their way out of the birth canal.

This thesis that war is a "birth experience" has now a bibliography of its own (277).

BIBLIOGRAPHY

1. Addington, Larry H. *The Patterns of War since the 18th Century.* Bloomington: Indiana University Press, 1984.
2. Adkins, Lesley and Adkins, Roy A. *A Handbook of British Archaeology.* London: Macmillan, Papermac, 1983.
3. Adler, Dorothy R. *British Investment in American Railways 1834-1898.* Charlottesville: University Press of Virginia, 1970.
4. Adler, Michael. *The Writing Machine. The History of the Typewriter.* London: Allen & Unwin, 1973.
5. Alcock, Leslie. *Arthur's Britain. History and Archaeology A.D. 367-634.* Allen Lane, The Penguin Press, 1971.
6. Aldcroft, Derek H. *The Development of British Industry and Foreign Competition 1875-1914.* London: George Allen & Unwin, 1968.
7. ――――. "The Economy, Management and Foreign Competition" in Roderick, Gordon, and Stephens, Michael (eds.) *Where Did We Go Wrong?* Lewes: The Falmer Press, 1981.
8. ――――. "Investment in and utilisation of manpower: Great Britain and her rivals 1870-1914" in Ratcliffe, B.M. (ed.) *Great Britain and Her World 1870-1914.* Manchester: Manchester University Press, 1975.
9. ――――. "McCloskey on Victorian Growth: A Commentary," *Economic History Review*, 27 (1974).
10. Allmand, C.T. (ed.). *Society at War. The Experience of England and France during the Hundred Years War.* Edinburgh: Oliver & Boyd, 1973.
11. ―――― (ed.). *War, Literature and Politics in the Late Middle Ages.* Liverpool: Liverpool University Press, 1976.
12. Allwood, John. *Great Exhibitions.* London: Studio Vista, 1977.
13. Almond, J.K. "Iron and Steel" in Roderick, Gordon and Stephens, Michael (eds.) *Where Did We Go Wrong?* Lewes: The Falmer Press, 1981.
14. Altschul, Michael. *Anglo-Norman England 1066-1154.* Cambridge: Cambridge University Press, 1969.
15. Anderson, M. *Family Structure in Nineteenth Century Lancashire.* Cambridge: Cambridge University Press, 1971.
16. Anderson, O. "The Growth of Christian Militarism in mid-Victorian Britain," *English Historical Review*, LXXXVI (1971).
17. Andriette, Eugene A. *Devon and Exeter in the Civil War.* Newton Abbot: David & Charles, 1971.
18. Anstey, Roger. *The Atlantic Slave Trade and British Abolition 1760-1810.* London: Macmillan, 1975.
19. Appleby, Joyce. *Economic Thought and Ideology in Seventeenth Century England.* Princeton, N.J.: Princeton University Press, 1978.
20. Armytage, W.H.G. "Battles for the Best: Some Educational Aspects of the Welfare-Warfare State in England" in Nash,

Paul (ed.) *The Educational Uses of the Past.* New York: Random House, 1970.
21. ─────. "Population and the Bio-Social Background" in Roderick, Gordon and Stephens, Michael (eds.) *Where Did We Go Wrong?* Lewes: The Falmer Press, 1981.
22. Arnold, Guy. *Held Fast for England: G.A. Henty, Imperialist Boys' Writer.* London: Hamish Hamilton, 1980.
23. Aston, Margaret. "Lollard Women Priests?," *Journal of Ecclesiastical History* (1981).
24. ─────. "Lollardy and Literacy," *History*, 62 (1977).
25. Aston, Michael and Rowley, Trevor. *Landscape Archaeology: An Introduction to Fieldwork Techniques on Post-Roman Landscapes.* Newton Abbot: David & Charles, 1974.
26. Bagwell, Philip S. and Mingay, G.F. *Britain and America 1850-1939.* London: Routledge & Kegan Paul, 1970.
27. Bailey, De Witt and Nie, Douglas A. *English Gunmakers: The Birmingham and Provincial Gun Trade in the 18th and 19th Centuries.* London: Arms and Armour Press, 1978.
28. Bailey, Peter. *Leisure and Class in Victorian England: Rational Recreation and the Contest for Control 1830-1885.* London: Routledge & Kegan Paul, 1978.
29. Baker, D. (ed.). *Medieval Women: Dedicated and Presented to Professor Rosalind M.T. Hill on the Occasion of her Seventieth Birthday.* Oxford, 1978.
30. Baker, W.J. *A History of the Marconi Company.* London: Methuen, 1970.
31. Baldwin, Mark and Burton, Antony (eds.). *Canals: A New Look. Essays in Honour of Charles Hadfield.* Chichester: Phillimore, 1984.
32. Ballhachet, Kenneth. *Race, Sex and Class under the Raj: Imperial Attitudes and Policies and their Critics 1793-1925.* London: Weidenfeld & Nicolson, 1980.
33. Bannister, Robert C. *Social Darwinism: Science and Myth in Anglo-American Social Thought.* Philadelphia: Temple University Press, 1979.
34. Barber, Malcolm. *The Trail of the Templars.* Cambridge: Cambridge University Press, 1978.
35. Barber, Richard. *The Figure of Arthur.* London: D.S. Brewer, 1976.
36. ─────. *The Knight and Chivalry.* London: Boydell Press, 1974.
37. ─────. *The Reign of Chivalry.* London: St. Martins Press, 1980.
38. Barclay, Glen St. John. *The Empire is Marching. A Study in the Military Effort of the British Empire 1800-1945.* London: Weidenfeld & Nicolson, 1976.
39. Barclay, M.W. and Hanson, R.P.C. (eds.). *Christianity in Britain 300-700.* Leicester: Leicester University Press, 1968.
40. Barlow, Frank. *The Norman Conquest and Beyond.* Hambledon Press, 1983.
41. Barnes, Barry, *Interests and the Growth of Knowledge.* London: Routledge & Kegan Paul, 1977.
42. Barnett, Correlli. *The Audit of War. The Illusion and Reality of Britain as a Great Nation.* London: Macmillan, 1986.

43. ―――――. *The Collapse of British Power*. London, 1972.
44. Barnie, John. *War in Medieval Society. Society Values and the Hundred Years War 1337-1399*. London: Weidenfeld & Nicolson, 1974.
45. Barrow, G.L. *The Emergence of the Irish Banking System 1820-1845*. Dublin: Gill & Macmillan, 1975.
46. Barter, Sarah. "The Board of Ordnance" in Charlton, John (ed.) *The Tower of London: Its Buildings and Institutions*. London: H.M.S.O., 1978.
47. Barthorpe, Michael. *The Armies of Britain 1485-1980*. London: National Army Museum, n.d.
48. Barlett, C.J. *Great Britain and her Sea Power 1818-1853*. Oxford: Clarendon Press, 1963.
49. Barton, Stuart. *Castles in Britain*. Worthing, Sussex: Lyle Publications, 1973.
50. Baumgart, Winfried. *Imperialism: The Idea and Reality of British and French Colonial Expansion*. Trans. by the Author with the Assistance of Ben V. Mast. Oxford: Oxford University Press, 1982.
51. Bauml, F.H. "Varieties and Consequences of Medieval Literacy and Illiteracy," *Speculum*, 55 (1980).
52. Baxter, Ian A. *A Brief Guide to Biographical Sources*. London: India Office, 1979.
53. Baxter, J.L. and Donnelly, E.K. "The Revolutionary Underground in the West Riding: Myth or Reality?" *Past and Present* (1974).
54. Bayley, C.C. *Mercenaries for the Crimea: The German, Swiss and Italian Legions in British Service 1854-1856*. Montreal: McGill-Queen's University Press, 1977.
55. Bayliss, Gwyn M. *Bibliographic Guide to Two World Wars*. London: Bowker, 1977.
56. Beals, C.S. (ed.). *Science, History and Hudson Bay*. vols. 1 & 2. Ottawa: Department of Energy, Mines and Resources, 1968.
57. Beaumont, Roger. *Sword of the Raj: The British Army in India 1747-1947*. Indianapolis: Bobbs-Merrill, 1977.
58. Beaver, Daniel R. "Cultural Change, Technological Development and the Conduct of War in the Seventeenth Century" in Weigley, Russell F. (ed.) *New Dimensions in Military History*. San Rafael: Presidio Press, 1975.
59. Beckett, James Camlin. *Confrontations: Studies in Irish History*, London: Faber & Faber, 1973.
60. Bédarida, François (trans. A.S. Foster). *A Social History of England*. London: Methuen, 1979.
61. Beeching, Jack. *The Chinese Opium Wars*. London: Hutchinson, 1975.
62. Beeching, William A. *Century of the Typewriter*. London: Heinemann, 1974.
63. Beeler, John H. *Warfare in Feudal Europe 730-1200*. Ithaca, New York: Cornell University Press, 1971.
64. Bell, Susan Groag. "Medieval Book Lovers: Arbiters of Lay Piety and Ambassadors of Culture," *Signs* 7 (1982).
65. Benson, Robert L. et al. (eds.). *Renaissance and Renewal in the Twelfth Century*. Cambridge: Harvard University Press, 1982.

66. Beresford, Maurice and Hurst, John G. (eds.). *Deserted Medieval Villages*. Lutterworth Press, 1971.
67. Berg, Maxine. *The Age of Manufactures: Industry, Innovation and Work in Britain 1700-1802*. London: Fontana, 1985.
68. ―――――. *The Machinery Question and the Making of Political Economy 1815-1848*. Cambridge: Cambridge University Press, 1980.
69. Berger, Carl. *The Sense of Power: Studies in the Ideas of Canadian Imperialism, 1867-1914*. Toronto: University of Toronto Press, 1970.
70. Berghahn, V.R. *Militarism: The History of an International Debate, 1861-1979*. Cambridge: Cambridge University Press, 1984.
71. Berman, Morris. *Social Change and Scientific Organization: The Royal Institution 1799-1844*. London: Heinemann Educational, 1978.
72. Berry, Sara S. *Cocoa, Custom and Socio-Economic Change in rural Western Nigeria*. Oxford: Oxford University Press, 1975.
73. Berton, Pierre. *The Great Railway: The National Dream*. Toronto: McClelland & Stuart, 1970.
74. Best, Geoffrey. *Humanity in Warfare: The Modern History of the International Law of Armed Conflicts*. London: Weidenfeld & Nicolson, 1980.
75. ―――――. *Mid-Victorian Britain*. London: Weidenfeld & Nicolson, 1971.
76. ―――――. "Militarism and the Victorian Public School" in Simon, B. and Bradley, I. (eds.) *The Victorian Public School*. Dublin: Gill & Macmillan, 1975, pp. 129-146.
77. ―――――. *War and Society in Revolutionary Europe, 1770-1870*. Leicester: Leicester University Press and Fontana Paperbacks, 1982.
78. Best, Geoffrey and Wheatcroft, Andrew (eds.). *War, Economy and the Military Mind*. London: Croom Helm, 1976.
79. Betts, Raymond F. *The False Dawn: European Imperialism in the Nineteenth Century*. Minneapolis: University of Minnesota Press, 1976.
80. Biddiss, Michael D. "Racial Ideas and Politics of Prejudice," *The Historical Journal*, 15 (1972).
81. Biddle, M. "Excavations at Winchester 1971. Tenth and Final Interim Report," *The Antiques Journal*, LV.
82. ―――――. "Planned Towns before 1066" in Barley, M.W. (ed.) *The Evolution of Towns*. Council for British Archaeology Urban Research Committee, Working Party on Town Plans and Topography, Leamington Spa, 1974.
83. Bienefeld, M.A. *Working Hours in British Industry: An Economic History*. London: Weidenfeld & Nicolson, 1972.
84. Birley, A.R. *The People of Roman Britain*. London: B.T. Batsford, 1979.
85. Birley, Robin. *Vindolanda: A Roman Frontier Post on Hadrian's Wall*. London: Thames & Hudson, 1977.
86. Bisson, T.N. "The Military Origins of Medieval Representation," *American Historical Review*, 71 (1966).
87. Biswas, A.K. *Science in India*. Calcutta: Firma, K.L. Mukhopodhyay, 1969.

88. Blackey, Robert. *Revolutions and Revolutionists: A Comprehensive Guide to the Literature.* Santa Barbara, California: ABC-CLIO, 1982.
89. Blackmore, H.L. *The Armouries of the Tower of London.* London: Ordnance, 1976.
90. Blainey, Geoffrey. *The Causes of War.* New York: Free Press, 1973.
91. Blake, John W. *West Africa: Quest for God and Gold 1454-1578.* London: Curzon Press, 1977.
92. Blakiston, Georgiana. *Woburn and the Russells.* London: Constable, 1980.
93. Blanchard, I. "Population Change, Enclosure and the Early Tudor Economy," *Economic History Review,* 23 (1970).
94. ─────. "English Lead and the International Bullion Crisis of the 1550's." in Coleman, D.G. and John, A.H. (eds.) *Trade, Government and Economy in Pre-Industrial England.* 1976.
95. Boahen, A.A. (ed.). *Africa under Foreign Domination 1880-1935.* London: Heinemann, 1985.
96. Bolt, Christine and Drescher, Seymour. *Anti-Slavery, Religion and Reform.* Folkestone: William Dawson, 1980.
97. Bond, B.J. *The Victorian Army and the Staff College, 1858-1914.* London: Eyre Methuen, 1972.
98. ───── (ed.). *Victorian Military Campaigns.* London: Hutchinson, 1967.
99. ─────. *War and Society in Europe 1870-1970.* Leicester: Leicester University Press, 1983.
100. ───── and Roy, Ian (eds.). *War and Society: A Handbook of Military History.* vol. 1, London: Croom Helm, 1975.
101. Bonser, Wilfred (ed.). *A Prehistoric Bibliography.* extended and edited by June Troy. Oxford: Basil Blackwell, 1976.
102. Booth, A. "Food Riots in North West England, 1790-1801," *Past and Present* (1977).
103. Bornstein, D. "Military Manuals in Fifteenth Century England," *Medieval Studies,* 37 (1975).
104. Bose, D.M., Sen, S.H. and Subbarayappa, B.V. (eds.). *A Concise History of Science in India.* New Delhi: Indian National Science Academy, 1971.
105. Bottigheimer, Karl S. *English Money and Irish Land: The "Adventurers" in the Cromwellian Settlement of Ireland.* Oxford: Oxford University Press, 1971.
106. Bowen, Daniel. *An Encyclopedia of War Machines.* London: Octopus Books, 1984.
107. Bowen, Desmond. *The Protestant Crusade in Ireland, 800-1870,* Dublin: Gill & Macmillan, 1978.
108. Bowen, H.C. and Fowler, P.J. *Early Land Allotment in the British Isles,* London: British Archaeological Reports, 1978.
109. Bowman, A.K. *Roman Writing Tablets from Vindolanda,* London: British Museum Publications, 1983.
110. Boyce, Gray Cowan (ed.). *Literature of Medieval History, 1930-1975;* A Supplement to Paetow's *Guide to the Study of Medieval History,* 5 vols., New York: Kraus International Publications, 1981.

111. Boynton, Lindsay. *The Elizabethan Militia, 1558-1638*, Newton Abbot: David & Charles, 1971.
112. Bradby, David et al. (eds.). *Performance and Politics in Popular Drama: Theatre, Film and Television, 1800-1976*, Cambridge University Press, 1980.
113. Bradley, Richard. *The Social Foundations of Prehistoric Britain*, London: Longman, 1984.
114. Branigan, Keith. *Roman Britain: Life in an Imperial Province*, London: The Reader's Digest Association Ltd., 1980.
115. ―――――. *The Roman Villa in South West England*, Bradford-on-Avon: Moonraker Press, 1977.
116. ―――――― and Fowler, Peter Jon. *The Roman West Country: Classical Culture and Celtic Society*, Newton Abbot: David & Charles, 1976.
117. Brantly, J.E., *History of Oil Well Drilling*, Houston: Texas Gulf Publishing Company, 1971.
118. Bratton, J.S. *The Victorian Popular Ballad*, London: Macmillan, 1975.
119. ―――――. "Theatre of War: The Crimea on the London Stage, 1854-5" in Bradby, David et al. (eds.) *ut supra*.
120. Breeze, David J. *The Northern Frontiers of Roman Britain*, New York: St. Martin's Press, 1982.
121. ―――――. *The Northern Frontiers of Rome*. London: B.T. Batsford, 1982.
122. ―――――― and Dobson, Brian. *Hadrian's Wall*, 2nd ed., Harmondsworth: Penguin, 1978.
123. Brereton, J.M. *The Horse in War*, Newton Abbot: David & Charles, 1976.
124. Brewer, Anthony. *Marxist Theories of Imperialism: A Critical Survey*, London: Routledge & Kegan Paul, 1980.
125. Brewer, J. and Styles, J. *An Ungovernable People: The English and their Law in the Seventeenth and Eighteenth Centuries*, London: Hutchinson, 1980.
126. Bridbury, A.R. "Before the Black Death," *Economic History Review*, 2nd Series, XXX, no. 3, (1977).
127. Briggs, A. *The Human Aggregate*, vol. I, pt. 1, vol. II, pt. 2, Brighton: Harvester Press, 1984.
128. Bristow, Edward J. *Vice and Vigilance: Purity Movements in Britain since 1700*, Totowa, New Jersey: Rowman & Littlefield, n.d.
129. Britton, Edward. *The Community of the Village*, Toronto: Macmillan of Canada, 1977.
130. Brock, P. *Pacifism in Europe to 1914*, Princeton University Press, 1972.
131. Brock, W.H. "The Spectrum of Scientific Patronage" in Turner, G.L.E. (ed.), *Patronage of Science in the Nineteenth Century*, Leyden: Noordhoff International, 1976.
132. Brockway, Lucile H. *Science and Colonial Expansion: the Role of the British Royal Botanic Gardens* (Studies in Social Discontinuity), New York: Academic Press, 1979.
133. Brodie, Bernard. "Technological Change, Strategic Doctrine and Political Outcome" in Knorr, Klaus (ed.), *Historical Dimensions of National Security Problems*, Lawrence: University Press of Kansas, 1976.

134. ———— and Brodie, Fawn M. *From Crossbow to H-Bomb*, Bloomington: Indiana University Press, 1973.
135. Brook, Fred and Allbutt, Martin. *The Shropshire Lead Mines*, Buxton: Moorland Publishing Company, 1973.
136. Brown, Elizabeth A.R. "Gascon Subsidies and the Finances of the English Dominions, 1315-1324," *Studies in Medieval and Renaissance History*, vol. VIII, Lincoln: University of Nebraska Press, 1971.
137. Brown, K.D. (ed.). *Essays in Anti-Labour History: Responses to the Rise of Labour in Britain*, Hamden, Conn.: Archon Books, 1984.
138. Brown, Lucy. *Victorian News and Newspapers*, Oxford University Press, 1985.
139. Brown, Michael B. "A Critique of Marxist Theories of Imperialism" in Owen, Roger and Sutcliffe, Bob (eds.), *Studies in the Theory of Imperialism*, London, 1972.
140. Brown, R.A. (ed.). *Battle Conference on Anglo-Norman Studies: Proceedings*, vol. i (1978), vol. ii (1979), vol. iii (1980), vol. iv (1981), vol. v (1983), vol. vi (1983), Woodbridge, Suffolk: Boydell Press, 1978-1983.
141. ————. *English Castles*, London, B.T. Batsford, 1976.
142. Bruce, Anthony. *The Purchase System in the British Army, 1660-1871*. London: Royal Historical Society, 1980.
143. Bruce, George. *The Burma Wars, 1824-1886*, London: Hart-Davis, MacGibbon, 1973.
144. Bruce, J. Collingwood. *Handbook to the Roman Wall*, 13th edition edited and enlarged by Charles Daniels, Newcastle-upon-Tyne: Harold Hill & Son, 1978.
145. Brunt, P.A. (ed.). *The Roman Economy: Studies in Ancient Economic and Administrative History* by A.H.M. Jones, Oxford: Basil Blackwell, 1974.
146. Buck, Mark. *Politics, Finance and the Church in the Reign of Edward II, Walter Stapledon, Treasurer of England*, Cambridge University Press, 1982.
147. Buckland, P. *Irish Unionism, 1885-1922: A Documentary History*, New York: Barnes & Noble, 1973.
148. Bugge, J. *Virginitas: An Essay on the History of a Medieval Ideal*, The Hague, 1975.
149. Bull, Edith. *Life and Thought in the Cotswolds*, London: J.M. Dent, 1973.
150. Bullough, D.A. "Games People Played: Drama and Ritual as Propaganda in Medieval Europe," *T.R.H.S.*, 5th series, XXVI (1974).
151. Bumke, Joachim (trans. W.T.H. and Erika Jackson), *The Concept of Knighthood in the Middle Ages*, New York: A.M.S. Press Inc., 1982.
152. Burgess, Keith. *The Challenge of Labour: Shaping British Society, 1850-1950*, London: Croom Helm, 1970.
153. ————. *The Origins of British Industrial Relations*, London: Croom Helm, 1975.
154. Burke, Peter. *Popular Culture in Early Modern Europe*, London: Temple Smith, 1978.
155. Burl, A. *Prehistoric Stone Circles*, Princes Risborough: Shire Publications, 1979.

156. ———. *The Stone Circles of the British Isles*, New Haven: Yale University Press, 1976.
157. Burnett, J. *A Social History of Housing, 1815-1970*, Newton Abbot: David & Charles, 1978.
158. Burroughs, Peter. "The Human Cost of Imperial Defence in the Early Victorian Age," *Victorian Studies*, XXIV (1980).
159. ———. "The Ordnance Department and Colonial Defence, 1821-1855," *Journal of Imperial and Commonwealth History*, vol. x (1982).
160. Burrow, John W. *Evolution and Society: A Study in Victorian Social Theories*, Cambridge University Press, 1966.
161. ———. *A Liberal Descent: Victorian Historians and the English Past*, Cambridge University Press, 1981.
162. Burton, J.E. *The Yorkshire Nunneries in the Twelfth and Thirteenth Centuries*, Borthwick Papers 56, York, 1979.
163. Butler, Richard Morley (ed.). *Soldier and Civilian in Roman Yorkshire*, Leicester University Press, 1971.
164. Buxton, Neil. "The Coal Industry" in Roderick, Gordon and Stephens, Michael (eds.), *Where Did We Go Wrong?*, Lewes: The Falmer Press, 1981.
165. Byatt, I.C.R. *The British Electrical Industry 1875-1914*, Oxford: Clarendon Press, 1979.
166. Bythell, Duncan. *The Sweated Trades: Outwork in Nineteenth Century Britain*, New York: St. Martin's Press, 1978.
167. Cafrey, Kate. *The Twilight's Last Gleaming: The British against America, 1812-1815*, New York: Stein & Day, 1977.
168. Cain, Peter J. *Economic Foundations of British Overseas Expansion, 1815-1914*, London, 1980.
169. Callahan, Raymond. *The East India Company and Army Reform, 1783-1798*, Cambridge, Mass.: Harvard University Press, 1973.
170. *Cambridge Economic History of Europe*, vol. VII, part 1 (1979).
171. Cameron, Kenneth. *Scandinavian Settlement in the Territory of the Five Boroughs: The Place Name Evidence*, University of Nottingham Press, 1965.
172. Campbell, R.H. *The Rise and Fall of Scottish Industry*, Edinburgh: John Donald, 1980.
173. Cannizzo, Cindy (ed.). *The Gun Merchants: Politics and Policies of the Major Arms Suppliers*, Oxford: Pergamon, 1980.
174. Cannon, Susan Faye, *Science in Culture: The Early Victorian Period*, New York: Dawson and Science History Publications, 1978.
175. Canny, Nicholas P. *The Elizabethan Conquest of Ireland: A Pattern Established, 1565-76*, New York: Barnes & Noble, 1976.
176. Capp, Bernard. *Astrology and the Popular Press: English Almanacs, 1500-1800*, London: Faber & Faber, 1979.
177. Cappon, Lester Jesse. "Geographers and Map-Makers British and American from about 1751 to 1785," *Proceedings of the American Antiquarian Society*, October 1971.
178. Cardwell, D.S.L. *Turing Points in Western Technology: A Study of Technology, Science and History*, New York: Neale Watson Academic Publishers, 1972.
179. Casey, Kathleen. "Women in Norman and Plantagenet England" in Kanner, Barbara (ed.), *The Women of England from Anglo-*

Saxon Times to the Present: Interpretative Bibliographical Essays, Hamden, Conn.: Archon Books, 1979.
180. Catto, J.I. (ed.). The History of the University of Oxford, vol. 1: The Early Oxford Schools, Oxford: Clarendon Press, 1984.
181. Cawood, J. "Terrestrial Magnetism and the Development of International Collaboration in the Early Nineteenth Century," Annals of Science, 34 (1977).
182. Chalklin, Christopher and Havinden, Michael. Rural Change and Urban Growth, 1500-1800, London: Longman, 1974.
183. Challis, C.E. The Tudor Coinage, New York: Barnes & Noble, 1978.
184. Chaloner, William Henry. The Movement for the Extension of Owen's College, 1865-1873, Manchester University Press, 1973.
185. Chamberlain, M.E. Decolonization: The Fall of European Empires, Historical Association Studies, Blackwell, 1985.
186. Chambers, J.D. Population, Economy and Society in Pre-Industrial England, Oxford University Press, 1972.
187. Chandler, David. The Art of Warfare in the Age of Marlborough, London: Batsford, 1976.
188. Chandos, John. Boys Together: English Public Schools, 1800-1860, Oxford University Press Paperback, 1982.
189. Chapman, Stanley. "The Textile Industries" in Roderick, Gordon and Stephens, Michael (eds.), Where Did We Go Wrong?, Lewes: The Falmer Press, 1981.
190. Chaudhuri, K.N. The Trading World of Asia and the East India Company, 1600-1760, Cambridge University Press, 1978.
191. Checkland, Sydney George. The Gladstones: A Family Biography, 1764-1851, Cambridge University Press, 1971.
192. ———. Scottish Banking: A History, 1695-1973, London: Collins, 1975.
193. Chesneaux, Jean, Bastid, Marianne and Bergere, Marie-Claire. China from the Opium Wars to the 1911 Revolution, New York: Pantheon, 1976.
194. Childs, John. The Army of Charles II, London: Routlege & Kegan Paul, 1976.
195. ———. Armies and Warfare in Europe, 1648-1789, Manchester University Press, 1975.
196. Chippendale, Christopher. "Stonehenge Astronomy: The Anatomy of a Modern Myth," Archaeology, vol. 39, no. 1 (Jan./Feb. 1986).
197. Chrimes, S.B., Ross, C.D. and Griffiths, R.A. (eds.). Fifteenth Century England, 1399-1509: Studies in Politics and Society, Manchester University Press, 1972.
198. Church, R.A. (ed.). The Dynamics of Victorian Business: Problems and Perspective to the 1970's, London: Allen & Unwin, 1980.
199. Clanchy, Michael T. From Memory to Written Record: England, 1066-1307, Cambridge, Mass., 1979.
200. Clark, Colin. Population Growth and Land Use, 2nd ed. London: Macmillan, 1967.
201. Clark, Peter. English Provincial Society from the Reformation to the Revolution: Religion, Politics and Society in Kent 1500-1640, Brighton: Harvester Press, 1977.

202. Clarke, I.F. *Pattern of Expectation, 1644-2001*, New York: Basic Books, 1979.
203. ――――. *Tale of the Future*, Library Association, 3rd edn., 1978.
204. Clarke, P.F. *Lancashire and the New Liberalism*, Cambridge University Press, 1971.
205. Clay, C. *Public Finance and Private Wealth: The Career of Sir Stephen Fox, 1627-1716*, Oxford University Press, 1978.
206. Clay, C.G.A. *Economic Expansion and Social Change: England, 1500-1700*, 2 vols. Cambridge University Press, 1984.
207. Clayton, Peter (ed.). *A Companion to Roman Britain*, Oxford: Phaidon, 1980.
208. Clegg, H.A., Fox, A. and Thompson, A.F. (eds.). *A History of British Trade Unions since 1889*, vol I: *To 1911*, vol. II: *1911-1933*, Oxford University Press, 1964 and 1978.
209. Clough, Cecil H. *Profession, Vocation and Culture in Later Medieval England*, University of Liverpool Press, 1982.
210. Coe, Brian. *Cameras from Daguerreotypes to Instant Pictures*, New York: Crown Publishers, 1978.
211. Cohen, Stephen P. *The Indian Army: Its Contribution to the Development of a Nation*, Berkeley: University of California Press, 1971.
212. Coleman, D.C. and John, A.H. (eds.). *Trade, Government and the Economy in Pre-Industrial England. Essays Presented to F.J. Fisher*, London: Weidenfeld & Nicolson, 1976.
213. ―――― and Mathias, Peter (eds.). *Enterprise and History. Essays in Honour of Charles Wilson*, Cambridge University Press, 1984.
214. Coleman, Janet. *Medieval Readers and Writers, 1350-1400*, New York: Columbia University Press, 1981.
215. Coles, J.M., Heals, V.E. and Orme, B.J. "The Use and Character of Wood in Prehistoric Britain and Ireland," *Proceedings of the Prehistory Society*, 44 (1978).
216. Collier, Basil. *Arms and the Men: The Arms Trade and Governments*, London: Hamish Hamilton, 1980.
217. Collingwood, R.G. and Richmond, Sir Ian. *The Archaeology of Roman Britain*, London: Methuen, 1969.
218. Connolly, Peter. *The Roman Army*, Macdonald Educ., 1975.
219. Contamine, Philippe (trans. Michael Jones), *War in the Middle Ages*, Oxford: Basil Blackwell, 1984.
220. Cooling, Benjamin Franklin (ed.). *War, Business and American Society: Historical Perspectives on the Military-Industrial Complex*, Port Washington, New York: Kennikat Press, 1977.
221. ――――. *War, Business and World Military-Industrial Complexes*, Port Washington, New York: Kennikat Press, 1982.
222. Cornwall, John. *Modern Capitalism: Its Growth and Transformation*, London: Martin Robertson, 1977.
223. ――――. "English Population in the Early Sixteenth Century," *Economic History Review*, second series, XXIII, no. 1 (1970).
224. Corran, H.S. *A History of Brewing*, Newton Abbot: David & Charles, 1975.

225. Corrigan, M. "Chaucer's Failure with Women: The Inadequacy of Criseyde," *Western Humanities Review* 23 (1969).
226. Corvisier, André. *Armies and Society in Europe, 1494-1789*, Bloomington: Indiana University Press, 1976 (trans. 1979 by Abigail T. Siddall).
227. Cottrell, P.L. *British Overseas Investment in the Nineteenth Century*, London: Macmillan, for the Economic History Society, 1975.
228. ―――. *Industrial Finance 1830-1914: The Finance and Organization of the English Manufacturing Industry*, London: Methuen, 1980.
229. ――― and Anderson, B.L. *Money and Banking in England: The Development of the Banking System, 1694-1914*, Newton Abbot: David & Charles, 1974.
230. Crafts, N.F.R. *Economic Growth During the British Industrial Revolution*, Oxford University Press, 1984.
231. Cranfield, G.A. *The Press and Society from Caxton to Northcliffe*, London, 1978.
232. Craton, M. (ed.). *Roots and Branches: Current Directions in Slave Studies*, Oxford: Pergamon, 1979.
233. ―――. *Sinews of Empire: A Short History of British Slavery*, London, Temple Smith, 1974.
234. ―――. *Testing the Chains: Slave Rebellions and Other Forms of Resistance in the British West Indies*, Ithaca, New York: Cornell University Press, 1976.
235. Cressy, David. "Educational Opportunity in Tudor and Stuart England," *History of Education Quarterly* 16 (1976).
236. ―――. "Levels of Illiteracy in England, 1530-1730," *Historical Journal* 20 (1977).
237. ―――. *Literacy and the Social Order: Reading and Writing in Tudor and Stuart England*, Cambridge University Press, 1980.
238. Crook, D.P. *Benjamin Kidd: Portrait of a Social Darwinist*, Cambridge University Press, 1984.
239. Crosland, Jessie. *Sir John Fastolfe: A Medieval Man of Property*, London: Peter Owen, 1970.
240. Crossick, Geoffrey. *An Artisan Elite in a Victorian Society: Kentish London, 1840-1880*, London: Croom Helm, Social History Series, 1978.
241. Crouzet, François. *The First Industrialists: The Problem of Origin*, Cambridge University Press, 1985.
242. ――― (trans. Anthony Forster). *The Victorian Economy*, London, Methuen, 1982.
243. Crowder, Michael (ed.). *West African Resistance: The Military Response to Colonial Occupation*, New York: Africana Pub. Corp., 1971.
244. Cruikshank, Marjorie. *Children and Industry: Child Health and Welfare in North West Textile Towns during the Nineteenth Century*, Manchester University Press, 1981.
245. Cullen, L.M.L. and Smout, T.C. (eds.). *Comparative Aspects of Irish and Scottish Economic and Social Development, 1600-1900*, Edinburgh: John Donald, 1977.
246. Cunliffe, Barry. *The Celtic World: Iron Age Communities in Britain*, New York: McGraw-Hill, 1979.

247. ─────. *Iron Age Communities in Britain: An Account of England, Scotland and Wales from the Seventh Century B.C. until the Roman Conquest*, London: Routledge & Kegan Paul, 1974.
248. Cunningham, Hugh. *Leisure in the Industrial Revolution*, New York: St. Martin's Press, 1980.
249. ─────. *The Volunteer Force: A Social and Political History, 1859-1908*, New York: St. Martin's Press, 1975.
250. ─────. "Jingoism in 1877-1878," *Victorian Studies*, xiv, no. 4 (1971).
251. Curran, J. "Capitalism and Control of the Press, 1800-1975" in Curran, J., Gurevitch, M. and Woollocott, J. (eds.), *Mass Communication and Society*, London: Edward Arnold, 1977.
252. Curtis, L.P. *Apes and Angels: The Irishman in Victorian Caricature*, Washington, D.C.: Smithsonian Institute, 1971.
253. Cuttino, G.R. "Kings Clerks and the Community of the Realm," *Speculum*, XXIX (April 1954).
254. Daaku, K.Y. *Trade and Politics on the Gold Coast, 1620-1720*, Oxford University Press, 1970.
255. Darby, H.C. *The Changing Fenland*, Cambridge University Press, 1983.
256. ─────. *The Medieval Fenland*, Newton Abbot: David & Charles, 1974.
257. ───── (ed.). *The Domesday Geography of Eastern England*, Cambridge University Press, 1971.
258. ───── and Terrett, I.B. (eds.). *The Domesday Geography of Midland England*, Cambridge University Press, 1971.
259. Darcy, C.P. *The Encouragement of the Fine Arts in Lancashire, 1760-1860*, Manchester University Press, 1976.
260. Davenport-Hines, R.P.T. *Dudley Docker: The Life and Times of a Trade Warrior*, Cambridge University Press, 1985.
261. Davidoff, L. "Mastered for Life: Servant and Wife in Victorian and Edwardian England," *Journal of Social History*, VII (1973-4).
262. Davidson, Roger. *Whitehall and the Labour Problem in Late Victorian and Edwardian Britain: A Study in Official Statistics and Social Control*, London: Croom Helm, 1985.
263. Davies, C.S.L. "Provisions for armies, 1509-60: A study in the effectiveness of early Tudor Government," *Economic History Review*, 2nd series, XVII, no. 2, (1964).
264. Davies, P.N. *Sir Alfred Jones: Shipping Entrepreneur Par Excellence*, London: Europa Publications, 1978.
265. Davies, R.R. *Lordship and Society in the March of Wales, 1282-1400*, Oxford: Clarendon Press, 1978.
266. Davin, Anna. "Imperialism and Motherhood," *History Workshop*, 5 (1978).
267. Davis, Ralph. *The Rise of the Atlantic Economies*, Ithaca, New York: Cornell University Press, 1973.
268. ─────. *The Industrial Revolution and British Overseas Trade*, Leicester University Press, 1978.
269. Deacon, Margaret. *Scientists and the Sea, 1650-1900: A Study of Marine Science*, London: Academic Press, 1971.
270. Dean, Sir Maurice. *The Royal Air Force and Two World Wars*, London: Cassell, 1979.

271. Deane, Phyllis and Cole, William Alan. *British Economic Growth, 1688-1959*, Cambridge University Press, 1967.
272. De Breffny, Brian (ed.). *The Irish World: The History and Cultural Achievements of the Irish People*, London: Thames & Hudson, 1977.
273. De Brisay, K. and Evans, K.A. (ed.). *Salt: The Study of an Ancient Industry--Conference Proceedings*, Colchester Archaeological Group, 1975.
274. Debus, Allen G. *Science and Education in the Seventeenth Century: The Webster-Ward Debate*, London: Macdonald, 1970.
275. Delbruck, Hans. *History of the Art of War*, vol. iii: *The Middle Ages*, Greenwood Press, 1982.
276. De Lotbiniere, S. "The Story of the English Gunflint," *Journal of the Arms and Armour Society*, vol. 9, no. 1 (1977).
277. De Mause, Lloyd et al. (eds.). *A Bibliography of Psychohistory*, New York: Garland Library of Social Science, 1977.
278. Dennis, R.J. *British Industrial Cities of the Nineteenth Century; A Social Geography*, Cambridge University Press, 1984.
279. Denoon, Donald. "Capital and Capitalists in the Transvaal in the 1890's and 1900's," *Historical Journal* 23 (1980).
280. *Department of the Army Ad Hoc Committee Report on the Army need for the Study of Military History*, 4 vols., West Point, 1971.
281. De Schveinitz, Karl Jr. *The Rise and Fall of British India*, London: Methuen, 1983.
282. Devorkine, D.H. "A Sense of Community in Astrophysics: Adopting a System of Spectral Classification," *Isis*, 72 (1981).
283. Dewey, Clive and Hopkins, A.G. (eds.). *The Imperial Impact: Studies in the Economic History of Africa and India*, London: Athlone Press, 1973.
284. Dharampal, S. (ed.). *Indian Science and Technology in the 18th Century: Some Contemporary European Accounts*, Delhi: Impex India, 1971.
285. Diamond, A. "Chaucer's Women and Women's Chaucer" in Diamond, A. and Edwards, L.R. (eds.), *The Authority of Experience: Essays in Feminist Criticism*, Amherst, Mass., 1977.
286. Dickinson, Gordon Cawood. *Statistical Mapping and the Presentation of Statistics*, London: Edward Arnold, 1973.
287. Dickson, P.G.M. *The Financial Revolution in England: A Study in the Development of Public Credit, 1688-1756*, London, 1967.
288. Dilke, O.A.W. *The Roman Land Surveyors: An Introduction to the Agrimensores*, Newton Abbot: David & Charles, 1971.
289. Dilks, David. *Curzon in India*, vols. 1 & 2, London: Rupert Hart Davis, 1969, 1970.
290. ———. *Neville Chamberlain*, vol. 1: *Pioneering and Reform, 1869-1929*, Cambridge University Press, 1984.
291. Dinwiddy, J.K. "The Early Nineteenth Century Campaign against Flogging in the Army," *English Historical Review* XCVII (1982).

292. Dobson, C.R. *Masters and Journeymen: A Pre-History of Industrial Relations, 1717-1800*, Croom Helm, 1980.
293. Dobson, R. Barrie. "Urban Decline in Late Medieval England" *T.R.H.S.*, 5th series, 27 (1977).
294. D'Ombrain, Nicholas. *War Machinery and High Policy: Defence Administration in Peacetime Britain*, Oxford University Press, 1973.
295. Donajgrodski, A.P. (ed.). *Social Control in Nineteenth Century Britain*, London: Croom Helm, 1977.
296. Donnelly, F.K. and Baxter, J.L. "Sheffield and the English Revolutionary Tradition, 1791-1820," *International Review of Social History* (1974).
297. Dottin, Georges (trans. David Macrae). *The Celts*, Geneva: Minerva, 1977.
298. Dougan, David. *The History of Lord Armstrong: The Great Gunmaker*, Newcastle-upon-Tyne: Frank Graham, 1970.
299. Douglas, David C. and Greenaway, G.W. *English Historical Documents, II: 1042-1189*, London: Eyre Methuen, 1981.
300. Drescher, Seymour. *Econocide: British Slavery in the Era of Abolition*, Pittsburgh: University of Pittsburgh Press, 1977.
301. Drudy, P.J. (ed.). *Irish Studies*, vols. I & II, Cambridge University Press, 1980 and 1982.
302. Duby, Georges (trans. C. Postan). *The Chivalrous Society*, London: Edward Arnold, 1977.
303. ─────. "The Culture of the Knightly Class: Audience and Patronage" in Benson, R.L. and Constable, G. (eds.), *Renaissance and Renewal in the Twelfth Century*, Cambridge, Mass., 1982.
304. ───── (trans. Howard B. Clarke). *The Early Growth of the European Economy: Warriors and Peasants from the Seventh to the Twelfth Century*, London: Weidenfeld & Nicolson, 1974.
305. Dudley, Donald R. *The World of Tacitus*, London: Secker & Warburg, 1968.
306. Dudley Edwards, R. *Ireland in the Age of the Tudors: The Destruction of Hiberno-Norman Civilization*, New York: Barnes & Noble, 1977.
307. Duiker, William J. *Cultures in Collision: The Boxer Rebellion*, San Rafael: Presidio Press, 1978.
308. Duminy, A.H. *The Capitalists and the Outbreak of the Anglo-Boer War*, Durban: University of Natal Press, 1977.
309. Duncan, T. Bentley. *Atlantic Islands: Madeira, the Azores and the Cape Verdes in Seventeenth Century Commerce and Navigation*, Chicago: University of Chicago Press, 1972.
310. Dupuy, Trevor Nevitt and Hammerman, Gay M. (eds.). *A Documentary History of Arms Control and Disarmament*, London: Bowker, 1973.
311. Dupuy, Col. Trevor N. *The Evolution of Weapons and Warfare*, London, 1980.
312. Dusgate, Richard H. *The Conquest of Northern Nigeria*, London: Frank Cass, 1985.
313. Dyer, D. *The City of Worcester in the Sixteenth Century*, Leicester University Press, 1973.

314. Dyos, H.J. and Aldcroft, D.H. *British Transport: An Economic Survey from the Seventeenth Century to the Twentieth*, Leicester University Press, 1969.
315. Edelstein, Michael. "Rigidity and bias in the British capital market, 1870-1930" in McClosekey, D.N. (ed.), *Essays on a Mature Economy: Britain after 1840*, London: Methuen, 1971.
316. ———. *Overseas Investment in the Age of High Imperialism*, London: Methuen, 1982.
317. Egan, Clifford L. "The Origins of the War of 1812: Three Decades of Historical Writing," *Military Affairs*, vol. 38, (1978).
318. Eggleston, Wilfrid. *National Research in Canada*, Toronto: Clarke, Irwin & Col., 1978.
319. Ehrenreich, Barbara and English, Deirdre. *Witches, Midwives and Nurses: A History of Women Healers*, London: Writers and Readers Publishing Co-operative, 1973.
320. Eicher, Carl K. and Liedholm, Carl. *Growth and Development of the Nigerian Economy*, Lansing: Michigan State University Press, 1970.
321. Eisenstein, Elizabeth L. *The Printing Press as an Agent of Change: Communications and Cultural Transformations in Early Modern Europe*, Cambridge University Press, 1978.
322. Eldridge, C.C. *England's Mission: The Imperial Idea in the Age of Gladstone and Disraeli, 1868-1880*, Chapel Hill: University of North Carolina Press, 1973.
323. ———. *Victorian Imperialism in the Nineteenth Century*, New York: St. Martins Press, 1984.
324. Eliot, M. "The Despard Conspiracy Reconsidered," *Past and Present* (1977).
325. Ellis, John. *The Social History of the Machine Gun*, London: Croom Helm, 1975.
326. Ellison, Mary. *Support for Secession: Lancashire and the American Civil War*, Chicago: University of Chicago Press, 1973.
327. Emsley, Clive. *British Society and the French Wars, 1793-1815*, London: Macmillan, 1979.
328. Emy, H.V. *Liberals, Radicals and Social Politics, 1892-1914*, Cambridge University Press, 1973.
329. Engels, Friedrich. *Engels as Military Critic: Articles Reprinted from the "Volunteer Journal" and the "Manchester Guardian" of the 1860's*: ed. By Chaloner, W.H. and Henderson, W.O., Manchester University Press, 1973.
330. English, Barbara. *The Lands of Holderness, 1086-1260: A Study in Feudal Society*, Oxford University Press, 1979.
331. Engstrand, Iris H.W. *Spanish Scientists and the New World: The Eighteenth Century Exhibitions*, Seattle: University of Washington Press, 1981.
332. Enser, A.G.S. *A Subject Bibliography of the First World War: Books in English, 1914-1975*, London: Andre Deutsch, 1979.
333. Erickson, C. and Casey, K. "Women in the Middle Ages: A Working Bibliography," *Medieval Studies* 37 (1975).
334. Esterhuyse, J.H. *South West Africa, 1880-1894*, Cape Town: C. Struick, 1965.
335. Eubanks, Cecil (ed.). *Karl Marx and Friedrich Engels: An*

Analytical Bibliography, New York and London: Garland Publishers Inc., 1977.
336. Evans, E.J. *The Contentious Tithe: The Tithe Problem and English Agriculture, 1750-1850*, London: Routledge & Kegan Paul, 1976.
337. ─────── (ed.). *Social Policy, 1830-1914: Individualism, Collectivism and the Origins of the Welfare State*, London: Routledge & Kegan Paul, 1978.
338. Evans, Ifor M. and Lawrence, Heather. *Christopher Saxton: Elizabethan Map Maker*, Wakefield Historical Publications and the Holland Press, 1979.
339. Evans, N.R. "Testators, Literacy, Education and Religious Belief," *Local Population Studies* 25 (1980).
340. Everitt, Alan M. (ed.). *Perspectives in English Urban History*, New York: Barnes & Noble, 1973.
341. Falkus, M.E. "The Early Development of the British Gas Industry, 1790-1815," *Economic History Review*, XXXV, no. 2 (May 1982).
342. Fallows, Marjorie R. *Irish Americans: Identity and Assimilation*, Englewood Cliffs, New Jersey: Prentice-Hall, 1979.
343. Farrar, Wildred V. "The Society for the Promotion of Scientific Industry, 1872-1876," *Annals of Science*, vol. 29 (1972).
344. Farrington, Anthony. *Guide to the Records of the India Office Military Department*, London: Foreign and Commonwealth Office, 1982.
345. Farwell, Byron. *The Great Anglo-Boer War*, Toronto: Fitzhenry and Whiteside, 1976.
346. ───────. *Mr. Kipling's Army*, New York: W.W. Norton & Co., 1981.
347. Fawcett, Trevor. "Popular Science in 18th Century Norwich," *History Today*, 22 (1972).
348. Fay, Peter Ward. *The Opium War*, Chapel Hill: University of North Carolina Press, 1975.
349. Fedorowicz, J.K. *England's Baltic Trade in the Early Seventeenth Century*, Cambridge University Press, 1980.
350. Feingold, Modecai. *The Mathematician's Apprenticeship: Science, Universities and Society in England, 1560-1640*, Cambridge University Press, 1984.
351. Fergusson, Thomas G. *British Military Intelligence, 1870-1914: The Development of a Modern Intelligence Organization*, Frederick, Md.: University Publications of America Inc., 1984.
352. Fernbach, D. (ed.). *Surveys from Exile*, Harmondsworth, 1973.
353. Ferrante, Joan M. *Woman as Image in Medieval Literature: From the Twelfth Century to Dante*, New York: Columbia University Press, 1975.
354. Ferrier, R.W. *The History of the British Petroleum Company*, Cambridge University Press, 1982.
355. Fesharaki, Fereidun. *The Development of the Iranian Oil Industry: International and Domestic Aspects*, New York: Praeger, 1976.
356. Ffrench Blake, R.L.V. *The Crimean War*, Leo Cooper, 1972.
357. Field, H. John. *Towards a Programme of Imperial Life: The*

British Empire at the Turn of the Century, Westport, Con.: The Greenwood Press, 1982.
358. Field, Henry M. History of the Atlantic Telegraph, Free Port, New York: Books for Libraries Press, 1972.
359. Fieldhouse, D.K. Economics and Empire, 1830-1914, Ithaca: Cornell University Press, 1973.
360. Finberg, H.P.R. (ed.). Scandinavian England: The Collected Papers of F.T. Wainwright, Chichester: Phillimore, 1978.
361. Finer, S.E. "State and Nation Building in Europe: The Role of the Military" in Tilly, C. (ed.), The Formation of National States in Western Europe, Princeton University Press, 1975.
362. Finlayson, Geoffrey B.A.M. The Seventh Earl of Shaftesbury, 1801-1885, London: Eyre Methuen, 1981.
363. Finley, M. The Ancient Economy, London: Chatto & Windus, 1981.
364. Fisher, Robin. Contact and Conflict: Indian/European Relations in British Columbia, 1774-1890, Vancouver: University of British Columbia Press, 1977.
365. Fisher, R.M. "Thomas Cromwell, Humanism and Educational Reform, 1530-40," Bulletin of the Institute of Historical Research 50 (1977).
366. Fletcher, Anthony. A County Community in Peace and War: Sussex, 1600-60, London: Longman, 1975.
367. Fletcher, Sheila. Women First: The Female Tradition in English Physical Education, 1880-1980, London: Athlone Press, 1984.
368. Flinn, M.W. British Population Growth, 1700-1850, London: Macmillan, 1970.
369. ─────. The History of the British Coal Mining Industry, vol. II: 1700-1830, Oxford: Clarendon Press, 1984.
370. ───── (ed.). Scottish Population History from the Seventeenth Century to the 1930's, Cambridge University Press, 1978.
371. ───── and Smout, T.C. (ed.). Essays in Social History, Oxford University Press, 1974.
372. Flint, John (ed.). The Cambridge History of Africa, vol. 5: From c. 1790 to c. 1870, Cambridge University Press, 1976.
373. Floud, Roderick. The British Machine Tool Industry, 1850-1914, Cambridge University Press, 1976.
374. Floud, R.C. and McCloskey, D.N. The Economic History of Britain since 1700, Cambridge University Press, 1981.
375. Foot, M.R.D. (ed.). War and Society: Essays in Memory of John Western, New York: Barnes & Noble, 1973.
376. Forde-Johnston, J. Hill Forts of the Iron Age in England and Wales: A Survey of the Surface Evidence, Liverpool University Press, 1976.
377. Foster, John. Class Struggle and the Industrial Revolution: Early Industrial Capitalism in Three English Towns, London: Macmillan, 1971.
378. Fowler, K.A. (ed.). The Hundred Years' War, London: Macmillan, 1971.
379. Francis, Daniel. Battle for the West: Fur Traders and the Birth of Western Canada, Edmonton: Hurtig Publishers, 1982.

380. Fraser, Brian and Springhall, J.O. *Sure and Steadfast: A History of the Boys' Brigade*, Glasgow, n.d.
381. Fraser, D. *The New Poor Law in the Nineteenth Century*, London: Macmillan, 1976.
382. ─────────. *Urban Politics in Victorian England: The Structure of Politics in Victorian Cities*, Leicester University Press, 1976.
383. Fraser, George Macdonald. *The World of the Public School*, London: Weidenfeld & Nicolson, 1977.
384. Fraser, W.H. *Trade Unions and Society: The Struggle for Acceptance, 1850-1880*, Allen & Unwin, 1974.
385. Frazer, Antony. *The Weaker Vessel: Women's Position in Society between Queen Anne and Queen Elizabeth*,
386. Freeman, Orville L. *Multinational Company: Instrument for World Growth*, Eastbourne: Praeger, 1981.
387. French, Peter J. *John Dee: The World of an Elizabethan Magus*, London: Routledge & Kegan Paul, 1972.
388. Frere, S.S. *Britannia: A History of Roman Britain*, 2nd edn., London: Routledge & Kegan Paul, 1978.
389. ───────── and St. Joseph, J.K.S. *Roman Britain from the Air*, Cambridge University Press, 1983.
390. Freund, Bill. *The Making of Contemporary Africa*, Bloomington: Indiana University Press, 1982.
391. Friesen, Gerald. *The Canadian Prairies: A History*, Toronto: University of Toronto Press, 1981.
392. Fritz, P.S. *The English Ministers and Jacobitism between the Rebellions of 1715 and 1745*, Toronto: University of Toronto Press, 1975.
393. Fryer, Peter. *Staying Power: The History of Black People in Britain*, London: Pluto Press, 1984.
394. Furber, Holden. *Rival Empires of Trade in the Orient, 1600-1800*, Minneapolis: University of Minnesota Press, 1976.
395. Furley, O.W. and Watson, T. *A History of Education in East Africa*, London: NOK Publishers, 1978.
396. Galbraith, John S. *Mackinnon and East Africa, 1878-1895: A Study of the "New Imperialism,"* Cambridge University Press, 1972.
397. Gann, L.H. and Duignan, Peter (eds.). *Colonialism in Africa, 1870-1960*, vol. 1: *The History and Politics of Colonialism, 1870-1914*, Cambridge University Press, 1969.
398. ───────── (eds.). *Colonialism in Africa, 1870-1960*, vol. 4: *The Economics of Colonialism*, Cambridge University Press, 1975.
399. ───────── (eds.). *Colonialism in Africa, 1870-1960*, vol. 5: *A Bibliographical Guide to Colonialism in Sub-Saharan Africa*, Cambridge University Press, 1974.
400. Gardner, Brian. *The East India Company*, London: Hart-Davis, 1971.
401. Gardner, Phil. *The Lost Elementary Schools of Victorian England*, London: Croom Helm, 1984.
402. Gathorne-Hardy, Jonathan. *The Public School Phenomenon*, London: Hodder & Stoughton, 1977.
403. Gemery, H. and Hogendorm, J. *The Uncommon Market: Essays in the Economic History of the Atlantic Slave Trade*, New York: Academic Press, 1978.

404. George, Betty Stein. *Education in Ghana*, DHEW Publication No. (OE) 75-19119, Washington, D.C.: Government Printing Office, 1976.
405. Gessen, Borish M. *The Social and Economic Roots of Newton's "Principia,"* with a new introduction by R.S. Cohen, New York: Fertig, 1971.
406. Gibbon, P. *Origins of Ulster Unionism*, Manchester University Press, 1975.
407. Gibbs-Smith, C.H. *Aviation: An Historical Survey*, London: H.M.S.O., 1985.
408. Gibson, Ian. *The English Vice: Beating, Sex and Shame in Victorian England and After*, London: Duckworth, 1978.
409. Gies, F. and Gies, J. *Women in the Middle Ages*, New York: Crowell, 1978.
410. Gifford, Prosser and Louis, William Roger. *France and Britain in Africa: Imperial Rivalry and Colonial Rule*, New Haven: Yale University Press, 1972.
411. Gill, Crispin. *Plymouth: A New History*, Newton Abbot: David & Charles, 1979.
412. Gillard, David. *The Struggle for Asia, 1828-1914: A Study in British and Russian Imperialism*, London: Methuen, 1977.
413. Gillingham, John. *The Wars of the Roses: Peace and Conflict in Fifteenth Century England*, London: Weidenfeld & Nicolson, 1981.
414. ———— and Holt, J.C. (eds.). *War and Government in the Middle Ages. Essays in Honour of J.O. Prestwich*, Ipswich: Boydell, 1984.
415. Given, J.B. *Society and Homicide in Thirteenth Century England*, Stanford, California, 1977.
416. Glover, Michael. *Velvet Glove: The Decline and Fall of Moderation in War*, London: Hodder & Stoughton, 1982.
417. Godechot, Jacques. *Les institutions de la France sous la révolution et l'Empire*, Paris, 1969.
418. Godwin, Sir Harry. *Fenland: Its Ancient Past and Uncertain Future*, Cambridge University Press, 1978.
419. Godwin, Sir Harry S. *The History of the British Flora: A Factual Basis for Phytogeography*, 2nd edn., Cambridge University Press, 1975.
420. Gooch, John. *Arms in Europe*, London: Routledge & Kegan Paul, 1980.
421. ————. *The Plans of War: The General Staff and British Military Strategy, c.1900-1916*, London: Routledge & Kegan Paul, 1974.
422. ———— and Perlmutter, Amos (eds.). *Military Deception and Strategic Surprise*, London: Frank Cass, 1982.
423. Goodburn, P. and Bartholomew, P. (eds.). *Aspects of the "notitia Dignitatum": Conference Papers*, British Archaeological Reports S15, 1976.
424. Goodman, A. *The Wars of the Roses: Military Activity and English Society, 1452-97*, London: Routledge & Kegan Paul, 1981.
425. Goodwin, A. *The Friends of Liberty: The English Democratic Movement in the Age of the French Revolution*, London: Hutchinson, 1979.

426. Goring, J.J. "Wealden Ironmasters in the Age of Elizabeth" in Ives, E.W., Knight, R.J. and Scarisbrick, J.J. (eds.), *Wealth and Power in Tudor England*, London, 1978.
427. Gorman, Mel. "Sir William O'Shaughnessy, Lord Dalhousie and the Establishment of the Telegraphic System in India," *Technology and Culture* 12 (1971).
428. Gottfried, Robert S. *Epidemic Disease in Fifteenth Century England: The Medical Response and the Demographic Consequences*, Brunswick: Rutgers University Press, 1978.
429. Gould, J.D. *The Great Debasement: Currency and Economy in mid-Tudor England*, Oxford: Clarendon Press, 1970.
430. Graber, G.S. *Mars and Minerva*, Baton Rouge: Louisiana State University Press, 1975.
431. Graff, Harvey J. (ed.). *Literacy and Social Development in the West: A Reader*, Cambridge University Press, 1982.
432. Graham, G.S. *The China Station War and Diplomacy, 1830-1860*, Oxford: Clarendon Press, 1978.
433. ―――――. *Tides of Empire. Discussions on the Expansion of Britain Overseas*, Montreal, 1972.
434. Gransden, Antonia. *Historical Writing in England, c.550 to 1307*, London: Routledge & Kegan Paul, 1974.
435. Grant, Edward. *Physical Science in the Middle Ages*, Cambridge University Press, 1971.
436. Gray, Richard (ed.). *The Cambridge History of Africa*, vol. 4: *From c. 1600-c. 1790*, Cambridge University Press, 1975.
437. Green, William A. *British Slave Emancipation: The Sugar Colonies and the Great Experiment, 1830-1865*, Oxford University Press, 1985.
438. Green, William A. *British Slave Emancipation: The Sugar Colonies and the Great Experiment, 1830-1865*, Oxford University Press, 1976.
439. Gregory, J.S. *Great Britain and the Taipings*, London: Routledge & Kegan Paul, 1969.
440. Griffiths, Sir Percival. *The British Impact on India*, 2nd edn., Ann Arbor: University of Michigan Press, 1972.
441. Griffiths, Ralph A. *The Reign of King Henry VI: The Exercise of Royal Authority, 1422-1461*, London: Ernest Benn, 1981.
442. Gruner, Wolf D. "The British Political, Social and Economic System and the Decision for Peace and War: Reflections on Anglo-German relations, 1800-1939," *British Journal of International Studies*, vol. VI, no. 3 (1980).
443. Guerlac, Henry. "An Augustan Monument: The "Optics" of Isaac Newton" in Hughes, Peter and Williams, David (eds.), *The Varied Pattern: Studies in the Eighteenth Century*, Toronto: Hakkert, 1975.
444. ―――――. *Essays and Papers in the History of Modern Science*, Baltimore: The Johns Hopkins University Press, 1977.
445. Guy, A.J. *Oeconomy and Discipline: Officership and Administration in the British Army, 1714-1763*, Manchester University Press, 1985.
446. Guy, J.J. "A Note on Firearms in the Zulu Kingdom," *Journal of African History*, 72 (1971).
447. Habbakuk, H.J. *Population Growth and Economic Development since 1750*, Leicester University Press, 1971.

448. Haber, L.F. *The Chemical Industry, 1900-30: International Growth and Technological Change*, Oxford University Press, 1971.
449. ―――――. "Chemical Innovations in Peace and War" in Bernhard, C.G., Crawford, Elisabeth and Sorborn, Per (eds.), *Science, Technology and Society in the Time of Alfred Nobel*, Oxford: Pergamon Press, 1982.
450. Hackett, General Sir John. *The Profession of Arms*, London: Sidgwick & Jackson, 1983.
451. Hadingham, Evan. *Circles and Standing Stones: An Illustrated Exploration of the Megalith Mysteries of Early Britain*, New York: Walker & Company, 1975.
452. Haigh, Christopher (ed.). *The Cambridge Historical Encyclopedia of Great Britain and Ireland*, Cambridge University Press, 1985.
453. Haines, Roy M. "Education in English Ecclesiastical Legislation of the Later Middle Ages" in Cuming, G.J. and Baker, D. (eds.), *Councils and Assemblies*, Cambridge University Press, Studies in Church History, vol. 7, 1971.
454. Hale, J.R. "Fifteenth and Sixteenth Century Public Opinion and War," *Past and Present*, XXII (1962).
455. ―――――. *Renaissance Fortification: Art or Engineering*, London: Thames & Hudson, 1978.
456. ―――――. "Sixteenth Century Explanations of War and Violence," *Past and Present*, LI (1971).
457. ―――――. *War and Society in Renaissance Europe*, London: Fontana, 1985.
458. Haley, Bruce. *The Healthy Body and Victorian Culture*, Cambridge: Harvard University Press, 1978.
459. Hall, Alan R. *The Export of Capital from Britain, 1870-1914*, London: Methuen, 1968.
460. Hall, A. Rupert. "What did the Industrial Revolution in Europe owe to Science?" in McKendrick, Neil (ed.), *Historical Perspectives: Studies in English Thought and Society in Honour of J.H. Plumb*, London: Europa Publications, 1974.
461. Hallam, H.E. *Rural England, 1066-1348*, London: Fontana, 1981.
462. Halstead, John P. *The Second British Empire: Trade, Philanthropy and Good Government, 1820-1890*, Westport, Conn.: Greenwood Press, 1982.
463. ――――― and Porcari, Serafino. *Modern Imperialism: A Bibliography of Books and Articles, 1815-1972*, Boston, 1972.
464. Hamer, W.S. *The British Army: Civil-Military Relations, 1885-1905*, Oxford University Press, 1970.
465. Hammack, James W. *Kentucky and the Second American Revolution: The War of 1812*, Lexington: University of Kentucky Press, 1976.
466. Hammersley, G. "The State and their English Iron Industry in the Sixteenth and Seventeenth Centuries" in Coleman, D.C. and John, A.H. (eds.), *Trade, Government and the Economy in Pre-Industrial England: Essays Presented to F.J. Fisher*, London: Weidenfeld & Nicolson, 1976.
467. Hammerton, A. James. *Emigrant Gentlewomen: Genteel Poverty and Female Emigration, 1830-1914*, London: Croom Helm, 1979.
468. Hamp, E.B. "Social Gradience in British Spoken Latin," *Britannia*, vi (1975).

469. Hanham, H.J. (ed.). *Bibliography of British History, 1851-1914*, Oxford University Press, 1976.
470. Hanson, William and Maxwell, Gordon. *Rome's North West Frontier: The Antonine Wall*, Edinburgh University Press, 1983.
471. Harley, C.K. "British Industrialization before 1841: Evidence of Slower Growth During the Industrial Revolution," *Journal of Economic History*, XLII, no. 2 (June 1982).
472. ─────. "Skilled Labour and the Choice of Technique in Edwardian Industry," *Explorations in Economic History*, II (1974).
473. Harnetty, Peter. *Imperialism and Free Trade: Lancashire and India in the mid-Nineteenth Century*, Manchester University Press, 1972.
474. Harries-Jenkins, Gwyn. *Armed Forces and the Welfare Societies*, London: Macmillan, 1982.
475. Harris, Jose. *William Beveridge: A Biography*, Oxford University Press, 1977.
476. Harrison, J.F.C. *The Birth and Growth of Industrial England, 1714-1867*, New York: Harcourt, Brace, Jovanovich, 1973.
477. Harriss, G.L. "War and the Emergence of the English Parliament, 1297-1360," *Journal of Medieval History*, 2 (1976).
478. Hartley, M. and Ingilby, Joan. *Life in the Moorlands of Northeast Yorkshire*, London: J.M. Dent, 1972.
479. Hartwell, R.M. (ed.). *The Industrial Revolution and Economic Growth*, London: Methuen, 1971.
480. ─────. "The Service Revolution" in Cipolla, Carlo M. (ed.), *The Industrial Revolution*, London: Collins, Fontana, Economic History of Europe Series, 1973.
481. Harvey, A.D. *Britain in the Early Nineteenth Century*, New York: St. Martins Press, 1978.
482. Harvey, Charles E. *The Rio Tinto Company: An Economic History of a Leading International Mining Concern*, London: Alison Hodge, 1981.
483. Hastings, Max (ed.). *Encyclopedia of Military Anecdotes*, Oxford University Press, 1985.
484. Haswell, Jock. *British Military Intelligence*, London: Weidenfeld & Nicolson, 1973.
485. Hatcher, John. *Plague, Population and the English Economy, 1348-1530*, London: Macmillan, 1977.
486. ─────. *Rural Economy and Society in the Duchy of Cornwall, 1300-1500*, Cambridge University Press, 1970.
487. Hatchey, Thomas E. *British and Irish Separatism from the Fenians to the Free State, 1867-1922*, Chicago: Rand-McNally, 1977.
488. Hay, J.R. *Origins of the Liberal Welfare Reforms, 1906-1914*, London: Macmillan, 1975.
489. Hayes, John R. (ed.). *The Genius of Arab Civilization Source of Renaissance*, New York: New York University Press, 1975.
490. Hayter, Tony. *The Army and the Crowd in Mid-Georgian England*, Totowa, New Jersey: Rowman and Littlefield, 1978.
491. Hayward, P.H.C. (ed.). *Jane's Dictionary of Military Terms*, London: Macdonald & Jane's, 1975.
492. Hechter, Michael. *Internal Colonisation: The Celtic Fringe in*

British National Development, 1536-1966, Berkeley: University of California Press,
493. Heggie, D.C. Megalithic Science: Ancient Mathematics and Astronomy in North West Europe, London: Thames and Hudson, 1981.
494. Helmholz, R.H. Marriage Litigation in Medieval England, Cambridge University Press, 1975.
495. Heningen, S.T. "Tudor Literature of the Physical Sciences," Huntingdon Library Quarterly, vol. 32 (1969).
496. Hennessey, Maurice H. The Wild Geese, Old Greenwich, Conn.: Devin-Adair, 1973.
497. Hennessey, R.A.S. The Electric Revolution, Newcastle-upon-Tyne: Oriel, 1972.
498. Henriques, U.R.Q. Before the Welfare State: Social Administration in Early Industrial Britain, London: Longman, 1979.
499. Herbert, Gilbert. Pioneers of Prefabrication: The British Contribution to the Nineteenth Century, Baltimore: Johns Hopkins University Press, 1978.
500. Hewitt, H.J. The Organization of War under Edward III, 1338-1362, Manchester University Press, 1966.
501. ─────. "The Organization of War" in Fowler, Kenneth (ed.), The Hundred Years' War, London: Macmillan, 1971.
502. Higham, Robin (ed.). Consolidated Author and Subject Index to the JRUSI, Ann Arbor, Michigan, UM TB00002 (1964).
503. Highman, B.W. Slave Populations of the British Caribbean, 1807-1934, London: Johns Hopkins University Press,
504. Hiles, Richard L. Power in the Industrial Revolution, Manchester University Press, 1970.
505. Hill, Christopher. Change and Continuity in Seventeenth Century England, London: Weidenfeld & Nicolson, 1975.
506. ─────. The Intellectual Origins of the English Revolution, Oxford University Press, 1965.
507. ─────. The World Turned Upside Down, London: Temple Smith, 1972.
508. Hill, C.W. Edwardian Scotland, Totowa, New Jersey: Rowman and Littlefield, 1976.
509. Hilton, Rodney H. Bond Men Made Free: Medieval Peasant Movements and the English Rising of 1381, London: Methuen, 1977.
510. Hilton, R.A. Medieval Society: The West Midlands at the End of the Thirteenth Century, London: Weidenfeld & Nicolson, 1967.
511. Hinde, Thomas (ed.). The Domesday Book, London: Victor Gollancz, 1985.
512. ─────. Forests of Britain, London: Victor Gollancz, 1985.
513. Hindley, Geoffrey. A History of Roads, London: Peter Davies, 1971.
514. Hirschmeier, Johannes and Yui, T. The Development of Japanese Business, Cambridge, Mass.: Harvard University Press, 1975.
515. Hobart, T.W.A. A Pictorial History of the Machine Gun, Shepperton: Ian Allen, 1971.
516. Hobsbawm, Eric John. The Age of Capital, 1848-75, London: Weidenfeld & Nicolson, 1975.

517. ——— and Ranger, Terence (eds.). *The Invention of Tradition*, Cambridge University Press, 1984.
518. Hodges, Richard. *Dark Age Economics: The Origins of Towns and Trade, A.D.600-1000*, New York: St. Martins Press, 1984.
519. Hodgson, Pat. *The War Illustrators*, London: Osprey, 1977.
520. Hodson, Howard. *Cheshire 1660-1780: The Restoration to the Industrial Revolution*, Chester: Cheshire Community Council, 1973.
521. Hogben, W. Murray. "British Civil-Military Relations on the North West Frontier of India" in Preston, Adrian and Dennis, Peter (eds.), *Swords and Covenants*, London: Croom Helm, 1976.
522. Hogg, A.H.A. "British Hill Forts: An Index," *B.A.R.*, British Series, 1979.
523. Holcombe, Lee. *Wives and Property: Reform of the Married Women's Property Law in Nineteenth Century England*, Oxford: Martin Robertson, 1983.
524. Holder, P.A. *The Roman Army in Britain*, London: B.T. Batsford, 1982.
525. Holmes, Clive. *The Eastern Association in the English Civil War*, Cambridge University Press, 1974.
526. Hoppen, K. Theodore. *The Common Scientist in the Seventeenth Century: A Study of the Dublin Philosophical Society, 1683-1708*, London: Routledge & Kegan Paul, 1970.
527. Hoskins, W.G. *The Age of Plunder: The England of Henry VIII, 1500-47*, London: Longman, 1976.
528. Houlding, J.A. *Fit for Service: The Training of the British Army, 1715-1795*, Oxford University Press, 1981.
529. Howard, Michael. *War in European History*, Oxford University Press, 1976.
530. ———. *War and the Liberal Conscience*, London: Maurice Temple Smith, 1978.
531. Howarth, Patrick. *Play Up and Play the Game: The Heroes of Popular Fiction*, London: Eyre Methuen, 1973.
532. Howe, Anthony. *The Cotton Masters, 1830-1860*, Oxford University Press, 1984.
533. Hsin-Pao Chang. *Commissioner Lin and the Opium War*, Cambridge, Mass.: Harvard University Press, 1962.
534. Hudson, Derek. *Thomas Barnes of "The Times"*; ed. Harold, Child, Greenwood Press, 1973.
535. Hudson, Kenneth. *Pawnbroking: An Aspect of British Social History*, London: Bodley Head, 1982.
536. Hueckel, G. "War and the British Economy: A General Equilibrium Analysis," *Explorations in Economic History*, X (1973).
537. Hughes, B.P. *Firepower: Weapons Effectiveness on the Battlefield, 1630-1850*, New York: Charles Scribner's Sons, 1974.
538. Hume, John R. and Moss, Michael S. *Beardmore: The History of a Scottish Industrial Giant*, London: Heinemann Educational Books, 1979.
539. Humphries, S. "Hurrah for England: Schooling and the Working Class in England," *Southern History*, 1 (1979).
540. Hunt, C.J. *The Leadminers of the Northern Pennines in the Eighteenth and Nineteenth Centuries*, Manchester University Press, 1970.

541. Hunt, E.H. *British Labour History, 1815-1914*, London: Weidenfeld & Nicolson, 1981.
542. Hunt, N. "Notes on the History of Benedictine and Cistercian Nuns in Britain," *Cistercian Studies*, 8 (1973).
543. Hunt, R.W. "The History of Grammar in the Middle Ages" in Burseill-Hall, G.L. (ed.), *Collected Papers*, Amsterdam, 1980. Additions and corrections to the foregoing by Gibson, M.T. and Hall, S.P., *Bodleian Library Record*, 11 (1982).
544. Hunt, William. *The Puritan Movement: The Coming of Revolution in an English County*, Cambridge, Mass.: Harvard University Press, 1983.
545. Hurt, J. *Education in Evolution: Church, State, Society and Popular Education, 1800-1870*, London: Routledge & Kegan Paul, 1970.
546. ————. *Elementary Schooling and the Working Classes*, London: Routledge & Kegan Paul, 1979.
547. Hutchinson, Thomas W. *Knowledge and Ignorance in Economics*, Oxford: Blackwell, 1978.
548. Huttenback, Robert A. *Racism and Empire: White Settlers and Colored Immigrants in the British Self-Governing Colonies, 1830-1971*, Ithaca, New York: Cornell University Press, 1976.
549. Hutton, Ronald. "The Royalist War Effort" in Morrill, John (ed.), *Reactions to the English Civil War*, London: Macmillan, 1982.
550. Hyams, Paul R. *Kings, Lords and Peasants in Medieval England: Common Law Villeinage in the Twelfth and Thirteenth Centuries*, Oxford University Press, 1980.
551. Hyde, C.K. *Technological Change and the British Iron Industry, 1700-1870*, New Jersey: Princeton University Press, 1977.
552. Hyman, Richard. *The Workers' Union, 1898-1929*, Oxford University Press, 1971.
553. Hynes, W.G. *The Economics of Empire: Britain, Africa and the New Imperialism, 1870-95*, London: Longman, 1979.
554. Ignatieff, M. *A Just Measure of Pain: The Penitentiary in the Industrial Revolution*, London: Macmillan, 1979.
555. Inglis, Brian. *Poverty and the Industrial Revolution*, London: Panther Books, 1970.
556. Inglis, Simon. *The Football Grounds of England and Wales*, London: Collins, Willow Books, 1985.
557. Ingrao, Charles. *The Hessian Mercenary State and the Industrial Revolution, Studies in History and Policy*, Bishops University, vol. IV, ed. Karl Schwayer and Jeremy Blick, Lennoxville, Quebec, 1985.
558. Inikort, J.E. "The Import of Firearms into West Africa, 1750-1807," *Journal of African History*, XVIII (1977).
559. Itzkowitz, D.C. *Peculiar Privilege: A Social History of English Fox Hunting, 1753-1885*, Brighton: Harvester Press, 1977.
560. Ive, Paul. *The Practice of Fortification*; introd. Martin Biddle, Gregg International, 1972.
561. Jackson, G. *Hull in the Eighteenth Century: A Study in Economic and Social History*, University of Hull Publications, 1972.

562. Jacob, J.R. *Robert Boyle and the English Revolution: A Study in Social and Intellectual Change*, New York: Burt Franklin, 1978.
563. Jacobs, Margaret C. *The Newtonians and the English Revolution, 1689-1720*, Brighton: Harvester Press, 1976.
564. Jaggi, Om Prakesh. *The History of Science and Technology in India*, 7 vols., Delhi: Atma Ram, 1969-1977.
565. Jamieson, Alan. *War and Peace, 1900-45*, London: Edward Arnold, 1979.
566. Janowitz, Morris. *Military Conflict: Essays in the Institutional Analysis of War and Peace*, London: Sage Publications, 1976.
567. ―――――. *Sociology and the Military Establishment*, London: Sage Publications, 1975.
568. Jarvis, R.C. *Collected Papers on the Jacobite Risings*, 2 vols., Manchester University Press, 1971 & 1972.
569. Jenkyns, Richard. *The Victorians and Ancient Greece*, Cambridge, Mass.: Harvard University Press, 1980.
570. Jensen, Gillian Fellows. "The Vikings in England: A Review," in Clemoes, P. and Hughes, K. (eds.), *England before the Conquest: Studies in Primary Sources presented to Dorothy Whitelock*, Cambridge University Press, 1971.
571. Jewell, Helen M. "The Cultural Interests and Achievements of the Secular Personnel of the Local Administration" in Clough, Cecil H. (ed.), *Profession, Vocation and Culture in Later Medieval England*, University of Liverpool Press, 1982.
572. Johnson, Anne. *Roman Forts of the First and Second Centuries A.D. in Britain and the Roman Province*, A. & C. Black, 1983.
573. Johnson, Richard. "Educational Policy and Social Control in Early Victorian England," *Past and Present*, no. 49 (1970).
574. Johnstone, Paul. *The Sea Craft of Pre-History*; prepared for publication by Sean McGrail, Cambridge, Mass.: Harvard University Press, 1980.
575. Jones, D.J.V. *The Last Rising: The Newport Insurrection of 1839*, Oxford: Clarendon Press, 1983.
576. Jones, D.K. "The Educational Legacy of the Anti-Corn Law League," *History of Education*, III (1974).
577. Jones, Gareth Elwyn. *Modern Wales: A Concise History, c.1485-1975*, Cambridge University Press, 1984.
578. Jones, Gareth Stedman. *Languages of Class: Studies in English Working Class History, 1832-1982*, Cambridge University Press, 1982.
579. Jones, Greta. *Social Darwinism and English Thought: The Interaction between Biological and Social Theory*, Brighton: Harvester Press, 1980.
580. Jones, Gwyn. *A History of the Vikings*, Oxford University Press, 1984.
581. Jones, T. *Chaucer's Knight: The Portrait of a Medieval Mercenary*, London: Eyre Methuen, 1982.
582. Jordan, W.C., McNab, B. and Ruiz, T.F. *Order and Innovation in the Middle Ages: Essays in Honour of Joseph R. Strayer*, Princeton University Press, 1976.

583. Joslin, David. *A Century of Banking in Latin America*, Oxford University Press, 1963.
584. Joyce, Patrick. *Work, Society and Politics: The Culture of the Factory in Later Victorian England*, London: Methuen, 1982.
585. Judd, Denis. *The Boer War*, London: Hart-Davis, 1977.
586. ―――――. *Radical Joe: A Life of Joseph Chamberlain*, London: Hamish Hamilton, 1977.
587. Kaeuper, Richard W. "The Frescobaldi of Florence and the English Crown," *Studies in Medieval and Renaissance History*, Lincoln: University of Nebraska Press, 1973.
588. Kanner, Barbara (ed.). *The Women of England from Anglo-Saxon Times to the Present: Interpretative Bibliographical Essays*, Hamden, Conn.: Archon Books, 1979.
589. Kapelle, William E. *The Norman Conquest of the North: The Region and its Transformation, 1000-1135*, London: Croom Helm, and Chapel Hill: University of North Carolina Press, 1979.
590. Kealey, E.J. *Medieval Medicus: A Social History of Anglo-Norman Medicine*, Baltimore: The Johns Hopkins University Press, 1981.
591. Kearney, Hugh Francis. *Scholars and Gentlemen: Universities and Society in Pre-Industrial Britain, 1500-1700*, London: Faber & Faber, 1970.
592. Keating, P. (ed.). *Into Unknown England, 1866-1913: Selections from the Social Explorers*, Manchester University Press, 1976.
593. Kee, Robert. *Ireland: A History*, London: Weidenfeld & Nicolson, 1981.
594. Keeler, M.F. (ed.). *Bibliography of British History, 1603-1714*, 2nd. rev. ed., Oxford University Press, 1976.
595. Keen, M.H. "Huizinga, Kilgour and the Decline of Chivalry," *Medievalia et Humanistica*, VII (1977).
596. ―――――. *Outlaws of Medieval Legend*, 2nd ed., London: Routledge & Kegan Paul, 1977.
597. Keeney, B.C. "Military Service and the Development of Nationalism in England, 1272-1327," *Speculum*, 22 (1947).
598. Keir, David. *The Bowring Story*, London: Bodley Head, 1962.
599. Kekewich, M. "Edward W., William Paxton and Literary Patronage in Yorkist England," *Modern Language Review*, (1971).
600. Kelly, H.A. "Marriage in the Middle Ages, 2: Clandestine Marriage and Chaucer's 'Troilus,'" *Viator*, 4 (1973).
601. Kelves, Daniel J. *In the Name of Eugenics: Genetics and the Uses of Human Heredity*, New York: Alfred A. Knopf, 1985.
602. Kemp, Anthony. *Weapons and Equipment of the Marlborough Wars*, Poole: Blandford Press, 1980.
603. Kemp, Tom. *Historical Patterns of Industrialization*, London: Longman, 1978.
604. Kennedy, Paul M. *The Rise of Anglo-German Antagonism, 1860-1914*, London: George Allen & Unwin, 1981.
605. ―――――. *The Realities behind Diplomacy: Background Influences on British External Policy, 1805-1980*, London: Allen & Unwin, 1981.
606. Kennedy, Robert E. *Irish: Emigration, Marriage and Fertility*, University of California Press, 1973.

607. Kennedy, W.P. "Institutional Response to Economic Growth: Capital Markets in Britain to 1914" in Hannah, L. (ed.), *Management Strategy and Business Development: An Historical and Comparative Study*, London: Macmillan, 1976.
608. Kent, Christopher. *Brains and Numbers: Elitism, Comtism and Democracy in Mid-Victorian England*, Toronto: University of Toronto Press, 1978.
609. Kershaw, I. "The Great Famine and Agrarian Crisis in England, 1315-1322," *Past and Present*, no. 59 (1973).
610. Kiernan, V.G. "Colonial Africa and its Armies" in Bond, B. and Roy, I (eds.), *War and Society: A Year of Military History*, vol. 2, London: Croom Helm, 1977.
611. Kieve, Jeffrey. *The Electric Telegraph: A Social and Economic History*, Newton Abbot: David & Charles, 1973.
612. King, E.J. *England, 1175-1425*, London: Routledge & Kegan Paul, 1979.
613. Kirby, R.G. and Musson, A.E. *The Voice of the People: John Doherty, Trade Unionist, Radical and Factory Reformer, 1798-1854*, Manchester University Press, 1975.
614. Kishlansky, M. *The Rise of the New Model Army*, Cambridge University Press, 1979.
615. Kittel, Ruth. "Women under the Law in Medieval England, 1066-1485" in Kanner, Barbara (ed.), *The Women of England from Anglo-Saxon Times to the Present: Interpretative Bibliographical Essays*, Hamden, Conn.: Archon Books, 1979.
616. Klapp, Orrin E. *Models of Social Order: Introduction to Sociological Theory*, Palo Alto: National Press Books, 1973.
617. Knight, P. "Women and Abortion in Victorian and Edwardian England," *History Workshop Journal*, IV (1977).
618. Koch, H.W. *The Rise of Modern Warfare, 1618-1815*, London: Hamlyn, 1981.
619. Korr, Charles P. *Cromwell and the New Model Foreign Policy: England's Policy Towards France, 1649-1658*, Berkeley & London: University of California Press, 1975.
620. Koss, Stephen E. *The Pro-Boers: The Anatomy of an Anti-War Movement*, University of Chicago Press, 1975.
621. Kostinen, Paul A.C. *The Military-Industrial Complex: A Historical Perspective*, New York: Praeger, 1980.
622. Kramnick, Isaac. "Children's Literature and Bourgeois Ideology" in Zagorin, Perez (ed.), *Culture and Politics from Puritanism to Enlightenment*, Berkeley: University of California Press, 1981.
623. Kubicek, Robert V. *Economic Imperialism in Theory and Practice: The Case of South African Gold Mining Finance, 1886-1914*, Durham, North Carolina: Duke University Press, 1979.
624. Labarge, Margaret Wade. *Gascony, England's First Colony, 1204-1453*, London: Hamish Hamilton, 1980.
625. Laing, Lloyd. *The Archaeology of Late Celtic Britain and Ireland, c. 400-1200 A.D.*, London: Methuen, 1975.
626. ———— and Laing, Jennifer. *The Origins of Britain*, London: Routledge & Kegan Paul, 1980.
627. Lander, J.R. *Conflict and Stability in Fifteenth Century England*, London: Hutchinson, 1969.

628. Landes, David S. *Unbound Prometheus: Technological Change and Industrial Development in Western Europe from 1750 to the Present*, Cambridge University Press, 1969.
629. Lang, Kurt (ed.). *Military Institutions and the Sociology of War: A Review of the Literature with Annotated Bibliography*, London: Sage Publications, 1972.
630. Langton, John and Morris, R.J. *Atlas of the Industrial Revolution*, London: Methuen, 1985.
631. Laqueur, Thomas W. "The Cultural Origins of Popular Literacy in England, 1500-1850," *Oxford Review of Education*, 2 (1976).
632. Laqueur, T.W. "Literacy and Social Mobility in the Industrial Revolution in England," *Past and Present*, 64 (August 1979).
633. Laslett, Peter and Wall, Richard (eds.). *Household and Family in Past Time*, Cambridge University Press, 1972.
634. Latouche, Robert. *The Birth of the Western Economy: Economic Effects of the Dark Ages*, London: Methuen, 1981.
635. Lawson, John and Silver, Harold. *A Social History of Education in England*, London: Eyre Methuen, 1973.
636. Lee, J.E. *The Modernisation of Irish Society, 1848-1918*, Dublin: Gill & Macmillan, 1973.
637. Lehmann, Joseph. *The First Boer War*, London: Jonathan Cape, 1972.
638. Lenman, Bruce. *The Jacobite Clans, 1649-1759*, London: Methuen, 1984.
639. ───────. *The Jacobite Risings in Britain, 1689-1746*, London: Methuen, 1980.
640. Le Patourel, H.E. Jean, "Les sites fossoyés et leurs problèmes: l'organisation de la recherche en Grand Bretagne," *Revue du Nord*, 58 (1976).
641. Levenson, Joseph R. *European Expansion and the Counter Example of Asia, 1300-1600*, Englewood Cliffs: Prentice Hall, 1967.
642. Levine, A.L. *Industrial Retardation in Britain, 1880-1914*, London: Weidenfeld & Nicolson, 1967.
643. Levy, Jack S. *War in the Modern Great Power System, 1495-1975*, Lexington: University of Kentucky Press, 1983.
644. Lewis, W.A. *Growth and Fluctuations, 1870-1913*, London: Allen & Unwin, 1978.
645. Liddington, J. and Norris, J. *One Hand Tied Behind Us: The Rise of the Women's Suffrage Movement*, London: Virago, 1978.
646. Lindsay, Jean. *The Canals of Scotland*. Newton Abbot: David & Charles, 1973.
647. Lis, H. and Soly, H. *Poverty and Capitalism in Pre-Industrial Europe*, Brighton: Harvester Press, 1979.
648. Liversidge, Douglas. *The Luddites: Machine-Breakers of the Early Nineteenth Century*, London: Watts, 1972.
649. Liversidge, Joan. *Britain in the Roman Empire*, London: Routledge & Kegan Paul, 1968.
650. Lloyd, Alan. *The Hundred Years' War*, London: Hart-Davis, 1977.
651. Lloyd, Ian. *Rolls Royce: The Growth of a Firm*, London: Macmillan, 1978.
652. Lloyd, Trevor. "Africa and Hobson's Imperialism," *Past and Present*, no. 58 (1972).

653. Longrigg, Roger. *The English Squire and His Sport*, London: Stanley Paul, 1975.
654. Louis, William Roger (ed.). *The Robinson and Gallagher Controversy*, New York: New Viewpoints, 1976.
655. Low, Donald Anthony. *The Lion Rampant: Essays in the Study of British Imperialism*, London: Frank Cass, 1973.
656. Loyn, H.R. "Towns in late Anglo-Saxon England: The Evidence and Some Possible Lines of Enquiry" in Clemoes, P. and Hughes, K. (eds.), *England Before the Conquest: Studies in Primary Sources Presented to Dorothy Whitelock*, Cambridge University Press, 1971.
657. Loyn, Henry Royston. *The Vikings in Britain*, London: B.T. Batsford, 1977.
658. ————. *The Vikings in Wales*, 1976.
659. Lucas, A.M. *Women in the Middle Ages: Religion, Marriage and Letters*, Brighton: Harvester Press, 1983.
660. Luttwak, Edward. *The Grand Strategy of the Roman Empire: From the First Century A.D. to the Third*, Baltimore: The Johns Hopkins University Press, 1977.
661. Luvass, Jay. *The Education of an Army: British Military Thought, 1815-1940*, Chicago: University of Chicago Press, 1964.
662. Lydon, James F. *The Lordship of Ireland in the Middle Ages*, Toronto: University of Toronto Press, 1972.
663. McBride, T.M. *The Domestic Revolution: The Modernisation of Household Service in England and France, 1820-1920*, London: Croom Helm, 1976.
664. McCaffrey, Lawrence J. *The Irish Diaspora in America*, Bloomington: Indiana University Press, 1976.
665. McCann, Philip (ed.). *Popular Education and Socialization in the Nineteenth Century*, London: Methuen, 1977.
666. McClean, I.W. "Anglo-American Engineering Competition 1870-1914: Some Third Market Evidence," *Economic History Review*, 29 (1976).
667. McCloskey, D.N. "Did Victorian Britain Fail?," *Economic History Review*, 23 (1970).
668. ————. *Economic Maturity and Entrepreneurial Decline: British Iron and Steel, 1870-1913*, Boston: Harvard University Press, 1973.
669. ———— (ed.). *Essays on a Mature Economy: Britain after 1840*, London: Methuen, 1971.
670. ————. "The Industrial Revolution, 1780-1860: A Survey" in Mokyr, Joel (ed.), *The Economics of the Industrial Revolution*, Totowa, New Jersey: Rowman & Littlefield, 1985.
671. Macdonald, Donald Farquhar. *The State and the Trade Unions*, London: Macmillan, 1976.
672. McElwee, William. *The Art of War: Waterloo to Mons*, London: Weidenfeld & Nicolson, 1975.
673. McFarlane, K.B. "England and the Hundred Years' War," *Past and Present*, no. 22 (July 1962).
674. ————. *England in the Fifteenth Century: Collected Essays*, Hambledon Press, 1981.
675. ————. *Lancastrian Kings and Lollard Knights*; ed. by

Highfield, J.R.L. and Harriss, G.I., Oxford University Press, 1972.
676. McGrail, Sean. *Woodworking Techniques before 1500*, British Archaeological Reports, April 1982.
677. Machin, G.I.T. *Politics and the Churches in Great Britain, 1832-1868*, Oxford University Press, 1977.
678. Mackay, Ruddock F. *Balfour: Intellectual Stateman*, Oxford University Press, 1985.
679. Mackenzie, J.M. *Propaganda and Empire: The Manipulation of British Public Opinion, 1880-1960*, Manchester University Press, 1984.
680. McKibbin, Ross. *The Evolution of the Labour Party, 1910-1924*, Oxford University Press, 1984.
681. Mackie, Euan. *The Megalith Builders*, London: Phaidon, 1977.
682. ―――. *Science and Society in Prehistoric Britain*, New York: St. Martins Press, 1977.
683. Mackinnie, Donald. "Eugenics in Britain," *Social Studies in Science*, 6 (1976).
684. McKisack, May. *Medieval History in the Tudor Age*, Oxford: Clarendon Press, 1971.
685. McLaren, Angus. *Birth Control in Nineteenth Century England*, London: Croom Helm, 1978.
686. ―――. *Reproductive Rituals: Perceptions of Fertility in Britain, 1500-1800*, London: Methuen, 1984.
687. MacLaren, Roy. *Canadians on the Nile, 1882-1898*, Vancouver: University of British Columbia Press, 1978.
688. Maclean, David. "Finance and 'Informal Empire' before the First World War," *Economic History Review*, 2nd series, 29 (1976).
689. Macleod, Roy M. and Collins, P. (eds.). *The Parliament of Science*, London; Science Reviews, 1981.
690. Macmillan, David S. "Scottish Enterprise in Australia, 1789-1879" in Payne, Peter L. (ed.), *Studies in Scottish Business History*, London: Frank Cass, 1967.
691. McNeill, William H. *Plagues and Peoples*, Oxford: Blackwell, 1977.
692. ―――. *The Pursuit of Power: Technology, Armed Force and Society since A.D.1000*, Chicago/London: University of Chicago Press, 1982.
693. MacPherson, F. *Anatomy of a Conquest: British Occupation of Zambia, 1884-1924*, London: Longman, 1981.
694. Maddicott, J.R. *The English Peasantry and the Demands of the Crown, 1294-1341*, Past and Present Supplement 1, 1975.
695. Magdoff, Harry. *Imperialism from the Colonial Age to the Present*, London: Monthly Review Press, 1978.
696. Majumdar, R.C. *Historiography in Modern India*, New York: Asia Publishing House, 1971.
697. ―――, Raychaudhuri, H.C. and Datta, K. *An Advanced History of India*, 2nd ed., London: Macmillan, 1981.
698. Malcolmson, Robert W. *Popular Recreations in English Society, 1700-1850*, Cambridge University Press, 1973.
699. Malone, Joseph J. *Pine Trees and Politics: The Naval Stores and Foreign Policy in Colonial New England, 1691-1775*, London: Longman, 1964.
700. Mandel, Ernest. *Late Capitalism*, London: Verso edition, 1978.

701. ──────. *Long Waves of Capitalist Development: Marxist Interpretation*, Cambridge University Press, 1981.
702. Mangan, J.A. *Athleticism in the Victorian and Edwardian Public School*, Cambridge University Press, 1981.
703. Mann, Jill. *Chaucer and Medieval Estates Satire: The Literature of Social Classes and the General Prologue to the "Canterbury Tales,"* Cambridge University Press, 1973.
704. Mann, J.C. "Spoken Latin in Britain as Evidenced by Inscriptions," *Britannia*, ii (1971).
705. Margary, Ivan D. *Roman Roads in Britain*, 2nd ed., London: John Baker, 1973. First published in German in 1972.
706. Marlowe, John. *Cecil Rhodes: The Anatomy of Empire*, London: Elek, 1972.
707. Marsden, P. *Roman Roads*, London: Thames & Hudson, 1980.
708. Marshall, P.J. *East Indian Fortunes: The British in Bengal in the Eighteenth Century*, Oxford: Clarendon Press, 1976.
709. Martin, G.W. "The Canadian Analogy in South Africa Union, 1870-1910," *South African Historical Journal*, 8 (1973).
710. Masek, Rosemary. "Women in an Age of Transition, 1485-1714" in Kanner, Barbara (ed.), *The Women of England from Anglo-Saxon Times to the Present: Interpretative Bibliographical Essays*, Hamden, Conn.: Archon Books, 1979.
711. Mason, Tony. *Association Football and English Society*, Eastbourne: Harvester Press, 1980.
712. Mather, F.C. "The General Strike of 1842" in Quinault, R. and Stevenson, J. (eds.), *Popular Protest and Public Order: Six Studies in British History, 1790-1920*, London: Allen & Unwin, 1974.
713. Mathias, Peter. *The First Industrial Nation: An Economic History of Britain, 1700-1914*, 2nd ed., London: Methuen, 1983.
714. ────── (ed.). *Science and Society, 1600-1900*, Cambridge University Press, 1972.
715. ──────. *The Transformation of England: Essays in the Economic and Social History of England and Wales in the Eighteenth Century*, London: Methuen, 1979.
716. Matthew, Donald. *The Medieval European Community*, London: B.T. Batsford, 1977.
717. Matthew, H.C.G. *Liberal Imperialists: The Ideas and Politics of a post-Gladstonian Elite*, Oxford University Press, 1973.
718. Mauskopf, Seymour H. (ed.). *The Reception of Unconventional Science*, A.A.A.S. Selected Symposium, Boulder, Colorado: West View Press, 1979.
719. May, E.R. (ed.). *Knowing One's Enemies: Intelligence Assessment Before the Two World Wars*, Princeton University Press, 1984.
720. Mayer, Hans Eberhard (trans. John Gillingham), *The Crusades*, Oxford University Press, 1972.
721. Mayer, Sydney Louis and Koenig, William (eds.). *The Two World Wars: A Guide to the Manuscript Collections in the United Kingdom*, London: Bowker, 1976.
722. Meacham, S. "The Sense of an Impending Clash: English Working Class Unrest before the First World War," *American Historical Review*, LXXVII (1972).

723. Meadows, Arthur Jack. *Science and Controversy: A Biography of Sir Norman Lockyer*, Cambridge, Mass.: M.I.T. Press, 1972.
724. Meek, Ronald L. *Social Science and the Ignoble Savage*, Cambridge University Press, 1976.
725. Megaw, J.V.S. and Simpson, D.P.A. *Introduction to British Prehistory*, University of Leicester Press, 1979.
726. Mellars, P.A. "The Palaeolithic and Mesolithic" in Renfrew, Colin (ed.), *British Prehistory: A New Outline*, London: Duckworth, 1974.
727. Meller, Helen. *Leisure and thee Changing City, 1870-1914: Bristol*, London: Routledge & Kegan Paul, 1976.
728. Merrifield, Ralph. *The Roman City of London*, London: Ernest Benn, 1965.
729. Midwinter, Eric C. *Social Administration in Lancashire, 1830-1860*, Manchester University Press, 1969.
730. Miers, S. "Notes on the Arms Trade and Government Policy in Southern Africa between 1870 and 1890," *Journal of African History*, 12 (1971).
731. Millburn, John R. "Benjamin Martin: Author, Instrument-Maker and 'Country Showman,'" *Science in History*, no. 2, Leyden: Noordhoff International Publishing, 1976.
732. Miller, Edward and Hatcher, John. "Medieval England: Rural Society and Economic Change, 1086-1348" in Briggs, Asa (ed.), *Social and Economic History of England*, vol. 1, London.
733. Minchinton, W.E. *Reactions to Social and Economic Change, 1750-1939*, University of Exeter, 1980.
734. Miskimin, Harry A. "The Impact of Credit on Sixteenth Century British Industry" in *The Dawn of Modern Banking*. Center for Medieval and Renaissance Studies, University of California, New Haven & London: Yale University Press, 1979.
735. ———, Herlihy, D. and Udovitch, A.L. (eds.). *The Medieval City*, New Haven: Yale University Press, 1977.
736. Mitchell, B.R. *Economic Development of the British Coal Industry, 1800-1914*, Cambridge University Press, 1984.
737. ——— and Jones, H.G. (eds.). *Second Abstract of British Historical Statistics*, Cambridge University Press, 1971.
738. Mitchison, R. *Lordship and Patronage: Scotland, 1603-1745*, London: Edward Arnold, 1983.
739. Mokyr, Joel (ed.). *The Economics of the Industrial Revolution*, Totowa, New Jersey: Rowman & Littlefield, 1985.
740. ———. "Stagflation in Economic Perspective: The Napoleonic Wars Revisited" in Uselding, P. (ed.), *Research in Economic History*, vol. 1 (1976).
741. Mommsen, W. and Mock, W. (eds.). *The Emergence of the Welfare State in Britain and Germany, 1850-1950*, London: Croom Helm, 1981.
742. Money, J. *Experience and Identity: Birmingham and the West Midlands, 1760-1800*, Montreal: McGill-Queens University Press, 1977.
743. Monteon, Michael. *Chile in the Nitrate Era: The Evolution of Economic Dependence*, Madison: University of Wisconsin Press, 1982.

744. Moody, T.W., Martin, F.K. and Byrne, F.J. (eds.). *A New History of Ireland*, vol. 3, Oxford: Clarendon Press, 1976.
745. Moran, J.A.H. *The Growth of English Schooling, 1340-1548: Learning, Literacy and Laicisation in Pre-Reformation York Diocese*, Princeton University Press, 1981.
746. Morgan, Kenneth O. *Rebirth of a Nation: Wales, 1880-1980*, Oxford University Press, 1981.
747. ―――. *Wales in British Politics, 1868-1922*, University of Wales Press, 1980.
748. Morrill, J.S. *Cheshire, 1630-1660: County Government and Society During the English Revolution*, Oxford University Press, 1974.
749. ―――. "The Northern Gentry and the Great Rebellion," *Northern History*, XV (1979).
750. ―――. "Provincial Squires and Middling Souls in the Great Rebellion," *Historical Journal*, 20 (1977).
751. ―――. *The Revolt of the Provinces: Conservatives and Radicals in the English Civil War, 1630-1650*, London: Allen & Unwin, 1977.
752. Morris, A.J.A. *The Scaremongers: The Advocacy of War and Rearmament, 1896-1914*, London: Routledge & Kegan Paul, 1984.
753. Morris, Desmond. *The Soccer Tribe*, London: Cape, 1981.
754. Morris, R.J. *Cholera 1832*, London: Croom Helm, 1976.
755. Morton, Desmond. *Ministers and Generals: Politics and the Canadian Militia, 1868-1904*, Toronto: University of Toronto Press, 1971.
756. Moseley, Leonard. *Power Play: The Tumultuous World of Middle East Oil, 1890-1973*, London: Weidenfeld & Nicolson, 1973.
757. Moss, Michael S. and Hume, John R. *Workshop of the British Empire: Engineering and Shipbuilding in the West of Scotland*, London: Heinemann Educational, 1977.
758. Muffett, D.J.M. *Empire Builder Extraordinary: Sir George Goldie, His Philosophy of Government and Empire*, Shearwater Press, 1978.
759. Mulligan, Lotte. "Puritans and English Science: A Critique of Webster," *Isis*, 71, no. 258 (1980).
760. Munro, John H. "Bullionism and the Bill of Exchange in England, 1271-1663" in *The Dawn of Modern Banking*, Center for Medieval and Renaissance Studies, University of California, Los Angeles, New Haven & London: Yale University Press, 1979.
761. Murphy, B.D. *History of the British Economy, 1086-1970*, London: Longman, 1973.
762. Murtaugh, D.M. "Women and Geoffrey Chaucer," *Journal of English Literary History*, 38 (1971).
763. Musgrave, P.W. "The Labour Force: Some Relevant Attitudes" in Roderick, Gordon and Stephens, Michael (eds.), *Where Did We Go Wrong?*, Lewes: The Falmer Press, 1981.
764. Musson, A.E. *The Growth of British Industry*, London: B.T. Batsford, 1978.
765. ―――. *Trade Union and Social Studies*, London: Frank Cass, 1974.
766. Mutero Chirenje, J. *A History of Northern Botswana*, London: Associated University Presses, 1977.

767. Namier, Sir Lewis. *The Structure of Politics at the Accession of George III*, London: Macmillan, 1979.
768. Needham, Joseph. *Clerks and Craftsmen in China and The West: Lectures and Addresses on the History of Science and Technology*, Cambridge University Press, 1970.
769. Nelson, L. *The Normans in South Wales, 1070-1171*, Houston: University of Texas Press, 1966.
770. Newark, Timothy. *Medieval Warfare*, London: Jupiter, 1979.
771. Newton, Douglas J. *British Labour, European Socialism and the Struggle for Peace, 1889-1914*, Oxford: Clarendon Press, 1985.
772. Niane, D.T. (ed.). *Africa from the Twelfth to the Sixteenth Century*, Heinemann, California: UNESCO, 1984.
773. Nicolson, Colin. "Edwardian England and the Coming of the First World War" in O'Day, Alan (ed.), *The Edwardian Age: Conflict and Stability, 1900-1914*, London: Macmillan, 1979.
774. Norman, A.V.B. and Pottinger, Don. *English Weapons for Warfare, 449-1660*, London: Arms and Armour Press, 1979 (1966).
775. Norman, E.R. *Church and Society in England, 1770-1970: A Historical Study*, Oxford: Clarendon Press, 1976.
776. Norman, Vesey. *The Medieval Soldier*, London: Arthur Baker, 1971.
777. North, D.C. *Structure and Change in Economic History*, New York: Norton, 1981.
778. Obelkevich, J. (ed.). *Religion and the People, 800-1700*, Chapel Hill: University of North Carolina Press, 1979.
779. O'Brien, D.P. and Presley, John R. *Pioneers of Modern Economics in Britain*, London: Macmillan, 1981.
780. O'Carroll, Maura. "The Educational Organization of the Dominicans in England and Wales, 1221-1348: A Multidisciplinary Approach," *Archivum Fratrum Praedicatorum*, 50 (1980).
781. O'Day, Rosemary. *Economy and Community: Economic and Social History of Pre-industrial England, 1500-1700*, London: A. & C. Black, 1975.
782. ─────. *Education and Society, 1500-1800: Social Foundations of Education in Early Modern Britain*, London: Longman, 1982.
783. O'Donaghue, Yolande. *William Roy, 1726-1790: Pioneer of the Ordnance Survey*, London: The British Library, 1977.
784. Ogot, B.A. (ed.). *Africa from the Sixteenth to the Eighteenth Century*, London: Heinemann, 1985.
785. Oliver, Roland (ed.). *The Cambridge History of Africa*, Cambridge University Press, 1985.
786. Orel, Harold (ed.). *Irish History and Culture*, Lawrence: University Press of Kansas, 1976.
787. Orme, Nicholas. *Education in the West of England, 1066-1548*, University of Exeter, 1976.
788. ─────. *English Schools in the Middle Ages*, London: Methuen, 1973.
789. ─────. *From Childhood to Chivalry: The Education of the English Kings and Aristocracy, 1066-1530*, London: Methuen, 1984.

790. ———. "Schoolmasters, 1307-1509" in Clough, H.C.H. (ed.), *Profession, Vocation and Culture in Later Medieval England*, Liverpool University Press, 1982.
791. O'Tuthaigh, Gearoid. *Ireland Before the Famine, 1798-1848*, Dublin: Gill & Macmillan [Gill History of Ireland], 1972.
792. Overy, R.J. *William Morris, Viscount Nuffield*, London: Europa Publications, 1976.
793. Paetow, Louis John. *A Guide to the Study of Medieval History;* errata compiled by Gray C. Boyce and with an addendum by Lynn Thorndike, New York: Kraus Reprint, 1980.
794. Page, Raymond Ian. *Life in Anglo-Saxon England*, London: B.T. Batsford, 1970.
795. Pakenham, Thomas. *The Boer War*, London: Weidenfeld & Nicolson, 1974.
796. Pakenham, Valerie. *The Noonday Sun: Edwardians in the Tropics*, London: Methuen, 1985.
797. Palliser, D.M. *The Reformation in York, 1534-1553*, Borthwick Papers no. 40, York: St. Anthony's Press, 1971.
798. ———. "Tawney's Century: Brave New World or Malthusian Prop?," *Economic History Review*, 2nd series, XXXI, no. 2 (1982).
799. Palmer, Susann. *Mesolithic Cultures of Britain*, Poole: Dolphin Press, 1977.
800. Parker, Vanessa. *The Making of King's Lynn: Secular Buildings from the 11th to 17th Centuries*, Chichester: Phillimore, 1971.
801. Parkes, M.B. "The Literature of the Laity" in Daiches, David & Thorlby, Anthony, K. (eds.), *Literature and Western Civilization*, vol. 2: *The Medieval World*, London: Aldus, 1973.
802. Parritt, Lt. Col. B.A.H. *The Intelligencers*, Ashford, Kent, 1971.
803. Partner, Nancy F. *Serious Entertainments: The Writing of History in Twelfth Century England*, Chicago: University of Chicago Press, 1977.
804. Paul, H. *The Sorcerer's Apprentice: The French Scientists' Image of German Science, 1840-1919*, Gainesville: University of Florida Press,
805. Pawlisch, H.S. *Sir John Davies and the Conquest of Ireland: A Study in Legal Imperialism*, Cambridge University Press, 1985.
806. Pawson, Eric. *Transport and Economy: The Turnpike Roads of Eighteenth Century Britain*, New York: Academic Press, 1977.
807. Payne, Peter L. (ed.). *Studies in Scottish Business History*, London: Frank Cass, 1967.
808. ———. "Industrial Entrepreneurship and Management in Great Britain" in Mathias, P. and Postan, M.M. (eds.), *The Cambridge Economic History of Europe*, vol. 7: *The Industrial Economies: Capital Labour and Enterprise*, Part 1: *Britain, France, Germany and Scandinavia*, Cambridge University Press,
809. Pearsall, Ronald. *Edwardian Life and Leisure*, Newton Abbot: David & Charles, 1973.

810. ―――. *Victorian Popular Music*, Newton Abbot: David & Charles, 1973.
811. Pelling, Henry. *History of British Trade Unionism*, London: Macmillan, 1976.
812. Penelope, Stanley J. and McGowan, C. "Woman and 'Wife': Social and Semantic Shifts in English," *Papers in Linguistics*, 12 (1979).
813. Pennington, Donald. "The War and the People" in Morrill, John (ed.), *Reactions to the English Civil War, 1642-1749*, London: Macmillan, 1982.
814. Penrose, Ernest Francis. *European Imperialism and the Partition of Africa*, London: Frank Cass, 1975.
815. Perceval-Maxwell, M. *Scottish Migration to Ulster in the Reign of James I*, London: Routledge & Kegan Paul, 1973.
816. Petree, J. Foster. "Charles Wye Williams (1779-1866): A Pioneer in Steam Navigation and Fuel Efficiency," *Trans Newcomen Society 1966-7*, vol. 39 (1970).
817. Plant, Marjorie. *The English Book Trade: An Economic History of the Making and Sale of Books*, London: Allen & Unwin, 1967.
818. Platt, Colin. *The Castle in Medieval England and Wales*, London: Secker & Warburg, 1982.
819. ―――. *Medieval England: A Social History and Archaeology from the Conquest to 1600 A.D.*, New York: Charles Scribner's Sons, 1978.
820. Platt, Desmond C. *Business Imperialism, 1840-1930: An Inquiry based on British Experience in Latin America*, Oxford University Press, 1977.
821. ―――. "Further Objections to an 'Imperialism of Free Trade,' 1830-60," *Economic History Review*, 2nd series, 26 (1973).
822. ―――. *Latin America and British Trade, 1806-1914*, London: A. & C. Black, 1972.
823. Pocock, J.G.A. (ed.). *Three British Revolutions: 1641, 1688, 1776*, Princeton University Press, 1981.
824. Polisensky, J.V. and Snider, F. *War and Society in Europe, 1618-1648*, Cambridge University Press, 1978.
825. Pollard, S. "Labour in Great Britain" in Mathias, P. and Postan, M.M. (eds.), *Cambridge Economic History of Europe*, vol. 7: *The Industrial Economies: Capital Labour and Enterprise, Part 1: Britain, France, Germany and Scandinavia*, Cambridge University Press.
826. Pollock, Linda A. *Forgotten Children: Parent-Child Relations from 1500-1900*, Cambridge University Press, 1983.
827. Ponko, Vincent R. *Ships, Seas and Scientists: United States Naval Exploration and Discovery in the Nineteenth Century*, Annapolis, Maryland: United States Naval Institute, 1974.
828. Pool, Ithiel De Sola (ed.). *The Social Impact of the Telephone*, London: M.I.T. Press, 1977.
829. Poole, J.B. and Andrews, Kay (eds.). *The Government of Science in Britain*, London: Weidenfeld & Nicolson, 1972.
830. Porteous, John Douglas. *Canal Ports: The Urban Achievement of the Canal Age*, New York: Academic Press, 1977.
831. Porter, A.N. *The Origins of the South African War: Joseph*

Chamberlain and the Diplomacy of Imperialism, Manchester University Press, 1980.
832. Porter, Bernard. *The Lion's Share: A Short History of British Imperialism, 1850-1970*, London: Longman, 1976.
833. ─────. *Britain, Europe and the World, 1850-1902: Delusions of Grandeur*, London: Allen & Unwin, 1982.
834. Post, John D. *The Last Great Subsistence Crisis in the Western World*, Baltimore: Johns Hopkins University Press, 1977.
835. Postan, M.M. *Essays on Medieval Agriculture and General Problems of the Medieval Economy*, Cambridge University Press, 1973.
836. ───── et al., *The Cambridge Economic History of Europe*, vols. 1-7, Cambridge University Press, 1963-1982.
837. Powell, Ellis T. *The Evolution of the Money Market, 1385-1915: An Historical and Analytical Study of the Rise and Development of Finance as a Centralised, Coordinated Force*, 3rd impression, , London: Frank Cass, 1966.
838. Power, Eileen. *Medieval Women*, ed. M.M. Postan, Cambridge University Press, 1975.
839. Power, E. "Some Women Practitioners of Medicine in the Middle Ages," *Proceedings of the Royal Society of Medicine*, 15 (1921-22).
840. Prebble, John. *Mutiny: Highland Regiments in Revolt, 1743-1804*, London: Secker & Warburg, 1975.
841. Preston, Richard Arthur. *Canada and "Imperial Defense": A Study of the British Commonwealth's Defense Organization, 1867-1919*, Toronto: University of Toronto Press, 1967.
842. ─────. *Canada's R.M.C.: A History of the Royal Military College*, Toronto: University of Toronto Press, 1970.
843. Prestwich, M. *The Three Edwards: War and the State in England, 1277-1377*, London: Methuen, 1981.
844. ─────. *War, Politics and Finance under Edward I*, London: Faber & Faber, 1972.
845. Price, Derek J. De Solla. *Science Since Babylon*, enlarged edition, Yale University Press, 1976.
846. Price, R. *An Imperial War and the British Working Class: Working Class Attitudes and Reactions to the Boer War, 1899-1902*, London: Routledge & Kegan Paul, 1982.
847. ─────. "Society, Status and Jingoism: The Social Roots of Lower Middle-Class Patriotism" in Crossick, G. (ed.), *The Lower Middle Class, 1870-1914*, London: Croom Helm, 1977.
848. Prior, Mary (ed.). *Women in English Society, 1550-1800*, London: Methuen, 1985.
849. Proudfoot, W.B. *The Origin of Stencil Duplicating*, London: Hutchinson, 1972.
850. Pugh, M. *Women's Suffrage in Britain, 1867-1928*, London: Historical Association Pamphlet, 1980.
851. Pugh, T.B. "The Magnates, Knights and Gentry" in Chrimes, S.B., Ross, C.D. and Griffiths, R.A (eds.), *Fifteenth Century England, 1399-1509: Studies in Politics and Society*, Manchester University Press, 1972.
852. Purves, J.G. and West, D.A. *War and Society in the Nineteenth Century Russian Empire*, Toronto: New Review Books, 1972.
853. Queller, Donald E. *The Fourth Crusade: The Conquest of*

Constantinople, 1201-1204, Leicester University Press, 1978.
854. Quinault, R. and Stevenson, J. (eds.). Popular Protest and Public Order: Six Studies in British History, 1790-1920, London: Allen & Unwin, 1974.
855. Raistrick, Arthur. The Lead Industry of Wensleydale and Swaledale, vol. 1: The Mines, vol. 2: The Smelting Mills, Moorland Publishing Company, 1975 and 1976.
856. Ramsey, Peter H. (ed.). The Price Revolution in Sixteenth Century England, London: Methuen, 1971.
857. Ray, Arthur J. The Early Fur Traders: A Study in Cultural Interaction, Toronto: McClelland & Stewart, 1976.
858. ———. Indians in the Fur Trade: Their Role as Trappers, Hunters and Middlemen in the Lands South West of Hudson Bay, Toronto: University of Toronto Press, 1975.
859. Read, Conyers. William Lambarde and Local Government, Ithaca, New York: Cornell University Press, 1962.
860. Reader, W.J. Bowater: A History, Cambridge University Press, 1981.
861. ———. Imperial Chemical Industries: A History, vol. 1: The Forerunners, 1870-1926, Oxford University Press, 1976.
862. ———. Macadam, The Macadam Family and Turnpike Roads, 1798-1861, London: Heinemann, 1980.
863. ———. Victorian England, London: B.T. Batsford, 1973.
864. Reeder, D.A. (ed.). Urban Education in the Nineteenth Century, New York: St. Martins Press, 1978.
865. Reel, Jerome V. (ed.). Index to Biographies of Englishmen, 1000-1485: Found in Dissertations and Theses, Greenwood Press Inc., 1975.
866. Rees, Gareth. "Copper Sheathing: An Example of Technological Diffusion in the English Merchant Fleet," Journal of Transport History, NS 1 (1971).
867. Rehna, T. "The Idea of Peace in the West, 500-1150," Journal of Medieval History, 6 (1980).
868. Reid, Stanford (ed.). The Scottish Tradition in Canada, Toronto: McClelland & Stewart, 1976.
869. Renfrew, Colin. Before Civilization: The Radiocarbon Revolution and Prehistoric Europe, London: Cape, 1973.
870. ——— (ed.). British Prehistory: A New Outline, London: Duckworth, 1974.
871. Renfrew, Colin. "Revolution in Prehistory," The Listener, vol. 84 (31 December 1970; 7 January 1971).
872. Reynolds, Peter J. Iron Age Farm: The Butser Experiment, London: Colonnade Books, 1979.
873. Reynolds, Terry S. Stronger than a Hundred Men: A History of the Vertical Waterwheel, Johns Hopkins Studies in the History of Technology, New Series no. 7, Baltimore: Johns Hopkins University Press, 1983.
874. Richards, Eric. The Leviathan of Wealth: The Sutherland Fortune in the Industrial Revolution, London: Routledge & Kegan Paul, 1973.
875. Riley-Smith, Louise and Riley-Smith, Jonathan. The Crusades: Idea and Reality, 1095-1274, London: Edward Arnold, 1981.
876. Rivet, A.L.F. and Smith, C. The Place Names of Roman Britain, London: B.T. Batsford, 1979.

877. Roberts, A.D. (ed.). *The Cambridge History of Africa*, vol. 7: c. 1905-1940, Cambridge University Press, 1985.
878. Roberts, Adam and Guelff, R. (eds.). *Documents on the Laws of War*, Oxford: Clarendon Press, 1982.
879. Roberts, David. *Paternalism in Early Victorian England*, London: Croom Helm, 1979.
880. Roberts, Robert. *The Classic Slum: Salford Life in the First Quarter of the Century*, Manchester University Press, 1971.
881. Robertson, John. *The Scottish Enlightenment and the Militia Issue*, Edinburgh: John Donald Publishers, 1985.
882. Robinson, Eric and McKie, Douglas (eds.). *Partners in Science: Letters of James Watt and Joseph Black*, Cambridge, Mass.: Harvard University Press, 1970.
883. Robinson, William. *Life and Tradition in the Lake District*, Lancaster: Dalesman Publishing Co., 1981.
884. Roderick, Gordon and Stephens, Michael (eds.). *Where Did We Go Wrong?*, Lewes: The Falmer Press, 1981.
885. Rodwell, Warwick and Rowley, Trevor (eds.). *The "Small Towns" of Roman Britain: Conference Papers*, British Archaeological Reports, 1975.
886. Roe, Derek A. *The Lower and Middle Palaeolithic Periods in Britain*, London: Routledge & Kegan Paul, 1981.
887. Rogers, Col. H.C.B. *The British Army of the Eighteenth Century*, London: George Allen & Unwin, 1977.
888. ———. *A History of Artillery*, New Jersey: The Citadel Press, 1975.
889. Roller, Duane H.D. *Perspective in the History of Science and Technology*, Norman: University of Oklahoma Press, 1972.
890. Rolt, Lionel T.C. *Victorian Engineering*, London: Allen Lane, 1970.
891. Ropp, Theodore. "Nineteenth Century European Military-Industrial Complexes" in Cooling, B.F. (ed.), *War, Business and American Society: Historical Perspectives on the Military-Industrial Complex*, Kennikat Press, 1977.
892. Rose, Michael E. *The English Poor Law, 1780-1930*, New York: Barnes & Noble, 1971.
893. ——— (ed.). *The Poor and the City: The English Poor Law in its Urban Context*, St. Martins Press, 1985.
894. Rosen, Andrew. *Rise Up, Women! The Militant Campaign of the Women's Social and Political Union, 1903-1914*, London: Routledge & Kegan Paul, 1974.
895. Rosenberg, Nathan. *Inside the Black Box: Technology and Economics*, Cambridge University Press, 1982.
896. ———. *Perspectives on Technology*, Cambridge University Press, 1976.
897. Roskill, Stephen Wentworth. *Hankey: Man of Secrets*, vol. 1, London: Collins, 1970.
898. Ross, Charles (ed.). *Patronage, Pedigree and Power in Later Medieval England*, Gloucester: Sutton, 1979.
899. Ross, Steven. *From Flintlock to Rifle: Infantry Tactics, 1740-1866*, London: Associated University Presses, 1981.
900. Rostow, Walt W. *The Stages of Economic Growth: A Non-Communist Manifesto*, rev. ed., Cambridge University Press, 1971.
901. Rothenberg, Gunther E. *The Art of Warfare in the Age of Napoleon*, London: B.T. Batsford, 1977.

902. Rothwell, W. "The Role of the French in Thirteenth Century England," *Bulletin of the John Rylands University Library*, 58 (1976).
903. Rousseau, G.S. "Science Books and Their Readers in the Eighteenth Century" in Rivers, Isabel (ed.), *Books and Their Readers in Eighteenth Century England*, Leicester University Press, 1982.
904. Rowland, B. (ed. and trans.). *Medieval Woman's Guide to Health: The First English Gynecological Handbook*, London, 1981.
905. Rowse, Alfred Leslie. *The Elizabethan Renaissance*, vol. 1: *The Life of the Society*, London: Macmillan, 1971.
906. Roy, Ian. "The Army and Its Critics in Seventeenth Century England" in bond, Brian and Roy, Ian (eds.), *War and Society: A Yearbook of Military History*, London: Croom Helm, 1977.
907. Russell, Colin Archibald and Goodman, D.C. *Science and the Rise of Technology since 1800*, London: John Wright & Sons in Association with the Open University Press, 1972.
908. Russell, Frederick H. *The Just War in the Middle Ages*, Cambridge University Press, 1975.
909. Russett, Bruce M. (ed.). *Peace, War and Numbers*, London: Sage Publications, 1972.
910. Sachse, William L. *The Colonial American in Britain*, Madison: University of Wisconsin Press, 1956.
911. ———. *Restoration England, 1660-1689*, Cambridge University Press, 1971.
912. Sadie, Stanley (ed.). *The New Grove Dictionary of Music and Musicians*, London: Macmillan, 1980.
913. Saenger, Paul. "Silent Reading: Its Impact on Late Medieval Script and Society," *Viator*, 13 (1982).
914. Sainty, J.C. *Lieutenants of Counties, 1585-1642*, University of London, Institute of Historical Research, 1970.
915. Salway, Peter. *Roman Britain*, Oxford University Press, 1981.
916. Sandberg, Lars G. *Lancashire in Decline: A Study in Entrepreneurship, Technology and International Trade*, Columbus: Ohio State University Press, 1974.
917. ———. "From Damnation to Redemption: Judgements on the Late Victorian Entrepreneur," *Explorations in Economic History*, 9 (1971).
918. Sanderson, J.M. *Universities and British Industry, 1850-1970*, London: Routledge & Kegan Paul, 1972.
919. Sanderson, M. *Education, Economic Change and Society in England, 1780-1870*, London: Macmillan, 1983.
920. ———. "Literacy and Social Mobility in the Industrial Revolution," *Past and Present*, 56 (1972).
921. Saul, S.B. (ed.). *Technological Change: The United States and Britain in the Nineteenth Century*, London: Methuen, 1970.
922. Sawyer, Peter (ed.). *The Domesday Book: A Reassessment*, London: Edward Arnold, 1985.
923. Sawyer, P.H. *Kings and Vikings: Scandinavia and Europe, A.D. 700-1100*, London: Methuen, 1982.
924. Sayers, R.S. *The Bank of England, 1891-1944*, 3 vols., Cambridge University Press, 1976.

925. Scarisbrick, J.J. Henry VIII, Berkeley: University of California Press, 1969.
926. Schapiro, Barbara. "The Universities and Science in 17th Century England," *Journal of British Studies*, 10, 7 (1971).
927. ———— and Frank, Robert G. Jr. *English Scientific Virtuosi in the Sixteenth and Seventeenth Centuries*, Los Angeles: University of California, William Andrews Clark Memorial Library, 1979.
928. Schlight, John. *Monarchs and Mercenaries: A Reappraisal of the Importance of Knight Service in Norman and Anglo-Saxon England*, Bridgeport, Conn. 1968.
929. Schnorrenberg, Barbara B. with Hunter, Jean E. "The Eighteenth Century Englishwoman" in Kanner, Barbara (ed.), *The Women of England from Anglo-Saxon Times to the Present: Interpretative Bibliographical Essays*, Hamden, Conn.: Archon Books, 1979.
930. Schofield, Robert E. *Mechanism and Materialism: British Natural Philosophy in an Age of Reason*, Princeton University Press, 1970.
931. Schofield, R.S. "Dimensions of Illiteracy, 1750-1850," *Explorations in Economic History*, vol. 10 (1973).
932. Schroeder, Paul W. *Austria, Great Britain and the Crimean War: The Destruction of the European Concert*, Ithaca, New York: Cornell University Press, 1973.
933. Schurman, D.M. *The Education of a Navy: The Development of British Strategic Naval Thought, 1867-1914*, London: Cresset, 1965.
934. Scott, A. *Every One a Witness*, London: Martins, 1970.
935. Scott, Samuel F. *The Response of the Royal Army to the French Revolution: Role and Development of the Line Army, 1787-93*, Oxford University Press, 1978.
936. Scouller, R.E. *The Armies of Queen Anne*, Oxford: Clarendon Press, 1966.
937. Scullard, H.H. *Roman Britain: An Outpost of the Empire*, London: Thames & Hudson, 1979.
938. Seaborne, Malcolm. *The English School: Its Architecture and Organisation*, vol. 1: *1370-1870*, London: Routledge & Kegan Paul, 1971.
939. Seaman, Lewis Charles Bernard. *Post-Victorian Britain, 1902-1951*, London: Methuen, 1967.
940. ————. *Victorian England: Aspects of English and Imperial History, 1837-1901*, London: Methuen, 1973.
941. Searle, G.R. *Eugenics and Politics in Britain, 1900-1914*, Science in History, no. 3, Leyden: Noordhoff, 1976.
942. ————. *The Quest for National Efficiency: A Study in British Politics and Political Thought, 1899-1914*, Berkeley: University of California Press, 1971.
943. Semmel, Bernard. *The Rise of Free Trade Imperialism: Classical Political Economy, the Empire of Free Trade and Imperialism, 1750-1850*, Cambridge University Press, 1970.
944. Sen, S.P. *Historians and Historiography in Modern India*, Calcutta: Institute of Historical Studies, 1973.
945. Senior, Hereward. *The Fenians and Canada*, Toronto: University of Toronto Press, 1978.

946. Setton, K.M. (ed. in chief). *A History of the Crusades*, Madison: University of Wisconsin Press, 1969.
947. ―――. *The Papacy and the Levant, 1204-1571*, Philadelphia, American Philosophical Society Memoirs, vol. 114, 1976.
948. Seymour, William. *Battles in Britain: Their Political Background*, vol. 1: *1066-1547*, vol. 2: *1547-1746*, London: Sidgwick & Jackson, 1976.
949. Seymour, W.A. (ed.). *A History of the Ordnance Survey*, Folkestone: Wm. Dawson, 1980.
950. Shahar, Shulamith. *The Fourth Estate: A History of Women in the Middle Ages*, London: Methuen, 1985.
951. Shapin, Steven A. "The Royal Society of Edinburgh: A Study of the Social Context of Hanoverian Science," *Diss. Abst. Int.*, 32 (1972).
952. Sharpe, Kevin (ed.). *Faction and Parliament: Essays on Early Stuart History*, London: Methuen, 1985.
953. Sheail, J. "The Distribution of Taxable Population and Wealth during the Early Sixteenth Century: A Commentary," *Transactions of the Institute of British Geographers*, 55 (1972).
954. Sheffield, James R. *Education in Kenya: An Historical Study*, New York: Columbia Teachers College Press, 1973.
955. Shelby, Lon R. "The Education of Medieval English Master Masons," *Medieval Studies*, 32 (1970).
956. Sherwig, John M. *Guineas and Gunpowder: British Foreign Aid in the Wars with France, 1793-1815*, Cambridge, Mass.: Harvard University Press, 1969.
957. Shirley, Rodney W. *Early Printed Maps of the British Isles: A Bibliography, 1477-1650*, revised ed., Holland Park Cartographies 5, London, 1980.
958. ―――. *The Mapping of the World: Early Printed World Maps, 1472-1700*, London: The Holland Press, 1983.
959. Simon, Joan. "Education" in Watson, G. (ed.). *The New Cambridge Bibliography of English Literature*, vol. 1: *600-1600*, Cambridge University Press, 1974.
960. ―――. *Education and Society in Tudor England*, Cambridge University Press, 1966.
961. ―――. *The Social Origins of English Education*, London: Routledge & Kegan Paul, 1970.
962. Sims, Geoffrey. "Engineering" in Roderick, Gordon and Stephens, Michael (eds.), *Where Did We Go Wrong?*, Lewes: The Falmer Press, 1981.
963. Singer, Charles et al. (eds.). *A History of Technology*, vol. 8: *Consolidated Indexes*, comp. Richard Raper, Oxford University Press, 1984.
964. Singer, Joel David and Small, Melvin M. *The Wages of War, 1816-1965: A Statistical Handbook*, Chichester: John Wiley, 1972.
965. Skelley, Alan Ramsay. *The Victorian Army at Home: The Recruitment and Terms and Conditions of the British Regular*, Montreal: McGill-Queens University Press, 1977.
966. Skelton, R.A. *Saxton's Survey of England and Wales*, Amsterdam, 1974.
967. Skipp, V.H.T. "Economic and Social Change in the Forest of Arden, 1530-1649," *Agricultural History Review*, 18 (1970).

968. Slavin, A.J. (ed.). *Tudor Men and Institutions: Studies in English Law and Government*, Baton Rouge, 1972.
969. Slocum, Robert B. *Biographical Dictionaries and Related Works*, Supplement (1972), Second Supplement (1978), Detroit: Gale Research Company.
970. Smail, R.C. *Crusading Warfare, 1097-1193*, Cambridge University Press, 1956.
971. Smeed, V. (ed.). *Encyclopedia of Military Models*, London: Octopus, 1981.
972. Smith, Alan G.R. *Science and Society in the Sixteenth and Seventeenth Centuries*, London: Thames & Hudson, 1972.
973. Smith, Barbara M.D. "The Galtons of Birmingham: Quaker Merchants and Bankers, 1702-1831," *Business History*, LX (1967).
974. Smith, Dennis. *Conflict and Compromise: Class Formation in English Society, 1830-1914*, London: Routledge & Kegan Paul, 1982.
975. Smith, I.F. "The Neolithic" in Renfrew, Colin (ed.), *British Prehistory: A New Outline*, London: Duckworth, 1974.
976. Smith, Philip. *The Treasure-Seekers: The Men Who Built Home Oil*, Toronto: Macmillan of Canada, 1978.
977. Smith, Richard M. (ed.). *Land, Kinship and the Life Cycle*, Cambridge University Press, 1985.
978. Smout, T.C. *A History of the Scottish People, 1560-1830*, London: Collins, 1969.
979. ———— (ed.). *The Search for Wealth and Stability: Essays in Economic and Social History Presented to M.W. Flinn*, London: Macmillan, 1979.
980. Smyth, A.P. *Warlords and Holy Men: Scotland, A.D. 800-1000, A New History of Scotland*, vol. 1, London: Edward Arnold, 1984.
981. Snell, K.D.M. *Annals of the Labouring Poor: Social Change and Agrarian England, 1660-1900*, Cambridge University Press, 1985.
982. Soffer, Rena N. *Ethics and Society in England: The Revolution in the Social Sciences, 1870-1914*, Berkeley: University of California Press, 1978.
983. Soldon, Norbert C. *Women in British Trade Unions, 1874-1976*, Dublin: Gill & Macmillan, 1978.
984. Solow, Barbara Lewis. *The Land Question and the Irish Economy, 1807-1903*, Cambridge, Mass.: Harvard University Press, 1972.
985. Soloway, R.A. *Prelates and People: Ecclesiastical Social Thought in England, 1783-1852*, London: Routledge & Kegan Paul, 1969.
986. Sorrell, Alan. *Roman London*, London: B.T. Batsford, 1969.
987. Southern, R.W. "Master Vacarius and the Beginning of an English Academic Tradition" in Alexander, J.J.G. and Gibson, Margaret Templeton (eds.), *Medieval Learning and Literature: Essays Presented to Richard William Hunt*, Oxford University Press, 1976.
988. Speck, W.A. *The Butcher: The Duke of Cumberland and the Suppression of the '45*, Oxford: Basil Blackwell, 1981.
989. Spiers, Edward M. *The Army and Society, 1815-1914*, London: Longman, 1980.

990. Springhall, J.O. "Boy Scouts, Class and Militarism, 1908-1930," *International Review of Social History*, XVI, part 2 (1971).
991. ─────────. *Youth, Empire and Society: British Youth Movements, 1883-1940*, Hamden, Conn.: Shoe String Press, 1977.
992. Stacey, C.P. *Canada and the British Army, 1846-71*, Toronto: University of Toronto Press, 1963.
993. Stafford, L.W.T. *The Modern Economy: A Theoretical Debate and its Practical Implications*, London: Longman, 1976.
994. Stahl, William H. *Roman Science: Origins, Development and Influence in the Later Middle Ages*, Madison: University of Wisconsin Press, 1962.
995. Stallard, Patricia Y. *Glittering Misery: Dependents of England's Fighting Army*, San Rafael: Presidio Press, 1978.
996. Stanley, George F.G. and Sylvestre, Guy (eds.). *Pioneers of Canadian Science*, Toronto: University of Toronto Press, 1967.
997. Steane, John. *The Archaeology of Medieval England and Wales*, London: Croom Helm, 1985.
998. Stearns, Peter N. *Lives of Labour: Work in a Maturing Industrial Society*, New York: Holmes & Meier, 1975.
999. ─────────. "The Working Class Women in Britain" in Vicinus, Martha J. (ed.), *A Widening Sphere: Changing Roles of Victorian Women*, Bloomington: Indiana University Press, 1977.
1000. Stearns, Raymond P. *Science in the British Colonies of America*, Urbana: University of Illinois Press, 1971.
1001. Steadman Jones, G. "Class Expression versus Social Control: A Critique of Recent Trends in the Social History of Leisure," *History Workshop*, 4 (1977).
1002. ─────────. *Outcast London: A Study in the Relations between Classes in Victorian Society*, Oxford: Clarendon Press, 1971.
1003. Steiner, Zara S. "Finance, Trade and Politics in British Foreign Policy, 1815-1914," *The Historical Journal*, 13 (1970).
1004. Stephens, Michael D. "Changing Attitudes to Education in England and Wales, 1833-1902: The Government Reports with Particular Reference to Science and Technical Studies," *Annals of Science*, 30 (1973).
1005. ───── and Roderick, Gordon W. "Education and Training for English Engineers in the late 19th and early 20th Centuries," *Annals of Science*, 27 (1971).
1006. Stevens, W.B. "Male Illiteracy in Devon on the Eve of the Civil War," *Devon Historian*, 11 (1975).
1007. Stevenson, J. *Popular Disturbances in England, 1700-1870*, New York: Longman, 1979.
1008. Stewart, Anthony Terence Quincey. *The Pagoda War: Lord Dufferin and the Fall of the Kingdom of Ava, 1885-86*, London: Faber & Faber, 1972.
1009. Stock, Brian. *The Implications of Literacy: Written Language and Models of Interpretation in the Eleventh and Twelfth Centuries*, Princeton University Press, 1983.
1010. Stocking, George W. *Middle East Oil: A Study in Political and*

Economic Controversy, Nashville: Vanderbilt University Press, 1970.
1011. Stone, Ian. *Canal Immigration in British India*, Cambridge University Press, 1984.
1012. Stone, Lawrence and Stone, Jeane C.F. *An Open Elite?: England, 1540-1880*, Oxford: Clarendon Press, 1976.
1013. ─────. *The Causes of the English Revolution, 1529-1642*, London: Routledge & Kegan Paul, 1972.
1014. ─────. *Schooling and Society: Studies in the History of Education*, Baltimore: Johns Hopkins University Press, 1977.
1015. Storch, Robert D. (ed.). *Popular Culture and Custom in Nineteenth Century England*, London: Croom Helm, 1982.
1016. Stover, Leon E. and Craig, Bruce. *Stonehenge: The Indo-European Heritage*, Chicago: Nelson Hall, 1978.
1017. Strachan, Hew. "The Early Victorian Army and the Nineteenth Century Revolution in Government," *English Historical Review*, XCV (1980).
1018. ─────. "Soldiers Strategy and Sebastopol," *Historical Journal*, XXI (1978).
1019. ─────. *Wellington's Legacy: The Reform of the British Army, 1830-54*, Manchester University Press, 1984.
1020. Strayer, J.R. "The Costs and Profits of War: The Anglo-French Conflict of 1290-1303" in Miskimin, H.A., Herligy, D. and Udovitch, A.L. (eds.), *The Medieval City*, New Haven: Yale University Press, 1977.
1021. Stuard, S.M. (ed.). *Women in Medieval Society*, Philadelphia: University of Pennsylvania Press, 1976.
1022. Summers, Anne. "Militarism in Britain before the Great War," *History Workshop*, 2 (1976).
1023. Sutherland, Gillian (ed.). *Education*; with an introduction by P. Ford and G. Ford, Government and Society in Nineteenth Century Britain: Commentaries on British Parliamentary Papers, Dublin: Irish Academic Press, 1977.
1024. Swift, Roger and Gilley, Sheridan. *The Irish in the Victorian City*, London: Croom Helm, 1985.
1025. Swinson, Arthur. *North West Frontier*, New York: Praeger, 1967.
1026. ───── (ed.). *A Register of the Regiments and Corps of the British Army*, London: Archive Press, 1972.
1027. Tarnes, Richard. *Isambard Kingdom Brunel, 1806-1859: An Illustrated Life*, London: Sage, 1972.
1028. Taylor, Arthur J. *Laissez-faire and State Intervention in Nineteenth Century Britain*, London: Macmillan, 1972.
1029. ─────. *The Standard of Living in Britain in the Industrial Revolution*, London: Methuen, 1975.
1030. Temple Patterson, A. *Portsmouth: A History*, Bradford-on-Avon: Moonraker Press, 1976.
1031. ─────. *Southampton*, London: Macmillan, 1970.
1032. Terraine, John. *The Smoke and the Fire: Myths and Anti-Myths of War, 1861-1945*, London: Sidgwick & Jackson, 1980.
1033. Thane, Pat, Crossick, Geoffrey and Floud, Roderick. *The Power of the Past: Essays for Eric Hobsbawm*, Cambridge University Press, 1984.
1034. ───── and Sutcliffe, Anthony. *Essays in Social History*, vol. 2, Oxford University Press, 1985.

1035. Thirsk, Joan (ed.). *The Agrarian History of England and Wales*, vol. 4: *1500-1640*, Cambridge University Press, 1967.
1036. ──────. *English Peasant Farming: An Agrarian History of Lincolnshire from Tudor to Stuart Times*, London: Methuen, 1981 (1957).
1037. ──────. *Horses in Early Modern England*, Stenton Lecture, University of Reading, 1978.
1038. Tholfsen, Trygve R. *Working Class Radicalism in the Mid-Victorian City*, New York: Columbia University Press, 1977.
1039. Thom, Alexander. *Megalithic Lunar Observatories*, Oxford University Press, 1971.
1040. ──────. *Megalithic Sites in Britain*, Oxford University Press, 1967.
1041. Thomas, Brinley. "Food Supply in the United Kingdom During the Industrial Revolution," *Agricultural History*, vol. 56, no. 1 (1982).
1042. ──────. *Migration and Economic Growth: A Study of Great Britain and the Atlantic Economy*, 2nd ed., Cambridge University Press, 1973.
1043. Thomas, Brinley. "Towards an Energy Interpretation of the Industrial Revolution," *Atlantic Economic Journal*, VII (1 March 1980).
1044. Thomas, R.H.G. *London's First Railway: The London and Greenwich*, London: B.T. Batsford, 1972.
1045. Thomas, R.P. and McCloskey, D.N. "Overseas Trade and Empire, 1700-1860" in Floud, R.C. and McCloskey, D.N. (eds.), *The Economic History of Britain since 1700*, vol. 1, Cambridge University Press, 1981.
1046. Thomis, M.I. *The Town Labourer and the Industrial Revolution: The British Experience, 1789-1850*, London: B.T. Batsford, 1974.
1047. Thompson, Allan. *The Dynamics of the Industrial Revolution*, London: Edward Arnold, 1973.
1048. Thompson, Edward Palmer. *Whigs and Hunters: The Origin of the Black Act*, New York: Pantheon Books, 1975.
1049. Thompson, Leonard Monteath. *Survival in Two Worlds: Moshoeshoe of Lesotho, 1786-1870*, Oxford University Press, 1976.
1050. Thompson, Noel W. *The People's Science: The Popular Political Economy of Exploitation and Crisis, 1816-1834*, Cambridge University Press, 1985.
1051. Thomson, Richard. *The Charity Commission and the Age of Reform*, London: Routledge & Kegan Paul, 1979.
1052. Thoumine, R.H. *Scientific Solider: A Life of General Le Marchant, 1766-1812*, Oxford University Press, 1968.
1053. Thrower, Rayner. *The Pirate Picture*, Chichester: Phillimore, 1980.
1054. Tiger, Lionel and Fox, Robin. *The Imperial Animal*, Toronto: McClelland & Stewart, 1971.
1055. Tilly, Charles. *As Sociology Meets History*, London: Academic Press, 1981.
1056. Titow, J.Z. "English Rural Society, 1200-1350" in Elton, G.R. (ed.), *Historical Problems: Studies and Documents*, 4, London: Allen & Unwin, 1969.
1057. ──────. *Winchester Yields: A Study in Medieval Agricultural Productivity*, Cambridge University Press, 1972.

1058. Tobin, R.B. "Vincent de Beauvais and the Education of Women," *Journal of the History of Ideas*, 35 (1974).
1059. Todd, M. *Roman Britain*, London: Fontana, 1981.
1060. Tomlinsin, H.C. *Guns and Government: The Ordnance Office under the Later Stuarts*, London: Royal Historical Society, 1979.
1061. Tooley, R.V. (compiler). *Tooley's Dictionary of Map-Makers*, New York: Alan R. Liss Inc., 1979.
1062. Towle, Philip. "The Debate on Wartime Censorship in Britain, 1902-1914" in Bond, Brian and Roy, Ian (eds.), *War and Society: A Yearbook of Military History*, London: Croom Helm, 1975.
1063. ———— (ed.). *Estimating Foreign Military Power*, London: Croom Helm, 1982.
1064. Trace, Keith. "The Chemical Industry" in Roderick, Gordon and Stephens, Michael (eds.), *Where Did We Go Wrong?*, Lewes: The Falmer Press, 1981.
1065. Tranter, Neil Lionel. *Population since the Industrial Revolution: The English Experience*, London: Croom Helm, 1973.
1066. Trebilcock, Clive. *The Industrialization of the Continental Powers, 1780-1914*, London: Longman, 1981.
1067. ————. "Legends of the British Armaments Industry: A Revision, 1890-1914," *Journal of Contemporary History*, V (1970).
1068. ————. "A Special Relationship: Government Rearmament and the Cordite Firms," *Economic History Review*, 2nd series, XIX, 1966.
1069. ————. "Spin-off in British Economic History: Armaments and Industry, 1760-1914," *Economic History Review*, 2nd series, XXII, no. 3 (Dec. 1969); "Spin-off: A Rejoinder," *ibid.*, XXIV (1971); "British Armaments and European Industrialization," *ibid.*, XXIV (1973).
1070. ————. *The Vickers Brothers: Armaments and Enterprise, 1854-1914*, London: Europa Press, 1977.
1071. Trinder, Barrie S. *The Industrial Revolution in Shropshire*, Chichester: Phillimore, 1973.
1072. Trustram, Myna. *Women of the Regiment: Marriage and the Victorian Army*, Cambridge University Press, 1984.
1073. Tuchman, Barabara W. *A Distant Mirror: The Calamitous Fourteenth Century*, New York: A.A. Knopf, 1978.
1074. Tucker, John and Winstock, Lewis S. *The English Civil War: A Military Handbook*, London: Arms and Armour Press, 1972.
1075. Tugendhat, C. *Oil: The Biggest Business*, London: Eyre & Spottiswoode, 1968.
1076. Turner, Frank M. "Public Science in Britain, 1880-1919," *Isis*, 77, no. 259 (1980).
1077. Turner, Hilary. *Town Defenses in England and Wales: An Architectural and Documentary Study, A.D.900-1500*, London: J. Baker, 1971.
1078. Turner, Mary. *Slaves and Missionaries: The Disintegration of Jamaican Slave Society, 1787-1834*, Champaign: University of Illinois Press, 1982.
1079. Turner, Ralph V. "The *Miles Literatus* in Twelfth and Thirteenth Century England: How Rare a Phenomenon?," *American Historical Review*, LXXXIII (1978).

1080. Tyler, Colin and Haining, John. *Ploughing by Steam: A History of Steam Cultivation over the Years*, Hemel Hempstead: Model & Allied Publications, 1970.
1081. Uden, Grant (ed.). *A Dictionary of Chivalry*, London: Longman, 1968.
1082. Underdown, David. *Revel, Riot and Rebellion: Popular Politics and Culture in England, 1603-1660*, Oxford University Press, 1985.
1083. ―――――. *Somerset in the Civil War and Interregnum*, Newton Abbot: David & Charles, 1973.
1084. Uselding, Paul J. "Henry Burden and the Question of Anglo-American Transfer in the 19th Century," *Journal of Economic History*, 30 (1970).
1085. Uzoigwe, Godfrey N. *Britain and the Conquest of Africa: The Age of Salisbury*, Ann Arbor: University of Michigan Press, 1972.
1086. Vale, M.G.A. *English Gascony, 1399-1453: A Study of War, Government and Politics during the Hundred Years' War*, Oxford University Press, 1970.
1087. ―――――. "New Techniques and Old Ideas: The Impact of Artillery on War and Chivalry at the End of the Hundred Years' War" in Allmand, C.T. (ed.), *War, Literature and Politics in the Late Middle Ages*, Liverpool University Press, 1976.
1088. ―――――. *Piety, Charity and Literacy among the Yorkshire Gentry, 1370-1480*, Borthwick Papers, no. 50, York: St. Anthony's Press, 1976.
1089. Van Creveld, Martin. *Supplying War: Logistics from Wallenstein to Patton*, Cambridge University Press, 1977.
1090. Van Gelder, Arthur Pine and Schlatter, Hugo. *History of the Explosives Industry in America*, New York: Arno Press, 1972.
1091. Van Doorn, Jacques (ed.). *Armed Forces and Society: Sociological Essays*, The Hague; Paris: Mouton, 1968.
1092. Van Horn, Kent Robertson (ed.). *Aluminum; Prepared by Engineers, Scientists and Metallurgists of the Aluminum Company of America*, Ohio: American Society for Metals, 1937.
1093. Verbruggen, J.F. (trans. Sumner Willard and S.C.M. Southern). *The Art of Warfare in Western Europe during the Middle Ages: From the Eighth Century to 1340*, Amsterdam: North Holland Publishing Company, 1977.
1094. Vicinus, Martha, J. (ed.). *Suffer and be Still: Women in the Victorian Age*, London: Methuen, 1980.
1095. ―――――― (ed.). *A Widening Sphere: Changing Roles of Victorian Women*, London: Methuen, 1980.
1096. Vine, P.A.L. *The Royal Military Canal*, Newton Abbot: David & Charles, 1972.
1097. Von Der Steinen, Karl. "The Discovery of Women in Eighteenth Century Political Life" in Kanner, Barbara (ed.), *The Women of England from Anglo-Saxon Times to the Present: Interpretative Bibliographical Essays*, Hamden, Conn.: Archon Books, 1979.
1098. Von Pivka, Otto. *Armies of the Napoleonic Era*, Newton Abbot: David & Charles.

1099. Von Tunzelmann, G.N. *Steam Power and British Industrialization to 1860*, Oxford University Press, 1978.
1100. Wacher, John S. *The Towns of Roman Britain*, London: B.T. Batsford, 1975.
1101. Wainwright, G.J. and Longworth, Ian H. *Durrington Walls: Excavations, 1966-1968*, London: Society of Antiquaries, 1971.
1102. Wall, Joseph Frazier. *Andrew Carnegie*, New York: Oxford University Press, 1971.
1103. Wallace-Hadrill, J.M. "War and Peace in the Early Middle Ages," *T.R.H.S.*, 5th series, 25 (1975).
1104. Walvin, James. *The People's Game: A Social History of British Football*, London: Allen Lane, 1975.
1105. Ward, Ralph T. *Pirates in History*, Baltimore: York Press, 1974.
1106. Ward, W.R. *Religion and Society in England, 1790-1850*, London: Batsford, 1972.
1107. Warner, Philip. *The Crimean War: A Reappraisal*, London: Arthur Barker, 1972.
1108. Warren, W. Lewis. *Henry II*, Berkeley: University of California Press, 1973.
1109. Warwick, Peter and Spies, S.B. *The South African War: The Anglo-Boer War, 1899-1902*, London: Longman, 1980.
1110. Watt, D. Cameron. *Succeeding John Bull: America in Britain's Place, 1900-1975*, Cambridge University Press, 1984.
1111. Webb, Henry J. *Elizabethan Military Science: The Books and the Practice*, Madison: University of Wisconsin Press, 1966.
1112. Webb, Malcolm C. "The Flag follows Trade: An Essay on the Necessary Interaction of Military and Commercial Factors in State Formation" in Sabloff, Jeremy and Lamberg-Karlovsky, C.C. (eds.), *Ancient Civilization and Trade*, Alberquerque: University of Mexico Press, 1973.
1113. Webster, Charles. *The Great Instauration: Science, Medicine and Reform, 1626-1660*, London: Duckworth, 1975.
1114. ———. *Samuel Hartlib and the Advancement of Learning*, Cambridge University Press, 1970.
1115. ———. "Science and the Challenge to the Scholastic Curriculum, 1640-1660" in "The Changing Curriculum," *History of Education Society*, 1971.
1116. Webster, Graham. *The Roman Imperial Army of the First and Second Centuries*, 2nd edn., London: A. & C. Black, 1979.
1117. Weigley, Russell F. (ed.). *New Dimensions in Military History*, San Rafael: Presidio Press, 1975.
1118. Weinroth, H. "The British Radicals and the Balance of Power, 1902-1914," *Historical Journal*, XXX, 3 (1974).
1119. ———. "Norman Angell and 'The Great Illusion,'" *Historical Journal*, XVII (1974).
1120. Weissman, H.P. "Anti-Feminism and Chaucer's Characterization of Women" in Economou, George D. (ed.), *Geoffrey Chaucer: A Collection of Original Articles*, New York: McGraw, 1976.
1121. Wells, R.A.E. *Dearth and Distress in Yorkshire, 1793-1802*, Borthwick Papers, no. 52, York: St. Anthony's Press, 1977.
1122. Wells, Roger. *Insurrection: The British Experience, 1795-1803*, Gloucester: Alan Sutton, 1983.

1123. West, Edwin George. *Education and the Industrial Revolution*, London: Batsford, 1975.
1124. ―――――. "Educational Slow Down and Public Intervention in Nineteenth Century England: A Study in the Economics of Bureaucracy," *Explorations in Economic History*, 12 (1975).
1125. ―――――. "Progress in Artisan Literacy" in Roderick, Gordon and Stephens, Michael (eds.), *Where Did We Go Wrong?*, Lewes: The Falmer Press, 1981.
1126. Western, J.R. *The English Militia in the Eighteenth Century*, London: Routledge & Kegan Paul, 1965.
1127. White, Gavin. "Firearms in Africa: An Introduction," *Journal of African History*, XII (1971).
1128. White, Lynn Jr. "The Crusades and the Technological Thrusts of the West" in Parry, V.J. and Yapp, M.E. (eds.), *War, Technology and Society in the Middle East*, Oxford University Press, 1975.
1129. Whitelock, Dorothy (ed.). *English Historical Documents*, vol. 1: *c. 500-1042*, 2nd ed., London: Eyre Methuen, 1979.
1130. Whittle, A.W.R. *The Earlier Neolithic of S. England and its Continental Background*, British Archaeological Report, Supplementary Series 35, 1977.
1131. Wiener, Martin S. *English Culture and the Industrial Spirit, 1850-1980*, Cambridge University Press, 1981.
1132. Wigham, Eric. *Strikes and the Government, 1893-1981*, London: Macmillan, 1982.
1133. Wilkinson, Bertie. *The High Middle Ages in England*, Cambridge University Press, 1978.
1134. Wilkinson, David. *Deadly Quarrels: Lewis F. Richardson and the Statistical Study of War*, Berkeley & London: University of California Press, 1981.
1135. Wilkinson, P. "English Youth Movements, 1908-1930," *Journal of Contemporary History*, 1969.
1136. Wilkinson-Latham, Robert. *British Artillery on Land and Sea, 1790-1820*, Newton Abbot: David & Charles, 1973.
1137. ―――――. *Phaedon Guide to Antique Weapons and Armour*, Oxford: Phaedon, 1981.
1138. Williams, Glydwr. "The Hudson's Bay Company and its Critics in the Eighteenth Century," *Transactions of the Royal Historical Society*, 5th series, vol. 20 (1970).
1139. Williams, Jac L. and Hughes, Gwilym Rees. *The History of Education in Wales*, Swansea: Christopher Davis, 1978.
1140. Williams, Judith B. *British Commercial Policy and Trade Expansion, 1750-1850*, Oxford University Press, 1972.
1141. Williamson, J.G. "Was the Industrial Revolution Worth It?: Disamenities and Death in Nineteenth Century British Towns," *Explorations in Economic History* XIX, no. 3 (July 1982).
1142. ―――――. "Why was British Growth so slow during the Industrial Revolution?," *Journal of Economic History*, XLIV, no. 3 (September 1984).
1143. Wills, Alfred J. *An Introduction to the History of Central Africa*, 3rd edn., Oxford University Press, 1974.
1144. Wilson, Andrew. "The Ever Victorious Army ..." (1876), Arlington Reprint by University Publications of America Inc., 1976.

1145. Wilson, Charles. *A History of Unilever*, London: Cassell, vol. 1, 1970.
1146. Wilson, David McKenzie (ed.). *The Archaeology of Anglo-Saxon England*, London: Methuen, 1976.
1147. Wilson, Keith. *Imperialism and Nationalism in the Middle East: The Anglo-Egyptian Experience.* London: Mansell Publishing, 1983.
1148. ————. *The Policy of the Entente: Essays on the Determination of British Foreign Policy, 1904-1914*, Cambridge University Press, 1985.
1149. Wilson, Richard George. *Gentlemen Merchants: The Merchant Community in Leeds, 1700-1830*, Manchester University Press, 1971.
1150. Wilson, Roger Burdett. *Memoirs and Diary of Daniel Gooch*, Newton Abbot: David & Charles, 1972.
1151. Wilson, Stephen. "For a Socio-Historical Approach to the Study of Western Military Culture," *Armed Forces and Society*, vol. 6 (1980).
1152. Winch, Donald. *Adam Smith's Politics: An Essay in Historiographic Revision*, Cambridge University Press, 1978.
1153. Winn, Peter. "British Informal Empire in Uruguay in the Nineteenth Century," *Past and Present*, no. 73 (1976).
1154. Winston, Alexander. *No Purchase, No Pay: Sir Henry Morgan, Captain William Kidd and Captain Woodes Rogers in the Great Age of Privateers and Pirates, 1665-1715*, London: Eyre & Spottiswoode, 1970.
1155. Winter, J.M. (ed.). *War and Economic Development: Essays in Memory of David Joslin*, Cambridge University Press, 1975.
1156. Wohl, Anthony S. *The Eternal Slum: Housing and Social Policy in Victorian England*, London: Edward Arnold, 1977.
1157. Wolf, Eric R. *Europe and the People without History*, Berkeley: University of California Press, 1982.
1158. Wolffe, Bertram. *Henry VI*, London: Eyure Methuen, 1981.
1159. Wolpert, Stanley. *A New History of India*, New York: Oxford University Press, 1977.
1160. Wood, Eric S. *Collins Field Guide to Archaeology in Britain*, London: Collins, 1979.
1161. Wood, John Cunningham. *British Economists and the Empire*, London: Croom Helm, 1983.
1162. Woodcock, George. *The Hudson's Bay Company*, Toronto: Collier Macmillan Canada, 1970.
1163. Woodruff, William. *America's Impact on the World: A Study of the Role of the United States in the World Economy, 1750-1970*, London: Macmillan, 1975.
1164. Woods, William. *England in the Age of Chaucer*, New York: Stein & Day, 1976.
1165. Woodward, Donald. "Swords into Ploughshares: Recycling in Pre-Industrial England," *Economic History Review*, 2nd series, XXXVIII, no. 2.
1166. Woodward, D.M. "The Assessment of Wages by the Justices of the Peace, 1563-1813," *The Local Historian*, 8 (1969).
1167. ————. "The Background of the Statute of Artificers: The Genesis of Labour Policy, 1558-63," *Economic History Review*, 2nd series, XXXIII, no. 1 (1980).

1168. Wootton, Grahame. *Pressure Groups in Britain, 1720-1970*, London: Allen Lane, 1975.
1169. Worthington, Ian. *Antecedent Education and Officer Recruitment: The Origin and Early Development of the Public School-Army Relationship*, Hull University Press, 1974.
1170. Wrightson, Keith. *English Society, 1580-1680*, London: Hutchinson, 1982.
1171. Wrigley, C.J. (ed.). *A History of British Industrial Relations*, Amherst: University of Massachusetts Press, 1982.
1172. Wrigley, E.A. *Population and History*, New York: McGraw-Hill, 1969.
1173. ———. "A Simple Model of London's Importance in Changing English Society and Economy, 1650-1750," *Past and Present*, 37 (1967).
1174. ——— and Schofield, R.S. *The Population History of England and Wales, 1541-1871*, London: E. Arnold, 1981.
1175. Wymer, J.J. "The Archaeology of Man in the British Quaternary" in Shotton, F.W. (ed.), *British Quaternary Studies: Recent Advances*, Oxford University Press, 1977.
1176. ——— (ed.). *Gazetteer of Mesolithic Sites of England and Wales*, C.B.A. Research Report no. 20, 1978.
1177. Yarmie, A.H. "Employers' Organizations in Mid-Victorian England," *International Review of Social History*, 25 (1980).
1178. Yates, Frances Amelia. *Astraea: The Imperial Theme in the Sixteenth Century*, Harmondsworth: Penguin, 1977.
1179. Yetman, Norman R. "The Irish Experience in America" in Orel, Harold (ed.), *Irish History and Culture*, Lawrence: University of Kansas Press, 1976.
1180. Youings, J.A. *The Dissolution of the Monasteries*, London: Allen & Unwin, 1972.
1181. Young, James D. *Women and Popular Struggles: A History of British Working Class Women, 1560-1984*, Edinburgh: Mainstream, 1986.
1182. Young, Leonard K. *British Policy in China, 1895-1902*, Oxford University Press, 1970.
1183. Young, Brigadier Peter and Holmes, Richard. *The English Civil War: A Military History of Three Civil Wars, 1642-1651*, London: Eyre Methuen, 1974.
1184. Youngson, A.J. *Economic Development in the Long Run*, London: Allen & Unwin, 1972.
1185. Ziegler, Philip. *The Black Death*, London: Collins, 1969.
1186. Zins, H. *England and the Baltic in the Elizabethan Era*, Manchester University Press, 1972.

III

MILITARY DEVELOPMENTS TO 1485

John Marshall Carter

Many of the problems of research into the pre-Tudor military history of England that were mentioned in Beeler's chapter in Higham's *Guide* persist. Source problems loom the largest still, particularly for the Roman and Anglo-Saxon periods. The way is made a little easier as the student pursues the post-Conquest period. Nevertheless, scholars since the 1960s have contributed important studies grounded in the available primary sources. Peter Clemoes' editing of *England Before the Conquest* (49) contains a number of valuable articles on Anglo-Saxon institutions. The Battle Conference on Anglo-Norman Studies and its *Proceedings* (30, 31, 32, 33) have yielded a number of important researches on the immediate pre-Conquest and post-Conquest periods. Journals such as *Albion* (6) and *Military Affairs* (108), while not devoted specifically to British military history, have quite often contained seminal articles on relevant topics. In addition, the student of the military history of the British Isles between Roman Britain and the dominance of the Tudors should find useful the pertinent sources collected in *Patrologia Latina* (121). Encyclopedic projects which should provide the student of medieval and early modern warfare with valuable reference information include *The Dictionary of the Middle Ages* (62) and *The International Military Encyclopedia* (136). Many general histories of medieval warfare have appeared since the early 1970s. John Beeler's *Warfare in Feudal Europe, 730-1200* (17) is a valuable narrative of the military developments in medieval Europe during the "classical age of feudalism," including the important English developments. As in his earlier work, Beeler's focus is on what happened to armies once they were mustered. H.W. Koch's *Medieval Warfare* (97), P. Newark's book by the same title (113), and Terence Wise's *Medieval Warfare* (145) contain valuable information on British developments and attest to the growing interest in medieval military history in the 1970s and 1980s.

For the English-speaking researcher, the translations of significant medieval military histories have been of extreme importance since 1970. Of particular usefulness are Walter J. Renfroe's translation of Delbrueck's classic, published in English as *History of the Art of War within the Framework of Political History* (58) and the translation of J.F. Verbruggen's *The Art of Warfare in Western Europe during the Middle Ages* (139). The most significant history of medieval warfare to date (1986) is Philippe Contamine's *War in the Middle Ages* (52). It is a magisterial history of medieval warfare

complete with one of the most extensive bibliographies on the subject.
Equally important for research into pre-Tudor military history has been the publication of the definitive editions of primary sources. M. Chibnall's six-volume edition of Orderic Vitalis' *Ecclesiastical History* (117) is indicative of the detailed craftsmanship with which a valuable source of history has been translated and edited. Orderic's position as an acute observer of twelfth-century Normandy and England makes his chronicle one of the most important sources for the study of Anglo-Norman military history. Although the printed sources which make up the *Ross Series* constitute one of the weightiest collections of primary materials for the study of medieval English warfare, the more recent definitive editions of chronicles, complete with scholarly apparatus of critical works and scholarship on the particular chronicle since its nineteenth century publication, represent a gigantic step forward for those interested in getting a clearer picture of their subject.
As Professor Beeler noted in his 1971 essay in Higham's *Guide*, the steady, albeit poorly publicized, work of British record societies continues to provide amateur and professional historian alike with bountiful supplies of edited and sometimes translated medieval and early modern sources. The Wiltshire Record Society, with its headquarters in Trowbridge, Wiltshire, is a case in point. Annually, the society produces an exacting work of scholarship-- usually an edited muster roll or monastic cartulary.
The long-awaited new edition of Gross' *A Guide to the Sources of English History to 1485* (84) is the most comprehensive guide to all aspects of English medieval historiography. An invaluable addition to the scholarly reference works is G.C. Boyce's *Literature of Medieval History, 1930-1975: A Supplement to Louis J. Paetow's "A Guide to the Study of Medieval History"* (147). Although many of the same problems confront the student of British military history to 1485, notable strides have been made in the period since Higham's *Guide* (1971) was published.
At this writing (1986), there remains a good deal of manuscript material which has not been published. The Public Record Office and the British Museum remain the principal repositories for these records. The medieval records remain at the Public Record Office at Chancery Lane while the modern records are housed at the PRO at Kew Gardens. The Bodleian Library at Oxford is also an important repository. The county record offices and the various cathedral libraries should be mentioned as record repositories, as should royal and noble residences such as Arundel Castle. Varying degrees of difficulty await the interested researcher.
Archaeology and anthropology have contributed significantly to a better understanding of the actions of primitive peoples. Although tremendous strides have been made by these disciplines and others, it is still very difficult to try to recreate the military history of prehistoric Britain. Nevertheless, those interested in pursuing such an intimidating, and no doubt frustrating, field would do well to consult Helen Clarke's *The Archaeology of Medieval England* (48) and Stanislav Andreski's *Military Organization and Society* (148).

The Roman Period. A somewhat clearer, but still murky, image of the military organization of Roman Britain remains. Specialized studies found in journals such as *The Journal of Roman Studies* (93) have helped to clear away some of the mists. Some relatively older works also provide insights into the military organization of Roman Britain. G.L. Cheesman's *The Auxilia of the Roman Imperial Army* (45), H.M.D. Parker's *The Roman Legions* (120), and Graham Webster's *The Roman Army* (143) are valuable for their work on the training, development, and deployment of the Roman army. R.E. Smith's *Service in the Post-Marian Army* (132) is also useful. Michael Grant's *The Army of the Caesars* (83) is a clear, descriptive narrative which contains valuable information about the Imperial Army in Britain. The interaction of legionnaires and the populace are investigated in Ramsay MacMullen's *Soldiers and Civilians in the later Roman Empire* (105). Very useful summaries of important people, institutions, and developments can be found in the detailed, multi-volumed work of Pauly-Wissowa, the *Real-Encyclopedie* (122).

Although a better picture of Roman Britain has emerged in the last two decades, Professor Beeler's picture of the military history of Roman Britain has not changed considerably. Archaeology will undoubtedly aid in the creation of a better understanding of the military history of Britain in the Roman period.

The Anglo-Saxon Age. The work of Delbrueck (58) and Verbruggen (139) contain valuable information about the military history of Anglo-Saxon England and, in particular, its comparison with continental developments. Beeler's *Warfare in Feudal Europe* (17) and Contamine's *War in the Middle Ages* (52) include valuable chapters on the organization of war in the pre-Conquest period.

This well-defined period of British History, ca. 450-1066, also suffers from some of the same historiographical problems as that of Roman Britain. The *Anglo-Saxon Chronicle* provides a usable framework and, in the entries for the eleventh and twelfth centuries, the detail increases. However, for the early Anglo-Saxon period, the sketchiness of the entries makes the writing of a military history nearly impossible. Stenton's *Anglo-Saxon England* remains the fullest account of operations by Anglo-Saxon armies, both before the amalgamation of the Anglo-Saxon Heptarchy and after. Some narrative histories of the transition period between the end of Roman Britain and the development of the petty Anglo-Saxon kingdoms have made clearer the rather dim picture of the early Anglo-Saxon period. Leslie Alcock's *Arthur's Britain: History and Archaeology* (1), in addition to its abundant bibliography, is a skillful synthesis of archaeological developments that shed some light on fortifications and other aspects of Anglo-Saxon military organization in the most shrouded period of all. H.P.R. Finberg (70) and D.J.V. Fisher (74) have contributed narrative histories of Anglo-Saxon England from the initial invasions to the time of the Norman Conquest. Making use of archaeological and literary evidence, they have given us two of the best pictures of pre-Conquest England since Stenton. N.P. Brooks (28) and Eric John (90) have focused on specific military campaigns in an effort to discern what they can about the organization of Anglo-Saxon society. John is one of the most ardent defenders of the Freeman School and its interpretation of Anglo-Saxon England as a feudalized state. John Morris (111) has done an admirable job of using Arthurian sources with other historical sources to create another mosaic of Anglo-Saxon England, the last two decades have not produced the caliber or quantity of work produced in the late 1950s and throughout the 1960s. There is little that ranks alongside the pioneering works of Hollister (*Anglo-Saxon Military Institutions*) and Michael Powicke (*Military Obligation in Medieval England*).

The Norman Conquest and Beyond. The two decades since the nine hundredth anniversary of the Battle of Hastings of October 14, 1066 have witnessed the continuation of the flood of studies on all aspects of the great battle and its aftermath called the Norman Conquest. Frank Barlow has assimilated much of the post-1966 materials into an admirable study of the Norman invasion in his *The Norman Conquest and Beyond* (10). David C. Douglas, one of the great students of the Conquest, continued his story of the Norman impact on Europe in *The Norman Fate, 1100-1154* (64). The Role of the Conquest in English historiography was traced by John Marshall Carter in "The Norman Conquest: Ten Centuries of Interpretation" (37). The Conquest played a vital role in English politics down to the twentieth century. The Normans have been perceived at various times as lawmakers and lawbreakers. John Le Patourel has viewed the Conquest in a European-wide context (101, 102).

The Battle of Hastings and the subsequent events continue to attract a wide array of writers both popular and professional. James Chambers' *The Norman Kings* (44) and Jack Lindsay's *The Normans and their World* (103) attest to the ever-increasing popularity of William the Conqueror and his descendants.

While the scholarly debate over the origins of English feudalism has not subsided, as witnessed in the work of R. Allen Brown (29), other aspects of the Norman Conquest have been investigated in the past two decades. W.A. Kapelle's *The Norman Conquest of the North* (94) follows the Norman army into northern England and Scotland in the century after the Battle of Hastings. The economic impact of the Norman Conquest has received a considerable amount of scholarly attention in the last fifteen years. H.C. Darby's *Domesday England* (56), R. Welldon Finn's *The Norman Conquest and its Effects on the Economy: 1066-1086* (72), and related studies have shown the relationship between war and the economy in post-Conquest England.

William the Conqueror has received scholarly biographical treatment from Edward A. Freeman, Frank Barlow, Frank Stenton, and David C. Douglas. Douglas' work ranks as definitive. What remains, among other necessary and vital studies, are biographies of other major players in the great Anglo-Norman drama of ca. 1042-1100. Odo of Bayeux, Eustace of Boulogne, William Fitzosbern, Robert of Mortain, and others among the Norman inner circle who exercised important military and political roles in post-Conquest England should provide present and future scholars with biographical potential. The famous Godwin family needs a biographer. Sidney Painter's biography of William Marshall (118) is a useful model of what can be done with other Anglo-Norman nobles. David R. Bates' work on Odo of Bayeux has already begun to bear fruit (15).

The century after the Norman Conquest has received biographical scholarship of note in the past two decades. Biographies containing the military careers of Henry II and Richard I have helped to illuminate further the great Angevin Age. W.L. Warren's majestic biography of Henry II contains much detail on Angevin military organization and also includes a very useful bibliography (142). Richard I has received steady attention from biographers since the 1960s, although his military career has nearly taken a backseat to his alleged prurient interests. James Brundage's *Richard Lion Heart* (35) and John Gillingham's *Richard the Lionheart* (78) are two competent biographies of the warlike Angevin king. Brundage makes the case that Richard's involvement in costly wars hurt England. Gillingham sees Richard as a competent ruler and administrator as well as a great and heroic crusader. Both are useful for further insights into his military career.

The military organization of Angevin England is a very complex undertaking. A useful, though old, work is James F. Baldwin's *The Scutage and Knight Service in England* (7).

The thirteenth century has not received the interest that the twelfth century has. F.M. Powicke's *The Loss of Normandy* (123) and Helena M. Chew's *The English Ecclesiastical Tenants-in-Chief and Knight Service: Especially in the Thirteenth and Fourteenth Centuries* (46), both old studies, remain valuable.

The Hundred Years War (1337-1453) dominated the military history of England in the Later Middle Ages and it seemingly dominates modern scholarship on English warfare. C.T. Allmand (2), C.A.J. Armstrong (4), and P. Contamine (50), among others, have contributed significantly to a better understanding of the military organization of England and France during the great war.

The Wars of the Roses have attracted their following among historians in the last twenty years. John Gillingham's *The Wars of the Roses: Peace and Conflict in Fifteenth Century England* (79) and A. Goodman's *The Wars of the Roses: Military Activity and English Society* (81) are valuable looks into the military exploits of the fifteenth century. Gillingham argues rather forcefully that the Wars of the Roses were not so destructive as had been once thought. Useful insights into various spheres of military activity in the fifteenth century are contained in K.B. McFarlane's *England in the Fifteenth Century* (104).

Generally, the picture of post-Conquest military history has been improved considerably by scholars since 1970. One significant trend has been fruitful research into the theme of "Warfare and Society." As the social history boom has reached almost all aspects of the discipline, many scholars have sought and now seek to understand better the relationship of the military sphere of pre-Tudor England with the other spheres of human existence.

A.B. Ferguson's attempt to understand the chivalric implications of pre-1485 warfare (69) was a pioneering effort, somewhat along Huizingan lines but specifically focusing on English developments. More recently, Richard Barber has investigated the relationships existing between the ideal knight and other aspects of medieval society (8). M.H. Keen has looked closely at the Huizingan notion of a chivalry in decline (96). In the last few years, Juliet Vale (138) has compared chivalric institutions in thirteenth and fourteenth century England with similar developments on the continent. She concluded that the creation of the Order of the Garter was a natural development within the context of northwestern European chivalric development.

Historians of pre-Tudor war and society have contributed substantially to our understanding of the "cost of war." Georges Duby's general study, *The Early Growth of the European Economy:*

Warriors and Peasants from the Seventh to the Twelfth Century, is a good general introduction to the history of war and the economy from a general European standpoint with considerable English material (65). A more specialized study of how the crown financed its martial activities is G.L. Harriss' *King, Parliament, and Public Finance in Medieval England to 1369* (86). E. Miller's studies (109, 110) are also quite useful. M. Prestwich has described the complex relationship between war and the economy in two commendable political histories, *War, Politics, and Finance under Edward I* (124), and *The Three Edwards: War and the State in England, 1272-1377* (125). Joseph R. Strayer has examined the costs of war in the Anglo-French conflict of 1294-1303 (135). A.R. Bridbury recreates the ravages of war and its impact on the economy before the Black Death (26).

Numerous studies which attempt to understand the impact of war on social institutions have appeared since the publication of Higham's *Guide*. John Barnie sought to understand the repercussions of the Hundred Years War on English institutions in his *War in Medieval English Society: Social Values and the Hundred Years War, 1337-1399* (11). War's impact on non-combatants has been investigated imaginatively by John Keegan (95) in a chapter on the Battle of Agincourt. His insights into the anxiety of battle among all classes of society and his innovative approach to the study of war psychology will make his book a useful model for some time to come. More recently, Ronald C. Finucane (73) has given us a very illuminating picture of war's devastating effect on women, minorities, and other non-combatants. *Soldiers of the Faith* contains some important chapters which convey vivid detail of the impact of the Crusades on the lives of "those who work." Barbara Hanawalt (85) devotes some coverage in her *Crime and Conflict in English Communities: 1300-1348* to the impact of war on the legal machinery of fourteenth century England. She concludes that the traditional view that crime increases during periods of political and military unrest was not supported by the fourteenth century data. The relationship between war and constitutional development has been an important theme of longstanding among historians of pre-Tudor England. Recently, J.A.P. Jones has reexamined this theme in *King John and Magna Carta* (91). The church's role in war and military organization has been reexamined by B. McNab in "Obligations of the Church in English Society: Military Arrays of the Clergy, 1369-1418" (106). On the whole, the last twenty years has been a very productive period for historians who have sought to understand the impact of war on social institutions.

The growth of social history since the 1960s has resulted in numerous sub-disciplines, each striving to find respectability. Although growing at a slow rate, sports history has found its champions. Still definitive is the seminal article by N. Denholm-Young, "The Tournament in the Thirteenth Century" (60). The tournament, according to the author, was the natural adjunct to war. It put the royal or noble household on a military footing. The tournament also had a constitutional role if it brought together noblemen for the purpose of sport but allowed them time to discuss other matters. Barber's *The Knight and Chivalry* (8) contains a useful discussion of the tournament. John Marshall Carter supplements Denholm-Young's approach in "Sport, War, and the Three Orders of Feudal Society" (41) and *Sports and Pastimes of the Middle Ages*

(40). Vale's *Edward the Third and Chivalry* (138) is probably the most important recent book on the interrelationship of sport and politics in later medieval England. Charles Young's *The Royal Forests of Medieval England* (146) addresses the impact of the Norman and Angevin periods on the development of the royal hunting preserves. This sub-discipline of history will surely grow within the next decade. The approach of correlating sport to war is a useful one that should produce illuminating studies.

The moral aspects of war have been investigated by some scholars in the period since 1970. P. Brock's general study, *Pacifism in Europe to 1914* (27) is a solid beginning to the study of war and morality. Interesting source material such as Philippe de Mezieres' *Letter to King Richard II* (107) add color and flavor to narratives of peace movements in pre-Tudor times. F.H. Russell's *The Just War in the Middle Ages* (128) is outstanding. Although a considerable amount of work has been done in this field of military history in the previous two decades, a good deal of it has been in languages other than English. Much work remains to be done on English, Scottish, Irish, and Welsh ideas on the "just war" in pre-Tudor Britain.

The period 1970 to 1986 has also witnessed the publication of some important studies on strategy and tactics in British warfare before 1485. D. Bornstein, for example, has combed medieval literature for information about strategy. His "Military Strategy in Malory and Vegetius' *De Re Militari*" (23) and "Military Manuals in Fifteenth Century England" (24) are vital contributions to the literature of later medieval English strategy. P. Contamine has also searched Froissart's manuscripts for evidence of strategy and tactics (51). Vegetius' influence on medieval warfare has been a subject of much disputation. The continued interest in this aspect of medieval English warfare has been sustained by C.R. Scrader's "The Ownership and Distribution of Manuscripts of the *De Re Militari* of Flavius Vegetius Renatus Before the Year 1300" (130).

Along tactical lines, the famous feigned flight at Hastings and the Anglo-Saxon reluctance (ignorance of?) to use cavalry at Hastings continues to find interested researchers. The feigned flight has been the subject of a mild controversy throughout the centuries. Bernard Bachrach investigated "The Feigned Retreat at Hastings" (5). John Marshall Carter concluded that the feigned retreat was not within the realm of tactical possibility at Hastings in his "The Feigned Flight at Hastings: Birth, Propagation, and Death of a Myth" (38). More recently, R. Allen Brown has fired a volley at those who doubt the feigned flight in *Proceedings of the Battle Conference on Anglo-Norman Studies*, III-1980 (32). The final word has not been written.

That the Anglo-Saxons either chose not to use cavalry at Hastings or were ignorant of its usefulness has generated a similar controversy through the twentieth century. Although the arguments have been rather one-sided in favor of Anglo-Saxon ineptitude and ignorance of the impact of cavalry, some creative counter arguments have been made. Possibly the best of these has been Richard Glover's "English Warfare in 1066" (80). Ransacking the poetry and prose fiction of Anglo-Saxon England, Glover rather cleverly demonstrated that cavalry was not only well known to pre-Conquest England but that it had been employed with success on numerous occasions prior to 1066.

Mustering and deploying an English army in the later Middle Ages have been the subjects of H.J. Hewitt's "The Organization of War" (88), J.S. Critchley's "Summonses to Military Service Early in the Reign of Henry III" (54), and A.E. Curry's "The First English Standing Army? Military Organization in Lancastrian Normandy, 1420-1450" (55). Hewitt has probably contributed the most to a better understanding of the organization of an English army in the thirteenth and fourteenth centuries. Whereas tactics and strategy and organization have been given serious scholarly attention in the past twenty years, there have been few, if any, attempts to deal with the very complex problem of the training of armies. Both Hollister, in *Anglo-Saxon Military Institutions*, and Beeler, in *Warfare in England, 1066-1189*, touched briefly on the training of Anglo-Saxon, Norman, and Anglo-Norman armies. They both agreed upon the speculative nature of attempting to trace the training of a medieval English army because of the paucity of sources. Where were knights trained and how did they learn tactical cohesion? Was it the "conrois," as Verbruggen (139), R. Allen Brown (32), and others have suggested? The conrois was a fundamental tactical unit usually composed of warriors from a particular feudatory. Had there been, for example, enough interaction (practice?) among the conrois in the feudal duchy of Normandy in 1066 to allow them to execute such a complex manoeuvre as the legendary feigned flight? And what about the tournament from the mid-eleventh century to the decline of feudalism? Was it a source of training and did it provide a military forum where the rules of war and the strategy and tactics of war were discussed and diffused? This area of the military history of pre-Tudor Britain seems relatively wide open for the creative researcher. However, as stated above, the problems of sources remain.

Armor and weapons have continued to interest both amateur and professional historians. Since the publication of Higham's *Guide* in 1971, several volumes have appeared that have added significantly to the knowledge of armor, weapons, and fortifications in Britain prior to 1485. Significant collections of pre-1485 armor and weapons are in the Tower of London, the Musee de l'Armée in Paris, the Schloss Churburg in Austria and other European repositories. John Beeler's "The John Woodman Higgins Armory" (18) demonstrates that historians of medieval and early modern English warfare might also investigate the massive holdings at the Higgins Armory in Worcester, Massachusetts. H.L. Blackmore's *The Armouries of the Tower of London* (21) should be consulted, as should the same author's *Hunting Weapons* (20). H.M. Larson discusses the armor business in the Middle Ages in an older, yet useful article (100). R.E. Oakeshott's *A Knight and his Armour* is an interesting study (116). Firearms in later medieval England are discussed in T.F. Tout's "Firearms in England in the Fourteenth Century" (137). There are other valuable illustrated books on armor and weapons that are accessible. Many of the most important ones were mentioned in Higham's *Guide*.

Since the 1960s, some valuable works on castles, siegecraft, and urban defense have been published. V. Anderson's *Castles of Europe* (3), J. Forde-Johnston's *Castles and Fortifications of Britain and Ireland* (75), and P.S. Fry's *British Medieval Castles* (77) are good examples. Still one of the most impressive bibliographies of post-Conquest fortifications is John Beeler's "The Military Significance of the English Castle, 1066-1175" (16). Philip Warner has followed up his outstanding volume on sieges with a look at the activities within a castle in his *The Medieval Castle: Life in a Fortress in Peace and War* (141). Urban defense in pre-1485 Britain has begun to interest a handful of scholars and probably will draw greater attention in the near future. M.W. Barley's "Town Defences in England and Wales After 1066" (9) is a case in point of what remains to be done with urban defense. This field will undoubtedly benefit from the detailed work of the county record societies, the valuable research and writing that go into the volumes of the Victoria County Histories, and the spadework of the archaeologist.

Many studies have appeared since the 1960s that have done much toward illuminating the military history of Scotland, Wales, and Ireland in the pre-1485 era. Scotland seems to have drawn the most attention. G.W.S. Barrow is probably the leading historian of medieval Scotland. His books such as *The Kingdom of the Scots: Government, Church, and Society from the Eleventh to the Fourteenth Century* (12); *The Anglo-Norman Era in Scottish History* (13), and *Kingship and Unity: Scotland, 1000-1306* (14) have contributed greatly to a better understanding of the military developments of medieval Scotland. To Barrow's impressive list should be added Archibald Duncan's *Scotland: The Making of a Kingdom* (66); Alexander Grant's *Independence and Nationhood: Scotland, 1306-1469* (82); Ranald Nicholson's *Scotland: The Later Middle Ages* (114), and Alfred P. Smyth's *Warlords and Holy Men: Scotland, A.D. 80-1000* (133). In addition to books which include Welsh and Irish military developments alongside their English counterparts, such as Kapelle's *The Norman Conquest of the North* (94) and M. Prestwich's *The Three Edwards: War and the State in England, 1272-1377* (125), specialized studies such as D.J. Cathcart King's "The Defence of Wales, 1067-1283: The Other Side of the Hill" (43) and J. Forde-Johnston's *Castles and Fortifications of Britain and Ireland* (75) prove illuminating.

Although great strides have been made towards a better understanding of the military history of Roman Britain, considerable research and writing remain to be done. The work of scholars like Graham Webster have illuminated some of the nuances of the Roman imperial army in Britain, but the military history of Roman Britain still warrants more attention. John Beeler had committed himself to the study of that topic at the time of his untimely death in 1985. At this writing (1986), there is no Sir Frank Stenton of the military history of Roman Britain.

The military history of the Anglo-Saxons has received a considerable, and justifiable, share of scholarly attention since the 1950s. However, the strides made over the past thirty-five years have not lifted the clouds that remain over the military history of Anglo-Saxon England.

Social history has won itself an accepted place in the historical pantheon. The impact of war on social institutions should be a goal for social historians as we head toward A.D. 2000 and beyond. A work such as John Keegan's *The Face of Battle*, only totally devoted to Roman Britain, Anglo-Saxon England, or a later medieval period would be a welcome contribution indeed. Ronald C. Finucane has come close to this type of social/military in his--although his focus is not specifically England--*Soldiers of the Faith* (73). More insights into war's impact on the non-combatant, the interaction of sport and war, the significance of peace movements in medieval society, and other relevant topics would be greatly beneficial for a better understanding of the military history of Britain from the Romans to the Tudors.

The military history of the fifteenth century, albeit the numerous studies on the Hundred Years War and the Wars of the Roses, is still a tenuous and treacherous period. More attention to the variety of military topics for the fifteenth century would produce important results.

The computer has proven its worth in fields many thought it could never penetrate. Quantitative studies of the military history of England from the Roman period to Bosworth Field would add immeasurably to our understanding of this all important topic of war.

BIBLIOGRAPHY

1. Alcock, Leslie. *Arthur's Britain: History and Archaeology, A.D. 367-634.* New York: St. Martin's Press, 1971.
2. Allmand, C.T. (ed.). *Society at War. The Experience of England and France During the Hundred Years War.* Edinburgh: Oliver and Boyd, 1973.
3. Anderson, V. *Castles of Europe: From Charlemagne to the Renaissance.* London: Elek, 1970.
4. Armstrong, C.A.J. *England, France and Burgundy in the Fifteenth Century.* London: Hambledon Press, 1983.
5. Bachrach, B.S. "The Feigned Retreat at Hastings," *Medieval Studies*, 33 (1971), pp. 264-267.
6. ———. "Henry II and the Angevin Tradition of Family Hostility," *Albion*, xvi (Summer, 1984), pp. 111-130.
7. Baldwin, James, F. *The Scutage and Knight Service in England.* Chicago: University of Chicago Press, 1897.
8. Barber, Richard. *The Knight and Chivalry.* London: Longmans, 1970.
9. Barley, M.W. "Town Defences in England and Wales After 1066," in *The Plans and Topography of Medieval Towns in England and Wales*, ed. M.W. Barley. pp. 57-71. London: Council for British Archaeology, 1976.
10. Barlow, Frank. *The Norman Conquest and Beyond.* London: Hambledon Press, 1983.
11. Barnie, John. *War in Medieval English Society: Social Values and the Hundred Years War, 1337-1399.* Ithaca and London: Cornell University Press, 1974.
12. Barrow, G.W.S. *The Kingdom of the Scots: Government, Church, and Society from the Eleventh to the Fourteenth Century.* London: Edward Arnold, 1973.
13. ———. *The Anglo-Norman Era in Scottish History.* Oxford: The Clarendon Press, 1980.
14. ———. *Kingship and Unity: Scotland, 1000-1300.* Toronto: University of Toronto Press, 1977.
15. Bates, David R. "The Character and Career of Odo, Bishop of Bayeux (1049/50-1097)," *Speculum*, L (January, 1975), pp. 1-20.
16. Beeler, John. "The Military Significance of the English Castle, 1066-1175." Diss. directed by Carl Stephenson. Cornell University, 1951.

17. ─────. *Warfare in Feudal Europe, 730-1200.* Ithaca, New York: Cornell University Press, 1971.
18. ─────. "The John Woodman Higgins Armory (Higgins Armory Museum)," *Military Affairs*, vol. XLVIV, no. 4, (October, 1985), pp. 198-202.
19. Bingham, Caroline. *The Crowned Lions: The Early Plantagenet Kings.* Totowa, N.J.: Rowman and Littlefield, 1978.
20. Blackmore, H.L. *Hunting Weapons.* London: Barrie and Jenkins, 1971.
21. ─────. *The Armouries of the Tower of London, I, Ordnance.* London: H.M. Stationery Office, 1976.
22. Bornstein, D. "The Scottish Prose Version of Vegetius' *De Re Militari.*" *Studies in Scottish Literature*, 8 (1971), pp. 174-183.
23. ─────. "Military Strategy in Malory and Vegetius' *De Re Militari.*" *Comparative Literature Studies*, 9 (1972), pp. 123-129.
24. ─────. "Military Manuals in Fifteenth Century England," *Medieval Studies*, 37 (1975), pp. 469-477.
25. Borst, Arno (ed.). *Das Rittertum im Mittelalter.* Darmstadt: Wissen schaftliche Buchgesellschaft Verlag), 1976.
26. Bridbury, A.R. "Before the Black Death," *Economic History Review*, 30 (1977), pp. 393-410.
27. Brock, P. *Pacifism in Europe to 1914.* Princeton: Princeton University Press, 1972.
28. Brooks, N.P. "England in the Ninth Century: The Crucible of Defeat," *Transactions of the Royal Historical Society* (5th series) 29 (1979), pp. 1-20.
29. Brown, R.A. *Origins of English Feudalism.* New York: Barnes and Noble, 1973.
30. ─────. *Proceedings of the Battle Conference on Anglo-Norman Studies, I-1978.* Totowa: Rowman and Littlefield, 1979.
31. ─────. *Proceedings of the Battle Conference on Anglo-Norman Studies, II-1979.* Woodbridge, Suffolk: The Boydell Press, 1980.
32. ─────. *Proceedings of the Battle Conference on Anglo-Norman Studies, III-1980.* Woodbridge, Suffolk: The Boydell Press, 1981.
33. ─────. *Anglo-Norman Studies V. Proceedings of the Battle Conference, 1982.* Woodbridge, Suffolk: The Boydell Press, 1983.
34. ─────. *The Normans.* New York: St. Martin's Press, 1984.
35. Brundage, James. *Richard Lion Heart.* New York: Scribner, 1974.
36. Campbell, J. (ed.). *The Anglo-Saxons.* Ithaca, New York: Cornell University Press, 1982.
37. Carter, John Marshall. "The Norman Conquest: Ten Centuries of Interpretation." Unpublished Master's Thesis. Directed by John Beeler. University of North Carolina at Greensboro, 1975.
38. ─────. "The Feigned Flight at Hastings: Birth, Propagation, and Death of a Myth," *San Jose Studies* (February, 1978), pp. 95-116.
39. ─────. "Warfare in England, 1150-1250," *San Jose Studies*, (February, 1981), pp. 40-61.

40. ——————. *Sports and Pastimes of the Middle Ages.* Columbus, Georgia: Brentwood Publishers, 1984.
41. ——————. "Sport, War, and the Three Orders of Feudal Society, 700-1300," *Military Affairs* (July, 1985), pp. 132-137.
42. ——————. *The Bayeux Tapestry as a Social Document.* Springfield, Mass.: Ginn Press, 1985.
43. Cathcart, King, D.J. "The Defence of Wales, 1067-1283: The Other Side of the Hill," *Archaeologia Cambrensis,* 126. (1977), pp. 1-16.
44. Chambers, James. *The Norman Kings.* London: Weidenfeld and Nicolson, 1981.
45. Cheesman, G.L. *The Auxilia of the Roman Imperial Army.* Oxford: The Clarendon Press, 1914.
46. Chew, Helena M. *The English Ecclesiastical Tenants-in-Chief and Knight Service: Especially in the Thirteenth and Fourteenth Centuries.* Oxford: Oxford University Press, 1932.
47. Chibnall, M. "Mercenaries and the Familia Regis Under Henry I," *History,* 62 (1977), pp. 15-23.
48. Clarke, Helen. *The Archaeology of Medieval England.* London: British Museum Publications, 1984.
49. Clemoes, Peter (ed.). *England before the Conquest: Studies in Primary Sources Presented to Dorothy Whitelock.* Cambridge: Cambridge University Press, 1971.
50. Contamine, P. "Crecy (1346) et Azincourt (1415): une comparaison," in *Divers Aspects du Moyen Age en Occident, Actes du Congres Tenu a Calais en Septembre 1974.* (Calais, 1977), pp. 29-44.
51. ——————. "Froissart: Art Militaire, Pratique et Conception de la Guerre," in *Froissart: Historian.* ed. J.J.N. Palmer. Woodbridge, Suffolk: Boydell Press, 1981.
52. ——————. *War in the Middle Ages.* Trans. Michael Jones. Oxford: Basil Blackwell, 1984.
53. Conway, Agnes. *Henry VII's Relations with Scotland and Ireland, 1485-1498.* New York: Octagon Books, 1972 (repr. of 1932 ed.).
54. Critchley, J.S. "Summonses to Military Service Early in the Reign of Henry III," *English Historical Review,* 85 (1971), pp. 79-95.
55. Curry, A.E. "The First English Standing Army? Military Organization in Lancastrian Normandy, 1420-1450," in *Patronage, Pedigree, and Power in Later Medieval England,* ed. Charles Ross. Totowa, N.J.: Rowman and Littlefield, 1979, pp. 193-214.
56. Darby, H.C. *Domesday England.* Cambridge: Cambridge University Press, 1977.
57. Darlington, R.R. *The Norman Conquest.* London: Athlone Press, 1963.
58. Delbrueck, Hans. *History of the Art of War within the Framework of Political History.* Trans. Walter J. Renfroe. Westport, Conn.: Greenwood Press, 1982.
59. Denholm-Young, N. "Feudal Society in the Thirteenth Century: The Knights," in *Collected Papers on Medieval Subjects.* Oxford: Basil Blackwell, 1946.
60. ——————. "The Tournament in the Thirteenth Century," in *Studies in Medieval History Presented to Frederick Maurice*

Powicke. ed. R.W. Hunt. Oxford: The Clarendon Press, 1948, pp. 240-268.
61. Denison, G. *A History of Cavalry.* 2 vols. Westport, Conn.: Greenwood Press, 1977.
62. *Dictionary of the Middle Ages.* ed. Joseph R. Strayer. 1982--in progress. New York: Scribner.
63. Douglas, David C. *The Norman Conquest and British Historians.* Glasgow: Jackson, 1946.
64. ─────. *The Norman Fate, 1100-1154.* Berkeley: University of California Press, 1976.
65. Duby, Georges. *The Early Growth of the European Economy: Warriors and Peasants from the Seventh to the Twelfth Century.* Trans. Howard B. Clarke. London: Weidenfeld and Nicolson, 1974.
66. Duncan, Archibald A.M. *Scotland: The Making of a Kingdom.* New York: Barnes and Noble, 1975.
67. Dupuy, R. Ernest and Dupuy, Trevor N. *The Encyclopedia of Military History: From 3500 B.C. to the Present.* New York: Harper and Row, 1970.
68. Erben, W. *Kriegsgeschichte Des Mittelalters.* Berlin: R. Oldenbourg, 1929.
69. Ferguson, A.B. *The Indian Summer of English Chivalry. Studies in the Decline and Transformation of Chivalric Idealism.* Durham, N.C.: Duke University Press, 1960.
70. Finberg, H.P.R. *The Formation of England, 550-1042.* St. Albans: Paladin, 1976.
71. Finer, S.E. "State and Nation-Building in Europe: The Role of the Military," in *The Formation of National States in Western Europe.* ed. C. Tilly. Princeton: Princeton University Press, 1975, pp. 84-163.
72. Finn, R. Welldon. *The Norman Conquest and its Effects on the Economy: 1066-1086.* Hamden, Conn.: Archon Books, 1971.
73. Finucane, Ronald C. *Soldiers of the Faith: Crusaders and Moslems at War.* New York: St. Martin's Press, 1984.
74. Fisher, D.J.V. *The Anglo-Saxon Age, ca. 400-1042.* London: Longman, 1973.
75. Forde-Johnston, J. *Castles and Fortifications of Britain and Ireland.* London: Dent, 1977.
76. Fowler, K.A. *The King's Lieutenant, Henry of Grosmont, First Duke of Lancaster, 1310-1361.* London: Elek, 1969.
77. Fry, P.S. *British Medieval Castles.* New York: A.S. Barnes, 1975.
78. Gillingham, John. *Richard the Lionheart.* New York: Time/Life Books, 1980.
79. ─────. *The Wars of the Roses: Peace and Conflict in Fifteenth Century England.* London: Weidenfeld and Nicolson, 1981.
80. Glover, Richard. "English Warfare in 1066," *English Historical Review*, 67 (1952), pp. 1-18.
81. Goodman, A. *The Wars of the Roses: Military Activity and English Society, 1452-97.* London: Routledge and Kegan Paul, 1981.
82. Grant, Alexander. *Independence and Nationhood: Scotland, 1306-1469.* London: Edward Arnold, 1984.

83. Grant, Michael. *The Army of the Caesars*. London: Weidenfeld and Nicolson, 1974.
84. Gross, Charles. *A Bibliography of English History to 1485*. Oxford: The Clarendon Press, 1975.
85. Hanawalt, Barbara. *Crime and Conflict in English Communities: 1300-1385*. Cambridge, Mass.: Harvard University Press, 1979.
86. Harris, G.L. *King, Parliament, and Public Finance in Medieval England to 1369*. Oxford: The Clarendon Press, 1975.
87. Henneman, J.B. *Royal Taxation in Fourteenth Century France*. 2 vols. Princeton: Princeton University Press, 1971-76.
88. Hewitt, H.J. "The Organization of War," in *The Hundred Years War*. ed. K.H. Fowler. London: St. Martin's Press, 1971, pp. 75-95.
89. *International Medieval Bibliography*. University of Minnesota. Minneapolis, Minn.: University of Minnesota Press, in progress.
90. John, Eric. "War and Society in the Tenth Century: The Maldon Campaign," *Transactions of the Royal Historical Society* (5th series) 27 (1977), pp. 173-195.
91. Jones, J.A.P. *King John and Magna Carta*. London: Longman, 1971.
92. Jones, Terry. *Chaucer's Knight: The Portrait of a Medieval Mercenary*. London: Methuen, 1980.
93. *Journal of Roman Studies*. Society for the Promotion of Roman Studies (London, 1911-).
94. Kapelle, W.A. *The Norman Conquest of the North*. Chapel Hill: University of North Carolina Press, 1979.
95. Keegan, John. *The Face of Battle*. London: Viking Press, 1976.
96. Keen, M.H. "Huizinga, Kilgour and the Decline of Chivalry," *Medievalia et Humanistica*. New series. 8 (Cambridge, 1977), pp. 1-20.
97. Koch, H.W. *Medieval Warfare*. London: Bison Books, 1978.
98. Kromayer, J. and Veith, G. *Antike Schlachtfelder*. Berlin: Weidmann, 1930-31.
99. Lander, J.R. "The Hundred Years' War and Edward IV's Campaign in France," in *Tudor Men and Institutions: Studies in English Law and Government*. ed. A.J. Slavin. Baton Rouge: Louisiana State University Press, 1972, pp. 70-100.
100. Larson, H.M. "The Armor Business in the Middle Ages," *Business History Review*, 14 (1940), pp. 49-64.
101. Le Patourel, John. *Normandy and England, 1066-1144*. Reading: University of Reading Press, 1971.
102. ———. *Feudal Empires Norman and Plantagenet*. London: Hambledon Press, 1984.
103. Lindsay, Jack. *The Normans and Their World*. London: Hart-Davis, MacGibbon, 1973.
104. McFarlane, K.B. *England in the Fifteenth Century: Collected Essays*. London: Hambledon Press, 1981.
105. MacMullen, R. *Soldiers and Civilians in the Later Roman Empire*. Cambridge, Mass.: Harvard University Press, 1963.
106. McNab, B. "Obligations of the Church in English Society: Military Arrays of the Clergy, 1369-1418," in *Order and Innovation in the Middle Ages: Essays in Honor of Joseph R.*

Strayer. ed. W.C. Jordan, B. McNab, and T.F. Ruiz. Princeton: Princeton University Press, 1976.
107. Mezieres, Philippe de. *Letter to King Richard II: A Plea made in 1395 for Peace Between England and France.* ed. and trans. G.W. Coopland. Liverpool: University of Liverpool Press, 1975.
108. *Military Affairs.* ed. Robin Higham. Kansas State University. Manhattan, Kansas.
109. Miller, E. *War in the North: The Anglo-Scottish Wars of the Middle Ages.* Hull: University of Hull Publication, 1960.
110. ―――――. "War, Taxation, and the English Economy in the Late Thirteenth and Early Fourteenth Century," in *War and Economic Development: Essays in Memory of David Joslin.* ed. J.M. Winter. Cambridge: Cambridge University Press, 1975.
111. Morris, John. *The Age of Arthur: A History of the British Isles from 350 to 650.* London: Weidenfeld and Nicolson, 1973.
112. Morton, C. and Munz, H. (eds.). *Carmen de Hastingae Proelio.* Oxford: The Clarendon Press, 1972.
113. Newark, P. *Medieval Warfare.* London: Weidenfeld and Nicolson, 1979.
114. Nicholson, Ranald. *Scotland: The Later Middle Ages.* New York: Barnes and Noble, 1974.
115. Nicolas, N. Harris. *History of the Battle of Agincourt and the Expedition of Henry the Fifth into France in 1415.* London: Edward Arnold, 1970 (repr. of 1832 ed.).
116. Oakeshott, R.E. *A Knight and His Armour.* London: Dufour, 1961.
117. Orderic Vitalis. *The Ecclesiastical History of Orderic Vitalis.* ed. M. Chibnall. 6 vols. Oxford: Oxford University Press, 1969-1980.
118. Painter, Sidney. *William Marshall.* Baltimore: Johns Hopkins University Press, 1933.
119. Palmer, J.J.N. *England, France and Christendom, 1377-1399.* Chapel Hill, N.C.: University of North Carolina Press, 1972.
120. Parker, H.M.D. *The Roman Legions.* Cambridge: W. Heffer and Sons, 1961.
121. *Patrologia Latina.* ed. J.P. Migne. 221 vols. (Paris, 1844-1882).
122. Pauly-Wissowa. *Real-Encyclopedie.* 1909--subsequent years. Stuttgart (J.B. Metzler).
123. Powicke, F.M. *The Loss of Normandy.* Manchester: Manchester University Press, 1961.
124. Prestwich, M. *War, Politics and Finance under Edward I.* London: Faber, 1972.
125. ―――――. *The Three Edwards: War and the State in England, 1272-1377.* London: Weidenfeld and Nicolson, 1980.
126. Prestwich, J.O. "The Military Household of the Norman Kings," *English Historical Review*, 96 (1981), pp. 1-35.
127. Rowley, Trevor. *The Norman Heritage, 1055-1200.* London: Routledge and Kegan Paul, 1983.
128. Russell, F.H. *The Just War in the Middle Ages.* Cambridge: Cambridge University Press, 1975.
129. Sandberger, D. *Studien Uber Das Rittertum in England,*

Vornehmlich Wahrend Des 14. Jahrhunderts. Berlin: Ebering, 1937.
130. Schrader, C.R. "The Ownership and Distribution of Manuscripts of the *De Re Militari* of Flavius Vegetius Renatus Before the Year 1300," *Dissertation Abstracts International, A,* 37, Ann Arbor, Michigan, 1976, pp. 3815-16.
131. Setton, Kenneth M. (ed.). *A History of the Crusades.* 5 vols. Madison, Wis.: University of Wisconsin Press, 1969-1979.
132. Smith, R.E. *Service in the Post-Marian Army.* Manchester: Manchester University Press, 1958.
133. Smyth, Alfred P. *Warlords and Holy Men: Scotland A.D. 80-1000.* London: Edward Arnold, 1984.
134. Springer, M. "Vegetius im Mittelalter," *Philologus,* 123 (1979), pp. 85-90.
135. Strayer, J.R. "The Costs and Profits of War: The Anglo-French Conflict of 1294-1303," in *The Medieval City.* ed. H.A. Miskimin, D. Herlihy, and A.L. Udovitch. New Haven, Conn.: Yale University Press, pp. 262-291.
136. *The International Military Encyclopedia (Time).* ed. John F. Sloan. Gulf Breeze, Fla.: Academic International Press, 1986--in progress.
137. Tout, T.F. "Firearms in England in the Fourteenth Century," *English Historical Review,* 26 (1911), pp. 666-702.
138. Vale, Juliet. *Edward III and Chivalry.* Totowa, N.J.: Rowman and Littlefield, 1983.
139. Verbruggen, J.F. *The Art of Warfare in Western Europe During the Middle Ages.* New York: North-Holland Publishing Company, 1977.
140. Wace, Robert. *Le Roman De Rou.* Eng. trans. E. Taylor. London: Pickering, 1837.
141. Warner, Philip. *The Medieval Castle: Life in a Fortress in Peace and War.* London: Barker, 1971.
142. Warren, W.L. *Henry II.* London: Methuen, 1973.
143. Webster, Graham. *The Roman Imperial Army of the First and Second Centuries.* New York: Funk and Wagnalls, 1970.
144. White, Lynn. *Medieval Religion and Technology.* Los Angeles: University of California Press, 1980.
145. Wise, Terence. *Medieval Warfare.* New York: Hastings House, 1976.
146. Young, Charles. *The Royal Forests of Medieval England.* Leicester: Leicester University Press, 1979.
147. Boyce, G.C. (ed.). *Literature of Medieval History, 1930-1975: A Supplement to Louis J. Paetow's "A Guide to the Study of Medieval History".* 5 vols. New York: Kraus, 1981.
148. Andreski, Stanislav. *Military Organization and Society.* London: Routledge & Kegan Paul, 1968; Berkeley: University of California Press, 1971.

Note: I would like to acknowledge the help given to me by the late Professor John H. Beeler. While I was an M.A. student of his and afterward, Professor Beeler was a fine scholar, teacher and friend. He had originally agreed to write this essay but his untimely death on April 10, 1985 prevented him from completing the task. J.M.C.

IV

THE ARMY, 1485-1689

John Childs

In 1485, national standing armies scarcely existed in western and eastern Europe; by 1702, all European states, from the very large to the minute, possessed regular, professional armed forces serving both in time of peace and in time of war. Through the pressures and protractions of the "century of religious war," the ad hoc renting of foreign mercenaries gradually gave way to the permanent retention of soldiers who were in the direct pay of the state. England developed along similar lines to France, Spain, the United Provinces, and Sweden, although at a slower pace. After the costly excesses of Henry VIII's overseas expeditions, the later Tudor and early Stuart monarchs grew exceedingly cautious and avoided involvement in foreign war. Elizabeth I's struggle against Spain was principally confined to naval warfare, with only modest commitments of land forces to the Dutch Republic, France, and Ireland. Although jolted by the Thirty Years' War, James I and Charles I succeeded in keeping England clear of the main conflicts and it was not until the advent of her own civil wars in 1642 that England began the rapid assimilation of continental military techniques and institutions. Once launched, progress was rapid. A decade of internal strife demanded large standing armies and the uncertain political power base of the regimes of the Interregnum continued that necessity. During the reigns of Charles II and James II, the concept that a standing army was vital to guarantee political stability at home and to give strength and weight to foreign policy became more accepted in English political life. To some extent, the two great constitutional crises of the seventeenth century--the period from 1640 to 1642, and the Glorious Revolution of 1688--revolved around the issue of the political control of the military. When England was dragged back into European warfare as the corollary of the Dutch invasion of 1688, she already possessed the standing army, the administration, the financial resources, and the grudging political will to make her full contribution to European development.

A glance down the bibliography printed by C.G. Cruickshank in the Higham *Guide*, reveals how few professional historians were then writing on the subject of the British army in the early modern era. This situation has altered, but not by very much. The military history of the sixteenth and seventeenth centuries remains dominated by "amateur" authors and fanatical laymen although there are some signs that an increasing appreciation of the role of armies both in building and maintaining the nation-states of the ancien regime is obliging more academically trained historians into taking military affairs into consideration. However, this trend ought not to be exaggerated. The following bibliography contains publications by one hundred and forty writers of whom fifty might qualify as professional historians.

Bibliographical services for the military historian have improved substantially since 1967. A.P.C. Bruce's *Bibliography of British Military History: From the Roman Invasions to the Restoration, 1660* (K.G. Saur, Munich, 1981), together with the early part of his second volume (1), is of great benefit with its comprehensive and annotated entries organized both thematically and chronologically. Another useful newcomer is John Morrill's selection of the principal new works on British seventeenth century history (4), although the author is sometimes prone to idiosyncratic judgements. Levine's (3) and Sachse's (6) bibliographies are simply lists of relevant works, whereas the older Oxford bibliographies combine thoroughness with scholarly annotation (2, 5).

In an age of rising travel costs, microfilm is assuming an increasing importance for the scholar. The Harvester Press of Hassocks, Brighton, has been outstandingly successful in microfilming important collections of manuscripts from the Public Record Office, the British Library, the House of Lords, and the Bodleian Library, Oxford. Some of these collections are only of passing interest to military historians (7, 10, 12, 15), but others are central. The papers of Sir William Clarke (9) are of vital importance in the study of Scottish affairs during the Interregnum, and the *London Gazette* (11) contains information on British military operations overseas as well as records of deserters and most royal orders and proclamations concerning the army. Until 1688, the State Papers Domestic in the Public Record Office, London, (13, 14, 16) form the bedrock source for any form of historical investigation of the British army and it is good to note that these collections have been microfilmed in their entirety. The jewel in the crown of these microfilmed sources is the Blenheim Collection in the British Library (8) but a word of caution must be offered; they have been subjected to judicious editing and as with all such procedures, one man's choice is another man's irrelevance.

With the emphasis on microfilming original manuscripts, less attention seems to have been paid to publishing printed editions of documents. The *Calendars of State Papers Domestic* for the reign of James II have been completed (18, 19, 20) in editions whose scholarship far exceeds that of the older calendars of the Restoration State Papers. The fourth volume of the Historical Manuscripts Commission's calendar of the Finch papers has been produced and it is of particular importance as it covers the papers of the 2nd Earl of Nottingham, secretary of state during the invasion scare of 1692, the Battle of La Hogue, the Battle of Steenkirk, and the abysmal attempt to raid the French coast (26). Similarly, six further volumes of the Salisbury Papers have been published, adding much to our knowledge of military affairs in the middle period of the reign of James I (27). David Chandler's edition of the memoirs of Robert Parker and Mérode Westerloo principally relates to the War of the Spanish Succession, but it does include some more general material dealing with the post-Restoration army (22). Clyve Jones and the Marquis of Cambridge have hunted down manuscript accounts of William of Orange's voyage to England in 1688 (21, 31), and Peter Young and Norman Tucker have edited two memoirs of the Civil Wars (39). *The Royalist Ordnance Papers* (37) are an important source for the history of Charles I's army at Oxford and also for military developments in the 1620s and 1630s. Walter Morgan's account of the faltering steps of the British auxiliaries in the United Provinces between 1572 and 1574 develops our knowledge considerably (33). The papers of Sir Paul Rycaut (38) provide a useful corroboration to the Earl of Clarendon's own letters about Tyrconnell's purge in Ireland, and Sheila Mulloy's edition of the *Franco-Irish Correspondence, 1688-1692* provides another invaluable source for the Jacobite Wars (34). Also included in the bibliography are some collections of documents which escaped the attention of C.G. Cruickshank in the Higham *Guide* (23, 24, 25, 29, 30, 35). At the time of writing, the Army Records Society has just begun work and military historians can anticipate some major record publications after the manner of the excellent products of the Navy Records Society.

The great bulk of secondary work published since 1967 has been devoted to the years between 1642 and 1702; offerings on army history during the sixteenth and first half of the seventeenth centuries are disappointingly thin. Building on the earlier work of C.G. Cruickshank (82), John Gilbert Millar has drawn our attention to the haphazard nature of Henry VII's armies, stressing their unreliability and the impossibility of achieving significant political goals with such inadequate resources (135, 136). C.S.L. Davies and D.L. Potter have cast light upon mid-Tudor diplomacy with the French (36, 83), whilst R.B. Wernham has linked military history with other branches of the discipline to produce a definitive account of the Elizabethan state and its foreign and military policy (194, 195). More insights into the workings of Elizabethan statecraft, patronage, and military operations are provided by H.A. Lloyd's monograph on the *Rouen Campaign* (126), and Nicholas Canny's study of the earlier stages of the conquest of Ireland (64). Geoffrey Parker's intriguing delve into "counter factual" history (154) shows how ill-prepared to face invasion England was in 1588, a line strongly supported by Jeremy Goring (98). The shorter writings of one of the most distinguished military historians of the sixteenth century, J.R. Hale, have now been collected into a single volume (101) which includes pieces on fortification, military education, drill, and the vexed question of clerical incitement to war. This thin scraping, although much of it is of high quality, represents the meagre results of eighteen years work on the history of the sixteenth century army.

G.R. Smith and M. Toynbee have compiled a biographical dictionary of some of the major military leaders of the Civil Wars (172) but the main recipient of biography has been Oliver Cromwell (93, 97, 206). Unfortunately, none of them are outstanding and cannot replace the earlier lives by C.H. Firth, John Morley, and Christopher Hill. James Sutherland's transcription of Colonel Hutchinson's memoirs (28) is welcome even if it does suffer slightly from having been edited by a scholar of English literature rather than by an historian. There have also been a number of biographies of lesser soldiers and commanders which have done much to amplify our detailed knowledge of Civil War military operations: Sir William Constable, Montrose, Troilus Turberville, Thomas Dalton, Robert Lilburne, and Sir Richard Grenville (61, 104, 81, 91, 100, 113, 138). John Wilson's biography of Thomas, Lord Fairfax (202) is competent if unexciting. John Adair's biographies of Sir William Waller (46) and John Hampden (47) and Vernon Snow's life of the Earl of Essex (174) are important, which is rather more than can be said for yet another clutch of biographies of Prince Rupert of the Rhine (49, 142, 178), none of which add significantly to our existing knowledge. Pride of place amongst biographers must go to P.R. Newman whose prosopography of royalist officers in England and Wales between 1642 and 1660 and its accompanying analysis will prove an invaluable tool of reference to future generations of historians (145, 147).

Joyce Malcolm has crossed swords with Peter Young and M.D.G. Wanklyn about the reliance placed by Charles I on Irish soldiers in the opening year of the Civil War (131, 132, 133, 189). This same concern about how a war which was wanted by no-one managed to start, lies within the focus of Ronald Hutton's pioneering study of the military administration in the royalist heartlands of the Thames Valley and the Welsh marches (115). General military histories of the Civil Wars have come from the pens of John Adair (45), J. Barbary (53), P. Haythornthwaite (108), and Peter Young and Richard Holmes (209), whilst P.R. Newman has drawn a cartographically dull atlas of the campaigns (149). Well illustrated and as good as any of the general accounts is Richard Ollard's *This War without an Enemy* (152), and H.C. Junge's review article surveys some of the recent developments in Civil War historiography from a unique angle (117).

Peter Young's book on Marston Moor (205) seemed to be definitive until P.R. Newman (146) challenged many of its basic assumptions about both the topography of the battlefield and the course of the action. Brigadier Young has since completed his trilogy of Civil War battle studies with *Naseby* (207). The battle of Rowton Heath (56) and the siege of Pontefract in 1645 (17) have received attention from John Barratt, and R.K.G. Temple has discovered new evidence on the battle of Maidstone (177). W.D. Pereira and Ian Roy have both investigated the siege of Gloucester, the former from a traditional, operational point-of-view, and the latter as an example of the contemporary conduct of war (155, 162). Dr. Roy has returned to this theme in "England turned Germany?" (164) and he has been supported in his findings by Stephen Porter (156) who places the English Civil Wars firmly within the context of the Thirty Years' War in Germany and the Netherlands.

Technical developments in weaponry have received little attention. The remarks by A. Kemp on the equipment of Marlborough's wars possess a good deal of relevance for much of this period (118), whilst Howard Tomlinson has demonstrated the shift in the location of the gunfounding industry from the Weald to the Midlands during the eighteenth century (182). The militia has been a little better served. W. Emberton's study of Philip Skippon and the London trained bands during the Civil Wars is of limited value (89); much more important are the articles by David Allen (48) and John Miller (140) which illustrate the crucial role played by the London militia in politics. Although mainly concerned with developments in the eighteenth century, John Western's *English Militia* (196) opens at the Restoration and dovetails with Lindsay Boynton's *Elizabethan Militia* (London: Routledge & Kegan Paul, 1967). The publication of the Norfolk Lieutenancy Journal (23) has provided some accessible source material for the late Stuart militia. The British army in the North

American and West Indian colonies during the seventeenth century has been the subject of two fine studies, one by Douglas Leach (124) and the other by Stephen Saunders Webb (192, 193). Not the least attraction of Webb's book (193) is the well-researched biographical appendix of British army officers who served as colonial governors between 1569 and 1727. The army of the East India Company comes under the microscope of G.J. Bryant (41) but his work is principally concerned with the middle years of the eighteenth century and he has little time to spare for the seventeenth century.

The history of fixed fortifications in Great Britain has received a massive boost with the publication of the *History of the King's Works* (78, 79). Not only are there chapters on forts, batteries, castles, and fieldworks, but also on the royal palaces and such military ephemera as the War Office, the Horse Guards, and the Royal Mews. Henry VIII's preparations for the defence of the south coast and the Thames estuary have been studied by B.M. Morley (141), a subject which has also received attention from J.R. Kenyon (119, 120). The latter author has also looked, with an archaeological emphasis, at some of the field fortifications thrown up during the Civil War (121). The history of the administration of the building of fortifications and the work of the Ordnance Office in general have formed the core of the works by Howard Tomlinson (180, 181, 183). As a sequel to A.D. Saunders, "Tilbury Fort and the Development of Artillery Fortifications in the Thames estuary," *The Antiquaries Journal*, xl. (1960), pp. 152-74, P.M. Wilkinson has reported on his excavation of this, the most modern in design of Charles II's exercises in fixed fortification (200). V.T.C. Smith has provided a similar service for Gravesend blockhouse which was intended to enfilade the passage of the river Thames in conjunction with Tilbury Fort (173).

After the termination of the Civil War in England in 1648, a number of new themes emerge through military historiography: the development of a standing army; the rise and growth of a professional officer corps; the close relationship between armed forces, political stability, and religious toleration; and the augmentation of the traditional English antipathy to permanent armed forces. David Underdown and Ian Gentles (95, 96, 187) have stressed the fundamental role of the New Model Army in creating, supporting, and then destroying various regimes in England between 1646 and 1660, but the key work is Mark Kishlansky's *Rise of the New Model Army* (123). With the accession of Charles II in 1660, a new, regular and professional army was established. It was small to begin with, but gradually it increased to reach a paper strength of forty thousand on the eve of the Dutch invasion in 1688. This process, in all its aspects, has been the focus of the continuing work of John Childs (71, 73). In addition he has studied the units of this army which saw action on foreign stations (69, 70, 74, 103) or served in the United Provinces with the Anglo-Dutch Brigade (25, 32, 75, 116). Because of the ties between the France of Louis XIV and both Charles II and James II of England, religion assumed a central position in Restoration politics; one of the major fears of the political nation was that the monarchy would move towards a militarized absolutism based on the Gallic example. There was little real danger of this until after the dissolution of the Oxford parliament in 1681 (72) although there were enough catholics in the Restoration officer corps to fuel these concerns (139). Under James II, and during the last four years of his brother's reign, an increasing centralization and authoritarianism did occur, much of it centered around the army, as John Western has observed (197). Lois Schwoerer has traced the growing anti-standing army movement which gave public expression to these anxieties (165, 166, 167).

Modern historians tend to see the invasion of William of Orange in 1688 and the resulting Glorious Revolution very much as a military campaign fought in a vacuum of political indifference. E.J. Priestley has investigated the episode of the "Portsmouth Captains" (157), an early indicator that all was not well within James II's army and this element of conspiracy forms a part of David Hosford's valuable study of *Nottingham, Nobles and the North* (112). William of Orange's organization of the defence of the United Provinces which freed elements of the Dutch army to engage in the expedition to England is a principal topic in John Carswell's *The Descent on England* (65), and some military history can be found in J.R. Jones, *The Revolution of 1688 in England* (London: Weidenfeld & Nicolson, 1972). Apart from the Dutch landing at Brixham on 5 November 1688, Monmouth's Rebellion in 1685 was the other military campaign of James II's short reign. Peter Earle and W.M. Wigfield have examined the political and social motivations of Monmouth's followers (84, 198, 199), David Chandler looks specifically at the campaign and battle of Sedgemoor (68), whilst Charles Trench (185), Robin Clifton (77), and J.N.P. Watson (191) have penned more broadly based studies of Monmouth, his politics, life, and rebellion.

The foundation of a regular army in England entailed the parallel emergence of a professional administration. G.A. Jacobsen's biography of *William Blathwayt* (New Haven: Yale University Press, 1932) pointed the way and the earlier history of the military elements in government administration has been included in Gerald Aylmer's monographs on the civil service during the first half of the seventeenth century (51, 52). Clive Holmes says a great deal about the military organization of the Eastern Association during the Civil War years (110). The financing and payment of the new army was the work of Sir Stephen Fox (76), whilst the artillery, fortifications, and supply came under the scrutiny of the Ordnance Office (183). Greater regularity brought the institutionalization of uniform (128) and the purchase system (40, 62, 63). Above all, the officer corps evolved from the status of an ad hoc occupation in time of war to a full-time profession for the sons of gentlemen and nobles. During the reigns of Elizabeth and the first two Stuarts, the English, Irish, and Scots who chose to earn their daily bread by offering their swords for hire were obliged to seek employment in foreign armies. Gradually a corps of trained, veteran British officers was formed in the Dutch, Swedish, French, and Germanic armies during the period of the Dutch Revolt against Spain and the Thirty Years' War (25, 30, 94, 99, 127, 145, 147, 186). On the outbreak of the Bishops' Wars, and more particularly in 1642, many of these officers returned to their native shores and served in the armies of the Civil Wars. The work of P.R. Newman and Ian Roy helps to illustrate this trend (145, 147, 37, 164). After the Restoration, professional officers could serve on a full-time basis with the establishments in England, Scotland, and Ireland, but as the number of commissions in all three was strictly limited until the expansion of the army in the summer of 1685, the majority of professional officers continued to serve overseas as mercenaries and auxiliaries in European armies. In 1685, most of these gentlemen flooded back into the British Isles to command the expanded forces of James II, removing once and for all the reserve of officers employed overseas. When the army was massively augmented in 1689 and 1690 for War of the Grand Alliance, a shortage of officers resulted. Geoffrey Holmes gives a chapter of his general study of the growth of the professions in England to the establishment of the army officer as a recognized, powerful, and socially accepted profession by the early eighteenth century (111).

The new reign of William III and Mary opened inauspiciously. The loyalty of the army was highly suspect and a wave of mutinies in March 1689 (86) led to the passing of the Mutiny Act (168). Thereafter, the threat of Jacobitism and internal insecurity were constant problems for the king, even if the physical risk of a French invasion died down after the Treaty of Limerick in 1691 and the defeat of the French fleet off Cape La Hogue in 1692 (50, 125, 130). William III was a warrior-prince in the grand European tradition. The standard biography, in English, by Stephen Baxter (57) is a little over-enthusiastic about William's martial abilities and the two later lives have borrowed heavily from this interpretation (159, 210). A prominent figure in William of Orange's continental alliances was the future George I of England, another fighting prince in the traditional, aristocratic mould (105). Ragnild Hatton and John Bromley have edited a collection of essays which cover numerous aspects of the relations between Louis XIV and William III--military, naval, and diplomatic (106, 179). The outstanding study of the Jacobite Wars in Ireland is by J.G. Simms (171), supplemented by the unpublished thesis of Wouter Troost (43). Having ransacked the Danish archives, K. Danaher and Dr. Simms have shed significant new light on the role and operations of the mercenary Danish corps in Ireland (24). Another important band of foreigners in William III's Irish army were the Huguenot refugees and something of their military contribution appears in the pages of Robin Gwynn's *Huguenot Heritage* (London: Routledge & Kegan Paul, 1985). The campaigns of the British army in Flanders have not yet been treated by modern scholarship. L.M. Waddell's unpublished doctoral thesis is a useful introduction to the field administration of the British corps (44) and D.G. Chandler has made sense out of the varying accounts of the actual size of the British presence with the allied army in the Low Countries (67). The army's reward at the conclusion of the War of the Grand Alliance at the Peace of Rijkswijk in 1697 was to suffer a massive disbandment as ingrained fears of the expense and political dangers inherent in a standing army overcame sanity, public spirit, and responsibility (165, 166, 167). It was to be the final victory of the anti-army lobby and, fortunately, the period of international peace was sufficiently short to avoid any permanent damage being inflicted upon the blossoming British regular army.

No historian has been brave enough to write a general military history of the entire early modern period, with one notable exception. Correlli Barnett's history of the British army from 1509 to 1970 (54) is generous in its allocation of space to the sixteenth and seventeenth centuries and forms a worthwhile introduction for students. Other than this, Ian Roy's review article (163) makes some broad remarks about seventeenth century army historiography and Lois

Schwoerer's *No Standing Armies!* (167) covers the entire 1600s. Some sort of scholarly overview would be most welcome.

Few of C.G. Cruickshank's suggestions for further research made at the end of his essay in the Higham *Guide* have been adopted. Eighteen years of historical writing has done little to advance our knowledge of the Tudor military world although more solid progress has been made in military history after 1600. The English Civil Wars have given birth to a long list of works of varying quality. John Childs is about to publish the third volume in his trilogy on the social and political history of the British army between 1660 and 1702 and this will complete a modern history of the embryonic standing army. Despite this, massive gaps remain within the whole early modern period. There is no scholarly and up-to-date general military history of the English Civil Wars or of the Bishops' Wars; Charles I's and Buckingham's martial exploits deserve attention; Cromwell has yet to find an adequate modern biographer; civil-military relations in England during the seventeenth century cry out for synthesis; and despite Childs' work there is no modern operational history of the British army during the War of the Grand Alliance. Much needs to be pulled together about the various British contributions to the Thirty Years' War and to the Dutch and Spanish armies during the Eighty Years' War. Although Jeremy Goring (98) has pointed to the decline in military interest and aptitude in the mid-Tudor years, there is virtually no writing on its revival in the form of chivalry and foreign service during Elizabeth I's reign apart from the brief remarks by Frances A. Yates in *Astraea: The Imperial Theme in the Sixteenth Century* (London: Routledge & Kegan Paul, 1975). Early modern army and navy history remains a field pregnant with opportunities for both young and established historians, particularly as more and more scholars are coming to the belated realization that the connections between the army, society, religion, and politics were extremely close throughout the seventeenth century.

BIBLIOGRAPHY

Bibliographies

1. Bruce, A.P.C. (ed.). *An Annotated Bibliography of the British Army, 1660-1914.* New York: Garland, 1975; 2nd. ed. K.G. Saur, Munich, 1985.
2. Davies, G., and Keeler, M.F. (eds.) *Bibliography of British History: The Stuart Period, 1603-1714.* Oxford: Clarendon Press, 1970.
3. Levine, Mortimer (ed.). *Tudor England, 1485-1603.* Cambridge: Cambridge University Press, 1968.
4. Morrill, J.S. (ed.). *Seventeenth Century Britain, 1603-1714.* Folkestone: Dawson, 1980.
5. Read, Conyers (ed.). *Bibliography of British History: The Tudor Period, 1485-1603.* Oxford: Clarendon Press, 2nd. ed., 1959.
6. Sachse, W.L. (ed.). *Restoration England, 1660-1689.* Cambridge: Cambridge University Press, 1971.

Microforms

7. Ballard MSS., selections from the Bodleian Library, Oxford. Harvester Microforms, Brighton.
8. Blenheim MSS., selections from the papers of the 1st Duke of Marlborough in the British Library. Harvester Microforms, Brighton.
9. Clarke, Sir William, MSS., 1640-1664, Worcester College, Oxford. Harvester Microforms, Brighton.
10. House of Lords MSS., main papers, 1509-1715. Harvester Microforms, Brighton.
11. London Gazette, 1665-1800. Clearwater Publishing, New York.
12. Rawlinson MSS., selections from the Bodleian Library, Oxford. Harvester Microforms, Brighton.
13. State Papers Domestic in the Public Record Office, London, 1547-1625. Harvester Microforms, Brighton.
14. State Papers Domestic in the Public Record Office, London, 1625-1702. Harvester Microforms, Brighton. The publication of this series has reached 1660 at the time of writing.
15. The Thomason Tracts in the British Library. Harvester Microforms, Brighton.
16. Unpublished State Papers of the Civil War and Interregnum in the Public Record Office, London. Harvester Microforms, Brighton.

Printed Source Material

17. Barratt, John. "A Royalist Account of the Relief of Pontefract, 1st March 1645," *Journal of the Society for Army Historical Research*, liii. (1975), pp. 159-69.
18. *Calendar of State Papers Domestic, 1685*. London: HMSO, 1960.
19. *Calendar of State Papers Domestic, 1686-7*. London: HMSO, 1964.
20. *Calendar of State Papers Domestic, 1687-9*. London: HMSO, 1972.
21. Cambridge, Marquis of. (ed.). "The March of William of Orange from Torbay to London--1688," *Journal of the Society for Army Historical Research*, xliv. (1966).
22. Chandler, D.G. (ed.). *Military Memoirs of Robert Parker and Comte de Mérode Westerloo*. London: Longman, 1968.
23. Cozens-Hardy, B. (ed.). *Norfolk Lieutenancy Journal, 1676-1701*. Norwich: Norfolk Record Society, 1961.
24. Danaher, K., and Simms, J.G. (eds.) *The Danish Force in Ireland, 1690-1691*. Dublin: Irish Manuscripts Commission, 1962.
25. Ferguson, James (ed.). *Papers illustrating the history of the Scots Brigade in the service of the United Provinces, 1572-1782*. 3 vols. Edinburgh: Scottish History Society, 1899-1901.
26. *Historical Manuscripts Commission, Finch MSS.*, iv. London: HMSO, 1965.
27. *Historical Manuscripts Commission, Salisbury MSS.*, xix.-xxiv. London: HMSO, 1965-76.
28. Hutchinson, Lucy. *Memoirs of the Life of Colonel Hutchinson*. ed. James Sutherland. Oxford: Oxford University Press, 1973.
29. James II, *The Memoirs of James II, his campaigns as Duke of York*. ed. A. Lytton Sells. London: Chatto & Windus, 1962.

30. Jennings, Brendan (ed.). *Wild Geese in Spanish Flanders, 1582-1700*. Dublin: Irish Manuscripts Commission, 1964.
31. Jones, Clyve, (ed.). "Journal of the voyage of William of Orange from Holland to Torbay, 1688," *Journal of the Society for Army Historical Research*, li. (1973), pp. 15-18.
32. Maclean, J. "Huwelijken van militairen, behorende tot het derde regiment van de Schotse Brigade in Nederland, ontleend aan de gereformeerde trouwboeken van 1674 tot 1708," *De Brabantse Leeuw*, xxi. (1972), pp. 90-113.
33. Morgan, Walter. *The Expedition in Holland, 1572-1574*. ed. Duncan Caldecott-Baird. London: Seely Service, 1976.
34. Mulloy, Sheila (ed.). *The Franco-Irish Correspondence, 1688-1692*. vol. 1. Dublin: Irish Manuscripts Commission, 1983.
35. Pollard, A.F. (ed.). *Tudor Tracts, 1532-1588*. New York: Cooper Square Publishers, 1964.
36. Potter, D.L. "Documents concerning negotiations of the Anglo-French Treaty of March 1550," *Camden Society*, 4th series xxix. (1984), pp. 58-180.
37. Roy, Ian (ed.). *The Royalist Ordnance Papers, 1642-6*. 2 vols. Oxford: Oxfordshire Record Society, 1964-75.
38. Rycaut, Sir Paul. "Sir Paul Rycaut's Memoranda and Letters from Ireland, 1686-1687," *Analecta Hibernica*, xxvii. (1972), pp. 123-82.
39. Young, Peter and Tucker, Norman (eds.) *Military Memoirs of Richard Atkyns and John Gwyn*. London: Longman, 1967.

Unpublished doctoral theses

40. Bassett, John Harvey. "The purchase system in the British army, 1660-1871," University of Boston, 1969.
41. Bryant, G.J. "The East India Company and its Army, 1600-1778," University of London, 1975.
42. Lucas, P.A. "Irish Armies in the 17th Century," University of Manchester, 1982.
43. Troost, Wouter. "William III and the Treaty of Limerick, 1691-1697," University of Leiden, 1983.
44. Waddell, L.M. "The Administration of the English Army in Flanders and Brabant from 1689 to 1697," University of North Carolina, 1971.

Books and articles

45. Adair, John. *By the Sword Divided*. London: Century Publishing, 1984.
46. ———. *Roundhead General: A Military Biography of Sir William Waller*. London: MacDonald, 1969.
47. ———. *A Life of John Hampden, The Patriot (1594-1643)*. London: MacDonald & Janes, 1976.
48. Allen, David. "The Role of the London Trained Bands in the Exclusion Crisis, 1678-1681," *English Historical Review*, lxxxvii. (1972), pp. 287-303.
49. Ashley, Maurice. *Rupert of the Rhine*. London: Hart Davis, 1976.
50. Aubrey, P. *The Defeat of James Stuart's Armada, 1692*. Leicester: Leicester University Press, 1979.

51. Aylmer, G.E. *The King's Servants: The Civil Service of Charles I, 1625-1642.* London: Routledge & Kegan Paul, 1961.
52. ———. *The State's Servants: The Civil Service of the English Republic, 1649-1660.* London: Routledge & Kegan Paul, 1973.
53. Barbary, J. *Puritan and Cavalier: The English Civil War.* London: Gollancz, 1977.
54. Barnett, Correlli. *Britain and Her Army, 1509-1970.* London: Allen Lane, 1970.
55. ———. *Marlborough.* London: Eyre Methuen, 1974.
56. Barratt, John. "The Battle of Rowton Heath, 1645," *Journal of the Society for Army Historical Research*, liv. (1976), pp. 208-24.
57. Baxter, S.B. *William III.* London: Longman, 1966.
58. Beckett, J.C. "The Irish Armed Forces, 1660-1685," in *Essays Presented to Michael Roberts.* eds. John Bossy and Peter Jupp. Belfast: Blackstaff Press, 1976.
59. Bence-Jones, M. *The Cavaliers.* London: Constable, 1976.
60. Bennett, M. "Henry Hastings and the Flying Army of Ashby-de-la-Zouch," *Leicestershire Archaeological and Historical Society Transactions*, cxxvi. (1982), pp. 62-70.
61. Bradley, N.B. "Sir William Constable's regiment, 1642-1655," *Journal of the Society for Army Historical Research*, lv. (1977), pp. 215-43.
62. Bruce, A.P.C. "The Early History of the Purchase System," *Army Quarterly*, cv. (1975), pp. 202-7.
63. ———. *The Purchase System in the British Army, 1660-1871.* London: Royal Historical Society, 1980.
64. Canny, Nicholas P. *The Elizabethan Conquest of Ireland: A Pattern Established, 1565-76.* Brighton: Harvester Press, 1976.
65. Carswell, John. *The Descent on England.* London: Barrie & Rockliff, 1969.
66. Chandler, D.G. *Marlborough as Military Commander.* London: Batsford, 1973.
67. ———. "Fluctuations in the strength of forces in English pay sent to Flanders during the Nine Years' War, 1688-1697," *War and Society*, i. (1983), pp. 1-19.
68. ———. *Sedgemoor, 1685: An Account and an Anthology.* London: Anthony Mott, 1985.
69. Childs, John. "Monmouth and the Army in Flanders," *Journal of the Society for Army Historical Research*, lii. (1974), pp. 3-12.
70. ———. "The British Brigade in Portugal, 1662-68," *Journal of the Society for Army Historical Research*, liii. (1975), pp. 135-47.
71. ———. *The Army of Charles II.* London: Routledge & Kegan Paul, 1976.
72. ———. "The Army and the Oxford Parliament of 1681," *English Historical Review*, xciv. (1979), pp. 580-7.
73. ———. *The Army, James II, and the Glorious Revolution.* Manchester: Manchester University Press, 1980.
74. ———. "The British Brigade in France, 1672-1678," *History*, lxix. (1984), pp. 384-97.

75. ―――――. "The Scottish Brigade in the Service of the Dutch Republic, 1689-1782," *Documentatieblad Werkgroep Achttiende Eeuw*, xvi. (1984), pp. 59-75.
76. Clay, Christopher. *Public Finance and Private Wealth: The Career of Sir Stephen Fox, 1627-1716*. Oxford: Clarendon Press, 1978.
77. Clifton, Robin. *The Last Popular Rebellion: The Western Rising of 1685*. London: Temple Smith, 1984.
78. Colvin, H.M. et. al. *The History of the King's Works 1485-1660*. 2 vols. London: HMSO, 1975-82.
79. ―――――. *The History of the King's Works, 1660-1782*. London: HMSO, 1976.
80. Costello, C. "Irish Military Surveys of the 17th Century," *An Cosantóir*, xxi. (1961), pp. 433-42.
81. Cowan, E.J. *Montrose, for Covenant and King*. London: Weidenfeld & Nicolson, 1977.
82. Cruickshank, C.G. *The English Occupation of Tournai, 1513-1519*. Oxford Clarendon Press, 1971.
83. Davies, C.S.L. "England and the French War, 1557-9," in *The Mid-Tudor Polity, c. 1540-1560*. eds. J. Loach and R. Tittler. London: Macmillan, 1980.
84. Earle, Peter. *Monmouth's Rebels: The Road to Sedgemoor, 1685*. London: Weidenfeld & Nicolson, 1977.
85. ―――――. *The Sack of Panama*. London: Jill Norman & Hobhouse, 1981.
86. Ellestad, Charles D. "The Mutinies of 1689," *Journal of the Society for Army Historical Research*, liii. (1975), pp. 4-21.
87. Ellis, P.B. *Hell or Connaught: The Cromwellian Colonisation of Ireland, 1652-1660*. London: Hamish Hamilton, 1975.
88. ―――――. *The Boyne Water: The Battle of the Boyne, 1690*. London: Hamish Hamilton, 1976.
89. Emberton, W. *Skippon's Brave Boys: The Origins, Development, and Civil War Service of London's Trained Bands*. Buckingham: Barracuda Books, 1984.
90. Fischer, Thomas A. *The Scots in Germany*. Edinburgh, 1902, reprinted John Donald, 1982.
91. Foster, M. *Troilus Turberville, Captain-lieutenant of the King's Life Guard (?1597-1645)*. London: Royal Stuart Society, 1980.
92. Francis, A.D. "The Grand Alliance in 1698," *Historical Journal*, x. (1967), pp. 352-60.
93. Fraser, Antonia. *Cromwell: Our Chief of Men*. London: Weidenfeld & Nicolson, 1973.
94. Garland, John L. "Irish officers in the Bavarian Service during the War of the Spanish Succession," *Irish Sword*, xiv. (1981), pp. 240-55.
95. Gentles, Ian. "The arrears of pay of the Parliamentary Army at the end of the first Civil War," *Bulletin of the Institute of Historical Research*, xlviii. (1975), pp. 52-63.
96. ―――――. "Arrears of Pay and Ideology in the Army Revolt of 1647," in *War and Society*. eds. Brian Bond and Ian Roy. London: Croom Helm, 1976.
97. Gillingham, J.B. *Cromwell: Portrait of a Soldier*. London: Weidenfeld & Nicolson, 1976.

98. Goring, Jeremy. "Social change and Military decline in Mid-Tudor England," *History*, lxxx. (1975), pp. 185-97.
99. Gouhier, Pierre. "Mercenaires Irlandais au service de la France," *Irish Sword*, vii. (1965), pp. 58-75.
100. Gratton, J.M. "Thomas Dalton of Thrunham: A Lancashire Royalist Colonel," *Recusant History*, xvi. (1982), pp. 89-90.
101. Hale, J.R. *Renaissance War Studies*. London: Hambledon Press, 1983.
102. Ham, R.E. "The Autobiography of Sir James Croft," *Bulletin of the Institute of Historical Research*, 1. (1977), pp. 48-57.
103. Hardacre, P.H. "The English contingent in Portugal, 1662-1668," *Journal of the Society for Army Historical Research*, xxxviii. (1960), pp. 112-25.
104. Hastings, M. *Montrose, The King's Champion*. London: Gollancz, 1977.
105. Hatton, Ragnild. *George I*. London: Thames & Hudson, 1978.
106. ———— and Bromley, J.S. (eds.) *William III and Louis XIV: Essays, 1680-1720, by and for Mark A. Thomson*. Liverpool: Liverpool University Press, 1968.
107. Hayes-McCoy, G.A. *Irish Battles*. London: Longman, 1969.
108. Haythornthwaite, P.J. *The English Civil War, 1642-1651: An Illustrated Military History*. Poole: Blandford Press, 1983.
109. Hebbert, F.J. "The Richards Brothers," *Irish Sword*, xii. (1975), pp. 200-11.
110. Holmes, Clive. *The Eastern Association*. Cambridge: Cambridge University Press, 1974.
111. Holmes, G.S. *Augustan England: Professions, State and Society, 1680-1730*. London: Allen & Unwin, 1982.
112. Hosford, David H. *Nottingham, Nobles and the North*. Hamden Conn.: Archon Books, 1976.
113. Howell, R. "The Army and the English Revolution: The Case of Robert Lilburne," *Archaeologia Aeliana*, 5th series ix. (1981), pp. 299-315.
114. Hussey, F. *Suffolk Invasion: The Dutch Attack on Landguard Fort, 1667*. Lavenham: Dalton, 1983.
115. Hutton, Ronald. *The Royalist War Effort, 1642-1646*. London: Longman, 1981.
116. Jones, G.H. "The Recall of the British from the Dutch Service," *Historical Journal*, xxv. (1982), pp. 423-35.
117. Junge, H.C. "'The fittest subject for a King's quarrel': Politik, Militär und Gesellschaft in England, 1640-1660," *Militärgeschichtliche Mitteilungen*, xxix. (1981), pp. 143-63.
118. Kemp, A. *Weapons and Equipment of the Marlborough Wars*. Poole: Blandford Press, 1980.
119. Kenyon, J.R. "Early Artillery Fortifications in England and Wales: A Preliminary Survey and Reappraisal," *Archaeological Journal*, cxxxviii. (1982), pp. 205-40.
120. ————. "Ordnance and the King's Fortifications in 1547-8: The Society of Antiquaries' MS. 129, folios 250-374r," *Archaeologia*, cvii. (1982), pp. 165-213.
121. ————. "The Civil War Earthworks around Raglan Castle,

Gwent: An Aerial View," *Archaeologia Cambrensis*, cxxxi. (1983), pp. 139-42.
122. Kightly, C. *Flodden: The Anglo-Scottish War of 1513*. London: Almark Publishing, 1975.
123. Kishlansky, M.A. *The Rise of the New Model Army*. Cambridge: Cambridge University Press, 1979.
124. Leach, D.E. *Arms for Empire: A Military History of the British Colonies in North America, 1607-1763*. New York: Macmillan, 1973.
125. Lenman, Bruce P. *The Jacobite Risings in Britain, 1689-1746*. London: Eyre Methuen, 1980.
126. Lloyd, Howell A. *The Rouen Campaign, 1590-92*. Oxford: Clarendon Press, 1973.
127. Loomie, A.J. "Gondomar's selection of English officers in 1622," *English Historical Review*, lxxxviii. (1973), pp. 574-81.
128. Lyndon, B. "Military Dress and Uniformity, 1680-1720," *Journal of the Society for Army Historical Research*, liv. (1976), pp. 108-20.
129. McGarth, P. *Bristol and the Civil War*. Bristol: Historical Association, 1981.
130. McLynn, F.J. *The Jacobites*. London: Routledge & Kegan Paul, 1985.
131. Malcom, Joyce Lee. "All the King's Men: The Impact of the Crown's Irish Soldiers on the English Civil War," *Irish Historical Studies*, xxi. (1977-8), pp. 239-64.
132. ———. "A King in Search of Soldiers: Charles I in 1642," *Historical Journal*, xxi. (1978), pp. 251-73.
133. ———. *Ceasar's Due: Loyalty and Charles I, 1642-1646*. London: Royal Historical Society, 1983.
134. Merriman, Marcus. "'The Epystle to the Queen's Majestie' and its 'Platte'," *Architectural History*, xxvii. (1984), pp. 25-32.
135. Millar, G.J. "Henry VIII's colonels," *Journal of the Society for Army Historical Research*, lvii. (1979), pp. 129-36.
136. ———. *Tudor Mercenaries and Auxiliaries, 1485-1547*. Charlottesville: University Press of Virginia, 1980.
137. Miller, A.C. "Joseph Lone's account of Cornwall during the Civil War," *English Historical Review*, xc. (1975), pp. 94-102.
138. ———. *Sir Richard Grenville of the Civil War*. London: Phillimore, 1979.
139. Miller, John. "Catholic Officers in the later Stuart Army," *English Historical Review*, lxxxviii. (1973), pp. 35-53.
140. ———. "The Militia and the Army in the Reign of James II," *Historical Journal*, xvi. (1973), pp. 659-79.
141. Morley, B.M. *Henry VIII and the Development of Coastal Defence*. London: HMSO, 1976.
142. Morrah, Patrick. *Prince Rupert of the Rhine*. London: Constable, 1976.
143. Muskett, P. "Military Operations against Smuggling in Kent and Sussex, 1698-1750," *Journal of the Society for Army Historical Research*, lii. (1974), pp. 89-110.
144. Newman, P.R. "The Defeat of Sir John Belasyse: Civil War in

Yorkshire, January--April 1644," *Yorkshire Archaeological Journal*, lii. (1980), pp. 123-33.
145. ——. *Royalist Officers in England and Wales, 1642-1660*. New York: Garland, 1981.
146. ——. *The Battle of Marston Moor*. Chichester: Bird, 1981.
147. ——. "The Royalist Officer Corps, 1642-1660: Army Command as a reflection of the Social Structure," *Historical Journal*, xxvi. (1983), pp. 945-58.
148. ——. "Aspects of the Civil War in Lancashire," *Transactions of the Lancashire and Chesire Antiquarian Society*, lxxxii. (1983), pp. 113-20.
149. ——. *Atlas of the English Civil War*. London: Croom Helm, 1985.
150. O'Callaghan, J.C. *History of the Irish Brigades in the Service of France*. Shannon: Irish Universities Press, 1969.
151. Ollard, R. L. *Man of War: Sir Robert Holmes and the Restoration Navy*. London: Hodder & Stoughton, 1969.
152. ——. *This War without an Enemy*. London: Hodder & Stoughton, 1976.
153. O'Neil, B.H. St. J. "Stephen von Haschenperg, an engineer to King Henry VIII, and his world," *Archaeologia*, xci. (1945), pp. 137-55.
154. Parker, Geoffrey. "If the Armada had landed," *History*, lxi. (1976), pp. 358-68.
155. Pereira, W.D. *The Siege of Gloucester*. Gloucester: Stoate & Bishop, 1983.
156. Porter, Stephen. "The Fire-raid in the English Civil War," *War and Society*, ii. (1984), pp. 27-40.
157. Priestley, E.J. "The Portsmouth Captains," *Journal of the Society for Army Historical Research*, lv. (1977), pp. 153-64.
158. Ridley, J. *The Roundheads*. London: Constable, 1976.
159. Robb, Nesca A. *William of Orange: A Personal Portrait*. 2 vols. London: Heinemann, 1966.
160. Robertson, John. *The Scottish Enlightenment and the Militia Issue*. Edinburgh: John Donald, 1985.
161. Rodger, N.A.M. "Ordnance Records and the Gunpowder Plot," *Bulletin of the Institute of Historical Research*, liii. (1980), pp. 124-5.
162. Roy, Ian. "The English Civil War and English Society," in *War and Society*, eds. Brian Bond and Ian Roy. London: Croom Helm, 1976.
163. ——. "The Army and its Critics in Seventeenth Century England," in *War and Society*, eds. Brian Bond and Ian Roy. London: Croom Helm, 1977.
164. ——. "England turned Germany? The Aftermath of the Civil War in its European context," *Transactions of the Royal Historical Society*, 5th series xxviii. (1978), pp. 127-44.
165. Schwoerer, Lois G. "The Literature of the Standing Army Controversy, 1697-1699," *Huntingdon Library Quarterly*, xxvii. (1965), pp. 187-212.
166. ——. "The Role of William III of England in the Standing Army Controversy--1697-1699," *Journal of British Studies*, v. (1966), pp. 74-94.

167. ——————. "No Standing Armies!": The Anti-Army Ideology in Seventeenth Century England. Baltimore: John Hopkins University Press, 1974.
168. Scouller, R.E. "The Mutiny Acts," Journal of the Society for Army Historical Research, 1. (1972), pp. 42-5.
169. Sweell, J.R. The Artillery Ground and Field in Finsbury: Two Maps of 1641 and 1705, with a commentary. London: London Topographical Society, 1977.
170. Silke, J.J. Kinsale. Liverpool: Liverpool University Press, 1970.
171. Simms, J.G. Jacobite Ireland, 1685-1691. London: Routledge & Kegan Paul, 1969.
172. Smith, G.R., and Toynbee M. Leaders of the Civil Wars, 1642-1648. Kineton: Roundwood Press, 1977.
173. Smith, V.T.C. "The Artillery Defences at Gravesend," Archaeologia Canatiana, lxxxix. (1974), pp. 141-68.
174. Snow, Vernon F. Essex the Rebel. Lincoln: University of Nebraska Press, 1970.
175. Stewart, R.W. "Arms Accountability in the Early Stuart Militia," Bulletin of the Institute of Historical Research, lvii. (1984), pp. 113-17.
176. Taylor, Clare. "The Phillipps Manuscript: A Chapter in Early Welsh Migration to the West Indies and to the United States," National Library of Wales Journal, xix. (1975-6), pp. 243-8.
177. Temple, R.K.G. "The Discovery of a Manuscript Eye-witness Account of the Battle of Maidstone," Archaeolgia Cantiana, xcvii. (1982), pp. 209-20.
178. Thomson, G.M. Warrior Prince: Prince Rupert of the Rhine. London: Secker & Warburg, 1976.
179. Thomson, M.A. "Louis XIV and William III, 1689-97," English Historical Review, lxxvi. (1961), pp. 37-58.
180. Tomlinson, Howard C. "The Ordnance Office and the King's forts, 1660-1714," Architectural History, xvi. (1973), pp. 5-25.
181. ——————. "Place and Profit: An Examination of the Ordnance Office, 1660-1714," Transactions of the Royal Historical Society, 5th series xxv. (1975), pp. 55-75.
182. ——————. "Wealden Gunfounding: An Analysis of its Demise in the Eighteenth Century," Economic History Review, 2nd series xxix. (1976), pp. 383-400.
183. ——————. Guns and Government: The Ordnance Office under the later Stuarts. London: Royal Historical Society, 1979.
184. Torntoft, Preben. "William III and Denmark-Norway, 1697-1702," English Historical Review, lxxxi. (1966), pp. 1-25.
185. Trench, Charles Chenevix. The Western Rising. London: Longman, 1966.
186. Tucker, Norman. "Volunteers in the Thirty Years' War," National Library of Wales Journal, xvi. (1969-70), pp. 61-76.
187. Underdown, David. Pride's Purge: Politics in the Puritan Revolution. Oxford: Clarendon Press, 1971.
188. Waddell, L.M. "The Paymaster Accounts of Richard Hill at Attingham Park," Journal of the Society for Army Historical Research, xlviii. (1970), pp. 50-9.
189. Wanklyn, M.D.G., and Young, Peter. "A King in search of

Soldiers: Charles I in 1642. A rejoinder," *Historical Journal*, xxiv. (1981), pp. 147-54.
190. Watson, I.B. "Fortifications and the 'idea' of Force in early East India Company relations with India," *Past and Present*, lxxxviii. (1980), pp. 70-87.
191. Watson, J.N.P. *Captain-General and Rebel Chief: The Life of James, Duke of Monmouth*. London: Allen & Unwin, 1979.
192. Webb, S.S. "Army Empire: English Garrison Government in Britain and America, 1596-1763," *William and Mary Quarterly*, 3rd series xxxiv. (1977), pp. 1-31.
193. ―――――. *The Governors-General: The English Army and the definition of Empire, 1569-1681*. Chapel Hill: University of North Carolina Press, 1979.
194. Wernham, R.B. *Before the Armada: The Growth of English Foreign Policy, 1485-1558*. London: Cape, 1966.
195. ―――――. *After the Armada: Elizabethan England and the Struggle for Western Europe, 1588-1595*. Oxford: Clarendon Press, 1984.
196. Western, J.R. *The English Militia in the Eighteenth Century*. London: Routledge & Kegan Paul, 1965.
197. ―――――. *Monarchy and Revolution: The English State in the 1680s*. London: Blandford Press, 1972; reprinted, MacMillan, 1985.
198. Wigfield, W. MacDonald. *The Monmouth Rebellion*. Bradford-on-Avon: Moonraker Press, 1980.
199. ―――――. *The Monmouth Rebels*. Gloucester: Alan Sutton, 1985.
200. Wilkinson, P.M. "The Excavations at Tilbury Fort, Essex," *Post-Medieval Archaeology*, xvii. (1983), pp. 111-62.
201. Williams, A.R. "A Technical Note on Some of the Armour of King Henry VIII and his contemporaries," *Archaeologia*, cvi. (1979), pp. 157-65.
202. Wilson, John. *Fairfax: A Life of Thomas, Lord Fairfax*. London: John Murray, 1985.
203. Woodward, D., and Cockerill, C. *The Siege of Colchester, 1648: A History and a Bibliography*. Chelmsford: Essex County Library, 1979.
204. Wroughton, John. *The Civil War in Bath and North Somerset, 1642-1650*. Bath: Victor Morgan, 1973.
205. Young, Peter. *Marston Moor, 1644*. Kineton: Roundwood Press, 1970.
206. ―――――. *Oliver Cromwell and His Times*. London: Severn House, 1975.
207. ―――――. *Naseby, 1645*. London: Century Publishing, 1985.
208. Young, Peter, and Emberton, W. *Sieges of the Great Civil War*. London: Bell & Hyman, 1978.
209. Young, Peter, and Holmes, Richard. *The English Civil War, 1642-1651*. London: Eyre Methuen, 1974.
210. Zee, Henri and Barbara van der. *William and Mary*. London: Macmillian, 1973.

ADDITIONS TO BIBLIOGRAPHY

211. Adair, John. *Cheriton, 1644.* Kineton: Roundwood Press, 1972.
212. Bennett, M. *The Battle of Bosworth.* Gloucester: Alan Sutton, 1985.
213. ―――――. "Leicester's Royalist Officers and the War Effort in the County, 1642-1646," *Journal of the Society for Army Historical Research*, lxii (1984), pp. 194-200.
214. Cogswell, Thomas. "Prelude to Ré: The Anglo-French struggle over La Rochelle, 1624-1627," *History*, lxxi (1986), pp. 1-21.
215. Hay, Millicent V. *The Life of Robert Sidney, Earl of Leicester, 1563-1626.* London and Toronto: Associated University Presses, 1984.
216. Hill, James Michael. *Celtic Warfare, 1595-1763.* Edinburgh: John Donald, 1986.
217. Hopkins, Paul. *Glencoe and the End of the Highland War.* Edinburgh: John Donald, 1986.
218. Lockyer, Roger. *Buckingham: The Life and Political Career of George Villiers, First Duke of Buckingham.* London: Longman, 1981.
219. Richmond, C. "The Battle of Bosworth, August 1485," *History Today*, xxxv no. 8 (1985), pp. 17-22.
220. Roy, Ian. "The British Army, 1500-1715: Recent Writing Reviewed," *Journal of the Society for Army Historical Research*, lxii (1984), pp. 194-200.
221. Wenham, L.P. *The Great and Close Siege of York, 1644.* Kineton: Roundwood Press, 1970.

V

THE NAVY TO 1714

Daniel A. Baugh
and
Geoffrey Scammell[1]

The original essay on "The Navy to 1714" commented on the manner in which Mahanite perspectives had tended to isolate naval history from maritime history; it noted that in the period before 1714 especially, "sea power was always a function of commerce, privateering and piracy, as well as of royal fleets." That essay did not pay sufficient tribute in this regard to the work of the late James A. Williamson, partly because it failed to take proper notice of his stimulating Ford Lectures for 1940, *The Ocean in English History* (9). It did, however, note the importance Kenneth Andrews' contributions, which have in some respects compelled a re-assessment of Williamson's views. Andrews' ongoing work, and the work of David B. Quinn and Geoffrey Scammell, continue to advance our understanding of Tudor and early Stuart maritime history, as will become quickly evident in this essay. Regarding the seventeenth-century development of the navy of England as an organized instrument of state power, research has been done, some of it in PhD dissertations not yet published, but the body of published monographs on this central topic remains remarkably slim.

As for surveys of broad scope, approximately twenty-five percent of Paul M. Kennedy's *The Rise and Fall of British Naval Mastery* (2), an admirable study of the geopolitics of naval power, deals with the Tudor and Stuart periods. Kennedy has bridged the gaps in the underlying monographic research with intelligence and virtuosity. Most important, he understands that "a survey of Britain's rise to naval mastery needs to concentrate as much upon peacetime as upon wartime developments" (p. 43)--a truth which traditional naval history acknowledged in theory but ignored in the actual recounting. Peter Padfield's *Tide of Empires* (5) is an unusual amalgam. Although it is filled with sea fights, it is framed in a general context of European development, the various national participants coming on stage according to a theory involving wealth, envy, and aggression. The theory is not worked into the history in much detail, but the study has two very considerable merits. First, the battle-and-breeze

---

[1]Essentially, Baugh has done the part after 1603, Scammell the parts before. We would like to thank Tim Grande for assistance in some preliminary compilations, and Linda M. Contento for typing the bibliography.

history is painted on a broad maritime-commercial canvas. Second, the adversaries' diplomatic and naval maneuverings are seen from both sides. A highly useful historical survey of the Admiralty as an institution by N.A.M. Rodger was published in 1979 (6).

General Bibliography and Archival Source Material. The fifth volume of the National Maritime Museum's printed catalogue of its library (3) provides a useful listing of printed books, with brief commentaries.

Basic research into certain areas of seventeenth-century English naval history can be greatly facilitated by the use of three published guides. The first is Eleanor S. Upton's subject guide to a large proportion of the volumes published by the Historical Manuscripts Commission (7). Although this guide extends only from 1603 to 1660, it is uniquely valuable. The H.M.C. reports that are not covered by it may be identified by consulting the list of reports (with brief descriptions) in the opening section of the *Bibliography of British History, 1603-1714*, 2nd edition (1). The second item is Peter Walne, *A Guide to Manuscript Sources for the History of Latin America and the Caribbean in the British Isles* (8); its superb index facilitates a rapid search (e.g. "West Indies, Naval, 17th cent."). Third, there is now a comprehensive printed guide to the naval administrative records preserved in the National Maritime Museum, prepared by R.J.B. Knight (4).

Finally, it should be noted that many of the State Papers Domestic and related Public Record Office series, which are key sources with regard to both later sixteenth and seventeenth-century naval transactions, may now be consulted away from the repository on microfilm; the Harvester Press series of State Papers Domestic is now filmed to 1660. The published calendars of these documents, long available in most research libraries, provide of course the best guide to their contents.

Before 1485. The history of England's naval forces and policies in the Middle Ages has still to be written. However, recent years have seen the appearance of several useful studies, mostly of severely limited chronological scope and often more concerned with the administrative rather than the maritime aspects of the subject. Michael Weir (79) patiently examines the attempts of the hapless Henry III to recover (1242-43) lands lost to France by his father. A.Z. Freeman's inquiries into the naval history of the later thirteenth century (27) focus particularly on the methods of defense against invasion (26). J.S. Kepler investigates the impact of the battle of Sluys on impressment for naval service in England 1340-43 (39). Timothy Runyan, who promises a large-scale work in the near future, has published articles that take an overall look at ships and seamen in late medieval England (59) and at the system for taking merchantmen into royal service (60); he has also produced a critical re-examination of a fourteenth-century cordage account for the royal ships (58). The crucially important naval side of the Hundred Years War has attracted some attention, but still lacks the definitive study it urgently needs. The subject is generally discussed by Colin Richmond (53). J.W. Sherborne has shown that the English defeat at the battle of La Rochelle resulted in vigorous measures by Edward III to reassert English prowess at sea (71). Sherborne has also inquired into the cost of naval (as well as military) forces in roughly the same period (73). The events of 1400-1403 are subjected to close scrutiny by C.J. Ford (25), whilst S.P. Pistono, following in the wake of Kingsford, examines the relations of Henry IV with pirates and privateers (46), notably the redoubtable John Hawley (47). J.A. Walker has written a careful and detailed account of the career of Henry V's celebrated soldier, John Holand, who among his many offices became Admiral in 1435 (76). Susan Rose had edited, with a detailed and valuable introduction, the accounts of William Soper, Keeper of the King's Ships, 1422-27 (54).

The characteristics of the combat ships, royal or otherwise, are still relatively neglected. Ships figure considerably in Richard Unger's densely packed, up-to-date and stimulating examination of Europe's medieval maritime economy (75). J.W. Sherborne has argued the importance of oared--and therefore maneuverable--barges and balingers in the late 1300s (72), and Susan Rose vigorously contests the generally held view that Henry V's *Grace à Dieu* was a "colossal technological mistake" (55).

1485-1603. The maritime and naval history of the Tudor Age, which has fascinated the English-speaking world since the days of Charles Kingsley and James Anthony Froude, has been particularly well served, with a number of eminent specialists publishing the conclusions of a lifetime's study of the period. Among historians who have addressed themselves to a broad chronological sweep, Peter Padfield, particularly interested in gunnery and tactics, examines the Tudor achievement in the context of European seapower (5), and Paul Kennedy contributes some valuable insights in his magisterial survey of the course of British naval history (2). Turning to studies that focus mainly on the Tudor period, David Quinn has written numerous scholarly papers on seamen, the beginnings of English oceanic enterprise, and American colonization, which have been substantially collected in a volume (51); he has also written, with A.N. Ryan, a probing survey of England's maritime history from 1550 to 1642 in which naval developments are critically and usefully summarized (52). Kenneth Andrews, drawing on decades of research on the period, revises some earlier interpretations in his splendid examination of English maritime enterprise from 1480 to 1630 (17). A study of "England and the French War, 1557-9" by C.S.L. Davies (23) is of considerable naval interest. R.B. Wernham continues his detailed and sympathetic appraisal of Elizabeth's cautious attitude toward the bold naval strategies advocated by some of her subjects (80, 81). G.V. Scammell discusses the maritime history of England in the broad context of Europe's penetration by sea of the wider world (65). The same author also draws attention to what the chartered trading companies, so much in evidence under Elizabeth and her successors, achieved or failed to achieve at sea (68).

It is not surprising that the bulk of the writing on this period has been concerned with the Elizabethan war at sea, in particular with the organization and impact of privateering on Spanish (and Portuguese) shipping and possessions, the evolution of an English oceanic strategy, and also the hesitant naval policies of the last years of the queen's reign. Tom Glasgow has continued his account of the pre-oceanic era of Tudor seapower (29, 30). G.V. Scammell sketches, in the context of the growth of European overseas empires in the sixteenth century, the emergence of the first oceanic strategies (61), and also examines the economic basis of the ideas of the well known Tudor propagandist of overseas expansion, Richard Hakluyt (64). A long admired article by David Waters on the Elizabethan Navy and the Armada is now available in booklet form (77), whilst the late Neville Williams, writing with intimate knowledge of the rich archives of the High Court of Admiralty, has left a colorful account of the history of piracy and privateering (82). Kenneth Andrews, who has made the transoceanic campaigns of England particularly his own, has given us a magisterial account of the century of war and trade in the Caribbean after 1530 (14), particularly important for its reappraisal of John Hawkins' activities and its critical approach to the writings of the late James Williamson. Andrews has also produced a galaxy of articles on various aspects of English privateering and oceanic ventures in this period (10, 12, 13). Among the most recent, there is a candid reevaluation of the motives and behavior of Humphrey Gilbert and Walter Raleigh (18), and a study of English attitudes toward possibilities in South America (15). Alan Haynes has presented a useful account of the Cadiz expedition of 1596 (36), and Ronald Pollitt has looked into the contentious early career of John Hawkins (48). A copy of Sir John Hawkins' instructions of 1590 has been brought to light by H.A. Lloyd (42), G.V. Scammell relates English penetration of Asia, ca. 1600, to the general privateering war (67), and in an examination of English activity in the Atlantic islands between ca. 1450 and 1650 traces the growth of English maritime strategy, suggesting that its implementation offered fewer difficulties than historians have commonly supposed (69).

R.W. Kenny has written a comprehensive account of the career of the Elizabethan Lord Admiral, Charles Howard (38), and there are useful shorter discussions of the activities of other naval figures, such as Richard Boulind's note on the Beestons and Tyrrells (20) and Rachel Lloyd's book on Christopher Carleill (43).

Some of the rich assortment of sources for the naval and maritime history of the period have been made available in either new or revised editions. John Hampden has brought together material on the career of Francis Drake (35). For the Hakluyt Society Mary F. Keeler has edited documents relating to Drake's West Indian voyage of 1585-6 (37) and K.R. Andrews those dealing with the disastrous last voyage of Drake and Hawkins (11). More light is shed on the abortive venture of Edward Fenton, in 1582, by E.S. Donno's edition of the Diary of Richard Madox, the erudite Oxford chaplain of the expedition (24).

Administration, Ships, and Naval Resources. Ships and their characteristics are discussed in the important work of Richard Unger already cited (75). Much attention has been lavished on the recently salvaged remnants of the Henrician *Mary Rose* (45, 56, 57). Tom Glasgow has written on the career of the royal ship *Tiger* and compiled a useful list of naval vessels 1539-1588 (28) (31). Richard Boulind has disentangled the histories of four craft in royal service in the sixteenth century (21), and J.E.G. Bennell has attempted a comprehensive survey of the undistinguished history of oared fighting ships in English service in the same period (19). A treatise by Sir Arthur Gorgas (1557-1625)--no great authority it must be admitted--on how ships were to be sailed, handled, kept afloat or brought into action, has been edited by Tom Glasgow (33). That most famous encounter, the Armada campaign, has been re-assessed by R.J. Lander and I.A.A. Thompson with results that take us back to the old view: the Spanish ships were bigger than those of the English, but the English had the advantage in guns and gunnery (40, 74).

Patterns of shipowning are examined by G.V. Scammell, with three broad social groups of owners identified--merchants, aristocrats, seamen--and their influence on governmental policy discussed (63). Many shipowners, of whom those of the Hawkins dynasty are the most celebrated, formed the backbone of such naval administration as the country possessed. Tom Glasgow has examined some interesting accounts of naval business, especially regarding the 1550s (34). He and Ronald Pollitt have each focussed some attention on the administratively important last years of Mary's and early years of Elizabeth's reign. Glasgow notes the importance of the Marquess of Winchester (32); Pollitt (50) detects the guiding spirit of the ubiquitously effective Sir William Cecil (later Lord Burghley). Pollitt has also re-examined the efforts to cope with the problems of the Armada campaign (49). The relatively unknown phenomenon of Elizabethan Ship Money was ably investigated fifty years ago by Ada H. Lewis (41) in a little volume that is now rather scarce.

The problem of finding crews both for merchantmen and warships, which so exercised contemporaries, is now receiving the attention it deserves from historians. There is some useful material in Christopher Lloyd's general survey of the history of the British seaman (175). G.V. Scammell investigates recruitment, skills, social background, age, and educational qualifications of those who served in merchant ships--and consequently from time to time in privateers and royal ships (62, 66). The same author has also made a preliminary survey of the manning of fighting ships in the century after 1550 (70). Further details are added by the articles of K.R. Andrews on the Elizabethan seaman (16) and Pauline Croft on English mariners trading to Spain and Portugal (22). J.J.N. McGurk displays and evaluates the methods used in attempting to man a coastal defence force in 1602 (44). Admiral Sir James Watt illuminates by his medical knowledge the story of the surgeons serving in the *Mary Rose* (78).

1603-1714. For reasons that could be matter for a separate essay, the development of English naval power is a subject that has benefitted very little from the lively interest in seventeenth-century England's role in the modernizing of the Western world. The present writer has briefly addressed the theme in an unpublished paper (95) the substance of which will be incorporated into a book of larger scope. The second chapter of Paul Kennedy's broad survey (2) is indispensable, and there are portions of Peter Padfield's *Tide of Empires* (5), particularly those touching the strategy and tactics of the Dutch wars, that bring matters neatly into focus. Still, the work of C.D. Penn on naval policy, published seventy years ago (197), remains valuable; Sir Julian Corbett's great, perhaps greatest, work, *England in the Mediterranean*, published eighty years ago (115), is still treasured for manifold reasons; and Sir Herbert Richmond's *The Navy as an Instrument of Policy, 1558-1727* (208) still offers the best comprehensive inquiry into strategies employed in seventeenth-century naval campaigns.

Among general surveys of imperial and foreign policy, the following are especially relevant to naval history. W.A. Speck's essay on the historiography of "The International and Imperial Context" of North American colonial policy (223) contains insights of broad scope. Klaus Knorr's older study of *British Colonial Theories, 1570-1850* has been rightly kept available by reprintings (166). A succinct and authoritative guide to *Stuart and Cromwellian Foreign Policy* (1603-1688) has been written by G.M.D. Howat (151). J.R. Jones, *Britain and the World 1649-1815* (154) links naval and foreign policy, and heavily accents seapower, but, though written by an expert, the book is not designed to assist research, because it provides no references and is rather thin on documentation; but it is an excellent book for broad orientation and contains a fine introductory bibliography.

For a broad view of the development of overseas trade, appropriate chapters of D.C. Coleman's judicious survey, *The Economy of England, 1450-1750* (112) are the first recourse. Ralph Davis's articles on the patterns of English trade (121) are indispensable. On English trade to the Mediterranean, Davis' brief survey (120) is still the best introduction. His general study of the Atlantic supplies a useful background (122); so does K.G. Davies, *The North Atlantic World in the Seventeenth Century* (119). For the Indian Ocean, see K.N. Chaudhuri's *The Trading World of Asia and the English East India Company, 1660-1760* (109). D.K. Bassett's article (92) on English trade and settlement in Asia, 1602-1690, is an excellent summary. A good introduction to geopolitics and navigation in the Pacific during the seventeenth century is the second volume of O.H.K. Spate's *The Pacific since Magellan* (222); its footnotes offered the best bibliographical entry to maritime transactions in the Pacific.

1603-1649. Very little of the talent and labor that has been lavished in recent years on English history in the first half of the seventeenth century has been directed toward naval matters. There have been some piecemeal additions to the historical catalog of operational failure. N.P. Bard has edited a tract that roundly criticized the management and execution of the Earl of Warwick's privateering voyage of 1627 (88); it touches on sea life, tactics and ship capabilities, and also, because its author was a tarpaulin, offers some interesting insights for historians of social class. Warwick's ventures at sea were scrutinized many years ago in an important article by Frank Craven (118). Donald Woodward has unearthed and published a chronicle of Sir Thomas Button's difficulties in trying to police Irish waters against various pirates, 1614-1622 (236). H. Barnby shows why forces were not marshalled to counter the raid on Baltimore (Co. Cork) in 1631 (90). An unpublished dissertation by J.C. Appleby (86) studies English privateering during the wars of the 1620s. J.S. Kepler has made an effort, on the basis of admittedly scant data, to determine whether the English gained or lost on the balance sheet of captures during hostilities in the 1624-1630 period (162). There was a good deal of naval activity in the 1620s, however inept in planning and execution it may have been. Because it treats the great man's objects and measures with a respect that many historians have been unwilling to accord them. Roger Lockyer's biography of *Buckingham* (176) provides a comprehensive and thoroughly researched introduction (replete with bibliographical and archival leads) to the naval plans, campaigns, and administrative problems of the decade; the powerful duke was Lord High Admiral from 1619 until his assassination, at Portsmouth, in 1628.

There is still a great deal that is not known about the growth and use of the navy during the civil war. However, M.L. Baumber has examined the uncertainties and expedients that led to the failure to maintain surveillance on the Irish coasts in the early years of the civil war (96). H.-C. Junge has published, with commentary on its political implications, a document that exhibits the names of ship-owners and mariners concerned with arming their vessels in the early years of the struggle (155). A surviving daybook kept by a Puritan chaplain has enabled Amos Miller to throw some light on the doings of a Parliamentary ship of war in 1644 (188); the cocksure and self-righteous chaplain stirred up a near mutiny onboard.

A number of excellent studies of politics and foreign policy provide essential background for the study of naval history in this period. The last three chapters of D.B. Quinn and A.N. Ryan, *England's Sea Empire* (52) give a good general view, and its opening bibliographical essay is valuable. Andrew's "Caribbean Rivalry and the Anglo-Spanish Peace of 1604" (12) treats an issue whose implications were momentous. Simon Adams' penetrating articles on foreign policy (83, 84) are of particular value. Also of naval interest are: Robert Ruigh's book on *The Parliament of 1624* (213); the portion of Conrad Russell's book that deals with the parliament of 1625 (214); and Thomas Cogswell's article exposing the extreme uncertainty of royal policy in 1625-26 on the eve of the La Rochelle expedition (111). Two articles appearing in the same number of *The Economic History Review*, one by Harland Taylor (228), the other by J.S. Kepler (161), offer particular illustrations of the role of the monarchy's policy of "neutrality" (which leaned toward helping Spain against the Dutch) in enhancing English maritime prosperity during the 1630s. Kepler's book on the entrepôt at Dover (160) contains material of naval interest and a good bibliography for the study of maritime trade and trade policy between 1620 and 1652. Robert Brenner's important and provocative articles (101, 102) probe the interrelationship of merchant groups, maritime enterprise, and political allegiance. George Edmundson's series of Ford Lectures of 1910, though thin on citations, remains the best survey of Anglo-Dutch rivalry prior to the Dutch wars (125).

1649-1660. The six volumes that were edited long ago for the Navy Records Society (133) still constitute the most important published collection of materials for the naval history of the First Dutch War; a volume of *Corrigenda*, by A.C. Dewar, was issued by the Society in 1932 (123). For day-to-day operations in the Mediterranean during the war the journal kept by Capt. John Weale, edited for the Society by J.R. Powell in 1952 (200), is also of value. Gardiner's *History of the Commonwealth and Protectorate* (134), which did not slight naval matters, remains in many ways the most useful survey of this period, although the author did not live to carry it beyond 1656. J.R. Powell's *Robert Blake* (201) provides reliable accounts of the great commander's campaigns, but its approach to strategic issues is rather simplistic. Powell has also contributed articles on Sir George Ayscue's expedition to Barbados in 1651 (202), and on John Bourne (203), who served as flagship captain in many campaigns; unfortunately the latter article does not reveal why rescuing Bourne's career from "the fog of war" is of any historical use. P. LeFevre's article on Ayscue (173) improves substantially upon the entry in the *D.N.B.* S.A.G. Taylor's book on the capture of Jamaica (229) is mostly military history, but not without naval interest. Of the three biographies of Prince Rupert that appeared in 1976 Patrick Morrah's (189) contains a good deal on Rupert's activities at sea and is unquestionably the one to which naval historians should turn.

Regarding naval policy in the aftermath of the civil war, a major study by Hans-Christoph Junge was published in 1980 under the title *Flottenpolitik und Revolution: Die Entstehung der englischen Seemacht während der Herrshaft Cromwells* (156). After more than five years the book has evidently not been reviewed in English. Junge's point of departure is fundamentally correct (in the opinion of the present writer); it is that England became a great maritime power in the mid-seventeenth century, not in the time of Hawkins and Drake. The book's thorough research is designed to show why the establishment of an effective naval policy should be seen as a logical consequence of the outcome of the English Civil War. The bibliography, though replete with minor flaws, is the best available on the middle part of the century. The navy's importance in shaping foreign policy is displayed in a well crafted study by Charles P. Korr entitled *Cromwell and the New Model Foreign Policy* (167); Korr's book also has a fine bibliography. In view of these bibliographies it is unnecessary to list the many interesting articles that have appeared within the last quarter century touching foreign policy during the Interregnum, but the following which are of particular maritime interest may be singled out: John F. Battick's on the relationship between the Western Design and the French Alliance (94), and also on the conception and objectives of the Western Design (93); James E. Farnell's on the influences of London merchant groups on the passage of the navigation ordinances and the contest with the Dutch (127); Michael Roberts' on Cromwell's Baltic policy (210); and R.C. Thompson's on the views of officers of the army and navy, and of London merchants, regarding foreign-policy decisions made under the Protectorate (230).

1660-1688. The character and methods of the Restoration navy are nicely captured in Richard Ollard's well researched biography of Sir Robert Holmes (192). C.R. Boxer's succinct account of *The Anglo-Dutch Wars of the 17th Century* (100) is especially valuable for its discussion of the Third Dutch War; its bibliography provides an avenue to both English and Dutch studies of the wars. A.W. Pearsall's illustrated booklet, *The Second Dutch War* (195) is a felicitous weaving of documents, some hitherto unpublished, into a coherent narrative of the campaigns. A first-hand glimpse of operations at sea during 1666 is available in *The Rupert and Monck Letter Book* (204); the volume also contains supplementary documents, many of which elucidate the strategic intentions. P.M. Bosscher's article on the "Four Days Battle" (98) is particularly valuable for its view of the condition and conduct of the Dutch forces. The

English naval catastrophe of 1667 is treated in a good book by P.G. Rogers, *The Dutch in the Medway* (211). J.R. Bruijn's article on Dutch privateering (106) in a useful introduction by a noted scholar and raises the question of how Dutch and English shipping losses may be compared. The participation of Scottish privateersmen in the second and third Dutch wars is addressed in an article by E.J. Graham (137).

A few historians have begun to pay attention to the navy and its activities during the last ten years of Charles II's reign--after the Dutch wars and after Samuel Pepys was no longer in office. The most important study is as yet unpublished, Sari Hornstein's dissertation (148) on the manner in which the English navy was used, mainly in the Mediterranean, to further the expansion of English trade by protecting it against predators. A portion of her findings will appear in the collection of published papers of the Seventh Naval History Symposium (149). P. LeFevre has studied Capt. John Tyrrell, who was frequently employed in Mediterranean operations in this epoch (174). Tyrrell also set forth for India, in 1684, a voyage to which W.E. May has devoted an article (181); May has also studied the navy's role in containing the Earl of Argyle's rebellion in 1682 (182). S. Mountfield has contributed a study of Capt. G. Collins (190), an officer whose hydrographic skills were put to good use by the Admiralty. M.J. Syndenham's article on Lord Dartmouth's fence-sitting posture in 1688 (227) suggests that strategic blundering and the 'Protestant wind' were probably not the main reasons why the king's navy failed to deter William of Orange's invasion.

The following studies of policy touch upon naval matters. A useful, brief overview is provided by J.L. Price's "Restoration England and Europe" (206). In Ronald Hutton's detailed study of the Restoration period down to 1667 (152) one may find a compressed account of the domestic political background of the Second Dutch War which throws fresh light on the causes of the war's calamitous denouement. On the politics behind the Third Dutch War, the best survey is in D.T. Witcombe, *Charles II and the Cavalier House of Commons, 1663-1674* (235). M.D. Lee has inquired into Arlington's role in the Treaty of Dover (172). C.R. Boxer's "Some Second Thoughts on the Third Anglo-Dutch War" (99) remains the indispensable guide to the movement of public opinion; it nicely complements the earlier, more extensive study by K.H.D. Haley, *William of Orange and the English Opposition* (138). Some chapters of Haley's recent biography of *Shaftesbury* (139) throw further light on the complex diplomatic shifts of the post-1668 period. Phyllis Lachs has offered a brief overview of the whole question of royal and parliamentary contentions about foreign policy during the Restoration (168). Useful background, though the book is not directly concerned with England, may be found in Alice Carter's *Neutrality or Commitment: The Evolution of Dutch Foreign Policy, 1667-1795* (108).

1689-1714. When one thinks of the tremendous demands imposed on the navy by the 1689-97 war, and the impressive growth of naval capabilities in response to those demands (and also the interpretations of English political development that have been based, to a considerable degree, upon the expansion of central government during the wars of 1689-97 and 1702-13), one can only wonder why naval history in this period has not received more scholarly attention in recent years.

Perhaps some students have concluded that John Ehrman's massive contribution, published in 1953 (126), left nothing further to be done. But strategic choices and operations at sea, though they figured in that book, were not its central concerns. *The Naval Side of King William's War* from November 1688 to June 1690 by Edward B. Powley (205) is a rambling monograph which contributes a detailed chronicle of the navy's role in subduing the Jacobite forces in Ireland. Philip Aubrey has provided a useful account of the turning away of the French invasion attempt of 1692 (87). J.S. Bromley's "The Jacobite privateers in the Nine Years War" (103) studies the activities of the raiders based at St. Malo, Brest, and Dunkirk, many of them Irish-born, who were commissioned by James II in exile to prey upon English shipping. No study of English seapower in the war of William III should overlook Geoffrey Symcox's first-rate analysis of French naval developments, *The Crisis of French Sea Power, 1688-1697* (226).

By assembling portions of more than ninety documents John Hattendorf provides a coherent narrative of Admiral Benbow's sea fight on the Spanish Main in 1702 as well as a glance at the subsequent court-martial proceedings (144). David Francis, *The First Peninsular War, 1702-1713* (132) is a valuable account of English naval as well as military operations. Stephen Gradish's article on seapower in the Mediterranean (136) is a useful summing up of that aspect of British strategy at the most important stage of its development. J.S. Kepler's article on an effort to hurry a battle squadron to the Mediterranean (163) is based mainly on a cache of Admiral Jennings' letter books and journals and provides a sequential account of the varied difficulties and delays involved in a major naval deployment. W.R. Meyer has used statistics found in the High Court of Admiralty papers to draw up a rough balance sheet of gains and losses from commerce warfare during the wars of 1689-97 (186) and 1702-13 (187). Parliament's concern for the provision of convoys is discussed by J.A. Johnston in "Parliament and the Protection of Trade, 1698-1694" (153).

Among background studies, the following are of particular interest to naval history. Henry Horwitz's examination of the Earl of Nottingham's career (150) throws fresh light on the development of naval policy in the early years of the war of William III, when Nottingham was First Lord. Also, the fourth volume of the Historical Manuscripts Commission's publication of the Finch MSS. (147) covered the year 1692; the volume is rich in naval material. There is an incisive rethinking of the question of the importance of Dunkirk, 1688-1713, in a paper by J.S. Bromley (105). Ian K. Steele's *Politics of Colonial Policy* (224) is mainly about the Board of Trade, but discusses the effort made to suppress piracy between 1697 and 1700, as well as issues of colonial defense in the period 1702-1706. A more broadly based inquiry into the navy's role in suppressing piracy in this epoch is provided by Robert Ritchie's book (209). A.D. Francis' book, *The Methuens and Portugal, 1691-1708* (129), especially Chapter 11, is highly relevant, as are his articles on "The Grand Alliance of 1698" (131) and Portugal's place in it (130). England's relations with the Dutch Republic during the 1702-13 war were of crucial importance; Douglas Coombs, *The Conduct of the Dutch* (114) is a first-class study of the factors that made the Dutch alliance a football of party politics. John Hattendorf illustrates the decision-making process in his article on the planning and execution of grand strategy in Queen Anne's reign (143). Henry L. Synder draws on memoranda of high-level conversations of 1707 to reveal more about the role of Lord Treasurer Godolphin in discussions of strategy and about the manifold options that were considered (220). Snyder's study of the political struggle over who should direct the Admiralty in 1709 exhibits an instance of the interaction of English political strife and war policy (221). Some valuable insights into Franco-Spanish financial sinews of war may be got from Henry Kamen's *The War of Succession in Spain, 1700-15* (157). Articles by A.D. MacLachlan (178) and B.W. Hill (146) focus some attention on the maritime concerns that arose in the diplomacy of peacemaking. Finally, Glyndwr Williams' essay on English projects and ventures in the South Seas (234) is especially relevant to an understanding of the mentality of maritime aggression in this period.

Piracy. By the early seventeenth century the line between privateering and piracy was becoming more clearly defined, at least in European waters. Nevertheless, an article by C.F. Senning (219) offers a striking instance of the triumph of expediency over legitimacy, wherein the peace-loving but money-hungry court of James I was quite prepared to arrogate to itself the plunder from a captured Portuguese merchantman and to claim simultaneously that the captors deserved no share at all because their action was of dubious legality. C.M. Senior's *A Nation of Pirates* (218) is a succinct and readable account of English piracy early in the century (ca. 1603-1615), and David Hebb has completed a PhD dissertation on "The English Government and the Problem of Piracy, 1616-1642" (145).

Sir Henry Morgan, whose highly irregular forces notoriously attacked the Spaniards but were also the only means of defending Jamaica in the decades after it was taken, has been the subject of two recent studies, a biography by Dudley Pope (199) and a detailed study of the expedition to Panama, by Peter Earle (124). Both books exhibit some original research, and Earle's contains a well considered Chapter 3 on the political and strategic considerations that allowed Morgan and the buccaneers their scope. The evidence in support of the maritime aspect of B.R. Burg's study of the sexual proclivities of sea-rovers (107) is thin and sometimes dubious. Students of the problem of piracy are pleased to learn that Robert Ritchie's study (209), which considers the seventeenth century generally and is particularly concerned in the closing chapters with the royal navy's role in suppression (ca. 1670-1730), will be soon published. For a bibliographical guide to piracy, the fourth volume of the National Maritime Museum's series of printed catalogues (191) is invaluable.

Administration, Ships, and Naval Resources. G.G. Harris, *The Trinity House of Deptford, 1514-1660* (142) has a chapter on "The Naval Affairs of the State." Evelyn Berckman, *Creators and Destroyers of the English Navy* (97) prints some choice fragments from the State Papers (1580s to 1660s), but its interpretations suffer from severe myopia. A notable contribution to the study of the period is the editing of the records of the official inquiries into the naval administrative inequities of James I's reign by A.P. McGowan (184); McGowan has also calendared a supplementary fragment (185). Linda

Peck has written a valuable article that delineates the political background of the 1608 inquiry (196). A short paper published in 1950 by M.C. Wren on the process of obtaining twenty ships for the navy from London in 1626-27 (237) is of naval as well as political interest. The same is true of R. Swales' excellent article on the Ship Money levy of 1628 (225). The Ship Money levies of the 1630s are largely a political subject, the government not being under specific wartime pressures; most of the studies are concerned with the problem of collection in particular counties, but it might be mentioned that Thomas Barnes' study of Somerset, recently reprinted (91), sets the broad context admirably, and that an article by N.P. Bard (89) has a national rather than a county focus. The most important figure in Early Stuart naval medicine was John Woodall, whose career as surgeon general and experimental inquiries into scurvy are reviewed in an essay by Sir Geoffrey Keynes (164). L.C. Martin provides a glance at the career of Charles I's surveyor of naval victualling, 1635-42 (180). Our knowledge of administration during the civil war and the early part of the Interregnum will always be restricted by a relative lack of surviving documents. But there are important details in Violet Rowe's study of the career of *Sir Henry Vane the Younger* (212), and there is an unpublished dissertation by W.N. Hammond on administration during the Interregnum (140).

In terms of published material, the study of Restoration naval administration still remains much in the condition that J.R. Tanner left it. Richard Ollard's *Pepys* (193) is a smoothly flowing biography that pays great attention to matters naval and political. Bernard Pool has provided a brief introduction to the great shipbuilding project of 1677, in which Pepys played a leading role (198). Pepys' role in the 1660s is made easier to trace by a new edition of the *Diary* (169), the last volume of which contains a subject index and a bibliography, both very useful. The role of Sir William Coventry remains largely overlooked, partly no doubt because of the overpowering fame of the great diarist. V. Vale's interesting analysis of Coventry's defense against Clarendon's accusations (233) provides a further reminder of how little has been published about this able man who was an important figure not only in naval administration, but also in the politics of maritime affairs. Now that the papers of the Coventry brothers, preserved at Longleat, are available on microfilm (117) it will be easier to mend this omission. During the seventeenth century the Navy Office was quartered in various parts of London; the locations and buildings are discussed briefly in T.F. Reddaway's study of "The Temporary Navy Office, 1673-84" (207). H.C. Tomlinson's monograph on the ordnance department from 1660 to 1714 (231) is of general administrative interest; his article on "The Ordnance Office and the Navy" (232) is a multifaceted analysis of the causes of the often frustrating delays in supplying ordnance and related stores to the fleet. Joseph J. Malone's important article on naval stores from the Baltic (179) is a well documented study of the situations before and after the bounty act of 1704-5. David Kirby also addresses the problem of naval stores in the reign of Anne (165).

Some compilations of personnel may be noted. R.C. Anderson's list of captains, 1642-60 (85), gives the specifics regarding their sea-service assignments. L. Gooch lists the Catholic officers in the fleet in 1688 (135) and reaches the conclusion that James II's policy did not favor them beyond the bounds of professional merit. J.C. Sainty's *Admiralty Officials* (215) and J.M. Collinge's *Navy Board Officials* (113) list everyone in the respective London offices, from the top authorities to the lowest clerks; the introductions of both books provide the best information available on the mechanics of appointments and promotions in the clerical ranks.

The history of the dockyards in the seventeenth century has not, for the most part, been intensively studied. Philip MacDougall's general history of the *Royal Dockyards* (177) is intended for non-specialist readers, but it is to be commended for its three chapters on the seventeenth century as well as its ground plans, illustrations, and bibliography. R.V. Saville's fine selection of documents pertaining to the management of the dockyards in the 1670s (216) gives an indication of the resources available for further research. There has been a great advance in recent years regarding the dockyard buildings and installations. Of the numerous studies by Jonathan Coad, his article on Devonport (Plymouth) is of most interest to students of the period before 1714 (110). The history of naval installations at home and overseas belongs largely to a later period, but T.W. Courtney's report on excavations at Woolwich dockyard (116) has much on the seventeenth century, especially in Part 2. The history of *Port Royal, Jamaica* by Michael Pawson and David Buisseret (194) is not to be missed: it is mostly concerned with the seventeenth century and contains a great deal that is relevant to naval history.

As for ship design and construction, Brian Lavery has done the necessary spade work (170) to get to the bottom of the function and usage of "rebuilding" (as opposed to building afresh)--concerning which the present writer once made some incorrect surmises. Sir Anthony Deane's treatise of naval architecture, written in 1670 and now available in a modern edition (171), is highly technical, but Lavery's introduction contains a historical commentary on both Deane's career and Restoration shipbuilding. Frank Fox's *Great Ships: The Battlefleet of King Charles II* (128) is beautifully illustrated, contains a good deal of useful history, and incorporates a list of Royal Navy ships of the period from 1660 to 1685 (which gives technical details and also reports the ultimate fate of each vessel). John Harland's *Seamanship in the Age of Sail* (141) is a clearly presented introduction to the technical aspects of maneuver, tracing the historical development as well as function of each aspect during the long span from 1600 to 1860.

Christopher Lloyd, *The British Seaman* (175) has three chapters that deal directly with the seventeenth century. Peter Kemp's *The British Sailor* (158) contains tasty and intriguing morsels, but the historical stitching is frequently ambiguous and largely out of date. Donald Kennedy's article on the Early Stuart monarchy's attitudes toward and treatment of seamen (159) is filled with interesting vignettes and insights. An article by Maxwell Schoenfeld (217) offers glimpses of the dreadful delays in disbursing pay to the navy's seamen during the Restoration period. The late J.S. Bromley's volume of selected pamphlets on *The Manning of the Royal Navy* (104) provides a penetrating longitudinal survey of an enduring problem; the first four pamphlets concern the period from 1689 to 1714. Bromley's knowledge and understanding of the maritime history of northwest Europe in this period was incomparable--an emblem of supreme scholarly devotion and integrity.

BIBLIOGRAPHY

Note: The following abbreviations are used:
B.I.H.R. Bulletin of the Institute of Historical Research
Hist. Jour. The Historical Journal
M.M. The Mariner's Mirror
N.R.S. Navy Records Society

General

1. Keeler, Mary Frear (ed.) *Bibliography of British History, Stuart Period, 1603-1714.* 2nd ed. Oxford: Clarendon Press, 1970.
2. Kennedy, Paul, M. *The Rise and Fall of British Naval Mastery.* 1st ed. 1976. 2nd ed. London and Basingstoke: Macmillan, 1983.
3. National Maritime Museum, Greenwich. *Catalogue of the Library. V: Naval History, Part One: The Middle Ages to 1815.* London: H.M.S.O., 1976.
4. ―――. *Guide to the Manuscripts. II: Public Records, Business Records and Artificial Collections,* ed. R.J.B. Knight. London: Mansell, 1980.
5. Padfield, Peter. *Tide of Empires: Decisive Naval Campaigns in the Rise of the West. I, 1481-1654: II, 1654-1763.* London: Routledge & Kegan Paul, 1979, 1983--in prog.
6. Rodger, N.A.M. *The Admiralty.* Lavenham, Suffolk: T. Dalton, 1979.
7. Upton, Eleanor Stuart. *Guide to the Sources of English History from 1603 to 1660 in Early Reports of the Royal Commission on Historical Manuscripts.* 2nd ed. New York and London: Scarecrow Press, 1964.
8. Walne, Peter. *A Guide to Manuscript Sources for the History of Latin America and the Caribbean in the British Isles.* Oxford: Oxford University Press, 1973.
9. Williamson, James A. *The Ocean in English History.* Oxford: Clarendon Press, 1941.

Before 1603

10. Andrews, Kenneth R. "Sir Robert Cecil and Mediterranean Plunder." *English Hist. Rev.,* 87 (1972), pp. 513-32.
11. ―――. *The Last Voyage of Drake and Hawkins.* London: Hakluyt Society, 1972.
12. ―――. "Caribbean Rivalry and the Anglo-Spanish Peace of 1604." *History,* 59 (1974), pp. 1-17.
13. ―――. "English Voyages to the Caribbean, 1596 to 1604: An Annotated List." *William and Mary Quarterly,* 31 (1974), pp. 243-54.
14. ―――. *The Spanish Caribbean: Trade and Plunder, 1530-1630.* New Haven: Yale Univ. Press, 1978.
15. ―――. "Beyond the Equinoctial: England and South America in

the Sixteenth Century." *Jour. of Imperial & Commonwealth Hist.*, X, 1 (1981), pp. 4-24.
16. ──────. "The Elizabethan Seaman." *M.M.*, 68 (1982), pp. 245-62.
17. ──────. *Trade, Plunder and Settlement: Maritime Enterprise and the Genesis of the British Empire, 1480-1630.* Cambridge: Cambridge University Press, 1984.
18. ──────. *Privateering and Colonisation in the Reign of Elizabeth I.* Exeter, 1985.
19. Bennel, J.E.G. "English Oared Vessels of the Sixteenth Century." *M.M.*, 60 (1974), pp. 9-26, 169-85.
20. Boulind, Richard. "Tudor Captains: The Beestons and the Tyrrells." *M.M.*, 59 (1973), pp. 171-8.
21. ──────. "Ships of Private Origin in the Mid-Tudor Navy." *M.M.*, 59 (1973), pp. 385-408.
22. Croft, Pauline. "English Mariners Trading to Spain and Portugal, 1558-1625." *M.M.*, 66 (1983), pp. 251-66.
23. Davies, C.S.L. "England and the French War, 1557-9," in *The Mid-Tudor Polity, c. 1540-1560*, ed. Robert Tittler and Jennifer Loach. London: Macmillan, and Totowa, N.J.: Rowman and Littlefield, 1980, pp. 159-85.
24. Donno, E.S. *An Elizabethan in 1582: The Diary of Richard Madox.* London: Hakluyt Society, 1976.
25. Ford, C.J. "Piracy or Policy: The Crisis in the Channel 1400-1403." *Trans. of the Royal Historical Society*, 5th ser. XXIX (1979), pp. 63-78.
26. Freeman, A.Z. "A Moat Defensive: The Coast Defense Scheme of 1295." *Speculum*, 42 (1967), pp. 442-62.
27. ──────. "Wooden Walls: The English Navy in the Reign of Edward I," in *Changing Interpretations and New Sources in Naval History: Papers from the Third Naval Academy History Symposium*, ed. Robert W. Love, Jr. New York and London: Garland, 1980, pp. 58-79.
28. Glasgow, Tom, Jr. "HMS *Tiger*." *North Carolina Historical Review*, 43 (1966), pp. 115-21.
29. ──────. "The Navy in the First Elizabethan Undeclared War, 1559-1560." *M.M.*, 54 (1968), pp. 23-37.
30. ──────. "The Navy in the French Wars of Mary and Elizabeth I, Part III: The Navy in the Le Havre Expedition, 1562-1564." *M.M.*, 54 (1968), pp. 281-96.
31. ──────. "List of Ships in the Royal Navy from 1539 to 1588." *M.M.*, 56 (1970), pp. 299-307.
32. ──────. "Maturing of Naval Administration, 1556-1564." *M.M.*, 56 (1970), pp. 3-26.
33. ──────. "Historical Document--Gorgas' Seafight." *M.M.*, 59 (1973), pp. 179-85.
34. ──────. "Vice Admiral Woodhouse and Ship-keeping in the Tudor Navy." *M.M.*, 63 (1977), pp. 253-63.
35. Hampden, J. (ed.) *Francis Drake Privateer: Contemporary Narratives and Documents.* London: Eyre Methuen, and University of Alabama Press, 1972.
36. Haynes, Alan. "The Cadiz Expedition, 1596." *History Today*, XXIII (1973), pp. 161-9.
37. Keeler, Mary F. *Sir Francis Drake's West Indian Voyage, 1585-86.* London: Hakluyt Society, 1981.

38. Kenny, R.W. *Elizabeth's Admiral: The Political Career of Charles Howard. Earl of Nottingham, 1536-1624*. Baltimore: Johns Hopkins Press, 1970.
39. Kepler, J.S. "The Effects of the Battle of Sluys upon the Administration of English Naval Impressment, 1340-1343." *Speculum*, XLVIII (1973), pp. 70-7.
40. Lander, R.J. "An Assessment of the Numbers, Sizes and Types of English and Spanish Ships Mobilized for the Armada Campaign." *M.M.*, 63 (1977), pp. 359-64.
41. Lewis, Ada Haeseler. *A Study of Elizabethan Ship Money, 1588-1603*. Philadelphia, 1928.
42. Lloyd, Howell A. "Sir John Hawkins' Instructions, 1590." *B.I.H.R.*, XLIV (1971), pp. 125-8.
43. Lloyd, Rachel. *Elizabethan Adventurer: A Life of Captain Christopher Carleill*. London: Hamilton, 1974.
44. McGurk, J.J.N. "A Levy of Seamen in Cinque Ports, 1602." *M.M.*, 66 (1980), pp. 137-44.
45. McKee, Alexander. *King Henry VIII's Mary Rose: Its Fate and Future*. New York: Stein and Day, 1974.
46. Pistono, S.P. "Henry IV and the English Privateers." *English Hist. Rev.*, 90 (1975), pp.322-30.
47. ————. "Henry IV and John Hawley, Privateer, 1399-1408." *Trans. of the Devonshire Association*, 111 (1979), pp. 145-63.
48. Pollitt, Ronald. "John Hawkins' Troublesome Voyages: Merchants, Bureaucrats, and the Origin of the Slave Trade." *Journal of British Studies*, XII (1973), pp. 26-40.
49. ————. "Bureaucracy and the Armada: The Administrator's Battle." *M.M.*, 60 (1974), pp. 119-32.
50. ————. "Rationality and Expedience in the Growth of Elizabethan Naval Administration," in *Changing Interpretations and New Sources in Naval History: Papers from the Third Naval Academy History Symposium*, ed. Robert W. Love, Jr. New York and London: Garland, 1980, pp. 68-79.
51. Quinn, David B. *England and the Discovery of America, 1481-1620*. London: Allen and Unwin, and New York: Knopf, 1974.
52. Quinn, David B. and Ryan, A.N. *England's Sea Empire 1550-1642*. London: Allen and Unwin, 1983.
53. Richmond, Colin F. "The War at Sea," in *The Hundred Years War*, ed. Kenneth Fowler. London: Macmillan, and New York: St. Martin's Press, 1971, pp. 99-121.
54. Rose, Susan. *The Navy of the Lancastrian Kings: Accounts and Inventories of William Soper, Keeper of the King's Ships, 1422-27*. London: N.R.S., 1982.
55. ————. "Henry V's *Grace à Dieu* and Mutiny at Sea: Some New Evidence." *M.M.*, 63 (1977), pp. 3-6.
56. Rule, M. *The Mary Rose*. London: Conway Maritime Press, 1982.
57. ————. "The Sinking of the *Mary Rose*." *History Today*, 32 (1982), pp. 27-36.
58. Runyan, Timothy J. "A Fourteenth-century Cordage Account for the King's Ships." *M.M.*, 60 (1974), pp. 311-28.
59. ————. "Ships and Mariners in Later Medieval England." *Journal of British Studies*, 16 (1977), pp. 1-17.

60. ———. "Merchantmen to Men-of-War in Medieval England," in *New Aspects of Naval History*, ed. Craig L. Symonds. Fourth Naval History Symposium, U.S. Naval Academy. Annapolis: Naval Institute Press, 1981, pp. 23-40.
61. Scammell, G.V. "The New Worlds and Europe in the Sixteenth Century." *Hist. Jour.*, XII, 3 (1969), pp. 389-412.
62. ———. "Manning the English Merchant Service in the Sixteenth Century." *M.M.*, 56 (1970), pp. 131-54.
63. ———. "Shipowning in the Economy and Politics of Early Modern England." *Hist. Jour.*, XV, 3 (1972), pp. 385-407.
64. ———. "Hakluyt and the Economic Thought of his Time," in *The Hakluyt Handbook*, ed. David B. Quinn. London: Hakluyt Society, 1974, pp. 15-22.
65. ———. *The World Encompassed: The First European Maritime Empires, c. 800-1650*. Berkeley and Los Angeles: Univ. of California Press, 1981.
66. ———. "European Seamanship in the Great Age of Discovery." *M.M.*, 68 (1982), pp. 357-76.
67. ———. "England, Portugal and the *Estado da India* c. 1500-1635." *Modern Asian Studies*, 16 (1982), pp. 177-92.
68. ———. *The English Chartered Trading Companies and the Sea*. London: H.M.S.O., 1983.
69. ———. "The English in the Atlantic Islands c. 1450-1650." *M.M.*, (forthcoming).
70. ———. "The Manning of the English Fighting Ships c. 1550-1650," in *Mélanges en l'honneur de Michel Mollat*. Paris: forthcoming.
71. Sherborne, J.W. "The Battle of La Rochelle and the War at Sea, 1372-5." *B.I.H.R.*, 42 (1969), pp. 17-29.
72. ———. "English Barges and Balingers of the Late Fourteenth Century." *M.M.*, 63 (1977), pp. 109-14.
73. ———. "The Cost of English Warfare with France in the Later Fourteenth Century." *B.I.H.R.*, 50 (1977), pp. 135-50.
74. Thompson, I.A.A. "Spanish Armada Guns." *M.M.*, 61 (1975), pp. 355-71.
75. Unger, Richard W. *The Ship in Medieval Economy, 600-1600*. London: Croom Helm, and Montreal: McGill-Queen's University Press, 1980.
76. Walker, J.A. "John Holand, a Fifteenth-Century Admiral." *M.M.*, 65 (1979), pp. 235-42.
77. Waters, David W. *The Elizabethan Navy and the Armada of Spain*. Greenwich: National Maritime Museum, 1975.
78. Watt, James. "Surgeons of the *Mary Rose*: The Practice of Surgery in Tudor England." *M.M.*, 69 (1983), pp. 3-18.
79. Weir, Michael. "English Naval Activities, 1242-1243." *M.M.*, 58 (1972), pp. 85-92.
80. Wernham, R.B. *The Making of Elizabethan Foreign Policy, 1558-1603*. Berkeley and Los Angeles: University of California Press, 1980.
81. ———. *After the Armada: Elizabethan England and the Struggle for Western Europe, 1588-1595*. Oxford: Clarendon Press, 1984.
82. Williams, Neville J. *The Sea Dogs: Privateers, Plunder and Piracy in the Elizabethan Age*. London: Weidenfeld and Nicolson, 1975.

1603-1714

83. Adams, Simon L. "Foreign Policy and the Parliaments of 1621 and 1624," in *Faction and Parliament: Essays on Early Stuart History*, ed. Kevin Sharpe. Oxford: Clarendon Press, 1978, pp. 139-72.
84. ———. "Spain or the Netherlands? The Dilemmas of Early Stuart Foreign Policy," in *Before the English Civil War*, ed. Howard Tomlinson. London: Macmillan, and New York: St. Martin's Press, 1983, pp. 79-101.
85. Anderson, Roger C. *List of English Naval Captains 1642-60*. London: Society for Nautical Research Occasional Publications, no. 8, 1964.
86. Appleby, John C. "English Privateering during the Spanish and French Wars, 1625-30." Unpublished. PhD dissertation, University of Hull, 1983.
87. Aubrey, Philip. *The Defeat of James Stuart's Armada, 1692*. Leicester University Press, and Totowa, N.J.: Rowman and Littlefield, 1979.
88. Bard, Nelson P. (ed.) "The Earl of Warwick's Voyage of 1627," in *The Naval Miscellany, V*, ed. N.A.M. Rodger. London: N.R.S., 1984, pp. 15-93.
89. Bard, Nelson P. "The Ship Money Case and William Fiennes, Viscount Saye and Sele." *B.I.H.R.*, 50 (1977), pp. 177-84.
90. Barnby, Henry. "The Algerian Attack on Baltimore 1631." *M.M.*, 56 (1970), pp. 27-31.
91. Barnes, Thomas G. *Somerset, 1625-1640: A County's Government during the 'Personal Rule'*. Chicago: University of Chicago Press, 1982. (Original ed. Harvard University Press, 1961.)
92. Bassett, D.K. "Early English Trade and Settlement in Asia, 1602-1690," in *Britain and the Netherlands in Europe and Asia*, ed. J.S. Bromley and E.H. Kossmann. London: Macmillan, and New York: St. Martin's Press, 1968, pp. 83-109.
93. Battick, John F. "A New Interpretation of Cromwell's Western Design." *Barbados Museum and Hist. Soc. Jour.*, 34 (1972), pp. 76-84.
94. ———. "Cromwell's Diplomatic Blunder: The Relationship Between the Western Design of 1654-55 and the French Alliance of 1657." *Albion*, V (1973), pp. 279-98.
95. Baugh, Daniel A. "Towards a 'Blue-Water' Defense Policy in Seventeenth-Century England: Its Political and Social Significance." Unpublished. Davis Center Seminar (Princeton University) paper. 1983.
96. Baumber, M.L. "The Navy and Civil War in Ireland 1641-1643." *M.M.*, 57 (1971), pp. 385-397.
97. Berckman, Evelyn. *Creators and Destroyers of the English Navy: As related by the State Papers Domestic*. London: Hamish Hamilton, 1974.
98. Bosscher, Philippus Meesse. "The Four Days Battle: Some Remarks and Reflections," *Royal United Service Institution Jour.*, 112 (1967), pp. 56-65.
99. Boxer, Charles R. "Some Second Thoughts on the Third Anglo-

Dutch War, 1672-1674." *Trans. Royal Historical Society*, 5th ser., 19 (1969), pp. 67-94.
100. ———. *The Anglo-Dutch Wars of the 17th Century, 1652-1674.* London: H.M.S.O., 1974.
101. Brenner, Robert. "The Social Basis of English Commercial Expansion, 1550-1650." *Journal of Economic History*, 32 (1972), pp. 361-84.
102. ———. "The Civil War Politics of London's Merchant Community." *Past & Present*, no. 58, (1973), pp. 53-107.
103. Bromley, John S. "The Jacobite Privateers in the Nine Years War," in *Statesmen, Scholars and Merchants: Essays in Eighteenth-Century History presented to Dame Lucy Sutherland*, ed. Anne Whiteman, J.S. Bromley, and P.G.M. Dickson. Oxford: Clarendon Press, 1973, pp. 17-43.
104. ——— (ed.) *The Manning of the Royal Navy: Selected Public Pamphlets, 1693-1873.* London: N.R.S., 1974.
105. ———. "The Importance of Dunkirk (1688-1713) Reconsidered," in *Course et Piraterie*, ed. M. Mollat. 15th Colloque International d'Histoire Maritime, I. Paris: Centre National de la Recherche Scientifique, 1975.
106. Bruijn, J.R. "Dutch Privateering during the Second and Third Anglo-Dutch Wars." *Acta Historiae Neerlandicae*, XI (1978), pp. 79-93.
107. Burg, B.R. *Sodomy and the Perception of Evil: English Sea Rovers in the Seventeenth-Century Caribbean.* New York University Press, 1983.
108. Carter, Alice Clare. *Neutrality or Commitment: The Evolution of Dutch Foreign Policy, 1667-1795.* London: Edward Arnold, 1975.
109. Chaudhuri, K.N. *The Trading World of Asia and the English East India Company, 1660-1760.* Cambridge: Cambridge University Press, 1978.
110. Coad, Jonathan. "Historic Architecture of H.M. Naval Base Devonport, 1689-1850." *M.M.*, 69 (1983), pp. 341-94.
111. Cogswell, Thomas. "Foreign Policy and Parliament: The Case of La Rochelle, 1625-1626." *English Hist. Rev.*, 99 (1984), pp. 241-67.
112. Coleman, D.C. *The Economy of England, 1450-1750.* Oxford: Oxford University Press, 1977.
113. Collinge, J.M. *Navy Board Officials, 1660-1832.* London: Institute of Historical Research, 1978.
114. Coombs, Douglas. *The Conduct of the Dutch: British Opinion and the Dutch Alliance during the War of the Spanish Succession.* The Hague: M. Nijhoff, 1958.
115. Corbett, Sir Julian S. *England in the Mediterranean: A Study of the Rise and Influence of British Power within the Straits, 1603-1713.* 2 vols. London: Longmans, 1904.
116. Courtney, T.W. "Excavations at the Royal Dockyard, Woolwich 1972-1973. Part One: The Building Slips; Part Two: The Central Area." *Post-Medieval Archaeology*, 8 (1974), pp. 1-28; 9 (1975), pp. 42-102.
117. *The Coventry Papers, Vols. 1-119 with appendix, catalogue and index.* From the Archives of the Marquess of Bath, Longleat. 84 reels. East Ardsley, Wakefield: Microform, Ltd.

118. Craven, W. Frank. "The Earl of Warwick, a Speculator in Piracy." *Hispanic American Hist. Rev.* 10 (1930), pp. 457-79.
119. Davies, Kenneth G. *The North Atlantic World in the Seventeenth Century*. Minneapolis: University of Minnesota Press, 1974.
120. Davis, Ralph. "England and the Mediterranean, 1560-1670," in *Essays in the Economic and Social History of Tudor and Stuart England*, ed. F.J. Fisher. Cambridge: Cambridge University Press, 1961.
121. ———. "English Foreign Trade, 1660-1700," and "English Foreign Trade, 1700-1774," in *The Growth of English Overseas Trade in the Seventeenth and Eighteenth Centuries*, ed. W.E. Minchinton. London: Methuen, 1969, pp. 78-120.
122. ———. *The Rise of the Atlantic Economies*. Ithaca, N.Y.: Cornell University Press, 1973.
123. Dewar, Capt. A.C. *Corrigenda to Papers Relating to the First Dutch War, 1652-54*. London: N.R.S., 1932.
124. Earle, Peter. *The Sack of Panama*. New York: Viking Press, 1982.
125. Edmundson, George. *Anglo-Dutch Rivalry during the First Half of the Seventeenth Century*. Oxford: Clarendon Press, 1911.
126. Ehrman, John. *The Navy in The War of William III: Its State and Direction*. Cambridge: Cambridge University Press, 1953.
127. Farnell, James E. "The Navigation Act of 1651, the First Dutch War, and the London Merchant Community." *Economic History Review*. 2nd ser., XVI (1964), pp. 439-54.
128. Fox, Frank. *Great Ships: The Battlefleet of King Charles II*. London: Conway Maritime Press, 1980.
129. Francis, Alan David. *The Methuens and Portugal 1691-1708*. Cambridge: Cambridge University Press, 1966.
130. ———. "Portugal and the Grand Alliance." *B.I.H.R.*, 38 (1965), pp. 71-93.
131. ———. "The Grand Alliance in 1698." *Historical Journal*, 10, 3 (1967), pp. 352-60.
132. ———. *The First Peninsular War, 1702-1713*. London: Macmillan, and New York: St. Martin's Press, 1975.
133. Gardiner, Samuel R. and C.T. Atkinson (eds.) *Letters and Papers Relating to the First Dutch War, 1652-1654*. 6 vols. London: N.R.S., 1899-1930.
134. Gardiner, Samuel R. *History of the Commonwealth and Protectorate, 1649-1660*. 3 vols. London: Longmans, 1894-1903.
135. Gooch, L. "Catholic Officers in the Navy of James II." *Recusant History*, 14 (1978), pp. 276-80.
136. Gradish, Stephen F. "The Establishment of British Seapower in the Mediterranean, 1689-1713." *Canadian Jour. of Hist.*, X, 1 (1975), pp. 1-16.
137. Graham, Eric J. "The Scottish Marine During the Dutch Wars." *Scottish Historical Review*, 61 (1982), pp. 67-74.
138. Haley, K.H.D. *William of Orange and the English Opposition, 1672-4*. Oxford: Clarendon Press, 1953.
139. ———. *The First Earl of Shaftesbury*. Oxford: Clarendon Press, 1968.
140. Hammond, Wayne N. "The Administration of the English Navy, 1649-1660." Unpublished PhD dissertation, University of British Columbia, 1974.

141. Harland, John. *Seamanship in the Age of Sail.* London: Conway Maritime Press, 1984.
142. Harris, G.G. *The Trinity House of Deptford, 1514-1660.* London: Athlone Press, 1969.
143. Hattendorf, John. "The Machinery for the Planning and Execution of English Grand Strategy in the War of the Spanish Succession, 1702-1713," in *Changing Interpretations and New Sources in Naval History,* ed. Robert W. Love, Jr. Third U.S.N.A. Hist. Symposium. New York and London: Garland, 1980, pp. 68-95.
144. ————. "Benbow's Last Fight: Documents relating to the battle off Cape Santa Marta, 19-24 August 1702," in *The Naval Miscellany, V,* ed. N.A.M. Rodger. London: N.R.S., 1984, pp. 143-206.
145. Hebb, David D. "The English Government and the Problem of Piracy, 1616-1642." Unpublished. PhD dissertation, University of London, 1985.
146. Hill, B.W. "Oxford, Bolingbroke, and the Peace of Utrecht." *Hist. Jour.,* 16, 2 (1973), pp. 241-63.
147. Historical Manuscripts Commission. *Report on the Manuscripts of the Late Allan George Finch, IV, 1692.* Ed. Francis Bickley. London: H.M.S.O., 1965.
148. Hornstein, Sari R. "The Deployment of the English Navy in Peacetime, 1674-1688." Unpublished. PhD dissertation, University of Leiden, 1985.
149. ————. "Convoys and Squadrons: English Naval Strategy and Deterrence, 1674-1688." U.S. Naval Academy, Seventh Naval History Symposium papers (forthcoming).
150. Horwitz, Henry. *Revolution Politicks: The Career of Daniel Finch, Second Earl of Nottingham, 1647-1730.* Cambridge University Press, 1968.
151. Howat, G.M.D. *Stuart and Cromwellian Foreign Policy.* London: Adam & Charles Black, 1974.
152. Hutton, Ronald. *The Restoration: A Political and Religious History of England and Wales, 1658-1667.* Oxford: Clarendon Press, 1985.
153. Johnston, J.A. "Parliament and the Protection of Trade, 1689-1694." *M.M.,* 57 (1971), pp. 399-413.
154. Jones, J.R. *Britain and the World 1649-1815.* Brighton: Harvester Press, and Atlantic Highlands, N.J.: Humanities Press, 1980.
155. Junge, Hans-Christoph. "'Trinity House' und die Vergabe von Artillerielizenzen für die Handelsschiffahrt im englischen Bürgerkrieg." *Militärgeschichtliche Mitteilungen,* 22 (1977), pp. 93-102.
156. ————. *Flottenpolitik und Revolution: Die Entstehung der englischen Seemacht während der Herrschaft Cromwells.* Stuttgart: Klett-Cotta, 1980.
157. Kamen, Henry. *The War of Succession in Spain, 1700-15.* Bloomington and London: Indiana University Press, 1969.
158. Kemp, Peter. *The British Sailor: A Social History of the Lower Deck.* London: Dent, 1970.
159. Kennedy, Donald. "The Crown and the Common Seamen in Early Stuart England." *Historical Studies: Australia and New Zealand,* XI (1964), pp. 170-7.

160. Kepler, Jon S. The Exchange of Christendom: The International Entrepôt at Dover, 1622-1641. Leicester University Press, 1976.
161. ———. "Fiscal Aspects of the English Carrying Trade during the Thirty Years War." Economic History Review. 2nd ser., XXV (1972), pp. 261-83.
162. ———. "The Value of Ships Gained and Lost by the English Shipping Industry During the Wars with Spain and France, 1624-1630." M.M., 59 (1973), pp. 218-221.
163. ———. "Sir John Jennings and the Preparations for the Naval Expedition to the Mediterranean of 1711-1713." M.M., 59 (1973), pp. 13-33.
164. Keynes, Sir Geoffrey. "John Woodall, Surgeon, His Place in Medical History." Jour. of the Royal College of Physicians of London, 2 (1967), pp. 15-33.
165. Kirby, David. "The Royal Navy's Quest for Pitch and Tar during the Reign of Queen Anne." Scandinavian Economic Hist. Rev., XXII, 2 (1974), pp. 97-116.
166. Knorr, Klaus E. British Colonial Theories, 1570-1850. Toronto: University of Toronto Press, 1944.
167. Korr, Charles P. Cromwell and the New Model Foreign Policy: England's Policy Toward France, 1649-1658. Berkeley and Los Angeles: University of California Press, 1975.
168. Lachs, Phyllis S. "Advise and Consent: Parliament and Foreign Policy under the Later Stuarts." Albion, VII (1975), pp. 41-54.
169. Latham, Robert and William Matthews (eds.) The Diary of Samuel Pepys. 11 vols. London: G. Bell, and Berkeley and Los Angeles: University of California Press, 1970-83.
170. Lavery, Brian. "The Rebuilding of British Warships, 1690-1740: Part One." M.M., 66 (1980), pp. 5-14.
171. ——— (ed.) Deane's Doctrine of Naval Architecture, 1670. London: Conway Maritime Press, 1981.
172. Lee, Maurice D. "The Earl of Arlington and the Treaty of Dover." Journal of British Studies, I (1961), pp. 58-70.
173. LeFevre, Peter. "Sir George Ayscue, Commonwealth and Restoration Admiral." M.M., 68 (1982), pp. 189-202.
174. ———. "John Tyrrell (1646-1692): A Restoration Naval Captain." M.M., 70 (1984), pp. 149-60.
175. Lloyd, Christopher. The British Seaman, 1200-1860: A Social Survey. London: Collins, 1968.
176. Lockyer, Roger. Buckingham: The Life and Political Career of George Villiers, First Duke of Buckingham, 1592-1628. London: Longman, 1981.
177. MacDougall, Philip. Royal Dockyards. Newton Abbot: David and Charles, 1982.
178. MacLachlan, A.D. "The Road to Peace, 1710-13," in Britain after the Glorious Revolution, 1689-1714, ed. Geoffrey S. Holmes. London: Macmillan, and New York: St. Martin's Press, 1969, pp. 197-215.
179. Malone, Joseph J. "England and the Baltic Naval Stores Trade in the Seventeenth and Eighteenth Centuries." M.M., 58 (1972), pp. 375-95.
180. Martin, L.C. "John Crane (1576-1660) of Loughton, Bucks--

Surveyor General of all Victuals for Ships, 1635-42." *M.M.*, 70 (1984), pp. 143-8.
181. May, W.E. "The 'Phoenix' in India, 1684-1687." *M.M.*, 57 (1971), pp. 193-202.
182. ———. "The Navy and the Rebellion of the Earl of Argyle." *M.M.*, 57 (1971), pp. 17-23.
183. ———. "Midshipmen Ordinary and Extraordinary." *M.M.*, 59 (1973), pp. 187-92.
184. McGowan, Alan P. (ed.) *The Jacobean Commissions of Enquiry, 1608 and 1618.* London: N.R.S., 1971.
185. McGowan, Alan P. "Further Papers from the Commission of Enquiry, 1608," in *The Naval Miscellany, V*, ed. N.A.M. Rodger. London: N.R.S., 1984, pp. 1-14.
186. Meyer, W.R. "English Privateering in the War of 1688 to 1697." *M.M.*, 67 (1981), pp. 259-72.
187. ———. "English Privateering in the War of the Spanish Succession, 1702-1713." *M.M.*, 69 (1983), pp. 435-46.
188. Miller, Amos C. "John Syms, Puritan Naval Chaplain." *M.M.*, 60 (1974), pp. 153-63.
189. Morrah, Patrick. *Rupert of the Rhine.* London: Constable, 1976.
190. Mountfield, Stuart. "Captain Greenvile Collins and Mr. Pepys." *M.M.*, 56 (1970), pp. 85-96.
191. National Maritime Museum. *Catalogue of the Library. IV: Piracy and Privateering.* London: H.M.S.O., 1972.
192. Ollard, Richard L. *Man of War: Sir Robert Holmes and the Restoration Navy.* London: Hodder and Stoughton, 1969.
193. ———. *Pepys: A Biography.* London: Hodder and Stoughton, 1974.
194. Pawson, Michael and David Buisseret. *Port Royal, Jamaica.* Oxford: Clarendon Press, 1975.
195. Pearsall, Alan W. *The Second Dutch War, 1665-1667.* London: H.M.S.O., 1967.
196. Peck, Linda Levy. "Problems in Jacobean Administration: Was Henry Howard, Earl of Northampton, a Reformer?" *Hist. Jour.*, 19, 4 (1976), pp. 831-58.
197. Penn, Christopher D. *The Navy under the Early Stuarts and its Influence on English History.* Leighton Buzzard and Manchester: Faith Press, 1913.
198. Pool, Bernard. "Pepys and the Thirty Ships." *History Today*, XX (1970), pp. 489-95.
199. Pope, Dudley. *Harry Morgan's Way: The Biography of Sir Henry Morgan, 1635-1684.* London: Secker and Warburg, 1977.
200. Powell, John R. "The Journal of John Weale, 1654-1656," in *The Naval Miscellany, IV.* London: N.R.S., 1952.
201. ———. *Robert Blake: General-at-Sea.* London: Collins, and New York: Crane, Russak, 1972.
202. ———. "Sir George Ayscue's Capture of Barbados in 1651." *M.M.*, 59 (1973), pp. 281-290.
203. ———. "John Bourne, Sometime Vice-Admiral." *M.M.*, 62 (1976), pp. 109-117.
204. Powell, John R. and Timings, E.K. (eds.) *The Rupert and Monck Letter Book, 1666.* London: N.R.S., 1969.
205. Powley, Edward B. *The Naval Side of King William's War.* London: John Baker, 1972.

206. Price, J.L. "Restoration England and Europe," in *The Restored Monarchy, 1660-1688*, ed. J.R. Jones. London: Macmillan, and Totowa, N.J.: Rowman and Littlefield, 1979.
207. Reddaway, Thomas F. "The Temporary Navy Office, 1673-84." *London and Middlesex Archaeological Soc. Trans.*, XIX, 2 (1957), pp. 90-4.
208. Richmond, Admiral Sir Herbert W. *The Navy as an Instrument of Policy, 1585-1727*. Posthumously publ. and ed. by E.A. Hughes. Cambridge: Cambridge University Press, 1953.
209. Ritchie, Robert F. *Captain Kidd and the War Against the Pirates*. Cambridge, Mass.: Harvard University Press, forthcoming 1986.
210. Roberts, Michael. "Cromwell and the Baltic." *English Hist. Rev.*, 76 (1961), pp. 402-46.
211. Rogers, Philip George. *The Dutch in the Medway*. Oxford: Oxford University Press, 1970.
212. Rowe, Violet A. *Sir Henry Vane the Younger: A Study in Political and Administrative History*. London: Athlone Press, 1970.
213. Ruigh, Robert E. *The Parliament of 1624: Politics and Foreign Policy*. Cambridge, Mass.: Harvard University Press, 1971.
214. Russell, Conrad. *Parliaments and English Politics, 1621-1629*. Oxford: Clarendon Press, 1979.
215. Sainty, J.C. *Admiralty Officials, 1660-1870*. London: Institute of Historical Research, 1975.
216. Saville, R.V. "The Management of the Royal Dockyards, 1672-1678," in *The Naval Miscellany, V*, ed. N.A.M. Rodger. London: N.R.S., 1984, pp. 94-142.
217. Schoenfeld, Maxwell P. "The Restoration Seaman and His Wages." *The American Neptune*, XXV (1965), pp. 278-87.
218. Senior, C.M. *A Nation of Pirates: English Piracy in its Heyday*. Newton Abbott: David & Charles, and New York: Crane, Russak, 1976.
219. Senning, C.F. "Piracy, Politics and Plunder under James I: The Voyage of the *Pearl* and its Aftermath, 1611-15." *Huntington Library Quarterly*, 46, 3 (1983), pp. 187-222.
220. Snyder, Henry L. "The Formulation of Foreign and Domestic Policy in the Reign of Queen Anne: Memoranda by Lord Chancellor Cowper of Conversations with Lord Treasurer Godolphin." *Hist. Jour.*, 11, 1 (1968), pp. 144-60.
221. ————. "Queen Anne versus the Junto: The Effort to place Orford at the Head of the Admiralty in 1709." *Huntington Library Quarterly*, XXXV (1972), pp. 323-42.
222. Spate, Oskar H.K. *The Pacific since Magellan. Vol. I: The Spanish Lake: vol. II: Monopolists and Freebooters*. Minneapolis: University of Minnesota Press, 1979, 1983.
223. Speck, William A. "The International and Imperial Context," in *Colonial British America*, ed. Jack P. Greene and John R. Pole. Baltimore and London: Johns Hopkins University Press, 1984, pp. 384-407.
224. Steele, Ian K. *Politics of Colonial Policy: The Board of Trade in Colonial Administration, 1696-1720*. Oxford: Clarendon Press, 1968.
225. Swales, Robin J.W. "The Ship Money Levy of 1628." *B.I.H.R.* 50 (1977), pp. 164-76.

226. Symcox, Geoffrey. *The Crisis of French Sea Power, 1688-1697: From the Guerre d'escadre to the Guerre de course.* The Hague: M. Nijhoff, 1974.
227. Syndenham, M.J. "The Anxieties of an Admiral: Lord Dartmouth and the Revolution of 1688." *History Today*, XII (1962), pp. 714-20.
228. Taylor, Harland. "Trade, Neutrality, and the 'English Road', 1630-1648." *Econ. Hist. Rev.* 2nd ser., XXV, 2 (1972), pp. 236-60.
229. Taylor, S.A.G. *The Western Design: An Account of Cromwell's Expedition to the Caribbean.* Kingston, Jamaica: Institute of Jamaica and Jamaica Historical Society, 1965.
230. Thompson, R.C. "Officers, Merchants, and Foreign Policy in the Protectorate of Oliver Cromwell." *Historical Studies: Australia and New Zealand*, XII (1966), pp. 149-65.
231. Tomlinson, H.C. *Guns and Government: The Ordinance Office under the later Stuarts.* London: Royal Hist. Soc., 1979.
232. ―――. "The Ordnance Office and the Navy." *English Hist. Rev.*, 90 (1975), pp. 19-39.
233. Vale, V. "Clarendon, Coventry, and the Sale of Naval Offices, 1660-8." *Cambridge Historical Jour.*, XII (1956), pp. 107-25.
234. Williams, Glyndwr. "'The Inexhaustible Fountain of Gold': English Projects and Ventures in the South Seas, 1670-1750," in *Perspectives of Empire: Essays presented to Gerald S. Graham*, ed. John E. Flint and G. Williams. London: Longman, 1973, pp. 27-53.
235. Witcombe, D.T. *Charles II and the Cavalier House of Commons, 1663-1674.* Manchester University Press, 1966.
236. Woodward, Donald (ed.) "Sir Thomas Button, the 'Phoenix' and the Defence of the Irish Coast 1614-1622." *M.M.*, 59 (1973), pp. 343-44.
237. Wren, Melvin C. "London and the Twenty Ships, 1626-1627." *American Hist. Rev.*, 55, 2 (1950), pp. 321-35.

VI

THE 18TH-CENTURY ARMY, 1702-1815

John Houlding

The last two decades have seen a remarkable burgeoning both in the scholarly and in the popular study of the eighteenth-century British Army, and there is much that can be added here to what was included by William A. Foote in his essay on the old army in Higham's *Guide*. However wide-ranging recent study may have been there have, nevertheless, been trends in this scholarship that might be noted here, and that should be considered by students embarking on further researches.

Perhaps the major stimulus to the studies of the 1960s and 1970s was the occasion of the bicentennial of the War for American Independence. This resulted in much good work, as will be evident below; and it is safe to say that, with the possible exception of the great French Wars, we now know more about the army of the 1770s--its administration and political guidance included--than of any other period during the years 1702-1815. There has in addition been a good deal of fruitful work done, during recent years, in the social history of the old army; and this approach, though to date it has tended to be focused almost entirely on the years after 1760, will doubtless continue to flourish so long as social history remains at centre stage in British studies generally. There has been, thirdly, something of a vogue for the study of the logistical arrangements and requirements of eighteenth-century campaigning, and the resulting work has been particularly revealing of the imperial army of an island power. Finally, and reflecting the concern of recent decades with policing and insurgency, much scholarly attention has been paid to the use of the regular army and reserve forces in aid of the civil authority; and as these studies continue it is to be expected that they will have a most significant impact not only on our understanding of the role of the army in society, but upon our larger conception of eighteenth-century constitutional history and of the social and political establishment of Hanoverian England.

A considerable variety of other work has been done since Higham's *Guide* first appeared, more traditional themes have still regularly been essayed, and many other avenues of approach have recently been scouted. This will be evident enough in the following lists. What is entered there is merely supplementary to the more extensive lists, and especially the archival directions, that formed part of Foote's chapter (and others) in Higham's *Guide*; and the reader is directed there for most of the older, major studies--those of Fortescue, Atkinson, Dalton, etc.--that are still basic to research into the eighteenth-century army.

Bibliographies and Guides. A variety of useful and important aids to the researcher have appeared during recent years. Along with Higham's *Guide*, of 1972, two other significant bibliographies have been published, of which Bruce's annotated bibliography (46) is the best in the field and should be among the first things consulted by any student embarking on a major research programme, while White's (395), though it is confined to books only and excludes articles and memoirs, is now the standard listing of regimental histories. These two are supplemented by the bibliographical articles of Hayter (184) and Neuburg (288), which are up-to-date surveys of the most recent work; and similar articles by Roy (323) and Strachan (356), though devoted to the periods just preceding and just following upon our own, may also be read with profit. It is hoped that this series will shortly produce a comparable essay on the recent bibliography of the French Wars of 1793-1815. The hundreds of historical and relevant archaeological research papers prepared for Parks Canada, of which several dozen deal with the army in the Canadas during our period, are available to researchers, and are catalogued in the publication *1984 Bibliography* (2nd Edition. Manuscripts and Publications, Research Divisions, Parks Canada), available from Ottawa. For the archives meanwhile, HMSO published in 1963 the most current catalogue of the PRO's holdings, as *Guide to the Contents of the Public Record Office*, London, 1963, an indispensable (and inexpensive) tool. Very useful too and also from HMSO is the recently revised sectional list of *Publications of the Royal Commission on Historical Manuscripts*, for all of the HMC's *Reports*. There have been two first-rate guides to archives in the United Kingdom, as *Record Repositories in Great Britain*, HMSO, 1973, and T. Wise, *A Guide to Military Museums*, 2nd Ed., Hemel Hempstead, 1971.

Doctoral dissertations completed in the British Isles and North America (and elsewhere) are most easily kept abreast of in *Dissertation Abstracts International*, and *Historical Research for University Degrees in the United Kingdom*, which appear annually and are in all research libraries. Very helpful too is A.R. Mitchell and B.R. Cooling, *Doctoral Dissertations in Military Affairs: A Bibliography*, Kansas State University, 1972, a listing which has been regularly updated with thirteen annual supplements appearing in regular numbers of the journal *Military Affairs*; and there are occasional lists of relevant theses, too, in the *Journal of the Society for Army Historical Research*.

Periodicals. Without question the most relevant periodical of British military history--indeed it is almost a primary source in itself for all aspects of the army's history--is the *Journal of the Society for Army Historical Research*, which has appeared since 1921. Perhaps three-fifths of its contents concern our period. Scholarly articles on the old army have been published with regularity in *Military Affairs*, since 1937, and in *The Irish Sword*, since 1949, and both must also be consulted. Of the older journals that deal primarily with contemporary British military affairs, the *Journal of the Royal United Service Institution*, since 1857, occasionally contains good historical articles, and the *Army Quarterly*, which succeeded the *United Service Magazine* in 1920, often does so; and both regularly review the literature. Among the corps publications, the *Journal of the Royal Artillery*, since 1858, and the *Journal of the Royal Army Medical Corps*, since 1903, will often be found of use. Weapons, uniforms, militaria and related subjects are dealt with in articles of varying quality in a variety of specialist journals and magazines, notable among which are the *Military Collector and Historian*, since 1951, and the *Canadian Journal of Arms Collecting*, from 1963. Seaborne activities, "conjunct expeditions" and the like are often treated in *The Mariner's Mirror*, from 1910, that most admirable of scholarly journals.

One always does well to check the eighteenth-century periodicals, which are easily accessible, notably *The Gentleman's Magazine*, from 1731, *The London Magazine*, from 1732, and *The Scots Magazine*, from 1739; and *The Annual Register*, since 1758, always repays study.

Military periodicals are listed in Higham's *Guide*, pp. 35-39; and of course the standard scholarly journals of British history must always be consulted.

References. A half-dozen important works of reference have been published of recent years, greatly assisting the student of the old army. Researchers will find especially invaluable Frederick's *Lineage Book* (124) which, though sometimes difficult to use, sets forth in great detail the dates of raising, amalgamation, disbandment, and name-changes of the regiments and corps of horse, foot, and marines during our period and beyond; and readers are reminded, too, of Laws' older work (235) which traces in great detail not only the lineages but also the locations and movements of all the troops and companies of the Royal Artillery. Regular reference will also be made to Leslie's lists (241) of the succession of colonels to the regiments (though not to those disbanded during the eighteenth century). Swinson's *Register* (361) and Ascoli's *Companion* (7) will be found valuable supplements to these other works. Two very useful references, Chandler's *Dictionary* (73) for the period of the great French Wars and Boatner's *Encyclopedia* (34) for the War for Independence, will be found very helpful, and it is to be hoped that comparable references will be compiled for the other wars of our period--indeed, a "DNB" for all of the noteworthy officers of the eighteenth century would form an admirable project.

Campaigns and Battles. There have been several broader, narrative histories, and a good many more particular analyses of aspects of the campaigns and battles of the period, in all advancing considerably our understanding of the army's, and hence of Britain's participation in the wars of the ancien regime. This scholarly concentration has, however, tended to be rather patchy, and as we noted above it is to the War for American Independence and the Napoleonic Wars that the lion's share of students have been attracted. It is hoped that future researchers will redress this imbalance, turning a great deal more attention to the Williamite wars in Ireland, the League of Augsburg campaigns in Flanders, and to the Austrian Succession and French Revolutionary wars generally. There are important theatres, too, that tend to be bypassed, notably so the West Indies, India, and the Mediterranean, and these remain rich in materials and wide open to research.

Scouller's landmark study (329) of administration, organization, and logistics has inspired a good deal of recent work on the War of the Spanish Succession, much of it in the scholarly tradition of Atkinson. Marlborough and his campaigns have been treated by Burton (53), Chandler (71), Bevan (26), and Francis (120), and there have been monographs on Oudenarde (24) and Blenheim (156, 378). Koontz has prepared important orders of battle for the British (222) and French (223) national contingents at Blenheim. Chandler (72) has contributed a fine study of the art of war in the earlier-eighteenth century, and Perjés has done a most important paper (300) on the period's logistical structures. Less attention, as usual, has been paid to Peterborough's army in the Iberian theatre; but Francis has written a model narrative history (121) to go with Kamen's study (208), and Scouller (330) has isolated the regiments involved. Students of the army of the 1702-12 campaigning are also likely to profit from Childs' forthcoming study of the army under William III; and they will also want to consult Waddell (381), who has provided us with a too-rare look at the administration of the army in the Low Countries during the 1690s, to which Chandler (74) has added a detailed article on the strength of the forces shipped out.

In contrast to the above, the interesting and by no means insignificant operations against the Spanish Bourbons, that marked the years of the long Walpole-Fleury peace, remain obscure. There were Spanish troops at Glenshiel, in 1719, and that same year saw a sizeable amphibious expedition to Vigo; Gibraltar was besieged in 1727; and Jenkins' Ear saw major operations in the Caribbean Seas from 1740. But none of this has been essayed for a long time; and even the major European and overseas campaigns of the War of the Austrian Succession, which swallowed up the Spanish struggle, have been overlooked by and large of late. For "Flanders," there has been only a monograph on Dettingen (291), though Morgan (279) has studied some of the war's effects upon administration, and the period has been investigated in detail on the Georgia frontier with Spanish Florida (202). The army's history during these years has, as always and quite ironically, been saved from oblivion by Jacobitism and the rebellions in Scotland. Several excellent works have appeared recently on the subject, notably Baynes' military history of the '15 (23) and Jarvis' detailed and delightful essays (207), notably those on Cope. Lenman (239) has written an important general history of the several risings, while McLynn (274) and Speck (340) have looked at the '45 in the field from opposite sides of the hill. Tomasson and Buist (372) is still the best military survey, and there is much that is useful in Taylor (367). But even for the '45, as indeed for the '15 (and not to mention the campaigns in Flanders and beyond), a detailed history of all the military operations, and especially of the locations and itineraries of the forces involved, remains unwritten; and it is essential before satisfactory conclusions can ever be drawn.

In contrast to the Austrian Succession, much research continues to be done on the Seven Years' War, though principally on the North American operations. Fregault (125), Steele (348), Bird (28), and Stanley (345) have written modern general histories of the conquest of New France, while Godfrey (153) and Parker (295) have looked in more detail at aspects of it, and there is general background information on the army in the Americas in Leach (237), Barker (16),

Stacey (344), and Hargreaves (172). Rogers (319) has considered the war's exacerbation of civil-military relations in America, and there is more on this theme (and others) in Shy (332) and in Anderson's study (3) of the allied Provincial forces. For single campaigns and battles in North America, Hamilton (171), Kopperman (224, 226, 227), Parker (295), and Yaple (410) are important on Braddock and the Monongahela, while Daudelin (94) has looked at Bushy Run, and Stacey (342, 343) and Grinnell-Milne (158) detail Wolfe's operations at Quebec. Further afield, Syrett (366) has dealt with the attack on Havana in 1762, and there have been articles on the assault landings at Louisbourg (189) and, more distantly, at Manila (374). On Europe, meanwhile, much less has been done. Savory's excellent history (327) of the campaigns in western Germany is a model of the detailed narrative lately out of fashion, but now needed more than ever for so many of the wars of the eighteenth century. Little's work (245) complements Savory's campaigns. Francis (119) has followed the short operations in Portugal, Hebbert (428) those in Belle-Ile, and Hackmann (169), supplemented by Boscawen (36), is essential for the descents on the French coast. Mackesy (256) is basic not only on Sackville's evil hour but for Minden itself, and there is a short account of that battle by Cole (81). Fraser (122) and Middleton (277, 278) are important for the strategic and policy background, Middleton's work in particular demolishing the old worship of Pitt as the omniscient organizer of victory. In two works, meanwhile, Lawford (233, 234) looked at Clive and the small British and Company forces in India at the mid-century.

As noted above, it is the American War for Independence that has received by far the most scholarly attention of late years, and this has made for a major advance (some might say imbalance) in our understanding of the old army. Civil-military relations, and the host of troubles that these brewed in mainland America, have been analysed for pre-war years in Shy's long, excellent study (332); and the subject reminds us once again of the need for a major, scholarly work on Amherst, and of the utility of Carter's edition (60) of Gage's correspondence. Mackesy's outstanding study (254) sees the world war from Whitehall, and follows--as should always be done, but very seldom is--the formative interplay of strategic direction and the movements of the forces in the field. The new strategic approaches to the war, deriving in large part from the recent wars of decolonialization, are put forward in Higginbotham (429), Gruber (424), Shy (333, 441), and Mackesy (434, 435), among others. Closer up, Gruber (159) details the relationship between the aims of the Howes as field commanders, and the actual flow of military events. Willcox (403) has followed the fascinating Clinton and, more regionally, Jackson (203) has looked at the Philadelphia operations, Cornwallis and the southern campaigns have been studied by the Wickwires (400), Lumpkin (250), Pancake (293), and Urwin (375), while Stanley (346), Hatch (179), and Reynolds (316) look at the 1775-76 invasion of Canada and its defence by Carleton. These recent works, taken together with the older studies of Gage's command, have made it possible for us to know more about Howe's headquarters and those of some others of the commanders in America, than we do about any others excepting Wellington's and, possibly, Marlborough's. Many of the individual campaigns in America have been freshly essayed, at least seven accounts of Saratoga appearing within works on Burgoyne by

Elting (108), Furneaux (130), Glover (147), Hargrove (173), Howson (196), Lunt (251), and Sweetman (360), while the admirable Freneau Press's bicentennial series includes excellent monographs not only on Saratoga (108) but on Bunker Hill (107), Princeton (337), and Long Island (258), among others. All known first-hand accounts of Lexington and Concord have been collected by Kehoe, in two handy volumes (214). There are three detailed works on the logistics of these campaigns, fought so far from their main source of supply, by Baker (13), Bowler (38), and Syrett (363). There is much on naval cooperation, and on the activities of the Marines too, in Clark's extensive collection of documents (80); and it needs to be added that not only in this but in all the wars of our period the subject of sea service is central to British operations, though neglected. Katcher (209) in a handy reference that should be copied for the army's other major wars lists the activities of each of the regular and loyalist regiments for 1775-83; and Watt (387), Allen (2), and Fryer (129) have studied in greater detail the histories of the loyalist corps from upper New York province. Weigley's (446), Calhoon's (415), and Smith's work (442, 443) is most important on the loyalists in the South, the crucial ingredient in all studies of the southern campaigning.

Where much has been done on the campaigning in mainland America, very little has been attempted (despite Mackesy's most recent display of their strategic importance) on operations elsewhere, during the American War. The crucial West Indian theatre has seen only Jamieson's work (206), still unpublished; and in Europe only the Gibraltar siege has been covered, by McGuffie (272) and Thompson (369), along with the defence of Jersey by Mayne (268). Curiously, amidst this plenty, no one save Higginbotham (188) has attempted a general narrative, in the vein of Savory, so that Ward (382) remains standard.

The great French Wars have continued, as ever, to receive plenty of attention; but as ever it is Wellington's army in the Peninsula that gets the limelight while operations elsewhere are overlooked, and the campaigns against the French Revolutionary forces sink further into oblivion even than those of 1740-48. Thus there have been surveys of Wellington's army, its organization and campaigns by Rogers (322), Park and Nafziger (294), Meyer (269), and by M. Glover (142, 143, 146, 148), while Brett-James (45) has looked at its daily life, Haswell (177) and Hyden (201) have considered the all-important but regularly overlooked subject of intelligence gathering and Redgrave--in another thesis (314) that should be published--has studied its logistical arrangements. All owe something to Ward's earlier study of its staff (383), and to R. Glover's work on the Duke of York's reforms (151). For the army's campaigns and battles there have recently been books on Salamanca (412), Vitoria (440), Badajoz (114), and Busaco (192), and another on the events surrounding the Convention of Cintra (144). Still in the Peninsula, Moore and Coruna have produced very different interpretations in Hibbert (186), Parkinson (296), and Davies (95); and, elsewhere, there have been studies of the Walcheren (35) and Helder (255) expeditions. Waterloo, as always, has remained a popular subject, and it has been described again by Lachouque (232), by Lord Chalfont and his contributors (70), and in a suggestive essay by Keegan (213), while there is a detailed new order of battle in Bowden (37), and an excellent article on d'Erlon's attack by Koontz (221). There are several Waterloo essays in Griffith (157). The fighting in Ireland around the great rising of 1798 is dealt with principally by Pakenham (292), but is touched on too by Ferguson (112) and Stoddard (352). Aspects of Britain's defence are considered by R. Glover (152).

Further afield, much remains to be studied. There were many significant campaigns in important theatres scarcely treated since Fortescue. The regular army's business in the Indian subcontinent became really considerable from this time, but we have had only the Wickwires' study of Cornwallis' earlier vice-royalty (401), Callahan (55) on the Company's armies, Bennell on the Maratha war (25), Weller on Wellington's early service (390), and Powell (308) on Ceylon. Nothing has been done on the African and South American campaigns, and (save for bits in the Moore biographies, and Marshall-Cornwall's article (265) on the 1801 Egyptian expedition) the Mediterranean is sadly ignored. There has been a new beginning to West Indian study with two fine, scholarly works, Buckley's (50) on the black regiments and Geggus' (134) on Saint-Domingue; and there are articles by Ashby (8) on Grenada and Duffy (101) on the broader theatre. In North America, the War of 1812 has enjoyed much good scholarly attention lately, with full narratives by Stanley (347), Mahon (257), and Horsman (191); and there have been monographs on Queenston Heights (396), Chateauguay (359, 417, 426), Mackinac (103), the New Orleans fiasco (315), and the burning of Washington (248).

There has, finally, been a useful survey of the many foreign regiments in British service during these years, by Yaple (411), and a study of one corps in particular be de Meuron (275), while Chandler's dictionary (73) is a useful reference throughout.

Memoirs, Journals, and Correspondence. There have been numerous additions to the already very extensive literature of published diaries, journals, memoirs, and correspondence written by officers and soldiers during our period; and as always the bulk of these are for the French Wars (and why this is so is a subject which, in itself, begs to be explored). There is not room here for them all, and we are fortunate in having good if not complete bibliographies of this work in Bruce (to 1975) (46) for the period as a whole, and for the French Wars in Brett-James (to 1972) (45) and in Vermieren (to 1982) (377).

For the Spanish Succession we have lately had Chandler's edition (76) of Private Deane's journal (and included is a listing of all of C.T. Atkinson's extensive work), along with Snyder's edition (339) of the Marlborough-Godolphin correspondence to go along with the older standard references of Murray (280) and Coxe (88), included here for convenience. For the mid-century Savory (328) edited a rare soldier's journal, while Whitworth (399) has published more of Wolfe's always rich letters, Kopperman (224) has added to those edited by Hamilton (171) on the Monongahela, and we have too the letters of an officer in one of the Troops of Horse Guards (123). Bouquet's papers are currently being published in an excellent, scholarly series (217). For the War for Independence we have, notably, the letters of officers edited by Ward (384) and by Balderston and Syrett (14), together with a fine soldier's journal by Bradford (40), and Klein and Howard (219) have recently edited General Robertson's letterbook. For the Napoleonic period there have been added, briefly, the letters or memoirs of at least one cavalry and three infantry officers edited by Haggard (170), M. Glover (150), Thompson (370), and Spurrier (341), together with those of a surgeon by Woodford (408) and of at least three private soldiers by Hibbert (187), Roy (324), and Webb-Carter (388). Most recently, we have had a collection of the Waterloo recollections of several officers and other ranks of the King's Dragoon Guards, edited by Mann (259).

The newly-formed Army Records Society, finally, will publish annually a volume of correspondence or papers on all aspects of the army's history, and some will be for our period. The ARS's first volume appeared in 1985.

Biography. There have of recent years appeared many biographies of distinguished British soldiers, some of them excellent and many, doubtless, inspired by Whitworth's fine study of Ligonier (398). Thus there have been several recent biographies of Marlborough, notably those of Bevan (26), Chandler (71), Cowles (87), Barnett (17), and Burton (53); but his lieutenants and soldier contemporaries have, curiously, continued to be overlooked as fit subjects, despite a spate of study of their operations. Cadogan, Orkney, Webb and the rest--not to mention Peterborough and Ormonde--need to be essayed. Neither have the soldiers of the mid-century been much considered. There has been a close enquiry into the maligned Sackville's behavior at Minden (256), and a biography of the 2nd Duke of Argyll (98), but otherwise nothing on the officers in the European theatres who, by and large, remain either vague and grey or figures of caricature, puffy-faced and puffy-eyed under their wigs. Overseas, Bradstreet is unlikeably grasping in Godfrey's scholarly study (153), and Bouquet is emerging from his extensively edited papers (217), while Clive has been admirably drawn (233). Among slightly older works, Cuneo (89) remains best on Robert Rogers, and Grinnell-Milne (158) is perceptive on Wolfe. More than most others, modern scholarly biographies are needed on Amherst and the Duke of Cumberland--although it is rumoured (and to be hoped) that Rex Whitworth may have a major biography of the Duke forthcoming. Officers of the War for Independence have received a good deal more attention than their predecessors, notably Burgoyne who has been variously portrayed by M. Glover (147), Howson (196), Hargrove (173) and, more convincingly, by Lunt (251). James Robertson's remarkable career is sketched by Klein and Howard (219), while Cornwallis' service in America is the subject of the Wickwires (400). Clinton too has been the subject of a fine biography (403), and there are shorter works on Carleton (41, 316). No one has replaced Alden on Gage (1), though there is a perceptive sketch of him by Shy (333); and there are outlines of others in Billias (27). It is to be regretted that the lack of collected papers of William Howe renders him so elusive, for his was the most crucial career in the American War. A new, scholarly study of Carleton would be of service, and so too would be biographies of Haldimand and Bouquet, among others.

For the great French Wars it is the later years that, as usual, have drawn the most attention--though the Wickwires have extended their biography of Cornwallis to his India and Ordnance years (401). Griffith's (157), Weller's (390) and Meyer's (269) new studies are the first major works on Wellington's years in the field to have appeared since Lady Longford's first volume (249) was published, but several of his senior officers have meanwhile been studied, namely Picton (283), Colville (82), Colquhoun Grant (177), Hill (368), Graham (44), Le Marchand (371), Murray (386), Harry Smith twice (174, 238), and MacGrigor (31). Blanco on MacGrigor and Ward (though brief) on Murray are the best of these. There has been at least one recent thesis on Beresford (379), and a modern biography of Moore (296).

Finally, students are reminded of the occasional utility of the older *Dictionary of National Biography* and the *Dictionary of American Biography*, both of which contain many short, biographical sketches of British officers, of varying quality. There are many better biographical sketches of officers who served in North America in the newer *Dictionary of Canadian Biography*, which has been appearing from 1966 to date; and, because its volumes are arranged by the dates of death of their subjects, it now covers most of our period.

Social History. The fascination of late decades with social history has so far produced nothing for the British Army of the calibre of A. Corvisier's work on the French, and *L'Armée française de la fin du XVIIe siècle au ministère de Choiseul: Le soldat*, Paris, 1964, still remains the model for the type. Although the surviving archival materials on the British Army are not so rich as those in France they do nevertheless constitute a vast trove for the social historian, and several important saps have recently been made. Yet the reader of much of this work cannot but feel that it tends to be arid, even antiquarian, and that it often seems devoid of usable conclusions; and the reviewer will be forgiven if he reminds researchers that, just as armies are for fighting, so military history is about soldiers *qua* soldiers. That much of the social history on the army is weak is due perhaps to the fact that it draws its intellectual framework and methodology from the sociology of rural villagers, artisans, town labourers, and communities, so that what normally results is more a study of the 'origins' of the soldiery than there current situation or military milieu. That this need not be the case is indicated again by Corvisier's work, sketching as it does the parameters of a société militaire into which one entered as a recruit and in which one participated as a soldier, with its own powerful coercive and normative factors, its own systems of law and discipline, its own expectations and rewards, values, routines, rhythms, etc. There has been too, during the last two decades especially and in the wake of S.L.A. Marshall's analyses, a significant flowering in the study of motivational systems, compliance, group cohesion, morale, esprit de corps, and combat effectiveness. All of this provides the context within which British soldiers might properly be analysed, a military sociology which would make it possible to deal with the soldiers in their own terms, rather than from a civil perspective which, too often, strikes air. Conclusions drawn from such work would not only be useful in their own right but would likely invigorate the study of operations, for instance, or regimental history; and would likely help to explain how it was that the army was usually skillful, why the bulk of the officers were careerist, and what it was that kept the other ranks with the colours.

There has nevertheless been much notable social history done on the army, of recent years. Several scholars have addressed the

British officer, though more for the later half of our period than for the earlier, and none have been so systematic in their approach as have historians of the Victorian officer. The question of purchase has had considerable attention, the mingling of property and authority having always boggled the bourgeois notion of the order of things. Bassett (22) and Bruce (47), the most detailed treatments, have described the mechanics of purchase, while Burton and Newman (54), and also M. Glover (145, and elsewhere) have shown it to have been very much less the normal means of promotion than used to be supposed. The tenor of this work has been to show purchase to have been at least as effective as any other manner of selection. Marshall (263), meanwhile, has much to say that is important in his scholarly study of the social origins, education, and careers of the non-purchase officers of the Royal Engineers; and it is to be wished that we had something comparable on the Royal Artillery, beyond Laws' important career sketches (236). In several complementary books (166, 168) and articles (164, 165, 167), Guy has studied in detail the pay and perquisites of regimental officers, and of the proprietary colonels too; and has considered also the relationship between the economics of proprietorship and dedication to the service. No one has attempted a major study (several could in fact be done) of the attitudes of officers to the service and to their profession, let alone of their larger world view, despite the fact that modern scholarly methods are providing methodological approaches. Classicism would be an admirable entré. Among subjects lately considered, Gilbert has looked at the officers' notions of honour (135), and Conway (85) and Gruber (425) at their political and career feelings in 1775-76. Jackson (203) has shown us the officers being sociable. In all, a great deal more needs to be done on the mass of regimental officers throughout the period; and for this there is no better source than the *Army Lists* whether printed or in manuscript, supplemented after 1759 with the Registers of commissions at the Public Record Office and, before 1740, with the recently-prepared manuscript Lists now available at the Old War Office Library.

If more needs to be done on the officers, this is even truer of the other ranks. Steppler's thesis (350) looks at the soldiers of the years 1760-93; and his forthcoming publication on the subject promises to be important. Steppler's work, and Frey's (126, 128) which contains much that is useful on many aspects of the soldier's service life, are together a large contribution to what we know of the common soldier during the second half of the eighteenth century; but what resemblance their clientele can have to the soldiers of the great French Wars at the end of our period, remains an open question. With the new requirements and the greatly expanded scope of recruiting after 1793, it seems apparent that things must have changed significantly--though this is yet to be explored. There is in contrast to the post-1760 decades remarkably little known about the common soldier prior to that time; and it is to be hoped that researchers will turn that way, despite the comparative paucity of surviving documents. There have been more general treatments of the soldier's service life in Hargreaves (172), Rogers (321), and Priestly (310), among others. More particularly, there has been a dissertation (84) on the interesting topic of military-civilian crime in America, over the years 1775-82, researches which should certainly be extended both in time and place; and there are important essays on the neglected topic of soldiers' wives legitimately with the army (228), and (forthcoming) on the major problem of alcohol in the army (230), and on the much-neglected subject of religion and its chaplains (231). Important too are the articles on recruiting (136) and deserting (139) by Gilbert, and the studies of Frey (127) and Gilbert (137, 141) on military law and its courts, admirably introduced by Ellestad (105). A major, detailed study of recruiting, looking at the numbers involved, regional and chronological fluctuations, and related social and economic factors, is badly needed; and so too is a study of law and discipline in the old army, which seem so extraordinary out of (and perhaps even in) their social context.

Finally, Winstock (406) has described and reprinted some of the music of the old army, a topic that, like those above and so many others--medicine, religion and its Wesleyan revival, quarters, diet, etc.--needs much further exploration.

The Army at Home. It is a measure not only of the significance so long accorded campaign history but also of Whiggish smugness that we still know so little about the condition and role of the eighteenth-century army when at home in the British Isles. There have recently, however, been a number of important studies of the Victorian army at home, and it is to be hoped that these will prove a catalyst for our period.

A beginning has been made in a number of specialist works which shed light partially, or peripherally; and it is perhaps not incidental that many of these have been concerned as much with the preservation of public order and even of established government, as with defence against external threats--though historians have been timid of extending conclusions far into the political and social realm.

Most work has been done on the army in England. Houlding (197) has described the rotation and distribution of the regiments about the kingdom, and sketched their activities in aid of the civil power. The most important study of the army's constant employment in suppressing riot and disorder is Hayter (183); and Shelton (331), Rogers (319), Boyd (39), and Emsley (110) have also recently contributed to the subject. Muskett's (281) is the main essay on anti-smuggling activities, though confined to the Kent and Sussex coasts. Emsley (109), in his survey of the great French Wars, has much to say in passing on the social and economic impact of the army at the end of our period, while Windibank (404) will look at the too neglected subject of the army and politics early in the century. R. Glover (152) is good on several aspects of the defense of Britain against Bonaparte. There is material in Emsley on the militia, volunteers, and other forces that played such a significant part in the country's life after 1793; but save for Western's fine work (394), detailed information on the reserves is only to be found in the older, standard references.

It is a curious fact that we know even less about the army in Scotland than in England, given the attention that continues to be devoted to Jacobitism; but it is to studies of that movement, nevertheless, that the student is obliged to turn for sketches of the army north of the border. The best of the most recent sketches will be found in Lenman (239, 240) and in the essays of Jarvis (207), not to overlook one of Prebble's colourful books (309). Taylor's first-rate monograph (367) on the building of military roads in Scotland, not just during Wade's tenure but for the century as a whole, is a model for the type and is without doubt one of the best monographs available on the peacetime army.

Just as Jacobitism and its suppression have focussed attention on the army in Scotland to the decades prior to the mid-century, so too in Ireland it is in the periods of trouble and rebellion that we know most about the army there. Thus there is a good deal on the distribution and activities, along with the purely active operations, of the army in Ireland, at both ends of our period, in Ferguson (112), and in Burns' first-rate essay (414) on the army in Ireland in 1775, while the years after 1790 are the special concern of Stoddard (352) and Kerrigan (218). The destruction of most of the central records of the eighteenth-century army in Ireland, in the Four Courts fire of 1922, has greatly impaired study through the quiet mid-century years; but Ferguson (112) has something to say on the long period and so too have Guy (163) and McLynn (273).

Regimental History. Regimental history has always been among the most popular and attractive approaches to the history of the army, but the quality of the resulting work has varied considerably, ranging from important documentary collections to hagiography. Considering the unique importance of the institution and the survival of so much in the way of its papers and artifacts, it is curious that regimental history has been the subject least penetrated by the 'new' military history--though it is not unlikely that it is on the verge of a scholarly renaissance. No student, nevertheless, should fail to consult the relevant works, since they are often a trove of detailed material; and many of the older works can be especially useful on corps serving in Ireland, where their authors had access to (and often reprinted) documents later destroyed in the 1922 Four Courts fire.

The literature is very large and only a sample of the work of recent years can be included here. Wise's booklet (407) is a handy list of all the regimental museums in the United Kingdom, with short descriptions of their highlights; while references like those of Frederick (124), Ascoli (7), and Swinson (361) will guide researchers through the confusion of amalgamations, disbandments, etc. White's bibliography (395), by regiment, carries the listing of titles down to 1965, and there is a selection of titles in Bruce (46). Just as it is recommended that the student check the relevant titles in Richard Cannon's seventy-one volumes of 1835-53, so it is wise to consult the appropriate work among the several dozen little introductory volumes on individual regiments in the *Famous Regiments* series, published since 1967 under the general editorship of Sir Brian Horrocks. Two of the more recent of these are Blaxland's on the Buffs (33) and Barker's on the East Yorks (15). Among the many more detailed, recent regimental histories, are Brereton on the 4th/7th Royal Dragoon Guards (43), Rigby on the 22nd, Cheshire Regiment (317), Sutherland on the Border Regiment (358), the Linklaters on the Black Watch (244), Vale on the South Staffs (376), and Bryant on the 95th Rifles (48). On certain of the old disbanded corps, there is Harper on Fraser's Highlanders (175); both Watt (387)

and Fryer (129) have looked recently at some of the loyalist corps of
1776-84; and some of the many foreign units in British service during
the French Wars are the subject of Yaple (411) and de Meuron (275).
Marshall's work (262, 263), though not regimental history properly
so-called, is important on the Royal Engineers. There have been two
articles, recently, on the reformation and the raising of old and new
regiments during the 1780s (304, 305); and we have had a doctoral
thesis on the Marine regiments of the 1739-48 war, and on the
independent Marine companies which were raised from 1755 (261).
Buckley's study (50) of the black West India Regiments is not only
definitive on those but adds much to our knowledge of West Indian
service. Katcher's handbook (209), with its thumbnail sketches of
the service histories of all of the regular and loyalist regiments
during the War for American Independence, is extremely useful, as are
the studies of Strach (353) and Dunnigan (102, 103) of the service
histories of regiments at Fort Niagara, and at the farther western
posts; something comparable should be done on the whole army for our
entire period.

Uniforms and Equipment. It will be appreciated that the study of the
dress and accoutrements of the British Army is a very popular
pastime, and that it is not practicable to mention here all of the
many short articles, booklets, painting guides, etc., that have
appeared on the subject in recent years. Many of the journals noted
above are regularly distinguished by the fine work of historians and
artist-historians like René Chartrand, W.Y. Carman, R.J. Marrion,
Philip Haythornthwaite, G.A. Embleton, R. Harris, Philip Katcher, D.
and B. Fosten, Pierre Turner, Michael Barthorp, Douglas Henderson,
A.W. Haarmann, Walter Dornfest, Charles Stadden, and others, and
their work must always be considered. In the Osprey series, the
booklets of Barthorp (19) on Marlborough's men and of May (266) on
the troops in the Americas during 1775-83, are useful, and
B. Fosten's four recent Napoleonic titles (115-118) are particularly
good. Among the many excellent articles deserving particular notice,
either for their quality or their suggestive use of sources, are
those of Chartrand (78) and Katcher (210, 211) on deserters'
descriptions, Mackay (253) on a colonial corps, and Caruana (66) on
the field dress of the Royal Artillery for 1775-83. Among more
detailed works, Barthorp's two volumes (20, 21) form an admirable
survey of the cavalry and infantry, while Campbell (57) on the
artillery is less useful for the eighteenth century than for later
periods. Strachan's volume (355) is a scholarly sourcebook for the
later-century, there is much good Peninsular material in Windrow and
Embleton (405), and Summers and Chartrand survey Canada (357).
Haswell-Miller and Dawnay (178) is an excellent source, notably for
Morier's paintings (if sadly in black-and-white), and Calver and
Bolton (56) is too often overlooked. Niemeyer and Ortenburg's book
(289) provides an example of what English-language publishers might
attempt, though something for the British Army on the scale of Hans
Bleckwenn's work on the Prussians will likely remain only the stuff
of which dreams are made. Otherwise, the familiar, older works of
Cecil C.P. Lawson, and of W.Y. Carman, remain generally the standard
references.

If there is a gap in this literature it is for the earlier
decades, c. 1689-1740; and even though the earlier pictorial evidence

is thin it is extra-ordinary that so little is known about the appearance of Marlborough's men, whose campaigns led to so many famous victories.

Military Medicine. Of all the factors affecting the history of the army in our period there was none more important--certainly so in wartime and perhaps so in peacetime too--than disease and its associated mortality. There are excellent bibliographical essays on the subject of military medicine and hygiene in Higham's *Guide* and in the present work, both for the army and the navy (where more work has been done); and it was indicated in Higham that the subject had for too long been neglected. With the appearance in recent years of a small number of important studies, however, there are grounds for hope that this neglect is ending. At the time of writing, Kopperman had in preparation a medical history of the army in America, c. 1755-1783; and planned too a larger, general treatment of medical philosophy and practice, hygiene, and other matters related to health in the eighteenth-century army, all of which promise to be a significant contribution. Much of Cantlie's long and detailed work (58) is relevant to our period, while Kopperman (225) has surveyed medical services--such as they were--within the army from the 1740s down to 1783, and Blanco (32) has traced military medicine through the French Wars. Blanco has also written an excellent, pioneering biography of Surgeon-General MacGrigor (31). There has been a particularly interesting exchange between Buckley (49) and Geggus (132, 133) on the appalling mortality and hospitalization rates in the West Indies, during 1793-1815; and (though it is just beyond our period) Burrough's important survey (51) extends this to other stations. A fascinating article by Gilbert (140), closely following two sample regiments through the long period of the French Wars, shows how the records may be used. But so much remains to be done on the subject of British military medicine that specific suggestions for future research will be superfluous.

Command, Administration, and Logistics. Although there have always been students of the formulation of policy and of the higher levels of command, whether by the generals in the field or by the politicians at home, there have been few attempts to pierce the confusion and complexity of the administrative machinery of the eighteenth-century British Army; and while both subjects need to be pursued it is to the latter, especially, that efforts need most to be directed, and there is scope for endless research. It is safe to say, indeed, that it is our having to rely on a few embarrassing generalizations to cover our limited knowledge of the army's administration, that precludes any major synthesis being written on the eighteenth-century army's history. There has nevertheless been some good work done lately in both spheres and, while some of the relevant studies come within the framework of campaign history or biography (and so have been noted above), several recent titles can be mentioned here.

It must be stated at the outset that the most important factor of all here, the royal command of the army, has not been considered in depth by anyone since Hayes sketched its outlines in an older essay (181), still quite useful--and this despite several 'biographies' of the Hanoverian monarchs. What might be done much more widely is shown by Gruber's excellent study (423) of the royal selection of Howe, Clinton, and Burgoyne for American command, in 1774-75. Much is hoped from Childs' forthcoming study of the army under William, to which the same author's work (79) on James II and the army remains an important introduction, however much the Glorious Revolution altered things. The biographies of eighteenth-century administrators, politicians, and ministers of the Crown are, of course, essential, though usually concerned more with the theatre of politics than with policies; but there has recently been some work that concentrates more closely on command and direction. For the earlier century we have lately had an edition of the Marlborough-Godolphin correspondence (339), and policy and strategy in the Peninsula form part of Francis' single-volume history (121). Middleton (277, 278) and Fraser (122) have done important work on the Pitt-Newcastle administration of the Seven Years' War, and Mackesy's history of the American War (254) is centred in Whitehall. Curiously, few if any historians studying the direction and command of British armies of the old regime have attempted to describe what ministers and generals deemed 'strategy' and strategic direction actually to be; and they, like most modern historians of diplomacy, can fairly be rapped for unconsciously and even overtly essaying the formulation of policy and campaign planning in Clausewitzian terms, without appreciating the mind set behind the unitary army operating on interior lines. There is thus room here for much insightful, and indeed exciting, work.

Work on the administrative machinery has been patchy too, lately. Many aspects of the administration of Anne's forces are discussed in Scouller's detailed and invaluable book (329), while Burton (52) and Tomlinson (373) have looked more particularly at the office of the Secretary at War, and the Ordnance. Hattendorf's short but excellent overview (180) of the governmental "machinery" behind the conduct of the 1702-12 war is relevant to later periods too; and comparable syntheses would be welcome for 1739-48, 1755-63, 1775-83, and 1793-1815. Morgan in an important thesis (279) has considered the impact of the neglected 1740-48 operations on various branches of administration, and Little (245, 246) looks at the Treasury and commissaries in the German campaigns of the Seven Year's War. The administration of the Marines, both the ten regiments of the 1739-48 war and the independent companies, in their three 'divisions', which followed from 1755, is the subject of another recent thesis (261). Syrett (363), Baker (13), and Bowler (38), in three important, complementary monographs noted earlier, have looked in detail at the role of the Treasury, the Navy Board, and the Ordnance in the supply and transportation of the army, its munitions and provisions, during the 1775-83 campaigns in North America. Pimlott (306), in an important thesis, has described in detail the army's administration at the time of the reforms of the 1780s, and some of this is continued through the 1790s and beyond in R. Glover's study (151) of the Duke of York's reforms. There is something on the Ordnance, at the end of the century, in Cornwallis' latest biography (401); and Condon (83) has studied the transport service between 1793 and the Amiens truce.

The very complex and important subject of the supply of the army, which enters not only into the fields of economic and administrative history but was also a crucial component of eighteenth-century generalship, has been much in vogue during recent years; and it has added significantly to our understanding of the army's operations. Probably the most important discussion available on the procurement, preparation, and land transport on forage and provisions in Early Modern campaigning is that of Perjes (300), chock full as it is of quantities, figures, and numbers that can be applied widely and, with care, used for general calculations. The commissaries themselves used comparable rules of thumb. Although the logistics of the 1704 march from the Low Countries to the Danube have been looked at by Francis (120) and are the subject of a forthcoming article by Phelan (302), and although much may be gleaned, passim, from two of Chandler's books (71, 72), we still have no general study of logistics of Marlborough's campaigns. Aspects of Flanders' campaigning, over 1689-1697, have been touched on by Waddell (381), and to the work of Little, Morgan, Syrett, Baker, and Bowler, noted above, has been added Redgrave's detailed study of supply in Wellington's Peninsular army (314). Further afield, Parker (295) studied the logistical difficulties hampering and, indeed, channeling operations in the primitive, frontier zones of North America.

Weapons, Drill, and Tactics. Some significant studies of the army's weapons have been made. To the standard work on longarms and pistols by Blackmore (30) has been added Rogers' survey (320), the two excellent monographs of Bailey (11) and Darling (90), and Gordon's essay (154) on cavalry pistols. Bailey (12) has in addition discussed in detail the Baker Rifle, while Darling has surveyed the peculiar arms of the Highland regiments (92); and edged weapons are the province of Darling again (91, 93), and of d'Arlington too (5). The heavier ordnance has likewise been recently studied, beginning with Peterson's survey (301) and Hughes' fine book (198). Wilkinson-Latham (402) has looked in detail at the guns used during 1790-1820, and Caruana (61, 63) has considered three species of battalion-gun. Hughes, Wilkinson-Latham, and Caruana all attempt classifications by size, weight, and construction, and if these were maintained through the period as a whole it would be of the greatest service to army historians. Jackson and de Beer (204) have published an attractive study on the manufacture in brass ordnance in the later-century.

Where arms have received much attention of recent years, this cannot be said of training in arms and their tactical use, and misuse. Modern nuclear-strategic studies, together with the social interests of the "new" military history, have elbowed aside the study of tactics; but the subject has begun to reassume its proper place. Hughes in two excellent works (199, 200) has examined the technical and tactical parameters of smoothbore longarms and ordnance. Cavalry is sadly overlooked by nearly everybody, despite its enormous significance throughout and well beyond our period. Myatt (284) has surveyed the infantry and Gates (131 and in a forthcoming monograph) has looked in more detail at the development of the light infantry of the great French Wars. Hubner (431) has found Burgoyne's light infantry admirably well trained, by the lights of the 1770s. Both Graves (155) and Caruana (61, 62) have something to say on artillery manuals and drill. Parker (295), Boscawen (36), and Syrett (364) have examined the tactical aspects of certain specialized operations. Arnold reminds us (6) of the methodological uncertainties with which the subject abounds, where nearly two centuries after the French Wars the Most basic of issues in linear tactics remain unresolved. R. Glover (151) has considered the preparation of the army to meet the Napoleonic legions, while Houlding (197) discusses the training of the army, its regulations and drillbooks from Marlborough's day down to that time. Kleinschmidt (220) has prepared an extensive list of extant British drillbooks, for our period and earlier, and there are others in Higham's *Guide* and in Bruce's bibliography (46).

The larger aspects of the army's tactical experience of wartime service in the Americas, in 1775-83 and much more seminally in 1754-63, are discussed finally in important essays by Paret (437, 438) and Mackesy (436): there is in these much food for thought for all students of later 18th-, and earlier 19th-century British and European military history.

BIBLIOGRAPHY

Note: The following abbreviations are used:

CJAC	*Canadian Journal of Arms Collecting*
JSAHR	*Journal of the Society for Army Historical Research*
MC&H	*Military Collector and Historian*
NAM	National Army Museum
OMMC	Organization of Military Museums of Canada
RUSI	Royal United Service Institution

1. Alden, John R. *General Gage in America.* Baton Rouge, 1968.
2. Allen, Robert S., ed. *The Loyal Americans: The Military Role of the Loyalist Provincial Corps and their Settlement in British North America, 1775-1784.* Ottawa, 1983.
3. Anderson, Fred. *A People's Army. Massachusetts Soldiers and Society in the Seven Years' War.* Chapel Hill, 1984.
4. Anon. Comp. *1984 Bibliography, 2nd Edition. Manuscripts and Publications, Research Divisions, Parks Canada.* Ottawa, 1985.
5. d'Arlington, John C. "The Pattern 1796 Light Cavalry Sabre." *CJAC*, 9 (1971), 127-34.
6. Arnold, James R. "A Reappraisal of Column Versus Line in the Napoleonic Wars." *JSAHR*, 60 (1982), 196-208.
7. Ascoli, David. *A Companion to the British Army, 1660-1983.* London, 1983.
8. Ashby, Timothy. "Fédon's Rebellion." *JSAHR*, 62 (1984), 155-68, 227-35; 63 (1985), 220-35.
9. Atkinson, C.T. "Material for Military History in the Reports of the Historical Manuscripts Commission." *JSAHR*, 21 (1943), 17-34.
10. Atwood, Rodney. *The Hessians. Mercenaries from Hessen-Kassel in the American Revolution.* Cambridge, 1980.
11. Bailey, D.W. *British Military Longarms, 1715-1815.* London, 1971.
12. ─────. "The Baker Rifle." *Guns Review, 13 (1973),* 188-91 et seq.
13. Baker, Norman. *Government and Contractors. The British Treasury and War Supplies, 1775-1783.* London, 1971.
14. Balderston, Marion, and Syrett, David, eds. *The Lost War. Let-*

ters from British Officers during the American Revolution. New York, 1975.
15. Barker, A.J. *The East Yorkshire Regiment (The 15th Regiment of Foot).* London, 1971.
16. ─────. *Redcoats.* London, 1976.
17. Barnett, Corelli. *Marlborough.* London, 1974.
18. Barthorp, Michael. *Wellington's Generals.* Osprey, London, 1978.
19. ─────. *Marlborough's Army.* Osprey, London, 1980.
20. ─────. *British Infantry Uniforms Since 1660.* Poole, 1982.
21. ─────. *British Cavalry Uniforms Since 1660.* Poole, 1984.
22. Bassett, J.H. "The Purchase System in the British Army, 1660-1870." Boston University PhD thesis, 1969.
23. Baynes, J. *The Jacobite Rising of 1715.* London, 1970.
24. Belfield, Eversley. *Oudenarde 1708.* London, 1972.
25. Bennell, A.S. "The Anglo-Maratha War of 1803-6." *JSAHR,* 63 (1985), 144-61.
26. Bevan, Bryan. *Marlborough the Man. A Biography of John Churchill, First Duke of Marlborough.* London, 1975.
27. Billias, G.A., ed. *George Washington's Opponents: British Generals and Admirals in the American Revolution.* New York, 1969.
28. Bird, Harrison. *Battle for a Continent. The French and Indian War, 1754-1763.* New York, 1965.
29. ─────. *Attack on Quebec. The American Invasion of Canada, 1775.* New York, 1968.
30. Blackmore, Howard L. *British Military Firearms, 1650-1850.* London, 18, 61.
31. Blanco, Richard L. *Wellington's Surgeon General. Sir James MacGrigor.* Durham, N.C., 1974.
32. ─────. "The Development of British Military Medicine, 1793-1814." *Military Affairs,* 38 (1974), 4-10.
33. Blaxland, Gregory. *The Buffs (Royal East Kent Regiment)(The Third Regiment of Foot).* London, 1972.
34. Boatner, M.M. *Encyclopedia of the American Revolution. (rev. ed.).* New York, 1974.
35. Bond, G.C. *The Grand Expedition. The British Invasion of Holland, 1809.* Athens, Georgia, 1979.
36. Boscawen, Maj. Hugh. "The Origins of the Flat-Bottomed Landing Craft 1757-58." *NAM Annual,* (1984), 23-36.
37. Bowden, S. *The Armies at Waterloo.* Arlington, Texas, 1983.
38. Bowler, R. Arthur. *Logistics and the Failure of the British Army in America, 1775-83.* Princeton, 1975.
39. Boyd, L.G. "The Role of the Military in Civil Disorders in England and Wales, 1780-1811." Univ. of Tennessee PhD thesis, 1977.
40. Bradford, S.S., ed. "The Common British Soldier--From the Journal of Thomas Sullivan, 49th Regiment of Foot." *Maryland Historical Magazine,* 62 (1967), 219-53.
41. Bradley, A.G. *Sir Guy Carleton (Lord Dorchester).* Toronto, 1966.
42. Brereton, J.M. "Sir John Fortescue, Historian of the British Army." *Blackwood's Magazine,* 319 (1976), 256-71.
43. ─────. *A History of the 4th/7th Royal Dragoon Guards and Their Predecessors.* Catterick, 1982.

44. Brett-James, Anthony. *General Graham, Lord Lynedoch*. London, 1959.
45. ―――――. *Life in Wellington's Army*. London, 1972.
46. Bruce, A.P.C. *An Annotated Bibliography of the British Army, 1660-1914*. New York, 1975.
47. ―――――. *The Purchase System in the British Army, 1660-1871*. London, 1980.
48. Bryant, Sir Arthur. *Jackets of Green*. London, 1972.
49. Buckley, Roger N. "The Destruction of the British Army in the West Indies, 1793-1815: A Medical History." *JSAHR*, 56 (1978), 38-58.
50. ―――――. *Slaves in Red Coats. The British West India Regiments, 1795-1815*. Yale, 1979.
51. Burroughs, Peter. "The Human Cost of Imperial Defence in the Early Victorian Age." *Victorian Studies*, 24 (1980), 7-32.
52. Burton, I.F. "The Secretary at War and the Administration of the Army During the War of the Spanish Succession." London PhD thesis, 1960.
53. ―――――. *The Captain-General. The Career of John Churchill, Duke of Marlborough, from 1702 to 1711*. London, 1968.
54. ―――――, and Newman, A. N. "Sir John Cope: Promotion in the Eighteenth-Century Army." *English Historical Review*, 78 (1963), 655-68.
55. Callahan, Raymond. *The East India Company and Army Reform, 1783-1798*. Harvard, 1972.
56. Calver, William L., and Bolton, R.P. *History Written with Pick and Shovel*. New York, 1950.
57. Campbell, D. Alistair. *The Dress of the Royal Artillery*. London, 1971.
58. Cantlie, Sir Neil. *History of the Army Medical Department*. 2 vols., London and Edinburgh, 1974.
59. Carman, W.Y. "The 25th Foot at Minorca." *NAM Annual 1973-74*, 10-14.
60. Carter, C.E., ed. *The Correspondence of General Thomas Gage*. 2 Vols., New Haven, 1933.
61. Caruana, Adrian. *The Light 6-Pounder Battalion Gun of 1776*. Bloomfield, Ont., 1977.
62. ―――――. "British Artillery Drill in the 18th Century." *CJAC*, 16 (1978), 46-60.
63. ―――――. *Grasshoppers and Butterflies: The Light 3-Pounders of Pattison and Townshead*. Bloomfield, Ont., 1979.
64. ―――――. "The Introduction of the Block Trail Carriage." *CJAC*, 18 (1980), 3-16.
65. ―――――. "Albert Borgard and British Artillery, 1675-1725." *CJAC*, 20 (1982), 77-94.
66. ―――――. "The Dress of the Royal Artillery in North America, 1775-1783." *M.C. & H*, 35 (1983), 124-29.
67. ―――――. "The Identification of British Muzzle-Loading Artillery. Part 1, The Designers." *CJAC*, 21 (1983), 131-37.
68. ―――――. "An Introduction to British Artillery in the Late XVII Century." *CJAC*, 22 (1984), 98-104.
69. ―――――, ed. *British Artillery Ammunition, 1780*. Bloomfield, Ont., 1979.

70. Chalfont, Arthur, Baron, ed. *Waterloo: Battle of Three Armies*. London, 1979.
71. Chandler, David. *Marlborough as Military Commander*. London, 1973.
72. ―――――. *The Art of Warfare in the Age of Marlborough*. London, 1976.
73. ―――――. *Dictionary of the Napoleonic Wars*. New York, 1979.
74. ―――――. "Fluctuations in the Strength of Forces in English Pay sent to Flanders during the Nine Years' War, 1688-1697." *War & Society*, 1 (1983), 1-19.
75. ―――――, ed. *Robert Parker and Comte de Mérode-Waterloo: The Marlborough Wars*. London, 1968.
76. ―――――, ed. *A Journal of Marlborough's Campaigns during the War of the Spanish Succession 1704-1711*. SAHR Special Publication No. 12, 1985.
77. Chartrand, René. "Notes on Bermuda Military Forces, 1687-1815." *MC&H*, 29 (1970).
78. ―――――. "British Army Deserter and Related Descriptions of Clothing, 1754-1763." *MC&H*, 35 (1983), 12-22.
79. Childs, John. *The Army, James II, and the Glorious Revolution*. Manchester, 1980.
80. Clark, William B., ed. *Naval Documents of the American Revolution*. 7 vols., USN History Division, Washington, D.C., 1964-76.
81. Cole, Howard N. *Minden, 1759*. London, 1972.
82. Colville, John. *Portrait of a General*. Salisbury, 1980.
83. Condon, Mary Ellen. "The Administration of the Transport System during the War against Revolutionary France." London PhD thesis, 1968.
84. Conway, S.R. "Military-Civilian Crime and the British Army in North America, 1775-81." London PhD thesis, 1982.
85. ―――――. "British Army Officers and the American War for Independence." *Wm & Mary Quarterly*, 41 (1984), 265-76.
86. ―――――. "The Recruitment of Criminals into the British Army, 1775-1781." *Bul. Instit. Hist. Research*, 58 (1985), 46-58.
87. Cowles, Virginia. *The Great Marlborough and His Duchess*. New York, 1983.
88. Coxe, William. *Memoirs of the Duke of Marlborough, with his Original Correspondence*. 3 vols., London, 1818-19.
89. Cuneo, J.R. *Robert Rogers of the Rangers*. New York, 1959.
90. Darling, Anthony D. *Red Coat and Brown Bess*. Bloomfield, Ont., 1970.
91. ―――――. "The British Infantry Hangers." *CJAC*, 8 (1970), 124-36.
92. ―――――. "Weapons of the Highland Regiments, 1740-80." *CJAC*, 8 (1970), 75-95.
93. ―――――. "The British Basket-Hilted Cavalry Sword." *CJAC*, 7 (1974), 79-96.
94. Daudelin, Rev. Don. "Numbers and Tactics at Bushy Run." *Western Pennsylvania Hist. Mag.*, 68 (1985), 153-79.
95. Davies, D.W. *Sir John Moore's Peninsular Campaign, 1808-1809*. The Hague, 1974.
96. Dean, C.G.T. *The Royal Hospital, Chelsea*. London, 1950.
97. Dickinson, H.T. "The Correspondence of Henry St. John and

Thomas Erle, 1705-08." *JSAHR*, 48 (1970), 205-24; 49 (1971), 3-9, 77-89.
98. Dickson, Patricia. *Red John of the Battles: John, 2nd Duke of Argyll and 1st Duke of Greenwich*. London, 1973.
99. Duffy, Christopher. *The Fortress in the Age of Vauban and Frederick The Great, 1660-1789*. London, 1985.
100. ———. *Fire and Stone. The Science of Fortress Warfare, 1660-1860*. Newton Abbot, 1975.
101. Duffy, Michael. "The British Army and the Caribbean Expeditions of the War against Revolutionary France, 1793-1801." *JSAHR*, 52 (1984), 65-73.
102. Dunnigan, Brian L. *King's Men at Mackinac: The British Garrisons, 1780-1796*. Mackinac Is. State Park Comm., 1973.
103. ———. *The British Army at Mackinac, 1812-1815*. Mackinac Is. State Park Comm., 1980.
104. Eccles, W.J. "The Battle of Quebec: A Reappraisal." *Proceedings of the 3rd Annual Meeting of the French Colonial Historical Society, 1977*, 70-81.
105. Ellestad, Charles D. "The Mutinies of 1689." *JSAHR*, 53 (1975), 4-12.
106. Ellis, Peter Berresford. *The Boyne Water. The Battle of the Boyne, 1690*. London, 1976.
107. Elting, John R. *The Battle of Bunker Hill*. Monmouth, N.J., 1975.
108. ———. *The Battles of Saratoga*. Monmouth, N.J., 1977.
109. Emsley, Clive. *British Society and the French Wars, 1793-1815*. London, 1979.
110. ———. "The Military and Popular Disorder in England, 1798-1801." *JSAHR*, 61 (1983), 10-12, 96-112.
111. Ferguson, James, ed. *Papers Illustrating the History of the Scots Brigade in the Service of the United Netherlands, 1572-1782*. 3 Vols., Edinburgh, 1899.
112. Ferguson, Kenneth P. "The Army in Ireland from the Restoration to the Act of Union." Trinity College Dublin PhD thesis, 1982.
113. ———. "Military Manuscripts in the Public Record Office of Ireland." *Irish Sword*, 15 (1982), 112-15.
114. Fletcher, I. *In Hell Before Daylight: The Siege and Storming of the Fortress of Badajoz, 16 March to 16 April 1812*. Tunbridge Wells, 1984.
115. Fosten, Bryan. *Wellington's Infantry (I)*. Osprey, London, 1981.
116. ———. *Wellington's Infantry (II)*. Osprey, London, 1982.
117. ———. *Wellington's Heavy Cavalry*. Osprey, London, 1982.
118. ———. *Wellington's Light Cavalry*. Osprey, London, 1982.
119. Francis, A.D. "The Campaign in Portugal, 1762." *JSAHR*, 59 (1981), 25-43.
120. ———. "Marlborough's March to the Danube." *JSAHR*, 50 (1972), 78-100.
121. ———. *The First Peninsular War, 1702-1713*. London, 1975.
122. Fraser, E.J.S. "The Pitt-Newcastle Coalition and the Conduct of the Seven Years' War, 1757-1760." Oxford D.Phil. thesis, 1976.
123. Frearson, C.E., ed. "'To Mr. Davenport', being Letters of Major Richard Davenport (1719-60) to his brother during service

in the 4th Troop of Horse Guards, 1742-60." *SAHR Special Publication No. 9*, 1968.
124. Frederick, J.B.M. *Lineage Book of the British Army. Mounted Corps and Infantry, 1660-1968.* Cornwallville, N.Y., 1969.
125. Frégault, Guy. *The War of the Conquest.* Toronto, 1969.
126. Frey, Sylvia. "The Common British Soldier in the Late Eighteenth Century: A Profile." *Societas*, 5 (1975), 117-31.
127. ―――. "Courts and Cats: British Military Justice in the Eighteenth Century." *Military Affairs*, 43 (1979), 5-11.
128. ―――. *The British Common Soldier in America. A Social History of Military Life in the Revolutionary Period.* Austin, Texas, 1981.
129. Fryer, Mary B. *King's Men: The Soldier Founders of Ontario.* Toronto, 1980.
130. Furneaux, Rupert. *Saratoga, the Decisive Battle.* London, 1971.
131. Gates, David. "The Creation and Training of the British Light Infantry Arm, c. 1790-1815.' Oxford D.Phil. thesis, 1985.
132. Geggus, David. "The Destruction of the British Army in the West Indies 1793-1815: Some Further Comments." *JSAHR*, 56 (1978), 238-40.
133. ―――. "Yellow Fever in the 1790s: The British Army in Occupied Saint-Domingue." *Medical History*, 23 (1979), 38-58.
134. ―――. *Slavery, War, and Revolution: The British Occupation of Saint-Domingue, 1793-1798.* Oxford, 1982.
135. Gilbert, Arthur N. "Law and Honour Among Eighteenth-Century British Army Officers." *Historical Journal*, 19 (1976), 75-87.
136. ―――. "Army Impressment during the War of the Spanish Succession." *The Historian*, 38 (1976), 689-708.
137. ―――. "The Regimental Courts Martial in the Eighteenth-Century British Army." *Albion*, 8 (1976), 50-66.
138. ―――. "Charles Jenkinson and the Last Army Press 1779." *Military Affairs*, 42 (1978), 7-11.
139. ―――. "Why Men Deserted from the Eighteenth-Century British Army." *Armed Forces & Society*, 6 (1980), 553-67.
140. ―――. "A Tale of Two Regiments: Manpower and Effectiveness in British Military Units during the Napoleonic Wars." *Armed Forces 7 Society*, 9 (1983), 275-292.
141. ―――. "The Changing Face of British Military Justice, 1757-83." *Military Affairs*, 49 (1985).
142. Glover, Michael. *Wellington's Peninsular Victories.* London, 1963.
143. ―――. *Wellington as Military Commander.* London, 1968.
144. ―――. *Britannia Sickens. Sir Arthur Wellesley and the Convention of Cintra.* London, 1970.
145. ―――. "Purchase, Patronage and Promotion in the Army at the Time of the Peninsular War." *Army Quarterly*, 103 (1972-3), 211-15, 355-62.
146. ―――. *The Peninsular War 1807-14.* Newton Abbot, 1974.
147. ―――. *General Burgoyne in Canada and America: Scapegoat for a System.* London, 1976.
148. ―――. *Wellington's Army in the Peninsula, 1808-1814.* Newton Abbot, 1977.

149. ———. *A Very Slippery Fellow: The Life of Sir Robert Wilson, 1777-1859.* Oxford, 1978.
150. ———, ed. *A Gentleman Volunteer. The Letters of George Hennell from the Peninsular War, 1812-1813.* London, 1979.
151. Glover, Richard. *Peninsular Preparation. The Reform of the British Army, 1795-1809.* Cambridge, 1963.
152. ———. *Britain at Bay. Defence Against Bonaparte, 1803-1814.* London, 1973.
153. Godfrey, William. *Pursuit of Profit and Preferment in Colonial North America: John Bradstreet's Quest.* Waterloo, Ont., 1982.
154. Gordon, Lewis H. "The British Cavalry and Dragoon Pistol." *CJAC*, 5 (1972), 11-18; 6 (1973), 10-13.
155. Graves, Donald E. "Louis de Tousard and his 'Artillerists Companion'; An Investigation of Source Material for Napoleonic Period Ordnance." *CJAC*, 5 (1972), 111-18; 6 (1973), 10-13.
156. Green, David. *Blenheim.* London, 1974.
157. Griffith, Paddy, ed. *Wellington Commander. The Iron Duke's Generalship.* Chichester, 1985.
158. Grinnell-Milne, Duncan. *Mad, Is He? The Character and Achievement of James Wolfe.* London, 1963.
159. Gruber, Ira D. *The Howe Brothers and the American Revolution.* New York, 1972.
160. Gurwood, Lt-Col John, ed. *The Dispatches of Field Marshal: the Duke of Wellington ...* New Edition. 13 Vols., London, 1837-
161. Guthorn, Peter. *British Maps of the American Revolutionary War.* Monmouth, N.J., 1973.
162. Guy, Alan J. "Drafts for Portugal, 1762. Recruiting for Rank at the End of the Seven Years' War." *NAM Annual 1977-78*, 29-34.
163. ———. "'A Whole Army Absolutely Ruined in Ireland': Aspects of the Irish Establishment, 1715-1773." *NAM Annual 1978-79*, 30-43.
164. ———. "'This Insulting Misfortune': Regimental Officers and the Problem of Personal Pay 1714-1775." *NAM Annual 1979-80*, 10-21.
165. ———. "'Oeconomy and Discipline': Regimental Officers and the Perquisites of Command 1714-1768." *NAM Annual 1980-81*, 32-40.
166. ———. *Regimental Agency in the British Standing Army, 1715-1763: A Study of Georgian Military Administration.* Manchester, 1980.
167. ———. "'The Colonel's Advantage': Regimental Proprietors and the Perquisites of Command, 1714-1763." *NAM Annual, 1981*, 29-37.
168. ———. *Oeconomy and Discipline. Officership and Administration in the British Army, 1714-63.* Manchester, 1985.
169. Hackmann, W.K. "English Military Expeditions to the Coast of France, 1757-1761." Univ. of Michigan PhD thesis, 1969.
170. Haggard, D.J., ed. "With the 10th Hussars in Spain. Letters of Edward Fox Fitzgerald." *JSAHR*, 44 (1966), 88-113.
171. Hamilton, C., ed. *Braddock's Defeat.* Norman, Okla., 1959.

172. Hargreaves, Reginald. *The Bloodybacks: The British Servicemen in North America and the Caribbean 1655-1783.* London, 1968.
173. Hargrove, Richard J. *General John Burgoyne.* Newark, N.J., 1983.
174. Harington, A.L. *Sir Harry Smith: Bungling Hero.* Cape Town, 1980.
175. Harper, J.R. *The 78th Fighting Frasers. A Short History of the Old 78th Regiment, or Fraser's Highlanders 1757-1763.* Laval, Quebec, 1966.
176. Harrington, Peter. "Images of Culloden." *JSAHR*, 63 (1985), 208-19.
177. Haswell, C.J.D. *The First Respectable Spy. The Life and Times of Colquhoun Grant, Wellington's Head of Intelligence.* London, 1969.
178. Haswell-Miller, A. E., and Dawnay, N. P. *Military Drawings and Paintings in the Royal Collection.* 2 Vols., Oxford, 1966-70.
179. Hatch, Robert. *Thrust for Canada: The American Attempt on Quebec in 1775-1776.* Boston, 1979.
180. Hattendorf, John B. "English Governmental Machinery and the Conduct of War, 1702-1713." *War & Society*, 3 (1985), 1-22.
181. Hayes, James. "The Royal House of Hanover and the British Army, 1714-1760." *Bul. John Rylands Libr.*, 40 (1957-8), 328-57.
182. Hayes-McCoy, G. A. *Irish Battles: A Military History of Ireland.* London, 1969.
183. Hayter, Tony. *The Army and the Crowd in Mid-Georgian England.* London, 1978.
184. ———. "The British Army 1713-1793: Recent Research Work." *JSAHR*, 63 (1985), 11-19.
185. Herbert, Brig. Charles. "Cocheath Camp 1778-1779." *JSAHR*, 45 (1967), 129-48.
186. Hibbert, Christopher. *Corunna.* London, 1967.
187. ———, ed. *The Recollections of Rifleman Harris.* London, 1970.
188. Higginbotham, Don. *The War of American Independence: Military Attitudes, Policies, and Practice, 1763-1789.* New York, 1971.
189. Hitsman, J.M., and Bond, C.C.J. "The Assault Landing at Louisbourg, 1758." *Canadian Historical Review*, 35 (1954), 314-30.
190. Hogg, O.F.G. *The Royal Arsenal: Its Background, Origin and Subsequent History.* 2 Vols., London, 1963.
191. Horsman, Reginald. *The War of 1812.* London, 1969.
192. Horward, D.D. *The Battle of Busaco: Masséna vs Wellington.* London, 1965.
193. ———. *Napoleon and Iberia: The Twin Sieges of Ciudad Rodrigo and Almeida, 1810.* Tallahassee, 1984.
194. ———. "'The Dreadful Day': Wellington and Masséna on the Coa, 1810." *Military Affairs*, 44 (1980), 163-70.
195. Howarth, David. *A Near Run Thing.* London, 1968.
196. Howson, Gerald. *Burgoyne of Saratoga.* New York, 1979.
197. Houlding, J.A. *Fit For Service. The Training of the British Army, 1715-1795.* Oxford, 1981.

198. Hughes, Maj-Gen B.P. *British Smooth-Bore Artillery.* Harrisburg, Pa., 1969.
199. ―――. *Firepower. Weapons Effectiveness on the Battlefield, 1630-1850.* New York and London, 1974.
200. ―――. *Open Fire. Artillery Tactics from Marlborough to Wellington.* Chichester, 1984.
201. Hyden, John S. "The Sources, Organisation and Uses on Intelligence in the Anglo-Portuguese Army 1808-1814." *JSAHR*, 52 (1984), 92-104, 169-75.
202. Ivers, L.E. *British Drums on the Southern Frontier: The Military Colonization of Georgia, 1733-49.* Chapel Hill, 1974.
203. Jackson, John W. *With the British Army in Philadelphia, 1777-1778.* San Rafael, Calif., 1979.
204. Jackson, Melvin H., and de Beer, Carel. *The Verbruggens at the Royal Brass Foundry.* Newton Abbot, 1973.
205. Jacobsen, G.A. *William Blathwayt: A Late Seventeenth-Century English Administrator.* Oxford, 1933.
206. Jamieson, A.G. "War in the Leeward Islands, 1775-1783." Oxford D.Phil. thesis, 1981.
207. Jarvis, Rupert C. *Collected Papers on the Jacobite Risings.* Vol. 1, Manchester, 1971.
208. Kamen, Henry. *The War of Succession in Spain, 1700-1715.* London, 1969.
209. Katcher, Philip R.N. *King George's Army 1775-1783. A Handbook of British, American, and German Regiments.* Reading, 1973.
210. ―――. "Military Notes and Deserter Descriptions from the Maryland Gazette and the Virginia Gazette, 1754-1760." *MC&H*, 33 (1981), 18-20.
211. ―――. "Military Notes and Deserter Descriptions from the Pennsylvania Gazette, 1755-1758." *MC&H*, 32 (1980), 66-69.
212. ―――. "Le Fantassin Britannique en Amerique du Nord, 1759." *Uniformes*, No. 62 (1981), 28-32; No. 63 (1981), 8-12.
213. Keegan, John D. *The Face of Battle.* London, 1976.
214. Kehoe, Vincent J.-R. *"We Were There!" April 19th 1775.* 2 Vols., Chelmsford, Mass., 1974.
215. Kemp, Alan. *The British Army in the American Revolution.* Almark, London, 1973.
216. Kemp, Anthony. *Weapons and Equipment of the Marlborough Wars.* Blandford, Dorset, 1980.
217. Kent, Donald H., et al, eds. *The Papers of Henry Bouquet.* 5 Vols. (to date, of eight projected). Harrisburg, Pa., 1976-.
218. Kerrigan, P.M. "The Defences of Ireland 1793-1815." *An Cosantoir*, 24 (1974), through 27 (1977), passim.
219. Klein, Milton M., and Howard, Ronald W., eds. *The Twilight of British Rule in Revolutionary America: The New York Letter Book of General James Robertson, 1780-1783.* New York, 1984.
220. Kleinschmidt, Harald. "Standortliste englischer Quellen zur Kriegskunst (1500-1799)." Typescript, Old War Office Library, 1983.
221. Koontz, John E. "Some Notes on d'Erlon's First Attack at Waterloo." *Empires, Eagles, & Lions*, No. 78 (1984), 47-55; No. 79 (1984), 19-44.

222. ―――. "British Infantry Units at Blenheim." *Gorget & Sash*, 1, No. 2 (n.d.), 21-26.
223. ―――. "Tallard's Army at Blindheim." *Gorget & Sash*, 1, No. 4 (n.d.), 22-27; 2, No. 1 (n.d.), 5-17.
224. Kopperman, Paul E. *Braddock at the Monongahela*. Pittsburgh, 1977.
225. ―――. "Medical Services in the British Army, 1742-1783." *Journal of the History of Medicine*, 34 (1979), 436-43.
226. ―――. "An Assessment of the Cholmley's Batman and British Journals of Braddock's Campaign." *Western Pennsylvania Hist. Mag.*, 62 (1979), 197-218.
227. ―――. "A British Officer's Journal of the Braddock Expedition." *Western Pennsylvanis Hist. Mag.*, 64 (1981), 169-87.
228. ―――. "The British Command and Soldiers' Wives in America, 1755-1783." *JSAHR*, 60 (1982), 14-34.
229. ―――. "The Stoppages Mutiny of 1763." *Western Pennsylvania Hist. Mag.*, 69 (1986), pp. 241-54.
230. ―――. "'The Cheapest Pay': Alcohol Abuse in the Eighteenth-Century British Army." (forthcoming; journal not yet known).
231. ―――. "Religion and Religious Policy in the British Army, c. 1700-1796." (forthcoming; journal not yet known).
232. Lachouque, Henri. *Waterloo*. London, 1975.
233. Lawford, James P. *Clive: Proconsul of India*. London, 1976.
234. ―――. *Britain's Army in India: From its Origins to the Conquest of Bengal*. London, 1978.
235. Laws, M.E.S. *Battery Records of the Royal Artillery, 1716-1859*. Woolwich, 1952.
236. ―――. "War Services of Officers of the Royal Artillery, 1716-1763." Typescript, Woolwich, 1974.
237. Leach, D.E. *Arms for Empire. A Military History of the British Colonies in North America, 1607-1763*. New York, 1973.
238. Lehmann, Joseph H. *Remember You Are An Englishman. A Biography of Sir Harry Smith, 1787-1860*. London, 1977.
239. Lenman, Bruce. *The Jacobite Risings in Britain, 1689-1746*. London, 1980.
240. ―――. *The Jacobite Clans of the Great Glen, 1650-1784*. London, 1985.
241. Leslie, N.B. *The Succession of Colonels of the British Army from 1660 to the Present Day*. SAHR Special Publication No. 11, 1974.
242. Lewis, Paul. *The Man Who Lost America. A Biography of Gentleman Johnny Burgoyne*. New York, 1973.
243. Liddell, R.S. *The Memoirs of the Tenth Royal Hussars*. London, 1981.
244. Linklater, E. and A. *The Black Watch*. London, 1977.
245. Little, H.M. "The Treasury, the Commissariat and the Supply of the Combined Army in Germany during the Seven Years' War (1756-1763)." London PhD thesis, 1981.
246. ―――. "The Emergence of a Commissariat During the Seven Years' War in Germany." *JSAHR*, 61 (1983), 201-14.
247. Livingstone, Alastair, et al., eds. *Muster Roll of Prince Charles Edward Stuart's Army 1745-46*. Aberdeen, 1984.
248. Lloyd, Allan. *The Scorching of Washington: The War of 1812*. Newton Abbot, 1974.

249. Longford, Elizabeth. *Wellington. The Years of the Sword.* London, 1969.
250. Lumpkin, Henry. *From Savannah to Yorktown. The American Revolution in the South.* Columbia, S.C., 1981.
251. Lunt, James. *John Burgoyne of Saratoga.* London, 1976.
252. MacIvor, Iain. *Fort George.* Edinburgh, 1970.
253. Mackay, Maj. Daniel S.C. "The Royal Canadian Volunteers." *OMMC Journal*, 6 (1977), 1-18.
254. Mackesy, Piers. *The War for America, 1775-1783.* London, 1964.
255. ─────. *The Strategy of Overthrow 1798-99. Statesmen at War.* London, 1974.
256. ─────. *The Coward of Minden. The Affair of Lord George Sackville.* London, 1979.
257. Mahon, John K. *The War of 1812.* Gainesville, Florida, 1972.
258. Manders, Eric. *The Battle of Long Island.* Monmouth, N.J., 1978.
259. Mann, Michael. *And They Rode On: The King's Dragoon Guards at Waterloo.* Salisbury, 1984.
260. Marini, A.J. "Parliament and the Marine Regiments, 1739." *Mariner's Mirror*, 62 (1976), 55-65.
261. ─────. "The British Corps of Marines, 1746-1771, and the United States Marine Corps, 1798-1818: A Comparative Study of the Early Administration and Institutionalization of Two Modern Marine Forces." Univ. of Maine PhD thesis, 1979.
262. Marshall, Douglas W. "The Military Engineers in America, 1755-1783." *JSAHR*, 51 (1973), 155-63.
263. ─────. "The British Military Engineers 1741-1783: A Study of Organization, Social Change, and Cartography." Univ. of Michigan PhD thesis, 1976.
264. ─────, and Peckman, Howard. *Campaigns of the American Revolution. An Atlas of Manuscript Maps.* Ann Arbor, 1976.
265. Marshall-Cornwall, Gen Sir James. "The First British Expeditionary Force to Egypt, 1801." *RUSI Journal*, 122 (1977), 52-55.
266. May, Robin. *The British Army in North America, 1775-1783.* Osprey, Reading, 1974.
267. ─────. *Wolfe's Army.* Osprey, Reading, 1974.
268. Mayne, Richard. *The Battle of Jersey.* Chichester, 1980.
269. Meyer, Jack A. "Wellington's Generalship: A Study of his Peninsular Campaigns." University of South Carolina PhD thesis, 1985.
270. McCardell, Lee. *Ill-Starred General. Braddock of the Coldstream Guards.* Pittsburgh, 1958.
271. McGuffie, T.H. "Recruiting the Ranks of the Regular Army during the French Wars: Recruiting, Recruits, and Methods of Recruitment." *JSAHR*, 34 (1956), 50-8, 123-32.
272. ─────. *The Siege of Gibraltar, 1779-1783.* London, 1965.
273. McLynn, F.J. "Ireland and the Jacobite Rising of 1745." *Irish Sword*, 113 (1979), 339-52.
274. ─────. *The Jacobite Army in England, 1745: The Final Campaign.* Edinburgh, 1983.
275. Meuron, Guy de. *Le regiment Meuron 1781-1816.* Lausanne, 1981.
276. Middleton, R. "A Reinforcement for America, Summer 1757." *Bul. Instit. Hist. Research*, 41 (1968), 58-72.

277. ———. "The Administration of Newcastle and Pitt: The Departments of State and the Conduct of the War, 1754-1760, with particular reference to the Campaigns in North America." Exeter Univ. PhD thesis, 1969.
278. ———. *The Bells of Victory. The Pitt-Newcastle Ministry and the Conduct of the Seven Years' War, 1757-1762.* Cambridge, 1985.
279. Morgan, G.W. "The Impact of War on the Administration of the Army, Navy and Ordnance in Britain, 1739-1754." Univ. of Leicester PhD thesis, 1977.
280. Murray, Gen Sir George, ed. *Letters and Dispatches of John Churchill, Duke of Marlborough, from 1702-1712.* 5 Vols., London, 1845.
281. Muskett, Paul. "Military Operations Against Smuggling in Kent and Sussex, 1698-1750." *JSAHR*, 52 (1974), 89-110.
282. Myatt, Frederick. *The Soldier's Trade: British Military Developments 1660-1914.* London, 1974.
283. ———. *Peninsular General. Sir Thomas Picton, 1758-1815.* Newton Abbot, 1980.
284. ———. *The British Infantry 1660-1945: The Evolution of a Fighting Force.* Poole, 1983.
285. Neace-Hill, W.B.R. "Brevet Rank." *JSAHR*, 48 (1970), 85-104.
286. Nelson, Paul D. *General Horatio Gates: A Biography.* Baton Rouge, 1976.
287. ———. "British Conduct of the American Revolutionary War: A Review of Interpretations." *Journal of American History*, 65 (1978), 623-53.
288. Neuburg, Victor E. "The British Army in the Eighteenth Century." *JSAHR*, 61 (1983), 39-47.
289. Niemeyer, Joachim, and Ortenburg, Georg. *The Hanoverian Army During the Seven Years' War. The "Gmunderer Prachtwerk."* Copenhagen, 1977.
290. Oatts, L.B. *The Emperor's Chambermaids. The Story of the 14th/20th King's Hussars.* London, 1973.
291. Orr, Michael. *Dettingen 1743.* London, 1972.
292. Pakenham, Thomas. *The Year of Liberty. The Story of the Great Irish Rebellion of 1798.* London, 1969.
293. Pancake, John S. *This Destructive War. The British Campaign in the Carolinas, 1780-82.* Univ. of Alabama Press, 1985.
294. Park, S.J., and Nafziger, G.F. *The British Military: Its System and Organization, 1803-1815.* Cambridge, Ont., 1983.
295. Parker, K.L. "Anglo-American Wilderness Campaigning, 1754-64; Logistical and Tactical Developments." Columbia Univ. PhD thesis, 1970.
296. Parkinson, R. *Moore of Corunna.* London, 1976.
297. Peckham, Howard. *Pontiac and the Indian Uprising.* New York, 1975.
298. ———, ed. *The Toll of Independence. Engagements and Battle Casualties of the American Revolution.* Chicago, 1974.
299. Pericoli, Ugo. *1815: The Armies at Waterloo.* London, 1973.
300. Perjés, G. "Army Provisioning, Logistics and Strategy in the Second Half of the 17th Century." *Acta Historica. Revue de l'Academie des Sciences de Hongrie*, 16 (1970), 1-51.
301. Peterson, Harold. *Round Shot and Rammers. An Introduction to*

Muzzle-Loading Land Artillery in the United States. Harrisburg, Pa., 1969.
302. Phelan, Ivan. "Marlborough as Logistician," *JSAHR*, 64 (1986-87 forthcoming).
303. Pickering, R.A. "The Plug Bayonet." *CJAC*, 10 (1972), 117-28.
304. Pimlott, J.L. "The Raising of Four Regiments for India, 1787-8." *JSAHR*, 52 (1974), 68-84.
305. ———. "The Reformation of the Life Guards, 1788." *JSAHR*, 52 (1974), 68-84.
306. ———. "The Administration of the British Army, 1783-93." Univ. of Leicester PhD thesis, 1975.
307. Porter, W., and Watson, C.M. *History of the Corps of Royal Engineers.* 3 Vols., London, 1889-1915.
308. Powell, G.S. *The Kandyan Wars. The British Army in Ceylon 1803-1818.* London, 1973.
309. Prebble, John. *Mutiny. Highland Regiments in Revolt 1743-1804.* London, 1975.
310. Priestly, E.J. "Army Life, 1757." *JSAHR*, 52 (1974), 197-208.
311. Rea, Robert T. "Graveyard for Britons, West Florida 1763-1781." *Florida Hist. Quarterly*, 47 (1969), 345-64.
312. ———. "Pensacola Under the British (1763-1781)," in McGovern, James R., ed. *Colonial Pensacola (Vol. 1),* Pensacola, Florida, 1974, pp. 57-87.
313. ———. "Life, Death, and Little Glory: The British Soldier on the Gulf Coast, 1763-1781," in Coker, W.S., ed. *The Military Presence on the Gulf Coast.* Pensacola, Florida, 1978, pp. 21-35.
314. Redgrave, T.M.O. "Wellington's Logistical Arrangements in the Peninsular War, 1809-1814." London PhD thesis, 1979.
315. Reilly, Robin. *The British at the Gates: The New Orleans Campaign in the War of 1812.* London, 1976.
316. Reynolds, Paul. *Guy Carleton. A Biography.* Toronto, 1980.
317. Rigby, Brig. Bernard. *Ever Glorious. The Story of the 22nd (Cheshire) Regiment.* Vol. 1, Chester, 1983.
318. Rioux, Christian. "The Royal Regiment of Artillery in Quebec City, 1759-1871." *History and Archaeology*, No. 57, (1982), 3-146.
319. Rogers, Alan. *Empire and Liberty: American Resistance to British Authority, 1755-1763.* New York, 1974.
320. Rogers, Col H.C.B. *Weapons of the British Soldier.* London, 1972.
321. ———. *The British Army of the Eighteenth Century.* London, 1977.
322. ———. *Wellington's Army.* London, 1979.
323. Roy, Ian. "The British Army 1500-1715: Recent Writing Reviewed." *JSAHR*, 62 (1984), 194-200.
324. Roy, R.H. "The Memoirs of Private James Gunn." *JSAHR*, 49 (1971), 90-120.
325. Rush, N. Orwin. *Spain's Final Triumph Over Great Britain in the Gulf of Mexico: The Battle of Pensacola, March 9 to May 8, 1781.* Tallahassee, 1966.
326. Russell, P. "Redcoats in the Wilderness: British Officers and Irregular Warfare in Europe and America, 1740 to 1760." *William & Mary Quarterly*, 35 (1978), 629-52.

327. Savory, Lt-Gen Sir Reginald. *His Britannic Majesty's Army in Germany, during the Seven Years' War.* Oxford, 1966.
328. ――――, ed. "John Tory's Journal, 1758-1762." *JSAHR*, 54 (1976), 70-95.
329. Scouller, Maj R.E. *The Armies of Queen Anne.* Oxford, 1966.
330. ――――. "The Peninsula in the War of the Spanish Succession." *JSAHR*, 54 (1976), 231-45; 55 (1977), 35-53.
331. Shelton, W.J. *English Hunger and Industrial Disorders. A Study of Social Conflict during the First Decade of George III's Reign.* Toronto, 1973.
332. Shy, John. *Toward Lexington. The Role of the British Army in the Coming of the American Revolution.* Princeton, 1965.
333. ――――. *A People Numerous and Armed. Reflections on the Military Struggle for American Independence.* New York, 1976.
334. Siborne, Maj-Gen T.H., ed. *Waterloo Letters.* London, 1891 (rpt. 1983).
335. Siborne, Capt William. *The Waterloo Campaign.* London, 1894.
336. Simms, J.G. *Jacobite Ireland.* London, 1969.
337. Smith, Samuel S. *The Battle of Princeton.* Monmouth, N.J., 1967.
338. ――――. *Fight For the Delaware, 1777.* Monmouth, N.J., 1974.
339. Snyder, H.L., ed. *The Marlborough-Godolphin Correspondence.* 3 Vols., Oxford, 1975.
340. Speck, W.A. *The Butcher. The Duke of Cumberland and the Suppression of the '45.* Oxford, 1981.
341. Spurrier, M.C., ed. "Letters of a Peninsular War Commanding Officer ... Sir Andrew Barnard." *JSAHR*, 47 (1969), 131-48.
342. Stacey, C.P. *Quebec 1759. The Siege and the Battle.* 2nd Ed, London, 1973.
343. ――――. "Generals and Generalship before Quebec, 1759-60." *The Canadian Historical Association, Report, 1959,* 1-15.
344. ――――. "The British Forces in North America during the Seven Years' War." *Dictionary of Canadian Biography.* Vol. iii. Toronto, 1974, xxiv-xxx.
345. Stanley, George F.G. *New France. The Last Phase, 1744-1760.* Toronto and London, 1968.
346. ――――. *Canada Invaded, 1775-1776.* Toronto, 1973.
347. ――――. *The War of 1812. Land Operations.* Ottawa, 1984.
348. Steele, Ian K. *Guerrillas and Grenadiers: The Struggle for Canada, 1689-1760.* Toronto, 1969.
349. Steppler, Glenn A. "British Military Artificers in Canada, 1760-1815." *JSAHR*, 60 (1982), 150-63.
350. ――――. "The Common Soldier in the Reign of George III, 1760-1793." Oxford D.Phil. thesis, 1984.
351. Stewart, Charles H. "The Service of British Regiments in Canada and North America." Typescript, DND Library, Ottawa, 1964.
352. Stoddard, Peter C. "Counter-Insurgency and Defence in Ireland, 1790-1815." Oxford D.Phil. thesis, 1972.
353. Strach, Stephen G. *The British Occupation of the Niagara Frontier, 1759-1796.* Niagara Falls, Ont., 1976.
354. ――――. "A Memoir of the Exploits of Captain Alexander Fraser and his Company of British Marksmen, 1776-1777." *JSAHR*, 63 (1985), 91-98., 164-79.

355. Strachan, Hew. *British Military Uniforms 1768-1796. The Dress of the British Army from Official Sources.* London, 1975.
356. ―――――. "The British Army, 1815-1856: Recent Writing Reviewed." *JSAHR*, 63 (1985), 68-79.
357. Summers, J.L., and Chartrand, René. *Military Uniforms in Canada, 1665-1970.* Ottawa, 1981.
358. Sutherland, D. *Tried and Valiant. The History of the Border Regiment (34th and 55th Regiments of Foot) 1702-1959.* London, 1972.
359. Suthren, Victor J.H. "The Battle of Chateauguay." *Canadian Historic Sites: Occasional Papers in Archaeology and History—No. 11.* Ottawa, 1974, pp. 95-150.
360. Sweetman, John. *Saratoga 1777.* London, 1972.
361. Swinson, Arthur. *A Register of the Regiments and Corps of the British Army.* London, 1972.
362. Syrett, David. "The British Landing at Havana: An Example of an Eighteenth-Century Combined Operation." *Mariner's Mirror*, 55 (1969), 325-31.
363. ―――――. *Shipping and the American War, 1775-83: A Study of British Transport Organization.* London, 1970.
364. ―――――. "The Methodology of British Amphibious Operations during the Seven Years' and American Wars." *Mariner's Mirror*, 58 (1972), 269-80.
365. ―――――. "Returns of His Majesty's Forces, 1768-1802." *JSAHR*, 60 (1982), 118-23.
366. ―――――, ed. *The Siege and Capture of Havana, 1762.* London, 1970.
367. Taylor, William. *Military Roads in Scotland.* Newton Abbot, 1976.
368. Teffeteller, Gordon. *The Supriser. The Life of Rowland, Lord Hill.* London, 1983.
369. Thompson, Brig. W.F.K. "The Great Siege of Gibraltar, 1779-1783." *Journal of the Royal Artillery*, 106 (1979), 88-113.
370. ―――――, ed. *An Ensign in the Peninsular War. The Letters of John Aitchison.* London, 1981.
371. Thoumine, R.H. *Scientific Soldier. A Life of General Le Marchant, 1766-1812.* London, 1968.
372. Tomasson, K., and Buist, F. *Battles of the '45.* London, 1967.
373. Tomlinson, H.C. *Guns and Government. The Office of Ordnance under the Later Stuarts.* London, 1979.
374. Tracy, Nicholas. "The Capture of Manila, 1762." *Mariner's Mirror*, 55 (1969), 311-23.
375. Urwin, Gregory J.W. "Cornwallis in Virginia: A Reappraisal." *MC & H*, 37 (1985), 111-26.
376. Vale, W. *History of the South Staffordshire Regiment.* Aldershot, 1969.
377. Vermieren, Roland A.L. "Memoirs Etc. by British Contemporaries." *Journal of the Napoleonic Association.* No. 21 (1982), 36-51.
378. Verney, Peter. *The Battle of Blenheim.* London, 1976.
379. Vichness, Samuel E. "Marshal of Portugal: The Military Career of William Carr Beresford, 1785-1814." Florida State Univ. PhD thesis, 1976.
380. Wace, Alan. *The Marlborough Tapestries at Blenheim Palace.* London, 1968.

381. Waddell, L.M. "The Administration of the English Army in Flanders and Brabant from 1689 to 1697." Univ. of North Carolina PhD thesis, 1971.
382. Ward, Christopher. *The War of the Revolution*. 2 Vols., New York, 1952.
383. Ward, S.G.P. *Wellington's Headquarters. A Study of Administrative Problems in the Peninsula, 1809-1814*. Oxford, 1957.
384. ———, ed. "The Letters of Captain Nicholas Delacherois, 9th Regiment." *JSAHR*, 51 (1973), 5-14.
385. ———, ed. "The Diary of Lieutenant Robert Woollcombe, RA, 1812-1813." *JSAHR*, 52 (1974), 161-80.
386. ———. "General Sir George Murray." *JSAHR*, 58 (1980), 191-208.
387. Watt, Gavin K., and Cruikshank, Ernest A. *The King's Royal Regiment of New York*. Toronto, 1984.
388. Webb-Carter, Brig. B.W. "The Letters of William Bell, 89th Foot, 1808-1810." *JSAHR*, 48 (1970), 66-84, 147-64.
389. Weller, Jac. *Wellington at Waterloo*. London, 1967.
390. ———. *Wellington in India*. London, 1972.
391. Wellington, 2nd. Duke of, ed. *Supplementary Despatches and Memoranda of Field Marshal Arthur Duke of Wellington, KG, ...* 15 Vols., London, 1858-72.
392. ———, ed. *Despatches, Correspondence and Memoranda ... in Continuation of the Former Series*. 8 Vols., London, 1867-80.
393. West, Jenny. "The Water-Powered Gunpowder Industry, as a Source of Ordnance 1700-1850." London, PhD thesis, 1985 (pending).
394. Western, J.R. *The English Militia in the Eighteenth Century*. London, 1965.
395. White, A.S. *Bibliography of Regimental Histories of the British Army*. London, 1965.
396. Whitfield, Carol. "The Battle of Queenston Heights." *Canadian Historic Sites: Occasional Papers in Archaeology and History--No. 11*. Ottawa, 1974, pp. 9-59.
397. ———. *Tommy Atkins: The British Soldier in Canada, 1759-1870*. Ottawa, 1981.
398. Whitworth, Maj-Gen R.H. *Field Marshal Lord Ligonier. A Story of the British Army, 1702-1770*. Oxford, 1958.
399. ———, ed. "Some Unpublished Wolfe Letters, 1755-1758." *JSAHR*, 53 (1975), 65-86.
400. Wickwire, Franklin and Mary. *Cornwallis and the War of Independence*. London, 1971.
401. ———. *Cornwallis: The Imperial Years*. Chapel Hill, 1980.
402. Wilkinson-Latham, R. *British Artillery on Land and Sea, 1790-1820*. Newton Abbot, 1973.
403. Willcox, William B. *Portrait of a General. Sir Henry Clinton in the War of Independence*. New York, 1964.
404. Windibank, Matthew. "The British Army and Politics in the Reign of George I." London PhD thesis, (pending, 1986).
405. Windrow, Martin, and Embleton, Gerry. *Military Dress in the Peninsular War, 1808-1814*. London, 1974.
406. Winstock, Lewis. *Songs and Music of the Redcoats ... 1642-1902*. London, 1970.

407. Wise, T. *A Guide to Military Museums.* 2nd Ed., Hemel Hempstead, 1971.
408. Woodford, L.W., ed. "War and Peace--The Experiences of an Army Surgeon, 1810-27." *JSAHR,* 49 (1971), 43-58.
409. Wyatt, R.J. "Wellington's Published Despatches and Correspondence." *JSAHR,* 62 (1984), 244-6.
410. Yaple, R.L. "Braddock's Defeat: The Theories and a Reconsideration." *JSAHR,* 46 (1968), 194-201.
411. ───. "The Auxiliaries: Foreign and Miscellaneous Regiments in the British Army, 1802-1817." *JSAHR,* 50 (1972), 10-28.
412. Young, Brig. Peter, and Lawford, Lt-Col J.P. *Wellington's Masterpiece: The Battle and Campaign of Salamanca.* London, 1973.

Supplement

413. Barlett, Thomas. "The Augmentation of the Army in Ireland, 1767-1769." *English Hist. Review,* 96 (1981), 540-59.
414. Burns, R.E. "Ireland and British Military Preparations for War in America in 1775." *Cithara,* 2 (1963), no. 2, 42-61.
415. Calhoon, Robert McCluer. *The Loyalists in Revolutionary America, 1760-1781.* New York, 1973.
416. Chandler, David, ed. "The Journal of Edward Heeley. Servant to Lt-Col Sir George Scovell, KCB, Assistant Quartermaster General to the British Army in the Campaign of 1815." *JSAHR,* 64 (1986), 94-117, 129-42.
417. Chartrand, René. "The Lower Canada Select Embodied Militia Battalions, 1812-15." *Military Illustrated,* 1 (1986), no. 4, 38-42.
418. Debor, Herbert W. "German Regiments in Canada, 1776-1783." *The German-Canadian Yearbook,* 2 (1975), 34-49.
419. Dunnigan, Brian. *Siege 1759: The Campaign Against Niagara.* Youngstown, N.Y., 1986.
420. Fry, Bruce W. *An Appearance of Strength: The Fortifications of Louisbourg.* 2 vols., Ottawa, 1984.
421. Gates, David. *The Spanish Ulcer. A History of the Peninsular War.* New York, 1986.
422. Graves, Donald E. "'Dry Books of Tactics': U.S. Infantry Manuals of the War of 1812 and After, Pt. 1." *MC&H,* 38 (1986), 50-61.
423. Gruber, Ira D. "George III Chooses a Commander in Chief," in R. Hoffman and P.J. Albert, eds., *Arms and Independence: The Military Character of the American Revolution.* Charlottesville, Va., 1984, pp. 166-90.
424. ───. "Britain's Southern Strategy," in W.R. Higgins, ed., *The Revolutionary War in the South: Power, Conflict, and Leadership.* Durham, N.C., 1979.
425. ───. "For King and Country: The Limits of Loyalty of British Officers in the War for American Independence," in Edgar Denton, ed., *Limits of Loyalty.* Waterloo, Ont., 1980, pp. 21-40.
426. Guitard, Michelle. *The Militia of the Battle of Chateauguay. A Social History.* Ottawa, 1983.
427. Haynes, Kenneth R. "The Race to Weitzel's Mill, 6 March 1781." *Gorget & Sash,* 3 (1986), 1-14.

428. Hebbert, F.J. "The Belle-Ile Expedition of 1761." *JSAHR*, 64 (1986), 81-93.
429. Higginbotham, Don. "Reflections on the War of Independence, Modern Guerrilla Warfare, and the War of Vietnam," in R. Hoffman and P.J. Albert, eds., (entry 423 above).
430. ─────, ed. *Reconsiderations on the Revolutionary War: Selected Essays*. Westport, Conn., 1978.
431. Hubner, Brian. "The Formation of the British Light Infantry Companies and their Employment in the Saratoga Campaign of 1777." Univ. of Saskatchewan MA thesis, 1986.
432. Leach, H.A. *The Founding of Fort Amherstburg (Malden), 1796*. Houston, 1985.
433. Luethy, Ivor C.E. "Swiss Mercenaries in the Service of the British Crown: The War of 1812." *SAHS Newsletter*, (Feb. 1985), 9-20.
434. Mackesy, Piers. *Could the British Have Won the War of Independence?* Worcester, Mass., 1976.
435. ─────. "The Redcoat Revived," in Wm. M. Fowler and Wallace Coyle, eds., *The American Revolution: Changing Perspectives*. Boston, 1979, pp. 171-88.
436. ─────. "What the British Army Learned," in R. Hoffman and P.J. Albert, eds., (entry 423 above), 191-215.
437. Paret, Peter. "Colonial Experience and European Military Reform at the end of the Eighteenth Century." *Bulletin of the Instit. of Hist. Research*, 37 (1964), 47-59.
438. ─────. "The Relationship Between the Revolutionary War and European Military Thought and Practice in the Second Half of the Eighteenth Century," in Don Higginbotham, ed., (entry 430 above).
439. Sarramon, Jean. *La bataille des Arapiles*. Toulouse, 1978.
440. ─────. *La bataille de Vitoria*. Toulouse, 1986.
441. Shy, John. "American Society and its War for Independence," in Don Higginbotham, ed., (entry 430 above), 72-82.
442. Smith, Paul H. *Loyalists and Redcoats: A Study of British Revolutionary Policy*. Chapel Hill, N.C., 1964.
443. ─────. "The American Loyalists: Notes on their Organisations and Numerical Strength." *William & Mary Quarterly*, 25 (1968), 259-77.
444. Smith, Samuel S. *The Battle of Brandywine*. Monmouth, N.J., 1976.
445. Washington, Ida and Paul. *Carleton's Raid*. Canaan, N.H., 1977.
446. Weigley, Russell F. *The Partisan War: The Southern Campaign*. Columbia, S.C., 1970.
447. Wyatt, R.J. "The Largest Military Bibliography in Existence in Great Britain." *JSAHR*, 64 (1986), 184-5.

VII

THE ROYAL NAVY, 1714-1860

Roger Knight
and
Alan Pearsall

Guides and Compilations. Access to documents and information about where they are and what they contain have improved over the last fifteen years. Useful as an initial guide in this respect for both administrative records and personal papers is the National Maritime Museum Guide to the Manuscripts (118). Access to the Public Records has been improved by new facilities at Kew as well as by a useful guide for genealogists (189), but also useful to others. The National Maritime Museum Library Catalogue can be used as a guide to printed sources (200), although it has not been updated. A number of listings have become indispensable. Most important among these must be the first reliable published list of ships of the Royal Navy by Colledge (34). Likewise, accurate lists of all Admiralty and Navy Board officials (not just the Commissioners) are now available (199, 35). Taylor's work on Sea Chaplains includes a list (225). A concise guide to events and to the ships involved is presented in an interesting and novel way (204).

Primary Sources. The activities of the two main record publishing bodies have continued. The Navy Records Society has produced five volumes relating wholly or in part to this period (6, 16, 76, 216 and *Naval Miscellany*, vol. V, individual contributions being noted separately). The U.S. Department of the Navy has continued its great *Naval Documents of the American Revolution* series (27, 158), and begun a new series on the War of 1812 (46). It has also published an interesting work on the editing of naval documents, including an important essay on historical aspects of the subject by Hattendorf (90). Finally, readers should note that documents are occasionally printed in the principal maritime historical journals, the *Mariner's Mirror* and *American Neptune*.

Histories. The one really important book encompassing the whole period and more is Paul Kennedy's general review of the rise and decline of British sea power (112). Graham outlines the association of sea power and empire (71), while Padfield is a useful detailed survey up to 1763 (169). Marcus adds a percipient study of eighteenth century sea war and maritime institutions (152).

Peacetime Policy and Diplomacy. Disappointingly little has been produced upon general naval and strategic policy, at least in book form. There are, however, numerous papers examining specific episodes and taking these by geographical area, a rather more satisfactory position is sometimes to be found. Barry Gough's three volumes (66-68), covering naval activities on the north west coasts of North America, are very thorough, while Graham on the China Seas (73) is a valuable contribution. The defense of India has also been usefully studied (105). More episodic are studies of the Baltic area (1, 49, 50), on the importance of Rio (7), on the reasons for the selection of Botany Bay (56, 57) and events in the Indian Ocean (103, 208). Haffenden (81) and Stout (210) outline naval influence on North America.

The importance of navies in peacetime as agents of diplomacy has been well discussed by the various papers of Tracy (231-234) and Webb (239, 241) for some of the lesser known but nevertheless illuminating diplomatic problems of the later eighteenth century. The few genuine "naval policy" essays are all nineteenth century. An account of one naval administration (8) adds to Hamilton's two thoughtful pieces (82, 85) and Rodger (186), while Lambert's "ship" book (124) must also be mentioned for its relations to naval policy.

War and Policy. While some useful work has been done on individual wars, nothing really significant has appeared, although important studies of parts of wars can be recorded. Perhaps most welcome is the work of Middleton on the higher command of the Seven Years' War (155-156), so long neglected by historians for no obvious reason except that Corbett apparently did his work so well as to be still highly regarded. The Revolutionary and Napoleonic Wars, also long without an overall review, have now been covered by Marcus' long awaited second volume (153), and by a welcome return to the naval field by C. Northcote Parkinson (170). Mahon's book on the War of 1812 (149) is, however, mainly military and its treatment of the sea war conventional. Padfield's contribution (168) is popular. In the second category, the parts of wars, we have two thorough volumes by Mackesy (144, 147) covering the years 1798-1802 and Glover's on the Napoleonic invasion threat (62), though the latter overlooks Keith's forces in the Channel. Both these authors tend to the military. For examinations of single campaigns, we have only one on the Nile campaign (132).

Articles, like the books, seem to ignore anything before 1756, a tendency also noticeable in other aspects of the subject. The exception is useful (148), pointing out the small effect of seapower on the 1745 rising. Neal (163) makes an attempt to arrive at the real cost of the Seven Years' War in both men and money. The American War, as always, has its adherents. Most interesting, perhaps, is Mackesy's speculation on whether the British could have won (145). Syrett has contributed a number of very useful papers on the early period (218-219, 221) and on logistical aspects (215, 218). Yeixa (246) discusses Samuel Graves' command in the early years. The long wars of 1793-1815 have produced a critical look at the effects of sea power (104), a study of sea power and the Peninsular War (99), two reviews of naval and commercial affairs in the North Sea and Baltic (196, 235), with a view of the neglected post-Trafalgar years (222), and an examination of Barham's management of the Admiralty (136). After 1815, the only new work has been a very interesting study (83) of the purposes of the Government in the Baltic campaign of 1854 and its relations with the Commander-in-Chief.

Tactics and Operations. The once-dominant topic of tactics and signals has only given rise to one recent work, Captain Creswell's useful book (38), while another of Syrett's papers outlines the general methods used in combined operations (217). Some of the articles do, however, touch upon tactical matters. Despite the popularity elsewhere of detailed examinations of celebrated or notorious events, only two fall within our scope, namely Bond on Walcheren (12) and Pope on Copenhagen 1801 (180), the latter a particularly comprehensive account of that famous occasion. Henderson has produced two books describing the activities of the somewhat neglected smaller types of warship in the 1793-1815 war (93-94). Once again, little is to be found prior to 1774; there is only an account, based on Spanish sources, of operations on the north coast of South America in 1743 (165) and a view of the Rochefort affair of 1757 (80).

A number of papers explore the detailed operations along the American coast during the 1770s (26, 36, 48, 157), whilst a useful, but unresolved, controversy developed over the events of the Battle of the Chesapeake and the other operations of Rodney, Hood and Thomas Graves (206-207, 14, 212). During the great wars of 1793-1815, the frigate position in 1798 is examined (5), some attention is deservedly given to the blockade of Brest (198, 201, 209), and to Nelson's doings in 1805 (226) and there is another Walcheren piece (25). In the War of 1812 attention is given to the British blockade and to what seemed at the time the horrific activities at New London (63-64), as well as a fresh view of Sir John Warren's squadron (137). Wood comments on Fortescue's view of Sir Alexander Cochrane in the New Orleans affair (245). The nineteenth century can only bring us a sound description of the little-known Parana operations of 1845-46 (122) and an account of the taking of the Taku Forts in 1858 (230).

Privateering; Defense of Trade. Some slight attention has been given to privateering, though the difficulty of finding sources appears to inhibit research in this field. Brown describes privateering activity in the Seven Years' War (21), but only one study of an individual port has appeared (229). Two contributions by Jamieson relate to American privateers in the West Indies in the American War (106-107). Raymond discusses the activities of Irish privateers on both sides, during the eighteenth century (184).

On the most important but somewhat neglected subject of the defence of trade, Crowhurst has written an interesting book, as well as a useful paper on convoys during the Seven Years' War (41-42). For the American War, Syrett has produced a book and two papers on subjects closely concerned with this topic (215, 218, 220). Finally, Jepsen includes interesting detail about the Baltic convoys in his examination of the disaster to the *St. George* and *Defence* in 1811 (108).

Manning and Personnel. The seemingly intractable problem of manning the Navy has been examined in detail and some of the press gang myths have been laid to rest. Bromley's N.R.S. publication of pamphlets (16) aired the intense political debate and he raised problems by shrewd questioning of current assumptions (17, 19). Gradish examined the political aspects in particular (69-70). A number of studies have looked at social conditions generally (4, 110) and some have looked at the more exotic (60-61, 188). Rodger's book (194) promises to be influential, containing many new ideas. However, all these studies have brought the subject away from the simplistic view of the uniformly harsh lot of the seaman. Rasor (182-183) takes the subject from the eighteenth century into the less fashionable nineteenth. An unusual work on religion in the Navy deserves wider circulation (11).

Little work has been done on naval medicine and health (248, 65), perhaps in the wake of Keevil, Lloyd and Coulter in the 1960s. Some gaps have been filled in naval education (213), and more is known about the Royal Naval Academy at Portsmouth (214, 228, 121), but this institution still lacks a general work and an assessment of its influence.

Administration and Dockyards. A much more complete picture is now emerging of the administrative base upon which the eighteenth and early nineteenth century navy operated. The post-1815 period, alas, still looks very bare. Work on the eighteenth century civil administration follows on from the pattern established by John Ehrman in the 1950s and Daniel Baugh in the 1960s. An authoritative and attractively-written survey of the Admiralty in general uses these ideas (185), while administration as a whole and the historians view of it has been considered in a bibliographical essay (119). Baugh has amplified his previous study of the Walpole period in a particularly full N.R.S. volume--a model of its kind (6). For the same period, an interesting thesis on the administration of the West Indies bases deserves publication (39). As with other aspects of the subject, the period of the American war has been well considered. The administrative effort of taking the war to America has been carefully examined (215). The dockyards have received a good deal of attention and Portsmouth has its own study for this period (121). More specialized aspects have also been examined including the visitations (78), task work and wage payments (79), appointments and promotions (114) and the always present problem of the government being relieved of its property by its employees (117). The period of peace between the American and Revolutionary Wars has been examined in relation to finance (240) and with reference to Charles Middleton (135), but a more general study needs to be done of this important period.

The dockyards in the Revolutionary and Napoleonic Wars have been comprehensively examined in a significant book by Morriss (162) which, put together with his other articles (159-161), leaves a good picture of a much more professional organization, particularly with the reform struggles of the St. Vincent period. An informative article on the politics of this period, confusing in the extreme, demonstrates the way in which the navy was at the very centre of British politics (15). Barham's part in them has also been reviewed (136). After this, little has been done though some pioneering studies of the mid nineteenth century of how the dockyard organizations were managed promise well for the future (24, 238).

An authoritative series of long articles by Coad (28-32) has established the industrial importance of dockyards much more widely than in the minds of mere scholars, a factor in the saving of Chatham dockyard when it closed as an operations base in 1984. These articles culminated in a book (33), though the authoritative scholarly study is still awaited. Evidence of a much wider public interest in dockyards is provided by the appearance of more general accounts of Chatham (141) and Devonport (22), while a general synthesis has also been attempted (142). Overseas, Halifax (205) and Port Royal, Jamaica (172) now have general histories.

Naval Stores. Since 1970 nothing to match the large studies of previous years, such as Bamford and Malone, can be reported, though economic historians, primarily Scandinavian, are producing very good work. Nothing, however, shakes the view that the Baltic was of the greatest significance for British naval power. Malone himself contributes to this view (150), while the shortage of hardwoods and Sir Robert Seppings' contribution has been examined (167). A useful illustrated booklet throws some light on the New England trade (151). A well documented thesis has been put forward that the search for new sources of timber and hemp affected the colonization of Australia (56).

Technical Developments. One of the most notable developments in the recent writing of naval history has been the analysis of ship design and shipbuilding. Moreover, in general, it has not been done for its own sake but related to strategic, political and naval considerations and out of this have come really worthwhile judgments on the state of British ship design, what the designers expected from their ships and how successful they were.
Early articles by Lavery on line-of-battle ships (127-128) and Gardiner on frigates (58-59) led to a major work by the former (129), which has already been influential and not only to technical historians. Howard provided a competent general survey (101). Special aspects such as masts and rigging (131), bomb vessels (174) and copper sheathing (115) fill the picture further, while useful general comments are found in Lyon (138). An unusual book, though slightly inaccurate, attempts to bring to life the building of a ship (43). The importance of one of the technical subjects in need of systematic treatment, that of naval ordnance, has been shown by a useful small work describing how vital improvements were made to British guns just before the Napoleonic Wars (3). A book on the building and working of the semaphore signalling system has been a valuable contribution (97). In the later period an important book describes the advent of the screw line of battleship (124), while articles on the introduction of the paddle frigate (123) and a review of British battleship design (20) are useful.

Biography. Biography has been disappointing. We have a further round of Nelson biographies (9, 13, 91, 133, 178, 237) of which Pocock might be mentioned for its attention to Nelson's earlier years, and two more on Cochrane, published simultaneously, and neither very satisfactory (74, 227). The explorers and surveyors have much the best of it, with books on Bligh (111), W.F.W. Owen (23) and Beaufort (55), the latter especially welcome. Other useful additions are on Peter Warren (75) and Hoste (177), while the naval service of William IV renders Ziegler's biography of that monarch (247) worthy of mention here. Otherwise only lesser figures are covered in articles (53, 96, 98, 109, 140, 171, 203).

Further Research. With the exception of Baugh's book on naval administration, admittedly comprehensive, the period up to the Seven Years War remains virtually untouched from almost every naval aspect, and still one has to turn to Richmond and Corbett. Thus the use of the navy in peacetime, always a weak subject in general, is particularly neglected in this period. Though there has been some useful work, more needs to be done on convoys and the protection of trade, while the present emphasis on social matters should surely not rule out further studies of operations, and even of tactics. Administratively, there are still questions to be resolved in the Seven Years War period, and in particular, the post-war administrations still offer many questions. Victualling, the Ordnance and the Treasurer of the Navy remain largely closed books. Modern biographies are still much needed for many of the principal figures, Wager, Norris, Boscawen, Kempenfelt, Howe, Jervis, Collingwwod and Duckworth all suggest themselves. Prize money and the finances and social background of sea officers would repay study, despite the articles of Bromley (18) and Fewster (52).

The post 1815 period has still received little attention, although general naval policy has been reviewed. Little is known about operations and the distribution of the navy and its support for the "Pax Britannica," the administrative developments, such as the abolition of the Navy Board and the reforms of Sir James Graham. The very large developments which took place in the dockyards and the application of steam power are largely unexplored. The flexibility and readiness of the Navy in adopting new ideas has been touched upon for the larger ships only, but it was the smaller vessels which were active.

BIBLIOGRAPHY

1. Aldridge, David. "Admiral Sir John Norris and the British naval expeditions to the Baltic Sea, 1715-1727." Unpublished London Ph.D. thesis, 1971.
2. Bach, John. "The Maintenance of Royal Navy Vessels in the Pacific Ocean, 1825-75." *Mariner's Mirror*, vol. 56 (1970), pp. 259-274.
3. Baker, H.A. *The Crisis in Naval Ordnance*. Greenwich: National Maritime Museum, 1983.
4. Barnett, Richard C. "The View from Below Deck: The British Navy, 1777-1781." *American Neptune*, vol. 38 (1978), pp. 92-100.
5. Barritt, M.K. "Nelson's Frigates, May to August 1798." *Mariner's Mirror*, vol. 58 (1972), pp. 281-295.
6. Baugh, Daniel A. *Naval Administration, 1715-1750*. London: Navy Records Society, 1977.
7. Bauss, Rudy. "Rio de Janeiro: Strategic Base for the Global Designs of the British Navy, 1777-1815," in *New Aspects of Naval History*. Craig L. Symonds, ed. Annapolis: Naval Institute Press, 1981, pp. 75-89.
8. Baxter, Colin F. "The Duke of Somerset and the creation of the British Ironclad Navy, 1859-66," *Mariner's Mirror*, vol. 63 (1977), pp. 279-284.

9. Bennett, Geoffrey. *Nelson the Commander*. London: Batsford, 1972.
10. ———. *The Battle of Trafalgar*. London: Batsford, 1977.
11. Blake, Richard Charles. "Aspects of Religion in the Royal Navy, c. 1770-c. 1870." University of Southampton M.Phil these 1980.
12. Bond, Gordon C. *The Grand Expedition*. Athens, Georgia: University of Georgia Press, 1979.
13. Bradford, Ernle. *Nelson: The Essential Hero*. London: Macmillan, 1977.
14. Breen, Kenneth. "Graves and Hood at the Chesapeake," *Mariner's Mirror*, vol. 66 (1980), pp. 53-65.
15. Breihan, John R. "The Addington Party and the Navy in British Politics, 1801-1806," in *New Aspects of Naval History*. Craig L. Symonds, ed. Annapolis: United States Naval Institute Press, 1981, pp. 163-189.
16. Bromley, J.S. *The Manning of the Royal Navy. Selected Public Pamphlets, 1693-1873*. London: Navy Records Society, 1974.
17. ———. "Away from Impressment; the idea of a Royal Naval Reserve, 1696-1896" in *Britain and the Netherlands* vol. 6, War and Society; Papers delivered to the sixth Anglo-Dutch Historical Conference, A.D. Duke & C.A. Tamse, ed., The Hague: Martinus Nighoff, 1978, pp. 168-188.
18. ———. "Prize Office and Prize Agency at Portsmouth, 1689-1748," in *Hampshire Studies*. John Webb, Nigel Yates and Sarah Peacock, eds. Portsmouth: City Records Office, 1981, pp. 168-188.
19. ———. "The British Navy and its Seamen after 1688: Notes for an Unwritten History" in *Charted and Uncharted Waters*, Sarah Palmer and Glyndwr Williams, eds. Greenwich: National Maritime Museum, 1981, pp. 148-163.
20. Brown, D.K. "British Battleship Design, 1840-1904," *Interdisciplinary Science Reviews*, vol. 6 (1981), pp. 79-93.
21. Brown, J.W. "British Privateering during the Seven Years War, 1756-1763," Exeter University M.A. thesis, 1978.
22. Burns, K.V. *The Devonport Dockyard Story*. Liskeard: Maritime Books, 1984.
23. Burrows, E.H. *Captain Owen of the African Survey, 1774-1857*. Rotterdam: A.A. Balkerma, 1979.
24. Casey, Neil. "An early organisational hegemony: methods of control in a Victorian naval dockyard," *Social Science Information*, vol. 23 (1984), pp. 677-700.
25. Christie, Carl. "The Royal Navy and the Walcheren Expedition of 1809" in *New Aspects of Naval History*, Craig L. Symonds, ed. Annapolis: Naval Institute Press, 1981, pp. 190-200.
26. Claderhead, William L. "British naval failure at Long Island: a lost opportunity in the American Revolution," *New York History*, vol. 57 (1976), pp. 321-338.
27. Clark, William Bell. *Naval Documents of the American Revolution*, vols. 1-4. Washington: Department of the Navy, 1964-1969 (see Morgan, William James).
28. Coad, Jonathan. "Chatham Ropeyard," *Post-Medieval Archaeology*, vol. 3, (1969), pp. 143-165.
29. ———. "The Chatham Mast Houses and Mould Loft." *Mariner's Mirror*, vol. 59 (1973), pp. 127-134.

30. ———. "Historic architecture of H.M. Naval Base, Portsmouth, 1700-1850." *Mariner's Mirror*, vol. 67 (1981), pp. 3-59.
31. ———. "Historic architecture of Chatham Dockyard, 1700-1850," *Mariner's Mirror*, vol. 68 (1982), pp. 133-188.
32. ———. "Historic architecture of H.M. Naval Base Devonport, 1689-1850," *Mariner's Mirror*, vol. 69 (1983), pp. 341-392.
33. ———. *Historic Architecture of the Royal Navy*. London: Gollancz, 1982.
34. Colledge, J.J. *Ships of the Royal Navy: An Historical Index*, vols. 1 & 2. Newton Abbot: David and Charles, 1969-70.
35. Collinge, J.M. *Office-Holders in Modern Britain, VII: Navy Board Officials, 1660-1832*. London: University of London, Institute of Historical Research, 1978.
36. Comtois, George. "The British Navy in the Delaware, 1775 to 1777," *American Neptune*, vol. 40 (1980), pp. 7-22.
37. Condon, Mary Ellen. "The Establishment of the Transport Board—A Subdivision of the Admiralty, 4 July 1794," *Mariner's Mirror*, vol. 58 (1972), pp. 69-84.
38. Creswell, John. *British Admirals of the Eighteenth Century: Tactics in Battle*. London: George Allen and Unwin, 1972.
39. Crewe, Duncan G. "British Naval Administration in the West Indies, 1739-48." Liverpool University Ph.D. thesis, 1978.
40. Crimmin, P.K. "Letters of Captain George Miller Mundy, 1797-1809," in *Naval Miscellany, V*, N.A.M. Rodger, ed. London: Navy Records Society, 1985, pp. 284-296.
41. Crowhurst, R.P. "The Admiralty and the Convoy System in the Seven Years War." *Mariner's Mirror*, vol. 57 (1971), pp. 163-173.
42. ———. *The Defence of British Trade, 1689-1815*. Folkestone: Dawson, 1977.
43. Dodds, James and Moore, James. *Building the Wooden Fighting Ship*. London: Hutchinson, 1984.
44. Douglas, W.A.B. "The Anatomy of Naval Incompetence: The Provincial Marine in the Defence of Upper Canada, before 1813." *Ontario History* (1979), pp. 3-25.
45. Duffy, Michael. "The Foundations of British Naval Power," in *The Military Revolution and the State, 1500-1800*, M. Duffy, ed. Exeter: Exeter University, 1980, pp. 49-85.
46. Dudley, William S. *The Naval War of 1812: A Documentary History*, vol. 1, Washington: Naval Historical Center, 1985.
47. Emsley, Clive. "The Recruitment of Petty Offenders during the French wars, 1793-1815." *Mariner's Mirror*, vol. 66 (1980), pp. 199-208.
48. Farley, M. Foster. "The Battle of Sullivan's Island, 1776." *History Today*, vol. 26 (1976), pp. 83-91.
49. Feldbaek, Ole. "The Anglo-Danish Convoy Conflict of 1800: A Study of Small Power Policy and Neutrality." *Scandinavian Journal of History*, vol. 2 (1977), pp. 161-182.
50. ———. *Denmark and the Armed Neutrality, 1800-1801*, Copenhagen: Akademisk Forlag, 1980.
51. Fellowes, J. "Shipbuilding at Sheerness: The Period 1750-1802." *Mariner's Mirror*, vol. 60 (1974), pp. 73-83.
52. Fewster, J.M. "Prize-money and the British Expedition to the

West Indies of 1793-4," *Journal of Imperial and Commonwealth History*, vol. 12 (1983-4), pp. 1-28.
53. Franks, R.D. "Admiral Sir Richard Onslow," *Mariner's Mirror*, vol. 67 (1981), pp. 327-337.
54. Frese, Joseph R. "Smuggling, the Navy and the Customs Service, 1763-1772," in *Seafaring in Colonial Massachusetts*, Frederick S. Allis Jr. ed. Boston: The Colonial Society of Massachusetts, 1980, pp. 199-212.
55. Friendly, Alfred. *Beaufort of the Admiralty. The Life of Sir Francis Beaufort*. London: Hutchinson, 1977.
56. Frost, Alan. "The Choice of Botany Bay: The Scheme to supply the East Indies with Naval Stores," *Australian Economic History Review*, 15 (1975), pp. 1-20.
57. ———. *Convicts and Empire: A Naval Question, 1776-1811*. Melbourne: Oxford University Press, 1980.
58. Gardiner, Robert. "The first English frigates," *Mariner's Mirror*, vol. 61 (1975), pp. 163-172.
59. ———. "The frigate designs of 1755-57," *Mariner's Mirror*, vol. 63 (1977), pp. 51-69.
60. Gilbert, Arthur N. "Buggery and the British Navy, 1700-1861," *Journal of Social History*, vol. 10 (1976), pp. 72-98.
61. ———. "Crime as Disorder: Criminality and the Symbolic Universe of the 18th century British Naval Officer" in *Changing Interpretations and New Sources in Naval History*, Robert William Love Jr., ed. New York and London: Garland Publishing Inc., 1980, pp. 110-122.
62. Glover, Richard. *Britain at Bay: Defence against Bonaparte, 1803-14*. London: George Allen and Unwin, 1973.
63. Goldenberg, Joseph A. "Blue lights and infernal machines: The British Blockade of New London," *Mariner's Mirror*, vol. 61 (1975), pp. 385-397.
64. ———. "The Royal Navy's blockade in New England waters, 1812-1815," *International History Review*, vol. 6 (1984), pp. 424-439.
65. Gordon, Eleanora C. "Scurvy and Anson's voyage round the world, 1740-1744: An Analysis of the Royal Navy's worst outbreak," *American Neptune*, vol. 44 (1984), pp. 155-166.
66. Gough, Barry M. *The Royal Navy and the North West Coast of North America, 1810-1914: A Study of British Maritime Ascendancy*. Vancouver: University of British Columbia, 1971.
67. ———. *Distant Dominion: Britain and the North West Coast of North America, 1579-1809*. Vancouver: University of British Columbia Press, 1980.
68. ———. *Gunboat Frontier: British Maritime Authority and the North West Coast Indians, 1846-1890*. Vancouver: University of British Columbia Press, 1984.
69. Gradish, Stephen F. "Wages and Manning: The Navy Act of 1758," *English Historical Review*, 93 (1978), pp. 46-67.
70. ———. *The Manning of the British Navy during the Seven Years War*. London: Royal Historical Society, 1980.
71. Graham, Gerald S. *Tides of Empire*. Montreal and London: McGill-Queens University Press, 1972.
72. ———. *The American War of Independence*. Greenwich: National Maritime Museum, 1976.

73. ――――. *The China Station: War and Diplomacy, 1830-1860*. Oxford: Oxford University Press, 1980.
74. Grimble, Ian. *The Sea Wolf: The Life of Admiral Cochrane*. London: Blond and Brigg, 1978.
75. Gwyn, Julian. *The Enterprising Admiral: The Personal Fortune of Admiral Sir Peter Warren*. Montreal and London: McGill Queens University Press, 1974.
76. ――――. *The Royal Navy and North America, 1736-1752*. London: Navy Records Society, 1976.
77. Haas, James M. "The Introduction of Task Work in Royal Naval Dockyards, 1775," *Journal of British Studies*, vol. 8 (1969), pp. 44-68.
78. ――――. "The Royal Dockyards: The Earliest Visitations and Reform, 1749-1778," *Historical Journal*, vol. 13 (1970), pp. 191-215.
79. ――――. "Methods of wage payment in the Royal Dockyards, 1775-1865," *Maritime History*, vol. 5 (1977), pp. 97-115.
80. Hackmann, W. Kent, "The British Raid on Rochefort, 1757," *Mariner's Mirror*, vol. 64 (1978), pp. 263-275.
81. Haffenden, P.S. "Community and Conflict: New England and the Royal Navy, 1689-1775," in *The American Revolution and the Sea*. Proceedings of the 14th International Conference of the International Commission for Maritime History. Greenwich: National Maritime Museum, 1974, pp. 84-93.
82. Hamilton, C.I. "The Royal Navy, Seapower and the screw ship of the line, 1845-60." University of Cambridge Ph.D. thesis, 1974.
83. ――――. "Sir James Graham, the Baltic campaign and War Planning at the Admiralty in 1854," *Historical Journal*, vol. 19 (1976), pp. 89-112.
84. ――――. "Naval Hagiography and the Victorian hero, *Historical Journal*, vol. 23 (1980), pp. 381-398.
85. ――――. "Naval power and diplomacy in the nineteenth century," *Journal of Strategic Studies*, vol. 3 (1980), pp. 74-88.
86. ――――. "Anglo-French seapower and the Declaration of Paris," *International History Review*, vol. 4 (1982), pp. 166-190.
87. ――――. "The Royal Navy, la Royale, and the militarisation of naval warfare, 1840-1870," *Journal of Strategic Studies*, vol. 6 (1983), pp. 182-212.
88. ――――. "Selections from the Phinn Committee of Inquiry, 1855," in *Naval Miscellany V*. N.A.M. Rodger, ed. London: Navy Records Society, 1985, pp. 371-438.
89. Harland, John. *Seamanship in the Age of Sail*. London: Conway Maritime Press, 1984.
90. Hattendorf, J.B. "Purpose and contribution in editing naval documents: A General Appreciation," in *Editing Naval Documents: An Historical Appreciation*. Washington: Naval Historical Center, 1984, pp. 43-61.
91. Hattersley, Roy. *Nelson*. London: Weidenfeld & Nicholson, 1974.
92. Heaps, Leo. *Log of the Centurion*. London: Hart-Davis, MacGibbon, 1973.
93. Henderson, James. *The Frigates: An Account of the Lesser Warships of the Wars from 1793 to 1815*. London: Adlard Coles, 1970.

94. ─────. *Sloops and Brigs: An Account of the Smallest Vessels of the Royal Navy during the Great Wars 1793-1815*. London: Adlard Coles, 1972.
95. Hills, B.F. "Shipbuilding for the Royal Navy at Sandwich in the Eighteenth Century," *Archaeologia Cantana*, vol. 94 (1978), pp. 195-230.
96. Hinchliffe, G. "Some Letters of Sir John Norris," *Mariner's Mirror*, vol. 56 (1970), pp. 77-84.
97. Holmes, T.W. *The Semaphore: The Story of the Admiralty-to-Portsmouth Shutter Telegraph and Semaphore Lines 1796 to 1847*. Ilfracombe: Arthur H. Stockwell, 1983.
98. Hopkinson, David. "The Naval Career of Jane Austen's brother," *History Today*, vol. 26 (1976), pp. 576-583.
99. Horward, Donald D. "British seapower and its influence upon the Peninsular War," *Naval War College Review*, vol. 31 (1978), pp. 54-71.
100. Hough, Richard. *Captain Bligh and Mr. Christian: The Men and the Mutiny*. London: Cassell, 1979.
101. Howard, Frank. *Sailing Ships of War, 1400-1860*. London: Conway Maritime Press, 1979.
102. Hughes, Quentin. *Britain in the Mediterranean and the Defence of her Naval Stations*. Liverpool: Penpaled Books, 1981.
103. Ingram, Edward. "A Scare of Seaborne Invasion: The Royal Navy at the Strait of Hormuz, 1807-1808," *Military Affairs*, vol. 46 (1982), pp. 64-68.
104. ─────. "Illusions of Victory: The Nile, Copenhagen and Trafalgar revisited," *Military Affairs*, vol. 48 (1984), pp. 140-143.
105. ─────. *In Defence of British India: Great Britain in the Middle East, 1775-1842*, London: Frank Cass, 1984.
106. Jamieson, Alan G. "Admiral James Young and the 'Pirateers', 1777," *Mariner's Mirror*, vol. 65 (1979), pp. 69-75.
107. ─────. "American privateers in the Leeward Islands, 1776-1778," *American Neptune*, vol. 43 (1983), pp. 20-30.
108. Jepsen, Palle Uhd. *St. George og Defence*. Esbjerg: Fiskeri og Søfartsmuseet, 1985.
109. Jones, A.G.E. "Sir Thomas Slade, 1703/4-1771," *Mariner's Mirror*, vol. 63 (1977), pp. 224-226.
110. Kemp, Peter K. *The British Sailor: A Social History of the Lower Deck*. London: Dent, 1971.
111. Kennedy, Gavin. *Bligh*. London: Duckworth, 1978.
112. Kennedy, Paul M. *The Rise and Fall of British Naval Mastery*. London: Allen Lane, 1976.
113. Keppel, Sonia. *Three Brothers at Havana 1762*. Salisbury: Michael Russell, 1981.
114. Knight, R.J.B. "Sandwich, Middleton and Dockyard Appointments," *Mariner's Mirror*, vol. 57 (1971), pp. 175-192.
115. ─────. "The Introduction of Copper Sheathing into the Royal Navy 1779-1786," *Mariner's Mirror*, vol. 59 (1973), pp. 299-309.
116. ─────. "The Performance of the Royal Dockyards in England during the American War of Independence," in *The American Revolution and the Sea*. Proceedings of the 14th International Conference of the International Commission for

Maritime History. Greenwich: National Maritime Museum, 1974, pp. 139-144.

117. ―――. "Pilfering and theft from the Dockyards at the time of the American War of Independence," *Mariner's Mirror*, vol. 61, pp. 215-225.

118. ―――. *Guide to the Manuscripts in the National Maritime Museum*, vol. I, *The Personal Collections*. London: Mansell, 1977, vol. II, *Public Records, Business Records and Artificial Collections*. London: Mansell, 1980.

119. ―――. "Civilians and the Navy, 1660-1832," in *Sea Studies: Essays in Honour of Basil Greenhill*, P.G.W. Annis, ed. Greenwich: National Maritime Museum, 1983, pp. 63-70.

120. ―――. "The Building and Maintenance of the British fleet during the Anglo-French Wars, 1685-1815," in *Marines de Guerre Europeenes XVII-XVIIIe siecles*. Martine Acerra, Jose Merino and Jean Meyer, ed. Paris: Presses de l'Universite de Paris-Sorbonne, 1985, pp. 35-50.

121. ―――. *Portsmouth Dockyard in the American War of Independence: the Dockyard Records, 1774-1783*. Portsmouth: City of Portsmouth, 1986.

122. Laing, E.A.M. "The Royal Navy in the River Parana during the Allied Intervention," *American Neptune*, vol. 36 (1976), pp. 125-143.

123. ―――. "The Introduction of Paddle Frigates into the Royal Navy," *Mariner's Mirror*, vol. 66 (1980), pp. 331-343.

124. Lambert, Andrew D. *Battleships in Transition: The Creation of the Steam Battlefleet, 1850-1860*. London: Conway Maritime Press, 1984.

125. ―――. "Sir Henry Keppel's Account, Capture of Bomarsund, August 1854," in *Naval Miscellany V*. N.A.M. Rodger, ed. London: Navy Records Society, 1985, pp. 354-370.

126. ―――. *H.M.S. Warrior*. London: Conway Maritime Press, 1986.

127. Lavery, Brian. "The Origins of the 74-gun ship," *Mariner's Mirror*, vol. 63 (1977), pp. 335-350.

128. ―――. "The Rebuilding of British Warships, 1690-1740, parts 1 & 2, *Mariner's Mirror*, vol. 66 (1980), pp. 5-14, 113-127.

129. ―――. *The Ship of the Line: The Development of the Battle Fleet 1650-1850*. 2 vols. London: Conway Maritime Press, 1983, 1984.

130. ―――. *The 74-gun ship Bellona*. London: Conway Maritime Press, 1985.

131. Lees, James. *The Masting and Rigging of English Ships of War, 1625-1860*. London: Conway Maritime Press, 1979.

132. Christopher Lloyd. *The Nile Campaign--Nelson and Napoleon in Egypt*. Newton Abbot: David & Charles, 1973.

133. ―――. *Nelson and Sea Power*. London: English University Press, 1973.

134. ―――. "Victualling of the Fleet in the Eighteenth and Nineteenth centuries," in *Starving Sailors*. J. Watt, E.J. Freeman and W.F. Bynum, ed., Greenwich: National Maritime Museum 1981, pp. 9-15.

135. Lloyd Philips, I. "The Evangelical Administrator: Sir Charles Middleton at the Navy Board, 1778-1790." University of Oxford Ph.D. thesis, 1974.

136. ―――. "Lord Barham at the Admiralty," *Mariner's Mirror*, vol. 64 (1978), pp. 217-233.
137. Lohnes, Barry J. "British Naval Problems at Halifax during the War of 1812," *Mariner's Mirror*, vol. 59 (1973), pp. 317-333.
138. Lyon, D.J. "British Warships: Types and Building Policy, 1688-1830," in *Les Marines de Guerre Europeennes XVII-XVIIIe siecles*, Martine Acerra, Jose Merino & Jean Meyer, ed., Paris: Presses de l'Universite de Paris-Sorbonne, 1985, pp. 147-164.
139. Maber, John M. "The Steam Engine and the Royal Navy," *Warship*, vol. 5 (1982), pp. 93-100.
140. McAteer, William. "Admiral Sir Charles Adam," *Mariner's Mirror*, vol. 63 (1977), pp. 264-278.
141. MacDougall, Philip. *The Chatham Dockyard Story*. Rochester: Rochester Press, 1981.
142. ―――. *Royal Dockyards*. Newton Abbot: David & Charles, 1982.
143. McGowan, A.P. "Captain Cook's Ships," *Mariner's Mirror*, vol. 65 (1979), pp. 109-118.
144. Mackesy, Piers. *Statesmen at War: The Strategy of Overthrow, 1798-1799*. London: Longman, 1974.
145. ―――. "Could the British have won the War of Independence?" Bland-Lee Lectures in History, *Clark University Journal* (1975), pp. 1-30.
146. ―――. "Problems of an Amphibious Power: Britain against France, 1793-1815," *Naval War College Review*, vol. 30 (1978), pp. 16-25.
147. ―――. *War without Victory: The Downfall of Pitt, 1799-1802*. Oxford: Clarendon Press, 1984.
148. McLynn, F.J. "Sea Power and the Jacobite Rising of 1745," *Mariner's Mirror*, vol. 67 (1981), pp. 163-172.
149. Mahon, John K. *The War of 1812*. Gainesville: University of Florida Press, 1972.
150. Malone, Joseph J. "England and the Baltic Naval Stores Trade in the Seventeenth and Eighteenth centuries," *Mariner's Mirror*, vol. 58 (1972), pp. 375-396.
151. Manning, Samuel F. *New England Masts and the King's Broad Arrow*. Greenwich: National Maritime Museum, 1980.
152. Marcus G.J. *A Naval History of England: The Age of Nelson*. London: Allen & Unwin, 1971.
153. ―――. *Heart of Oak. A Survey of British Sea Power in the Georgian Era*, Oxford: Oxford University Press, 1975.
154. May, W.E. *The Boats of Men of War*. Greenwich: National Maritime Museum, 1975.
155. Middleton, Richard. "Pitt, Anson and the Admiralty, 1756-1761," *History*, vol. 55 (1970), pp. 189-198.
156. ―――. *The Bells of Victory: The Pitt-Newcastle Ministry and the Conduct of the Seven Years' War, 1757-1762*. Cambridge: University Press, 1985.
157. Millar, John F. (ed.) "A British Account of the Siege of Rhode Island, 1778," *Rhode Island History*, vol. 83 (1979), pp. 79-85.
158. Morgan, William James. (ed.) *Naval Documents of the American Revolution*, vols. 5-8 (1776-1777) and atlas, Washington:

Department of the Navy, 1970-1980 (see Clark, William Bell).
159. Morriss, Roger A. "Labour Relations in the Royal Dockyards, 1801-1805," *Mariner's Mirror*, vol. 62 (1976), pp. 337-346.
160. ————. "Samuel Bentham and the Management of the Royal Dockyards," *Bulletin of the Institute of Historical Research*, vol. 54 (1981), pp. 226-240.
161. ————. "St. Vincent and Reform, 1801-1804," *Mariner's Mirror*, vol. 69 (1983), pp. 269-290.
162. ————. *The Royal Dockyards during the Revolutionary and Napoleonic Wars*. Leicester: University Press, 1983.
163. Neal, Larry D. "Interpreting Power and Profit in Economic History: A Case Study of the Seven Years' War," *Journal of Economic History*, vol. 37 (1977), pp. 20-35.
164. ————. "The Cost of Impressment during the Seven Years' War," *Mariner's Mirror*, vol. 64 (1978), pp. 45-62.
165. Ogelsby, J.C.M. "The British Attacks on the Caracas Coast 1743," *Mariner's Mirror*, vol. 58 (1972), pp. 27-40.
166. Oppenheim, M.M. *The Maritime History of Devon*. Exeter: University of Exeter, 1968.
167. Packard, J.J. "Sir Robert Seppings and the Timber Problem," *Mariner's Mirror*, vol. 64 (1978), pp. 145-156.
168. Padfield, Peter. *Nelson's War*. London: Hart-Davis, MacGibbon, 1976.
169. ————. *Tide of Empires: Decisive Naval Campaigns in the Rise of the West*, vol. II, *1654-1763*. London: Routledge & Kegan Paul, 1982.
170. Parkinson, C. Northcote. *Britannia Rules: The Classic Age of Naval History, 1793-1815*. London: Weidenfeld & Nicholson, 1977.
171. Parry, Ann. *The Admirals Fremantle*. London: Chatto & Windus, 1971.
172. Pawson, Michael and Buisseret, David. *Port Royal, Jamaica*. Oxford: Clarendon Press, 1975.
173. Pearsall, A.W.H. "The Bombardment of Acre, November 3 1840," *Sefunin*, vol. 2 (1967-8), pp. 50-55.
174. ————. "Bomb Vessels" *Polar Record*, vol. 16 (1973), pp. 781-788.
175. ————. "Lord Anson: Sailor-Statesman or Not?" in *Actes du 7e Coloque International d'Histoire Militaire*, Abigail T. Siddall, ed., Manhattan, Kansas: Sunflower University Press, 1984, pp. 270-279.
176. ————. "Naval Aspects of the Landings on the French Coast, 1758" in *Naval Miscellany V*, N.A.M. Rodger ed., London: Navy Records Society, 1985, pp. 207-243.
177. Pocock, Tom. *Remember Nelson: The Life of Captain Sir William Hoste*. London: Collins, 1977.
178. ————. *The Young Nelson in the Americas*. London: Collins, 1980.
179. Poole, Eric. "The Letters of Midshipman E.A. Noel, 1818-1822," in *Naval Miscellany V*, N.A.M. Rodger ed., London: Navy Records Society, 1985, pp. 330-353.
180. Pope, Dudley. *The Great Gamble: Nelson at Copenhagen*. London: Weidenfeld & Nicolson, 1972.

181. ─────. *Life in Nelson's Navy.* London: George Allen & Unwin, 1981.
182. Rasor, Eugene L. *Reform in the Royal Navy: A Social History of the Lower Deck, 1850-1880.* Hamden, Connecticut: Archon Books, 1976.
183. ─────. "The Manning Question in the Royal Navy in the Early Ironclad Era," in *Changing Interpretations and New Sources in Naval History.* Robert William Love Jr. ed., New York and London: Garland Publishing Inc., 1980, pp. 208-215.
184. Raymond R.J. "Privateers and privateering off the Irish coast in the Eighteenth Century," *Irish Sword,* vol. 18 (1977), pp. 60-69.
185. Rodger, N.A.M. *The Admiralty.* Lavenham: Terence Dalton, 1979.
186. ─────. "British Naval Thought and Naval Policy, 1820-1890: Strategic Thought in an era of Technological Change," in *New Aspects of Naval History.* Craig L. Symonds ed., Annapolis: Naval Institute Press 1981, pp. 140-152.
187. ─────. *Articles of War: The Statutes which Governed our Fighting Navies 1661, 1749 and 1886.* Portsmouth: Kenneth Mason, 1982.
188. ─────. "Stragglers and Deserters from the Royal Navy during the Seven Years' War," *Bulletin of the Institute of Historical Research,* vol. 57 (1984), pp. 56-79.
189. ─────. *Naval Records for Genealogists.* London: Public Records Office, 1984.
190. ─────. "The Victualling of the British Navy during the Seven Years' War," *Bulletin du Centre d'Histoire des Espaces Atlantiques,* no. 2 (1985), pp. 37-53.
191. ─────. "Patronage and competence," in *Les Marines de Guerres Europeennes XVII-XVIIIe siecles.* Martine Acerra, Jose Merino and Jean Meyer, ed., Paris: Presses de l'Universite de Paris-Sorbonne, 1985, pp. 237-248.
192. ─────. "The Douglas Papers, 1760-1762," in *Naval Miscellany V,* N.A.M. Rodger, ed., London: Navy Records Society, 1985, pp. 244-283.
193. ─────. "Le Scorbut dans le Royal Navy pendant le Guerre de Sept Ans," in *L'homme et la me dans l'Europe du Nord Quest de l'Antiquite á nos jours.* Alain Lottin, Jean-Claude Hocquet & Stephane Lebecq. *Nevue du Nord,* estra no, 1986.
194. ─────. *The Wooden World: An Anatomy of the Georgian Navy.* London: Collins, 1986.
195. Roland, A. *Underwater Warfare in the Age of Sail.* Bloomington and London: Indiana University Press, 1978.
196. Ryan, A.N. "Trade Between Enemies: Maritime Resistance to the Continental System in the Northern Seas, 1808-1812," in *The North Sea.* Arne Bang Anderson, Basil Greenhill and Egil Harald Grude, ed., Oslo: Norwegian University Press, 1985, pp. 181-194.
197. ─────. "Documents relating to the Copenhagen operation, 1807," in *Naval Miscellany V,* N.A.M. Rodger ed., London: Navy Records Society, 1985, pp. 297-329.
198. ─────. "The Royal Navy and the Blockade of Brest, 1689-1805: Theory and Practice," in *Les Marines de Guerre Europeennes XVII-XVIIIe siecles.* Martine Acerra, Jose Merino and Jean

Meyer, ed., Paris: Presses de l'Universite de Paris-Sorbonne, 1985, pp. 175-193.
199. Sainty, J.C. *Office-holders in Modern Britain: IV: Admiralty Officials, 1660-1870.* London: Institute of Historical Research, The Athlone Press, 1975.
200. Sanderson, Michael. *Catalogue of the Library of the National Maritime Museum. Naval History: Part 1.* London: Her Majesty's Stationery Office, 1976.
201. Schaber, J.R. "Admiral Sir William Cornwallis and the Blockade of Brest, 1801-1806," University of Oxford B.Litt., thesis, 1977.
202. Servies, James A. (ed.) *The Log of H.M.S Mentor 1780-1781.* Pensacola: University Presses of Florida, 1982.
203. Severn, Derek. "Nelson's Hardy," *History Today*, vol. 27 (1977), pp. 505-512.
204. Shrubb, R.E.A. and Sainsbury, A.B. *The Royal Navy Day by Day.* Fontwell: Centaur Press, 1979.
205. Smith, Marilyn Gurney. *The King's Yard: An Illustrated History of the Halifax Dockyard.* Halifax: Nimbus Publishing, 1985.
206. David Spinney. "Sir Samuel Hood at St. Kitts: A Reassessment," *Mariner's Mirror*, vol. 58 (1972), pp. 179-182.
207. ———. "Rodney and the Saints: A Reassessment," *Mariner's Mirror*, vol. 68 (1982), pp. 377-389.
208. Spray, William A. "British Surveys in the Chagos Archipelago and Attempts to form a settlement at Diego Garcia in the late 18th Century," *Mariner's Mirror*, vol. 56 (1970), pp. 59-76.
209. Steer, D.M. "The Blockade of Brest by the Royal Navy, 1793-1805," unpublished University of Liverpool M.A. thesis, 1971.
210. Stout, Neil R. *The Royal Navy in America 1760-1775.* Annapolis: Naval Institute Press, 1973.
211. Stuart, Vivian and Eggleston, George T. *His Majesty's Sloop-of-War 'Diamond Rock'.* London: Robert Hale, 1978.
212. Sulivan, J.A. "Graves and Hood," *Mariner's Mirror*, vol. 69 (1983), pp. 175-194.
213. Sullivan, F.B. "The Naval Schoolmaster during the Eighteenth century and the early Nineteenth century," *Mariner's Mirror*, vol. 62 (1976), pp. 311-326.
214. ———. "The Royal Academy at Portsmouth, 1729-1806," *Mariner's Mirror*, vol. 63 (1977), pp. 311-326.
215. Syrett, David. *Shipping and the American War 1775-1783: A Study of British Transport Organisation.* London: Athlone Press, 1970.
216. ———, (ed.) *The Siege and Capture of Havana 1762.* London: Navy Records Society, 1971.
217. ———. "The Methodology of British Amphibious Operations during the Seven Years' and American Wars," *Mariner's Mirror*, vol. 58 (1972), pp. 269-280.
218. ———. "Lord George Germain and the Protection of Military Storeships 1775-1778," *Mariner's Mirror*, vol. 60 (1974), pp. 395-405.
219. ———. "The Royal Navy's role in the attempt to suppress the revolt in America, 1775-1776," in *The American Revolution and the Sea.* Proceedings of the 14th International Confer-

ence of the International Commission for Maritime History. Greenwich: National Maritime Museum, 1974, pp. 10-22.
220. ―――. "The Organisation of British Trade Convoys during the American War, 1775-1783," *Mariner's Mirror*, vol. 62 (1976), pp. 169-181.
221. ―――. "Defeat at Sea: The Impact of American naval operations upon the British, 1775-1778," in *Maritime Dimensions of the American Revolution*. Washington: Naval History Division, Department of the Navy, 1977, pp. 13-22.
222. ―――. "The Role of the Royal Navy in the Napoleonic Wars after Trafalgar, 1805-1814," *Naval War College Review*, vol. 32 (1979), pp. 71-94.
223. ―――. "A Checklist of Admiral Lord Howe manuscripts in United States Archives and Libraries," *Mariner's Mirror*, vol. 67 (1981), pp. 273-284.
224. ―――. *Neutral Rights and the War in the Narrow Seas, 1778-1782*. Fort Leavenworth, Kansas: Combat Studies Institute, 1985.
225. Taylor, Gordon. *The Sea Chaplains*. Oxford: Oxford Illustrated Press, 1978.
226. Terraine, John. *Trafalgar*. London: Sidgwick & Jackson, 1976.
227. Thomas, Donald. *Cochrane, Britannia's Last Sea King*. London: Andre Deutsch, 1978.
228. Thomas, J.H. "Portsmouth Naval Academy: An Educational Experiment examined," *Portsmouth Archives Review*, vol. 3 (1978), pp. 10-39.
229. Timewell, H.C. "Guernsey Privateers," *Mariner's Mirror*, vol. 56 (1970), pp. 199-218.
230. ―――. "The First Reduction of the Taku Forts, 1858," *Mariner's Mirror*, vol. 63 (1977), pp. 163-171.
231. Tracy, Nicholas. "Parry of a Threat to India 1768-74," *Mariner's Mirror*, vol. 59 (1973), pp. 35-48.
232. ―――. "The Gunboat Diplomacy of the Government of George Grenville 1764-1765: the Honduran, Turk's Island and Gambian Incidents." *Historical Journal*, vol. 17 (1974), pp. 711-731.
233. ―――. "The Administration of the Duke of Grafton and the French Invasion of Corsica in 1768." *Eighteenth Century Studies*, vol. 8 (1974), pp. 169-182.
234. ―――. "The Falklands Islands crisis of 1770; Use of Naval Force." *English Historical Review*, vol. 90 (1975), pp. 40-75.
235. Trulsson, Sven G. *British and Swedish policies and strategies in the Baltic after the Peace of Tilsit in 1807: A Study of Decision-Making*. Lund: Bibliotheca Historica Lundensis, 1976.
236. Unger, Richard W. "Design and Construction of European Warships in the Seventeenth and Eighteenth Centuries," in *Les Marines de Guerre Europeennes XVII-XVIIIe siecles*. Martine Acerra, Jose Merino and Jean Meyer, ed., Paris: Presses de l'Université de Paris-Sorbonne, 1985, pp. 21-34.
237. Walder, David. *Nelson*. London: Hamish Hamilton, 1978.
238. Waters, Mavis. "The Dockyard Work-force: A picture of Chatham Dockyard ca. 1860," *Archaeologia Cantiana*, vol. 97 (1981), pp. 79-94.

239. Webb, Paul L.C. "The Naval Aspects of the Nootka Sound Crisis," *Mariner's Mirror*, vol. 61 (1975), pp. 133-154.
240. ⸻. "The Rebuilding and Repair of the Fleet, 1783-1793," *Bulletin of the Institute of Historical Research*, vol. 50 (1977), pp. 194-209.
241. ⸻. "Seapower in the Ochakov Affair of 1791," *International History Review*, vol. 2 (1980), pp. 13-33.
242. Whiteley, W.H. "The British Navy and the Siege of Quebec, 1775-1776," *Canadian Historical Review*, vol. 61 (1980), pp. 3-27.
243. Williams, Glyndwr (ed.) *A Voyage round the World, by George Anson*. Oxford: University Press, 1974.
244. Winton, John. *Hurrah for the Life of a Sailor*. London: Michael Joseph, 1977.
245. Wood, G.N. "The Admiral should have been court-martialled and shot," *Army Quarterly*, vol. 106 (1976), pp. 236-242.
246. Yeixa, Donald A. "Vice-Admiral Samuel Graves and the North American squadron 1774-1776," *Mariner's Mirror*, vol. 62 (1976), pp. 371-385.
247. Ziegler, Philip. *King William IV*. London: Collins, 1972.
248. Zuckerman, Arnold. "Scurvy and the Ventilation of Ships in the Royal Navy: Samuel Sutton's Contribution," *Eighteenth Century Studies*, vol. 10 (1976), pp. 222-234.
249. Zulueta, Julian de, "Trafalgar--the Spanish view," *Mariner's Mirror*, vol. 66 (1980), pp. 293-318.

VIII

THE ROYAL NAVY, 1860-1919

Jon Tetsuro Sumida

Many books and articles on the Royal Navy in the late nineteenth and early twentieth century had been written by 1971. Naval officers, naval journalists, and politicians associated with naval affairs generated a host of memoirs, biographies of near contemporaries, and other works. To these must be added the contributions of naval historians, a number of whom deserve mention here. G.A. Ballard (101), Oscar Parkes, Edgar March, James Phinney Baxter, and Bernard Brodie wrote important studies of naval technology. William Ashworth published a pioneering article that examined economic aspects of British naval administration (1). Frederic Manning, A. Temple Patterson, Geoffrey Bennett, Peter Padfield, Martin Gilbert, and Richard Hough produced significant naval biographies. D.M. Schurman gave serious consideration to the development of British naval strategic thought. Sir Julian Corbett and Sir Henry Newbolt covered naval operations during the First World War in a multi-volume official history that is recognized as a classic. Arthur J. Marder, A. Temple Patterson, Peter Kemp, Martin Gilbert, Stephen Roskill, and E.W.R. Lumby edited valuable collections of documents. G.S. Graham formulated a provocative analysis of the political context of Britain's nineteenth century maritime ascendancy. The distinguished scholarly monographs of Arthur J. Marder provided a detailed and wide-ranging account of British naval policy from the 1880s to 1919, aspects of which were given fuller treatment in an article by R.T.B. Langhorne (46) and in books by Paul Halpern (135) and Samuel Williamson (213). (Full references can be found in the chapters written by Ruddock F. Mackay and Arthur J. Marder in the parent to this volume, except for those accompanied by numbered references to the bibliographical listing of the present work.)

Since 1971, the historical literature on the Royal Navy from 1860 to 1919 has undergone substantial growth. Works on naval materiel, in particular, have proliferated. Historians such as D.K. Brown (10, 12, 108), Ian Buxton (112), N.J.M. Campbell (13-17, 113-114), Norman Friedman (129), Antony Preston (175, 176), John Roberts (185-186), and Stanley Sandler (82, 193), have produced first-rate studies of warship design based in large part upon careful archival research and informed in some cases by professional technical training and experience. Willem Hackman (134), Sir Arthur Hezlet (138), Peter Hodges (139), Peter Padfield (167), and Geoffrey Till (206) have published books and Alan Cowpe (18) and Nathan Okun (67-69) informative articles on naval weaponry and other equipment.

J.J. Colledge and F.J. Dittmar (125), Robert Gardiner and Randal Gray (130), and Chesneau and Eugene M. Kolesnik (117) have compiled or edited reference volumes that provide comprehensive coverage of the warships of the Royal Navy. Three warship pictorial series--*Warships in Profile*, *Warship Monographs*, and *Ensign*--were begun and then sadly discontinued, but a fourth series, *Anatomy of the Ship*, whose first release by John Roberts was devoted to H.M.S. *Hood* (186), is well underway, and *Warship* and *Warship International*, two fine quarterly journals that have published a good deal on the Royal Navy in the late nineteenth and early twentieth century, continue to flourish.

Several historical works on naval materiel by authors mentioned above deserve special comment. Sandler's scholarly account of the development of the Royal Navy's ironclad fleet during the 1860s fills a wide gap in the literature. Friedman's historical study of the factors that determined the design of capital ships provides even the technically inexperienced reader with an accessible introduction to a complex and significant subject. Campbell's comparative study of British and German battle cruiser development (114) and Buxton's monograph on big-gun monitors are outstanding examples of warship studies that combine generous illustration, informed technical discussion, and perceptive operational history. Hodges' monograph on battleship main armament, Willem Hackmann's treatise on the development of sonar, and Nathan Okun's articles on warship armor have established new standards of technical sophistication and detail for writing on naval equipment. Padfield's history of naval gunnery was based upon considerable archival research and remains the best general study of naval gunnery, its popular and pictorial format notwithstanding. Conway Maritime Press should be recognized not only for its publication of many of the excellent works on naval materiel that have appeared since 1970 but in particular for their series of warship reference volumes, *Conway's All the World's Fighting Ships* (117, 130), which provide comprehensive coverage, detailed statistical information, and useful historical discussion, with relatively few errors.

Several biographies of major naval figures have appeared since 1971. Ruddock Mackay's biography of Sir John Fisher, the centrally important and highly controversial naval administrator (154), supercedes the earlier works by Reginald Bacon and Richard Hough. Although there is more to be said on the subject of Fisher's technical, tactical, and strategic thinking and its effect on Admiralty policy, Mackay's meticulously researched and carefully reasoned account is likely to remain standard for a long time to come. Studies of Winston Churchill by William Manchester (158), Ted Morgan (161), and Henry Pelling (171), have not extended the work of Randolph Churchill's authorized biography insofar as his father's career as First Lord before and during the First World War is concerned. John Winton's biography of Sir John Jellicoe, a wartime commander of the Grand Fleet and First Sea Lord, is certainly readable and not without insight (215), but serious readers should consult the scholarly biography by A. Temple Patterson. Stephen Roskill's biography of Sir David Beatty, the commander of the battle cruiser force at Jutland and afterwards Jellicoe's successor as commander of the Grand Fleet, on the other hand, was based upon the subject's private papers, which had previously not been freely available to scholars, and is the first critical study of a naval officer about whom there has been much debate (192). Roskill's last book reveals much about Beatty's personal life that had not been known though perhaps surmised, and provides an account of the battle of Jutland that was well-informed by the recent work of other historians. And A. Temple Paterson has contributed a solid account of the life of Sir Reginald Tyrwhitt, the energetic commodore of the Harwich force from 1914 to 1918 (170).

In addition, there have been a number of notable works published on less familiar but nevertheless significant persons connected with the Royal Navy. D.M. Schurman's biography of Sir Julian Corbett, the influential naval historian and theorist (195), and Barry Hunt's biography of Admiral Sir Herbert Richmond, the naval officer and scholar (148), provide needed accounts of men who were deeply concerned with the intellectual development of the service. Paul Halpern's first of three volumes for the Navy Record Society on the papers of Admiral Roger Keyes, who is best known for his leading part in the famous raid at Zeebrugge, contains a large quantity of material covering the years 1914-1918, which has been edited with exemplary care and industry (136). Anthony Pollen's biography of his father, Arthur Hungerford Pollen, is the first book-length study of a brilliant inventor and Britain's leading naval journalist of the First World War (174). Pollen's evaluations of his father's accomplishments and his analyzes of naval operations during the First World War, which were based upon long and careful reading of the many private and official papers that were kept by his family, deserve the most serious consideration. The author of this bibliographical essay has published an annotated edition of Arthur Hungerford Pollen's privately printed and circulated works on the subject of naval gunnery under the auspices of the Navy Records Society (203).

Aspects of British naval politics and administration have been covered in a number of works worthy of note. Gerald Jordan (38), Howard Weinroth (94), and F.W. Wiemann (97) have written articles on radical opposition in Parliament to spending on naval armaments between 1906 and 1914. N.A.M. Rodgers' introductory history of the Admiralty for the *Offices of State* series has no pretensions to great depth, but the author's critical perspective and knowledge of official documents make it more valuable to the serious scholar than might at first be apparent (189), while his three articles for the *Mariner's Mirror* on the Admiralty from 1869 to 1885 give detailed treatment to an important period (75-77). Eugene Rasor's study of the Admiralty's reform of personnel policy between 1850 and 1880 (179, 180), J.S. Bromley's edition of documents on manning the Royal Navy (107), and Henry Baynham's popular social history of the common seaman during the *Dreadnought* era (102) have substantially increased knowledge about a major subject that has been for the most part ignored. Articles by Donald Gordon (28) and Hugh Lyon (54), and one of the chapters in a book on British shipbuilding by Sidney Pollard and Paul Robertson (173), examine aspects of the Royal Navy's relations with private industry, a pair of articles by Mavis Waters provides an outline history of changes in the work force at the Royal Dockyards at Chatham (92, 93), while articles on the Board of Invention and Research by Jack Gusewelle (29) and the team of Roy MacLeod and E. Kay Andrews (59) focus on the Royal Navy's support of scientific research during the First World War. D.K. Brown, the Assistant Director of Naval Construction, has written a semi-official volume on the Royal Corps of Naval Constructors (108). And Philip Macdougall (153), Geoffrey Penn (172), and John G. Wells (211) have produced book-length histories of various Royal Navy shore establishments.

Much has been written about naval tactics, strategy, policy, and planning. Nicholas d'Ombrain's excellent monograph on the Committee on Imperial Defence from 1902 to 1914 has a good deal to say about the part played by the navy in the formulation of British grand strategy, such as it was, before the First World War (126). C.I. Hamilton's article on the impact of changing technology on the strategy and tactics of the British and French navies between 1840 and 1870 is highly informative (32). N.A.M. Rodger's perceptive and provocative article on the impact of technological change on British naval strategic thinking between 1820 and 1890 (80) and Bryan Ranft's important article on British trade defense policy from 1860 to 1906 (72) should be read and considered carefully by every serious student of the naval history of the period. Philip Towle's articles on the effect of the Russo-Japanese War on British naval technical, tactical, and strategic thought (90, 91), and H.I. Lee's article on strategy in the Mediterranean between 1908 and 1912 (52) are also recommended. Paul Haggie's article provides a brief critical account of war planning, or the lack of it, at the Admiralty between 1904 and 1910 (30). Avner Offer's article on the effect which concern over the possibility of working class unrest in the event of food shortages had on British naval planning is intriguing, but by no means convincing (66). And an article by the author of this bibliographical essay puts forward a revisionist interpretation of British naval policy during the decade before the First World War (87).

There have been a few additions to the voluminous literature on naval operations during the First World War. Arthur J. Marder's revision of his volume on the battle of Jutland, the third of his quintet on the Royal Navy from 1904 to 1919, incorporates some new information of interest, but his basic interpretation of the action and its aftermath remain unchanged (159). N.J.M. Campbell's long awaited detailed account of Jutland contains much valuable technical information drawn from official records, although his analysis has not taken the latest work on fire control into consideration (115). James Goldrick's book on the naval war in the North Sea from August 1914 to February 1915, is informed by extensive archival research and the author's experience as a serving naval officer, and is particularly distinguished by its perceptive analysis of the effect that problems with materiel and the structure of command had on the performance of the opposing fleets (131). Alan Coles' book on the sinking of three British armored cruisers in September 1914 by the German submarine *U9* is a carefully considered account inspired by a long-time fascination with the event and based upon careful study (118). Redmond McLaughlin's book provides a straight-forward examination of the *Goeben* affaire (155), but a proper evaluation of Admiral Troubridge's decision not to engage awaits a technically informed reconsideration of the gunnery issues. Colin Simpson's sensationalist expose of the *Lusitania* affair (196) has been severely challenged--not to say demolished--by a book on the same subject jointly authored by Thomas A. Bailey and Paul B. Ryan (100) and in Patrick Beesly's revealing monograph on British naval intelligence during the First World War, which may well be the best that can be achieved on an extremely difficult subject, although the absence of reference notes--in spite of the extensive use of archival sources-- is a drawback (104).

Technical change and its effects, great power naval rivalry, and naval aspects of the First World War have been the subject of a number of broad histories. Peter Padfield's *The Battleship Era*, a study of the relationship between British naval strategy and the development of the armored steam battleship, has been somewhat dated by the more recent work on naval materiel already described, but can still be read with profit (166). His *Rule Britannia* (169), along with Richard Humble's *Before the Dreadnought* (146), offer narrative accounts for the general reader of the Royal Navy during the nineteenth and early twentieth century. Padfield's *The Great Naval Race*, a history of the Anglo-German naval rivalry, usefully incorporates the recent work of leading scholarly authorities (168). John Lambelet's quantitative approach to the Anglo-German naval rivalry in a trio of articles has been much admired by some, but the technical data problem is by no means as simple as it is made out to be and the central issue of finance is practically ignored (43, 44, 45). Richard Hough's *The Great War at Sea*, which was intended as an updated one volume derivative of Marder's five volume history of the Royal Navy from 1904 to 1919, is marred by significant errors of fact, questionable judgements, and the failure to incorporate much recent work of significance (143). Paul Kennedy's *The Rise and Fall of British Naval Mastery* persuasively challenges Mahanian explanations of Britain's naval development by considering her naval affairs in relation to a larger political, military, and economic context (150). William McNeill's *The Pursuit of Power* has much to say that is stimulating about British industry and naval armaments in the course of a wide-ranging examination of the evolution of the modern military-industrial complex (156). For those interested in the Royal Navy during the period under review, Kennedy's three chapters covering the years between 1859 to 1918 and McNeill's two chapters on the late nineteenth and early twentieth centuries are essential reading.

The naval papers on the period held by the Public Record Office, which were described in the Higham *Guide* have been moved from London to Kew. No changes have been made in the indexing or arrangement of the Admiralty collections, but significant material on the navy can be found in the papers of the Royal Commission on Awards to Inventors which were not made available until the mid 1970s, and important documents on technical subjects--such as the internal memoranda of the Naval Ordnance Department--have been in storage at Bath and may eventually find their way to the P.R.O. The private papers of a number of prominent naval figures, which in several instances include official documents unavailable elsewhere, have been added to the collections of British archives. For an up-to-date record of the location of private papers, readers should consult the Historical Manuscripts Commission at Quality Court, London. Special attention should be drawn, however, to the Archive Center at Churchill College, Cambridge, whose acquisition of the papers of Fisher, Churchill, Frederic Dreyer, Arthur Pollen and others, have made it a research center on naval matters of the first rank.

Insofar as further historical investigation is concerned, the large quantity and good quality of work accomplished so far notwithstanding, much remains to be done. A scholarly study of British naval administration in the late nineteenth and early twentieth century comparable to that of Daniel Baugh's fine work on the mid-eighteenth century, which would include detailed treatment of such neglected subjects as the dockyards, overseas bases, victualling, and naval finance, has yet to be written. Little is known about such critically important subjects as tactical development, training and maneuvers, the naval officer corps, the naval reserve system, or the evolution of the technical departments. There is still a great deal more to be learned about various naval technical subjects, including gunnery (as distinct from the study of ordnance), steam engineering (the water-tube boiler controversy, for example), capital ship protection (especially during the *Dreadnought* period), and communications (strategic and tactical), to name only a select few. The Mediterranean Fleet, for so long the most important British naval command, and other fleets, deserve serious study. Advances in these and other areas will undoubtedly lead to major reappraisals of what have been regarded as authoritative works on naval policy and operations. In this regard, what P.G.M. Dickson wrote about the historical literature in his own field is probably just as true, if not more so, for that on the Royal Navy from 1860 to 1919. "Insufficient is as yet known about the eighteenth century, in England or Europe," he observed in the preface to his *The Financial Revolution in England*, "to bear the weight of generalization with which historians have normally loaded it, and which only detailed monographs can modify and render more supportable."

BIBLIOGRAPHY

A Select List of Essays and Articles

1. Ashworth, William. "Economic Aspects of Late Victorian Naval Administration," *Economic History Review*, 22 (December, 1969): 491-505.
2. Ballard, Admiral George Alexander. "Admiral Ballard's Memoirs, Part 1: Burney's and H.M.S. *Britannia*," *Mariner's Mirror*, 61 (November, 1975): 345-50.
3. ———. "Admiral Ballard's Memoirs, Part 2: Midshipman," *Mariner's Mirror*, 62 (February, 1976): 23-32.
4. ———. "Admiral Ballard's Memoirs, Part 3: Around the World 1880-1882," *Mariner's Mirror*, 62 (May, 1976): 129-33.
5. ———. "Admiral Ballard's Memoirs, Part 4: Greenwich, Excellent, Vernon and Hecla 1882-84," *Mariner's Mirror*, 62 (August, 1976): 249-52.
6. ———. "Admiral Ballard's Memoirs, Part 5: Temeraire, Cruiser and Woodlark 1884-1885," *Mariner's Mirror*, 62 (November 1976): 347-52.
7. ———. "Admiral Ballard's Memoirs, Part 6: Up the Irrawaddy to Mandalay," *Mariner's Mirror*, 63 (February, 1977): 25-31.
8. Baynham, Henry. "Commander R.H.D. Townshend, Royal Navy (1879-1916)," *Naval Review*, 72 (July, 1984): 250-3.
9. Bennett, N.R. "The Naval Pivot of Asia: An Examination of the Place of Hong Kong in British Far Eastern Strategy, 1900-

1914," *Journal of Oriental Studies*, 7 (January, 1969): 63-75.
10. Brown, David K. (D.K.). "William Froude," *Warship*, 2 (1978): 212-3.
11. ————. "Technical Topics: Roughness and Fouling," *Warship*, 3 (1979): 283-6.
12. ————. "Attack and Defence," Part 3: *Warship*, 6 (1982): 285-91.
13. Campbell, John (N.J.M.). "Cordite," *Warship*, 2 (1978): 138-40.
14. ————. "British Super-Heavy Guns." Parts 1-4, *Warship*, 3 (1979): 66-70, 135-42, 196-201.
15. ————. "British Naval Guns, 1880-1945." Parts 1-4, *Warship*, 5 (1981): 59-61, 96-7, 200-2, 254-5.
16. ————. "British Naval Guns, 1880-1945." Parts 5-7, *Warship*, 6 (1982): 43-5, 214-7, 282-4.
17. ————. "British Naval Guns 1880-1945." Parts 8-11, *Warship*, 7 (1983): 40-3, 119-20, 170-2, 240-3.
18. Cowpe, Alan. "The Royal Navy and the Whitehead Torpedo," in *Technical Change and British Naval Policy, 1860-1939*, pp. 23-36. ed. Bryan Ranft. London: Hodder and Stoughton, 1977.
19. Dale, George F. "Stability of Nitrocellulose-based Powder," *Warship International*, 17 (1980): 349-58.
20. Dandeker, Christopher. "Bureaucracy Planning and War: The Royal Navy, 1880 to 1918," *Armed Forces and Society*, 11 (Fall, 1984): 130-46.
21. d'Ombrain, Nicholas J. "Churchill at the Admiralty and the Committee of Imperial Defense, 1911-14," *Journal of the Royal United Service Institution*, 115 (March, 1970): 38-41.
22. Douglas, Commander W.A.B. "The R.N.A.S. in Combined Operations, 1914-1915," in *Dreadnought to Polaris: Maritime Strategy Since Mahan: Papers from the Conference on Strategic Studies at the University of Western Ontario, March 1972*, pp. 19-29. ed. A.M.J. Hyatt. Toronto: Copp Clark, 1973.
23. ————. "Canadian Naval Historiography," *Mariner's Mirror*, 70 (November, 1984): 349-62.
24. Ekoko, A.E. "British Naval Policy in the South Atlantic, 1874-1914," *Mariner's Mirror*, 66 (August, 1980): 209-23.
25. English, Major J.A. "The Trafalgar Syndrome: Jutland and the Indecisiveness of Modern Naval Warfare," *Naval War College Review*, 32 (May-June 1979): 60-77.
26. Fairbanks, Charles H., Jr. "Arms Races: The Metaphor and the Facts," *The National Interest*, 1 (Fall, 1985): 75-90.
27. Goldrick, J.V.P. (ed.). "The Memoirs of Captain J.B. Foley," in *The Naval Miscellany, Volume V*, pp. 499-531. ed. N.A.M. Rodger. London: George Allen and Unwin for the Navy Records Society, 1984.
28. Gordon Donald C. "The Lengthy Shadow of H.H. Mulliner," in *Changing Interpretations and New Sources in Naval History: Papers from the Third United States Naval Academy History Symposium*, pp. 309-24. ed. Robert William Love, Jr. New York: Garland, 1980.
29. Gusewelle, Jack K. "Science and the Admiralty during World War I: The Case of the Board of Invention and Research," in

Naval Warfare in the Twentieth Century, 1900-1945, pp. 105-17. ed. Gerald Jordan. London: Croom Helm, 1977.
30. Haggie, Paul. "The Royal Navy and War Planning in the Fisher Era," *Journal of Contemporary History*, 8 (July 1973): 113-30.
31. Halpern, Paul G. "De Robeck and the Dardanelles Campaign," in *The Naval Miscellany, Volume V*, pp. 439-98. ed. N.A.M. Rodger. London: George Allen and Unwin for the Navy Records Society, 1984.
32. Hamilton, C.I. "The Royal Navy, la Royale, and the Militarisation of Naval Warfare, 1840-1870," *Journal of Strategic Studies*, 6 (June 1983), 182-212.
33. Hamilton, W. Mark. "The 'New Navalism' and the British Navy League, 1895-1914," *Mariner's Mirror*, 64 (February, 1978): 37-44.
34. Higgins, Maria S. "Winston S. Churchill's Legacy to the Royal Navy, 1911-1915," *Naval War College Review*, 27 (November-December, 1974): 67-77.
35. Higham, Robin. "The Peripheral Weapon in Wartime: A Case Study," in *Naval Warfare in the Twentieth Century, 1900-1945*, pp. 90-104. ed. Gerald Jordan. London: Croom Helm, 1977.
36. Hone, Thomas C. "Game Theory and Symmetrical Arms Competition: The Dreadnought Race," *Journal of Strategic Studies*, 7 (June, 1984): 169-77.
37. Jones, Archer, and Keogh, Andrew J. "The Dreadnought Revolution: Another Look," *Military Affairs*, 44 (July, 1985): 124-31.
38. Jordan, Gerald. "Pensions not Dreadnoughts: The Radicals and Naval Retrenchment," in *Edwardian Radicalism, 1900-1914: Some Aspects of British Radicalism*, pp. 162-79. ed. A.J.A. Morris. London: Routledge and Kegan Paul, 1974.
39. Jurens, W.R. "Exterior Ballistics with Microcomputers," *Warship International*, 21 (1984): 49-72.
40. Kemp, Peter. "From Tryon to Fisher: The Regeneration of a Navy," in *Naval Warfare in the Twentieth Century, 1900-1945*, pp. 16-31. ed. Gerald Jordan. London: Croom Helm, 1977.
41. Kennedy, Paul M. "Strategic Aspects of the Anglo-German Naval Race," in *Marine und Marinepolitik im kaiserlichen Deutschland 1871-1914*, ed. H. Schottelius and W. Deist (Dusseldorf, 1972). Reprinted in Paul M. Kennedy, *Strategy and Diplomacy 1870-1945: Eight Studies*, pp. 127-60. London: George Allen and Unwin, 1983.
42. ———. "Fisher and Tirpitz: Political Admirals in the Age of Imperialism," in *Naval Warfare in the Twentieth Century, 1900-1945*, pp. 45-59. ed. Gerald Jordan. London: Croom Helm, 1977. Reprinted in Paul M. Kennedy, *Strategy and Diplomacy 1870-1945: Eight Studies*, pp. 109-26. London: George Allen and Unwin, 1983.
43. Lambelet, John C. "The Anglo-German Dreadnought Race, 1905-1914," in *The Papers of the Peace Science Society (International)*, 22 (1974): 1-45.
44. ———. "A Numerical Model of the Anglo-German Dreadnought

Race," in *The Papers of the Peace Science Society (International)*, 24 (1975): 29-48.
45. ──────. "A Complementary Analysis of the Anglo-German Dreadnought Race," in *The Papers of the Peace Science Society (International)*, 26 (1976): 49-66.
46. Langhorne, R.T.B. "The Naval Question in Anglo-German Relations, 1912-1914," *Historical Journal*, 14 (June, 1971): 359-70.
47. Lant, Jeffrey L. "The Spithead Naval Review of 1887," *Mariner's Mirror*, 62 (February, 1976): 67-79.
48. Lautenschlager, Karl. "Technology and the Evolution of Naval Warfare," *International Security*, 8 (Fall, 1983): 3-51.
49. ──────. "A Majestic Revolution." Parts I-II, *Warship*, 7 (1983): 44-50, 110-18. (For a critique of this series, see the letter by Ralph I. Cook in *Warship*, 8 (1984): 69.) Greenwich: Conway Maritime Press, 1983.
50. Layman, R.D. "Furious and the Tondern Raid," *Warship International*, 10 (1973): 374-85.
51. ──────. "Air vs. Sea in World War I," *Warship International*, 19 (1982): 215-22.
52. Lee, H.I. "Mediterranean Strategy and Anglo-French Relations, 1908-1912," *Mariner's Mirror*, 57 (August, 1971): 267-85.
53. Lyon, D.J. "Torpedo Warfare: A Successful Prediction," *Warship*, 7 (1983): 146-53.
54. Lyon, Hugh. "The relations between the Admiralty and private industry in the development of warships," in *Technical Change and British Naval Policy, 1860-1939*, pp. 37-64. ed. Bryan Ranft. London: Hodder and Stoughton, 1977.
55. Maber, John. "The Steam Engine and the Royal Navy," *Warship*, 6 (1982): 93-100.
56. Mackay, Ruddock F. "The Admiralty, the German Navy, and the Redistribution of the British Fleet, 1904-1905," *Mariner's Mirror*, 56 (May 1970): 341-6.
57. ──────. "Historical Reinterpretations of the Anglo-German Naval Rivalry, 1897-1914," in *Naval Warfare in the Twentieth Century, 1900-1945*, pp. 32-44. ed. Gerald Jordan. London: Croom Helm, 1977.
58. Mackenzie, John. "The Tanganyika Naval Expedition of 1915-1916," *Mariner's Mirror*, 70 (November, 1984): 397-410.
59. MacLeod, Roy M., and Andrews, E. Kay. "Scientific advice in the War at Sea, 1915-1917: The Board of Invention and Research," *The Journal of Contemporary History*, 6 (1971): 3-40.
60. McDonald, J. Kenneth. "Lloyd George and the Search for a Postwar Naval Policy, 1919," in *Lloyd George: Twelve Essays*, pp. 191-222. ed. A.J.P. Taylor. New York: Atheneum, 1971.
61. Mannix, Rear Admiral Daniel P. "The Great North Sea Mine Barrage," *American Heritage*, 34 (April/May 1983): 36-47.
62. Marder, Arthur J. "The Dardanelles Revisited: Further Thoughts on the Naval Prelude," in *Dreadnought to Polaris: Maritime Strategy Since Mahan; Papers from the Conference on Strategic Studies at the University of Western Ontario, March 1972*, pp. 30-46. ed. A.M.J. Hyatt. Toronto: Copp Clark, 1973. Revised and expanded version with the same title in Arthur J. Marder, *From the Dardanelles to Oran:*

Studies of the Royal Navy in War and Peace, 1915-1940, pp. 1-32. London: Oxford University Press, 1974.

63. ―――. "The Influence of History on Sea Power: The Royal Navy and the Lessons of 1914-1918," *Pacific Historical Review*, 75 (June 1970): 1327-56. Reworked and expanded version with the same title in Arthur J. Marder, *From the Dardanelles to Oran: Studies of the Royal Navy in War and Peace, 1915-1940*, pp. 33-63. London: Oxford University Press, 1974.

64. May, William Edward. "Notes for Historical Research on the Royal Navy," *Military Affairs*, vol. 40 (December, 1976): 186-7.

65. Mountbatten, Earl, of Burma. "The Battle of Jutland," *Mariner's Mirror*, 66 (May, 1980): 99-111.

66. Offer, Avner. "The Working Classes, British Naval Plans and the Coming of the Great War," *Past and Present*, no. 107 (May 1985): 204-26.

67. Okun, Nathan. "Armor and its Application to Warships, Part One," *Warship International*, 13 (1976): 115-22.

68. ―――. "Armor and its Application to Warships, Part Two," *Warship International*, 14 (1977): 98-103.

69. ―――. "Armor and its Application to Warships, Conclusion," *Warship International*, 15 (1978): 284-93.

70. Parnell, Commander Charles L. "Lawrence of Arabia's Debt to Seapower," *United States Naval Institute Proceedings*, 105 (August, 1979): 75-83.

71. Preston, Antony. "The End of the Victorian Navy," *Mariner's Mirror*, 60 (November, 1974): 363-81.

72. Ranft, Bryan. "The protection of British seaborne trade and the development of systematic planning for war, 1860-1906," in *Technical Change and British Naval Policy, 1860-1939*, pp. 1-22. Edited by Bryan Ranft. London: Hodder and Stoughton, 1977.

73. Rasor, Eugene L. "The Manning Question in the Royal Navy in the Early Ironclad Era," in *Changing Interpretations and New Sources in Naval History: Papers from the Third United States Naval Academy History Symposium*, pp. 208-15. ed. by Robert William Love, Jr. New York: Garland, 1980.

74. Rodger, N.A.M. "The Design of the Inconstant," in *Mariner's Mirror*, 61 (February 1975): 9-22.

75. ―――. "The Dark Ages of the Admiralty, 1869-1885, Part I: 'Business Methods,' 1869-1874," *Mariner's Mirror*, 61 (November, 1975): 331-4.

76. ―――. "The Dark Ages of the Admiralty, 1869-1885, Part II: Change and Decay, 1874-1880," *Mariner's Mirror*, 62 (February, 1976): 33-6.

77. ―――. "The Dark Ages of the Admiralty, 1869-1885, Part III: Peace, Retrenchment and Reform, 1880-1885," *Mariner's Mirror*, 62 (May, 1976): 121-8.

78. ―――. "British Belted Cruisers," *Mariner's Mirror*, 64 (February, 1978): 23-36.

79. ―――. "The First Light Cruisers," *Mariner's Mirror*, 65 (August, 1979): 209-30.

80. ―――. "British Naval Thought and Naval Policy, 1820-1890: Strategic Thought in an Era of Technological Change," in

New Aspects of Naval History: Selected Papers presented at the Fourth Naval History Symposium, United States Naval Academy, 25-26 October 1979, pp. 140-52. ed. Craig L. Symonds, Annapolis, Maryland: Naval Institute Press, 1981.

81. St. John, Captain (U.S.A.) Ronald B. "European Naval Expansion and Mahan, 1889-1906," *Naval War College Review*, 23 (March, 1971): 74-83.

82. Sandler, Stanley. "In Deference to Public Opinion--The Loss of H.M.S. *Captain,*" *Mariner's Mirror*, 59 (April, 1973): 57-68.

83. Schofield, Brian. "'Jacky' Fisher, H.M.S. *Indomitable* and the Dogger Bank Action: A Personal Memoir," in *Naval Warfare in the Twentieth Century, 1900-1945*, pp. 60-9. ed. Gerald Jordan. London: Croom Helm, 1977.

84. Schurman, D.M. "An Historian and the Sublime Aspects of the Naval Profession," in *Dreadnought to Polaris: Maritime Strategy Since Mahan*, pp. 1-22. ed. by A.M.J. Hyatt. Toronto: Copp Clark, 1973.

85. Sims, Engineer Lieutenant S.H. "An Eye-Witness at the Battle of Jutland," *Naval Review*, 72 (April, 1984): 126-30.

86. Slessor, John. "Admiralty Command Policy in Two World Wars: Reflections Based on Arthur Marder's Story of Jutland," in *Naval Warfare in the Twentieth Century, 1900-1945*, pp. 118-27. ed. by Gerald Jordan. London: Croom Helm, 1977.

87. Sumida, Jon Tetsuro. "British Capital Ship Design and Fire Control in the *Dreadnought* Era: Sir John Fisher, Arthur Hungerford Pollen, and the Battle Cruiser," *The Journal of Modern History*, 51 (June, 1979): 205-30.

88. ─────. "The Royal Navy and Technological Change, 1815-1945," in *Men, Machines and War*. ed. by Ronald Haycock. Waterloo: Wilfrid Laurier University Press, 1987.

89. Sweetman, Jack. "Coronel: Anatomy of a Disaster," in *Naval Warfare in the Twentieth Century, 1900-1945*, pp. 70-89. ed. Gerald Jordan. London: Croom Helm, 1977.

90. Towle, Philip A. "The Effect of the Russo-Japanese War on British Naval Policy," *Mariner's Mirror*, 60 (November, 1974): 383-94.

91. ─────. "The evaluation of the experience of the Russo-Japanese War," in *Technical Change and British Naval Policy, 1860-1939*, pp. 65-79. ed. Bryan Ranft. London: Hodder and Stoughton, 1977.

92. Waters, Mavis. "Changes in the Chatham Dockyard Workforce, 1860-1890. Part I. From Wood to Iron: Change and Harmony, 1860-87," *Mariner's Mirror*, 69 (February, 1983): 55-63.

93. ─────. "Changes in the Chatham Dockyard Workforce, 1860-1890. Part II. From Iron To Steel: Change and Suspicion, 1887-1890," *Mariner's Mirror*, 69 (May, 1983): 165-173.

94. Weinroth, Howard. "Left-Wing Opposition to Naval Armaments in Britain before 1914," *Journal of Contemporary History*, 6 (1971): 93-120.

95. Wells, Anthony. "Naval Intelligence and decision making in an era of technical change," in *Technical Change and British Naval Policy, 1860-1939*, pp. 123-45. ed. Bryan Ranft. London: Hodder and Stoughton, 1977.

96. White, Ensign (U.S.N.R.) Donald G. "The Misapplication of a

Weapons System: The Battle Cruiser as a Warship Type," *Naval War College Review*, 22 (January, 1970): 42-57.
97. Wiemann, F.W. "Lloyd George and the Struggle for the Navy Estimates of 1914," in *Lloyd George: Twelve Essays*, pp. 71-91. ed. A.J.P. Taylor. New York: Atheneum, 1971.
98. Wilson, Michael. "The First Submarines for the Royal Navy," *Warship*, 6 (1982): 266-70.

Books and Doctoral Dissertations

99. Anderson, Russell W. "The Abandonment of British Naval Supremacy, 1918-1920," unpublished PhD dissertation, University of Kentucky, 1974.
100. Bailey, Thomas A. and Ryan, Paul B. *The Lusitania Disaster: An Episode in Modern Warfare and Diplomacy*. London: Collier Macmillan, 1975.
101. Ballard, Admiral G.A. (ed. G.A. Osbon and N.A.M. Rodger). *The Black Battlefleet*. (An opulently produced reprint of a series of articles from the *Mariner's Mirror* published beginning in 1929.) Annapolis: Naval Institute Press, 1980.
102. Baynham, H. *Men from the Dreadnoughts*. London: Hutchinson, 1976.
103. Beatty, Charles. *Our Admiral: A Biography of Admiral of the Fleet Earl Beatty, 1871-1936*. London: W.H. Allen, 1980.
104. Beesly, Patrick. *Room 40: British Naval Intelligence 1914-18*. London: Hamish Hamilton, 1982.
105. Blumenthal, Harvey. "W.T. Stead's Role in Shaping Official Policy: The Navy Campaign of 1884," unpublished PhD dissertation, George Washington University, 1984.
106. Breyer, Siegfried. *Battleships of the World, 1905-1970*. Greenwich: Conway Maritime Press, 1980.
107. Bromley, J.S. (ed.). *The Manning of the Royal Navy: Selected Public Pamphlets 1693-1873*. Publications of the Navy Records Society, vol. 119. London: Navy Records Society, 1974.
108. Brown, D.K. *A Century of Naval Construction: The History of the Royal Corps of Naval Constructors 1883-1983*. London: Conway Maritime Press, 1983.
109. Bullen, J.R. "The Royal Navy and the Baltic 1918-20," unpublished PhD dissertation, University of London, 1983.
110. Burt, R.A. and Trotter, W.P. *Battleships of the Grand Fleet: A Pictorial Review of British Battleships and Battlecruisers 1906-1921*. Annapolis: Naval Institute Press, 1982.
111. Burt, R.A. *British Battleships of World War One*. Annapolis: Naval Institute Press, 1986.
112. Buxton, Ian. *Big Gun Monitors: The History of the Design, Construction and Operation of the Royal Navy's Monitors*. Annapolis: Naval Institute Press, 1978.
113. Campbell, John (N.J.M.). *Queen Elizabeth Class*. Warship Monographs. Greenwich: Conway Maritime Press, 1972.
114. Campbell, N.J.M. *Battlecruisers: The Design and Development of British and German Battlecruisers of the First World War Era*. Greenwich: Conway Maritime Press, 1978.
115. ―――. *Jutland: An Analysis of the Fighting*. Annapolis: Naval Institute Press, 1986.

116. Carew, A.B. "The Royal Naval Lower Deck Reform Movement, 1900-39," unpublished PhD dissertation, University of Sussex, 1980.
117. Chesneau, Roger, and Kolesnik, Eugene M. (eds.). *Conway's All the World's Fighting Ships, 1860-1905.* Greenwich: Conway Maritime Press, 1979.
118. Coles, Alan. *Three Before Breakfast.* Havant, Hants.: Kenneth Maron, 1979.
119. Costello, John, and Hughes, Terry. *Jutland 1916.* New York: Holt, Rinehart and Winston, 1976.
120. Cowburn, Philip M. "The Royal Navy and the Australian Colonies, 1859-1891," unpublished PhD dissertation, University of New South Wales, 1975.
121. Cowpe, Alan. "Underwater Weapons and the Royal Navy, 1869-1918," unpublished PhD dissertation, University of London, 1980.
122. Cunninghame-Graham, Admiral Sir Angus. *Random Naval Recollections.* Dunbartonshire: by the author, 1979.
123. Davis, G.M., compiler. *The Loss of H.M.S. Montagu: Lundy, 1906.* Atworth: by the compiler, 1981.
124. Dingman, Roger. *Power in the Pacific: The Origins of Naval Arms Limitation, 1914-1922.* Chicago: University of Chicago Press, 1976.
125. Dittmar, F.J., and Colledge, J.J. *British Warships, 1914-1919.* London: Ian Allan, 1972.
126. d'Ombrain, Nicholas. *War Machinery and High Policy: Defence Administration in Peacetime Britain, 1902-1914.* London: Oxford University Press, 1973.
127. Elliott, Peter. *The Cross and the Ensign: A Naval History of Malta 1798-1979.* [London?]: Patrick Stephens, 1980.
128. Fock, Harald. *Fast Fighting Boats, 1870-1945: Their Design, Construction, and Use.* Annapolis: Naval Institute Press, 1978.
129. Friedman, Norman. *Battleship Design and Development, 1905-1945.* Greenwich: Conway Maritime Press, 1978.
130. Gardiner, Robert, and Gray, Randal. *Conway's All the World's Fighting Ships 1906-1921.* London: Conway Maritime Press, 1985.
131. Goldrick, James. *The King's Ships Were at Sea: The War in the North Sea, August 1914-February 1915.* Annapolis: Naval Institute Press, 1984.
132. Griffin, Rose T. "Official British Reaction to the German Threat, 1911-1914," unpublished PhD dissertation, St. Louis University, 1972.
133. Gusewelle, Jack Keeney. "The Board of Invention and Research: A Case Study in the Relations between Academic Science and the Royal Navy in Great Britain during the First World War," unpublished PhD dissertation, University of California, Irvine, 1971.
134. Hackmann, Willem. *Seek and Strike: Sonar, Anti-Submarine Warfare and the Royal Navy, 1914-54.* London: Her Majesty's Stationery Office, 1984.
135. Halpern, Paul G. *The Mediterranean Naval Situation 1908-1914.* Cambridge, Mass.: Harvard University Press, 1971.

136. Halpern, Paul G. (ed.). *The Keyes Papers: Selection from the Private and Official Correspondence of Admiral of the Fleet Baron Keyes of Zeebrugge*, volume I: *1914-1918*. Publications of the Navy Records Society, vol. 117. London: George Allen and Unwin, 1972.
137. Hayward, Victor. *H.M.S. Tiger at Bay*. London: William Kimber, 1977.
138. Hezlet, Vice-Admiral Sir Arthur. *Electronics and Sea Power*. New York: Stein and Day, 1975.
139. Hodges, Peter. *The Big Gun: Battleship Main Armament, 1860-1945*. Annapolis: Naval Institute Press, 1981.
140. Hogg, Ian and Batchelor, John. *Naval Gun*. Poole Doreset: Blandford Press, 1978.
141. Horsfield, John Arnold. "The Art of Leadership in War: The Royal Navy from the Age of Nelson through World War II as a Case History," unpublished PhD dissertation, University of California, Irvine, 1977.
142. ―――――. *The Art of Leadership in War: The Royal Navy from the Age of Nelson to the End of World War II*. Westport, Conn.: Greenwood Press, 1980.
143. Hough, Richard. *The Great War at Sea, 1914-1918*. Oxford: Oxford University Press, 1983.
144. ―――――. *The Greatest Crusade: Roosevelt, Churchill, and the Naval Wars*. New York: William Morrow, 1986.
145. Hughes, Quentin. *Britain in the Mediterranean and the Defence of her Naval Stations*. Liverpool: Penpaled Books, 1981.
146. Humble, Richard. *Before the Dreadnought: The Royal Navy from Nelson to Fisher*. London: Macdonald and Jane's, 1976.
147. ―――――. *Fraser of North Cape: The Life of Admiral of the Fleet Lord Fraser (1888-1981)*. London: Routledge and Kegan paul, 1983.
148. Hunt, Barry D. *Sailor-Scholar: Admiral Sir Herbert Richmond, 1871-1946*. Waterloo, Canada: Wilfrid Laurier University Press, 1982.
149. Jenkins, Commander C.A. *H.M.S. Furious 1917-1925*. Warship in Profile. Windsor: Profile Publications, 1973.
150. Kennedy, Paul M. *The Rise and Fall of British Naval Mastery*. New York: Charles Scribner's Sons, 1976 (paperback edition with comment on events up to September 1982, London: Macmillan, 1983).
151. Leather, John. (Photographs by Beken of Cowes). *World's Warships in Review 1860-1906*. Annapolis: Naval Institute Press, 1976.
152. Lutrin, Carl E. "The Trident in Politics: The Royal Navy as an Interest Group," unpublished PhD dissertation, University of Missouri-Columbia, 1972.
153. Macdougall, Philip. *Royal Dockyards*. Newton Abbot: David and Charles, 1982.
154. Mackay, Ruddock F. *Fisher of Kilverstone*. Oxford: Clarendon Press, 1973.
155. McLaughlin, R. *The Escape of the Goeben*. London: Seeley Service, 1974.
156. McNeill, William H. *The Pursuit of Power: Technology, Armed Force, and Society since A.D. 1000*. Chicago: University of Chicago Press, 1982.

157. Macpherson, Ken, and Burgess, John. *The Ships of Canada's Naval Forces, 1910-1981.* Annapolis: United States Naval Institute Press, 1982.
158. Manchester, William. *The Last Lion: Winston Spencer Churchill's Visions of Glory, 1874-1932.* Boston: Little, Brown, 1983.
159. Marder, Arthur J. *From the Dreadnought to Scapa Flow: The Royal Navy in the Fisher Era, 1904-1919.* Vol. III: *Jutland and After (May 1916-December 1916)*, second edition, revised. London: Oxford University Press, 1978.
160. Melville, Thomas R. "Canada and Sea Power: Canadian Naval Thought and Policy, 1860-1910," unpublished PhD dissertation, Duke University, 1981.
161. Morgan, Ted. *Churchill: Young Man in a Hurry, 1874-1915.* New York: Simon and Schuster, 1982.
162. Northcott, Maurice P. *Hood: Design and Construction.* Ensign. Special. London: Bivouac Books, 1975.
163. ―――. *Renown and Repulse.* Ensign, no. 8. London: Battle of Britain Prints, 1978.
164. Oram, H.P.K. *Ready for Sea.* London: Seeley, Service and Co., 1974.
165. Owen, Charles. *No More Heroes: The Royal Navy in the Twentieth Century: Anatomy of a Legend.* London: George Allen and Unwin, 1975.
166. Padfield, Peter. *The Battleship Era.* London: Rupert Hart-Davis, 1972.
167. ―――. *Guns at Sea.* London: Hugh Evelyn, 1973.
168. ―――. *The Great Naval Race: Anglo-German Naval Rivalry, 1900-1914.* New York: David McKay, 1974.
169. ―――. *Rule Britannia: The Victorian and Edwardian Navy.* London: Routledge and Kegan Paul, 1981.
170. Patterson, A. Temple. *Tyrwhitt of the Harwich Force.* London: MacDonald, 1973.
171. Pelling, Henry. *Winston Churchill.* London: Macmillan, 1974.
172. Penn, Geoffrey. *H.M.S. Thunderer: The Story of the Royal Naval Engineering College Keyham and Manadon.* Emsworth: Kenneth Mason, 1984.
173. Pollard, Sidney, and Robertson, Paul. *The British Shipbuilding Industry, 1870-1914.* Harvard Studies in Business History, vol. 30. Cambridge, Mass.: Harvard University Press, 1979.
174. Pollen, Anthony. *The Great Gunnery Scandal: The Mystery of Jutland.* London: Collins, 1980.
175. Preston, Antony. *'V & W' Class Destroyers, 1917-1945.* London: Macdonald, 1971.
176. ―――. *Battleships of World War I: An Illustrated Encyclopedia of the Battleships of all Nations, 1914-1918.* Harrisburg, Pennsylvania: Stackpole Books, 1972.
177. Price, Alfred. *Aircraft versus Submarine: The Evolution of the Anti-Submarine Aircraft, 1912 to 1980.* London: Jane's Publishing Company, 1973.
178. Putsipher, Lewis E. "Aircraft and the Royal Navy, 1908-1918," unpublished PhD. dissertation, Duke University, 1981.
179. Rasor, Eugene L. "The Problem of Discipline in the Mid-19th Century Royal Navy," unpublished PhD dissertation, University of Virginia, 1972.

180. ——. *Reform in the Royal Navy: A Social History of the Lower Deck, 1850-1880.* Hamden, Connecticut: Archon Books, 1976.
181. Raven, Alan, and Roberts, John. *Queen Elizabeth Class Battleships.* Ensign, no. 4. London: Bivouac Books, 1975.
182. ——. *British Battleships of World War Two: The Development and Technical History of the Royal Navy's Battleships and Battlecruisers from 1911 to 1946.* London: Arms and Armour Press, 1976.
183. ——. *'V' and 'W' Class Destroyers.* Man O'War series, Edward Valerio, ed. London: Arms and Armour Press, 1979.
184. ——. *British Cruisers of World War Two.* [Begins with 'Arethusa' class of 1912.] Annapolis: United States Naval Institute Press, 1980.
185. Roberts, John. *Invincible Class.* Warship Monographs. Greenwich: Conway Maritime Press, 1972.
186. ——. *The Battlecruiser Hood.* Anatomy of the Ship. Greenwich: Conway Maritime Press, 1982.
187. Robertson, Paul L. "The Management of Manpower in British Shipbuilding 1870-1914: A Study in the Organization of Human Resources Under Conditions of Changing Technology," unpublished PhD dissertation, University of Wisconsin, 1972.
188. Robertson, R.G. *H.M.S. Hood/Battle-Crusier 1916-1941.* Warships in Profile. Windsor: Profile Publications, 1973.
189. Rodger, N.A.M. *The Admiralty.* Offices of State series. Lavenham: Terence Dalton, 1979.
190. Roskill, Stephen. *Hankey: Man of Secrets*, vol. I: *1877-1918.* New York: St. Martin's Press, 1970.
191. ——. *Churchill and the Admirals.* London: Collins, 1977.
192. ——. *Admiral of the Fleet Earl Beatty: The Last Naval Hero: An Intimate Biography.* London: Collins, 1980.
193. Sandler, Stanley. *The Emergence of the Modern Capital Ship.* Newark: University of Delaware Press, 1979.
194. Sainty, J.C. (compiler). *Admiralty Officials, 1660-1870.* Vol. IV in the series: Office-Holders in Modern Britain. London: Athlone Press, 1975.
195. Schurman, Donald M. *Julian S. Corbett, 1854-1922: Historian of British Maritime Policy from Drake to Jellicoe.* London: Royal Historical Society, 1981.
196. Simpson, Colin. *The Lusitania.* Boston: Little, Brown, and Co., 1972.
197. Smith, Peter Charles. *Hard Lying: The Birth of the Destroyer, 1893-1913.* Annapolis: Naval Institute Press, 1971.
198. ——. *Hit First, Hit Hard: The Story of H.M.S. Renown 1916-48.* London: William Kimber, 1979.
199. Smith, Stephen R.B. "British Nationalism, Imperialism, and the City of London, 1880-1900," unpublished PhD dissertation, University of London, 1985.
200. Stokesbury, James L. *Navy and Empire.* New York: William Morrow, 1983.
201. Storr, F. "The Development of the Marine Compound Steam Engine, c. 1870-90," unpublished PhD dissertation, Council for National Academic Awards, 1983.

202. Sumida, Jon Tetsuro. "Financial Limitation, Technological Innovation, and British Naval Policy, 1904-1910," unpublished PhD dissertation, University of Chicago, 1982.
203. Sumida, Jon Tetsuro (ed.). *The Pollen Papers: The Privately Circulated Printed Works of Arthur Hungerford Pollen 1901-1916*. Publications of the Navy Records Society, vol. 124. London: George Allen and Unwin, 1984.
204. Taylor, Gordon. *London's Navy: A Story of the Royal Naval Volunteer Reserve*. London: Quiller Press, 1983.
205. Thetford, Owen. *British Naval Aircraft since 1912*. London: Putnam, 1958, 1971, 1977, 1978, 1982.
206. Till, Geoffrey. *Air Power and the Royal Navy, 1914-1945*. London: Jane's Publishing Company, 1979.
207. Trotter, Wilfrid Pym. *The Royal Navy in Old Photographs*. Annapolis: Naval Institute Press, 1975.
208. Vale, Vivian. *The American Peril: Challenge to Britain on the North Atlantic, 1900-1904*. Manchester: Manchester University Press, 1984.
209. van der Vat, Dan. *The Grand Scuttle: The Sinking of the German Fleet at Scapa Flow in 1919*. Annapolis: Naval Institute Press, 1985; first published 1982.
210. Wells, A.R. "Studies in British Naval Intelligence, 1880-1945," unpublished PhD dissertation, University of London, 1972.
211. Wells, Captain John G. *Whaley: The Story of H.M.S. Excellent 1830 to 1980*. Portsmouth: H.M.S. Excellent, 1980.
212. White, Colin. *The Heyday of Steam*. Annapolis: Naval Institute Press, 1983.
213. Williamson, Jr., Samuel R. *The Politics of Grand Strategy: Britain and France Prepare for War, 1904-1914*. Cambridge, Mass.: Harvard University Press, 1969.
214. Wingate, John. *H.M.S. Dreadnought*. Warships in Profile. Windsor: Profile Publications, 1971.
215. Winton, John. *Jellicoe*. London: Michael Joseph, 1981.
216. ———. *Convoy: The Defence of Sea Trade, 1890-1990*. London: Michael Joseph, 1983.

Supplement to Bibliography

217. Coad, J.G. *Historic Architecture of the Royal Navy: An Introduction*. London: Victor Gollancz, 1983.
218. Halpern, Paul G. *The Naval War in the Mediterranean, 1914-1918*. London: George Allen and Unwin, 1987.
219. Lambert, Andrew. *Warrior: The World's First Ironclad, Then and Now*. Annapolis: Naval Institute Press, 1987.
220. Semmel, Bernard. *Liberalism and Naval Strategy: Ideology, Interest, and Sea Power During the Pax Britannica*. London: Royal Historical Society, 1981.
221. Sumida, Jon Tetsuro. *In Defence of Naval Supremacy: Finance, Technology and British Naval Policy, 1889-1914*. London: Allen & Unwin, forthcoming (1988).
222. Tarrant, V.E. *Battlecruiser Invincible: The History of the First Battlecruiser, 1909-1919*. Annapolis: Naval Institute Press, 1987.
223. Watton, Ross. *The Battleship Warspite*. Series: *Anatomy of the Ship*. Annapolis: Naval Institute Press, 1986.

224. Williams, R.H. "Arthur Balfour, Sir John Fisher and the Politics of Naval Reform, 1904-10," *Historical Research* 60 (1987).

Note: I wish to acknowledge the assistance of Professors Paul Kennedy and Gerald Jordan, who suggested the inclusion of a number of entries that I had overlooked.

IX

THE ARMY IN THE NINETEENTH CENTURY

Albert Tucker

In the last fifteen years a rich and abundant harvest has come to the student of the nineteenth-century army. The high quality of monographs and articles which have appeared since the end of the 1960s is a tribute to a new generation of scholars whose work removes the earlier notion that the army had been neglected, its place treated as a marginal subject of history within the more vital components of Victorian society. We have now a whole new body of scholarly studies written by trained historians whose power of reflection moves readily between problems of military organization and those areas that study the army as a social institution. The very breadth of this new interest, while it has produced new and creative insights, has also demonstrated the challenge facing the socio-military historian who would project the questions and methods of research onto problems that no longer isolate but include the army within the larger social structure.

The Army in Society and Politics. In 1980 Edward Spiers completed a survey of army and society from the end of the Napoleonic Wars to the outbreak of World War I (51). Published in the Longman series, "Themes in British Social History," the book met a need that had long been felt by scholars and teachers of Victorian society. After one chapter on officers and one on the other ranks, the book follows a chronological rather than a thematic treatment, under conventional headings such as "Wellington's Army," "The Crimean War," "The South African War" and "The Haldane Reforms." Within this arrangement the author gives to the reader insights that arise not only from extensive reading in secondary sources but from original research into private and official papers, so that the book is not simply a survey text.

Some of his findings are derived from a mix of parliamentary papers and autobiographies, leading to a number of clear statistical tables. One, on the origins of the officer corps, demonstrates the continuing dominance of landed families from the south, a subject explored in an earlier sociological article by C.B. Otley (42). Other charts on recruiting are integrated into Spiers' statement that figures and tables do not support a necessary correlation with cycles of unemployment and pauperism, that "hunger and poverty were not the sole motives for enlistment," despite assumptions to that effect even within the army itself. At a more impressionistic level, from the reading of soldiers' autobiographies, Dr. Spiers has to admit that "unemployment prompted many men to offer themselves for enlistment."

Of those who did, most were casual laborers and "the least skilled sections of the working class." The conclusions are not new or startling but they are placed in more interesting ways than ever before within the context of the whole society. One of his tables for every five years from 1815 to 1910 shows that the number of men under arms consistently numbered fewer than 2% of the total male population in the United Kingdom.

Spiers' book was influenced by two studies with similar themes which appeared in the 1970s; one by Alan Skelley (49), a contemporary of Spiers as a graduate student at the University of Edinburgh, the other by Gwyn Harries-Jenkins (31), a sociologist with a special interest in armed forces and social structures. This latter book concentrates its argument almost entirely on the officers, who numbered some 6,000 in total. Chapter six of Harries-Jenkins' book contains an account of the various tasks of the Victorian army, with a focus on maintaining an empire through the mounting of small detachments which constituted a "guardian force." The empirical nature of preparing these small expeditions inspired little urgency about large-scale organization or planning and direction by a General Staff, leaving too little incentive for developing a continuous imperial strategy.

As a result, British officers were not subjected to rigorous professional training that would give them a functional status beyond that of gentlemen. Yet they possessed resources in the form of arms and organization that were greater than those of any other institution in society. Why, then, did they never constitute a threat to the civil power? The reason, according to Harries-Jenkins, derived not only from social origins, from aristocratic family connection and the role of the gentleman, but equally from politics, from political participation at every level of government. Chapter seven of his book is a perceptive essay on officers in politics, some holding a variety of offices by civil appointment while others were elected to parliamentary seats in numbers that sometimes totalled 15% of the House of Commons.

The army as a social organization is studied at another level by Alan Skelley (49) who concentrates entirely on men in the ranks, arguing that the ordinary soldier experienced a steady improvement in living and training conditions in the last four decades of the nineteenth century. Skelley's book is divided into chapters on health, education, crime and discipline, pay, pensions and problems of recruiting, with chapters broken into subdivisions that enable him to discuss topics as diverse as barracks and medical care, venereal disease, literacy, marriage and the education of soldiers' children. From time to time he relates the treatment of these issues in the army to similar problems in civil society, equating barracks with working-class housing, or placing questions of prisons and military punishment within the context of contemporary theories of criminology. On the whole, however, the book has limitations in its treatment of the army as a reflection of other issues within Victorian society. Parallels between military conditions and those of civilian institutions are treated as facts with frequent footnote references, but explanation and discourse are not developed on the same level as the honesty of Skelley's extensive research.

More directly interpretive on army reform is an article by Hew Strachan, who has taken the army as a case study in the wider debate over the nineteenth-century revolution in government (54). Pointing to the challenge of meeting costs in 1847 when the army absorbed 30% of central-government expenditure, to overlapping departments and confused administration, to conditions within the ranks and the accumulation of statistics, Strachan argues that "The direct influence of Bentham on army reform was ... non-existent." Even the reform pamphlets of Sir Charles Trevelyan in the 1860s were arguments for the military participation not of the middle class of commerce and industry, but of the sons of farmers and those "who received a liberal education, the clergy, the medical profession and upwards."

It would be misleading for the historian, however, to conclude that reform was motivated solely by circumstance and events, that ideas were marginal if not irrelevant. The impact of war overseas fused with the interplay of social and political tensions to question specific traditions of military organization, leading to the influence of other groups than the Benthamites and the Utilitarians. This statement may become clearer through a chronological division of historical writing around the Crimean and the Boer Wars.

The Crimean War: Before and After. The article by Strachan was but a prelude to the book that he had been preparing for some time, which he published in 1984 and which now must be considered the definitive study of the pre-Crimean army (54). There is an element of confusion in the title, for *Wellington's Legacy* did not accord with attempts at military reform through the quarter century from 1830 to 1854, yet reform is the dominant argument of the author. Aside from this quibble, however, the book is rich in its knowledge of politics and high command, illustrated in particular by the role of Viscount Hardinge as commander-in-chief and by that of Lord Frederick Fitzclarence as Lieutenant Governor of Portsmouth after 1847. There are lucid commentaries also on the military press and its influence, on officers and their regiments, and on the soldier's life in terms of discipline and equipment, food and accommodation, punishment and rewards, with a section on education that illustrates the fundamental tension between schools and teachers supervised by central military authority and the historic independence of the regiments. The conclusion here is that "the army was serving as a microcosm of society in the great arguments of church and state."

While there is a ring of truth to this statement, it reflects the influence of Strachan's sources which include little of observation from the soldiers themselves. The limitation is inevitable given the absence of letters and the nature of the periodicals and the printed parliamentary papers. By supplementing these with the rigorous use of archives and a wide-ranging bibliography, the author argues convincingly the case for a reform movement in being well before the Crimean War.

The lines of that interpretation are not straight and unmodified, however. Conditions for the soldier are described in terms of particular experience in Waterfield (57) and Pearman (3); punishment and flogging are given specialized attention by Hopkins (33) and Dinwiddy (22); while Peter Burroughs (19) examined the soldier stationed at overseas garrisons who was subject to mismanagement and indifference in the various departments responsible for the army. Despite the enlightened efforts at the War Office of the young Lord Howick, subsequently the third Earl Grey, and his use of statistical studies on disease and death through the talents of Henry Marshall and Lieutenant Alexander Tulloch, Burroughs concludes that "military complacency and traditionalism survived without serious challenge until the Crimean War."

Whatever the deficiencies in military administration or the scale of reforms, it was a principal object of the army to fight and conquer as well as hold on to overseas territory, a feature of the period that is especially evident in the new biography of Sir Harry Smith (37). Through the nineteenth century the British army was engaged in more than 190 military expeditions and small wars, a selection of which are recounted by Byron Farwell in a book that informs the reader with biographical accounts of high-ranking officers who led a few of these expeditions (24). His sources are all secondary but the writing and the judgments are lively and the book contains an interesting essay on the British regiment which should be read in conjunction with a similar essay by John Keegan (34). Farwell's chapter on the Crimean War, however, reads like marginal commentary by comparison with recent books by A.J. Barker (8), R.L.V. ffrench Blake (14) and Philip Warner (56). Blake in particular does a service to the student of tactics and strategy; he puts aside the debate over maladministration and Russell's despatches in favor of concentration on military action, a focus to be found also in the Strachan article (54) and in the Hodge diary (4).

Blake's book was favorably reviewed by Brison Gooch (27) in an essay that praised also the recently published letters from the Crimea of the soldier-surgeon, Dr. Douglas Reid (10), a book that should be placed with Richard Blanco's study of Sir James McGrigor (16) and the more general survey of army medical services by Sir Neil Cantlie (20). Any study of medicine and hospitals should also include F.B. Smith's short biography of Florence Nightingale which reads like a well documented but prolonged essay in relentless criticism of her purpose and her methods in using people (50). While confirming her decisive role in army sanitary reform, Smith cannot agree that achieving public good mitigates her complex pursuit of self-satisfaction as a "tricky, dogmatic, wheedling manipulator" (p. 198). The book was considered seriously enough to warrant two long critical reviews, one by Richard Shannon in the *Times Literary Supplement* (48), the other by Eileen and David Spring in the *Bulletin of the History of Medicine* (52). Inevitably, the debate has also been informed by a scholar of psychohistory (1).

Less controversial are specialized studies that concentrate on one aspect of military organization, such as the role of mercenaries in the Crimea by Bayley (11) and a number of books that single out the British cavalry. Apart from a new general account of the cavalry by Warner (56), we now have both the short monograph on Captain Nolan by Bartlett (9), and the extended five-volume history by the Marquess of Anglesey on the nineteenth-century cavalry from 1816 to 1919 (5). Three volumes have so far appeared covering the years from 1816 to 1898. They have chapters not only on organization, campaign and horses, but on the putting down of riot, distinctions between cavalry and yeomanry, courts martial and punishment among the rank and file, and the system of purchase among the officers. These accounts of the cavalry at home are sometimes more interesting than the narrative of imperial campaigns, which gives to the work an uneven quality; but

Anglesey's study is nevertheless the most comprehensive history in print of this pre-eminent section of the army.

His research is based largely on secondary printed sources but in the course of preparing his reading Anglesey edited two books of memoirs and letters of soldiers who recounted actual battle experiences. The first was the journal of a non-commissioned officer, Sergeant Pearman (3); the second the letters from the Crimea of Colonel Edward Hodge, commander of the 4th Dragoon Guards, describing conditions in the field as well as his part in the battle of Balaclava, an action that the editor clarifies with his own short essay (4). The biography by Edward Spiers of another officer, General de Lacy Evans, is less satisfying because Evans left so few private papers, served so briefly in the Crimea and spent so much of his life as a member of parliament (51). The "radical" quality of his career was more political than military, and the student is left wondering if an essay would have been more appropriate, concentrating on Evans and reform in the pre-Crimean army.

Certainly the essay form helps to explain the success of two authors on subjects that confirm the breadth of interest which has enlarged the socio-military focus of the Crimean War. Using the training of the art historian, Matthew Lalumia has explored illustrations, sketches and painting that reveal another expression of criticism, largely in the form of satire, against aristocratic leadership of the army (36). Reaction was often founded on humanitarian criteria, specifically within modes of thinking that were shaped by an evangelical faith. Olive Anderson argued the particular impact of religion in public reaction against the Crimean War, finding some of her evidence in the careers of officers such as Headly Vicars, Hope Grant and Henry Havelock, men whose command over others reflected Protestant Christian conversions (2). She found also that from outside the army a remarkable number of middle-class women began to take an interest in the conditions of the soldier, primarily from a missionary attitude that was parallel with the activities of other women in housing, prisons and contagious diseases.

Women who lived more within the army, as the wives of soldiers, have become subjects of two books. The first, by Veronica Bamfield, is the more conventional and anecdotal but it is also lively in style and informed in judgment because of the author's experience as an officer's wife and member of a military family (7). The wives of the "other ranks" tend to be filtered through this experience but the insights are those of a woman involved intimately in regimental life, who knew first-hand the anxieties of unwanted pregnancies: "one woman who lived to over 80 had no fewer than six pregnancies terminated in an Indian bazaar" (p. 26). The narrative captures the gregarious quality of living in or near barracks, the hazards of travel by ship and by marching, the dread of women searching the battlefield for dead husbands, and the general improvements that came for the army wife after the Crimean War.

The thirty years after that war are the chronological frame for Myna Trustram's very different book on marriage and the Victorian army (55). It is analytical, reflective, scholarly, placing its subject in the main stream of feminist studies through a perspective of some originality. Acknowledging recent literature on the patriarchal family as the basis for an ordered society, Dr. Trustram concludes: "what we see are attempts by the military authorities to negotiate a lifestyle in keeping with civilian morality and family demands, but one not endangering military efficiency" (p. 4). One large ramification from these attempts involved loyalty to the regiment itself as a substitute for family, driving army commanders to support restrictions on marriage and to prefer a place for prostitutes in proximity to barracks, thereby coming into conflict with the dominant Victorian ideology that prescribed correct forms for sexual and moral relations strictly within the family. These views of the author are developed more strikingly than are statements from army wives themselves. They hardly emerge from the sustained research but the lack is minor by comparison with the significance of the book for a deeper understanding of the army within the structural problems of writing Victorian social history.

This challenge should now include other subjects such as the army and social control, an issue which has so far been simply touched upon in Mather's older study of public order (38), and in a more recent essay on riots by D. Philips (45). J.E. King has studied what he calls "collective violence" in Lancashire, pointing to public dislike not only of the police but of the Militia (35). Distinctions between the Militia and the Volunteers are central to the books by Ian Beckett (12) and Hugh Cunningham (21), and to the article by Patricia Morton (41), all of whom interpret the Volunteer Movement in relation to class divisions, local price, and an amateur form of militarism, a subject that is also explored in a slight essay by Geoffrey Best (13).

More confined to the regular army, though it had large social ramifications, was the subject of commission by purchase. While the practice seemed to be sanctioned by the need to keep the army free from the insidious influences of seniority and patronage, in fact both were present and purchase did little to nourish professional criteria or staff training. Reform was frequently debated but the buying and selling of commissions persisted until the Royal Warrant of 1871. The issues surrounding the system are closely examined by Anthony Bruce in a short book that is based on his PhD thesis at the University of Manchester (18). The book concentrates on the nineteenth century with one chapter going beyond abolition of purchase to discuss selection and promotion of officers in the late Victorian army. Unfortunately the focus on parliamentary debates and the parliamentary papers leads to few fresh conclusions, and the role of army agency or banks such as Cox and Company is omitted entirely. It would have been innovative to include some study of purchase as a business related to banking. Strictly in terms of military history, however, Dr. Bruce dwells on the adverse moral effects for the officer corps and on the close ties between purchase and regimental loyalties, ties that are basic in recent studies of the army after 1870.

From 1870 to 1914. Attachment to the regiment continued long after the abolition of purchase but regimental feeling had to be reconciled with larger issues of staff training. The challenge to ideas of strategy and organization became acute with technological change and distance from the center of empire. Small wars became more complex than historians have appreciated, according to Howard Bailes in an interpretive essay on the Zulu war of 1879 and the Egyptian expedition of 1882 (6). Imperial control had nevertheless to be placed in context with the military resurgence of Prussia and designs of Russia on the northwest frontier of India. These issues were very much in the minds of a number of scholars who have recently advanced our knowledge of the Staff, of Military Intelligence, and changes in relations between army and government.

Two important studies were published in the early 1970s, one by W.S. Hamer, the other by Brian Bond. Hamer's study filled a gap between the Cardwell Reforms and the Boer War (29). Concentrating on civil-military relations, assuming civilian predominance and the pervasive role of inquiry by committee and commission, together with the exigencies of party politics and cabinet government, Hamer examined not only a wealth of parliamentary papers but the larger collections of private papers that were just being opened in the 1960s. His study is an admirable work of research, leading him to conclude that closer co-operation and understanding were steadily developing between the more intelligent and professional senior officers on the one hand, and civilian political reformers on the other. This relationship was becoming embodied in formal boards and commissions, and their functioning was crucial to modernization of the British army before World War I.

At the heart of this change, however, was the spirit of education and professional training, raising the gradual recognition of the army staff officer as one entitled to respect over the relative parochialism of the regiment. Brian Bond concentrated on the history of the Staff College as one way of explaining the "transformation which took place in the character of the British Army" between 1854 and 1914 (17). The need for special training of officers in a central academy was slow to take root; some regiments persisted in frowning on two-year leaves for study. Nor, until 1904 did a General Staff exist for posting. But Bond's book makes it clear that if the Staff College at Camberley was slow to develop in the 1860s, by the nineties it was becoming a center for study, placing a premium on intellect over connection or birth and encouraging a new type of professional officer, many of whom would be ready to take command of divisions and corps in the British Expeditionary Force in 1914.

The careers of most of these commanders included some familiarity with the comparatively new Intelligence Section which is the subject of a remarkably thorough, probing and scholarly book by Thomas Fergusson (25). Based on a PhD thesis at Duke University, and on experience as an officer in the United States' Army, Fergusson's study closely analyses the origins of the Military Intelligence Division after the Crimean War, recognizing the role of the Topographical and Statistical Section but arguing that War-Office Intelligence came into being only after the Cardwell Reforms. From 1873 the story is a continuous one, with fluctuations related to broader questions of War-Office organization but leading to the establishment of a secure department as an outcome of the Esher Report in 1904, when Intelligence came under the Director General of Military Operations. On the way to this achievement, Fergusson includes the role of such gifted officers as Henry Brackenbury, David Henderson, William Nicholson, William Robertson and James Grierson. Their place in the book enlivens what is sometimes an account of intricate administrative history in which the Boer War marks a dividing line between the Cardwell Reforms and World War I.

These two important studies by Brian Bond and Thomas Fergusson emphasize once again that the pace of reform was dramatically stimulated by the war in South Africa. Before 1895 staff training and Intelligence operations were hindered not only by economy but by the weight of tradition, particularly around the Duke of Cambridge, whose retirement as commander-in-chief is described as "Dislodging the Duke" by John Wilson in his biography of Campbell-Bannerman (59). During the war from October 1899 to May 1902, weaknesses of training and leadership were placed in context with much larger problems that are superbly recounted in Thomas Pakenham's major study (43). Into a book of 700 pages he distills the fruits of eight years of research and writing, examining archives on both sides in three languages, comprehending the confusions of imperial as well as military policy, listening to the stories of soldiers and through the reading of unpublished diaries and letters bringing a fresh perspective to the Boer War, including fascinating biographical sketches of the prominent men involved, whether civilians such as Chamberlain and Milner, or military figures such as Wolseley and Roberts. On Sir Redvers Buller, Pakenham brings new sympathetic insight that forms a prominent theme of the book, and he places leadership in conjunction with what he calls "basic handicaps" for the British--"weak intelligence and poor mobility" (p. 194). The grasp of complex relationships and the breadth of conception make Pakenham's a superior comprehensive work of history that should be considered for some time the definitive one-volume study of the Boer War. By comparison the recent book by Byron Farwell, based on wide reading in secondary printed sources, contains some fine writing on the details of battles but few new insights on the significance of the war (24).

For the student of modern British military history, the outcome of that war is still a central point of transition into the twentieth century. The reports of commissions and committees together with an immense resource of private papers form the base for the study by John Gooch of formation of the General Staff, the central military council that was essential to British planning in the decade before World War I (28). The background of imperial debate between German plans in Europe and Russian designs on India were examined by Adrian Preston (44), but the intricate web of military strategy, imperial policy and party politics has been woven into the theme of grand strategy by Nicholas d'Ombrain (23), S.R. Williamson (58), Geoffrey Searle (47), and John McDermott (39). The broad sweep of their work assumes the more specialized examination of army reform by Satre (46), the book on the Haldane reforms by Spiers (51), and the article on the politics of those reforms by Anthony Morris (40). Finally Viscount Esher, a central figure through all of these debates, is the subject of a biography by Peter Fraser, who writes incisively on the constitutional questions involved in relations between the Esher Committee, the crown, the Committee of Imperial Defence and the General Staff (26).

The formal structure of these institutions, the large questions of strategy involved, and the quality of professional training all mark a fundamental change from the early nineteenth to the early twentieth century. The bearing of private papers on this remarkable change need not be listed here; it is evident in the bibliographies of such comprehensive scholarly studies as those of Strachan, Fergusson, Pakenham and Gooch.

BIBLIOGRAPHY

1. Allen, Donald R. "Florence Nightingale: Toward a Psycho-historical Interpretation." *Journal of Interdisciplinary History*, VI (Summer, 1975).
2. Anderson, Olive. "The Growth of Christian Militarism in Mid-Victorian Britain." *English Historical Review*, LXXXIV (1971), 46-72.
3. Anglesey, Marquess of (ed.). *Sergeant Pearman's Memoirs*. London: Cape, 1968.
4. ———— (ed.). *Little Hodge: Being Extracts from the Diaries and Letters of Colonel Edward Cooper Hodge written during the Crimean War, 1854-1856*. London: Leo Cooper, 1971.
5. ————. *A History of the British Cavalry, 1816 to 1919*. London: Secker & Warburg. vol. I, 1816-1850 (1973). vol. II, 1851-1871 (1975). vol. III, 1872-1898 (1983).
6. Bailes, Howard. "Technology and Imperialism: A Case Study of the Victorian Army in Africa." *Victorian Studies*, XXIV (1980), 83-104.
7. Bamfield, Veronica. *On the Strength: The Story of the British Army Wife*. London: Charles Knight, 1974.
8. Barker, A.J. *The Vainglorious War, 1854-56*. London: Weidenfeld and Nicholson, 1970.
9. Bartlett, H. Moyse. *Louis Edward Nolan and his Influence on the British Cavalry*. London: 1971.
10. Baylen, Joseph O. and Conway, Alan (eds.). *Soldier-Surgeon: The Crimean War Letters of Dr. Douglas A. Reid*. Knoxville: University of Tennessee Press, 1968.
11. Bayley, Charles C. *Mercenaries for the Crimea: The German, Swiss, and Italian Legions in British Service, 1854-1856*. Montreal: McGill-Queen's University Press, 1977.
12. Beckett, Ian F.W. *Rifleman Form: A Study of the Rifle Volunteer Movement 1859-1908*. Aldershot: Ogilby Trusts, 1982.
13. Best, Geoffrey. "Militarism and the Victorian Public School" in Brian Simon and Ian Bradley (eds.) *The Victorian Public School*. Dublin: Gill and Macmillan, 1975.
14. Blake, R.L.V. ffrench. *The Crimean War*. London: Leo Cooper, 1971. Sphere Books, 1973.
15. Blanco, Richard L. "Reform and Wellington's Post-Waterloo Army 1815-54." *Military Affairs*, 29 (1965), 123-31.
16. ————. *Wellington's Surgeon General: General Sir James McGrigor*. Durham, North Carolina: Duke University Press, 1974.
17. Bond, Brian. *The Victorian Army and the Staff College, 1854-1914*. London: Methuen, 1972.
18. Bruce, Anthony. *The Purchase System in the British Army, 1660-1871*. London: Royal Historical Society, 1980.
19. Burroughs, Peter. "The Human Cost of Imperial Defence in the early Victorian Age," *Victorian Studies*, XXIV (1980), 7-32. "The Ordnance Department and Colonial Defence, 1821-1855,"

Journal of Imperial and Commonwealth History, X (1982), 125-49.
20. Cantlie, Neil (Sir). A History of the Army Medical Services. 2 vols. Edinburgh: Churchill Livingstone, 1974.
21. Cunningham, Hugh. The Volunteer Force. London: Croom Helm, 1975.
22. Dinwiddy, J.K. "The Early Nineteenth Century campaign against Flogging in the Army," English Historical Review, XCVII (1982), 308-31.
23. d'Ombrain, N.J. War Machinery and High Policy: Defence Administration in Peacetime Britain, 1902-1914. London: Oxford University Press, 1973.
24. Farwell, Byron. Queen Victoria's Little Wars. New York: Harper and Row, 1973. The Great Anglo-Boer War. New York: Harper and Row, 1976.
25. Fergusson, Thomas G. British Military Intelligence, 1870-1914. Frederick, Md.: University Publications of America, 1984.
26. Fraser, Peter. Lord Esher: A Political Biography. London: Hart-Davis, 1973.
27. Gooch, Brison D. "Recent Literature on Queen Victoria's Little Wars," Victorian Studies, XVII (Dec. 1973), 217-24.
28. Gooch, John. The Plans of War: The General Staff and British Military Strategy, 1900-1916. London: Routledge and Kegan Paul, 1974. The Prospect of War: Studies in British Defence Policy, 1847-1942. London: Cass, 1981.
29. Hamer, W.S. The British Army: Civil Military Relations, 1885-1905. London: Oxford University Press, 1970.
30. Hanham, H.J. "Religion and Nationality in the mid-Victorian Army," in M.R.D. Foot (ed.) War and Society: Historical Essays in Honour of J.R. Western. London: Elek, 1973.
31. Harries-Jenkins, Gwyn. The Army in Victorian Society. London: Routledge and Kegan Paul. Toronto and Buffalo: University of Toronto Press, 1977.
32. Haswell, Jock. British Military Intelligence. London: Weidenfeld and Nicolson, 1973.
33. Hopkins, Harry. The Strange Death of Private White: A Victorian Scandal that made History. London: Weidenfeld and Nicolson, 1977.
34. Keegan, John. "Regimental Ideology," in Geoffrey Best and Andrew Wheatcroft (eds.) War, Economy and the Military Mind. London: Croom Helm, 1976.
35. King, J.E. "'We could eat the Police!': Popular Violence in the North Lancashire cotton strike of 1878," Victorian Studies, XXVIII (Spring, 1985), 439-71.
36. Lalumia, Matthew. "Realism and anti-aristocratic sentiment in Victorian depictions of the Crimean War," Victorian Studies, XXVII (Autumn, 1983), 25-51.
37. Lehmann, Joseph H. Remember You Are an Englishman: A Biography of Sir Harry Smith, 1787-1860. London: Cape, 1977.
38. Mather, F.C. Public Order in the Age of the Chartists. Manchester: Manchester University Press, 1959.
39. McDermott, John. "The Revolution in British Military Thinking from the Boer War to the Moroccan crisis," Canadian Journal of History, IX (1974), 159-77.

40. Morris, Anthony. "Haldane's Army Reforms 1906-1908: The Deception of the Radicals," *History*, 56 (Feb. 1971), 17-34.
41. Morton, Patricia. "Another Victorian Paradox: Anti-militarism in a jingoistic society," *Historical Reflections*, VIII (1981), 169-89.
42. Otley, C.B. "The Social Origins of British Army Officers," *Sociological Review*, XVIII (July, 1970), 213-39.
43. Pakenham, Thomas. *The Boer War*. New York: Random House, 1979.
44. Preston, Adrian. "Wolseley, the Khartoum relief expedition and the defence of India, 1885-1900," in Adrian Preston and Peter Dennis (eds.) *Swords and Covenants*. London: Croom Helm, 1976.
45. Quinault, Roland and Stevenson, John (eds.). *Popular Protest and Public Order: Six Studies in British History*. London: Allen and Unwin, 1974.
46. Satre, Lowell J. "St. John Brodrick and Army Reform 1901-1903," *Journal of British Studies*, XV (1976), 117-39.
47. Searle, Geoffrey. *The Quest for National Efficiency: A Study in British Politics and Political Thought, 1899-1914*. Oxford: Blackwell, 1971.
48. Shannon, Richard. "An Icon and Her Intrigues: Review of F.B. Smith, *Florence Nightingale*," in *Times Literary Supplement* (28 May 1982), 571-72.
49. Skelley, Alan R. *The Victorian Army at Home: The Recruitment and Terms and Conditions of the British Regular, 1859-1899*. London: Croom Helm. Montreal: McGill-Queen's University Press, 1977.
50. Smith, F.B. *Florence Nightingale: Reputation and Power*. New York: St. Martin's Press, 1982.
51. Spiers, Edward M. *Haldane: An Army Reformer*. Edinburgh: Edinburgh University Press, 1980. *The Army and Society, 1815-1914*. London: Longman, 1980. *Radical General: Sir George deLacy Evans, 1787-1870*. Manchester: Manchester University Press, 1983.
52. Spring, Eileen and David. "The Real Florence Nightingale: An Essay Review," *Bulletin of the History of Medicine* (Summer, 1983), 285-90.
53. Stevenson, John. *Popular Disturbances in England, 1700-1870*. London: Longman, 1979.
54. Strachan, Hew. "Soldiers, Strategy and Sebastopol," *Historical Journal*, XXI (1978), 303-25. "The early Victorian army and the nineteenth-century revolution in government," *English Historical Review*, XCV (1980), 782-809. *Wellington's Legacy: The Reform of the British army, 1830-1854*. Manchester: Manchester University Press, 1984.
55. Trustram, Myna. *Women of the Regiment: Marriage and the Victorian Army*. New York: Cambridge University Press, 1984.
56. Warner, Philip. *The British Cavalry*. London: Dent, 1984.
57. Waterfield, R. *Memoirs of Private Waterfield*. ed. A. Swinson and D. Scott. London: Cassell, 1968.
58. Williamson, S.R. *The Politics of Grand Strategy*. Cambridge, Mass.: Harvard University Press, 1969.
59. Wilson, John. *C.B.: A Life of Sir Henry Campbell-Bannerman*. New York: St. Martin's Press, 1973.

X

POLITICS AND THE HIGH COMMAND, 1899-1965

David French

The politics and administration of British defense policy in the first half of the twentieth century has attracted considerable interest since Higham's *Guide* was published. Perhaps because the literature has grown so quickly we are still without an up-to-date account of the development of British defence policy. Michael Howard's seminal Ford Lectures (125) were given in 1971 and parts of it have now become a little dated. They can be supplemented by Gooch (102), Beckett and Gooch (14) and Kennedy (143). Wilson is an indispensable guide to the Cabinet archives but unfortunately no similar guides have yet been published for the service departments. Hazlehurst and Woodland have published a guide to the Papers of Cabinet ministers and Cook has edited two volumes describing the papers of selected public servants (277, 119, 51, 52). Mayer and Koenig have compiled a guide to manuscripts collections relating to the two world wars held in repositories in the United Kingdom (179).

1899-1914. The origins and consequences of Britain's involvement in the second Boer War can be traced through Porter (212) and Pakenham (200) supplemented by the Papers of Midleton (384), Roberts (403), Buller (307) and White (425). Attempts by Balfour's Unionist government to reform the army are briefly surveyed by Zebel (285), Mackay (167), Bertie (20) and Satre (235). Matthew (177) shows how the war alerted the Liberal Imperialist wing of the Liberal Party to the gaps in British defences. D'Ombrain (69) explains why the prewar Committee of Imperial Defence failed to co-ordinate defence policy before 1914 and three of its most prominent members, Lord Esher, Sir George Clarke and Maurice Hankey are portrayed by Fraser (83), Gooch (100) and Roskill (223). Further illumination of the prewar activities of the CID can be gained from the papers of Esher (341) and one of its assistant secretaries, Adrian Grant Duff (353).

The diplomatic context within which defence planners worked has attracted considerable attention. The works by Steiner (250), Kennedy (142) and Hinsley (121) are essential reading for an understanding of the European context as are Nish (197) and Lowe (161) for Britain's changing position in the Far East. Watt charts the course of Anglo-American relations, a matter of growing importance to the British as the century progressed (272). Robbins' biography of Grey is the standard life of the Liberal Foreign Secretary (221). Wilson presents a novel and controversial interpretation of why Britain went to war in 1914 (276). Williamson (275) has written a brilliant account of the development of the Anglo-French military Entente before 1914 and this can be supplemented by the works of Coogan and McDermott (50, 180). Spiers (247), Bond (22), Fergusson (79) and Gooch (99) each illustrate aspects of how the army was modernized after the Boer War. The origins and prewar activities of the General Staff can also be traced in the Ellison, (339) Lyttleton (378), Ewart (343), Mottistone (391) and Wilson (426) papers. Andrew provides a full account of the growing pains of the secret service (5). Mackay (166) and Haggie (110) look at the efforts of Lord Fisher to prepare the navy for a war against Germany. There is also some evidence on this question in the Cawdor (311), Selborne (405), Tweedmouth (420) and Crease (322) papers. Fisher's own papers have been deposited at Churchill College, Cambridge (344), and a microfilm of the papers of one of his successors as First Sea Lord, Prince Louis of Battenberg, is available in the Imperial War Museum (385). French (85) tried to synthesize naval, military and economic planning for war.

1914-1918. The most convenient introduction to the development of central government during the war is Burk (30). The Hankey papers shed considerable light on the inner workings of the government during and after the war (358). The activities of the Asquith Liberal government between August 1914 and May 1915 are best approached through Hazlehurst (118) and Fraser (84) and the published diary of Sir Charles Hobhouse (62). There is still no adequate account of the way in which high politics and strategy were intertwined during the war. Stubbs (253) is rightly critical of Lord Beaverbrook's *Politicians and the War, 1914-16* but there is nothing yet to replace it. Turner has provided a good account of the functions of Lloyd George's "garden suburb" (265, 266) and Leo Amery's published diaries illuminate the activities of the Lloyd George Coalition (9, 293). The Lothian papers contain extensive files on Lothian's work as one of Lloyd George's private secretaries between 1917-21 (377). Asquith's role as a war leader is best approached through Jenkins (135), Hazlehurst (117), Koss (149) and the letters he wrote to various lady friends (28, 294). Grigg is excellent on Lloyd George's climb to the Premiership but stops in December 1916 and has disappointingly little that is new to say about his role as a strategist (109). Lloyd George's own assessment of his policies can be found in his mistress' diary (255). Churchill's wartime career has been the subject of two massive volumes by Gilbert (95, 96). Royle's biography of Kitchener is a considerable improvement on its predecessors but must be supplemented by Neilson (40, 230, 191). The papers of Sir Herbert Creedy, Kitchener's private secretary, are now open for inspection (323). Mackay briefly reconsiders Balfour's work at the Admiralty and Foreign Office (167). Although both the Curzon and Derby papers are available there are still no satisfactory accounts of their wartime work (325, 330). Those papers once held in the Beaverbrook Library have now been transferred to the House of Lords Record Office. A small collection of papers relating to Milner's activities in the War Cabinet are now in the Public Record Office (387).

The concluding chapters of Hinsley (121) provide the best introduction to the diplomatic context within which British strategists operated between 1914-16. The development of British war aims has attracted a growing body of research. Most of it has concentrated on the final two years of the war and is based on a detailed analysis of diplomatic and political papers. Rothwell (228) is of fundamental importance. Bridge, Calder and Fest (27, 34, 80) have examined British policy towards eastern Europe and the Habsburg Empire; Egerton has investigated British attitudes towards the creation of the League of Nations (77) and Fest (81), Cooper (53) and Kernek (144) have considered the possibility of a negotiated peace. Bunselmeyer has looked at the origins of reparations (29) and Jaffe says much of interest about British attitudes towards the postwar balance of power (134).

Woodward presents a highly traditional view of the debate between the "easterners" and "westerners" but supports it with much new research (281, 282). This view has been challenged, initially by Gooch (101), and subsequently by Neilson (193) and French (88). Both of the latter have pointed to the significant constraints placed on British policy-makers by their need to bow to the wishes of their allies. Other works which have highlighted the significance of Britain's relationship with her allies are Dutton (75, 76), Burk (31) and Cassar (39). Several British liaison officers with the allies have left papers relating to their work (301, 306, 316, 400, 411).

Holmes' biography of Sir John French, based to a considerable extent on French's own unpublished papers, was a revelation and a successful rebuttal of the "donkey" school of military historians. Cassar concentrates on his career between 1914-15 (124, 345, 349, 41). Haig still awaits a full-scale scholarly biography examining not just his wartime but his pre-and postwar careers. The works by Sixsmith and Marshall-Cornwall add little to our knowledge (241, 175). Additional information about Haig's career can be gleaned from the papers of three members of his staff, Davidson, Butler, Boraston, and from a small collection of letters Haig wrote after the war to the Reverend G.S. Duncan (327, 308, 303, 355). The papers of three other Western Front commanders, Monro, Smith-Dorrien and Horne are now open to researchers (409, 366, 388). The inner history of the development of the War Office remains to be written although there is plenty of material upon which to base it (323, 380, 383, 393, 421). Nancy Maurice provides an interesting account of the Maurice Case which might have toppled Lloyd George in 1918 but the evidence upon which Maurice based his arguments is challenged by Woodward (178, 282). Maurice's papers have been deposited at King's College London (383).

Much still remains to be written concerning the war against the Turks. The origins and course of the Dardanelles campaign have been reassessed by Gilbert (95) and French (86), whilst Prior (215) brilliantly demolishes Churchill's own tendentious account in *The World Crisis*. Several of the leading actors, including Hamilton, Birdwood and Limpus have left extensive collections of papers (357, 302, 374). Hamilton has been the subject of a biography by his nephew (112). The course of events in Mesopotamia up to the fall of Kut has been re-examined by Galbraith (91) but the story of the strategical direction of the war in the Middle East after 1916 has not yet been told. Lord Allenby still lacks a good modern biography although the material for it is available (292). The Imperial War Museum has acquired some of the papers of his predecessor, Sir Archibald Murray (314, 393). Britain's tangled relations with the Arabs and Jews has been analyzed by Kedourie and Friedman (141, 89) and T.E. Lawrence has been the subject of several new biographies

(148, 165, 252). Sir Mark Sykes, co-author of the Sykes-Picot agreement is the subject of a biography by Adelson (1, 415).

Before his death Arthur Marder was able to complete his seminal work on the Royal Navy during the war and to publish a revised and enlarged edition of the third volume (168, 172). The availability of new collections of papers led to two new assessments of Earl Beatty (12, 227, 299, 300, 348). The National Maritime Museum has acquired a collection of letters written by Jellicoe to E.E. Bradford between 1914-17, together with the diaries of Sir Charles Madden, Jellicoe's Chief of Staff between 1914-16 and subsequently second in command of the Grand Fleet (370, 381). Lord Wester Wemyss' papers have now been deposited at Churchill College (424).

Although a considerable body of documentary material is available, the debate about the proper role of air power during the war has not yet attracted the attention it deserves. Cooper and Sweetman provide useful introductions (54, 254). The Royal Air Force Museum houses the papers of Sir David Henderson (Director General of Military Aeronautics, 1913-18 and Vice-President of the Air Council, 1918), Lord Trenchard (Chief of Air Staff, 1918 and 1919-29) and Sir Frederick Sykes (Chief of Air Staff, 1918-19) (362, 414, 419). The papers of Lord Weir, the President of the Air Board, are at Churchill College and he has been the subject of a biography by Reader (216, 423).

Historians of British intelligence during the war are still hampered by the government's illogical insistence that much of the evidence must be kept secret even after material relating to the Second World War has been released. But, perhaps encouraged by the Publication of several volumes of the official history of British secret intelligence during the Second World War, historians of British strategy during the First World War have also recently begun to investigate the influence of intelligence on decision-making. The Edmonds papers contain some material about the origins of the War Office's secret service (338), Hiley has examined the failure of British espionage against Germany (120), French has used the Kirke papers to show how G.H.Q. improvised a secret intelligence service on the Western front in 1914-15 (87, 372) and Beesly has provided a useful account of Room 40, the Admiralty's intelligence and codebreaking organization (15). Andrew has synthesized all of this and added much that is new (5). Some of the private papers upon which he based his work are now housed at Churchill College (315, 329, 356). The Kell papers contain a memoir by his wife of the first head of MI5 (371). The relationship between strategy and propaganda has been illustrated by Sanders, Sanders and Taylor and Neilson (233, 234, 192).

1919-1939. There is no single volume surveying the higher direction of British defence policy between the wars. Gibbs (94) concentrates on the latter half of the 1930s and presents only some brief comments on the period before 1932. Watt (271) has fitted the dilemmas of Britain's defence planners into a European context and Roskill's volumes on Hankey's career after 1919 contain a mass of invaluable information about the deliberations of the Cabinet and the Committee of Imperial Defence (223). Welch has examined the origins and development of the Chiefs of Staff Sub-committee (273). The most important classes of Cabinet papers for the inter-war period are

CAB 23 and 24 (Cabinet Minutes and Memoranda to 1939), CAB 29 (International Conference), CAB 30 (Washington Disarmament Conference), CAB 32 (Imperial Conferences to 1939), CAB 53 (Chiefs of Staff Committee), CAB 54 (Deputy Chiefs of Staff Committee), CAB 55 (Joint Planning Committee), CAB 56 (Joint Intelligence Committee) and CAB 64 (Minister for the Co-ordination of Defence: Registered files).

Morgan's history of the Lloyd George Coalition government is disappointingly thin on defence policy (187). Dockrill and Goold have written an excellent account of British Policy at the peace conferences (68). The best guides to the brief period between 1919-21 when the British tried and failed to run their empire like a military fief are by Jeffrey (136) and Darwin (60, 61). Townshend has provided a perceptive account of the British army's failure in Ireland between 1919-21 (262) and Orde has surveyed the development of British security policy until the mid-19120s (198).

The biographies of Baldwin by Hyde and MacDonald by Marquand both have something of interest to say about their protagonist's attitudes towards defence policy. Marquand has made extensive use of MacDonald's papers and is particularly instructive on the limits of his pacificism (174, 129, 379). Baldwin's papers are thin for his third government but the Vincent manuscripts contain some references to his views on defence policy (297, 421). Carlton has investigated the disarmament policy of the second Labour government (37) and Kyba has examined the way in which Public opinion constrained defence planning in the early 1930s (150). Dilks' biography of Chamberlain has at the time of writing (1986) not gone beyond 1929, so students of Chamberlain's defence policy must have recourse to existing biographies, Fuchser's study of Chamberlain and appeasement, Middlemas' and Douglas' studies of diplomacy and defence policy in the late 1930s, Colvin's account of the Chamberlain Cabinet and Chamberlain's own papers (48, 70, 71, 90, 183, 312). Parkinson was one of the first historians to write an account of Cabinet policy between Munich and Dunkirk based on newly released Cabinet papers (205). Two Foreign Secretaries in the 1930s, Hoare and Eden, have attracted recent biographers but Lord Halifax has not (38, 57, 363). Rose has written a sympathetic biography of Lord Vansittart (222).

The central dilemma of British defence Planners in the 1930s was that Britain faced a multiplicity of threats in the short and medium term with inadequate resources and too few reliable friends. Lippincott has investigated the strategy of appeasement in the late 1930s (159). Wasserstein and Cohen have examined the significance of Britain's Mandate commitment in Palestine (44, 270) and Pratt looked at the threat to Britain's position in the Middle East posed by Italy (214). Louis, Lee and Lowe examined the background to Britain's interests in the Far East posed by the growing threat from Japan whilst Nedipath and McIntyre assess the failure of the Singapore naval base to deter the Japanese (160, 152, 162, 181, 190). MacDonald, Ovendale and Reynolds have each underlined the extent to which Chamberlain's policies were designed to win and retain the support of the Dominions and the United States (164, 199, 219). Taylor and Short showed how a growing awareness of their material weaknesses encouraged British governments to rely on propaganda to bolster their position abroad (240, 256, 257).

The policies of the three services have each been the subject of considerable research. Roskill has characterized naval policy between 1930-39 as being a period of reluctant rearmament (225). Marder (169) has analyzed why the Admiralty failed to learn some of the most important lessons of the First World War and traced their reactions to the growing menace posed by the Japanese in the Far East (173). The papers of several First Lords of the Admiralty, including Long, Alexander, Chatfield and Hoare are open to researchers, together with those of a number of senior staff officers (290, 313, 332, 333, 335, 348, 376, 394). An edition of Lord Bridgeman's papers is being prepared (305).

Bond has written an excellent study of British military policy between the wars as well as editing the diaries of Sir Henry Pownall, who was both an Assistant Secretary of the CID and later Director of Military Operations and Intelligence at the War Office (23, 26, 402). The Derby papers contain interesting insights into the War Office's reaction to the period of retrenchment the army faced after 1919 and the Hore-Belisha and Haydon papers are important sources for any study of the army in the late 1930s (330, 360, 365). Milne is the only inter-war CIGS to have found a recent biographer (195, 386) although some of the papers of several of his predecessors and successors, including Cavan, Deverell and Montgomery-Massingberd are available to researchers (310, 331, 390). Jeffrey has published a selection of Wilson's papers emanating from his period as CIGS (137, 318, 426). Trythall has written a short account of Hoare-Belisha's fall from Power (263) and Dilks has looked briefly at the influence of the General Staff in shaping foreign policy in 1930s (66). There is still no adequate study of the reactions of the War Office to the problems posed by rearmament in the late 1930s. Bond, Reid and Tyrthall have provided perceptive studies of Sir Basil Liddell Hart and Major-General J.F.C. Fuller, two of the most influential intellectual critics of defence policy between the wars (25, 217, 264). Liddell Hart's own papers are an indispensable source for any study of defence policy between the wars (373).

The development of air policy between the wars has attracted much more attention from historians of the inter-war period than it has from those of the First World War. Smith, Hyde and Powers have each written general studies and they can be supplemented by the papers of Hoare, Trenchard, Salmond, Newall and Dowding (130, 213, 243, 244, 245, 337, 395, 404, 419). Cross has published a biography of Lord Swinton (58, 413). Churchill's part in urging the government towards greater efforts in the area of air rearmament is analyzed by Gilbert (97) and Bialer has suggested that fear of air attack persuaded the Cabinet to give priority to the RAF rather than to the other two services when they began to rearm (21). The work of the service intelligence branches in discovering, and sometimes exaggerating, the extent of German rearmament, has been analyzed by Andrew, Hinsley, Wark and in several of the essays in Andrew and Dilks (5, 6, 122, 267, 268, 269).

The relationship between the economy, rearmament and defence policy in 1930s is best approached through the studies by Dunbabin, Coghlan, Parker and Peden (74, 43, 201, 203, 209). Peden has done much to absolve the Treasury from the suspicion that they were more interested in ensuring that Britain had enough money left to pay an indemnity to the victors after Britain had lost the war than in ensuring that she spent sufficient money on defence to ensure that she would win the war (208). Shay and Parker have examined, inter-

High Command and Modern War 249

alia, the influence of businessmen and trade unionists in determining the pace of rearmament policy (203, 239). Dennis has explained why the Chamberlain government introduced conscription in peacetime for the first time in 1939 (63). Murray compared Britain's achievements with those of her friends and rivals (189).

1939-1945. A single volume making available to students the burgeoning literature on the development of British strategy during the Second World War is badly needed. The War Cabinet files in the Public Record Office (CAB 65--CAB 127) together with those of the Prime Minister's private office files (PREM 1, 2, and 3) are an indispensable source. The third volume of Roskill's biography of Hankey includes a chapter on the Chamberlain War Cabinet (223). Many of the principal telegrams and memoranda emanating from the War Cabinet between 1940-43 have already been published (104, 105, 106, 107) and further glimpses of its activities can be gleaned from the papers of Attlee (295), Chatfield (313), Ismay, (368), Jacob (369), Lindemann, (375), Nicholl (396), Sinclair (406), and Tizard (417). Wingate's biography of Ismay only serves as a starting point for the full-scale biography he deserves (279) and Attlee's biographer, like his protagonist, has little to say about grand strategy (115).

The period of the "Phoney War" and British policy towards Scandinavia has been studied by Munch-Petersen and Parker. (188, 202) Douglas analyzed the policies of the Chamberlain government in the winter and spring of 1939-40 (71), Bayer (10) has written briefly about British policy towards the Russo-Finnish war of 1939-40 and work is now in progress about the development of British war aims before the fall of France. Bond, Dilks, Gates and Johnson have investigated the collapse of the Anglo-French alliance in the summer of 1940 (24, 65, 93, 138) and Thomas and Spears have examined the development of Anglo-French relations after the fall of France (246, 258).

The wartime career of Winston Churchill has predictably attracted considerable attention. At the time of writing Gilbert's official biography has reached 1941 (98). Schoenfeld examined the structure of the Churchill Cabinet (237), Colville has anatomized the "Churchillians" and portrayed Churchill himself in his diaries (46, 47, 317), and Cosgrave, Lewin and Thompson tried to assess Churchill's abilities as a strategist (55, 155, 260). Roskill and Marder have conducted a sometimes acrimonious debate about Churchill's relationship with his admirals (170, 224).

The development of British foreign policy during the war can best be approached through the five volume official history by Woodward (283) supplemented by the biography of Eden by Carlton cited above and the published diaries of three senior Foreign Office officials, Bruce Lockhart, Cadogan and Harvey (64, 116, 284). Beitzell and Douglas have examined the uneasy relationship which existed between the three major wartime allies (18, 72, 73). Reynolds has written brilliantly about the origins of the Anglo-American alliance (219) and Thorne has written equally brilliantly about the competitive co-operation in the war against Japan (261). The origins of the secret Churchill-Roosevelt correspondence has been uncovered by Leutze (153) and it has been edited and published by Kimball and by Loewenheim and his collaborators (147, 163). Sainsbury has investigated the significance of the Moscow, Cairo and

Teheran conferences of 1943 (232). Beaumont has written perceptively about British economic aid to Russia and Kersaudy has analysed British relations with de Gaulle and the Free French (13, 145). British relations with de Gaulle and the Free French (13, 145). Rothwell has written at very great length about the Foreign Office's war aims (229). His work can usefully be supplemented by the more detailed studies by Reiss on the Churchill-Stalin "Percentages" agreement and Sharp on the issue of the division of Germany (218, 238).

The official history of British grand strategy during the war has been completed by Howard (126) and the United Kingdom Military Series has almost been completed with a series of volumes on the Mediterranean campaign (184, 185). The official histories can be supplemented by Parkinson's two volumes (205, 206). M.R.D. Foot's official history of S.O.E. in France should be complemented by Stafford, the relevant chapters in Pimlott and the works by Auty and Clogg who have investigated British policy towards resistance movements in the Balkans (8, 210, 248, 249). Sainsbury, Jackson, Lawlor and Pitt have each written about aspects of Britain's involvement in North Africa and the Mediterranean between 1940-43 (132, 151, 211, 231). Grigg has argued provocatively that timidity robbed the western allies of victory in 1943 (108). Jackson is on much firmer ground in his assessment of Operation "Overlord" (133). Callahan and Allen have written accounts of the forgotten war in Burma and the Far East (3, 4, 35).

The publication of successive volumes in the official history of British intelligence during the war has been the most important development in the literature during the last decade (122). Writing books about Ultra and Enigma and memoirs about work at Bletchley Park has become a minor industry. The best accounts include those by Lewin (157), Bennett (19), Kahn (140), Welchman (274), Garlinski (92), Jones (139) and Stengers (251). The work of Professor Hinsley and his colleagues should be supplemented by Beesly on the Admiralty's Operational Intelligence Centre and his biography of Admiral Godfrey (15, 16, 352). Masterman has written a brief account of the double-cross system which turned and ran captured German agents in Britain and Cruickshank has written illuminatingly about the work of the Political Warfare Executive (59, 176).

The War Office files in the Public Record Office relating to the higher direction of the war are voluminous. The most important include WO 32 (Registered Papers, General Series), WO 106 and WO 193 (Director of Military Operations), WO 163 (War Office Council and Army Council), WO 165--WO 179 (War Diaries), WO 197--WO 205 (Military Headquarters Papers) and WO 208 (Director of Military Intelligence). Senior military commanders have drawn their fair share of attention. Hamilton had access to Montgomery's own private papers, an advantage denied to his earlier biographers, and Montgomery's brother throws some interesting light on the Field Marshal's early life (42, 113, 114, 154, 186). Lewin's work on Slim is a model of how military biographies should be written and he has also written an excellent volume on Wavell (36, 156, 158). The latter can be supplemented by the second volume of Connell's biography of Wavell which examined his role as Supreme Allied Commander in South East Asia (49).

Alexander, Auchinleck, Gort and Alanbrooke have also attracted biographers (82, 131, 196, 207). The papers of Ironside (367), Dill

(334, 361), Alanbrooke (289), Acland (288), Slim (408), Auchinleck (296), Alexander (291), Montgomery (389), de Guingand (351), Dempsey (328), Gale (350), Davidson (326), Adam (287), Strong (412) and Percival (399) have survived and most are available for research.

Since the publication of Higham's Guide the Air Ministry files have been transferred to the Public Record Office. The development of the strategy of air warfare can be investigated in AIR 6 (Meetings of the Air Board and Air Council), AIR 8 (Chief of Air Staff), AIR 9 (Director of Plans), AIR 14 (Headquarters, Bomber Command), AIR 15 (Headquarters, Coastal Command), AIR 16 (Headquarters, Fighter Command), AIR 23 (Headquarters, Overseas Commands), AIR 40 (Director of Intelligence), AIR 42 (Combined Operations Planning Committee), AIR 46 (Air Missions) and AIR 47 (Combined Operations Planning Staff). Portal and Harris have attracted good recent biographers but Dowding has not (182, 220, 236). The papers of a clutch of Airmarshals, including Douglas (336), Dowding (337), Portal (401), Slessor (407), Tedder (416), Evill (342), Freeman (347), Holinghurst (364), Leigh-Mallory (382), Elmhirst (340), Peirse (398) and Bottomley (304) are now open.

Much work still remains to be done on the Admiralty during the war. Slessor has castigated Admiralty command policy in both world wars as "woefully lacking in imagination" (242). A start can be made in assessing this judgement by examining the Admiralty's files in the Public Record Office. The most important are those in classes ADM 1, ADM 116 and ADM 178 (Admiralty and Secretariat papers and cases), ADM 167 (Minutes and Memoranda of the Board of Admiralty) and ADM 205 (Papers of the First Sea Lord). These must be supplemented by the papers of North (397), Somerville (410), Cunningham (324), Mountbatten (392), Tovey (418), Fraser (346). Halpern has edited a volume of the Keyes Papers covering his activities during the Second World War (111), and Zeigler and Humble have written lives of Mountbatten and Fraser (128, 286).

BIBLIOGRPAHY

Published Works

1. Adelson, R. *Mark Sykes: Portrait of an Amateur*. London: Jonathan Cape, 1975.
2. Allen, H.R. *The Legacy of Lord Trenchard*. London: Cassell, 1972.
3. Allen, L. *Singapore, 1941-42*. London: Davis-Poynter, 1977.
4. ———. *Burma: The Longest War, 1941-1945*. London: J.M. Dent, 1984.
5. Andrew, C. *Secret Service: The Making of the British Intelligence Community*. London: Heinemann, 1985.
6. Andrew, C. and Dilks, D. (eds.) *The Missing Dimension: Governments and Intelligence Communities in the Twentieth Century*. London: Macmillan, 1984.
7. Aster, S. *Anthony Eden*. London: Weidenfeld & Nicolson, 1976.
8. Auty, P. and Clogg, R. (eds.) *British Policy towards Wartime Resistance in Yugoslavia and Greece*. London: Macmillan, 1975.
9. Barnes, J. and Nicholson, D. *The Leo Amery Diaries*, Vol. 1 (1896-1929). London: Hutchinson, 1980.

10. Bayer, J.A. "British Policy towards the Russian-Finnish Winter War, 1939-40," *Canadian Journal of History*, vol. 16 (1980).
11. Baylis, J. *Anglo-American Defence Relations 1939-80: The Special Relationship*. London: Macmillan, 1981.
12. Beatty, C. *Our Admiral: A Biography of Admiral of the Fleet Earl Beatty*. London: W.H. Allen, 1980.
13. Beaumont, J. *Comrades in Arms: British Aid to Russia, 1941-1945*. London: Davis-Poynter, 1980.
14. Beckett, I. and Gooch, J. *Politicians and Defence: Studies in the Formation of British Defence Policy 1845-1970*. Manchester: Manchester University Press, 1981.
15. Beesly, P. *Very Special Intelligence: The Story of the Admiralty's Operational Intelligence Centre, 1939-1945*. London: Hamish Hamilton, 1977.
16. ―――――. *Very Special Admiral: a Biography of Admiral John Henry Godfrey*. London: Hamish Hamilton, 1980.
17. ―――――. *Room 40: British Naval Intelligence 1914-1918*. London: Hamish Hamilton, 1982.
18. Beitzell, R.E. *The Uneasy Alliance: America, Britain and Russia, 1941-43*. New York: Knopf, 1972.
19. Bennett, R. "Ultra and Some Command Decisions," *Journal of Contemporary History*, vol. 16 (1981).
20. Bertie, J. "H.O. Arnold-Forster at the War Office, 1903-1905." [Unpublished Liverpool University Ph.D., 1974.]
21. Bialer, U. *The Shadow of the Bomber: The Fear of Air Attack and British Politics, 1932-1939*. London: Royal Historical Society, 1981.
22. Bond, B. *The Victorian Army and the Staff College, 1854-1914*. London: Eyre Methuen, 1972.
23. ―――――. (ed.) *Chief of Staff: The Diaries of Lieutenant General Sir Henry Pownall*, vols. 1-2. London: Leo Cooper, 1972-4.
24. ―――――. *France and Belgium, 1939-40*. London: Davis-Poynter, 1975.
25. ―――――. *Liddell Hart: A Study of his Military Thought*. London: Cassell, 1977.
26. ―――――. *British Military Policy Between the Two World Wars*. Oxford: Clarendon Press, 1980.
27. Bridge, F.R. "The British Declaration of War on Austria-Hungary in 1914," *Slavonic and East European Review*, vol. 47 (1969).
28. Brock, M. and E. (eds.) *H.H. Asquith: Letters to Venetia Stanley*. London: Oxford University Press, 1982.
29. Bunselmeyer, R.E. *The Cost of the War, 1914-1918: British Economic War Aims and the Origins of Reparations*. Hamden, Conn.: Archon, 1975.
30. Burk, K. (ed.) *War and the State: The Transformation of British Government, 1914-1919*. London: Allen & Unwin, 1982.
31. Burk, K. *Britain, America and the Sinews of War*. London: Allen & Unwin, 1985.
32. Butler, J.R.M. (ed.) *Grand Strategy*, vols. 1-6. London: H.M.S.O., 1956-1972.
33. Cabinet Office, *War Cabinet Memoranda: General Index of GT Papers 1-8412 (December 1916-October 1919)*. London: List and Index Society, vol. 156.

34. Calder, K.J. *Britain and the Origins of the New Europe, 1914-1918*. Cambridge: Cambridge University Press, 1976.
35. Callahan, R. *Burma, 1942-1945*. London: Davis-Poynter, 1978.
36. Calvert, M. *Slim*. New York: Ballantine, 1973.
37. Carlton, D. *MacDonald versus Henderson: The Foreign Policy of the Second Labour Government*. London: Macmillan, 1970.
38. ―――. *Anthony Eden: a Biography*. London: Allen Lane, 1981.
39. Cassar, G.H. *The French and the Dardanelles: A Study in the Failure in the Conduct of War*. London: Allen & Unwin, 1971.
40. ―――. *Kitchener: Architect of Victory*. London: William Kimber, 1977.
41. ―――. *The Tragedy of Sir John French*. Newark, New Jersey: University of Delaware Press, 1985.
42. Chalfont, A.L. *Montgomery of Alamein*. London: Weidenfeld & Nicolson, 1976.
43. Coghlan, F. "Armaments, Economic Policy and Appeasement: Background to British foreign policy, 1931-37," *History*, vol. 57 (1972).
44. Cohen, M.J. *Palestine--Retreat from the Mandate: The Making of British Policy, 1936-1945*. London: Elek, 1978.
45. Colville, J. *Man of Valour: Field Marshal Lord Gort VC*. London: Collins, 1972.
46. ―――. *The Churchillians*. London: Weidenfeld & Nicolson, 1981.
47. ―――. *The Fringes of Power: Downing Street Diaries 1939-55*. London: Hodder and Stoughton, 1985.
48. Colvin, I.G. *The Chamberlain Cabinet: How the Meetings in 10 Downing Street, 1937-1939, led to the Second World War*. London: Gollancz, 1971.
49. Connell, J. and Roberts, Brigadier M. *Wavell: Supreme Commander, 1941-43*. London: Collins, 1969.
50. Coogan, J.W. and Coogan, P.F. "The British Cabinet and the Anglo-French staff talks, 1905-1914: who knew what and when did he know," *Journal of British Studies*, vol. 24 (1985).
51. Cook, C. (ed.) *Sources in British Political History 1900-1951*. vol. 2. *A Guide to the Private Papers of Selected Public Servants*. London: Macmillan, 1975.
52. ―――. *Sources in British Political History 1900-1951*. vol. 6. *First Consolidated Supplement*. London: Macmillan, 1985.
53. Cooper, J.M. "The British Response to the House-Grey Memorandum: New Evidence and New Questions," *Journal of American History*, vol. 59 (1973).
54. Cooper, M. "A House Divided: Rivalry and Administration in British Military Air Command, 1914-1918," *Journal of Strategic Studies*, vol. 3, (1980).
55. Cosgrave, P. *Churchill at War*. vol. 1. *Alone, 1939-40*. London: Collins, 1974.
56. Crampton, R.J. *The Hollow Detente: Anglo-German Relations in the Balkans, 1911-1914*. London: George Prior, 1980.
57. Cross, J.A. *Sir Samuel Hoare, a Political Biography*. London: Jonathan Cape, 1977.
58. ―――. *Lord Swinton*. Oxford: Clarendon Press, 1982.

59. Cruickshank, C.G. *Deception in World War Two.* London: Oxford University Press, 1979.
60. Darwin, J.G. "The Chanak Crisis and the British Cabinet," *History*, vol. 65 (1980).
61. ———. *Britain, Egypt and the Middle East: Imperial Policy in the Aftermath of War.* London: Macmillan, 1981.
62. David, E. (ed.) *Inside Asquith's Cabinet: From the Diaries of Charles Hobhouse.* London: Murray, 1977.
63. Dennis, P. *Decision by Default. Peacetime Conscription and British Defence Policy 1919-1939.* London: Routledge & Kegan Paul, 1972.
64. Dilks, D. ed. *The Diaries of Sir Alexander Cadogan, 1938-1945.* London: Cassell, 1971.
65. ———. "The Twilight War and the Fall of France: Chamberlain and Churchill in 1940," *Transactions of the Royal Historical Society*, vol. 28 (1978).
66. ———. "'The Unnecessary War?': Military Advice and Foreign Policy in Great Britain, 1931-1939," in A. Preston (ed.) *General Staffs and Diplomacy before the Second World War.* London: Croom Helm, 1978.
67. ———. (ed.) *Retreat from Power: Studies in British Foreign Policy in the Twentieth Century*, vols. 1-2. London: Macmillan, 1981.
68. Dockrill, M.L. and Goold, J.D. *Peace Without Promise: Britain and the Peace Conferences, 1919-1923.* London: Batsford, 1981.
69. d'Ombrain, N. *War Machinery and High Policy.* London: Oxford University Press, 1973.
70. Douglas, R. *In the Year of Munich.* London: Macmillan, 1977.
71. ———. *The Advent of War, 1939-40.* London: Macmillan, 1978.
72. ———. *New Alliances, 1940-41.* London: Macmillan, 1982.
73. ———. *From War to Cold War, 1942-48.* London: Macmillan, 1981.
74. Dunbabin, J.P.D. "British Rearmament in the 1930s: A Chronology and Review," *Historical Journal* vol. 18 (1975).
75. Dutton, D.J. "The Calais Conference of December 1915," *Historical Journal*, vol. 21 (1978).
76. ———. "The deposition of King Constantine of Greece, June 1917: An Episode in Anglo-French Diplomacy," *Canadian Journal of History*, vol. 12 (1978).
77. Egerton, G.W. *Great Britain and the Creation of the League of Nations: Strategy, Politics and International Organisation, 1914-1919.* London: Scolar Press, 1979.
78. Farrar-Hockley, A. *Goughie: The Life of General Sir Hubert Gough.* London: Hart-Davis, 1975.
79. Fergusson, T.G. *British Military Intelligence, 1870-1914.* London: Arms and Armour Press, 1984.
80. Fest, W.B. *Peace or Partition: The Habsburg Monarchy and British Policy 1914-1918.* London: Prior, 1978.
81. ———. "British War Aims and German Peace Feelers during the First World War (December 1916--November 1918)," *Historical Journal*, vol. 15 (1978).
82. Fraser, D. *Alanbrooke.* London: Collins, 1982.
83. Fraser, P. *Lord Esher. A Political Biography.* London: Hart-Davis, MacGibbon, 1973.

84. ———. "British War Policy and the Crisis of Liberalism in May 1915," *Journal of Modern History*, vol. 54 (1982).
85. French, D. *British Economic and Strategic Planning, 1905-1915.* London: Allen & Unwin, 1982.
86. ———. "The Origins of the Dardanelles Campaign Reconsidered," *History*, vol. 68 (1983).
87. ———. "Sir John French's Secret Service on the Western Front, 1914-1915," *Journal of Strategic Studies*, vol. 7 (1984).
88. ———. *British Strategy and War Aims, 1914-1916.* London: Allen & Unwin, 1986.
89. Friedman, I. *The Question of Palestine 1914-1918. British-Jewish-Arab Relations.* London: Routledge & Kegan Paul, 1973.
90. Fuchser, L.W. *Neville Chamberlain and Appeasement: A Study in the Politics of History.* New York: Norton, 1982.
91. Galbraith, J.S. "No man's child: the campaign in Mesopotamia 1914-1916," *International History Review*, vol. 6 (1984).
92. Garlinski, J. *Intercept: The Enigma War.* London: J.M. Dent, 1979.
93. Gates, E.M. *End of the Affair: The Collapse of the Anglo-French Alliance, 1939-40.* London: Allen & Unwin, 1981.
94. Gibbs, N.H. *Grand Strategy*, vol. 1. *Rearmament Policy.* London: H.M.S.O., 1976.
95. Gilbert, M. *Winston S. Churchill*, vol. 3: *1914-1916.* London: Heinemann, 1971.
96. ———. *Winston S. Churchill*, vol. 4: *1916-1922.* London: Heinemann, 1975.
97. ———. *Winston S. Churchill*, vol. 5: *1922-1939.* London: Heinemann 1976.
98. ———. *Finest Hour: Winston S. Churchill, 1939-1941.* London: Heinemann, 1983.
99. Gooch, J. *The Plans of War: The General Staff and British Military Strategy c. 1900-1916.* London: Routledge & Kegan Paul, 1974.
100. ———. "Sir George Clarke's Career at the Committee of Imperial Defence, 1904-1907," *Historical Journal*, vol. 18 (1975).
101. ———. "Soldiers, Strategy and War Aims in Britain, 1914-1918," in B. Hunt and A. Preston (eds.) *War Aims and Strategic Policy in the Great War 1914-1918.* London: Croom Helm, 1977.
102. ———. *The Prospect of War: Studies in British Defence Policy 1847-1942.* London: Frank Cass, 1981.
103. Graves, R.P. *Lawrence of Arabia and his World.* London: Thames and Hudson, 1976.
104. Great Britain, Cabinet Office. *Principal War Telegrams and Memoranda, 1940-1943. Middle East.* Nendeln, Lichtenstein: Kraus-Thomson Organisation in association with H.M.S.O., 1976.
105. ———. *Principal War Telegrams and Memoranda, 1940-1943. Washington, America, U.K. and Europe.* Nendeln, Lichtenstein: Kraus-Thomson Organisation in association with H.M.S.O., 1976.

106. ―――. *Principal War Telegrams and Memoranda, 1940-1943. India*. Nendeln, Lichtenstein: Kraus-Thomson Organisation in association with H.M.S.O., 1976.
107. ―――. *Principal War Telegrams and Memoranda, 1940-1943. Miscellaneous*. Nendeln, Lichtenstein: Kraus-Thomson Organisation in association with H.M.S.O., 1976.
108. Grigg, J. *1943. The Victory that Never Was*. London: Eyre Methuen, 1980.
109. ―――. *Lloyd George: From Peace to War, 1912-1916*. London: Methuen, 1985.
110. Haggie, P. "The Royal Navy and War Planning in the Fisher era," *Journal of Contemporary History*, vol. 8 (1971).
111. Halpern, P.G. (ed.) *The Keyes Papers*, vol. 3. London: Allen & Unwin, 1981.
112. Hamilton, I. *The Happy Warrior: A Life of General Sir Ian Hamilton*. London: Cassell, 1966.
113. Hamilton, N. *Monty: The Making of a General, 1887-1942*. London: Hamish Hamilton, 1982.
114. ―――. *Monty: Master of the Battlefield, 1942-1944*. London: Hamish Hamilton, 1983.
115. Harris, K. *Attlee*. London: Weidenfeld & Nicolson, 1982.
116. Harvey, J. (ed.) *The War Diaries of Oliver Harvey*. London: Collins, 1978.
117. Hazlehurst, C. "Asquith as Prime Minister, 1908-1916," *English Historical Review*, vol. 85 (1970).
118. ―――. *Politicians at War, July 1914 to May 1915: A Prologue to the Triumph of Lloyd George*. London: Jonathan Cape, 1971.
119. ――― and Woodland, C. *A Guide to the Papers of British Cabinet Ministers, 1900-1951*. London: Royal Historical Society, 1974.
120. Hiley, N.P. "The Failure of British Espionage against Germany, 1907-14," *Historical Journal*, vol. 26 (1983).
121. Hinsley, F.H. (ed.) *British Foreign Policy under Sir Edward Grey*. Cambridge: Cambridge University Press, 1977.
122. Hinsley, F.H. et al. *British Intelligence in the Second World War. Its influence on Strategy and Operations*, vols. 1-3. London: H.M.S.O., 1979-1981.
123. H.M.S.O. *The Second World War. A Guide to the Documents in the Public Record Office*. London: H.M.S.O., 1972.
124. Holmes, R. *The Little Field Marshal: Sir John French*. London: Jonathan Cape, 1981.
125. Howard, M. *The Continental Commitment. The Dilemma of British Defence Policy in the Two World Wars*. London: Temple Smith, 1972.
126. ―――. *Grand Strategy*, vol. IV. *August 1942--September 1943*. London: H.M.S.O., 1972.
127. ―――. "British Military Preparations for the Second World War," in Dilks ed. *Retreat From Power*, vol. 1.
128. Humble, R. *Fraser of the North Cape: The Life of Admiral of the Fleet Lord Fraser of the North Cape, 1888-1981*. London: Routledge and Kegan Paul, 1983.
129. Hyde, H.M. *Baldwin: The Unexpected Prime Minister*. London: Hart-Davis, MacGibbon, 1973.

130. ———. *British Air Policy between the Wars, 1918-1939.* London: Heinemann, 1976.
131. Jackson, W.G.F. *Alexander of Tunis as Military Commander.* London: Batsford, 1971.
132. ———. *The North African Campaign, 1940-43.* London: Batsford, 1975.
133. ———. *"Overlord." Normandy 1944.* London: Davis-Poynter, 1978.
134. Jaffe, L.S. *The Decision to Disarm Germany: British Policy towards Postwar German Disarmament, 1914-1919.* London: Allen & Unwin, 1985.
135. Jenkins, R. *Asquith.* London: Collins, revised edition, 1978.
136. Jeffery, K. *The British Army and the Crisis of Empire, 1918-1922.* Manchester: Manchester University Press, 1984.
137. ———. (ed.) *The Military Correspondence of Field Marshal Sir Henry Wilson, 1918-1922.* London: Bodley Head for the Army Record Society, 1985.
138. Johnson, D.W.J. "Britain and France in 1940," *Transactions of the Royal Historical Society,* vol. 22 (1972).
139. Jones, R.V. *Most Secret War: British Scientific Intelligence 1939-1945.* London: Hamish Hamilton, 1978.
140. Kahn, D. "Codebreaking in World Wars I and II: The major successes and failures, their causes and their effects," *Historical Journal,* vol. 23 (1980).
141. Kedourie, E. *In the Anglo-Arab Labyrinth: The McMahon-Husayn Correspondence and its Interpretations, 1914-1939.* Cambridge: Cambridge University Press, 1976.
142. Kennedy, P.M. *The Rise of the Anglo-German Antagonism, 1860-1914.* London: Allen & Unwin, 1980.
143. ———. *The Realities Behind Diplomacy: Background Influences on British External Policy 1865-1980.* London: Allen & Unwin, 1981.
144. Kernek, S.J. "Distractions of Peace during War: the Lloyd George Government's Reactions to Woodrow Wilson, December 1916--November 1918," *Transactions of the American Philosophical Society,* vol. 65 (1975).
145. Kersaudy, F. *Churchill and de Gaulle.* London: Collins, 1981.
146. Kettle, M. *Russia and the Allies, 1917-1920,* vol. 1. *The Allies and the Russian collapse, March 1917--March 1918.* London: Andre Deutsch, 1979.
147. Kimball, W.F. *Churchill and Roosevelt. The Complete Correspondence,* vols. 1-3. Princeton, New Jersey: Princeton University Press, 1984.
148. Knightly, P. *Lawrence of Arabia.* London: Sidgwick & Jackson, 1976.
149. Koss, S. *Asquith.* London: Allen Lane, 1976.
150. Kyba, P. *Covenants Without Swords: Public Opinion and British Defence Policy 1931-1935.* Waterloo, Ontario: Wilfreid Laurier University Press, 1983.
151. Lawlor, S. "Greece, March 1941: The politics of British Military Intervention," *Historical Journal,* vol. 25 (1982).
152. Lee, B.A. *Britain and the Sino-Japanese War, 1937-1939. A Study in the Dilemmas of British Decline.* London: Oxford University Press, 1973.

153. Leutze, J. "The Secret of the Churchill-Roosevelt Correspondence, September 1939--May 1940," *Journal of Contemporary History*, vol. 10 (1970).
154. Lewin, R. *Montgomery as Military Commander*. London: Batsford, 1971.
155. ———. *Churchill as Warlord*. London: Batsford, 1973.
156. ———. *Slim, the Standardbearer: A Biography of Field Marshal the Viscount Slim*. London: Cooper, 1976.
157. ———. *Ultra Goes to War: The Secret Story*. London: Hutchinson, 1978.
158. ———. *The Chief: The Biography of Field Marshal Lord Wavell*. London: Hutchinson, 1980.
159. Lippincott, J.M. "The Strategy of Appeasement: The Formulation of British Defence Policy, 1934-1939." [Unpublished Oxford University D. Phil., 1976.]
160. Louis, Wm. Roger. *British Strategy in the Far East, 1919-39*. Oxford: Clarendon Press, 1971.
161. Lowe, P. *Great Britain and Japan, 1911-1915: A Study of British Far Eastern Policy*. London: Macmillan and St. Martin's Press, 1969.
162. ———. *Great Britain and the Origins of the Pacific War: A Study of British Policy in East Asia, 1937-1941*. Oxford: Clarendon Press, 1977.
163. Lowewenheim, F.L., Langley, H.D. and Jonas, M. (eds.). *Roosevelt and Churchill: Their Secret Wartime Correspondence*. London: Barrie and Jenkins, 1975.
164. Macdonald, C.A. *The United States, Britain and Appeasement, 1936-1939*. London: Macmillan, 1981.
165. Mack, J.E. *A Prince of our Disorder: The Life of T.E. Lawrence*. London: Weidenfeld & Nicolson, 1976.
166. Mackay, R.F. *Fisher of Kilverstone*. Oxford: Clarendon Press, 1973.
167. ———. *Balfour: Intellectual Statesman*. London: Oxford University Press, 1985.
168. Marder, A.J. *From the Dreadnought to Scapa Flow: The Royal Navy in the Fisher Era*, vol. 5. *Victory and Aftermath. (January 1918 to June 1919)*. London: Oxford University Press, 1970.
169. ———. "The Influence of History on Sea Power: The Royal Navy and the Lessons of 1914-1918," *Pacific History Review*, vol. 41 (1972).
170. ———. *Winston is Back: Churchill at the Admiralty*. English Historical Review Supplement no. 5 (1972).
171. ———. *Operation "Menace": The Dakar Expedition and the Dudley North Affair*. London: Oxford University Press, 1976.
172. ———. *From the Dreadnought to Scapa Flow: The Royal Navy in the Fisher Era*, vol. 3. *Jutland and After (May 1916--December 1916)*. London: Oxford University Press, second edition, revised and enlarged, 1978.
173. ———. *Old Friends, New enemies*, vol. 1. *Strategic Illusions, 1936-41*. Oxford: Clarendon Press, 1981.
174. Marquand, D. *Ramsay MacDonald*. London: Jonathan Cape, 1977.
175. Marshall-Cornwall, Sir J. *Haig as Military Commander*. London: Batsford, 1973.

176. Masterman, Sir J. *The Double-Cross System in the War of 1939 to 1945.* New Haven, Conn: Yale University Press, 1972.
177. Matthew, H.C.G. *The Liberal Imperialists: The Ideas and Politics of a Post-Gladstonian Elite.* London: Oxford University Press, 1973.
178. Maurice, N. (ed.) *The Maurice Case: From the papers of Major General Sir F. Maurice.* London: Leo Cooper, 1972.
179. Mayer, S.L. and Koenig, W.J. *The Two World Wars. A Guide to the Manuscript Collections in the United Kingdom.* London: Bowker, 1976.
180. McDermott, J. "The revolution in British military thinking from the Boer War to the Moroccan crisis," *Canadian Journal of History,* vol. 9 (1974).
181. McIntyre, D. *The Rise and Fall of the Singapore Naval Base, 1919-1942.* London: Macmillan, 1979.
182. Messenger, C. *Bomber Harris and the Strategic Bombing Offensive, 1939-1945.* London: Arms and Armour Press, 1984.
183. Middlemas, K. *Diplomacy of Illusion: The British Government and Germany, 1937-1939.* London: Weidenfeld and Nicolson, 1972.
184. Molony, C.J.C. et al. *The Mediterranean and Middle East,* vol. V. *The Campaign in Sicily 1943 and the Campaign in Italy,* 3rd. September 1943 to 31 March 1944. London: H.M.S.O., 1973.
185. ———. *The Mediterranean and Middle East,* vol. VI. *Victory in the Mediterranean.* Part 1. 1st. April to 4 June 1944. London: H.M.S.O., 1984.
186. Montgomery, B. *A Field Marshal in the Family.* London: Constable, 1974.
187. Morgan, K.O. *Consensus and Disunity: The Lloyd George Coalition Government, 1918-1922.* Oxford: Clarendon Press, 1979.
188. Munch-Peterson, T. *The Strategy of the Phoney War: Britain, Sweden and the Iron Ore Question, 1939-1940.* Stockholm: Militarhistoriska Forlaget, 1981.
189. Murray, W. *The Change in the European Balance of Power, 1938-1939: The Path to Ruin.* Princeton, New Jersey: Princeton University Press, 1984.
190. Nedipath, J. *The Singapore Naval Base and the Defence of Britain's Eastern Empire, 1919-1941.* Oxford: Clarendon Press, 1981.
191. Neilson, K. "Kitchener: A Reputation Refurbished," *Canadian Journal of History,* vol. 15 (1980).
192. ———. "Joy rides"? British Intelligence and Propaganda in Russia, 1914-1917," *Historical Journal,* vol. 24 (1981).
193. ———. *Strategy and Supply: the Anglo-Russian Alliance, 1914-1917.* London: Allen & Unwin, 1984.
194. Newman, S. *March 1939, the British Guarantee to Poland: A Study in the Continuity of British Foreign Policy.* Oxford: Clarendon Press, 1976.
195. Nicol, G. *Uncle George: Field Marshal Lord Milne of Salonika and Rubislaw.* London: Reedminster Publications, 1976.
196. Nicolson, N. *Alex: The Life of Field Marshal Earl Alexander of Tunis.* London: Weidenfeld & Nicolson, 1973.
197. Nish, I.H. *Alliance in Decline: A Study in Anglo-Japanese Relations 1908-1923.* London: Athlone Press, 1972.

198. Orde, A. *Great Britain and International Security, 1920-1926.* London: Royal Historical Society, 1978.
199. Ovendale, R. *Appeasement and the English Speaking World: Britain, the United States, the Dominions and the Policy of Appeasement, 1937-1939.* Cardiff: University of Wales Press, 1975.
200. Pakenham, T. *The Boer War.* London: Weidenfeld & Nicolson, 1979.
201. Parker, R.A.C. "Economics, Rearmament and Foreign Policy: The United Kingdom before 1939--a preliminary study." *Journal of Contemporary History*, vol. 10 (1975).
202. ―――――. "Britain, France and Scandinavia, 1939-40," *History*, vol. 61 (1976).
203. ―――――. "British Rearmament 1936-1939: Treasury, Trade Unions and Skilled Labour," *English Historical Review*, vol. 96 (1981).
204. ―――――. "The Pound Sterling, the American Treasury and British Preparations for War, 1938-39," *English Historical Review*, vol. 98 (1983).
205. Parkinson, R. *Peace For Our Time: Munich to Dunkirk--The Inside Story.* London: Hart-Davis, 1971.
206. ―――――. *Blood, Toil, Tears and Sweat: The War History from Dunkirk to Alamein based on the War Cabinet Papers of 1940-1942.* London, Hart-Davis, MacGibbon, 1973.
207. ―――――. *The Auk: Auchinleck, Victor at Alamein.* London: Hart-Davis, MacGibbon, 1977.
208. Peden, G.C. *British Rearmament and the Treasury, 1932-39.* Edinburgh: Scottish Academic Press, 1979.
209. ―――――. "The Burden of Imperial Defence and the Continental Commitment Reconsidered," *Historical Journal*, vol. 27 (1984).
210. Pimlott, B. *Hugh Dalton.* London: Cape, 1985.
211. Pitt, B. *The Crucible of War. The Western Desert 1941.* London: Cape, 1980.
212. Porter, A.N. *The Origins of the South African War: Joseph Chamberlain and the Diplomacy of Imperialism, 1895-1899.* Manchester: Manchester University Press, 1980.
213. Powers, B.D. *Strategy Without Slide-Rule: British Air Strategy, 1914-1939.* London: Croom Helm, 1976.
214. Pratt, L.R. *East of Malta, West of Suez: Britain's Mediterranean Crisis, 1936-1939.* Cambridge: Cambridge University Press, 1975.
215. Prior, R. *Churchill's "World Crisis" as History.* London: Croom Helm, 1983.
216. Reader, W.R. *Architect of Air Power. The Life of the First Lord Weir of Eastwood, 1877-1959.* London: Collins, 1968.
217. Reid, B.T.H. "The Development of the Military Thought of Major-General J.F.C. Fuller, 1878-1966" [Unpublished London University Ph.D. 1983].
218. Reiss, A. "The Churchill--Stalin "Percentages" Agreement on the Balkans, Moscow, October 1944," *American Historical Review*, vol. 83 (1978).
219. Reynolds, D. *The Creation of the Anglo-American Alliance: A Study in Competitive Cooperation.* London: Europa, 1981.

220. Richards, D. *Portal of Hungerford: The Life of Marshal of the Royal Air Force Viscount Portal of Hungerford.* London: Heinemann, 1977.
221. Robbins, K. *Sir Edward Grey.* London: Cassell, 1970.
222. Rose, N. *Vansittart: Study of a Diplomat.* London: Heinemann, 1978.
223. Roskill, S.W. *Hankey: Man of Secrets*, vols. 1-3. London: Collins, 1970-74.
224. ―――. "Marder, Churchill and the Admiralty, 1939-42," *Journal of the Royal United Services Institute*, vol. 117 (1972).
225. ―――. *Naval Policy Between the Wars*, vol. 2: *The Period of Reluctant Rearmament, 1930-39.* London: Collins, 1976.
226. ―――. *Churchill and the Admirals.* London: Collins, 1977.
227. ―――. *Admiral of the Fleet Earl Beatty, the Last Naval Hero: an Intimate Biography.* London: Collins, 1980.
228. Rothwell, V.H. *British War Aims and Peace Diplomacy, 1914-1918.* Oxford: Clarendon Press, 1971.
229. ―――. *Britain and the Cold War, 1941-1947.* London: Cape, 1982.
230. Royle, T. *The Kitchener Enigma.* London: Michael Joseph, 1985.
231. Sainsbury, K. *The North African Landing, 1942: A Strategic Decision.* London: Davis-Poynter, 1976.
232. ―――. *The Turning Point. Roosevelt, Stalin, Churchill and Chiang-Kai-Shek, 1943. The Moscow, Cairo and Tehran Conferences.* London: Oxford University Press, 1985.
233. Sanders, M.L. "Wellington House and British Propaganda during the First World War," *Historical Journal*, vol. 18 (1975).
234. ―――, and Taylor, P.M. *British Propaganda during the First World War, 1914-1918.* London: Macmillan, 1982.
235. Satre, L.J. "St. John Brodrick and Army Reform, 1901-1903," *Journal of British Studies*, vol. 15 (1976).
236. Saward, D. *"Bomber" Harris.* London: Cassell and Buchan and Enright Publishers, 1984.
237. Schoenfeld, M.P. *The War Ministry of Winston Churchill.* Ames, Iowa: Iowa State University Press, 1972.
238. Sharp, T. *The Wartime Alliance and the Zonal Division of Germany.* London: Oxford University Press, 1976.
239. Shay, R.P. *British Rearmament in the Thirties: Politics and Profits.* Princeton, New Jersey: Princeton University Press, 1977.
240. Short, K.R.M. *Film and Radio Propaganda in World War Two.* London: Croom Helm, 1983.
241. Sixsmith, E.K.G. *Douglas Haig.* London: Weidenfeld & Nicolson, 1976.
242. Slessor, J. "Admiralty Command Policy in Two World Wars: Reflections based on Arthur Marder's story of Jutland," in G. Jordan (ed.) *Naval Warfare in the Twentieth Century, 1900-1945.* London: Croom Helm, 1977.
243. Smith, M. "The Royal Air Force, Air Power and British Foreign Policy, 1932-1937," *Journal of Contemporary History*, vol. 12 (1976).
244. ―――. "A matter of Faith: British Strategic Air Doctrine before 1939," *Journal of Contemporary History*, vol. 15 (1980).

245. ─────. *British Air Strategy between the Wars*. Oxford: Clarendon Press, 1984.
246. Spears, Sir E. *Fulfillment of a Mission: The Spears Mission to Syria and Lebanon, 1941-1944*. London: Leo Cooper, 1977.
247. Spiers, E.M. *Haldane: An Army Reformer*. Edinburgh: Edinburgh University Press, 1980.
248. Stafford, D. "The Detonator Concept: British Strategy, SOE and European Resistance after the Fall of France," *Journal of Contemporary History*, vol. 10 (1975).
249. ─────. *Britain and European Resistance, 1940-1945: A Survey of the Special Operations Executive, with Documents*. London: Macmillan, 1979.
250. Steiner, Z. *Britain and the Origins of the First World War*. London: Macmillan, 1977.
251. Stengers, J. "Enigma, the French, the Poles and the British, 1931-1940," in C. Andrew and D. Dilks (eds.) *The Missing Dimension*.
252. Stewart, D. *T.E. Lawrence*. London: Hamish Hamilton, 1977.
253. Stubbs, J.O. "Beaverbrook as Historian: *Politicians and the War, 1914-1916* reconsidered," *Albion*, vol. 14 (1982).
254. Sweetman, J. "The Smuts Report of 1917: Merely Political Window Dressing?" *Journal of Strategic Studies*, vol. 4 (1981).
255. Taylor, A.J.P. (ed.) *Lloyd George: A Diary by Frances Stevenson*. London: Hutchinson, 1971.
256. Taylor, P.M. "'If War should come': Preparing the Fifth Arm for total war, 1935-1939," *Journal of Contemporary History*, vol. 16 (1981).
257. ─────. *The Projection of Britain: British Overseas Publicity and Propaganda, 1919-1939*. Cambridge: Cambridge University Press, 1981.
258. Thomas, T.R. *Britain and Vichy: Dilemma of Anglo-French Relations, 1940-42*. London: Macmillan, 1979.
259. Thompson, N. *The Anti-appeasers: Conservative Opposition to Appeasement in the 1930s*. Oxford: Clarendon Press, 1971.
260. Thompson, R.W. *Generalissimo Churchill*. London: Hodder and Stoughton, 1974.
261. Thorne, C. *Allies of a Kind: The United States, Britain and the War against Japan, 1941-45*. London: Hamish Hamilton, 1978.
262. Townshend, C. *The British Campaign in Ireland, 1919-1921: The Development of Political and Military Policies*. London: Oxford University Press, 1975.
263. Trythall, A.J. "The Downfall of Leslie Hore-Belisha," *Journal of Contemporary History*, vol. 16 (1981).
264. ─────. *"Boney" Fuller; The Intellectual General*. London: Cassell, 1977.
265. Turner, J.A. "The Formation of Lloyd George's 'Garden Suburb': 'Fabian-like Milner Penetration?'" *Historical Journal*, vol. 20 (1977).
266. ─────. *Lloyd George's Secretariat*. Cambridge: Cambridge University Press, 1980.
267. Wark, W.K. "British Intelligence on the German Airforce and Aircraft Industry, 1933-1939," *Historical Journal*, vol. 25 (1982).
268. ─────. "Baltic Myths and Submarine Bogeys: British Naval

Intelligence and Nazi Germany," *Journal of Strategic Studies*, vol. 6 (1983).
269. ————. "British Military and Economic Intelligence: Assessments of Nazi Germany before the Second World War," in C. Andrew and D. Dilks (eds.) *The Missing Dimension*.
270. Wasserstein, B. *The British in Palestine: The Mandatory Government and the Arab-Jewish Conflict 1917-1929*. London: Royal Historical Society, 1978.
271. Watt, D.C. *Too Serious a Business: European Armed Forces and the Approach to the Second World War*. London: Temple Smith, 1975.
272. ————. *Succeeding John Bull: America in Britain's Place, 1900-1975*. Cambridge: Cambridge University Press, 1984.
273. Welch, H.G. "The Origins and Development of the Chiefs of Staff sub-committee of the Committee of Imperial Defence, 1923-1939" [Unpublished London University Ph.D., 1974].
274. Welchman, G. *The Hut Six Story: Breaking the Enigma Codes*. London: Allen Lane, 1982.
275. Williamson, S. *The Politics of Grand Strategy: Britain and France Prepare for War, 1904-1914*. Cambridge, Mass.: Harvard University Press, 1969.
276. Wilson, K.M. *The Policy of the Entente: Essays on the Determinants of British Foreign Policy 1904-1914*. Cambridge: Cambridge University Press, 1984.
277. Wilson, S.S. *The Cabinet Office to 1945*. London: H.M.S.O., 1975.
278. Wilson, T. "Britain's 'Moral commitment' to France in August 1914," *History*, vol. 64 (1979).
279. Wingate, Sir R. *Lord Ismay: a Biography*. London: Hutchinson, 1970.
280. Winterbotham, F.W. *The Ultra Secret*. London: Weidenfeld & Nicolson, 1974.
281. Woodward, D.R. "Britain in a Continental War: the Civil-Military debate over the Strategical Direction of the Great War 1914-1918," *Albion*, vol. 12 (1980).
282. ————. *Lloyd George and the Generals*. Newark: University of Delaware Press, 1983.
283. Woodward, Sir L. *British Foreign Policy in the Second World War*, vols. 1-5. London, H.M.S.O., 1970-1976.
284. Young, K. ed. *The Diaries of Sir Robert Bruce Lockhart*, vol. 2, *1939-1965*. London: Macmillan, 1981.
285. Zebel, S.H. *Balfour: A Political Biography*. Cambridge: Cambridge University Press, 1973.
286. Zeigler, P. *Mountbatten: The Official Biography*. London: Collins, 1985.

Primary Sources

287. The Adam Papers. The papers of General Sir R.F. Adam (Adjutant General, 1942-6) are in the Liddell Hart Centre for Military Archives, King's College, Strand, London WC2R 2LS. Write to the Archivist.
288. The Acland Papers. The papers of Lieutenant-General A.N.F. Acland (Military Secretary to the Secretary of State for War, 1940-42) may be placed in the Imperial War Museum in due course. Write to the Keeper, the Department of

Documents, the Imperial War Museum, Lambeth Road, London SE1 6HZ.
289. The Alanbrooke Papers. The papers of Field Marshal Viscount Alanbrooke. His correspondence whilst CIGS between 1941-46 is in the Public Record Office (WO 216). Other papers have been deposited at the Liddell Hart Centre for Military Archives, King's College, London.
290. The A.V. Alexander Papers. The Papers of A.V. Alexander, Earl of Hillsborough, are at Churchill College Cambridge. Write to the Archivist, Churchill College, Cambridge CB3 ODS.
291. The Alexander Papers. The papers of Field Marshal Viscount Alexander are the Public Record Office (WO 214).
292. The Allenby Papers. The papers of Field Marshal Viscount Allenby, including his Boer War letters and papers covering his service during World War One, are in the Liddell Hart Centre for Military Archives, King's College, London.
293. The Amery Papers. The papers of Leopold Amery are in the hands of his son, the Rt. Hon. Julian Amery PC. MP., 112 Eaton Square, London SW1 and are not generally available for research.
294. The Asquith Papers. The letters Asquith wrote to Sylvia Laura Henley between 1915-19 have been deposited in the Bodleian Library. Write to the Keeper, the Department of Western Manuscripts, the Bodleian Library, Oxford OX1 3BG.
295. The Attlee Papers. The papers of Viscount Attlee are in the Bodleian Library.
296. The Auchinleck Papers. The papers of Field Marshal Sir C.J.E. Auchinleck are in the John Rylands Library of the University of Manchester, Deansgate, Manchester M13 3EH.
297. The Baldwin Papers. The papers of Earl Baldwin are in Cambridge University Library. Write to the Archivist, Cambridge University Library, West Road, Cambridge CB3 9DR.
298. The Balfour Papers. The papers of Earl Balfour at Whittinghame Tower, East Lothian, Scotland supplement those deposited in the British Library.
299. The Beatty Papers. The papers of Admiral of the Fleet Earl Beatty are in the National Maritime Museum. Write to the Department of Documents, the National Maritime Museum, Greenwich, London, SE 10.
300. The Bellairs Papers. The papers of Rear Admiral R.M. Bellairs (War Staff Officer to the C-in-C Grand Fleet, 1917-18) are in the Naval Library, Ministry of Defence. Write to the Naval Library, Ministry of Defence, Empress State building, Lille Road, Fulham, London.
301. The Benson Papers. The papers of Lt. Col. Sir Reginald Benson (liaison officer between GHQ, GQG and Groupe des Armees du Nord) are in the Liddell Hart Centre for Military Archives, King's College, London.
302. The Birdwood Papers. The papers of Field Marshal Lord Birdwood are in the Imperial War Museum.
303. The Boraston Papers. The papers of Lt. Col. J.H. Boraston (private secretary to Sir Douglas Haig) are in the Imperial War Museum.
304. The Bottomley Papers. The papers of Air Chief Marshal Sir N.H. Bottomley (Assistant Chief of Air Staff (Operations)

1942-3 and Deputy Chief of Air Staff 1943-5) are in the Royal Air Force Museum, Hendon. Write to the Archivist, the Royal Air Force Museum, RAF Hendon, The Hyde, London NW9 5LL.

305. The Bridgeman Papers. The papers of 1st Viscount Bridgeman are in the Shropshire Record Office. Write to the Shropshire Record Office, The Shirehall, Abbey Foregate, Shrewsbury SY2 6ND.

306. The Bromhead Papers. The diaries of Lt. Col. A.C. Bromhead (member of the special mission to the Russian armies, 1916 and Commander, Special Mission to the Italian Army, 1918-19) are in the University of London Library. Write to the Librarian, University of London Library, Senate House, Malet Street, London WC1E 6HU.

307. The Buller Papers. The papers of General Sir R.H. Buller are in the Public Record Office (WO 132/25-26).

308. The Butler Papers. The papers of Lt. Gen. Sir R.H.K. Butler (Deputy CCGS at GHQ) are in the Imperial War Museum.

309. The Campbell-Bannerman Papers. A collection of letters written by Sir Henry Campbell-Bannerman to Sir Guy Fleetwood-Wilson of the War Office between 1892-1907 has been deposited in the British Library (Add. Mss 59846Q). Write to the Department of Manuscripts, the British Library, Great Russell Street, London WC1B 3DG.

310. The Cavan Papers. A copy of the memoirs of Field Marshal Lord Cavan is at Churchill College, Cambridge. Other papers relating to the period 1916-23 are in the Public Record Office (WO 79).

311. The Cawdor Papers. The bulk of the papers of the Third Earl Cawdor are in the Carmarthenshire County Record Office. Write to Dyfed Archive Service, Carmarthenshire Record Office, County Hall, Carmarthen SA31 1JP. One additional volume has been deposited at the Ministry of Defence Library (Navy).

312. The Chamberlain Papers. The papers of both Austen and Neville Chamberlain are in Birmingham University Library. Write to the Librarian, PO Box 363, the University, Edgbaston, Birmingham B15 2TT.

313. The Chatfield Papers. The papers of Lord Chatfield are in the National Maritime Museum.

314. The Cheetham Papers. The papers of Sir M. Cheetham are in the Middle Eastern Centre, St. Anthony's College, Oxford. Write to the Librarian, St. Anthony's College, 137 Banbury Road, Oxford OX2 6JF.

315. The Clarke Papers. The papers of W.F. Clarke are in Churchill College, Cambridge.

316. The Clive Papers. The papers of Lt. Gen. Sir G.S. Clive (the head of the British military mission to GQG) are in the Liddell Hart Centre for Military Archives, King's College, London.

317. The Colville Papers. The papers of Sir John Colville (private secretary to Winston Churchill 1940-41 and 1943-45) are in Churchill College, Cambridge.

318. The Congreve Papers. The letters between Gen. Sir W.N. Congreve

and Sir Henry Wilson between 1919-1922 are in the Imperial War Museum.
319. The Corbett Papers. The papers of Sir Julian Corbett are in the National Maritime Museum.
320. The Courtney Papers. The papers of Air Chief Marshal Sir C.L. Courtney (Director of Operations and Intelligence and Deputy Chief of Air Staff 1935-6 and Air Member for Supply and Organisation, 1940-45) have been deposited at the Royal Air Force Museum, Hendon.
321. The Cowans Papers. The papers of Gen. Sir J.S. Cowans (Quarter Master General, 1912-19) are in the Imperial War Museum.
322. The Crease Papers. The papers of Captain T.E. Crease (Fisher's Naval Secretary, 1905-10 and 1914-15) are in the Naval Library, Ministry of Defence.
323. The Creedy Papers. The papers of Sir H.J. Creedy (Kitchener's private secretary 1914-16) are divided between the Imperial War Museum and the Public Record Office (WO 159).
324. The Cunningham Papers. The papers of Viscount Cunningham of Hyndhope have been deposited in the British Library and at Churchill College, Cambridge.
325. The Curzon Papers. A further collection of papers of Viscount Curzon was made at the India Office Library in 1977. Write to the Librarian, India Office Library, European Manuscripts Section, Foreign and Commonwealth Office, 197 Blackfriars Road, London SE1 8NG.
326. The Davidson Papers. The papers of Maj. Gen. F.H.N. Davidson (Director of Military Intelligence, 1940-44) are in the Liddell Hart Centre for Military Archives, King's College, London.
327. The Davidson Papers. The papers of Maj. Gen. Sir J.H. Davidson (Director of Military Operations at GHQ, 1916-18) are in the National Library of Scotland. Write to the Keeper, the Department of Documents, the National Library of Scotland, George IV Bridge, Edinburgh EH1 1EW.
328. The Dempsey Papers. The papers of General Sir M. Dempsey are in the Public Record Office (WO 285).
329. The Denniston Papers. The papers of A.G. Denniston are at Churchill College, Cambridge.
330. The Derby Papers. The papers of 17th Earl of Derby have been deposited in the Liverpool Record Office (write to the Archivist, Liverpool Record Office, City Libraries, William Brown Street, Liverpool L3 8EW) and the Public Record Office (WO 137).
331. The Deverell Papers. Some letters by Deverell can be found in the papers of Brig. Gen. H. Sandilands at the Liddell Hart Centre for Military Archives, King's College, London.
332. The Dewar Papers. The papers of Vice Admiral K.G.B. Dewar (Assistant Director, Plans division, Naval Staff, 1917 and Deputy Director N.I.D. 1925-7) are in the National Maritime Museum.
333. The Dickens Papers. The papers of Admiral Sir G.C. Dickens (Deputy Director Plans Division, Admiralty, 1920-22 and D.N.I., 1932-5) are in the hands of his son, Captain Peter Dickens RN, Lye Green Forge, Crowborough, Susex TN6 1UU.

334. The Dill Papers. The papers of Field Marshal Sir John Dill, mostly relating to his career in World War One, have been deposited in the Liddell Hart Centre for Military Archives, King's College, London. The Public Record Office possess papers relating to his period as GOC Palestine between 1936-7 and as CIGS between 1940-41 (WO 282).
335. The Domville Papers. The papers of Admiral Sir B.E. Domville (Director of Plans Division, Admiralty, 1920-22 and Director of N.I.D., 1927-30) are in the National Maritime Museum.
336. The Douglas Papers. The papers of Marshal of the Royal Air Force Baron Douglas are in the Imperial War Museum.
337. The Dowding Papers. The papers of Air Chief Marshal Baron Dowding are in the Royal Air Force Museum, Hendon.
338. The Edmonds Papers. The papers of Brigadier General Sir James Edmonds (the official historian of British military operations on the western front, 1914-1918) are in the Liddell Hart Centre for Military Archives, King's College, London.
339. The Ellison Papers. The papers of Lt. Gen. Sir G.F. Ellison (secretary of the War Office Reconstitution Committee and private secretary to Lord Haldane 1905-8) are in the possession of his stepson, Mr. Simon Spencer, the Red House, Burnham, Bucks.
340. The Elmhirst Papers. The papers of Air Marshal Sir T. Elmhirst (Deputy Director Intelligence Section, Air Ministry, 1940 and Assistant Chief of Air Staff (Intelligence) 1945-7), are at Churchill College, Cambridge.
341. The Esher Papers. The papers of the 1st Viscount Esher are at Churchill College, Cambridge.
342. The Evill Papers. The papers of Air Chief Marshal Sir Douglas Evill (Vice Chief of Air Staff, 1943-6) are in the Royal Air Force Museum, Hendon.
343. The Ewart Papers. The papers of Lt. Gen. Sir J.S. Ewart (Director of Military Operations, 1906-10 and Adjutant-General, 1910-14) are in the possession of Mr. Hector Monro and have been catalogued by the National Register of Archives (Scotland).
344. The Fisher Papers. The papers of Admiral of the Fleet Lord Fisher are at Churchill College, Cambridge.
345. The Fitzgerald Papers. The papers of Lt. Col. B.J.H. Fitzgerald (Private Secretary to Sir John French, 1914-15) are in the Imperial War Museum.
346. The Fraser Papers. The papers of Lord Fraser of the North Cape are in the National Maritime Museum.
347. The Freeman Papers. The papers of Air Chief Marshal Sir W.R. Freeman (Vice Chief of Air Staff, 1940-2) are in the Public Record Office (AVIA 10).
348. The Fremantle Papers. The papers of Admiral Sir S.R. Fremantle (Deputy Chief of Naval Staff, 1918-19) are in the National Maritime Museum.
349. The French Papers. The papers of Field Marshal Lord French are in the Imperial War Museum.
350. The Gale Papers. The papers of Lt. Gen. Sir H. Gale are in the Liddell Hart Centre for Military Archives, King's College, London.

351. The Guingand Papers. The papers of Maj. Gen. Sir. F. de Guingand (Chief of Staff 8 Army and 21 Army Group) are in the Liddell Hart Centre for Military Archives, King's College, London.
352. The Godfrey Papers. The papers of Admiral J.H. Godfrey (Director of Naval Intelligence 1939-42) are in the National Maritime Museum and the Naval Library, Ministry of Defence.
353. The Grant Duff Papers. The papers of Lt. Col. A. Grant Duff (Assistant Secretary, Committee of Imperial Defence, 1910-14) are at Churchill College, Cambridge.
354. The Grigg Papers. The papers of Sir John Grigg are at Churchill College, Cambridge.
355. The Haig Papers. The National Library of Scotland has acquired seventeen letters Haig wrote to the Reverend G.S. Duncan between 1918-1926 to supplement its existing collection of Haig papers.
356. The Hall Papers. The papers of Admiral Sir W.R. Hall (Director of Naval Intelligence, 1914-18) are at Churchill College, Cambridge.
357. The Hamilton Papers. The papers of General Sir I.S.M. Hamilton are in the Liddell Hart Centre for Military Archives, King's College, London.
358. The Hankey Papers. The private papers and diaries of Lord Hankey are at Churchill College Cambridge. His Cabinet Office papers are in the Public Record Office. (CAB 63).
359. The Harington Papers. A small collection of the papers of General Sir C. Harington (GOC Army of the Black Sea, 1920-21 and GOC Allied Occupation Force in Turkey 1921-22) relating to the Chanak crisis are in the Museum of the King's Regiment (Liverpool), City of Liverpool Library, William Brown Street, Liverpool 3.
360. The Hayden Papers. The papers of Maj. Gen. J.C. Hayden (Military Assistant to Hore-Belisha, 1938-39) are in the Imperial War Museum.
361. The Headlam Papers. The papers of Lt. Col. Sir C.M. Headlam, held in the Durham County Record Office, PO Box Durham, County Hall, Durham, DH1 5UL, contain some letters written by Sir John Dill.
362. The Henderson Papers. The papers of Lt. Gen. Sir D. Henderson (Director General of Military Aeronautics, 1913-18 and Vice-President of the Air Council, 1918), are in the Royal Air Force Museum, Hendon.
363. The Hoare Papers. The papers of Sir Samuel Hoare (Viscount Templewood) are in Cambridge University Library.
364. The Hollinghurst Papers. The papers of Air Chief Marshal Sir L. Hollinghurst (Director General of Organisation, 1941-43) are in the Royal Air Force Museum.
365. The Hore-Belisha Papers. The papers of Leslie Hore-Belisha are at Churchill College, Cambridge.
366. The Horne Papers. The papers of General Lord Horne are in the Imperial War Museum.
367. The Ironside Papers. The papers of Field Marshal Viscount Ironside are in the possession of his son, the Second Viscount, at Broomwood Manor, Chignal St. James,

Chelmsford, Essex and are not generally available for research.
368. The Ismay Papers. The papers of General Lord Ismay are in the Liddell Hart Centre for Military Archives, King's College, London.
369. The Jacob Papers. The papers of Lt. Gen. Sir. I.C. Jacob (Military Assistant Secretary to the Committee of Imperial Defence, 1938 and to the War Cabinet, 1939-46) remain in his possession.
370. The Jellicoe Papers. The National Maritime Museum has a collection of letters Earl Jellicoe wrote to E.E. Bradford between 1914-17.
371. The Kell Papers. The papers of Maj. Gen. Sir V. Kell are in the Imperial War Museum.
372. The Kirke Papers. The papers of General Sir Walter Kirke relating to his command of the secret service on the western front between 1914-17 are in the Imperial War Museum. Kirke's papers relating to his period as Deputy Chief of the General Staff in India between 1926-29 are in the India Office Records Office and other papers relating to his career between the wars are in the Liddell Hart Centre for Military Archives, King's College, London.
373. The Liddell Hart Papers. The papers of Sir Basil Liddell Hart are now in the Liddell Hart Centre for Military Archives, King's College, London.
374. The Limpus Papers. The papers of Admiral Sir A. Limpus, including his diaries, are now in the National Maritime Museum.
375. The Lindemann Papers. The papers of F.A. Lindemann, Viscount Cherwell, are in Nuffield College, Oxford. Write to the Librarian, Nuffield College, Oxford OX1 1NF.
376. The Long Papers. The papers of Walter Long, 1st Viscount Long, are in the British Library.
377. The Lothian Papers. The papers of Philip Kerr, 11th Marquis of Lothian, are in the Scottish Record Office.
378. The Lyttelton Papers. The Boer War papers of Gen. Sir N.G. Lyttelton are in the Liddell Hart Centre for Military Archives, King's College, London. The remainder of his papers, including those relating to his period as CIGS between 1904-8 are at Westfield College, London. Write to the Librarian, Westfield College, University of London, Kidderpore Ave., London NW3.
379. The MacDonald Papers. The papers of J.R. MacDonald are in the Public Record Office (PRO 30/69).
380. The MacDonogh Papers. The papers of Lt. Gen. Sir G.M. MacDonogh (Director of Military Intelligence, War Office, 1916-18) are in the Public Record Office (PRO WO 106/1510-1517).
381. The Madden Papers. The papers of Admiral of the Fleet Sir C.E. Madden (Chief of Staff to Jellicoe, 1914-16 and second in command of the Grand Fleet, 1917-18) are in the National Maritime Museum.
382. The Mallory Papers. The papers of Air Chief Marshal Sir T. Leigh-Mallory (AOC in C, Fighter Command, 1942; Air C in C Allied Expeditionary Air Forces, 1943-44) are in the Royal Air Force Museum, Hendon.

383. The Maurice Papers. The papers of Maj. Gen. Sir F. Maurice (Director of Military Operations, War Office, 1916-18) are in the Liddell Hart Centre for Military Archives, King's College, London.
384. The Midleton Papers. The papers of W. St. John Broderick, First Earl of Midleton, are in the Public Record Office (PRO 30/67).
385. The Milford Haven Papers. A microfilm of the papers of Prince Louis of Battenberg, First Marquis of Milford Haven, is in the Imperial War Museum.
386. The Milne Papers. The papers of Field Marshal Lord Milne are in the Liddell Hart Centre for Military Archives, King's College, London.
387. The Milner Papers. A small collection of papers relating to Viscount Milner's activities as a member of Lloyd George's War Cabinet are in the Public Record Office (PRO 30/30).
388. The Monro Papers. The papers of Gen. Sir C. Monro (C in C, India, 1916-20) are in the India Office Record Office.
389. The Montgomery Papers. The papers of Field Marshal Viscount Montgomery are in the Imperial War Museum.
390. The Montgomery-Massingberd Papers. The papers of Field Marshal Sir A.A. Montgomery-Massingberd are in the Liddell Hart Centre for Military Archives, King's College, London.
391. The Mottistone Papers. The papers of J.E.B. Seely, First Baron Mottistone, are in Nuffield College, Oxford.
392. The Mountbatten Papers. The papers of Admiral of the Fleet Earl Mountbatten are owned by the Broadlands Archives Trust, Broadlands, Romsey, Hants. Write to the Archivist.
393. The A.J. Murray Papers. The papers of General Sir A.J. Murray (CGS to the BEF, 1914-15, CIGS 1915 and GOC Egyptian Expeditionary Force 1916-17) are in the Imperial War Museum and the Public Record Office (PRO WO 79/69-72).
394. The O. Murray Papers. A collection of letters by Sir O. Murray (Permanent Secretary to the Admiralty) to Sir V. Baddeley on the re-organization of the Admiralty Secretariat in 1920-21 are in the Public Record Office (ADM 225).
395. The Newall Papers. The papers of Marshal of the Royal Air Force Sir C.L.N. Newall (Chief of Air Staff, 1937-40) are in the Royal Air Force Museum, Hendon and the Public Record Office (AIR 8/235-299).
396. The Nicholl Papers. The papers of Rear Admiral A.D. Nicholl (Naval Assistant Secretary of the Committee of Imperial Defence, 1936-39; Naval Assistant Secretary to the War Cabinet, 1939-41) are in the Imperial War Museum.
397. The North Papers. The papers of Admiral Sir D. North are at Churchill College, Cambridge.
398. The Peirse Papers. The papers of Air Chief Marshal Sir R.E.C. Peirse (Deputy Chief of Air Staff, 1937-40; Vice Chief of Air Staff, 1940; AOC in C Bomber Command, 1940-42) are in the Royal Air Force Museum, Hendon.
399. The Percival Papers. The papers of Lt. Gen. A.E. Percival (GOC Malaya 1941-42) are in the Imperial War Museum.
400. The Phillimore Papers. The papers of Admiral Sir R. Phillimore (head of the British Naval Mission to Russia, 1915-16) are in the Imperial War Museum.

401. The Portal Papers. The private papers of Marshal of the Royal Air Force Viscount Portal of Hungerford (AOC in C Bomber Command, 1940; Chief of Air Staff, 1940-45) are in the possession of Viscountess Portal, West Ashling House, Chichester, Sussex. Portal's letters to Winston Churchill are in Christ Church College, Oxford.
402. The Pownall Papers. The papers of Lt. Gen. Sir H. Pownall are in the Liddell Hart Centre for Military Archives, King's College, London.
403. The Roberts Papers. The Boer War papers of Field Marshal Lord Roberts are in the Public Record Office. (WO 105). Other papers are held by the National Army Museum. Write to the Librarian, the National Army Museum, Royal Hospital Road, London SW3 4HT.
404. The Salmond Papers. The papers of Marshal of the Royal Air Force Sir J.M. Salmond (Chief of Air Staff, 1930-3) are in the Royal Air Force Museum, Hendon.
405. The Selborne Papers. The papers of 2nd Earl Selborne are in the Bodleian Library.
406. The Sinclair Papers. The papers of Sir Archibald Sinclair, 1st. Viscount Thurso, are in the Public Record Office (AIR 19/73-557).
407. The Slessor Papers. The papers of Marshal of the Royal Air Force Sir J. Slessor (Director of Plans, Air Ministry, 1937-41; AOC-in-C Coastal Command, 1943; AOC-in-C Mediterranean and Middle East, 1944-45) are in the Royal Air Force Museum, Hendon.
408. The Slim Papers. The papers of Field Marshal Viscount Slim are in Churchill College Cambridge. A series of letters he wrote to Lt. Col. H.R.K. Gibbs between 1942-62 are in the Imperial War Museum.
409. The Smith-Dorrien Papers. The papers of Gen. Sir H. Smith-Dorrien (GOC 2 Army Corps, 1914; COC 2 Army 1915) are in the Imperial War Museum and the British Library.
410. The Somerville Papers. The papers of Admiral of the Fleet Sir J.F. Somerville (C in C Eastern Fleet 1942-44) head of British Admiralty delegation to Washington, 1944-45) are in Churchill College, Cambridge.
411. The Spears Papers. The papers of Maj. Gen. Sir. E. Spears (head of the British Military Mission to Paris, 1917-20) are in the Liddell Hart Centre for Military Archives, King's College, London.
412. The Strong Papers. The papers of Maj. Gen. Sir K.W.D. Strong (Head of Intelligence, Home Forces, 1942; head of Intelligence, SHAEF, 1943-45) are in the Liddell Hart Centre for Military Archives, King's College, London.
413. The Swinton Papers. The papers of Viscount Swinton are in the Public Record Office (AIR 19/23, 24 and 522).
414. The Sykes Papers. The papers of Maj. Gen. Sir F.H. Sykes (Chief of Air Staff, 1918-19) are in the Royal Air Force Museum, Hendon.
415. The Sykes Papers. The papers of Sir Mark Sykes are in the Brynmor Jones Library, the University, Hull, Humberside HU6 7RX and in the Public Record Office (PRO FO 800/208).

416. The Tedder Papers. The papers of Marshal of the Royal Air Force Sir A. Tedder (Deputy Supreme Commander AEF, 1943-45) are in the Royal Air Force Museum, Hendon.
417. The Tizard Papers. The papers of Sir H.T. Tizard are in the Imperial War Museum.
418. The Tovey Papers. The papers of Admiral of the Fleet Baron Tovey (C in C Home fleet, 1940-43) are in the National Maritime Museum.
419. The Trenchard Papers. The correspondence of Marshal of the Royal Air Force Viscount Trenchard (Chief of Air Staff 1918 and 1919-29) for the period 1919-25 are in the Royal Air Force Museum, Hendon. Further papers relating to his earlier career are in the possession of the 2nd. Viscount Trenchard, Abdale House, North Mymms, Hatfield, Herts, AL9 7T.
420. The Tweedmouth Papers. The papers of Edward Marjoribanks, 2nd. Baron Tweedmouth are in the Naval Library, Ministry of Defence Library.
421. The Vincent Papers. The papers of Sir H.G. Vincent (private secretary to Baldwin and MacDonald, 1928-34; principle private secretary 1934-36; principle assistant secretary, Committee of Imperial Defence, 1936-39) are in the Brotherton Library, University of Leeds. Write to the Librarian, Brotherton Library, University of Leeds, Leeds LS2 9JT.
422. The von Donop Papers. The papers of Maj. Gen. Sir S. von Donop (Master General of the Ordnance 1913-16) are in the Public Record Office (WO 79) and the Imperial War Museum.
423. The Weir Papers. The papers of Sir W.D. Weir, 1st. Viscount Weir (President of the Air Board, 1918-19) are in Churchill College, Cambridge.
424. The Wester Wemyss Papers. The papers of Admiral of the Fleet Baron Wester Wemyss (First Lord of the Admiralty 1917-19) are in Churchill College, Cambridge.
425. The White Papers. The papers of Field Marshal Sir G.S. White are in the India Office Library.
426. The Wilson Papers. The papers of Field Marshal Sir Henry Wilson (Director of Military Operations, War Office, 1910-14; CIGS 1918-22) are in the Imperial War Museum.
427. The Worthington Evans Papers. The papers of Sir L. Worthington Evans, 1st. Baron Worthington Evans (Secretary of State for War 1921-22) are in the Bodleian Library, Oxford.

I am most grateful to Dr. Brian Holden Reid of the Royal United Services Institute for Defence Studies, London, for his comments on an earlier draft of this article.

XI

THE FIRST WORLD WAR ON LAND

Dominick Graham

Historians have developed counter-views about the performance of the British Army in the First World War to the one that still prevailed when M.J. Williams published his essay. But the new work has largely centred on the Western Front. Certainly, the Dardanelles/Gallipoli has attracted scholars, but new interpretations of the campaign have not resulted from their work, nor has the consensus that the Westerners were correct been reversed by it.

Accepting that as a datum, scholars have started, at last, to analyze how the Western strategy was executed. They are beginning to incorporate the debate about war aims which was stirred up by Fritz Fischer's *Germany's Aims in the First World War* (25), into a broad review of how the purposes of the war were related to the battlefield. Perhaps there is a consensus that the links were weak or non-existent? That prevailing view is part and parcel of a conviction that the war was unnecessary and military operations aimless, but may simply reflect the compartments in which diplomatic, political, military and other historians tend to specialize. The break-down of specialisms is the dynamic of all new works, and at the level of policy that is indicated by several titles. We have Barry Hunt and Adrian Preston (editors) *War Aims and Strategic Policy in the Great War, 1914-18* (31), David Stevenson, *French War Aims Against Germany, 1914-19* (50), Gerhard Ritter's *The Sword and the Scepter* (45), V.H. Rothwell's *British War Aims and Peace Diplomacy, 1914-1918* (47), Paul Guinn's *British Strategy and Politics* (27), a better book than Williams allowed (his p. 3), Steven E. Miller (ed.), *Military Strategy and the Origins of the First World War* (42). The task for the historian of the war on land is to explain what were the assumptions under which soldiers and politicians laboured during the war, although the familiar literature on frocks and brass-hats suggests that they seldom laboured together (60).

The lack of political purpose in continuing the war after 1916, its unnecessariness in the first place, underlay the fashionable view of the fighting that still prevailed when Williams wrote. This, what may be called the established view from the thirties until almost the present, acknowledged the great ordeals and achievements of British manhood--how could it not?--but declared the Army's methods to have been not only futile but also unprogressive. Nothing was learned by the commanders from battle to battle, except that they needed more and more matériel. There was no change, no movement on the ground and no growth in perception for historians to study and record. Obviously, the Army's leaders had not risen to the demands placed on them; Sir Douglas Haig, as C-in-C from the end of 1915, epitomized the shortcomings of the High Command. Basil Liddell Hart was only mildly critical of the High Command in his *History of the World War, 1914-18* (Williams 71), published in 1930, and in that book did not express the opinions that are to be found in his letters and conversations during the thirties. (See Liddell Hart Centre for Military Archives below.) However, in *The Donkeys* (18), Alan Clark, representing a post-1945 view-point on the Western Front when the events were being raked over again in the Press, stepped in where angels had feared to tread. Instead of being content to adopt the confident, disapproving tone of the mainstream historians who avoided specifics (see Taylor below), he used hidden axioms and unverified statements to develop a fresh head of sarcasm and contemptuous indignation against British military leadership. *The Donkeys*, although still quoted, is so full of errors that it is a polemic and not history. Yet the dead-weight of misguided opinion that the book seemed to voice provoked some historians to restore the balance. *The Donkeys* was published in the same year as Terraine's *Haig* (see below) and represents, to extreme, the opposite and prevailing view to Terraine's of Haig and his generals.

Earlier, in the thirties, the received view that the Army's commanders had been incompetent, that the war should not have been fought at all and, if it had been unavoidable, should not have been fought by the British Army on the Continent, suited the pacifism and isolationist tendencies of politicians on both sides of the House of Commons at that time. Politicians believed that they were in step with a majority of the people in rejecting an unpopular notion that the Army ought to be able to fight on the Continent again. Furthermore, it served the policies of the Treasury during the Depression to economize on defense, particularly on the Army. Never again!, a sentiment being expressed not only by pacifists and appeasers but by Liddell Hart and some senior soldiers as well by 1937, appeared to be rational, popular and a virtuous necessity (Brian Bond, *British Military Policy Between the Two World Wars* (8)).

It is remarkable that this thirties view of the, by then, not so recent war was different from that of the twenties, before the Depression had set in and before the shadows of another war made people frightened to analyze the last one objectively. Indeed the difference between the twenties and thirties in this respect may be seen in the service journals. The controversial final volumes of the official campaign histories were not published until the late forties (Williams 29). Their appearance drew fresh attention to the war and strengthened thirties opinion of it. Another war had come and gone by then. The Second one suggested to most historians that it had been better conducted in the field and in the councils than the First, and that it had been less wasteful in life: casualty figures had been, in large measure, the yardstick by which the First War had been judged (Williams 125, for instance). Indeed, the impression that casualties had been comparatively light contributed to a view that the Second War was not only a "Just War" and a better war but had even been a "good war." The British people had entered it reluctantly, unlike the First, but as they supported the war effort they fought more effectively. For a time, there was a predisposition to look upon its conduct benignly, in marked contrast to the First.

Contrasting the conduct of the wars in this fashion served to reinforce negative views of the latter.

In the vanguard of those who contested the established view was John Terraine, who published his *Douglas Haig: The Educated Soldier* in 1963 (52). Terraine continued to write about the Western Front until recently. His *The Western Front 1914-18* (1964) (53) expressed his general view but his more recent books have followed the historiographical trend described below by showing the progressive methods used towards the end of the war (*To Win a War* in 1978, 56 *The Smoke and the Fire* in 1980, 54 and *White Heat* in 1982, 57). Terraine pointed out that there had been no alternative to the campaign on the Western Front, nor, given the unpreparedness of Britain in 1914 and 1915 for such a war, to the manner in which it was fought. After 1915 the two sides were so equally balanced that a war of attrition was bound to result. Terraine was, in effect, reiterating the statement of Sir Douglas Haig in his final despatch on 21 March 1919 (9). Terraine later pointed out, on several occasions, that Britain was only saved from a similar situation in 1940 by being so weak that her army was soundly defeated and thrown off the Continent. However, many young men of the new generation were yet to suffer their father's fate, not on a new Western Front on land but in the skies over Germany. Meanwhile, the Soviet Union suffered the experience of the French and British on the 1914-18 Western Front in defending their Motherland from 1941 to 1945. It was unhistorical and insular, argued Terraine, for the British to bewail the casualties of 1914-18 when all other belligerents suffered still more heavily than they: furthermore, the Russians had more killed in 1941-45 than the total casualties of all belligerents from all causes in 1914-18. How could the Second War be called a "Good War" except from a grossly distorted point of view?

In this last insight is the inspiration for historians who compare rather than contrast the two wars and who endeavour to incorporate both experiences in a more sophisticated general history of warfare and of war and society. Necessarily, therefore, the subject of the British Army in the First World War cannot be treated as discretely as formerly. Eventually, the light-weight treatment of military events by political historians and of political events by military historians will be corrected in a new synthesis. In the meanwhile the influence of the main-stream political historians will dominate, as it has since the thirties.

The tone of Keith Robbins' *The First World War* (46), is derisive and humorously dismissive as it assumes that its readers will agree with his point of view while at the same time not take him literally. A book of the cynical eighties, perhaps, but it represents the rational *status quo ante* Terraine that is still the established view. It was well represented by A.J.P. Taylor two decades ago in his *English History, 1914-1945* (51). He repeated the undocumented and undated comment that Haig had observed that "two machine guns per battalion were more than sufficient," and described Terraine's *Haig* as " ... an essay in vindication; educated courtier would be a more appropriate title." Norman Dixon, not a historian, devotes a chapter to Haig in his *On the Psychology of Military Incompetence* (19), and Martin van Creveld in *Command in War* (62), who is a military historian, presents Haig and his subordinates in a similarly critical fashion, although neither avoided errors copied from general historians who, clearly, had not examined the documentary sources themselves.

Terraine's approach has been seen as reactionary, not revisionist at all, by those who object to his partiality to their *bête noir* Sir Douglas Haig, to his serving up a new version of Sir James Edmonds' apologia for the Old Army's officer corps and for using published sources deriving from Edmonds almost exclusively. Also, he shared with Haig the opinion that the politicians who committed the Country to war unprepared should shoulder the blame for what happened on the Western Front; it was because of them that so many young men met their calvary there. Of course, the implicit suggestion that if the cap fitted the political community of 1914 it ought to be worn by the "Guilty Men" of 1939 as well was unwelcome, for it pointed a finger at a generation of men and women with a vested interest and responsibility for interpretations that Terraine attacked--those of teachers in a school of disenchantment and defeatism purveying an intellectual viewpoint--a sort of *trahison des clercs*--associated with appeasement. Nevertheless, some historians tried to bridge the gap between Terraine and the rest working from both ends. While luke-warm on Haig and objecting to Terraine's apparent determinism about the events on the Western Front (6, 20, 21, 22, 34, 51, 59, 60) they embraced the idea of comparing rather than contrasting the two world wars. They examined more closely than Terraine had yet done the nature of the fighting on the Western Front, the tactics, technology and techniques in one direction and in the other, the psychological, social and political anatomy of the army of human material that Haig handled. Their idea was to find out first how the war on the Western Front was fought and then to answer the question was there an alternative?

From these beginnings there have emerged not one but two lines of development. It is too early to call them separate schools of thought but the expressions "neo-establishment" and "revisionist" may serve, at least, to differentiate one from the other. The former shares many of the assumptions of the established interpretation deriving from the thirties, while the latter uses Terraine's revisionism as starting point. They both look at battle as a political event but seek to explain it in terms usually associated with social history. Indeed, whereas Terraine and his opponents are mainly political historians of traditional stamp, the new military historians are predominantly social historians, in their methodology at least. To explain the how and the why is more important to them than what happened and who won. The revisionists, for instance, are reacting to the dominant historians' tendency to treat the fighting impressionistically at best, superficially at worst, and to emphasize results which they usually express in terms of ground won or casualties suffered and inflicted. Whether it was by design or not, these criteria necessarily reduced descriptions of fighting to the level of the absurd or to black humour. In the meanwhile the real links between the fighting soldier and his commander in terms of doctrine, training, organization, morale, weapons capability and psychology, to mention some of the professional concerns in all battles, were omitted. Perhaps these subjects had been considered too boring and to have had only tenuous connections with reality? Perhaps the way battles were being recounted was itself a reaction to the battle sequences in the official campaign histories which were as readable as railway timetables? Or, in the political direction, to distance the writers from the "drum and trumpet" school which seemed to glorify battles and leaders and make sense out of what ought to remain a muddle and was certainly not glorious. Those who did not call themselves military historians, a branch of their discipline not considered quite respectable, saw no reason to learn about the profession of arms, had little sympathy for the material and preferred to write about the stupendous military struggle from a political standpoint--as it were from the central safety of the Cabinet supplemented by fleeting visits to the chateaux of France. Exceptions to the rule like Basil Liddell Hart and Cyril Falls (Williams 71-77 and 35-6) were successful in bridging the gap between political and military history but at the price of treating superficially the social links mentioned above. The new writers were part of a wider movement, of whom Michael Howard was the pioneer and leader, that was integrating military history with the main streams, the history of the British Army with war history, and the history of the First War on land with British history.

Perhaps the two new schools may be differentiated from each other by describing the point of origin of the neo-establishment as the society from which the soldiers came. It takes the civilian's point of view. The revisionists take the Army as their point of origin. They start with the event--the battle--and work back to causes in an empirical fashion, taking a professional view. Clausewitz described the approach in "Method and Routine" and "Critical Analysis" (30). The two meet on the battlefield, as it were, entering from different directions and with different assumptions, each contributing to the other's understanding.

The revisionists have looked at the reforms in British tactics and equipment in the years between 1904 and 1914, noted that they were occurring simultaneously in other armies, and have followed the brisk pace of change and experimentation during the war itself. They have shown that far from the Western Front being tactically and technologically stagnant, it was there that land/air warfare had its origins and that by the middle of 1918 methods were in use that were not to be rediscovered and developed until 1942. Their close attention to methodology and equipment focuses attention on the middle levels of command where the motivation for innovation originated. The papers of officers at this level showed that they were not the stereotypes depicted by writers like Clark. Caught in a period of rapid change in techniques and technology, for which they themselves were partly responsible, these officers had to grapple with new ideas, sometimes with success sometimes not, while fighting a war which was consuming their human seed corn--15,000 men a month in quiet periods and 100,000 during great battles.

This argument has been developed in detail by Shelford Bidwell and Dominick Graham in *Fire-Power: British Army Weapons and Theories of War, 1904-45* (6). They treat the two wars as a unit, explaining the problems of effecting change in terms of institutional rivalry, conflicting doctrinal assumptions and staff procedures for command and control. On the other hand they explain the technical limitations on the development of weapons systems and tactics and the eventual evolution of sophisticated procedures in order to present a more judicious critique of the High Command. These subjects are the theme, the battles the historical examples. They condemn Haig for placing strategic conditions on all his battles that hindered his commanders from making proper use of the new techniques that were available to them by 1917--techniques that he did not fully understand himself. John A. English's *A Perspective on Infantry* (22), is an excellent professional's history of infantry tactics which supports the belief that to understand what happens on a battlefield, its components must be studied in detail. Unlike *Fire-Power*, *A Perspective on Infantry* does not attempt the institutional approach. Suggestions pointing in the direction taken by these writers were made by John P. Campbell in "Refighting Britain's Great Patriotic War," *International Journal* 1970-71 (12). Several articles by T.H.E. Travers use similar explanations and answer similar questions, particularly "The Hidden Army: Structural Problems in the British Officer Corps, 1900-1918" in the *Journal of Contemporary History*, 1982 (58), and "Learning and Decision-making on the Western Front, 1915-18," *Canadian Journal of History*, 1983 (59). It is of interest, that this trend in historiography is not restricted to one war and one service, for similar methods for answering similar questions have been used by Marc Milner in his examination of the Royal Canadian Navy and the Royal Navy in the Battle of the Atlantic in *North Atlantic Run* (43). In the future we can expect that a functional approach to history, more typical of social and economic than of political historians, will carry military historians across service and national boundaries, and, to some extent, across the boundaries of time marking essentially political historians' conceptions of periodization.

Work from the other direction is still being inspired by the thirties' revulsion against war when the poetry, diaries and memoirs of literary figures were so popular. It was given fresh impetus and new directions by the mood of the sixties which was anti-establishment, socially sensitive and was expressed by people who had not fought in either war. The point of view is that of the soldier as an individual rather than as a soldier *per se*. Here, the influence of sociologists is evident, particularly, that of the Chicago school, Morris Janowitz and Charles Moskos for instance, Moskos paying particular attention to the ranks, and of Marxian historians and sociologists. There is a hint of fascination with war, a kind of love-hate symbiosis between the writer and his subject, the writer at times treating his subject as fiction as much as history.

The seminal historical work is probably John Keegan's *The Face of Battle* (33), in which he describes his dissatisfaction with the state of military history and sets out to demonstrate an alternative. Keegan deals with the experience of battle--Agincourt and Waterloo as well as the Somme--and is concerned to explain what happens to men on the battlefield rather than to proclaim who wins and who loses or why. For instance, he describes what happens when infantrymen advance against machine-guns or through defensive artillery fire. Ultimately, though, he argues for the thesis that the individual has become increasingly powerless in face of more and more efficient killing machines in the hands of men who are concealed behind cover and may never see, let alone come face to face with, those that they kill. Since the opening days of the battle of the Somme, when few soldiers came to grips with an enemy, war has become ever more impersonal, with all that implies. Martin Middlebrook's *The First*

Day on the Somme (40), uses oral evidence to recapture the horrific hours on 1 July 1916 when the British Army suffered nearly 60,000 casualties. The men in the battalions had no concern with or knowledge of strategy, staff doctrine, the techniques of artillery support or the problems of mounting battles. It is not Middlebrook's concern to put the battle into its general military context; his subject is a portrait of the members of the volunteer units which were destroyed so quickly and uselessly after months of cheerful, willing preparation. Lynn Macdonald in *Somme* (36) and *They Called it Passchendaele* (37), uses the recollections of participants to recount the whole of a campaign, which is more satisfactory for the historian but is still open to the objection that memory is an unreliable guide, even when an experience is recorded a few days after a shocking event. It is particularly unreliable after a subject has talked to other people, compared notes and repeated his story many times. By then, he may no longer tell truth from fiction. Indeed, sharpness of definition seems less important than color to these writers. That is quite a different perspective to that of S.L.A. Marshall, the pioneer of oral military history, who used immediate after-action interviews to help commanders in the field to correct mistakes and also to collect material for his own books and for the official histories of the Second World war (38). His observations on the use and abuse of oral evidence need to be taken to heart by those who, a generation at least after an event, present their notebooks and tape recordings of participants as factual evidence. Provided the aim is to recall ambience, poetry rather than prose, to be the artist rather than the scientist, historians play to the strength of this source of information. Examples are Tony Ashworth's *Trench Warfare, 1914-18: The Live and Let Live System* (2), about passive and active policies on different parts of the front, voluntary or involuntary, and their effects, and John Ellis' *Eye-deep in Hell: The Western Front, 1914-18* (20). Both are analytical studies from the point of view of the soldier as a civilian in uniform rather than the professional concerned primarily with defeating his enemy.

Paradoxically, these studies tend to carry a message about the writers' attitude to war which reflects the after-taste rather than the reality of war. Yet in this dichotomy lies its mystery and its tragedy. The subject of morale is, perhaps, the meeting point of the two "schools" for it must be discussed by both. Morale is both a personal and a professional matter; civil and military. However, it is a subject that can be infected by sentiment, either from those who admire the regimental system to excess or those who cannot treat the subject of war dispassionately. Since John Baynes wrote his *Morale* (Williams, 9), the medical studies of the First War have been augmented by a few excellent works on the Second and some that cover both wars. The approximately 23% of casualties that were due to battle stress in the Second War make the subject important, and it is yet another way in which the history of the two wars are linked. The contribution of the medical profession is, of course, decisive. For instance Robert H. Ahrenfeldt's *Psychiatry in the British Army in the Second World War* (1), is a landmark. Clearly professionals are the more likely to treat the continuities in the subject than those who are simply addressing a single campaign in one war. Frank Richardson, chief medical officer of a division, wrote *Fighting*

Spirit (44) and Anthony Kellett *Combat Motivation* (34); both look at the performance of soldiers under stress from a professional soldier's vantage point. Kellett's book has a good bibliography. Work is still needed to up-date books written on "shell shock" and "war neuroses" immediately after the First War. Here, two unpublished theses should be mentioned: P.J. Lynch, "The exploitation of courage in the British Army, 1914-18" (35) and Brent Wilson "The Morale and Discipline of the BEF, 1914-18" (65). It will be noted below, however, that research into morale has been handicapped by the restrictions that have been placed on scholars' access to official sources.

The twin urges to discover how battles were fought and to describe what the fighting was really like for the soldiers, eyeball to eyeball with their enemy counter-part, is leading historians to study training, in the United Kingdom and in France and Belgium, in the wider sense of preparation for battle. Peter Simkins has work in progress on the training of the Kitchener Armies, and the subject is touched on in *A Nation in Arms: A Social Study of the British Army in the First World War*, of which Ian F.W. Beckett and Keith Simpson are the editors (5). There is Denis Winter's *Death's Men: Soldiers of the Great War* (66), which takes the recruit from enlistment to the front line. Winter's assumption that all had similar experiences and universally disliked it is a weakness in his book. Although memoirs, which are mainly of officers, generally treat periods of training with scant attention or light-heartedly, perhaps indicating the irrelevance of much of it to later experience, it would be wrong to assume that the training machine was unprogressive. Yet, it ought to be examined from the point of view of the trainers as well as the trained, and we ought to know the staff's organization for managing training and on its rationale. This work could be combined with wider studies of the staff system and its doctrine (for which Haig had been largely responsible prior to 1914) comparing it to that of the Germans. The logistics of the Western Front has been approached by Martin van Creveld in his *Supplying War* (62), as part of a wider study, but as engineer services, recovery and repair, transport and supply were decisive in deciding how the war on the Western Front was fought, it is time that a definitive study on the subject was written. Command, control and communications are in need of treatment as well (62).

The literature of the war, which colored the views of it prevalent in the thirties and subsequent decades and expressed the shock, often delayed in its effects, which war experience had on the writers, is clearly of a different order from that of the Second War. Some of the work is still alive and well; for instance that of Siegfried Sassoon (Williams 107), Robert Graves (Williams 51), Edmund Blunden (*Undertones of War*, 1930) and of Wilfred Owen still enjoys reissues. It is, of course, part of the popular literature of nostalgia, escapism and pacifism. To the original corpus has been added the diaries and memoirs of men who served in both wars, and there has been a surge of newly discovered diaries of the trenches of which *The Journal of Private Fraser*, edited by Reginald Roy (48) and P.J. Campbell's *The Ebb and Flow of Battle* (13) and the sequel *In the Cannon's Mouth* are recent examples (14). Paul Fussell's *The Great War and Modern Memory* (26), described by the author as "about the British experience on the Western Front," and *Vain Glory* (17), Guy

Chapman's familiar collection first published in 1937--"not an anthology ... an attempt to display the War of 1914-18 through the eyes of those who took an active part in it"--are both excellent.

Biographies of the important senior commanders continue to appear. Anthony Farrar Hockley's *Goughie: The Life of General Sir Hubert Gough* (24), Jeffery Williams' sympathetic and readable *Byng of Vimy* (64), Richard Holme's *The Little Field-Marshal: Sir John French* (28), George Cassar's *Kitchener: Architect of Victory* (15) and his recent *The Tragedy of Sir John French* (16), and Edward Spiers' *Haldane: An Army Reformer* (49), should be noted. Biographies of the commanders of the Second War, most of whom had fought at the rank of major or lieutenant-colonel in the First, a few, Bernard Freyberg for instance, commanding brigades, may be added to the list. In a different category are Anthony Trythall's *Boney Fuller: The Intellectual General* (61), and Brian Bond's invaluable *Liddell Hart: A Study of his Military Thought* (7), because they did not, of necessity, follow the general rule of biographers not to emphasize historiographical issues lest they upset the balance of their work. However, when the biographer's subject is caught up in them, as for instance was Farrar-Hockley's *Goughie* (24) in the controversy over the writing of *Volume II, Military Operations France and Belgium, 1917,* concerning Passchendaele, he ought to deal with it (Williams 29, 30 and "Strategy"). Gough, Sir John Davidson, G.C. Wynne, the narrator, James Edmonds and Neil Malcolm provided evidence that reflected badly on Haig and also on Plumer, who otherwise emerged from the war unscathed, but less badly on Gough. Wynne was not unbiased and seemed not to grasp the significance of the evidence in his own files and those of Edmonds. But the compromise that eventually appeared in print did not satisfy him, and he refused to allow his name to appear on the volume's title page. it was, in consequence, "completed and edited" by James Edmonds (Williams 127, 128 and Graham 70). It is of interest to note that John Terraine's *The Road to Passchendaele* (55) presents evidence in favor of Haig's management of the battle and against Lloyd George's role in it, but does not penetrate to the required level of analysis that Goughie's biographer might have reached.

The main archives have extended their collections and private papers markedly. An aging veteran population which has deposited documents, "the demand for military history," remarked upon by Michael Howard in a *Times Literary Supplement* article (29) of that title as long ago as 1969, in particular public appetite for books on the two wars, and vigorous action by Keepers, particularly at the Imperial War Museum and the Centre for Military Archives at King's College, London, are providing historians with the materials for their books. As a result of the expansion, guides such as those of S.L. Mayer and W.J. Koenig, *The Two World Wars: A Guide to Manuscript Collections in the United Kingdom* (39), and Gwyn M. Bayliss, *Bibliographic Guide to the Two World Wars: An Annotated Survey of English-Language Reference Materials* (4), can never be taken as the final answer. Most of the principal archives will provide, sometimes for a small charge, an up-to-date list of their holdings. As to published works, this essay is but a guide to the directions which research and writing has taken and it mentions only some of the important work related to recent endeavors. However, small annotated bibliographies should be sought out such as that in *A Nation in Arms*

(5). Peter Simkins has one forthcoming to coincide with the publication of the proceedings of the International Commission of Military History's Stuttgart symposium in 1985. There is Anthony Bruce, *A Bibliography of the British Army, 1660-1914* (11), which includes work from the pre-1914 years, and A.G.S. Enser's *A Subject Bibliography of the First World War: Books in English 1914-1978* (23), which contains a list of divisional and regimental histories.

The Public Record Office issues information leaflets periodically, of which number six, "Operational Records of the British Army in the War of 1914-19," dated June 1983, number 37, "Access to Public Records," and "Records of Officers and Soldiers who have served in the British Army," dated 1985, are useful. Some guidance to the War Office and Cabinet Office series in addition to that in M.J. Williams' essay may be found in pages 309-10 of *Fire-Power* (6), with a guide to periodical sources and some of the private documentary ones. Attention should be drawn to Cabinet 45, now open until 1945, which contains correspondence concerning drafts of the official histories between the participants in battle sequences and the narrators. This correspondence is not available for the 1917 and 1918 battles which were prepared when the Cabinet Offices were short of staff. Those that exist contain much information on current field tactics and techniques as well as critical comments on the way the battles were managed. Much of this incidental material did not find its way into the published volumes.

Records of courts-martial will be opened from 1990, but WO 154 (Documents removed from war diaries) remains closed for 100 years. It may be noted that the records of the Ministry of Pensions contain material on pension awards and have been used as demographic evidence by J.M. Winter for his important studies on the effect of heavy casualties on the war generation, and of the shift in purchasing power due to their employment from men to the women in the family. ("Britain's 'lost generation' of the First World War" in *Populations Studies*, 1977 (68), "Army and Society: The Demographic context" in *A Nation in Arms* (5) and his recent *The Great War and the British People* (67)). Unfortunately, documentation on subjects under the jurisdiction of the Adjutant-General, that is manpower, discipline, health, recruitment and morale, amongst others, is restricted because of closed or lost files. Tony Babington's *For the Sake of Example: Capital Courts-Martial 1914-1920* (3), is an attempt to cover the subject despite restrictions on sources. Nevertheless, on this and other subjects, researchers should always enquire whether files listed as closed may be seen under restricted circumstances.

The many new acquisitions of the Department of Documents, the Imperial War Museum, Lambeth may be determined by writing to the Keeper, presently Dr. R.W.A. Suddaby. They include the following, which are mentioned because of their general interest. A collection of letters of FM Sir John French, January to December 1915, additional papers and correspondence 1914-21 and diaries 1900-1921; the papers of Sir Henry Wilson are now supported by Keith Jeffery's *The Military Correspondence of FM Sir Henry Wilson 1918-22* (32); the papers of Sir Archibald Murray, of General Sir Walter Kirke concerning his direction of MI16, the clandestine intelligence section at GHQ, 1914-17, and papers of FM Viscount Montgomery, 1887-1976. There are additional Smith-Dorrien papers in the form of a typescript copy of a diary of his command of II Corps and Second Army, 1914-15, and a notebook compiled by Sir Cyril Deverell, a post-war CIGS, while commanding 20th Infantry Brigade in 1916. The Museum has the war diaries of Robert Erskine Childers, the working drafts of Siegfried Sassoon's *Memoirs of an Infantry Officer* (Williams 108), a short series of letters from Robert Graves between 1914 and 1919 and a diary kept by Dennis Wheatley the novelist, during the spring retreat in 1918.

Running the IWM a close second in its holdings is the Liddell Hart Centre for Military Archives, King's College, London. An up-to-date consolidated list of accessions may be obtained for a small sum from the College Archivist and Archivist in the Centre, presently Patricia Methven, together with "Notes for Readers." The collection, like that of the IWM, is growing apace. Its foundation is the collection of Sir Basil Liddell Hart consisting of 1,000 boxes. Apart from valuable material on tanks, the drafts and reviews and correspondence concerning his numerous publications and his posts as Military Correspondent of the *Daily Telegraph*, 1925-35 and *The Times*, 1935-39, Liddell Hart communicated with almost everyone who had played a part in the First War and its aftermath. Particularly illuminating is his correspondence with Sir James Edmonds which includes records of their table-talk at regular lunches in the early thirties when the Somme volumes were being written and when Liddell Hart had published his own *History of the World War*, and was helping David Lloyd George write his *Memoirs* (Williams 79). The value of this part of his papers is increased by the presence in the archive of the Edmonds and Wynne Papers as well. The researcher is made aware that the Liddell Hart Centre archive is a historian's collection, which lends it special appeal.

Notable items that have arrived since Mayer and Koenig published their guide include the following. FM Viscount Allenby's papers, FM Sir John Dill's, Major-General Charles Foulkes' (Director of Gas Services 1914-18), a box of letters from Liddell Hart to Robert Graves, 1939-44, and some post-1918 papers of General Sir Walter Kirke, the chairman of the Kirke Committee. Also the papers of FM Lord Milne, whose long career included service in France and Salonika and as CIGS 1926-33; Major John North, who served in France, 1914-18 and in the Second War and has papers concerning his work *Gallipoli: The Fading Vision* (nm), and Major-General Sir Charles Townshend (of Kut-el-Amara) whose papers include correspondence with Lieutenant-Colonel A.J. Barker and others concerning the latter's *The Neglected War*, 1967, and *Townshend of Kut*, 1967 (Williams 5 and 6).

Churchill College, Cambridge issues a guide obtainable for a small sum from the Archivist. (Churchill's holdings include the generally closed papers of Sir Winston Churchill, although those covering the 1914-18 war may be viewed on a restricted basis.) Additions since Mayer and Koenig published are a box of Sir Frederick Maurices' papers concerning the Lloyd George-Maurice crisis over reinforcements in 1918, and 1 box of xeroxed copies of Marshal of the Royal Air Force Viscount Trenchard's correspondence with Winston Churchill 1917-27.

The Haig Papers are in the National Library of Scotland, George IV Bridge, Edinburgh, and a summary of other holdings in the Department of Manuscripts may be obtained from the Keeper.

The National Army Museum has added the papers of Lieutenant-General Sir Reginald Savory, which includes letters and diaries from Gallipoli, Egypt and Vladivostok.
Access to the Ministry of Defence, Whitehall, Library is restricted and it no longer issues yearly accession lists. Army Council Instructions can be seen there or in the PRO. The Library has a collection of peace and war establishments and printed War Office publications. The Royal United Services Institute Library is maintained on behalf of the RUSI by the MOD Library and is available to members only, although it may be used by appointment for general reference.
The Army Records Society has been formed to publish original records describing the development, organization, administration and activities of the British Army from early times. The first volume issued has been the military correspondence of Sir Henry Wilson by Keith Jeffery (32). Further volumes will include one on the Curragh Incident. The ARS may be contacted through the National Army Museum, Royal Hospital Road, Chelsea, London SW34HT.

BIBLIOGRAPHY

1. Ahrenfeldt, Robert H. *Psychiatry in the British Army in the Second World War.* London: Routledge and Kegan Paul, 1958.
2. Ashworth, Tony. *Trench Warfare, 1914-1918: The Live and Let Live System.* London: Macmillan, 1980.
3. Babington, Anthony. *For the Sake of Example: Capital Courts Martial 1914-1920.* New York: St. Martin's Press, 1983.
4. Bayliss, Gwyn M. *Bibliographic Guide to the Two World Wars: An Annotated Survey of English Language Reference Materials.* London: Bowker, 1977.
5. Beckett, Ian F.W. and Simpson, Keith. *A Nation in Arms: A Social Study of the British Army in the First World War.* Manchester: Manchester University Press, 1985.
6. Bidwell, Shelford and Graham, Dominick. *Fire-Power: British Army Weapons and Theories of War, 1904-1945.* London: Allen and Unwin, 1982 (pb. edition 1985).
7. Bond, Brian. *Liddell Hart: A Study of his Military Thought.* London: Cassell, 1977.
8. ─────. *British Military Policy Between the Two World Wars.* Oxford: Clarendon Press, 1980.
9. Boraston, J. H. (ed.) *Sir Douglas Haig's Despatches.* London: Dent, 1979.
10. Brown, Tom. "Shell Shock in the Canadian Expeditionary Force" in Charles B. Roland (ed.) *Health, Disease and Medicine: Essays in Canadian History.* Toronto: The Hannah Institute for the History of Medicine, 1984.
11. Bruce, Anthony P.C. *A Bibliography of the British Army, 1660-1914.* London: Saur, 1985.
12. Campbell, John, P. "Refighting Britain's Great Patriotic War," *International Journal*, vol. 26 (1970-1).
13. Campbell, P.J. *The Ebb and Flow of Battle.* London: Hamish Hamilton, 1977.
14. ─────. *In the Cannon's Mouth.* London: Hamish Hamilton, 1979.

15. Cassar, George H. *Kitchener: Architect of Victory.* London: Kimber, 1977.
16. ―――. *The Tragedy of Sir John French.* Newark: University of Delaware Press, 1985.
17. Chapman, Guy. *Vain Glory: A Miscellany of the Great War 1914-18 Written by Those Who Fought in it on Each Side and On All Fronts.* London: Cassell, 1937.
18. Clark, Alan. *The Donkeys.* London: Hutchinson, 1963.
19. Dixon, Norman F. *On the Psychology of Military Incompetence.* London: Cape, 1976.
20. Ellis, John. *Eye-deep in Hell: The Western Front, 1914-18.* London: Croom Helm, 1976.
21. ―――. *The Sharp End: The Fighting Man in World War II.* New York: Scribner's, 1980.
22. English, John A. *A Perspective on Infantry.* New York: Praeger, 1981.
23. Enser, A.G.S. *A Subject Bibliography of the First World War: Books in English, 1914-1978.* London: Andre Deutsch, 1979.
24. Farrar-Hockley, Anthony. *Goughie: The Life of General Sir Hubert Gough.* London: Hart Davis MacGibbon, 1975.
25. Fischer, Fritz. *Germany's Aims in the First World War.* London: Chatto and Windus, 1967.
26. Fussell, Paul. *The Great War and Modern Memory.* Oxford: Oxford University Press, 1975.
27. Guinn, Paul. *British Strategy and Politics, 1914-1918.* Oxford: Clarendon Press, 1965.
28. Holmes, Richard. *The Little Field-Marshal: Sir John French.* London: Cape, 1981.
29. Howard, Michael. "The Demand for Military History," *Times Literary Supplement*, 1214 (13 November 1969).
30. ―――, and Paret, Peter (eds., and trs.). Carl von Clausewitz *On War.* Princeton, N.J.: Princeton University Press, 1976.
31. Hunt, Barry, and Preston, Adrian (eds.). *War Aims and Strategic Policy in the Great War, 1914-18.* London: Croom Helm, 1978.
32. Jeffery, Keith (ed.). *The Military Correspondence of FM Sir Henry Wilson 1918-22.* London: The Army Records Society/Bodley Head, 1985.
33. Keegan, John. *The Face of Battle.* London: Cape, 1976.
34. Kellett, Anthony. *Combat Motivation: The Behaviour of Soldiers in Battle.* Boston: Kluwer-Nijhoff Publishing, 1982.
35. Lynch, P.J. "The Exploitation of Courage: Psychiatric Care in the British Army, 1914-1918," unpublished M. Phil, London U., 1977.
36. Macdonald, Lynn. *Somme.* London: Michael Joseph, 1983.
37. ―――. *They Called it Passchendaele.* London: Michael Joseph, 1978.
38. Marshall, S.L.A. *Men Against Fire.* New York: Morrow, 1947. Marshall wrote many books of which *Porkchop Hill* is an example of his methods.
39. Mayer, S.L. and Koenig, W.J. *The Two World Wars: A Guide to the Manuscript Collections in the United Kingdom.* London: Bowker, 1976.

40. Middlebrook, Martin. *The First Day of the Somme.* London: Allen Lane, 1971.
41. ―――――. *Battle, 21 March 1918: The First Day of the German Spring Offensive.* London: Allen Lane, 1978.
42. Miller, Steven E. (ed.). *Military Strategy and the Origins of the First World War.* Princeton, N.J.: Princeton University Press, 1985,
43. Milner, Marc. *North Atlantic Run.* Toronto: University of Toronto Press, 1985.
44. Richardson, F.M. *Fighting Spirit: A Study of Psychological Factors.* London: Leo Cooper, 1978.
45. Ritter, Gerhard. *The Sword and the Sceptre.* London: Allen and Lane, 1970-73.
46. Robbins, Keith. *The First World War.* Oxford: Oxford University Press, 1984.
47. Rothwell, V.H. *British War Aims and Peace Diplomacy, 1914-18.* Oxford: Oxford University Press, 1971.
48. Roy, Reginald. *The Journal of Private Fraser, 1914-1918.* Victoria, B.C.: Sono Nis Press, 1985.
49. Spiers, Edward M. *Haldane: An Army Reformer.* Edinburgh: Edinburgh University Press, 1980.
50. Stevenson, David. *French War Aims Against Germany, 1914-1918.* Oxford: Oxford University Press, 1982.
51. Taylor, A.J.P. *English History, 1914-45.* Oxford: The Clarendon Press, 1965.
52. Terraine, John. *Douglas Haig; The Educated Soldier.* London: Hutchinson, 1963.
53. ―――――. *The Western Front, 1914-19.* London: Hutchinson, 1964.
54. ―――――. *The Smoke and the Fire: Myths and Anti-Myths of War, 1861-1945.* London: Sidgwick and Jackson, 1980.
55. ―――――. *The Road to Passchendaele, the Flanders Offensive of 1917: A Study in Inevitability.* London: Leo Cooper, 1977.
56. ―――――. *To Win a War; 1918 The Year of Victory.* London: Sidgwick and Jackson, 1978.
57. ―――――. *White Heat: The New Warfare 1914-18.* London: Guild Publishing, 1982.
58. Travers, T.H.E. "The Hidden Army: Structural Problems in the British Officer Corps, 1900-1918," *Journal of Contemporary History*, 17 (1982), pp. 523-44.
59. ―――――. "Learning and Decision-making in the Western Front, 1915-18: The British example," *Canadian Journal of History* (April 1983), pp. 87-97.
60. ―――――. "The Offensive and the problem of innovation in British Military thought, 1870-1915," *Journal of Contemporary History*, 13 (1978).
61. Trythall, Anthony. *Boney Fuller: The Intellectual General.* London: Cassell, 1977.
62. van Creveld, Martin. *Supplying War; Logistics from Wallenstein to Patton.* Cambridge: Cambridge University Press, 1977.
63. ―――――. *Command in War.* Cambridge, Mass.: Harvard University Press, 1985.
64. Williams, Jeffrey. *Byng of Vimy: General and Governor-General.* London: Leo Cooper/Secker and Warburg, 1983.

65. Wilson, Brent J. "The Morale and Discipline of the BEF, 1914-18," unpublished thesis, University of New Brunswick, Canada, 1978.
66. Winter, Denis. *Death's Men: Soldiers of the Great War*. London: Allen Lane, 1978.
67. Winter, Jay M. *The Great War and the British People*. London: Macmillan, 1986.
68. ―――――. "Britain's 'lost generation' of the First World War," *Population Studies*, 31, 3 (1977), pp. 449-66.
69. Woodward, David. *Lloyd George and the Generals*. London & Toronto: A.U.P., 1983.
70. Wynne, G.C. See Williams 127 and 128. On the subject of the official history volumes see David French, "'Official but not History?' Sir James Edmonds and the Official History of the Great War," *R.U.S.I.*, 131 (March 1986), pp. 58-63, and Jay Luvaas, "The First British Official Historians" in Robin Higham (ed.) *Official Histories: Essays and Bibliographies from around the World*. Manhattan, Ks.: Kansas State University, 1970.

XII

THE HOME FRONT IN THE FIRST WORLD WAR

David R. Woodward

World War I, Great Britain's first total war, considerably magnified the importance of the "home front," an expression which first came into being during this war. Victory could not be won on the battlefield alone. Historians now recognize more than ever that the fortunes of Great Britain depended upon a multiplicity of factors involving all of society. The popularity of themes such as war and society, war and economy and civil-military relations, in combination with a wealth of newly available primary materials in the late 1960s, have resulted in an astonishing output of books and articles. Some of the brightest young British historians have explored various aspects of the British home front during the past twenty years with impressive results.

Surveys. T. Wilson's long awaited *The Myriad Faces of War: Britain and the Great War* (295) is scheduled for publication in 1986. An entertaining but superficial comparative survey by J. Williams (290) on the home fronts of Britain, France and Germany does not supplant the authoritative *The War Behind the War, 1914-1918: A History of the Political and Civilian Fronts* by F.P. Chambers. Excellent for its illustrations and broad coverage is *The Marshall Cavendish Illustrated Encyclopedia of World War I* (184). A. Briggs and A. Marwick are among the distinguished contributors. Syntheses dealing with political, administrative and social history that should not be overlooked for their perspective in *la longue durée* are by M. Beloff (12), R. Blake (15), W.H. Greenleaf (97), T.O. Lloyd (152), M.D. Pugh (222), K. Robbins (230), K. Burgess (22), B.B. Gilbert (88) and J. Stevenson (252). The social history by Stevenson is especially good for the 1914-1919 period.

Wartime Politics. Although there was strong Liberal opposition in both Cabinet and Parliament, Britain chose to march with France and Russia in August 1914. The position of David Lloyd George, who would have been a formidable leader of any peace party, is best analyzed by C. Hazlehurst (112) and B.B. Gilbert (89). That Britain had a "moral obligation" to fight is questioned by T. Wilson (293). The recently published diaries of J.A. Pease (291), Charles Hobhouse (54) and Leo Amery (8) are important new primary political sources on either Britain's entry into the war or the first months of the conflict. The published letters from H.H. Asquith to Venetia Stanley (19) constitute an even more valuable source. Although many of Asquith's letters have appeared in previous works in bowdlerized form, including Asquith's memoirs, this collection serves as the best record available for the first nine months of the wartime government.

No political subject has attracted as much interest as the shifting fortunes of the Liberal and Labour parties in general and the Asquith-Lloyd George relationship in particular. The spell cast by Lord Beaverbrook has been broken by extremely critical assessments of his *Politicians and the War, 1914-1916*. The breach first gently opened in Beaverbrook's scholarship by A.J.P. Taylor (259) has been widened with zest by J.M. McEwen (164), P. Fraser (80) and J.O. Stubbs (254). Although Beaverbrook's account of politics is shown to have many flaws, including bias and misuse of sources, his preference for Lloyd George over Asquith receives strong support in the modern literature. Hazlehurst (111) has written a damning assessment of Asquith and S. Koss (139), although more sympathetic, finds him a poor war leader. As Asquith's reputation declines, that of Lloyd George rises. Asquith certainly suffers by comparison in J. Grigg's masterful *Lloyd George: From Peace to War, 1912-1916* (100) and C. Hazlehurst's *Politicians at War July 1914 to May 1915: A Prologue to the Triumph of Lloyd George* (112).

New sources continue to add to our understanding of Lloyd George, who has been rightly characterized as a bundle of contradictions. The publication of Lloyd George's family letters (194) and the diary and love letters of his mistress and later wife Frances Stevenson (260, 261) offer revealing glimpses of him, as do the works of a growing army of Lloyd George scholars. P. Rowland (237) covers his entire career but neglects many archival sources. K.O. Morgan's illustrated biography (193) is aimed at the general audience but is balanced and insightful; an article (195) by Morgan provides an excellent survey of Lloyd George's premiership. Many facets of Lloyd George's wartime service have now been given detailed scrutiny: his work in the Ministry of Munitions (1), his views on foreign affairs before 1917 (86), his conflict with the generals (311) and his relations with the labor movement (314). Of these works, Grigg comes closest to portraying the whole man.

Contemporaries could agree on little about the political crises of May 1915 and December 1916. This is equally true of modern accounts. S. Koss (141), aggressively opposed by Hazlehurst (112), finds an anti-Asquith conspiracy led by Winston Churchill during the May 1915 crisis. M.D. Pugh (220), from a wider perspective, argues that Asquith was trying to avoid a General Election. P. Fraser (76, 77) places emphasis on war policy as the catalyst and D. French (83) provides the military background for the "shell crisis" of May 1915. The most provocative (and questionable) account of Asquith's fall in December 1916 is by R.J. Scally (243), who sees the Lloyd George coalition of 1916 as a crisis of democratization dating back to the Boer War which had a parallel in counter-revolutionary regimes on the Continent. Better supported by the sources and less ambitious in their scope are accounts by J.M. McEwen (159, 163, 167, 169), J.D. Fair (69, 71) and P. Lowe (154).

As Asquith faltered so also did the Liberals whose position in British politics was taken by Labour. Whether Labour's displacement of Liberalism would have occurred when it did without the war remains an open question. P.F. Clarke (39) finds the health of Liberals to be robust in Lancashire on the eve of war, even enjoying success in working class districts. K. Laybourn and J. Reynolds (149) conclude that the opposite was true in West Yorkshire. Their picture of growing prewar Labour inroads on Liberalism lends support to R.I. McKibbin's thesis (173) that the war had no significant part to play in Labour's rise. The development of a working-class consciousness and the 1918 Franchise Act and not the war were largely responsible for Labour's electoral success according to McKibbin. Two useful surveys on Labour's rise are by S. Pierson (217) and R. Moore (190). P. Stansky (251) has compiled a collection of documents on the Labour Party during the war.

The Liberal response to the growing influence of Labour is one of the themes found in Brown's collection of essays (20); M. Bentley (13) argues in his intellectual history that the Liberal preference for principle over power contributed to the party's decline. Liberalism after 1916 can be followed in studies by R. Douglas (61), who is good on both the December 1916 crisis and the Coupon Election, E. David (54), who provides the Liberal voting record, 1916-1918, K.O. Morgan (192) and D.M. Creiger (51, 52).

Parliament's influence on either the executive or the management of the war effort was usually quite insignificant (79). In other areas, especially electoral reform, however, the effect of its deliberations could be dramatic. The electorate rose from less than 8,000,000 in the last prewar election in 1910 to more than 21,000,000 in the Coupon Election of 1918. J.D. Fair (69) has written a solid volume on interparty conferences, including the Irish Convention of 1917-1918 and conferences on electoral reforms between 1916-1918. M.D. Pugh's important study of electoral reform (221) discounts the war's influence on democratizing British society. D.H. Close (43) argues the opposite. Electoral reform has been the subject of detailed studies in part because of its alleged relationship to the rise of Labour and the decline of Liberalism. In contrast to M. Hart (107), H.C.G. Matthew, R.I. McKibbin and J.A. Kay (185) argue that the new franchise was at least as responsible as the war for the fall of Liberalism. D. Tanner (258) and P.F. Clarke (40) have also made contributions to this debate. Women's suffrage, an important element in electoral reform, is examined at the Cabinet level by D. Morgan (191). Fair (70) links the giving of the franchise to sailors and soldiers to suffrage for women, who could hardly be ignored under the circumstances. The Coupon Election, with emphasis on its background, has been treated by R. Douglas (60), B. McGill (170) and J. Turner (272).

The stock of biographies on World War I personalities continues to grow. S. Roskill's biography (235) of Maurice Hankey, the most important behind-the-scenes individual in the government, is one of the most significant modern books on Britain's involvement in the war. It serves as a corrective to some aspects of Hankey's memoirs and reflects a rare understanding of the political and diplomatic events of the war. K. Rose (233) revises in some important ways the standard biography of George V by Sir H. Nicholson. D. Judd's *Lord Reading* (129), D. Dutton's *Austen Chamberlain: Gentleman in Politics* (64) and J. Campbell's *F.E. Smith, First Earl of Birkenhead* (28) fill a void. K. Robbins' biography of Sir Edward Grey (231) is not as complete on the war years as one would wish, but nine of the nineteen contributions in *British Foreign Policy under Sir Edward Grey* (114) deal with war-related subjects. Pride of place for those who have written on Churchill belongs to M. Gilbert (90, 91, 92, 93). His detailed and well informed narrative is an essential source for the war as well as for Churchill; the companion volumes are packed with raw material. Churchill's famous *World Crisis* has been subjected by R. Prior (219) to a detailed and revealing analysis based on the new materials now available, an exercise which one would also like to see applied one day to Lloyd George's memoirs. P. Fraser (78) offers interesting insight on Lloyd George's publication of Cabinet documents and other official information. H. Pelling's *Winston Churchill* (215) has the advantage of covering Churchill's life in one volume, but it does not reflect the depth of archival research found in Gilbert. The political careers of Austen Chamberlain and Lord Curzon are included in D.R. Thorpe's *The Uncrowned Prime Ministers* (267). A.J. Balfour, who held Cabinet rank for twenty-seven years, longer than any other British political leader, is the subject of three new biographies (66, 171, 316). The great Tory proconsul Lord Milner has been most recently analyzed by J. Marlowe (177) and T.H. O'Brien (205), the latter attempting to uncover his more human side. D. Marquand (178) tries to rehabilitate Ramsay MacDonald in a study that gives some emphasis to his contributions to the creation of a Parliamentary Labour Party.

Grand Strategy and Civil-Military Relations. The often differing perspectives of the military and civilian authorities continue to generate controversy among historians. D.R. Woodward (311) has written the only comprehensive account based on the new archival sources of Lloyd George's stormy relationship with the generals. Until recently the historical judgement on Lord Kitchener's war leadership was that he was a national disaster. This view, however, has been brought into question by modern scholarship. Essays by P. Simkins (247), P. Fraser (76) and K. Neilson (202) and a book by G.H. Cassar (31) paint a sympathetic picture of the British Secretary for War, 1914-1916. He is shown to be sensible rather than incoherent and vacillating, with underlying and basically sound policies. Sir Henry Wilson (128) continues to be his own worst enemy as the publication of his military correspondence while C.I.G.S. reveals. Sir John French has been the subject of careful analysis by R. Holmes (117) and G.H. Cassar (32); both are in agreement that French was not up to the great task of commanding the B.E.F. T.H.E. Travers (269) promises to portray Sir Douglas Haig's generalship in a different light in a forthcoming book. R. Hough (121) and R.F. Mackay (172) have written biographies of John Arbuthnot Fisher, the First Sea Lord, 1914-1915. Mackay is the better reference for the war years; the Dardanelles venture and the Fisher-Churchill relationship are skillfully handled. Sir John Jellicoe, First Sea Lord, 1916-1917, is treated favorably by A.T. Patterson (212), but his cautious and pessimistic nature still emerges. Lord Esher, who often had a role to play in civil-military relations because of his society and military contacts, is the subject of a biography by P. Fraser (81).

No subject divided the civilians and soldiers more than grand strategy. J. Gooch has made contributions of considerable value to this subject, an essay, "Soldiers, Strategy and War Aims in Britain," (96) and *The Plans of War: The General Strategy c. 1900-1916* (95). The latter is exceptional in its treatment of civil-military decision making during the first months of the war. The influence of two

Dominion leaders, J.C. Smuts and Sir Robert Borden, on British grand strategy has been examined respectively in articles by D.R. Woodward (310) and G.L. Cook (48). Woodward has also surveyed Britain's Continental commitment in an article (305). K. Neilson's *Strategy and Supply: The Anglo-Russian Alliance, 1914-1917* (203) approaches the strategical debate from a somewhat different emphasis: the influence of allies on the formulation of grand strategy. J. Terraine (264) examines the pros and cons of the decision to launch the most controversial British offensive of the war, the so-called Passchendaele Offensive, through contemporary records. This collection of documents speaks for itself, but Terraine's editorial intervention make clear his view that the pros for this offensive outweighed the cons. The manpower crisis in the B.E.F. at the beginning of 1918 which Sir Frederick Maurice blamed on the Lloyd George ministry can be explored in an article by D.R. Woodward (308) and *The Maurice Case: From the Papers of Major-General Sir Frederick Maurice* (186) by N. Maurice.

War Objectives and Anti-War Sentiment. The publication of Fritz Fischer's monumental work in the 1960s on German war objectives, *Germany's War Aims in the First World War*, sparked an interest in British as well as German war objectives. In 1971, V.H. Rothwell (236) produced a pioneer study of the formulation of British war aims based on impressive research in official British archives. Publications on specific aspects of British war objectives soon followed. British policy toward Eastern Europe has been explored by W. Fest (74), W.R. Callott (27) and K.J. Calder (26). L.S. Jaffe (126) and R.E. Bunselmeyer (21) describe respectively the development of British plans to disarm Germany and the evolution of the policy to extract compensation for the war-related losses of the British Empire. The role played by British radicals and liberals in the creation of the League of Nations is described by G.W. Egerton (65). Lord R. Cecil's role is given by H. Cecil (36). Economic rivalry between the United States and Britain is highlighted in a flawed study by E.B. Parsons (211). P. Kennedy has interesting speculations on the connection between industrial and financial power, military strength, and imperial benefits and responsibilities in his *The Realities Behind Diplomacy: Background Influences on British External Policy, 1865-1980* (131). One of his four sections is on total war and its impact, 1914-1919.

Efforts to end the ruinous conflict through negotiation have attracted increased scholarly attention. President Wilson's efforts at mediation are explored by D.R. Woodward (309) and J.M. Cooper (49), who focus on the House-Grey Memorandum of early 1916, and by S.J. Kernek (136, 137), who examines Anglo-American relations, December 1916-November 1918. The possibility of a negotiated peace between Berlin and London are analyzed by D.R. Woodward (307, 312) and W.B. Fest (73). The British military's reactions to considerations of a compromise peace, 1916-1918, is the subject of an article by D.R. Woodward (306).

Other scholars have gone beyond official discussions of peace negotiations. Their focus is on individuals or groups against the war as a whole or conscription in particular. M. Ceadel's work (34) on British pacifism, although stronger for the 1930s and 1940s than for the 1914-1918 period, should not be overlooked. J. Vellacott's study of Bertrand Russell (279) examines both his public life and the pacifist movement. The No-Conscription Fellowship, which Russell chaired, receives definitive treatment by T.C. Kennedy (133). The government's reaction to conscientious objectors has been treated in a solid administrative history of J. Rae (223). The public's reactions to COs is given by T.C. Kennedy (132, 134, 135), who, along with L.R. Tucker (271), has subjected the Quakers to scholarly scrutiny. The political role of the Union of Democratic Control, launched in September 1914 by opponents of Britain's entry into the war, is examined by M. Swartz (256). The secretary of the U.D.C., E.D. Morel, has found a biographer in C.A. Cline (41). Two broad studies of the anti-war movement are by K. Robbins (229) and H. Weinroth (286). Robbins shows that the loose collection of peace groups and societies had no cohesive or clear-cut peace program. Like Swartz, Robbins relates the decline of the Liberal Party to Liberal defections over official war aims. One disillusioned left-wing Liberal who did not join either the U.D.C. or Labour was L.T. Hobhouse (249). Two other sources of anti-war sentiment--Suffragists and the working class--are scrutinized by J.V. Newberry (204) and K. Weller (287) respectively. The very limited influence of the anti-war groups, which most studies reflect, is one of the themes of a comparative study by F.L. Carsten (30).

Press and Propaganda. The radio in 1914 was still in the future, making the press for all practical purposes the sole medium of communication. When the political parties declared a wartime truce in Parliament, the political battleground tended to shift from Westminster to Fleet Street. Editors, journalists and proprietors such as Northcliffe, Rothermere and Beaverbrook were soon exercising considerable influence over public affairs and meddling in civil-military relations. Fleet Street's impact on public affairs has not always received the attention that it merits until recently. The much acclaimed work by S. Koss (142) devotes some 100 out of 686 pages of text to the Great War. Based extensively on manuscript collections, Koss' volume is excellent in examining the tenuous relationship between the press and political parties. The involvement of the press in politics for the first half of the war has also been described by S. Inwood (125). Five superior articles by J.M. McEwen (160, 162, 165, 166, 167), however, provide the best and most complete coverage of the wartime national press. Press censorship has been studied by C.J. Lovelace (153); C. à C. Repington, one journalist whom the Lloyd George ministry would have loved to muzzle, is the subject of an article by W.M. Ryan (238). The edited diaries of C.P. Scott (296) and Sir George Riddell (168), the last mentioned only recently opened, shed light on the relationship between the press and Lloyd George. D. Ayerst (6) is good on the influence of the liberal Scott, who was both owner and editor of the *Manchester Guardian*. A.G. Gardiner (140), editor of the *Daily News*, H.N. Brailsford (151), socialist journalist, H.W. Massingham (110), editor of the *Nation*, J.L. Garvin, editor of the *Observer*, and Beaverbrook (Sir Max Aitken, 259), who had a controlling interest in the *Express*, have all been the subject of recent works. A running pictorial record of social changes during the war can be found in the periodical best noted for its photographs, the *Illustrated London News* (14).

It is the rare and foolhardy modern scholar who writes on British wartime politics without extensive research in the contemporary press. Many British wartime newspapers can be researched in north London at the British Library's Newspaper Library in Colindale, which houses some 650,000 volumes and 14,000 reels of microfilm of nineteenth and twentieth century newspapers.

Since modern propaganda came into existence in World War I, the British, not surprisingly, were poorly equipped initially to fight this crucial war of paper bullets. With only the secret Foreign Office propaganda organization aimed at enemy and neutral opinion at Wellington House, newspapers, especially the Northcliffe press, played the central role in whipping up hysteria against the enemy. Combining their efforts, the press and Wellington House (239) eventually produced perhaps the most outrageous propaganda charge against the Germans: that Allied corpses were being utilized by a corpse-conversion works for oils and fats. The continued stalemate in the trenches and growing war weariness meant increased emphasis on propaganda in 1917-1918. A Department of Information (later made into a ministry) was created to coordinate Wellington House, a Cinema Division, a Political Intelligence Division and a News Division. Two recent books have added to our understanding of British propaganda: M.L. Sanders and P.M. Taylor (240) on official foreign propaganda and C. Haste (108) on domestic propaganda. Specific aspects of propaganda and its effects can be explored in articles. T. Wilson (294), through an examination of the Bryce Report, shows how decent Englishmen had their views colored by the doctrine of state necessity. P.M. Taylor (262) describes the usually unhappy relationship between Foreign Office officials and the propagandists; N. Reeves (224, 225) examines the neglected subject of film propaganda; and A.G. Marquis (179) makes some interesting comparisons and contrasts between German and British propaganda.

Britain's propaganda machine exploited German air attacks by the Zeppelin ('baby-killers') and the twin-engined Gotha, which introduced the British public to a new element in warfare: strategic bombing. This war on civilians created panic in some quarters and also provoked xenophobia. In addition to its psychological impact, German air attacks led to the development of a sophisticated British system of air defense. Works by C. Cole and E.F. Cheesman (44), H.G. Castle (33), D.G. Collyer (46) and R. Rimell (228) all contribute to our understanding of this important chapter of the history of the home front.

War Socialism and its Impact. The prewar state exercised little control over the ordinary citizen. Other than the post office, "board school," tax man and policeman, the typical Englishman had little contact with the state. Total war changed all of this. Victory largely depended upon the government's success in mobilizing the nation's resources for war. That Britain was ill prepared to fight a total war of any duration is shown by D. French (82, 84) and C. Trebilcock (270). Liberal laissez-faire attitudes, according to French, were much less responsible for this unpreparedness than the illusion of a short war and prewar planning that concerned only token British involvement in a Continental conflict. The "shells scandal" led to the creation of the Ministry of Munitions in May 1915. During the remainder of the war this new ministry expanded its influence and control throughout the entire economy. By the end of the war, the Ministry of Munitions had a staff of 65,000 men and women and controlled over 3,500,000 workers; 250 factories, quarries and mines were under its direct control and 20,000 establishments were being supervised by it. R.J.Q. Adams (1, 2) and C. Wrigley (314) in recent studies give Lloyd George high marks for his leadership of the Ministry of Munitions. One of Lloyd George's innovations was to utilize businessmen rather than civil servants. How businessmen reacted to state intervention is examined from a broad perspective in an essay by J. Turner (276). Government intervention, Turner argues, was usually resisted by businessmen unless it was in line with their own ideas and politics.

The Great War had a profound influence on science and science-based industries. The Munitions Inventions Department, which received some 50,000 suggestions during the war, is examined by M. Pattison (213, 214). Science and the Admiralty is the subject of essays by J.K. Gusewelle (101) and R.M. MacLeod and E.K. Andrews (176). The government's relationship to the scientists and technologists can be followed in works by L.F. Harber (102, 103), R. Mcleod (175) and J. Reinharz (227).

Control of the food supply serves as another important example of the government's intervention during the war. J. Harris (104) has studied the role of bureaucrats and businessmen in controlling the food supply; and P.E. Dewey had demonstrated that money was still to be made even after the government intervened to reduce profits in agriculture. See also the recently edited papers of Lord Crawford (280).

No less than four British armies fought in the war: the regular army, the Territorials, Kitchener's volunteer New Army, and the conscript army which followed the introduction of compulsion in 1916. The dramatic expansion of the army is an important subject that has finally received the scholarly attention it merits. I. Beckett provides a solid introduction in his essay, "The Nation in Arms, 1914-1918" (11). Various aspects of the voluntary recruiting movement have been explored by J.M. Osborne (209), C. Hughes (123) and R. Douglas (63). Conscription, a divisive policy that divided the country, is examined by R.J.Q. Adams and P.P. Poirier (3). The problem of military manpower was a part of the larger question of the efficient utilization of manpower for both civilian and military requirements. Recruiting's impact on the labour force in industry and agriculture is explained by P.E. Dewey (56, 58) in two articles. Demographic or social aspects of the army are the subject of two superior essays by J.M. Winters (297) and P. Simkins (248).

The efforts to allocate manpower effectively through National Service fell short of expectations. D. Dilks (59) points to some of the failures of this administrative innovation, but he fails in his biography to pinpoint the individual responsibility of Neville Chamberlain, the first Director-General of National Service.

The war's impact on women has been discussed by G. Braybon (18), A. Marwick (183), M. Kozak (144) and N.A. Ferguson (72). Marwick's conclusions on the relationship between war and the position of women are questioned by Braybon and Ferguson. Braybon writes from a critical feminist-socialist perspective and succeeds in showing how contemporary attitudes affected women in the work place. Ferguson joins Braybon in arguing that the war's impact on the employment of skilled and unskilled women was short lived. Kozak, on the other hand, sees an interrelationship between war and social change.

The government had perhaps no more delicate issue on the home front than its relationship with labour. An important addition to the literature is C. Wrigley's balanced examination (314) of Lloyd George's handling of government intervention in industrial relations. The successes and especially the failures of Lloyd George's new Ministry of Labour are well described in an essay by R. Lowe (156). The activities and significance of the War Emergency Workers' National Committee are explored by Harrison (106). Worker support of the war effort depended to a considerable degree on the equitable sharing of all classes of the war-imposed sacrifices on the British people. B.A. Waites (282) has some interesting comments on the "moral economy" of the working class.

Ramsay MacDonald's opposition notwithstanding, the Labour leadership overwhelmingly supported the government once Britain was at war. Arthur Henderson (122) replaced MacDonald as leader of the parliamentary party and later joined the War Cabinet. Many other Labour Party and national union leaders accepted government positions. As the expanding war economy began to undermine established wages, hours and union practices, the rank and file began to look to shop stewards' organizations for leadership rather than their former leaders who had been coopted by bureaucratic state socialism. The growing radicalism of many workers can be followed in the writings of J. Hinton (115, 116), S. Pollard (218) and J. Bush (24). Hinton examines the war's impact on skilled engineering craftsmen in the munitions industry and Bush shows how the war gave Labour many opportunities for political power and organization among the some one million workers in east London. A study of how the war affected one trade union leader is the J. Schneer biography of Ben Tillett (244). The British Workers' League (known in the Coupon Election as the National Democratic Party) is the subject of essays by R. Douglas (62) and J.O. Stubbs (255).

The success of communism in Russia in 1917 encouraged the more militant Labour elements. M.H. Cowden (50) details relations between the Soviets and British Labour, and R. Challinor (37) examines the origins of British Bolshevism. J.M. Winter (298) has an enlightening essay on the Russian Revolution's influence on Henderson and the reconstruction of the Labour Party into a national party with a socialist program. In his history of both the wartime Labour Party and the evolution of socialist thought, Winter (303) focuses on the socialist theories of the Webbs (285), R.H. Tawney (265) and G.D.H. Cole (29, 313). The Webbs emerge as the heroes of his book. A new socialist ideology was not created, Winter notes, but some aspects of socialist thought had a wider acceptance because of the conflict.

Whether the Great War had important long-run consequences for the course of British history and the welfare of the people remains an argument without end. A central problem is to separate the changes directly attributable to the war from evolutionary changes that would have occurred anyway. A. Marwick leads the way in seeing a positive interrelationship between World War I and social change in Britain. His comparative study, *War and Social Change in the Twentieth Century* (182), introduces a new methodology to establish the critical influence of war in promoting social change. He examines four dimensions of war: war as *destruction*; war as a *test* of existing institutions; war as a creator of *participation* for underprivileged groups; and war as a *psychological* experience. More recently he has written a vigorous defense of his ideas in *Britain in our Century: Images and Controversies* (181). His dissenters, which include R. McKibbin, M.D. Pugh and G. Braybon, to name only a few, remain unconvinced, arguing that the long-range effects on social change were either insignificant or negative in their effect. A.S. Milward's survey (189) of the economic effects of the war expands the discussion to include the international repercussions of the war on the British economy and society, which he concludes had the greater impact on Britain's development.

A revisionist study, *War and the State: The Transformation of British Government, 1914-1919* (23), takes a fresh look at the extreme changes in the organization and role of the British government. This administrative history takes exception with the idea that Lloyd George's rise to the premiership represented the triumph of war socialism over laissez-faire Liberalism. A.M. Gollin (94), however, makes a good case that A.J.P. Taylor's "freedom" vs. "control" theme continues to offer the best means of analyzing British wartime politics.

The new administrative machinery created by the war did not constitute a lasting revolution for the interwar period with the exception of the strengthened position of the Treasury and the new Cabinet Secretariat. The Secretariat, which contributed greatly to the development of the presidential prime ministership, has been minutely examined by J. Turner (274, 275) and J.F. Naylor (200, 201). Turner (273) takes a revisionist position on the Lloyd George ministry, concluding that its administrative achievements have been considerably exaggerated. The primary difference between the ministries of Asquith and Lloyd George, he asserts, was political and not administrative.

Ireland. The divisive Irish question created bad blood on both sides of the Irish Sea and poisoned British politics. P. Jalland and J. Stubbs (127) describe well the bitter controversy over Home Rule in August and September 1914 which led the Conservatives to believe that Liberalism could never be trusted on Ulster; the Liberals for their part thought that some Conservatives were using Ireland to bludgeon Liberalism. S. Lawlor (148) M. Laffan (145) and G. Dangerfield (53) have written general surveys. Dangerfield's brilliant book has the most appropriate title, *The Damnable Question: A Study in Anglo-Irish Relations*. Laffan's study is judicious and balanced; only some thirty pages are devoted to the pre-1918 period in Lawlor's account.

The failure of British policy in Ireland has been analyzed from many perspectives. Lloyd George, a central figure in Irish negotiations, does not emerge blameless in essays by D.G. Boyce (17), D.W. Savage (241) and A.J. Ward (284). R.B. McDowell (158) focuses on the Irish Convention, 1917-1918. In contrast to those who treat this attempt at compromise as a pseudo-event, McDowell believes that it probably represented the last chance for a united Ireland. The impact of the Irish question on Liberalism during the war is the subject of an article by J.M. McEwen (161). An analysis of the role of Augustine Birrell, the Chief Secretary for Ireland, and Dublin

Castle, the nerve center of Irish administration, in the 1916 rising can be found in books by L. O'Broin (206, 207). D.G. Boyce (16) examines the war's influence on Irish compromise. He argues that British policy failed in the end because it was based on the exigencies of the war instead of on long-term considerations. R. Casement, the Ulster Protestant who became a martyr to Irish nationalists following his execution at Pentonville in 1916, continues to attract biographers. His divided character has been most recently scrutinized by B. Inglis (124), B.L. Reid (226) and R. Sawyer (242). The unification of the Sinn Fein ("Ourselves Alone") in 1917 and Irish politics during war and revolution in Country Clare have been treated respectively by M. Laffan (146) and D. Fitzpatrick (75).

Society. The Sound Records Department of the Imperial War Museum contains an important World War I oral history collection. Recorded since 1972, this collection concerns subjects such as war work and conscientious objectors. *The Edwardians: The Remaking of British Society* (266) by P. Thompson is a standard work on British society that utilizes oral interviews. Examining the impact of the war on all social classes, Thompson concludes that the old country aristocracy and gentry were adversely affected by the war. J.M. Winter (299) demonstrates that the "lost generation" was no myth for the social elite. A. Lambert (147) has written an illuminating book on the pinnacle of British high society in London during the war. Despite the obvious political importance of Lord Curzon and Balfour, who are included in Lambert's elite British aristocratic circle known as "the souls," there remain serious questions about A.J. Mayer's revisionist conclusions concerning the position and importance of the British aristocracy down to the war (187). B.A. Waites (281, 283) has explored class and status during the war.

Wartime rural life receives recent attention. The incredibly detailed and voluminous diary of A. Clark, the Rector of Great Leighs in Essex, has been edited by J. Munson (38). Clark's complete diary can be found in the Bodleian Library. P. Horn (120), who focuses on tenant farmers and laborers, concludes that changes in agricultural life were accelerated rather than begun by the war. M. Moynihan (199) makes extensive use of materials in the Imperial War Museum to give the war record of the citizens of the coastal town of Southwold, which was on the direct path of Zeppelins in route to London. The mood of the country when war broke out can be found in popular accounts by K. McLeod (174) and J. Terraine (263). British hysteria about enemy spies, which contributed to the breakdown of public order in some instances, is the subject of an article by D. French (85).

A. Wilkinson's *The Church of England and the First World War* (289) shows that the church's response to war was really quite varied and complex, although it is true that nonconformists were more likely to be conscientious objectors than Anglicans. The gulf between Anglican chaplains and the common soldiers is also stressed. A. Marrin's work (180), which gives some consideration to denominations other than the Church of England, complements Wilkinson's study. J.M. Winter (301, 302) has shown that the standards of health did not really decline in wartime Britain. He also cautions the researcher against relying on the report of the Ministry of National Service Medical Boards as a source for the health of Britain's male

population. Winter's recent social and demographic history, *The Great War and the British People* (300), is a most important addition to the literature. An administrative history which reveals Lloyd George's genuine interest in the nation's health is *The Struggle for the Ministry of Health 1914-1919* by F. Honigsbaum (118).
English Education, Social Change and War: 1911-1920 by G. Sherington (245) debunks the view of a direct relationship between war and social change. Bureaucratic continuity, he argues, proved to be more prominent than war-influenced political and social change. The 1918 Education Act is thoroughly evaluated by L. Andrews (4). British public housing, 1915-1921, is the subject of a book by L.F. Orbach (208), who argues that a strong motivation for public housing was fear of worker unrest. The role of Lloyd George's chief agent for domestic radical politics, C. Addison, can be followed in Orbach's study and a biography by K. and J. Morgan (196).

Cultural. The postwar British novel in its different forms is analyzed by H. Cecil (35). H. Klein (138) has compiled a collection of critical essays with a comparative emphasis on war fiction. The poetry of the trench writers can be found in the useful collection by J. Silkin (246). The life of perhaps Britain's best known Great War poet, Wilfred Owen, has been described by J. Stallworthy (250).
Some superior cultural histories on the interrelationship between ideas, action and historical memory have recently been published. P. Fussell's *The Great War and Modern Memory* (87) is a masterful analysis of the British experience in the trenches of France and Flanders as seen through the eyes of writers. The literary response to the war, of course, should never be used as documentary evidence. While Fussell focuses on literary and linguistic responses, E.J. Leed's *No Man's Land: Combat & Identity in World War I* (150) describes psychological responses. The intellectual impact of the war can be found in *The Generation of 1914* (304) by R. Wohl and *Redemption by War: The Intellectuals and 1914* (253) by R.N. Stromberg.

Research Opportunities. The opening of the official records for the 1914-1922 period in 1965 and important private collections such as the Lloyd George Papers in the last half of the 1960s roughly coincided with the editor's deadline (October 1967) for contributors to *A Guide to the Sources of British Military History*. Since then historians have mined the wealth of new materials. Most existing literature has been significantly revised. The suggestions for future research made by Paul Guinn in his essay on the home front have been exhausted. This is not to assert that research on the home front is now sterile. Far from it. New primary materials, however, are certain to be relatively rare and gaps in the literature more difficult to discern. Local history remains one inviting area for research. There is also a need for works of synthesis which incorporate the findings of detailed archival research. A work that gives an overview of the political history of the war years, for example, is yet to be written.

BIBLIOGRAPHY

GUIDES TO THE SOURCES

Before delving into the mass of evidence relating to British history since 1914, searchers would be well advised to begin their efforts with the common sense discussion by C.L. Mowat (198) of some of the pitfalls of working with such contemporary sources as the *Parliamentary Debates*, newspapers, official papers and unpublished private papers. The indispensable six-volume reference work for political history (47), primarily compiled by C. Cook, directs the searcher to the papers of members of Parliament, selected public servants, writers, intellectuals and publicists, and the archives of organizations and societies. Private papers made available since Cook's volumes can be found in the annual list of Accessions to Repositories published by H.M. Stationery Office for the Historical Manuscript Commission. See C. Hazlehurst and C. Woodland (113) for the papers of cabinet ministers; S.L. Mayer and W.J. Koenig (188) are of particular value to the new school of military historians, for their guide to manuscript collections includes political and diplomatic records that are relevant to the war's course and outcome. The National Register of Archives, maintained by the Historical Manuscript Commission, Quality House, Quality Court, Chancery Lane, London XC2A 1HP, remains an essential listing of private papers. History theses, 1971-1980, can be found in J.M. Horn (119); works in progress and theses completed after 1980 can be located in the Institute of Historical Research's annual publications, *Theses in Progress* and *Theses Completed*. The guide by S.S. Wilson (292) provides Cabinet Office (CAB) references for the multifarious cabinet committees, international conferences and imperial conferences. Not to be overlooked are the bibliographical guides by A.F. Havighurst (109) and A.G.S. Enser (68) and the helpful survey of reference materials by G.M. Bayliss (10).

1. Adams, R.J.Q. *Arms and the Wizard: Lloyd George and the Ministry of Munitions, 1915-1916.* College Station: Texas A&M University Press, 1978.
2. ————. "Delivering the Goods: Reappraising the Ministry of Munitions, 1915-1916." *Albion*, 7 (1975): 232-4.
3. ———— and Philip P. Poirier. *The Conscription Controversy in Great Britain, 1900-18.* Columbus: Ohio State University Press, forthcoming.
4. Andrews, Lawrence. *The Education Act, 1918.* London: Routledge & Kegan Paul, 1976.
5. Ayerst, David. *Garvin of the Observer.* Dover, N.H.: Croom Helm, 1985.
6. ————. *The Manchester Guardian: Biography of a Newspaper.* Ithaca: Cornell University Press, 1971.
7. Bagwell, Philip S. "The Triple Alliance, 1913-1922" in *Essays in Labour History 1886-1923*, edited by Asa Briggs and John Saville, pp. 96-129. Hamden, Conn.: Archon Books, 1971.
8. Barnes, John and David Nicholson. *The Leo Amery Diaries.* vol. 1: *1896-1929.* London: Hutchinson, 1980.
9. Barnett, L. Margaret. *British Food Policy During the First World War.* Winchester, Ma.: George Allen & Unwin, 1985.

10. Bayliss, Gwyn M. *Bibliographic Guide to the Two World Wars: An Annotated Survey of English-Language Reference Materials.* London: Bowker, 1977.
11. Beckett, Ian. "The Nation in Arms, 1914-1918" in *A Nation in Arms: A Social Study of the British Army in the First World War*, edited by Ian F.W. Beckett and Keith Simpson, pp. 1-35. Manchester: Manchester University Press, 1985.
12. Beloff, Max. *Wars and Welfare, Britain 1914-1945.* London: Edward Arnold, 1984.
13. Bentley, Michael. *The Liberal Mind 1914-29.* New York: Cambridge University Press, 1977.
14. Bishop, James. *The Illustrated London News Social History of the First World War.* London: Angus & Robertson, 1982.
15. Blake, Robert. *The Decline of Power 1915-1964.* New York: Oxford University Press, 1985.
16. Boyce, David G. "British Opinion, Ireland, and the War, 1916-1918." *Historical Journal*, 17 (1974): 575-93.
17. ─────. "How to Settle the Irish Question: Lloyd George and Ireland 1916-21" in *Lloyd George: Twelve Essays*, edited by A.J.P. Taylor, pp. 137-64. New York: Atheneum, 1977.
18. Braybon, Gail. *Women Workers in the First World War.* London: Croom Helm, 1981.
19. Brock, Michael and Eleanor (eds.). *H.H. Asquith: Letters to Venetia Stanley.* New York: Oxford University, 1982.
20. Brown, Kenneth D. (ed.). *Essays in Anti-Labour History: Responses to the Rise of Labour in Britain.* Hamden, Conn.: Archon Books, 1974.
21. Bunselmeyer, Robert E. *The Cost of the War, 1914-1919: British Economic War Aims and the Origins of Reparation.* Hamden, Conn.: Archon Books, 1975.
22. Burgess, Keith. *The Challenge of Labour: Shaping British Society 1850-1930.* New York: St. Martin's, 1980.
23. Burk, Kathleen. "The Treasury: From Impotence to Power" in *War and the State: The Transformation of British Government, 1914-1919*, edited by Kathleen Burk, pp. 84-107. London: George Allen & Unwin, 1982.
24. Bush, Julia. *Behind the Lines: East London Labour 1914-1919.* London: Merlin Press, 1985.
25. Cahalan, Peter. *Belgian Refugee Relief in England during the Great War.* New York: Garland Publishing, 1982.
26. Calder, Kenneth J. *Britain and the Origins of the New Europe 1914-1918.* London: Cambridge University Press, 1976.
27. Callott, W.R. "The Last War Aim: British Opinion and the Decision for Czechoslovak Independence, 1914-1919." *Historical Journal*, 27 (1984): 979-89.
28. Campbell, John. *F.E. Smith, First Earl of Birkenhead.* London: Jonathan Cape, 1983.
29. Carpenter, L.P. *G.D.H. Cole: An Intellectual Biography.* New York: Cambridge University Press, 1973.
30. Carsten, F. L. *War Against War: British and German Radical Movements in the First World War.* Berkeley: University of California Press, 1982.
31. Cassar, George H. *Kitchener: Architect of Victory.* London: William Kimber, 1977.

32. ———. *The Tragedy of Sir John French.* Newark, N.J.: University of Delaware Press, 1985.
33. Castle, H.G. *Fire Over England: The German Air Raids of World War I.* London: Leo Cooper/Secker & Warburg, 1982.
34. Ceadel, Martin. *Pacificism in Britain 1914-1945: The Defending of a Faith.* New York: Oxford University Press, 1980.
35. Cecil, Hugh. "The Literary Legacy of the Wars: The Post-War British War Novel--a Select Bibliography" in *Home Fires and Foreign Fields: British Social and Military Experience in the First World War,* edited by Peter H. Liddle, pp. 205-30. London: Brassey's Defence Publishers, 1985.
36. ———. "Lord Robert Cecil and the League of Nations during the First World War in *Home Fires and Foreign Fields: British Social and Military Experience in the First World War,* edited by Peter H. Liddle, pp. 69-81. London: Brassey's Defence Publishers, 1985.
37. Challinor, Raymond. *The Origins of British Bolshevism.* Totowa, N.J.: Rowman & Littlefield, 1977.
38. Clark, Andrew. *Echoes of the Great War.* Edited by James Munson. New York: Oxford University Press, 1985.
39. Clarke, P.F. *Lancashire and the New Liberalism.* New York: Cambridge University Press, 1971.
40. ———. "Liberals, Labour and the Franchise." *English Historical Review,* 92 (1977): 582-90.
41. Cline, Catherine Ann. *E.D. Morel, 1873-1924: The Strategies of Protest.* Belfast, N.I.: Blackstaff Press, 1980.
42. Cline, Peter. "Winding Down the War Economy: British Plans for Peacetime Recovery, 1916-19" in *War and the State: The Transformation of British Government, 1914-1919,* edited by Kathleen Burk, pp. 157-81. London: George Allen & Unwin, 1982.
43. Close, David H. "The Collapse of Resistance to Democracy: Conservatives, Adult Suffrage, and Second Chamber Reform, 1911-1918." *Historical Journal,* 20 (1977): 893-918.
44. Cole, Christopher and E.F. Cheesman. *The Air Defence of Britain 1914-1918.* London: Putnam, 1984.
45. Coleman, D.C. "War Demand and Industrial Supply: The 'Dope Scandal,' 1915-19" in *War and Economic Development: Essays in Memory of David Joslin,* edited by J.M. Winter, pp. 205-27. New York: Cambridge University Press, 1975.
46. Collyer, David G. *Kent's Listening Ears: Britain's First Early Warning System.* David Collyer, 25 Pilot's Avenue, Deal, Kent.
47. Cook, Chris, etc. (eds.). *Sources on British Political History 1900-1951.* 6 vols. London: Macmillan, 1975-1985.
48. Cook, George L. "Sir Robert Borden, Lloyd George and British Military Policy, 1917-1918." *Historical Journal,* 14 (1971): 371-95.
49. Cooper, John Milton, Jr. "The British Response to the House-Grey Memorandum: New Evidence and New Questions." *Journal of American History,* 59 (1973): 958-71.
50. Cowden, Morton H. *Russian Bolshevism and British Labour, 1917-1921.* Boulder, Colo.: East European Monographs; distributed by Columbia University Press. New York, 1984.

51. Creiger, Don M. *Chiefs without Indians: Asquith, Lloyd George and the Liberal Remnant, 1916-1935.* Washington, D.C.: University Presses of America, 1982.
52. ——————. *The Decline of the British Liberal Party: Why & How.* Murray, Ky.: Lorrah & Hitchcock Publishers, 1985.
53. Dangerfield, George. *The Damnable Question: A Study in Anglo-Irish Relations.* Boston: Little, Brown & Co, 1976.
54. David, Edward. (ed.). *Inside Asquith's Cabinet: From the Diaries of Charles Hobhouse.* London: John Murray, 1977.
55. ——————. "The Liberal Party Divided, 1916-18." *Historical Journal*, 13 (1970): 509-32.
56. Dewey, P.E. "Agricultural Labour Supply in England and Wales During the First World War." *Economic History Review*, 28 (1975): 100-12.
57. ——————. "British Farming Profits and Government Policy During the First World War." *Economic History Review*, 37 (1984): 373-90.
58. ——————. "Military Recruiting and the British Labour Force During the First World War." *Historical Journal*, 27 (1984): 199-223.
59. Dilks, David. *Neville Chamberlain*, vol. 1. *Pioneering and Reform, 1869-1929.* New York: Cambridge University Press, 1984.
60. Douglas, Roy. "The Background to the 'Coupon' Election Arrangements." *English Historical Review*, 86 (1971): 318-56.
61. ——————. *The History of the Liberal Party.* Cranbury, N.J.: Thomas Yoseloff of A.S. Barnes & Co., 1971.
62. ——————. "The National Democratic Party and the British Workers' League." *Historical Journal*, 15 (1972): 533-52.
63. ——————. "Voluntary Enlistment in the First World War and the Work of the Parliamentary Recruiting Committee." *Journal of Modern History*, 42 (1970): 564-85.
64. Dutton, David. *Austen Chamberlain: Gentleman in Politics.* Boston: Ross Anderson Publications, 1983.
65. Egerton, George W. *Great Britain and the Creation of the League of Nations: Strategy, Politics, and International Organizations, 1914-1919.* Chapel Hill: The University of North Carolina Press, 1979.
66. Egremont, Max. *Balfour: A Life of Arthur James Balfour.* London: Collins, 1980.
67. Englander, David and James Osborne. "Jack, Tommy and Henry Dubb: The Armed Forces and the Working Class." *Historical Journal*, 21 (1978): 593-621.
68. Enser, A.G.S. *A Subject Bibliography of the First World War: Books in English 1914-1978.* London: Andre Deutsch, 1979.
69. Fair, John D. *British Interplay Conferences: A Study of the Procedure of Conciliation in British Politics, 1867-1921.* New York: Clarendon Press, 1980.
70. ——————. "The Political Aspects of Women's Suffrage During the First World War." *Albion*, 8 (1976): 274-95.
71. ——————. "Politicians, Historians and the War: A Reassessment of the Political Crisis of December 1916." *Journal of Modern History*, 49 (1977), on-demand supplement.

72. Ferguson, Neal A. "Women's Work: Employment Opportunities and Economic Roles, 1918-1939." *Albion*, 7 (1975): 55-68.
73. Fest, W.B. "British War Aims and German Peace Feelers During the First World War (December 1916-November 1918)." *Historical Journal*, 15 (1972): 285-308.
74. Fest, Wilfried. *Peace or Partition: The Habsburg Monarchy and British Policy, 1914-1918*. New York: St. Martin's Press, 1978.
75. Fitzpatrick, David. *Politics and Irish Life 1913-21: Provincial Experience of War and Revolution*. Dublin: Gill & Macmillan, 1977.
76. Fraser, Peter. "The British 'Shells Scandal' of 1915." *Canadian Journal of History*, 18 (1983): 69-86.
77. ———. "British War Policy and the Crisis of Liberalism in May 1915." *Journal of Modern History*, 54 (1982): 1-26.
78. ———. "Cabinet Secrecy and War Memoirs." *History*, 70 (1985): 397-409.
79. ———. "The Impact of the War of 1914-1918 on the British Political System" in *War and Society*, edited by M.R.D. Foot, pp. 123-39. New York: Barnes & Noble, 1973.
80. ———. "Lord Beaverbrook's Fabrications in Politicians and the War, 1914-1916." *Historical Journal*, 25 (1982): 147-66.
81. ———. *Lord Esher: A Political Biography*. London: Hart-Davis, MacGibbon, 1973.
82. French, David. *British Economic and Strategic Planning, 1905-1915*. London: George Allen & Unwin, 1982.
83. ———. "The Military Background to the 'Shell Crisis' of May 1915." *Journal of Strategic Studies*, 2 (1979): 192-205.
84. ———. "The Rise and Fall of 'Business as Usual'" in *War and the State: The Transformation of British Government, 1914-1919*, edited by Kathleen Burk, pp. 7-31. London: George Allen & Unwin, 1982.
85. ———. "Spy Fever in Britain, 1900-1915." *Historical Journal*, 21 (1978): 355-70.
86. Fry, Michael G. *Lloyd George and Foreign Policy*, vol. 1: *The Education of a Statesman, 1890-1916*. Montreal: McGill-Queen's University Pres, 1977.
87. Fussell, Paul. *The Great War and Modern Memory*. New York: Oxford University Press, 1975.
88. Gilbert, Bentley B. *British Social Policy 1914-1939*. London: Batsford, 1970.
89. ———. "Pacifist to Interventionist: David Lloyd George in 1911 and 1914. Was Belgium an Issue?" *Historical Journal*, 28 (1985): 863-85.
90. Gilbert, Martin. *Winston S. Churchill*, vol. 3: *1914-1916*. London: Heinemann, 1971.
91. ———. *Winston S. Churchill*, vol. 4: *1917-1922*. London: Heinemann, 1971.
92. ———. *Winston S. Churchill. Companion Volume III. Part I August 1914--April 1915, Part II May 1915--December 1916*. 2 vols. London: Heinemann, 1972.
93. ———. *Winston S. Churchill, Companion Volume IV. Part I January 1917--June 1919*. London: Heinemann, 1978.

94. Gollin, Alfred M. Review of David French, *British Economic and Strategic Planning, 1905-1915* in *Albion*, 15 (1983): 259-65.
95. Gooch, John. *The Plans of War: The General Staff and British Military Strategy c. 1900-1916*. London: Routledge & Kegan Paul, 1974.
96. ─────. "Soldiers, Strategy and War Aims in Britain 1914-1918" in *War Aims and Strategic Policy in the Great War 1914-1918*, edited by Barry Hunt and Adrian Preston, pp. 21-40. London: Croom Helm, 1977.
97. Greenleaf, W.H. *The British Political Tradition*, vol. 1: *The Rise of Collectivism*; vol. 2: *The Ideological Heritage*. London: Methuen, 1983.
98. Griffin, Nicholas J. "The Response of British Labor to the Importation of Chinese Workers: 1916-1917." *Historian*, 40 (1978): 252-70.
99. Grigg, John. "Lloyd George and Ministerial Leadership in the Great War" in *Home Fires and Foreign Fields: British Social and Military Experience in the First World War*, edited by Peter H. Liddle, pp. 1-8. London: Brassey's Defence Publishers, 1985.
100. ─────. *Lloyd George: From Peace to War, 1912-1916*. Berkeley: University of California Press, 1985.
101. Gusewelle, J.K. "Science and the Admiralty During World War I: The Case of the BIR" in *Naval Warfare in the Twentieth Century*, edited by G. Jordan, pp. 107-17. London: Croom Helm, 1977.
102. Harber, L.F. *The Chemical Industry 1900-1930*. Oxford: Clarendon Press, 1971.
103. ─────. *The Poisonous Cloud: Chemical Warfare in the First World War*. New York: Oxford University Press, 1985.
104. Harris, Jose. "Bureaucrats and Businessmen in British Food Control, 1916-1919" in *War and the State: The Transformation of British Government, 1914-1919*, edited by Kathleen Burk, pp. 135-56. London: George Allen & Unwin, 1982.
105. ─────. *William Beveridge: A Biography*. New York: Oxford University Press, 1977.
106. Harrison, Royden. "The War Emergency Workers' National Committee, 1914-1918" in *Essays in Labour History 1886-1923*, edited by Asa Briggs and John Saville, pp. 211-59. Hamden, Conn.: Archon Books, 1971.
107. Hart, Michael. "The Liberals, the War and the Franchise." *English Historical Review*, 97 (1982): 820-32.
108. Haste, Cate. *Keep the Home Fires Burning: Propaganda in the First World War*. London: Allen Lane, 1977.
109. Havighurst, Alfred F. *Modern England 1901-1970*. London: Cambridge University Press, 1976.
110. ─────. *Radical Journalist: H.W. Massingham (1860-1924)*. London: Cambridge University Press, 1974.
111. Hazlehurst, Cameron. "Asquith as Prime Minister, 1908-1916." *English Historical Review*, 85 (1970): 502-31.
112. ─────. *Politicians at War July 1914 to May 1915: A Prologue to the Triumph of Lloyd George*. New York: Alfred A. Knopf, 1971.

113. ———— and Christine Woodland. *Guide to the Papers of British Cabinet Ministers 1900-1951*. London: Royal Historical Society, 1974.
114. Hinsley, F.H. (ed.). *British Foreign Policy Under Sir Edward Grey*. London: Cambridge University Press, 1977.
115. Hinton, James. "The Clyde Workers' Committee and the Dilution Struggle" in *Essays in Labour History 1886-1923*, edited by Asa Briggs and John Saville, pp. 152-84. Hamden, Conn.: Archon Books, 1971.
116. ————. *The First Shop Stewards' Movement*. London: George Allen & Unwin, 1973.
117. Holmes, Richard. *The Little Field Marshal: Sir John French*. London: Jonathan Cape, 1981.
118. Honigsbaum, Frank. *The Struggle for the Ministry of Health 1914-1919*. Occasional Papers on Social Administration, no. 37. London: G. Bell & Sons, 1970.
119. Horn, J.M. *History Theses, 1971-80: Historical Research for Higher Degrees in the Universities of the United Kingdom*. London: Institute of Historical Research, 1984.
120. Horn, Pamela. *Rural Life in England in the First World War*. New York: St. Martin's, 1985.
121. Hough, Richard. *Admiral of the Fleet: The Life of John Fisher*. New York: Macmillan, 1970.
122. Howard, Christopher. "MacDonald, Henderson, and the Outbreak of War, 1914." *Historical Journal*, 20 (1977): 871-91.
123. Hughes, Clive. "Army Recruitment in Gwynedd, 1914-1916." M.A. thesis, University of Wales, 1983.
124. Inglis, Brian. *Roger Casement: The Biography of a Patriot who Lived for England, Died for Ireland*. New York: Harcourt Brace Jovanovich, 1973.
125. Inwood, S. "The Role of the Press in English Politics During the First World War, with Special Reference to the Period 1914-1916." PhD dissertation, Oxford University, 1971.
126. Jaffe, Lorna S. *The Decision to Disarm Germany: British Policy Toward Postwar German Disarmament, 1914-1919*. Boston: George Allen & Unwin, 1985.
127. Jalland, Patricia and John Stubbs. "The Irish Question After the Outbreak of War in 1914: Some Unfinished Party Business." *English Historical Review*, 96 (1981): 778-807.
128. Jeffrey, Keith (ed.). *The Military Correspondence of Field Marshal Sir Henry Wilson 1918-1922*. London: Bodley Head for the Army Records Society, 1985.
129. Judd, Denis. *Lord Reading: Rufus Isaacs, First Marquess of Reading, Lord Chief Justice, and Viceroy of India, 1860-1935*. London: Weidenfeld & Nicolson, 1982.
130. Kendle, John. "Federalism and the Irish Problem in 1918." *History*, 56 (1971): 207-30.
131. Kennedy, Paul. *The Realities behind Diplomacy: Background Influences on British External Policy, 1865-1980*. London: George Allen & Unwin, with Fontana, 1981.
132. Kennedy, Thomas C. "Fighting about Peace: The No-Conscription Fellowship and the British Friends' Service Committee, 1915-1919." *Quaker History*, 69 (1980): 2-22.
133. ————. *The Hound of Conscience: A History of the No*

Conscription Fellowship, 1914-1919. Fayetteville: Arkansas University Press, 1981.
134. ———. "Public Opinion and the Conscientious Objector, 1915-1919." Journal of British Studies, 12 (1973): 105-19.
135. ———. "The Quaker Renaissance and the Origins of the Modern British Peace Movement, 1895-1920." Albion, 16 (1984): 243-72.
136. Kernek, Sterling J. "The British Government's Reactions to President Wilson's 'Peace' Note of December, 1917." Historical Journal, 13 (1970): 721-66.
137. ———. Distractions of Peace During War: The Lloyd George Government's Reactions to Woodrow Wilson December, 1916--November, 1918. Philadelphia: American Philosophical Society, 1975.
138. Klein, Holger (ed.). The First World War in Fiction. London: Macmillan, 1976.
139. Koss, Stephen. Asquith. New York: St. Martin's, 1976.
140. ———. Fleet Street Radical: A.G. Gardiner and the Daily News. London: Allen Lane, 1973.
141. ———. Lord Haldane: Scapegoat for Liberalism. New York: Columbia University Press, 1969.
142. ———. The Rise and Fall of the Political Press in Britain, vol. 2: The Twentieth Century. Chapel Hill: The University of North Carolina Press, 1984.
143. ———. Nonconformity in Modern British Politics. Hamden, Conn.: Archon Books, 1975.
144. Kozak, Marion. "Women Munition Workers during the First World War." PhD dissertation, University of Hull, 1977.
145. Laffan, Michael. The Partition of Ireland, 1911-1925. Dublin: Dublin Historical Association, 1983.
146. ———. "The Unification of Sinn Fein in 1917." Irish Historical Studies, 17 (1971): 353-79.
147. Lambert, Angela. Unquiet Souls: A Social History of the Illustrious, Irreverent, Intimate Group of British Aristocrats Known as "The Souls." New York: Harper & Row, 1984.
148. Lawlor, Sheila. Britain and Ireland 1914-23. Totowa, N.J.: Barnes & Noble Books, 1983.
149. Laybourn, Keith and Jack Reynolds. Liberalism and the Rise of Labour 1890-1918: The Yorkshire Labour Movement, Old Liberalism and New Liberalism. New York: St. Martin's, 1984.
150. Leed, Eric J. No Man's Land: Combat & Identity in World War. New York: Cambridge University Press, 1979.
151. Leventhal, F. M. The Last Dissenter: H.N. Brailsford and His World. New York: Oxford University Press, 1985.
152. Lloyd, T.O. Empire to Welfare State: English History 1906-1967. London: Oxford University Press, 1970.
153. Lovelace, C.J. "Control and Censorship of the Press during the First World War." PhD dissertation, University of London, 1982.
154. Lowe, Peter. "The Rise to the Premiership, 1914-1916" in Lloyd George: Twelve Essays, edited by A.J.P. Taylor, pp. 95-133. New York: Atheneum, 1971.

155. Lowe, R. "Welfare Legislation and the Unions during and after the First World War." *Historical Journal*, 25 (1982): 437-41.
156. Lowe, Rodney. "The Erosion of State Intervention in Britain, 1917-24." *Economic History Review*, 31 (1978): 270-86.
157. ―――. "The Ministry of Labour, 1916-19: A Still, Small Voice?" in *War and the State: The Transformation of British Government, 1914-1919*, edited by Kathleen Burk, pp. 108-34. London: George Allen & Unwin, 1982.
158. McDowell, R.B. *The Irish Convention 1917-18*. London: Routledge & Kegan Paul, 1970.
159. McEwen, J.M. "A Churchill Story: Dinner at F.E. Smith's 5 December 1916." *Queen's Quarterly*, 83 (1976): 273-77.
160. ―――. "'Brass-Hats' and the British Press During the First World War." *Canadian Journal of History*, 18 (1983): 43-67.
161. ―――. "The Liberal Party and the Irish Question During the First World War." *Journal of British Studies*, 12 (1972): 109-31.
162. ―――. "Lloyd George's Acquisition of the Daily Chronicle in 1918." *Journal of British Studies*, 22 (1982): 127-44.
163. ―――. "Lloyd George's Liberal Supporters in December 1916: A Note." *Bulletin of the Institute of Historical Research*, 53 (1980): 265-72.
164. ―――. "Lord Beaverbrook: Historian Extraordinary." *Dalhousie Review*, 59 (1979): 129-43.
165. ―――. "The National Press during the First World War: Ownership and Circulation." *Journal of Contemporary History*, 17 (1982): 459-86.
166. ―――. "Northcliffe and Lloyd George at War, 1914-1918." *Historical Journal*, 24 (1981): 651-72.
167. ―――. "The Press and the Fall of Asquith." *Historical Journal*, 21 (1978): 863-83.
168. ――― (ed.). *The Riddell Diaries, 1908-1923*. London: Athlone Press, forthcoming.
169. ―――. "The Struggle for Mastery in Britain: Lloyd George versus Asquith, December 1916." *Journal of British Studies*, 18 (1978): 131-56.
170. McGill, Barry. "Lloyd George's Timing of the 1918 Election." *Journal of British Studies*, 14 (1974): 109-24.
171. Mackay, Ruddock F. *Balfour: Intellectual Statesman*. New York: Oxford University Press, 1985.
172. ―――. *Fisher of Kilverstone*. New York: Clarendon Press, 1973.
173. McKibbin, Ross. *The Evolution of the Labour Party, 1910-1924*. New York: Oxford University Press, 1974.
174. McLeod, Kristy. *The Last Summer: May to September 1914*. New York: St. Martin's, 1983.
175. MacLeod, Roy and Kay. "War and Economic Development: Government and the Optical Industry in Britain, 1914-1918" in *War and Economic Development: Essays in Memory of David Joslin*, edited by J.M. Winter, pp. 165-203. New York: Cambridge University Press, 1975.
176. MacLeod, R.M. and E.K. Andrews. "Scientific Advice in the War at Sea 1915-1917: The Board of Inventions and Research." *Journal of Contemporary History*, 6 (1971): 3-40.

177. Marlowe, John. *Milner: Apostle of Empire*. London: Hamish Hamilton, 1976.
178. Marquand, David. *Ramsay MacDonald*. London: Jonathan Cape, 1977.
179. Marquis, Alice Goldfarb. "Words as Weapons: Propaganda in Britain and Germany during the First World War." *Journal of Contemporary History*, 13 (1978): 469-98.
180. Marrin, Albert. *The Last Crusade: The Church of England in the First World War*. Durham, N.C.: Duke University Press, 1974.
181. Marwick, Arthur. *Britain in our Century: Images and Controversies*. New York: Thomas & Hudson, 1984.
182. ―――――. *War and Social Change in the Twentieth Century: A Comparative Study of Britain, France, Germany, Russia and the United States*. New York: St. Martin's, 1975.
183. ―――――. *Women at War, 1914-1918*. London: Croom Helm, 1977.
184. *Marshall Cavendish Illustrated Encyclopedia of World War I*. 12 vols. Freeport, N.Y.: Marshall Cavendish Corporation, 1984.
185. Matthew, H.C.G.; R.I. McKibbin; and J.A. Kay. "The Franchise Factor in the Rise of the Labour Party." *English Historical Review*, 91 (1976): 723-52.
186. Maurice, Nancy (ed.). *The Maurice Case: From the Papers of Major-General Sir Frederick Maurice, C.C.M.G., C.B.* Hamden, Conn.: Archon Books, 1972.
187. Mayer, Arno J. *The Persistence of the Old Regime: Europe to the Great War*. New York: Pantheon, 1981.
188. Mayer, S.L. and W.J. Koenig. *The Two World Wars: A Guide to Manuscript Collections in the United Kingdom*. Epping: Bowker, 1976.
189. Milward, Alan S. *The Economic Effects of the Two World Wars on Britain*. 2nd. ed., rev. London: Macmillan, 1984.
190. Moore, Roger. *The Emergence of the Labour Party, 1880-1924*. London: Hodder & Stoughton, 1978.
191. Morgan, David. *Suffragists and Liberals: The Politics of Woman Suffrage in England*. Totowa, N.J.: Rowman & Littlefield, 1974.
192. Morgan, Kenneth O. *The Age of Lloyd George*. New York: Barnes & Noble, 1971.
193. ―――――. *Lloyd George*. London: Weidenfeld & Nicolson, 1974.
194. ――――― (ed.). *Lloyd George Family Letters, 1865-1936*. New York: Oxford University Press, 1973.
195. ―――――. "Lloyd George's Premiership: A Study in 'Prime Ministerial Government.'" *Historical Journal*, 13 (1970): 130-57.
196. ――――― and Jane. *Portrait of a Progressive: The Political Career of Christopher, Viscount Addison*. New York: Clarendon Press, 1980.
197. Mowat, C.L. "Ramsay MacDonald and the Labour Party" in *Essays in Labour History 1886-1923*, edited by Asa Briggs and John Saville, pp. 129-51. Hamden, Conn.: Archon Books, 1971.
198. ―――――. *Great Britain Since 1914*. Ithaca, N.Y.: Cornell University Press, 1971.
199. Moynihan, Michael (ed.). *People at War, 1914-1918*. Newton Abbot: David & Charles, 1973.

200. Naylor, John F. *A Man and an Institution: Sir Maurice Hankey, the Cabinet Secretariat and the Custody of Cabinet Secrecy.* New York: Cambridge University Press, 1984.
201. ———. "The Establishment of the Cabinet Secretariat." *Historical Journal,* 14 (1971): 783-803.
202. Neilson, Keith. "Kitchener: A Reputation Refurbished." *Canadian Journal of History,* 15 (1980): 207-27.
203. ———. *Strategy and Supply: The Anglo-Russian Alliance, 1914-1917.* London: George Allen & Unwin, 1984.
204. Newberry, Jo Vellacott. "Anti-War Suffragists." *History,* 62 (1977): 411-25.
205. O'Brien, Terence H. *Milner: Viscount Milner of St. James' and Cape Town, 1854-1925.* London: Constable, 1979.
206. O'Broin, Leon. *The Chief Secretary: Augustine Birrell in Ireland.* Hamden, Conn.: Archon Books, 1970.
207. ———. *Dublin Castle and the 1916 Rising.* New York: New York University Press, 1971.
208. Orbach, Laurence F. *Homes for Heroes: A Study of the Evolution of British Public Housing, 1915-1921.* London: Seeley, Service, 1977.
209. Osborne, John Morton. *The Voluntary Recruiting Movement in Britain, 1914-1916.* New York: Garland Publishing, 1982.
210. Oxbury, Harold. *Great Britons: Twentieth Century Lives.* New York: Oxford University Press, 1985.
211. Parsons, Edward B. *Wilsonian Diplomacy: Allied-American Rivalries in War and Peace.* St. Louis, Mo.: Forum Press, 1978.
212. Patterson, A. Temple. *Jellicoe: A Biography.* London: Macmillan, 1969.
213. Pattison, Michael. "The Munitions Inventions Department: A Case Study in the State Management of Military Science, 1915-1919." PhD dissertation, Teeside Polytechnic, 1981.
214. ———. "Scientists, Government and Invention: The Experience of the Inventions Boards 1915-1918" in *Home Fires and Foreign Fields: British Social and Military Experience in the First World War,* edited by Peter H. Liddle, pp. 83-100. London: Brassey's Defence Publishers, 1985.
215. Pelling, Henry. *Winston Churchill.* New York: D.P. Dutton, 1974.
216. Perry, F.W. "Manpower and Organisational Problems in the Expansion of the British and Other Commonwealth Armies During the Two World Wars." PhD dissertation, University of London, 1982.
217. Pierson, Stanley. *British Socialists: The Journey from Fantasy to Politics.* Cambridge, Mass.: Harvard University Press, 1979.
218. Pollard, Sidney. "The Foundation of the Co-operative Party" in *Essays in Labour History 1886-1923,* edited by Asa Briggs and John Saville, pp. 185-210. Hamden, Conn.: Archon Books, 1971.
219. Prior, Robin. *Churchill's World Crisis as History.* London: Croom Helm, 1983.
220. Pugh, Martin D. "Asquith, Bonar Law and the First Coalition." *Historical Journal,* 17 (1974): 813-36.

221. ———. *Electoral Reform in War and Peace, 1906-18.* London: Routledge & Kegan Paul, 1978.
222. ———. *The Making of Modern British Politics 1867-1939.* Oxford: Basil Blackwell, 1982.
223. Rae, John. *Conscience and Politics: The British Government and the Conscientious Objector to Military Service, 1916-1919.* New York: Oxford University Press, 1970.
224. Reeves, Nicholas. "Film Propaganda and its Audience: The Example of British Official Films during the First World War." *Journal of Contemporary History,* 18 (1983): 463-94.
225. ———. "Official British Film Propaganda during the First World War." PhD dissertation, University of London, 1981.
226. Reid, B.L. *The Lives of Roger Casement.* New Haven, Conn.: Yale University Press, 1976.
227. Reinharz, Jehuda. "Science in the Service of Politics: The Case of Chaim Weizmann during the First World War." *English Historical Review,* 100 (1985): 572-603.
228. Rimell, Ray. *Zeppelin! A Battle for Air Supremacy in World War I.* London: Conway Maritime Press, 1984.
229. Robbins, Keith. *The Abolition of War. The 'Peace Movement' 1914-19.* Cardiff: University of Wales Press, 1976.
230. ———. *The Eclipse of a Great Power: Modern Britain, 1870-1975.* London: Longman, 1983.
231. ———. *Sir Edward Grey: A Biography of Lord Grey of Fallodon.* London: Longman, 1971.
232. Rolf, David. "Origins of Mr. Speaker's Conference during the First World War." *History,* 64 (1979): 36-46.
233. Rose, Kenneth. *King George V.* London: Weidenfield & Nicolson, 1983.
234. Rose, M.E. "The Success of Social Reform? The Central Control Board (Liquor Traffic) 1915-21" in *War and Society,* edited by M.R.D. Foot, pp. 71-84. New York: Barnes & Noble, 1973.
235. Roskill, Stephen. *Hankey Man of Secrets,* vol. 1: *1877-1918.* London: Collins, 1970.
236. Rothwell, V.H. *British War Aims and Peace Diplomacy 1914-1918.* New York: Oxford University Press, 1971.
237. Rowland, Peter. *David Lloyd George: A Biography.* New York: Macmillan, 1975.
238. Ryan, W. Michael. "From 'Shell Scandal' to Bow Street: The Denigration of Lieutenant-Colonel Charles à Court Repington." *Journal of Modern History,* 50 (1978), on-demand supplement.
239. Sanders, M.L. "Wellington House and British Propaganda during the First World War." *Historical Journal,* 18 (1975): 119-46.
240. ——— and Philip M. Taylor. *British Propaganda during the First World War, 1914-1918.* London: Macmillan, 1982.
241. Savage, David W. "'The Parnell of Wales has Become the Chamberlain of England': Lloyd George and the Irish Question." *Journal of British Studies,* 12 (1972): 86-108.
242. Sawyer, Roger. *Casement: The Flawed Hero.* London: Routledge & Kegan Paul, 1984.
243. Scally, Robert J. *The Origins of the Lloyd George Coalition: The Politics of Social-Imperialism, 1900-1918.* Princeton, N.J.: Princeton University Press, 1975.

244. Schneer, Jonathan. *Ben Tillett: Portrait of a Labour Leader*. Urbana: University of Illinois Press, 1982.
245. Sherington, Geoffrey. *English Education, Social Change and War: 1911-20*. Manchester: Manchester University Press, 1983.
246. Silkin, Jon. *Out of Battle: The Poetry of the Great War*. New York: Oxford University Press, 1972.
247. Simkins, Peter. "Kitchener and the Expansion of the Army" in *Politicians and Defence: Studies in the Formulation of British Defence Policy, 1846-1970*, edited by Ian F.W. Beckett and John Gooch, pp. 87-109. Manchester: Manchester University Press, 1981.
248. ———. "Soldiers and Civilians: Billeting in Britain and France" in *A Nation in Arms: A Social Study of the British Army in the First World War*, edited by Ian F.W. Beckett and Keith Simpson, pp. 164-91. Manchester: Manchester University Press, 1985.
249. Smith, Harold. "World War I and British Left Wing Intellectuals: The Case of Leonard T. Hobhouse." *Albion*, 5 (1973): 261-73.
250. Stallworthy, Jon. *Wilfred Owen*. London: Oxford University Press, 1974.
251. Stansky, Peter (ed.). *The Left and the War: The British Labour Party and World War I*. New York: Oxford University Press, 1969.
252. Stevenson, John. *British Society, 1914-1945*. London: Allen Lane & Pelican Books, 1984.
253. Stromberg, Roland N. *Redemption by War: The Intellectuals and 1914*. Lawrence: Regents Press of Kansas, 1982.
254. Stubbs, John O. "Beaverbrook as Historian: 'Politicians and the War, 1914-1916' Reconsidered." *Albion*, 14 (1982): 235-53.
255. ———. "Lord Milner and Patriotic Labour, 1914-1918." *English Historical Review*, 87 (1972): 717-54.
256. Swartz, Marvin. *The Union of Democratic Control in British Politics during the First World War*. New York: Oxford University Press, 1971.
257. Sweet, David. "The Domestic Scene: Parliament and People" in *Home Fires and Foreign Fields: British Social and Military Experience in the First World War*, edited by Peter H. Liddle, pp. 9-19. London: Brassey's Defence Publishers, 1985.
258. Tanner, Duncan. "The Parliamentary Electoral System, the Fourth Reform Act and the Rise of Labour in England and Wales." *Bulletin of the Institute of Historical Research*, 56 (1983): 205-19.
259. Taylor, A.J.P. *Beaverbrook*. London: Hamish Hamilton, 1972.
260. ——— (ed.). *Lloyd George: A Diary by Frances Stevenson*. London: Hutchinson, 1971.
261. ——— (ed.). *My Darling Pussy: The Letters of Lloyd George and Frances Stevenson, 1913-1914*. London: Weidenfeld & Nicolson, 1975.
262. Taylor, Philip M. "The Foreign Office and British Propaganda During the First World War." *Historical Journal*, 23 (1980): 875-98.
263. Terraine, John. *Impacts of War, 1914 & 1918*. London: Hutchinson, 1970.

264. ―――――. *The Road to Passchendaele. The Flanders Offensive of 1917: A Study in Inevitability.* London: Leo Cooper, 1977.
265. Terrill, Ross. *R.H. Tawney and His Times: Socialism as Fellowship.* Cambridge, Mass.: Harvard University Press, 1973.
266. Thompson, Paul. *The Edwardians: The Remaking of British Society.* Bloomington: Indiana University Press, 1975.
267. Thorpe, D.R. *The Uncrowned Prime Ministers.* London: Darkhorse Publishing, 1980.
268. Tomlinson, J.D. "The First World War and British Cotton Piece Exports to India." *Economic History Review*, 32 (1979): 494-506.
269. Travers, T.H.E. *The Killing Ground: The British Army, the Western Front, and the Emergence of Modern Warfare, 1900-1918.* London: George Allen & Unwin, forthcoming.
270. Trebilcock, Clive. "War and the Failure of Industrial Mobilisation: 1879-1914" in *War and Economic Development: Essays in Memory of David Joslin*, edited by J.M. Winter, pp. 139-64. New York: Cambridge University Press, 1975.
271. Tucker, Leigh Robert. "English Quakers and World War I." PhD dissertation, University of North Carolina, 1972.
272. Turner, John. "The British Commonwealth Union and the General Election of 1918." *English Historical Review*, 93 (1978): 528-58.
273. ―――――. "Cabinets, Committees and Secretariats: The Higher Direction of War" in *War and the State: The Transformation of British Government, 1914-1919*, edited by Kathleen Burk, pp. 57-83. London: George Allen & Unwin, 1982.
274. ―――――. "The Formation of Lloyd George's 'Garden suburb': 'Fabian-like Milnerite Penetration?'" *Historical Journal*, 20 (1977): 165-84.
275. ―――――. *Lloyd George's Secretariat.* New York: Cambridge University Press, 1980.
276. ―――――. "The Politics of 'Organised Business' in the First World War" in *Businessmen and Politics: Studies of Business Activity in British Politics, 1900-1945*, edited by John Turner, pp. 33-49. London: Heinemann, 1984.
277. ―――――. "State Purchase of the Liquor Trade in the First World War." *Historical Journal*, 23 (1980): 589-615.
278. Veitch, Colin. "'Play Up! Play Up! and Win the War!' Football, the Nation and the First World War 1914-15." *Journal of Contemporary History*, 20 (1985): 363-78.
279. Vellacott, Jo. *Bertrand Russell and the Pacifists in the First World War.* Brighton: Harvester Press, 1980.
280. Vincent, John (ed.). *The Crawford Papers.* Manchester: Manchester University Press, 1984.
281. Waites, B.A. "The Effect of the First World War on Class and Status in England 1910-20." *Journal of Contemporary History*, 11 (1976): 27-48.
282. ―――――. "The Government of the Home Front and the 'Moral Economy' of the Working Class" in *Home Fires and Foreign Fields: British Social and Military Experience in the First World War*, edited by Peter H. Liddle, pp. 175-93. London: Brassey's Defence Publishers, 1985.

283. ―――――. "Some Aspects of Class and Status in England, 1910-1920." PhD dissertation, Open University, 1982.
284. Ward, Alan J. "Lloyd George and the 1918 Irish Conscription Crisis." *Historical Journal*, 17 (1974): 107-29.
285. Webb, Beatrice Potter. *The Power to Alter Things, 1905-1924*. Edited by Norman and Jeanne MacKenzie. Cambridge, Mass.: Harvard University Press, 1984.
286. Weinroth, H. "Peace by Negotiation and the British Anti-War Movement, 1914-1918." *Canadian Journal of History*, 10 (1975): 369-92.
287. Weller, Ken. *'Don't be a Soldier!' The Radical Anti-War Movement in North London 1914-1918*. 97 Ferme Park, Crouch End, London: Journeyman Press, 1985.
288. Whiteside, Noelle. "Welfare Legislation and the Unions during the First World War." *Historical Journal*, 23 (1980): 857-74.
289. Wilkinson, Alan. *The Church of England and the First World War*. London: S.P.C.K., 1978.
290. Williams, John. *The Home Fronts: Britain, France and Germany 1914-1918*. Chicago: Regnery, 1972.
291. Wilson, K. M. "The Cabinet Diary of J.A. Pease, 24 July--5 August." *Leeds Phil. and Lit. Soc. Proceedings*, 19 (1983): n.p.
292. Wilson, S.S. *The Cabinet Office to 1945*. Public Record Office Handbook No. 17. London: HMSO, 1975.
293. Wilson, Trevor. "Britain's Moral Commitment to France in August, 1914." *History*, 114 (1979): 380-90.
294. ―――――. "Lord Bryce's Investigation into Alleged German Atrocities in Belgium, 1914-15." *Journal of Contemporary History*, 14 (1979): 369-83.
295. ―――――. *The Myriad Faces of War: Britain and the Great War*. Oxford: Polity Press, forthcoming.
296. ―――――. (ed.). *The Political Diaries of C.P. Scott, 1911-1928*. London: Collins, 1970.
297. Winter, J.M. "Army and Society: The Demographic Context" in *A Nation in Arms: A Social Study of the British Army in the First World War*, edited by Ian F.W. Beckett and Keith Simpson, pp. 193-209. Manchester: Manchester Press, 1985.
298. ―――――. "Arthur Henderson, the Russian Revolution, and the Reconstruction of the Labour Party." *Historical Journal*, 15 (1972): 753-73.
299. ―――――. "Britain's 'Lost Generation' of the First World War." *Population Studies*, 31 (1977): 449-66.
300. ―――――. *The Great War and the British People*. Cambridge, Mass.: Harvard University Press, 1986.
301. ―――――. "The Impact of the First World War on Civilian Health in Britain." *Economic History Review*, 30 (1917): 487-507.
302. ―――――. "Military Fitness and Civilian Health in Britain during the First World War." *Journal of Contemporary History*, 15 (1980): 211-44.
303. ―――――. *Socialism and the Challenge of War: Ideas and Politics in Britain, 1912-1918*. London: Routledge & Kegan Paul, 1974.
304. Wohl, Robert. *The Generation of 1914*. Cambridge, Mass.: Harvard University Press, 1979.

305. Woodward, David R. "Britain in a Continental War: The Civil-Military Debate over the Strategical Direction of the Great War of 1914-1918." *Albion*, 12 (1980): 37-65.
306. ―――――. "Britain's 'Brass Hats' and the Question of a Compromise Peace, 1916-1918." *Military Affairs*, 35 (1971): 63-68.
307. ―――――. "David Lloyd George, a Negotiated Peace with Germany, and the Kühlmann Peace Kite of September, 1917." *Canadian Journal of History*, 6 (1971): 75-93.
308. ―――――. "Did Lloyd George Starve the British Army of Men Prior to the German Offensive of 21 March 1918?" *Historical Journal*, 27 (1984): 241-52.
309. ―――――. "Great Britain and President Wilson's Efforts to End World War I in 1916." *Maryland Historian*, 1 (1970): 45-58.
310. ―――――. "The Imperial Strategist: Jan Christiaan Smuts and British Military Policy, 1917-1918." *Military History Journal*, 5 (1981): 131-45, 148, 153.
311. ―――――. *Lloyd George and the Generals*. Newark, N.J.: University of Delaware Press, 1983.
312. ―――――. "The Origins and Intent of David Lloyd George's January 5 War Aims Speech." *Historian*, 34 (1971): 22-39.
313. Wright, A.W. *G.D.H. Cole and Socialist Democracy*. New York: Oxford University Press, 1979.
314. Wrigley, Chris. *David Lloyd George and the British Labour Movement: Peace and War*. New York: Barnes & Noble, 1976.
315. ―――――. "The Ministry of Munitions: An Innovatory Department" in *War and the State: The Transformation of British Government, 1914-1919*, edited by Kathleen Burk, pp. 32-56. London: George Allen & Unwin, 1982.
316. Zebel, Sydney H. *Balfour: A Political Biography*. Cambridge: Cambridge University Press, 1973.

XIII

THE ROYAL NAVY SINCE 1919

Barry D. Hunt

Since 1972 and the institution of the thirty-year rule governing access to state papers in the PRO, scholarly interest in the post-World War I Royal Navy undoubtedly has quickened. Much of that interest, however, has been concerned with the higher direction of national policy and inter-service matters. The Navy's history very largely remains the preserve of more popular writers whose battle accounts, ship histories and pictorial series continue to fill the booksellers' shops. Some of these latter works are eminently worthwhile and, in terms of their use of new evidence or enlivenment of events, deserve wide recognition. Others are of more uncertain quality. The seeming reluctance of younger scholars to even enter the field may also have something to do with its continued domination by Professor Arthur Marder and Captain Stephen Roskill, at least until their recent deaths (Marder in December 1980 and Roskill, in November 1982). Their olympian presence was made all the more daunting by the acrimonious personal feud that attended their later years. But as much as their friends regretted their combativeness-- and their public exchanges did make unpleasant reading--it seems now that naval history must be the better for it. Their broadsides laid bare important features of the Royal Navy's twentieth century record with which their names inevitably will be linked. Thankfully, they composed their differences shortly before Marder's passing. Their final exchanges were "very cordial" according to Roskill who, in his own final work on Admiral Beatty (219), paid warm tribute to his counterpart's unusual accomplishments.

Their quarrel centred on Winston Churchill's leadership and, more particularly, the extent and effect of his interventions in strategy making and actual operations as First Lord in 1939-1940. Roskill saw them as excessive and dangerous interferences. Marder, generally, disagreed. This difference of opinion also colored their assessments of other naval leaders--notably of Admiral Sir Dudley Pound as First Sea Lord, 1939-1943--as well as their interpretations of new evidence from official sources, personal papers and memories. The wider bases of their disagreements are less easily pinned down. Perhaps, as their historical preoccupations shifted away from the periods on which their reputations were established--Marder on the Navy of the Victorian-Edwardian and Fisher age and his magisterial five-volume *Dreadnought to Scapa Flow* (160), and Roskill for his three-volume official history of the Second World War at sea (214)-- into the interwar period, and beyond, some friction was inevitable.

Marder crossed that divide in the final volume of *Dreadnought to Scapa Flow*. Its Conclusion, "Reflections on an Era," summed up what was right and what was not about the Royal Navy at the apex of its power and laid out the political, doctrinal and organizational legacies of the Great War that would shape naval attitudes and developments in the years ahead. Some of these themes were expanded upon in his next book, a collection of essays entitled *From the Dardanelles to Oran: Studies of the Royal Navy in War and Peace, 1915-1940* (162). In "The Dardanelles Revisited" he took a fresh look at the ships alone prelude in light of the Mitchell Report and Group Captain H.A. Williamson's unpublished memoirs, concluding provocatively that the whole operation was much closer run than more recent convention has allowed. In "The Influence of History Upon Sea Power" he enquired why more systematic investigations of the Fleet's 1914-1918 experiences were not undertaken or encouraged suggesting why so many of the hard-won lessons in tactics, anti-submarine warfare, convoys and combined operations had to be rediscovered after 1939. This is followed by an examination of the Navy's basic strategic dilemma laid bare by the 1935 Ethiopian Crisis when competing concerns for German and Japanese threats forced the Admiralty under Chatfield towards the appeasement of Italy. In "Winston is Back"—an expanded version of his controversial 1974 *English Historical Review* article, together with a long addendum entitled "Musing on a Bolt from Olympus"—Marder set out his version of Churchill's eight months as First Lord in the Chamberlain War Cabinet. The final essay on the 1940 attack on French ships at Oran provided, in classic Marder style, the first thoroughly documented account of the diplomatic and operational aspects of that tragic episode. In his next book, *Operation "Menace"* (163), he retraced the story of the sequel Dakar expedition as an authoritative case study of an operational plan and all that can go wrong with it, underscoring again Churchill's part in strategy direction and its effects on some of the expedition's main figures, notably Admirals Sir Dudley North and Sir James Somerville.

Old Friends, New Enemies (164) was Marder's first sortie into Pacific and Japanese naval affairs. Tragically, it was also his last. The manuscript for this the first of a projected two-volume major study was barely finished before his death. (The sequel, based on his notes and incomplete chapter drafts, hopefully will be completed by someone else.) In Part I of *Old Friends*, Marder traced out the steps by which the close ties between the Royal and Imperial Japanese Navies were gradually eroded after 1921. He also examined the rationales for the fortified base at Singapore, the strategy of despatching the main fleet to operate from it and the unsuccessful attempts to secure Dominion and United States cooperation which, in the final wartime crisis, led to the sending out of the ill-fated Force Z based on only the *Prince of Wales* and *Repulse*. In all of this he reveals that both navies suffered from failures to develop commonly understood general policies and too frequently from wishful thinking that did not keep pace with strategic developments. In Part II, he examined the origins of these defects by contrasting the two navies' educational systems, doctrine, materiel, intelligence assessments and professional thinking. This section is one of the more useful descriptions available of the interwar Royal Navy's internal leadership and management. Part III recounts the tragedy of Force Z's encounter with the Japanese invasion force in December

1941. Though little new material is offered, it is so well told as to make it--much as was his rendering of Jutland in volume III of *Dreadnought To Scapa Flow*--the standard account against which others must now be judged. In all, *Old Friends* is a fitting capstone to Marder's unusually rich contribution to naval history that set standards of scholarship and presentation surpassing even Mahan's and perhaps Corbett's. *Naval Warfare in the Twentieth Century* (120), a collection of essays by some of Marder's friends and students and edited by Gerald Jordan, was published in 1977 to mark his formal retirement from university life.

Captain Roskill's historical interests also shifted in the 1960s with no less impressive or important results. Aided by his research assistant on the official war history, Commander Geoffrey Hare, Roskill began editing for the Navy Records Society materials on the Fleet Air Arm's administrative and organizational history. The first massive volume of that project, *The Naval Air Service, 1908-1918* (215), was published in 1969. He continued collecting materials for projected successor volumes that were intended to carry the record through World War II. His major work at this time, however, was his much needed study *Naval Policy Between the Wars* (216) the first volume of which ("The Period of Anglo-American Antagonism, 1919-1929") was released in 1968. His insights into the critical problems of naval disarmament, Singapore and Empire defence, the battleship versus aircraft and submarines controversies and, most especially, the bitterness and constancy of Anglo-U.S. rivalry at every level make this the authoritative work on the period. Publication of Volume II ("The Period of Reluctant Rearmament, 1930-1939") was delayed until 1976 by PRO access problems and by Roskill's decision in the interim to write the authorized life of Lord Hankey (217). This second *Naval Policy* volume, based on similarly meticulous research of British and American archives, also displayed a markedly increased sensitivity to the impact of personality and domestic politics that may reflect Roskill's greater personal knowledge of the 1930s, the availability of more survivors and, perhaps, the experience of handling the Hankey project. His chapters on the Invergordon Mutiny, its aftermath under Admiral Sir John Kelly, Admiral Chatfield's "new look" navy, the Ethiopian crisis and problems of strategic over-stretch have set the stage for important follow-up works by others. Read in conjunction with Professor Norman Gibbs' Volume I of the official history's Grand Strategy series (75)--also published in 1976--it is an invaluable introduction to the now open official records.

Roskill's decision to attempt a full-scale life of Maurice Hankey was important, of course, not only in terms of his personal development as an historian. The ubiquitous Cabinet Secretary's extensive papers had never been systematically exploited. They cover areas that were either ignored or deleted in his own published memoirs, and are unquestionably one of the most important collections in existence. They are now deposited, along with the other valuable collections that Roskill played such a major role in acquiring for the remarkable Churchill College Archives Centre at Cambridge. By any standard, the resultant three-volume *Hankey, Man of Secrets* (217) was an impressive achievement. Roskill's last two books were more controversial.

Churchill and the Admirals (218), released in 1977, covers Winston's associations with the Navy from 1911, though with most of the emphasis on the Second World War. Written very largely in response to Marder's contentions, it is highly polemical in places and does not represent Roskill at his best, though it would be difficult to fault his industry or the light he casts on senior naval personalities who would otherwise remain obscure figures. His Appendix, "A Historical Controversy," usefully summarizes his arguments with Marder especially on the value of verbal evidence. Roskill's last book, *Admiral of the Fleet Earl Beatty. The Last Naval Hero: An Intimate Biography* (219) also has shortcomings some of which--mainly difficulties with the Admiral's descendants--were beyond his powers to correct, while others reflect the intricacies of Beatty's character and private existence. If Roskill's is not the last word, his own mature judgments and reluctant admiration for Beatty's achievements as wartime commander and as First Sea Lord under the testing circumstances of postwar run down, disarmament and the extended Jutland "controversy," do provide the most complete portrait so far. The Beatty papers, previously unorganized and stored in trunks at Chicheley Hall, were purchased by the National Maritime Museum, Greenwich, in 1981.

Biographies and Memoirs. Apart from those already mentioned and the latest of Martin Gilbert's volumes on Churchill (76), scholarly examinations of leading naval figures are still very much needed. Beatty's postwar career has also been touched upon by his nephew Charles in *Our Admiral: A Biography of Admiral of the Fleet Earl Beatty, 1871-1936* (14) although in this essentially personal portrait or family memoir Beatty's professional activities are lesser considerations. In *Jellicoe* (279), John Winton includes coverage of his subject's 1919 Empire tour and Governor-Generalship of New Zealand. Professor A. Temple Patterson similarly traces the later career of another of the Great War's few outstanding admirals in *Tyrwhitt of the Harwich Force* (193). His long expected biography of Chatfield is presumably still in progress. Three volumes of *The Keyes Papers* (86) covering that intrepid Admiral's long and distinguished career from 1914 to 1945 have been completed by Paul Halpern for the Navy Records Society. *Mountbatten: Hero of Our Time* (110) by Richard Hough is overly harping and sensationalist and therefore disappointing. Philip Ziegler's *Mountbatten: The Official Biography* (283), on the other hand, is everything an excellent biography should be. Its comprehensive coverage of Lord Louis' unusual achievements includes some of the few available insights into the workings of post-1945 naval affairs when he was First Sea Lord and then the first effective Chief of the Defence Staff. In this latter respect, Richard Humble's *Fraser of North Cape* (113) is disappointing. His coverage of Lord Fraser's distinguished career before and during the war, particularly his Pacific Fleet appointment is solid; that given to his postwar, NATO and Korean War responsibilities is less so. Patrick Beesly's *Very Special Admiral: The Life of Admiral J.H. Godfrey, CB* (17) is an excellent portrayal of the difficult genius whose outstanding achievements as DNI proved so vital in World War II. His career, including postwar command of the Royal Indian Navy, is fully canvassed. But it was his work in rebuilding and directing the NID until his highly questionable summary dismissal that is the central focus. It should be read in tandem with Beesly's earlier and widely acclaimed account of the NID's Operational Intelligence centre entitled, *Very Special Intelligence* (16), discussed below.

Professor Donald Schurman's study of Britain's leading civilian maritime strategic thinker that was contained in his earlier groundbreaking work, *The Education of a Navy* is extended and completed in *Julian S. Corbett, 1854-1922* (226). Most of this biography treats Corbett's work prior to 1918, but the last chapter, which recounts his difficulties as the official historian of the war at sea, provides an unique insider's perspective on early postwar service politics during Beatty's time. Corbett's achievements in overcoming Admiralty interference and clear differences concerning history's use in protecting individual reputations, adds a good deal to our understanding of the Jutland controversy and its pervasive impact on professional thinking. Interwar naval politics are also a major focus of Barry Hunt's *Sailor-Scholar: Admiral Sir Herbert Richmond, 1871-1945* (114). As Corbett's disciple, Richmond went on to establish his own reputation as Britain's other leading naval historian and theorist. As leader of the so-called "Young Turks" of the Grand Fleet, he also became the navy's most outspoken champion of anti-materialist thought and activist for educational, doctrinal and organizational reform. Based on a wide range of private and official primary sources, this study records Richmond's successes and failures within the context of post-Fisher defense politics.

Other useful new biographies include: Richard Baker's *The Terror of Tobermory* (6), a life of Vice-Admiral Sir Gilbert Stephenson, the legendary Commodore Western Isles; and *Dry Ginger* (7) of Admiral of the Fleet Sir Michael Le Fanu; S.W.C. Pack's *Cunningham the Commander* (186); Charlotte and Dennis Plimmer, *A Matter of Expediency: The Jettison of Admiral Sir Dudley North* (196); Oliver Warner's *Admiral of the Fleet: The Life of Sir Charles Lambe* (260). Autobiographical works include, Roger Hill, *Destroyer Captain* (102); Basil Jones, *And So to the Baltic: A Sailor's Story* (119); Charles Lamb, *War in a Stringbag* (137); G.E. Livock, *To The Ends of the Air* (148); A.B. Palmer, *Pedlar Palmer of Tobruk* (188); R. Ransome Wallis, *Two Red Stripes: A Naval Surgeon at War* (259); C.W.F. Simpson, *Periscope View: A Professional Autobiography* (229).

General Histories. For general overviews of post-1919 developments, Professor Paul Kennedy's *The Rise and Fall of British Naval Mastery* (125) is a solid starting point. In this balanced and readable reconsideration of Mahanian "Blue Water" conventions, Kennedy explains the relationships that existed between Britain's naval preeminence and the growth and decline of her financial, economic and industrial world standing. The last three chapters carry his arguments through to the present demonstrating how a reluctance to face and then to deal with the implications of this decline circumscribed Britain's ability to exploit her traditional maritime and continental strategic options. Some naval aspects of this theme are also treated in his subsequent books, *The Realities Behind Diplomacy: Background Influences on British External Policies, 1865-1980* (126), and *Strategy and Diplomacy 1870-1945: Eight Studies* (127). Geoffrey Till's *Maritime Strategy and the Nuclear Age* (248), though not primarily historical nor exclusively British in its treatment, does with contributions from various experts in the field provide an excellent introduction to the ideas of the leading thinkers and to applications of major concepts in the field of modern maritime strategy. Bryan Ranft has also edited an important collection of essays, *Technical Change and British Naval Policy, 1860-1939* (204), several of which bear on the interwar Admiralty's responses to technical innovations and relations with private industry. Also useful as a general introduction to this area are Vice-Admiral Hezlet's *The Submarine and Sea Power* (97), *Aircraft and Seapower* (98), and *The Electron and Seapower* (99). Several autobiographical studies by early pioneers of naval aviation, submarines and ASW have appeared but the best scholarly treatment is Geoffrey Till's *Air Power and the Royal Navy, 1914-1945* (247), which thoroughly exploits the official sources and recollections of key participants. Till's careful analysis of this difficult struggle over the impact of aircraft on sea power and the prolonged clash of ideas concerning their control suggests that the Fleet Air Arm's problems were, at root, a reflection of Britain's general defense predicament following 1918 and less directly, or simplistically, the legacy of official shortsightedness or obscurantism.

Officer education and naval leadership generally are still badly neglected topics. The following, however, are helpful: on leadership, John Horsfield's *The Art of Leadership in War: The Royal Navy from The Age of Nelson to the End of World War II* (108) and Charles Owen's *No More Heroes--The Royal Navy in the Twentieth Century: Anatomy of a Legend* (183); on education, E.L. Davies and E.J. Groves' *Dartmouth: Seventy-Five Years in Pictures* (51) and *The Royal Naval College, Dartmouth* (52); on training establishments, Admiral Schofield's *Navigation and Direction: The Story of HMS Dryad* (225) and Captain J.G. Wells' *Whaley: The Story of HMS Excellent, 1830-1980* (266).

The Interwar Years. The interwar period has been well covered by an impressive range of new studies of Britain's imperial and global problems. The broader context of defense policy and planning is set out in Professor Norman Gibbs' first volume of the official *Grand Strategy* series (75) and in such works as Corelli Barnett, *The Collapse of British Power* (9), Brian Bond, *British Military Policy Between the Two World Wars* (21) and Michael Howard, *The Continental Commitment: The Dilemma of British Defence Policy in the Era of the Two World Wars* (111). Donald Cameron Watts' *Too Serious a Business: European Armed Forces and the Approach of the Second World War* (262) is useful for contrasting naval thinking with that of the other services. His *Succeeding John Bull: America in Britain's Place* (263) is particularly important for Anglo-US relations and contains a good deal about interwar professional attitudes in both navies. In *The Second Baldwin Government and the United States, 1924-1929: Attitudes and Diplomacy* (169), Brian McKercher concentrates more closely on Austen Chamberlain, the Foreign Office and British policy generally in attempting to resolve the deadlock associated with the 1927 Geneva Naval Conference and the ongoing Belligerent versus Neutral Rights question. Michael Fry's *Illusions of Security* (69) investigates the earlier postwar debates between leading British and Dominion "Atlanticists" and their opponents prior to the 1921-22 Washington talks, while Roger Dingman's *Power in the Pacific: The Origins of Naval Arms Limitation, 1914-1922* (55) compares British, U.S. and

Japanese approaches. The latter is particularly interesting for his extensive multi-archival research and emphasis on the political processes of national disarmament policy development.

The Pacific and Far Eastern dimensions of British policy and strategy have been comprehensively scouted in works such as: Stephen Endicott, *Diplomacy and Enterprise: British China Policy 1933-1937* (61); Bradford Lee, *Britain and the Sino-Japanese War, 1937-1939* (140); W.R. Louis, *British Strategy in the Far East* (150) and *Imperialism at Bay* (151); Peter Lowe, *Britain in the Far East* (154) and *Great Britain and the Origins of the Pacific War* (153); M. Murfett, *Fool-Proof Relations* (178a); Ian Nish, *Alliance in Decline: Anglo-Japanese Relations, 1908-1923* (180), as editor, *Anglo-Japanese Alienation* (181); Aron Shai, *Origins of the War in the East* (227); Christopher Thorne, *The Limits of Foreign Policy* (245) and *Allies of a Kind: The United States, Britain and the War Against Japan, 1941-45* (246); and Ann Trotter, *Britain and East Asia, 1933-1937* (250).

On the issue of Singapore, good introductory treatments can be found in C. Mary Turnbull, *A History of Singapore* (251), and David McIntyre, *The Rise and Fall of the Singapore Naval Base* (168). *Britannia at Bay* (83), by Paul Haggie retraces the origins of the fortified base policy and the "Main Fleet to Singapore" strategy through the 1920s and provides a sustained analysis of Foreign Office and Admiralty thinking that, after 1931, failed to fully reconsider basic assumptions in the light of financial restraints and new threats closer to home in the Mediterranean. This persistence in an overtaken strategy, for which he blames Chatfield and an unwillingness to the more hard-nosed about foregoing promises to the Pacific Dominions, Haggie suggests reflected a general lack of leadership and ability in navy and government circles. James Neidpath covers much the same ground in *The Singapore Naval Base and the Defence of Britain's Eastern Empire* (179) though more specifically from a defense and especially naval perspective. The first half emphasises the genesis of the Singapore scheme and includes interesting references to some of its earliest and more prescient critics including Admiral Richmond and Field Marshal Smuts, as well as later studies on the problems of reinforcing Malaya and defending it from overland attack. A much needed Commonwealth perspective on Singapore and on Imperial Defence generally comes from Ian Hamill, *The Strategic Illusion: The Singapore Strategy and the Defence of Australia and New Zealand, 1919-1942* (87) and I.C. McGibbon's official New Zealand history *Blue Water Rationale: The Naval Defence of New Zealand 1914-1942* (167).

This is perhaps the place to mention some of the new works that take these developments through to their wartime climax. In *Singapore, 1941-42* (3), Louis Allen gives a detailed rendering of the Malayan campaign. The latter half of his book is particularly appealing for his examination of both pre- and post-war appreciations and apologias for what went wrong and suggests that recognition of the broader problem of defending Malaya and not just Singapore could have mitigated if not averted the final disaster. Noel Barber's *Sinister Twilight* (8) and S. Woodburn Kirby's *Singapore: Chain of Disaster* (129) very ably fill out the human side of the saga as does Martin Middlebrook's and Patrick Mahoney's *Battleship: The Loss of* the *Prince of Wales* and *Repulse* (172) an excellent treatment of Force Z's story that should be read in tandem with Marder's.

In *East of Malta, West of Suez: Britain's Mediterranean Crisis, 1936-1939* (202), Larry Pratt has tied these issues of Far Eastern defense back to developments closer to home illustrating how Mussolini's Ethiopian adventure and flaunting of the League exposed the full extent of Britain's commitments-capabilities gap. Approaching the crisis much as Chamberlain's government had to, that is as a crisis in overall Empire defense, Dr. Pratt explores the many facets of the situation which more established "guilty men" interpretations of the Appeasement period have simply ignored. He is therefore able to explain why, in the face of Japanese, German and then Italian threats, decisions to pursue rearmament and appeasement policies simultaneously did make strategic sense. He also reveals much about the mentality and quality of defence planners and of the bureaucratic decision-making process. Its conclusions, he suggests, were acted upon by Chamberlain in line with basic policy departures decided upon as early as 1933 when it had become obvious that the Washington system of detente and arms controls was visibly collapsing. Stephen Pelz, in *Race to Pearl Harbor* (195), contrasts British, American and Japanese reactions to that breakdown at the 1935 London Naval Conference. There, he argues, British and U.S. determination to preserve the battleship's status played into the hands of the Japanese who, contrary to their public posturing, wanted the Washington system ended. There is some useful material on the Admiralty's part in the processes of rearmament and the approach of war in Robert Shay's *British Rearmament in the 1930s* (228) and George Peden's *British Rearmament and the Treasury, 1933-1939* (194). Otherwise, the best scholarly treatments are Roskill's and Gibbs' (216 and 75).

The navy's internal history in this period remains an open field. Glimpses into individuals' activities and life on overseas stations can be found in: James Cable *The Royal Navy and the Seige of Bilbao* (30), the second half of Gregory Haines' *Gunboats on the Great River: A History of the Royal Navy on the Yangtse* (84) and Martin Brice *The Royal Navy and the Sino-Japanese Incident, 1937-1941* (24). New investigations of the Invergordon "mutiny" by David Divine (56), Len Wincott (272) and Alan Ereira (64) have also appeared. Anthony Carew's *The Lower Deck of the Royal Navy, 1900-1939: The Invergordon Mutiny in Perspective* (35) uses PRO documentation, private papers and contemporary and later writings to explain the mutiny in broader social and political terms of why, despite important reform initiatives by personalities such as Fisher and Churchill, official attitudes towards the lower deck took so long to change and how, when the need for technically better trained sailors became so obvious, the sailor's own efforts to improve their lot met suspicion and indifference.

The Second World War. In the Higham *Guide*, Peter Kemp accurately predicated the impact of the thirty-year rule on World War II writing. What he could not have foreseen in 1972 was the release that same year of Sir John Masterman's *Double-Cross System* and in 1974 Group Captain F.W. Winterbotham's *The Ultra Secret*. These books broke the silence on Britain's best-kept and most important wartime intelligence secrets and laid the groundwork for some radical recastings of the war's historiography. The early results were sufficiently uneven in their quality and perspectives as to move the authorities in 1977 to release much of the formerly highly classified intelligence records to scholarly purview. Their hope that more thorough and even-handed assessments would result, on the whole is being fulfilled and these are discussed in Chapter XXII. Those works that bear more or less directly on naval affairs or operations are included in this section.

Apart from the PRO's published and unpublished listings, several recently released guides are now available to steer students through the newer materials including, C. Hazlehurst and C. Woodland, *A Guide to the Papers of British Cabinet Ministers, 1900-1951* (96); Christopher Cook, et. al., *Sources in British Political History* (44) especially Vol. I, *The Archives of Selected Organisations and Societies*, and Vol. II, *Private papers of Selected Public Servants*, and Vol. VI, *First Consolidated Supplement* that cover many senior naval figures. Alan Reid's *Concise Encyclopedia of the Second World War* (208) has some introductory information on senior individuals and various operations. Indispensible for references to books, bibliographies and archives are: Gwyn Bayliss, *A Bibliographic Guide to the Two World Wars: An Annotated Survey of English Language Reference Materials* (13); A.G.S. Ensor, *A Subject Bibliography of the Second World War* (63); S.L. Mayer and W.J. Koenig, *The Two World Wars: A Guide to Manuscript Collections in the United Kingdom* (166); and Myron Smith, *World War II at Sea: A Bibliography of Sources in English* (231).

In completing outstanding volumes in the various official histories, authors have been able to cite all the sources directly as opposed to the earlier practice of annotations that gave leads to the unpublished documents. Professor Michael Howard's monumental Volume VI covering the period August 1942 to September 1943 (112) and Norman Gibbs' Volume I covering rearmament policy (75) round off the Grand Strategy series. The Campaign Series has added volumes on *The Mediterranean and Middle East* (175) and *The War Against Japan* (128). Also complete is Sir Llewellyn Woodward's impressive five-volume *British Foreign Policy in the Second World War* (281). Most important are the volumes on *British Intelligence in the Second World War: Its Influences on Strategy and Operations* (105). That the coverage of naval as well as other service matters is so authoritative can be attributed not only to the distinguished academic credentials of Professor Hinsley and his co-authors but also to their personal intelligence experience. Hinsley served throughout the war as deputy head of the Naval Section at Bletchley Park.

For general naval histories, Peter Kemp's *Victory at Sea* (121) is still important. Originally published in 1957 with Admiralty encouragement as a more "popular" companion to Roskill's official volumes, it was re-issued in 1976. Also useful are Geoffrey Bennett, *Naval Battles of World War II* (18) and Donald Macintyre *The Naval War Against Hitler* (157). Roger Parkinson has used War Cabinet records and war diaries to produce a detailed though unanalytical three-volume chronology (189-191) of policy development at the highest levels. An interesting counterpoint, invaluable for placing naval events in context, is provided by Jurgen Rohwer's and Gerhard Hummelchen's two-volume *Chronology of the War at Sea, 1939-1945* (211).

Some of the most important research of the last decade has been concerned with the so-called "special relationship" between Britain and the U.S. and the politics of their wartime alliance building, planning and direction. James Leutze's *Bargaining for Supremacy: Anglo-American Naval Collaboration, 1937-1941* (142) is the most important and useful for the naval side of things. Unlike earlier interpretations that more or less accepted Winston Churchill's descriptions of the alliance as a natural extension of an underlying cultural unity and partnership--an idealistic conception largely unchallenged in Joseph P. Lash, *Roosevelt and Churchill, 1939-1941: The Partnership that Saved the West* (139)--Leutze's account demonstrates that the links were always more tentative and hard-nosed, and the limits of the Grand Alliance more clearly understood. David Reynold's *The Creation of the Anglo-American Alliance, 1937-1941: A Study in Competitive Cooperation* (209) and Christopher Thorne's *Allies of a Kind* (246) provide similarly "realist" perspectives on the relationship's wider aspects. Mark Stoler's book, *The Politics of the Second Front: American Military Planning and Diplomacy in Coalition Warfare, 1941-1943* (241) is revealing about the Americans' attitudes and reactions to their British allies. Also instructive on Allied naval relations and planning are A.L. Funk, *The Politics of Torch* (71), and Keith Sainsbury, *The North African Landings, 1942* (221). The latter is part of an excellent series of concise operational studies edited by Noble Frankland and Christopher Dowling and published by Davis-Poynter.

Comparatively few of the many new works on wartime intelligence, deception and other special operations have been specifically naval in focus. The most important of these is Patrick Beesly's *Very Special Intelligence: The Story of the Admiralty's Operational Intelligence Centre, 1939-1945* (16). Relying heavily on British and German official records including O.I.C. files, the private papers of Vice-Admiral Sir Norman ("Ned") Denning (the principal architect of the Centre's staff) and his own experiences as one of its earliest members and, from 1942 to 1945, as assistant director of the Submarine Tracking Room, Beesly has judiciously and affectionately explained the OIC's evolution into the remarkable source of dependable and rapidly deployed information that so well served not just the Navy, but all the services and most especially the RAF. Beesly's biography of Sir John Godfrey who as wartime DNI was responsible for the OIC's efforts has already been mentioned (17). Another approach to Godfrey is contained in Edwin Montagu's autobiography *Beyond Top Secret U* (176). As department head of Section 17M, Montagu worked closely with Godfrey. Unfortunately, more is revealed here about their love-hate relationship than about Montagu's responsibilities that included involvement in a variety of special intelligence activities and membership, as the Navy's representative, on the XX Committee that controlled double agents' activities. Navy-related intelligence activities are also developed in: Aileen Clayton, *The Enemy is Listening: The Story of the Y Service* (39); Basil Collier, *Hidden Weapons: Allied Secret or Undercover Services in World War II* (42); A. Cecil Hampshire, *The Secret Navies* (89) and *Undercover Sailors: Secret Operations of World War Two* (91); and C.M. Waddington, *OR in World War II: Operational Research Against the U-Boat* (258). Ronald Lewin's impressive study of the connections between "Ultra" intelligence and actual operations in *Ultra Goes to War* (144) includes coverage on the war in the Atlantic. The Pacific theatre is covered in his follow-up book(s) *The Other Ultra* (145) and *The American Magic: Codes Ciphers and the Defeat of Japan* (146).

Much painstaking research remains to be done on specific operations in the Battle of the Atlantic to complete our understanding of how intelligence efforts, cypher breaking, radio interception, high frequency direction finding as well the interplay of weather, circumstance and human judgement ultimately did affect the struggle against the U-Boat. The best starting point is Jurgen Rohwer's remarkable book *The Critical Convoy Battles of March 1943* (212) and his *Axis Submarine Successes, 1939-1945* (213). His collaboration with Dr. Alec Douglas of the Canadian Forces in "'The Most Thankless Task' Revisited: Convoys, Escorts and Radio Intelligence in the Western Atlantic, 1941-1943" published in James Boutilier's *The RCN in Retrospect* (23) should also be consulted for its use of the now accessible British and German operational naval records. The latter are housed at the Bundesarchiv-Militararchiv Freiburg, and the Bibliothek fur Zeitgeschicte in Stuttgart. Microfilms of U-Boat logs and English translations of the BdU War Diaries are retained by the MOD's naval historical section in London. The Directorate of History at National Defence Headquarters, Ottawa, also holds copies of the BdU diaries. Of the PRO's Admiralty an Air Ministry records, the most useful are the monthly anti-submarine reports and Reports of Proceedings (Adm.199 series), naval intelligence records (Adm.233 series), and Enigma decrypts from Bletchley Park (DEFE series). Also important are Ultra related materials in the US Navy's Operational Archives in Washington (OP-20-G, Final Report Series on the Battle of the Atlantic).

The already extended list of popular literature on the Atlantic war continues to grow with books such as those by Costello and Hughes and by Barrie Pitt of the same titles (48). Captain Donald McIntyre's 1956 book *U-Boat Killer* (158) has been reissued making the perspective of one of that battle's more gallant and successful commanders available to a later generation. Specific convoy actions during the March 1943 turning point period analyzed by Rohwer have also been dramatically recreated in Peter Gretton *Crisis Convoy: The Story of HX231* (79) and Martin Middlebrook *Convoy: The Battle for Convoys SC122 and HX229* (170). These books' concerns for illustrating the human experiences and outcomes on both sides are nicely complemented by Rohwer's emphasis on strategic and tactical control problems. The Canadians' important part in the struggle has now been given the serious attention it has long needed. Marc Milner's *North Atlantic Run: The Royal Canadian Navy and the Battle of the Convoys* (174) is a thorough, scholarly account that throws as much light on British and American strengths and deficiencies as it does on those of the RCN. In *U-Boats Against Canada: German Submarines in Canadian Waters* (82), Professor Michael Hadley has exploited the German records with the same thoroughness and balanced judgement to lay out the enemy's perspective.

The best general treatment of the Murmansk runs is given in Admiral Brian Schofield's *The Arctic Convoys* (224) which incorporates much of the new material to update his earlier *Russian Convoys* (1964). Why David Irving's *The Destruction of Convoy PQ17* (115) has also been reissued is less easy to explain. When it was first released in 1968 it immediately became the subject of a successful litigation action brought by Captain Broome, commander of the escort group involved. Since then "Jacky" Broome has published his own account of the action in *Convoy is to Scatter* (26), Paul Lund and Harry Ludlam have written an excellent eyewitness account in *PQ17, Convoy to Hell*, and of course the whole controversy surrounding the Admiralty's handling of things has been examined by Beesly, Roskill and Hinsley. On other aspects, *Arctic Victory* (234), by Peter C. Smith is a chronicle of Convoy PQ18's struggles based on British and German sources; *Arctic Destroyers* by G.G. Connell traces the actions of the 'O' Class destroyers through some seventy-five convoys in the worst of conditions; and Per Hansson in *One in Ten Had to Die* (92) recounts one Norwegian ship's experience on three of these runs.

Other operations in Home and Northern Waters have been reconsidered in works such as: Peter Smith's *Hold the Narrow Seas* (236) covering larger surface unit operations in the English Channel throughout the war; on the torpedoing of HMS *Royal Oak* in October 1939 by Gerald Snyder, *The Royal Oak Disaster*, (239) and H. Weaver, *Nightmare at Scapa Flow* (265); on the Norwegian campaign, Edward Brookes *Prologue to a War* (25), Captain Peter Dickens *Narvik: Battles in the Fiords* (53); on Dunkirk, Robert Jackson, *Dunkirk: The British Evacuation 1940* (117). Probably the most impressive and exciting popular account is Ludovic Kennedy's *Pursuit: The Chase and Sinking of the Bismarck* (123). It should be read along with the German viewpoint found in Baron von Mullenheim-Rechberg's memoir *Battleship Bismarck: A Survivor's Story* (178), and of a British survivor (out of only 3), Ted Briggs, who with Alan Coles has written *Flagship HOOD: The Fate of Britain's Mightiest Warship* (40). Kennedy's no less successful *Menace: The Life and Death of the Tirpitz* (124) incorporates Ultra materials that amplify earlier accounts and sheds somewhat different light on the Admiralty's direction of all shipping activities, including PQ17, that were effected by the great ship's presence. Her eventual demise is the subject of G. Frere-Cook's concise account, *The Attacks on the Tirpitz* (68). The saga of the battle cruisers' *Scharnhorst* and *Gneisenau* February 1942 passage up the Channel and the shortcomings they revealed in RN and RAF defenses have been re-examined in P.G. Cooksley, *Operation Thunderbolt: The Nazi Warships' Escape, 1942* (45); Peter Kemp, *Escape of the Scharnhorst and Gneisenau* (122); and J.D. Potter's *Fiasco* (201). Their ultimate fate is handled in John Austin and Nick Carter, *The Man Who Hit the Scharnhorst* (5), Richard Garrett, *Scharnhorst and Gneisenau* (73); and John Winton's *The Death of the Scharnhorst*. The latter's account of the Admiralty's relationships with the CinC at sea (in this case Fraser) and use of OIC materials derived from Bletchley Park decodes demonstrates how well the lessons of the PQ17 disaster had been learned.

On Mediterranean naval operations, Warren Tute's *The Deadly Stroke* (253) and John Williams' *The Guns of Dakar: Operation Menace, September 1940* (269), are popular reconstructions overtaken by Marder's account (163). Admiral Schofield has written *The Attack on Taranto* (222) and Captain Pack has extended his 1961 Batsford series study *The Battle of Matapan* with some of his own recollections in *Night Action off Cape Matapan* (184). Peter C. Smith has added to his short studies, *Destroyer Leader* of 1968 and *Task Force 57* of 1969, with *Pedestal: The Malta Convoy of August 1942* (233) and (with Edwin

Walker) *The Battle of the Malta Striking Forces* (237). The latter--from the Ian Allen series "Sea Battles in Closeup"--records the achievements of the main surface forces (D14, D5 and Force K) operating from Malta in 1941. Other Malta titles include: George Hogan, *Malta: The Triumphant Years, 1940-1943* (107); and Kenneth Poolman, *Night Strike from Malta: 830 Squadron RN and Rommel's Convoys* (198). On the eastern Mediterranean, there is S.W.C. Pack's *The Battle for Crete* (185), Smith and Walker *The War in the Aegean* (238), and David A. Thomas *Crete 1941: The Battle at Sea* (244).

The Navy's Pacific theatre operations, though always secondary from a strategic and Allied perspective to those in the Mediterranean, apparently have been more appealing to recent writers. John Costello's *The Pacific War* (49) and John Winton's *War in the Pacific: Pearl Harbor to Tokyo Bay* (276) are useful general treatments. Winton's compact but reliable coverage nicely complements his earlier account of the actions of Britain's Pacific forces in *The Forgotten Fleet* (274). He has also written a concise account of the risky but exciting final destroyer action of the war in *Sink the Haguro* (277). The most ambitious reassessment of the war is Ned Willmott's *Empires in the Balance: Japanese and Allied Pacific Strategies February to April 1942* (270), and *The Barrier and the Javelin: Japanese and Allied Pacific Strategies to June 1942* (271). Based on enough of the newly opened primary sources (including untapped Japanese records) to sustain his frequently critical appraisals, these volumes are also important for their sustained synthesis of the existing literature and intelligent probing of its many discrepancies. Though advertised as strategic analysis, these volumes are as much operational history that may with completion of the successor volume(s) shape up as the major unofficial treatment of the war. *The Battle of the Java Sea* (257) by F.C. Van Oosten, provides a Dutch perspective on Allied cooperation and use of intelligence following the creation of a joint command structure.

Combined Operations, Materiel, Technical Developments. New books on Combined Operations include: A. Cecil Hampshire, *The Beachhead Commandos* (92); Major-General J.L. Moulton, *The Royal Marines* (177); and J.D. Ladd, *The Royal Marines 1919-1980: An Authorised History* (133), *Royal Marine Commando: The History of Britain's Elite Fighting Force* (134) and *SBS: The Invisible Raiders. The History of the Special Boat Squadron, World War Two to the Present* (135). Ladd's *Assault From the Sea, 1939-1945* (132) is a technical description of assault craft illustrated with examples from the war. Particular operations are covered in: Ronald Atkin, *Dieppe 1942: The Jubilee Disaster* (4); S.W.C. Pack *Operation Husky: The Allied Invasion of Sicily* (187); and P.W. Warner, *The D-Day Landings* (261). *D-Day* (254) by Warren Tute, John Costello and Terry Hughes is a good pictorial record. *Code Name MULBERRY* (94), by Guy Hartcup, considers the planning, construction and operation of the artificial harbors that helped to facilitate the follow up operations. The best concise treatment of the naval side of OVERLORD is Admiral Brian Schofield's *Operation NEPTUNE* (223).

The need for scholarly histories of individual ships, ship types and classes, and of naval materiel generally continues while popular accounts and photographic records abound. Some of the more important of these are, on naval aviation--David Brown, *Carrier Operations in*

World War II, vol. 1, *The Royal Navy*, vol. II, *The Pacific Navies* (27); Nathan Miller, *The Naval Air War, 1939-1945* (173); R.T. Partridge, *Operation Skua* (192); Kenneth Poolman, *Escort Carriers 1941-1945: An Account* (197); John Winton, *Air Power at Sea, 1939-1945* (275) and *Find, Fix and Strike: The Fleet Air Arm at War, 1939-1945* (278). On various surface vessels there are: Captain Peter Dickens, *Night Action: MTB Flotilla at War* (54); Peter Elliot, *Allied Escort Ships of World War II* (59) and *Allied Minesweeping in World War II* (60); W.H. Garzki and R.O. Dulin, *British, Soviet, French and Dutch Battleships of World War II* (74); Gregory Haines, *Cruisers at War* (85); Peter Hodges and Norman Friedman, *Destroyer Weapons of World War II* (106); Alan Rover, *British Battleships of World War II: The Development and Technical History of the Royal Navy's Battleships and Battlecruisers from 1911 to 1946* (206), and *British Battle Cruisers of World War II* (207); T.W. Ross, *The Best Way to Destroy a Ship: The Evidence of European Naval Operations in World War II* (220); Peter C. Smith, *The Great Ships Pass: British Battleships at War, 1939-1945* (235) and *Hard Lying: The Birth of the Destroyers* (232). On submarines, Erminio Bugnasco, *Submarines of World War II* (28); Richard Compton-Hall, *The Underwater War, 1939-1945* (43); and Kenneth Poolman, *Periscope Depth: Submarines at War* (199) are useful.

The Navy Since World War II. The post-1945 Navy still awaits its major historians. Certainly in comparison to those chronicling the Army's activities during Britain's transition from world to middle power status, books specifically devoted to the Navy's fortunes are rare. Purists may suggest that only now, as the thirty-year rule has advanced to encompass the 1956 Suez turning point, can historians begin to make their impact. Of course, this ignores the fact that historians of the Cold War and Detente periods have already passed through their so-called "revisionist" and "post-revisionist" phases. Why the Navy has been neglected is not easy to explain for, by its very nature, naval history has always been international history. Perhaps loss of Empire may have constricted publishers' horizons as much as anyone's.

Britain's general defense problems have been thoroughly addressed since the war although mainly by political scientists, strategic studies specialists and journalists for whom policy prescription or criticism rather than historical analysis, is the main concern. The accumulated contemporary literature is now vast and begins itself to become historical evidence. Picking one's way through press and periodical commentaries, and various publications of The Royal Institute of International Affairs, The International Institute of Strategic Studies, The Royal United Services Institute and others listed in Chapter XXII of the Higham *Guide* remains a daunting prospect. That burden has been eased considerably, however, by Julian Lider's long though somewhat cumbersome treatment in his book *British Military Thought After World War II* (147). His argument that British military thinkers' general failure to take more systematic approaches in developing a coherent military doctrine accounts for the essentially unplanned and costly nature of the withdrawal from the world stage may not be entirely convincing and not least because of Lider's own failure to be more discriminating concerning the quality of individual contributions. Still, the book is a genuine mine of information; its notes and bibliography alone provide a comprehensive listing of references that might otherwise escape notice.

The general background to Britain's postwar defense situation has been thoroughly reconsidered in Professor C.J. Bartlett's, *The Long Retreat: A Short History of British Defence Policy, 1945-1970* (10); Peter Calvocoressi, *The British Experience, 1945-1975* (33); Phillip Darby, *British Defence Policy East of Suez, 1947-1968* (50); Lawrence Martin, *British Defence Policy: The Long Recessional* (165); and F.S. Northedge, *Descent from Power: British Foreign Policy, 1945-1973* (182). The military-political realities of Britain's relations with her allies are covered in John Baylis, *Anglo-American Defence Relations, 1939-1979: The Special Relationship* (12) and his edited work, *British Defence Policy in a Changing World* (11); Michael Chichester and John Wilkinson, *The Uncertain Ally: British Defence Policy, 1960-1990* (37); Laurence Freedman, *Britain and Nuclear Weapons* (67); A.J.R. Groom, *British Thinking about Nuclear Weapons* (80); Admiral of the Fleet Sir Peter Hill-Norton, *No Soft Options* (103); I.S. Macdonald, *Anglo-American Relations Since the Second World War* (156); and R.B. Manderson-Jones, *The Special Relationship: Anglo-American Relations and Western European Union, 1947-1956* (159).

A. Cecil Hampshire's *The Royal Navy Since 1945: Its Transition to the Nuclear Age* (88) is a readable and well-illustrated chronicle of the major changes that have occurred in the Navy up to 1975. Desmond Wettern's *The Decline of British Seapower* (268) is a much longer treatment though disappointing in that it does not venture beyond a cataloguing of annual events using extracts and paraphrases from estimates, parliamentary debates and personal notes, though not PRO materials. It does expose some interesting aspects of naval planning and management associated with materiel and manpower problems.

New book length studies of post war operational activities such as those associated with the unsung Beira Patrol, or the Cod War, remain to be done. *The Corfu Incident* (141) by Eric Leggett is an interesting account by a journalist who in October 1946 was serving in one of the cruisers involved. Glimpses of the Navy's part in the 1956 Suez operation can be found in Roy Fullick and Geoffrey Powell, *Suez: The Double War* (70); Robert Jackson, *Suez 1956: Operation Musketeer* (118); Selwyn Lloyd, *Suez 1956: A Personal Account* (149); and K. Love, *Suez: The Twice Fought War* (152).

The 1982 Falklands-Malvinas conflict and the rush to get into print has produced an ever growing list of books whose value will be better appreciated once and if access to government dossiers, operations orders and signal logs is granted. The "official" perspective on these actions has been set out in *The Falklands Campaign: The Lessons* (65) and in *Falkland Islands Review: A Report of a Committee of Privy Counsellors* (the so-called Franks Report) (66). In the conclusion to the second (1984) edition of *Maritime Strategy and the Nuclear Age* (248), Geoffrey Till has added a brief but balanced assessment of the operations and of the extent to which they may confirm or call into question accepted strategic wisdom. A similar approach, though with a somewhat wider focus, is contained in Alberto Coll's and Anthony Arend's edited collection of essays, *The Falklands War: Lessons for Strategy, Diplomacy and International Law* (41). Of the popular accounts, Martin Middlebrooke's *Operation Corporate* (171) is probably the best to date. Essentially a campaign study based on extensive interviews with British participants, it provides a vivid and straightforward account of the land and naval fighting free of obvious personal or political bents. Other accounts now available include: P. Bishop and J. Witherow (of *The Observer* and *The Times*), *The Winter War: The Falklands Conflict* (20); Pat Eddy and Magnus Linklater, *The Falklands War* (58); Adrian English and Anthony Watts, *Battle for the Falklands: Naval Forces* (62); Arthur L. Gorshov, *The Sinking of the Belgrano* (77); Max Hastings and Simon Jenkins, *The Battle for the Falklands* (95); John Laffin, *Fight for the Falklands* (136); Roger Villar, *Merchant Ships at War: The Falklands Experience* (256); the *Sunday Times* of London Insight Team, *War In The Falklands: The Full Story* (242); and Geoffrey Underwood, *Our Falklands War* (255).

Finally, mention should be made of some British studies which though concerned mainly with contemporary or future naval developments do also refer to the recent past and provide helpful leads to the periodical and journal literature. These would include: Adelphi Paper (Nos. 122-124) *Power at Sea*, published by the IISS; Ken Booth, *Navies and Foreign Policy* (22); Sir James Cable, *Gunboat Diplomacy: The Political Application of Limited Naval Force* (29), *Britain's Naval Future* (31), and *Diplomacy at Sea* (32); Rear-Admiral J.R. Hill, *The Royal Navy Today and Tomorrow* (100), and *British Seapower in the 1980s* (101); Admiral of the Fleet the Lord Hill-Norton, *Sea Power* (104); Geoffrey Till, *The Future of British Sea Power* (249); and M.B.F. Ranken (ed.), *Britain and the Sea: Future Dependence—Future Opportunities* (205).

BIBLIOGRAPHY

1. Adelphi Paper. *Power at Sea* (Nos. 122-24). London: International Institute of Strategic Studies, 1976.
2. Allen, Louis. *The End of the War in Asia*. London: Hart Davis MacGibbon, 1976.
3. ———. *The Politics and Strategy of the Second World War—Singapore 1941-1942*. London: Davis Poynter, 1977.
4. Atkin, Ronald. *Dieppe 1942: The Jubilee Disaster*. London: Macmillan, 1980.
5. Austin, J. and Carter, N. *The Man Who Hit the Scharnhorst*. London: Seeley Service, 1974.
6. Baker, Richard. *The Terror of Tobermory*. London: W.H. Allen, 1972.
7. ———. *Dry Ginger: The Biography of Admiral of the Fleet Sir Michael Le Fanu*. London: W.H. Allen, 1977.
8. Barber, Noel. *Sinister Twilight: The Fall and Rise Again of Singapore*. London: Collins, 1968.
9. Barnett, Correlli. *The Collapse of British Power*. London: Eyre Methuen, 1972.
10. Bartlett, C.J. *The Long Retreat: A Short History of British Defence Policy, 1945-1970*. London: Macmillan, 1972.
11. Baylis, John (ed.). *British Defence Policy in a Changing World*. London: Croom-Helm, 1977.
12. ———. *Anglo-American Defence Relations 1939-1979: The Special Relationship*. London: Macmillan, 1981.

13. Bayliss, Gwyn M. *A Bibliographic Guide to the Two World Wars: An Annotated Survey of English Language Reference Materials.* London: Bowker, 1977.
14. Beatty, Charles. *Our Admiral: A Biography of Admiral of the Fleet Earl Beatty, 1871-1936.* London: W.H. Allen, 1980.
15. Beaver, Paul. *Encyclopedia of the Modern Royal Navy, Including the Fleet Air Arm and Royal Marines.* London: Patrick Stephens, 1982.
16. Beesly, Patrick. *Very Special Intelligence: The Story of the Admiralty's Operational Intelligence Centre, 1939-1945.* London: Hamish Hamilton, 1977.
17. ―――. *Very Special Admiral: The Life of Admiral J.H. Godfrey, CB.* London: Hamish Hamilton, 1980.
18. Bennett, Geoffrey. *Naval Battles of World War II.* London: Batsford, 1977.
19. Bennett, Ralph. *Ultra in the West: The Normandy Campaign of 1944-1945.* London: Hutchinson, 1979.
20. Bishop, P. and Witherow, J. *The Winter War: The Falklands Conflict.* London: Quartet, 1982.
21. Bond, Brian. *British Military Policy Between the Two World Wars.* Oxford: Clarendon Press, 1980.
22. Booth, Ken. *Navies and Foreign Policy.* London: Croom-Helm, 1977; New York: Crane Russak, 1977; Holmes & Meier, 1979.
23. Boutilier, James (ed.). *The RCN in Retrospect, 1910-1968.* Vancouver: UBC Press, 1982.
24. Brice, Martin. *The Royal Navy and the Sino-Japanese Incident, 1937-1941.* London: Allan, 1973.
25. Brookes, Edward. *Prologue to a War.* London: White Lion, 1977.
26. Broome, Captain Jack. *Convoy is to Scatter.* London: William Kimber, 1972.
27. Brown, David. *Carrier Operations in World War II.* Vol. 1. *The Royal Navy;* Vol. 2. *The Pacific Navies.* London: Ian Allen, 1974.
28. Bugnasco, Erminio. *Submarines of World War Two.* London: Arms and Armour, 1977.
29. Cable, Sir James. *Gunboat Diplomacy: The Political Application of Limited Naval Force.* London: Chatto & Windus, for the IISS, 1971.
30. ―――. *The Royal Navy and the Seige of Bilbao.* New York: Cambridge University Press, 1979.
31. ―――. *Britain's Naval Future.* London: Macmillan, 1983.
32. ―――. *Diplomacy at Sea.* London: Macmillan, 1985.
33. Calvocoressi, Peter. *The British Experience, 1945-1975.* London: Bodley Head, 1978.
34. ―――. *Top Secret Ultra.* London: Cassell, 1980.
35. Carew, Anthony. *The Lower Deck of the Royal Navy 1900-1939: The Invergordon Mutiny in Perspective.* Manchester University Press, 1981.
36. Connell, G.G. *Arctic Destroyers: The 17th Flotilla.* London: Kimber, 1982.
37. Chichester, M. and Wilkinson, J. *The Uncertain Ally: British Defence Policy, 1960-1990.* Aldershot: Gower, 1982.
38. Clark, Ronald W. *The Man Who Broke "Purple": The Life of the World's Greatest Cryptologist, William F. Friedman.* London: Weidenfeld & Nicolson, 1977.

39. Clayton, Aileen. *The Enemy is Listening: The Story of the Y-Service*. London: Hutchinson, 1980.
40. Coles, Alan and Briggs, Ted. *Flagship Hood: The Fate of Britain's Mightiest Warship*. London: Robert Hale, 1979.
41. Coll, Alberto and Arend, Anthony C. (eds.). *The Falklands War: Lessons for Strategy, Diplomacy and International Law*. London: Allen & Unwin, 1985.
42. Collier, Basil. *Hidden Weapons: Allied Secret or Undercover Services in World War II*. London: Hamish Hamilton, 1982.
43. Compton-Hall, Richard. *The Underwater War, 1939-1945*. Poole: Blandford Press, 1982.
44. Cook, Chris, et al. *Sources in British Political History, 1900-1951*. London: Macmillan, 1975-78. Vol. 1. *A Guide to the Archives of Selected Organisations and Societies*. Vol. 2. *A Guide to the Private Papers of Selected Public Servants*. Vol. 6. *First Consolidated Supplement*.
45. Cooksley, P.G. *Operation Thunderbolt: The Nazi Warships' Escape, 1942*. London: Hale, 1981.
46. Corse, Robert. *A Cold Corner of Hell: The Story of the Murmansk Convoys, 1941-1945*. New York: Doubleday, 1969.
47. Cosgrove, Patrick. *Churchill at War*. Vol. I. *Alone, 1939-1940*. London: Collins, 1974.
48. Costello, John and Hughes, Terry. *The Battle of the Atlantic*. London: Collins, 1977.
49. Costello, John. *The Pacific War*. New York: Rawson, 1981.
50. Darby, Phillip. *British Defence Policy East of Suez, 1947-1968*. London: Oxford University Press, 1973.
51. Davies, E.L. and Groves, E.J. *Dartmouth: Seventy-Five Years in Pictures*. Portsmouth: Gieves & Hawkes, 1980.
52. ----------. *The Royal Naval College, Dartmouth*. Portsmouth: Gieves & Hawkes, 1981.
53. Dickens, Captain Peter. *Narvik: Battles in the Fiords*. London: Ian Allen, 1974.
54. ----------. *Night Action: MTB Flotilla at War*. Annapolis: Naval Institute Press, 1974.
55. Dingman, Roger. *Power in the Pacific: The Origins of Naval Arms Limitation, 1914-1922*. Chicago: University of Chicago Press, 1976.
56. Divine, David. *Mutiny at Invergordon*. London: Macdonald, 1970.
57. Doughty, Martin. *Merchant Shipping and War. A Study of Defence Planning in Twentieth Century Britain*. Royal Historical Society Studies in History Series, No. 31, 1982.
58. Eddy, Pat and Linklater, Magnus. *The Falklands War*. London: Sphere, 1982.
59. Elliot, Peter. *Allied Escort Ships of World War II*. London: Macdonald and Janes, 1977.
60. ----------. *Allied Minesweeping in World War II*. London: Patrick Stephens, and Annapolis: Naval Institute Press, 1979.
61. Endicott, Stephen. *Diplomacy and Enterprise: British China Policy, 1933-1937*. Vancouver: U.B.C. Press, 1975.
62. English, A. and Watts, A. *Battle for the Falklands: Naval Forces*. London: Osprey, 1982.
63. Ensor, A.G.S. *A Subject Bibliography of the Second World War: Books in English, 1939-1974*. London: Deutsch, 1977.

64. Ereira, Alan. *The Invergordon Mutiny.* London: Routledge & Kegan Paul, 1981.
65. *The Falklands Campaign: The Lessons.* London: HMSO, 1982.
66. *Falkland Islands Review. A Report of a Committee of Privy Counsellors.* (The Franks Report). London: HMSO, 1983.
67. Freedman, Lawrence. *Britain and Nuclear Weapons.* London: Macmillan, 1980.
68. Frere-Cook, Gervis. *The Attacks on the Tirpitz.* London: Ian Allen, 1973.
69. Fry, Michael. *Illusions of Security: North Atlantic Diplomacy, 1918-1922.* Toronto: University of Toronto Press, 1972.
70. Fullick, Roy and Powell, Geoffrey. *Suez: The Double War.* London: Hamish Hamilton, 1979.
71. Funk, A.L. *The Politics of TORCH: The Allied Landings and the Algiers Putsch, 1942.* Lawrence: University Press of Kansas, 1974.
72. Garlinski, Joseph. *Intercepts: Secrets of the Enigma War.* London: J.M. Dent, 1979.
73. Garrett, Richard. *Scharnhorst and Gneisenau.* London: David & Charles, 1979.
74. Garzki, W.H. & Dulin, R.O. *British, Soviet, French and Dutch Battleships of World War II.* London & Sydney: Jane's, 1981.
75. Gibbs, Norman H. *History of the Second World War, Grand Strategy,* Vol. 1, *Rearmament Policy.* London: HMSO, 1976.
76. Gilbert, Martin. *Winston S. Churchill.* London: Heinemann. Vol. 111: *1914-1916* (1971); Vol. IV: *1917-1922* (1975); Vol. V: *1923-1939* (1976); Vol. VI: *1939-1941* (1983). *Companion* to Vol. 111, Nos. 1 & 2 (1972); to Vol. IV, Nos. 1, 2 & 3 (1977); to Vol. V, Nos. 1 & 2 (1981), No. 3 (1982).
77. Gorshov, Arthur L. *The Sinking of the Belgrano.* London: Secker, 1984.
78. Gretton, Peter. *Former Naval Person: Winston Churchill and The Royal Navy.* London: Cassell, 1968.
79. ―――――. *Crisis Convoy: The Story of HX 231.* London: Peter Davies, 1974.
80. Groom, A.J.R. *British Thinking About Nuclear Weapons.* London: Frances Pinter, 1974.
81. Hackmann, William. *Seek and Strike: Sonar, Anti-Submarine Warfare and the Royal Navy, 1914-1934.* London: HMSO, 1984.
82. Hadley, Michael L. *U-Boats Against Canada: German Submarines in Canadian Waters.* Montreal: McGill-Queen's University Press, 1985.
83. Haggie, Paul. *Britannia at Bay: The Defence of the British Empire Against Japan, 1931-1941.* Oxford: Clarendon Press, 1981.
84. Haines, Gregory. *Gunboats on the Great River: A History of the Royal Navy on the Yangtse.* London: Macdonald & Jane's, 1975.
85. ―――――. *Cruisers at War.* London: Ian Allen, 1978.
86. Halpern, Paul G. (ed.). *The Keyes Papers. Selections From the Private and Official Correspondence of Admiral of the Fleet Baron Keyes of Zeebrugge.* Vol. 1, *1914-1918.* Greenwich: Navy Records Society, 1972. Vol. 11, *1919-1938,* and

Vol. 111, *1939-1945*. London: George Allen & Unwin for the Navy Records Society, 1980 and 1981.
87. Hamill, Ian. *The Strategic Illusion: The Singapore Strategy and the Defence of Australia and New Zealand, 1919-1942*. Singapore: University of Singapore Press, 1981.
88. Hampshire, A. Cecil. *The Royal Navy Since 1945: Its Transition to the Nuclear Age*. London: William Kimber, 1975.
89. ─────. *The Secret Navies*. London: William Kimber, 1978.
90. ─────. *The Blockaders*. London: William Kimber, 1980.
91. ─────. *Undercover Sailors. Secret Operations of World War II*. London: William Kimber, 1981.
92. ─────. *The Beachhead Commandos*. London: William Kimber, 1983.
93. Hansson, Per. *One in Ten Had to Die*. London: George Allen & Unwin, 1970.
94. Hartcup, Guy. *Code Name Mulberry*. London: David & Charles, 1977.
95. Hastings, Max and Jenkins, Simon. *The Battle for the Falklands*. London: Michael Joseph, 1983.
96. Hazlrm musiehurst, C. and Woodland, C. *A Guide to the Papers of British Cabinet Ministers, 1900-1951*. London: Royal Historical Society, 1974.
97. Hezlet, Vice-Admiral Sir Arthur. *The Submarine and Sea Power*. London: Peter Davies, 1967.
98. ─────. *Aircraft and Sea Power*. London: Peter Davies, 1970.
99. ─────. *The Electron and Sea Power*. London: Peter Davies, 1975.
100. Hill, Rear-Admiral J.R. *The Royal Navy Today and Tomorrow*. London: Ian Allen, 1981.
101. ─────. *British Sea Power in the 1980s*. London: Ian Allen, 1986.
102. Hill, Roger. *Destroyer Captain*. London: William Kimber, 1979.
103. Hill-Norton, Admiral of the Fleet Sir Peter. *No Soft Options*. London: Hurst, 1978.
104. ─────. *Sea Power*. London: Faber & Faber, 1982.
105. Hinsley, F.H., et. al. *British Intelligence in the Second World War: Its Influence on Strategy and Operations*. 3 vols. London: HMSO, 1979, 1982, 1984.
106. Hodges, Peter and Friedman, Norman. *Destroyer Weapons of World War Two*. Greenwich: Conway, 1978.
107. Hogan, George. *Malta: The Triumphant Years, 1940-1943*. London: Robert Hale, 1978.
108. Horsfield, John. *The Art of Leadership in War: The Royal Navy From the Age of Nelson to the End of World War II*. Westport, Conn.: Greenwood Press, 1980.
109. Hough, Richard. *The Great Admirals*. London: Weidenfeld & Nicolson, 1981.
110. ─────. *Mountbatten: Hero of Our Time*. London: Weidenfeld & Nicolson, 1981.
111. Howard, Michael E. *The Continental Commitment: The Dilemma of British Defence Policy in the Era of the Two World Wars*. London: Maurice Temple Smith, 1972.
112. ─────. *History of the Second World War, Grand Strategy*. Vol. IV, *August 1942-September 1943*. London: Routledge & Kegan Paul, 1984.

113. Humble, Richard. *Fraser of North Cape: The Life of Admiral of the Fleet Lord Fraser, 1888-1981*. London: Routledge & Kegan Paul, 1984.
114. Hunt, Barry D. *Sailor-Scholar: Admiral Sir Herbert Richmond, 1871-1946*. Waterloo: Wilfrid Laurier University Press, 1982.
115. Irving, David. *The Destruction of Convoy PQ17*. London: William Kimber, 1980.
116. Jackson, Robert. *Strike From the Sea: A Survey of British Naval Air Operations, 1900-1969*. London: Baker, 1970.
117. ─────. *Dunkirk: The British Evacuation 1940*. London: Baker, 1976.
118. ─────. *Suez 1956: Operation Musketeer*. London: Ian Allen, 1980.
119. Jones, Captain Basil. *And So to the Baltic: A Sailor's Story*. Privately published, 1980.
120. Jordan, Gerald (ed.). *Naval Warfare in the Twentieth Century, 1900-1945: Essays in Honour of Arthur Marder*. London: Croom-Helm, 1977.
121. Kemp, Peter K. *Victory at Sea 1939-1945*. London: White Lion, 1976.
122. ─────. *Escape of the Scharnhorst and Gneisenau*. London: Ian Allen, 1975.
123. Kennedy, Ludovic. *Pursuit: The Chase and Sinking of the Bismarck*. London: Collins, 1974.
124. ─────. *Menace: The Life and Death of the Tirpitz*. London: Sidgwick & Jackson, 1979.
125. Kennedy, Paul. *The Rise and Fall of British Naval Mastery*. London: Allen Lane, 1976 (New York: Scribner). Reissued, Krieger Reprints, 1982.
126. ─────. *The Realities Behind Diplomacy: Background Influences on British External Policies, 1865-1980*. London: Allen Unwin, 1981.
127. ─────. *Strategy and Diplomacy 1870-1945: Eight Studies*. London: Allen & Unwin, 1984.
128. Kirby, Stanley W. *The Official History of the War Against Japan*. vol. V. London: HMSO, 1970.
129. ─────. *Singapore: Chain of Disaster*. London: Cassell, 1971.
130. Kirkpatrick, Lyman B. *Captains Without Eyes: Intelligence Failures in World War II*. London: Hart Davis, 1970.
131. Kozaczuk, Wladyslaw. *Enigma, How the German Machine Cipher Was Broken and How it Was Read by the Allies in World War II*. University Publications of America, 1984.
132. Ladd, J.D. *Assault from the Sea 1939-1945*. Newton Abbot: David and Charles, 1976.
133. ─────. *The Royal Marines 1919-1980: An Authorised History*. London: Jane's, 1981.
134. ─────. *Royal Marine Commando: The History of Britain's Elite Fighting Force*. London: Hanlyn, 1982.
135. ─────. *SBS: The Invisible Raiders. The History of the Special Boat Squadron, World War Two to the Present*. London: Arms & Armour, 1983.
136. Laffin, John. *Fight for the Falklands*. London: Sphere Books, 1982.

137. Lamb, Commander Charles. *War in a Stringbag*. London: Cassell, 1977.
138. Lamb, James B. *The Corvette Navy: True Stories from Canada's Atlantic War*. Toronto: Macmillan, 1977.
139. Lash, Joseph P. *Roosevelt and Churchill, 1939-1941: The Partnership that Saved the West*. New York: Norton, 1976.
140. Lee, Bradford. *Britain and the Sino-Japanese War, 1937-1939*. Stanford University Press, 1973.
141. Leggett, Eric. *The Corfu Incident*. London: Seeley, 1974.
142. Leutze, James R. *Bargaining for Supremacy: Anglo-American Naval Collaboration, 1937-1941*. Chapel Hill: University of North Carolina Press, 1977.
143. Lewin, Ronald. *Churchill as Warlord*. London: Batsford, 1973.
144. ―――――. *Ultra Goes to War*. London: Hutchinson, 1978.
145. ―――――. *The Other Ultra*. London: Hutchinson, 1982.
146. ―――――. *The American Magic: Codes, Ciphers and the Defeat of Japan*. New York: Farrar, 1982.
147. Lider, Julian. *British Military Thought After World War II*. Aldershot: Gower, 1985.
148. Livock, Group Captain G.E. *To the Ends of the Air*. London: HMSO, 1973.
149. Lloyd, Selwyn. *Suez 1956: A Personal Account*. London: Jonathan Cape, 1978.
150. Louis, W.R. *British Strategy in the Far East, 1919-1939*. Oxford: Clarendon Press, 1971.
151. ―――――. *Imperialism at Bay: The United States and the Decolonization of the British Empire*. Oxford: Clarendon Press, 1977.
152. Love, K. *Suez: The Twice Fought War*. London: Longmans, 1970.
153. Lowe, Peter. *Great Britain and the Origins of the Pacific War: A Study of British Policy in East Asia 1937-1941*. Oxford: Clarendon Press, 1977.
154. ―――――. *Britain in the Far East: A Survey From 1919 to the Present*. London: Longmans, 1981.
155. MacDonald, C.A. *The United States, Britain and Appeasement, 1936-1939*. New York: St. Martin's, 1981.
156. Macdonald, I.S. *Anglo-American Relations Since the Second World War*. Newton Abbott: David and Charles, 1974.
157. Macintyre, Captain Donald. *The Naval War Against Hitler*. London: Batsford, 1971; New York: Scribners, 1974.
158. ―――――. *U-Boat Killer*. London: Seeley Service; Annapolis: Naval Institute Press, 1974.
159. Manderson-Jones, R.B. *The Special Relationship: Anglo-American Relations and Western European Union, 1947-1956*. London: Weidenfeld and Nicolson, 1972.
160. Marder, Arthur J. *From the Dreadnought to Scapa Flow: The Royal Navy in the Fisher Era, 1904-1919*. London: Oxford University Press, 1961-1970. 5 vols. Vol. III, *Jutland and Aftermath* (revised and enlarged, 1978).
161. ―――――. *Winston is Back: Churchill at the Admiralty, 1939-1940*. London: Longmans, 1972.
162. ―――――. *From the Dardanelles to Oran: Studies of the Royal Navy in War and Peace, 1915-1940*. London: Oxford University Press, 1974.

163. ──────. *Operation "Menace": The Dakar Expedition and the Dudley North Affair.* London: Oxford University Press, 1976.
164. ──────. *Old Friends, New Enemies: The Royal Navy and the Imperial Japanese Navy--Strategic Illusions, 1936-1941.* Oxford: Clarendon Press, 1981.
165. Martin, L.W. *British Defence Policy: The Long Recessional.* IISS, Adelphi Paper No. 61, 1969.
166. Mayer, S.L. and Koenig, W.J. *The Two World Wars: A Guide to Manuscript Collections in the United Kingdom.* London: Bowker, 1976.
167. McGibbon, I.C. *Blue-Water Rationale: The Naval Defence of New Zealand, 1914-1942.* Wellington: Government Printing Office, 1981.
168. McIntyre, W. David. *The Rise and Fall of the Singapore Naval Base, 1919-1942.* London: Macmillan, 1979.
169. McKercher, Brian. *The Second Baldwin Government and the United States, 1924-1929: Attitudes and Diplomacy.* Cambridge: Cambridge University Press, 1984.
170. Middlebrook, Martin. *Convoy: The Battle for Convoys SC122 and HX229.* London: Allen Lane, 1976; New York: Morrow, 1977.
171. ──────. *Operation Corporate.* London: Penguin, 1985.
172. ────── and Mahoney, Patrick. *Battleship: The Loss of the Prince of Wales and Repulse.* London: Allen Lane, 1977.
173. Miller, Nathan. *The Naval Air War, 1939-1945.* London: Conway Maritime Press, 1980.
174. Milner, Marc. *North Atlantic Run: The Royal Canadian Navy and the Battle of the Convoys.* Toronto: University of Toronto Press, 1985.
175. Molony, Brigadier C.J.C., et. al. *History of the Second World War: The Mediterranean and the Middle East.* Vol. V. London: HMSO, 1973.
176. Montagu, E. *Beyond Top Secret U.* London: Peter Davis, 1977.
177. Moulton, Major-General J.L. *The Royal Marines.* RM Museum, 1982.
178. von Mullenheim-Rechberg, Baron Burkard. *Battleship Bismarck.* London: The Bodley Head, 1981.
178. (a) Murfett, Malcolm. *Fool-Proof Relations: The Search for Anglo-American Naval Cooperation during the Chamberlain Years, 1937-1940.* Singapore: Singapore University Press, 1984.
179. Neidpath, James. *The Singapore Naval Base and the Defence of Britain's Eastern Empire, 1919-1941.* Oxford: Clarendon Press, 1981.
180. Nish, Ian. *Alliance in Decline: Anglo-Japanese Relations 1908-1923.* London: Athlone Press, 1972.
181. ────── (ed.). *Anglo-Japanese Alienation: Papers of the Anglo-Japanese Conference on the History of the Second World War.* Cambridge: Cambridge University Press, 1982.
182. Northedge, F.S. *Descent from Power: British Foreign Policy 1945-1973.* London: Allen and Unwin, 1974.
183. Owen, Charles. *No More Heroes: The Royal Navy in the Twentieth Century: Anatomy of a Legend.* London: George Allen & Unwin, 1975.

184. Pack, Captain S.W.C. *Night Action Off Cape Matapan*. London: Ian Allen, 1972.
185. ―――. *The Battle for Crete*. London: Ian Allen, 1974.
186. ―――. *Cunningham the Commander*. London: Batsford, 1974.
187. ―――. *Operation Husky: The Allied Invasion of Sicily*. Newton Abbott: David and Charles, 1977.
188. Palmer, A.B. *Pedlar Palmer of Tobruk: An Autobiography*. Roebuck Series, Australia, 1981.
189. Parkinson, Roger. *Peace for Our Time: Munich to Dunkirk--The Inside Story*. London: Hart Davis, 1971.
190. ―――. *Blood, Toil, Tears and Sweat: The War History from Dunkirk to Alamein Based on War Cabinet Papers of 1940 to 1942*. London: Hart Davis, MacGibbon, 1973.
191. ―――. *A Day's March Nearer Home: The War History from Alamein to VE Day Based on the War Cabinet Papers of 1942 to 1945*. London: Hart Davis, MacGibbon, 1974.
192. Partridge, R.T. *Operation Skua*. Fleet Air Arm Museum, 1983.
193. Patterson, A. Temple. *Tyrwhitt of the Harwich Force*. London: Macdonald, 1973.
194. Peden, George C. *British Rearmament and the Treasury, 1932-1939*. Edinburgh: Scottish Academic Press, 1979.
195. Pelz, Stephen E. *Race to Pearl Harbor: The Failure of the Second London Naval Conference and the Onset of World War II*. Boston: Harvard University Press, 1984.
196. Plimmer, Charlotte and Dennis. *A Matter of Expediency: The Jettison of Admiral Sir Dudley North*. London: Quartet Books, 1978.
197. Poolman, Kenneth. *Escort Carriers, 1941-1945: An Account of British Escort Carriers and Trade Protection*. London: Allen, 1972.
198. ―――. *Night Strike from Malta: 830 Squadron RN and Rommel's Convoys*. London: Jane's, 1980.
199. ―――. *Periscope Depth: Submarines at War*. London: William Kimber, 1981.
200. Popham, Hugh. *Into the Wind: A History of British Naval Flying*. London: Hamish Hamilton, 1969.
201. Potter, John Deane. *Fiasco*. London: Heinemann; New York: Stein & Day, 1970.
202. Pratt, Lawrence R. *East of Malta, West of Suez: Britain's Mediterranean Crisis, 1936-1939*. Cambridge and New York: Cambridge University Press, 1975.
203. Price, Alfred. *Aircraft versus Submarine: The Evolution of the Anti-Submarine Aircraft, 1912-1972*. London: Kimber, 1973.
204. Ranft, Bryan (ed.). *Technical Change and British Naval Policy, 1860-1939*. London: Hodder & Stoughton, 1977.
205. Ranken, M.B.F. (ed.). *Britain and the Sea: Future Dependence--Future Opportunities*. Edinburgh: Scottish Academic Press, 1984.
206. Rover, Alan and Roberts, John. *British Battleships of World War II: The Development and Technical History of the Royal Navy's Battleships and Battlecruisers from 1911 to 1946*. Annapolis: Naval Institute Press, 1976; London: Arms and Armour, 1976.
207. ―――. *British Cruisers of World War II*. London: Arms and Armour; Annapolis: Naval Institute Press, 1980.

208. Reid, Alan. *A Concise Encyclopedia of the Second World War*. London: Osprey, 1974.
209. Reynolds, David. *The Creation of the Anglo-American Alliance, 1937-1941: A Study in Competitive Cooperation*. Chapel Hill: University of North Carolina Press, 1981.
210. Rhodes James, Robert. *Churchill: A Study in Failure, 1900-1939*. London: Weidenfeld & Nicolson, 1970.
211. Rohwer, Jurgen and Hummelchen, Gerhard. *Chronology of the War at Sea, 1939-1945*. 2 vols. London: Ian Allen, and New York: Archon Books, 1972-74.
212. ———. *The Critical Convoy Battles of March 1943*. London: Ian Allen, 1977.
213. ———. *Axis Submarine Successes, 1939-1945*. Annapolis: Naval Institute Press, 1983.
214. Roskill, Captain Stephen W. *The War at Sea 1939-1945*. 3 vols. London: HMSO, 1954-1962.
215. ———. *The Naval Air Service*. Vol. 1. *1908-1918*. The Navy Records Society, 1969.
216. ———. *Naval Policy Between the Wars*. Vol. I. *The Period of Anglo-American Antagonism, 1919-1929*; Vol. II. *The Period of Reluctant Rearmament, 1930-1939*. London: Collins, 1968, 1976.
217. ———. *Hankey: Man of Secrets*. Vol. 1, *1877-1918*; Vol. 11, *1919-1931*; Vol. 111, *1931-1963*. London: Collins, 1970, 1972, 1974.
218. ———. *Churchill and the Admirals*. London: Collins, 1977.
219. ———. *Admiral of the Fleet Earl Beatty. The Last Naval Hero: An Intimate Biography*. London: Collins, 1980.
220. Ross, T.W. *The Best Way to Destroy a Ship: The Evidence of European Naval Operations in World War II*. Manhattan Kansas: MA/AH Publishing, 1980.
221. Sainsbury, K. *The North African Landings 1942: A Strategic Decision*. London: Davis-Poynter, 1976.
222. Schofield, Vice-Admiral Brian B. *The Attack on Taranto*. London: Ian Allen, 1973.
223. ———. *Operation NEPTUNE*. London: Ian Allen, 1974.
224. ———. *The Arctic Convoys*. London: MacDonald & Jane's, 1977.
225. ———. *Navigation and Direction: The Story of HMS Dryad*. London: Morgan, 1977.
226. Schurman, Donald M. *Julian S. Corbett, 1854-1922: Historian of British Maritime Policy from Drake to Jellicoe*. London: Royal Historical Society, 1981.
227. Shai, Aron. *Origins of the War in the East: Britain, China and Japan, 1937-1939*. London: Croom Helm, 1976.
228. Shay, Robert P. *British Rearmament in the 1930s: Politics and Profits*. Princeton: University Press, 1977.
229. Simpson, Rear-Admiral C.W.G. *'Periscope View': A Professional Autobiography*. London: Macmillan, 1972.
230. Smith, Dan. *The Defence of the Realm in the 1980s*. London: Croom Helm, 1980.
231. Smith, Myron J. *World War II at Sea: A Bibliography of Sources in English*. Metuchen, N.J.: Scarecrow Press, 1976.
232. Smith, Peter. *Hard Lying: The Birth of the Destroyers*. London: William Kimber, 1971.

233. ———. *Pedestal: The Malta Convoy of August 1942.* London: William Kimber, 1971.
234. ———. *Arctic Victory: The Story of Convoy PQ18.* London: William Kimber, 1975.
235. ———. *The Great Ships Pass: British Battleships at War, 1939-1945.* London: William Kimber, 1977.
236. ———. *Hold The Narrow Sea: Naval Warfare in the English Channel, 1939-1945.* London: Moorland; Annapolis: Naval Institute Press, 1984.
237. ——— and Walker, Edwin. *The Battle of the Malta Striking Forces.* London: Ian Allan, 1974.
238. ———. *War in the Aegean.* London: William Kimber, 1974.
239. Snyder, Gerald S. *The Royal Oak Disaster.* London: William Kimber, 1976. San Rafael, Calif: Presidio Press, 1978.
240. Stokesbury, James L. *Navy and Empire.* New York: Morrow, 1983. London: Hale, 1984.
241. Stoler, Mark A. *The Politics of the Second Front: American Military Planning and Diplomacy in Coalition Warfare, 1941-1943.* Westport: Greenwood, 1977.
242. Sunday Times of London, Insight Team. *War in the Falklands: The Full Story.* London: Andre Deutsch, 1982.
243. Swettenham, J. *Canada's Atlantic War.* Toronto: Stevens, 1979.
244. Thomas, David A. *Crete 1941: The Battle at Sea.* London: Deutsch, 1972.
245. Thorne, Christopher. *The Limits of Foreign Policy. The West, the League and the Far Eastern Crisis of 1931-1933.* London: Hamish Hamilton, 1972.
246. ———. *Allies of a Kind: The United States, Britain and the War Against Japan, 1941-1945.* London: Hamish Hamilton, 1978.
247. Till, Geoffrey. *Air Power and the Royal Navy 1914-1949: A Historical Survey.* London: Jane's, 1979.
248. ———. et. al. *Maritime Strategy and the Nuclear Age.* London: Macmillan, 1982; second edition, 1984.
249. ——— (ed.). *The Future of British Sea Power.* London: Macmillan, 1984.
250. Trotter, Ann. *Britain and East Asia, 1933-1937.* London and New York: Cambridge University Press, 1975.
251. Turnbull, Constance Mary. *A History of Singapore, 1819-1975.* London, Kuala Lampur, New York: Oxford University Press, 1978.
252. Turnbull, Patrick. *Dunkirk: Anatomy of a Disaster.* London: Holmes & Meier, 1979.
253. Tute, Warren. *The Deadly Stroke.* London: Collins, 1973.
254. ———, Costello, John and Hughes, Terry. *D-Day.* London: Sidgwick and Jackson, 1974.
255. Underwood, Geoffrey. *Our Falklands War.* London: Maritime Books, 1983.
256. Villar, Roger. *Merchant Ships at War: The Falklands Experience.* Annapolis: Naval Institute Press, 1984.
257. Van Oosten, F.C. *The Battle of the Java Sea.* London: Ian Allan, 1976.
258. Waddington, C.M. *OR in World War II: Operational Research Against the U-Boat.* London: Elek Science, 1973.

259. Wallis, R. Ransome. *Two Red Stripes: A Naval Surgeon at War*. London: Ian Allan, 1973.
260. Warner, Oliver. *Admiral of the Fleet: The Life of Sir Charles Lambe*. London: Sidgwick and Jackson, 1969.
261. Warner, P. *The D-Day Landings*. London: William Kimber, 1980.
262. Watt, D. Cameron. *Too Serious a Business: European Armed Forces and the Approach of the Second World War*. London and Berkeley: 1974.
263. ———. *Succeeding John Bull: America in Britain's Place, 1900-1975*. Cambridge University Press, 1984.
264. Watts, Anthony. *The U-Boat Hunters*. London: Macdonald and Jane's, 1976.
265. Weaver, H.J. *Nightmare at Scapa Flow: The Truth About the Sinking of HMS Royal Oak in Scapa Flow in 1939*. London: Creerelles, 1981.
266. Wells, Captain J.G. *Whaley: The Story of HMS Excellent, 1830-1980*. HMS Excellent, 1980.
267. Welshman, Gordon. *The Hut Six Story: Breaking the Enigma Codes*. London: Allen Lane, 1983.
268. Wettern, Desmond. *The Decline of British Seapower*. London: Jane's, 1982.
269. Williams, John. *The Guns of Dakar: Operation Menace, September 1940*. London: Heineman, 1976.
270. Willmott, H.P. *Empires in the Balance: Japanese and Allied Pacific Strategies to April 1942*. Annapolis: Naval Institute Press, 1982.
271. ———. *The Barrier and the Javelin: Japanese and Allied Pacific Strategies, February to June 1942*. Annapolis: Naval Institute Press, 1983.
272. Wincott, Len. *Invergordon Mutineer*. London: Weidenfeld & Nicolson, 1974.
274. Winton, John. *The Forgotten Fleet*. London: Michael Joseph, 1969.
275. ———. *Air Power at Sea, 1939-1945*. London: Sidgwick & Jackson, 1976.
276. ———. *The War in the Pacific: Pearl Harbor to Tokyo Bay*. London: Sidgwick & Jackson, 1976.
277. ———. *Sink the Haguro!: The Last Destroyer Action of the Second World War*. London: Seeley, 1979.
278. ———. *Find, Fix and Strike! The Fleet Air Arm at War, 1939-1945*. London: Batsford, 1980.
279. ———. *Jellicoe*. London: Michael Joseph, 1981.
280. ———. *Convoy: Defence of Sea Trade*. London: Michael Joseph, 1983.
281. Woodward, Sir Llewellyn. *British Foreign Policy in the Second World War*. 5 vols. London: HMSO, 1970-1976.
282. Young, John. *A Dictionary of Ships of the Royal Navy of the Second World War*. Cambridge: Patrick Stephens, 1975.
283. Ziegler, Philip. *Mountbatten: The Official Biography*. London: Collins, 1985.

XIV

THE DEVELOPMENT OF THE ROYAL AIR FORCE, 1909 - 1945

Stephen Harris and Norman Hillmer

When the first edition of the *Guide* appeared almost two decades ago, the study of modern British history was undergoing a revolution. The fifty-year rule which had controlled access to government documents had been replaced by a thirty-year rule, which itself would soon be modified to ensure that files relating to the Second World War would all be released together, and earlier than originally scheduled. Then it was decided that highly classified files about the most secret aspects of intelligence and electronic warfare could also be made available to the public. Here was the stuff that would allow scholarly examination of the Royal Air Force in the last years of peace and in the crucible of the Second World War. Here too was the documentary framework for revisionist criticism of the major studies that already existed.

Air history, however, remains underdeveloped as a field, and suffers badly in comparison with army and naval history. Despite the wealth of new material and the passage of time, many of the gaps in RAF history identified by Robin Higham in the first *Guide* have not been filled. The inter-war years have been studied in considerable detail, to be sure: mistakes and misperceptions made between 1919 and 1939 shaped the war in the air, and they are seen as convenient bases for new and critical assessments of the RAF in action. But other important areas remain unexplored. There is no sound single volume history of the RAF. A history of the Air Council has yet to be written, and while there are individual biographies of a number of the principal actors, very few do justice to their subject. There is no adequate collective treatment of the RAF's senior officers, what might be called the air force's 'general staff.' Nor is there any comprehensive account of air force training or the way in which the RAF managed its personnel resources. The Empire Air Training Scheme, also known as the British Commonwealth Air Training Plan, is the subject of Hatch's *Aerodrome of Democracy* (129), but the focus of the book is understandably on the development of the training programme in Canada, where most aircrew training took place. Social historians have ignored the RAF, so that questions about the composition of the air force, and personnel selection processes, are largely unanswered, while those relating to morale and discipline continue to be matters of conjecture. We still have a long way to go before our knowledge of the RAF as an institution and of its performance at the tactical and grand tactical (or operational) levels of war can in any way be considered complete.

Recent interest and research naturally centres on the Second World War, which has replaced the First as 'Grandfather's War.' There is a growing sense of nostalgia about the conflict; much of the suffering has been forgotten, and the period 1939-1945 had emerged as a kind of Golden Age. It was no accident that the Royal Navy sailed to the Falklands amidst talk of a renewed 'Spirit of Dunkirk,' reflecting a longing for a time when right and wrong and a sense of duty were apparently simple, straightforward concepts. Veterans, feeling such emotions keenly and now largely retired from their postwar careers, are taking the time available to set down what they remember. There is a lucrative market for books about familiar campaigns, weapons, personalities.

Nostalgia, fortunately, is not the only impulse produced by the passing of four decades since the last bombs fell on Germany and Japan, and since the last Spitfire shot down a Messerschmitt or Focke Wulf. A healthy skepticism is rampant forty years on. Critical assessments are appearing on the large issues--policy, and the conduct of operations at the highest level--and the work of Max Hastings (127), Martin Middlebrook (193) and the better memoir writers (113, 214, 278) is providing often scathing and always complex views of the war from below. Accordingly, while books like *The Dam Busters* appeared in the 1950s, today we expect works like John Sweetman's study of *Operation Chastise* (272), which not only questions the origins of the raid, but also asks whether it was all worth while. Similarly, the best of the current Battle of Britain literature (6, 172, 180, 206A) pays the compulsory homage to the heroism of 'The Few,' but it also acknowledges that they belonged to a flawed organization, Fighter Command, which was combatting an even more seriously flawed *Luftwaffe*. The lesson, perhaps, is that forty percent efficiency will beat thirty per cent efficiency most of the time, and that Fighter Command did not so much win the battle as it failed to lose it.

Journals. There are few additions to the list gathered by Robin Higham in the first *Guide*. Although not devoted to RAF history, both the *Journal* of the Royal United Services Institute and the American *Aerospace Historian* have included serious scholarly articles on British air power. First World War enthusiasts display their wares in the several national *Cross & Cockade Journals*.

Public and Private Papers. The main development here is the release of the AIR and related collections at the Public Record Office, Kew, and of similar documents in archives around the Commonwealth. The Air Historical Branch monographs, a partial list of which appears in the bibliographies of Terraine (275) and Hyde (139), are being made available and private papers are beginning to turn up. The biographers of Harris (190, 256) and Portal (242) certainly had access to their subject's files and those of colleagues, but researchers must still travel many miles in the United Kingdom, and write many letters, to locate and receive permission to use such collections. Although its listings are difficult to use and incomplete, the National Register of Archives in London is an invaluable point of departure. In Ottawa, the Canadian Public Archives and the Directorate of History, National Defence Headquarters, hold important collections, while in Canberra the Australian War Memorial is the place to begin.

Official Histories. The most important British official history to emerge since 1970 is the multi-volume work on intelligence in progress by F.H. Hinsley (131A). An essential corrective to Winterbotham's over-dramatized memoir (290), it makes clear the importance of 'special' signals and electronic intelligence in the prosecution of World War II. For the RAF 'Ultra' was of less use than it was for the navy, in the main because the *Luftwaffe* was able to use landlines for most of its internal communications, but snippets of information about the enemy order of battle and equipment were available form this source from time to time especially from units stationed in the Balkans, where landlines did not exist. Far more important was electronic and signals intelligence, particularly for the bomber offensive. Until April 1944 at least, Air Chief Marshal Harris was convinced that Bomber Command could obtain air superiority indirectly--not by fighting for it, but by evading the German night-fighter force. Once the latter was equipped with radar, evasion became a game of electronic hide and seek in which the technological balance could shift very suddenly and decisively. It was therefore crucial to know what measures the other side was employing in order to develop counters to them. Hinsley is an essential source on this, but R.V. Jones (156), Alfred Price (229), Martin Streetly (271), Aileen Clayton (69), W.E. Jones (157) and Brian Johnson (152) should be read in conjunction with it.

Parts of other recent official histories contain useful information. Volumes by Norman Gibbs (107) and Michael Howard (136) complete the *Grand Strategy* set in the United Kingdom Military Series. Payton-Smith (212) deals with the supply of oil and aviation fuel to the RAF. Mellor (187) adds data on casualties and the RAF medical service. Of a demi-official nature is the RAF Museum Series, reprints from official air publications (59, 60, 92, 138, 163, 201, 269).

Canada's multi-volume Official History of the Royal Canadian Air Force is now being published. Its belated appearance has allowed the authors to say things which might have been left unsaid if they were writing soon after the events they were describing, and to give complete references for all statements. Volume I, by S.F. Wise (292), is the history of Canadian airmen in the First World War, but since there was no operational Canadian air force at the time, and personnel from the Dominion were scattered through the British flying services, it is essentially a history of the RAF (and its predecessors), and of the air war, 1914-1919. It is also revisionist, and demonstrates that the doctrine of area bombing, which admitted that the enemy's civilian population was a legitimate target, was practiced during the Great War--and may have owed more to Sir Frederick Sykes than Lord Trenchard. The book is also quite the best study to appear on close support operations during the war, and illustrates that the RAF had stumbled onto a doctrine for the tactical use of air power which it then ignored for the next twenty years.

The second volume, by W.A.B. Douglas (87) has more purely Canadian content, but a good half of the book is part and parcel of RAF history. The process by which Commonwealth aircrews were trained in Canada on a massive scale is told in substantially different terms than F.J. Hatch (129), and the section on the Battle of the Atlantic is an essential supplement to anything so far written about Coastal Command. In particular, Douglas makes complete use of the intelligence available to both sides in their analysis of the fight for individual convoys between Allied and German naval and air forces.

General Histories. The single synthesizing history of the RAF Robin Higham called for has not appeared. A five-volume set on pre-1939 British aviation by Harold Penrose (215-219) scarcely counts because of its bulk, and it is really a catalogue of events, personalities, prototypes, and production. Although Sir Maurice Dean (83) promises much, written as it is by a former senior official in the Air Ministry, it too is disappointing. The to-and-fro of policy-making in the 1930s is glossed over, while the work of the Air Ministry during the war is treated in a completely uncritical (and unconvincing) fashion. Only two books, not general histories but studies of the second air war, 1939-1945, come close to the ideal: one is R.J. Overy's broad history of the war in the air (208) and the other is the monumental required study of the RAF by John Terraine (275).

The First World War. There is little in the way of analytical history of aerial operations in World War I besides Wise (292). Most recent books have been memoirs, by Winter (289), Insall (141), Voss (281), Kinney (162), and Lewis (169). Christopher Cole (70, 71) offers a reproduction of Royal Flying Corps Communiqués. MacMillan (181) highlights the operations of the British flying services in a little-known theatre of war.

The Inter-War Years. Montgomery-Hyde (139), Powers (223) and Smith (266) are the obvious sources, but the history of British air policy and strategy cannot be divorced from the history of British foreign and military policy in general. Doubts about the wisdom of ever again making a continental commitment, the power of the Treasury, and the belated (and confused) rush to rearm affected all three services, and often cause inter-service rivalries in the fight for larger budgets. Bond (24), Gibbs (107), Howard (135), Shay (259), and Peden (213) are all important in this respect. The RAF's doctrine of the bomber as deterrent was acceptable to government interested in defense on the cheap. Then the same politicians, alerted to the growing power of Germany, began to fear the capabilities claimed for the *Luftwaffe*. As a result they demanded that the RAF remained wedded to the concept of strategic bombing, making for dissonance between government and service policy. Uri Bialer (23) elaborates nicely on this point, and successfully communicates the atmosphere of the 1930s when fear of cataclysmic attack dominated thinking in Whitehall and throughout the United Kingdom.

The same story, from a service point of view, is told in the early chapters of Terraine (275), Verrier (283), Hastings (127) and Saward (256), and in Allen's *Legacy of Lord Trenchard* (5), by far the most critical of the lot. All of them show how, to one degree or another, the RAF's adoption of the false doctrine that strategic bombing was a war-winner in itself blinded the service to alternate uses of air power, and condemned escort fighters, anti-shipping forces, air transport, close air support, and very nearly Fighter Command, to oblivion. Because of this RAF was in no position to intervene effectively in the Battle of France. The Air Historical Branch narratives are particularly useful for this period.

Second World War. General. Apart from highly illustrated primers there are few general histories of the RAF 1939-1945, and two of them are especially disappointing: Dean's survey (83), and Richards' study of Portal (242), a biography which is essentially a history of the RAF at war. The former is uncritical (13) while the latter, an authorized biography, verges on hagiography. This is unfortunate. 'Peter' Portal was an impressive man, and does not need to be protected by an account in which the higher direction of the air war appears to have been completely harmonious, all sweetness and light. Mistakes were made, some under Portal's stewardship. He was Chief of the Air Staff when Dowding was sacked, somewhat unceremoniously, and when open disloyalty to a higher commander was rewarded with Leigh-Mallory's transfer to 11 Group to take over from Park. It was also under Portal, first as AOC-in-C of Bomber Command, and then as CAS, that the bombing offensive grew into a costly campaign very likely directed against the wrong target systems and that Fighter Command wasted itself on Rhubarbs and Circuses over France.

John Terraine's major study (275) corrects this rosy view. Relying in the main on Air Historical Branch narratives and published accounts, he shatters many of the myths about the Royal Air Force, and does not hesitate to be critical. But it is his overall theme that is most intriguing. Known for his spirited defense of Field Marshal Sir Douglas Haig during the Great War--one of the few British generals, the prolific author would argue, who ever defeated a main enemy army in a major continental war--Terraine draws an implicit analogy between the position of Haig's armies and the RAF. Until 1917, at least, Haig knew that the French Army was the preponderant Allied force, and because of this subordinated his plans to what the French were doing. Once the French had mutinied, Haig had to fight battles to prove that Britain was still in the war. The same was true of the RAF between the fall of France and the opening of the Second Front. It was the only means at Britain's disposal to attack Germany and, at the same time, to prove to the countries of Occupied Europe and to the USSR that the United Kingdom would see the war through. Because of this higher purpose, Terraine suggests, the options open to the Air Staff and to Bomber Command were limited, just as they had been for Haig.

September 1939-June 1940. The RAF's war before the Battle of Britain was at first uninspiring, and then calamitous. Bombers dropped feeble propaganda leaflets by night in the opening months, and were devastated by day bombing operations against military targets in Germany and the German Army in France. The fighters and light-bombers of the Advanced Air Striking Force and the Fighter Command reinforcements flown to France were also shattered. Terraine's (275) chapters on these months are good, but necessarily brief, and his conclusion that the calamitous Battle of France was the pay-off for all that the RAF had ignored about army support between the wars is unassailable. Goddard (110), Passmore (211), Franks (96), Bowyer (56) and Halliday (117) add colour to this story, with Goddard, the

Air Officer in charge of administration in the expeditionary forces air component, and Bowyer being the best at evoking the sense of despair and desperation among the British airmen in France.

Battle of Britain. Despair turned to a strange sense of relief once France had fallen and Britain stood alone, and the Battle of Britain has become one of the great events in the country's military history, ranking with Waterloo and Trafalgar. Little wonder, therefore, that so many histories of the battle, complete with heroes and moments of high drama, continue to be written and to sell well. Bushby (65), Cooksley (76), Halliday (117), Parkinson (210) and especially Price (225) and Ramsey (235) are good examples of this genre.

Yet there was another side to the battle, a sad story of discord and disharmony, first acknowledged at length in Derek Wood and Derek Dempster's *The Narrow Margin*, published in 1961. The extent, however, to which the crisis in Fighter Command may have influenced the conduct and outcome of the Battle of Britain has become the object of bitter argument rather more recently. The first shots were fired by Robert Wright (293), stout defender of Air Chief Marshal Dowding and Keith Park, Air Officer Commanding 11 Group. It was Dowding, after all, who had been responsible for the Spitfire and Hurricane design competition; he had pioneered the development of radar-assisted ground control interception; he had stood up to Churchill to prevent the attrition of Britain's fighter resources in the Battle of France; and with Park's complete cooperation he had husbanded the resources of Fighter Command so that it could rise and fight again, and in the process prevent the Germans from achieving the air superiority over Southern England which was essential to their invasion plans. The removal of Dowding after winning this victory, seen by Wright as the result of behind-the-scenes manoeuvering by Leigh-Mallory and Douglas Bader, is presented as one of the most distasteful episodes in RAF history. Vincent Orange's recent biography of Sir Keith Park (206A) looks at the same events with a similar bias but from the viewpoint of Dowding's loyal subordinate.

Wing Commander H.R. Allen (6) leads the opposition to this point of view. Having initiated the Spitfire/Hurricane competition, Allen argues, Dowding subsequently promulgated fighter specifications that lagged far behind British design and engineering potential in the late 1930s. And then, despite his conviction that the enemy bomber formations must be intercepted before they reached their target, he chose to keep his Hurricane squadrons forward while the Spitfires, with appreciably better rates of climb, were held farther back. Finally, in Allen's view, Dowding suffered from tragic flaws in personality. Not only were his relations with the Air Staff and Air Ministry unnecessarily difficult, but he also failed to intervene early in the dispute between Park and Leigh-Mallory which threatened to unhinge the air defense of Southern England. Whether or not one accepts the arguments put forward by Lucas (172) and Turner (280)--that the 'Big Wing' tactics advocated by Bader and Leigh-Mallory were preferable to those employed by Park--it is difficult to challenge Allen's conclusions that something was wrong with Britain's air defenses. Either because of lack of coordination within fighter command, or because of Air Ministry policies which gave priority to

training bomber crews, 11 Group appears to have been unnecessarily hammered in the summer of 1940.
The historian receives little assistance on these issues from the memoirs of Battle of Britain pilots. Their loyalties to Park or Leigh-Mallory typically depend on the Group in which they served. Fighter pilot memoirs from the Battle of Britain are rarely reflective, perhaps because there was little reason to question what they were doing, and this lack of context and critical questioning carries over to the 1941-42 period, when Fighter Command's sweeps over France failed to win air superiority there. Instead, most memoirs deal with three aspects of the fighter pilot's life: aerial combat at 15,000 feet, mess life, and the dispassionate way in which the loss of friends and colleagues had to be handled.
Certainly none of the recent 'fighter' memoirs achieves the poetry of Richard Hillary's *The Last Enemy*, mentioned in the first edition of this *Guide*, but Barclay (14), Godefroy (113), Kent (160), and Bartley (19) are good reading. Of the biographies of Fighter Command pilots Lucas (172) stands ahead of Smith (268) and Stokes (270) because it addresses the larger issues of tactics and command. Lucas (173), Franks (102), and Halliday (118) provide snapshots of the battle.

Bomber Command. If the Battle of Britain was the single most dramatic moment for the RAF, the bomber offensive was the test of its resolve over the long haul. Was it also the RAF's greatest mistake, morally and militarily? The official history of the bomber offensive by Sir Charles Webster and Noble Frankland deserves the accolades it received in the first edition of this *Guide*. Webster and Frankland write 'true history.' The bomber offensive is not depicted as a smooth, coherent, and well-coordinated military campaign, but as it was--an often muddled and improvised effort to send enough aircraft to Germany, without grievous losses, in order to bring the Reich to its knees before a long slogging match on land became necessary. Bomber Command failed to meet this objective, and Webster and Frankland have no difficulty in saying so; nor do they cover up its losses, or make exaggerated claims for the contribution bombing made to the final defeat of Germany. They do not always address the issue of target selection, or the alternate employment of heavy bombers, as candidly as they might have, and since theirs is an official history of policy and command decisions at the highest level, it is also somewhat antiseptic. Individual aircrews, squadrons, and groups, except for the specialists, rarely appear.
The general histories of the bomber offensive which have appeared since the last *Guide* conform, in the main, to the conclusions reached by the official historians but add more human content. Jackson (142, 143, 148), Morrison (200), and Longmate (171), fall into this category. Other historians have dissected individual raids. Messenger's short, but complete, history of Cologne (191), Sweetman's (272) study of the Dams raid, and Musgrove's account of Hamburg (202) stand out. Messenger is particularly good at describing the state of the German air defenses in mid-1942, while Sweetman provides a corrective to the romance of the *Dambusters* book and film. Building upon the model he used for his fascinating study of the *First Day on the Somme*, Martin Middlebrook's three books on Hamburg, Peenemünde, and Nuremberg (192,

193, 194) make fascinating reading because of their first-person testimony. Cooper's *Berlin* (78) and McKee's *Dresden* (179) are similar, but less dramatic. Although all of these books to some extent criticize specific aspects of the bomber offensive, none is a sustained study of Bomber Command's problems in doctrine, tactics, equipment, or morale.

Wing Commander H.R. Allen's scathing indictment of Trenchardian ideas, left as a legacy to Portal and Harris (5), centres on one idea: 'The Bomber School indulged in the wishful thinking that the German nation consisted of a poor dispirited people, ground underfoot by the Gestapo' and ready for collapse as soon as it was put to the test. The bombing of German cities was this test, but when it became apparent that the destruction of cities was not achieving what it was supposed to, Bomber Command and the Air Staff dissembled rather than admit the error of their original assumptions. In the view of Allen, an RAF planner and Battle of Britain veteran, thousands of Allied airmen died attacking the wrong targets, for the wrong reasons.

Anthony Verrier (283) had, about ten years earlier, made a similar case, less emotionally and in more difficult prose. The real value of his book was the way in which it addresses, first of all, the merits of bombing different target systems, and, secondly, the question of air superiority. Bomber Command could not, he says, maintain an efficient offensive, with affordable casualty rates, until the German air defenses were mastered. But to this end Bomber Command contributed little. The Germans lost their early warning networks only because of the advance of the Allied armies in France, a neat and ironic twist to the doctrine that Bomber Command might make land battles unnecessary. Just as important, the German night fighters became ineffective because they ran out of fuel, but this happened only when the Americans, attacking the 'panacea' targets Harris abhored and escorted by the long-range fighters the Air Staff had declared were a technological impossibility, shot the *Luftwaffe* out of the sky and won the freedom to turn their attention to the German oil industry. Hansell (124) agrees.

Max Hastings (127) has a narrower focus. Where Verrier, the official historians, and most other writers have glossed over or rationalized the morality of area bombing, Hastings has attacked the question directly. It is his contention that British statesmen and military leaders had both the wherewithal and the responsibility to plan and build a bomber force that was capable of something other than a campaign of terror aimed at the enemy's women and children.

Saward (256), Messenger (190), and Richards author of the popular official history of the RAF (243), express contrary views, with Messenger declaring that any questioning of the morality of the bomber offensive is 'cheap sarcasm.' Richards is completely unsatisfactory in explaining the nature of the relationship between Portal and Harris, and makes what appears to be a less than honest attempt to create distance between the Chief of the Air Staff and the area bombing policies adopted by Bomber Command. The two biographies of Harris complement each other, although that by Saward, the 'authorized' version, is clearly less critical of its subject. Both, however, offer ample evidence that while Harris rarely left his headquarters, and almost never visited his men, he nevertheless cared deeply about them, and was more open-minded about improving the defensive armament of bomber aircraft than is generally acknowledged.

Yet readers will still come away from these three books unsure about why bomber crews displayed the loyalty they did to their commander. Terraine (275) and Hastings (127) both address the question of morale in Bomber Command.

There are some excellent monographs about Bomber Command. Musgrove (202) is a history of the Pathfinder Force, while Streetly (271), Jones (156), Jones (157), and Price (229) are essential to understand the importance of electronic warfare in bombing operations. Michael Bowyer (56) is good on 2 Group. Middlebrook has done all historians of the bomber offensive a remarkable service with his *Bomber Command War Diaries* (195), a review of every night's activity including number of aircraft sent, number lost, nature of bombing, and *Luftwaffe* defensive efforts.

Perhaps because, as Terraine suggests, the Bomber Command experience was analogous to the trench war of 1914-1918, the veterans of the bomber offensive have produced memoirs that approach the quality of those from the Great War. They show more critical thinking and reflection than any others coming out of the RAF. Murray Peden (214) is by far the best, but Thompson (278) is also useful for the way in which it points out how good crews managed to survive. Bushby (64), Raymond (238), Currie (82), Renaut (241), Powell (222), and Wainwright (285) are all worth reading. Unfortunately, Bramson's biography of "Pathfinder" Bennett (58) tells us less than Bennett's own memoirs, recently republished (21). Hamilton's biography of Pickard (123), read in conjunction with Jackson (147), highlights the work of Bomber Command personnel on special operations.

Perhaps it is night-flying that makes aircrews introspective. In the event, although there is no history of RAF night-fighter and intruder operations to equal Aders' study of Bomber Command's main opponent (1), the memoirs of those involved in bomber support operations--McIntosh (177), Chisholm (67), and Alcorn (4)--are surprisingly good.

Other Commands and Theatres. John Terraine (275) believes that the contribution of Coastal Command and the anti-shipping squadrons to final victory has received less attention that it deserves, and he is undoubtedly correct. There is no general analytical history beyond his own few chapters on the subject, and Bowyer (31), Nesbit (203, 204), Jones(153), Rawlings (236) and Hendrie (130) are not nearly so good as the best books on Bomber Command. Price (224) is superb on the development of tools and techniques to combat the German U-Boats, and is easier to read than Waddington (284). A naval point of view is provided in Till (279). The failure of the RAF to find and sink *Prinz Eugen, Scharnhorst* and *Gneisenau* is told in Cooksley (75). There are several interesting memoirs, however, Nesbit (205), McVicar (182, 184) and Jaworzyn (151) being the best. Fraser (103) is useful for its story of the Leigh Light.

Ferry Command also has no history of its own, but Powell (222), Bramson (58), McVicar (183) and Bennett (21) provide some insights. British and Commonwealth air operations in South East Asia are the subject of Melnyk (188) Beauchamp (20), Innes (140), Kelly (158) and Franks (99).

The most neglected area in the history of the RAF is the tactical air story, from the experience gained in the Great War to the agony of 1940, to the heady days of the Desert Air Force and cab rank in Italy, to the disharmony of Normandy. Bowyer (40, 49) on the Desert Air Force is not analytical enough but is helped by Lavigne and Edwards (166). Shores (261) is a good beginning for 2nd TAF, and Scott (258) is a reasonably good memoir. Franks (101) offers little more than glimpses. Mead (185) is extremely valuable on the specific subject of air observation and aerial reconnaissance.

Miscellany. Aviation medicine is finally receiving some attention, in Gibson and Harrison (109), Robinson (251), and in parts of Mellor (187). The important work of Boscombe Down, the RAF's experimental establishment, is dealt with by Johnson (152). The story of the RAF Regiment is told in its own history (254).

So-called serious historians often sneer at the 'buttons and bows' and 'buff' authors, who are criticized for setting down more than anyone wants to know about the minutiae of military history. But in their eagerness to deal with large, contentious issues serious historians often ignore minor details, get the facts wrong, and then repeat each other often enough that these mistakes become received wisdom. It is the careless historian indeed, therefore, who ignores the work of these specialists writing in his field.

Histories of bases and airfields abound--Ashworth (9, 10), Bowyer (52, 53), Dickson (85), Smith (264, 265), Flint (94), Fraser (104), Halpenny (119-122), and Haslam (126), are just some examples-- and are most useful for those who wish to delve into the air war from below. Squadron histories are also plentiful. Those by Brookes (60A), Halley (114) Lewis (170), Rawlings (236, 237) and Russell (255) are perhaps less interesting for the general reader than Cooper's (77, 79) two-volume account of 617 Squadron or Hunt (137) on the Royal Air Force Auxiliary units. The technical specialists come into their own, however, when it comes to the histories of specific aeroplanes, manufacturers, or types of aircraft, and books on these subjects are legion. Out list, we are sure, is incomplete, but worth noting are Hardy (125), Merrick (189), Robertson (246, 248), Thetford (276), Weal (287) and the two Bowyers (25, 30, 38, 42, 44, 46, 48, 50, 54, 57).

Future Research. Some areas requiring further research have already been mentioned in passing. Higham's plea for books on training, 'air control' in the Middle East, the Air Council, and the RAF officer corps has not been answered. There is no good history of the development of British policy on tactical air, and the tactical/grand tactical (operational) side of the bomber offensive has been ignored. A comparative history of the way the different Bomber Command groups approached their task would be useful, if only to explain why, in late 1944, the *Luftwaffe* thought that 5 Group *and* 6 Group rated better than the rest. Research into questions of aircraft serviceability, and of replacement policy and its implementation, is needed. We should know much more about how the RAF made use of operational research, in particular to discover whether Freeman Dyson (89) was telling the complete story when he declared that submissions from junior members of the OR staff somehow got lost whenever they were at odds with the prevailing opinions at Bomber Command Headquarters. Neither Ferry Command nor Coastal Command have the histories they deserve; the ground staffs and ground crews remain practically invisible; and there is little on RAF contributions in the two great regional theatres--the Middle East and South East Asia. Relations with the Commonwealth air forces, and the conflicting demands of operational efficiency and national identity, have not been studied thoroughly. What should be obvious is that, despite all the books to have appeared since 1968, there is a remarkable amount of work still to do.

BIBLIOGRAPHY

1. Aders, Gebhard. *History of the German Night Fighter Force 1917-1945*. London: Jane's, 1978.
2. Adkin, Fred. *From the Ground Up: To Service Ground Crew Everywhere*. Shrewsbury: Airlife, 1983.
3. *Airfield Plans*. Battle of Britain International. Ongoing series.
4. Alcorn, Douglas, with Souster, Raymond. *From Hell to Breakfast*. Toronto: Intruder, 1980.
5. Allen, H.R. *The Legacy of Lord Trenchard*. London: Cassell, 1972.
6. ─────. *Who Won the Battle of Britain?* London: Barker, 1974.
7. Allinson, Les. *Canadians in the Royal Air Force*. Roland, Man.: Les Allinson, 1978.
8. Allward, Maurice. *Hurricane Special*. London: Ian Allan, 1975.
9. Ashworth, Chris. *Military Airfields of the Central South and South-East*. Cambridge: Stephens, 1985.
10. ─────. *Military Airfields of the South-West*. Cambridge: Stephens, 1982.
11. Bader, Douglas. *Fight for the Sky*. London: Sidgwick & Jackson, 1973.
12. Baker, Anne, and Ivelaw, Sir Ronald. *Wings Over Kabul*. London: Kimber, 1976.
13. Balfour of Inchyre, 1st Baron of Shefford, Harold Harrington Balfour. *Wings over Westminster*. London: Hutchinson, 1973.
14. Barclay, George. *Fighter Pilot: A Self-Portrait*. Edited by Humphrey Wynn. London: Kimber, 1976.
15. Barker, Ralph. *The Hurricats*. London: Pelham, 1978.
16. ─────. *The RAF at War*. Alexandria, Va.: Time-Life, 1981.
17. Baring, Maurice. *Flying Corps Headquarters 1914-1918*. Edinburgh: Blackwood, 1968.
18. Barnes, C.H. *Handley Page Aircraft Since 1907*. London: Putnam, 1976.
19. Bartley, Anthony. *Smoke Trails in the Sky: From the Journals of a Fighter Pilot*. London: Kimber, 1985.
20. Beauchamp, Gerry. *Mohawks over Burma*. Stittsville, Ont.: Canada's Wings, 1985.
21. Bennett, D.C.T. *Pathfinder: A War Autobiography*. London: Goodall, 1983.
22. Benson, John. *Birds Don't Fly at Night*. Cobalt, Ont.: Highway Book Shop, 1983.
23. Bialer, Uri. *The Shadow of the Bomber: The Fear of Air Attack and British Politics 1932-1939*. London: Royal Historical Society, 1980.

24. Bond, Brian. *British Military Policy Between the Two World Wars.* Oxford: O.U.P., 1980.
25. Bowyer, Chaz. *Air War Over Europe 1939-45.* London: Kimber, 1981.
26. ———. *Airmen of World War One: Men of the British and Empire Air Forces in Old Photographs.* London: Arms & Armour, 1975.
27. ———. *Beaufighter at War.* London: Ian Allan, 1976.
28. ———. *Bomber Barons.* London: Kimber, 1983.
29. ———. *Bomber Group at War.* London: Ian Allan, 1981.
30. ———. *Bristol Blenheim.* London: Ian Allan, 1984.
31. ———. *Coastal Command at War.* London: Ian Allan, 1979.
32. ———. *Eugene Esmonde, VC, DSO.* London: Kimber, 1984.
33. ———. *Fighter Command, 1936-1968.* London: Dent, 1980.
34. ———. *Fighter Pilots of the R.A.F. 1939-1945.* London: Kimber, 1984.
35. ———. *The Flying Elephants: A History of No. 27 Squadron, Royal Flying Corps--Royal Air Force, 1915-1969.* London: Macdonald, 1972.
36. ———. *For Valour: The Air VCs.* London: Kimber, 1978.
37. ———. *Guns in the Sky: The Air Gunners of World War Two.* London: Dent, 1979.
38. ———. *Hampden Special.* London: Ian Allan, 1976.
39. ———. *History of the Royal Air Force.* Feltham: Hamlyn, 1977.
40. (a) ———. *Images of the Air War, 1939-45.* London: Batsford, 1983.
40. ———. *Men of the Desert Air Force, 1940-1943.* London: Kimber, 1984.
41. ———. *Mosquito: Squadrons of the Royal Air Force.* London: Ian Allan, 1984.
42. ———. *Mosquito at War.* London: Ian Allan, 1973.
43. ———. *Path Finders at War.* London: Ian Allan, 1977.
44. ———. *Royal Air Force: The Aircraft in Service Since 1918.* Feltham: Hamlyn, 1981.
45. ———. *Royal Air Force Handbooks, 1939-1945.* London: Ian Allan, 1984.
46. ———. *Sopwith Camel--King of Combat.* Falmouth: Glasney, 1978.
47. ———. *Surviving World War Two Aircraft.* London: Batsford, 1981.
48. ———. *Wellington at War.* London: Ian Allan, 1982.
49. Bowyer, Chaz, and Shores, Christopher F. *Desert Air Force at War.* London: Ian Allan, 1981.
50. Bowyer, Michael F. *Aircraft for the Royal Air Force.* London: Faber, 1980.
51. ———. *Fighting Colours: RAF Fighter Camouflage and Markings 1937-1975.* Cambridge: Stephens, 1975.
52. ———. *Military Airfields of the Cotswolds and the Central Midlands.* Cambridge: Stephens, 1983.
53. ———. *Wartime Military Airfields of East Anglia, 1939-45.* Cambridge: Stephens, 1979.
54. ———. *Stirling Bomber.* London: Faber, 1980.
55. ———. *Squadron Codes, 1937-56.* Cambridge: Stephens, 1979.

56. ─────. *2 Group RAF: A Complete History, 1936-1945.* London: Faber, 1974.
57. Bowyer, Michael J.F. and Philpott, Bryan. *Mosquito.* Cambridge: Stephens, 1980.
58. Bramson, Alan. *Master Airman: A Biography of Air Vice-Marshal Donald Bennett, CB, CBE, DSO.* Shrewsbury: Airlife, 1985.
59. *British Aviation Colours of World War Two: The Official Camouflage Colours and Markings of RAF Aircraft, 1939-1945.* RAF Museum Series, vol. 3. Hendon: Arms & Armour, 1976.
60. *British Military Aircraft of World War One: The Official Technical and Rigging Notes for RFC and RNAS Fighting and Training Aeroplanes, 1914-1918.* RAF Museum Series, vol. 4. London: Arms & Armour, 1976.
60. (a) Brookes, Andrew. *Bomber Squadron at War.* London: Ian Allan, 1983.
61. Brown, Don L. *Miles Aircraft Since 1925.* London: Putnam, 1970.
62. Brown, George, and Lavigne, Michael. *Canadian Wing Commanders of Fighter Command in World War II.* Langley, B.C.: Battleline Books, 1984.
63. Bruce, J. M. *The Bristol Fighter.* London: Arms & Armour, 1986.
64. Bushby, John R. *Gunner's Moon: A Memoir of the RAF Night Assault on Germany.* London: Ian Allan, 1972.
65. ─────. *Air Defence of Great Britain.* London: Ian Allan, 1973.
66. Chajkowsky, William E. *Royal Flying Corps: Borden to Texas to Beamsville.* Cheltenham, Ont.: Boston Mills, 1979.
67. Chisholm, Roderick. *Cover of Darkness.* Morley: Elmfield Press, 1976.
68. Clark, Ronald W. *The Role of the Bomber.* London: Sidgwick & Jackson, 1977.
69. Clayton, Aileen. *The Enemy is Listening.* London: Hutchinson, 1980.
70. Cole, Christopher, ed. *Royal Air Force, 1918.* London: Kimber, 1968.
71. ─────, ed. *Royal Flying Corps 1915-1916.* London: Kimber, 1969.
72. Collier, Basil. *A History of Airpower.* London: Weidenfeld and Nicolson, 1974.
73. Congdon, Philip. *Behind the Hangar Doors.* Woodhall Spa, Lincolnshire: Sonik Books, 1985.
74. Cooke, Ronald C., and Nesbit, Roy Conyers. *Target: Hitler's Oil; Allied Attacks on German Oil Supplies 1939-1945.* London: Kimber, 1985.
75. Cooksley, Peter G. *Operation Thunderbolt: The Nazi Warship Escape 1942.* London: Hale, 1981.
76. ─────. *1940: The Story of No. 11 Group Fighter Command.* London: Hale, 1983.
77. Cooper, Alan W. *Beyond the Dams to the Tirpitz: The Later Operations of 617 Squadron.* London: Kimber, 1983.
78. ─────. *Bombers over Berlin: The RAF Offensive November 1943-March 1944.* London: Kimber, 1985.
79. ─────. *The Men Who Breached the Dams: 617 Squadron 'The Dambusters'.* London: Kimber, 1982.
80. Copp, De Witt S. *Forged in Fire: Strategy and Decisions in the Air War Over Europe 1940-45.* New York: Doubleday, 1982.

81. Crawley, Aidan. *Escape from Germany: The Methods of Escape Used by RAF Airmen during the Second World War.* London: HMSO, 1985.
82. Currie, Jack. *Lancaster Target: The Story of a Crew who Flew from Wickenby.* London: New English Library, 1977.
83. Dean, Sir Maurice. *The Royal Air Force and Two World Wars.* London: Cassell, 1979.
84. Deighton, Len. *Fighter: The True Story of the Battle of Britain.* London: Cape, 1977.
85. Dickson, Charles. *Croydon Airport Remembered: An Aviation Artist Looks Back.* London: London Borough of Sutton Libraries and Arts, 1986.
86. Dodds, Ronald. *The Brave Young Wings.* Stittsville, Ont.: Canada's Wings, 1980.
87. Douglas, W.A.B. *The Creation of a National Air Force. The Official History of the Royal Canadian Air Force.* Vol. 2. Toronto: University of Toronto Press, 1986.
88. Duncan Smith, W.G.G. *Spitfire into Battle.* London: Murray, 1981.
89. Dyson, Freeman. *Disturbing the Universe.* New York: Harper and Row, 1979.
90. Fairhead, R. *An Airman's Diary.* Bognor Regis: New Horizon, 1982.
91. Ferguson, Aldon Patrick. *A History of Royal Air Force, Shawbury.* Liverpool: Merseyside Aviation Society, 1977.
92. *Fighting in the Air: The Official Combat Technique Instructions for British Fighter Pilots, 1916-1945.* RAF Museum Series, vol. 7. London: Arms & Armour, 1978.
93. *Fighter Squadron at War.* London: Ian Allan, 1980.
94. Flint, Peter. *RAF Kenley.* Lavenham: Dalton, 1985.
95. Foxley-Norris, Christopher, ed. *Royal Air Force at War.* London: Ian Allan, 1983.
96. Franks, Norman L.R. *The Air Battle of Dunkirk.* London: Kimber, 1983.
97. ─────. *The Battle of the Airfields: 1st January 1945.* London: Kimber, 1982.
98. ─────. *Fighter Leader: The Story of Wing Commander Ian Gleed.* London: Kimber, 1978.
99. ─────. *First in Indian Skies.* Lincoln Life Productions, 1981.
100. ─────. *Sky Tiger: The Story of "Sailor" Malan.* London: Kimber, 1980.
101. ─────. *Typhoon Attack.* London: Kimber, 1984.
102. ─────. *Wings of Freedom: Twelve Battle of Britain Pilots.* London: Kimber, 1980.
103. Fraser, Donald A. *Live to Look Again: Memoirs of a Canadian Pilot with the RAF during WW II.* Belleville, Ont.: Mika, 1984.
104. Fraser, W. *The Story of the Royal Air Force--Manston.* Manston: RAF, 1972.
105. Garbett, Mike, and Goulding, Brian. *Lancaster at War.* No. 1. London: Ian Allan, 1971. No. 2. London: Ian Allan, 1979.
106. ─────. *Lincoln at War, 1944-66.* London: Ian Allan, 1979.
107. Gibbs, Norman H. *Grand Strategy.* Vol. 1. *Rearmament Policy.*

History of the Second World War. United Kingdom Military Series. London: HMSO, 1976.
108. Gibbs-Smith, Charles H. *Aviation: An Historical Survey from its Origins to the End of World War II.* London: HMSO, 1970.
109. Gibson, T.M. and Harrison, M.H. *Into Thin Air: A History of Aviation Medicine in the RAF.* London: Hale, 1984.
110. Goddard, Sir Victor. *Skies to Dunkirk: A Personal Memoir.* London: Kimber, 1982.
111. Golley, John. *The Day of the Typhoon: Flying with the RAF Tankbusters in Normandy.* Wellingborough: Stephens, 1986.
112. Goulding, J., and Moyes, P.J.R. *RAF Bomber Command and its Aircraft 1941-1945.* London: Ian Allan, 1980.
113. Godefroy, Hugh Constant. *Lucky Thirteen.* Stittsville, Ont.: Canada's Wings, 1983/London: Croom Holm, 1983.
114. Halley, James J. *Famous Maritime Squadrons of the R.A.F.* Vol. 1. Windsor: Hylton Lacy, 1973.
115. ―――. *Royal Air Force Unit Histories.* 2 vols. Hutton, Brentwood: Air-Britain, 1969-73.
116. ―――. *The Squadrons of the Royal Air Force.* Tonbridge: Air-Britain, 1980.
117. Halliday, Hugh A. *No. 242 Squadron, the Canadian Years: The Story of the RAF's "All-Canadian" Fighter Squadron.* Stittsville, Ont.: Canada's Wings, 1982.
118. ―――. *The Tumbling Sky.* Stittsville, Ont.: Canada's Wings, 1978.
119. Halpenny, Bruce Barrymore. *Military Airfields of Greater London.* Cambridge: Stephens, 1984.
120. ―――. *Military Airfields of Yorkshire.* Cambridge: Stephens, 1982.
121. ―――. *To Shatter the Sky: Bomber Airfield at War.* Cambridge: Stephens, 1984.
122. ―――. *Wartime Military Airfields of Lincolnshire and the East Midlands.* Cambridge: Stephens, 1981.
123. Hamilton, Alexander. *Wings of Night: The Secret Missions of Group Captain Charles Pickard, DSO and 2 Bars.* London: Kimber, 1977.
124. Hansell, Haywood S. *The Air Plan that Defeated Hitler.* Atlanta: Privately Published, 1972.
125. Hardy, M.J. *The de Havilland Mosquito.* New York: Arco, 1977.
126. Haslam, E.B. *The History of Royal Air Force Cranwell.* London: HMSO, 1982.
127. Hastings, Max. *Bomber Command.* London: Joseph, 1979.
128. Haswell, Jock. *British Military Intelligence.* London: Weidenfeld and Nicolson, 1973.
129. Hatch, F.J. *Aerodrome of Democracy: Canada and the British Commonwealth Air Training Plan 1939-1945.* Ottawa: Minister of Supply and Services, 1983.
130. Hendrie, Andrew. *Seek and Strike: The Lockheed Hudson in World War II.* London: Kimber, 1983.
130. (a) Higham, Robin. *Air Power: A Concise History.* London: Macdonalds and New York: St. Martin's Press, 1973; revised and expanded edition, Manhattan, Ks.: Sunflower University Press, 1984.
130. (b) ―――. *Diary of a Disaster: British Aid to Greece, 1940-1941.* Lexington: University Press of Kentucky, 1986.

131. Hill, Robert. *The Great Coup*. London: Arlington, 1977.
131. (a) Hinsley, F.H. et. al. *British Intelligence in the Second World War: Its Influence on Strategy and Operations*. 3 vols. in 4 parts to date. London: HMSO, 1979-
132. Hogg, Ian V. *Anti-Aircraft: A History of Air Defence*. London: Macdonald and Jane's, 1978.
133. Hooton, Ted. *Spitfire Special*. London: Ian Allan, 1972.
134. Horrocks, Sir Brian, ed. *The Red Devils: The Story of British Airborne Forces*. London: Cooper, 1973.
135. Howard, Michael. *The Continental Commitment: The Dilemma of British Defence Policy in the Era of the Two World Wars*. London: Temple Smith, 1972.
136. ―――. *Grand Strategy*. Vol. IV. *August 1942-September 1943*. History of the Second World War. United Kingdom Military Series. London: HMSO, 1972.
137. Hunt, Leslie. *Twenty-One Squadrons: The History of the Royal Auxiliary Air Force: 1925-1957*. London: Garnstone, 1972.
138. *The Hurricane II Manual: The Official Air Publication for the Hurricane IIA, IIB, IIC, IID, IV and Sea Hurricane IIB and IIC, 1941-1945*. RAF Museum Series, vol. 2. London: Arms & Armour, 1976.
139. Hyde, H. Montgomery. *British Air Policy Between the Wars 1918-1939*. London: Heinemann, 1976.
140. Innes, David J. *Beaufighters over Burma: No. 27 Squadron, RAF, 1942-45*. Poole: Blandford, 1985.
141. Insall, A.J. *Observer: Memoirs of the RFC 1915-1918*. London: Kimber, 1970.
142. Jackson, Robert. *Before the Storm: The Story of Royal Air Force Bomber Command, 1939-42*. London: Barker, 1972.
143. ―――. *Bomber! Famous Bomber Missions of World War Two*. London: Barker, 1980.
144. ―――. *Fighter Pilots of World War II*. London: Corgi, 1978.
145. ―――. *Fighter! Story of Air Combat, 1936-1945*. London: Barker, 1979.
146. ―――. *Hawker Hunter*. London: Ian Allan, 1982.
147. ―――. *The Secret Squadrons: Special Duty Units of the RAF and USAAF in the Second World War*. London: Robson, 1983.
148. ―――. *Storm from the Skies: The Strategic Bombing Offensive, 1943-1945*. London: Barker, 1974.
149. ―――. *V-Bombers*. London: Ian Allan, 1981.
150. James, Derek N. *Gloster Aircraft Since 1917*. London: Putnam, 1971.
151. Jaworzyn, J.F. *No Place to Land: A Pilot in Coastal Command*. London: Kimber, 1984.
152. Johnson, Brian, and Heffernan, Terry. *A Most Secret Place: Boscombe Down 1939-45*. London: Jane's, 1982.
153. Jones, Geoffrey P. *Attacker: The Hudson and its Flyers*. London: Kimber, 1980.
154. ―――. *Night Flight: Halifax Squadrons at War*. London: Kimber, 1981.
155. ―――. *Raider: The Halifax and its Flyers*. London: Kimber, 1978.
156. Jones, R.V. *Most Secret War*. London: Hamish Hamilton, 1978.
157. Jones, W.E. *Bomber Intelligence: 103, 150, 166, 170 Squadrons*

Operations & Techniques, '42-'45. Leicester: Midland Counties Publications, 1983.
158. Kelly, Terence. *Hurricane over the Jungle.* London: Kimber, 1977.
159. Kennerly, Byron. *The Eagles Roar!: A Fighter Pilot's Story of World War II with the American Eagle Squadron.* Washington: Zenger, 1980.
160. Kent, J.A. *One of the Few.* London: Kimber, 1971.
161. King, H.F. *Armament of British Aircraft 1909-1939.* London: Putnam, 1971.
162. Kinney, Curtis, with Titler, Dale M. *I Flew a Camel.* Philadelphia: Dorrance, 1972.
163. *The Lancaster Manual: The Official Air Publication for the Lancaster Mk.1 and III, 1942-1945.* RAF Museum Series, vol. 5, London: Arms & Armour, 1977.
164. Lamb, Charles. *War in a Stringbag.* London: Cassell, 1977.
165. Lambert, Bill. *Combat Report.* London: Kimber, 1973.
166. Lavigne, J.P.A. Michel and Edwards, J.F. *Kittyhawk Pilot: Wing Commander J.F. (Stocky) Edwards.* Battleford, Sask.: Turner Warwick Publications, 1983.
167. Lee, Arthur. *Open Cockpit: A Pilot of the Royal Flying Corps.* London: Jarrolds, 1969.
168. Lewin, Ronald. *Ultra Goes to War.* London: Hutchinson, 1978.
169. Lewis, Gwilyn H. *Wings Over the Somme 1916-1918.* Edited by Chaz Bowyer. London: Kimber, 1976.
170. Lewis, Peter H. *Squadron Histories, R.F.C., R.N.A.S. and R.A.F. since 1912.* London: Putnam, 1968.
171. Longmate, Norman. *The Bombers: The RAF Offensive against Germany 1939-1945.* London: Hutchinson, 1983.
172. Lucas, P.B. (Laddie). *Flying Colours: The Epic Story of Douglas Bader.* London: Hutchinson, 1981.
173. ———, ed. *Wings of War: Airmen of All Nations Tell Their Stories, 1939-1945.* London: Macmillan, 1983.
174. Lumsden, Alec. *Wellington Special.* London: Ian Allan, 1974.
175. Lyall, Gavin, ed. *The War in the Air: The Royal Air Force in World War II.* New York: Morrow, 1969.
176. McCarthy, John. *Australia and Imperial Defence 1918-1939: A Study in Air and Sea Power.* St. Lucia, Queensland: University of Queensland Press, 1976.
177. McIntosh, Dave. *Terror in the Starboard Seat.* Markham, Ont.: Paperjacks, 1981.
178. McKinty, Alec. *The Father of British Airships: A Biography of E.T. Willows.* London: Kimber, 1970.
179. McKee, Alexander. *Dresden 1945: The Devil's Tinderbox.* London: Souvenir Press, 1982.
180. MacMillan, Norman. *Into the Blue.* London: Jarrolds, 1969.
181. ———. *Offensive Patrol: The Story of the RNAS, RFC and RAF in Italy 1917-18.* London: Jarrolds, 1973.
182. McVicar, Don. *A Change of Wings.* Shrewsbury: Airlife, 1984.
183. ———. *Ferry Command.* Shrewsbury: Airlife, 1981.
184. ———. *North Atlantic Cat.* Shrewsbury: Airlife, 1983.
185. Mead, P. *The Eye in the Air: History of Air Observation and Reconnaissance for the Army, 1785-1945.* London: HMSO, 1983.

186. Meager, George. *My Airship Flights 1915-1930*. London: Kimber, 1970.
187. Mellor, W. Franklin, ed. *Casualties and Medical Statistics. History of the Second World War. United Kingdom Medical Series*. London: HMSO, 1972.
188. Melnyk, T.W. *Canadian Flying Operations in South East Asia 1941-1945*. Ottawa: Minister of Supply and Services, 1976.
189. Merrick, K.A. *Halifax: An Illustrated History of a Classic World War II Bomber*. London: Ian Allan, 1980.
190. Messenger, Charles. *'Bomber' Harris and the Strategic Bombing Offensive 1939-1945*. London: Arms & Armour, 1984.
191. ————. *Cologne: The First 1000-Bomber Raid*. London: Ian Allan, 1982.
192. Middlebrook, Martin. *The Battle of Hamburg: Allied Bomber Forces Against a German City in 1943*. London: Allen Lane, 1980.
193. ————. *The Nuremberg Raid, 30-31 March 1944*. London: Allen Lane, 1973.
194. ————. *The Peenemünde Raid, The Night of 17-18 August 1943*. London: Allen Lane, 1982.
195. Middlebrook, Martin and Everitt, Chris. *The Bomber Command War Diaries: An Operational Reference Book, 1939-1945*. Harmondsworth: Penguin, 1985.
196. Mitchell, William. *No Medals for the Airmen*. Aylmer, Ont.: Northwood Pub., 1982.
197. Moyes, Philip J.R. *Bomber Squadrons of the Royal Air Force*. Revised edition by John D.R. Rawlings. London: Macdonald, 1976.
198. Morpurgo, J.E. *Barnes Wallis: A Biography*. London: Longman, 1972.
199. Morris, Alan. *First of the Many: The Story of the Independent Force, RAF*. London: Jarrolds, 1968.
200. Morrison, Wilbur H. *Fortress Without a Roof: The Allied Bombing of the Third Reich*. New York: St. Martin's, 1982.
201. *The Mosquito Manual: The Official Air Publications for the Mosquito F. Mk.II, N.F. Mk. XII, and N.F. Mk. XVI, 1941-1945*. RAF Museum Series, vol. 6. London: Arms & Armour, 1977.
202. Musgrove, Gordon. *Operation Gomorrah: The Hamburg Firestorm Raid*. London: Jane's, 1981.
202. (a) ————. *Pathfinder Force: A History of 8 Group*. London: Macdonald and Jane's, 1976.
203. Nesbit, Roy Conyers. *The Strike Wings: Special Anti-Shipping Squadrons, 1942-1945*. London: Kimber, 1984.
204. ————. *Torpedo Airmen: Missions with British Beauforts 1940-42*. London: Kimber, 1983.
205. ————. *Woe to the Unwary: A Memoir of Low-Level Bombing Operations*. London: Kimber, 1981.
206. Nolan, Brian. *Hero: The Buzz Beurling Story*. Toronto: Lester & Orpen Dennys, 1981.
206. (a) Orange, Vincent. *Sir Keith Park*. London: Methuen, 1986.
207. Ormes, Ian and Ormes, Ralph. *Clipped Wings*. London: Kimber, 1973.
208. Overy, D.J. *The Air War 1939-1945*. London: Europa, 1980.
209. Oxspring, Bobby. *Spitfire Command*. London: Kimber, 1985.

210. Parkinson, Roger. *Summer 1940: The Battle of Britain.* New York: David McKay, 1977.
211. Passmore, Richard. *Blenheim Boy.* London: Harmsworth, 1981.
212. Payton-Smith, D.J. *Oil: A Study of Wartime Policy and Administration.* History of the Second World War. United Kingdom Civil Series. London: HMSO, 1971.
213. Peden, G.C. *British Rearmament and the Treasury: 1932-1939.* Edinburgh: Scottish Academic Press, 1979.
214. Peden, Murray. *A Thousand Shall Fall.* Stittsville, Ont.: Canada's Wings, 1979.
215. Penrose, Harold. *British Aviation: The Adventuring Years, 1920-1929.* London: Putnam, 1973.
216. ──────. *British Aviation: The Great War and Armistice 1915-1919.* London: Putnam, 1969.
217. ──────. *British Aviation: The Ominous Skies, 1935-1939.* London: HMSO, 1980.
218. ──────. *British Aviation: The Pioneer Years, 1903-1914.* London: Putnam, 1967.
219. ──────. *British Aviation: Widening Horizons, 1930-1934.* London: HMSO, 1979.
220. Peskett, S. John. *Strange Intelligence: From Dunkirk to Nuremberg.* London: Hale, 1981.
221. Popham, Hugh. *Into The Wind: A History of British Naval Flying.* London: Hamish Hamilton, 1969.
222. Powell, Griffith. *Ferryman.* Shrewsbury: Airlife, 1982.
223. Powers, Barry D. *Strategy Without Slide-Rule: British Air Strategy 1914-1939.* London: Croom Helm, 1976.
224. Price, Alfred. *Aircraft Versus Submarine: The Evolution of the Anti-Submarine Aircraft 1912 to 1972.* London: Kimber, 1973.
225. ──────. *Battle of Britain: The Hardest Day 18 August 1940.* London: Macdonald and Jane's, 1979.
226. ──────. *The Blitz on Britain.* London: Ian Allan, 1977.
227. ──────. *The Bomber in World War II.* London: Macdonald and Jane's, 1976.
228. ──────. *Spitfire: A Documentary History.* London: Macdonald and Jane's, 1977.
229. ──────. *Instruments of Darkness: The History of Electronic Warfare.* London: Macdonald and Jane's, 1977.
230. ──────. *The Spitfire Story.* London: Jane's, 1982.
231. ──────. *Spitfire at War.* London: Ian Allan, 1974.
232. ──────. *Spitfire at War: 2.* London: Ian Allan, 1985.
233. ──────. *World War Two Fighter Conflict.* London: Macdonald, 1975.
234. Price, Alfred, and Ethell, Jeffrey. *Target Berlin: Mission 250, 6 March 1944.* London: Jane's, 1981.
235. Ramsey, Winston G., ed. *The Battle of Britain Then and Now.* London: After the Battle Magazine, 1980.
236. Rawlings, John D.R. *Coastal, Support and Special Squadrons of the RAF and their Aircraft.* London: Jane's, 1982.
237. ──────. *Fighter Squadrons of the R.A.F. and their Aircraft.* London: Macdonald, 1969.
238. Raymond, Robert S. *A Yank in Bomber Command.* New York: Hippocrene Books, 1977.

239. Reader, W.J. *Architect of Airpower: The Life of the First Viscount Weir.* London: Collins, 1968.
240. Reed, Arthur and Beaumont, Roland. *Typhoon and Tempest at War.* London: Kimber, 1974.
241. Renaut, Michael. *Terror by Night: A Bomber Pilot's Story.* London: Kimber, 1982.
242. Richards, Denis. *Portal of Hungerford: The Life of Marshal of the Royal Air Force Viscount Portal of Hungerford KG, GCB, OM, DSO, MC.* London: Heinemann, 1977.
243. Richards, Denis, and Saunders, Hillary St. George. *The Royal Air Force 1939-1945.* London: HMSO, 1974.
244. Richey, Paul. *Fighter Pilot.* London: Jane's, 1980.
245. Roberts, R.N. *The Halifax File.* London: Air-Britain and British Aviation Archaeological Council, 1982.
246. Robertson, Bruce. *Beaufort Special.* London: Ian Allan, 1976.
247. ————. *British Military Aircraft Serials 1912-1969.* London: Ian Allan, 1969.
248. ————. *Lysander Special.* London: Ian Allan, 1977.
249. ————. *The RAF--A Pictorial History.* London: Hale, 1978.
250. ————. *Wheels of the RAF.* Cambridge: Stephens, 1983.
251. Robinson, Douglas H. *The Dangerous Sky: A History of Aviation Medicine.* Seattle: University of Washington Press, 1973.
252. Robinson, Frank. *The British Pensacola Battalion: A Flight Log Representing the British Flight Battalion U.S. Naval Air Station, Pensacola, Florida, 1941-1944.* Manhattan, Kan.: Sunflower University Press, 1984.
253. Rochford, Leonard H. *I Chose the Sky.* London: Kimber, 1977.
254. *The Royal Air Force Regiment--A Short History.* RAF Regiment Fund, 1982.
255. Russell, Wilfrid. *The Friendly Firm: A History of 194 Squadron, R.A.F.* London: 194 Squadron, RAF Association, 1972.
256. Saward, Dudley. *'Bomber' Harris: The Story of Marshal of the Royal Air Force, Sir Arthur Harris, Bt., GCB, OBE, AFC, LLD, Air Officer Commanding-in-Chief, Bomber Command, 1942-1945.* London: Cassell, 1984.
257. Sawyer, Tom. *Only Owls and Bloody Fools Fly at Night.* London: Kimber, 1982.
258. Scott, Desmond. *Typhoon Pilot.* London: Secker & Warburg, 1982.
259. Shay, Robert Paul. *British Rearmament in the 1930s: Politics and Profits.* Princeton, N.J.: Princeton University Press, 1977.
260. Shores, Christopher F. *Ground Attack Aircraft of World War II.* London: Macdonald and Jane's, 1977.
261. ————. *2nd TAF.* Reading: Osprey, 1970.
262. Slessor, Sir John Cotesworth. *These Remain: A Personal Anthology, Memories of Flying, Fighting and Field Sports.* London: Joseph, 1969.
263. Smith, D. *Spitfire into Battle.* London: Murray, 1981.
264. Smith, David J. *Military Airfields of Scotland, the North-East and Northern Ireland.* Cambridge: Stephens, 1983.
265. ————. *Military Airfields of Wales and the North West.* Cambridge: Stephens, 1981.
266. Smith, Malcolm. *British Air Strategy Between the Wars.* Oxford: O.U.P., 1984.

267. Smith, Peter C. *Impact: The Dive Bombers Speak.* London: Kimber, 1981. Also published as *The History of Dive Bombing.* Annapolis, Maryland: Nautical & Aviation, 1981.
268. Smith, Sydney. *Wings Day. The Man Who Led the R.A.F.'s Epic Battle in German Captivity.* London: Collins, 1968.
269. *The Spitfire V Manual: The Official Air Publication for the Spitfire F.V.A., F.V.B., F.V.C., LD.VA., LF.VB., and LF.VC., 1941-1945.* RAF Museum Series, vol. 1. London: Arms & Armour, 1976.
270. Stokes, Doug. *Paddy Finucane--Fighter Ace.* London: Kimber, 1983.
271. Streetly, Martin. *Confound and Destroy: 100 Group and the Bomber Support Campaign.* London: Macdonald and Jane's, 1978.
272. Sweetman, John. *The Dams Raid: Epic or Myth, Operation Chastise.* London: Jane's, 1982.
273. Taylor, John W.R., and Moyes, Philip J.R. *Pictorial History of the Royal Air Force.* 2 vols. London: Ian Allan, 1980.
274. Taylor, Sir Patrick Gordon. *Sopwith Scout 7309.* London: Cassell, 1968.
275. Terraine, John. *The Right of the Line: The Royal Air Force in the European War 1939-45.* London: Hodder & Stoughton, 1985. Also published as *A Time for Courage: The Royal Air Force in the European War 1939-1945.* New York: Macmillan, 1985.
276. Thetford, Owen, *Aircraft of the Royal Air Force Since 1918.* New York: Funk & Wagnalls, 1968.
277. Thomas, C.H. *The Typhoon File.* London: Air Britain and British Aviation Archaeological Council, 1981.
278. Thompson, Walter R. *Lancaster to Berlin.* London: Goodall, 1985.
279. Till, Geoffrey. *Air Power and the Royal Navy 1914-1945: A Historical Survey.* London: Jane's, 1979.
280. Turner, John Frayn. *The Bader Wing.* Tunbridge Wells: Midas Books, 1981.
281. Vee, Roger [Vivian Voss]. *Flying Minnows: Memoirs of a World War One Fighter Pilot, from Training in Canada to the Front Line, 1917-1918.* London: Arms & Armour, 1977.
282. Verity, Hugh. *We Landed at Midnight: Secret RAF Landings in France 1940-44.* London: Ian Allan, 1979.
283. Verrier, Anthony. *The Bomber Offensive.* London: Batsford, 1968.
284. Waddington, C.H. *O.R. in World War 2: Operational Research Against the U-boat.* London: Elek Science, 1973.
285. Wainwright, John. *Tail-end Charlie.* London: Macmillan, 1978.
286. Wallace, G.F. *The Guns of the Royal Air Force 1939-1945.* London: Kimber, 1972.
287. Weal, Elke C.; Weal, John F.; and Barker, Richard F. *Combat Aircraft of World War Two.* London: Arms & Armour, 1977.
288. Whitehouse, Arch. *The Military Airplane: Its History and Development.* New York: Doubleday, 1971.
289. Winter, Denis. *The First of the Few.* London: Allen Lane, 1982.
290. Winterbotham, F.W. *The Ultra Secret.* London: Weidenfeld and Nicolson, 1974.

291. Williams, Geoffrey. *Wings Over Westgate.* Maidstone, Kent: Privately Published, 1986.
292. Wise, S.F. *Canadian Airmen and the First World War. The Official History of the Royal Canadian Air Force.* Vol. 1. Toronto: University of Toronto Press, 1980.
293. Wright, Robert. *Dowding and the Battle of Britain.* London: Macdonald, 1969.
294. Wright, Robert, and Deighton, Len. *Battle of Britain.* London: Cape, 1980.
295. Wynn, H., and Young, S. *Prelude to Overlord.* Shrewsbury: Airlife, 1983.

XV

THE BRITISH ARMY, 1919-1945

Keith Neilson

Writing in Higham's *Guide*, John Keegan remarked on the "unworked character" of research on the British army in the inter-war period. "It will indeed," he concluded, "for some time be difficult to know where to begin" the research necessary to clarify matters. In the same volume, M.J. Williams, writing on the period from 1939 to 1945, echoed Keegan's assessment, noting that "scholarly research is needed in almost every sphere." Such is no longer the case. In the last fifteen years, the opening of the British archives and the greater academic attention paid to military history have yielded an impressive flow of works that have enlarged our knowledge of military affairs for the period from 1919 to 1945 enormously.

The amount of primary sources now available is substantial (and somewhat intimidating). While there is no adequate substitute for a visit to the Public Record Office (PRO) at Kew, the following gives a general indication of the riches held there. For the period of World War II, the PRO itself has produced a booklet outlining its holdings (158). The following classes of papers are useful for the inter-war period: in the Cabinet (Cab) papers, Cab 2 (Committee of Imperial Defence minutes), Cab 4 (CID miscellaneous memoranda), Cab 16 (CID sub-committees), Cab 21 (registered files), Cab 23 (Cabinet minutes), Cab 24 (Cabinet papers), Cab 27 (Cabinet committees), Cab 29 (conference reports and notes), Cab 53 (meetings and memoranda of Chiefs of Staff), Cab 55 (meetings and memoranda of the Joint Planning Sub-Committee); in the War Office (WO) papers, WO 32 (general series), WO 33 (miscellaneous), WO 106 (Directorate of Military Operations and Intelligence), WO 163 (minutes of the Army Council). This is but a brief overview. There is much material of interest in the Foreign Office (FO) records (particularly in FO 371, the political files for individual countries), the official papers of the prime ministers (PREM files), the Treasury files and, collaterally for the army, the papers of the other two (Admiralty and Royal Air Force) services. For those who are interested in the army from the point of view of foreign affairs, there is an excellent published guide to sources on foreign policy by Sidney Aster (8). The papers of private individuals are now available in plenitude. There are three repositories of significance: the Liddell Hart Centre for Military Archives, King's College; the collection at Churchill College, Cambridge and that at the Imperial War Museum. The archivists at all three centres can provide up-to-date information, but there is an invaluable published guide available in Chris Cook's series of volumes (43).

The shape of historical work concerning the British army in the inter-war era was set in 1972. In that year, Michael Howard argued that British defence policy was faced by a constant dilemma: whether to focus on defending the Empire or to concentrate on a "continental commitment" (85). The more detailed discussions that have followed in general have utilized this dilemma as the framework for their discussions, although not all of Howard's contentions have been accepted (150). By far the best look at military affairs, 1918-1939, is Brian Bond's superb *British Military Policy between the Two World Wars* (26). Based on the author's own wide-ranging investigations, and those of a large number of his graduate students, Bond's survey puts all historians in his debt and serves as the best starting point for any would-be researcher. Bond has placed his own work in a wider context with a second book, *War and Society in Europe, 1870-1970* (30), a volume that stands as the most useful general study available. D. Cameron Watt's stimulating look at European armed forces from 1919 to 1939 provides a wider perspective for the purely British case (188), while there are some interesting essays in the collection edited by Adrian Preston (157). The first volume of the British official history on grand strategy, by N.H. Gibbs, covers much of the same ground as Bond's *British Military Policy*, but in the wider context of national strategy (67). Correlli Barnett has added two controversial and important books. The first, a survey of the British army since 1509, trumpets the value of the army--as opposed to the navy--to Britain over the course of three and a half centuries (14). The second, concentrating on the modern era, remains the most determined argument for a continental commitment yet presented (15). A useful interpretative essay on British defense policy by Hew Strachan helps put the controversies of the subject in intelligible order (173).

While 1918 brought the end of World War I, it did not bring an end to the fighting for the British army. The next four years saw a continuing need for a military effort, one pursued perforce with diminished resources. Keith Jeffery's excellent volume, *The British Army and the Crisis of Empire 1918-22*, makes it clear just how far responsibilities outran resources and explains how attempts were made to cope with this problem (91). Jeffery has rendered two other valuable services with his editorial work on the correspondence of Sir Henry Wilson, the Chief of the Imperial General Staff (CIGS), 1918-1922 (93) and with his fine article on the post-war army (94). The problems for the British army were geographically wide-ranging. The British intervention in Russia can be followed to its inglorious conclusion in the final two volumes of Ullman's trilogy on Anglo-Soviet relations (181), while there is much of interest in the published diaries of Lord Ironside dealing with his various tasks after leaving the Russian imbroglio (89). Nor were British problems confined to Russia. The Irish problem was at least as controversial, if not as ideological. Here, the work of D.G. Boyce (31) and, in particular, Charles Townshend (176, 177, 178) make clear the military dimensions of this problem. There is also useful information about the troubles in Ireland in Richard Holmes' fine biography of Sir John French (84). British military problems stretched also into the Middle East and India. Two works by B.C. Busch, on the Arabs and the west Asian frontier respectively (32, 33), make it clear that the task far exceeded the tools available. John Darwin's concise study illustrates that British problems in Egypt were closely linked to the Middle East generally (47). While Aden was not a major problem for British defense planners, R.J. Gavin shows that it had a continuing influence for a century and a quarter (66). Marian Kent's fine book on Mesopotamia illustrates that economic concerns were often intertwined with military considerations, particularly when it came to oil concessions (101a).

From 1922 to 1939, as conflicting priorities chased diminished resources, the army found itself in competition with the other service ministries. The major works that have been written about the inter-war defense problems reflect this fact. So, too, do they reflect the changing nature of military history. More and more, recent studies have moved away from what may be called the "purely military" aspects of the complicated issue of national defense towards studies that embrace the economic, financial, political and technological aspects of military matters. While many of the following works are concerned with the army only partially, or indirectly, they are essential for a rounded understanding of more purely terrene matters.

For the Royal Navy, the late Stephen Roskill's two volumes on policy provide a comprehensive guide (163). Roskill's final two volumes of his biography of Lord Hankey are important for naval--indeed for all defense--matters (162). Air policy has received extensive coverage. The best of these is also the most recent, Malcolm Smith's, *British Air Strategy between the Wars*. which illustrates clearly the relationship between doctrine, finance and general defense policy (170). Also useful are two other studies that cover the period as a whole, Hyde's *British Air Policy between the Wars, 1918-1939* (87) and Powers' *Strategy without Slide-rule: British Air Strategy, 1914-1939* (155). A more specific study by Uri Bialer concentrates on the influence that the possibility of air attack had for British policy (22). Of rather marginal value are two volumes by H. Penrose (152, 153).

We have been well served with respect to the economic realities behind military policy. The inability of the army to squeeze more money out of the Treasury is explicated fully in two fine works, G.C. Peden's *British Rearmament and the Treasury 1932-1939* (149) and Robert Shay, Jr., *British Rearmament in the Thirties: Politics and Profits* (169). Of the two, Peden tends to see the situation more in the context of limited choices, while Shay is critical of the choices made without suggesting alternatives that were both possible and politically acceptable. Paul Kennedy's wide-ranging look at the realities behind diplomacy is useful in this context (100). Shay and Peden's works should be augmented by a number of articles that deal with some of the details surrounding the economic and financial preparations for war. Peden himself has contributed a close look at Sir Warren Fisher's attitudes (151), while R.A.C. Parker has looked at the Treasury's relationship with labor (147) and the American government's views on sterling (148). Also of interest are two German works, one dealing with the economic aspects of British policy towards Germany (190); the other with British defense policy generally, but with a political scientists' eye (130). There is a useful discussion of the literature on this subject by J. Dunabin (51).

The general question of defense policy in the 1930s is tied, willy-nilly, to the question of appeasement. In addition to the studies in the previous paragraphs, there are a number of important works dealing with these two general themes. One of the best is Larry Pratt's superb study of British policy in the Mediterranean (156). Peter Dennis uses the issue of conscription to illustrate how British defense planners were caught between preparing a large army for a "continental commitment" and a smaller one for a war of "limited liability" (48). Patrick Kyba illustrates nicely that British public opinion failed to move in favor of rearmament as late as 1935 (106), while Maurice Cowling shows that the shadow of Hitler was pervasive in British policy making (44). With this in mind, David Carlton's biography of Eden should be consulted (37). Also important is Keith Middlemas, *Diplomacy of Illusion* (133), while his biography of Baldwin, written with John Barnes, is thorough if not always revealing (134).

The question of appeasement itself has been put in its longer perspective in an illuminating article by Paul Kennedy (101). D. Cameron Watt has provided two useful review articles summarizing the trends in the historiography and suggesting new avenues of approach (186, 187). There is a very good detailed survey of appeasement in the English-speaking world by Ritchie Ovendale, that shows the context in which British thinking on the subject had to operate (146). A useful study by C.A. Macdonald looks closely at American attitudes towards appeasement and shows just how well informed the White House was of British attitudes (121).

On the more purely military side of things, there are two important books that delineate clearly, although they do not agree with each other, some of the thinking that shaped the military contribution to the immediate pre-war political decisions. Wesley Wark's look at British military intelligence appreciations of German strength in the 1930s shows clearly that preconceived ideas determine conclusions just as much as do the data actually gathered (185). Wark's subtle and nuanced approach finds little sympathy in Williamson Murray's controversial look at the balance of power prior to 1939 (137a). In hanging judge fashion, Murray is sharply critical of the British for crediting Germany with a power greater than she possessed, and argues that Germany's relative weakness was evident. On the whole, Wark's approach seems more likely to explain what actually, as opposed to what should have, happened, a fact that a close reading of the diaries of Sir Henry Pownall--who as assistant and then deputy secretary to the CID and later as Director of Military Operations and Intelligence was well-placed to know such matters--confirms (27).

The inter-war army can not be left before taking a look at those thinkers who attempted to shape its approach to war. Once again, we owe a debt of thanks to Brian Bond for his study of Liddell Hart's varied contributions to military history and defense debate (29). There is a good survey of the British military intellectuals by Robin Higham (82), but this must be supplemented by the more detailed work below. Lord Carver has produced a thin volume on armored warfare (38), while the details of Fuller's theories on armored warfare have been developed clearly by Brian Holden Reid (159). Reid should be read in conjunction with Trythall's biography of Fuller (180), a book that makes clear the difficulties faced by a man who wished to champion radical reform in a period of financial restraint. Charles Messenger, in a wider look at blitzkrieg, has something of interest for those concerned with British military theorists, albeit in a European-wide context (129). Ronald Lewin's study of Vyvyan Pope suggests that Britain had at least one commander who fully appreciated the value of the tank, but his premature death leaves this as conjecture (112). Of immense value, and wide scope, is Bidwell and Graham's *Fire-Power*, a book that looks at both weapons and theories of war in the period from 1904 to 1945 (24).

The army was concerned not only with external but also with internal enemies in the period between the wars. Often, although not nearly as frequently as many of its continental counterparts, the army spent its energies giving aid to the civil power. The special case of Ireland has been discussed above, but there were others. Jeffery and Hennessy's excellent survey of the use of the military against strikers is essential reading (95). This should be supplemented by some specific studies. Rothstein on 1919 is an uneven personal account (164). The reliability of the army itself as an instrument against social unrest needs further study, although there is a good look at it for the period from 1917 to 1921 (55). That the army was well aware of the problems that giving aid to the civil power engendered is clear from Keith Jeffery's fine article (92), while Peter Dennis demonstrates that plans to use the Territorials in such a role foundered as a result of fears for the latter's unreliability (49). The fear of Bolshevism among ex-servicemen was widespread according to S.R. Ward (183), who has also written penetratingly on the fate of former military men (184).

Until recently, intelligence was the "missing dimension" in diplomatic and military studies. Fortunately, this is no longer the case. Wark's book, cited above, has shown just how important knowledge of one's enemies is for the formulation of defense policy. The fine collection of essays, edited by Ernest May, lets us know just how much (or how little) the various powers knew of the military capacities of their likely opponents (127). Christopher Andrew's witty and erudite look at the British secret service has much of interest for the military historian, and provides an excellent bibliography of both primary and secondary source materials pertaining to intelligence (7). There is much dealing with the inter-war period in the first volume of F.H. Hinsley's official history of intelligence in World War II (83). This is an area of growth for researchers, who should be aware that there is a new journal specifically devoted to matters of intelligence (88).

The British defense position in the Far East has been a particular favorite of historians. Echoing Howard's dilemma of Imperial versus Continental commitment, these studies tend to show that limited resources resulted in limited defense capability. The first intimation that Britain had to some extent written off the Far East came with the decision not to renew the Anglo-Japanese alliance, a decision that Ian Nish has delineated clearly (143). The subsequent decline in Anglo-Japanese relations can be followed in Peter Lowe (118) and in a collection of essays edited by Nish (144). On the naval side of the Anglo-Japanese rivalry, Marder's *Old Friends, New Enemies* (125) is essential. The larger picture of British defense planning in this region can be found in W.R. Louis' fine study, *British Strategy in the Far East 1919-1939* (116).

A number of special studies offer differing conclusions--
although all agree that the problem was one of limited resources--as
to what Britain should have done to defend her position in the Far
East. Paul Haggie's examination of the British response to the
Japanese threat concludes that commitments should have been cut to
fit resources (74). Neidpath's definitive study of the defense of
Singapore (138) suggests that the naval reductions agreed to at
London in 1930 meant that defense against Japan was impossible, while
McGibbon's study of the defense of New Zealand suggests that there
was little alternative to the policy actually followed (122). As to
the British position in China, a number of fine studies show how
military weakness dictated policy. Of particular note are the books
by Bradford A. Lee (110), Anne Trotter (179), S.L. Endicott (54) and
Aron Shai (168).

Many of the preceding books also figure closely on the origins
of the war. There are some specific studies, though, that are
important for military historians as well as for those interested in
the purely diplomatic issues. Sidney Aster's account of 1939 has
stood the test of recent archival work and remains a lucid survey
(9). Another fine account is Adamthwaite (1), while Kaiser has
looked at economic interests in eastern Europe to provide a new slant
on war origins (97). The reasoning behind the British guarantee to
Poland has been clearly outlined by Newman (140), although here
Wark's (185) study on military appreciations of military strength
provides a corrective.

Writings on World War II have multiplied endlessly during the
last fifteen years. One of the ways in which this has been evidenced
is in the emergence of some fine surveys. Perhaps the best of these,
which takes a wide look at the conflict, is *Total War* by Calvocoressi
and Wint (36). A more purely military view of events can be found in
Liddell Hart's *History of the Second World War* (115). Henri Michel
provides a view of the war largely from the French perspective (131),
while John Lukacs concentrates on the effect that the war had on
European society (120). There have also appeared some bibliographic
and reference books, although it should be made clear that none of
them are entirely satisfactory and must be supplemented by the
bibliographies in the major works cited below. A.G.S. Ensor has
published a useful work, dealing with works in English written
between 1939 and 1974 (56). Well organized is Gwyn Bayliss' volume,
which has the added advantage of covering both world wars (18), while
John Keegan's encyclopedia of World War II is an accurate, if
limited, source (98). Also helpful is the guide to manuscripts
compiled by Mayer and Koenig (128), although this must be
supplemented by Cook (43). A very good volume, although one that
concentrates heavily on American matters, is compiled by Myron J.
Smith Jr. (171).

Once the war began, there was little initially for the army to
do. The German threat to Scandinavia provided an early question
concerning just what the army was capable of doing. The Russo-
Finnish war, and the allied response to it, is covered well in Jukka
Nevakivi (139), although this should be supplemented by Bayer's
recent article on British deliberations (17). The Norwegian campaign
has not attracted recent attention, but a joint Norwegian work (in
English) allows a wider perspective to be taken, and introduces the
non-English literature (5). A recent article on allied attitudes to

Scandinavia as a whole makes it clear that the attitude of the Soviet Union underpinned all thinking (11). There is a fine study that deals with the issue of Sweden and iron ore for Germany which is of use (137).

The war in France has produced several fine studies. Pride of place goes to Brian Bond for his graceful account of that campaign (28), although Eleanor Gates has also written trenchantly on the subject (65). There is a lucid, popular account of the battle for the Channel ports (69), and Colville's biography of Gort saves that soldier from charges of incompetence (40). The above works focus on the British perspective and for balance it is necessary to consult some more French-oriented studies. The background to the French collapse is presented masterfully by Duroselle (52) in a telling indictment of pre-war French society. François Bédarida looks at the effort (or, rather, the lack of effort) to co-ordinate Anglo-French defense plans during the phoney war (20), while Jeffrey Gunsburg takes a sympathetic look at the problems of the French high command (72). There are valuable essays in the collection edited by Preston (157), but the best look at the French military position is that of Young (192). Of course, Anglo-French relations did not end with the creation of Vichy, and here R.T. Thomas' *Britain and Vichy* shows how the existence of two French governments created a wide range of diplomatic problems for the British (174). The factors that influenced Churchill to carry on the war after the fall of France have been examined with some detail by David Reynolds (160).

It is important to remember that Britain fought the war in the context of a coalition. The Anglo-Soviet alliance was an awkward one, complicated as it was by severe ideological differences as well as by the usual quarrels involving differing national interests. Gabriel Gorodetsky outlines clearly the initial problems between the two partners through a look at the ambassadorship of Sir Stafford Cripps (70). Sheila Lawlor points out just how little confidence the British had in the Soviet Union's military capacity (109), a belief that events initially confirmed. The Anglo-Soviet alliance was one that centered to a great extent around economic co-operation, and here Joan Beaumont is definitive on the purely British contribution to the Soviet war effort (19). As American aid to Stalin became intertwined with that of Britain, Beaumont should be read in conjunction with a fine study of American aid to the U.S.S.R. by George C. Herring (80) and an interesting account of the initial Anglo-American economic mission to Moscow (108). The Soviet alliance was not an easy one for Britain, and Lothar Kettenacker traces the strains on the partnership caused by differing views as to the post-war fate of Germany (102). For an excellent account of how the Soviet Union viewed the support of its allies, John Erickson's two volumes (57, 58) are essential reading. The road to the Cold War, including its war-time antecedents can be found in two valuable books, by Rothwell from the British perspective (165) and by Mastny from the Soviet (126).

The other great alliance was the Anglo-American one. Its pre-1941 roots have been elegantly laid bare by David Reynolds (161). There are two superb books that both examine, although from different angles, similar aspects of the Anglo-American relationship. Christopher Thorne's *Allies of a Kind* shows that the two English-speaking allies were pursuing rather different ends in their war with

Japan (175), while W.R. Louis demonstrates that the United States looked with hostility upon the continuing existence of the British Empire (117). Warren Kimball is very good on lend-lease (104), but there is no definitive study of Anglo-American economic relations and how they influenced military decisions. The views of the British embassy in Washington are available in published form (141), although this must be seen as subordinate to the complete records available at the PRO. A good book, although one concentrating on establishing the reasons for diminished Anglo-American co-operation after the war is Hathaway's suitably entitled, *Ambiguous Partnership* (79). Another useful book in this genre is Anderson (6). When the next volume of Gilbert's biography of Churchill (68)--now complete to 1941--is published, undoubtedly much more of the "special relationship" will be revealed, although there has already been a massive amount of the Churchill-Roosevelt correspondence published (103). On the military side of the alliance, much of the day to day functioning at the higher policy levels can be followed in David Fraser's biography of Alanbrooke (63).

The war in North Africa has been one where the efforts of biographers have largely held sway. From the publication of Correlli Barnett's *The Desert Generals* in 1960 until 1981 the Auchinleck school dominated. The reaction against Montgomery's claims for his own importance was typified nicely by Alun Chalfont (34), who pointed out the Field Marshal's inability to share credit. The publication of the first volume of the official biography of Montgomery in 1981 challenged such views (76). Since that time, the Montgomery school has dominated concerning North Africa, with Barnett's attempt at rebuttal in a new and enlarged (but not a second edition) of *The Desert Generals* (16) largely unconvincing. Of value for this campaign, as it is for both Italy and Burma, is Nigel Nicolson's biography of Alexander of Tunis (142). Barry Pitt (154) and James Lucas (119) have written recent books on Alamein.

Italy and the Mediterranean have been looked at more thoroughly than before. Michael Howard's volume in the Grand Strategy series is essential (85a), but Keith Sainsbury provides a fuller understanding of the strategic controversy surrounding the landings in North Africa (166, 167). The invasion of Sicily and the struggle in Italy to the spring of 1944 can be found in C.J.C. Molony (136). There is a clear, if popular, account of the Salerno landings by Hickey and Smith (81). The battle for Cassino has received what is likely to be the definitive account by John Ellis (53). There is a fine new survey of the entire Italian campaign by Dominick Graham and Shelford Bidwell that brings the researcher up to date with the latest developments at the same time as providing a clear explanation of what happened (71). The special case of the defense of Malta has received a sympathetic study focussing on the plight of the Maltese (96).

But as would be expected, the efforts of historians have concentrated on the Normandy landings and the subsequent campaign in Europe. Thanks to Hinsley's volumes on intelligence, we have learned a great deal about the value of codebreaking and deception for the success of Overlord (83). While Hinsley largely subsumes earlier, incomplete studies, there is still much of value in Bennett (21), Cruickshank (45) and Lewin (114). Intelligence aside, there have been a number of excellent books written about Normandy. Perhaps the best survey is that of Carlo D'Este (50), although John Keegan's *Six Armies in Normandy* is a fascinating account (99). The final two volumes of Hamilton's biography of Montgomery attempt to vindicate their subject, but with rather less success than with respect to North Africa (75, 77). Despite determined efforts by Hamilton, the picture of Montgomery provided by Lamb is more convincing (107). For an American perspective, Ambrose is essential on Eisenhower (4), and Russell Weigley provides a superb look at Eisenhower's lieutenants (189). Max Hastings has provided a very readable account of the campaign, largely in touch with recent work (78). For those interested in polemics, the prolific David Irving has provided a controversial look at the personalities involved (90).

The war in the Far East has also received attention. The fateful Singapore campaign has had three valuable studies. The first done, by S.W. Kirby (105), is also the best, while Stanley Falk (59) and Louis Allen (3) add useful detail. The Burma campaign is now much more comprehensible. Ronald Lewin's biography of Slim reveals much of the inter-allied squabbling that the latter was too reticent to include in his memoirs (113). Raymond Callaghan has written a useful account of the entire campaign (35), while Shelford Bidwell has contributed a good study of the Chindits (23). Ziegler's biography of Mountbatten (193) has material of interest. By far the best study available is Louis Allen's *Burma, The Longest War* (2), which utilizes both British and Japanese sources to provide a comprehensive look at the war.

For much of the war, Britain's military contribution to the campaign in Europe made itself felt by means of air attack and through the related matters of SOE and resistance movements. With respect to the air, R.J. Overy provides an excellent overview (145). On SOE, a debt is owed to M.R.D. Foot, who has supplemented his official history with a valuable overview (61) and an evaluation of SOE's usefulness (62). Cruickshank shows the problems that SOE encountered in attempting to work on the European model in the Far East (46), while there is an interesting collection of articles on resistance in Yugoslavia and Greece that has much of value for SOE (10). On resistance, the best study from the British perspective is David Stafford (172). For the wider perspective, Jørgen Haestrup is essential (73), while Foot (60) is also important. On south-eastern Europe, Barker (12) shows the tangle that the Balkans created for British policy makers.

The development and expansion of the British army during the war is a neglected topic. David Fraser is good on the men themselves (64), but more is needed on the growth of the high command. Martin van Creveld strikes a blow for the value of the study of logistics in the understanding of strategy (182), while Alan Milward outlines the effect of the war on the British economy (135). Correlli Barnett (13) savages the effort of the wartime economy in a book more designed to explain the present-day difficulties of Britain. On the subject of things technical, William H. McNeill's brilliant look at technology and armed force has much to say about the war (124) and is essential reading.

While much has been done in the fifteen years since the precursor of this volume was published, there is still room for further work. For the inter-war period, the era of the 1920s is still relatively under studied. A look at the effect of the

Treasury's attempts to control the civil service would be of value, as would more detailed examinations of the various attempts at arms control. For the war, much needs to be written to integrate what we now know about intelligence with previous writings about strategy. More work, too, needs to be done on matters technical, especially in an effort to show how closely they were linked with the rarefied heights of grand strategy.

BIBLIOGRAPHY

1. Adamthwaite, Anthony. *The Making of the Second World War*. London: Allen and Unwin, 1977.
2. Allen, Louis. *Burma, The Longest War, 1941-45*. London: J.M. Dent, 1984.
3. —————. *Singapore 1941-1942*. London: Davis-Poynter, 1977.
4. Ambrose, Stephen E. *The Supreme Commander: The War Years of General Dwight D. Eisenhower*. London: Cassell, 1968.
5. Andenaes, Johs.; Riste, Olav; and Skodvin, Magne. *Norway and the Second World War*. 3rd. ed. Tanum: Norli, 1983.
6. Anderson, Terry H. *The United States, Great Britain, and the Cold War, 1944-1947*. Columbia, Miss.: University of Missouri Press, 1981.
7. Andrew, Christopher. *Secret Service: The Making of the British Intelligence Community*. London: Heinemann, 1985.
8. Aster, Sidney. *British Foreign Policy, 1918-1945: A Guide to Research and Research Materials*. Wilmington, Del.: Scholarly Resources Inc., 1984.
9. —————. *1939: The Making of the Second World War*. London: Andrew Deutsch, 1973.
10. Auty, Phyllis and Clogg, Richard (eds.). *British Policy Towards Wartime Resistance in Yugoslavia and Greece*. New York: Barnes and Noble, 1975.
11. Barclay, Glen St. J. "Diversion in the East: The Western Allies, Scandinavia, and Russia, November 1939-April 1940." *Historian*, 41, 3 (1979), 483-98.
12. Barker, Elisabeth. *British Policy in South-East Europe in the Second World War*. New York: Barnes and Noble, 1976.
13. Barnett, Correlli. *The Audit of War*. London: Macmillan, 1986.
14. —————. *Britain and Her Army, 1509-1970: A Military and Political Survey*. London: Allen Lane, 1970.
15. —————. *The Collapse of British Power*. London: Eyre Methuen, 1972.
16. —————. *The Desert Generals*. Bloomington, Ind.: Indiana University Press, 1982 [new and enlarged reprint of 1960 edition].
17. Bayer, J.A. "British Policy Towards the Russo-Finnish Winter War 1939-40." *Canadian Journal of History*, 16, 1 (1981), 27-65.
18. Bayliss, Gwyn. *Bibliographic Guide to the Two World Wars: An Annotated Survey of English-Language Reference Materials*. New York: Bowker, 1977.
19. Beaumont, Joan. *Comrades in Arms: British Aid to Russia 1941-1945*. London: Davis-Poynter, 1980.

20. Bédarida, François. *La stratégie secrète de la drôle de guerre: Le Conseil Suprême Interallié, Septembre 1939-Avril 1940.* Paris: Presses de la Foundation Nationale des Sciences Politiques et Editions du CNRS, 1979.
21. Bennett, Ralph. *Ultra in the West: The Normandy Campaign of 1944-45.* London: Hutchinson, 1979.
22. Bialer, Uri. *The Shadow of the Bomber: The Fear of Air Attack and British Politics, 1932-1939.* London: Royal Historical Society, 1980.
23. Bidwell, Shelford. *The Chindit War.* London: Hodder and Stoughton, 1979.
24. ———— and Graham, Dominick. *Fire-Power: British Army Weapons and Theories of War 1904-1945.* London: Allen and Unwin, 1982.
25. Bidwell, R.G. *Gunners at War.* London: Arms and Armour Press, 1970.
26. Bond, Brian. *British Military Policy between the Two World Wars.* Oxford: Clarendon Press, 1980.
27. ———— (ed.). *Chief of Staff: The Diaries of Lieutenant-General Sir Henry Pownall.* 2 volumes. London: Leo Cooper, 1972-1974.
28. ————. *France and Belgium, 1939-1940.* London: Davis-Poynter, 1975.
29. ————. *Liddell Hart: A Study of His Military Thought.* London: Cassell, 1977.
30. ————. *War and Society in Europe, 1870-1970.* Leicester: Leicester University Press, 1984.
31. Boyce, D.G. *Englishmen and Irish Troubles.* London: Jonathan Cape, 1972.
32. Busch, Briton Cooper. *Britain, India and the Arabs.* Berkeley and London: University of California Press, 1971.
33. ————. *Mudros to Lausanne: Britain's Frontier in West Asia, 1918-1922.* Albany, N.Y.: State University of New York Press, 1976.
34. Chalfont, Alun. *Montgomery of Alamein.* New York: Atheneum, 1976.
35. Callaghan, Raymond. *Burma 1942-1945.* London: Davis-Poynter, 1978.
36. Calvocoressi, Peter and Wint, Guy. *Total War: The Story of World War II.* New York: Pantheon Books, 1972.
37. Carlton, David. *Anthony Eden: A Biography.* London: Allen Lane, 1981.
38. Carver, Field Marshal Lord. *The Apostles of Mobility: The Theory and Practice of Armoured Warfare.* London: Weidenfeld and Nicolson, 1979.
39. Ceadal, Martin. *Pacifism in Britain, 1914-1945: The Defining of a Faith.* London and New York: Oxford University Press, 1980.
40. Colville, J.R. *Man of Valour: Field Marshal Lord Gort, V.C.* London: Collins, 1972.
41. Connell, John. *Wavell, Scholar and Soldier: To June 1941.* London: Collins, 1964.
42. ————. *Wavell, Supreme Commander, 1941-1943.* London: Collins, 1969.

43. Cook, Chris. *Sources in British Political History 1900-1951.* 6 vols. London: Macmillan, 1975-1985.
44. Cowling, Maurice. *The Impact of Hitler. British Politics and British Policy, 1933-1940.* Cambridge: Cambridge University Press, 1975.
45. Cruickshank, Charles. *Deception in World War II.* Oxford: Oxford University Press, 1979.
46. ———. *SOE in the Far East.* Oxford: Oxford University Press, 1984.
47. Darwin, John. *Britain, Egypt and the Middle East.* London: Macmillan, 1975.
48. Dennis, Peter. *Decision by Default: Peacetime Conscription and British Defence 1919-1939.* London: Routledge and Kegan Paul, 1972.
49. ———. "The Territorial Army in Aid of the Civil Power in Britain, 1919-1926." *Journal of Contemporary History,* 16 (1981), 705-24.
50. D'Este, Carlo. *Decision in Normandy.* New York: E.P. Dutton, 1983.
51. Dunabin, J. "British Rearmament in the 1930s: A Chronology and Review." *Historical Journal,* 18, 3 (1975), 587-609.
52. Duroselle, Jean-Baptiste. *La décadence, 1932-1939.* Paris: Imprimerie Nationale, 1979.
53. Ellis, John. *Cassino: The Hollow Victory.* New York: McGraw-Hill, 1984.
54. Endicott, S.L. *Diplomacy and Enterprise: British China Policy 1933-1937.* Manchester: Manchester University Press, 1977.
55. Englander, David and Osborne, James. "Jack, Tommy, and Henry Dubb: The Armed Forces and the Working Class." *Historical Journal,* 21, 3 (1978), 593-621.
56. Ensor, A.G.S. *A Subject Bibliography of the Second World War: Books in English 1939-1974.* London: Andre Deutsch, 1977.
57. Erickson, John. *The Road to Berlin. Stalin's War With Germany.* Volume II. London: Weidenfeld and Nicolson, 1983.
58. ———. *The Road to Stalingrad: Stalin's War With Germany.* Volume I. London: Weidenfeld and Nicolson, 1975.
59. Falk, Stanley. *Seventy Days to Singapore.* New York: G.P. Putnam's Sons, 1975.
60. Foot, M.R.D. *Resistance.* London: Eyre Methuen, 1976.
61. ———. *SOE: An Outline History of the Special Operations Executive, 1940-46.* London: British Broadcasting Corporation, 1984.
62. ———. "Was SOE any Good?" *Journal of Contemporary History,* 16 (1981), 167-81.
63. Fraser, David. *Alanbrooke.* London: Collins, 1982.
64. ———. *And We Shall Shock Them: The British Army in the Second World War.* London: Stodder and Houghton, 1983.
65. Gates, Eleanor M. *End of the Affair: The Collapse of the Anglo-French Alliance, 1939-40.* Berkeley and Los Angeles: University of California Press, 1981.
66. Gavin, R.J. *Aden Under British Rule 1839-1967.* London: C. Hurst, 1975.
67. Gibbs, N.H. *Grand Strategy.* Volume I. London: HMSO, 1976.
68. Gilbert, Martin. *Finest Hour: Winston S. Churchill, 1939-1941.* London: Heinemann, 1983.

69. Glover, Michael. *The Fight for the Channel Ports*. London: Leo Cooper, 1985.
70. Gorodetsky, Gabriel. *Stafford Cripps' Mission to Moscow, 1940-1942*. Cambridge: Cambridge University Press, 1984.
71. Graham, Dominick and Bidwell, Shelford. *Tug of War: The Battle for Italy, 1943-45*. London: Hodder and Stoughton, 1986.
72. Gunsburg, Jeffrey A. *Divided and Conquered: The French High Command and the Defeat of the West 1940*. Westport and London: Greenwood Press, 1979.
73. Haestrup, Jørgen. *Europe Ablaze: An Analysis of the European Resistance Movements, 1939-45*. Odense: Odense University Press, 1978.
74. Haggie, Paul. *Britannia at Bay: The Defence of the British Empire Against Japan 1931-1941*. Oxford: Clarendon Press, 1981.
75. Hamilton, Nigel. *Monty: Master of the Battlefield, 1942-1944*. London, Hamish Hamilton, 1983.
76. ―――. *Monty: The Making of a General, 1887-1942*. London: Hamish Hamilton, 1981.
77. ―――. *Monty: The Field-Marshal, 1944-1976*. London: Hamish Hamilton, 1986.
78. Hastings, Max. *Overlord: D-Day and the Battle for Normandy*. London: Michael Joseph, 1984.
79. Hathaway, Robert M. *Ambiguous Partnership: Britain and America, 1944-1947*. New York: Columbia University Press, 1981.
80. Herring, George C., Jr. *Aid to Russia 1941-1946: Strategy, Diplomacy, The Origins of the Cold War*. New York and London: Columbia University Pres, 1973.
81. Hickey, Des and Smith, Gus. *Operation Avalanche: The Salerno Landings, 1943*. London: Heinemann, 1983.
82. Higham, Robin. *The Military Intellectuals in Britain, 1918-1939*. New Brunswick, N.J.: Rutgers University Press, 1966.
83. Hinsley, F.H., et al. *British Intelligence in the Second World War: Its Influence on Strategy and Operations*. 3 vols. London: HMSO, 1979-1984.
84. Holmes, Richard. *The Little Field Marshal: Sir John French*. London: Jonathan Cape, 1981.
85. Howard, Michael. *The Continental Commitment: The Dilemma of British Defence Policy in the Era of Two World Wars*. London: Temple Smith, 1972.
85. (a) ―――. *Grand Strategy*. vol. IV. *August 1942-Sept. 1943*. London: HMSO, 1970 [1972].
86. ―――. *War and the Liberal Conscience*. London: Oxford University Press, 1981.
87. Hyde, H. Montgomery. *British Air Policy between the Wars, 1918-1939*. London: Heinemann, 1976.
88. *Intelligence and National Security*. London: Frank Cass, 1986-
89. Ironside, Lord (ed.). *High Road to Command: The Diaries of Maj.-Gen. Sir Edmund Ironside 1920-22*. London: Leo Cooper, 1972.
90. Irving, David. *War between the Generals*. London: Allen Lane, 1981.
91. Jeffery, Keith. *The British Army and the Crisis of Empire, 1918-1922*. Manchester: Manchester University Pres, 1984.

92. ———. "The British Army and Internal Security 1919-1939." *Historical Journal*, 24, 2 (1981), 377-97.
93. ——— (ed.). *The Military Correspondence of Field Marshal Sir Henry Wilson 1918-1922*. London: Army Records Society, 1985.
94. ———. "The Post-War Army," in *A Nation in Arms: A Social Study of the British Army in the First World War*. edited by I.F.W. Beckett and Keith Simpson. Manchester: Manchester University Press, 1985, 211-34.
95. ——— and Hennessy, Peter. *States of Emergency: British Governments and Strikebreaking since 1919*. London: Routledge and Kegan Paul, 1983.
96. Jellison, Charles A. *Besieged: The World War II Ordeal of Malta 1940-1942*. Hanover, N.H.: University Press of New England, 1984.
97. Kaiser, David E. *Economic Diplomacy and the Origins of the Second World War: Germany, Britain, France and Eastern Europe, 1930-1939*. Princeton: Princeton University Press, 1980.
98. Keegan, John. *Rand McNally Encyclopedia of World War II*. Chicago: Rand McNally, 1977.
99. ———. *Six Armies in Normandy*. London: Jonathan Cape, 1982.
100. Kennedy, Paul. *The Realities Behind Diplomacy: Background Influences on British External Policy, 1865-1980*. London: Allen and Unwin, 1980.
101. ———. "The Tradition of Appeasement in British Foreign Policy 1865-1939." *British Journal of International Studies*, 2 (1976), 195-215.
101. (a) Kent, Marian. *Oil & Empire: British Policy & Mesopotamian Oil 1900-1920*. London: Macmillan, 1976.
102. Kettenacker, Lothar. "The Anglo-Soviet Alliance and the Problem of Germany, 1941-1945." *Journal of Contemporary History*, 17 (1982).
103. Kimball, Warren F. *Churchill and Roosevelt: The Complete Correspondence*. 3 volumes. Princeton: Princeton University Press, 1984.
104. ———. *The Most Unsordid Act: Lend-Lease 1939-1941*. Baltimore: Johns Hopkins Press, 1969.
105. Kirby, S.W. *Singapore: The Chain of Disaster*. London: Cassell, 1971.
106. Kyba, Patrick. *Covenants without the Sword: Public Opinion and British Defence Policy, 1931-1935*. Waterloo, Ontario: Wilfrid Laurier University Press, 1983.
107. Lamb, Richard. *Montgomery in Europe, 1943-1945: Success or Failure?* New York: Franklin Watts, 1983.
108. Langer, John Daniel. "The Harriman-Beaverbrook Mission and the Debate over Unconditional Aid for the Soviet Union, 1941." *Journal of Contemporary History*, 14 (1979), 463-82.
109. Lawlor, Sheila. "Britain and the Russian entry into the War," in *Diplomacy and Intelligence during the Second World War Essays in Honour of F.H. Hinsley*. edited by Richard Langhorne. Cambridge: Cambridge University Press, 1985 168-83.
110. Lee, Bradford A. *Britain and the Sino-Japanese War, 1937-1939*

A Study in the Dilemmas of British Decline. Stanford: Stanford University Press, 1973.
111. ─────. "Strategy, Arms and the Collapse of France 1930-40," in *Diplomacy and Intelligence during the Second World War: Essays in Honour of F.H. Hinsley.* edited by Richard Langhorne. Cambridge: Cambridge University Press, 1985, 43-67.
112. Lewin, Ronald. *Man of Armour: A Study of Lieut.-General Vyvyan Pope.* London: Leo Cooper, 1976.
113. ─────. *Slim the Swordbearer.* London: Leo Cooper, 1976.
114. ─────. *Ultra Goes to War.* London: Hutchinson, 1978.
115. Liddell Hart, B.H. *History of the Second World War.* New York: G.P. Putnam's Sons, 1971.
116. Louis, Wm. Roger. *British Strategy in the Far East, 1919-1939.* Oxford: Clarendon Press, 1971.
117. ─────. *Imperialism at Bay: The United States and the Decolonization of the British Empire, 1941-1945.* Oxford: Clarendon Press, 1977.
118. Lowe, Peter. *Great Britain and the Origins of the Pacific War: A Study of British Policy in East Asia, 1927-1941.* Oxford: Clarendon Press, 1977.
119. Lucas, James. *The War in the Desert: The Eighth Army at El Alamein.* London: Arms and Armour Press, 1982.
120. Lukacs, John. *The Last European War: September 1939-December 1941.* Garden City, N.Y.: Anchor Press, 1976.
121. Macdonald, C.A. *The United States, Britain and Appeasement, 1936-1939.* New York: St. Martin's Press, 1981.
122. McGibbon, I.C. *Blue-Water Rationale: The Naval Defence of New Zealand 1914-1942.* Wellington: Government Printing Office, 1982.
123. Macksey, Kenneth. *A History of the Royal Armoured Corps and its Predecessors 1914 to 1975.* Beaminster: Newton Publications, 1983.
124. McNeill, William H. *The Pursuit of Power: Technology, Armed Force, and Society since A.D. 1000.* Chicago: University of Chicago Press, 1982.
125. Marder, Arthur J. *Old Friends, New Enemies: The Royal Navy and the Imperial Japanese Navy. Strategic Illusions, 1936-1941.* Oxford: Clarendon Press, 1981.
126. Mastny, Vojtech. *Russia's Road to the Cold War: Diplomacy, Warfare and the Politics of Communism, 1941-1945.* New York: Columbia University Press, 1979.
127. May, Ernest R. (ed.). *Knowing One's Enemies: Intelligence Assessment before the Two World Wars.* Princeton: Princeton University Press, 1984.
128. Mayer, S.L. and Koenig, W.J. *The Two World Wars: A Guide to the Manuscript Collections in the United Kingdom.* New York: Bowker, 1976.
129. Messenger, Charles. *The Art of Blitzkrieg.* London: Ian Allen, 1976.
130. Meyers, Reinhard. *Britische Sicherheitspolitik, 1934-1938: Studien zur aussen-und sicherheitspolitischen Entscheidungsprozess.* Düsseldorf: Droste Verlag, 1976.
131. Michel, Henri. *The Second World War.* New York: Praeger, 1975.

132. ———. *The Shadow War: European Resistance 1939-1945.* translated by Richard Barry. New York: Harper and Row, 1972.
133. Middlemas, Keith. *Diplomacy of Illusion: The British Government and Germany 1937-39.* London: Weidenfeld and Nicolson, 1972.
134. ——— and Barnes, John. *Baldwin: A Biography.* London: Weidenfeld and Nicolson, 1969.
135. Milward, Alan. *War, Economy and Society, 1939-1945.* London: Allen Lane, 1977.
136. Molony, C.J.C. *The Mediterranean and the Middle East.* volume V. London: HMSO, 1973.
137. Munch-Petersen, Thomas. *The Strategy of the Phoney War: Britain, Sweden and the Iron Ore Question 1939-1940.* Stockholm, 1981.
137. (a) Murray, Williamson. *The Change in the European Balance of Power, 1938-1939: The Path to Ruin.* Princeton: Princeton University Press, 1984.
138. Neidpath, James. *The Singapore Naval Base and the Defence of Britain's Eastern Empire, 1919-1941.* Oxford: Clarendon Press, 1981.
139. Nevakivi, Jikka. *The Appeal That Was Never Made: The Allies, Scandinavia and the Finnish Winter War, 1939-1940.* Montreal: McGill-Queen's University Pres, 1976.
140. Newman, Simon. *March 1939: The British Guarantee to Poland.* Oxford: Oxford University Press, 1976.
141. Nicholas, H.G. (ed.). *Washington Despatches, 1941-1945: Weekly Political Reports from the British Embassy.* Chicago: University of Chicago Press, 1981.
142. Nicolson, Nigel. *Alex: The Life of Field Marshal Earl Alexander of Tunis.* New York: Atheneum, 1973.
143. Nish, Ian H. *Alliance in Decline: A Study in Anglo-Japanese Relations, 1908-23.* London: Athlone, 1972.
144. ——— (ed.). *Anglo-Japanese Alienation, 1919-1952.* Cambridge: Cambridge University Press, 1982.
145. Overy, R.J. *The Air War, 1939-1945.* London: Europa, 1980.
146. Ovendale, Ritchie. *'Appeasement' and the English Speaking World: Britain, the United States, the Dominions and the Policy of 'Appeasement', 1937-1939.* Cardiff: The University of Wales Press, 1975.
147. Parker, R.A.C. "British Rearmament, 1936-1939: Treasury, Trade Unions and Skilled Labour." *English Historical Review,* 96 (1981), 306-43.
148. ———. "The Pound Sterling, the American Treasury and British Preparations for War, 1938-1939." *English Historical Review,* 98 (1983), 261-79.
149. Peden, G.C. *British Rearmament and the Treasury 1932-1939.* Edinburgh: Scottish Academic Press, 1979.
150. ———. "The Burden of Imperial Defence and the Continental Commitment Reconsidered." *Historical Journal,* 27, 2 (1984), 405-23.
151. ———. "Sir Warren Fisher and British Rearmament against Germany." *English Historical Review,* 94 (1979), 29-47.
152. Penrose, H. *British Aviation: Ominous Skies, 1935-1939.* London: HMSO and the Royal Air Force Museum, 1980.

153. ———. *British Aviation: Widening Horizons, 1930-1934*. London: HMSO and the Royal Air Force Museum, 1979.
154. Pitt, Barrie. *The Crucible of War: Year of Alamein 1942*. London: Jonathan Cape, 1982.
155. Powers, Barry D. *Strategy without Sliderule: British Air Strategy 1914-1939*. London: Croom Helm, 1976.
156. Pratt, Lawrence R. *East of Malta, West of Suez. Britain's Mediterranean Crisis, 1936-1939*. Cambridge: Cambridge University Press, 1975.
157. Preston, Adrian (ed.). *General Staffs and Diplomacy before the Second World War*. London: Croom Helm, 1978.
158. Public Record Office. *The Second World War: A Guide to the Documents in the Public Record Office*. London: HMSO, 1972.
159. Reid, Brian Holden. "J.F.C. Fuller's Theory of Mechanized Warfare." *Journal of Strategic Studies*, 1, 3 (1978), 295-312.
160. Reynolds, David. "Churchill and the British 'Decision' to fight on in 1940: Right Policy, Wrong Reason," in *Diplomacy and Intelligence during the Second World War: Essays in Honour of F.H. Hinsley*. edited by Richard Langhorne. Cambridge: Cambridge University Press, 1985, 147-67.
161. ———. *The Creation of the Anglo-American Alliance, 1937-1941: A Study in Competitive Co-operation*. London: Europa, 1981.
162. Roskill, Stephen. *Hankey. Man of Secrets*. 3 volumes. London: Collins, 1970-1974.
163. ———. *Naval Policy between the Wars*. 2 volumes. London: Collins, 1968-1976.
164. Rothstein, Andrew. *The Soldiers' Strikes of 1919*. London: Macmillan, 1980.
165. Rothwell, Victor. *Britain and the Cold War, 1941-1947*. London: Jonathan Cape, 1982.
166. Sainsbury, Keith. *The North African Landings 1942: A Strategic Decision*. London: Davis-Poynter, 1976.
167. ———. "'Second Front in 1942'--A Strategic Controversy Revisited." *British Journal of International Studies*, 4 (1978), 47-58.
168. Shai, A. *Origins of the War in the East: Britain, China and Japan 1937-1939*. London: Croom Helm, 1976.
169. Shay, Robert Paul, Jr. *British Rearmament in the Thirties: Politics and Profits*. Princeton: Princeton University Press, 1977.
170. Smith, Malcolm. *British Air Strategy between the Wars*. Oxford: Clarendon Press, 1984.
171. Smith, Myron J., Fr. *World War II: The European and Mediterranean Theatres. An Annotated Bibliography*. New York and London: Garland, 1984.
172. Stafford, David. *Britain and European Resistance 1940-1945*. London: Macmillan, 1980.
173. Strachan, Hew. "The British Way in Warfare Revisited." *Historical Journal*, 26, 2 (1983), 447-61.
174. Thomas, R.T. *Britain and Vichy: The Dilemma of Anglo-French Relations 1940-42*. London: Macmillan, 1979.
175. Thorne, Christopher. *Allies of a Kind: The United States,*

Britain and the War against Japan 1941-1945. London: Hamish Hamilton, 1978.
176. Townshend, Charles. The British Campaign in Ireland, 1919-1921: The Development of Political and Military Policies. Oxford: Oxford University Press, 1975.
177. ―――――. "The Irish Insurgency, 1918-21: The Military Problem," in Regular Armies and Insurgency. edited by Ronald Haycock. London: Croom Helm, 1979, 32-52.
178. ―――――. "The Irish Republican Army and the Development of Guerrilla Warfare, 1916-1921." English Historical Review, 94 (1979), 318-45.
179. Trotter, Anne. Britain and East Asia, 1922-1937. Cambridge: Cambridge University Press, 1975.
180. Trythall, Anthony John. "Boney" Fuller: Soldier, Strategist and Writer, 1878-1966. New Brunswick, N.J.: Rutgers University Press, 1977.
181. Ullman, Richard H. Anglo-Soviet Relations, 1917-1921. 3 volumes. Princeton: Princeton University Press, 1961-1973.
182. van Creveld, Martin. Supplying War: Logistics from Wallenstein to Patton. Cambridge: Cambridge University Press, 1978.
183. Ward, S.R. "Intelligence Surveillance of British Ex-Servicemen, 1918-1920." Historical Journal, 16, 1 (1973), 179-88.
184. ―――――. The War Generation: Veterans of the First World War. Port Washington, N.Y.: Kennikat, 1975.
185. Wark, Wesley. The Ultimate Enemy: British Intelligence and Nazi Germany, 1933-1939. Ithaca, N.Y.: Cornell University Press, 1985.
186. Watt, Donald Cameron. "Appeasement: The Rise of a Revisionist School?" Political Quarterly, 36 (1965), 191-213.
187. ―――――. "The Historiography of Appeasement," in Crisis and Controversy: Essays in Honour of A.J.P. Taylor. edited by A. Sked and C. Cook. New York: St. Martin's, 1976.
188. ―――――. Too Serious a Business: European Armed Forces and the Approach to the Second World War. London: Temple Smith, 1975.
189. Weigley, Russell F. Eisenhower's Lieutenants: The Campaigns of France and Germany, 1944-1945. Bloomington, Ind.: Indiana University Press, 1981.
190. Wendt, B.-J. Economic Appeasement: Handel und Finance in der britische Deutschlandpolitik, 1933-39. Düsseldorf: Droste, 1971.
191. Wheeler, Mark C. Britain and the War for Yugoslavia, 1940-1943. New York: Columbia University Press, 1980.
192. Young, Robert J. In Command of France: French Foreign Policy and Military Planning, 1933-1940. Cambridge, Mass. and London: Harvard University Press, 1978.
193. Ziegler, Philip. Mountbatten. New York: Alfred A. Knopf, 1985.

XVI

THE HOME FRONT IN THE SECOND WORLD WAR

Harold L. Smith

This chapter includes materials published since 1969 which fall into the categories of political, social, diplomatic, or cultural-intellectual history. In light of the enormous outpouring of studies bearing on the Second World War, it necessarily is selective rather than exhaustive. It is intended to provide a guide to the major works of scholarship in the four areas within the purview of this chapter, and to identify other bibliographies and guides likely to be of interest to a researcher. Items mentioned in the original bibliography by Margaret Gowing and A.H.K. Slater are not repeated as it is assumed the reader will use their bibliography in conjunction with this one.

Several bibliographic guides to the Second World War have been issued since the Gowing and Slater essay appeared. The volumes by Bayliss (19), Enser (71, 72), and Ziegler (226) are especially helpful. Researchers planning to examine files in the Public Record Office should consult two P.R.O. handbooks: *The Second World War: A Guide to Documents in the Public Record Office* (164) and *The Cabinet Office to 1945* (166). The List and Index Society has sponsored the printing of guides to several classes of records in the Public Record Office; the guides to War Cabinet Memoranda (35, 36), for example, should not be overlooked by anyone concerned with policy-making at the highest level of government. Scholars who intend to use collections of private papers will find the multi-volume *Sources in British Political History 1900-1951*, edited by Chris Cook and Jeffrey Weeks, indispensable. Narrower in scope, but also worth consulting, are Janet Percival's (160) guide to the archives and manuscript collections in the University of London, the guide to the Modern Records Centre at the University of Warwick edited by Richard Storey and Janet Druker (193), and the guide to the Churchill College Archives Centre issued by Churchill College (44). Finally, anyone engaged in research on the Second World War should contact the Imperial War Museum Department of Documents; its holdings include unpublished materials on a wide variety of civilian as well as military topics.

When Gowing and Slater wrote their essay there were few studies of wartime political life. The opening of the public records and many collections of private papers to researchers since then has made possible considerable improvement in this area. Of special importance is Paul Addison's (5) *The Road to 1945* which provides the fullest narrative account of the transformation of British politics during the war. *The Churchill Coalition* by J.M. Lee (118) is a perceptive brief study focusing on the administrative machinery of government with topical rather than chronological chapters. Henry Pelling's (158) *Britain and the Second World War* is a well-informed comprehensive study which draws attention to the connections between the domestic and military aspects of the war. Addison (2) and A.J.P. Taylor (199) have contributed chapters on the coalition government in separate volumes of essays. Although only portions of the volumes by Keith Middlemas (143) and Maurice Cowling (56) discuss wartime politics, both books have stimulated much controversy and should be noted. John Ramsden (167) provides some information on the Conservative Party, while Trevor Burridge (32) draws attention to the Labour Party's influence on wartime foreign policy. David Howell (100) is useful on the discussion of domestic policy within the Labour Party. The records of the Conservative (50, 51, 52) and the Labour Party (112, 113, 114) have been published, as have the Fabian Society's (73) Executive Committee minutes and some correspondence. Wartime by-elections have been studied by Addison (3), while Pelling (156) and William Harrington (83) should be consulted on the 1945 general election.

Our understanding of wartime political life has benefited considerably from biographies of prominent political figures. Martin Gilbert (79), in the sixth volume of the authorized biography of Churchill, provides a detailed account of Winston Churchill's activities during the critical years 1939 through 1941. Addison's (4) chapter on Churchill in a volume devoted to British Prime Ministers is well worth careful study. Pelling's (159) biography of Churchill devotes seven chapters to the war years, but it was published before many of the relevant records became available. Several other studies also discuss Churchill's wartime role (39, 48, 54, 103, 122, 205).

Other cabinet ministers have also been the subject of major biographical works. The volumes by Kenneth Harris (88) and Burridge (33) enhance Clement Attlee's reputation, while Ben Pimlott's (162) life of Hugh Dalton draws upon Dalton's Second World War diary, as well as other sources, in developing a sympathetic portrait of a complex personality. Bernard Donoughue and G.W. Jones (66) have reconstructed Herbert Morrison's career from limited sources. Elizabeth Barker (17) has drawn attention to the stormy relationship between Churchill and Anthony Eden. Eden's life is critically examined by David Carlton (40); Lord Beaverbrook receives a more sympathetic treatment from Taylor (201). Brendan Bracken (26, 128), Maurice Hankey (150, 174), Samuel Hoare (59), and Harold Macmillan (75) have also been the subject of recent biographies. Other prominent political figures whose biographies have been written include Lord Swinton (60), Christopher Addison (147), Harold Nicolson (120), Ellen Wilkinson (211), Lady Astor (197), and John Strachey (203). Jose Harris' (87) study of William Beveridge clarifies the assumptions underlying the views of one of the most important individuals outside the government.

The autobiographies, diaries, and letters of politically active individuals provide a rich source for students of wartime politics. Especially valuable is the diary of John Colville (49), Churchill's private secretary, which offers a revealing behind-the-scenes portrait of Churchill as Prime Minister, as well as impressions of those who were part of Churchill's inner circle of advisors. It is rivaled in importance only by Dalton's diary (161) which documents at length the infighting within the coalition government. Other works within this group which should be consulted on wartime politics include those by R.A. Butler (34), Robert Boothby (23), John Reith (194), Tom Driberg (68), Douglas Jay (104), Lionel Robbins (171), Harold Balfour (14), Duff Cooper (53), David Eccles (70), George Wigg (217), Oliver Harvey (91), and Alexander Cadogan (64).

Considerable attention has been devoted to the various agencies concerned with shaping public opinion during the war. Ian McLaine's (141) study of the Ministry of Information has much to say about public attitudes as well as government efforts to influence public opinion. Michael Balfour (15), Ken Short (181), Nicholas Pronay (163), and Francis Thorpe (207) should also be consulted on the government's propaganda. The Home Intelligence reports edited by Addison (1) are packed with information about wartime public opinion on a considerable variety of topics. Also useful on public opinion are the Mass Observation (90) reports, now available on microfiche; a selection of the reports has been edited by Angus Calder (38). The results of some of the more important Gallup polls have been published in book form (77). The wartime news media have attracted considerable attention from historians. Two studies by Asa Briggs (27, 28) make good use of BBC archival material in tracing the wartime development of that institution; the works by Gerald Mansell (134) and Andrew Boyle (25) contain additional information of the BBC. The typescripts used by newsreaders for the BBC (30) *Home Service Nine O'Clock News* program are now available on microfiche. Donald McLachlan (140), David Ayerst (11), A.J.P. Taylor (198), and C.H. Rolph (173) shed new light on the editors of *The Times*, the *Observer*, the *Manchester Guardian*, and the *New Statesman* respectively. Other studies of the press include Ayerst (12) on the *Manchester Guardian*, Tom Hopkinson (98) on the *Picture Post*, and Cecil King (107) on the *Daily Mirror*. Finally, Stephen Koss' (110) history of the changing role of twentieth century newspapers includes two important chapters on the wartime press.

Although some important work has been done on social history since Gowing and Slater wrote their essay, Calder's (37) earlier study remains the best general history of British society during the war. John Stevenson's (192) *British Society 1914-1945* provides a valuable analysis of inter-war social trends, some of which continued after 1939, but is rather brief on the war itself. Alan Milward's *War, Economy and Society 1939-1945* (144) focuses rather more on economics than social history. The volumes by Susan Briggs (29) and Arthur Marwick (139) make extensive use of photographs to illustrate wartime social change. Marwick's two essays (136, 137) develop the thesis that the war was a watershed in British social history. Most of the contributors to *War and Social Change: British Society in the Second World War*, edited by Harold L. Smith (185), find Marwick's view unconvincing. The volume contains interpretive essays on areas in which the war is thought to have initiated lasting changes: Penny Summerfield discusses social class, Jay Winter demography, Deborah Thom education, Harold L. Smith women, Dan Fox the health service, John Stevenson the planning movement, John Macnicol the evacuation of schoolchildren, Henry Pelling the Labour Party, R.J. MacLeod employment policy, and Jose Harris political ideas and the concept of the Welfare State. The studies by Norman Longmate (123, 125), Tom Harrison (89), and George Beardmore (20) convey a sense of what everyday life was like for civilians during the war. These accounts may be supplemented by the diaries of Nella Last (31), Doris White (216), Clara Milburn (65), Barbara Pym (97), and Vera Hodgson (96). Longmate's (124) account of the G.I.'s in Britain suggests how Britons were affected by the presence of a foreign army in their country. On other topics John Macnicol (132) and Hilary Land (115) discuss the campaign for family allowances, Edward Smithies (188) comments on wartime crime, Arthur Marwick (138) traces the changing image of class, Elizabeth Merson (142) suggests how children were affected by the war, Joanna Mack (129) and Leonard Mosley (148) describe the war's impact on London, Travis Crosby (58) examines the civilian evacuation from urban centers, and Jay Winter (221) considers the war's effect on infant mortality. The *Bibliography of British Economic and Social History* edited by W.H. Chaloner (43) and R.C. Richardson should be consulted for additional works relevant to this area.

Several studies shed new light on the wartime changes in health care and education. On the origins of the National Health Service the works by Dan Fox (76), Rudolf Klein (108), and John E. Pater (155) deserve special mention. Much of the writing on education is concerned with the origins and nature of the 1944 Education Act. P.H.J.H. Gosden's (82) volume should be the starting point for investigations into the evolution of wartime education policy. Readers concerned with the origins of the Education Act should also consult the articles by Jeffereys (105) and Wallace (212). Brian Simon (182) provides a stimulating account of the political struggle over educational reform at the beginning of the war.

Considerable progress has been made during the past fifteen years in our understanding of the war's effect on women. Penny Summerfield's (196) study of women workers and government policy toward them is of special interest. The histories of trade union women by Sheila Lewenhak (121) and Sarah Boston (24) include valuable chapters on the attitude of trade unions toward women workers. Two articles by Harold L. Smith (186, 187) describe the efforts by feminist groups to widen employment opportunities for women and to obtain equal pay for them. Margaret Allen (9) makes explicit some of the contradictions in the cultural assumptions underlying the government's womanpower policies. Denise Riley (169, 170) draws attention to the ambivalence in the government's attitude toward working mothers. The records of the Labour Party Women's Group (111) include some information on the views of Labour women on women's issues as well as other matters. Elizabeth Wilson (220) has drawn attention to the implications of the Beveridge Report and wartime social policy for the position of women. On the issue of family planning during the war the reader should consult Audrey Leathard (117). John Costello (55) provides information on marriage and sexuality during the war in *Love Sex and War: Changing Values 1939-1945*. Raynes Minns (145) devotes considerable attention to housewives in her discussion of the domestic front. The autobiographies of Dora Russell (179), Leah Manning (133), and Jennie Lee (119) enable the reader to trace the effect of the war on individual women in greater detail. The Fawcett Library, which specializes in materials on women's history, holds the papers of several feminist groups active during the war. A catalogue of the Fawcett Library's (74) collection of printed materials is available on microfiche. The *Biographical Dictionary of British Feminists*, vol. 2. *1930-1945* by Olive Banks is scheduled for publication late in 1986 and should be very helpful in identifying feminists active during the Second World War.

A good general study of the trade unions and industrial relations during the war is lacking. The appropriate chapters in Henry Pelling's (157) history of the trade unions and Ross Martin's (135) account of the TUC provide a summary of major developments. These should be supplemented by Walter Citrine's (45) account of his activities, and especially by Richard Croucher's (61) stimulating volume on engineers at war. The records of the TUC General Council (209, 210) and its major committees (208) are now available, as are the Ministry of Labour (165) records on industrial disputes and industrial relations policy. Eric Wigham (219) has a good, although brief, chapter on wartime industrial relations. James Hinton (94) reviews Communist influence among Coventry factory workers. Henry Parris (153), Eric Wigham (218), and Alan Clinton (46) should be consulted on civil service unions during the war. The extensive bibliographies by G.S. Bain (13) and Harold Smith (184) will be useful to anyone wishing to go further into this area.

Other studies have covered a wide range of subjects relating to the war. Pacifism has been examined by Rachel Barker (18), Martin Ceadel (42), and Francis Partridge (154), civil liberties by Neil Stammers (191), British policy toward the European Jews by Bernard Wasserstein (214), the treatment of internees by Miriam Kochran (109), Oswald Mosley by Robert Skidelsky (183), the political activities of exiles in Britain by Anthony Glees (80), the British Armed Forces education program by Penny Summerfield (195), London firemen by Neil Wallington (213), film censorship by James Robertson (172), and the wartime role of Political and Economic Planning by Michael Young (225).

Although excellent work has been done on some topics, there is no outstanding general study of wartime cultural and intellectual developments. Robert Hewison (93) comes closest, but his volume is restricted to literary figures. Bernard Crick's (57) biography is good on George Orwell's wartime activities, including his difficulties in finding a publisher willing to risk the government's wrath by publishing his controversial book, *Animal Farm*. There have been several valuable studies of Labour intellectuals: Margaret Cole (47) and Luther Carpenter (41) are best on G.D.H. Cole, Ross Terrill (202) on R.H. Tawney, and Granville Eastwood (69) on Harold Laski. Linda Shires (180) should be consulted on wartime poetry, Anthony Aldgate and Jeffrey Richards (7) on the cinema, and Alan Ross (175) on war art. But for information on many wartime intellectuals their own letters and diaries are the best source. See, for example, the letters of Sidney and Beatrice Webb (130) and Virginia Woolf (151), and the diaries of Evelyn Waugh (63), Beatrice Webb (131), and Virginia Woolf (21). The autobiographies of Malcolm Muggeridge (149) and A.J.P. Taylor (200) are also of some interest.

Sir Llewellyn Woodward's (222) five volume work is the official history of British wartime foreign policy. Warren Kimball's (106) edition of the Churchill-Roosevelt correspondence documents diplomatic activity at the highest level. Also contributing to our understanding of U.S.-British relations are the studies by Robert Hathaway (92), Joseph Lash (116), Roger Louis (126), David Reynolds (168), Christopher Thorne (206), and Donald C. Watt (215). P.M.H. Bell (22), Eleanor Gates (78), Roger Parkinson (152), and R.T. Thomas

(204) are useful on British policy toward France. British-Russian relations are discussed by Gabriel Gorodetsky (81), Graham Ross (176), and Victor Rothwell (177). On British policy toward South-Eastern Europe see G.M. Alexander (8) and Elizabeth Barker (16). Peter Lowe (127) and R.J. Moore (146) should be consulted by those interested in British policy in Asia. Specialists in diplomatic history will find the extensive annotated bibliography provided by Sidney Aster (10) very helpful.

Several sources are useful in keeping abreast of new research on the Second World War. One of the best is the *Annual Bulletin of Historical Literature* issued by the Historical Association of Great Britain (95). The Royal Historical Society (178) also publishes an annual bibliography, but, unlike that provided by the Historical Association, it is not annotated. The Society for the Study of Labour History (190) provides an annual bibliography in its *Bulletin* which includes a wide range of materials beyond what might be construed as "labour" history in the narrowest sense of the term. The *Newsletter* of the Social History Society of Great Britain (189) should be consulted, as well as the annual bibliographies in the *Economic History Review* and the *English Historical Review*. Two annual publications by the Institute of Historical Research (101, 102) are especially helpful in monitoring research by young scholars: *Theses in Progress* and *Theses Completed*. Robert Donovan's (67) volume lists research projects on British Studies in progress by North American scholars. Finally, Keith Robbins' bibliography of British history for the period since 1914 in the Oxford University Press series (jointly sponsored by the American Historical Association and the Royal Historical Society of Great Britain) is forthcoming and should be of considerable value to researchers.

Several areas requiring additional research have been indicated in the preceding pages. In addition to these there is a need for a study of the wartime Conservative Party making use of its archives, which are now available at the Bodleian Library; for biographies of R.A. Butler and Stafford Cripps; for an account of reconstruction planning and demobilization using P.R.O. files; and for a full-scale examination of the effect which American troops stationed in Britain had on British culture. Also, we are still lacking studies of women white-collar workers; the wartime feminist movement; the family, including marital relationships; and the debate over the population question which led to the appointment during the war of a Royal Commission on Population. Finally, it would be very useful to have a social history of wartime Britain focused explicitly on categories of social analysis, such as social class and social structure, and drawing upon the new sources which have become available since Calder's *The People War* was published.

BIBLIOGRAPHY

1. Addison, Paul (ed.). *The British People and World War II: Home Intelligence Reports on Opinion and Morale 1940-1944.* Brighton: Harvester Press, 1978 (microfiche).
2. Addison, Paul. "Journey to the Centre: Churchill and Labour in Coalition, 1940-1945" in Alan Sked and Chris Cook (eds.)

Crisis and Controversy: Essays in Honour of A.J.P. Taylor. London: Macmillan, 1976.
3. ―――――. "The By-Elections of the Second World War" in Chris Cook and John Ramsden (eds.) By-Elections in British Politics. London: Macmillan, 1973.
4. ―――――. "Winston Churchill" in John P. Mackintosh (ed.) British Prime Ministers in the Twentieth Century, vol. 2. Churchill to Callaghan. London: Weidenfeld and Nicolson, 1978.
5. ―――――. The Road to 1945. London: Jonathan Cape, 1975.
6. Agar, Herbert. Britain Alone, June 1940-June 1941. London: Bodley Head, 1972.
7. Aldgate, Anthony and Jeffrey Richards. Britain Can Take It: The British Cinema in the Second World War. Oxford: Blackwell, 1985.
8. Alexander, G.M. The Prelude to the Truman Doctrine: British Policy in Greece, 1944-1947. Oxford: Clarendon Press, 1982.
9. Allen, Margaret. "The Domestic Ideal and the Mobilization of Womanpower in World War II," Women's Studies International Forum, VI (1983).
10. Aster, Sidney. British Foreign Policy: A Guide to Research and Materials. Wilmington: Scholarly Resources, 1984.
11. Ayerst, David. Garvin of the "Observer." London: Croom Helm, 1985.
12. ―――――. The Manchester Guardian: Biography of a Newspaper. London: Collins, 1971.
13. Bain, G.S. (ed.). A Bibliography of British Industrial Relations. Cambridge: Cambridge University Press, 1979.
14. Balfour, Harold. Wings Over Westminster. London: Hutchinson, 1973.
15. Balfour, Michael. Propaganda in War, 1939-1945: Organizations, Politics and Publics in Britain and Germany. London: Routledge, 1979.
16. Barker, Elizabeth. British Policy in Southeast Europe in the Second World War. London: Macmillan, 1976.
17. ―――――. Churchill and Eden at War. London: Macmillan, 1978.
18. Barker, Rachel. Conscience, Government and War: Conscientious Objection in Great Britain, 1939-45. London: Routledge, 1982.
19. Bayliss, Gwyn. A Bibliographic Guide to the Two World Wars. London: Bowker, 1977.
20. Beardmore, George. Civilians at War: Journals 1938-1946. London: Murray, 1984.
21. Bell, Anne O. (ed.). The Diary of Virginia Woolf. Vol. 5, 1936-1941. London: Hogarth Press, 1984.
22. Bell, P.M.H. A Certain Eventuality: Britain and the Fall of France. Farnborough: Saxon House, 1974.
23. Boothby, Robert. Boothby: Recollections of A Rebel. London: Hutchinson, 1978.
24. Boston, Sarah. Women Workers and the Trade Union Movement. London: Davis-Poynter, 1980.
25. Boyle, Andrew. Only the Wind Will Listen: Reith of the BBC. London: Hutchinson, 1972.

26. ―――――. *Poor Dear Brendan. The Quest for Brendan Bracken.* London: Hutchinson, 1974.
27. Briggs, Asa. *A History of Broadcasting in the United Kingdom,* vol. III. *The War of Words.* London: Oxford University Press, 1970.
28. ―――――. *The BBC: The First Fifty Years.* Oxford: Oxford University Press, 1985.
29. Briggs, Susan. *Keep Smiling Through: The Home Front 1939-1945.* London: Weidenfeld and Nicolson, 1975.
30. British Broadcasting Corporation. *The Home Service Nine O'Clock News 1939-1945.* Cambridge: Chadwyck-Healey, microfiche.
31. Broad, Richard and S. Fleming (eds.). *Nella Last's War: A Mother's Diary 1939-45.* Bristol: Falling Wall Press, 1981.
32. Burridge, Trevor. *British Labour and Hitler's War.* London: Deutsch, 1976.
33. ―――――. *Clement Attlee: A Political Biography.* London: Cape, 1986.
34. Butler, Lord. *The Art of the Possible: The Memoirs of Lord Butler.* London: Hamish Hamilton, 1971.
35. Cabinet Office. *List of War Cabinet Memoranda (CAB 66) 1939 Sept.-1945 July.* London: Swift, 1977.
36. ―――――. *List of War Cabinet Memoranda (CAB 67 and 68) 1939 Sept.-1942 Dec..* London: Swift, 1978.
37. Calder, Angus. *The People's War.* London: Jonathan Cape, 1969.
38. ―――――― and Dorothy Sheridan (eds.). *Speak for Yourself: A Mass-Observation Anthology, 1937-49.* London: Jonathan Cape, 1984.
39. Callahan, Raymond. *Churchill: Retreat from Empire.* Wilmington: Scholarly Resources, 1984.
40. Carlton, David. *Anthony Eden.* London: Allen Lane, 1981.
41. Carpenter, Luther. *G.D.H. Cole: An Intellectual Biography.* Cambridge: Cambridge University Press, 1973.
42. Ceadel, Martin. *Pacifism in Britain, 1914-1945: The Defining of a Faith.* Oxford: Oxford University Press, 1981.
43. Chaloner, W.H. and R.C. Richardson (eds.). *A Bibliography of British Economic and Social History.* Manchester: Manchester University Press, 1984.
44. Churchill College. *A Guide to the Holdings of the Churchill College Archives Centre.* Cambridge: Churchill College, 1980.
45. Citrine, Lord [Walter]. *Two Careers.* London: Hutchinson, 1967.
46. Clinton, Alan. *The Post Office Workers: A Trade Union and Social History.* London: Allen and Unwin, 1984.
47. Cole, Margaret. *The Life of G.D.H. Cole.* London: Macmillan, 1971.
48. Colville, John. *The Churchillians.* London: Weidenfeld and Nicolson, 1981.
49. ―――――. *The Fringes of Power: 10 Downing Street Diaries 1939-1955.* London: Hodder and Stoughton, 1985.
50. Conservative and Unionist Party. *Executive Committee Minutes of the National Union of Conservative Associations, 1897-1956, together with Central Council Minutes and Annual Reports.* Brighton: Harvester, microfiche.
51. ―――――. *Minutes and Reports of the Conservative Party Conferences, 1867-1946.* Brighton: Harvester, microfilm.

52. ―――. *Pamphlets and Leaflets. Part 5: 1938-1949.* Brighton: Harvester, microfiche.
53. Cooper, Artemis (ed.). *A Durable Fire: The Letters of Duff and Diana Cooper, 1913-1950.* London: Collins, 1983.
54. Cosgrave, Patrick. *Churchill at War.* London: Collins, 1974.
55. Costello, John. *Love Sex and War: Changing Values 1939-45.* London: Collins, 1985.
56. Cowling, Maurice. *The Impact of Hitler: British Politics and British Policy 1933-1940.* London: Cambridge University Press, 1975.
57. Crick, Bernard. *George Orwell: A Life.* London: Secker and Warburg, 1980.
58. Crosby, Travis. *The Impact of Civilian Evacuation in the Second World War.* London: Croom Helm, 1986.
59. Cross, John A. *Sir Samuel Hoare: A Political Biography.* London: Cape, 1977.
60. ―――. *Lord Swinton.* Oxford: Oxford University Press, 1982.
61. Croucher, Richard. *Engineers at War 1939-1945.* London: Merlin, 1982.
62. Davenport, Nicholas. *Memoirs of a City Radical.* London: Weidenfeld and Nicolson, 1974.
63. Davie, Michael (ed.). *The Diaries of Evelyn Waugh.* London: Weidenfeld and Nicolson, 1976.
64. Dilks, David. *The Diary of Sir Alexander Cadogan 1938-1943.* London: Cassell, 1971.
65. Donnelly, Peter. *Mrs. Milburn's Diaries: An Englishwoman's Day-to-Day Reflections, 1939-1945.* London: Harrup, 1979.
66. Donoughue, Bernard and G.W. Jones. *Herbert Morrison.* London: Weidenfeld and Nicolson, 1973.
67. Donovan, Robert K. (ed.). *Current Research in British Studies.* Manhattan, Kansas: MA-AH Publishers, 9th ed., 1986.
68. Driberg, Tom. *Ruling Passions.* London: Cape, 1977.
69. Eastwood, Granville. *Harold Laski.* Oxford: Mowbray, 1977.
70. Eccles, David. *By Safe Hand: The Wartime Letters of David and Sybil Eccles.* London: Bodley Head, 1982.
71. Enser, A.G.S. *A Subject Bibliography of the Second World War: Books in English 1939-1974.* London: Deutsch, 1977.
72. ―――. *A Subject Bibliography of the Second World War: Books in English 1975-1983.* Aldershot: Gower, 1985.
73. Fabian Society. *Archives of the Fabian Society. Part 2: Minutes of the Executive Committee, 1919-1960. Part 3: Correspondence of Eminent Persons, 1881-1959.* Brighton: Harvester Press, microfilm.
74. Fawcett Library. *Bibliofem.* London: Fawcett Library, microfiche.
75. Fisher, Nigel. *Harold Macmillan: A Biography.* London: Weidenfeld and Nicolson, 1982.
76. Fox, Dan. *Health Policies, Health Politics: The Experience of Britain and America, 1911-1965.* Princeton: Princeton University Press, 1986.
77. Gallup, George (ed.). *The Gallup International Public Opinion Polls, Great Britain, 1937-1975.* London: Greenwood, 1977.
78. Gates, Eleanor. *End of the Affair: The Collapse of the Anglo-French Alliance, 1939-1940.* Berkeley: University of California Press, 1981.

79. Gilbert, Martin. *Winston S. Churchill*, vol. 6. *Finest Hour, 1939-1941*. London: Heinemann, 1983.
80. Glees, Anthony. *Exile Politics During the Second World War: German Social Democrats in Britain*. London: Oxford University Press, 1982.
81. Gorodetsky, Gabriel. *Stafford Cripps' Mission to Moscow, 1940-1942*. Cambridge: Cambridge University Press, 1984.
82. Gosden, P.H.J.H. *Education in the Second World War: A Study in Policy and Administration*. London: Methuen, 1976.
83. Harrington, William and Peter Young. *The 1945 Revolution*. London: Davis-Poynter, 1978.
84. Harris, Jose. "Did British Workers Want the Welfare State? G.D.H. Cole's Survey of 1942," in Jay Winter (ed.) *The Working Class in Modern British History*. Cambridge: Cambridge University Press, 1983.
85. ―――. "Social Planning in War-time: Some Aspects of the Beveridge Report," in Jay Winter (ed.) *War and Economic Development*. Cambridge: Cambridge University Press, 1975.
86. ―――. "Some Aspects of Social Policy in Britain During the Second World War," in W.J. Mommsen (ed.) *The Emergence of the Welfare State in Britain and Germany 1850-1950*. London: Croom Helm, 1981.
87. ―――. *William Beveridge*. Oxford: Clarendon Press, 1977.
88. Harris, Kenneth. *Attlee*. London: Weidenfeld and Nicolson, 1982.
89. Harrison, Tom. *Living Through the Blitz*. London: Collins, 1976.
90. ―――. *The Tom Harrison Mass-Observation Archive*. Part 1. *File Reports, 1937-1941*, Part 2: *File Reports, 1942-1949*. Brighton: Harvester, microfiche.
91. Harvey, John (ed.). *The War Diaries of Oliver Harvey*. London: Collins, 1978.
92. Hathaway, Robert. *Ambiguous Partnership: Britain and America, 1944-1947*. New York: Columbia University Press, 1981.
93. Hewison, Robert. *Under Siege: Literary Life in London 1939-45*. London: Weidenfeld and Nicolson, 1978.
94. Hinton, James. "Coventry Communism: A Study of Factory Politics in World War Two," *History Workshop Journal*, 10 (1980).
95. Historical Association. *Annual Bulletin of Historical Literature*. (1911-).
96. Hodgson, Vera. *Few Eggs and No Oranges: A Diary Showing How Unimportant People in London and Birmingham Lived through the War Years, 1940-45*. London: Dobson, 1976.
97. Holt, Hazel and Hilary Pym (eds.). *A Very Private Eye. An Autobiography in Diaries and Letters: Barbara Pym*. London: Macmillan, 1984.
98. Hopkinson, Tom (ed.). *"Picture Post," 1938-50*. London: Chatto, 1984.
99. ―――. *Of This Our Time: A Journalist's Story 1905-50*. London: Hutchinson, 1982.
100. Howell, David. *British Social Democracy*. London: Croom Helm, 1980.
101. Institute of Historical Research (University of London). *Theses Completed*. (1953-).
102. ―――. *Theses in Progress*. (1954-).

103. James, Robert Rhodes (ed.). *Winston S. Churchill: His Complete Speeches, 1897-1963*, 8 vols. New York: Chelsea House, 1974.
104. Jay, Douglas. *Change and Fortune: A Political Record*. London: Hutchinson, 1980.
105. Jeffereys, K.R.A. "Butler, the Board of Education and the 1944 Education Act," *History*, 69 (1984).
106. Kimball, Warren (ed.). *Churchill and Roosevelt: The Complete Correspondence*. Princeton: Princeton University Press, 1984.
107. King, Cecil. *With Malice Toward None*. London: Sidgwick and Jackson, 1970.
108. Klein, Rudolf. *The Politics of the National Health Service*. London: Longman, 1983.
109. Kochran, Miriam. *Britain's Internees in the Second World War*. London: Macmillan, 1983.
110. Koss, Stephen. *The Rise and Fall of the Political Press in Britain*, vol. 2. *The Twentieth Century*. London: Hamish Hamilton, 1984.
111. Labour Party. *Conference Reports and Publications of the Labour Party Women's Group, 1918-1972*. Brighton: Harvester, microfilm.
112. ―――――. *General Correspondence and Political Records*. Part 5. *Subject Files (2-3), 1917-1943*. Brighton: Harvester, microfilm.
113. ―――――. *National Executive Committee Minutes*. Part 2: *1927-1939*, Part 3. *1940-1951*. Brighton: Harvester, microfiche.
114. ―――――. *Pamphlets and Leaflets*. Part 3: *1940-1952*. Brighton: Harvester, microfiche.
115. Land, Hilary. "The Introduction of Family Allowances," in P. Hall (ed.) *Change, Choice and Conflict in Social Policy*. London: Heinemann, 1975.
116. Lash, Joseph. *Roosevelt and Churchill, 1939-1941: The Partnership that Saved the West*. New York: Norton, 1976.
117. Leathard, Audrey. *The Fight for Family Planning: The Development of Family Planning Services in Britain, 1921-1974*. London: Macmillan, 1980.
118. Lee, J.M. *The Churchill Coalition 1940-1945*. London: Batsford, 1980.
119. Lee, Jennie. *My Life with Nye*. London: Jonathan Cape, 1980.
120. Lees-Milne, James. *Harold Nicolson: A Biography*, vol. 2. *1930-1968*. London: Chatto and Windus, 1981.
121. Lewenhak, Sheila. *Women and Trade Unions: An Outline History of Women in the British Trade Union Movement*. London: Ernest Benn, 1977.
122. Lewin, Ronald. *Churchill as Warlord*. London: Batsford, 1973.
123. Longmate, Norman. *How We Lived Then: A History of Everyday Life During the Second World War*. London: Arrow, 1973.
124. ―――――. *The G.I.'s: The Americans in Britain, 1942-1945*. London: Hutchinson, 1975.
125. ―――――. *The Home Front: An Anthology of Personal Experience 1938-1945*. London: Chatto and Windus, 1981.
126. Louis, Roger. *Imperialism at Bay: The United States and the Decolonization of the British Empire, 1941-1945*. London: Oxford University Press, 1978.

127. Lowe, Peter. *Great Britain and the Origins of the Pacific War: A Study of British Policy in East Asia, 1937-1941.* Oxford: Clarendon Press, 1977.
128. Lysaght, Charles. *Brendan Bracken.* London: Allen Lane, 1979.
129. Mack, Joanna and S. Humphries. *London at War: The Making of Modern London 1939-45.* London: Sidgwick and Jackson, 1985.
130. MacKenzie, Norman (ed.). *The Letters of Sidney and Beatrice Webb*, vol. III. *Pilgrimage 1912-1947.* Cambridge: Cambridge University Press, 1978.
131. ———— and Jeanne MacKenzie (eds.). *The Diary of Beatrice Webb*, vol. IV. *"The Wheel of Life," 1924-1943.* London: Virago, 1985.
132. Macnicol, John. *The Movement for Family Allowances, 1918-45: A Study in Social Policy Development.* London: Heineman, 1980.
133. Manning, Leah. *A Life for Education: An Autobiography.* London: Gollancz, 1970.
134. Mansell, Gerald. *Let Truth Be Told: Fifty Years of BBC External Broadcasting.* London: Weidenfeld and Nicolson, 1982.
135. Martin, Ross. *TUC: The Growth of a Pressure Group 1868-1976.* Oxford: Clarendon Press, 1980.
136. Marwick, Arthur. "People's War and Top People's Peace? British Society and the Second World War," in Alan Sked and Chris Cook (eds.) *Crisis and Controversy.* London: Macmillan, 1976.
137. ————. "Problems and Consequences of Organizing Society for Total War," in N.F. Dreisziger (ed.). *Mobilization For Total War: The Canadian, American and British Experience 1914-1918, 1939-1945.* Waterloo, Ontario: Wilfred Laurier University Press, 1981.
138. ————. *Class: Image and Reality in Britain, France and the USA Since 1930.* London: Collins, 1980.
139. ————. *The Home Front: The British and the Second World War.* London: Thames and Hudson, 1976.
140. McLachlan, Donald. *In the Chair: Barrington-Ward of "The Times" 1927-1948.* London: Weidenfeld and Nicolson, 1971.
141. McLaine, Ian. *Ministry of Morale.* London: Allen and Unwin, 1979.
142. Merson, Elizabeth. *Children in the Second World War.* Harlow: Longman, 1983.
143. Middlemas, Keith. *Politics in Industrial Society.* London: Deutsch, 1979.
144. Milward, A.S. *War, Economy and Society 1939-1945.* London: Allen Lane, 1977.
145. Minns, Raynes. *Bombers and Mash, The Domestic Front 1939-45.* London: Virago, 1980.
146. Moore, R.J. *Churchill, Cripps, and India: 1939-1945.* Oxford: Oxford University Press, 1979.
147. Morgan, Kenneth and Janet Morgan. *Portrait of a Progressive: The Political Career of Christopher, Viscount Addison.* Oxford: Oxford University Press, 1980.
148. Mosley, Leonard. *Backs to the Wall: London Under Fire, 1939-1945.* London: Weidenfeld and Nicolson, 1971.
149. Muggeridge, Malcolm. *Chronicles of Wasted Time*, vol. 2. London: Collins, 1973.

150. Naylor, John. *A Man and an Institution: Sir Maurice Hankey, the Cabinet Secretariat and the Custody of Cabinet Secrecy*. Cambridge: Cambridge University Press, 1984.
151. Nicolson, Nigel and Joanne Trautmann (eds.). *The Letters of Virginia Woolf*, vol. 6. *Leave the Letters Till We're Dead, 1936-1941*. London: Hogarth, 1984.
152. Parkinson, Roger. *Peace for Our Time: Munich to Dunkirk--The Inside Story*. London: Hart-Davis, 1971.
153. Parris, Henry. *Staff Relations in the Civil Service: Fifty Years of Whitleyism*. London: Allen and Unwin, 1973.
154. Partridge, Francis. *A Pacifist's War*. London: Hogarth, 1978.
155. Pater, John E. *The Making of the National Health Service*. Oxford: Oxford University Press, 1982.
156. Pelling, Henry. "The 1945 General Election Reconsidered," *The Historical Journal*, 23 (June 1980).
157. ―――. *A History of British Trade Unionism*. London: Macmillan, 3rd ed., 1976.
158. ―――. *Britain and the Second World War*. London: Collins, 1970.
159. ―――. *Winston Churchill*. London: Macmillan, 1974.
160. Percival, Janet (ed.). *A Guide to Archives and Manuscripts in the University of London*, 2 vols. London: University of London, 1983-84.
161. Pimlott, Ben (ed.). *The Second World War Diary of Hugh Dalton 1940-1945*. London: Cape, 1986.
162. ―――. *Hugh Dalton*. London: Jonathan Cape, 1985.
163. Pronay, Nicholas and D. W. Spring (eds.). *Propaganda, Politics, and Film, 1918-1945*. London: Macmillan, 1982.
164. Public Record Office. *The Second World War: A Guide to Documents in the Public Record Office*. London: HMSO, 1972.
165. ―――. *Conflict and Consensus in British Industrial Relations 1916-1946. Part 1: Government Industrial Relations Policy, 1921-1946; Part 2: Industrial Disputes, 1921-1946; Part 3: Conciliation Officers Weekly Reports, 1940-1946*. Brighton: Harvester, microfilm.
166. ―――. *The Cabinet Office to 1945*. London: HMSO, 1975.
167. Ramsden, John. *The Making of Conservative Party Policy: The Conservative Research Department Since 1929*. London: Longman, 1981.
168. Reynolds, David. *The Creation of the Anglo-American Alliance, 1937-1941: A Study in Competitive Co-operation*. London: Europa, 1981.
169. Riley, Denise. "The Free Mothers: Pronatalism and Working Mothers in Industry at the End of the Last World War in Britain," *History Workshop Journal*, 11 (Spring 1981).
170. ―――. *War in the Nursery: Theories of the Child and Mother*. London: Virago, 1983.
171. Robbins, Lionel. *Autobiography of An Economist*. London: Macmillan, 1971.
172. Robertson, James C. *The British Board of Film Censors: Film Censorship in Britain 1896-1950*. London: Croom Helm, 1985.
173. Rolph, C.H. *Kingsley: The Life, Letters and Diaries of Kingsley Martin*. London: Gollancz, 1973.
174. Roskill, Stephen. *Hankey: Man of Secrets*, vol. 3, *1931-1963*. London: Hutchinson, 1980.

175. Ross, Alan. *Colours of War: War Art, 1939-1945*. London: Cape, 1983.
176. Ross, Graham (ed.). *The Foreign Office and the Kremlin: British Documents on Anglo-Soviet Relations, 1941-1945*. Cambridge: Cambridge University Press, 1984.
177. Rothwell, Victor. *Britain and the Cold War, 1941-1947*. London: Cape, 1982.
178. Royal Historical Society. *Annual Bibliography of British and Irish History*. (1976-).
179. Russell, Dora. *The Tamarisk Tree*. Part 2. *My School and the Years of War*. London: Virago, 1981.
180. Shires, Linda. *British Poetry of the Second World War*. New York: St. Martin's Press, 1985.
181. Short, Ken (ed.). *Film and Radio Propaganda in World War II*. London: Croom Helm, 1983.
182. Simon, Brian. *The Politics of Educational Reform, 1920-1940*. London: Lawrence and Wishart, 1974.
183. Skidelsky, Robert. *Oswald Mosley*. London: Macmillan, 1975.
184. Smith, Harold. *The British Labour Movement to 1970: A Bibliography*. London: Mansell, 1980.
185. Smith, Harold L. (ed.). *War and Social Change: British Society in the Second World War*. Manchester: Manchester University Press, 1986.
186. ―――. "The Problem of 'Equal Pay for Equal Work,'" in Great Britain during World War II," *Journal of Modern History*, 53 (December 1981).
187. ―――. "The Womanpower Problem in Britain during the Second World War," *The Historical Journal*, 27 (December 1984).
188. Smithies, Edward. *Crime in Wartime*. London: Allen and Unwin, 1982.
189. Social History Society. *Newsletter*. (1976-).
190. Society for the Study of Labour History. *Bulletin*. (1960-).
191. Stammers, Neil. *Civil Liberties in Britain During the Second World War*. London: Croom Helm, 1983.
192. Stevenson, John. *British Society 1914-1945*. Harmondsworth: Penguin, 1984.
193. Storey, Richard and Janet Druker (eds.). *Guide to the Modern Records Centre, University of Warwick Library*. Warwick: University of Warwick, 1977.
194. Stuart, C.H. (ed.) *The Reith Diaries*. London: Collins, 1975.
195. Summerfield, Penny. "Education and Politics in the British Armed Forces in the Second World War," *International Review of Social History*, 26 (1981).
196. ―――. *Women Workers in the Second World War*. London: Croom Helm, 1984.
197. Sykes, Christopher. *Nancy: The Life of Lady Astor*. London: Collins, 1972.
198. Taylor, A.J.P. (ed.). *W.P. Crozier: Off the Record: Political Interviews 1933-1943*. London: Hutchinson, 1973.
199. ―――. "1932-1945" in David Butler (ed.) *Coalitions in British Politics*. London: Macmillan, 1978.
200. ―――. *A Personal History*. London: Hamish Hamilton, 1983.
201. ―――. *Beaverbrook*. London: Hamish Hamilton, 1972.
202. Terrill, Ross. *R.H. Tawney and His Times*. Cambridge, Mass.: Harvard University Press, 1973.

203. Thomas, Hugh. *John Strachey*. London: Eyre and Methuen, 1973.
204. Thomas, R.T. *Britain and Vichy: The Dilemma of Anglo-French Relations, 1940-1942*. New York: St. Martin's Press, 1979.
205. Thompson, R.W. *Generalissimo Churchill*. London: Hodder and Stoughton, 1973.
206. Thorne, Christopher. *Allies of a Kind: The United States, Britain and the War Against Japan, 1941-1945*. London: Oxford University Press, 1978.
207. Thorpe, Francis. *British Official Films of the Second War: A Descriptive Catalogue*. London: Clio, 1980.
208. Trades Union Congress. *Committee Minutes and Papers, 1922-1950*. Part 1 *Economic Committee, Finance and General Purposes Committee, etc.* Part 2 *Colonial Advisory Committee, etc.* Brighton: Harvester, microfilm.
209. ————. *General Council Minute Books*. Part 2. *1932-1946*. Brighton: Harvester, microfiche.
210. ————. *Pamphlets and Leaflets*. Part 2. *1931-1947*. Brighton: Harvester, microfiche.
211. Vernon, Betty. *Ellen Wilkinson*. London: Croom Helm, 1982.
212. Wallace, R.G. "The Origins and Authorship of the 1944 Education Act," *History of Education*, 10 (1981).
213. Wallington, Neil. *Firemen at War: The Work of London's Fire-Fighters in the Second World War*. Newton Abbot: David and Charles, 1981.
214. Wasserstein, Bernard. *Britain and the Jews of Europe, 1939-1945*. Oxford: Clarendon Press, 1979.
215. Watt, Donald C. *Succeeding John Bull: America in Britain's Place, 1900-1975*. Cambridge: Cambridge University Press, 1984.
216. White, Doris. *D for Doris, V for Victory*. Milton Keynes: Oakleaf Books, 1981.
217. Wigg, George. *George Wigg*. London: Michael Joseph, 1972.
218. Wigham, Eric. *From Humble Petition to Militant Action: A History of the Civil and Public Services Association 1903-1978*. London: Civil and Public Services Association, 1980.
219. ————. *Strikes and the Government 1893-1974*. London: Macmillan, 1976.
220. Wilson, Elizabeth. *Women and the Welfare State*. London: Tavistock, 1977.
221. Winter, Jay. "Unemployment, Nutrition and Infant Mortality in Britain, 1920-1950," in Jay Winter (ed.) *The Working Class in Modern British History*. Cambridge: Cambridge University Press, 1983.
222. Woodward, Llewellyn. *British Foreign Policy in the Second World War*, 4 vols. London: HMSO, 1970-1975.
223. Yass, Marion. *This Is Your War: Home Front Propaganda in the Second World War*. London: HMSO, 1983.
224. Young, Kenneth (ed.) *The Diaries of Sir Robert Bruce Lockhart, II. 1939-65*. London: Macmillan, 1981.
225. Young, Michael. "The Second World War," in John Pinder (ed.) *Fifty Years of Political and Economic Planning: Looking Forward 1931-1981*. London: Heinemann, 1981.
226. Ziegler, Janet. *World War II: Books in English, 1945-65*. Stanford, CA: Hoover Institution Press, 1971.

XVII

THE DOMINION SERVICES:

AUSTRALIA AND NEW ZEALAND

Ronald Haycock

Much has changed in the writing of Australian military history since Robin Higham lamented in 1970 that after two years of trying he could not even get someone to assess what little had been done to that date. Moreover, what had been written was dominated by the monumental works of the remarkable C.W. Bean, the official historian of Australia's role in the Great War. Yet part of the change is due to the vastly improved organization of archival sources, especially of the Australian Archives in Melbourne and the newer facility at Mitchell in Canberra. Recently the Central Studies Establishment of the Defence Ministry also based in the capital has done some interesting historical work on munitions and weapons acquisition. So too the Australian War Memorial, always the locus of support for the official war histories, remains more than ever the prime mover in military history as well as being a major repository.

There are now a few more valuable bibliographies and guides. Three of these which will be very useful are Jean Fielding and Robert O'Neill's, *A Select Bibliography of Australian Military History, 1891-1939* (1978) (32) and Michael Piggott's, *A General Guide to the Library Collections and Archives*, (1982) (90) followed by his *Guide to the Personal, Family and Official Papers of C.E.W. Bean* (1983) (91). The latter is especially useful for those who wish to explore Bean's strong personality and Australia's fighting relationship with British forces.

Australian military history has not escaped the introspection evident in the other Dominions. But in the last fifteen years, study has broadened well beyond that of the official histories. While the national pride in the Australian effort in war (second in the empire only to New Zealand's) remains, challenges to the sanctity of the digger legend, identification of the colonial cringe, re-examinations of relationships with the forces and governments of the Mother Country, domestic, social and political explorations--all have added a far wider dimension of Australia's connection with war and British arms. Regimental, unit, popular battlefield studies and militaria works have proliferated. Since few of them are analytical, however, few are mentioned herein. Nevertheless the reader should be aware of their existence if for no other reason that most of them contribute on the side of evidence rather than interpretation.

The expert in the Australian colonial period is Brigadier General M. Austin. In particular, his *The Army in Australia, 1840-*

1850: Prelude to the Golden Years (1979), (4) not only looks at the colonial and British forces in the colonies, but casts this view against the more general story of those colonies and their relationship with Britain. Yet, a major theme of Australia's military history long past the colonial era is fighting beyond her shores and usually in loyal service with Great Britain. One of the first involvements, described in K.S. Inglis' *The Rehearsal: Australians at War in the Sudan 1885* (1985) (56) was the 900 man contingent sent to join the British force avenging the death of "Chinese" Gordon at Khartoum. Many of the themes and forces described here in miniature reached greater proportions during the second Anglo-Boer War. First, R.L. Wallace's *The Australians at the Boer War* (1976) (109) is largely a competent operational history; then there is L.M. Field's *The Forgotten War: Australian Involvement in the South African Conflict of 1899-1902* (1979) (31), a more balanced and broader view challenging many of the assumptions of the colonials' willingness to go and Imperial willingness to have them.

Substantial gains have been made in the writing on the First World War. Bean's classic is currently being republished by the University of Queensland. Both Dudley McCarthy *Gallipoli to the Somme: The Story of C.E.W. Bean* (1983) (73) and Kevin Fewster (ed.) *Gallipoli Correspondent: The Frontline Diary of C.E.W. Bean* (30) focus on the historian himself and the latter work points out the differences between Bean's diary observations and the image of the digger he portrayed in his official history. Renewed interest in the Bean myth and mateship reached its most influential and popular levels in Bill Gammage's *The Broken Years* (1974) (37). A wealth of information on the private lives of soldiers, the book offers little new interpretations. Where new outlooks come are with social and political interpretations of particular war questions beyond mateship and empire loyalty. The debate over conscription and recruitment in the 1914-1918 period, inextricably connected to the nation's painful Viet Nam experience a half-century later, is covered in J.N.I. Dawes and L.L. Robson's (eds.) *Citizen to Soldier: Australia Before the Great War: Recollections of Members of the First AIF* (1977) (22), a supplement to the latter's early *The First AIF: A Study of its Recruitment 1914-1918* (1970) (96). Unemployment, social malaise, and public acceptance are all reasons explored for compulsory military service in a democratic society in J.M. Main's *Conscription: The Australian Debate 1907-1970* (1970) (69), John Barrett's *Falling In: Australians and 'Boy Conscription', 1911-1915* (1979) (6) and T.W. Tanner's *Compulsory Citizen Soldier* (1980) (106). The Diggers themselves recorded aspects of their naiveté, repugnance, and disillusionment with the British Army. William Harney, *Bill Harney's War* (1983) (44), A.B. Facey, *A Fortunate Life* (1981) (27) and R. East's (ed.), *The Gallipoli Diary of Sergeant Lawrence of the Australian Engineers--1st A.I.F.* (1981) (25) cover most of these emotions as well as the traditional and optimistic ones.

Social studies of this conflict have produced interesting results in showing the complicated and diverse domestic response of Australians to British Military endeavours. Michael McKernan's *The Australian People and the Great War* (1980) (77) and Marilyn Lake, *A Divided Society: Tasmania During World War One* (1975) (62) are good starts. That the Great War was a turning point in Australia's relationship with Great Britain and indeed that the country had already developed a defense direction of its own, are made clear in several social-military studies such as Suzanne Welborn's *Lords of Death: A People, A Place, A Legend* (1982) (111) or in the policy and political studies of Neville Meany, *A History of Australian Defence and Foreign Policy, 1901-1923*, vol. 1, *The Search For Security in the Pacific, 1901-1914* (1976) (72) or L.F. Fitzhardinge, *William Morris Hughes: A Political Biography*, Vol. II, *The Little Digger, 1914-1952* (1979) (35). The commanders themselves have undergone substantial first or sometimes a second examination in recent years. A.J. Hill's full scale biography of Sir Harry Chauvel (1978) (47) of Light Horse fame established Sir Harry as a true Australian commander by attitude and temperament. Conversely particular was the definitive study of Sir John Monash by Geoffrey Serle, *John Monash: A Biography* (1982) (101), which in Hill's terms, makes this great German-Jewish Australian General seem atypical yet well explained. D.M. Horner, a serving-soldier historian, in *The Commanders: Australian Military Leadership in the Twentieth Century* (1984) (50) has examined sixteen commanders, five of them from the Great War (Bridges, White, Creswell, Chauvell and Monash), while looking for a distinctive Australian style. That answer eluded him perhaps because the essays make no model or outside examples with which comparisons can be made.

John McCarthy's *Australia and Imperial Defence, 1918-1939: A Study in Air and Sea Power* (1976) (74) and Jane Ross' *The Myth of the Digger: The Australian Soldier in Two World Wars* (1985) (97) are ideally suited to make the transition from one world war to the other. Again, both underscore the major themes of Australia's military history, the British connection and the special and national qualities of the soldiers. However, both are critical. The former looks at the nation's reliance on the doomed Singapore Strategy while the latter concludes that these improbably national heroes, the diggers, have enjoyed far more prominence in the development of society than they deserved. Whatever the case, the official histories series *Australia in the War of 1939-1945* was completed in 1977, adding three more titles since Higham's original list: Paul Hasluck, *The Government and the People, 1942-1945* (1970) (45), G. Hermon Gill, *Royal Australian Navy 1942-1945* (1968) (39) and finally S.J. Butlin and C.B. Schedvin, *War Economy, 1942-1945* (1977) (12). This twenty-two volume series has not had the popularity of Bean's earlier effort. However, like Bean, Gavin Long compiled before he died a single volume about the war. *The Six Years War: A Concise History of Australia in the 1939-1945 War* (1973) (66) is an honest, straight-forward account which unfortunately avoids larger questions such as Australia's relationship with her major allies. That neglect no doubt spawned John Robertson's *Australia at War, 1939-1945* (1981) (95), a comprehensive war study which not only raises the larger issues but whose battle and strategic analysis is written with clarity and brevity. Once more questions of the psychology of the commanders, army intrigues and alliance policy are dealt with by David Horner in his *Crisis of Command: Australian Generalship and the Japanese Threat 1941-1943* (1978) (49) and *High Command: Australia and Allied Strategy 1939-1945* (1982) (51). Finally, the researcher cannot forget the wealth of documentary material published in the several volumes of H. Kenway, H.J.W. Stokes and P.G. Edwards (eds.), *Documents in Australian Foreign Policy, 1937-1949* (24).

As in the earlier conflict, the wartime society has its students. Michael McKernan, *All In! Australia During the Second World War* (1983) (78), is a true social history. It may be that the very little bit on war administration, domestic politics and munitions production is the author's deference to the official historians of the domestic scene like Hasluck, Butlin or Mellor. The vital part played by women in the various roles is examined by Patsy Adam-Smith in *Australian Women at War* (1984) (2). While it ignores many of the main issues of female position in society, it is full of useful information. Attempts to do for the 2/AIF what Gammage did for the first are made in Peter Charlton's popular but worthwhile *The Thirty-Niners* (1981) (16) which covers the lives of early volunteers who served in the Middle East, Greece and Crete.

Several specialized studies, memoirs and biographies dealing with the war period and more have also recently appeared. Edwin Ride, *British Army Aid Group: Hong Kong Resistance, 1942-1945* (1982) (94), details the fascinating episodes of the BAAG's Australian commander, Colonel Lindsay Ride's assistance in securing allied escapes and providing intelligence. The American popular historian, Walter Lord, has given an anecdotal yet hair-raising account of the coast watchers in the Pacific Islands in his *Lonely Vigil: Coastwatchers of the Solomons* (1977) (67). Major-General Hopkins examines the development of Australian armoured force well before the war until well after it, concentrating on the events, doctrinal debates and policy changes which affected its fortunes, in *Australian Armour: A History of the Royal Australian Armoured Corps, 1927-1972* (1978) (48). Air Marshal Sir Richard Williams was Chief of the Air Staff for much of the important interwar period. His memoir, *These are the Facts* (1978) (112) at times tests its title. Rowell's story, *Full Circle* (1974) (98) also reveals a fascinating military life from his injury at Gallipoli through his service in World War Two until he was made Chief of the General Staff in the 1950s. His versions of the political battles over the years are most interesting. Biographies have also added much about famous soldiers and airmen such as Blamey, Herring, Mackay and Scherger in the last fifteen years.

Many of these people of course reached career heights after the war. Yet many Australian military men and public figures seem reluctant to publish and some left little in the way of papers. But the major military events of the post-war period are again addressed by official historians. Korea got two volumes, both published under the auspices of the Australian War Memorial in Robert O'Neill's *Australia in the Korean War, 1950-1953*, vol. 1, *Strategy and Diplomacy* (1981) (85) and vol. 2, *Combat Operations* (1984) (86). Recently, another official history series covering Australian involvement in the Malayan Emergency and in Vietnam has been commissioned and, as in the past, the War Memorial has chosen prominent historians from the country's universities to do the job. For instance, Peter Dennis of the Australian Defence Force Academy (The University of New South Wales) is presently carrying out research for the volume on operations in Malaya. Separately, military education, at least the land forces' side of it, are covered fully in C.D. Coulthard-Clark's recently published history of RMC Duntroon (20).

As in the case with other countries in this survey, by the late 1950s Australian military endeavours, save for a few specialized and progressively more isolated incidents, have separated themselves from their British military connections. The literature, for instance, on Australia and Viet Nam or the Australian American alliance grows apace, but it is beyond our scope. While this quick survey shows that great progress has been made since Higham first undertook the task in 1968, there are plenty of areas left untouched. Many deserving military figures still need exploration. Little has been done on the changing relationship between Australia and Britain, on training, supply, and organization between their military forces. There is even less on the internal administrative and the various defence reorganizations or equipment purchases in Australia over the years, although in the latter area of munitions, Andrew Ross of the Central Studies Establishment of the Defence Department is doing valuable work on Australian munitioning. Finally, the researcher cannot ignore the many higher degree theses Australian scholars like T.B. Miller's "History of Defence Forces of Port Phillip and District and the Colony of Victoria, 1836-1900" (MA: Melbourne, 1957) (79) or L.D. Atkinson's "Australian Defence Policy: A Study in Empire and Nation, 1897-1910" (Ph.D.: ANU, 1964) (3) represent. Moreover the country's journals are full of very good articles on all aspects of Australian military history where it touches the British story.

New Zealanders have not been generally as enthusiastic about writing their military history as have Australians. The foundations of the country were laid in a much different manner than those in the far larger and more diverse Australian colonies. Outside of the Maori Wars of the mid-19th century, and the occasional Russian Pacific scare, New Zealand's military history belongs to the 20th century beginning with the Boer War. And mostly these monumental efforts were closely entwined with Australia's. In times of peace, distance and British Admiralty protection shielded New Zealanders from many external military problems.

As might be expected, the Maori Wars--recently dubbed the "land wars" by New Zealand historians no doubt to reflect cause rather than race--have been the focal point of writing about 19th century military events. In comparative terms, the struggles were minor fights between regular British soldiers and sailors, volunteer settlers and Maori on both sides. Most had to do with the sharp practices of European settlers on native lands and other grievances. Generally, the conflicts were the encroachments of a more advanced society on another less so. Also part of Queen Victoria's little wars, the New Zealand domestic hostilities provided experience for many an imperial soldier such as Sir Fred Middleton who served there, in the Indian Mutiny and most notably in Canada's North-West Rebellion.

There are several works available to the student of the Maori Wars, but they did not come quickly. In 1937, A.J. Harrop produced *England and the Maori Wars* (27), then in 1950 his *New Zealand After Five Wars* (29). By 1962, Keith Sinclair had analysed their background and causes in *The Origins of the Maori Wars* (62). From there, scholarship in the next decade quickened. Edgar Holt, *The Strangest War* (1962) (31) surveyed all of the conflicts from 1843 until 1872; B.J. Dalton, *War and Politics in New Zealand, 1855-1870* (1967) (18) looked at the domestic political scene and civil-military relations in the last fifteen years of the troubles, while Ian Ward, *The Shadow of the Land* (1968) (68) interpreted the first years of fighting in a study of British policy and racial conflict. By 1969, James Cowan produced his two volume study on the Maori conflict. *The New Zealand Wars* (14) remains one of the most exhaustive on the subject. A much more popular survey came from Tom Gibson, *The Maori Wars: The British Army in New Zealand, 1840-1872* (1974) (22). And finally in 1979, Michael Barthorp skillfully compiled *To Face the Daring Maoris* (5), an account of the first conflict, 1845-1849, from familiar sources and long forgotten past narratives. British policy toward the Island colony has been explored by W.P. Morrell, *British Colonial Policy in the Mid-Victorian Age: South Africa, New Zealand, the West Indies* (1969) (45) and by Peter Adams, *Fatal Necessity: British Intervention in New Zealand, 1830-1847* (1977) (1).

In spite of these books, much needs to be done on the land wars. For instance, Sir George Grey, participant, governor, politician and New Zealand Prime Minister, all over a half century, has only two biographical studies: G.W. Henderson's *Sir George Grey: Pioneer of Empire in Southern Lands* in 1907 (30) and J. Rutherford's *Sir George Grey* in 1961 (60). In the end one of the values of such studies should be to see how the imperial garrisons functioned in social as well as military terms. What is also needed then is more study on their community activities, on civil-military relations and on settlement contributions.

Furthermore, while the National Archives of New Zealand contains plenty of material about military fortifications, equipment, organization, threat perceptions and subsequent policy (the latter mostly reactive and ad hoc such as with the Russian scare of the late 1870s), little has been written from it. Three decades of peace in New Zealand ended with the Boer War. For the next seventy-five years, and mostly as a very junior partner of the British, New Zealand fought and suffered proportionately more than nearly all the others in the Empire-Commonwealth. But the written history of these great events is uneven. The official history of the Boer War was not produced until 1949: D.O.W. Hall, *The New Zealanders in South Africa, 1899-1902* (26). As far as the Island's position in the scheme of Imperial defense, the researcher must rely on D.C. Gordon, *The Dominion Partnership in Imperial Defense, 1870-1914* (1965) (24), R.A. Preston, *Canada and Imperial Defence* (1964) (57) and J.E. Kendle, *The Colonial and Imperial Conferences, 1887-1911, A Study in Imperial Organization* (1963) (35). But plenty of material in the raw form remains stuck in New Zealand's archives and in Great Britain. In terms of Prime Ministers' and Defence Ministers' and important soldiers' contributions to the knowledge of British and New Zealand arms, there is a great deal to be done.

The degree of New Zealand's participation and subsequent casualties in the First World War staggers the outsider. Forty percent of the male population between the ages of 20 and 45 served overseas. Nearly twenty percent were killed. But in spite of this huge national effort; the same outsider can not help but note the lack of histories on the war. From 1920 until recently historiography was mostly non-existent. No doubt more pressing concerns of economic depression, international disillusionment and, in 1939, a new, even larger conflict overshadowed the story of the Kiwi in the Great War. In part due to lack of interest by the government of the day, the "official" story of the 1914-1918 conflict remains four unofficial volumes of popular campaign history published under the auspices of the Army after 1919. Their authors were serving soldiers assigned the task in addition to their normal regimental duties. Higham's *Guide* lists all of these. As for the other writing, it is mostly of the unit type often produced by enthusiastic participants and it is generally unanalytical, patriotic and cautious. Nevertheless, these works of the 1920s and 30s remain the primary historical record of New Zealand's participation in the First World War. Many of these are in the accompanying list (1a, 2, 3, 8, 10, 11, 13, 14, 16, 19, 20, 38, 44, 46, 47, 49, 50, 54, 59, 64, 67); a few should be mentioned. The most important is O.E. Burton's *The Silent Division: New Zealanders at the Front, 1914-1919* (1935) (9). It was the only single volume on the first New Zealand Expeditionary Force until Christopher Pugsley's *Gallipoli: The New Zealand Story* (1984) (56). The latter is an important reassessment which makes substantial use of personal letters and diaries. There are a very few biographical accounts of the war; most notable of them are Robin Hyde's *Passport to Hell* (1936) (33) and James Gasson's, *Travis V.C.: Man in No Man's Land* (1966) (21).

In spite of chronic lack of interest in historical military research at New Zealand Universities, the last few years have seen kindled a small interest in the subject of World War One. The studies are of the social type and usually are in the form of journal articles and university theses. For instance, P.S. O'Connor has looked at the problems of venereal disease as well as the recruitment of Maori soldiers and conscientious objectors (51, 52, 53). There are others (7, 12, 15, 25, 32, 34, 36, 37, 39, 43, 67) and at this writing Christopher Pugsley is preparing a companion history to his earlier Gallipoli, this time on the New Zealand Expeditionary Force in France and Flanders, 1916-1918.

Scholarly works on military policy covering the inter-war period are even scarcer than those on the Great War. But there are two important and excellent studies produced on naval and defense matters. Ian McGibbon's *Blue Water Rationale* (1981) (40) is a masterly study of defense policy from the outbreak of World War One but primarily in the interwar period to the collapse of Singapore in 1942. Argued with precision and clarity and based on British and New Zealand sources, McGibbon's work shows New Zealand's increasing doubts about England's Pacific policy. The dilemma, especially for the Labour government elected in 1935, was that while disliking the dependence on the Royal Navy, a manifestation of what they considered outdated colonial control, they, like other governments before and after, could find no alternative to the increasingly unreliable Singapore strategy. David MacIntyre's *The Rise and Fall of the Singapore Naval Base 1919-1942* (1979) (42) is also an excellent survey of the British Pacific policy written by a New Zealander. Currently MacIntyre is working on a much needed history of military policy between the wars.

In comparison to the apparent official disinterest in Great War history, the enthusiastic government sponsorship of the record of New Zealand's massive World War Two effort is quite obvious. Higham's volume also lists this splendid series which covers air, land, sea and civil subjects, both in narrative and document form. It was produced by the Department of Interior's War History Branch. There are over seventy titles. And Ian McGibbon notes that the last of the official volumes of the war, *The Home Front* by Nancy M. Taylor will appear in early 1986 (66). One wonders if such a marvelous official effort has not had a similar effect as Bean's history of the Great War had on Australian writing where its commanding presence might have discouraged others from efforts in the area. Of course, the difference with the New Zealand project is that it has not been dominated by any one personality. Whatever the case, the New Zealand official history is essential reading for the student of British military affairs.

As for the post-1945 period, not much has yet come out of activities in these years. However, Ian McGibbon is working on the official history of New Zealand in the Korean War. This augers well for a start. One might also recommend to the researcher the artifactual and some documentary evidence at the Queen Elizabeth II Army Memorial Museum in Waiour. The best repository, however, remains the National Archives in Wellington.

In summary, New Zealanders have not been as enthusiastic as have others in the Commonwealth to write about military organization, policy, defense industries and social and political aspects of their military past. These areas are mostly untouched. Some of the reasons have already been mentioned. But an important one remains that unlike South Africa, Canada and Australia, there is no New Zealand equivalent to institutions such as their military colleges which provide an interest in and an even focus on such studies. Recent scholarship from men like McGibbon and Pugsley comes not from the universities but from the armed services and the Department of the Interior's historical section. Here may be the very genesis of a new interest in military studies.

BIBLIOGRAPHY

The author would like to thank Peter Dennis and Jeffrey Grey in Australia, and Ian McGibbon in New Zealand for their invaluable contributions to this chapter. One should note the Dennis and Grey article, "Australian and New Zealand Writing on the First World War" in *Neue Forschungen zum Ersten Weltkreig*, Jurgen Rohwer ed., Bernard und Graefe Verlay Koblenz, 1985.

Australia

1. Adam-Smith, Patsy. *The Anzacs.* Melbourne: Nelson and Sons, 1978.
2. ―――. *Australian Women at War.* Melbourne: Nelson, 1984.
3. Atkinson, L.D. "Australian Defence Policy: A Study in Empire and Nation, 1897-1910." Ph.D.: Australian National University, 1964.
4. Austin, M. *The Army in Australia, 1840-1850. Prelude to the Golden Years.* Canberra: Australian Government Publishing Service, 1979.
5. Barclay, Glen St. J. *The Empire is Marching: A Study in the Military Effort of the British Empire, 1800-1945.* London: Weidenfeld and Nicolson, 1976.
6. Barrett, John. *Falling In: Australians and 'Boy Conscription' 1911-1915.* Sydney: Hale and Iremonger, 1979.
7. Bean, C.E.W. *Two Men I Knew: William Bridges and Brudenell*

White, *Founders of the A.I.F.* Sydney: Angus and Robertson, 1957.
8. ─────. *Anzac to Amiens: A Shorter History of Australian Fighting Services in the First World War.* Canberra: Australian War Memorial, 1946.
9. ─────. *The Official History of Australia in the War of 1914-1918*, vol. I, *The Story of Anzac.* St. Lucia: University of Queensland Press, 1981.
10. Bridges, B.J. *New South Wales and the Anglo-Boer War, 1899-1902.* 2 vols. Ph.D.: University of South Africa, Pretoria, 1981.
11. Brugger, Suzanne. *Australians and Egypt, 1914-1919.* Carlton: Melbourne University Press, 1980.
12. Butlin, Sydney James and C.B. Schedvin. *War Economy, 1942-1945.* Canberra: Australian War Memorial, 1977.
13. Carnegie, Margaret and Frank Shield. *In Search of Breaker Morant: Balladist and Bushveldt Carbineer.* [no publisher] 1979.
14. Champ, Jack and Colin Burgess. *Diggers of Colditz.* Sydney: Allen and Unwin, n.d.
15. Chapman, Ivan. *Iven G. Mackay. Citizen and Soldier.* Melbourne: Melway, 1975.
16. Charlton, Peter. *The Thirty-Niners.* Melbourne: Macmillan, 1981.
17. Clarke, Hugh V. *Twilight Liberation: Australian Prisoners of War between Hiroshima and Home.* Sydney: Allen and Unwin, n.d.
18. Clark, R. *First Queensland Mounted Infantry in the South African War, 1899-1900.* [no publisher] 1971.
19. Coulthard-Clark, C.D. *The Citizen General Staff: The Australian Intelligence Corps, 1907-1914.* Canberra: Military History Society of Australia, 1976.
20. ─────. *Duntroon: The Royal Military College of Australia, 1911-1986.* Sydney: Allen and Unwin, 1986.
21. ─────. *A Heritage of Spirit: A Biography of Major-General Sir William Throsby Bridges, K.C.B., C.M.G.* Carlton: Melbourne University Press, 1979.
22. Dawes, J.N.I. and L.L. Robson, (eds.). *Citizen to Soldier: Australia before the Great War: Recollections of Members of the First A.I.F.* Carlton: Melbourne University Press, 1977.
23. Denton, Kit. *The Breaker: A Novel with a Selection of Verse by Harry (The Breaker) Morant.* Sydney: Angus and Robertson, 1980.
24. *Documents in Australian Foreign Policy, 1937-1949.* Vol. 3, January to June 1940. H. Kenway, H.J.W. Stokes and P.G. Edwards, (eds.). Canberra: Australian Government Publishing Service, 1979.
25. East, Sir Ronald, (ed.). *The Gallipoli Diary of Sergeant Lawrence of the Australian Engineers--1st A.I.F.* Carlton: Melbourne University Press, 1981.
26. Edwards, Cecil. *John Monash.* Melbourne: State Electricity Commission of Victoria, 1970.
27. Facey, A.B. *A Fortunate Life.* Fremantle: Fremantle Arts Centre Press, 1981.

28. Festberg, A.F. and B.J. Videon. *Uniforms of the Australia Colonies*. Melbourne: Hill of Content, 1972.
29. Festberg, Alfred. *Australian Army Guidons and Colours*. Australia: Allara Publishing, 1972.
30. Fewster, Kevin, (ed.). *Gallipoli Correspondent: The Frontline Diary of C.E.W. Bean*. Sydney: George Allen and Unwin, 1983.
31. Field, L.M. *The Forgotten War: Australian Involvement in the South African Conflict of 1899-1902*. Carlton: Melbourne University Press, 1979.
32. Fielding, Jean and Robert O'Neill. *A Select Bibliography of Australian Military History, 1891-1939*. Canberra: Australian Dictionary of Biography, 1978.
33. Firkins, Peter C. *The Australians in Nine Wars: Waikato to Long Tan*. London: Robert Hale and Co., 1972.
34. ─────. *Of Nautilus and Eagles: History of the Royal Australian Navy*. Stanmore, N.S.W.: Cassell Australia, 1975.
35. Fitzhardinge, L.F. *William Morris Hughes: A Political Biography*, vol. 2, *The Little Digger, 1914-1952*. Sydney: Angus and Robertson, 1979.
36. Forward, Roy and Bob Reece. *Conscription in Australia*. St. Lucia: University of Queensland Press, 1968.
37. Gammage, Bill. *The Broken Years: Australian Soldiers in the Great War*. Canberra: Australian National University Press, 1974.
38. ─────. *An Australian in the First World War*. Cambridge: Cambridge University Press, 1977.
39. Gill, George Hermon. *Royal Australian Navy, 1942-1945*. Canberra: Australian War Memorial, 1968.
40. Glen, Frank. *For Glory and a Farm: The Story of Australia's Involvement in the New Zealand Wars of 1860-1866*. Whakatane: Whakatane and District History Society, 1984.
41. Goler, Geoffrey, (ed.). *Eureka: Rebellion Beneath the Southern Cross*. Adelaide: Rigby Ltd., n.d.
42. Gow, N. "The Formulation of Australian Defence Policy, 1918-1923." MA: University of Western Australia, 1972.
43. Hamill, Ian. *The Strategic Illusion: The Singapore Strategy and the Defence of Australia and New Zealand, 1919-1942*. Singapore: Singapore University Press, 1981.
44. Harney, W. *Bill Harney's War*. 1983 (as cited in: Kent, D.A. "From the Sudan to Saigon: A Critical Review of Historical Works," *Australian Literary Studies*. vol. 12, no. 2, Oct. 1986, p. 159.
45. Hasluck, Paul. *The Government and the People, 1942-1945*. Canberra: Australian War Memorial, 1970.
46. Hetherington, John. *Blamey: Controversial Soldier*. Canberra: Australian War Memorial and Australian Government Publishing Service, 1973.
47. Hill, A.J. *Chauvel of the Light Horse: A Biography of General Sir Harry Chauvel, G.C.M.G., K.C.B.* Carlton: Melbourne University Press, 1978.
48. Hopkins, Major-General R.W.L. *Australian Armour. A History of the Royal Australian Armoured Corps 1927-1972*. Canberra:

Australian War Memorial and Australian Government Publishing Service, 1978.
49. Horner, D.M. *Crisis of Command: Australian Generalship and the Japanese Threat, 1941-1943.* Canberra: Australian National University Press, 1978.
50. ———— (ed.). *The Commanders: Australian Military Leadership in the Twentieth Century.* Sydney: George Allen and Unwin, 1984.
51. ————. *High Command: Australia and Allied Strategy, 1939-1945.* Sydney: George Allen and Unwin, 1982.
52. Horton, D.C. *Ring of Fire: Australian Guerilla Operations Against Japan in World War 2.* London: Leo Cooper, 1983.
53. Hudson, W.J. *Billy Hughes in Paris: The Birth of Australian Diplomacy.* Sydney: Nelson and the Australian Institute of International Affairs, 1978.
54. Inglish, K.S. "The Anzac Tradition," in *Meanjin.* vol. XXIV, no. 1 (1965), pp. 25-44.
55. ————. *C.E.W. Bean, Australian Historian.* St. Lucia: University of Queensland Press, 1970.
56. ————. *The Rehearsal: Australians at War in the Sudan 1885.* Adelaide: Rigby Ltd., 1985.
57. Isaacs, Wing Commander Keith. *Military Aircraft of Australia, 1909-1918.* Canberra: Australian War Memorial, 1971.
58. Jenkins, G.K. *Songs of the Breaker; Lyrics by Henry Morant.* Adelaide: Book Agencies of Adelaide, 1980.
59. Laffin, John. *Anzacs at War; The Story of Australian and New Zealand Battles.* London: Abelard Schumann, 1965.
60. ————. *The Australian Army at War, 1899-1975.* Reading, Berks.: Osprey, n.d.
61. Laird, J.T., (ed.). *Other Banners: An Anthology of Australian Literature of the First World War.* Canberra: Australian War Memorial and Australian Government Publishing Service, 1971.
62. Lake, Marilyn. *A Divided Society: Tasmania During World War One.* Carlton: Melbourne University Press, 1975.
63. Lawson, Alan. "Acknowledging Colonialism: Revisions of the Australian Tradition," *Australia and Britain: Studies in a Changing Relationship.* A.F. Madden and W.H. Morris-Jones (eds.). London: Frank Cass in association with Institute of Commonwealth Studies, University of London, 1980.
64. Lewis, Brian B. *Our War: Australia During World War I.* Melbourne University: International Scholarly Book Services, 1980.
65. Livingston, William. *Australia, New Zealand and the Pacific Islands Since the First World War.* Austin: University of Texas Press, 1979.
66. Long, Gavin. *The Six Years War: A Concise History of Australia in the 1939-45 War.* Canberra: Australian War Memorial and Australian Government Publishing Service, 1973.
67. Lord, Walter. *Lonely Vigil: Coastwatchers of the Solomons.* New York: Viking Press, 1977.
68. Madden, A.F. and W.H. Morris-Jones, (eds.). *Australia and Britain: Studies in a Changing Relationship.* London: Frank Cass in association with Institute of Commonwealth Studies, University of London, 1980.

69. Main, J.M. *Conscription: The Australian Debate, 1907-1970.* Melbourne: Cassell Australia Ltd., 1970.
70. Manning, Frederic. *Her Privates We.* London: Peter Davies, 1977.
71. Mayo, L. *Bloody Buma: The Campaign That Halted the Japanese Invasion of Australia.* New York: Doubleday, 1974.
72. Meany, Neville. *A History of Australian Defence and Foreign Policy, 1901-1923.* vol. I, *The Search for Security in the Pacific, 1901-1914.* Sydney: Sydney University Press, 1976.
73. McCarthy, Dudley. *Gallipoli to the Somme: The Story of C.E.W. Bean.* Sydney: John Ferguson, 1983.
74. McCarthy, John. *Australia and Imperial Defence, 1918-1939: A Study in Air and Sea Power.* St. Lucia: Queensland University Press, 1976.
75. McKernan, Michael. *Australian Chaplains in Gallipoli and France.* Sydney: Allen and Unwin, n.d.
76. ————. *Australian Churches at War: Attitudes and Activities of the Major Churches, 1914-1918.* Sydney and Canberra: Catholic Theological Faculty and Australian War Memorial, 1980.
77. ————. *The Australian People and the Great War.* Melbourne: Nelson, 1980.
78. ————. *All In! Australia During the Second World War.* Melbourne: Thomas Nelson, 1983.
79. Miller, T.D. "History of the Defence Forces of Port Phillip and District and the Colony of Victoria, 1836-1900." MA: University of Melbourne, 1957.
80. Miller, T.B. *Australia in Peace and War: External Relations, 1788-1977.* London: C. Hurst, 1978.
81. Monash, John. *The Australian Victories in France in 1918.* London: Hutchison, 1920.
82. Mooreland, Alan. *Gallipoli.* London: Hamish Hamilton, 1956.
83. Nelson, Hank. *Prisoners of War: Australians Under Nippon.* 1985 (as cited in: Kent, D.A. "From the Sudan to Saigon: A Critical Review of Historical Works," *Australian Literary Studies.* vol. 12, no. 2 (Oct. 1985), p. 163.
84. Nicholls, Bob. *Blue Jackets and Boxers: Australia's Naval Expeditions to the Boxer Uprising.* Sydney: Allen and Unwin, n.d.
85. O'Neill, Robert. *Australia in the Korean War, 1950-1953.* vol. 1, *Strategy and Diplomacy.* Canberra: The Australian War Memorial and the Australian Government Publishing Service, 1981.
86. ————. *Australia in the Korean War, 1950-1953,* vol. 2, *Combat Operations.* Canberra: Australian War Memorial, 1984.
87. Parkinson, Roger. *The Auk: Victory at El Alamein.* London: Granada Publishing, 1977.
88. Paull, R. *Retreat from Kokoda: The Australian Campaign in New Guinea, 1942.* Melbourne: William Heinemann, 1983.
89. Pedersen, P.A. *Monash as Military Commander.* Carlton: Melbourne University Press, 1985.
90. Piggott, Michael. *A General Guide to the Library Collections and Archives.* Canberra: Australian War Memorial, 1982.

91. ─────. *A Guide to the Personal, Family and Official Papers of C.E.W. Bean*. Canberra: Australian War Memorial, 1982.
92. Rayner, Harry. *Scherger: A Biography of Air Chief Marshal Sir Frederick Scherger*. Canberra: Australian War Memorial, 1984.
93. Richelson, Jeffrey and Desmond Ball. *The Ties That Bind: Intelligence Co-operation Between UKUSA Countries*. Sydney: Allen and Unwin, n.d.
94. Ride, Edwin. *British Army Aid Group: Hong Kong Resistance, 1942-1945*. Hong Kong: Oxford University Press, 1982.
95. Robertson, John. *Australia at War, 1939-1945*. Melbourne: William Heinemann, 1981.
96. Robson, L.L. *The First A.I.F.: A Study of its Recruitment, 1914-1918*. Carlton: Melbourne University Press, 1970.
97. Ross, Jane. *The Myth of the Digger: The Australian Soldier in Two World Wars*. Sydney: Hale and Iremonger, 1985.
98. Rowell, S.F. *Full Circle*. Melbourne: Melbourne University Press, 1974.
99. Sayers, Stuart. *Ned Herring: A Life of Sir Edmund Herring*. Canberra: Hyland House and Australian War Memorial, 1980.
100. Serle, G. "The Digger Tradition and Australian Nationalism" in *Meanjin*, vol. XXIV no. 2 (1965), pp. 149-158.
101. ─────. *John Monash: A Biography*. Carlton: Melbourne University Press, 1982.
102. Sissons, D.C. *Attitudes to Japan and Defence, 1890-1923*. MA Thesis: University of Melbourne, 1956.
103. Smith, F. B. *The Conscription Plebiscites in Australia, 1916-1917*. Melbourne: Victorian Historical Association, 1965.
104. Smithers, A.J. *Sir John Monash*. London: Leo Cooper, 1973.
105. *South African War, 1899-1902*. Australian War Memorial. Canberra: Australian War Memorial, 1974.
106. Tanner, Thomas. *Compulsory Citizen Soldier*. Sydney: Alternative Publishing Cooperative Ltd., 1980.
107. Turner, Ian. *"1914-19." A New History of Australia*. F.K. Crowley (ed.). Melbourne: William Heinemann, 1974.
108. Walker, Richard and Helen Walker. *Curtin's Cowboys: Australia's Secret Bush Commandos*. Sydney: Allen and Unwin, n.d.
109. Wallace, R.L. *The Australians at the Boer War*. Canberra: Australian War Memorial and Australian Government Publishing Service, 1976.
110. Wedd, Monty. *Australian Military Uniforms, 1800-1982*. Kenthurst, N.S.W.: Kangaroo Press, 1982.
111. Welborn, Suzanne. *Lords of Death: A People, A Place, A Legend*. Fremantle: Fremantle Arts Centre Press, 1982.
112. Williams, Richard. *These are the Facts: The Autobiography of Air Marshal Sir Richard Williams*. Canberra: Australian War Memorial, 1978.

New Zealand

1. Adams, Peter. *Fatal Necessity: British Intervention in New Zealand, 1830-1847*. Auckland: Auckland University Press, 1977.
1. (a) Allen, S.S. *To Auckland, 1918, being a partial Record of the War Service in France of the 2/Auckland Regiment during the Great War*. Auckland: Whitcombe and Tombs Ltd., 1920.

2. [Annabel, Norman]. *Official History of the New Zealand Engineers during the Great War, 1914-1919*. Wanganui: Evans, Cobb and Sharp, 1927.
3. Austin, Lieutenant-Colonel W.S. *The Official History of the New Zealand Rifle Brigade (The Earl of Liverpool's Own)*. Wellington: L.T. Watkins Ltd., 1924.
4. Barber, Laurie. *Redcoat to Jungle Green, New Zealand's Army in Peace and War*. Lower Hutt: INL Print, 1984.
5. Barthorp, Michael. *To Face the Daring Maoris*. London: Hodder and Stoughton, 1979.
6. Bennett, Neville. "Consultation or Information: Britain, the Dominions and the Renewal of Anglo-Japanese Alliance, 1911." *New Zealand Journal of History*, IV, no. 2 (Oct. 1970), pp. 178-194.
7. Boyd, Mary. "The Military Administration of Western Samoa, 1914-1919." *New Zealand Journal of History*, II no. 2 (1968), pp. 148-164.
8. Burton, 2/Lieut. O.E. *The Auckland Regiment, being an account of the doings on Active Service of the First, Second and Third Battalions of the Auckland Regiment*. Auckland: Whitecombe and Tombs Ltd., 1922.
9. Burton, O.E. *The Silent Division, New Zealanders at the Front, 1914-1919*. Sydney: Angus and Robertson, 1935.
10. Byrne, Lieut. A.E. *Official History of the Otago Regiment NZEF in the Great War, 1914-1918*. Dunedin: J. Wilkie and Col., 1921.
11. Byrne, Lieut. J.R. *New Zealand Artillery in the Field, 1914-1918*. Auckland: Whitcombe and Tombs Ltd., 1922.
12. Cain, D.L. "Perceptions of War, 1914-18," unpublished research essay, University of Canterbury, 1981.
13. Carberry, Lieut. Col. A.D. *The New Zealand Medical Services in the Great War, 1914-1918, Based on Official Documents*. Auckland: Whitcombe and Tombs Ltd., 1924.
14. Cowan, James. *The Maoris in the Great War: A History of the New Zealand Native Contingent and Pioneer Battalion*. Auckland: Whitcombe and Tombs Ltd., 1926.
14a. Cowan, James. *The New Zealand Wars*. 2 vols., New York: AMS Press Inc., 1969.
15. Cumming, R. "New Zealand's Role in the First World War," unpublished research essay, University of Auckland, 1971.
16. Cunningham, W.H., C.A.L. Treadwell and J.S. Hanna. *The Wellington Regiment N.Z.E.F., 1914-1919*. Wellington: Ferguson and Osborn, 1928.
17. Dalton, B.J. "The Military Reputation of Sir George Grey: The Case of Wereroa." *New Zealand Journal of History*, IX (No. 2, Oct. 1975), pp. 126-141.
18. Dalton, B.J. *War and Politics in New Zealand, 1855-1870*. Sydney: Sydney University Press, 1967.
19. Ellis, Roy Findlayson. *By Wires to Victory: Describing the Work of the New Zealand and Divisional Signal Company in the 1914-1918 War*. Auckland: 1st NZEF Divisional Signal Company War History Committee, 1968.
20. Ferguson, Capt. David. *The History of the Canterbury Regiment NZEF, 1914-1918*. Auckland: Whitcombe and Tombs Ltd., 1921.

21. Gasson, James. *Travis V.C.: Man in No Man's Land*. Wellington: A.H. and A.W. Reed, 1966.
22. Gibson, Tom. *The Maori Wars: The British Army in New Zealand, 1840-1892*. London: Leo Cooper, 1974.
23. Glen, Frank. *For Glory and a Farm. The Story of Australia's Involvement in the New Zealand Wars of 1860-1866*. Whakatane: Whakatane and District Historical Society, 1984.
24. Gordon, D.C. *The Dominion Partnership in Imperial Defense, 1870-1914*. Baltimore: Johns Hopkins, 1965.
25. Graham, J.M. "The Voluntary System: Recruiting, 1914-1916." Unpublished MA Thesis, University of Auckland, 1972.
26. Hall, D.O.W. *The New Zealanders in South Africa, 1899-1902*. Wellington: Department of Internal Affairs, 1949.
27. Harrop, A.J. *England and the Maori Wars*. London: Unwin, 1937.
28. ————. *England and New Zealand*. London: Meuthuen, 1962.
29. ————. *New Zealand After Five Wars*. London: Jarrolds, 1950.
30. Henderson, G.C. *Sir George Grey: Pioneer of Empire in Southern Lands*. London: Dent, 1907.
31. Holt, Edgar. *The Strangest War: The Story of the Maori Wars in New Zealand, 1843-1872*. London: Putnam and Co., 1962.
32. Hucker, G.J. "Patriot Organizations in the First World War," unpublished thesis, Massey University, 1979.
33. Hyde, Robin. *Passport to Hell, The Story of James Douglas Stark, Bomber, Fifth Regiment, New Zealand Expeditionary Forces*. London: Hurst and Blackott Ltd., 1936.
34. Josephson, M. "Gallipoli and the New Zealand Press," unpublished research essay, University of Otago, 1978.
35. Kendle, J.E. *The Colonial and Imperial Conferences, 1887-1911: A Study in Imperial Organization*. London: Longman's, 1967.
36. Kiklerr, G.A. "The Invasion of Samoa, August, 1914," unpublished research essay, University of Otago, 1978.
37. Laytham, J.R. "Gallipoli: The New Zealand Experience," unpublished research essay, University of Otago, 1978.
38. Luxford, Major J.H. *With the Machine Gunners in France and Palestine: The Official History of the New Zealand Machine Gun Corps in the Great War, 1914-1918*. Auckland: Whitcombe and Tombs Ltd., 1923.
39. Mathieson, K.H. "A Study of Auckland Society in the First Years of the Great War August 1914--August 1915," unpublished research essay, University of Auckland, 1979.
40. McGibbon, I.C. *Blue Water Rationale: The Naval Defence of New Zealand, 1914-1942*. Wellington: Government Printer, 1981.
41. McIntyre, W.D. *The Imperial Frontier in the Tropics, 1865-1875*. London: Macmillan, 1967.
42. ————. *The Rise and Fall of the Singapore Naval Base, 1919-1942*. Hamden, Conn.: Archon Books, 1979.
43. Mcleod, J.C. "Activities of New Zealand Women during World War I," unpublished research essay, University of Otago, 1978.
44. Moore, A.B. *The Mounted Riflemen in Sinai and Palestine: The Story of New Zealand's Crusaders*. Auckland: Whitcombe and Tombs, 1920.
45. Morrell, W.P. *British Colonial Policy in the Mid-Victorian Age: South Africa, New Zealand, the West Indies*. Oxford: Clarendon Press, 1969.

46. Napier, Capt. W.E.L. *With the Trench Mortars in France.* Auckland: Alpe Bros. and Co., n.d.
47. Neill, J.C., (ed.). *The New Zealand Tunnelling Company 1915-1919.* Auckland: Whitcombe and Tombs, 1922.
48. *New Zealand Expeditionary Force: Roll of Honour.* Wellington: Government Printer, 1924.
49. Nicol, Sergt. C.G. *The Story of Two Campaigns, Official War History of the Auckland Mounted Rifles Regiment, 1914-1919.* Auckland: Wilson and Horton, 1921.
50. "Officers." *Regimental History of the New Zealand Cyclist Corps in the Great War, 1914-1918.* Auckland: Whitcombe and Tombs Ltd., 1922.
51. O'Connor, P.S. "The Awkward Ones--Dealing with Conscience, 1916-1918." *New Zealand Journal of History*, VIII, no. 2 (1974), pp. 118-136.
52. ———. "The Recruitment of Maori Soldiers, 1914-1918." *Political Science*, XIX, no. 2, (1967), pp. 48-83.
53. ———. "Venus and the Lonely Kiwi: The War Effort of Miss Ettie A. Rout." *New Zealand Journal of History.* I, no. 1, (1967), pp. 11-32.
54. Powles, Colonel C.G. (ed.) *The History of the Canterbury Mounted Rifles, 1914-1919.* Auckland: Whitcombe and Tombs, 1928.
55. Pugh, Michael C. "The New Zealand Legion, 1932-1935," *New Zealand Journal of History*, V, no. 1 (Apr., 1971), pp. 49-69.
56. Pugsley, Christopher. *Gallipoli, The New Zealand Story.* Auckland: Hodder and Stoughton, 1984.
57. Preston, R.A. *Canada and 'Imperial Defense': A Study of the Origins of the British Commonwealth's Defence Organization 1867-1919.* Durham, N.C.: Duke University Press, 1967.
58. Richardson, Len. "Politics and War: Coal Miners and Conscription, 1914-1918," in Philip R. May, ed. *Miners and Militants: Politics in Westland, 1865-1918.* Christchurch: Whitcoulls Ltd., 1975, pp. 128-155.
59. Robertson, John. *With the Cameliers in Palestine.* Dunedin: A.H. and A.W. Reed, 1938.
60. Rutherford, J. *Sir George Grey.* London: Cassell, 1961.
61. Searight, Sarah. "The Treaty of Waitangi," *History Today*, XXII, no. 2 (Feb., 1972), pp. 111-119.
62. Sinclair, K. *The Origins of the Maori Wars.* Wellington: New Zealand University Press, 1962.
63. Sinclair, Keith, ed. *A Soldier's View of Empire: The Reminiscences of James Bodell, 1831-1892.* London: The Bodley Head, 1982.
64. Smith, Stephen John. *The Samoa (NZ) Expeditionary Force, 1914-1915: An Account based on Official Records of the Seizure and Occupation by New Zealand of the German Islands of Western Samoa.* Wellington: Ferguson and Osborn Ltd., 1924.
65. Stanborough, P.E. "Fire in the Ferns, the Maori Wars 1843-1872." Honours B.A. History Thesis, The Royal Military College of Canada, 1985.
66. Taylor, Nancy M. *The Home Front.* Wellington: War History Branch Government Printer, expected 1986.

67. Van Boxtel, J.M. "The Soldier Advocate: The Foundation Years of New Zealand Returned Soldiers Association, 1915-1919," unpublished research essay, University of Otago, 1978.
68. Ward, Ian. *The Shadow of the Land: A Study in British Policy and Racial Conflict in New Zealand, 1832-1852.* Wellington: Government Printer, 1968.
69. Wilkie, Major A.H. *Official War History of the Wellington Mounted Rifles Regiment, 1914-1919.* Auckland: Whitcombe and Tombs Ltd., 1924.

XVIII

THE DOMINION SERVICES:

CANADA

Ronald Haycock

British military endeavours on the North American continent have had a longer history than in many of the other Dominions. The English and French struggle for the continent, the centuries of Indian Wars and the strategic aspects of economic competition are some of those events. So too are the American War of Independence and the War of 1812. Continued fear of the United States, rebellions and Fenian invasions form parts of a whole host of 19th century involvements of a new Dominion for imperial planners and Canadian politicians. These culminated in the monumental efforts of the country as part of British arms in the two great wars of this century. Like other parts of the Empire, human and physical resources, imperialism, increasing self-awareness, race, and politics are all part of the story.

When J. Mackay Hitsman compiled his original list of Canadian publications it contained only twenty-three entries. Things have changed. Particularly important is the growth in labour-saving bibliographic services. Without a doubt the best single military work is Owen A. Cooke's *The Canadian Military Experience, 1867-1983: A Bibliography* (1984, 2nd edition) (35). In over three hundred pages, the author has listed every conceivable printed and other source, the finding of which is made simple by good internal organization and an ample index of subjects, persons and services down to the unit level. Cooke also provides a handy summary of other bibliographies. Among them are the early attempts at gathering material, especially C.E. Dornbusch's several compilations on the Canadian Army from the Crimean War to the 1960s (43, 44). For the general reader, there is much to be found in D.A. Muise: *A Reader's Guide to Canadian History 1: Beginnings to Confederation* and J.L. Granatstein and Paul Steven's *A Reader's Guide to Canadian History 2: Confederation to the Present*, both appearing in 1982 (72, 152). However, the essential volume remains Cooke's.

There are several excellent general surveys on Canadian military history. The classic remains G.F.G. Stanley's *Canada's Soldiers; The Military History of an Unmilitary People* (1974, 3rd edition) (215). It is best at battle and unit history and covers the ground from the Ancien Régime to unification. Far newer, more analytical and wider in scope are Desmond Morton's *Canada and War; A Military and Political History* (1981) and his popular survey, *A Military History of Canada* (1985) (145, 148). The latter covers three centuries of

Canadian military events and should be read in concert with Stanley. The dean of Canadian military historians is Colonel C.P. Stacey and his *The Military Problems of Canada* (1940) is still a good introduction to the unique set of Canadian circumstances as is his *Introduction to the Study of Military History for Canadian Students* (1953) (202, 209). Collectively, the papers compiled by Michael Cross and Robert Bothwell entitled *Policy by Other Means: Essays in Honour of C.P. Stacey* (1972) (39) focus on a wide range of Canada's military past. A far less scholarly effort is D.J. Goodspeed's brief centennial celebration for the non-specialist of the three Canadian services: *The Armed Forces of Canada: A Century of Achievement* (1967) (62). Lastly, for those who want to see what these centuries of soldiers dressed like, Brigadier-General J.L. Summer's and René Chartrand's study, *Military Uniforms in Canada, 1665-1970* (1981) can not be bettered (220).

A great deal has been written about French military events which remains outside the purview of this essay. Yet where the Ancien Régime touches British or Anglo-American fortunes, there is much to describe. The themes are of struggle and survival, of imperial fortune and North American events and, as I.K. Steele has written, of *Guerillas and Grenadiers: The Struggle for Canada, 1689-1760* (1969) (217). Even if its author does not seem to know the difference between irregular and guerilla warfare, with its useful bibliography, this work shows how France survived a century in North America by practicing "petite guerre" and because the English colonial forces were neither better nor as unified. But the main reason was that the British did not decide to give North America overwhelming military support until 1754. Faced with fighting British regulars attacking the main French garrisons, there was never any doubt about the outcome.

The "Red Coat" service in North America during this and later periods is well-described in Reginald Hargreave's *The Bloodybacks* (1968) and A.J. Barker's *Redcoats* (1976) (83, 5) but perhaps best by Parks Canada historian, Carol Whitfield's *Tommy Atkins: The British Soldier in Canada, 1759-1870* (1981) (238). One of the "centres of gravity" for the British regular and the Anglo-American alike was the great French garrison of Louisbourg guarding the vital portal of the St. Lawrence. The most meritorious of the several recent publications on the fortress is Christopher Moore's *Louisbourg Portraits: Life in an Eighteenth-Century Garrison Town* (1982) (138). Raymond Baker's *A Campaign of Amateurs: The Siege of Louisbourg, 1745* (1978) (4) shows clearly that the New Englanders took it readily because the French never gave serious consideration to proper defensive installations. G.A. Rawlyk in *Yankees at Louisbourg* (1967) (176) considers this feat to be the most important military achievement of the American colonists prior to the War of the Revolution.

Those who are concerned with British military policy for North America in the two decades after the Treaty of Aix-la-Chapelle will benefit from a re-issue of documents from the Duke of Cumberland's papers edited in 1969 by S.M. Pargellis entitled *Military Affairs in North America, 1748-1765; Selected Documents from the Cumberland Papers in Windsor Castle* (originally published in 1936) (164). The actual military events, the end result of strategic decisions made well in London and badly in Versailles are analysed by George Stanley in *New France: The Last Phase: 1744-1760* (1968) (213). French-Canadian historian Guy Frégault, first in French in 1955 then in English in 1969, claimed in *Canada: The War of the Conquest* (56) that the British conducted the Seven Years' War solely for colonial conquest--a dubious proposition considering European events and Pitt's grand strategy.

There are many particular studies on the British forces. General Wolfe at Quebec has received the "Lion's Share." Oliver Warner in *With Wolfe to Quebec* (1972) (236) applauds the General's tactical and leadership ability but faults his sense of strategy. In reading Gordon Donaldson's *Battle for a Continent: Quebec 1759* (1973) (42), it becomes apparent that if one wants scholarship above entertainment then go elsewhere, especially to C.P. Stacey's *Quebec, 1759: The Siege and the Battle* (1959) (204). It provides both. Wolfe had many faults. So did the French commanders but Quebec was taken more by cooperation of land and sea effectives than anything else. Brian Connell has brought out a new edition of Captain John Knox's classic *Historical Journal of the Campaigns in North America for the Years 1757, 1758, 1759 and 1760* first published in 1769. Now called *The Siege of Quebec* (1979) (102), it replaces A.G. Doughty's almost unreadable three volume monument to turn-of-the-century scholarship on Knox's journal.

No attempt is being made here to go too deeply into the enormous area of the American Revolution. John Shy, Ira Gruber and Richard Ketchum, among others, have published widely in the area of the British Army in America (76, 77, 101, 196, 197). For recent research, especially theses relating to the British Army in the eighteenth century, one should consult Tony Hayter's article in the *Journal of the Society for Army Historical Research* (Spring, 1985) (91).

During the American rebellion, patriot forces conducted a daring attempt to snatch Canada from British rule. It failed. Canadians did not support the revolution and mostly the reasons were far more complex than conventional loyalty to the British. Gustave Lanctot's *Canada and the American Revolution, 1774-1783* (1967) (105) does not detail or analyse the military campaign as well as G.F.G. Stanley's *Canada Invaded, 1775-1776* (1973) (214). This is a story covered again by Robert Hatch in *Thrust for Canada: The American Attempt on Quebec in 1775-1776* (1979) (86). Both are well-written and researched works; the former concentrates on the Anglo-Canadian defense, the latter on the American attack.

Lord Dorchester, Sir Guy Carleton, was not only the architect of the Quebec Act of 1774, one cause of the American Rebellion, but as Governor of Canada, he ultimately became responsible for its defense. Paul Reynolds, *Guy Carleton: A Biography* (1980) (179) falls short of a true biography. It concentrates mostly on the events of 1775-76 and 1782-83. One is still dependent on A. Burt's classic work on Dorchester, *Guy Carleton, Lord Dorchester, 1724-1808* (1957) (29). Ultimately, Carleton became bitter when French-Canadians did not flock to British colours in the Revolution. *Revolution Rejected, 1775-1776* edited by G.A. Rawlyk (1968) (175) explores why Nova Scotia's and Quebec's population refused to join the rebels or actively support the British forces. Professor Rawlyk is the author of several other works which look at maritime British North America's reaction to the War of Independence and its historical relationship with the New England regions. These studies help unravel the complex forces which British administrations and soldiers in the eighteenth century so frequently seemed to be insensitive to or unaware of.

Recently scholarship on one of these soldiers, who in the past has usually been accredited with losing Great Britain her American colonies, has undergone substantial revision. Lieutenant-General John Burgoyne has been vindicated by Michael Glover in *General Burgoyne in Canada and America* (1976) (60). Colonel James Lunt's *John Burgoyne of Saratoga* (1976) (110) sifts fact from fiction and provides the reader with an objective re-appraisal of the General's military career in North America.

The American revolution cost Britain thirteen of her North American colonies and profoundly changed the nature of the remaining ones in British North America. For Canadians, the United States became the enemy. Continued British involvement in the western districts, Indian troubles and the influx of loyalists with their claims against the new Republic continued to temper British North America and U.S. relations (25, 162, 198). By 1812 war occurred again. Fought mostly in the Upper Canadian theatre, it has provided the stuff for substantial literature. In 1964 Morris Zaslow and W.B. Turner edited a series of essays, *The Defended Border: Upper Canada and the War of 1812* (248) that initiated the re-interest in the subject. The following year, J. Mackay Hitsman produced his meticulously researched *The Incredible War of 1812: A Military History* (1965) (94). This book is one of the best and should be read together with G.F.G. Stanley's more recent *The War of 1812: Land Operations* (1983) (216). At the onset of the conflict, as both men show, Anglo-Canadian discipline prevailed over American numbers. Montreal was the key to the Canadian defence system, a fact which US soldiers and strategists were slow to realize. In the United States, the most scholarly work comes from John K. Mahon who provides some analysis of the effect on the North American war of Britain's involvement with Napoleon (124). Walter Lord has added another title to his list of popular war histories with *The Dawn's Early Light* (1972) (109). From Britain Kate Caffrey's *The Twilight's Last Gleaming: Britain vs America, 1812-1815* (1977) (31) has done the same for a British general audience, many of whom associate 1812 more with Tchaikovsky than any Anglo-American conflict. Back in Canada, journalist-historian Pierre Berton's two volumes, *The Invasion of Canada, 1812-1813* (1980) and *Flames Across the Border, 1813-1814* (1981) brings the conflict grippingly alive for his readers by giving attention to the personal experience of those involved (10, 11). Like the more scholarly historians, Berton dispels many of the myths created by nineteenth century militiamen and loyalists, pointing out that the British regular did most of the real fighting in this war. Another very useful aspect of Berton's, Stanley's and Hitsman's works is that their bibliographies contain very valuable periodical literature old and new, about particular groups, events and units, Indian and French-Canadian participation not the least among them. Two of these, in book form, are worth mentioning. Parks Canada historian Michelle Guitard gives impressive details on militia administration, organization and recruiting in her *The Militia of the Battle of Chateauguay: A Social History* (1983) (78). Finally, of all the diverse battlegrounds of 1812, those in the Champlain Valley have received scant attention. Britain used that valley to invade the

United States in 1814. Such is Professor Allan Everest's scenario in *The War of 1812 in the Champlain Valley* (1981) (54). Long on scholarship and short on human drama, the author's research is impeccable.

The War of 1812 only demonstrated to Canadians and British soldiers alike that the United States would be the main enemy in the foreseeable future. Defense was expensive and the British taxpayer and regular soldier were bearing most of the real burden. As well as the obvious defense factors, George Raudzens points to the economic and social implications of the British military construction that took place after the war in *The British Ordnance Department and Canada's Canals 1815-1855* (1979) (173). By reproducing sources and providing historiographical comment, Peter Burroughs has analysed the times in *British Attitudes Towards Canada, 1822-1849* (1971) (28). His study covers the vital years when the costs of colonial protection were escalating and many Britons were questioning the basic political and economic ideas which had underpinned the Empire for decades. Ultimately such questions would have grand implications for the continuance of the British Army in North America, to which both the pioneering findings of Hitsman's *Safe-guarding Canada, 1763-1871* (1967) (95) and Stacey's *Canada and the British Army, 1846-1871* (1936) (201) attest.

As imperial administrators were rethinking their positions on the colonies, many of the colonies themselves were undergoing internal crises. In Canada's case, the constitutional struggle for responsible government led to rebellion in 1837. In the past a great deal has been written about the uprisings. Joseph Schull's *Rebellion: The Rising of French Canada, 1837* (1971) (191) is one of them. But until Elinor Senior's *Redcoats and Patriotes: The Rebellions in Lower Canada 1837-1838* (1985) (194), no one has viewed them from the perspective of the British Garrison. Mrs. Senior's pioneering study is an extension of her two earlier works, *British Regulars in Montreal: An Imperial Garrison, 1832-1854* and *Roots of the Canadian Army: Montreal District, 1846-1870*. Both books appearing in 1981 analyse the very important role which British garrison troops had on the day-to-day life of pre-Confederation Canadians and on the nation's long term evolution (192, 193).

It was the military crises that provided some important reasons for the Confederation of British North America in 1867. The aggravated Anglo-American relations arising out of the U.S. Civil War, Fenian invasions, and increasingly more influential arguments for withdrawing imperial troops, forced the new Dominion to bear reluctant responsibility for its own defense. The next four decades saw remarkable military growth and no lack of thorny relations between Canadians and British soldiers and politicians alike. It is this intriguing process that forms the basis of Desmond Morton's fascinating interpretation of military politics, in *Ministers and Generals: Politics and the Canadian Militia, 1868-1904* (1970) (142). Logically his research is the extension of Stacey's and Hitsman's earlier volumes. This thoroughly-researched book analyses the effects of the new imperialism and national aspirations on defense matters; it exposes the politics-riddled military system and explores the conceptual debate between advocates of a part-time force as opposed to those favouring professional cadres (or a combination of both) for the defense of the country. Morton concludes that by 1904, Canada developed a military system modelled on the British pattern but adapted to Canadian needs. Moreover, the British and the Canadians both slowly learned something about self-government. Many of the ideas initiated in Morton's first book are examined with the particular experiences of his famous ancestor, William Otter in *The Canadian General: Sir William Otter* (1974) (144).

There were, of course, many other specific events that allowed a closer examination of defense. Richard Preston's *The Defence of the Undefended Border: Planning for War in North America* (1977) carefully sifts the plans for war by Canadians and Americans against each other until the eve of the Second World War (172). This sort of isolated but serious thinking went on well after the British--at least those in England and excluding some of their officers serving in Canada such as Lord Dundonald--had given up any hope of being able or wanting to defend Canada. The reasons such plans continued so long likely had more to do with political if not institutional and nationalistic reasons.

There were many events that made Canadian and even British soldiers nervous. Some of the earliest involved Fenian invasions. These raids were the first serious external military crises involving the new Dominion. Over the years several articles and books have been written on the subject. One should note several excellent articles by C.P. Stacey on Fenians and the military listed in Granatstein's and Steven's bibliography. More recently, there is Brian Jenkins' *Fenians and Anglo-American Relations During Reconstruction* (1969) (98) and W.S. Neidhardt's *Fenianism in North America* (1975) (155). The latter includes an examination of the mostly neglected Canadian response to the problem while Canadian historian Hereward Senior, in *The Fenians and Canada* (1978) (195) stays almost exclusively with Canadian settings and sources.

The Riel Rebellions of 1869-70 and 1885 have received a substantial amount of study. The latter event, at least, represents the first time the Canadian militia successfully took to the field without major British help. G.F.G. Stanley's *Birth of Western Canada; A History of the Riel Rebellions* (1936) is not a purely military study but provides much information about the background, social conditions and the campaigns (211). Unquestionably the best source for military analysis is Desmond Morton's *The Last War Drum* (1972) (143). It should be supplemented by his and Reginald Roy's compilation of documents *Telegrams of the North-West Campaign* (1972) (149). Thomas Flanagan, again not a military historian, has provided in his *Riel and the Rebellion: 1885 Reconsidered* (1983) a useful corrective to the exercises in hagiography which have typified much of the writing on Riel (55). At least one brave historian, Walter Hildebrandt, has tried to make the connexion between other colonial conflicts and the Métis in his well-illustrated *The Battle of Batoche: British Small Warfare and the Entrenched Métis* (1985) (92). For an overall survey of the general campaign, C.P. Stacey has produced several monographs and articles noted in Hildebrandt's bibliography. Lastly it would be difficult not to include at least one book on the North West Mounted Police. This is so because they were involved in the rebellion and in other wars and carried the "Queen's Commission." Importantly, the Canadian government consciously chose police over military forces to avoid the bloody experience of the American frontier. The best of several works is

R.C. Macleod's *The N.W.M.P. and Law Enforcement, 1873-1905* (1976) (120).
To understand much of the imperial fervour which fuelled Canadians, Carl Berger's *The Sense of Power: Studies in the Ideas of Canadian Imperialism, 1867-1914* (1970) (9) is essential reading. So is Ramsay Cook's (and others) compilation of papers entitled *Imperial Relations in the Age of Laurier* (1969) (34). Indeed, some Canadians did go as volunteers to imperial adventures abroad. C.P. Stacey's article on the Canadian Nile voyagers appeared in the *Canadian Historical Review* in 1952. Seven years later he published *Records of the Nile Voyageurs* for the Champlain Society (203, 205). Recently, Roy MacLaren dealt with the same subject with the very Victorian title *Canadians on the Nile 1882-1898; Being the Adventures of the Voyageurs on the Khartoum Relief Expedition and Other Exploits* (1978) (118). The best is still Stacey.
Canadians were not exempt from the passions about and participation in the Anglo-Boer War in 1899. The debate nearly split the country, provoked a constitutional crisis and led to the dismissal of another British General Officer Commanding the Canadian Militia. All of this, and there is no book-length scholarly study of Canada's military role in that war. The histories of the various regiments which went--The Royal Canadian Regiment, the Royal Canadian Dragoons and Lord Strathcona's Horse, for instance, say something, (75, 210) but the most thorough, modern analyses remains those chapters in Desmond Morton's *Otter* and his *Ministers and Generals* already mentioned. In understanding the imperial politics relating to the war and military matters, one should read Carman Miller's *The Canadian Career of the Fourth Earl of Minto* (1980) (135). Paul Stevens and John Saywell have edited and introduced this Governor-General's papers in two volumes entitled *Lord Minto's Canadian Papers: A Selection of the Public and Private Papers of the Fourth Earl of Minto*, (1981) (218). Richard A. Preston's *Canada and "Imperial Defense"* (1967) is still the best single examination of the entire topic of imperial defense from Confederation through the Great War, (169) although Norman L. Penlington's *Canada and Imperialism, 1896-1899* (1965) can be read with much profit (166).
Like all of the other Dominions and colonies in 1914, when Britain was at war Canada was at war. The question was what form would that participation take. For over a decade it had already been obvious to Britain that Canada was no longer simply a place in which to serve. Instead Canada's own forces, her growing imperial-nationalism and capability coupled with the hard reality of the international situation dictated that the Dominion would be a resource for British arms. Perhaps this was the logical consequence of the steady military Anglicization process of the previous years. Clearly the scope of British military history becomes increasingly wider and more diverse. The Canadian literature on both the World Wars is already immense and growing rapidly. Since Owen Cooke's bibliography records nearly everything printed on those conflicts, this guide attempts only to note some of the newer, more important and some of the more worthy older ones.
The fighting formation of the Great War was the Canadian Corps. There are two official histories of the Canadian forces; the first, a proposed multi-volume series was never completed. In 1925 Sir Andrew MacPhail produced *The Medical Services* story first. It contains a

great deal about politics, scandal and the relationship of Canadian Medical units with the larger British organization (121). Only in 1938, did A.F. Duguid's *Official History of the Canadian Forces in the Great War, 1914-1919* appear. This single volume covered just the first full year of the conflict for the Expeditionary Force (CEF). Its narrative is sound but not very analytical. Of particular value is its accompanying volume of notes and appendices (48). Years later, a new team of Army Headquarters historians under Colonel G.W.L. Nicholson completed the project in 1962 under one cover: *Official History of the Canadian Army in the First World War: The Canadian Expeditionary Force, 1914-1919* (156). Since then there have been a series of publications some of them better than others on the Corps. John Swettenham's *To Seize Victory* (1965) (221) remains a good well-written if somewhat opinionated work. And others worthy of mention are D.J. Goodspeed's *The Road Past Vimy: The Canadian Corps, 1914-1918* (1969) (63), Herbert Fairlie Wood's *Vimy!* (1967) (246) and recently Pierre Berton's *Vimy* (1986) (12). Of the leaders--soldiers and citizens--more and more gets published. Canada's most famous soldier, and the first native son to command the Corps, Sir Arthur W. Currie, has had two biographers besides Colonel H.M. Urquhart's admiring *Arthur Currie: The Biography of a Great Canadian* (1950) (232). The more critical treatment of his military talent comes out of A.M.J. Hyatt's doctoral dissertation, "The Military Career of Sir Arthur Currie" (Duke: 1965), soon expected in book form (97). Those in search of a Canadian hero will be attracted by Daniel Dancocks' *Sir Arthur Currie: A Biography* (1985) (41). Hyatt and Desmond Morton have produced several good articles on Sir Arthur Currie in various learned journals. Currie's predecessor, English General Sir Julian Byng, was a man of common sense, decency and good humour, well-loved by his Canadians. Unfortunately, his only biographer is hampered by an absense of Byng's papers. Nevertheless, Jeffrey Williams' *Byng of Vimy: General and Governor-General* (1983) is a good read (242). Andrew McNaughton's career reached its pinnacle in the next German war yet the formative stages during World War One are analysed in John Swettenham's *McNaughton* (1968-69) (223).

Perhaps predictably, the civilians of the Great War have received more attention than individual soldiers. Much is to be learned about Anglo-Canadian relations and domestic war administration from R.C. Brown's two volumes on Prime Minister Robert Borden: *Robert Laird Borden: A Biography* (1975 and 1980) (23, 24). Sam Hughes, the Minister of Militia and Defence was the early war's most visible politician and one who caused British war leaders and soldiers in particular no end of concern. This compiler's *Sam Hughes: The Public Career of a Controversial Canadian, 1853-1916* (1986) attempts to balance this man's amazing career (90). Understanding the nature of Canadian politics is seminal to understanding much of Canada's role in the war. John English's *The Decline of Politics: The Conservatives and the Party System 1901-20* (1977) (53) and Desmond Morton *A Peculiar Kind of Politics: Canada's Overseas Ministry in the First World War* (1982) (147) are the valuable works in this regard.

Much of value concerning mobilization can be found in Fred Dreisziger's (ed.) *Mobilization for Total War: The Canadian, American and British Experience, 1914-1918, 1939-1945* (1981) (47) and about the effects of war on North American society in J.L. Granatstein and

R.D. Cuff (eds.) *War and Society in North America* (1971) (70) and Michael Cross and Robert Bothwell, (eds.) *Policy by Other Means: Essays in Honour of C.P. Stacey* (1972) (39). Great debate effecting British arms has centered around specific issues. Not the least is manpower and conscription. The definitive work is Granatstein's and Hitsman's *Broken Promises: A History of Conscription in Canada* (1977) (71). Michael Bliss competently and sensitively unravels Canada's contribution to the munitions effort, one reflecting most of the larger British problems, in *A Canadian Millionaire: The Life and Times of Sir Joseph Flavelle Bart* (1978) (15). All sorts of myths and rumours remain about Canada's infamous Ross rifle in the hands of Canadian and British soldiers alike. The best technical description on this weapon is Frank Dupuis' and others, *The Ross Rifle Story* (1984) (49). But an analysis of the politics, policy and acquisition process comes from Ronald Haycock "Early Canadian Weapons Acquisition--'That Damned Ross Rifle'," in *Canadian Defence Quarterly* (1985) (89). The themes of manpower and munitions in the regions of Canada are well-handled in Barbara Wilson, *Ontario and the First World War* (1977) and John Herd Thompson, *The Harvests of War: The Prairie West, 1914-1918* (1979) (228, 243).

Personal remembrances of the Great War abound; some, like *The Journal of Private Fraser, 1914-1918: Canadian Expeditionary Force* (1985) edited by R.H. Roy, are excellent documents (188). Others such as Gordon Reid's *Poor Bloody Murder: Personal Memoirs of the First World War* (1980) are carelessly compiled (178). The war was full of heroes. John Swettenham has compiled biographical sketches including reprints of the citations for all of Canada's Victoria Cross and George Cross winners in *Valiant Men: Canada's Victoria Cross and George Cross Winners* (1973) (225). One of them, later to serve as defense minister in the 1950s, has his own biography written by R.H. Roy: *For Most Conspicuous Bravery: A Biography of Major-General George R. Pearkes, V.C., Through Two World Wars* (1977) (186). Canadians did not always fight on the western front or under British command. Some saw service in Russia. Actor Raymond Massey wrote a gripping account of his CEF and Siberian experiences in *When I Was Young* (1976) (129) and historians John Swettenham, *Allied Intervention in Russia, 1918-1919* (1967) and Roy Maclaren, *Canadians in Russia, 1918-1919* (1976) have described that adventure in full detail (117, 222).

Soon after the Armistice was struck in 1918, the Canadian Army rapidly began to demobilize. For most of the interwar years, it was not much larger than its pre-1914 levels. Military development was hampered by insensitive and parsimonious governments, by a fear of involvement, by constitutional nationalism, world depression, and a shift of the international power balance from Britain to the USA. In the armed forces simple survival seemed the basic posture. James Eayrs' multi-volume series *In Defence of Canada*, Vol. 1, *From the Great War to the Great Depression* (1964) and Vol. 2 *Appeasement and Rearmament* (1965), points out the confusion in management with Mackenzie King being the villain (51). A military understanding needs an appreciation of external policy. C.P. Stacey, *Canada and the Age of Conflict, A History of Canadian External Policies, Vol. II, 1921-1948: The Mackenzie King Era* (1981) (208) has a more balanced view of events than Eayrs' but one no less flattering of the times. R.A. Preston's *Defence of the Undefended Border* tries to explain what Colonel J. Sutherland Brown was doing in happily planning for strikes against the United States while hoping for aid from Great Britain (172). Swettenham's biography of McNaughton also provides much useful information on a far-sighted soldier who could play his own political defence games in hard times. One particular body born out of them was the Conference of Defence Associations created in 1932, largely to watch out for the interests of the part-time soldiers as the Militia's prestige and military importance declined before professional needs. Its history is well laid out by Lieutenant-Colonel W.A. Morrison's MA thesis, "The Conference of Defence Associations and the Evolution of the Office of Major-General of Reserves" (1980) (140).

As mentioned, no attempt is being made here to cover all of the material published in Canada on the Second World War. Cooke's and other bibliographies do that. Indeed substantial critical commentary is provided in W.A.B. Douglas' and Brereton Greenhous' article in *Military Affairs*, "Canada and the Second World War: The State of Clio's Art" (1978) (46). In all, the literature varies from official history through personal memoirs and units and from excellent to bad. Ironically, it was this six years of crises that produced Canada's most involved moment with British arms and at the same time put the country and her forces on a path moving irrevocably away from that traditional connexion. In the 1970s, no doubt aided by bicultural forces, painful memories of the Viet Nam conflict and increasing links with the United States' North American military fortune, a new generation of interest has produced substantial writing about the Second World War. Moreover, the thirty year rule on much of the military material has been lifted.

The place to begin for all wartime topics is in the Mackenzie King diaries. All his papers in the Public Archives of Canada are now open, but J.W. Pickersgill's, (ed.), *The Mackenzie King Record* (1960-1970) covers the period from 1939 to 1948 (167). When read with the very best of the official war histories, C.P. Stacey's *Arms, Men and Governments: The War Policies of Canada, 1939-1945* (1970) one gets possibly the finest synthesis of Canada's war policy obtainable (206). Two works on political parties and the attitude toward the war relationship with England and matters like conscription, supply and finances belong to the prolific and able J.L. Granatstein; *Canada's War: The Politics of the Mackenzie King Government, 1939-1945* (1975) (68) and *The Politics of Survival: The Conservative Party, 1939-1945* (1967) (67), cover both sides. He makes it clear in *Canada's War* that the nation stopped fighting for Britain and started fighting for herself. On the conscription issue, his *Broken Promises* (71) is the standard work while much can be gathered from Swettenham's *McNaughton* (223) and Roy's biography of Pearkes (186).

On the military-diplomatic side, Maurice Pope's memoirs, *Soldiers and Politicians* (1962) gives a good account of alliance warfare and co-operation with British and American Supply Missions in the United States from a man who was there (168). Much of what went on in Ottawa in King's dealing with Britain and other allies come from his double capacity as Minister of External Affairs as well as Prime Minister. J.L. Granatstein's *A Man of Influence: Norman A. Robertson and Canadian Statecraft 1929-1968* (1981) details the career of probably the most important civil servant in Ottawa during the war (69). The wartime careers of Vincent Massey, Charles Ritchie, Lester

Pearson and George Vanier also add dimension to Canada's relations with British strategic decision makers and military events (130, 180, 154, 200).

W.A.B. Douglas and Brereton Greenhous have brought the overall view of Canada's successes and failures in the Second World War home to a general Canadian readership in their *Out of the Shadows: Canada in the Second World War* (1977) (45). The first popular account, it surveys the campaigns, industrial and the political fronts showing how King was wary of generals who had a different view of his concept of a limited war for Canada. The British, or the Americans for that matter, gave little strategic weight to Canadian counsels. Yet the million Canadian soldiers involved and the massive industrial expansion in those six years thrust a confident and more mature nation "out of the shadows."

In 1977 these same authors commented in "The State of Clio's Art" that military history of the war has not claimed as much attention from the historians as other areas especially in tactical and technical fields (46). Happily the situation has improved. The newer works concentrate on the great and often bloody high points of Canada's military effort. The debacle at Hong Kong in December 1941 has always had a passionate place in the Canadian mind. Sacrificing 2000 Canadians on the altar of Imperial defense seems naive. Carl Vincent places the blame squarely on Canadian leaders, both military and political, in *No Reason Why: The Canadian Hong Kong Tragedy--An Examination* (1981) (234). The historiography of the entire affair is discussed in Lieutenant-Colonel W.A. Morrison's excellent review of Vincent's work in *Canadian Defence Quarterly* (1982) (141).

Dieppe has had more ink applied than Hong Kong. Much like Australians and New Zealanders, Canadians seem to be able to create heroes out of bloody defeat. The first attempts, Terence Robertson *The Shame and the Glory: Dieppe* (1962) is an applaudable attempt (183); John Mellor's *Forgotten Heroes; the Canadians at Dieppe* (1975) (133) is not. The only real analysis appearing from any pen is the brief but packed monograph from Lieutenant-Colonel T. Murray Hunter, *Canada at Dieppe* (1982) (96). Canadians were "left pretty much in the dark by the British as to what operations they intended against the enemy in 1942," and Canadian higher authorities had a vague feeling they wanted their troops committed after their long, tedious training wait in England. The lessons did not warrant the losses because there was precious little thinking among Canadian soldiers as to why or how Dieppe could be assaulted successfully.

While some Canadians went to fight with British forces in Italy in 1943, the largest effort remained against Europe from the Atlantic side. Normandy has, in W.J. McAndrew's words, received its "roses and thorns" in current books (111). Canadians had their own beach in June 1944. Forty years after that fateful assault Reg Roy's *1944; The Canadians in Normandy* (1984) (187) and J.L. Granatstein's and Desmond Morton's *Bloody Victory, Canadians and the D-Day Campaign* (1984) (73) rectified the naively arrogant British and American authors' tendencies to forget Juno Beach and later events with anything more than throw away lines about Canadians. The more traditional military narrative, Roy's *1944*, is packed full of details at what Roy does best, of moving units through chaos and the fog of war. Morton and Granatstein, on the other hand, have combined lots of good photographs with a well-written and researched text. This popular history is not meant to be a criticism as much as praise and understanding for Canada's citizen-soldiers who "deserve to be remembered by their country."

These histories were, indeed, predated over a year by Terry Copp and Robert Vogel's series of books intended to be a detailed study of the operational history of the First Canadian Army in North West Europe from the D-Day landing until the end of the war. Called the *Maple Leaf Route*, the series started with *Caen* (1983) and *Falaise* (1983) then *Antwerp* (1984). Generally applauded as solid history, thereby belying their coffee table format, they mix photographs, maps, and unit diaries with critical text based on sound documentation (36, 37, 38). More of the mainstream formula for military history is Shelagh and Denis Whitaker's *Tug of War* (1984). It is a straightforward narrative of the strategy and tactics of the problem-riddled Scheldt campaign (237).

Many biographies, autobiographies and memoirs of Canada's soldiers have come about since the end of the war. Unfortunately this does not apply to the most senior of the Canadian commanders. E.L.M. Burns, *General Mud* (1970) (27), Swettenham's biography of McNaughton and Roy's of Pearkes already cited, are the exception. Little is heard about, for example, H.D. Crerar, Guy Simonds or Chief of the General Staff, Kenneth Stuart. General Chris Vokes, with journalist J.P. Maclean, finally produced his outspoken memoir, *Vokes* (1985), but it lacks substance and analysis that could have explained much of what was going on around one of Canada's most colourful battle leaders (235). Other senior officers have made their contribution. Colonel R.S. Malone was attached to Montgomery's HQ at the end of the Sicilian Campaign as the Canadian public relations officer, and produced *Missing from the Record* (1946). Besides giving personal glimpses of Monty's Headquarters, the memoir provided important information in 1946 about McNaughton's firing, Defence Minister J.L. Ralston's resignation, conscription, and the sometimes bitter relations between Crerar and Montgomery. But Malone's next book, *A Portrait of War, 1939-1943* (1983), thirty-seven years later, adds little to the story, relying instead too much on memory and too little on research (125, 126).

There are other personal stories from and about the veterans available. Most do not and were not intended to satisfy the scholars but nearly all will contribute something to the raw stuff of history. Owen Cooke lists all of this genre published to 1983. But a few of the more recent ones are worth mentioning. One of the best is Fred Cederberg's *The Long Road Home* (1984) (32a). He has produced an excellent worm's eye-view of an infantryman which Ben Greenhous thinks should be required reading for junior infantry officers. Former Deputy Secretary of NATO (1964-1968) James Alan Roberts has done the same in his memoir, *The Canadian Summer: The Memoirs of James Alan Roberts* (1981) (182). In *Memoires du Général Jean V. Allard* (with Serge Bernier, 1985) the General's early chapters tell the story of a French-Canadian's pre-war and war-time service in Italy, Holland and Germany, as part of the proving ground for his later career as the Chief of the Defence Staff responsible for the Armed Forces unification in the late sixties (1). One of the most moving stories comes from the pen of novelist Farley Mowat, *And No Birds Sang* (1979) (151). It chronicles Mowat's personal experiences in the Hasting and Prince Edward Regiment. His earlier history of that unit, *The Regiment* (1955) (150) has been described as the most enjoyable regimental history of the war. Strome Galloway, *The General Who Never Was* (1981) (58) and Brian Nolan's *Hero; the Buzz Beurling Story* (1981) (161) depict war in the field and the air with men who loved and practiced the military role in different ways. Hopefully there will be more such memoirs published, for the veterans are getting old; the public and the historians should not be denied their evidence.

There are far more monographs of the regimental type. The total continues to grow each year. Their quality varies and their focus is mostly too narrow. Yet, used in conjunction with campaign histories they give valuable perspectives. Some relate only the Second World War events; others are truly regimental histories. Some examples are Mowat's aforementioned *The Regiment*, Kim Beattie's *Dileas: History of the 48th Highlanders of Canada, 1929-1956* (1959) (8), D.J. Goodspeed's, *Battle Royal: A History of the Royal Regiment of Canada, 1869-1962* (1962) (61), G.F.G. Stanley's, *In the Face of Danger: The History of the Lake Superior Regiment* (1960) (212), Reg Roy's *Sinews of Steel: The History of the British Columbia Dragoons* (1965) (184), and his *The Seaforth Highlanders of Canada, 1919-1965* (1969) (185), G.W.L. Nicholson's, *The Gunners of Canada* (1967-1972) and *More Fighting Newfoundlanders* (1969) (157, 158) and Brereton Greenhous' *Semper Paratus: The History of the Royal Hamilton Light Infantry (Wentworth Regiment), 1862-1977* (1977) and *Dragoons: The Centennial History of the Royal Canadian Dragoons, 1883-1983* (1983) (74, 75). The best two histories of French-Canadian units are C-M Boissonault's *Histoire du Royal 22e Régiment* (1964) (16) and Gérard Marchand's *Le Régiment du Maisonneuve vers la victoire, 1944-1945* (1980) (127). Nearly all of these authors bring high scholarship and military knowledge to their product.

In 1945 Canada had the world's fourth largest air force. Unfortunately, the official history of the Canadian air force has as yet only Wise's volume covering the Great War, although the next two due to appear shortly will offer much to the historian interested in the 1939-1945 period. So far there are only a few titles reflecting scholarly substance on the air effort, yet much is printed. Cooke lists several hundred items. Most are squadron, technical or documentary in nature. There are exceptions to this group. Perhaps one of the last gasps of the imperial defense co-operation was the British Commonwealth Air Training Plan. F.J. Hatch's *The Aerodrome of Democracy* (1983) is now the definitive study on this very important scheme (85). Part of the research put into the official air force history has produced T.W. Melnyk's *Canadian Flying Operations in South East Asia, 1941-1945* (1976) (134). A dozen years ago, Carl Vincent started a series dedicated to looking at particular aircraft and squadrons. From these beginnings it has blossomed and now encompasses a lot of air history titles. There are also several surveys of military aviation coming out of Vincent's publishing house and the Canadian War Museum. Four of these are Samuel Kostenuk and John Griffin, *RCAF Squadron Histories and Aircraft 1924-1968* (1977) (103), H.A. Halliday, *Chronology of Canadian Military Aviation* (1975) (80), F.H. Hitchens' *Air Board, Canadian Air Force and Royal Canadian Air Force* (1972) (93) and K.M. Molson and H.A. Taylor, *Canadian Aircraft Since 1909* (1982) (137). One that looks at Canadians serving in British air service is Les Allison's *Canadians in the*

Royal Air Force (1978) (2). Recent titles about individual airmen include Nolan's *Hero* already mentioned, and Douglas Harvey's *Boys, Bombs and Brussels Sprouts: A Knees-Up, Wheels-Up Chronicle of World War II* (1981) (84). Murray Peden's *A Thousand Shall Fall* (1979) (165) reminds the reader of what it was like to go through the myriad and risky process of becoming a captain in Bomber Command.

The Royal Canadian Navy was perhaps the most British of all Canadian armed services. Certainly it stayed that way longer. Its history, like the air force, is much scarcer than the land forces. The only official histories by Tucker and Schull were written thirty-five years ago (190, 230). Not until James Boutilier compiled his *The RCN in Retrospect, 1910-1968* (1982) (19) has there been a worthy attempt to examine specific aspects of naval history under one cover. A good general history of the navy remains to be written. Few sailors, especially of the higher ranks, have written memoirs. But there are some. Jeffry Brock, *With Many Voices* (1981-1983), is interesting for its information and a first class account of the war at sea but also the anglification of the Canadian service (22). So is Hal Lawrence's *A Bloody War; One Man's Memories of the Canadian Navy, 1939-1945* (1979) (106) and H. Nelson Lay *Memoirs of a Mariner* (1982) (107). For years little effort was given to the RCN's major Second World War effort, the North Atlantic. James Lamb, *The Corvette Navy: True Stories from Canada's Atlantic War* (1977) (104) has put together some of the heroic and otherwise events. John Swettenham and Fred Gaffen open the subject wider in *Canada's Atlantic War* (1979) (226). Yet six years had to go by before two works, Marc Milner's *North Atlantic Run: The Royal Canadian Navy and the Battle for the Convoys* (1985) and Michael Hadley's *U-Boats Against Canada; German Submarines in Canadian Waters* (1985) finally set the standards against which what follows must be set. Readable and well-researched, these studies are critical of British, American and Canadian naval policy alike. They tell the story of how a poorly equipped, sometimes poorly led from Halifax and Ottawa, and rapidly expanding force overcame these impediments to carry the main burden of the North Atlantic War by 1944 (136, 79). In spite of Hadley's and Milner's fine efforts much remains to be done.

So too it is with Canada's industrial and economic contribution to the war effort. Within the Empire-Commonwealth, Canada was the major provider to Great Britain of war stuff. King had even envisaged this role as one way of building an industrial base and so avoiding the bloody field commitment of the earlier conflict. In spite of this very little has been produced about the process itself or about policy and co-operation with Great Britain. There is an official history: J. de N. Kennedy's *History of the Department of Munitions and Supply* (1950) but it is nothing more than a list of agencies (100). Stacey's *Arms, Men and Government* (1970) (206) has much of value, pointing out that in spite of being ignored by Britain and the United States on strategic munitioning policy Canadians got lots done at lower levels. Robert Bothwell and William Kilbourn's *C.D. Howe* (1979) provides a good overview of Howe's war production mobilization (18).

Canada's relationship to Britain was far different after the war than before it. Gone was the dependence in mind and fact. Reflecting this change the Canadian armed forces underwent a shift in manners and equipment from the British pattern to others, much of it to that of the United States. Perhaps it is fair to say the Korean War speeded up events and that de-Anglification had its greatest moment in integration and unification in the sixties. Whatever the case, the evolution caused a search for identity that still goes on. Perhaps the passage is best recorded in some of the general surveys of Canada's defense and foreign policy. James Eayrs' further volumes *In Defence of Canada* carry the process to the Vietnam War. *Peacekeeping and Deterrence* (1972), *Growing Up Allied* (1980) and *Indochina: The Roots of Complicity* (1984) (51). Also important are Desmond Morton's chapters in *Canada and War* and a *Military History of Canada* (145, 148). Along with Hector Massey's *Canadian Military--A Profile* (1972), the various later articles in *Canada as a Military Power* (1982) and R.B. Byers and Colin Gray's *Canadian Military Professionalism: The Search for Identity* (1973) also shed light on the changing scene (128, 146, 30). Another interesting way to examine Canada's changing role is to read R.A. Preston's *Canada's RMC: A History of the Royal Military College* (1969) (170). H.F. Wood's, *Strange Battleground* (1966) (245) and T. Thorgrimsson and E.C. Russell's *Canadian Naval Operations in Korean Waters, 1950-1955* (1965) (229) are official histories covering the military events in Korea.

This rather long list on Canadian works which illuminate British military history only skims the surface. Researchers are cautioned to give full play to the bibliographic sources mentioned at the onset. Canadian military history is at an expansive and exciting stage. And there remains a lot to do.

BIBLIOGRAPHY

1. Allard, Gen. Jean V. avec Serge Bernier. *Memoirs du Général Jean V. Allard.* Boucherville, P.Q.: Les Editions de Montagne, 1985.
2. Allison, Les. *Canadians in the Royal Air Force.* Roland, Manitoba: privately printed, 1978.
3. Allison, Sydney. *The Bantams: The Untold Story of World War I.* Oakville, Ont.: Mosaic Press, 1982.
4. Baker, Raymond. *A Campaign of Amateurs: The Siege of Louisbourg, 1745.* Ottawa: Parks Canada, 1978.
5. Barker, A.J. *Redcoats.* London: Gordon and Cremonesi, c. 1976.
6. Barratt, G.R.V. *Russian Shadows on the British Northwest Coast of North America, 1810-1890: A Study of Rejection of Defence Responsibilities.* Vancouver: University of British Columbia, 1983.
7. Beal, Bob and Rod Macleod. *Prairie Fire: The 1885 North-West Rebellion.* Edmonton: Hurtig, 1984.
8. Beattie, Kim. *Dileas: History of the 48th Highlanders of Canada, 1929-1956.* Toronto: privately printed, 1957.
9. Berger, Carl. *The Sense of Power: Studies in the Ideas of Canadian Imperialism 1867-1914.* Toronto: University of Toronto Press, 1970.
10. Berton, Pierre. *The Invasion of Canada, 1812-1813.* Toronto: McClelland and Stewart, c. 1980.
11. ———. *Flames Across the Border, 1813-1814.* Toronto: McClelland and Stewart, c. 1981.

12. ———. *Vimy*. Toronto: McClelland and Stewart, 1986.
13. Bindon, Kathryn M. *More Than Patriotism*. Don Mills, Ont.: Nelson, 1979.
14. Bird, Will R. *Ghosts Have Warm Hands*. Toronto: Clarke, Irwin and Co., 1968.
15. Bliss, Michael. *A Canadian Millionaire: The Life and Times of Sir Joseph Flavelle, Bart*. Toronto: Macmillan, 1978.
16. Boissonault, C-M. *Histoire du Royal 22ᵉ Régiment*. Quebec: Editions du pélican, 1964.
17. ———. *Histoire politico-militaire des Canadiens français (1763-1967)*. Trois-Rivières, P.Q.: Edition du Bien public, 1967.
18. Bothwell, Robert and William Kilbourn. *C.D. Howe: A Biography*. Toronto: McClelland and Stewart, 1979.
19. Boutilier, James A., (ed.). *The RCN in Retrospect, 1910-1968*. Vancouver: University of British Columbia Press, 1982.
20. Bowler, Arthur. *The War of 1812*. Toronto: Holt, Rinehart and Winston, 1973.
21. Broadfoot, Barry. *Six Years, 1939-1945; Memories of Canadians at Home and Abroad*. Toronto: Doubleday, 1974.
22. Brock, Jeffry V. *With Many Voices*. Toronto: McClelland and Stewart, 1981-83 (2 vols.).
23. Brown, Robert Craig. *Robert Laird Borden: A Biography, volume I: 1854-1914*. Toronto: Macmillan, 1975.
24. ———. *Robert Laird Borden: A Biography, vol. 2: 1914-1937*. Toronto: Macmillan, 1980.
25. Brown, Wallace. *The View at Two Hundred Years: The Loyalists of the American Revolution*. Worcester, Mass.: American Antiquarian Society, 1970.
26. Burns, E.L.M. *Manpower in the Canadian Army, 1939-1945*. Toronto: Clarke Irwin, 1956.
27. ———. *General Mud: Memoirs of Two World Wars*. Toronto: Clarke Irwin, 1970.
28. Burroughs, P. *British Attitudes Towards Canada, 1822-1849*. Scarborough: Prentice-Hall, 1971.
29. Burt, A.L. *Guy Carleton, Lord Dorchester, 1724-1808*. (The Canadian Historical Association, Historical Booklets, no. 5), Ottawa: 1957.
30. Byers, R.B. and Colin S. Gray, (eds.). *Canadian Military Professionalism: The Search for Identity*. Toronto: Canadian Institute of International Affairs, 1973.
31. Caffrey, Kate. *The Twilight's Last Gleaming: Britain vs. America, 1812-1815*. New York: Stein and Day, 1977.
32. Cassar, George. *Beyond Courage: The Canadians at Ypres*. Ottawa: Oberron Press, 1985.
32. a. Cederberg, Fred. *The Long Road Home: The Autobiography of a Canadian Soldier in Italy in World War II*. Don Mills, Ont.: General Publishing, 1984.
33. Chappell, M. *The Canadian Army at War*. New York: Osprey, 1985.
34. Cooke, Ramsay, et. al. (eds.). *Imperial Relations in the Age of Laurier*. Toronto: University of Toronto Press, 1969.
35. Cooke, O.A. *The Canadian Military Experience, 1867-1983: A Bibliography*. Second edition. Ottawa: Directorate of History, Department of National Defence, 1984.

36. Copp, Terry and Robert Vogel. *Maple Leaf Route: Caen*. Alma, Ont.: Maple Leaf Route, 1983.
37. ———. *Maple Leaf Route: Falaise*. Alma, Ont.: Maple Leaf Route, 1983.
38. ———. *Maple Leaf Route: Antwerp*. Alma, Ont.: Maple Leaf Route, 1984.
39. Cross, Michael and Robert Bothwell, (eds.). *Policy by Other Means: Essays in Honour of C.P. Stacey*. Toronto: Clarke Irwin, 1972.
40. Cuff, R.D. and J.L. Granatstein. *Canadian-American Relations in Wartime: From the Great War to the Cold War*. Toronto: Hakkert, 1975.
41. Dancocks, Daniel. *Sir Arthur Currie: A Biography*. Toronto: Methuen, 1985.
42. Donaldson, Gordon. *Battle for a Continent: Quebec 1759*. Toronto: Doubleday, 1973.
43. Dornbusch, C.E. *The Canadian Army 1855-1958: Regimental Histories and a Guide to the Regiments*. Cornwallville, N.Y.: Hope Farm Press, 1959.
44. ———. *The Canadian Army 1855-1965: Lineages: Regimental Histories*. Cornwallville, N.Y.: Hope Farm Press, 1965.
45. Douglas, W.A.B. and Brereton Greenhous. *Out of the Shadows: Canada in the Second World War*. Toronto: Oxford University Press, 1977.
46. ———. "Canada and the Second World War: The State of Clio's Art," *Military Affairs*. vol. 42, no. 1 (February 1978), pp. 24-28.
47. Dreisziger, N.F. (ed.). *Mobilization for Total War: The Canadian, American and British Experience 1914-1918, 1939-1945*. Waterloo: Wilfrid Laurier University Press, 1981.
48. Duguid, A.F. *Official History of the Canadian Forces in the Great War, 1914-1919*. vol. 1 and appendices. Ottawa: King's Printer, 1938.
49. Dupuis, Frank, R. Phillips and J. Chadwick. *The Ross Rifle Story*. Sydney, published by John A. Chadwick, 1984.
50. Easton, Allan. *50 North: An Atlantic Battleground*. Toronto: Ryerson Press, 1963.
51. Eayrs, James. *In Defence of Canada*. 5 vols. Toronto: University of Toronto Press, 1964-83.
52. Elliot, S.R. *Scarlet to Green; a History of Intelligence in the Canadian Army, 1903-1963*. Toronto: privately printed, 1981.
53. English, John. *The Decline of Politics: The Conservatives and the Party System 1901-20*. Toronto: University of Toronto Press, 1977.
54. Everest, Allan S. *The War of 1812 in the Champlain Valley*. Syracuse: Syracuse University Press, 1981.
55. Flanagan, Thomas. *Riel and the Rebellion: 1885 Reconsidered*. Saskatoon: Western Producer Prairie Books, 1983.
56. Frégault, Guy. *Canada: The War of the Conquest*. M.M. Cameron (trans.). Toronto: Oxford University Press, 1969.
57. Frost, Leslie. *Fighting Men*. Toronto: Clarke, Irwin and Co., 1967.
58. Galloway, Strome. *The General Who Never Was*. Bellville: Mika Publishing, 1981.

59. Garrett, Richard. *General Wolfe*. London: Barker, c. 1975.
60. Glover, Michael. *General Burgoyne in Canada and America: Scapegoat for a System*. London: Gordon and Cremonesi, 1976.
61. Goodspeed, D.J. *Battle Royal: A History of the Royal Regiment of Canada, 1862-1962*. Toronto: privately printed, 1962.
62. ─────. *The Armed Forces of Canada, 1867-1967: A Century of Achievement*. Ottawa: Queen's Printer, 1967.
63. ─────. *The Road Past Vimy: The Canadian Corps, 1914-1918*. Toronto: Macmillan, 1969.
64. Gough, Barry M. *The Royal Navy and the Northwest Coast of North America, 1810-1914: A Study of British Maritime Ascendency*. Vancouver: University of British Columbia Press, 1971.
65. ─────. *Distant Dominion: Britain and the Northwest Coast of North America, 1579-1809*. Vancouver: University of British Columbia Press, 1980.
66. ─────. *Gunboat Frontier: British Maritime Authority and Northwest Coast Indians, 1846-1890*. Vancouver: University of British Columbia Press, 1984.
67. Granatstein, J.L. *The Politics of Survival: The Conservative Party, 1939-1945*. Toronto: University of Toronto Press, 1967.
68. ─────. *Canada's War: The Politics of the Mackenzie King Government, 1939-1945*. Toronto: Oxford University Press, 1975.
69. ─────. *A Man of Influence: Norman A. Robertson and Canadian Statecraft, 1929-1968*. Ottawa: Deneau Publishers, 1981.
70. ───── and R.D. Cuff, (eds.). *War and Society in North America*. Toronto: T. Nelson, 1971.
71. ───── and J.M. Hitsman. *Broken Promises: A History of Conscription in Canada*. Toronto: Oxford University Press, 1977.
72. ───── and P. Stevens, (eds.). *A Reader's Guide to Canadian History, 2: Confederation to the Present*. Toronto: University of Toronto Press, 1982.
73. ───── and Desmond Morton. *Bloody Victory; Canadians and the D-Day Campaign 1944*. Toronto: L. and O. Dennys, 1984.
74. Greenhous, Brereton. *Semper Paratus: The History of the Royal Hamilton Light Infantry (Wentworth Regiment) 1862-1977)*. Hamilton: privately printed, 1977.
75. ─────. *Dragoons: The Centennial History of the Royal Canadian Dragoons, 1883-1983*. Ottawa: Guild of the RCD, 1983.
76. Gruber, Ira D. *The Howe Brothers and the American Revolution*. New York: Atheneum, 1972.
77. ─────. "For King and Country: The Limits of Loyalty of British Officers in the War for American Independence" in Edgar Denton III, *The Limits of Loyalty*. Waterloo: Wilfrid Laurier University Press, 1980.
78. Guitard, Michelle. *The Militia of the Battle of Chateauguay: A Social History*. Ottawa: National Parks and Sites Branch, Parks Canada, 1983.
79. Hadley, Michael J. *U-Boats Against Canada; German Submarines in Canadian Waters*. Montreal and Kingston: McGill-Queen's University Press, 1985.

80. Halliday, H.A. *Chronology of Canadian Military Aviation.* Ottawa: Queen's Printer, 1975.
81. ――――. *No. 242 Squadron; the Canadian Years; The Story of the RAF's "All-Canadian" Fighter Squadron.* Stittsville, Ont.: Canada's Wings, 1978.
82. ――――. *The Tumbling Sky.* Stittsville, Ont.: Canada's Wings, 1978.
83. Hargreaves, Reginald. *The Bloodybacks: British Servicemen in North America and the Caribbean, 1655-1783.* London: Hart-Davis, 1968.
84. Harvey, J. Douglas. *Boys, Bombs and Brussels Sprouts: A Knees-Up, Wheels-Up Chronicle of World War II.* Toronto: McClelland and Stewart, 1981.
85. Hatch, F.J. *The Aerodrome of Democracy: Canada and the British Commonwealth Air Training Plan, 1939-1945.* Ottawa: Directorate of History, Department of National Defence, 1983.
86. Hatch, Robert M. *Thrust for Canada: The American Attempt on Quebec in 1775-1776.* Boston: Houghton Mifflin, 1979.
87. Haycock, Ronald G. "The American Legion in the Canadian Expeditionary Force, 1914-1917: A Study in Failure," *Military Affairs,* vol. 43, no. 3 (Oct., 1979), pp. 115-119.
88. ――――. "The Myth of Imperial Defence: Australian-Canadian Bilateral Military Co-operation, 1942," *War and Society,* vol. 2, no. I (May, 1984), pp. 65-84.
89. ――――. "Early Canadian Weapons Acquisition: 'That Damned Ross Rifle'," *Canadian Defence Quarterly,* vol. 14, no. 3 (Winter, 1984/85), pp. 48-57.
90. ――――. *Sam Hughes: The Public Career of a Controversial Canadian, 1853-1916.* Waterloo: Wilfrid Laurier University Press, 1986.
91. Hayter, Tony. "The British Army, 1713-1793: Recent Research Work," *Journal of the Society for Army Historical Research.* vol. 63, no. 253 (Spring, 1985), pp. 11-19.
92. Hildebrandt, Walter. *The Battle of Batoche: British Small Warfare and the Entrenched Métis.* Ottawa: Parks Canada, 1985.
93. Hitchens, F.H. *Air Board, Canadian Air Force and Royal Canadian Air Force.* Ottawa: Queen's Printer, 1972.
94. Hitsman, J. MacKay. *The Incredible War of 1812: A Military History.* Toronto: University of Toronto Press, 1965.
95. ――――. *Safeguarding Canada, 1763-1871.* Toronto: University of Toronto Press, 1967.
96. Hunter, T. Murray. *Canada at Dieppe.* Ottawa: Balmuir, 1982.
97. Hyatt, A.M.J. "The Military Career of Sir Arthur Currie." Ph.D.: Duke University, 1965.
98. Jenkins, Brian. *Fenians and Anglo-American Relations During Reconstruction.* Ithaca, N.Y.: Cornell University Press, 1969.
99. Kaufman, David and Michiel Horn. *A Liberation Album; Canadians in the Netherlands, 1944-45.* Toronto: McGraw-Hill Ryerson, 1980.
100. Kennedy, J. de N. *History of the Department of Munitions and Supply: Canada in the Second World War.* 2 vols. Ottawa: King's Printer, 1950.

101. Ketchum, Richard B. *The Winter Soldiers.* Garden City, N.Y.: Doubleday, 1973.
102. Knox, John. *The Siege of Quebec.* edited by Brian Connell. Mississauga: Pendragon House, 1979.
103. Kostenuk, Samuel and John Griffin. *RCAF Squadron Histories and Aircraft, 1924-1968.* Toronto: S. Stevens, Hakkert, 1977.
104. Lamb, James B. *The Corvette Navy: True Stories from Canada's Atlantic War.* Toronto: Macmillan, 1977.
105. Lanctot, Gustave. *Canada and the American Revolution, 1774-1783.* Margaret M. Cameron (trans.). London: Harrap, 1967.
106. Lawrence, Hal. *A Bloody War; One Man's Memories of the Canadian Navy, 1939-1945.* Toronto: Macmillan, 1979.
107. Lay, H. Nelson. *Memoirs of a Mariner.* Stittsville: Canada's Wings, 1982.
108. Leckie, Robert. *The Wars of America.* 2 vols. New York: Harper and Row, 1981.
109. Lord, Walter. *The Dawn's Early Light.* New York: Norton, 1972.
110. Lunt, James. *John Burgoyne of Saratoga.* London: Macdonald and Jane's, 1976.
111. McAndrew, W.J. "Book Essay: Roses and Thorns in Normandy," *Canadian Defence Quarterly*, vol. 14, no. 1 (Summer, 1984), pp. 51-53.
112. Macdonald, Lyn. *They Call it Passchendaele.* Toronto: Nelson, 1978.
113. MacIntosh, Dave. *Terror in the Starboard Seal.* Don Mills, Ont.: General Publishing, 1980.
114. MacIntyre, D.E. *Canada at Vimy.* Toronto: P. Martin, 1967.
115. McKee, Fraser M. *The Armed Yachts of Canada.* Erin, Ont.: Boston Mills Press, 1983.
116. Macksey, Kenneth. *The Shadow of Vimy Ridge.* Toronto: Ryerson, 1965.
117. McLaren, Roy. *Canadians in Russia, 1918-19.* Toronto: Macmillan, 1976.
118. ―――――. *Canadians on the Nile, 1882-1898; Being the Adventures of the Voyageurs on the Khartoum Relief Expedition and Other Exploits.* Vancouver: University of British Columbia Press, 1978.
119. ―――――. *Canadians Behind Enemy Lines, 1939-1945.* Vancouver: University of British Columbia Press, 1981.
120. MacLeod, R.C. *The N.W.M.P and Law Enforcement, 1873-1905.* Toronto: University of Toronto Press, 1976.
121. MacPhail, Sir Andrew. *The Medical Services.* Ottawa: King's Printer, 1925.
122. Macpherson, K.R. *Canada's Fighting Ships.* Toronto: Hakkert, 1975.
123. ――――― and John Burgess. *The Ships of Canada's Naval Forces, 1910-1981: A Complete Pictorial History of Canadian Warships.* Toronto: Collins, 1981.
124. Mahon, John K. *The War of 1812.* Gainesville, Florida: University of Florida Press, 1972.
125. Malone, Richard S. *Missing From the Record.* Toronto: Collins, 1946.
126. ―――――. *A Portrait of War, 1939-1943.* Toronto: Collins, 1983.

127. Marchand, Gérard. *Le Régiment du Maisonneuve vers la victoire, 1944-1945*. Montréal: Les Presses Libres, 1980.
128. Massey, Hector J. *The Canadian Military--A Profile*. Toronto: Copp Clark, 1972.
129. Massey, Raymond. *When I Was Young*. Toronto: McClelland and Stewart, 1976.
130. Massey, Vincent. *What's Past is Prologue*. Toronto: Macmillan, 1963.
131. Mathieson, William D., (ed.). *My Grandfather's War; Canadians Remember the First World War, 1914-1918*. Toronto: Macmillan, 1981.
132. Moyne, J.W. *Operational Research in the Canadian Armed Forces during the Second World War*. 2 vols. ORAE Report R68, Ottawa: DND, 1978.
133. Mellor, John. *Forgotten Heroes: The Canadians at Dieppe*. Toronto: Methuen, 1975.
134. Melnyk, T.W. *Canadian Flying Operations in South-East Asia, 1941-1945*. Ottawa: Queen's Printer, 1976.
135. Miller, Carman. *The Canadian Career of the Fourth Earl of Minto: The Education of a Viceroy*. Waterloo: Wilfrid Laurier University Press, 1980.
136. Milner, Marc. *North Atlantic Run: The Royal Canadian Navy and the Battle for the Convoys*. Toronto: University of Toronto Press, 1985.
137. Molson, K.M. and H.A. Taylor. *Canadian Aircraft Since 1909*. Stittsville, Ont.: Canada's Wings, 1982.
138. Moore, Christopher. *Louisbourg Portraits: Life in an Eighteenth Century Garrison Town*. Toronto: Macmillan, 1982.
139. Morris, David. *The Canadian Militia from 1855: An Historical Summary*. Erin, Ont.: Boston Mills Press, 1983.
140. Morrison, W.A. "The Conference of Defence Associations and the evolution of Major General of Reserves." War Studies M.A. Thesis. Royal Military College of Canada, Kingston, Ontario, 1980.
141. ————. "Book Essay: The Hong Kong Tragedy," *Canadian Defence Quarterly*. vol. 12, no. 2 (Autumn, 1983), pp. 54-56.
142. Morton, Desmond. *Ministers and Generals: Politics and the Canadian Militia, 1868-1904*. Toronto: University of Toronto Press, 1970.
143. ————. *The Last War Drum: The North-West Campaign of 1885*. Toronto: Hakkert, 1972.
144. ————. *The Canadian General: Sir William Otter*. Toronto: A.M. Hakkert, 1974.
145. ————. *Canada and War: A Military and Political History*. Toronto: Butterworths, 1981.
146. ———— and others. *Canada as a Military Power*. No. 51 of the International Review of Military History. Ottawa: Canadian Commission of Military History, 1982.
147. ————. *A Peculiar Kind of Politics: Canada's Overseas Ministry in the First World War*. Toronto: University of Toronto Press, 1982.
148. ————. *A Military History of Canada*. Edmonton: Hurtig Publishers, 1985.
149. ———— and Reginald H. Roy, (eds.). *Telegrams of the North-West Campaign*. Toronto: Champlain Society, 1972.

150. Mowat, Farley. *The Regiment*. Toronto: McClelland and Stewart, 1955.
151. ―――――. *And No Birds Sang*. Toronto: McClelland and Stewart, 1979.
152. Muise, D.A., (ed.). *A Reader's Guide to Canadian History. I: Beginnings to Confederation*. Toronto: University of Toronto Press, 1982.
153. Munro, Iain R. *Canada and the World Wars*. Toronto: Wiley, 1979.
154. Munro, J.A. and A.I. Inglis, (eds.). *Mike: The Memoirs of the Right Honourable Lester B. Pearson*. 3 vols. Toronto: University of Toronto Press, 1972-1975.
155. Neidhardt, W.S. *Fenianism in North America*. London: Pennsylvania State University Press, 1975.
156. Nicholson, (Col.) G.W.L. *Official History of the Canadian Army in the First World War: The Canadian Expeditionary Force, 1914-1919*. Ottawa: Queen's Printer, 1962.
157. ―――――. *The Gunners of Canada: The History of the Royal Regiment of Canadian Artillery*. 2 vols. Toronto: McClelland and Stewart, 1967-1972.
158. ―――――. *More Fighting Newfoundlanders: A History of Newfoundland's Fighting Forces in the Second World War*. St. John's: Government of Newfoundland, 1969.
159. ―――――. *Canada's Nursing Sisters*. Toronto: S. Stevens, Hakkert, 1975.
160. ―――――. *Seventy Years of Service: A History of the Royal Canadian Army Medical Corps*. Ottawa: Borealis Press, 1977.
161. Nolan, Brian. *Hero: The Buzz Beurling Story*. Toronto: Lester and Orpen, Dennys, 1981.
162. Norton, Mary Beth. *The British-Americans: The Loyalist Exiles in England, 1774-1789*. Toronto: Little Brown, 1972.
163. Paret, Peter. "Colonial Experience and European Military Reform at the End of the Eighteenth Century," *Bulletin of the Institute of Historical Research*. vol. 37 (1964), pp. 47-59.
164. Pargellis, Stanley McCrory, (ed.). *Military Affairs in North America, 1748-1765: Selected Documents from the Cumberland Papers in Windsor Castle*. Hamden, Conn.: Archon Books, 1969.
165. Peden, Murray. *A Thousand Shall Fall*. Stittsville: Canada's Wings, 1979.
166. Penlington, Norman L. *Canada and Imperialism, 1869-1899*. Toronto: University of Toronto Press, 1965.
167. Pickersgill, J.W., (ed.). *The Mackenzie King Record*. 4 vols. Toronto: University of Toronto Press, 1960-1970.
168. Pope, Maurice. *Soldiers and Politicians: The Memoirs of Lt.-Gen. Maurice A. Pope, C.B., M.C.* Toronto: University of Toronto Press, 1962.
169. Preston, Richard A. *Canada and 'Imperial Defense': A Study of the Origins of the British Commonwealth's Defense Organization, 1867-1919*. Durham: Duke University Press, 1967.
170. ―――――. *Canada's R.M.C.: A History of the Royal Military College*. Toronto: University of Toronto Press, 1969.
171. ―――――. *Canadian Defence Policy and the Development of the*

Canadian Nation, 1867-1917. Ottawa: Canadian Historical Association, 1970.

172. ──────. The Defence of the Undefended Border: Planning for War in North America, 1867-1939. Montreal: McGill-Queen's University Press, 1977.

173. Raudzens, George. The British Ordnance Department and Canada's Canals, 1815-1855. Waterloo: Wilfrid Laurier Press, 1979.

174. Rawlyk, George A. Nova Scotia's Massachusetts: A Study of Massachusetts--Nova Scotia Relations, 1630 to 1784. Montreal: McGill-Queen's University Press, 1973.

175. ────── (ed.). Revolution Rejected, 1775-1776. Toronto: Prentice-Hall, 1968.

176. ──────. Yankees at Louisbourg. Orono: University of Maine Press, 1967.

177. Read, Daphne, (ed.). The Great War and Canadian Society: An Oral History. Toronto: New Hogtown Press, 1978.

178. Reid, Gordon, (ed.). Poor Bloody Murder: Personal Memoirs of the First World War. Oakville: Mosaic Press, 1980.

179. Reynolds, Paul. Guy Carleton: A Biography. Toronto: Gage, 1980.

180. Ritchie, C. The Siren Years: A Canadian Diplomat Abroad, 1937-45. Toronto: Macmillan, 1974.

181. Robbins, Keith. 417 Squadron History. Stittsville, Ont.: Canada's Wings, 1983.

182. Roberts, James Alan. The Canadian Summers: The Memoirs of James Alan Roberts. Toronto: University of Toronto Bookroom, 1981.

183. Robertson, Terence. The Shame and the Glory: Dieppe. Toronto: McClelland and Stewart, 1962.

184. Roy, Reginald. Sinews of Steel: The History of the British Columbia Dragoons. Brampton, Ont.: privately printed, 1965.

185. ──────. The Seaforth Highlanders of Canada, 1919-1965. Vancouver: Evergreen Press, 1969.

186. ──────. For Most Conspicuous Bravery: A Biography of Major-General George R. Pearkes, V.C., through Two World Wars. Vancouver: University of British Columbia Press, 1977.

187. ──────. 1944: The Canadians in Normandy. Ottawa: Macmillan, 1984.

188. ────── (ed.). The Journal of Private Fraser, 1914-1918: Canadian Expeditionary Force. Victoria: Sono Nisi Press, 1985.

189. ──────. "The Battle for Courcelette, September, 1916: A Soldier's View," Journal of Canadian Studies, vol. 16 (Fall-Winter, 1984), pp. 56-67.

190. Schull, Joseph. The Far Ships: An Official Account of the Canadian Naval Operations in the Second World War. Ottawa: King's Printer, 1950.

191. ──────. Rebellion: The Rising of French Canada, 1837. Toronto: Macmillan, 1971.

192. Senior, Elinor Kyte. British Regulars in Montreal: An Imperial Garrison, 1832-1854. Montreal: McGill-Queen's University Press, c. 1981.

193. ──────. Roots of the Canadian Army: Montreal District, 1846-

1870. Montreal: Montreal Military and Maritime Museum, 1981.
194. ———. *Redcoats and Patriotes: The Rebellions in Lower Canada, 1837-1838*. Stittsville: Canada's Wings, 1985.
195. Senior, Hereward. *The Fenians and Canada*. Toronto: Macmillan, 1978.
196. Shy, John. *Toward Lexington: The Role of the British Army in the Coming of the American Revolution*. Princeton: Princeton University Press, 1965.
197. ———. *A People Numerous and Armed: Reflections on the Military Struggle for American Independence*. New York: Oxford University Press, 1976.
198. Smith, Paul H. *Loyalists and Redcoats: A Study in British Revolutionary Policy*. Chapel Hill: University of North Carolina Press, 1964.
199. Snowie, J. Allan. *Bloody Buron Normandy, 08 July, 1944*. Erin, Ont.: Boston Mills Press, 1984.
200. Speaight, Robert. *Vanier: Soldier, Diplomat and Governor General*. Toronto: Collins, 1970.
201. Stacey, C.P. *Canada and the British Army, 1846-1871: A Study in the Practice of Responsible Government*. London: Longmans, Green, 1936.
202. ———. *The Military Problems of Canada: A Survey of Defence Politics and Strategic Conditions Past and Present*. Toronto: Ryerson Press, 1940.
203. ———. "Canada and the Nile Expedition of 1884-85," *Canadian Historical Review*, vol. 33 (December 1952), pp. 319-40.
204. ———. *Quebec, 1759: The Siege and the Battle*. Toronto: Macmillan, 1959.
205. ———. *Records of the Nile Voyageurs, 1884-1885: The Canadian Voyageur Contingent in the Gordon Relief Expedition*. Toronto: Champlain Society, 1959.
206. ———. *Arms, Men and Government: The War Policies of Canada, 1939-1945*. Ottawa: Queen's Printer, 1970.
207. ———. *Canada and the Age of Conflict: A History of Canadian External Policies, vol. I: 1867-1921*. Toronto: Macmillan, 1977.
208. ———. *Canada and the Age of Conflict: A History of Canadian External Policies, vol. II, 1921-1948: The Mackenzie King Era*. Toronto: Macmillan, 1981.
209. ——— (ed.). *Introduction to the Study of Military History for Canadian Students*. Ottawa: Directorate of Military Training, 1953.
210. ——— and Ken Bell. *100 Years: The Royal Canadian Regiment, 1883-1983*. Don Mills, Ont.: Collins, Macmillan Canada, 1983.
211. Stanley, G.F.G. *Birth of Western Canada: A History of the Riel Rebellions*. London: Longmans Green, 1936.
212. ———. *In the Face of Danger: The History of the Lake Superior Regiment*. Port Arthur, Ont.: privately printed, 1960.
213. ———. *New France: The Last Phase, 1744-1760*. Toronto: McClelland and Stewart, 1968.
214. ———. *Canada Invaded, 1775-1776*. Toronto: Hakkert, 1973.

215. ———. *Canada's Soldiers: The Military History of an Unmilitary People*. 3rd edn. Toronto: Macmillan, 1974.
216. ———. *The War of 1812: Land Operations*. Toronto: Macmillan of Canada in collaboration with the National Museum of Man, National Museums of Canada, c. 1983.
217. Steele, I.K. *Guerillas and Grenadiers: The Struggle for Canada, 1689-1760*. Toronto: Ryerson Press, 1969.
218. Stevens, Paul and John Saywell (eds.). *Lord Minto's Canadian Papers: A Selection of the Public and Private Papers of the Fourth Earl of Minto*. Toronto: Champlain Society, 1981.
219. Stewart, Gordon and G.A. Rawlyk. *A People Highly Favoured of God--The Nova Scotia Yankees and the American Revolution*. Toronto: Macmillan, 1972.
220. Summers, J.L. and R. Chartrand. *Military Uniforms in Canada, 1665-1970*. Ottawa: National Museum of Man, 1981.
221. Swettenham, John. *To Seize Victory: The Canadian Corps in World War I*. Toronto: Ryerson Press, 1965.
222. ———. *Allied Intervention in Russia, 1918-1919, and the Part Played by Canada*. Toronto: Ryerson Press, 1967.
223. ———. *McNaughton*. 3 vols. Toronto: Ryerson Press, 1968-1969.
224. ———. *Canada and the First World War*. Toronto: Ryerson Press, 1969.
225. ——— (ed.). *Valiant Men: Canada's Victoria Cross and George Cross Winners*. Toronto: Hakkert, 1973.
226. ——— and Fred Gaffen. *Canada's Atlantic War*. Toronto: Samuel-Stevens, 1979.
227. Thistle, Mel, (ed.). *The Mackenzie--McNaughton Wartime Letters*. Toronto: University of Toronto Press, 1975.
228. Thompson, John Herd. *The Harvests of War: The Prairie West, 1914-1918*. Toronto: McClelland and Stewart, 1979.
229. Thorgrimsson, Thor and E. C. Russell. *Canadian Naval Operations in Korean Waters, 1950-1955*. Ottawa: Queen's Printer, 1965.
230. Tucker, Gilbert N. *The Naval Service of Canada: Its Official History*. 2 vols. Ottawa: King's Printer, 1952.
231. Upton, L.F.S. (ed.). *The United Empire Loyalists: Men and Myths*. Toronto: Copp Clark, 1967.
232. Urquhart, H.M. *Arthur Currie: The Biography of a Great Canadian*. Toronto: Dent, 1950.
233. Vincent, Carl. *The Blackburn Shark*. Stittsville: Canada's Wings, 1974.
234. ———. *No Reason Why: The Canadian Hong Kong Tragedy--An Examination*. Stittsville, Ont.: Canada's Wings, 1981.
235. Vokes, (General) Chris with J.P. Maclean. *Vokes: My Story*. Ottawa: Gallery Books, 1985.
236. Warner, Oliver. *With Wolfe to Quebec: The Path to Glory*. Toronto: Collins, 1972.
237. Whitaker, Denis W. and Shelagh. *Tug of War: The Canadian Victory that Opened Antwerp*. Toronto: Stoddart Publishing, 1984.
238. Whitfield, Carol M. *Tommy Atkins: The British Soldier in Canada, 1759-1870*. Ottawa: National Historic Parks and Sites Branch, Parks Canada, 1981.

239. Wickwire, Franklin and Mary. *Cornwallis: The American Adventure*. Boston: Houghton Mifflin, 1970.
240. Wigley, Philip G. *Canada and the Transition to Commonwealth: British-Canadian Relations, 1917-1926*. Cambridge: Cambridge University Press, 1977.
241. Williams, Jeffrey. *The Princess Patricia's Canadian Light Infantry*. London: Leo Cooper, 1972.
242. ──────. *Byng of Vimy: General and Governor-General*. London: Leo Cooper, 1983.
243. Wilson, Barbara M., (ed.). *Ontario and the First World War, 1914-1918: A Collection of Documents*. Toronto: Champlain Society, 1977.
244. Wise, S.F. *The Official History of the Royal Canadian Air Force*, volume 1, *Canadian Airmen and the First World War*. Toronto: University of Toronto Press in cooperation with the Minister of Supply and Services Canada, 1980.
245. Wood, H.F. *Strange Battleground: The Operations in Korea and Their Effects on the Defence Policy of Canada*. Ottawa: Queen's Printer, 1966.
246. Wood, Herbert Fiarlie. *Vimy!* Toronto: Macmillan, 1967.
247. Worthington, Larry. *Amid the Guns Below: The Story of the Canadian Corps, 1914-1919*. Toronto: McClelland and Stewart, 1965.
248. Zaslow, Morris and W.B. Turner, (eds.). *The Defended Border: Upper Canada and the War of 1812*. Toronto: Macmillan, 1964.

XIX

THE DOMINION SERVICES:

SOUTH AFRICA

Ronald Haycock

Of all the old self-governing Dominions, South Africa represents several complications for the study of British Military History. As Colonel Neil Orpen noted seventeen years ago, there was then and still is the semantical problem of what is British and what is South African or colonial-dominion military history. For our purposes the answer must be that as long as South Africa remained in the Commonwealth then any point of contact with British military fortunes remains a legitimate consideration. Of course what had not bothered Orpen was the massive proliferation of historical works since he drafted his contribution. Moreover, the wealth of information has been augmented by Afrikaner military historians who have brought a different view, one often from the "other side of the hill" and one reflecting the national emergence of the Afrikaner himself both in race and institutions. There is also a much wider scope in the latest writing, varying from consideration of Blacks and the Boer War to bibliographic and international strategic considerations. The basic categories into which the newer major works fall, however, seem to sustain those of earlier writing: the two Anglo-Boer wars, the various other campaigns, official histories of World War Two, military biography and the histories of various units and arms.

Before launching into any study one should consider the many bibliographic aids available. One of the simplest and best ways for any student to become familiar with the bibliography and the agencies that preserve, organize and list resources is to read "Historiography" in *South Africa 1985: The Official Yearbook of the Republic of South Africa* (97). Beyond this there are several valuable resources covering military history. The remarkable industry of historians is ably recorded in C.F.J. Muller, et. al., *South African History and Historians: A Bibliography* (1979) (63). It contains over 4,500 titles. The University of the Orange Free State's History Department at Bloemfontein specializes in South African military writing. The Sanlam Library of the University of South Africa (Pretoria) has prepared several useful military bibliographies including "The Boer War 1899-1902" (1983) (88), "Lord Chelmsford and the Anglo-Zulu War" (1984) (88a), "Australian and New Zealand Literature with Special Emphasis on the Anglo-Boer War, 1899-1902" (1983) (21) and "The Zulu War: A Short Bibliography" (1985) (89). There is also the Military Information Bureau of the South African Defence Force in Pretoria. This organization holds many valuable military records and contains a battery of archivist-historians who frequently publish in the South African Defence Force journal *Militaria*. Finally, the Human Sciences Research Council (Institute of Research Development, Pretoria) maintains a list of graduate theses and dissertations submitted to South African universities over the years. There is much here to reward the researcher.

As might be expected, the literature relating to British arms still finds a major focal point in the two great Anglo-Boer conflicts, especially the last one, ending in 1902. Afrikaner historians writing in their own language and largely viewing the conflicts from the Boer side and in the nationalist terms of freedom wars have added immensely to the literature. Professor J.E.H. Grobler in an article in *Historia* (1980) arising out of research for his doctoral thesis (University of Pretoria 1981: it is presently being prepared for publication in English) shows how the Transvaal, having failed to achieve independence from Britain, finally forced negotiations by defeating the British three times between December 1880 and March 1881 (37). Colonel George Duxbury, the Director of the South African Museum of Military History (Saxonwold, Transvaal, 2132), has also examined the war in his *David and Goliath: The First War of Independence* (1981) (25). The standard interpretation by a British historian remains Joseph Lehmann, *The First Boer War* (1972) (49).

But writing about this earlier conflict is nowhere near the vast output about the second Boer War. The researcher is well-advised to consult D.E. Rowse's excellent annotated bibliography on this conflict ("The Boer War, 1899-1902," Sanlam Library) not only for the books assessed but for the South African and international journal literature (88). Some samples will suffice; Howard Bailes', "Technology and Imperialism: A Case Study of the Victorian Army in Africa" (*Victorian Studies*, 1980) (5) and T.H.E. Travers, "Technology, Tactics and Morale: Jean De Bloch, The Boer War and British Military Theory, 1900-1914" (*Journal of Modern History*, 1979) (104) examines how the British Army generally rejected both De Bloch's writing and the lessons of the Boer War, espousing instead the power of the offensive.

Looking at the war as a whole, the definitive work in Afrikaans is J.H. Breytenbach's monumental 4 volumes, *Die geskiedenis van die Tweede Vryheidsoorlog in Suid-Afrika 1899-1902* (1960-1981) (13). And Rowse's bibliography lists many more. But in the last twenty years, writing about this unfortunate conflict has also proliferated, no doubt because of the war's size and the state of the British Army going into and coming out of it. Moreover, the studies are far more balanced in their interpretation and coverage than older works. A most recent and well-rounded survey remains the collection of essays by various authorities covering such diverse topics as Black participation through technology, tactics and economics. Edited by Peter Warwick *The South African War: The Anglo-Boer War, 1899-1902* (1980) is a collection which not only gives a more complete look but offers a revitalized Roberts and a view of more inflexible Boers whatever their individual talents. The British public was willing to accept the draconian ways of Kitchener because they felt that their own country's success was buttered by colonial expansion. And there is a refreshing look at the literary legacy of the period (107).

Byron Farwell, *The Great Boer War* (1977) (27) and Thomas Pakenham *The Boer War* (1979) (76) are both massively scholarly and revisionist. Both cast a wide net of personalities, politics, battles, disease and concentration camps. Lord Pakenham rehabilitates the much maligned Sir Redvers Buller by putting him in the context of the Victorian Army rivalry and War Office incompetence. He also makes a firm connexion between imperial aims of the British government and the interest of the mining magnates.

From the general treatment of the war, the literature concentrates on individuals, and, specific campaigns and diplomacy. In 1963 Julian Symons in his *Buller's Campaign* (102) began the revision of Redvers Buller. It was a reassessment carried on by O. Ransford in *The Battle of Spion Kop* (1969) (85). He concluded that the Devon General was the victim of contemporary training of the British Army whose officers were afraid to make bold decisions. Finally, Buller's resuscitation was accomplished by Pakenham. Philip Bateman's short study gives brief sketches of the then leading soldiers on both sides in *Generals of the Anglo-Boer War* (1977) (6). Individual studies of Boer generals are found in several works. Among them are D.M. Moore's brief study of Botha: *General Louis Botha's Second Expedition to Natal During the Anglo-Boer War, September to October 1901* (1979) (61) and F. Meintjies' *The Commandant General* (1971) (57). These works, both popular and scholarly, take advantage of the historical material available only in South Africa.

There is also a large number of publications in both languages that deal with particular campaigns. W. Baring Pemberton's, *Battles of the Boer War* (1964 and 1969) (78) in part helped perpetuate the stereotype that the British Army was incompetent prior to 1899. But his five-battle study does show how that army learned the painful and basic lessons of shooting straight, taking cover and manoeuvering. Brian Gardiner, the journalist-historian strips the apocrypha from Baden Powell's performance in his *Mafeking: A Victorian Legend* (1967) (32); R. Chisholm's *Ladysmith* (19) (1979) and Kenneth Griffith's hard-to-read *Thank God We Kept the Flag Flying* (1974) (36) details the trials of those in and out of besieged Ladysmith.

Specialized studies covering such areas as war courses, policy, race, diplomacy and public opinions are not as prevalent as the more narrowly military works. Yet they are there. Elizabeth Longford's *Jameson's Raid* (1982) (50) is a revised text of her earlier work and concludes that such an event was the end of aggressive imperial freebooting and filibustery as well as an obvious act of British misjudgment. *The Origins of the South African War: Joseph Chamberlain and the Diplomacy of Imperialism, 1895-1899* (1980) (79) by A.N. Porter exhonorates Chamberlain from "extensive culpability or special guilt." Peter Warwick unseats the myth of the "White Man's War" in his ground-breaking *Black People and the South African War, 1899-1902* (1983) (106). He shows that the Blacks gained very little in freedom or better living conditions under the British than they had under the Boers. Finally, one should read A.M. Grundlingh's fine book review in *Kleio* (1978) (38). In commenting on S.P. Spies' *Methods of Barbarism? Roberts and Kitchener and Civilians in the Boer Republics, January 1900-May 1902* (1978) (100), Grundlingh gives a good historiographical survey of the works previously published on the subject.

Opposition to British military effort against the Boers has received more consideration in the last twenty years. Two doctoral dissertations cover the Pro-Boer (J.W. Auld, "The Pro-Boer Liberals in Britain During the Boer War, 1899-1902," Stanford University, 1970) and the British anti-war movement (Patricia Ann Shaw Ashman, "Anti-War Sentiment in Britain During the Boer War," St. Louis University, 1972) (3, 4). The next year there were two more titles added to publishers' lists of the same genre. Richard Price studied the British working classes' attitude to the war and found plenty of support for it: *An Imperial War and the British Working Class* (1972) (82). Stephen Koss edited a collection of documents illustrating the opinions and activities of British liberals strongly opposed to the British position in the conflict: *The Pro Boers: The Anatomy of an Anti-War Movement* (1973) (47). Such literature not only reflects the anti-war mood of the 1970s but also the willingness of historians to carry their studies beyond the confines of the narrowly military.

While the bulk of the studies have centered in the great Anglo-Boer conflicts, other aspects of British arms in South Africa are well represented. Of the general literature covering colonial campaigning, C.E. Callwell's *Small Wars: Their Principles and Practice* (1896) (18) is still a seminal work after ninety years. Brian Bond has written and edited several good pieces including his essay "Colonial Wars and Primitive Expeditions, 1856-1899" in Brigadier Peter Young's and Lt. Col. J.P. Lawford's *History of the British Army* (1970) (11). There is also Bond's own earlier collection, *Victorian Military Campaigns* (1967) (10). Denis Judd took a fascinating, however superficial, look at the British Army's notable failures in *Someone Has Blundered: Calamities of the British Army in the Victorian Age* (1973) (43). Fortunately, the topic was saved the same year by Byron Farwell's good survey, *Queen Victoria's Little Wars* (1973) (28). This last work remains more impartial than Dr. Victor Kiernans' 1980 effort, *European Empires from Conquest to Collapse 1815-1960* (46). His observations that many British armies were full "of third-rate human materials" whose smashing victories over Africans and Asians "imply the thews and fury of the heroes of Valhalla in an army of ill-fed, disease ridden alcoholics" seems cynically over-simplified (p. 36).

The "native" wars, if that word is any longer usable, have their place. A.J. Smithers surveyed the conflict of first the Boers then the British Army with the Kaffirs in his *The Kaffir Wars, 1779-1877* (1973) (94). But it is the Zulu Wars, probably because of their length and unexpected difficulties for British arms, that continue to fascinate historians. The aforementioned University of South Africa's bibliographies "The Zulu War: A Short Bibliography" (1985) and "Lord Chelmsford in the Anglo-Zulu War" (1984) are vital, especially for periodical and dissertation studies (89, 88a). Of the published works, Donald Morris' *The Washing of the Spears* (1966) (62) still dominates the field even though F.W.D. Jackson's series of articles in the *Society for Army Historical Research Journal* (Vol. 43, 1965) entitled "Isandhlwana, 1879: The Sources Re-examined" (1965) (41) is a very scholarly analysis. In the next decade, there were several other relevant interpretations for the period including David Clammer's *The Zulu War* (1973) (20), Michael Glover's *Rorke's Drift: A Victorian Epic* (1975) (33) and Frank Emery's *The Red Soldier: Letters from the Zulu War* (1977) (26) which is based on letters from all ranks there. Finally, in 1981 there was a compilation by editors Andrew Duminy and Charles Ballard, *The Anglo-Zulu War: New Perspectives* (24).

One of the dominant figures of the Victorian Army was Sir Garnet Wolseley whose career included substantial South African service. The African material in Joseph Lehmann's *All Sir Garnet: A Life of Field Marshal Lord Wolseley* (1964) (48) is relevant and Adrian Preston has published much perceptive and interesting material on Sir Garnet including *The South African Diaries of Sir Garnet Wolseley 1875* (1971) and in 1973, *The South African Journal of Sir Garnet Wolseley, 1879-1880* (80, 81).

As Colonel Orpen pointed out in the original edition, beyond John Buchan's description of the South African Infantry Brigade in World War One published under the title *The History of the South African Forces in France* (1920) (17), this conflict is sadly neglected in the historiography. In 1924 the South African General Staff published *The Union of South Africa and the Great War, 1914-1918* (1924) (96) and just before the second German war J.J. Collyer produced for the Union Government, *The Campaign in German South West Africa, 1914-1915* (1937) and *The South Africans with General Smuts in South East Africa, 1916* (1939) (22, 23). Little has been produced since then. The British official history of the Great War remains the major resource for South Africa's valiant efforts on the Somme, at Ypres, Delville Wood and elsewhere in Europe, Africa and Palestine.

Such is not the case with the story of World War Two. Yet in the matter of official history, it was nearly so. After that war, the Union War Histories section of the Prime Minister's office was created to write a multi-volume official story of the conflict. Hailed as the most authoritative work yet produced on the North African campaigns 1941-1942, J.A.I. Agar-Hamilton's and L.C.F. Turner's *Crisis in the Desert, May-July 1942* (1952) (1) and *The Sidi Rezegh Battles, 1941* (1957) (2), were all that had appeared when Prime Minister Vorster shut down the War Histories Section in 1961. It seemed that South Africa might enjoy the unenviable distinction of failing to produce a record of her part in World War Two. Ex-servicemen felt they had been given short shrift. In response to the closure, an unofficial body, the South African War Histories Advisory Committee was charged to complete the series. By 1982, the end result was that nine more volumes appeared. Mostly under the prolific and able authorship of Colonel Neil D. Orpen with the general title *South African Forces in World War Two* (1968-1982) (15, 16, 55, 56, 67, 71, 72, 73, 74), the titles cover most facets of the war. Volume seven, *South Africa at War* (1979) (56) details the domestic war effort, including military, social and industrial mobilization. It is particularly critical of the heavy hand of the Chief of the General Staff, General Sir Pierre van Ryneveld. There has been some criticism of the series. For instance, the intensity of the research has left some of the volumes with a fascination for details and structures. And there is nowhere any major assessment of Field Marshal J.C. Smuts' contribution to the grand strategic direction of the war. Perhaps it was felt that Sir Keith Hancock's two earlier volumes: *Smuts* (1962-1968) (39), had said enough on the great man. In spite of this, however, the entire publishing effort of the story of World War Two remains a testament to the authors' productivity and South African veterans' determination to tell their own war story.

As the official and semi-official histories were coming out, forces, some of them similar to those effecting the other Dominions, were separating South Africa's national forces from its historical connexions with British Arms. Yet there continues to be much written especially unit and particular arms history showing the British links. Neil Orpen himself is responsible for several. Among them are his *Gunners of the Cape* (1965) (68), *Prince Alfred's Guard* (1967), (70), *The Cape Town Highlanders 1885-1970* (1970) (66), and *The History of the Transvaal Horse Artillery, 1904-1974* (1975) (69). A.C. Martin has produced the definitive history of *The Durban Light Infantry* (Vol. 1, 1854-1934; Vol. 2, 1935-1960) (53, 54), and as might be expected, the Military Information Branch of the Central Documentation Service continues to publish pieces such as the late Brigadier-General W. Otto's *The Special Service Battalion* (1973) (75), R.J. Bouch's collection, *Infantry in South Africa, 1652-1976* (1977) (12) and Colonel F.J. Jacob's history of the *South African Corps of Signals* (42). Finally, the researcher will always find many valuable sketches and bibliographic material in the professional journal of the South African Defence Force, *Militaria*.

The last fifteen years has seen great gains made in the writing of British military history in South Africa. However much needs to be done. There remains a fascination with the Anglo-Boer Wars, no doubt explained by the Afrikaner nationalism born in them and reaffirmed by the trials of subsequent involvement in British wars, the declaration of the Republic and reactions to recent international pressures. This fascination has been to the detriment of other studies. World War One and the Korean Conflict need detailed analyses. More light should be shed on important personalities like Smuts or various defence ministers and chiefs of staff. Little has been done, for instance, about the influence of South Africa on British strategy in peace or war. There is less on the routine relationships between South Africa and British soldiers in terms of education, social influences, training or the equipping of armies. Explorations of the military implications of the High Commissioners, or the Governors-General is untapped. There is a handful of military enthusiasts, who continue to work on British military history in that country, but the field still remains ripe for the exploration.

BIBLIOGRAPHY

The author would like to thank Colonel J.A. Combrinck, J.E.H. Grobler, Deon Fourie, D.E. Rowse, Colonel George Duxbury and Andrew Duminy, all of South Africa, for their generous help in compiling this list.

1. Agar-Hamilton, J.A.I. and L.C.F. Turner. *Crisis in the Desert, May-July 1942*. Cape Town: Oxford University Press, 1952.
2. ─────. *The Sidi Rezegh Battles, 1941*. Cape Town: Oxford University Press, 1957.
3. Ashman, Patricia Ann Shaw. "Anti-War Sentiment in Britain During the Boer War." PhD: St. Louis University, 1972.

4. Auld, J.W. "The Pro-Boer Liberals in Britain During the Boer War, 1899-1902." PhD: Stanford University, 1970.
5. Bailes, Howard. "Technology and Imperialism: A Case Study of the Victorian Army in Africa," *Victorian Studies*, vol. 24, no. 1 (1980), pp. 83-104.
6. Bateman, P. *Generals of the Anglo-Boer War*. Cape Town: South African Historical Mint, 1977.
7. Belfield, E. *The Boer War*. London: Leo Cooper, 1975.
8. Bellairs, Lady (ed.). *The Transvaal War, 1880-1881*. Cape Town: Struik, 1972.
9. Benyon, John. *Proconsul and Paramountcy in South Africa: The High Commission, British Supremacy and the Sub-Continent, 1866-1910*. Pietermaritzburg: University of Natal Press, 1980.
10. Bond, Brian (ed.). *Victorian Military Campaigns*. London: Hutchinson, 1967.
11. ————. "Colonial Wars and Primitive Expeditions, 1856-1899," in Peter Young and J.P. Lawford (eds.), *History of the British Army*. London: Barker, 1970.
12. Bouch, R.J. (ed.). *Infantry in South Africa, 1652-1976*. Pretoria: Documentation Service, SADF, 1977.
13. Breytenbach, J.H. *Die geskiedenis, van die Tweede Vryheidsoorlog in Suid-Afrika, 1899-1902*. 4 vols., Pretoria: Staatsdrukker, 1960-1981.
14. ———— and Ploeger, J. *Majuba Gedenkbock: uitgegee ter herdenking van die Boere se strydter verkryging van hul onafhanklikheid'n eeu gelede*. Roodepoort: Cum Boecke, 1980.
15. Brown, J.A. *Eagles Strike*; vol. 4 of *South African Forces in World War II*. Cape Town: Purnell, 1974.
16. ————. *A Gathering of Eagles*; vol. 2 of *South African Forces in World War II*. Cape Town: Purnell, 1970.
17. Buchan, John. *The History of the South African Forces in France*. London: Nelson, 1920.
18. Callwell, C.E. *Small Wars: Their Principles and Practice*. London: Harrison and Sons, 1896.
19. Chisholm, R. *Ladysmith*. Bramfontein: Jonathan Ball, 1979.
20. Clammer, David. *The Zulu War*. Newton Abbot: David and Charles, 1973.
21. Colenbrander, H. and le Roux, L. (compilers). "Australian and New Zealand Literature with a Special Emphasis on the Anglo-Boer War (1899-1902) as a Theme." Sanlam Library, The University of South Africa, 1983.
22. Collyer, J.J. *The Campaign in German South West Africa, 1914-1915*. Pretoria: Government Printer, 1937.
23. ————. *The South Africans with General Smuts in South East Africa, 1916*. Pretoria: Government Printer, 1939.
24. Duminy, Andrew and Charles Ballard (eds.). *The Anglo-Zulu War: New Perspectives*. Pietermaritzburg: University of Natal Press, 1981.
25. Duxbury, Colonel G.R. *David and Goliath: The First War of Independence 1880-1881*. Johannesburg: South African National Museum of Military History, 1981.
26. Emery, Frank. *The Red Soldier: Letters from the Zulu War, 1879*. London: Hodder and Stoughton, 1977.

27. Farwell, Byron. *The Great Boer War*. London: Allen Lane, 1977.
28. ———. *Queen Victoria's Little Wars*. London: Allen Lane, 1973.
29. Featherstone, Donald. *Captain Carey's Blunder: The Death of the Prince Imperial*. London: Leo Cooper, 1973.
30. Fitzpatrick, Sir Percy. *South African Memories: Scraps of History*. Johannesburg: A.D. Donker, 1979.
31. Flint, John E. *Cecil Rhodes*. London: Hutchinson, 1976.
32. Gardner, Brian. *Mafeking: A Victorian Legend*. New York: Harcourt, Brace and World, 1967.
33. Glover, Michael. *Rorke's Drift: A Victorian Epic*. Cape Town: Purnell, 1975.
34. Goosen, J.C. *South Africa's Navy: The First Fifty Years*. Cape Town: W.J. Flesch, 1973.
35. Gordon, C.T. *The Growth of Boer Opposition to Kruger, 1890-95*. Oxford: Oxford University Press, 1970.
36. Griffith, Kenneth. *Thank God We Kept the Flag Flying: The Siege and Relief of Ladysmith, 1899-1900*. London: Hutchinson, 1974.
37. Grobler, J.E.H. "Militere Verset Teen Britse Bestuur: Die Eerste Vryheidsoorlog, 1880-1891," *Historia*, vol. 25 (no. 2, 1980), pp. 29-41.
38. Grundlingh, A.M. "New Perspectives on Britain's Conduct of the Anglo-Boer War," *Kleio*, vol. 10, nos. 1 and 2 (1978), pp. 39-46.
39. Hancock, W.K. *Smuts*. 2 vols. Cambridge: Cambridge University Press, 1962-1968.
40. Harington, A.L. *Sir Harry Smith - Bungling Hero*. Cape Town: Tafelberg, 1980.
41. Jackson, F.W.D. "Isandhlwana, 1879: The Sources Reexamined," *Society for Army Historical Research Journal*, vol. 43 (March, Sept. and Dec. 1965), pp. 30-43, 113-132 and 169-183.
42. Jacobs, F.J. et. al. *South African Corps of Signals*. Pretoria: Documentation Service, SADF, Publication No. 4.
43. Judd, Denis. *Someone Has Blundered: Calamities of the British Army in the Victorian Age*. London: Barker, 1973.
44. ———. *The Boer War*. L. Kennedy (ed.). London: Hart-Davis, MacGibbon, 1977.
45. Kandyba-Foxcroft, E. *Russia and the Anglo-Boer War, 1899-1902*. Roodepoort: Cum Books, 1981.
46. Kiernan, Victor G. *European Empires From Conquest to Collapse, 1815-1960*. Bungay: Fontana, 1982.
47. Koss, Stephen (ed.). *The Pro-Boers: The Anatomy of an Anti-war Movement*. Chicago: University of the Chicago Press, 1973.
48. Lehmann, Joseph H. *All Sir Garnet: A Life of Field Marshal Lord Wolseley*. London: Jonathan Cape, 1964.
49. ———. *The First Boer War*. London: Jonathan Cape, 1972.
49. (a) ———. *Remember You are an Englishman*. London: Jonathan Cape, 1977.
50. Longford, Elizabeth. *Jameson's Raid*. London: Weidenfeld and Nicholson, 1982.
51. McNab, R. *French Colonel: Villebois-Mereuil and the Boers, 1899-1900*. Cape Town: Oxford University Press, 1975.

52. Marlowe, John. *Cecil Rhodes: The Anatomy of Empire*. London: Elek, 1972.
53. Martin, A.C. *The Durban Light Infantry:* vol. 1, *1854-1934*. Durban: Durban Light Infantry Association, 1969.
54. ———. *The Durban Light Infantry:* vol. 2, *1935-1960*. Durban: Durban Light Infantry Association, 1969.
55. Martin, H.J. and Neil Orpen. *Eagles Victorious*, vol. 6 of *South African Forces in World War II*. Cape Town: Purnell, 1977.
56. ———. *South Africa at War*, vol. 7 of *South African Forces in World War II*. Cape Town: Purnell, 1979.
57. Meintjies, F. *The Commandant-General: The Life and Times of Petrus Jacobus Joubert of the South African Republic, 1831-1900*. Cape Town: Tafelberg, 1971.
58. Meintjies, Johannes. *The Voortrekkers: The Story of the Great Trek and the Making of South Africa*. London: Cassell, 1973.
59. ———. *The Anglo-Boer War, 1899-1902*. Cape Town: Struik, 1976.
60. Milton, J.R.L. *The Edges of War: A History of the Frontier Wars, 1702-1878*. Cape Town: Juta, 1983.
61. Moore, D.M. *General Louis Botha's Second Expedition to Natal, During the Anglo-Boer War, September to October 1901*. Cape Town: Historical Publication Society, 1979.
62. Morris, Donald R. *The Washing of the Spears*. London: Jonathan Cape, 1966.
63. Muller, C.F.J. et. al., (eds.). *South African History and Historians: A Bibliography*. Pretoria: University of South Africa, 1979.
64. Noer, Thomas J. *Briton, Boer and Yankee: The United States and South Africa, 1870-1914*. Kent, Ohio: Kent State University Press, 1979.
65. Nutting, Anthony. *Scramble for Africa: The Great Trek to the Boer War*. London: Constable, 1970.
66. Orpen, Neil. *The Cape Town Highlanders, 1885-1970*. Cape Town: CTH Historical Committee, 1970.
67. ———. *East Africa and Abyssinian Campaigns*, vol. 1 of *South African Forces in World War II*. Cape Town: Purnell, 1968.
68. ———. *Gunners of the Cape: The Story of the Cape Field Artillery*. Cape Town: Standard Press, 1965.
69. ———. *The History of the Transvaal Horse Artillery, 1904-1974*. Johannesburg: The Transvaal Horse Regimental Council, 1975.
70. ———. *Prince Alfred's Guard*. Cape Town: Books of Africa, 1967.
71. ———. *Victory in Italy*, vol. 5 of *South African Forces in World War II*. Cape Town: Purnell, 1975.
72. ———. *War in the Desert*, vol. 3 of *South African Forces in World War II*. Cape Town: Purnell, 1972.
73. ——— and H.J. Martin. *Salute the Sappers: Part I*, vol. 8 of *South African Forces in World War II*. Johannesburg: Sappers Association, 1981.
74. ———. *Salute the Sappers: Part 2*, vol. 9 of *South African Forces in World War II*. Johannesburg: Sappers Association, 1982.

75. Otto, Brigadier W. *The Special Services Battalion.* Pretoria: Documentation Service, SADF, 1973.
76. Pakenham, Thomas. *The Boer War.* London: Weidenfeld and Nicolson, 1979.
77. Parsons, Neil. *A New History of Southern Africa.* London: Macmillan, 1982.
78. Pemberton, W. Baring. *Battles of the Boer War.* London: Pan Books, 1969.
79. Porter, A.N. *The Origins of the South African War: Joseph Chamberlain and the Diplomacy of Imperialism, 1895-1899.* Cape Town: David Phillip, 1980.
80. Preston, Adrian W. (ed.). *The South African Diaries of Sir Garnet Wolseley, 1875.* Cape Town: A.A. Balkema, 1971.
81. ———— (ed.). *The South African Journal of Sir Garnet Wolseley, 1879-1880.* Cape Town: A.A. Balkema, 1973.
82. Price, Richard. *An Imperial War and the British Working Class: Working Class Attitudes and Reactions to the Boer War.* London: Routledge and Kegan Paul, 1972.
83. Rands, F.W.U. *With 'Bobs' and Kruger.* N.P., 1977.
84. Ransford, Oliver. *The Battle of Majuba Hill: The First Boer War.* London: Murray, 1967.
85. ————. *The Battle of Spion Kop.* London: John Murray, 1969.
86. Reckitt, B.N. *The Lindley Affair: The Diary fo the Boer War.* Hull: A. Brown and Sons, 1972.
87. Ross, Edward. *Diary of the Siege of Mafeking October 1899--May 1900.* Cape Town: van Riebeck Society, 1980.
88. Rowse, D.E. (compiler). "The Boer War, 1899-1902," Pretoria: Sanlam Library, the University of South Africa, 1983.
88. (a) ———— and E. de Lange (compilers). "Lord Chelmsford and the Anglo-Zulu War," Pretoria: Sanlam Library, the University of South Africa, 1984.
89. ———— et. al. (compilers). "The Zulu War: A Short Bibliography," Pretoria: Sanlam Library, the University of South Africa, 1985.
90. Schreuder, D.M. *The Scramble for Southern Africa, 1877-1895: The Politics of Partition Reappraised.* Cambridge: Cambridge University Press, 1980.
91. Selby, John. *The Boer War: A Study in Cowardice and Courage.* London: Arthur Barker, 1969.
92. Sharpe, Gerald. *The Siege of Ladysmith.* London: Macdonald and Jane's, 1976.
93. Siwundhla, H.T. "The Participation of Non-European in the Anglo-Boer War, 1899-1902." PhD: Claremont Graduate School, 1977.
94. Smithers, A.J. *The Kaffir Wars, 1779-1877.* London: Leo Cooper, 1973.
95. *South Africa Field Force Casualty List, 1899-1902.* Essex: Oaklands Book Division, 1972.
96. South Africa. General Staff. *The Union of South Africa and the Great War, 1914-1918.* Official History. Pretoria: The Government Printing and Stationery Office, 1924.
97. *South Africa 1985: The Official Yearbook of the Republic of South Africa.* 11th edition, Pretoria: Government Printer, 1985.

98. *The South Africa War Casualty Roll, 1899-1902.* 2 vols. London: J.B. Hayward and Son, 1972.
99. *South African War Honours and Awards, 1899-1902: Officers and Men of the Army and Navy Mentioned in Despatches.* London: Arms and Armour Press, 1971.
100. Spies, S.B. *Methods of Barbarism? Roberts and Kitchener and Civilians in the Boer Republics, January 1900--May 1902.* Cape Town: Human and Rousseau, 1978.
101. ─────. *The Origins of the Boer War.* London: Edward Arnold, 1972.
102. Symons, Julian. *Buller's Campaign.* London: Cresset Press, 1963.
103. Todd, P. and D. Fordham. *Private Tucker's Boer War Diary: The Transvaal War of 1899, 1900, 1901, 1902.* London: Elm Tree Books, 1980.
104. Travers, T.H.E. "Technology, Tactics and Morale: Jean de Bloch, The Boer War and British Military Theory, 1900-1914," *Journal of Modern History*, vol. 51, no. 2 (1979), pp. 264-286.
105. Uys, Ian. *Heidelbergers of the Boer War.* Heidelberg: Ian Uys, 1981.
106. Warwick, Peter. *Black People and the South African War, 1899-1902.* Cambridge: Cambridge University Press, 1983.
107. ───── (ed.). *The South African War: The Anglo-Boer War, 1899-1902.* London: Longmans, 1980.
108. Wilkinson-Latham, Christopher. *The Boer War.* London: Osprey, 1977.
109. Witton, G. *Scapegoats of the Empire.* Melbourne: Angus and Robertson, 1982.
110. Wright, John B. *Bushman Raiders of the Drakensberg, 1840-1870: A Study of Their Conflict with Stock-Keeping Peoples in Natal.* Pietermaritzburg: University of Natal Press, 1971.

XX

BRITISH ARMS IN INDIA

Ronald Haycock

The historiography of the British Army, as Hew Strachan has recently noted, has too long been Euro-centric. That posture suggests the Army was doing little in the 19th century save participating in the Crimean and the Boer Wars nearly a half century apart and not very well at that. The long peace, it is commonly held, produced inertia, incompetence and little or no doctrine. But this opinion ignores the large colonial military experience. The lack of attention to it is not hard to understand. There emerged, for instance, no major spokesman for the doctrine of the Army's colonial activities. Still British arms were undergoing a substantial and particular development. Most of this experience was gained in India.

For the general reader more about the Army in India is gained by reading the novels of M.M. Kaye, Paul Scott or John Masters. And it is not a bad way of acquiring enjoyably basic knowledge about a fascinating past. But for the historian the process is much more complicated. All literature about British arms has grown immensely in the past two decades. Western, mostly British, and some Indian scholars have substantially widened the view of the entire Indian military experience. Of all the repositories of primary material, the India Office Library contains as much about the Crown's regiments as it does those of the East India Company and yields more than materials in the Public Record Office. There are now several excellent bibliographic guides to the Indian literature, some more formal than others. Partly as a hangover of their colonial past when the Indian Army was regarded by the majority of Indian intellectuals as the despised servant of the British and partly due to the anti-militarist attitudes of many of the educated Indians, military history has not received adequate attention from its scholars. However, S.N. Prasad, *The Military History of India* (1976) (151) has gone a long way in breaking through this impasse. Published under the aegis of the Indian Council of Historical Research his effort surveys the work done on Indian military history "since the earliest times." In England, Anthony Bruce's *Annotated Bibliography of the British Army, 1660-1914* (1975) (22) has much of value as do two book surveys by M.E. Yapp, "Recent Books on Modern Indian History" (1975) and "Recent Books on India" (1982) (188, 189). Philip Amos has gathered a long list of all of the publications on the strategic Indian concerns in his "Recent Works on the Great Game in Asia"

(1980) (5).* Such guides are necessary beginnings for any researcher.

Also indispensible are the general surveys of the British Army, not the least being Sir John Fortesque's monumental *History of the British Army*. Inspite of the obvious biases and evidential reliances, the work, whose last three volumes cover the colonial period, remains the pillar stone of campaign history (60).

Historians obviously prefer to study the period after the 1857 Mutiny. Yet there is much written about India before that unhappy event. Malcolm Yapp, *Strategies of British India: Britain, Iran and Afghanistan, 1798-1850* (1980) details the British policies and looks at how they were shaped and misshaped in the first half of the 19th century (190). Early aspects of what ultimately became the "Great Game," is explored by Edward Ingram, *The Beginning of the Great Game in Asia, 1828-1834* (1970) (86). Ingram departs from the usual orthodoxy that free trade and laissez-faire dictated strategies in India by showing that the real invincibility of the British there was that their military machine should not fight and that trade therefore was geared to fit this strategum. P.J. Marshall has two books that look at policy and the activators of it within the East India Company: *Problems of Empire: Britain and India 1757-1813* (1968) and *East Indian Fortunes: The British in Bengal in the Eighteenth Century* (1976) (114, 115). By 1794, Whitehall had come to perceive the Company's army as an imperial force. Yet amalgamation with the British Army was met with a storm of protest. Raymond Callahan, *The East India Company and Army Reform, 1783-1798* (1972) gives a good analysis of the 18th century Indian army officers' perspective on many of these forces (28). The central event of British military history in India before the Mutiny is, of course, Plassey and along with that Clive. This moody but masterful man has been the subject of no less than five books in a two year period. The best are James Lawford's *Clive: Proconsul of India* (1976) (98) and Mark Bence-Jones, *Clive of India* (1974) (14). Both agree that without Clive it was at least open to doubt that the British would have maintained their foothold in Madras and Bengal. Lawford has also explored a larger military theme in *Britain's Army in India: From Its Origins to the Conquest of Bengal* (1978) with clarity and precision, noting that discipline and scientific military superiority gave the minority European soldiers, namely those of the East India Company, dominance (97).

Once Clive and his generation laid the foundations for British India many others, both soldiers and civilians, added to the edifice. Jac Weller completed his trilogy on Wellington with *Wellington in India* (1972) (181), a very full account of the young man's confusing early career on the sub-continent. Weller never loses sight of how Wellington's experiences prepared him for his campaigns in the Peninsula and Flanders. C.H. Philip's *The Young Wellington in India* (1973) (147) complements Weller's but the relevant chapters in Elizabeth Longford's first volume *Wellington: Years of the Sword* (1972) (105), add little new. Michael Edwardes, *Glorious Sahibs: The Romantic as Empire Builder* (1968) (48) tries to assign the common

---

*One should also note the bibliographic surveys mentioned in previous chapter by H. Strachan and E. M. Spiers.

ideology of romanticism to an analysis of his sahibs: David Ochterlony, Charles Metcalfe, John Malcolm and Mountstuart Elphinstone. Unfortunately, the attempt ignores the multiplicity of other motives. One thing is sure however: these men did expand British influence and subordinate Indian rulers. More insight into the minds of various lesser sahibs comes out of K.K. Dyson, *A Various Universe: A Study of the Journals and Memoirs of British Men and Women in the Indian Sub-Continent 1765-1856* (1978) (45). From these works, the social-military historian in particular can learn a great deal about specific events, shifting attitudes of British rule, and British-Indian relationships.

Individuals, particularly governors, have received much attention. D.N. Panigrahi, *Charles Metcalfe in India: Ideas and Administration, 1806-1835* (1968) (141), C.H. Philips (ed.), *The Correspondence of Lord William Bentinck, Governor-General of India, 1828-1835* (1977) (146), and B.J. Hasrat (ed.), *The Punjab Papers: Selection from the Private Papers of Lord Auckland, Lord Ellenborough, Viscount Hardinge and the Marquis of Dalhousie, 1836-1849, on the Sikhs* (1970) (74) cover much of the ground. But beyond providing overwhelming documentation and in the case of Sir Cyril Philips' compilation, a sense of the urgency of the times, little beyond policy questions illuminates British arms. Other lesser notables of the period have published journals or found biographers. N.K. Barooah, *David Scott in North-East India, 1802-1831: A Study in British Paternalism* (1970) (11) and D.G.E. Hall, *Henry Burney: A Political Biography* (1974) (71) details the careers of two of the John Company's administrators and diplomat-soldiers. And there are reprints or new editions of books concerning four common soldiers that give good descriptions of active service under the Company's banners: Arthur Swinson and Donald Scott (eds.), *The Memoirs of Private Waterfield* (1968) (177); C.J. Stranks (ed.), *The Path of Glory: The Memoirs of John Shipp* (1969) who served in the ranks in India from 1801 to 1825 (176); N.W. Bancroft, *From Recruit to Staff Sergeant* (1979) (10) and James Lunt's new edition of Sita Ram's 1873 classic, *From Sepoy to Subedar* (106). The last two memoirs explain much about the true causes of the 1857 Mutiny.

There appears to be no end to the demand for books on Britain's small wars especially about Indian ones. Now not of much importance as history, G.B. Malleson, *The Decisive Battles of India From 1746 to 1849* first published in 1883 and reprinted recently (1974) (112) still has value as a statement of historical philosophy. John Pemble, *The Invasion of Nepal--John Company at War* (1971) (143) is a well-researched analysis of the war against the Gurkhas in 1814-1816. Perhaps the toughest wars fought by the John Company were those against the Sikhs. The best of a series on these conflicts is H.C.B. Cook's *The Sikh Wars, 1845-6, 1848-9* (1975) (37). Not only are the arduous campaigns well-described but so too is the difficult relationship between Hardinge and Gough. There is also Donald Featherstone, *At Them With the Bayonet! The First Sikh War* (1968) (58), a scissor and paste compilation of Sir John Fortesque's narrative interlarded with interesting contemporary accounts. George Bruce, *Six Battles for India: The Anglo-Sikh Wars* (1969) (24) points out lessons in command, administration and tactics that were not learned for later wars. A well-written and documented but decidedly anti-British assessment of imperial influence in the Punjab can be read in Niranyan Khilnani's *British Power in the Punjab* (1972) (93), and military events there are covered by R.H. Haigh and P.W. Turner, *Episodes in Punjab Military History in the Mid-19th Century Culminating in the Indian Mutiny of 1857* (1979) (70). Barbara English, *John Company's Last War* (1971) (52) points out how the last campaign, the one against the contemptible Persians, was casually undertaken and poorly led. Not all Company generals served their arms well; however, Major-General B.P. Hughes, *The Bengal Horse Artillery 1800-1861: The Red Men--a 19th Century Corps d'élite* (1971) (83) shows that many formations did and for a long time.

The Mutiny of 1857 shattered the John Company rule and changed the very nature of the British presence in India. There are many periods in British history better known through popular myth than historical fact. The Indian Mutiny is one of these. Traditionally, many historians have recounted the bloody affair from the British side and nearly always in terms of British arms for good or bad with scant attention paid to the other side of the hill. Problems with documentation account for some of that. Recently scholars such as the late Eric Stokes in such articles as "Traditional Elites in the Great Rebellion of 1857" in Edmund Leach and S.N. Mukherjee, *Elites in South Asia* (1970) (99), and his later book *The Peasant and the Raj: Studies in Agrarian Society and Peasant Rebellion in Colonial India* (1978) (173) have changed the perspective in the study of British Indian history. Even earlier Sir John Smyth, *The Rebellious Rani* (1966) (168) had nice things to say about at least one rebel leader, and he even casts doubts that the massacre of Jhansi was her fault. However, many other recent works follow traditional paths. Michael Edwardes, *Red Year: The Indian Rebellion of 1857* tries to probe the motives of the Indian leaders but fails (49). In Christopher Hibbert, *The Great Mutiny, India 1857* (1977), the causes of the rebellion are laid out but with no definitive judgement made on them even though no Briton or Indian comes out very well (79). John Pemble, *The Raj: The Indian Mutiny and the Kingdom of Oudh, 1810-1859* (1977) (144) presents a superbly written, sometimes highly critical assessment of the defenders of the Lucknow Residency but one which still fails to explore the nature of Oudh society or to touch on questions surrounding leadership, organization or changing composition of the Lucknow rebels. More popular and conventional portrayals are given by Alexander Llewellyn, *The Siege of Delhi* (1977) (103) and Christopher Wilkinson-Latham, *The Indian Mutiny* (1977) (185). Both can point to the shortcomings of British policy and the failure of many British officers to understand their Indian charges.

Fortunately, many of the contemporary witnesses accounts of the grisly events of 1857 are published. Michael Edwardes has edited Sir William Russell's account, *My Indian Mutiny Diary* (1957) (160); James Hewitt has compiled a collection of *Eyewitnesses to the Indian Mutiny* (1973) (78) while David Hutchinson has edited and shortened N.A. Chick's popular post-mutiny serial *Annals of the Rebellion, 1857-58* (1974) (34). In 1977 Oxford University Press reprinted Sir George Scott Robertson's 1898 classic, *Chitral: The Story of a Minor Siege* (159). In all, the researcher is well-served by these sources but only on the British side.

The bulk of the historical writing about India deals with the Mutiny and after. Sheer size of the Indian Army and the massive efforts of the First and Second World Wars made the wealth of literature, especially memoirs and regimental histories, predictable. Yet the study of the Victorian Army and the colonial influence remains a relatively recent phenomenon. Outside of Colonel C.E. Callwells' *Small Wars: Their Principles and Practice* (1896) (29) there were few spokesmen for doctrinal development. And there were few historians willing to examine the field. Not until Brian Bond's pioneering work in 19th century military studies in the 1960s were serious attempts made to do so. His editorship of *Victorian Military Campaigns* (1967) (20), his contribution to Young and Lawford's *History of the British Army* (1970) (191) and his *The Victorian Army and the Staff College, 1854-1914* (1972) (19) opened the field for later scholars such as Byron Farwell, *Queen Victoria's Little Wars* (1973) (57); E.M. Spiers, *The Army and Society, 1815-1914* (1980) (170); Hew Strachan *Wellington's Legacy: The Reform of the British Army, 1830-1854* (1984) (175), his *From Waterloo to Balaclava: Tactics, Technology and the British Army, 1815-1854* (1985) (174) and Howard Bailes, "The Influence of Continental Examples and Colonial Warfare Upon the Reform of the Late Victorian Army," (Ph.D., London, 1984) (8). All of these along with Jay Luvaas' seminal work, *The Education of an Army: British Military Thought, 1815-1940* (1964) (108) are vital background for understanding British arms in India.

The centre piece of British colonial arms was the Indian Army. As memories of the Raj fade, it is fortunate that the history of this successful institution is being told. The two best works are T.A. Heathcote, *The Indian Army: The Garrison of British Imperial India, 1822-1922* (1974) (77) and Philip Mason, *A Matter of Honour* (1974) (117). Both studies examine British policies, recruitment, training, equipment and organization. Heathcote's is the more tightly focussed with good statistics and chapters on the Indian soldier and the reserves as well as officers and command. Unfortunately, Mason's volume contains no footnotes. From here the scope and quality of the efforts become somewhat limited. Boris Mollo's, *The Indian Army* (1981) (126), does not supercede Heathcote or Mason but should be read in conjunction with both. Stephen Cohen, *The Indian Army: Its Contribution to the Development of the Indian Nation* (1971) (35) examines the broad base of the Indian components but has little regard for the British aspect. K.M.L. Saxena, *The Military System of India (1850-1900)* concludes that the post mutiny British methods of recruitment, training, equipping and officering produced an organization both efficient and politically safe (161). H.S. Bhatia, *Political, Legal and Military History of India* (1977) (18) has tried to make sense out of fragmented and diverse military history but construction and source weaknesses have undermined the value of his work. V. Longer, *Red Coats to Olive Green: A History of the Indian Army, 1660-1974* (1974) (104) covers ground already tread but is not an academic effort and has no documentation. In spite of its failure to provide either footnotes or bibliography, Byron Farwell's, *Mr. Kipling's Army* (1984) (56) is a delightful example of popular social military history with all of the pitfalls of the type. Other works of limited or specific use are W. Golant, *The Long Afternoon: British India, 1601-1947* (1975) (67); N.B. Leslie, *The Battle Honours of the British and Indian Armies, 1695-1914* (1970) (102) and Michael Glover, *An Assemblage of Indian Army Soldiers and*

Uniforms from the Original Paintings of the Late Paul Charter (1973) (66). A central consideration for the Crown's forces in Asia was the "Great Game" and India was its focus. Philip Amos' bibliography on strategic concerns indicates that much has already been written, and since his list came out there are more. As mentioned, Edward Ingram, *The Beginning of the Great Game in Asia 1828-1834* (1979) (86), his *Commitment to Empire: Prophecies of the Great Game in Asia, 1779-1800* (1981) (87) and M.E. Yapp, *Strategies of British India: Britain, Iran and Afghanistan, 1798-1850* (1980) (190) cover the pre-Mutiny period. Soundly based on archival material, these works range beyond the frontiers of India and present different interpretations of events. Gerald Morgan's semi-popular *Anglo-Russian Rivalry in Central Asia, 1810-1895* (1981) (132) can be compared with David Gillard's earlier *The Struggle for Asia, 1828-1914: A Study in British and Russian Imperialism* (1977) (64). Keith Jeffrey, "The Eastern Arc of Empire: A Strategic View, 1850-1950," in *Journal of Strategic Studies* (1982) (91) surveys the entire post-Mutiny period to independence. Charles Miller, *Khyber: The Story of an Imperial Migraine* (1977) (125) brightly narrates the history of Afghanistan and the North-West frontier. His analysis goes well beyond his title. The Afghan Wars--sometimes so disastrous for British military enterprise but always part of the strategic game--are well surveyed by T.A. Heathcote in *The Afghan Wars, 1839-1919* (1980) (76). It is a far more scholarly effort than Robert Wilkinson-Latham's popular potted history, *North-West Frontier, 1837-1947* (1977) (186). Leigh Maxwell, *My God--Maiwand!: The Operations of the South Afghanistan Field Force, 1878-1880* (1979) (122) gives a lucid analysis of the military and political events surrounding the disaster of Maiwand during the Second Afghan War. Several personal remembrances of service on the North-West frontier have augmented an appreciation of what life was like there. There is a reprint of Sir Robert Warburton's *Eighteen Years in the Khyber, 1879-1898*, originally published in 1900 (180). Francis Stockdale, *Walk Warily in Waziristan* (1983) (172) is a joyful narration of the personal reminiscences of a young sapper officer in 1919 and 1920. Brigadier R.C.B. Bristow's, *Memoirs of the British Raj: A Soldier in India* (1974) (21) and David Lee's, *Never Stop the Empire When It's Hot* (1983) (101) are worthwhile reading. André Singer, *Lords of the Khyber: The Story of the North-West Frontier* (1984) (164) has provided an anecdotal account of the colourful figures who played key roles in British military and political events along the Afghanistan-India border in the 19th and 20th centuries. For those who want to see the historical images of the North-West Frontier, Michael Barthorp does this in an interesting compilation, *The North-West Frontier: British India and Afghanistan: A Pictorial History, 1839-1947* (1982) (13). Interestingly, there is little written on the North-East Frontier. However, Alistair Lamb, *The McMahon Line* (1966) (96) and Indian scholar, Shotam Mehra, *The McMahon Line and After* (1976) (123) have looked at the North-East Frontier Agency. Both are scholarly works dealing with the complex inter-relationship between British India, Tibet and China from 1904 to 1947. The latter work has the advantage of including many Indian sources.

What is also surprising is that outside of official history, some memoirs and Indian Army surveys, few works have recently been produced on India during the Great War. No doubt this area is rich for the tilling. Dewitt Ellinwood and S.D. Pradhan, *India and World War I* (1978) (51) is one exception. The book deals with the impact of the Great War on the Indian social fabric and peripherally on the politics of the period. Much remains to be done on such areas as personal stories, unit histories and industrial responses.

The literature of the next world conflict is far larger but many of the same omissions remain. Philip Ziegler's prize winning official biography *Mountbatten: The Official History* (1985) (192) explains much about this amazing man's personal contribution to the war strategy as well as his remarkable rôle in the creation of an independent India and Pakistan. Sir Ronald Wingate, *Lord Ismay* (1970) (187) details the early life of Ismay as an Indian Army officer and describes his involvement in policy making in the years after 1936. There are others who have had their India stories told. Tom Pocock, *Fighting General* (1973) (149) covers the crusty and tough Sir Walter Walker's career before, during and after the war. And more experiences come out of Brigadier John Prendergast's own story *Prender's Progress* (1979) (153). In *Laughter at the Door: A Continued Autobiography* (1974) (179), Geoffrey Trease tells what it was like to serve in the Army Educational Corps at a small hill station in India, while Patrick Davis, *A Child in Arms* (1970) (40) has recorded his memories of training in India and his introduction to war with the 4th Battalion, 8th Gurkhas.

The number of campaign and unit histories covering the Second World War has proliferated. Many of the authors themselves had first hand knowledge of their subject. Brigadier E.D. Smith, *Even the Brave Falter* (1978) (167) provides a very real picture of platoon and company warfare with the 7th Gurkha Rifles in Northern Italy in 1944-45; this book is the final one of three by Smith about the famous soldiers from Nepal. His other two, *Britain's Brigade of Gurkhas* (1973) (165) and *East of Katmandu: The Story of the 7th Duke of Edinburgh's Own Gurkha Rifles* (1976) (166) pays tribute to the Brigade tracing its history from the raising of the 2nd, "Gods Own" in 1815 to the Borneo confrontation a century and a half later. During the Second World War, the Gurkhas met some of their severest trials in Burma. Denis Sheil-Small, *Green Shadows: A Gurkha Story* (1982) (163) recounts his Burma service with Walker's 4/8th Gurkhas, as does Eric Nield, *With Pegasus in India: The Story of 153 Gurkha Parachute Battalion* (c. 1971) (137). He was then the Medical Officer with that unit in the bitter fighting of the "Sancol" column which operated for six weeks behind Japanese lines in Burma. The 111th Long Range Penetration Brigade of Wingate's Special Force was a persistently unlucky group that suffered badly in Burma. Richard Rhodes James gives his own perceptive and penetrating account of that searing experience in *Chindit* (1980) (158). One different memoir of the Burma experience is Charles Carfrae *Chindit Column* (1985) (30), different because Carfrae commanded not British or Gurkhas there, but soldiers from a Nigerian regiment. More about their Burma experience needs to be written. Pat Carmichael, *Mountain Battery* (1983) (31), at the time a subaltern in the 23rd Mountain Battery, describes his unit's role in Burma early in that war and Louis Allen, *Sittang: The Last Battle* (1973) (4) gives a good account of the Indian Army's single-handed destruction of Japan's abandoned 28th Army at the conflict's end.

The outbreak of war did not stop the internal political process attempting to gain Indian independence, and the enemy was quick to exploit the times. K.K. Ghosh, *The Indian National Army: Second Front of the India Independence Movement* (1969) (62) sees the collaboration of that force with the Japanese in 1942 as a means of serving the cause of independence. Greater emphasis on the Japanese relationship comes from Joyce C. Lebra in *Jungle Alliance: Japan and the Indian National Army* (1972) (100). All of the salient events of that unfortunate experiment are repeated by G.H. Corr in *The War of the Springing Tiger* (1975) (38). A good assessment of the Nazi strategy for India comes from Milan Hauner, *India in Axis Strategy: Germany, Japan and Indian Nationalists in the Second World War* (1981) (75).

Of all of the Indian Army formations, the Gurkhas have received more printer's ink than any other. The explanation is their courage and remarkable record; and in 1947 they cast their lot with the British Army not the new Indian one. As noted previously one of their chief historians has been E.D. Smith, but others have contributed. Harold James and Denis Sheil-Small, *A Pride of Gurkhas* (1975) (90) carries the history of the 2nd past 1947 in Malaya, Hong Kong and Borneo, and Byron Farwell, *The Gurkhas* (1984) (55) retraces their spectacular and long history in a popular and exciting account that is not hindered by scholarly apparatus. For anyone interested in photographs of these soldiers, Major Robin Adshead has compiled over 200 in *Gurkha: The Legendary Soldier* (1971) (1).

Other units have their histories as well. Pakistani Major General Shahid Hamid records the story of the Indian cavalry in *So They Rode and Fought* (1983) (72). He began his own career under the Raj in the 3rd Cavalry. D.K. Palit has edited a *History of the Regiment of Artillery, Indian Army* (1972) (139) which traces the Indian artillery from well before the formation of the Regiment in 1936 to the recent clashes with Pakistan and China on India's borders. An anthology of actions and anecdotes of the Indian Mountain Artillery comes from C.H.T. MacFetridge and J.P. Warren, *Tales of the Mountain Gunners* (1973) (110). Finally, K.C. Praval *India's Paratroopers* (1975) (152) presents a clear and detailed account of the 50th Indian Parachute Brigade since its formation in 1941.

Of the Governors General of India between 1819 and 1919 all but nine of them had military experience. Their relationship to policy and the Indian Army make them important for the study of British Arms. There are two general surveys of the Governors of India. Philip Mason, *The Men Who Ruled India* (1953) (118) has been republished in 1985 and M. Bence-Jones, *The Viceroys of India* (1982) (16) has collected biographies of them from Canning to Mountbatten. But it is the individual studies that would be of most value.

Edward Moulton, *Lord Northbrook's Indian Administration, 1872-1876* (1968) (133) concludes that this former under-secretary for war developed the formula of political inactivity and low taxation in India. Even though vitally interested in the defence of the North-West Frontier, Northbrook knew that turning the taxation screw for hiring more troops which expansion of Raj would entail, ultimately would produce more disaffection than the countervailing force. No such military-political policy was followed by his successor, Lord Lytton. Unfortunately, Mary Lutyens, *The Lyttons in India: An*

Account of Lord Lytton's Viceroyalty (1979) (107) gives bare mention to army reform or other of her grandfather's policies, or indeed of recent scholarship which shows that Lytton deliberately precipitated the crisis which dragged a reluctant British cabinet into the Afghan invasion. Lord Ripon's Administration in India (1972) (121) by P. Mathur is a useful if not very exciting work. George Curzon was Viceroy of India at the very apogee of expansive imperialism. David Dilk's two volumes, Curzon in India (1969-1970) (42) points out that Curzon thought India the lynch-pin of the Empire. He wanted to use the gem as a strategic chessman of British foreign policy, to reform Indian administration and to subordinate the Indian Army to these policies. Much of the personal Curzon is portrayed in journalist Peter King's compilation of photos and extracts from the Viceroy's writings in *A Viceroy's India: Leaves from Lord Curzon's Notebook* (1984) (39). The notebook entries deal mostly with Curzon's perceptions as a travel writer. Linlithgow is the subject of G. Rizvi's, *Linlithgow and India: A Study of British Policy and the Political Impasse in India 1936-1943* (1978) (157). It details many of the problems of governing India in wartime but sees them mostly from the constitutional impasse rather than the military perspective. But Linlthgow's son, John Glendevon, *The Viceroy at Bay* (1971) (65) has portrayed a more sympathetic picture of his father's attempts to face both war and nearly insurmountable political problems. Penderel Moon, *Wavell: The Viceroy's Journal* (1973) (127) has edited his subject's diaries, making complicated events clearer and giving more understanding to an often-criticised man. Finally, as mentioned before Philip Ziegler has given us an assessment of the last of the Viceroys in *Mountbatten* (192). Obviously more study needs to be made of the British rulers of India at the Viceregal and Lieutenant Governor levels.

Part of the complicated duties of the rulers of India dealt with British foreign policy relevant to the subcontinent and the relations with India's princely states. Briton Cooper Busch, *Britain, India and the Arabs, 1914-1921* (1971) (26) and his *Mudros to Lausanne: Britain's Frontier in West Asia, 1918-1923* (1976) (27) analyses the particular view the government of India and the Indian Army had of the defeat of the Turkish Empire. Ultimately the "Indian lobby" did not dominate British foreign policy but it was a powerful force. Professor Busch's scholarly analysis makes some sense out of the controversies and machinations passing between Whitehall and Simla. Internally, the Raj was also concerned with the one third of the Indian territory not under its rule. After the Mutiny and because of it, as Ajit K. Neogy's detailed and scholarly study, *The Paramount Power and the Princely States of India, 1858-1881* (1979) (136) suggests, British policy toward the Princes changed fundamentally. No longer fearing annexation, these states took their place along side the British provinces hence elaborating for the first time the concept of India as a single unit. Always important in peace and war for British arms, policy toward the princely states is analysed in the twentieth century by Barbara Ramusack, *The Princes of India in the Twilight of Empire: Dissolution of a Patron-Client System, 1914-1939* (1978) (156), and S.R. Ashton, *British Policy Toward the Indian States 1905-1939* (1982) (7). Particularly interesting is the Princes' role in the Great War.

As Indian nationalism grew, the Indian Army and police were often thrust into central and controversial roles. Helen Fein's *Imperial Crime and Punishment: The Massacre of Jalianwala Bagh and British Judgement, 1919-1920* (1977) (59) is a sociological study of the Amritsar disturbances and an analysis of the subsequent inquiry. Alfred Draper, *Amritsar: The Massacre That Ended the Raj* (1981) (44) details the incredible conduct of Brigadier General Dyer whose misjudgment caused this unhappy and bloody episode. *The Punjab Mail Murder* (c. 1980) (145) by Roger Perkins tells the story of Lt. George Hext who served with the 8th Punjab Regiment until he was murdered by political extremists in 1931. Of the Indian Police, there is one recent survey: *To Guard My People: The History of the Indian Police* (1971) (69) by Sir Percival Griffith.

General or social commentaries on the Raj in India are important for understanding the British-Indian military phenomenon. There are several works of varying quality which provide this background. Michael Edwardes' detailed and readable *British India 1792-1947: A Survey of the Nature and Effect of Alien Rule* (1967) (47) is a good place to start. By meticulous research M.E. Chamberlain, *Britain and India: The Interaction of Two Peoples* (1974) (32) provides answers to such questions as whether the British intended originally to conquer and hold India. Peter Mudford, *Birds of a Different Plumage* (1974) (134) and William Golant, *The Long Afternoon* (1975) (67) are welcome companions to a reprint of Dennis Kincaid's pioneering exposé of the relations Britons had with India, *British Social Life in India, 1608-1937* (1938 and 1973) (94). Of particular interest is Kenneth Ballhatchet's *Race, Sex and Class Under the Raj* (1980) (9). The author studies the Indian government's attempts to prevent the ravages of venereal disease among British soldiers through the supply of healthy Indian prostitutes. It was a proposition that offended many Victorian English minds. Equally fascinating is Peter Burrough's look at medical care of the British Army in "The Human Cost of Imperial Defence in the Early Victorian Age" (1980) (25). But further studies in these areas are needed.

The recent wave of interest in the Raj has also produced some very good and not so good popular productions. Charles Allen's and Michael Mason's edition of the BBC radio series, *Plain Tales from the Raj* (1975) (3) is not as well done as the radio version. But Allen's *Raj: A Scrapbook of British India, 1877-1947* (1977) (2) gives interesting portraits of the imperial presence. British fictional literature and the popular view of British India are interpreted by Allan Greenberger, *The British Image of India* (1969) (68), Benita Parry, *Delusions and Discoveries: Studies on India in the British Imagination* (1972) (142), and Shamsul Islam, *Chronicles of the Raj* (1979) (89). Ray Desmond has compiled early photographs of all aspects of British India in *Victorian India in Focus: A Selection of Early Photographs from the Collection in the India Office Library and Records* (1982) (41), while Mark Bence-Jones, *Palaces of the Raj* (1973) (15) approaches the subject of British social life through a study of government buildings and residency houses.

Quitting India was painful and complicated for the British. Not the least because of historical attachments of British arms and the Indian Army. It is beyond the scope of this essay to comment on the various analyses leading up to and including that departure. Many of the more important works are included in the attached list. And one should always refer to Yapp's bibliographical essays. However, the majestic twelve volume series, Transfer of Power, 1942-1947 (1970-1983) (113) edited by Nicholas Mansergh, E.W.R. Lumley and Penderel Moon is a special case. This indispensible set contains hitherto unpublished official and private documents arranged to tell the story of the last years in India. Students of British military history will find much of value.

BIBLIOGRAPHY

1. Adshead, Robin. *Gurkha: The Legendary Soldier.* Singapore: Asia Pacific Press, 1971.
2. Allen, Charles. *Raj: A Scrapbook of British India 1877-1947.* London: Andre Deutsch, 1977.
3. ———— and Michael Mason (eds.). *Plain Tales from the Raj: Images of British India in the Twentieth Century.* London: Andre Deutch, 1975.
4. Allen, Louis. *Sittang: The Last Battle; the End of the Japanese in Burma, July-August 1945.* London: Macdonald, 1973.
5. Amos, Philip. "Recent Works on the Great Game in Asia," in *International History Review.* vol. 2, no. 2 (1980), pp. 308-320.
6. Anglesey, Marquis of. *A History of the British Cavalry, 1816-1919.* 3 Volumes. London: Leo Cooper, 1973.
7. Ashton, S.R. *British Policy Towards the Indian States 1905-1939.* London: Curzon Press, 1982.
8. Bailes, Howard H.R. "The Influence of Continental Examples and Colonial Warfare Upon the Reform of the late Victorian Army," Ph.D. thesis: King's College, University of London, 1984.
9. Ballhatchet, Kenneth. *Race, Sex and Class under the Raj.* London: Weidenfeld and Nicolson, 1980.
10. Bancroft, N.W. *From Recruit to Staff Sergeant.* London: Ian Henry Publications, 1979.
11. Barooah, N.K. *David Scott in North-East India, 1802-1831: A Study in British Paternalism.* New Delhi: Munshiram Manoharial, 1970.
12. Barr, Pat and Ray Desmond. *Simla: A Hill Station in British India.* London: Scribners, 1978.
13. Barthorp, Michael. *The North-West Frontier: British India and Afghanistan: A Pictorial History 1839-1947.* Dorset: Blandford Press, 1982.
14. Bence-Jones, Mark. *Clive of India.* London: Constable, 1974.
15. ————. *Palaces of the Raj.* London: Allen and Unwin, 1973.
16. ————. *The Viceroys of India.* London: Constable, 1982.
17. Bhatia, H.S. (ed.). *Military History of India.* New Delhi: Deep and Deep, 1977.
18. ———— (ed.). *Political, Legal and Military History of India.* 5 Volumes. New Delhi: Deep and Deep, 1984.
19. Bond, Brian. *The Victorian Army and the Staff College 1854-1914.* London: Eyre Methuen, 1972.
20. ———— (ed.). *Victorian Military Campaigns.* London: Hutchinson, 1967.

21. Bristow, Brigadier R.C.B., OBE. *Memoirs of the British Raj: A Soldier in India.* London: Johnson, 1974.
22. Bruce, Anthony. *An Annotated Bibliography of the British Army, 1660-1914.* New York: Garland, 1975.
23. Bruce, George. *The Burma Wars, 1824-1886.* London: Hart-Davis MacGibbon, 1973.
24. ―――. *Six Battles for India: The Anglo-Sikh Wars: 1845-6.* London: Arthur Barker, 1969.
25. Burroughs, Peter. "The Human Cost of Imperial Defence in the Early Victorian Age," *Victorian Studies*, XXIV (1980), pp. 7-32.
26. Busch, B.C. *Britain, India and the Arabs, 1914-1921.* Berkeley: University of California Press, 1971.
27. ―――. *Mudros to Lausanne: Britain's Frontier in West Asia, 1918-1923.* Albany: State University of New York Press, 1976.
28. Callahan, Raymond. *The East India Company and Army Reform 1783-1798.* London: Oxford University Press, 1972.
29. Callwell, Colonel C.E. *Small Wars: Their Principles and Practice.* London: H.M.S.O., 1896, reprinted in 1976.
30. Carfrae, Charles. *Chindit Column.* London: William Kimber, 1985.
31. Carmichael, Pat. *Mountain Battery.* Bournemouth: Devin Books, 1983.
32. Chamberlain, M.E. *Britain and India: The Interaction of Two Peoples.* Hamden, Conn.: Archon, 1974.
33. Chaughur, Nirad C. *Clive of India: A Political and Psychological Essay.* London: Barrie and Jenkins, 1975.
34. Chick, N.A. (Compiler) and David Hutchinson (ed.). *Annals of the Rebellion, 1857-58.* London: Charles Knight, 1974.
35. Cohen, Stephen P. *The Indian Army: Its Contribution to the Development of the Indian Nation.* Berkeley: University of California Press, 1971.
36. Collier, Richard. *The Sound of Fury: An Account of the Indian Mutiny.* London: Collins, 1963.
37. Cook, H.C.B. *The Sikh Wars, 1845-6, 1848-9.* London: Leo Cooper, 1975.
38. Corr, Gerald H. *The War of the Springing Tiger.* London: Osprey, 1975.
39. Curzon, Marquess, of Kedleston. *A Viceroy's India: Leaves from Lord Curzon's Note-Book.* Peter King ed. London: Sidgwick and Jackson, 1984.
40. Davis, Patrick. *A Child in Arms.* London: Hutchinson, 1970.
41. Desmond, Ray. *Victorian India in Focus: A Selection of Early Photographs From the Collection of the India Office Library and Records.* London: Her Majesty's Stationery Office, 1982.
42. Dilks, David. *Curzon in India,* 2 Volumes. London: Holt Davis, 1969-70.
43. Dobbin, Christine E., (ed.). *Basic Documents in the Development of Modern India and Pakistan, 1835-1947.* London: Van Nostrand Reinhold, 1970.
44. Draper, Alfred. *Amritsar: The Massacre That Ended the Raj.* London: Cassell, 1981.

45. Dyson, K.K. *A Various Universe: A Study of the Journals and Memoirs of British Men and Women in the Indian Subcontinent, 1765-1856.* Delhi: Oxford University Press, 1978.
46. Eden, Emily. *Up the Country: Letters from India.* London: Virago, 1983.
47. Edwardes, Michael. *British India, 1772-1947: A Survey of the Nature and Effect of Alien Rule.* London: Sidgwick and Jackson, 1967.
48. ―――. *Glorious Sahibs: The Romantic as Empire-Builder, 1799-1838.* London: Eyre and Spottiswoode, 1968.
49. ―――. *Red Year: The Indian Rebellion of 1857.* London: Hamish Hamilton, 1973.
50. ―――. *A Season in Hell: The Defence of the Lucknow Residency.* London: Hamish Hamilton, 1973.
51. Ellinwood, Dewitt C. and S.D. Pradhan. *India and World War One.* Columbia, Mo.: South Asia Books, 1978.
52. English, Barbara. *John Company's Last War.* London: Collins, 1971.
53. Farrell, James Gordon. *The Hill Stations.* London: Weidenfeld and Nicolson, 1981.
54. ―――. *The Siege of Krishnapur.* London: Weidenfeld and Nicolson, 1973.
55. Farwell, Byron. *The Gurkhas.* New York: Norton, 1984.
56. ―――. *Mr. Kipling's Army.* New York: Norton, 1981.
57. ―――. *Queen Victoria's Little Wars.* London: Allen Lane, 1973.
58. Featherstone, Donald. *At Them with the Bayonet! The First Sikh War.* London: Jarrolds, 1968.
59. Fein, Helen. *Imperial Crime and Punishment: The Massacre at Jalianwala Bagh and British Judgement, 1919-1920.* Honolulu: University Press of Hawaii, 1977.
60. Fortesque, Sir John. *History of the British Army.* London: Macmillan, 1899-1913. (13 Vols.).
61. Garrett, Richard. *Robert Clive.* London: Barker, 1976.
62. Ghosh, K.K. *The Indian National Army: Second Front of the India Independence Movement.* Meerut, Uttar Pradesh: Meenaksh Prakashan, 1969.
63. Ghosh, Suresh Chandra. *Dalhousie in India, 1848-1856: A Study of His Social Policy as Governor-General.* Columbia, Mo.: South Asia Books, 1973.
64. Gillard, David. *The Struggle for Asia, 1828-1914: A Study in British and Russian Imperialism.* London: Methuen, 1977.
65. Glendevon, John Hope. *The Viceroy at Bay: Lord Linlithgow in India, 1936-1943.* London: Collins, 1971.
66. Glover, Michael. *An Assemblage of Indian Army Soldiers and Uniforms from the Original Paintings by the Late Paul Charter.* London: Perpetua Press, 1973.
67. Golant, W. *The Long Afternoon: British India 1601-1947.* London: Hamish Hamilton, 1975.
68. Greenberger, Allen J. *The British Image of India.* London: Oxford University Press, 1969.
69. Griffith, Sir Percival, KBE. *To Guard My People: The History of the Indian Police.* London: Edward Benn, 1971.

70. Haigh, R.H. and P.W. Turner. *Episodes in Punjab Military History in the Mid-19th Century, Culminating in the Indian Mutiny of 1857.* Manhattan, Kansas: MA/AH Publishers, c. 1979.
71. Hall, D.G.E. *Henry Burney: A Political Biography.* London: Oxford University Press, 1974.
72. Hamid, Major-General S. Shahid. *So They Rode and Fought.* Tunbridge Wells, Kent: Midas Books, 1983.
73. Harris, John. *The Indian Mutiny.* London: Hart-Davis, MacGibbon, 1973.
74. Hasrat, B.J. (ed.). *The Punjab Papers: Selections from the Private Papers of Lord Auckland, Lord Ellenborough, Viscount Hardinge, and the Marquis of Dalhousie, 1836-1849, on the Sikhs.* Hoshiarput: V.V. Research Institute Book Agency, 1970.
75. Hauner, Milan. *India in Axis Strategy: Germany, Japan and Indian Nationalists in the Second World War.* Stuttgart: Klett-Cotta, 1981.
76. Heathcote, T.A. *The Afghan Wars, 1839-1914.* London: Osprey, 1980.
77. ―――. *The Indian Army: The Garrison of British Imperial India, 1822-1922.* London: David and Charles, 1974.
78. Hewitt, James (ed.). *Eye-Witnesses to the Indian Mutiny.* Reading, Berkshire: Osprey, 1972.
79. Hibbert, Christopher. *The Great Mutiny, India 1857.* London: Allen Lane, 1978.
80. Hilton, Richard. *The Indian Mutiny: A Centenary History.* London: Hollis and Carter, 1957.
81. Hodson, Henry Vincent. *The Great Divide: Britain--India--Pakistan.* London: Hutchinson, 1969.
82. Houlding, J.A. *Fit for Service: The Training of the British Army, 1715-1795.* Oxford: Clarendon Press, 1981.
83. Hughes, Major-General B.P. *The Bengal Horse Artillery, 1800-1861: 'The Red Men'--a Nineteenth Century Corps d'élite.* London: Arms and Armour Press, 1971.
84. Hunt, R. and J. Harrison. *The District Officer in India.* London: Scolar Press, 1980.
85. Hutchins, Francis G. *India's Revolution: Gandhi and the Quit-India Movement.* Cambridge: Cambridge University Press, 1973.
86. Ingram, Edward. *The Beginning of the Great Game in Asia, 1828-1834.* Oxford: Clarendon Press, 1979.
87. ―――. *Commitment to Empire: Prophecies of the Great Game in Asia, 1797-1800.* Oxford: Clarendon Press, 1981.
88. ――― (ed.). *Two Views of British India: The Private Correspondence of Mr. Dundas and Lord Wellesley: 1798-1801.* Somerset: Adams and Dart, 1970.
89. Islam, Shamsul. *Chronicles of the Raj.* London: Macmillan, 1979.
90. James, Harold and Denis Sheil-Small. *A Pride of Gurkhas.* London: Leo Cooper, 1975.
91. Jeffrey, Keith. "The Eastern Arc of Empire: A Strategic View, 1850-1950," *Journal of Strategic Studies*, 5, no. 4 (Dec. 1982), pp. 531-545.
92. Kaye, M.M. *The Far Pavilions.* New York: St. Martin's c. 1978.

93. Khilnani, N.M. *British Power in the Punjab, 1839-1858.* New York: Asia Publishing House, c. 1972.
94. Kincaid, Dennis. *British Social Life in India, 1608-1937.* London: Routledge and Kegan Paul, 1973.
95. Knightley, P. *The First Casualty: The War Correspondent as Hero, Propagandist and Myth Maker from the Crima to Vietnam.* London: Andre Deutsch, 1975.
96. Lamb, Alastair. *The McMahon Line: A Study in the Relations Between India, China and Tibet, 1904 to 1947.* London: Routledge and Kegan Paul, 1966.
97. Lawford, James P. *Britain's Army in India: From Its Origins to the Conquest of Bengal.* London: Allen and Unwin, 1978.
98. ——————. *Clive: Proconsul of India.* London: George Allen and Unwin, 1976.
99. Leach, Edmund and S.N. Mukherjee. *Elites in South Asia.* Cambridge: Cambridge University Press, 1970.
100. Lebra, Joyce C. *Jungle Alliance: Japan and the Indian National Army.* Singapore: Asia Pacific Press, 1972.
101. Lee, David. *Never Stop the Engine When It's Hot.* London: Harmsworth, c. 1983.
102. Leslie, N.B. *The Battle Honours of the British and Indian Armies 1695-1914.* London: Leo Cooper, 1970.
103. Llewellyn, Alexander. *The Siege of Delhi.* London: Macdonald and Jane's, 1977.
104. Longer, V. *Red Coats to Olive Green: A History of the Indian Army, 1600-1974.* Bombay: Allied Publishers, 1974.
105. Longford, Elizabeth. *Wellington.* 2 vols. London: Weidenfeld and Nicholson, 1969-1972.
106. Lunt, James, (ed.). *From Sepoy to Subedar, being the Life and Adventures of Subedar Sita Ram, a Native Officer of the Bengal Army, Written and Related by Himself.* London: Routledge and Kegan Paul, 1970.
107. Lutyens, Mary. *The Lyttons in India: An Account of Lord Lytton's Viceroyalty 1876-80.* London: John Murray, 1979.
108. Luvaas, Jay. *The Education of An Army: British Military Thought, 1815-1940.* Chicago: University of Chicago Press, 1964.
109. Macfarlane, Iris. *The Black Hole; or, The Makings of a Legend.* London: Allen and Unwin, 1975.
110. MacFetridge, C.H.T. and J.P. Warren, (eds.). *Tales of the Mountain Gunners: An Anthology Compiled by Those Who Served With Them.* Edinburgh: Blackwood, 1973.
111. Malcolm, Sir John. *The Political History of India, 1784-1823.* K.N. Panikkar, (ed.). New Delhi: Associated Publishing House, 1970.
112. Malleson, G.B. *The Decisive Battles of India from 1746 to 1849 Inclusive.* New Delhi: Associated Publishing House, c. 1974.
113. Mansergh, N., E.W.R. Lumley and P. Moon, (eds.). *The Transfer of Power, 1942-1947.* 12 vols. London: H.M.S.O., 1970-1983.
114. Marshall, P.J. *East Indian Fortunes: The British in Bengal in the Eighteenth Century.* Oxford: Clarendon Press, 1976.
115. ——————. *Problems of Empire: Britain and India, 1757-1813.* New York: Allen and Unwin, 1968.

116. Masih Uddin Khan, Mohammad. *British Aggression in Awadh; Being the Treatise of M. Mohammad Masih Uddin Khan Bahadur entitled Oude, Its Princes, and Its Government Vindicated; Printed by John Davy and Sons, London, in 1857 and Suppressed by the British Government*. Meerut: Meenaksh: Prakashan, 1969.
117. Mason, Philip. *A Matter of Honour: An Account of the Indian Army, Its Officers and Men*. London: J. Cape, 1974.
118. ———. *The Men Who Ruled India*. London: J. Cape, 1985. (Originally published 1953-54.)
119. Masson, Charles. *Narrative of Various Journeys in Baluchistan, Afghanistan, the Punjab and Kalat*. Karachi: Oxford University Press, 1977.
120. Masters, John. *Nightrunners of Bengal*. New York: Viking Press, 1951.
121. Mathur, P. *Lord Ripon's Administration in India*. New Delhi: S. Chand, 1972.
122. Maxwell, Leigh. *My God--Maiwand!: The Operations of the South Afghanistan Field Force, 1878-1880*. London: Leo Cooper, 1979.
123. Mehra, Shotam. *The Mcmahon Line and After: A Study of the Triangular Contest on India's North-Eastern Frontier Between Britain, China, and Tibet, 1904-1947*. Columbus, Mo.: South Asia Books, 1976.
124. Mill, James. *The History of British India*. Chicago: University of Chicago Press, 1975.
125. Miller, Charles, *Khyber: The Story of an Imperial Migraine*. New York: Macmillan, 1977.
126. Mollo, Boris. *The Indian Army*. Poole, Dorset: Blandford Press, 1981.
127. Moon, Penderel, (ed.). *Wavell: The Viceroy's Journal*. Oxford: Oxford University Press, 1973.
128. Moore, Robin James. *Churchill, Cripps, and India, 1939-1945*. Oxford: Clarendon Press, 1979.
129. ———. *The Crisis of Indian Unity, 1917-1940*. Oxford: Clarendon Press, 1974.
130. ———. *Escape from Empire: The Attlee Government and the Indian Problem*. Oxford: Clarendon Press, 1983.
131. Moorhouse, Geoffrey. *India Britannica*. New York: Harper and Row, c. 1983.
132. Morgan, Gerald. *Anglo-Russian Rivalry in Central Asia 1810-1895*. London: Cass, 1981.
133. Moulton, Edward C. *Lord Northbrook's Indian Administration, 1872-1876*. London: Asia Publishing House, 1968.
134. Mudford, Peter. *Birds of a Different Plumage: A Study of British Indian Relations from Akbar to Curzon*. London: Collins, 1974.
135. Napier, Priscilla. *Revolution and the Napier Brothers, 1820-1840*. London: Joseph, 1973.
136. Neogy, Ajit K. *The Paramount Power and the Princely States of India, 1858-1881*. Calcutta: K.P. Bagchi and Company, 1979.
137. Nield, Eric. *With Pegasus in India: The Story of 153 Gurkha Parachute Battalion*. Privately published, c. 1971.
138. Page, David. *Prelude to Partition: The Indian Muslims and the*

Imperial System of Control, 1920-1932. Delhi: Oxford University Press, 1982.
139. Palit, D.K. (ed.) History of the Regiment of Artillery, Indian Army. London: Leo Cooper, 1972.
140. Pandey, B.N. The Break-Up of British India. London: Macmillan, 1969.
141. Panigrahi, D.N. Charles Metcalfe in India: Ideas and Administration, 1806-1835. New Delhi: Manshiram Manoharial, 1968.
142. Parry, Benita. Delusions and Discoveries: Studies on India in the British Imagination, 1880-1930. London: Allen Lane, 1972.
143. Pemble, John. The Invasion of Nepal--John Company at War. London: Oxford University Press, 1971.
144. ―――――. The Raj: The Indian Mutiny and the Kingdom of the Oudh, 1810-1859. Hassocks: Harvester Press, 1977.
145. Perkins, Roger. The Punjab Mail Murder. Privately printed, c. 1980.
146. Philips, C.H. (ed.)., The Correspondence of Lord William Bentinck, Governor-General of India, 1828-1835. Oxford: Oxford University Press, 1977.
147. ―――――. The Young Wellington in India. London: Athlone Press, 1973.
148. ――――― and Mary Doreen Wainwright (eds.). Partition of India: Policies and Perspectives, 1935-1947. Boston: MIT Press, 1970.
149. Pocock, Tom. Fighting General: The Public and Private Campaigns of General Sir Walter Walker. London: Collins, 1973.
150. Powell, Geoffrey. The Kandyan Wars, the British Army in Ceylon, 1803-1818. London: Leo Cooper, 1973.
151. Prasad, S.N. A Survey of Work Done on the Military History of India. Calcutta: K.P. Bagchi, 1976.
152. Praval, K.C. India's Paratroopers. London: Leo Cooper, 1975.
153. Prendergast, John. Prender's Progress. London: Cassell, 1979.
154. Preston, A.W. "Frustrated Great Gamesmanship: Sir Garnet Wolseley's Plan for War against Russia, 1873-1880," International History Review, 2, no. 2 (1980), pp. 239-365.
155. ―――――. "Wolseley, the Khartoum Relief Expedition and the Defence of India, 1885-1900," The Journal of Imperial and Commonwealth History, 6, no. 3 (May 1978), pp. 254-280.
156. Ramusack, Barbara N. The Princes of India in the Twilight of Empire: Dissolution of a Patron-Client System, 1914-1939. Columbus: Ohio State University Press, c. 1978.
157. Rizvi, Gowher. Linlithgow and India: A Study of British Policy and the Political Impasse in India, 1936-43. London: Royal Historical Society, 1978.
158. Rhodes James, Richard. Chindit. London: John Murray, 1980.
159. Robertson, Sir George S. Chitral: The Story of a Minor Siege. London: Methuen and Co., 1898; reprinted London: Oxford University Press, 1977.
160. Russell, Sir William Howard. My Indian Mutiny Diary. Michael Edwardes (ed.). London: Cassell, 1957.
161. Saxena, K.M. The Military System of India (1850-1900). New Delhi: Sterling Publishers, 1974.
162. Scott, Paul. The Jewel in the Crown. New York: Morrow, 1966.

163. Sheil-Small, Denis. *Green Shadows: A Gurkha Story*. London: Kimber, 1982.
164. Singer, Andre. *Lords of the Khyber: The Story of the North-West Frontier*. London: Faber and Faber, 1984.
165. Smith, E.D. *Britain's Brigade of Gurkhas: The 2nd K.E.O. Gurkha Rifles, the 6th Gurkha Rifles and the 10th P.M.O. Gurkha Rifles*. London: Leo Cooper, 1973.
166. ―――――. *East of Katmandu: The Story of the Duke of Edinburgh's Own Gurkha Rifles*. London: Leo Cooper, 1976.
167. ―――――. *Even the Brave Falter*. London: Hale, 1978.
168. Smyth, Sir John. *The Rebellious Rani*. London: Frederic Muller, 1966.
169. Spear, Percival. *Master of Bengal: Clive and His India*. London: Thames and Hudson, 1975.
170. Spiers, E.M. *The Army and Society, 1815-1914*. London: Longman, 1980.
171. Stewart, A.T.Q. *The Pagoda War: Lord Dufferin and the Fall of the Kingdom of Ava, 1885-6*. London: Faber and Faber, 1972.
172. Stockdale, Francis (Tim). *Walk Warily in Waziristan*. London: Arthur Stockwell, 1983.
173. Stokes, Eric. *The Peasant and the Raj: Studies in Agrarian Society and Peasant Rebellion in Colonial India*. Cambridge: Cambridge University Press, 1978.
174. Strachan, Hew. *From Waterloo to Balaclava: Tactics, Technology and the British Army, 1815-1854*. Cambridge: Cambridge University Press, 1985.
175. ―――――. *Wellington's Legacy: The Reform of the British Army, 1830-54*. Manchester: Manchester University Press, 1984.
176. Stranks, C.J. (ed.). *The Path of Glory: The Memoirs of John Shipp*. London: Chatto and Windus, 1969.
177. Swinson, Arthur and Donald Scott (eds.). *The Memoirs of Private Waterfield*. London: Cassell, 1968.
178. Towle, Philip. "The Russo-Japanese War and the Defense of India," *Military Affairs*, 44, no. 3, (1980), pp. 111-117.
179. Trease, Geoffrey. *Laughter at the Door: A Continued Autobiography*. London: Macmillan, 1974.
180. Warburton, Sir Robert, edited by Mary Cecil, Lady Warburton. *Eighteen Years in the Khyber, 1879-1898*. Oxford: Oxford University Press, 1970. (Originally published by John Murray, 1900.)
181. Weller, Jac. *Wellington in India*. London: Longman, 1972.
182. Wilkes, Captain John. *The Bengal Native Infantry, 1757-1796; Continued to 1816 By a Brother Officer*. London: Muller, 1970.
183. Wilkinson, T. *Two Monsoons*. London: Duckworth, 1976.
184. Wilkinson-Latham, Robert. *From Our Special Correspondent: Victorian War Correspondents and Their Campaigns*. London: Hodder and Stoughton, 1979.
185. ―――――. *The Indian Mutiny*. London: Osprey, 1977.
186. ―――――. *North-West Frontier, 1837-1947*. London: Osprey, 1977.
187. Wingate, Sir Ronald. *Lord Ismay*. London: Hutchinson, 1970.
188. Yapp, M.E. "Recent Books on Modern Indian History," *British Book News* (August 1975), pp. 525-30.

189. ———. "Recent Books on India," *British Book News* (March 1982), pp. 134-139.
190. ———. *Strategies of British India: Britain, Iran and Afghanistan, 1798-1850*. London: Oxford University Press, 1980.
191. Young, Peter and J.P. Lawford (eds.). *History of the British Army*. London: Arthur Baker, 1970.
192. Ziegler, Philip. *Mountbatten. The Official History*. New York: Knopf, 1985.

XXI

SCIENCE, TECHNOLOGY AND ECONOMICS IN THE TWENTIETH CENTURY

David Edgerton and Philip Gummett

This essay is wider in scope than R.W. Clark's contribution to Higham's *Guide*. It covers a longer period, from the beginning of the First World War to the present day, and includes the category of economics, here taken to mean the economics of war, the economic effect of armament production in war and peace, and the employment of professional economists in Government for purposes connected with defense. There is also a significant difference in content. Clark's survey necessarily covered principally official and semi-official works, biographies and material from service and technical journals. Since 1968 a growing, but still small, number of military, economic and business historians, as well as historians of science and technology, have turned their attention to questions of war and armaments. For the period since 1945, the importance of science, technology and economics to defense matters has become increasingly obvious and consequently the amount of secondary material is vast. The above differences have required the adoption of a different format to that used by Clark, but it must be stressed that this essay in no way supersedes Clark's, which remains indispensable both in its content and in its advice to researchers in this difficult field.

It is only in recent years that the relationship between science, technology, economics and war has begun to receive the attention from historians that it deserves. Two very useful survey articles by J.M. Winter and Merritt Roe Smith are worth noting as attempts to bring together the disparate literatures on these themes and to indicate the importance of the subject (315, 279). Interesting and broad-ranging arguments about this complex relationship have been put forward, notably in the works of Kaldor, Pearton and Sen (158, 226, 267).

Science and Technology: Organization and Policy. The key point to make about the overall organization of, and policy towards, science and technology in British government since the Second World War is that policy continued to be formulated and implemented on a departmental basis, according to the principle of the responsibility of ministers for the work of their own departments. There has been continued resistance to the notion of any over-arching organization for bringing together the research and development (R&D) programs and policies of the different departments, and so defence R&D policy has operated largely independently of civil. It is true that there have occasionally been official reports which have sought to take stock across the board, such as the Gibb-Zuckerman report on *The Management* and *Control of Research and Development* in 1961, (217) but these have been the exception rather than the rule.

The organization of science and technology in the First World War, has not been the subject of an official history. For the interwar and Second World War periods there is coverage in summary form by the official historian of the Second World War (236). Recent studies have taken an interest in science and technology in the First World War and in defence in the interwar years (234, 255), but work has concentrated on the origins of the Department of Scientific and Industrial Research (182, 208, 209, 301), which was primarily a civil organization. Of the secondary literature, Gummett's historical introduction to his *Scientists in Whitehall* is the best guide and has extensive references to biographical and other material (100). A great deal of biographical material is also relevant, for example (41, 42, 93, 318).

With respect to biographical material, we should single out for special attention that relating to Lord Zuckerman. Zuckerman, played a major part in both defense and civil science policy throughout the post-war period, as Deputy Chairman of the Advisory Council on Scientific Policy, Chief Scientific Adviser in the Ministry of Defence, and Chief Scientific Adviser to the Cabinet. At the time of writing he continues to play an active part in the House of Lords Select Committee on Science and Technology. He has published the first volume of his autobiography (318) covering the period to 1946, and a second volume is in preparation. Zuckerman has also published a trenchant critique of the role of nuclear weapons scientists in the arms race (319). His papers are becoming available in the Library of the University of East Anglia (320). The papers of other scientists who have been influential in the post-war period are also becoming available. The best single source of information about these is the archive held at the University of Oxford (37).

A useful survey of the scientific records of the Public Record Office has been prepared; it indicates the difficulties likely to be encountered as well as providing valuable advice (157). The papers of the official historians, now available in the Public Record Office, are very useful.

The effect on scientists of participation in war has been the subject of very interesting work in recent years. The promotion of trade unionism among scientists in wartime has been the subject of work by MacLeod (183) for the First World War. A notable work covering this question among many others, especially the Second World War, is Werskey's collective biography of socialist scientists of the 1930s (309). The wartime experience of scientists is dealt with in the literature on the freedom versus planning in science debate of the 1940s (178, 281). Hodges' study of Alan Turing is very sensitive to political questions and raises the interesting question of the effect of the cold war on left-inclined scientists (125). More specific questions about the effect of war on science are covered in a Royal Society symposium (257).

In terms of government organization of military R&D, the establishment of the Ministry of Defence in 1947 did not take the process of integration of the separate Service interests very far, as was amply demonstrated in the report by the Committee, chaired by Air Chief Marshal Sir Guy Garrod, on the organization and work of the scientific branches of the Ministry of Supply and the Admiralty, in

1951. This report, and the associated documents, are available in the Public Record Office and present a fascinating picture of confusion, duplication of effort, and general over-commitment (239c). Despite the availability of this body of material, the Public Record Office is a little disappointing as a source of material on central organization for the early post-war years. For example, the main records of the key Defence Research Policy Committee, the principal scientific advisory body on defense research policy, are closed, although the assiduous researcher can find many of the minutes and memoranda of the Committee attached as appendices to other items, such as the records of the Chiefs of Staff Committee and the Cabinet's Defence Committee.

Another important element of the arrangements for military R&D is the defense research establishments. There is no general history of their activities, and much useful material could be obtained for the first post-war decade from material in the Public Record Office, particularly the ADM, AIR and AVIA series. For the position through the 1960s, the 1969 report from the Select Committee on Science and Technology (139) is invaluable. In the late 1970s, pressure to rationalise the establishments, as part of general economies in civil service staffing levels, coupled with concern about whether the establishments were not too committed to development work at the expense of longer-term research, led to the establishment of an inquiry under Lord Strathcona. The resulting report is available as an Open Government document from the Ministry of Defence (201). The continued process of reduction in numbers of staff and numbers of establishments is documented in the Council for Science and Society's report on UK Military R&D (48), and the position as of 1985 is summarised in the *Statement on the Defence Estimates 1985* (200). There are very few studies of specific research establishments. Vick has written about the first two decades of the Atomic Energy Research Establishment, Harwell, during part of which it was, of course, a major defence research establishment (303), and much more on Harwell and on the Atomic Weapons Research Establishment, Aldermaston, is to be found in Margaret Gowing's official history (95). Putley has written on the Royal Signals and Radar Establishment, Malvern (240), and Kinsey on Orfordness (163). A number of works discuss the activities of the Royal Aircraft Establishment (168, 306, 317), and Thayer's book on the arms trade also makes some observations about defense research establishments (292).

The 1970s have seen the release of information on scientific intelligence, notably in the work of R.V. Jones (151, 155, 156, 167). Scientific exchange with the Soviet Union has been dealt with by Beardsley (18).

Procurement: Organization and Policy. No comprehensive study of procurement policy is available, though for the First World War the semi-official Carnegie histories, of which the important ones, listed by Milward (198), are invaluable, as is the *History of the Ministry of Munitions* (204). The political importance of Lloyd George, Christopher Addison and Winston Churchill has also focussed attention on the Ministry of Munitions (1, 2, 3, 83, 91, 206). For the interwar period, Gibbs (89) has a great deal on the organization of supply, including the role of the Principal Supply Officers' Committee, as does Reader's biography of Lord Weir (243); Peden's important contribution to the wider debate on rearmament (45, 227, 229, 231); and Cross' biography of Lord Swinton (50). For the wartime years, Scott and Hughes' Official History, *Administration of War Production*, remains essential, as do Postan, and Postan, Hay and Scott (235, 236, 266). The Public Record Office papers of War Office, Admiralty, Ministry of Munitions, Ministry of Supply, and Ministry of Aircraft Production are in different states of confusion and therefore the narratives produced by the official historians, and their correspondence, are valuable sources. For the immediate post-war years two theses should be consulted (273, 314).

The best studied procurement policies have been those of the Air Ministry in the rearmament period (11, 50, 68, 75, 76, 77, 78, 123, 124, 227, 243, 250, 270, 277, 278, 286). The best known wartime procurement minister remains the first Minster of Aircraft Production, Lord Beaverbrook, who has been the subject of an appreciative biography (288) and an overdue critical analysis of his effect on British aircraft production in the Battle of Britain by Robertson (252). Overy's comparative study is very useful (218). The Ministry of Supply and the Admiralty have provoked much less interest among historians.

The full history of procurement policy for the post-war period has still to be written. Useful starting places are, however, Bartlett's history of British defense policy, 1945-70 (17) and Johnson's work on the Ministry of Defence, 1944-74 (152). Gummett's piece on defense research policy of 1984 (101), and the 1986 report from the Council for Science and Society on *UK Military R&D* (48) are also useful, as is Angus' paper on the organization of defense procurement and production (7).

For the 1960s, two very different sources are the book by Reed and Williams on Denis Healey, which surveys the defense cuts introduced by the Labour Government in the mid-60s (246), and the report on defense research from the Select Committee on Science and Technology of the House of Commons in 1969 (139). The Select Committee's report, and the Government's response (58), provide a very detailed description of the organization of the various agencies for defense research, development and procurement. That dissatisfaction with the organizational arrangements continued was recognized in the early stages of the Conservative Government of 1970-74 when an inquiry into the government organization for defence procurement and civil aero-space was set up under the chairmanship of Sir Derek (now Lord) Rayner (94). The Rayner report led to the formation within the Ministry of Defence of an organization called the Procurement Executive. This very large organization became responsible for the running of the defense research establishments, for the design, development and production for nuclear weapons, for overseeing the development and design of all weapons systems and weapons platforms, and for placing contracts with, and managing the relationship with, the defense manufacturers. The Procurement Executive itself became the subject of a substantial report by the Commons Select Committee on Defence in 1982 (131).

In the context of increasing doubts in some quarters about the value and survivability of the surface navy, a White Paper by the Secretary of State for Defence, John Knott, in 1981 (299) presaged a fairly major shift in Britain's defense posture, and in particular reduced the proposed size of the fleet. The consequences which this might have brought about for overall procurement policy were, however, swept away by the incidence of the Falklands crisis in 1982. The next occasion for a major change in the organization of the Ministry of Defence was the arrival of Mr. Heseltine as Secretary of State in 1983. Mr. Heseltine brought with him from his previous post a preference for a particular managerial style. This led to a change in the central organization for defense (36), which, amongst other things, slightly reduced the formal status of the Chief Scientific Advisor. This and other consequences for the scientific and technological activities of the Ministry were taken up in a report from the Commons Defence Committee (132).

A number of themes have become important in discussions of defense procurement in recent years. One of these is the question of value for money. Much emphasis has been put by government since the general election of 1979 on increasing competition among defense contractors. A defense Open Government document of 1983 specifically addressed the question of value for money in defense equipment procurement (203). A second important theme has been that of international collaboration in the design, development and procurement of defense equipment. Much tension continues to exist, both about the desirability of collaboration in the first place, and about the relative attractions of trans-Atlantic versus European collaboration. Many valuable book-length reviews and shorter, more specific, discussions have been written (70, 73, 118, 259, 274, 290, 312). A third prominent policy issue has been the question of the economic implications of Britain's commitment to defense research and development. With approximately 50% of government spending on research and development going to the Ministry of Defense, this money being spent partly in the defense research establishments, but mainly in industry, questions have arisen about the balance between the government's civil and defense commitments to science and technology, and about the impact of this heavy commitment to the defense sector on the capacity of British industry to remain competitive in international civil markets, especially those which depend upon scientists and technologists who may be being drawn preferentially into the defense sector. A report by Sir Ieuan Maddock, formerly Chief Scientist in the Department of Industry, on the civil exploitation of defense technology in the electronics sector, was extremely critical of practice as of the early 1980s (175). At around the same time the Ministry of Defence itself held a seminar on the transfer of technology from defense R&D to the civil sector (202), and the House of Lords Select Committee on Science and Technology, in an inquiry into engineering research and development, also offered some critical observations (140). At the time of writing, the Lords Committee was conducting hearings into civil research and development in Britain, one aspect of which was to be the question of the impact of defense R&D on the civil sector. A more general critique of the problems of technical change in the defense industry has been offered by Kaldor (159). There is, however, a shortage in Britain of detailed case studies of the influence of Ministry of Defence funding on specific areas of research and development. One exception is Dickson's study of the part played by the Ministry of Defence in semi-conductor research and development (63). A general review of arguments on this subject is contained in the Council for Science and Society's report on UK military R&D (48).

On the related subject of conversion of defense facilities to civil purposes, see the papers prepared for the Labour Party Defence Study Group in 1979 (160). Finally, for two other sources which contain some useful material on procurement and R&D matters, see Freedman (84) and the proceedings of an academic-Ministry of Defence seminar on defense planning and weapons technology held in the University Southampton in 1969 (81).

Economic History, Economics and Economists. The economic history of war has appropriately been called a 'no-man's land' (315). The same might be said of war preparations. Partly because of this, the Carnegie economic and social histories of the First World War, and the official histories of the Second World War remain essential. Some of the latter are being republished with references. The official histories of the Second World War were censored to prevent the Russians obtaining sensitive information about industrial capacity, and should therefore now be used in conjunction with the papers of the official historians in the Public Record Office. The histories should not be regarded as the last word as at least two studies have shown (51, 68): Milward's comments on the histories should also be noted (197).

The annual listing of publications in the *Economic History Review* is a convenient guide to new literature. The financial aspects of war and rearmament have been increasingly studied. The First World War is covered by Burk (30, 31, 32, 33). The economic aspects of rearmament have been re-examined by Peden and Parker (221, 222, 223, 227, 229, 231). The economic impact is covered by Thomas and Robertson (294, 251). The economics of war remain relatively unexplored by historians (16, 197, 198), so reference needs to be made to the official historians (9, 19, 49, 112, 113, 114, 115, 128, 130, 142, 143, 186, 216, 220, 225, 235, 236, 263, 264, 266, 280); and a volume produced by the Oxford Institute of Statistics (219); and the volume edited by Chester (39). The question of state-industry relations has until recently been untouched. Useful sources are Rogow and Shore (254). Longstreth (173), Peden (228) and Edgerton (68). Another neglected aspect is the provision of capital to the munitions industry and the disposal of assets after the war: the best study remains the official history (130).

The employment by Government of professional economists was very much the product of the Second World War. There have been recent studies of the establishment of the Economic Section and the Central Statistical Office and more generally of this important, and lasting, change in the machinery of Government (23, 36, 43). The role of the Economic Section in establishing Keynesian economics in the government machinery is now well covered (21). Much less well covered is what these economists actually did during the war, especially in economic planning at Cabinet level, and at Ministry level. The classic work on this is Devons' reflections on his experiences at the Ministry of Aircraft Production (60, 61), and this may be compared with the more polemical pieces by other wartime planners provoked by the debate on economic planning of 1947-48, for example (82, 120, 185).

The economics of defense in the post-war years has been attracting a great deal of attention in recent years, but the main thrust of the argument has been over the overall effect of defense spending on the economy. Kennedy's book is a useful starting point (161).

Business History and Armaments. The increasing popularity of business history has resulted in the availability of a number of scholarly histories of firms involved in the production of armaments. Many gaps remain, although these can increasingly be made good by consulting the ever increasing 'enthusiast' literature. There are also an increasing number of biographies and autobiographies of business men as well as scientists, technologists and designers working in the industry. The *Dictionary of Business Biography* is indispensible here as a source and guide to the literature (150). The journals *Business History* and the *Business History Review* should be consulted. Increasing attention has been given to certain enduring themes in consideration of the arms industry: profiteering in the First World War (23, 44); the effect on the arms industry of low arms spending in the interwar years (53); and the 'Merchants of Death' controversy of the early 1930s (27, 53, 68, 187, 215). Profiteering in the 1930s has also been discussed (270). The importance of the First World War in forcing the state to establish new industries and safeguard them after the war has also been a significant theme. The overall conclusion has been that Britain was as a result much better placed, scientifically, technologically and industrially in 1939 than in 1914 (35, 44, 107, 119, 168, 214, 244, 262).

The best covered armaments firm remains Vickers, although J.D. Scott's history should now be supplemented by the work of Trebilcock for the early period (296), and of Davenport-Hines for most of the interwar years (53, 72). New material is also available on Beardmore, BSA and Armstrong-Whitworth (53, 54, 65, 141).

There is a vast amount of material on the aircraft industry, only a small part of which is scholarly work, for example the work of Fearon on the interwar period, and on the firm of Handley-Page in particular (74, 75, 76, 77, 78, 179, 260, 268, 293). The Putnam histories of particular firms are designed for enthusiasts but are meticulously done and contain invaluable information (14, 15, 146, 147, 176 are examples). Penrose's history of British aviation also contains much valuable information although the index is unreliable, and is disgracefully biased politically despite having been published by HMSO (232). Reading Griffith's account of fellow travellers of the right provokes an interesting explanation (98). Quill's account of the Spitfire is very useful (241). The biography of Barnes Wallis is a useful corrective to the famous film *The Dambusters* (207). For the War years, the official historians remain essential (235, 236). Mensforth's contemporary work is also very helpful (189, 190, 191). Aero-engine production is covered by a study of Rolls-Royce and some biographies and autobiographies (103, 129, 170, 171, 172). On the technical development of aviation and aero-engines, see (13, 47, 90, 196).

For the important work of electrical firms in both wars, but particularly for the Second World War, there are a variety of useful sources (12, 24, 153, 164, 194, 214, 313). For the chemical industry the best source is the history of Imperial Chemical Industries and its predecessors by Reader, which may be supplemented by other less

comprehensive material (195, 244). On the motor industry, see (40), and the oil companies, see (154).
For the post war years the business history coverage is much less good, but once again the aircraft industry is the most accessible (59, 87, 177, 199, 247, 316).
The arms trade in the interwar years is usefully covered by Sampson's work and by recent more detailed studies (27, 55, 80, 261). The *Minutes of Evidence taken by the Royal Commission on the Private Manufacture of and Trading in Arms, 1935-36* is an important source (256). For the post-war years see Sampson and Thayer (261, 292).

The Use of the Products of Science and Technology, and Industry, by the Armed Services. The armed services are highly conservative socially, but at least in wartime have been forced to adapt and to use new technology. The adoption of new weaponry is an area of study which needs developing. A good example of the work that has now been done is Ellis' study of the machine-gun (71, 291). For the interwar period there is Hacker's work on mechanization of the army (20, 108, 109, 166), as well as Kaldor's book, *The Baroque Arsenal*, which develops an institutional model for explaining innovation in the defense sector (158).

Cross-Service Weapons. The development and use of radar has continued to attract attention. The amount of scholarly work remains small, however, despite the mass of material available in archives and in the secondary literature (144, 145, 167, 287). Electronic warfare is covered by (56, 122, 237). Chemical warfare is better served, as the recent work of Haber on the First World War shows (10, 105, 106).

An important indication of the perceived prospects in June 1945 for new weapons is contained in a report by an *ad hoc* committee chaired by Sir Henry Tizard, and submitted to the Chiefs of Staff Committee. Entitled, "Future Development in the Weapons and Methods of War," the report is interesting not only for the review which it offers but also for the ignorance of its authors of the precise state of development of atomic weapons (239a). One of the important new developments was, of course, guided weapons. Here the Public Record Office is again unhelpful because so many of the key documents are closed. But one useful source is a memorandum by the Minister of Defence to the Cabinet Defence Committee entitled "Guided Weapons Research and Development" of 1949 (239b). Some rather more journalistic discussion of early guided weapons work is contained in Worcester (317).

The major weapons development in the immediate post-war years was, of course, the atomic bomb. Here the definitive source is the magisterial official history by Margaret Gowing which covers the period to 1952. In two volumes, she discusses in very great detail the policy making and policy execution processes (95). Rather longer time periods are covered, albeit less authoritatively, by Groom (99) and Pierre (233). After Gowing, the best single volume on the British atomic energy programme is that by John Simpson (271). This book goes into remarkable detail (remarkable considering the lack of access to official papers) on the post-1952 period, and is especially valuable on the question of Anglo-American nuclear relations, including the vexed question of Anglo-US trade in military nuclear materials. Simpson's book takes us from the V-bomber program through the discussions over Skybolt, on into Polaris and thence to Chevaline and Trident. Anglo-American relations have also been discussed by Wheeler (310) and Dillon (64), and Simpson himself has also published an earlier work on the procurement of Polaris (272). Of studies of more recent British nuclear politics, specifically the Chevaline and Trident decisions, the best single source is Freedman (85). Also useful are (134, 135, 136, 211, 275), while for an ingenious attempt to assess the scale of the current nuclear stockpile, see Gallacher (86).

Concern about nuclear weapons has, from time to time, and especially in recent years, generated a search for alternative means of defense. Some of these have pressed for fully non-nuclear defense (6, 212, 238) while others have sought means of combining new conventional technologies (the so-called "emerging technologies") with new defense strategies to reduce dependence upon nuclear weapons, especially in Europe (25, 67, 104, 282).

Science, Technology and Development of New Weapons and New Technologies. Here once again is an area where scholarly work is very limited in quantity for the period 1914-1945 in general. For the First World War Cardwell and Pattison are very useful (35, 181, 224). On the optical glass situation see MacLeod's detailed study (180). For the Second War questions of design and development are best covered in the official histories (see above). Hartcup covers major inventions made during the Second World War covering land, sea and air in a popular way (116). There is very little on army weapons (52, 308), though the history of artillery by Hogg (126, 127) deserves mention. On the tank, see (193).

As far as the navy is concerned there are useful studies of various aspects of the application of scientific and technical knowledge by Hackmann, MacLeod, Waddington and Waters (110, 111, 304, 307). More recently, the design and procurement of warships was investigated by the Public Accounts Committee in 1985 (138). A history of the origin of torpedoes exists (97). Recent problems with cost overruns in the torpedo program have been the subject of Parliamentary enquiries (133, 137) and some relevant information may be found in (29).

The great quantities of material on the airforce have already been referred to. On air weapons, the V-bomber force has been discussed by several authors (28, 102, 148). Edmonds provided a useful examination of the future of manned aircraft in the mid-1960s (69). TSR-2 (311) and Tornado (8, 305) have also been well served, as has the Harrier both before and after the Falklands (88, 177, 210). We should also mention Charnley's review of current influences and trends in aeronautical research published in 1982 (38).

Journals. A number of journals and periodical publications provide useful, if sometimes only occasional, material for scholars in this field. In recent years, military science and technology has been increasingly covered in journals dealing with the history and sociology of science and technology, notably, *Isis, Technology & Culture* (both of which produce invaluable annual bibliographies), *Social Studies of Science, Minerva*, and *Notes and Records of the Royal Society of London*. Of particular importance are the publications of the International Institute for Strategic Studies (4, 283, 284). Also valuable are the Yearbook of the Royal United Services Institute (258) the excellent Report of the Armament and Disarmament Information Unit at Sussex University (5), *Jane's Defence Weekly* (149)--an erratic and occasionally politically outlandish trade weekly with a strong technical bias, *Science in Parliament* (265)--a digest of scientific (including defense) matters in Parliament, and *Defence Analysis*, a fairly new journal spanning many areas of defense policy including the technological (57).

BIBLIOGRAPHY

1. Adams, R.J.Q. *Arms and the Wizard: Lloyd George and the Ministry of Munitions.* London: Cassell, 1978.
2. Addison, Christopher. *Four and a Half Years: A Personal Diary from June 1914 to January 1919.* London: Hutchinson, 1934.
3. ———. *Politics from Within, 1911-1918.* 2 vols. London: Herbert Jenkins, n.d.
4. *Adelphi Papers.* London: International Institute for Strategic Studies, periodic, 1966-
5. *ADIU Report.* Sussex University: Armament and Disarmament Information Unit, 1979-
6. Alternative Defence Commission. *Defence Without the Bomb.* London: Taylor and Francis, 1983.
7. Angus, R. *The Organisation of Defence Procurement and Production in the United Kingdom.* Aberdeen: Aberdeen Studies in Defence Economics, no. 13, 1979.
8. ———. "The Tornado Project" in M. Edmonds (ed.). *International Arms Procurement: New Directions.* New York: Pergamon, 1981.
9. Ashworth, W. *Contracts and Finance.* London: HMSO, 1953.
10. Ayerst, R.P., McLaren-Permi, M. and Liddell, D. "The Role of Chemical Engineering in Providing Propellants and Explosives for the UK Armed Forces" in William F. Furter (ed.). *History of Chemical Engineering.* Washington: American Chemical Society, 1980, pp. 367-391.
11. Bailer, Uri. *The Shadow of the Bomber: The Fear of Air Attack and British Politics 1932-1939.* London: Royal Historical Society, 1980.
12. Baker, W. *A History of the Marconi Company.* London: Methuen, 1970.
13. Banks, F.R. (Rod). *I Kept No Diary.* Shrewsbury: Airlife, 1978.
14. Barnes, C.H. *Bristol Aircraft Since 1910.* London: Putnam, 1964.
15. ———. *Shorts' Aircraft Since 1900.* London: Putnam, 1967.
16. Barnett, Corelli. *The Audit of War.* London: Macmillan, 1986.
17. Bartlett, C.J. *The Long Retreat: A Short History of British Defence Policy, 1945-70.* London: Macmillan, 1972.
18. Beardsley, E.H. "Secrets between Friends: Applied Science Exchange between the Western Allies and the Soviet Union during World War II," *Social Studies of Science*, 7 (1977).
19. Behrens, C.B.A. *Merchant Shipping and the Demands of War.* London: HMSO, 1955.

20. Bidwell, S. and Graham, D. *Fire-power: British Army Weapons and Theories of War, 1904-1945.* London: Allen and Unwin, 1982.
21. Booth, Alan. "The 'Keynesian Revolution' in Economic Policy-Making," *Economic History Review,* XXXVI (1983).
22. Booth, A. and Coats, A.W. "Some Wartime Observations on the Role of Economists in Government," *Oxford Economic Papers,* XXXII (1980).
23. Boswell, J.S. and Johns, B.R. "Patriots or Profiteers? British Businessmen and the First World War," *Journal of European Economic History,* XI (1982).
24. British Thomson-Houston Co. Ltd. *BTH Reminiscences: Sixty Years of Progress.* The British Thomson-Houston Co. Ltd., 1946.
25. British Atlantic Committee. *Diminishing the Nuclear Threat: NATO's Defence and New Technology.* London: The British Atlantic Committee, 1984.
26. Brockway, A.F. and Mullally, F. *Death Pays a Dividend.* London: Gollancz, 1944.
27. Brockway, A.F. *The Bloody Traffic.* London: Gollancz, 1933.
28. Brookes, A. *V-Force: The History of Britain's Airborne Deterrent.* London: Jane's, 1982.
29. Bryson, Admiral Sir Lindsay. "All at sea," inaugural address as President of the Institution of Electrical Engineers. *IEE Proceedings* Part A, vol. 133, no. 1 (January 1986).
30. Buckley, M.E. *Bibliographical Survey of Contemporary Sources for the Economic and Social History of the War.* Oxford: Clarendon Press, 1922.
31. Burk, K. "J.M. Keynes and the Exchange Rate Crisis of July 1917," *Economic History Review,* XXXII (1979).
32. ———. *Britain, America and the Sinews of War, 1914-1918.* London: Allen and Unwin, 1984.
33. ——— (ed.). *War and the State: The Transformation of British Government, 1914-1919.* London: Allen and Unwin, 1982.
34. Cairncross, Sir Alec. "An Early Think-tank: The Origins of the Economic Section," *Three Banks Review,* 144 (1984).
35. Cardwell, D.S.L. "Science and Technology in World War One," *Proceedings of the Royal Society,* A, 342 (1975).
36. *The Central Organisation for Defence.* Cmnd. 9315. London: HMSO, 1984.
37. Centre for Contemporary Scientific Archives, University of Oxford.
38. Charnley, Sir John. "Aeronautical Research: Some Current Influences and Trends," *The Aeronautical Journal* (October 1982), pp. 282-93.
39. Chester, D.N. (ed.). *Lessons of the British War Economy.* Cambridge: Cambridge University Press, 1951.
40. Church, R.A. *Herbert Austin: The British Motor Car Industry to 1941.* London: Europa, 1979.
41. Clark, R.W. *J.B.S.: The Life and Work of J.B.S. Haldane.* London: Hodder and Stoughton, 1968.
42. ———. *Sir Edward Appleton.* Oxford: Pergamon, 1971.
43. Coats, A.W. "Economists in Government: Britain. The Rise of the Specialists," *History of Political Economy,* XIII (1981).

44. Coleman, D.C., article in J.M. Winter (ed.). *War and Economic Development*. Cambridge: Cambridge University Press, 1975.
45. Coghlan, F. "Armaments, Economic Policy and Appeasement, 1931-1937," *History*, 57 (1972).
46. Collier, B. *Arms and the Man*. London: Hamish Hamilton, 1980.
47. Constant, Edward. *The Turbojet Revolution*. Baltimore: The Johns Hopkins University Press, 1980.
48. Council for Science and Society. *UK Military R&D: Report of a Working Party, Council for Science and Society*. Oxford: Oxford University Press, 1986.
49. Court, W.H.B. *Coal*. London: HMSO, 1951.
50. Cross, J.A. *Lord Swinton*. Oxford: Clarendon Press, 1982.
51. Croucher, R. *The Engineers at War, 1939-1945*. London: Merlin, 1982.
52. Crow, H.D. *British Armoured Fighting Vehicles 1919-40*. Windsor: Profile, 1970.
53. Davenport-Hines, R.P.T. "The British Armaments Industry during Disarmament." PhD thesis, Cambridge University, 1979.
54. ─────. *Dudley Docker: The Life and Times of a Trade Warrior*. Cambridge: Cambridge University Press, 1984.
55. ─────. "Vickers' Balkan Conscience: Aspects of Anglo-Romanian Armaments, 1918-1939," *Business History*, XXV (1983).
56. Dawn, R. "Colossus-Progenitor of the Electronic Computer," *Industrial Archeology*, 17 (1984).
57. *Defence Analysis*. London: Brassey's, 1985-
58. *Defence Research and Development*. Cmnd. 4236. London: HMSO, 1969.
59. Devons, E. "The Aircraft Industry: in D. Burn (ed.). *Structure of British Industry*. vol. 2. Cambridge: Cambridge University Press, 1958.
60. ─────. "Economic Planning in War and Peace," *Manchester School*, XVI (1948).
61. ─────. *Planning in Practice: Essays in Aircraft Planning in Wartime*. Cambridge: Cambridge University Press, 1950.
62. ─────. *Papers on Economic Planning and Management*. ed. A.K. Cairncross. Manchester: Manchester University Press, 1970.
63. Dickson, Keith. "The influence of Ministry of Defence funding on semi-conductor research and development in the United Kingdom," *Research Policy*, vol. 12 (1983), pp. 113-120.
64. Dillon, G.M. *Dependence and Deterrence: Success and Civility in the Anglo-American Special Nuclear Relationship 1962-1982*. Aldershot: Gower, 1983.
65. Douglas, D. *The Great Gun Maker*. Newcastle-upon-Tyne, 1970.
66. Dunbabin, J.P.D. "British Rearmament in the 1930s: A Chronology and Review," *Historical Journal*, XVIII (1975).
67. Economist Intelligence Unit. *Defence Papers: A Trans-Atlantic Debate over Emerging Technologies and Defence Capabilities*. London: Economist Intelligence Unit, 1984.
68. Edgerton, D.E.H. "Technical Innovation, Industrial Capacity and Efficiency: Public Ownership and the British Military Aircraft Industry, 1935-48," *Business History*, XXVI (1984).
69. Edmonds, M. "The Future of Manned Aircraft" in J. Erickson et. al. (eds.). *The Military-Technical Revolution--Its Impact*

on Strategy and Foreign Policy. London: Pall Mall Press, for the Institute for the Study of the USSR, Munich, 1966.
70. ———— (ed.). International Arms Procurement: New Directions. New York: Pergamon, 1981.
71. Ellis, J. The Social History of the Machine Gun. London: Croom Helm, 1975.
72. Evans, Sir Harold. Vickers Against the Odds, 1956-1977. London: Hodder and Stoughton, 1978.
73. Facer, R. The Alliance and Europe: Part III: Weapons Procurement in Europe--Capabilities and Choices. London: International Institute for Strategic Studies, 1975.
74. Fearon, P. "The Formative Years of the British Aircraft Industry, 1913-24," Business History Review, XLIII (1969).
75. ————. "The British Airframe Industry and the State, 1918-35," Economic History Review, XXVII (1974).
76. ————. "The British Airframe Industry and the State in the Interwar Period: A Reply," Economic History Review, XXVIII (1975).
77. ————. "The Vicissitudes of a British Aircraft Company: Handley Page Ltd. between the Wars," Business History, XX (1978).
78. ————. "Aircraft Manufacturing" in N.K. Buxton and D.H. Aldcroft (eds.) British Industry between the Wars. London: Scolar, 1979.
79. (No entry)
80. Ferris, John. "A British 'Unofficial' Aviation Mission and Japanese Naval Developments, 1919-1929," Journal of Strategic Studies, 5 (1982).
81. Feuchtwanger, E.J. (ed.). Defence Planning and Weapons Technology. Southampton: University of Southampton, Department of Extra-Mural Studies, 1969.
82. Franks, O. Central Planning and Control in War and Peace. London: London School of Economics and Political Science, 1947.
83. Fraser, P. "The British 'Shells Scandal' of 1915," Canadian Journal of History, XVIII (1983).
84. Freedman, L. Arms Production in the United Kingdom: Problems and Prospects. London: Royal Institute of International Affairs, 1978.
85. ————. Britain and Nuclear Weapons. London: Macmillan, 1980.
86. Gallacher, J. Nuclear Stocktaking: A Count of Britain's Warheads. University of Lancaster: Bailrigg Paper on International Security, No. 5, 1982.
87. Gardner, C. British Aircraft Corporation: A History. London: Batsford, 1981.
88. Gehting, M.J. Harrier. London: Arms and Armour, 1983.
89. Gibbs, N.H. Rearmament. London: HMSO, 1976.
90. Gibbs-Smith, C.H. Aviation: An Historical Survey from its Origins to the End of World War II. London: HMSO, 1970.
91. Gilbert, M. Winston S. Churchill, vol. IV, 1916-1922. London: Heinemann, 1975 and vol. IV, Companion, Part I, London: Heinemann, 1977.
92. Gedden, J. (ed.). Harrier: Ski-Jump to Victory. London: Brassey's, 1983.

93. Goldsmith, M. *Sage: A Life of J.D. Bennal.* London: Hutchinson, 1980.
94. *Government Organisation for Defence Procurement and Civil Aerospace* (Rayner report). London: HMSO, Cmnd. 4641, 1971.
95. Gowing, M. *Independence and Deterrence: Britain and Atomic Energy 1945-1952,* vol. 1: *Policy Making.* vol. II: *Policy Execution.* London: Macmillan, 1974.
96. Grady, H.F. *British War Finance.* New York: Columbia University Press, 1927.
97. Gray, E.A. *The Devil's Device: The Story of Robert Whitehead, Inventor of the Torpedo.* London: Seeley Service, 1975.
98. Griffiths, R. *Fellow Travellers of the Right: British Enthusiasts for Nazi Germany 1933-39.* London: Constable, 1980.
99. Groom, A.J.R. *British Thinking About Nuclear Weapons.* London: Pinter, 1974.
100. Gummett, P. *Scientists in Whitehall.* Manchester: Manchester University Press, 1980.
101. ―――――. "Defence Research Policy" in M. Goldsmith (ed.). *UK Science Policy: A Critical Review of Policies for Publicly Funded Research.* Harlow: Longman, 1984.
102. Gunston, Bill. *Bombers of the West.* London: Ian Allan, 1973.
103. ―――――. *By Jupiter! The Life of Sir Roy Fedden.* London: Royal Aeronautical Society, 1978.
104. Gutteridge, W.F. and Taylor, T. (eds.). *The Dangers of New Weapon Systems.* London: Macmillan, 1983.
105. Haber, L.F. *Gas Warfare, 1916-1945: The Legend and the Facts.* London: 1976.
106. ―――――. *The Poisonous Cloud: Chemical Warfare in the First World War.* Oxford: Clarendon Press, 1985.
107. ―――――. "Government Intervention at the Frontiers of Science: British Dyestuffs and Synthetic Organic Chemicals," *Minerva,* 11 (1973).
108. Hacker, Barton C. "Imaginations in Thrall: The Social Psychology of Military Mechanisation 1919-39," *Parameters,* 12 (1982).
109. ―――――. "Resistance to Innovation: The British Army and the Case Against Mechanisation, 1919-1939," *Actes du XIIIe Congres International d'Histoire des Sciences,* 12 (1971: pub. 1974).
110. Hackmann, W.D. "Underwater Acoustics and the Royal Navy, 1893-1930," *Annals of Science,* 36 (1979).
111. ―――――. *Seek and Strike: Sonar Anti-Submarine Warfare and the Royal Navy, 1914-54.* London: HMSO, 1984.
112. Hall, H.D. *North American Supply.* London: HMSO, 1955.
113. ――― and C. C. Wrigley. *Studies of Overseas Supply.* London: HMSO, 1956.
114. Hancock, W.K., and Gowing, M.M. *British War Economy.* London: HMSO, 1949.
115. Hargreaves, E.L., and Gowing, M.M. *Civil Industry and Trade.* London: HMSO, 1952.
116. Hartcup, G. *The Challenge of War, Scientific and Engineering Contributions to World War II.* Newton Abbot: David and Charles, 1970.

117. Hartley, K. *A Market for Aircraft.* London: Institute of Economic Affairs, 1974.
118. ————. *NATO Arms Cooperation: A Study in Economics and Politics.* London: Allen and Unwin, 1983.
119. Heath, Sir Frank and Hetherington, A.L. *Industrial Research and Development in the United Kingdom.* London: Faber, 1946.
120. Henderson, Sir H.D. *The Uses and Abuses of Economic Planning.* Cambridge: Cambridge University Press, 1947.
121. Hendry, J. "Prolonged Negotiations: The British Fast Computer Project and the Early History of the British Computer Industry," *Business History*, XXVI (1984).
122. Hezlet, Sir Arthur. *The Electron and Sea Power.* New York: Stein and Day, 1975.
123. Higham, R. "Quantity Versus Quality: The Impact of Changing Demand on the British Aircraft Industry," *Business History Review*, XLII (1968).
124. ————. "Government, Companies and National Defense: British Aeronautical Experience, 1918-45 as the Basis for a Broad Hypothesis," *Business History Review*, 39 (1965).
125. Hodges, A. *Alan Turing: The Enigma of Intelligence.* London: Burnett, 1983.
126. Hogg, I.V. *A History of Artillery.* London: Hamlyn, 1974.
127. ———— and Thurston, L.F. *British Artillery Weapons and Ammunition, 1914-1918.* London: Ian Allen, 1972.
128. Hohan, C.M. *Works and Buildings.* London: HMSO, 1952.
129. Hooker, Sir S. *Not Much of an Engineer: An Autobiography.* Shrewsbury: Airlife, 1984.
130. Hornby, W. *Factories and Plant.* London: HMSO, 1958.
131. House of Commons, Select Committee on Defence, Session 1981-82, Second Report. *Ministry of Defence Organisation and Procurement: Report and Minutes of Evidence.* London: HMSO, HC 22, 1982.
132. House of Commons, Third Report from the Defence Committee, Session 1983-4. *Ministry of Defence Reorganisation.* London: HMSO, HC 584, 1984.
133. House of Commons, Defence Committee, Session 1980-81. *The Sting Ray Lightweight Torpedo.* London: HMSO, 1981.
134. House of Commons, Fourth Report from the Defence Committee, Session 1980-81. *Strategic Nuclear Weapons Policy.* London: HMSO, HC 36 and HC 674 (1979-80) 1981.
135. House of Commons, Sixth Report from the Expenditure Committee, Session 1978-79. *The Future of the United Kingdom's Nuclear Weapons Policy.* London: HMSO, HC 348, 1979.
136. House of Commons, Ninth Report of the Committee of Public Accounts, Session 1981-82. *Ministry of Defence: Chevaline Improvement to the Polaris Missile System.* London: HMSO, HC 269, 1982.
137. House of Commons, Twenty-eighth Report from the Committee of Public Accounts, Session 1984-85. *The Torpedo Programme.* London: HMSO, HC 391, 1985.
138. House of Commons, Thirty-fifth Report from the Committee of Public Accounts, Session 1984-85. *Design and Procurement of Warships.* London: HMSO, HC 452, 1985.
139. House of Commons, Second Report from the Select Committee on Science and Technology, Session 1968-69. *Defence Research:*

Report, Minutes of Evidence, Appendices and Index. London: HMSO, HC 213, 1969.
140. House of Lords, Select Committee on Science and Technology, Session 1982-83. *Engineering Research and Development*. London: HMSO, HL 89, 1983.
141. Hume, J.M. and Moss, M.S. *Beardmore: The History of a Scottish Industrial Giant*. London: Heinemann Educational, 1979.
142. Hurtsfield, J. *The Control of Raw Materials*. London: HMSO, 1953.
143. Inman, P. *Labour in the Munitions Industries*. London: HMSO, 1957.
144. Institution of Electrical Engineers. *Proceedings Part A* 132 (1985), no. 6. (Special Issue of Historical Radar), contains papers most of which are reprints of internal documents prepared by radar pioneers.
145. Institution of Electrical Engineers. *History of Radar Development to 1945*. London: Institution of Electrical Engineers, 1985.
146. James, D.N. *Gloster Aircraft Since 1917*. London: Putnam, 1971.
147. Jackson, A.J. *Blackburn Aircraft Since 1909*. London: Putnam, 1968.
148. Jackson, R. *V-Bombers*. London: Ian Allen, 1981.
149. *Jane's Defence Weekly*. London: Jane's, 1983-
150. Jeremy, D.J. (ed.). *The Dictionary of Business Biography*. London: Butterworths, 1984-
151. Johnson, B. *The Secret War*. London: BBC, 1978.
152. Johnson, F. A. *Defence by Ministry: The British Ministry of Defence 1944-1974*. London: Duckworth, 1980.
153. Jones, R., and Marriott, O. *Anatomy of a Merger*. London: Cape, 1970.
154. Jones, G. "Admirals and Oilmen: The Relationship Between the Royal Navy and the Oil Companies, 1900-1924" in S. Palmer and G. Williams (eds.), *Charted and Uncharted Waters*. London: National Maritime Museum and Queen Mary College, 1982.
155. Jones, R.V. *Most Secret War*. London: Hamish Hamilton, 1978.
156. ———. "Alfred Ewing and 'Room 40'," *Notes and Records of the Royal Society of London*, 34 (1979).
157. Jubb, Michael. "Scientific Records in the British Public Record Office," *History of Science*, XXIII (1985).
158. Kaldor, M. *The Baroque Arsenal*. London: Deutsch, 1982.
159. ———. "Technical Change in the Defence Industry," in K. Pavitt (ed.), *Technical Innovation and British Economic Performance*. London: Macmillan, 1980.
160. ———, Smith, D. and Vines, S. (eds.). *Democratic Socialism and the Cost of Defence: The Report and Papers of the Labour Party Defence Study Group*. London: Croom Helm, 1979.
161. Kennedy, Gavin. *Defense Economics*. London: Duckworth, 1982.
162. Kerr, T.H. "The Role of the Research Establishments in the Developing World of Aerospace," *The Aeronautical Journal*, vol. 86 (Dec. 1982), pp. 359-69.
163. Kinsey, G. *Orfordness, Secret Site: A History of the Establishment, 1915-1980*. Lavenham: Terence Dalton, 1981.

164. Kraus, J. "The British Electron-Tube and Semi-conductor Industry, 1935-62," *Technology and Culture*, 9 (1968).
165. Lee, J.M. "The British Civil Service and the War Economy: Bureaucratic Conceptions of the 'Lessons of History' in 1918 and 1945," *Transactions of the Royal Historical Society*, 5th Series, XXX (1980).
166. Lewin, Ronald. *Man of Armour: A Study of Lt. General Vyvyan Pope and the Development of Armoured Warfare*. London: Leo Cooper, 1976.
167. ———. *Ultra Goes to War*. New York: McGraw-Hill, 1978.
168. Lighthill, M.J. "The Royal Aircraft Establishment" in *The Organisation of Research Establishments*. ed. Sir John Cockcroft. London: Cambridge University Press, 1966.
169. (No entry)
170. Lloyd, Ian. *Rolls-Royce: The Growth of a Firm*. London: Macmillan, 1978.
171. ———. *Rolls-Royce: The Merlin at War*. London: Macmillan, 1978.
172. ———. *Rolls-Royce: The Years of Endeavour*. London: Macmillan, 1978.
173. Longstreth, F. "The City, Industry and the State" in C. Crouch (ed.), *State and Society in Contemporary Capitalism*. London: Croom Helm, 1979.
174. Lowe, R. "The Erosion of State Intervention in Britain, 1917-24," *Economic History Review*, XXXI (1978).
175. Maddock, Sir Ieuan. *Civil Exploitation of Defence Technology: Report to the Electronics Economic Development Council and Observations by the Ministry of Defence*. London: National Economic Development Office, 1983.
176. Mason, F.K. *Hawker Aircraft Since 1920*. 2nd edition. London: Putnam, 1971.
177. ———. *Harrier*. 2nd edn. Cambridge: Stephens, 1983.
178. McGucken, W. *Scientists, Society and the State: The Social Relations of Science Movement in Great Britain, 1931-1947*. Columbus, Ohio: Ohio State University Press, 1984.
179. McKinnon Wood, R. *Aircraft Manufacture: A Description of the Industry and Proposals for its Socialisation*. London: New Fabian Research Bureau, 1935.
180. MacLeod, R.M. and MacLeod, E.K. "War and Economic Development: Government and the Optical Industry in Britain 1914-1918" in J.M. Winter (ed.), *War and Economic Development*. Cambridge: Cambridge University Press, 1975.
181. ——— and Andrews, E. Kay. "Scientific Advice in the War at Sea, 1915-1917," *Journal of Contemporary History*, 6 (1971).
182. ———. "The Origins of DSIR: Reflections on Men and Ideas, 1915-16," *Public Administration*, 48 (1970).
183. ——— and McLeod, K. "The Contradictions of Professionalism: Scientists' Trade Unions and the First World War," *Social Studies of Science*, 9 (1979).
184. Mead, Peter. *The Eye in the Air: History of Air Observation and Reconnaissance for the Army since 1785*. London: HMSO, 1983.
185. Meade, J.E. *Planning and the Price Mechanism*. London: Allen and Unwin, 1948.

186. Medlicott, W.N. *Economic Blockade*, 2 vols. London: HMSO, 1952, 1959.
187. Melada, I. *Guns for Sale: War and Capitalism in English Literature, 1851-1939*. Jefferson, N.C.: McFarland, 1983.
188. Melville, Sir Harry. *The DSIR*. London: Allen and Unwin, 1962.
189. Mensforth, E. and Petter, W.E.W. "The Design and Production of Airframes," *Journal of the Royal Aeronautical Society*, 48 (1944).
190. ———. "Airframe Production," *Proceedings of the Institutions of Mechanical Engineers*, 156 (1947).
191. ———. "The British Airframe Industry," *Proceedings of the Institution of Mechanical Engineers*, 156 (1947).
192. ———. *Family Engineers*. London: Ward Lock, 1981.
193. Metcalf, M. and Edmonds, M. "RSI and the Main Battle Tank 1970-1980," in M. Edmonds (ed.), *International Arms Procurement: New Directions*. New York: Pergamon, 1981.
194. Metropolitan-Vickers Electrical Company Ltd. *Contribution to Victory*. Manchester: Metropolitan Vickers Electrical Company Ltd., 1947.
195. Miles, F.D. *A History of Research in the Nobel Division of ICI*. ICI, 1955.
196. Miller, R. and Sawers, D. *The Technical Development of Modern Aviation*. London: Routledge and Kegan Paul, 1968.
197. Milward, A.S. *War, Economy and Society, 1939-1945*. London: Allen Lane, 1977.
198. ———. *The Economic Effects of Two World Wars on Britain*. 2nd edn. London: Macmillan, 1984.
199. Ministry of Aviation. *Report of the Committee of Inquiry into the Aircraft Industry*. Cmnd. 2853 (1965).
200. Ministry of Defence. *Statement on the Defence Estimates, 1985*. Cmnd. 9430, (2 vols.). London: HMSO, 1985.
201. Ministry of Defence. *Steering Group on Research and Development Establishments*. Strathcona Report. London: Ministry of Defence, 1980.
202. Ministry of Defence, Procurement Executive. *The Transfer of Technology from Defence R&D to the Civil Sector: Proceedings of a Seminar held in the Ministry of Defence on 8 July 1982*. London: Ministry of Defence, (mimeo), 1982.
203. Ministry of Defence. *Value for Money in Defence Equipment Procurement*. Defence Open Government Document 83/01. London: Ministry of Defence, 1983.
204. *History of the Ministry of Munitions*, 12 vols. London: HMSO, 1920-1922.
205. More, C. "Armaments and Profits: The Case of Fairfield," *Business History*, XXIV (1982).
206. Morgan, K.O. and Morgan, J. *Portrait of a Progressive: The Political Career of Christopher, Viscount Addison*. Oxford: Clarendon Press, 1980.
207. Morpurgo, J.E. *Barnes Wallis: A Biography*. London: Longmans, 1972.
208. Moseley, R. "Government Science and the Royal Society: The Control of the National Physical Laboratory in the Inter-War Years," *Notes and Records of the Royal Society of London*, 35 (1980).

209. ———. "Tadpoles and Frogs: Some Aspects of the Professionalisation of British Physics, 1870-1939," *Social Studies of Science*, 7 (1977).
210. Myles, B. *Jump Jet: The Revolutionary V/STOL Fighter*. 2nd. edn. London: Brassey's, 1985.
211. Nailor, P. and Alford, J. *The Future of Britain's Deterrent Force*. Adelphi Paper, no. 156. London: International Institute for Strategic Studies, 1980.
212. Neild, R. *How to Make Up Your Mind About the Bomb*. London: Deutsch, 1981.
213. New Left Review (eds.). *Exterminism and Cold War*. London: Verso, 1982.
214. Nibblett, Chris. "Images of Progress: Three Episodes in the Development of Research Policy in the UK Electrical Engineering Industry," PhD Thesis, University of Manchester, 1980.
215. Noel Baker, P. *The Private Manufacture of Armaments*. London: Gollanz, 1936.
216. O'Brien, T.H. *Civil Defence*. London: HMSO, 1955.
217. Office of the Minister for Science. *Report of the Committee on the Management and Control of Research and Development*. Gibb-Zuckerman Report. London: HMSO, 1961.
218. Overy, R.J. *The Air War 1939-1945*. London: Europa, 1980.
219. Oxford Institute of Statistics. *Studies in War Economics*. Oxford: Blackwell, 1947.
220. Parker, H.M.D. *Manpower*. London: HMSO, 1957.
221. Parker, R.A.C. "Economics, Rearmament and Foreign Policy: The United Kingdom before 1939--a Preliminary Study," *Journal of Contemporary History*, 10 (1975).
222. ———. "British Rearmament 1936-1939: Treasury Trades Unions and Skilled Labour," *English Historical Review*, XCVI (1981).
223. ———. "The Pound Sterling, the American Treasury and British Preparations for War, 1938-1939," *English Historical Review*, 98 (1983).
224. Pattison, M. "Scientists, Inventors and the Military in Britain, 1915-19: The Munitions Invention Department," *Social Studies of Science*, 13, 4 (1983).
225. Payton Smith, D.J. *Oil*. London: HMSO, 1971.
226. Pearton, Maurice. *The Knowledgeable State: Diplomacy, War and Technology since 1830*. London: Burnett, 1982.
227. Peden, G.C. *British Rearmament and the Treasury 1932-1939*. Edinburgh: Scottish University Press, 1979.
228. ———. "Arms and the Businessman" in J. Turner (ed.), *Businessmen and Politics*. London: Heinemann, 1984.
229. ———. "Sir Warren Fisher and British Rearmament Against Germany," *English Historical Review*, 94 (1979).
230. ———. "Keynes, The Treasury and Unemployment in the Later Nineteen-Thirties," *Oxford Economic Papers*, 32 (1980).
231. ———. "A Matter of Timing: The Economic Background to British Foreign Policy, 1937-1939," *History*, 69 (1984).
232. Penrose, Harald. *British Aviation: The Pioneering Years, 1903-1914* (London: Putnam); *British Aviation: The Great War and Armistice* (London: Putnam); *British Aviation: The Adventuring Years 1920-1929* (London: Putnam, 1973); *British*

Aviation: Widening Horizons, 1930-1934 (London: HMSO, 1979); British Aviation: The Ominous Skies, 1935-1939 (London: HMSO, 1980).
233. Pierre, A. Nuclear Politics: The British Experience with an Independent Strategic Force, 1939-1970. London: Oxford University Press, 1972.
234. Poole, J.B. and Andrews, K. (eds.). The Government of Science in Britain. London: Weidenfeld and Nicholson, 1972.
235. Postan, M.M. British War Production. London: HMSO, 1952.
236. ———, Hay, D. and Scott, J.D. Design and Development of Weapons. London: HMSO, 1964.
237. Price, Alfred. Instruments of Darkness: The History of Electronic Warfare. London: MacDonald and Jones, 1977.
238. Prins, G. (ed.). Defended to Death: A Study of the Nuclear Arms Race from the Cambridge University Disarmament Seminar. Harmondsworth: Penguin, 1983.
239. Public Record Office,
a) CAB 80/94, Chiefs of Staff Committee, Future Development in Weapons and Methods of War. Report by Sir Henry Tizard's "Ad Hoc" Committee, 1945;
b) CAB 131/7, Cabinet Defence Committee, Guided Weapons Research and Development. Memorandum by the Minister of Defence, 1949;
c) DEFE 7/282 Report by the Committee on the Organisation and Work of the Scientific Branches of the Ministry of Supply and the Admiralty (Chairman: Air Chief Marshal Sir Guy Garrod), 1951.
240. Putley, E.H. "The History of the RSRE," Physics in Technology, vol. 16, no. 1 (1985).
241. Quill, Jeffrey. Spitfire. London: Arrow, 1985.
242. Ranft, Bryan. Technical Change and British Naval Policy, 1860-1939. London: Hodder and Stoughton, 1977.
243. Reader, W.J. Architect of Air Power: The Life of The First Viscount Weir of Eastwood, 1877-1959. London: Collins, 1968.
244. ———. Imperial Chemical Industries: A History. 2 vols. London: OUP, 1970, 1975.
245. ———. "ICI and the State," in B. Supple (ed.). Essays in British Business History. Oxford: Clarendon Press, 1977.
246. Reed, B. and Williams, G. Denis Healey and the Policies of Power. London: Sidgwick and Jackson, 1971.
247. Reed, A. Britain's Aircraft Industry: What Went Right? What Went Wrong? London: Dent, 1973.
248. Reid, R.W. Tongues of Conscience: War and The Scientists' Dilemma. London: Constable, 1969.
249. Richards, Denis. Portal of Hungerford: The Life of Marshal of the Royal Air Force Viscount Portal of Hungerford KG, GCB, OM, DSO, MC. London: Heinemann, 1977.
250. Robertson, A.J. "The British Airframe Industry and the State in the Interwar Period: A Comment," Economic History Review, XXVIII (1975).
251. ———. "British Rearmament and Industrial Growth, 1935-1939," in P. Helding (ed.), Research in Economic History, 8 (1983).

252. ─────. "Lord Beaverbrook and the Supply of Aircraft, 1940-1941," in A. Slaven and D.H. Aldcroft (eds.), *Business, Banking and Urban History: Essays in Honour of S.G. Checkland*. Edinburgh: John Donald, 1982.
253. Robinson, D.M. "British Microwave Radar, 1939-41," *Proceedings of the American Philosophical Society*, 27 (1983).
254. Rogow, A.A. *The Labour Government and British Industry, 1945-1951*. Oxford: Blackwell, 1955.
255. Rose, H. and Rose, S. *Science and Society*. London: Allen Lane, 1969.
256. *Report of the Royal Commission on the Private Manufacture of an Trading in Arms 1935-36* Cmnd. 5292, Parliamentary Papers 1935/36, vol. VII; *Statement Relating to the Report of the Royal Commission on the Private Manufacture and Trading in Arms 1935-36*, Cmnd. 5451, Parliamentary papers 1936/37, vol. XXI.
257. Royal Society of London. *Proceedings of the Royal Society*, A, 342 (1975).
258. Royal United Services Institute & Brassey's. *Defence Yearbook*. Oxford: Pergamon, annual.
259. Royal United Services Institute. *Weapons Procurement, Defence Management and International Collaboration*. London: RUSI, 1972.
260. Ryder, R.F. "The Economic History of the Aircraft Industry." MSc thesis, University of Southampton, 1958.
261. Sampson, A. *The Arms Bazaar: The Companies, the Dealers, the Bribes: From Vickers to Lockheed*. London: Hodder and Stoughton, 1977.
262. Sanderson, M. "Research and the Firm in British Industry, 1919-1939," *Science Studies*, 2 (1972).
263. Savage, C.L. *Inland Transport*. London: HMSO, 1957.
264. Sayers, R.S. *Financial Policy, 1939-54*. London: HMSO, 1956.
265. *Science in Parliament: A Periodical Summary Relating to Scientific and Technical Matters dealt with in Parliament*. London: Parliamentary and Scientific Committee, 1975-
266. Scott, J.D., and Hughes, R. *The Administration of War Production*. London: HMSO, 1955.
267. Sen, G. *The Military Origins of Industrialisation and International Trade Rivalry*. Brighton: Francis Pinter, 1984.
268. Sharp, M. *The History of de Havilland*. Shrewsbury: Airlife, 1982.
269. Shaw, Martin (ed.). *War, State and Society*. London: Macmillan, 1984.
270. Shay, R.P. *British Rearmament in the Thirties: Politics and Profits*. Princeton: Princeton University Press, 1977.
271. Simpson, J. *The Independent Nuclear State: The United States, Britain and the Military Atom*. London: Macmillan, 1983; 2nd edition. 1986.
272. ─────. "The Polaris Executive: A Case Study of a Unified Hierarchy," *Public Administration*, 48, (1970).
273. Simpson, John. "Understanding Weapon Acquisition Processes: A Study of Naval Anti-Submarine Aircraft Procurement in Britain, 1945-55." PhD Thesis, University of Southampton, 1976.

274. ——— and Gregory, Frank. "West European Collaboration in Weapons Procurement," *Orbis*, vol. 16 (Summer 1972), pp. 435-61.
275. Smart, Ian. *The Future of the British Nuclear Deterrent: Technical, Economic and Strategic Issues.* London: Royal Institute of International Affairs, 1977.
276. Smith, M.S. "Rearmament and Deterrence in Britain in the 1930s," *Journal of Strategic Studies*, 1 (1978).
277. Smith, M. *British Air Strategy Between the Wars.* Oxford: Clarendon Press, 1984.
278. ———. "The Air Ministry, the Aircraft Industry and the Building of the Bomber Force," *Business History Review*, LIV (1980).
279. Smith, Merritt Roe (ed.). *Military Enterprise and Technological Change: Perspectives on the American Experience.* Cambridge, Mass.: The MIT Press, 1985.
280. *Statistical Digest of the War.* London: HMSO, 1951.
281. Stewart, F. and Wield, D. "Science, Planning and the State," in G. McLennan et. al., *State and Society in Contemporary Britain.* Cambridge: Polity, 1984.
282. Strachan, H. "Conventional Defence in Europe," *International Affairs*, vol. 61, no. 1 (1984/85).
283. *Strategic Survey.* London: International Institute for Strategic Studies, 1968, annual.
284. *Survival.* London: International Institute for Strategic Studies, 1962.
285. Swann, J.P. "The Search for Synthetic Penicillin during World War II," *British Journal for the History of Science*, 16 (1983).
286. Swinton, Viscount. *I Remember.* London: Hutchinson, 1948.
287. Swords, S.S. *A Technical History of the Beginnings of Radar.* Dublin: Trinity College, 1983; to be published February 1986 by the IEE History of Technology, series 5.
288. Taylor, A.J.P. *Beaverbrook.* London: Hamish Hamilton, 1972.
289. Taylor, H.A. *Fairey Aircraft since 1915.* London: Putnam, 1974.
290. Taylor, Trevor. *Defence, Technology and International Integration.* London: Pinter, 1982.
291. Terraine, J. *White Heat: The new Warfare 1914-1918.* London: Sidgwick and Jackson, 1982.
292. Thayer, G. *The War Business: The International Trade in Armaments.* London: Weidenfeld and Nicolson, 1969.
293. Thetford, O. *Aircraft of the Royal Air Force since 1918.* London: Putnam, 1968.
294. Thomas, Mark. "Rearmament and Economic Recovery in the Late 1930s," *Economic History Review*, 36 (1983).
295. Trebilcock, R.C., article in J.M. Winter (ed.). *War and Economic Development.* Cambridge: Cambridge University Press, 1975.
296. ———. *The Vickers Brothers.* London: Europa, 1977.
297. ———. "Spin-off in British Economic History: Armaments and Industry, 1760-1914," *Economic History Review*, XXII (1969).
298. Turner, P.W. and Haigh, R.H. *The Growth of Industrialism and its Effects on Military Tactics and Technology.* Sheffield: Polytechnic, 1983.

299. *The UK Defence Programme: The Way Forward.* Cmnd. 8288. London: HMSO, 1981.
300. United States Airforce Academy. *Science, Technology and Warfare Proceedings of the Third Military History Symposium.* Washington, 1969.
301. Varcoe, Ian. "Scientists and Organised Research in Great Britain, 1914-1916: The Early History of the DSIR," *Minerva*, 9 (1970).
302. ─────. "Cooperative Research Associations in British Industry, 1918-1934," *Minerva*, 19 (1981).
303. Vick, F.A. "The Atomic Energy Research Establishment, Harwell" in *The Organisation of Research Establishments.* ed.: Sir John Cockcroft. London: Cambridge University Press, 1966.
304. Waddington, C.H. *OR in World War 2: Operational Research against the U-boat.* London: Elek, 1973.
305. Walker, William. "The Multi-role Combat Aircraft: A Case Study in European Collaboration," *Research Policy*, vol. 2 (1974), pp. 280-305.
306. Walter, Percy B. *Early Aviation at Farnborough: The History of the Royal Aircraft Establishment.* London: MacDonald, 1971-74.
307. Waters, D.W. "Seamen, Scientists, Historians and Strategy," *British Journal for the History of Science*, XIII (1980).
308. Weeks, John. *Men against Tanks: A History of Anti-Tank Warfare.* Newton Abbott: David & Charles, 1975.
309. Werskey, P.G. *The Visible College: A Collective Biography of British Scientists and Socialists of the 1930s.* London: Allen Lane, 1978.
310. Wheeler, N.J. "British Nuclear Weapons and Anglo-American Relations, 1945-54," *International Affairs*, vol. 62, no. 1 (1985/86).
311. Williams, G., Gregory, F. and Simpson, J. *Crisis in Procurement: A Cast Study of the TSR-2.* London: Royal United Services Institute, 1970.
312. Williams, Roger. *European Technology: The Politics of Collaboration.* London: Croom Helm, 1973.
313. Wilson, John. "The Ferrantis and the Growth of the Electrical Industry 1882-1952." PhD Thesis, Manchester University, 1980.
314. Winston, Philip. "The British Government and Defence Production, 1943-1950." PhD thesis. Cambridge University, 1982.
315. Winter, J.M. (ed.). *War and Economic Development.* Cambridge: Cambridge University Press, 1975.
316. Wood, D. *Project Cancelled.* London: Macdonald and Janes, 1975.
317. Worcester, Richard. *Roots of British Air Policy.* London: Hodder and Stoughton, 1966.
318. Zuckerman, S. *From Apes to Warlords: The Autobiography (1904-1946) of Solly Zuckerman.* London: Hamish Hamilton, 1978.
319. ─────. *Nuclear Illusion and Reality.* London: Collins, 1982.
320. ─────. *Collected Papers.* Norwich: Library of University of East Anglia.

XXII

INTELLIGENCE SINCE 1900

Wesley K. Wark

The modern British intelligence system is a twentieth century creation. It first took shape at the turn of the century, when the strategic confidence of the nineteenth century finally gave way to the strategic anxieties of the new age. In response to new international tensions, states began to place a premium on the possession of good quality intelligence, so as to be able to measure the power and threat manifested by potential enemies. By the outbreak of the First World War, although a great deal of innocence surrounded the nature and conduct of intelligence, a specialized intelligence bureaucracy had begun to emerge in Britain. Its main components were the service attachés stationed abroad, small intelligence directorates in London, and the two secret service bureaus (the forerunners of MI5 and MI6). From 1914 onward, the British intelligence system would undergo massive mobilizations and demobilizations to meet war and peacetime conditions, would reflect changes in the circumstances of British power, and would be forced to respond to unimagined technological change in both the weapons of war and in the means to collect and process intelligence. But it would never be dismantled.

Intelligence as an instrument of statecraft in both war and peace thus has a respectably long pedigree. It is as old as the machine gun, battleship, submarine or aeroplane; older than blitzkrieg or the atom bomb. Yet intelligence, until recently, attracted comparatively little scholarly attention. Robin Higham's *A Guide to the Sources of British Military History*, although considered the standard reference work after its publication in 1971, contained no separate chapter on intelligence, few references to the subject, and gave little indication that research was needed or would be useful in the area. Higham's authors, a high-powered team, in their neglect of intelligence were expressing the conventional wisdom.

Poor research opportunities, a weak literature, and a popular caricature of intelligence as the underworld adventures of master spies, combined to hold scholarship at arm's length. The situation began to change in the late 1960s, when parts of the British archival record became open to research under the new thirty-year rule. Subsequently, exciting new evidence about the historical contribution of intelligence in the Second World War, and a contemporary prominence achieved by national intelligence agencies in the Watergate and Church committee eras, brought renewed scholarly attention to bear. Of these factors, perhaps the greatest stimulus was provided by the revelation of the "Ultra Secret"--the story of Allied code-breaking successes against the Axis powers in World War Two. Ultra may be the last, and best, new story about the Second World War. But even before the dimensions of Ultra began to be revealed, some historians were already speculating on the intellectual puzzles involved in understanding intelligence. Mario Toscano, a leading Italian diplomatic historian, pointed the way in a 1950 paper, reprinted in English in 1970, which described the negative potential of mistaken intelligence to support wrong policies and to misdirect government leaders, in this case Mussolini (182).

Dramatic new stories like Ultra will continue to fuel research into intelligence. Hopefully, long-run interest will be assured by the fascination involved in attempting to research a difficult story (the historian becomes his own intelligence officer), and in attempting to understand how government and military authorities pictured the world. Writing about intelligence, in this sense, requires a careful deconstruction of the images they employed and a careful analysis of the process by which intelligence affected decision-making and events. It is this wider definition of intelligence which is used here to guide the selection of titles for inclusion.

Bibliographies and Guides. One aspect of the recent coming of age of intelligence studies has been the production of bibliographies. Consulting them can save considerable time, especially as the conventional Library of Congress system for book classification ensures that intelligence histories will be scattered widely through a library's holdings. Two massive, comprehensive bibliographies appeared in 1968, by William Harris (71), and by Max Gunzenhäuser (69). More recent are the three volumes by Myron Smith (170) and the bibliography of the unique Russell J. Bowen collection (167) at Georgetown University. The annotated bibliographies by George Constantinides (33), Walter Pforzheimer at the U.S. Defence Intelligence College (40), and Paul Blackstock (20) are all valuable. These works can be consulted for further information on topics not covered here in any detail, such as resistance, propaganda, deception, technical intelligence, counter-insurgency, and domestic espionage.

For a comprehensive description of research materials in Britain and a broader listing of works encompassing diplomatic history, readers should use the excellent guide by Sidney Aster (4), which has a section on intelligence. Chris Cook's six volumes (35) are an indispensable guide to archives and private papers in Britain.

Primary Sources. The principal center for research into intelligence subjects in the United Kingdom is the Public Record Office (PRO) at Kew Gardens (154). The holdings of intelligence-related records at the PRO are vast, but research in the field is not without its pitfalls. For one thing, there has never been a centralized office of intelligence assessment in Great Britain, and for that reason, no centralized intelligence archive exists. The closest one comes to this is the Foreign Office, with its monopoly on political intelligence, and its control of the channels of reporting from embassies abroad. The PRO record class FO 371 (Foreign Office General Correspondence) is particularly valuable and reasonably well-indexed, though rather daunting in size. Political intelligence, amateur agent reporting, attaché material, service intelligence analysis, and occasionally secret service information can all be found here. In addition to the Foreign Office papers, researchers can also explore the records of the intelligence directorates of the three service departments, Admiralty, Air Ministry, and War Office. Unfortunately, these records, though considerable for the Second World War, are very incomplete for other periods. Intelligence at the highest echelons of government can be followed in the various classes of records in the Cabinet Office series, especially the papers of the Chiefs of Staff, the senior military advisers to the government. Papers from the Prime Minister's Office also occasionally shed light on the reception of intelligence at the top. A special class, 'DEFE 3', has been created for the recently released World War Two 'Ultra' material. To date, none of the comparable records of British signals intelligence in the Far East have been released, but these are promised in due course. Looking further back, researchers interested in an introductory sketch of military intelligence in World War One might consult WO 32/10776, 'Historical Sketch of the Directorate of Military Intelligence during the Great War,' dated May, 1921 (192). Some intelligence materials, including pre-First World War attaché reports, are still to be found in the various branches of the Ministry of Defence Libraries in London (134).

It should be noted that certain classes of government records remain inaccessible. Those of the Secret Service (SIS or MI6), and of the Security Service (MI5) are under permanent closure, as are the records (with the exception of the Ultra decrypts) of the signals intelligence establishment, the Government Code and Cypher School (GC & CS), renamed Government Communications Headquarters (GCHQ) after World War Two. The same condition holds true for the papers of the Joint Intelligence committee, created in 1936, upon which sat representatives of MI6 and MI5. Many post-1945 military intelligence papers have been removed from classes opened under the provisions of the thirty year rule. Other, more peculiar, instances of closed records abound. Naval intelligence division files for the interwar period have not been released. The papers of the Industrial Intelligence Centre (which ceased to exist in 1939) languish in record class CAB 48 under a fifty or seventy-five year security clampdown, awaiting their twenty-first century historian. Research into some areas of intelligence can thus be frustrating.

Further afield, a number of research archives hold private papers of interest to the intelligence historian. These include, notably, Churchill College archives (29), the Imperial War Museum (86), the Intelligence Corps Museum (87), the Liddell Hart Centre for Military Archives (119), the National Maritime Museum (144), and the RAF Museum (165). Special mention might be made of the Air Photo Library at the University of Keele, which holds much of the print collection of the World War Two Allied Central Interpretation Unit (188). Details on holdings at these archives can be obtained by writing direct to the archivist, or by consulting the volumes of the Chris Cook series (35).

Printed primary documents relating to intelligence are, unfortunately, almost non-existent. The series, *Documents on British Foreign Policy* (67) is disappointing for its failure to reproduce service attaché reports in any systematic way. It is too early to tell whether the fault will recur in the new series covering the post-1945 period, *Documents on British Overseas Policy* (66).

The better-endowed University libraries have an opportunity to acquire 'Ultra' material and its Pacific 'Magic' counterpart on microfilm, supplied by commercial microform companies in Britain and the United States. Several universities in North America have availed themselves of this chance to acquire an intelligence archive and to stimulate their own research in the area. A listing of some of the American universities offering teaching in the field of intelligence can be found in *Teaching Intelligence in the 1980s* (177).

Official Histories and Command Papers. Although British governments were assiduous in compiling official histories on many aspects of the First and Second World War efforts, none relating to intelligence were ever released. Fortunately, the government agreed to authorize, in the 1970s, publication of an official history of British intelligence in World War Two. Written by a team of historians headed by F.H. Hinsley, a veteran of the wartime Government Code and Cypher School, the official history has appeared in three volumes, with a final volume forthcoming in 1987 (79). This work is, in its way, a masterpiece of the official historian's art. It is extremely scholarly, and very thoroughly researched, making no concessions to easy reading or superficial analysis. It provides an invaluable source on the history of British wartime intelligence and is an essential text for all students of the 'Ultra' story. The final, forthcoming volume will contain a detailed bibliography which should be a considerable aid to study.

Also worth mentioning here is the sole British government 'command paper' released on matters relating to military intelligence. Students of intelligence failures in general, and of the Falkland Islands affair in particular, will find something to ponder in the Franks Report (65).

General Surveys. One difficulty associated with understanding the role and importance of intelligence in the twentieth century has been the lack of reliable general accounts which set intelligence into a historical context and offered explanations for its evolution. An earlier generation of popular histories, like those of R.W. Rowan (164) and Richard Deacon (39) read like adventure stories. Nigel West's various works on the history of MI5 (196, 197) and MI6 (198) showed a flair for investigative reporting and advanced our knowledge of selected episodes, but provided little in the way of historical analysis. John Bulloch's book on MI5 (24) exhibited the same sorts of strengths and weaknesses. Jock Haswell's work on *British Military Intelligence* (73) in fact largely restricted itself to a history of the army's intelligence corps. Major General Sir Kenneth Strong provided a gallery of intelligence heroes, some sketched valuably from his own long experience as a career intelligence officer (174). Still in a popular vein was the work by David Wise and Thomas Ross, *The Espionage Establishment* (207), which concentrated on contemporary intelligence matters and included only a brief section on British intelligence which was hardly authoritative. Better, but still brief, was Harry Howe Ransom's chapter in *The Intelligence Establishment* (157).

A breakthrough came with the appearance of David Kahn's impressively researched *The Codebreakers* (99). Kahn's book was a pioneering study, the first documented history of code-breaking activities. Two recent works provide the reader with a thorough grounding in the history of twentieth century British intelligence. Walter Laqueur's book, *A World of Secrets* (115), explores some of the major conceptual problems raised by a study of intelligence. Christopher Andrew's *Secret Service* (2) is unlikely to be surpassed as a general history of the British intelligence community. It is both witty and scholarly, a Gibbonesque treat. Careful attention should be paid to the author's account of the evolution of the British SIS, in which the secret service ultimately escaped from its amateur past. The accompanying bibliography is useful.

Thanks to Andrew, Laqueur and Kahn the novice reader and researcher can now enter the arcane world of intelligence with some confidence. The literature has ceased to be dominated by ahistorical histories and undocumented narratives.

Essay Collections. It is perhaps indicative of the newness of intelligence history that much of the best writing on the subject as yet takes the shape of essays and articles. Although relatively ephemeral, the essay formula allows research methods and ideas to be tested and interim findings to be aired. A collected volume of essays serves a useful function by providing a variety of entries into the study of intelligence.

Two of the most substantial of these collections of essays appeared in 1984. One is an eclectic volume edited by Christopher Andrew and David Dilks entitled, *The Missing Dimension* (3). It ranges in subject matter from Japanese intelligence at the turn of the century, through consideration of code-breaking in both World Wars, to aspects of British intelligence, a brief history of the CIA, to end with a piece on the decline of British security censorship. The second major collection of essays, *Knowing One's Enemies*, is edited by Ernest May from conference papers originally read at Harvard University (132). It is more unified in subject matter, focusing on the nature of intelligence assessments among the great powers on the eve of the First and Second World Wars. Ernest May's own introduction and conclusion to the volume should be read for their insights into the factors which affect intelligence assessments. Bureaucratic politics and preconceived ideas both loom large in this account.

David Kahn collected many of his shorter pieces on intelligence in *Kahn on Codes* (101). Richard Langhorne's *festschrift* for Professor F.H. Hinsley contains a number of fine essays treating intelligence themes (113). Other essays are more widely dispersed. An introduction to the history of naval intelligence appears in Bryan Ranft's collection (156). A preview of Christopher Andrew's ideas on the importance of wartime mobilization in the development of British intelligence can be found in N.F. Dreisziger (43). David Dilks contributed an important essay on 'Appeasement and Intelligence' to a volume he edited (42). Walter Laqueur's *The Second World War* contains essays reprinted from the *Journal of Contemporary History*, including several on intelligence (114).

Intelligence before World War One. Prior to 1914 the British intelligence system was in its infancy. Little government direction or finances were provided, expertise was limited, agents and sources few in number. W.C. Beaver explores the nineteenth century origins of the military intelligence division (11). This history can be traced down to 1914 in the works of Thomas Fergusson (50) and B.A.H. Parritt (146), both of which are well documented and cover much the same ground, giving greatest attention to the organizational developments in British military intelligence. John Gooch provides some valuable material on the intelligence function as part of the growth of the General Staff structure in Britain (63). Alfred Vagts' general history, *The Military Attaché*, gives an account of the European practice of the military attaché system (189). Paul Kennedy draws attention to the importance of the British system of imperial communications before World War One in his edited volume, *The War Plans of the Great Powers* (103). In the May volume, Kennedy recounts the strengths and weaknesses of British intelligence assessments before 1914, particularly in the naval sphere (132).

Some feel for the amateur conditions of British intelligence in this pre-war era can be gained from a reading of memoirs by Baden-Powell (7), Lord Gleichen (60), and General Waters (194). A contemporary manual of intelligence practices, based on experiences derived from the Boer War, is David Henderson's *Field Intelligence* (75).

World War One. The First World War saw a tremendous, ad-hoc mobilization of British resources in intelligence. Part of that mobilization occurred to meet the pressing demands for intelligence at the front and behind the enemy lines in France. Ultimately more significant was the effort to exploit new technological opportunities in signals intelligence and in aerial photo reconnaissance. Breakthroughs in these areas assured intelligence a new importance in wartime and released it from dependence on information supplied by the inherently slower and less reliable agent networks.

Studies which attempt to examine the impact of new forms of intelligence on the conduct of the war are still few in number. There are no general histories which devote themselves to First World War intelligence; the literature is dominated by a few valuable specialized studies and a mass of older memoir and biographical material largely of the 'ace spy' variety.

Discussion of World War One code-breaking can be found in essays by Christopher Andrew and David Kahn, in *The Missing Dimension* (3). These should be supplemented by reference to Kahn's survey, *The Codebreakers* (99). The most famous episode of wartime code-breaking, the British reading of German telegrams announcing the onset of unrestricted submarine warfare and an effort at alliance building directed towards Mexico and Japan in 1917, has attracted considerable attention. The best introduction is provided by Barbara Tuchman in the *Zimmermann Telegram* (187), which should be read in conjunction with Patrick Beesly's excellent study of British naval intelligence, *Room 40* (12). American cryptographers William Friedman and Charles Mendelsohn wrote a manuscript on the Zimmermann telegram for private circulation, which is now published (56). Friedrich Katz explored the Mexican and American backgrounds to the affair in his *The Secret War in Mexico* (102). Still useful are the older works by Yves Glyden (61) and R.E. Priestley (153), though both must be considered rare library holdings.

Only the Royal Navy's intelligence service has been subjected to any historical scholarship. By far the best book on the subject is that by Patrick Beesly (12), himself a Second World War naval intelligence officer. Eunan O'Halpin's skillful essay on "British

Intelligence in Ireland" reveals the disastrous incursions of naval intelligence into political matters (3). Admiral Sir William James' biography of the Director of Naval Intelligence, Admiral "Blinker" Hall, is still valuable (92). Older studies which are still of some use include A.W. Ewing's biography of the founder of the navy's cryptographic bureau, Sir Alfred Ewing (46), Hoy's work, *40 O.B.* (83), and the journalistic, contemporary account by Hector Bywater and H.C. Ferraby, *Strange Intelligence* (26). Robert Grant provides a detailed account of aspects of the submarine war in *U-Boat Intelligence*, written largely from German documents (64). Lawson's book, *Tales of Aegean Intrigue* (116) is an unusual account by a naval intelligence officer working in the Mediterranean.

Turning to continental espionage, Christopher Andrew provides the context and a valuable general sketch in *Secret Service* (2). The only book on military intelligence is Haswell's unsatisfactory text (73). Perhaps the best memoir is that by Sir Ivone Kirkpatrick, detailing his exploits in constructing an intelligence network behind German lines in Flanders (106). Compton Mackenzie's story of his activities in the secret service, *Greek Memories* provoked a government lawsuit under the Official Secrets Act when it first appeared in 1932 (124). Works by the former senior security intelligence chief, Sir Basil Thomson, including the *Allied Secret Service in Greece* (180) and his memoirs, *Queer People* (181), slipped through more quietly. Some information on John Buchan's (Lord Tweedsmuir's) activities as MI5 press chief, can be found in Janet Adam Smith's biography (169), and in Buchan's memoirs (23). Some further insight into the conduct of secret service work on the continent can be gleaned from the memoirs by Sir George Aston (5), Sir George Cockerill (31), and Marthe McKenna (123). Nicholas Everitt's story, *British Secret Service during the Great War* (45), and Henry Landau's three volumes (110, 111, 112) also provide tidbits.

Outside the European arena, studies of intelligence are extremely scarce. Winstone's book on British intelligence in the Middle East, *The Illicit Adventure*, is the only work of its kind and is very valuable (204). Hugh Trevor-Roper (Lord Dacre) contributed an astonishing account of amateur (and fraudulent) espionage in China in his *Hermit of Peking*, a biography of sinologist and sensational liar, Sir Edmund Backhouse (185). An account which dramatizes German intelligence and British counter-intelligence in the United Kingdom is Felstead's *German Spies at Bay* (48). Two works cover the activities of British intelligence missions in the United States. W.B. Fowler is the best work on British intelligence director Sir William Wiseman (55). Arthur Willert's study, *The Road to Safety* (203) is also useful.

The British intelligence effort to assess conditions in Russia, particularly after the Bolshevik revolution removed the country from the list of effective allies, has not yet found its historian. However, Christopher Andrew should be consulted (2). A whole host of memoirs provide further details. These include works by the naval officer, Captain Augustus Agar (1), the future Cabinet Minister Sir Samuel Hoare (Lord Templewood) (81), the Foreign Office's man in Moscow, Sir Robert Bruce Lockhart (120), and accounts by three of Britain's more adventurous secret agents, Sir Paul Dukes (44), George A. Hill (76), and the ill-fated Sidney Reilly (159). To these can be added the book by Dorian Blair and C.H. Dand, *Russian Hazard* (21).

Two biographies, both largely undocumented, by Michael Kettle (105) and Robin Bruce Lockhart (121), attempt to explore the improbable career of ace and freelance spy, Sidney Reilly, in his attempts to overthrow the Bolshevik regime. Ted Morgan's biography of Somerset Maugham provides a brief account of the writer's unproductive mission as an intelligence officer to Russia in 1916 (140).

The Inter-War Years, 1918-1939. Demobilization of the intelligence system was the order of the day after 1918. The key elements of the intelligence directorates and the secret service, survived but were crippled in efficiency. The only positive development was the creation of a centralized code-breaking organization, the Government Code and Cypher School. But GC & CS, too, was strapped for funds and personnel.

Much of intelligence system's concentration in the 1920s was focused on the Soviet Union and the activities of the Comintern. Christopher Andrew recounts the successes of GC & CS against Soviet codes in the 1920s and the government's injudicious use of signals intelligence intercepts, which ultimately stalemated GC & CS's efforts (2). The Middle East remained a trouble spot, and some 1920s events are described in Winstone (204). The frustrations of trying to monitor German disarmament in the 1920s are described in Brigadier General J.H. Morgan's *Assize of Arms* (139). Major General Temperley provides an account of his experiences as a military man at the League of Nations in Geneva (178).

Not until the 1930s arrived did British intelligence have to respond to a serious threat to national security. That threat was posed by Nazi Germany, in the first instance, with Japan and Italy in the wings. Wesley K. Wark's, *The Ultimate Enemy*, provides the only detailed examination of military and economic intelligence assessments of Nazi Germany in the 1930s (193). A briefer introduction to the subject is presented by Wark in an essay in *The Missing Dimension* (3). A more broad-ranging survey of British intelligence in Europe before 1939 can be found in D.C. Watt's essay in May's *Knowing One's Enemies* (132). Peter Lowe contributed a piece on British assessments of Japan before 1941 to the same volume (132). Authoritative, but brief chapters on the pre-war SIS and GC & Cs can be found in F.H. Hinsley's official history, volume one (79). Two essays by David Dilks provide additional valuable material. His 'Appeasement and Intelligence' in the volume *Retreat from Power* (42), is the best short survey of political intelligence; while his piece on British security lapses in *The Missing Dimension* (3) shows the inadequacy of inter-war practices. The successes achieved by the German Forschungsamt in monitoring the communications of the British embassy in Berlin are detailed in David Irving's *Breach of Security* (90). Norman Baillie-Stewart tells how own story of his brief career in treason in *The Officer in the Tower* (8).

Naval intelligence in the 1930s is surveyed in Patrick Beesly's *Very Special Intelligence* (14) and in his biography of Admiral Godfrey, *Very Special Admiral* (13). Donald McLachlan's earlier study of Second World War naval intelligence, *Room 39* (125) also has some background information. Arthur Marder contributed a stimulating chapter on British naval intelligence on Japan in *Old Friends, New Enemies* (127). The Admiralty's outlook on the German navy is explored in a chapter in Wark's *The Ultimate Enemy* (193).

The threat of a knock-out blow from the air was taken very seriously by the British authorities in the interwar period, especially once the Luftwaffe began its rapid expansion. The contemporary outlook is evident in the memoirs of the RAF's director of plans during the 1930s, Sir John Slessor's *The Central Blue* (168). Air intelligence chief Sir Victor Goddard also provides useful insights in his memoir, *Skies to Dunkirk* (62). Uri Bialer explores some dimensions of the British fear of surprise air attack (19). Wark's account has two chapters devoted to the air intelligence picture of the Luftwaffe (193).

Military intelligence was the largest of the inter-war service directorates. Memoirs by two British military attachés to Germany, James Marshall-Cornwall's *Wars and Rumours of Wars* (128), and Sir Kenneth Strong's *Intelligence at the Top* (173) provide valuable insights into the nature of attaché reporting. Ewan Butler has written a biography of the most flamboyant of the inter-war military attachés, General Sir Noel Mason-Macfarlane (25). Readers are fortunate in having two very forthright diaries in print from which some idea of the reception of military intelligence in London can be gained. These are the diaries of Lieutenant General Sir Henry Pownall, edited by Brian Bond (22), and *The Ironside Diaries*, edited by Macleod and Kelly (126). Wark's *The Ultimate Enemy* summarizes military intelligence assessments of the Third Reich from 1933 to 1939 (193).

Evidence of the reception by the Foreign Office of intelligence is analyzed in Andrew's *Secret Service* (2) and in Dilk's essay, "Appeasement and Intelligence" (42). Norman Rose's biography of Vansittart gives a brief sketch of Vansittart's private intelligence network (163). Two major diaries are in print, both kept by senior Foreign Office officials in the 1930s: *The Diaries of Sir Alexander Cadogan*, edited by David Dilks (41), and the *Diplomatic Diaries of Oliver Harvey* (72).

On the secret service in the inter-war period, the essential account is by Andrew (2). This can be augmented by critical reference to Nigel West's history (198) and to two memoir accounts, both of proven veracity, by former SIS officers: Frederick Winterbotham's *The Nazi Connection* (205), and John Whitwell's *British Agent* (202). On MI5 in this period one can also consult Nigel West (197) and John Bulloch (24).

In an era when intelligence resources were limited, the British system came to rely to a considerable extent on amateur agents and volunteered information. T.P. Conwell-Evans wrote a biography of one of Britain's most accomplished private intelligence officers, retired RAF Group Captain Malcolm Graham Christie, who passed information to the British from Germany (34). A.P. Young was an industrialist used by Vansittart as a go-between in contacts with Nazi German dissidents. His story is told in *The 'X' Documents*, edited by Sidney Aster (211). Information from foreign intelligence services was also highly prized. General Frantisek Moravec's memoirs, *Master of Spies*, gives good account of the nature of intelligence collaboration between Britain and Czechoslovakia before the latter's demise in 1939 (138). Castellan's *Le Réarmement Clandestin du Reich* has some material on Anglo-French collaboration (28).

World War Two. British intelligence came of age in the Second World War, achieving a new pre-eminence as a vital tool of decision-making and a major instrument of war. Not surprisingly, the Second World War has attracted more writing on intelligence subjects than any other period. This phenomenon has to do, in part, with the unlocking of the "Ultra Secret" and the impact which the story of Allied code-breaking achievements has had on the accepted picture of the war.

A good introduction to the history of signals intelligence in World War Two is provided by Ronald Lewin in an essay in Walter Laqueur's collection (114), and by David Kahn in *The Missing Dimension* (3). Beyond these works, one enters a still rapidly expanding literature. Approached historiographically, the first account in English was written by a former SIS officer, Group Captain Frederick Winterbotham, who pioneered the system for handling Ultra intelligence--the Special Liaison Units. Winterbotham's *The Ultra Secret* was written from memory and suffers from the usual defects of such accounts (206). Following Winterbotham came the first scholarly work, an excellent study by Ronald Lewin, *Ultra Goes to War* (118). A conference held in Germany on the subject provoked amazed responses from former German intelligence officers and military historians. The papers were published by Jürgen Rohwer and Eberhard Jäckel (161).

Beginning in 1979 the volumes of the British official history of intelligence by F.H. Hinsley were published (79). This multi-volume work must be considered the most comprehensive account. Drawing on Hinsley for most of his evidence, Basil Collier has written a more general book on wartime intelligence, *Hidden Weapons* (32). Two accounts written by GC & CS practitioners have now appeared. Gordon Welchman's *The Hut Six Story* (195) and Peter Calvocoressi's *Top Secret Ultra* (27) both give valuable portraits of Bletchley Park (the wartime headquarters of GC & CS). Penelope Fitzgerald's *The Knox Brothers* (51) provides a brief biographical account of one of GC & CS's veterans, Dilwyn Knox. Andrew Hodges' *Alan Turing* (82) is a full-scale biography of a major figure at Bletchley and a pioneer of mathematical and computer systems to aid in code-breaking.

The contribution of foreign intelligence services to Allied code-breaking is discussed in Jean Stengers' article on "Enigma" in *The Missing Dimension* (3). Józef Garliński's survey, *Intercept* (58), gives some information on the Polish code-breaking effort. More controversial is Wladyslaw Kozaczuk's book, *Enigma* (109), which makes high claims for the Polish work in cryptography as the foundation for all subsequent Allied breakthroughs. French signals intelligence is described in Gustave Bertrand's *Enigma* (16).

Ralph Bennett's *Ultra in the West* (15) is a detailed case study of the contribution of Ultra to the Normandy landings and the offensive in north west Europe after D-Day. It is to be followed by a forthcoming volume on the Italian campaign. On Ultra and D-Day see also the book by Haswell (74). Ronald Lewin's, *The Other Ultra* (117) is the best available survey of signals intelligence, including Brian Johnson's *The Secret War* (94), Ewen Montagu's *Beyond Top Secret U* (136) and Robert A. Haldane's *The Hidden War* (70). David Kahn's *The Codebreakers* provides the essential context for understanding the historical evolution of signals intelligence (99).

Compared to code-breaking, less attention has been paid to the other sources of signals intelligence, such as direction finding and traffic analysis. The only book on the subject is Aileen Clayton's

The Enemy is Listening (30), an interesting account of her career in the British "Y" service.

The Battle of the Atlantic was profoundly influenced by the signals intelligence war waged between Britain and Nazi Germany. For the German side of the story see the essay by Jürgen Rohwer in *The Missing Dimension* (3). Hinsley is essential reading for British naval intelligence (79). The official history should be supplemented by the accounts contained in Beesly's two works, *Very Special Intelligence* (14) and *Very Special Admiral* (13), and by the earlier, but thoughtful book by McLachlan, *Room 39* (125).

Aerial photo reconnaissance techniques had to be learned virtually from scratch, owing to the RAF's failure to sustain any expertise in the field after World War One. A useful general history is Ursula Powys-Lybbe, *The Eye of Intelligence* (152). Constance Babington-Smith's *Evidence in Camera* (6) is a valuable memoir, and can be supplemented by Geoffrey Millington's *The Unseen Eye* (133). Ralph Barker provides a biographical portrait of one of the pioneers of air photo reconnaissance in World War Two, Sidney Cotton (10).

The story of scientific and technical intelligence is told by the SIS's wartime director of the program, R.V. Jones in *Most Secret War* (95). David Irving's *The Mare's Nest* (91) and James McGovern's *Crossbow and Overcast* (122) provide more specific studies of Allied intelligence on the German rocket projects. S. John Peskett's *Strange Intelligence* (149) is an unusual memoir by an RAF officer in charge of examining captured enemy aircraft and equipment.

The highly successful use of captured and "doubled" enemy agents to purvey false reports to the enemy is told by J.C. Masterman in *The Double Cross System in the War of 1939-1945* (130), an official account drawn up after the war, which Masterman succeeded in publishing only in 1972. Gunther Peis' work on the same subject is based on oral evidence (147). Two highly readable memoirs by agents of the double cross system have appeared: Dusko Popov's *Spy/Counterspy* (151) and Juan Pujol's *Garbo* (155). A.W. Sansom gives an account of British counter-intelligence in Cairo (166).

The contribution of intelligence to strategical and tactical deception operations in the Second World War has a small literature. The best survey is by Charles G. Cruickshank, *Deception in World War Two* (37). David Mure's two works focus on the Middle East (142, 143). Dennis Wheatley, horror story writer turned intelligence officer, explores the background to deception schemes prior to D-Day in *The Deception Planners* (200). Ewen Montagu tells the story of one of the most famous, if rather grisly, deception operations of the war in *The Man who Never Was* (137).

Intelligence in support of resistance operations and as conducted by the SIS's sometimes rival, the Special Operations Executive (SOE), can be traced in a number of works. There are two officially sanctioned histories, both excellent: M.R.D. Foot's *SOE in France* (52) and the more recent work by Charles Cruickshank, *SOE in the Far East* (38). SOE operations in Malaya are recounted by Ian Trenowden (184). Bickham Sweet-Escott's memoirs are particularly valuable for their account of liaison between the British and American services (175). Jean Overton Fuller explores security lapses in the SOE which led to tragedy (57). Further information on the duel between Allied agents and German counter-intelligence can be found in Ladislas Farago (47), Herman Giskes (59) and Charles Whiting (201). David

Kahn's, *Hitler's Spies* is the best account of German military intelligence in World War Two (100).
David Stafford's survey of SOE is especially valuable for its account of the origins of this clandestine service (171). Some of the amateur flavor accompanying early sabotage operations in Europe is captured in Merlin Minshall's *Guilt-Edged* (135) and John Toyne's *Win Time for Us* (183).

The activities of British intelligence in the western hemisphere, run by an organization known as British Security Co-Ordination (BSC) has attracted much public attention, but little scholarship. The most carefully documented study, by Stanley Hilton, deals only peripherally with BSC operations in its coverage of German espionage in South America (78). Two popular, but unsatisfactory biographies are in print of BSC's director, Sir William Stephenson. The best of the pair is by H. Montgomery Hyde (85), the worst is by the Canadian journalist William Stevenson (172).

A number of memoirs and biographies of wartime intelligence officers exist to help flesh out the story of intelligence work. Major General Sir Kenneth Strong's book (173) is an important account by Eisenhower's chief intelligence officer. Philip Johns provides a rare inside account of the SIS station in Lisbon (93). Sigismund Payne Best tells the painful story of his entrapment by German intelligence in the early days of the war (17). David Hunt (84) and David Walker (191) provide accounts of intelligence at various Allied headquarters. Graham Greene's memoirs contain a brief sketch of his intelligence career in West Africa (68). Malcolm Muggeridge's memoirs of wartime intelligence are in a similar vein (141). George Martelli's book, *Agent Extraordinary* (129) is a useful account of espionage networks on the French channel coast. Two former senior officers of the service charged with aiding escapers and evaders in occupied Europe give its history in *MI9* (53). R.W. Thompson provides some details of the relationship between Sir Winston Churchill and his one-time intelligence chief Sir Desmond Morton (179). Anthony Read and David Fisher have contributed a recent, if rather exaggerated biography of the SIS's deputy chief, Claude Dansey (158).

Surprisingly, only three works have discussed the issue of wartime intelligence failures in general. The earliest work appeared in 1941, written by Sidney T. Felstead (49). It was followed many years later by Lyman Kirkpatrick's work (107), the best available study. More recent, but thin, is Nigel West's *Unreliable Witness* (199).

General essays on a variety of subjects touching on intelligence matters can be found in Walter Laqueur's *The Second World War* (114) and in Richard Langhorne's *Diplomacy and Intelligence during the Second World War* (113). Essays in the latter collection by Ronald Zweig on intelligence in Palestine and by David Reynolds on the British dilemma upon the fall of France are particularly noteworthy.

Intelligence after 1945. The main lines of the post-Second World War intelligence effort derived from the lessons of the war, especially as they identified signals intelligence and aerial photo reconnaissance as the most lucrative and advanced forms of information collection. Britain joined the top-secret UKUSA Pact in 1947, committing herself to a signals intelligence-sharing arrangement with the U.S.A., Canada, Australia and New Zealand which is maintained to this day. The actual work of the Government Communications Headquarters at Cheltenham is one of the state's most closely guarded secrets. Some general information on postwar code-breaking can be found in David Kahn's *The Codebreakers* (99), in Christopher Andrew's epilogue to *Secret Service* (2) and in the investigative book by James Bamford, *The Puzzle Palace*, which looks at the activities of the American National Security Agency, responsible for signals intelligence (9).

Postwar developments in aerial reconnaissance from the U-2 to spy satellites can be followed in John Taylor and David Monday, *Spies in the Sky* (176) and in Philip Klass' highly regarded *Secret Sentries in Space* (108).

While high technology has increasingly dominated intelligence work since 1945, public attention remains firmly fixed on the traditional realm of the spy. Lack of documentation rules out any proper historical analysis, but Anthony Verrier, an SIS veteran, comes closest to a convincing portrait of the secret service in its postwar days (190). Kermit Roosevelt provides an informative story of the successful Anglo-American operation to overthrow the Iranian regime in 1953 (162). Colonel William Kennedy discusses the varieties of contemporary intelligence in a knowledgeable way (104). Two memoirs by former service attachés in Moscow, Richard Hilton (77) and Anthony Courtney (36) indicate the difficulties posed by overt intelligence collection in the Soviet Union.

Perhaps the SIS's single most important success in HUMINT (human intelligence) occurred with the running of Soviet GRU Colonel Oleg Penkovsky in 1961 and 1962. *The Penkovsky Papers* (148) are of disputed parentage; further information on the episode can be gained from Greville Wynne's two volumes of memoirs (209, 210).

Perhaps the worst disaster suffered by British intelligence after 1945 was its penetration by a succession of Soviet 'moles' or double-agents. Kim Philby was the most notorious of these, especially given the high-ranking position he enjoyed in SIS. Nicholas Bethell discusses Philby's role in the failure of the Anglo-American operation against Albania between 1949 and 1954 in *The Great Betrayal* (18). Philby's own memoirs are silent on this episode (150). The literature on the Philby affair and on the British moles (Burgess, Maclean, Blunt et al.) is easily accessible and not particularly relevant to this volume. Interested readers should start with Hugh Trevor-Roper's short monograph, *The Philby Affair* (186), and with the essay by Robert Cecil in *The Missing Dimension* (3). Nigel West contributes a general history of the postwar MI5 in *A Matter of Trust* (196).

Curiously, there are no monograph studies of British intelligence operations in any of the small wars fought since 1945. Perhaps the Falkland Islands conflict will attract an intelligence historian, if not readers will have to rely on the Franks report (65).

Journals. *Intelligence and National Security* (88), which brought out its first number in January 1986--a special issue on code-breaking-- is the first scholarly journal to devote itself solely to intelligence topics. A number of major historical journals regularly print articles on intelligence including *The Historical Journal* (80), *The Journal of Contemporary History* (96), the *International History Review* (89), and the *Journal of Strategic Studies* (98). Occasional pieces can be found in *The Journal of the Royal United Services*

Institute (97), and the *Revue d'Histoire de la Deuxième Guerre Mondiale* (160). More contemporary scholarly issues relating to intelligence are covered in *World Politics* (208), *Orbis* (145), and *Foreign Affairs* (54).

Research Opportunities. The study of intelligence has undoubtedly acquired scholarly legitimacy, but is yet in its infancy. Much of twentieth century intelligence remains a "missing dimension" and offers exciting opportunities for research. The Second World War period will surely continue to attract a large number of scholars, due to the massive available documentation and the revisionistic impact of Ultra and Magic. The early decades of the Cold War beckon, as the archives become available to researchers. Studies are needed of the role of intelligence in such international crises as Berlin, Korea, Indochina, Suez and Cuba; to which might be added specific British security problems that accompanied decolonialization in such places as Malaya and Aden. A study of British intelligence assessments of the Soviet threat after 1945 is badly needed.

Further back in time, it is to be hoped that enterprising scholars will attempt studies of the impact of intelligence on the land and air campaigns of the First World War, though the archival record is admittedly fragmentary. Research into colonial intelligence and into intelligence related to the Middle East would be valuable additions to the literature. For the interwar period much remains to be done. A history of the Government Code and Cypher School in the period would be extremely valuable, but is perhaps ruled out by the closure of documents. There are no monograph accounts of British intelligence on Japan or on Italy, where the documentary record is certainly large. Further studies of the nature of intelligence failures in war and peace would be useful, as would investigations into the nature of Second World War and postwar intelligence alliances in the West.

All in all, the opportunities for research and writing appear limitless. Such studies will only prove useful, however, to the extent that they manage to transcend an obsession with organizational history and narrative story-telling, and explore the central question of the role of images and preconceptions in the shaping and use of intelligence.

BIBLIOGRAPHY

1. Agar, Captain Augustus. *Baltic Episode*. London: Hodder and Stoughton, 1963.
2. Andrew, Christopher. *Secret Service: The Making of the British Intelligence Community*. London: Heinemann, 1985.
3. Andrew, Christopher and David Dilks (eds.). *The Missing Dimension: Governments and Intelligence Communities in the Twentieth Century*. London: Macmillan, 1984.
4. Aster, Sidney. *British Foreign Policy 1918-1945: A Guide to Research and Research Materials*. Wilmington, Delaware: Scholarly Resources, 1984.
5. Aston, Sir George. *Secret Service*. London: Faber & Faber, 1930.

6. Babington-Smith, Constance. *Evidence in Camera*. London: Chatto and Windus, 1958. (U.S. title: *Air Spy: The Story of Photo Intelligence in World War Two.*)
7. Baden-Powell, Lieutenant-General Sir Robert. *My Adventures as a Spy*. London: C.A. Pearson, 1915.
8. Baillie-Stewart, Norman. *The Officer in the Tower*. London: Frewin, 1967.
9. Bamford, James. *The Puzzle Palace: A Report on America's Most Secret Agency*. Boston: Houghton Mifflin, 1982.
10. Barker, Ralph. *Aviator Extraordinary: The Sidney Cotton Story*. London: Chatto and Windus, 1969.
11. Beaver, William C. "The Development of the Intelligence Division and Its Role in Aspects of Imperial Policing." Oxford D. Phil. dissertation, 1976.
12. Beesly, Patrick. *Room 40: British Naval Intelligence 1914-1918*. London: Hamish Hamilton, 1982.
13. ———. *Very Special Admiral: The Life of Admiral J.H. Godfrey*. London: Hamish Hamilton, 1980.
14. ———. *Very Special Intelligence: The Story of the Admiralty's Operational Intelligence Center, 1939-1945*. London: Hamish Hamilton, 1977.
15. Bennett, Ralph. *Ultra in the West: The Normandy Campaign of 1944-1945*. London: Hutchinson, 1979.
16. Bertrand, Gustave. *Enigma ou la Plus Grande Énigme de la Guerre, 1939-1945*. Paris: Plon, 1973.
17. Best, Sigismund Payne. *The Venlo Incident*. London: Hutchinson, 1951.
18. Bethell, Nicholas. *The Great Betrayal*. London: Hodder and Stoughton, 1984.
19. Bialer, Uri. *The Shadow of the Bomber: Fear of Air Attack and British Politics 1932-1939*. London: Royal Historical Society, 1980.
20. Blackstock, Paul W. *Intelligence, Espionage, Counterespionage, and Covert Operations: A Guide to Information Sources*. Detroit: Gale, 1978.
21. Blair, Dorian and C.H. Dand. *Russian Hazard: The Adventures of a British Secret Service Agent in Russia*. London: R. Hale, 1937.
22. Bond, Brian (ed.). *Chief of Staff: The Diaries of Lieutenant-General Sir Henry Pownall*. 2 vols. London: Leo Cooper, 1972.
23. Buchan, John (Lord Tweedsmuir). *Memory Hold the Door*. London: Hodder and Stoughton, 1941.
24. Bulloch, John. *MI5: The Origin and History of the British Counter-Espionage Service*. London: A. Baker, 1963.
25. Butler, Ewan. *Mason-Mac: The Life of Lieutenant-General Sir Noel Mason-Macfarlane*. London: Macmillan, 1972.
26. Bywater, Hector C. and H.C. Ferraby. *Strange Intelligence: Memoirs of Naval Secret Service*. London: Constable, 1931.
27. Calvocoressi, Peter. *Top Secret Ultra*. London: Cassell, 1980.
28. Castellan, Georges. *Le Réarmement Clandestin du Reich, 1930-1935: vu par le deuxième bureau de l'etat-major Français*. Paris: Plon, 1954.
29. Churchill College Archives, Cambridge CB3 OD5, England.

30. Clayton, Aileen. *The Enemy is Listening.* London: Hutchinson, 1980.
31. Cockerill, Sir George. *What Fools We Were.* London: Hutchinson, 1944.
32. Collier, Basil. *Hidden Weapons: Allied Secret or Undercover Services in World War Two.* London: Hamish Hamilton, 1982.
33. Constantinides, George. *Intelligence and Espionage: An Annotated Bibliography.* Boulder, Colorado: Westview Press, 1983.
34. Conwell-Evans, T.P. *None So Blind.* London: Harrison & Sons, 1947.
35. Cook, Chris et al. *Sources in British Political History, 1900-1951.* 6 vols. London: Macmillan, 1975-1985.
36. Courtney, Anthony. *Sailor in a Russian Frame.* London: Johnson, 1968.
37. Cruickshank, Charles G. *Deception in World War Two.* Oxford: Oxford University Press, 1979.
38. ————. *SOE in the Far East.* Oxford: Oxford University Press, 1983.
39. Deacon, Richard (Donald McCormick). *A History of the British Secret Service.* London: F. Muller, 1969.
40. Defence Intelligence College. *Bibliography of Intelligence Literature: A Critical and Annotated Bibliography of Open Source Literature.* Walter Pforzheimer, ed. 8th edition. Washington, D.C.: Defence Intelligence College, 1985.
41. Dilks, David (ed.). *The Diaries of Sir Alexander Cadogan, 1938-1945.* London: Cassell, 1971.
42. ————. *Retreat from Power: Studies in Britain's Foreign Policy of the Twentieth Century.* Vol. 1: *1906-1939.* London: Macmillan, 1981.
43. Dreisziger, N.F. (ed.). *Mobilization for Total War: The Canadian American and British Experience, 1914-18, 1939-45.* Waterloo, Ontario: Wilfrid Laurier University Press, 1981.
44. Dukes, Sir Paul. *The Story of "ST 25": Adventure and Romance in the Secret Intelligence Service in Red Russia.* London: Cassell, 1938.
45. Everitt, Nicholas. *British Secret Service during the Great War.* London: Hutchinson, 1920.
46. Ewing, A.W. *The Man of Room 40: The Life of Sir Alfred Ewing.* London: Hutchinson, 1939.
47. Fargo, Ladislas. *The Game of the Foxes: The Untold Story of German Espionage in the United States and Great Britain during World War Two.* London: Hodder and Stoughton, 1974.
48. Felstead, Sidney Theodore. *German Spies at Bay: Being an Actual Record of the German Espionage in Great Britain During the Years 1914-18, Compiled from Official Sources.* London: Hutchinson, 1920.
49. ————. *Intelligence: An Indictment of a Colossal Failure.* London: Hutchinson, 1941.
50. Fergusson, Thomas G. *British Military Intelligence, 1870-1914: The Development of a Modern Intelligence Organization.* London: Arms and Armour Press, 1984.
51. Fitzgerald, Penelope. *The Knox Brothers.* London: Macmillan, 1977.

52. Foot, M.R.D. *SOE in France: An Account of the Work of the British Special Operations Executive in France 1940-1944*. London: HMSO, 1966.
53. Foot, M.R.D. and J.M. Langley. *MI9: The British Secret Service that Fostered Escape and Evasion 1939-1945 and its American Counterpart*. London: Bodley Head, 1979.
54. *Foreign Affairs*. New York, 1922-. Five issues per year.
55. Fowler, W.B. *British-American Relations 1917-1918. The Role of Sir William Wiseman*. Princeton: Princeton University Press, 1969.
56. Friedman, William F. and Charles J. Mendelsohn. *The Zimmermann Telegram of January 16, 1917 and its Cryptographic Background*. Laguna Hills, California: Aegean Park Press, 1976.
57. Fuller, Jean Overton. *The German Penetration of SOE: France 1941-1944*. London: William Kimber, 1975.
58. Garliński, Józef. *Intercept: The Enigma War*. London: J.M. Dent, 1979. (U.S. title: *The Enigma War*.)
59. Giskes, Herman. *London Calling North Pole*. London: William Kimber, 1953.
60. Gleichen, Lord Edward. *A Guardsman's Memoirs. A Book of Recollections*. London: Blackwood, 1932.
61. Gylden, Yves. *The Contribution of the Cryptographic Bureaus in the World War*. Washington, D.C.: Government Printing Office, 1935.
62. Goddard, Sir Victor. *Skies to Dunkirk: A Personal Memoir*. London: William Kimber, 1982.
63. Gooch, John. *The Plans of War: The General Staff and British Military Strategy, 1900-1916*. London: Routledge and Kegan Paul, 1974.
64. Grant, Robert. *U-Boat Intelligence 1914-1918*. London: Putnam, 1969.
65. Great Britain. "Falkland Islands Review: Report of a Committee of Privy Counsellors." (Franks Report.) CMD 8787. London: HMSO, 1983.
66. Great Britain, Foreign and Commonwealth Office. *Documents on British Overseas Policy*. Edited by Rohan Butler and Roger Bullen. London: HMSO.
67. Great Britain, Foreign Office. *Documents on British Foreign Policy*. Edited by Sir Llewellyn Woodward, Rohan Butler, W.N. Medlicott et al. London: HMSO, 1946-
68. Greene, Graham. *Ways of Escape*. London: Bodley Head, 1980.
69. Gunzenhäuser, Max. *Geschichte des Geheimen Nachrichtendienstes (Spionage Sabotage und Abwehr. Literaturbericht und Bibliographie)*. Frankfurt am Main: Bernard & Graefe, 1968.
70. Haldane, Robert A. *The Hidden War*. New York: St. Martin's Press, 1978.
71. Harris, William R. *Intelligence and National Security: A Bibliography with Selected Annotations*. Rev. ed. Cambridge, Mass.: Harvard University Center for International Affairs, 1968.
72. Harvey, John (ed.). *The Diplomatic Diaries of Oliver Harvey, 1937-1940*. London: Collins, 1970.
73. Haswell, Jock. *British Military Intelligence*. London: Weidenfeld & Nicolson, 1973.

74. ———. *D-Day: Intelligence and Deception.* London: Batsford, 1979.
75. Henderson, David. *Field Intelligence: Its Principles and Practises.* London: HMSO, 1904.
76. Hill, George A. *Go Spy the Land: Being the Adventures of I.K.8 of the British Secret Service.* London: Cassell, 1932.
77. Hilton, Richard. *Military Attaché in Moscow.* London: Hollis and Carter, 1949.
78. Hilton, Stanley E. *Hitler's Secret War in South America: German Military Espionage and Allied Counter-espionage in Brazil, 1939-1945.* Baton Rouge, Louisiana: LSU Press, 1981.
79. Hinsley, F.H. et al. *British Intelligence in the Second World War.* 3 vols. London: HMSO, 1979, 81, 84. (Vol. 1: 1939 to mid-1941; Vol. 2: mid-1941 to mid-1943; Vol. 3, pt. 1: mid-1943 to summer 1944; Vol. 3, pt. 2: summer 1944 to 1945, still in progress.)
80. *The Historical Journal.* Cambridge, 1958-. Quarterly since 1969.
81. Hoare, Sir Samuel. *The Fourth Seal: The End of a Russian Chapter.* London: W. Heinemann, 1930.
82. Hodges, Andrew. *Alan Turing: The Enigma of Intelligence.* London: Hutchinson, 1983.
83. Hoy, Hugh Cleland. *40 O.B.* London: Hutchinson, 1932.
84. Hunt, David. *A Don at War.* London: William Kimber, 1966.
85. Hyde, H. Montgomery. *The Quiet Canadian.* London: Hamish Hamilton, 1962. (U.S. title: *Room 3603: The Story of the British Intelligence Center in New York during World War Two.*)
86. Imperial War Museum. Lambeth Road, London SE1 6HZ, England.
87. Intelligence Corps Museum. Ashford, Kent, England.
88. *Intelligence and National Security.* London, 1986-. Quarterly.
89. *International History Review.* Simon Fraser University, Burnaby, British Columbia, 1981-. Quarterly.
90. Irving, David. *Breach of Security: The German Secret Intelligence File on Events leading up to the Second World War.* London: William Kimber, 1968.
91. ———. *The Mare's Nest.* London: William Kimber, 1964.
92. James, Admiral Sir William. *The Eyes of the Navy: A Biographical Study of Admiral Sir Reginald Hall.* London: Methuen, 1955. (U.S. title: *The Codebreakers of Room 40: The Story of Admiral Sir Reginald Hall, The Genius of British Counter-espionage.*)
93. Johns, Philip. *Within Two Cloaks: Missions with Secret Intelligence Service and Special Operations Executive.* London: William Kimber, 1979.
94. Johnson, Brian. *The Secret War.* London: BBC Publications, 1978.
95. Jones, R.V. *Most Secret War: British Scientific Intelligence 1939-1945.* London: Hamish Hamilton, 1982. (U.S. title: *The Wizard War.*)
96. *Journal of Contemporary History.* London, 1966-. Quarterly.
97. *Journal of the Royal United Services Institute.* London, 1857-. Quarterly.
98. *Journal of Strategic Studies.* London, 1978-. Quarterly.

99. Kahn, David. *The Codebreakers.* London: Weidenfeld and Nicolson, 1967.
100. ─────. *Hitler's Spies: German Military Intelligence in World War Two.* New York: Macmillan, 1978.
101. ─────. *Kahn on Codes.* New York: Macmillan, 1983.
102. Katz, Friedrich. *The Secret War in Mexico.* Chicago: University of Chicago Press, 1981.
103. Kennedy, Paul. *The War Plans of the Great Powers, 1880-1914.* London: Allen and Unwin, 1979.
104. Kennedy, Colonel William V. *The Intelligence War.* London: Salamander, 1983.
105. Kettle, Michael. *Sidney Reilly: The True Story.* London: Corgi books, 1983.
106. Kirkpatrick, Sir Ivone. *The Inner Circle: Memoirs of Ivone Kirkpatrick.* New York: St. Martin's Press, 1959.
107. Kirkpatrick, Lyman B. Jr. *Captains without Eyes: Intelligence Failures in World War Two.* New York: Macmillan, 1969.
108. Klass, Philip J. *Secret Sentries in Space.* New York: Random House, 1971.
109. Kozaczuk, Wladyslaw. *Enigma.* Frederick, Md.: University Publications of America, 1984.
110. Landau, Henry. *All's Fair: The Story of the British Secret Service behind the German Lines.* New York: G.P. Putnam's, 1934.
111. ─────. *Secrets of the White Lady.* New York: G.P. Putnam's 1935.
112. ─────. *Spreading the Spy Net: The Story of a British Spy Director.* London: Jarrolds, 1938.
113. Langhorne, Richard (ed.). *Diplomacy and Intelligence during the Second World War: Essays in Honour of F.H. Hinsley.* Cambridge: Cambridge University Press, 1985.
114. Laqueur, Walter (ed.). *The Second World War: Essays in Military and Political History.* London: Sage, 1982.
115. ─────. *A World of Secrets: The Uses and Limits of Intelligence.* New York: Basic Books, 1985.
116. Lawson, John Cuthbert. *Tales of Aegean Intrigue.* New York: Dutton, 1921.
117. Lewin, Ronald. *The Other Ultra.* London: Hutchinson, 1982. (U.S. title: *American Magic.*)
118. ─────. *Ultra Goes to War.* London: Hutchinson, 1978.
119. The Liddell Hart Centre for Military Archives. King's College, Strand, London WC2R 2LS, England.
120. Lockhart, Sir Robert H. Bruce. *Memoirs of a British Agent.* London: Putnam, 1932.
121. Lockhart, Robin Bruce. *Reilly--Ace of Spies.* London: Futura, Macdonald, 1967.
122. McGovern, James. *Crossbow and Overcast.* New York: Morrow, 1964.
123. McKenna, Marthe. *I Was a Spy.* London: Jarrolds, n.d.
124. Mackenzie, Compton. *Greek Memories.* London: Chatto and Windus, 1939.
125. McLachlan, Donald. *Room 39: A Study in Naval Intelligence.* London: Weidenfeld and Nicolson, 1968.
126. Macleod, Colonel Roderick and D. Kelly (eds.). *The Ironside Diaries, 1937-1940.* London: Constable, 1962.

127. Marder, Arthur J. *Old Friends, New Enemies: The Royal Navy and the Imperial Japanese Navy: Strategic Illusions, 1936-1941.* Oxford: Clarendon Press, 1981.
128. Marshall-Cornwall, James. *Wars and Rumours of Wars.* London: Leo Cooper, 1984.
129. Martelli, George. *Agent Extraordinary.* London: Collins, 1960.
130. Masterman, J.C. *The Double-Cross System in the War of 1939-1945.* New Haven, Conn.: Yale University Press, 1972.
131. Masters, Anthony. *The Man who was M: The Life of Maxwell Knight.* Oxford: Basil Blackwell, 1984.
132. May, Ernest R. *Knowing One's Enemies: Intelligence Assessment before the Two World Wars.* Princeton: Princeton University Press, 1984.
133. Millington, Geoffrey. *The Unseen Eye.* London: Gibbs and Phillips, 1961.
134. Ministry of Defence Libraries. Including the Air Library, Adastral House, Theobalds Road, London WC1X 8RU; Naval Historical Library. Empress State Building, Lillie Road, Fulham, London SW6 1TR.
135. Minshall, Merlin. *Guilt-Edged.* London: Bachamn & Turner, 1975.
136. Montagu, Ewen. *Beyond Top Secret U.* London: P. Davies, 1977.
137. ———. *The Man who Never Was: The Story of Operation Mincemeat.* London: Evans, 1953.
138. Moravec, General Frantisek. *Master of Spies.* London: Bodley Head, 1975.
139. Morgan, Brigadier General J. H. *Assize of Arms.* London: Methuen, 1945.
140. Morgan, Ted. *Maugham.* New York: Simon & Schuster, 1980.
141. Muggeridge, Malcolm. *The Infernal Grove.* Vol. 2 of *Chronicles of Wasted Time.* London: Collins, 1973.
142. Mure, David. *Master of Deception: Tangled Webs in London and in the Middle East.* London: William Kimber, 1980.
143. ———. *Practice to Deceive.* London: William Kimber, 1977.
144. National Maritime Museum. Romney Road, Greenwich, London SE10 9NF, England.
145. *Orbis.* Philadelphia, 1957-. Quarterly.
146. Parritt, B.A.H. *The Intelligencers: The Story of British Military Intelligence up to 1914.* Ashford, Kent: Intelligence Corps Museum, 1971.
147. Peis, Gunther. *The Mirror of Deception.* London: 1976.
148. Penkovsky, Oleg. *The Penkovsky Papers.* New York: Doubleday, 1965.
149. Peskett, S. John. *Strange Intelligence: From Dunkirk to Nuremburg.* London: Robert Hale, 1981.
150. Philby, Kim. *My Silent War.* London: MacGibbon and Kee, 1968.
151. Popov, Dusko. *Spy/Counter-Spy.* London: Weidenfeld and Nicolson, 1974.
152. Powys-Lybbe, Ursula. *The Eye of Intelligence.* London: William Kimber, 1983.
153. Priestley, R.E. *The Signal Service in the European War of 1914 to 1918 (France).* Chatham: Royal Army Signal Corps, 1921.
154. Public Record Office. Ruskin Avenue, Kew, Richmond, Surrey, TW9 4DU, England.
155. Pujol, Juan, with Nigel West. *Garbo.* London: Weidenfeld and Nicolson, 1985.

156. Ranft, Bryan (ed.). *Technical Change and British Naval Policy 1860-1939*. London: Hodder and Stoughton, 1977.
157. Ransom, Harry Howe. *The Intelligence Establishment*. Cambridge, Mass.: Harvard University Press, 1970.
158. Read, Anthony and David Fisher. *Colonel Z: The Secret Life of a Master of Spies*. London: Hodder and Stoughton, 1984.
159. Reilly, Sidney G. *The Adventures of Sidney Reilly, Britain's Master Spy*. London: Mathews and Marrot, 1931. (U.S. title: *Britain's Master Spy*.)
160. *Revue d'Histoire de la Deuxième Guerre Mondiale*. Paris, 1950-. Quarterly.
161. Rohwer, Jürgen and Eberhard Jäckel (eds.). *Die Funkauflärung und ihre Rolle im Zweiten Weltkrieg*. Stuttgart: Motorbuch- -Verlag, 1979.
162. Roosevelt, Kermit. *Counter-Coup: The Struggle for Control of Iran*. New York: McGraw-Hill, 1979.
163. Rose, Norman. *Vansittart: Study of a Diplomat*. London: Heinemann, 1978.
164. Rowan, Richard, Wilmer. *The Story of Secret Service*. New York: Garden City Publishing Co., 1939.
165. Royal Air Force Museum. Aerodrome Road, Hendon, London, NW9 5LL, England.
166. Sansom, A.W. *I Spied Spies*. London: George Harrap, 1965.
167. *Scholar's Guide to Intelligence Literature: Bibliography of the Russell J. Bowen Collection*. Frederick, Md.: University Publications of America, 1983.
168. Slessor, Marshal of the RAF Sir John. *The Central Blue*. London: Cassell, 1956.
169. Smith, Janet Adam. *John Buchan: A Biography*. Boston: Little, Brown, 1965.
170. Smith, Myron J. Jr. *The Secret Wars: A Guide to Sources in English*. 3 vols. Santa Barbara, California: ABC-Clio, 1980-81.
171. Stafford, David. *Britain and European Resistance 1940-1945: A Survey of the Special Operations Executive, with Documents*. London: Macmillan, 1983.
172. Stevenson, William. *A Man Called Intrepid: The Secret War*. New York: Harcourt, Brace, Jovanovich, 1976.
173. Strong, Major-General Sir Kenneth. *Intelligence at the Top*. London: Cassell, 1968.
174. ———. *Men of Intelligence: A Study of the Roles and Decisions of Chiefs of Intelligence from World War One to the Present Day*. New York: St. Martin's Press, 1971.
175. Sweet-Escott, Bickham. *Baker Street Irregular*. London: Methuen, 1965.
176. Taylor, John W.R. and David Monday. *Spies in the Sky*. New York: Scribners, 1972.
177. *Teaching Intelligence in the 1980s*. Edited by Marjorie Cline et al. Washington, D.C.: National Intelligence Study Center, 1985.
178. Temperley, Major-General A.C. *The Whispering Gallery of Europe*. London: Collins, 1938.
179. Thompson, R.W. *Churchill and Morton*. London: Hodder and Stoughton, 1976.

180. Thomson, Sir Basil H. *The Allied Secret Service in Greece.* London: Hutchinson, 1931.
181. ―――――. *Queer People.* London: Hodder and Stoughton, 1922.
182. Toscano, Mario. *Designs in Diplomacy: Pages from European Diplomatic History in the Twentieth Century.* Baltimore, Md.: Johns Hopkins University Press, 1970.
183. Toyne, John. *Win Time for Us.* Toronto: Longmans, Canada, 1962.
184. Trenowden, Ian. *Operations Most Secret: SOE, the Malayan Theatre.* London: William Kimber, 1978.
185. Trevor-Roper, Hugh. *Hermit of Peking: The Hidden Life of Sir Edmund Backhouse.* Harmondsworth, England: Penguin, 1978.
186. ―――――. *The Philby Affair: Espionage, Treason, and Secret Services.* London: William Kimber, 1968.
187. Tuchman, Barbara W. *The Zimmermann Telegram.* New York: Macmillan, 1958.
188. University of Keele, Air Photo Library. Department of Geography, University of Keele, Keele, Staffordshire, ST5 5BG, England.
189. Vagts, Alfred. *The Military Attaché.* Princeton: Princeton University Press, 1967.
190. Verrier, Anthony. *Through the Looking Glass: British Foreign Policy in the Age of Illusions.* London: Jonathan Cape, 1983.
191. Walker, David E. *Lunch with a Stranger.* London: Wingate, 1957.
192. War Office. "Historical Sketch of the Directorate of Military Intelligence during the Great War," May 1921, WO 32/10776. Public Record Office.
193. Wark, Wesley K. *The Ultimate Enemy: British Intelligence and Nazi Germany, 1933-1939.* Ithaca, N.Y.: Cornell University Press, 1985.
194. Waters, Brigadier-General W.H.H. *'Secret and Confidential': The Experiences of a Military Attaché.* London: John Murray, 1926.
195. Welchman, Gordon. *The Hut Six Story: Breaking the Enigma Codes.* London: Allen Lane, 1982.
196. West, Nigel (R. Allison). *A Matter of Trust: MI5, 1945-1972.* London: Weidenfeld and Nicolson, 1982.
197. ―――――. *MI5: British Security Service Operations 1909-1945.* London: Bodley Head, 1981.
198. ―――――. *MI6: British Secret Intelligence Service Operations, 1909-1945.* London: Weidenfeld and Nicolson, 1983.
199. ―――――. *Unreliable Witness: Espionage Myths of World War Two.* London: Weidenfeld and Nicolson, 1984. (U.S. title: A Thread of Deceit.)
200. Wheatley, Dennis. *The Deception Planners: My Secret War.* London: Hutchinson, 1980.
201. Whiting, Charles. *The Battle for Twelveland: An Account of Anglo-American Intelligence Operations within Nazi Germany, 1939-1945.* London: Leo Cooper, 1975.
202. Whitwell, John (A. Leslie Nicholson). *British Agent.* London: William Kimber, 1966.
203. Willert, Arthur. *The Road to Safety: A Study in Anglo-American Relations.* London: Derek Verschoyle, 1952.
204. Winstone, H.V.F. *The Illicit Adventure: The Story of Political*

and *Military Intelligence in the Middle East from 1898 to 1926.* London: Jonathan Cape, 1982.
205. Winterbotham, Frederick. *The Nazi Connection.* London: Weidenfeld and Nicolson, 1978.
206. ─────. *The Ultra Secret.* New York: Harper and Row, 1974.
207. Wise, David and Thomas B. Ross. *The Espionage Establishment.* New York: Random House, 1967.
208. *World Politics.* Princeton, N.J., 1948-. Quarterly.
209. Wynne, Greville. *The Man from Moscow: The Story of Wynne and Penkovsky.* London: Hutchinson, 1967. (U.S. title: Contact on Gorky Street.)
210. ─────. *The Man from Odessa.* London: Robert Hale, 1981.
211. Young, Arthur P. *The 'X' Documents.* Edited by Sidney Aster. London: Andre Deutsch, 1974.

XXIII

MEDICINE IN THE SERVICES

Rosalie Stott

The major bibliographic sources of work on the history of British naval and military medicine are the *Bibliography of the History of Medicine* and *Recent Work in the History of Medicine*. Essays are most likely to be found in the *Journal of the History of Medicine and Allied Sciences*, the *Bulletin of the History of Medicine*, *Medical History*, *Military Medicine*, *Military Affairs*, the *Mariner's Mirror*, the *Journal of the Society for Army Historical Research*, the *Historical Journal*, the *Journal of the Royal Army Medical Corps*, the *Journal of the Royal Naval Medical Service, Aviation, Space and Environmental Medicine*, and the *Proceedings of the Royal Society of London*. In addition to the collections by Poynter (251) and Lloyd (184) there are sections on military and naval medicine in Bruce (47) and in Garrison and Morton (234).

Poynter (251) commented on the relative neglect of military medical history in 1968; Richard Blanco (32) came to a similar conclusion in 1974. By 1986 some important books have made the situation a little less bleak. Prominent amongst these books must be Lt. Gen. Cantlie's history of the British Army Medical Department from the time of the New Model Army to the foundation of the R.A.M.C. in 1898 (59). First and foremost an account of medical service in the field, concentrating particularly upon the Revolutionary and Napoleonic Wars and the Crimean War, Cantlie also deals extensively with the progressive changes in organization and administration during the period; the reforms at the turn of the nineteenth century, the subsequent work of Sir James McGrigor, Director-General from 1815 until 1851, the agitations for reform during and following the Crimean War and the reorganization of the 1870s.

Cantlie's book begins in the mid-seventeenth century because it is only from that point that one can begin to speak of an organized medical service as an integral part of an army. Historians have written extensively about the ways military and naval surgeons have in the past coped with the changing methods of mutilating soldiers and seamen, but not always to emphasize how strategically insignificant their work was in earlier times (see, for example, 24, 95, 279-83, 316, 317, 320, 322-24). Awareness of the utility of the military surgeon in modern times can perhaps be traced to the military surgical literature of the sixteenth century, generated by Paré's book (244), in which British surgeons with continental experience and education began to participate from the mid-century (9, 92, 189, 321). Largely through the influence such eminent surgeons, when in military service, could exert with their commanding officers, by the seventeenth century surgeons and hospitals had "proved their value" and become a regular part of the establishment whenever an army was raised.

All this is apparent in the secondary literature already cited in Bruce (47). Not a great deal has been done since then. Webster (326) has touched briefly on how military hospitals could provide a vehicle for medical innovation during the Civil War and Interregnum, and there has been some work on John Woodall, the Surgeon-General of the H.E.I.C. in the early seventeenth century (166), whose manual *The Surgeon's Mate* (1617), written as a general guide for surgeons serving with the H.E.I.C., has recently been reprinted (335). In showing Woodall's close ties intellectually with Paracelsian medical theories (74) and economically with Stuart commerce (6) we can now understand better his manual to enhance the utility of the naval surgeon.

We have to look to the Enlightenment, however, to the time when human activity began to accumulate significant material value, to record the real development of an awareness of the strategic value of the military surgeon. In military terms such ideas can be translated into a recognition by commanders of the need to preserve the ability of men to function effectively in prescribed environments; when preventive as well as curative medical therapies were seen to have a value. This recognition can be traced to the military and naval medical literature of the eighteenth century promoting naval and military sanitary reform (150). A relatively complete list of this material can be obtained by combining the collections of Blanco (32), Poynter (251) and Lloyd (184). Some important early pieces--to balance an emphasis on late-eighteenth century material--need adding (1, 8, 113, 133, 148, 149, 233, 273).

Historiographically, emphasis has often been placed on the individuals promoting these reforms; to the literature in the collections already cited can be added work on Sir John Pringle, for example (119, 146, 254, 278, 289), Gilbert Blane (176, 268) and Thomas Trotter (267). Leonard Gillespie (99, 100-01, 161) and Hamilton Dickson (173) have been added to the list more recently, and there have been two new studies of John Hunter (78, 258-59). There has been some revision here; Qvist (258) is obviously very annoyed with "irresponsible" past narratives of John Hunter's work, and Jacyna (153) invites us to think hard about heroes generally in his essay on the creation of the mythology of John Hunter.

James Lind of Haslar--there are two, see (21)--is, of course, the biggest hero, to this day the symbol of the utility and excellence of the naval medical service (122). Until Carpenter's account of the history of scurvy (62), commentary on Lind's work was generally uninquisitive (104, 137, 226, 266, 293), although Stockman's readiness (299) to explore the contradictions between historical and contemporary recognition of Lind's work—why *did* it take over thirty years for the Admiralty to accept what to modern ears is Lind's conclusive proof of the efficacy of citrus fruits in preventing scurvy?—Hughes' audacity (138) in questioning Lind's scientific method (but see Wyatt (339)) and Troehler's focus (312) on Lind's other statistical work, are welcome exceptions. Lloyd (185) sees the cause of Admiralty indifference to Lind's work in the report it had commissioned from Captain Cook (who was himself indifferent to, or ignorant of, Lind's work (320)), which eschewed nutritional remedies for shipboard sickness in favour of greater shipboard sanitary discipline. And it must not be forgotten that Cook, who publicized his opinions (67), had considerable contemporary support from, for example, Pringle (255) and was echoed by Blane just a few years later (35). Lorenze (187-88) reminds us that Lind was not alone in his interest in scurvy, and Zuckerman (340) shows that conjecture about scurvy was not limited to problems of nutrition. Others have described naval surgeons interested in the problem of syphilis (40, 90, 292, 320), of wound management (36, 164, 186) and the endemic eighteenth century study of natural history (40, 90, 162, 163, 334).

A sailor incapacitated by syphilis could return to duty; one dead from scurvy could not. Previously disparate work on naval health has been brought together by Gradish (112) within the context of naval problems of manning (45) and administration (18-19) in the eighteenth century. Gradish argues that the work of Lind and others searching for a cure for scurvy, the introduction of sanitary measures and the establishment of naval hospitals are all explainable within the context of the Admiralty's acceptance in the mid-eighteenth century of the novel idea, owing much to the influence of Anson, of the strategic benefits of conserving manpower. (And within this framework, of course, the failure of the Admiralty to identify the "right" cure for scurvy is immaterial.)

Gradish shows the increasing naval dissatisfaction by mid-century with the "sick quarters" on land, usually contracted out to private individuals, to which sick seamen had traditionally been consigned. It was argued that if permanent naval hospitals were erected then the widespread problems in such establishments of desertion, and the dangers of fever and of drunkenness and immorality could be circumscribed. Such arguments throw into relief that distinctive naval cultural trait which equates land with contamination, either in the medical context of disease or in a more general context of anxiety about security and/or immorality. (See also (257)) It is a theme which might well be developed, because it is clear that as naval hospitals developed the medical and security aspects of confinement continued to be interrelated. In the reorganization of naval hospitals at the end of the eighteenth century, for example, security was clearly paramount (143, 156, 256). In the stationary hospital ships of the nineteenth century, on the other hand, confinement was seen as a medical therapy, providing an atmosphere more conducive to speedy recovery for sick sailors (108, 201). And in the 1860s, when confinement came to replace corporal punishment, it is not clear precisely why special facilities on land had to be provided for naval prisoners "to save our seamen from the contamination of prisoners in civil jails" (261).

As we approach the period of the Revolutionary and Napoleonic Wars, historical commentary on the innovative nature of preventive health measures in the military increases (52, 80, 86, 288). Like Gradish, Peter Mathias sees these innovations as a result of the greater premium on health apparent in the army and navy by the end of the century and, looking at these developments from the nineteenth century, he sees them as the forerunner of the improvements in hygiene, diet and clothing considered crucial determinants of lower morbidity at the end of that century (205). Troehler (311) has pointed to the statistical nature of these new therapeutic ideas, and Stott (300) sees them being promoted primarily by Scottish-trained medical officers. Frey (91) anachronistically uses an environmental/social etiology of disease as a vehicle for discussing the life of the British soldier in North America in the late eighteenth century without pointing to the innovative nature of such ideas.

We are learning more about the administration of the army medical department in the eighteenth century; about avenues of recruitment, for example, mainly into regiments (37), although general hospitals and medical staff officers, unattached to a regiment, were beginning to be formed at mid-century (169). Information about medical administration within the regiment could be developed from Guy (117), and it would be interesting to know the extent, if any, to which the regimental medical officer contributed towards making the men "fit for service" in the earlier eighteenth century (135).

Historical assessment of the utility of the military medical officer becomes possible by the turn of the nineteenth century. The consensus: not much. Mortality in the West Indies in the 1790s has been modified by Geggus (96) but is still an enormous 60%. Mortality there remained high throughout the wars (49) and recruitment was slow (98). However, indigenous regiments were raised on the strength of medical theories proposing the black soldier's perceived immunity to local disease and alcohol abuse (50). The work of the first and only Inspector of Health for Land Transport--Sir Jeremiah Fitzpatrick--had only minimal impact on conditions of travel for troops (33, 192) although naval surgeons, legislated into the slave trade at the end of the century (38), brought qualified improvements to the conditions of slaves in transit (286-87), but see Northrop (239). Wellington was well satisfied with his surgeons generally (105) and with his Surgeon-General in particular (32). We learn something of the realities of surgery on the Peninsular battlefields from Brett-James

(43), Walter Henry (123) and Woodford (336). Crowe places reform of the Army Medical Board in 1810 in a context larger than the specific response to the Walcheren episode (70), and documents extreme peculation in the commissariat (69).

Parliamentary papers on the health of the army and navy in the 1830s--the first large-scale statistical health studies undertaken in England (71)--were, in the case of the army (no recent work has been done on the navy reports) the distillation of army medical reports instituted by Sir James McGrigor after he took command of the reformed Army Medical Department in 1815 (32, 34). In contrast to proposals for reform based on these reports, Burroughs (54) and Blanco (31) conclude how very little was actually achieved in the 1830s and 40s, particularly in foreign postings. The mechanisms of reform documented in these recent historical essays fit well into Strachan's conclusions (301) that reform in the Victorian army followed the McDonagh model of administrative growth (191), although while Strachan places the generation of reform at the regimental level Burroughs locates it within administrative circles.

Health and welfare reform was supposed to act as a deterrent within the larger context of discipline; although not expected to replace the need for flogging, it *was* expected to reduce the desire to desert (55). Flogging was condemned as an humanitarian (30, 77) and political (295) offense. In bringing medical and military principles into such acute conflict it seems likely that flogging, and malingering too (93) would have been seen by some as a medical offense, although no-one has yet investigated this question.

There is not a great deal of recent work on the Crimean War. Cantlie's detailed look (59) at the administrative problems there is generally impartial but shows irritation with the insensitivity of the civilian critics to the medical department's multiple sources of command there. Lalumia (170) discusses the impact of emotive portraiture of wounded soldiers on Victorian public opinion, although Sweetman (306) rejects the idea of popular pressure influencing the quintessentially political task of administration. Sweetman (307) finds the formation of the Medical (later Hospital) Staff Corps--albeit a corps without officers--the only evidence of medical administrative reform arising out of the war.

Florence Nightingale continues to command more attention from historians (2, 20, 145, 243, 271-72, 291, 296) than all other women in the Crimea at the time (110, 139, 151). The best recent work on the women there has been done by Summers (304) who has distinguished different motivations and objectives between paid nurses and the lady volunteers. An important account by her of nurses in the British Army in the second half of the nineteenth century can be expected (305). In a category entirely distinct one would have to place the career of Dr. James Barrie, a transvestite now labelled "female," who pursued an entirely successful military career in South Africa, the Crimea and briefly in Canada (269).

Skelley's analysis of military health statistics from 1856 to 1899 (290) shows the significant steady decline of mortality and admissions to hospital in the army during that period, although he fails to explain why; none of the factors he chose to highlight improved appreciably during this period. Alcohol abuse incapacited but did not kill many soldiers or sailors in the nineteenth century (195) and venereal disease received significant public protection through opposition to the Contagious Diseases Acts, from their first introduction in the 1860s (27, 290), in Indian cantonments in the 1880s (160) and again during World War I (51).

Organized military medical education in Britain is generally dated from the establishment of the Army Medical School at Chatham in 1860 (moving to Netley in 1863), although a chair in military medicine had been established in Edinburgh in 1805 (11, 227). But see Woodford (337). Skelly (290) reminds us of the European reputation the school quickly acquired, although little has been written about it. Cantlie (59) is the best source. A few articles have discussed work at Chatham: Sir David Bruce's introduction there of the first course in bacteriology to be taught in England (72, 314); the contribution of Dr. Edward Parkes, first professor of hygiene at Chatham, to community medicine in general, and to the work of Sir John Simon, Medical Officer to the Privy Council (171, 270); and the career of Dr. Thomas Longmore, first professor of military surgery and author of the influential *A Treatise on the Transport of Sick and Wounded Troops* (1869).

Cantlie attributes the enormous disruption and dissatisfaction within the Army Medical Department in the post-Crimean period to medical officers' lack of military status and to the abandonment of the regimental hospital system in 1873 (59), problems which were not resolved until the establishment of the R.A.M.C. in 1898 (207). Medical officers also had to adjust to the expansion of army medical services occasioned by the introduction of nurses (248, 330), and by the adoption of the Geneva Convention in 1864, although the Red Cross and St. John's Ambulance were slow establishing national organizations in Britain (10, 65, 89). Pollock (249) and Nicholls (238) provide useful guides to the field organization of medical services at the time of World War I. The R.A.M.C. was ill-prepared for war in 1914; regular officers were swamped with administrative responsibilities (124). Martin (196) is a useful contemporary account of the procedures which took practicing and student doctors anxious to enlist--from Britain and the Dominions--in to military and immediately into active service as "temporary lieutenants" in the R.A.M.C.

Contemporaries thought sailors much healthier than soldiers in the nineteenth century (71), an impression borne out by recent social histories of life below deck (165, 242, 261, 333) which have little to say about sickness amongst sailors. Moreover, historiography of naval medical officers in the nineteenth century continues to find them more distinguished for their geomorphic than their medical successes (5, 68, 116, 142, 157, 158, 181). And new work only serves to confirm Lloyd & Keevil's conclusions as to the desultory nature of naval medical education in the nineteenth century (174); a naval medical school was not established until 1912 (237). All of which adds up to a rather different medical experience than is found in the army, and suggests that the well-known story, recently retold (252), of naval recalcitrance over the question of the introduction of tropical medicine into the military medical education programme at the end of the nineteenth century might well be written as another manifestation of tension between maritime and continental war strategies (292). The medical problems of Imperial defence have, in fact, received little attention. McDonald (204) is too brief, and Hunt (140) provides only a rather predictable account of medical service in India. The mechanics of the drug trade operated by the H.E.I.C. in the eighteenth and nineteenth centuries is interestingly told by Leigh (177).

There has been no recent work on the administration of naval medical service in the nineteenth century. There is room for a study of Sick Berth attendants and of naval nursing. Sick berth attendants were appointed for the first time in the 1830s, and in 1854 were introduced into Haslar and Plymouth to replace what were seen as the unsatisfactory females employed there. In 1884 reorganization brought into being the Sick Berth Branch at the same time that female nurses were reintroduced into Haslar and Plymouth, later to become the Q.A.R.N.N.S. (63, 121, 152, 247). As with the R.A.M.C., the naval medical service was ill-prepared for World War I and a new category--surgeon-probationers--was created from final year medical students who were made temporary Sub-Lieutenants in the R.N.V.R. (3,4).

"Abundant lack of agreement and clarity about roles for women" in World War I generally (107) was particularly true in regard to medical service. Initially told to "go home and sit still" (175) women physicians were allowed in 1916, without rank, into the R.A.M.C. (231). (Nor did they achieve rank in World War II.) The large majority of women involved in the war effort (206), however, learned "to turn themselves quickly into charity appeal organizers" (23) and formed the numerous V.A.D.'s, generally under the sponsorship of the Red Cross. Vera Brittain's book (44) is only the most eloquent testimony of the great variety of female experience in medical war service, some extremely courageous--Edith Cavell (64) comes immediately to mind--some more self-consciously noble (197), but most seeing the war as an opportunity to make the suffrage case (297). Two recent essays demonstrate the cultural framework within which women had to operate; Winter (332) shows the eugenicist bias--equating height with health--in assessing fitness of recruits in 1917, and Greenhut (115) shows the lengths to which military authorities went to try to prevent white women nursing the Indian Army when it came to Europe in World War I.

It is a truism that technology has revolutionized medical practice in the twentieth century. Always immediately available to the battlefield--anaesthesia was used in the Naval Hospital at Malta in the 1840s (285) and in the Crimea (284, 73); diagnostic radiotherapy appeared in the South African Wars (22, 57, 260)--much of that technology has benefitted surgical practice most directly. Cope's volume in the official medical history of the war (223) shows the extent of surgical expertise by World War II, and the author succinctly summarizes the benefits to men in war generally and to surgical effectiveness in particular of a more mechanized society. In the transportation of blood, the development of plastic surgery (16, 26, 129, 294) and of medical support staffs such as dentistry and rehabilitation (15, 41, 106, 120, 276, 319, 329), and in the utilization of technological and pharmacological advances in eradicating some of the most tenacious infectious diseases such as tuberculosis (109, 253) and venereal disease (88, 136) (although qualification has to be recorded against successes in controlling other diseases, such as malaria (48)) it is clear that Michael Howard is correct in suggesting that advances in medical technology have contributed to a greater toleration of war. By the same token, however, it is also true, that technological progress has made military medical practice an integral part of military strategy, bringing with it the inevitable conflict and tensions between professional responsibility and military obligation (313).

Nowhere are these tensions more apparent than in the development of the other area of medical speciality which has paralleled medical technological advance, which is of course psychiatry. Two recent essays (46, 84), each containing substantial bibliographies, discuss the neuroses of war, Ellis' essay showing the growth of literature and treatment of conditions we would now label neurotic in armies since before the American Civil War, while Brown focuses specifically on developments in World War I. Both papers linger, without offering judgement, on what is probably the most controversial aspect of World War I psychiatry in the British Army--critics claiming that "circumstances of war overrode any purely medical ethics"--which was the "faradic" treatment of Dr. Yealland at the National Hospital, Queen's Square, a form of disciplinary treatment involving confinement and electro-shock therapy to extract obedience to medical orders.

Psychiatric literature in World War II moved beyond diagnosis and treatment of mental illness to work in identifying psychologically unfit military candidates and in assisting in the maintenance of a high morale in both military and civilian populations (102, 228, 230, 235, 262). There has been no secondary literature to supercede Ahrenfeldt, but any future work on morale in World War II would have to include the work of Philip Mitchiner, responsible for the organization of civilian doctors in 1938 in preparation for war (232). A surgeon and medical officer in the Territorials, Mitchiner inspired a whole generation of surgeons in World War II (17). One of them (325), outlining surgical problems of World War II, unwittingly characterized Mitchiner in his description of the revolution in blood transfusion at that time, which, he said, made the replacement of blood "as simple as refuelling a car."

The strategic necessity of ensuring the ability of human beings to function effectively in prescribed environments has clearly taken on new meaning with the development of the means to travel and work undersea and in space. Medical problems in these environments are no longer those of human beings in groups, i.e. sanitation and infectious disease; nor are they problems of physical inefficiency. They are quintessentially questions of preventive medicine--"enabling more pilots to remain fit to fly"--(66, 190, 200, 202) and they are questions of environmental and psychological stress on individuals (13, 97, 128, 131, 167). Moreover, since as the Director-General of the R.A.F. Medical Services pointed out in 1978 "the first priority is the health of the air crew" (76) military medical research would appear to be moving away from egalitarian health principles and thus no longer to be compared with, equated with, civilian medical practice (76, 122).

What future historians will see in these changes remains to be seen. What is clear is that the growing affective military history is bringing suffering in war into much greater focus. Undoubtedly, such a point of view will ensure that military medical historical records will be used increasingly in the future, although serious historical analysis of the medical role in the context of that suffering in twentieth century warfare is still, to a large extent, waiting to be written.

BIBLIOGRAPHY

1. Addington, A. *An Essay on the Sea-Scurvy*. Reading: M. Cooper, 1753.
2. Allen, D.R. "Florence Nightingale: Towards a Psychohistorical Interpretation." *J. Inst. Hist.*, 6 (1975), 23-45.
3. Allison, R.S. *The Surgeon Probationers*. Belfast: Blackstaff Press Ltd., 1976.
4. ―――――. "Surgeon Probationers: The Young Medical Students who served in the Royal Navy during the First Great War of 1914-1918." *J. R. Nav. Med. Serv.*, 62, no. 2 (Summer 1976), 121-31; 62, no. 3 (Winter 1976), 176-186; 63, no. 1 (Spring 1977), 41-54.
5. Anon. "Two Naval Medical Explorers." *J. R. Nav. Med. Serv.*, 63, no. 3 (Winter 1977), 149-56.
6. Appleby, J.H. "New Light on John Woodall, Surgeon and Adventurer." *Med. Hist.*, 25, no. 3 (July 1981), 251-68.
7. Armstrong, H.G. "The William K. Stewart memorial lecture--1969. Anglo-American Military Aviation Medicine." *Aerosp. Med.*, 40 (Nov. 1969), 1169-75.
8. Aubrey, T., MD. *The Sea-Surgeon, Or the Guinea Man's Vade Mecum in which is laid down, the Method of curing such Diseases*

as usually happen Abroad, especially on the Coast of Guinea; with the best way of treating Negroes, both in Health and in Sickness. Written for the use of young Sea Surgeons London: J. Clarke, 1729.
9. Baker, George. *The composition or making of the most excellent and pretious oil called oleum magistrale ... with the maner how to apply it particularly. The which oyl cureth these disseases folowing. That is to say, wouds, contusios, hargubush shot.* ... London: John Alde, 1574.
10. Balgarnie, B. "The Workers of Voluntary Aid Detachments." *J. R. Army Med. Corps*, 22 (1914), 54-64.
11. Ballingall, G.A. "Memoir of Sir Geo. Ballingall." *J. R. Army Med. Corps*, 6 (1906), 59-66.
12. Barkley, K.T. *The Ambulance: The Story of Emergency Transportation of Sick and Wounded through the Centuries.* Hicksville, New York: 1978.
13. Barnard, E.E. "Physiological aspects of Naval Problems." *J. R. Nav. Med. Serv.*, 66, no. 1 (Spring 1980), 23-5.
14. Barnes, Elinor and James A. Barnes (eds.) *Naval Surgeon: The Diary of Dr. Samuel Pellman Boyer.* Introduction by Allan Nevins, Ann Arbor, Mich.: University Microfilms International, 1981.
15. Barry, C.B. "Rehab. in the Services. III. The Royal Airforce." *Rheumatol. Phys. Med.*, 10 (Nov. 1970), 431-34.
16. Battle, R.J. "Plastic surgery in the two world wars and in the years between." *J. R. Soc. Med.*, 71, no. 11 (Nov. 1978), 844-8.
17. ———. "Major-General P.H. Mitchiner, C.B., C.B.E., M.D., M.S., F.R.C.S. (1888-1952). His Life and Teaching." *J. R. Army Med. Corps*, 115 (1969), 78-86.
18. Baugh, Daniel A. (ed.) *Naval Administration 1715-1750.* London: Navy Record Society, 1977.
19. ———. *British Naval Administration in the Age of Walpole.* Princeton, N.J.: Princeton University Press, 1965.
20. Baylen, J.O. "The Florence Nightingale/Mary Stanley Controversy: Some Unpublished Letters." *Med. Hist.*, 18 (April 1974), 186-93.
21. Bebbington, W.G. "Dr. James Lind (1736-1812) a friend of Shelley." *Notes & Queries*, 205, pp. 83-93.
22. Benton, E.H. "British Surgery in the South African War: The Work of Major Frederick Porter." *Med. Hist.*, 21, no. 3 (July 1977), 275-90.
23. Berry, James Dickinson Berry, F. May and Blease, W. Lyon. *The Story of a Red Cross Unit in Serbia.* London: Churchill, 1916.
24. Billroth, Theodor. *Historical Studies on the Nature of Treatment of Gunshot Wounds from the 15th Century to the Present Time.* trans. C.P. Rhoads. New Haven, Conn.: Yale University Press, 1933.

25. Bird, J.R. "Group approaches and Army Health." *J. R. Army Med. Corps*, 126 (1980), 112-19.
26. Bishop, E. *The Guinea Pig Club*. London: Macmillan, 1973.
27. Blanco, R.L. "The Attempted Control of Venereal Disease in the Army of Mid-Victorian...." *Jour. Soc. Army His. Res.*, 45 (1967).
28. ———. "Sir James McGrigor and the Army Medical Corps." *History Today*, 21 (1971), 132-40.
29. ———. "Army Recruiting Reforms, 1861-67." *Jour. Soc. Army Hist. Res.*, 46 (1968).
30. ———. "Attempts to Abolish Branding and Flogging in the Army of Victorian England." *Jour. Soc. Army His. Res.*, 46 (1968).
31. ———. "Reform & Wellington's Post-Waterloo Army." *Military Affairs*, 29 (1965), 123-131.
32. ———. *Wellington's Surgeon General: Sir James McGrigor*. Durham: Duke U.P., 1974.
33. ———. "The Soldier's Friend--Sir Jeremiah Fitzpatrick, Inspector of Health for Land Forces." *Med. Hist.*, 20, no. 4 (Oct. 1976), 402-21.
34. ———. "Henry Marshall (1775-1851) and the Health of the British Army." *Med. Hist.*, 14 (1970), 260-276.
35. Blane, Sir Gilbert. *A Short Account of the Most Effectual Means of Preserving the Health of Seamen*. London: 1780.
36. Boog-Watson, W.N. "Thomas Robertson, Naval Surgeon, 1793-1828." *Bull. Hist. Med.*, 46 (Mar.-Apr. 1972), 131-49.
37. ———. "Four Monopolies and the Surgeons of London and Edinburgh." *J. Hist. Med.*, 25 (July 1970), 311-22.
38. ———. "The Guinea Trade and Some of its Surgeons." *Jour. Roy. Coll. Surg. Engl.*, 14 (1969), 203-214.
39. Bornmann, R.C. "Doctors at Greenwich." *J. R. Nav. Med. Serv.*, 57 (Winter 1971), 145-9.
40. Bowen, E.G. *David Samwell 1751-1798*. Cardiff: CSP Ltd., 1974.
41. Bradlaw, R. "The Royal Army Dental Corps." *Br. Dent. J.*, 16, 130 (Feb. 1971), 173-6.
42. Brereton, F.S. *The Great War and the R.A.M.C.* London: Constable, 1919.
43. Brett-James, Antony. *Life in Wellington's Army*. London: Allen & Unwin, 1972.
44. Brittain, Vera. *Testament of Youth*. London: Gollancz, 1933. (Reprinted Virago 1978 with preface by Shirley Williams.)
45. Bromley, J.S. (ed.) *The Manning of the Royal Navy: Selected Public Pamphlets, 1693-1873*. London: Navy Records Society, 1974.
46. Brown, Tom. "Shell Shock in the Canadian Expeditionary Force 1914-1918: Canadian Psychiatry in the Great War." in Charles G. Roland (ed.) *Health, Disease and Medicine*. Toronto: The Hannah Institute, 1984.

47. Bruce, A.P.C. *A Bibliography of British Military History: From the Roman Invasions to the Restoration.* New York: K.G. Saur, 1981.
48. Bruce-Chwatt, L.J. "Mosquitos, Malaria and War: Then and Now." *J. R. Army Med. Corps,* 131 (1985), 85-99.
49. Buckley, R.A. "The Destruction of the British Army in the West Indies 1793-1815: A Medical History." *Jour. Soc. Army Hist. Res.,* 56, no. 226 (1978), 79-94.
50. Buckley, Roger N. *Slaves in Red Coats: The British West Indies Regiments, 1795-1815.* New Haven & London: Yale University Press, 1981.
51. Buckley, Suzanne. "The Failure to Resolve the Problem of Venereal Disease among the Troops in Britain during World War I" in Brian Bond & Ian Roy (eds.) *War & Society: A Yearbook of Military History.* vol. II. London: Croom Helm, 1977, 65-85.
52. Buer, Mabel C. *Health, Wealth and Population in the Early Days of the Industrial Revolution.* London: Routledge & Kegan Paul, 1968.
53. Burne, J.C. "The Long Reach Hospital Ships and Miss Willis." *Proc. R. Soc. Med.,* 66 (Oct. 1973), 1017-21.
54. Burroughs, P. "The Human Cost of Imperial Defence in the Early Victorian Age." *Victorian Studies,* 24, no. 1 (1980), 7-32.
55. ———. "Tackling Army Desertion in British North America." *Can. Hist. Rev.,* LXI (1980), 28-68.
56. ———. "Crime and Punishment in the British Army 1815-1870." *Eng. Hist. Review,* 100 (1985), 545-571.
57. Burrows, E.H. "The First Use of X Rays in War." *Br. J. Radiol.,* 45 (May 1972), 393-4.
58. Caldwell, R. *Military Hygiene.* London: Bailliere, Tindall & Cox, 1910.
59. Cantlie, Lt. Gen. Sir N. *A History of the Army Medical Department.* 2 vols. London: Churchill Livingstone, 1974.
60. ———. "Inspector-General of Hospitals Robert Jackson (1750-1827), Army Medical Department." *Proc. R. Soc. Med.,* 65 (Dec. 1972), 1123-6.
61. Caria, Mendes J. "John Hunter, his travels in Portugal, and his probable influence on Portuguese medicine." in *Proceedings of the XXIII International Congress of the History of Medicine,* London: 1974, p. 772-3.
62. Carpenter, Kenneth J. *The History of Scurvy and Vitamin C.* Cambridge: Cambridge University Press 1986.
63. Clark, S.G. "Farewell to the SBA." *J. R. Nav. Med. Serv.,* 70 (1984), 3-8.
64. Clarke-Kennedy, A.E. *Edith Cavell. Pioneer and Patriot.* London: Faber & Faber, 1965.
65. Clifford, J. *For the Service of Mankind: Furley, Lechmere and Duncan St. John Ambulance Founders.* London: Hale, 1971.

66. Cole, Howard N. *On Wings of Healing: The Story of the Airborne Medical Services, 1940-1960.* Edinburgh & London: Blackwood, 1963.
67. Cook, J. "The Method taken for preserving the Health of the crew of His Majesty's Ship the Resolution during her late Voyage round the World." *Phil. Trans. Roy. Soc.* 1776.
68. Cree, Edward H. *Naval Surgeon: The Voyages of Dr. Edward H. Cree, Royal Navy, as related in his private journals 1837-1856 illustrated by the author.* Edited and with an introduction by Michael Levieu. New York: 1982.
69. Crowe, K.E. "Thomas Burn Cathewood and the Medical Department of Wellington's Army, 1809-1814." *Med. Hist.*, 20, no. 1 (Jan. 1976), 22-40.
70. ─────. "The Walcheren Expedition and the New Army Medical Board: A Reconsideration." *Eng. Hist. Rev.*, 88 (Oct. 1973), 770-85.
71. Cullen, M.J. "The Health of the Armed Forces." in *The Statistical Movement In Victorian England.* New York: Barnes and Noble, 1975.
72. Davies, M. "A Bibliography of the Work of Sir David Bruce, 1887-1924." *J. R. Army Med. Corps*, 101 (1955), 122-129.
73. Davison, M.H. and Wynne N.A. "The Decline in the Popularity of Chloroform." *Int. Anesthesiol. Clin.*, 8 (Summer 1970), 189-201.
74. Debus, A. "John Woodall, Paracelsian Surgeon." *Ambix*, 10 (1962).
75. Derby, Earl of. "Presidential Address." *Journal of the Royal Sanitary Institute*, 35 (1914), 277-286.
76. Dhenin, Sir E. "The State of British Medicine. Medicine in the Armed Forces." *Proc. R. Soc. Med.*, 71 (1978), 558-561.
77. Dinwiddy, J.R. "The Early 19th Century Campaign against Flogging in the Army." *Eng. Hist. Rev.*, 97 (1982), 308-331.
78. Dobson, J. *John Hunter.* Edinburgh: 1969.
79. Douglas, John. *Medical Topography of Upper Canada.* London: 1819, reprinted with an introduction by Charles G. Roland, Science History Publications, 1985.
80. Drew, Maj. Gen. W.R.M. "The Challenge of the Rickettsial Diseases." *J. R. Army Med. Corps*, (1965), 95-105.
81. Dunant, Jean Henri. *Un souvenir de Solferino.* Genève: F.G. Fick, 1862.
82. Dunbar-Miller, R.A. "Alcohol and the Fighting Man--An Historical Review." *J. R. Army Med. Corps*, 130 (1984), 117-21.
83. Elkington, H.P. "Some Episodes in the Life of James Goodall Elkington." *J. R. Army Med. Corps*, 16 (1911), 79-104.
84. Ellis, R.S. "The Origins of the War Neuroses." *J. R. Nav. Med. Serv.*, 70, 3 (1984), 168-177 and, 71, 1 (1985), 32-44.
85. Fauntleroy, Surg. A.M. U.S. Navy. *Report on the Medico-Military Aspects of the European War.* Washington, 1915.

86. Flinn, M.W. "Introduction" to *Report on The Sanitary Condition of the Labouring Population of Gt. Britain by Edwin Chadwick 1842.* Edinburgh: Edinburgh University Press, 1965.
87. Forbes, T.R. "Coroners' Inquisitions on the Deaths of Prisoners in the Hulks at Portsmouth, England, in 1817-27." *J. Hist. Med. Allied Sci.*, 33, no. 3 (July 1978), 356-66.
88. Fraser, I. "Penicillin: Early Trials in War Casualties." *Br. Med. J.* [Clin Res], 289 (Dec. 22-29, 1984), 1723-5.
89. Fraser, I. "Sir William MacCormack and his Times." *Ann. R. Coll. Surg. Engl.*, 65, no. 5 (Sept. 1983), 339-46.
90. Fraser-Harris, D.F. "Some Account of David Samwell, The Welsh Surgeon, Eye-Witness of the Murder of Cpt. Cook Feb., 14, 1779." *Ann. Med. History*, 7, 509-512.
91. Frey, Sylvia R. *The British Soldier in America: A Social History of Military Life in the Revolutionary Period.* Austin: University of Texas Press, 1981.
92. Gale, Thomas. *An Excellent Treatise of Wounds made with Gonneshot.* London: R. Hall, 1563.
93. Gandevia, B. "Malingering in the Penal Service: Its Epidemiology and Social Implications, with Contemporary Observations by Dr. James Stuart." in H. Attwood and G. Kenny (eds.) *Festschrift for Kenneth Fitzpatrick Russell.* Victoria, N.S.W.: Queensbury Hill Press, 1978.
94. Gask, G.E. "The Treatment of Wounds of the Thorax during the War of 1914-1918." in *Essays in the History of Medicine.* London: Butterworth, 1950, 157-166.
95. ―――――. "Historical Sketch of the Methods of Treating Wounds of the Chest in War From AD 1300-1900." in *Essays in the History of Medicine.* London: Butterworth, 1950, 145-156.
96. Geggus, D. "Yellow Fever in the 1790s: The British Army in Occupied Saint Domingue." *Med. Hist.*, 23, no. 1 (Jan. 1979), 38-58.
97. Gibson, T.M. & Harrison, M.H. *Into Thin Air: A History of Aviation Medicine in the RAF.* London: Robert Hall, 1984.
98. Gilbert, Arthur N. "A Tale of Two Regiments." *Arm. For. Soc.*, 9 (1982-83), 275-90.
99. Gillespie, J.P. "The Diet & Health of Seamen in the W.I. at the End of the 18th c. Some remarks on the work of Leonard Gillespie, MD." *J. R. Nav. Med. Serv.*, 37 (1951), 187-192.
100. Gillespie, L. *Observations on Diseases prevailed on Board H.M. Squadron in Leeward Islands Station 1794-6.* London: J. Cathell, 1800.
101. ―――――. *Advice to Commanders and Officers of H.M. Fleet serving in West Indies.* 1798.
102. Gillespie, R.D. *Psychological Effects of War on Citizen and Soldier.* New York: Norton, 1942.
103. Glass, A.J. "The Role of Military Psychiatry in the development

of Community Mental Health Centers." *Milit. Med.*, 135 (May 1970), 345-55.
104. Glass, J. "James Lind MD & 18th century naval medical hygiene." *J. R. Nav. Med. Serv.*, 35 (1949), 68-86.
105. Glover, M. "The Doctors of Wellington's Army." *Practitioner*, 213, 1274 (Aug. 1974), 233-40.
106. Godden, L.J. (ed.) *History of the Royal Army Dental Corps.* Aldershot: Purnell, 1971.
107. Goldman, Nancy L. (ed.) *Female Soldiers--Combatants or Non-Combatants.* Westport, Conn.: Greenwood Press, 1982.
108. Goldsmith, E. and McBride, A.G. "Dreadnought Seamen's Hospital." *Br. Med. J.*, 6024 (June 1976), 1511-3.
109. Goldsworthy, B.M. "The End of an Era: The Story of Mass Miniature Chest Radiography in the Royal Navy." *J. R. Nav. Med. Serv.*, 67, no. 1 (1981), 32-6.
110. Gordon, J.E. "Mary Seacole: A Forgotten Nurse Heroine of the Crimea." *Midwife Health Visit*, 11, no. 2 (Feb. 1975), 46-50.
111. Gordon, Maurice Bear. *Naval and Maritime Medicine during the American Revolution.* N.J.: Ventro Pub., 1978.
112. Gradish, S.F. *The Manning of the British Navy During the Seven Years' War.* London: Royal Historical Society, 1980.
113. Grainger, James. *An Essay on the More Common West Indian Diseases.* 1764.
114. Greeley, P.W. "The Influence of War on the Development of a Major Subspecialty." *Milit. Med.*, 138 (April 1973).
115. Greenhut, Jeffrey. "Race, Sex and War: The Impact of Race and Sex on Morale and Health Services for the Indian Corps on the Western Front 1914." *Military Affairs*, 45 (1981), 71-74.
116. Gruber, J.W. "Who was the Beagle's naturalist?" *Br. J. Hist. Sci.*, 4 (June 1969), 266-82.
117. Guy, Alan J. *Oeconomy and Discipline: Officership and Administration in the British Army, 1714-63.* Manchester: Manchester University Press, 1985.
118. Haigh, R.R. *The Long Carry: The Journal of Stretcher Bearer Frank Dunham 1916-1918.* New York: Pergamon Press, 1970.
119. Hamilton, D. "Sir John Pringle." *J. R. Army Med. Corps*, 110 (1984), 138-47.
120. Hardy, J.H. "Royal Dental Corps Diamond Jubilee (1921-1981)." *Br. Dent. J.*, 151, no. 10 (Nov. 1981), 351-2.
121. Harland, Kathleen M. "A Short History of Queen Alexandra's Royal Naval Nursing Service." *J. R. Nav. Med. Serv.*, 70 (1984), 59-65.
122. Harrison, J.A. "Military Medicine in the United Kingdom: Similarities and Differences with respect to the United States and other NATO allies." *J. R. Nav. Med. Serv.*, 66, no. 3 (Winter 1980), 173-9.

123. Hayward, P. (ed.). *Surgeon Henry's Trifles; Events of a Military Life.* London: Chatto & Windus, 1970.
124. Herrington, Maj. Gen. Sir Wilmot. *A Physician in France.* London: Arnold, 1919.
125. Hess, A.F. *Scurvy, Past and Present.* London: J.B. Lippincott Co., 1920.
126. Hill, B. "Mrs. Somerville's husband William Somerville, M.D., F.R.S." *Practitioner,* 206 (1971), 555-58.
127. ———. "In war and peace Sir Charles Blagden, M.D.Ed., F.R.S. (1748-1820)" *Practitioner,* 217, no. 1297 (July 1976), 126-31.
128. Hill, Leonard. *Caisson Sickness and the Physiology of Work in Compressed Air.* London: E. Arnold, 1912.
129. Hillary, Richard. *The Last Enemy.* London: Macmillan, 1943.
130. Hoeppli, R. "Early Navigation and the spread of Parasitic Diseases." *Episteme,* 5, no. 3 (1971), 201-217.
131. Hoff, E.C. & Fulton, J.F. (eds.). *A Bibliography of Aviation Medicine,* Baltimore: Yale Medical Library, 1942.
132. Holford, J.M. "Some highlights of Naval Medical History." *J. R. Nav. Med. Serv.,* 5, 2 & 3 (1965), 51-57.
133. Home, Francis. *Medical Facts and Experiments.* London: A. Millar, 1759.
134. Horrocks, B. "Colonel Sir William Heaton Horrocks, KCMG, CB." *J. R. Army Med. Corps,* 131, no. 2 (June 1985), 62-4.
135. Houlding, J.A. *Fit for Service: The Training of the British Army, 1715-1795.* Oxford: Clarendon, 1981.
136. Howie, J. "Gonorrhoea: A Question of Tactics." *Br. Med. J.,* 2 (Dec. 22-29, 1979), 1631-2.
137. Hudson & Hebert. "Lind on Shipboard Sanitation." *J. Hist. Med. Allied Sci.,* (1956).
138. Hughes, R.E. "James Lind and the Cure of Scurvy: An Experimental Approach." *Med. Hist.,* no. 19 (1975), 342-351.
139. Hughes, Sister Marie Jeanne D'Arc. *Crimean Diary of Mother M. Francis Bridgman.* Unpubd. doctoral thesis, Catholic University of America.
140. Hunt, Richard. *The Shadowless Lamp: Memoires of an R.A.M.C. Surgeon.* London: Wm. Kimer, 1971.
141. Hunter, J.T.S. "Discussion in the problem of Blast Injuries." *Proc. R. Soc. Med.,* 34 (1940-41), 171-192.
142. Huntley, M.A., R.E. Johnson & A.P. Bell. "A Bibliography of Sir John Richardson (1787-1865) in articles in Learned Journals." *J. Soc. Bibliogr. Nat. Hist.,* 6 (1972), 98-117.
143. Hurford, A. "The Early History of Plymouth Hospital." *J. R. Nav. Med. Serv.,* 21 (1935), 40-47; 138-151; 249-252.
144. Hurst, Arthur F. *Medical Diseases of the War.* London: E. Arnold, 1917.
145. Huxley, E. *Florence Nightingale.* London: 1975.
146. Hutchinson, B. *Biographia Medica: or Historical and Critical*

       Memoirs of the Lives and Writings of the Most Eminent Medical Characters. London: J. Johnson, 1799.
147. Hutchinson, Woods. *The Doctor in War*. New York: Houghton Mifflin Co., 1918.
148. Huxham, John. *An Essay on Fevers*. London: S. Austen, 1750.
149. ———. "A Method for Preserving the Health of Seamen in long Cruizes and Voyages." *Gentlemen's Magazine*, 17 (1747), 467-69.
150. Irving, James. "A Concise View of the Progress of Military Medical Literature in this Country." *Edin. Med. and Surg. Jour.*, 63 (1846), 285-302; 64 (1845), 83-98, 115-129, 375-389; 65 (1846), 34-39.
151. Iveson-Iveson, J. "A Balaclava Nurse." *Nursing Mirror*, 158, no. 21, 27-9.
152. ———. "History of the Navy Nurses: A Life on the Ocean Waves." *Nursing Mirror*, 153, no. 1 (July 1, 1981), 22-4.
153. Jacyna, L.S. "Images of John Hunter." *Hist. Sci.*, 21 (1983), 85-108.
154. James, P.R. "A Naval Surgeon's Log 1781-83." *J. R. Nav. Med. Serv.*, 19 (1933), 221-240.
155. Johnson, J. "Extract from "The Oriental Voyage 1807." *J. R. Nav. Med. Serv.*, 24 (1933), 178-183.
156. Johnson, R. "The Diary of the First Governor of Plymouth Hospital." *J. R. Nav. Med. Serv.*, 2 (1916), 191-199.
157. Johnson, R.E. *Sir John Richardson: Arctic explorer, natural historian, naval surgeon*. London: Taylor & Francis, 1976.
158. Jones, A.G. "Dr. W.H.B. Webster, 1793-1875: Antarctic scientist." *Polar Rec.* (Gr Brit), 17, no. 107 (1974), 143-5.
159. Jones, D.R. "Aeromedical transportation of psychiatric patients: Historical review and present management." *Aviat. Space Environ. Med.*, 51, no. 7 (July 1980), 709-16.
160. Kaminsky, A.P. "Morality legislation and British troops in late nineteenth century India." *Military Affairs*, 43, no. 2 (1979), 78-83.
161. Keevil, J.J. "Leonard Gillespie, M.D. 1758-1842." *Bull. Hist. Med.*, 28 (1954), 301-332.
162. ———. "William Anderson 1748-1778, Master Surgeon RN." *J. R. Nav. Med. Serv.*, 21 (1935), 124-138.
163. ———. "A. Menzies 1754-1842." *Bull. Hist. Med.*, 22 (1948), 796-811.
164. ———. "Ralph Cuming." *J. R. Nav. Med. Serv.*, 36 (1950).
165. Kemp, P. *The British Sailor: A Social History of the Lower Deck*. London: J.M. Dent, 1970.
166. Keynes, Sir G. "John Woodall, Surgeon, his place in Medical History." *Jour. Roy. Coll. Phys.*, 2 (1967).
167. Kindwall, E.P. "A Short History of Diving and Diving Medicine." in Strauss, R.H. (ed.): *Diving Medicine*. New York: Grune & Stratton, 1976, p. 1-12.

168. Kirkup, J. (ed.). *Several Chirurgical Treatises.* Bath: Kingsmead Press, 1977.
169. Koppelman, P.E. "Medical Services in the British Army, 1742-1783." *J. Hist. Med. Allied Sci.*, 34, no. 4 (Oct. 1979), 428-55.
170. Lalumia, M. "Realism and Anti-Aristocratic Sentiment in Victorian depictions of the Crimean War." *Victorian Studies*, 27 (1983), 25-51.
171. Lambert, R. *Sir John Simon 1816-1904 and English Social Administration.* London: 1963.
172. Lankford, N.D. "The Victorian Medical Profession and Military Practice: Army Doctors and National Origins." *Bull. Hist. Med.*, 54, no. 4 (Winter 1980), 511-28.
173. Lattimore, M.I. "Sir David James Hamilton Dickson, M.D. (1780-1850)." *J. R. Nav. Med. Serv.*, 67, no. 2 (1981), 92-100.
174. ―――――. "Early Naval Medical Libraries, Personal and Corporate." *J. R. Nav. Med. Serv.*, 69, no. 2 (Summer 1983), 107-11.
175. Lawrence, Margot. *Shadow of Swords: A Biography of Elsie Inglis.* London: Joseph, 1971.
176. Leach, R.D. "Sir Gilbert Blane, Bart, M.D., F.R.S. (1749-1832)." *Ann. R. Coll. Surg. Engl.*, 62, no. 3 (May 1980), 232-9.
177. Leigh, D. "Medicine, the City and China." *Med. Hist.*, 18 (Jan. 1974), 51-67.
178. Lelean, P.S. *Sanitation in War.* London: J. & A. Churchill, 1915.
179. Lewis, H.E. "Medical aspects of Polar Exploration: Sixtieth anniversary of Scott's last expedition." *Proc. R. Soc. Med.*, 65 (Jan. 1972), 39-42.
180. Lewis, Michael. *A Social History of the Navy, 1793-1815.* London: Allen & Unwin, 1980.
181. ―――――. *The Navy in Transition.* London: Hodder & Stoughton, 1965.
182. Lister, Joseph. "A Method of Antiseptic Treatment applicable to Wounded Soldiers in the present War." *Br. Med. J.*, 2 (1980), 243-44.
183. Livingston, St. Clair. *Under Three Flags: With the Red Cross in Belgium, France and Serbia.* London: Macmillan, 1916.
184. Lloyd, C. "The Evolution of Naval Medicine," in Robin Higham (ed.) *A Guide to the Sources of British Military History* Berkeley: University of California Press, 1971.
185. ―――――. "Cook and scurvy." *Mariners' Mirror*, 65 (Feb. 1979), 23-8.
186. Long, W.H. "Journal of Navy Surgeon 1758-1763." *Naval Yarns.* 1899, pp. 61-107.
187. Lorenz, J. "Some Pre-Lind writers on Scurvy." *Proc. Nutrition Soc.*, 12 (1953), 306-324.

188. ———. "The Conquest of Scurvy." *J. Am. Diet Ass.*, 30 (1954), 665-670.
189. Lowe, Peter. *A Discourse of the Whole Art of Chirurgerie ...* London, 1599.
190. Lumley, E.A. *Army and Air Force Doctor.* London: Cooper, 1971.
191. MacDonagh, Oliver. "The Nineteenth-Century Revolution in Government: A Reappraisal." *Historical Journal*, 1 (1958), 52-67.
192. ———. *Inspector General: Sir Jeremiah Fitzpatrick and the Politics of Social Reform 1783-1802.* London: Croom Helm, 1981.
193. Macdonald, L. *The Roses of No Man's Land.* London, 1980.
194. MacKenna, R.M. "Robert M.B. MacKenna." *J. Am. Acad. Dermatol.*, 6, no. 1 (Jan. 1982), 135-44.
195. Marjot, D.H. "Delirium Tremens in the Royal Navy and British Army in the 19th century." *J. Stud. Alcohol*, 38 (1977), 1613-23.
196. Martin, Arthur A. *A Surgeon in Khaki.* London: Arnold, 1915.
197. Martin-Nicholson, Mrs. Mary E. L. *My Experience on Three Fronts.* London: Allen & Unwin, 1916.
198. Mathews, M. & Harris, M. "The Royal Navy Medical Air Evacuation Unit." *J. R. Nav. Med. Serv.*, 66, no. 2 (Summer 1980), 147-51.
199. Mathias, Peter. "Swords & Ploughshares: The Armed Forces, Medicine & Public Health in the late 18th Century" in Winter, J.M. (ed.) *War and Economic Development.* London: 1975.
200. Maxwell, V.B. "The first 2 years: A Brief History of the British Association of Aviation Medical Examiners." *Aviat. Space Environ. Med.*, 54, no. 5 (May 1983), xiii-xiv.
201. Mayberry, J.F. "The Hamadryad Hospital Ship for Seamen 1866-1905." *Br. Med. J.*, (Dec. 1980), 1690-2.
202. Maycock, R. *Doctors in the Air.* London: Allen & Unwin, 1957.
203. McBryde, B. "A Nurse's War." *Nursing Times*, 75, no. 26 (June 28, 1979), 1084-6; 75, no. 27 (July 5, 1979), 1150-2.
204. McDonald, Donald. *Surgeons Two and A Barber: Being Some Account of the Life and Work of the Indian Medical Service, 1600-1947.* London: Heinemann, 1950.
205. McKeowen, T. and R.G. Brown. "Medical Evidence Related to English Population Changes in the Eighteenth Century" in Michael Drake (ed.) *Population in Industrialization*, London, Methuen: 1969.
206. McLaren, Barbara. *Women of the War.* London: Hodder & Stoughton, 1917.
207. McLaughlin, R. *The Royal Army Medical Corps.* London: 1972.
208. McLeod, Geo H. *Notes on the Surgery of the War in the Crimea, with Remarks on the Treatment of Gunshot Wounds.* London: J. Churchill, 1858.

209. McNalty, Sir Arthur S. (ed.). *History of the Second World War. United Kingdom Medical Series.* London: H.M.S.O., 1952-: see 210-225.
210. Coulter, J.L.S. *The Royal Naval Medical Service. Vol. I Administration.* London: H.M.S.O., 1954.
211. ―――. *The Royal Naval Medical Service, Vol. II Operations.* London: H.M.S.O., 1966.
212. Crew, F.A.E. *The Army Medical Services. Administration 2 vols.* London: H.M.S.O., 1952 and 1955.
213. ―――. *The Army Medical Services, Campaigns. 5 vols.* London: H.M.S.O., 1956, 1957, 1959, 1962 and 1966.
214. Rexford-Welch, S.C. *The Royal Air Force Medical Services. Vol. I Administration.* London: H.M.S.O., 1954.
215. ―――. *The Royal Air Force Medical Services. Vol. II Commands.* London: H.M.S.O., 1955.
216. ―――. *The Royal Air Force Medical Services. Vol. III Campaigns.* London: H.M.S.O., 1958.
217. Dunn, C.L. *The Emergency Medical Services. Vol. I England and Wales.* London: H.M.S.O., 1952.
218. ―――. *The Emergency Medical Services. Vol. II Scotland, Northern Ireland and the Principal Air Raids on Industrial Centres in Gt. Britain.* London: H.M.S.O., 1953.
219. McNalty, Sir Arthur S. *The Civilian Health & Medical Services. Vol. I England & Wales.* London, H.M.S.O., 1958.
220. ―――. *The Civilian Health & Medical Services. Vol. II Scot, Northern Ireland, the Colonies.* London, H.M.S.O., 1958.
221. Green, F.H.K. & Covell, Maj. Gen. Sir G. *Medical Research.* London: H.M.S.O., 1953.
222. Cope, V. Zachary. *Medicine & Pathology.* London: H.M.S.O., 1952.
223. ―――. *Surgery.* London: H.M.S.O., 1953.
224. McNalty, Sir Arthur S. and Mellor, W. Franklin (eds.). *Medical Services in War: The Principal Medical Lessons of the Second World War.* London: H.M.S.O., 1968.
225. Mellor, W.J. (ed.). *Casualties & Medical Statistics.* London: H.M.S.O., 1972.
226. Meicklejohn, A.P. "The Curious Obscurity of Dr. James Lind." *J. Hist. Med.*, (1954), 304-310.
227. "Memoir on the Life of John Thomson" in John Thomson, *An Account of the Life, Lectures and Writings of William Cullen, M.D.* 2 vols. London: Blackwood 1859.
228. Miller, E. (ed.). *The Neuroses in War.* New York: Macmillan, 1940.
229. Miller, G. *The Adoption of Inoculation for Smallpox in England and France.* University of Pennsylvania Press: 1957.
230. Mira, E. *Psychiatry in War.* New York: Norton, 1943.

231. Mitchell, A.M. "Medical Women & the Medical Services of the First World War" in H. Attwood and G. Kenny (eds.) *Festschrift for Kenneth Fitzpatrick Russell*. Victoria, N.S.W., 1978.
232. Mitchiner, P.H. & Cowell, E.M. *Medical Organization and Surgical Practice in Air Raids*. London: Churchill, 1939.
233. Monro, Donald. *An Account of the Diseases which were most frequent in the British Military Hospitals in Germany, from January 1761, till the return of the Troops to England in March 1763: to which is added, An Essay on the Means of Preserving the Health of Soldiers, and Conducting Military Hospitals*. London: A. Millar, 1764.
234. Morton, Lester T. *A Medical Bibliography (Garrison & Morton)*. fifth edn. Aldershot: Gower, 1983.
235. Mott, F.W. *War Neuroses and Shell Shock*. London: Hodder & Stoughton, 1919.
236. Mussen, Surg. Rear-Adm. R.W. *The Story of a Naval Doctor*. priv. printed.
237. ―――――. "The Royal Naval Medical School" *J. R. Nav. Med. Serv.*, 33, no. 2 (1947), 61-67.
238. Nicholls, T.B. *Organization, Strategy and Tactics of the Army Medical Services in War*. London: Bailliere, Tindall & Cox, 1937.
239. Northrup, D. "African Mortality in the Suppression of the Slave Trade: The case of the Bight of Biafra." *J. Interdiscip. Hist.*, 9, no. 1 (1978), 47-64.
240. Oliver, T.P. "67 years ago: The Journal of the Royal Naval Medical Service." Vol. 1, No. 1, *J. R. Nav. Med. Serv.*, 68, no. 2 (1982), 98-101.
241. ―――――. "67 years ago: The Journal of the Royal Naval Medical Service." Vol. 1, *J. R. Nav. Med. Serv.*, 68, no. 3 (Winter 1982), 167-70.
242. Padfield, Peter. *Rule Britannia: The Victorian and Edwardian Navy*. London: Routledge & Kegan Paul, 1981.
243. Palmer, I.S. *Florence Nightingale. Reformer, Reactionary, Researcher*. Washington: 1976.
244. Paré, Ambroise. *La méthode de traicter les playes faictes par hacquebutes et aultres bastons à feu, et de celles qui sont faictes par flêches, dardz et semblables*. Paris, Ches viuant Gaulterot, 1545.
245. Parker, Geoffrey. *The Black Scalpel*. London: Wm. Kimber, 1968.
246. Patterson, T.J. "Mr. Lucas and the B.L. letter (Colley Lyon Lucas)." *Plast. Reconstr. Surg.*, 48 (July 1971), 68-71.
247. Paul, R.W.F., et al. "The Royal Naval Medical Staff School." *J. R. Nav. Med. Serv.*, 70 (1984), 9-14.
248. Piggott, J. *Queen Alexandra's Royal Army Nursing Corps*. London: Cooper, 1975.
249. Pollock, Maj. C.E. "A Comparison of Foreign Army Medical Methods with those of the British Army, with spec. ref. to

the Territorial Force." *J. R. Army Med. Corps*, 22 (1914), 35-53.
250. Pope, Dudley. *Life in Nelson's Navy*. Annapolis, Md.: Naval Institute Press, 1981.
251. Poynter, F.N.L. "The Evolution of Military Medicine" in Robin Higham (ed.) *A Guide to the Sources of British Military History*. Berkeley: University of California Press, 1971, 591-605.
252. Preston, P.J. "The Royal Naval contribution to a 'Strange pathology.'" *J. Trop. Med. Hyg.*, 76 (August 1973), 198-202.
253. Price, S.H. "A history of mass radiography of the chest in the Royal Naval Barracks Portsmouth." *J. R. Nav. Med. Serv.*, 56 (Winter 1970), 265-72.
254. Pringle, Sir J. *Six Discourses delivered by Sir J.P. when President of the R.S.; To which is prefixed the Life of the Author by Andrew Kippis*. London: 1783.
255. ―――――. *A discourse upon some late improvements of the means for preserving the health of mariners* delivered at the Anniversary Meeting of the Royal Society, November 30, 1776.
256. Pugh, P.D. "History of the Royal Naval Hospital, Plymouth." *J. R. Nav. Med. Serv.*, 58 (Summer 1972), 78-94; (Winter 1972), 207-26.
257. ―――――. "The planning of Haslar." *J. R. Nav. Med. Serv.*, 62, no. 2 (Summer 1976), 103-20.
258. Qvist, G. "Some controversial aspects of John Hunter's life and work." *Ann. R. Coll. Surg. Engl.*, 61, no. 3 (May 1979), 219-23.
259. ―――――. *John Hunter 1728-1793*. London: 1982.
260. Ramsey, L.J. "Bullet wounds and X-Rays in Britain's little wars." *Jour. Soc. Army Hist. Res.*, (Summer 1982), 91-102.
261. Rasor, Eugene L. *Reform in the Royal Navy: A Social History of the Lower Deck 1850 to 1880*. Hamden, Archon, 1976.
262. Rees, J.R. *The Shaping of Psychiatry by War*. New York: Norton, 1945.
263. Reid, R.L. "The British Crimean medical disaster--ineptness or inevitability?" *Milit. Med.*, 140, no. 6 (June 1975), 420-6.
264. *Review of War Surgery and Medicine, 1918-1919*, U.S. Office of Surgeon General.
265. Riddell, W.J. "Dr. Duncan McArthur (1773-1855)--physician to the fleet." in *Proceedings of the XXIII International Congress of the History of Medicine*. London, 1974, p. 1155-61.
266. Rolleston, Sir H.D. "James Lind, Pioneer of Naval Hygiene." *J. R. Nav. Med. Serv.*, 1 (1915), 181-190.
267. ―――――. "Thomas Trotter, M.D...." *J. R. Nav. Med. Serv.*, 5 (1919), 412-19.

268. ———. "Sir Gilbert Blane M.D." *J. R. Nav. Med. Serv.*, 2 (1916), 72-81.
269. Rose, J. *The Perfect Gentleman: The Remarkable Life of Dr. James Miranda Barry, the Woman who served as an Officer in the British Army from 1813 to 1859.* London: Hutchinson, 1977.
270. Rosen, G. "Edmund A. Parkes in the development of hygiene." *J. R. Army Med. Corps*, 122 (1976), 187-91.
271. Roxburgh, R. "Miss Nightingale and Miss Clough: Letters from the Crimea." *Victorian Studies*, 13, no. 1 (1969), 71-89.
272. ———. "Miss Clough, Miss Nightingale and the Highland Brigade." *Victorian Studies*, 15 (1971), 75-9.
273. Russell, Alexander. *The Natural History of Aleppo.* London: 1756.
274. Russell, M.W. "Sir James McGrigor." *J. R. Army Med. Corps*, 13 (1909), 117-152.
275. Saunders, Hilary St. George. *The Red Cross and the White: A Short History of the Joint War Organization of the British Red Cross Society and the Order of St. John of Jerusalem during the War 1939-1945.* London: Holle & Carter, 1949.
276. Scholfield, B.B. & Martyn, L.F. *The Rescue Ships.* Edinburgh & London: Blackwood, 1968.
277. Scott, J. "The Journal of Dr. James Scott, M.D., R.N., Bristol-Cape, 1839." *Q. Bull. S. Afr. Libr.*, 31, no. 3 (1977), 49-60.
278. Selwyn, Sydney. "Sir John Pringle--Hospital Reformer, Moral Philosopher & Pioneer of Antiseptics." *Med. Hist.*, 10 (1866), 266-273.
279. Senn, N. "Ancient Military Surgery." *Surg. Gyn. Obst.*, 4 (1906), 690-699.
280. ———. "Medieval Military Surgery." *Surg. Gyn. Obst.*, 5 (1907), 613-622.
281. ———. "The Period of Awakening of Military Surgery." *Surg. Gyn. Obst.*, 6 (1908), 379-384.
282. ———. "The Dawn of Modern Military Surgery." *Surg. Gyn. Obst.*, 6 (1909), 477-482.
283. ———. "The Evolution of the Military Surgeon." *Surg. Gyn. Obst.*, 8 (1909), 393-400.
284. Shepherd, J.A. "The smart of the knife--early anaesthesia in the services." *J. R. Army Med. Corps*, 131 (1985), 109-115.
285. ———. *Spencer Wells.* Edinburgh, 1965.
286. Sheridan, R.B. *Doctors and Slaves: A Medical and Demographic History of Slavery in the British West Indies 1680-1834.* Cambridge: Cambridge University Press, 1985.
287. ———. "The Guinea Surgeons on the Middle Passage: The provision of Medical Services in the British Slave Trade." *Int. J. Afr. Hist. Stud.*, 14, no. 4 (1981), 601-25.
288. Singer, Charles & E.A. Underwood. *A Short History of Medicine.* Oxford: Clarendon Press, 1962.

289. Singer, Dorothy W. "Sir John Pringle and His Circle." *Ann. Science.*, 6 (1849-50), 127-180, 229-61.
290. Skelley, A.R. *The Victorian Army at Home: The Recruitment and Terms and Conditions of the British Regular 1859-1899.* London: Croom Helm, 1977.
291. Smith, F.B. *Florence Nightingale. Reputation and Power.* London: Croom Helm, 1982.
292. Smith, H.M. "The Introduction of Venereal Disease into Tahiti: A Re-examination." *J. Pac. Hist.*, 10, no. 1 (1975), 38-45.
293. Southwell-Sander, G.H.C. "The Development of Naval Preventive Medicine." *J. R. Nav. Med. Serv.*, 63 (1957), 54-71.
294. Stark, R.B. "The History of Plastic Surgery in Wartime," in R.B. Stark (ed.) *Symposium on War Injuries.* London: Phil Saunders, 1975.
295. Steiner, E.E. "Separating the soldier from the citizen: Ideology and criticism of corporal punishment in the British Army, 1790-1815." *Social History*, (1983), 19-35.
296. Stewart, P. *Florence Nightingale.* London, 1973.
297. Stobart, Mrs. St. Clair. *War and Women.* London: G. Bell & Sons, 1913.
298. Stock, P.G. "The Problem of the Air-Raid Shelter." *Proc. Roy. Soc. Med.*, 34 (1940-41), 125-138.
299. Stockman, R. "James Lind & Scurvy." *Edin. Med. Jour.*, n.s.33 (1926), 329-350.
300. Stott, R. "The Scottish dimension of Enlightenment Medicine: The Political Economy of Health." *Soc. Soc. Hist. Med. Bull.*, (London), 25 (Dec. 1979), 41-4.
301. Strachan, Hew. "The Early Victorian Army and the Nineteenth-century Revolution in Government." *Eng. Hist. Rev.*, XCV (1980), 782-809.
302. ―――――. *Wellington's Legacy: The Reform of the British Army, 1830-54.* Manchester: Manchester University Press, 1984.
303. ―――――. "The British Way in Warfare Revisited." *Historical Journal*, 26, no. 2 (1983), 447-461.
304. Summers, A. "Pride and Prejudice: Ladies and Nurses in the Crimean War." *History Workshop*, 16 (1983), 32-56.
305. ―――――. "Women as Military Nurses in Gt. Britain between 1856 and 1899." [Abst.] *Hist. Nurs. Grp. Roy. Coll. Nurs. Bull.*, no. 5 (1984), 14.
306. Sweetman, John. *War and Administration.* Edinburgh: Acadia Press, 1984.
307. ―――――. "The Crimean War and the formation of the Medical Staff Corps." *Jour. Soc. Army Hist. Res.*, 53, no. 214 (1975), 113-19.
308. Tidy, Maj. Gen. Sir Henry Letheby and Kutschbach, J.M. Browne (eds.). *Inter-Allied Conferences on War Measures 1942-45*, Convened by the Royal Society of Medicine, London, 1947.
309. Tilghman, R.C. "Captain James Cook (1728-1779)." *Trans. Am. Clin. Climatol Assoc.*, 92 (1980), 1-15.

310. Till, A.S. "Gordon-Taylor, war surgeon and historian." *Ann. R. Coll. Surg. Engl.*, 54 (Jan. 1974), 33-47.
311. Troehler, N. "Qualification in British Medicine and Surgery 1750-1830 with special reference to its introduction into therpeutics." Unpub. PhD, London, 1978.
312. Troehler, U. "Towards clinical investigation on a numerical basis: James Lind at Haslar Hospital, 1758-1783." in *International Congress of the History of Medicine, 27th Barcelona, 1980 Actast*. Barcelona: Acadèmia de Ciències Médiques de Catalunya i Balears, 1981. 414-9.
313. Vastyan, E.A. "Warriors in White: Some Questions about the Nature and Mission of Military Medicine." *Tex. Rep. Biol. Med.*, 32, no. 1 (Spring 1974), 327-42.
314. Vella, E.E. "Brucellosis (the Corps disease)." *J. R. Army Med. Corps*, 129 (1983), 97-100.
315. ―――――. "The development of pathology in the RAMC." *Proc. R. Soc. Med.*, 68, no. 5 (May 1975), 321-6.
316. Wakeley, Sir C. "Surgeons and the Navy." *Ann. R. Coll. Surg. Engl.*, 21 (1957), 267-289.
317. Wangensteen, O.H., J. Smith and S.D. Wangensteen. "Some Highlights in the History of Amputation Reflecting Lessons in Wound Healing." *Bull. Hist. Med.*, 41 (1967), 97-131.
318. *War Medicine*: 1917-1919. Army Red Cross, Paris, For Medical Officers of the American Exped. Force.
319. Ward, F.G. "Rehabilitation in the services. I. The Royal Navy." *Rheumatol. Phys. Med.*, 10 (Nov. 1970), 425-8.
320. Watt, J. "Medical Aspects and Consequences of Cook's Voyages" in R. Fisher & H. Johnston (eds.), *Captain Cook and His Times*, 1978, 129-157.
321. ―――――. "Surgeons of the Mary Rose: The Practice of Surgery in Tudor England." *Mariner's Mirror*, 69 (1983), 3-18.
322. ―――――. "The Injuries of Four Centuries of Naval Warfare." *Ann. R. Coll. Surg. Engl.*, 57 (1975), 3-24.
323. ―――――. Lettsomian Lectures "Medical Perspectives of some Voyages: Patterns of Discovery." *Trans. Med. Soc. Lond.*, 95 (1979), 61-91.
324. ―――――. "Some forgotten contributions of Naval Surgeons." *J. R. Soc. Med.*, 78 (1985), 753-62.
325. Watts, J.C. *Surgeon at War*. London: Allen & Unwin, 1955.
326. Webster, Charles. *The Great Instauration Science, Medicine and Reform 1626-1660*. London: Duckworth, 1975.
327. Wellcome Institute of the History of Medicine. "Medicine and Surgery in the Great War, 1914-1918; An Exhibition to commemorate the 50th anniversary of the Armistice. Nov. 11, 1918." London, 1968, 48 p. (Its Publications Exhibition catalogues, no. 4).
328. Whipple, Allen O. *The Story of Wound Healing & Wound Repair*. Springfield: 1963.

329. Whittaker, V.B. "Rehabilitation in the Services. II. The Army." *Rheumatol. Phys. Med.*, 10 (Nov. 1970), 428-30.
330. Wickes, H.L. "History of Nursing in the Army: Behind the Lines." *Nursing Mirror*, 153, no. 2 (July 8, 1981), 23-4.
331. Williams, E. "Diary of a VAD 1940-49." *Nursing Mirror*, 153 (1981), passim.
332. Winter, J.M. "Military fitness and civilian health in Britain during the first World War." *J. Contemp. Hist.*, 15, no. 2 (1980), 211-44.
333. Winton, J. *Hurrah for the Life of a Sailor: Life on the Lower Deck of the Victorian Navy*. London: Michael Joseph, 1977.
334. Winton, R.R. "Surgeons and Health on the Endeavour." *Med. J. Aust.*, 26, no. 2 (Sept. 1970), 567-73.
335. Woodall, J. *The Surgeon's Mate*. Facsimile of 1617 edn., edited by J. Kirkup. Bath: Kingsmead Press, 1978.
336. Woodford, L.W. (ed.). *A Young Surgeon in Wellington's Army: The Letters of William Dent*. Old Woking, Surrey: Unwin, 1976.
337. ―――. "A Medical Student's Career in the early Nineteenth Century." *Med. Hist.*, 24 (Jan. 1970), 90-5.
338. Wright, David S. "The History and Development of the Medical Services of H.M. Dockyard, Chatham, 1625-1966." *J. R. Nav. Med. Serv.*, 54 (1968), 25-68.
339. Wyatt, H.V. "James Lind and the Prevention of Scurvy." *Med. Hist.*, 20, no. 4 (Oct. 1976), 433-8.
340. Zuckerman, A. "Scurvy and the Ventilation of Ships in the Royal Navy: Samuel Sutton's contribution." *Eighteenth Century Studies*, 10 (1976-77), 222-34.

Supplement to Bibliography

341. Borrie, John. *Despite Captivity: A Doctor's Life as Prisoner of War*. London: Kimber, 1975.
342. Bowie, Donald C. "Captive Surgeon in Hong Kong: The Story of the British Military Hospital, Hong Kong 1942-45" *Journal of the Hong Kong Branch of the Royal Asiatic Society*, 15 (1975), 150-290.
343. Daniel, Paul. *Surgeon at Arms*. London: Heinemann, 1958.
344. *"Doc": A History of the R.N. Sick Berth Service*. London: H.M.S.O., 1986.
345. Douglas, Keith. *From Alamein to Zem Zem*. London: Bantam, 1985.
346. Ellis, John. *The Sharp End of War*. Newton Abbot: David & Charles, 1980.
347. ―――. *Eye-Deep in Hell*. London: Croom Helm, 1976.
348. Hamilton, J. *Soldier Surgeon in Malaya*. London: Angus & Robertson, 1958.
349. Keegan, J. *The Face of Battle*. London: Jonathan Cape, 1976.
350. ―――. *Soldiers: A History of Men in Battle*. London: Viking, 1986.
351. Kessel, L. *Surgeon at Arms*. London: Heinemann, 1958.
352. Rose, A. *Who Dies Fighting*. London: Jonathan Cape, 1944.

353. Rodgers, N.A.M. *The Wooden World: An Anatomy of the Georgian Navy.* London: Collins, 1986.
354. Seagrave, G. *Burma Surgeon.* London: Gollancz, 1943.
355. ─────. *Burma Surgeon Returns.* London: Gollancz, 1946.
356. Stevenson, W.F. *Wounds in War.* London: Longman, 1897.

XXIV

THE HISTORY OF MILITARY AND MARTIAL LAW

F.H. Dean

In what follows, the corresponding chapter in Professor Higham's *A Guide to the Sources of British Military History* will be referred to as 'the original chapter', and the volume edited by Professor Higham will be described as 'the parent volume'. This chapter is likely to be considerably shorter than some which will appear in the present volume. This is because its sole purpose is to guide the reader to the recent literature relating to its subject, and such material is in fact scanty. The original sources for the study of the history of military and martial law, of necessity, are unchanged.

The outline of the subject, together with its references to the source materials, contained on pages 613 to 622 of the parent volume, requires no changes or amplification. The process of regular revision of the service disciplinary legislation, which was described on pages 621 and 622 of the parent volume, has continued, and several important innovations and developments have occurred. There have been detailed reviews of the Army Act 1955 (see the bibliography printed at the end of this chapter (item 1(a)) and of the Air Force Act 1955 (1(b)) at five-yearly intervals, carried out by Select Committees of the House of Commons, and from 1970 onwards this review has also extended to the Naval Discipline Act 1957 (1(c)). Virtually all of the recommendations made by these Committees have been accepted by the House of Commons and have been enacted in the Armed Forces Acts of 1971, 1976, 1981 and 1986 respectively (1(f), 1(h), 1(i), 1(j)). It is therefore to these statutes, and to the Select Committee Reports on which they are based, that students must turn to find what significant developments have occurred since the original chapter appeared. All of these documents are cited in the bibliography at the end of the chapter (2(a), 2(b), 2(c), 2(d), 2(e), 2(f), 2(g)).

The development of most constitutional importance must be the bringing of the Naval Discipline Act 1957 into line with the other two service discipline Acts, involving also the subjection to quinquennial review of the naval code of discipline at the same time as the review of the army and the Royal Air Force. Thus a distinction which extended far back into history (see the original chapter, pages 621-2) has disappeared. This change was effected by the Armed Forces Act 1971, as recommended by the Select Committee of that year.

Another major development recommended by that Select Committee, and carried into law by the Armed Forces Act 1971, was the provision of a unified code of offenses and punishments applicable to all three services. The definitions of offenses within the jurisdiction of service disciplinary tribunals, and the range of punishments which could be awarded, had been virtually identical so far as the army and the Royal Air Force were concerned since the latter was established in 1917, but substantial differences in form, and a few in substance, existed between these and the provisions applicable to the naval forces. The introduction of the unified code may be said to be in line with the policy of standardising the administration of the three fighting services, and the assimilation of their organization, which found expression during the 1960s in the abolition, as separate entities, of the Admiralty, the War Office and the Air Ministry and the creation of the Ministry of Defence. This process has not yet reached its conclusion, however, since the three services still maintain a separate existence under the general direction of the Ministry, a situation which may be contrasted with the complete assimilation of the three branches of the armed forces now existing in Canada.

Among changes of lesser importance recommended to Parliament and effected by the Armed Forces Act 1971, were some alterations in the law relating to the limited jurisdiction of service tribunals over civilians, the creation of a right of appeal by civilians against sentences of courts-martial, and the effect of the existence of the situation defined as active service.

Further important developments were recommended by the Select Committee of the House of Commons of 1975-76, and enacted by the Armed Forces Act 1976. The most significant of these was perhaps the creation of a new criminal court, akin to magistrates' courts in England, to deal with civilians outside the United Kingdom who are liable to trial under the Army Act 1955 or the Air Force Act 1955. It had long been recognized that courts-martial were not suitable tribunals, in many instances, for the trial of such cases, especially where the offense alleged was relatively minor and the accused was a juvenile or a woman. Among other difficulties was the fact that the range of punishments available to courts-martial was frequently found to be unsuitable for infliction on juveniles. The new courts are termed Standing Civilian Courts. Trials may be directed to be held before such courts only within an area specified by the Secretary of State for Defence with the approval of the Lord Chancellor, and up to the present time the only areas for which the use of Standing Civilian Courts has been authorized are the Federal Republic of Germany, the Netherlands, Belgium and Berlin. The trial is held before a legally qualified civilian magistrate appointed by the Lord Chancellor from among the assistants to the Judge Advocate General, and for the trial of juveniles the magistrate may sit with two assessors (who have no vote) or members (who are actual members of the court and have a vote). Among other limitations upon the range of offenses which may be tried is the prohibition of the trial by a Standing Civilian Court of any offence which a magistrates' court would be unable to try if it were alleged to have been committed in England or Wales. Standing Civilian Courts have a specified range of punishments and orders available to them, including restitution orders. Their findings, sentences or orders can be reviewed by service reviewing officers, and there is a right of appeal to a court-marital and thus, ultimately, to the Courts-Martial Appeal Court. Evidence was given to the Select Committee as to the arrangements contemplated to assist Standing Civilian Courts, for instance by the provision in Germany of a senior probation officer selected by the Home Office, who can assist in the preparation of cases and prepare social enquiry reports on persons coming before the courts. It should be emphasized that the system of Standing Civilian Courts does not extend to the trial of civilians who are subject only to the Naval Discipline Act 1957, since the naval authorities have not found a need for such facilities.

Another innovation of some importance made by the Armed Forces Act 1976, and applicable to juvenile civilian offenders convicted under any of the three service discipline Acts, was the introduction of reception orders, authorizing the offender to the removed to the United Kingdom and there received by any local government authority in England or Wales, after which 'care proceedings' (which are not criminal in their nature) can be instituted in any part of the United Kingdom. It is evident that the purpose of all these measures is to secure to civilians (and especially to those of them who are juveniles) protections, and a range of penalties appropriate to their status and age, which will as far as possible be equivalent to those which are applicable in ordinary civilian life.

The Armed Forces Act 1976 also made an important change in the powers of commanding officers in the army and the Royal Air Force to award sentences of detention and fines to N.C.O.'s, soldiers and airmen tried summarily before them. In the Royal Navy, commanding officers had for a long period had considerably greater powers of summary punishment than their equivalents in the other services, because of the practical difficulty of assembling courts-martial on board ships at sea. The Act of 1976 has increased the period of detention which may be awarded summarily in the army and the Royal Air Force from 28 days to 60 days, subject to the right of the accused to elect to be tried by court-martial, and the adoption of a more formal system of summary trial, which must include the preparation of a written summary of the evidence, the consent of higher authority to the use of the extended power, and the limitation of its use to cases where the accused does not dispute the facts. The level of fines which may be awarded by an army or Royal Air Force commanding officer has also been increased. There is, however, no requirement that the accused shall be represented.

The changes made by the Armed Forces Act 1981 were not so far-reaching as those which resulted from the Act of 1976. Attention may be called, however, to the provision placing young service offenders on the same footing as their civilian counterparts under the Act of 1976, by empowering courts-martial to sentence them to detention in a civilian corrective establishment instead of to imprisonment or detention in a service corrective establishment. Another provision enables children of persons subject to service law overseas, who are believed to be at risk of ill-treatment or in moral danger, to be held temporarily in a place of safety while attempts are made to provide for their safety and welfare. The Select Committee were told that if in such a case the most secure future for the child was adjudged to be within the care of a United Kingdom local authority, the child's parents would be sent back to the United Kingdom by administrative action, after which the child could be taken into care pursuant to English law. Other provisions related to the improvement of powers to deal with persons who while overseas suffer from mental disorder, and to the completion of the assimilation of the women's services into the armed forces of the Crown. The Select Committee also discussed a number of matters on which immediate legislation was not proposed, but which were recommended for future consideration. These included the existing proscription of homosexuals within the armed forces (on which evidence was given by representatives of the Campaign for Homosexual Equality), alcoholism and drug abuse in the armed forces, and the composition of courts-martial (with reference to whether those below commissioned rank should be eligible to sit as members of such courts).

The most recent developments are those proposed by the Select Committee of the House of Commons which sat in 1985-86 and which were carried into law by the Armed Forces Act 1986. This Act appears, perhaps not surprisingly, to mark a pause in the phase of rapid change during the period of nearly thirty years between 1952 and 1981. Indeed this latest in the series of Armed Forces Acts, like those of 1961 and 1966 (1(d) and 1(e)) was in the main a tidying-up operation, and thus less likely to be of interest to students than its three immediate predecessors. However, there are some significant provisions in it which may repay attention. The provisions, mentioned above, of the 1981 Act affecting children at risk have been strengthened: whereas under the earlier Act where an order for the temporary removal of such a child had been made, there was no statutory provisions for its removal to the United Kingdom so as to bring it within the ambit of U.K. law, this gap has now been filled by the Act of 1986. The intention, foreshadowed in 1976, to strengthen the powers of Standing Civilian Courts once experience in the working of their original powers had been gained, has now been fulfilled, if only to a minor extent, by conferring on these courts a power to defer sentence. The Select Committee hinted, moreover, that this process might usefully be carried further, by giving Standing Civilian Courts a power to suspend, or partially suspend, a sentence actually awarded, and to activate suspended sentences awarded by United Kingdom civilian courts, which in turn would be empowered to exercise a similar power with regard to Standing Civilian Courts' suspended sentences. It became clear, however, that detailed discussion of the practical arrangements which these proposals would entail would be necessary between the Ministry of Defence and the Home Office, and consequently no provisions on these lines have been enacted as yet.

Apart from the statutory changes made by the 1986 Act, some students may find it rewarding to study some other matters discussed by the Select Committee but not recommended as subjects for legislation. These included the question whether persons charged under the service discipline Acts receive adequate guidance as to their rights, and whether in the army and the Royal Air Force accused persons dealt with summarily are adequately represented: the Committee recommended that arrangements resembling these already existing in the Royal Navy should be introduced in the other two services. The scope of the death penalty was also considered. There now remain five service offenses for which that penalty may be awarded, and the Committee, remarking that each of these involves a positive act of treachery or of deliberate assistance to, or impeding of operations against, the enemy, did not suggest that any alteration in the law should be made. The incidence of homosexuality and of drug abuse, in the armed forces was again considered, and for the first time there was discussion as to the extent to which service personnel should be permitted not merely to join trade unions, but to participate actively in their affairs, e.g. by joining in strike action. Again no alteration in the existing rules was recommended. Finally, it was suggested that as there is now a permanent Standing Defence Committee of the House of Commons, the periodical reviews of the service discipline Acts and the consideration of Armed Forces Bills might well be left in future to that Committee: matters needing urgent attention could then be considered as and when they arose and not have to await the next quinquennial review, and the appointment of a Select Committee would cease to be necessary.

Very few cases involving questions of military law have been decided in the civil courts in recent years; even these in the Courts-Martial Appeal Court (which is itself a civil court, of equivalent status to the criminal division of the (civil) Court of Appeal and manned by civilian judges, thus resembling its counterpart in the United States) have seldom related to matters of general legal importance. However, the provisions of the three service discipline Acts permitting the trial by service courts of most civil offenses (see the Army Act 1955 and the Air Force Act 1955, section 70, and the Naval Discipline Act 1955 and the Air Force Act 1955, section 70, and the Naval Discipline Act 1955, section 42) have been considered in several cases: see R. v. Page (14); Cox v. The Army Council (ibid., item 9); Secretary of State for Defence v. Warn (15); R. v. Kirkup (12); and R. v. Gordon-Finlayson (11). Two interesting cases on the scope of the offense of conduct to the prejudice of good order and service discipline (see the Army Act 1955 and the Air Force Act 1955, section 69, and the Naval Discipline Act 1957, section 39) have been decided by the Courts-Martial Appeal Court: see R. v. Miller (13) on the necessity for proof of *mens rea*, and R. v. Davies and R. v. Hamilton (10) on the question whether misbehaviour occurring away from any service establishment and not directly connected with service duties or affairs, can come within the scope of the offence. There has also been a decision of the House of Lords, on appeal from the Courts-Martial Appeal Court, on the question whether a soldier can be brought to trial by Court-Martial after the day on which he would ordinarily have been discharged or transferred to the reserve, for an offense allegedly committed before that date, if at that date the offense had come to light and was being investigated, although he had not actually been charged (16).

Since the original chapter was written, the Fourth Edition of *Halsbury's Laws of England* has been published, and in it the title *Royal Forces* has been to a great extent re-written and expanded (4). The constitutional position of the armed forces, and the relationship between civil and military law are treated at some length, and the law relating to visiting forces is fully covered. Among the recent legislation having an impact on members of the armed forces is the Rehabilitation of Offenders Act 1974 (1(g), which provides for certain criminal convictions to become 'spent' by lapse of time, after which, with certain limitations, they cannot be referred to in future proceedings, and need not be disclose when seeking employment, etc.: the impact of these provisions upon service disciplinary proceedings and other aspects of service life, e.g. promotion and appointments to sensitive positions, is examined. The modern developments stemming from the work of the recent Select Committees and effected by the series of Armed Forces Acts, which have been covered earlier in this chapter, are fully described. Students may therefore find this title of *Halsbury's Laws* a useful source of detailed information. It is kept up to date by the publication of annual supplements. It should be used in conjunction with the corresponding title in *Halsbury's Statutes of England* (5) which is also kept up to date by supplements and continuation volumes issued each year.

Students studying the penal system of the British armed forces may find valuable information in Judge Babington's recent book *For the Sake of Example: Capital Courts-Martial 1914-1920* (3). Much has been written on the subject of the trial of soldiers charged with capital offenses such as cowardice, desertion in the face of the enemy and such-like offenses during the first world war, but most of this has generated more heat than light. Babington's book is the first whose author has had access to a great deal of new and original information not previously available, and thus for the first time a full and accurate account of the subject has been made possible. Of especial interest is the account of the concern which the trials aroused even during the war and more so afterwards, and of how this led, not only to alterations in the actual law, but to changed attitudes to the appropriate treatment of behavior previously regarded as calling only for punishment. The volume contains a useful Bibliography.

The official *Manuals* of army and air force law continue (6 and 7) and there is now a *Manual of Naval Law* (8). The periodicals cited in the Bibliography at the end of the original chapter also continue and should be searched by students for articles relating to their own fields of work.

BIBLIOGRAPHY

The Bibliography which follows is intended only to supplement the one printed at the end of the original chapter in the parent volume on pages 624-630 and not to supersede it. For this reason, the sections of the latter entitled 'Useful Libraries', 'Bibliographical Volumes', 'Original Records' and 'Periodicals' are not reprinted here. It may be mentioned, however, that the address of the Judge Advocate General is now: 22 Kingsway, London WC26 6LE (telephone 01-430-5335).

Printed Sources other than Periodicals and Text-Books

1. Acts of Parliament. Those cited in the present chapter are the following:
   - (a) Army Act 1955 (3 & 4 Eliz. 2, c. 18)
   - (b) Air Force Act 1955 (3 & 4 Eliz. 2, c. 19)
   - (c) Naval Discipline Act 1957 (5 & 6 Eliz. 2, c. 53)
   - (d) Army and Air Force Act 1961 (1961, c. 52)
   - (e) Armed Forces Act 1966 (1966, c. 52)
   - (f) Armed Forces Act 1971 (1971 c. 33)
   - (g) Rehabilitation of Offenders Act 1974 (1974 c. 53)
   - (h) Armed Forces Act 1976 (1976 c. 52)
   - (i) Armed Forces Act 1981 (1981 c. 55)

(j) Armed Forces Act 1986 (1986 c. 21)
2. Reports of Select Committees of the House of Commons. Those cited in the present chapter are the following:
  (a) Select Committee on the Army Act and the Air Force Act: 4 Reports with Evidence, etc., Sessions 1952-1954 (H.C. Papers Nos. 244 and 331 of 1952, 289 of 1953, and 223 of 1954).
  (b) Select Committee on the Army and Air Force Bill: Report with Evidence etc., Session 1961 (H.C. Papers No. 162 of 1961).
  (c) Select Committee on the Armed Forces Bill: Report with Evidence, etc., Session 1966-1967 (H.C. Papers No. 202 of 1966-1967).
  (d) Select Committee on the Armed Forces Bill: Report with Evidence, etc., Session 1970-1971 (H.C. Papers No. 367 of 1970-1971).
  (e) Select Committee on the Armed Forces Bill: Report with Evidence, etc., Session 1975-1976 (H.C. Papers No. 429 of 1975-1976).
  (f) Select Committee on the Armed Forces Bill: Report with Evidence, etc., Session 1980-1981 (H.C. Papers No. 253 of 1980-1981).
  (g) Select Committee on the Armed Forces Bill: Report with Evidence, etc., Session 1985-1986 (H.C. Papers No. 170 of 1985-1986).
All these Reports are published by H.M.S.O., London.

Printed Books

3. Babington (Judge). *For the Sake of Example: Capital Courts-Martial 1914-1920*, London: Secker and Warberg 1983.
4. *Halsbury's Laws of England*, 4th edn., vol. 41, title *Royal Forces*, by J. G. Morgan-Owen, F. H. Dean and others. London: Butterworths 1983; together with annual Cumulative Supplements.
5. *Halsbury's Statutes of England*, vol. 29, title *Royal Forces*, London: Butterworths 1971, with annual Cumulative Supplements and Continuation Volumes. When needing to refer to Acts of Parliament, students are advised to use these publications rather than the Statutes as officially published, because Halsbury's Statutes contain copious notes and cross-references. A 4th edition of this work is now in course of publication, but the volume containing the title "Royal Forces" has not yet been issued.
6. *Manual of Air Force Law*, 3 vols., London: H.M.S.O., various dates. Vol. 1 (6th edition, 1983) contains the Air Force Act 1955, the Rules of Procedure, and other regulations in daily use, with notes; Vol. 2 contains other material of less day to day importance, but includes an historical chapter; Vol. 3 relates to the trial of civilians by court-martial and the Standing Civilian Court.
7. *Manual of Military Law*, 3 vols., London: H.M.S.O., various dates. Part I (12th edition 1972) the contents of which are equivalent to those in volume 1 of the *Manual of Air Force Law*, plus a Civilian Supplement, separately bound, equivalent to volume 3 of the *Manual of Air Force Law*.

Part 2, containing a section on the History of Military Law and others dealing with the Reserve Forces, the Women's Forces, the application of the civil law to the armed forces, the employment of troops in aid of the civil power, etc., some of these have not been kept up to date. Part 3 deals with the international law of war.

8. *Manual of Naval Law*, London: H.M.S.O., 1982. All the Service legal *Manuals* are frequently amended, and in using them students should check to see that their copy has been amended up to date. Major amendments are issued by H.M.S.O. in packets of loose leaf pages to be inserted in place of those to be discarded; these bundles also contain lists of minor amendments to be copied into the volumes by hand in the holder's copies.

All the above are available in all significant law libraries, except the Service Manuals, which are less widely available but are kept in the Bodleian Law Library at Oxford and in the libraries of the Services and of the Judge Advocate General listed in the Bibliography to the original chapter in the parent volume.

Decided Cases

9. Cox v. The Army Council (1963) A C 48, (1962) 1 All E.R. 880, 46 Cr App Rep 258 (House of Lords).
10. R. v. Davies, R. v. Hamilton (1980) Crim L R 582, (C-MAC).
11. R. v. Gordon-Finlayson (1941) 1 K B 171 (D.C.).
12. R. v. Kirkup (1950) 34 Cr App Rep 150 (C C A).
13. R. v. Miller (1983) The Times Newspaper, 6th June (C-MAC).
14. R. v. Page (1954) 1 Q B 170, 2 All E.R. 1355, 37 Cr App Rep 189 (C-MAC).
15. Secretary of State for Defence v. Warn (1970) A C 394, (1968) 2 All E.R. 300, 52 Cr App Rep 366 (House of Lords).
16. R. v. Garth (1986) 268 (House of Lords).

The meaning of the abbreviations used in the above citations is as follows:

A C = The House of Lords Appeal Cases series in the (demi-official) Law Reports.
All E.R. = The All England Law Reports.
Cr App Rep = The Criminal Appeal Reports.
C C A = Court of Criminal Appeal (now replaced by the Criminal Division of the Court of Appeal).
Crim L R = The Criminal Law Review.
C-MAC = The Courts-Martial Appeal Court.
D.C. = The Divisional Court of the King's or Queen's Bench Division.
K B, Q B = The King's/Queen's Bench Division series in the demi-official Law Reports.

XXV

BRITISH DEFENSE POLICY AND PRACTICE 1945-85

Martin Edmonds
and
David Weston

University of Manchester

INTRODUCTION: A BIBLIOGRAPHICAL OVERVIEW OF DEFENSE SOURCES

In the Chapter on British Defence Policy in the Higham volume innovation in British military thinking, the high rate of technological change in weaponry and the problems of coming to terms with the "Retreat from Empire" were highlighted. The same observation holds true for the period since 1970, the year that the chapter was completed, with the qualification that broad strategic thinking on deterrence has remained constant and the retreat from Empire has almost been accomplished except for a few--and in the case of the Falklands, notable,--minor outposts. The focus of attention among scholars, commentators and analysts has shifted somewhat to issues associated with Britain's membership of the Atlantic Alliance, military procurement, the impact of defense spending on the British economy, and, inevitably, the conflicts in which the British Armed Forces have been engaged.

The earlier survey also made a point which remains valid today, and perhaps even more so as the tendency of successive Governments has been to be ever more secret about defense policy issues and content; this is the relative paucity of primary sources on British defense policy since 1945, and certainly since 1970. The Thirty Year Rule, which frequently covers longer periods where defense and strategic issues are concerned, is as fixed and immutable as ever. Furthermore, as such scandals as the Ponting affair and that of Sarah Tysdale have demonstrated, the nature of Section II of the Official Secrets Acts, 1911, 1920 and 1939, has become more and more inclusive and a Freedom of Information Act less and less a realistic possibility in all but the distant future. Thus researchers into British defense policy and practice since 1945, if their interest is after 1956, have to depend on leaks from within Whitehall (34), illuminating memoirs and biographies of the less discreet, such as that of Mountbatten (162), and the painstaking work of constant investigation, careful collation and deduction. One excellent example of what can be achieved in this respect is the work of Duncan Campbell, and in particular his expose of United States defense and security interests in Britain (30).

In these general respects, little has changed since 1970; but in specifics there have been significant developments. In particular retired servicemen have not been afraid to put pen to paper, not in recounting their past exploits in war, but in contributing to current debates on British defense strategy and policy, men such as Hill-Norton (90), Carver (32), Cameron (29), and Beach (14). Nor have civil servants always retained their traditional reserve, with Cooper (41) and Hockaday (92) making useful contributions. It is a paradox that with greater secrecy on the one side, there has been a widening of the policy debate on the other. One explanation is that the debate tends to revolve around general issues and personal opinion, articulated with the usual disclaimers, rather than the hard empirical realities of defense plans and capabilities.

The hallmark of the period since 1970 for the researcher has been the rapid expansion of interest in British defense *per se* and the content of defense policy, an interest which draws on and correspondingly stimulates, more and more journals and magazines, many of them with high technical content. This, however, does not take into account the occasional papers of the various research Institutes that have a specific interest in defense issues which they did not have previously, such as Chatham House (RIIA) (294). Since 1970 Institutes that have expanded their existing defense interests include the International Institute for Strategic Studies (IISS) (287), the Royal United Services Institution (RUSI) (295), and the Royal College of Defence Studies (296). Then there are the publications of the several new ones that have been established over the past fifteen years in British universities with the assistance of external (mostly American) finance, such as the Centre for Defence Economics (Aberdeen) (286), the Centre for the Study of Arms Control and International Security (Lancaster) (288), the Peace Studies Department (Bradford) (292), the Arms Control and Disarmament Intelligence Unit (Sussex) (215), the Richardson Institute (Lancaster) (293), and the Centre for Defence Studies (Edinburgh) (297). Several new independent defense-related research organizations have also been established during this period, whose occasional papers and publications must also be included including the Council for Arms Control (290), British Atlantic Committee (289), and the Institute for European Defence and Strategic Studies (291). For a survey of teaching and research in defense throughout the United Kingdom, see Edmonds and Gooch (53), or Reychler and Rudney (130).

Two other developments since 1970 regarding sources on British defense should be noted. The first is the steady increase in the number of journals and magazines that have been added to the total that existed in 1960. It is perhaps significant that very few journals before 1960 have ceased publication, articles on British defense policy have been taken by journals that previously did not give space to defense issues, and journals that carried defense related articles before 1970 are carrying more than ever. Articles on British defense are also being increasingly accepted in defense journals published outside the country. A list of the more important journals with significant interest in defense and edited or published in Britain is included in the Bibliography (214).

The dividing line between what is a journal and what is a magazine is a difficult one; using the rough distinction of what constitutes an article as opposed to a report, the number of magazines with extensive or significant, defense reportage has also increased. Frequently these sources, focusing as they do on military technology and the services, unearth more factual material than is likely to be found in journal articles. The more useful ones are also listed in the bibliography (214), and are not restricted to British publications. Weapons and military technology have indeed now assumed an almost international character.

The list of journals and magazines contained in the bibliographical appendix have been selected for their emphasis on defense issues, irrespective of whether or not that emphasis is technical or policy-related, or supportive or critical of British defense policy. But because of the eclectic nature of the subject and its wide impact on so many aspects of society, many important articles on British defense appear in journals and magazines whose emphasis is not primarily on defense. There are too many such articles to list comprehensively, but those journals with an occasional useful discussion of British defense and security policy are included below (271). For a useful initial search for these articles the standard indexes should be used (298). However, reflecting the increasing interest in defence and the number of articles written on it, some indexes devoted exclusively to defense have recently been produced and these should be consulted first (300, 306).

The amount of information disseminated about British defense and defense related issues has proliferated since the late 1960s, of which books and articles have taken full advantage. Some of the additional information has been a consequence of a symbiotic process of public interest on the one side and newspaper coverage on the other. As defense commands greater public attention, which should be expected since the Ministry of Defence is a major spending department with far-reaching economic, social and in particular technological impact, so newspapers, particularly the so-called 'quality' press, has given it increasing coverage. The trend has been further stimulated by mounting concern within the population at large about the relevance and efficacy of nuclear deterrence, heightened perception of super-power rivalry inside and outside Europe, the global arms race, successive defense expenditure scandals, such as the Chevaline (192), Stingray (184), Nimrod, and MBT 80 (54), weapons programmes, and operational ambiguities as in the case of the ill famed "Belgrano Affair" (74, 127). For quick and easy access to Press and Magazine coverage of British defense, other than the standard *Times* (316), and other newspaper indexes (301), the Press Libraries of the International Institute for Strategic Studies (a duplicate of which from 1967 until 1983 is held at Lancaster University (288)), the Royal Institute of International Affairs (294), or the Ministry of Defence War Office Library (342) should be consulted.

Despite this widening interest in British defense and strategic issues, one somewhat disturbing trend has emerged in recent years: this is the propensity of British scholars and commentators on defense, particularly those attached to International Institutes but also in Universities to be primarily concerned with the strategic problems and "debates" of the super-powers. This has been encouraged by the opportunity to do so being opened and funded by outside--mostly American--institutions. The intention is for these studies to be 'policy-oriented', and relevant to either American or Western security problems.

In becoming drawn into these debates, and putting effort into the security problems of others--even though they impinge on

Britain's defense and security interests--these scholars have given less and less of their time to Britain's defense policy problems and practices. More seriously, they have tended to become embroiled in the broader, global, strategic debates yet have done so with limited or restricted access to data. This has forced them into higher and higher levels of speculation and arm-chair theorizing, of little or no immediate value to pressing British defence problems. The highly speculative discussion of the American "Star Wars" (SDI) initiative and the imaginative opinions *a priori* articulated over the Soviet-American arms control talks, for example, have tended to dominate the contents of British defense oriented journals. On balance they have been superficial and distanced from Britain's real defense problems.

Information on contemporary British defense issues ultimately comes from either the Services, the Ministry of Defence, or Whitehall. It is perhaps here, within the Ministry of Defence, more than anywhere else that the stimulus for wider knowledge and understanding of defense issues can be traced. If any one person, or any one decision, widened the dissemination of defense information can be isolated, that of Mr. Healey in the mid 1960s to expand the content of the annual Defence White Paper and to release more defense information must be the strongest contender (129). A brief comparison of the 1985 Statement on the Defence Estimates (plus statistics) (167)--albeit at exorbitant expense--with the earlier Defence White Paper speaks for itself. It is refreshing to see how extensively used this greater sharing of defense information has been, and with what beneficial effect.

The Statement on the Defence Estimates has not been the only instance of widened Government dissemination of defense information. The frequency with which successive Governments have had to relate defense commitments with diminishing resources has produced numerous Defence Reviews (168) and Ministry of Defence Command Papers, the more significant of which are included below (165). Both Command (Cmnd) (166) and House of Commons (HC) (178) Papers, of course, are also issued by the Ministry of Defence in response to Parliamentary enquiry into defense policy planning and spending. Parliamentary interest over the past twenty years has expanded considerably, and it is, arguably, here, more than anywhere, that the most valuable sources of defense information have become available.

There are two reasons for this increase: first, defense, which hithertofore was not generally considered either a vote-catching or career-enhancing area of government concern became so, as both the nuclear deterrent issue and defense procurement expenditure assumed new dimensions; and, second, changes in the committee structure in the House of Commons led, initially, to defense being included as an area of public expenditure with foreign policy (179) and, later, after the reforms of 1979, as an area in its own right with its own specialist Parliamentary Committee (183). This meant that whereas in the late 1960s defense was but one of a number of areas to which the Commons Committee on National Expenditure could turn its attention, it is today accorded an annual examination, with up to four specific defense topics of concern reported on in any one year. In recent years other specialist committees of the House of Commons have also turned their attention to defense problems, including those primarily concerned with Science and Technology (196), Foreign Affairs (197), and the Treasury (198).

Nor have other Committees of the House of Commons been idle in defense matters during the past twenty years. In particular the Public Accounts Committee (189), frequently as a consequence of persistent over-runs in weapons procurement, has probed specific aspects of defense expenditure with illuminating results. Three reports in particular were highly revealing: first there was the one billion pounds Chevaline Polaris A3 warhead improvement programme which had been hidden from the public and parliament for almost ten years (192), then the widely challenged Polaris nuclear deterrent replacement programme with the Trident system (193), and lastly the report on Government contracting for Defence (194). Full details of all House of Commons Committee Reports and Hearings are not possible here; but what should be noted is that they do offer the student of British defense policy a much more fruitful and rewarding source than hithertofore.

Finally, there are the open government documents (Green Papers) on defense issues prepared and published by the Ministry of Defence (199) and others (209) which bear on defense issues published by other administrative departments. Defense publications of this type are distributed on the initiative of the Secretary of State for public consumption and are designed to provide background material on current or future Ministry of Defence or services' policy or practices. This can be illustrated from four recent examples, each of which coincides with the government's defense policy. One was a paper outlining the reorganization of the Ministry of Defence itself and its adoption of new internal management (MINIS) procedures (207); a second was a paper on the expansion of the Territorial Army (206); a third on the future of the Royal Dockyards, as part of the Thatcher government's policy of privatization (208), and the last on the UK Trident programme (204).

To these Departmental sources should also be added the more traditional source of information from parliamentary debates, both in the Lords and Commons (210). Whilst there is no obvious indication that the standard or substance of defense debates have improved, the extent of participation and the frequency of questions on defense issues in parliament, suggest that parliamentary affairs are a source to be given serious attention. For a full guide to all government and parliamentary material, the Annual (monthly) Government Publications list, from 1945, should be used (213).

Turning to non-governmental and secondary sources on British defense policy and practice, the sheer number and bulk of publications on defense acquired from journal, magazine and government and parliamentary sources precludes specific references in this chapter, except where they have been identified as being particularly significant or influential. For non-British scholars, however, and especially those from America, considerable caution should be exercised to avoid attributing the same significance to either parliamentary committee hearings and defense articles in journals as their equivalents in the United States. Very seldom, even in the more respectable national newspapers or major journals, are articles and contributions published as part of, or an input into, the defense policy planning process, or as a means of exercising influence or pressure on defense planners. The Official Secrets Acts, despite recent examples of unofficial, and even official, leaks, effectively prevents such a thing happening and normally serves to ensure that even articles written by authoritative people are normally anodine, often platitudinous, and couched in bland generalities.

This effectively leaves the researcher with secondary sources, especially books, of which there have been a number both single authored and edited. Compared with the period 1945-67, the period 1967 to the present day is replete with publications. Not only is the quantity greater, but the range of subjects within the defense subject area has also expanded, making the categories used in the first edition of this volume difficult to carry over to the later period. However, the broad categories can be retained, though the specific areas within these have been amended to reflect shifts in scholarly and public interest, concern and attitude towards defense. Finally, an extra category has been added to cover the enormous attention that has been given, understandably, to the role of the services in Northern Ireland, and during the Falklands War.

STRATEGIC AND DEFENSE POLICY ISSUES

(1) Nuclear Strategic Issues and the Independent Deterrent. Before 1967, books and articles published on British defence policy were few and far between with such emphasis as there was being given to theoretical problems relating to deterrence and nuclear weaponry. By 1967 most of those debates had either been resolved or exhausted in broad terms, though the specifics and minutiae of policy or capability continued to offer scope for further discussion and speculation and publication. Several books, starting where Rosencrance (134), left off, have chronicled these debates, two of which stand out, but for different reasons. Freedman's *Evolution of Nuclear Strategy* (69) is one, but here Britain's strategic debates are placed within a broader, and more general international framework. For this reason his more specific *Britain and Nuclear Weapons* (70) is a better place to start. A more detailed and empirical study is Pierre's examination of the British experience with an independent strategic force 1939-70 (126) both from the point of view of defense policy and military practicality. In this context, Smart's study of the future of the British nuclear deterrent (138) and that of Alford and Nailor make thought provoking reading (2).

To these must also be added McLean and the Oxford Research Group's comparative study of how nuclear decisions are made (119), Simpson's close investigation of the interelationship of civil and military nuclear power (137), McMahan's study of Britain's Nuclear Deterrent (115) and Gowing and Arnold's companion volume (77) to *Britain and Atomic Energy 1939-45* (76) which set the background to Britain's decision, or absence of it, first to develop a nuclear warhead. Finally, there is Dillon's detailed study of the origins and performance of the British Polaris programme (49) which is a book that would equally be at home amongst those concerned with either the Anglo-US special relationship, such as Baylis' *Anglo American Defence Relations 1939-80* (12) or weapons procurement studies such as Menaul's (120) and Brookes' (24) studies of Britain's airborne deterrent.

(2) General Works on British Defense Policy. Until 1967 only two general volumes concerned with British defense policy had been published, that of Rosecrance, above, and Snyder (140). Both authors are American, so it was a welcome change when Barnett's historical account of British defense policy from 1945-1970 was published in 1972 (9). This was followed one year later by Darby's study of Britain's defense policy East of Suez to 1968 (46) since when only two general books on British defense policy have been produced, those of Baylis (11) and Edmonds (57). Single authored books, but with partisan points of view, include those of Smith (139), Chichester and Wilkinson (36), Owen (123), and Baylis (13). As an exercise in intelligent speculation of where British defense policy might point in the future, there is Roper's recently edited volume (132).

(3) The Protest Movement. Compared with earlier studies of the protest movement in the 1950s those of the 1970s and 1980s were concerned less with the movement itself and more with the arguments for and against nuclear weapons and deterrence theory. In this sense, the nuclear disarmers had grown up and come of age, recognizing that British defense policy as far as the strategic element was concerned had to be confronted not on emotional grounds but on the same terms, with the same logic and terminology as those advocating deterrence. Thus there was, at the time of the decision in the later 1970s to find a replacement for the aging Polaris system in the 1990s and to strengthen the theatre nuclear forces in Europe, consequent upon Russian deployment of new bomber and intermediate range nuclear missiles, a rash of books challenging both the theories behind these decisions and their relevance to Britain's security. Prominent among these was Smith and Thompson's widely read, and therefore influential, book *Protest and Survive* (150). To this the Bishop of Salisbury's *The Church and the Bomb* (6) should be added, along with Edmonds' study (56), the Labour Party's thinking on the nuclear deterrent (108), Cox's *Overkill* (42), and Zuckerman's balanced appraisal (164).

The decision to deploy nuclear cruise missiles in Europe prompted a more specific outburst of protest, one that focused more widely than on Britain's independent nuclear deterrent role. Nonetheless, Britain, as a member of NATO, and one of the countries to receive cruise missiles as part of the theatre nuclear weapon improvement programme immediately became part of the debate. It therefore was prominently included in the wider European protest, of which the Alternative Defence Commission Report (3) and the various contributions of Kaldor and Smith (100) and Coates and Duff (40), are the better known.

(4) Britain and the Western Alliance. Reference has already been made to two serious works by Dillon and Baylis on the importance of the special relationship between Britain and the United States to Britain's defense. The implication of that relationship and Britain's place in the force structure of a Western Alliance heavily dependent on United States material were starkly and critically drawn in Campbell's *The Unsinkable Aircraft Carrier* (30). Whilst revealing in technical terms and with reference to US facilities in Britain the interdependence of the two countries, it also pointed to Britain's subservience, suggesting implications that linked with those whose attention has been drawn (below) to civil defense and internal security operations.

The special relationship is but one of many facets of the NATO Alliance, a subject which has attracted several scholars' attention both in respect of Alliance policy and strategy, weapons procurement and in speculating about future conflict in Europe (79). In respect of the first, most volumes on NATO have tended to be edited collections, with the majority of contributors from the United States. Among these volumes some of the better known are those of Fedder (64), Twitchett (153), Broadhurst (23), Myers (121), Windass (160) and Brady and Kaufman (21). But for a sound retrospective study of NATO's origins as well as a timely reminder of its original objectives, de Staerke's recent study should be consulted (142).

Books on arms collaboration within the Alliance have been a mixture of those that have stressed the economies of collaboration and those concerned with the political and security dimensions. Neither, of course, is mutually exclusive. Volumes by Edmonds (54), Hartley (87), Taylor (149) and Kennedy (103), look not merely at the general issues concerning weapons collaboration within NATO, but more especially at Britain's commitment to and experience of it.

DEFENSE: SUBSTANTIVE ISSUES IN RESPECT OF POLICY, SYSTEM, AND ENVIRONMENT

(1) **Policy**. Britain's defense policy, despite all the reviews that have been undertaken since 1945 (168, 174), has remained fairly consistent. The independent nuclear deterrent and the Western/North Atlantic Alliance have remained two foundations upon which it has been based since 1949. These have been covered above in respect of the broader strategic objectives of British defense policy. At a lower level of analysis British defense policy at the conventional level is translated into commitments to NATO through the British Army of the Rhine and RAF Germany and the protection of shipping from potential submarine attack in the Eastern Atlantic, to ensure the reinforcement of Europe from the United States in time of crisis or war. It is worth saying here that neither BAOR and RAF Germany, nor the Navy's anti-submarine, Eastern Atlantic roles have attracted much scholarly attention, and remain largely unexplored and under-researched fields. All three commitments, however, are subsumed under a wider rubric concerning the roles of air power and sea power as, for example, in books by Mason (117) and James Cable (26) or in more general volumes such as Edmonds' *Defence Equation* (57).

The fourth component in Britain's defense policy which has remained constant has been that of home defense. By and large it has been the cinderella element, involving Britain's reserves and civil defense. Among books that have given any serious attention to home defense considerations the one that stands out is Laurie's *Beneath the City Streets* (109), a revealing expose of the preparations and provisions for internal security and protection in the event of invasion or all-out war. Ackroyd's co-written volume (1), whilst addressing a different subject entirely, also offers some insights into the background of home defense contingency planning in Britain. Combined with Campbell's study (above), the three books paint a potentially disturbing picture of the potential for abuse of home defense preparations within Britain in times of non-war, peace, or in the battle against terrorism.

The last consistent element in Britain's defense policy commitments is what today is referred to as "out-of-area operations." It is a policy element that in the pre-1970 days was referred to as "East of Suez" policy, the commitment to the Commonwealth and Empire, or Britain's overseas dependencies. In the cut-back in defense commitments in the 1960s through economic stringency, it has been the overseas element that has been cut, freeing resources primarily for European, alliance and independent nuclear deterrent roles. This has been well chronicled up to 1968 by Darby (46); since then the subject has not received close attention until, that is, the Falklands crisis of 1982. This topic will be considered in detail below, under operations.

(2) **The Defense System.** One area that has attracted some attention of late is that of the Ministry of Defence and the defense decision-making process. Incorporated within this is not merely the structure of the higher defense organization of defense but the process by which policy decisions are made and the necessary budget allocations decided (190). First in this field was F.A. Johnson, whose volume on the central organization of defense in Britain from 1945 to 1974 is the most comprehensive (98). To these should be added the contributions by Martin (116), Edmonds (55), Edmonds and Beaumont (52), Hobkirk (91), Beckett and Gooch (15) and Howard (94). Although these volumes address themselves specifically to the questions of central defense decision-making, none would make quite so much sense without the benefit of Ziegler's biography of Mountbatten (162), or Reed and William's portrait of Denis Healey whilst he was Secretary of State for Defence (129).

The central organization of defense is, however, only at the hub of a structure which contains the three armed services: Army, Navy and Air Force. All three services receive constant attention, mostly in the technical journals and in the service oriented magazines and periodicals. They also have good coverage at a fairly low level of analysis focusing on weapons, units or uniforms. Very little, however, except Edmonds' recent volume (57), has been written which looks at the services as a whole, as an interdependent, integrated defense force, or as individual fighting systems. Nor has much attention been given to their separate, and sometimes shared, problems concerning recruitment, retention, education, training, pay, unionization, women's service contributions, command and control, and so on. The attention given to these sorts of issues in the United States is not paralleled in Britain. Occasionally an article or monograph will appear on any one of these subjects--unions were a big issue in the mid 1970s as Harries-Jenkins' study reflected (84), as was the role of women--but not in books. Downes (51) will be one exception when her study of the military academies is published.

(3) **The Services.** There have, nevertheless, been general books published since 1967 on the services during the post war period which warrant mention. Taking the services in order of seniority, the navy is the focal subject matter of D. Rodger's study of the *Admiralty* (131), an unusual book in that it concentrates on the central command structure of a service, rather than the service as a whole. A general survey of how the navy has fared since 1945 can be found in Hampshire's volume published in 1975 (81); it is a useful background to the subsequent reductions in the navy over the past ten years.

The Falklands War, in which the navy played a major role, stimulated interest in naval policy and the future of the Royal Navy. In particular, Speed, one-time Minister responsible for the navy, used the opportunity to press home his argument that the navy should not, after the savage cuts it was expected to sustain after the 1981 Defence Review, be allowed to diminish (141). In more temperate, analytical terms, Cable's study of Britain's naval future (27) makes better reading, though would not have had the same political impact as Williams and Richard's discussion of the future relevance of the navy's Eastern Alliance role in European security (157).

Turning next to the army, the attention generated by the Falklands, Northern Ireland, and regimental reorganization inevitably has led to a number of lengthy books. Perhaps the most comprehensive is Stanhope's *The Soldiers* (143), to which should be added Barnett's historical survey (8), and Barker's volume (5). On the regimental system today, two short studies stand out, those of Keegan (102) and Weston (156); both help to clarify many of the misrepresentations that exist about what the regiment is and where it figures in the British Army. On the regimental system before the drastic cuts of the 1970s, Blaxland should be referred to (18).

One very useful series which provides an insight both into the British Army and into post war operations in which particular units have served, is that of the *Famous Regiments*, under the overall editorship of General Horrocks (62). Published by Leo Cooper, there have been too many to list here and to select some rather than others would risk accusation of partiality or unwarranted selectivity. As a whole, they are a colorful and important record. There are numerous other lengthy studies on army regiments of which Geraghty's insight into the SAS (75) and Macksey's look at the cavalry (113) warrant mention.

Finally there is the Royal Air Force. Though the junior service, it is the one that has attracted most attention. In part this can be explained by the high technological content of its equipment and also for the close individual association that equipment has with men that operate them. The books on the history of the air force cover the post-war years comprehensively, those of Trevenan-James (152) and Brett (22), supplemented by Lee's examinations of the RAF in the Middle East (110) and in Germany (111) and Brookes' (24) and Menaul's (120) studies of the RAF's contribution to Britain's deterrent. Numerous books have been written on aircraft from which an understanding of the RAF and its policy on air power can be induced; Myles' detailed history of the Harrier jump jet is a representative example (122).

(4) Defense Economics. The fundamental problem of British defense policy in the post-war period has been one of matching resources to commitments; periodic reviews and the adjustment of commitments to meet financial and economic constraints has been a constant feature of the conduct of defense policy in Britain. Britain spends markedly more on defense as a proportion of GNP than the majority of her NATO allies. This has lead to pressures for a reduction, pressures that are likely to increase since the 1979 NATO commitment to a 3% real growth in defense spending ended in 1985. From 1986, the MOD is almost certain to face a period of, at best, zero growth and it is unlikely that present commitments and weapons projects will be matched by projected resources. Difficult choices will have to be made in the near future.

The centrality of economics has meant that it is almost a requirement that general books on defense policy in Britain have at least one chapter on the economic constraints that British policymakers face. A general introduction to the subject of defense economics and the British experience is provided by Kennedy (104) and a general picture of the relationship between policy and public expenditure decisions is provided by Heclo and Wildavsky (89). The budgetary process with regard to defense has been analysed by Greenwood (78), Hobkirk (91), Hartley (86) and Burt (25).

Equipment-related expenditure accounts for nearly half the total defense budget and there is, therefore, considerable interest in the process of procurement and its impact on industry and the economy. The government and the MOD itself is currently concerned to get the best deal for its money and the Defence Committee (186) and the Committee of Public Accounts (194) have both been critical of the MOD's method of procurement and project management. The MOD has itself been sufficiently concerned with the manner in which the system works to suggest reforms particularly in the tendering of contracts (173, 201, 205). The process of procurement has also been studied by Isaac and Courtney (95) and Wood (161) has put it within the framework of the handling of government projects in general. Details of the procurement process can also be found in the occasional papers *Asides* (286) and *Adelphi Papers* (287).

Details of the defense industry can be obtained from a variety of sources; one of the principal ones is that published by Jordan's (232), a survey of the top 500 or so defense contracts collected every 3-4 years (now in its 3rd edition). Information on the defense industry can be kept up to date through *Jane's Defence Weekly* (230) and technical trade periodicals such as the *Engineer* (263). There have also been changes in the structure of the government's own defense production sector; for example, the Royal Ordnance Factories are to be fully privatized by 1986 (203) and so in due course are British Shipbuilders and British Aerospace. The Bradford University School of Peace Studies (292) and the Science Policy Research Unit (215) at the University of Sussex also hold information on the British defense industries.

Defense spending has effects on the economy beyond the immediate impact of spending on specific industries (125). Bellini and Pattie argue that defense spending stimulates industrial activity (16), and studies by the Labour Party Defence Group (108, 99) have come to the opposite conclusion examining in depth the deleterious effect that defense expenditure has on investment, employment, research and on the economy in general. They argue that more employment and improved economic performance would follow from defense cutbacks and an industrial conversion programme. Chalmers (35) has looked not simply at the contemporary period but has also argued that a factor in Britain's decline throughout the whole of the twentieth century has been her overly large annual defense expenditure.

The argument that defense spending is bad for the economy is countered largely by reference to two factors, the phenomena of "spin-off," that is to say the transfer of technology--products or processes--from the military sector to the civil sector, and the contribution to the balance of payments of arms exports. The debate remains largely anecdotal since there is not at present any effective measurement of its extent or form. The result is that few works have concentrated on "spin-off," although others have focused on military R and D to which it can be related. The organization and nature of the British defense R and D effort has been recorded by a Council on Science and Society Report (163) which is critical of the lack of the readily available data on the subject and hence the lack of effective accountability. Of the 2.2 billion spent by the MOD on R and D in 1984-85 about a third is spent within the MOD on research establishments which have themselves been undergoing a process of reorganization (202). The only available statistics on the allocation of R and D resources to industry can be found in the *Annual Review of Government R and D* (209). Kaldor (101) has analysed the effect of military R and D and concludes that it has inhibited economic growth by diverting resources from civil enterprises and that its military effect has been to produce equipment that is increasingly expensive and too complex. Directly concerned with spin-off, but in the electronics sector, the Maddock report (114) found that industry was inadequately organized to be able to fully exploit spin-off potential.

Britain ranks fourth among the world's arms exporters and accounts for some 25-30% of all arms production in the UK with an estimated 3.5% by value of external trade. Nevertheless there is no single work covering British arms sales. There is, however, coverage in many of the works that deal with the defense industry and arms production including that of Freedman (68). Other works include a RUSI Seminar on Defence Policy and Arms Sales (135) and chapters in several books dealing with arms sales in general (31, 136) as well as numerous articles in the defense related journals and periodicals.

The belief that Britain spends more than it ought on defense has led to several authors suggesting means of reducing the defense burden either by reducing commitments or by changing the manner by which Britain purchases her equipment. At one end of the spectrum there is the "conversion" literature found in several journals, occasional papers (293) and books (30) which aim to reduce substantially Britain's defense commitments by proposing a non-nuclear posture and a reduction in overseas obligations; this would then release the defense industry for civil production. Others accept that major commitments are unlikely to change very much and recognize that the need is therefore for less elaborate or less expensive equipment--quantity rather than quality (13, 139). Collaboration is one road down which the production of defense equipment might go and this option has been analysed by Hartley (87), Freedman (68) and Edmonds (54). Williams (159) has considered the prospects of European collaboration in general and the broader issues it raises. Buying "off the shelf" is an option that has been advocated by Hartley, and one that, as Britain falls further and further behind in an increasing number of technological fields, would appear to be an increasing possibility. Whatever the choices are made the economic environment is likely to remain the fundamental problem area for British defense planners.

(5) **Operations.** Since 1969 two operations directly involving the British Armed Forces have dominated: these are Northern Ireland and the Falklands War, and will be treated separately below. Nonetheless, other operations since 1945 have attracted scholarly or publishers' interest, though the thirty year rule has precluded any work

based on primary source material after 1955. Suez has been of constant interest, and to the numerous books published before 1970 Fullick (72) and Love (112) can be included. Nothing of significance has appeared of colonial "fire fighting" operations in, for example, Kenya, Malaya, or Cyprus though Gavin's account of the British in Aden (73), James and Sheil-Small's study of Borneo (96), and Jeapers' "look at the SAS in Oman" (97) at least are reminders of Britain's involvement outside Europe since 1945.

In a more general context Harbottle (83), Kitson (105) and Carver (33), each at one time having become a senior ranking officer in the army, offer an insight into the British Army in the execution of their duties as colonial policemen. As an insight into the British imperial past, they provide a useful personal account and perspective; one day they may even serve in historical research as a good indicator of the restraint, impartiality and temperance of the British soldier on colonial duty.

Northern Ireland. A vast amount of literature has been published about the situation in Northern Ireland and it is not the intention here to cover all these works. The object is to cover those books which are concerned directly with the conduct of the security operations in the province. For those who wish to study the Northern Ireland situation in greater detail the books by Rose (133), Darby (45), Stewart (144), Farrell (63), Uttley (154), *The Sunday Times* (147) and Flackes (65) are recommended as well as the numerous government reports (168).

Between 1969-84, 385 British soldiers had been killed whilst serving in Northern Ireland; serving with the Ulster Defence Regiment, a part-time regiment of the British Army raised exclusively in the early 1970s for duties in the province (172), 145 members have to date lost their lives. Of the local police force, the Royal Ulster Constabulary, 208 members have been killed in the same period. The number of troops stationed in the North peaked in July 1972 when it reached 21,000; today there are less than 7,000, but this is still three times more than when the current troubles began in 1969.

General books on Northern Ireland or terrorism that include sections on the security situation include Wilkinson (158) and Watt (155); both include some useful descriptive accounts. By far the most useful work to any student of the British Army in Northern Ireland are the four volumes by David Barzilay (10) chronicling the activities of the British Army in Ulster from 1969 to 1980. Lt. Col. Michael Dewar (48) has also published an account of the army in Northern Ireland, although this is a somewhat selective work aiming largely, it would seem, to portray the army in the best possible light. Other ex-soldiers have tackled Northern Ireland: Clarke's pictorial account (37) of his time there conveys a sense of the sort of conditions with which the army was confronted, as does a book by Patrick chronicling the activities of the bomb disposal squad (124). Ex RGJ Robin Evelegh's work (60) is more thoughtful as he engages in a discussion on the rights of the soldier in situations of civil unrest and the sort of legal machinery the military believe that they require to conduct properly an internal security role in Northern Ireland. In a more general study Bonner (19) has undertaken a detailed legal analysis of the powers available to the security forces during an emergency, both to combat terrorism and to deal with essential services. Riot control is one of the most difficult areas, and in work carried out by Deanne-Drummond (47) he recommends the use of baton-rounds (his study was sponsored by Schemerly Ltd., a manufacturer of internal security equipment) and video taping to provide evidence. Bomb disposal is another, graphicly described from personal experience by Styles (145).

More critical to army operations but still largely supportive of their role is a book by Hamill (80). This is useful work since it goes into much detail over the nature of Army-RUC relations which is really at the crux of internal security operations in the province. If there is a middle-ground in the literature of the army in Northern Ireland then Hamill's work is probably it. On the anti-establishment side is a work by a French journalist, Roger Faligot (61) who approaches the operations of the army from the viewpoint of trying to establish that their conduct in Northern Ireland was an attempt to put into practice the theories of General Sir Frank Kitson (106). Patsy McArdle (118) has also considered the evidence against the army with regard to illegal activities, notably border-crossing.

Some writers have gone beyond the Northern Ireland context and considered the army's role in internal security in a wider framework. Clutterbuck (38) has expressed concern over the growth of political violence in the UK, particularly during industrial disputes, but argues against using the army to support the police in the maintenance of public order. Northern Ireland, he agrees, was different in that both the rioters and the police were armed, and a large proportion of the Catholic minority accepted neither the law nor its upholders, the RUC. The dilemma of liberal societies in tackling terrorism has been approached by Wilkinson (158), but he believes that some aspects of a liberal legal system have to be suspended e.g. non-jury courts, special powers of detention--exclusion, if the terrorists are to be combatted effectively.

Clutterbuck, Wilkinson and others (39) are strong advocates of media control in terrorist conflicts both as a means of denying a valuable propaganda weapon to the terrorists but also as a means of putting over the government's position most effectively. In a Northern Irish context Curtis (43) has argued that media manipulation is the apotheosis of the conflict.

The present conflict in Northern Ireland has been a running sore in the side of the British Army and the British Government in general since 1969. Although the extent of the "troubles" is now very low compared with the peak of 1971-72, it shows no signs of abating fully. Much has been written on the conflict already, and it is likely that still more remains to be written.

The Falklands. Like the Vietnam war, the Falklands conflict was fought--despite the government's attempts to control the flow and content of information--in a daily blaze of publicity in the press and, of course, on the television. It was inevitable, therefore, given both the successful outcome to the war and the height of public interest--if not xenophobia--in the war that in its wake there should have been a substantial number of books and memoirs about the conflict and those who served in it. In the scramble to be first into print, and therefore the most successful, commercially, the accuracy and judgement of many of the books produced left much to be desired. However, the sheer number of them in a short period virtually ensured that scarcely any aspect of the conflict was ignored or overlooked. And for those who have lost the habit of reading, there were also the video tapes produced by both the BBC and the Independent Television channels.

First into print were books by those journalists who had reported on the war for their respective newspapers, and who had accompanied the task force to the South Atlantic. The very first was a joint endeavour by Dobson, et al. (50) who managed to get into print before the war had even ended. High among this group of journalists are the general accounts of the war of Fox (67), Bishop and Witherow (17), Hastings and Jenkins (88) Hanrahan and Fox (82), and the *Sunday Times* Insight Team (148). For a pictorial record, and one which is full of topographical interest, there is the *Sunday Express Magazine* collection of photographs (146), and the commissioned drawings of the official war artist, Kitson (107).

The particular contribution of the services in the conflict have not been ignored, though have tended to take a little longer to appear. Most accounts have come out in article form in journals, but a number of books have emerged since 1982. The three Osprey "Men at War" series books on the Navy, Army and Air Force in the Falklands by English and Watts (58), Fowler (66), and Braybrook (20) warrant mention. On the naval contribution, specifically, and the lessons of the conflict for future naval operations,--and assuming these lessons were not patently evident after the *Prince of Wales* experience--there is the Ministry of Defence's own Report (175) and Preston's *Sea Combat off the Falklands* (128). Other service based books are those of Speed (141), Frost (71) and Ethell (59).

The Falklands war was not without its critics. Robert Harris' analysis of the relationship between the media and the government (85) is a valuable analysis of a difficult subject, to which the Ministry of Defence's own Report on the Protection of Military Information, the House of Commons Defence Committee Enquiry (187) and Hooper's more conceptual study of the military and the media (93) should be added. Equally valuable, and no less objectively and constructively critical is the report of the committee of enquiry into the Falklands crisis chaired by Lord Franks (176) and the Report of the House of Commons Defence Committee (187). Political opposition to the war may be found in the books and monographs by Barnett (7), Dalyell (44) and Arblaster (4). For an account of the sinking of the *Belgrano*, and the political repurcussions, Ponting's case (127) and the more general study by Gavshon and Rice (74) should be consulted.

Without question the most poignant rejection of the war and the motives behind it, at least in the judgement of the author, must be Hugh Tinker's testament to his son, Lieutenant David Tinker RN, who was killed whilst serving on HMS *Glamorgan* in the last few days of the war (151).

With the benefit of time to reflect, relieved of the commercial pressures to rush into print, the judged analysis of Calvert (28) should be mentioned. With further time to look back on the episode and to check to various accounts, the International Institute for Strategic Studies has commissioned a thorough study of the Falklands war, with a view to its publication in 1987.

Conclusion. Compared with the period up to 1968, the last seventeen years has witnessed a prolifery of books, articles, reports, studies and pamphlets on British defense policy and practice. In a manner of speaking, this should have been expected as the constraints of the thirty year rule cease to apply up to the period ending 1955. However, little seems to have been done which takes advantage of the public record. Scarcely anything has been done, for example, on the Korean War, or the post-war rearmament programme, the various colonial conflicts, such as Palestine, though the release of public documents on the Suez crisis might generate interest.

The marked expansion of defense literature, therefore, has to be directly related to a general recognition that defense has become a major public issue, and one that extends beyond the purely parochial concerns of the British Isles. Britain is still a major military power with an independent nuclear capability. It has alliance commitments in Europe and maintains a presence beyond the NATO area. There is also the concern for home defense, an increasingly disturbing issue in the light of international terrorist developments and a marked increase in militancy at home in industrial and political disputes. At the same time, Britain has declined economically as the cost of its defense commitments has increased, with the effect that something, sometime, will have to give. It will be a matter of choices, and where there are choices, there is political interest. Without doubt, the literature on British defense policy and practice has a promising future; but how much of it will be of a scholarly nature must remain an imponderable.

BIBLIOGRAPHY

Books

1. Ackroyd, C., K. Margolis et al. *The Technology of Political Control*. London: Pelican Books, 1977.
2. Alford, J., and P. Nailors. *The Future of Britain's Deterrent Force*. London: IISS, 1980.
3. Alternative Defence Commission. *Defence without the Bomb*. London: Taylor and Francis, 1983.
4. Arblaster, A. *The Falklands: Thatcher's War*. London: Socialist Society, 1982.
5. Barker, D. *Soldiering On*. London: Deutsch, 1981.
6. Barker, J. (Bishop of Salisbury). *The Church and the Bomb*. London: Hodder and Stoughton, 1982.
7. Barnett, A. *Iron Britannia*. London: Alison and Busby, 1982.
8. Barnett, C. *Britain and her Army*. London: Allen Lane, 1970.
9. ———. *The Long Retreat*. London: MacMillan, 1972.
10. Barzilay, D. *The British Army in Ulster*. vols. 1-4. London: Century, 1983.
11. Baylis, J. (ed.) *British Defence Policy in a Changing World*. London: Croom Helm, 1977.
12. ———. *Anglo American Defence Relations 1939-80*. London: MacMillan, 1981.
13. ———. *Alternative Approaches to British Defence Policy*. London: MacMillan, 1984.
14. Beach, H. "British Forces in Germany" in Martin Edmonds *The Defence Equation*. London: Brassey's, 1986.

Defence Policy and Practice

15. Beckett, F.W., and J. Gooch. *Politicians and Defence.* Manchester: Manchester University Press, 1981.
16. Bellini, J., and G. Pattie. *A New World Role for the Medium Power: The British Opportunity.* London: RUSI, 1978.
17. Bishop, P., and J. Witherow. *The Winter War.* London: Quartet, 1982.
18. Blaxland, G. *The Regiments Depart.* London: Kimber 1971.
19. Bonner, D. *Emergency Powers in Peacetime.* London: Street Maxwell, 1985.
20. Braybrook, R. *Air Forces.* London: Osprey, 1982.
21. Brady, L., and J. Kaufman. *NATO in the 1980s.* New York: Praeger, 1985.
22. Brett, J. *A Short History of the RAF.* London: HMSO, 1984.
23. Broadhurst, A. *The Future of European Alliance Systems.* Boulder: Westview, 1982.
24. Brookes, A. *V Force: The History of Britain's Airborne Deterrent.* London: Janes, 1982.
25. Burt, R. *Defence Budgeting.* London: IISS, 1975.
26. Cable, J. *Gunboat Diplomacy.* London: Chatto and Windus, 1971.
27. ———. *Britain's Naval Future.* London: Macmillan, 1983.
28. Calvert, P. *The Falklands Crisis.* London: Pinter, 1982.
29. Cameron, N. (Chairman). *Diminishing the Nuclear Threat.* London: BAC, 1984.
30. Campbell, D. *The Unsinkable Aircraft Carrier.* London: Joseph, 1984.
31. Canizzo, C. *The Gun Merchants.* New York: Pergamon, 1980.
32. Carver, Lord. *A Policy for Peace.* London: Faber, 1982.
33. ———. *War Since 1945.* London: Wiedenfeld, 1980.
34. Chapman, L. *Your Disobedient Servant.* London: Chatto and Windus, 1978.
35. Chalmers, M. *Paying for Defence.* London: Pluto, 1985.
36. Chichester, M., and J. Wilkinson. *The Uncertain Ally: British Defence Policy 1960-1990.* London: Gower, 1982.
37. Clarke, A. *Contact.* London: Pan, 1984.
38. Clutterbuck, R. *Britain in Agony.* London: Faber, 1978.
39. ———. *Media and Political Violence.* London: MacMillan, 1981.
40. Coates, K., P. Duff et al. *Eleventh Hour for Europe.* London: Spokesman, 1981.
41. Cooper, F. "Perhaps Minister: Political and Military Relations Today and in the Future," *RUSI Journal*, vol. 128, no. 1 (March 1983), pp. 3-6.
42. Cox, J. *Overkill.* London: Penguin, 1977.
43. Curtis, L. *Northern Ireland. The Propaganda War.* London: Pluto, 1984.
44. Dalyell, T. *One Man's Falklands.* London: Woolf, 1982.
45. Darby, J. *Conflict in Northern Ireland.* Dublin: Gill and Macmillan, 1976.
46. Darby, P. *British Defence Policy East of Suez 1947-68.* London: Oxford University Press, 1973.
47. Deanne-Drummond, A. *Riot Control.* London: Bartholomew, 1975.
48. Dewar, M. *The British Army in Northern Ireland.* London: Arms and Armour Press, 1985.
49. Dillon, M. *Dependency and Deterrence.* Aldershot: Gower, 1983.

50. Dobson, C. *The Falklands Conflict*. London: Hodder and Stoughton, 1982.
51. Downes, C. "Officer Education and Training." Lancaster, Unpublished PhD, 1983.
52. Edmonds, M., and R. Beaumont. *War in the Next Decade*. London: MacMillan, 1971.
53. ———, and J. Gooch. "Military Studies in the United Kingdom" in Colin Milner (ed.) *Conflict Studies in Higher Education*. Romford: ISCCS, 1981.
54. ——— (ed.) *International Arms Procurement*. New York: Pergamon, 1981.
55. ——— (ed.) *Central Organizations of Defence*. London: F. Pinter, 1985.
56. ———. *Peace Movements in Contemporary Europe: Britain*. Pittsburgh: UCIS, 1984.
57. ——— (ed.) *The Defence Equation*. London: Brasseys, 1986.
58. English, A., and A. Watts. *Naval Forces*. London: Osprey, 1982.
59. Ethell, J., and A. Price. *Air War South Atlantic*. London: Sidgwick and Jackson, 1983.
60. Evelegh, R. *Peacekeeping in a Democratic Society*. London: Hurst, 1979.
61. Faligot, R. *British Military Strategy in Northern Ireland*. London: Zed Press, 1983.
62. *Famous Regiments Series*. (ed. Gen. Horrocks) London: Leo Cooper.
63. Farrell, M. *Northern Ireland, the Orange State*. London: Pluto, 1980.
64. Fedder, E. *Defence Politics of the Atlantic Alliance*. New York: Praeger, 1980.
65. Flackes, W. *Northern Ireland: A Political Directory*. London: Aeriel, 1984.
66. Fowler, W. *Land Forces*. London: Osprey, 1982.
67. Fox, R. *Eyewitness Falklands*. London: Methuen, 1982.
68. Freedman, L. *Arms Production and Prospects in the United Kingdom*. London: RIIA, 1978.
69. ———. *Evolution of Nuclear Strategy*. London: MacMillan, 1980.
70. ———. *Britain and Nuclear Weapons*. London: MacMillan, 1980.
71. Frost, J. *2 Para Falklands*. London: Buchan and Knight, 1983.
72. Fullick, R., and G. Powell. *Suez, the Double War*. London: Hamish Hamilton, 1979.
73. Gavin, J. *Aden under British Rule 1839-1967*. London: Hurst, 1976.
74. Gavshon, A., and B. Rice. *Sinking the Belgrano*. London: Secker and Warburg, 1984.
75. Geraghty, A. *Who Dares, Wins*. London: Arms and Armour, 1980.
76. Gowing, Margaret. *Britain and Atomic Energy*. London: MacMillan, 1964.
77. Gowing, Margaret, and L. Arnold. *Independence and Deterrence*. volumes I and II. London: MacMillan, 1974.
78. Greenwood, D. *Budgeting for Defence*. London: RUSI, 1972.
79. Hackett, Sir John. *The Third World War*. London: Sphere, 1978.
80. Hamill, D. *Pig in the Middle: The Army in Northern Ireland*. London: Methuen, 1985.

Defence Policy and Practice

81. Hampshire, C. *The Royal Navy Since 1945*. London: Kimber, 1975.
82. Hanrahan, B. and R. Fox. *I Counted Them All Out And I Counted Them All Back*. London: BBC, 1982.
83. Harbottle, M. *The Impartial Soldier*. London: Oxford, 1969.
84. Harries-Jenkins, G. *Trade Unions in Armed Forces*. Hull: IUS, 1976.
85. Harris, R. *Gotcha: The Media, the Government, and the Falklands Crisis*. London: Faber, 1983.
86. Hartley, K. "The British Experience" in G. Harries-Jenkins (ed.) *Armed Forces and Welfare Societies*. London: MacMillan, 1982.
87. ————. *NATO Arms Cooperation*. London: Allen and Unwin, 1983.
88. Hastings, M., and S. Jenkins. *The Battle for the Falklands*. London: Joseph, 1983.
89. Heclo, H. and A. Wildavsky. *The Private Government of Public Money*. London: Macmillan, 1974.
90. Hill-Norton, P. *No Soft Options*. London: Hurst, 1977.
91. Hobkirk, M. *The Politics of Defence Budgeting*. London: MacMillan, 1984.
92. Hockaday, A. "Budgeting for Defence," *RUSI Journal*. volume 124, no. 4 (1979), pp. 3-10.
93. Hooper, A. *The Military and the Media*. Aldershot: Gower, 1983.
94. Howard, M. *The Central Organisation of Defence*. London: RUSI, 1970.
95. Isaac, P., and K. Courtney, "Procurement for the Armed Forces, I and II" *Procurement*, Jan./Feb. 1975.
96. James, H., and D. Sheil-Small. *The Undeclared War*. London: Leo Cooper, 1970.
97. Jeapes, A. *SAS, Operation Oman*. London: Kimber, 1980.
98. Johnson, F.A. *Defence by Ministry*. London: Duckworth, 1979.
99. Kaldor, M., D. Smith and S. Vires (eds.) *Democratic Socialism and the Cost of Defence*. London: Croom Helm, 1979.
100. ————, and D. Smith. *Disarming Europe*. London: Merlin, 1982.
101. ————. *The Baroque Arsenal*. London: Deutsch, 1982.
102. Keegan, J. "Regimental Ideology" in G. Best and A. Wheatcroft *War, Economy and the Military Mind*. London: Croom Helm, 1976.
103. Kennedy, G. *Burden Sharing in NATO*. London: Duckworth, 1979.
104. ————. *Defence Economics*. London: Cowman and Litchfield, 1975.
105. Kitson, F. *Bunch of Fives*. London: Faber, 1977.
106. ————. *Low Intensity Operations*. London: Faber, 1971.
107. Kitson, L. *The Falklands War: A Visual Diary*. London: Mitchell Beasley, 1982.
108. Labour Party Study Group. *Sense about Defence*. London: Quartet, 1977.
109. Laurie, P. *Beneath the City Streets*. London: Panther, 1979.
110. Lee, D. *Flight from the Middle East*. London: HMSO, 1980.
111. ————. *The RAF in Germany 1945-78*. London: HMSO, 1982.
112. Love, K. *Suez--Twice Fought War*. London: Longmans, 1970.
113. Macksey, K. *The Tanks: History of the RTR 1945-75*. London: Arms and Armour, 1979.

114. Maddock, I. Civil Exploitation of Defence Technology. London: NEDO, 1983.
115. McMahan, J. British Nuclear Weapons. London: Junction Books, 1981.
116. Martin, L. (ed.) Defence Management. London: MacMillan, 1976.
117. Mason, R.A. Readings in Air Power. Bracknell: RAF Staff College, 1980.
118. McArdle, P. The Secret War. Cork: Mercer Press, 1985.
119. McLean, S. How Nuclear Weapons Decisions Are Made. London: MacMillan, 1986.
120. Menaul, S. Countdown. Britain's Strategic Forces. London: Hale, 1980.
121. Myers, K. NATO. The Next Thirty Years. Boulder: Westview, 1979.
122. Myles, B. Jump jet--The Revolutionary V/S TOL Fighter. London: Brasseys, 1978.
123. Owen, D. The Politics of Defence. London: Cape, 1972.
124. Patrick, D. Fetch Flix. London: Hamilton, 1980.
125. Pavit, K. (ed.) Technical Change and British Economic Performance. London: MacMillan, 1980.
126. Pierre, A. Nuclear Politics. London: Oxford University Press, 1972.
127. Ponting, C. The Right to Know. London: Sphere, 1985.
128. Preston, A. Sea Combat off the Falklands. London: Willow, 1982.
129. Reed, B., and G. Williams. Dennis Healey and the Policies of Power. London: Sidgwick and Jackson, 1971.
130. Reychler, L., and R. Rudney. Directory Guide of European Security and Defense Research. New York: Pergamon Brassey's, 1985.
131. Rodger, D. The Admiralty. Lavenham: T. Daltrey, 1979.
132. Roper, J. (ed.) The Future of British Defence Policy. Aldershot: Gower, 1985.
133. Rose, R. Governing without Consensus. Boston: Beacon, 1971.
134. Rosencrance, R. Defense of the Realm. New York: Columbia University Press, 1968.
135. Royal United Services Institution. Weapons Procurement, Defence Management and International Collaboration. London: RUSI, 1972.
136. Sampson, A. The Arms Bazaar. London: Hodder and Stoughton, 1977.
137. Simpson, J. The Independent Nuclear State. London: MacMillan, 1984.
138. Smart, I. The Future of the British Nuclear Deterrent. London: RIIA, 1977.
139. Smith, D. The Defence of the Realm in the 1980s. London: Croom Helm, 1980.
140. Snyder, W. The Politics of British Defence Policy. London: Benn, 1964.
141. Speed, K. Sea Change. Bath: Ashgrove, 1982.
142. Staerke, A. de. NATO's Anxious Birth. London: Hurst, 1985.
143. Stanhope, H. The Soldiers. London: Hamish Hamilton, 1979.
144. Stewart, A. The Narrow Ground. London: Faber, 1977.
145. Styles, G. Bombs Have no Pity. London: Luscombe, 1975.

146. Sunday Express Magazine. *War in the Falklands*. London: Weidenfeld and Nicolson, 1982.
147. Sunday Times Insight Team. *Ulster*. Harmondsworth: Penguin, 1972.
148. ―――――. *The Falklands War*. London: Sphere, 1982.
149. Taylor, T. *Defence Technology and International Integration*. London: F. Pinter, 1982.
150. Thompson, E.P. *Protest and Survive*. London: Penguin, 1980.
151. Tinker, H. *Last Message from the Falklands*. London: Penguin, 1983.
152. Trevenan-James, A. *The RAF: The Past 30 Years*. London: MacDonald and James, 1976.
153. Twitchett, K. *International Security*. London: Oxford University Press, 1970.
154. Uttley, T. *Lessons of Ulster*. London: Dent, 1985.
155. Watt, D. (ed.) *The Constitution of Northern Ireland*. London: Heinemann, 1981.
156. Weston, D. "Mother, Sister, Mistress?: The British Regiment" in M. Edmonds *The Defence Equation*. London: Brasseys, 1986.
157. Williams, G. Lee., I. Richard et al. *Europe or the Open Sea*. London: Knight, 1970.
158. Wilkinson, P. (ed.) *British Perspectives on Terrorism*. London: Allen and Unwin, 1981.
159. Williams, R. *European Technology*. London: Croom Helm, 1973.
160. Windass, S. (ed.) *Avoiding Nuclear War*. London: Brassey's, 1985.
161. Wood, D. *Project Cancelled*. London: MacDonald, 1976.
162. Ziegler, P. *Mountbatten*. London: Guild, 1985.
163. Ziman, J. et al. *British Military Research and Development*. London: Council on Science and Society and Oxford University Press, 1986.
164. Zuckerman, S. *Nuclear Illusion and Reality*. London: Collins, 1982.

Official Sources

165. Command Papers
166.   *MOD Responses to Commons Committee Reports* 1945
167.   *Statements on the Defence Estimates* 1968--Published Annually.
168.   *Supplementary Statements on the Defence Estimates* 1968-- Issued intermittantly: 1970, Cmnd 4521
169.   *Disturbances in Northern Ireland* (Cameron Report) Belfast 1969, Cmnd 532.
170.   *Structure and Composition of the RUC* (Hunt Report) Belfast 1969, Cmnd 535.
171.   *Violence and Disturbance in Northern Ireland* (Scarman Report) Belfast 1969, Cmnd 566.
172.   *Formation of the Ulster Defence Regiment*. London 1969, Cmnd 4641.
173.   *Government Organisation for Defence Procurement and Aerospace* (Rayner Report) London 1971, Cmnd 4641.
174.   *The United Kingdom Defence Programme: The Way Forward*. London 1981, Cmnd 8288.
175.   *The Falklands Campaign: The Lessons*. London 1982, Cmnd 8758.

176. Falkland Islands, Review (Franks Report) 1983, Cmnd 8787.
177. The Central Organisation of Defence. London, Cmnd 9315.
178. House of Commons Papers
179. (1) Select Committee on Expenditure: Defence and External Affairs sub-Committee 1963-1979 (HMSO London).
180. 5th Report Defence Cuts 1973/4 HC208.
181. 2nd Report The Defence Review Proposals 1974/5 HC259.
182. 8th Report Defence Expenditure 1977-8 HC600.
183. (2) Defence Committee 1979--present.
184. 3rd Report Stingray Torpedo 1980/81 HC218 and Government Response HC 473.
185. Special Report Nuclear Weapons Policy 1980/81 HC130.
186. 2nd Report Ministry of Defence Organisation and Procurement 1981/2 HC22.
187. 1st Report Handling of Press and Public Information during the Falklands Crisis. 1982/3 HC17.
188. 3rd Report Ministry of Defence Reorganisation 1983/4 HC584.
189. (3) Public Accounts Committee 1945--present.
190. (a) Appropriation Accounts (Defence) with the Report of the Comptroller and Auditor General thereon, 1945--present.
191. (b) Public Accounts Committee Reports.
192. 9th Report The Chevaline Improvement to the Polaris Missile System 1981/2 HC269.
193. 19th Report The UK Trident Programme 1983/4 HC348.
194. 25th Report Profit Formula for non-Competitive Government Contracts: Ministry of Defence 1984/5 HC390.
195. (4) Other Commons Committees
196. (i) Science and Technology
Defence Research 1967-8 HC137 I-XXII
197. (ii) Foreign Affairs
5th Report Falkland Islands 1983/4 HC268 I and II.
198. (iii) Treasury and Civil Service
3rd Report Efficiency and Effectiveness in the Civil Service 1981/2 HC326 Vols 1-111.
199. (5) Government Department Publications/Consultative Documents (Green Papers).
200. (i) Ministry of Defence
201. Study into the Financial Security of Defence Requirements 1979. 81/8.
202. R and D Establishments (Strathcona Report) MOD 1980.
203. The Future of the Royal Ordnance Factories 1981 81/28.
204. The UK Trident Programme 1982 82/01.
205. Value for Money in Defence Procurement 1983 83/01.
206. Territorial Army Expansion 1986-90 1984 84/02.
207. MINIS and the Development of the Organisation for Defence 1984 84/03.
208. The Future of the Royal Dockyards 1985 85/01.
209. (ii) The Cabinet Office
——————— Government R and D
210. (6) Parliamentary Debates
211. Hansard: House of Commons Debates 1945
House of Lords Debates 1945
212. (7) Government Publications
213. Monthly List, London: HMSO.

Periodicals (With first date of Publication, place of publication and where indexed.)

214. (i) <u>With significant interest in British Defence Issues</u>
215. *ADIU Report.* Falmer, SPRU Sussex University. 1979-- (Not indexed).
216. *Arms Control.* London, 1980--(Not indexed).
217. *Armed Forces.* London, 1982--(DMT; PROMT).
218. *Atlantic Quarterly.* London, 1983--(SSHI).
219. *Army Quarterly and Defence Journal.* Tavistock, 1829-- (CML; AULI; PAIS; PROMT).
220. *Brassey's Defence Yearbook.* London, 1886--(CML).
221. *Defence Analysis.* London, 1985--(CML).
222. *Defence Attache.* London, 1960--(CML).
223. *Defence Communications and Security Review.* London, (No Date) (CML).
224. *Defence.* Windsor, 1970--(CML; DMT; PROMT).
225. *Defence Helicopter World.* London, 1982--(CML).
226. *Defence Materiel.* London, 1976--(CML; DMT; PROMT).
227. *International Affairs.* London, 1922--(BHI; PAIS; MPI; SSHI; IBSS).
228. *International Law Enforcement.* Eton, (No Date) (CML).
229. *Interstate.* Aberystwyth, (No Date) (CML).
230. *Jane's Defence Weekly.* London, 1984--(CML; DMT).
231. *Jane's Military Review.* London, (No Date) (CML).
232. *Jordan's British Defence Industry.* London, (not indexed).
233. *Journal of Strategic Studies.* London, 1978--(CML; CC).
234. *Military Affairs.* Manhattan, KS, 1937--(CML; AULI; CC; HA).
235. *Military Technology.* Bonn, 1976--(CML; PROMT).
236. *Miltronics.* Maidenhead, 1983--(CML; DMT; PROMT).
237. *NATO Review.* London, 1953--(CML; DMT).
238. *NATO's 16 Nations.* Farnborough 1956 (AULI; CML; DMT; MPI).
239. *Navy International.* Hazelmere, 1895--(DMT; PROMT).
240. *Royal United Services Institute Journal.* London, 1857--(PAIS; BHI; AULI; DMT).
241. *Sanity.* London, 1961--(CML).
242. *Survival.* London, 1959--(CML).
243. (ii) <u>Major Service Journals/Service Publications of Significance</u>
244. *Air Clues.* London, 1946--(not indexed).
245. *Army Quarterly and Defence Journal.* London, 1829-- (AULI; PAIS; PROMT).
246. *British Army Review.* London, 1967--(CML).
247. *Globe and Laurel.* Southsea, 1892--(CML).
248. *Hawk.* Cranwell, 1982--(not indexed).
249. *Journal of the Royal Signals Institute.* London, (No Date) (CML).
250. *Naval Forces.* Farnborough, 1980--(CML; DMT; PROMT).
251. *RAF Quarterly.* London, 1930--(AULI).
252. *Royal Artillery Journal.* Woolwich, 1858--(CML).

253. *Royal Engineers Journal.* Chatham, 1870--(CML; CA; EI).
254. *REME Journal.* Arborfield, (No Date) (CML).
255. *Tank.* London, 1919--(CML).
256. *Waggoner.* (and RCT Review) Aldershot, 1891--(CML).
257. Plus Regimental Journal and Service Establishment in-house publications. Including: *Claymore*, (1950); *Devonport News*, (1969); *Fusilier*, (1969); *Guards Magazine* (1862); *Kingsman*, (1970); *Lioness*, (1945); *Pegasus*, (1946); *Provost Parade*, (1947); *Queens Own Highlander*, (1961); *Royal Army Pay Corps Journal*, (1931); *Royal Military Police Journal*, (1950); *Royal Pioneer*, (1942); and *Torch*, (1967).

(iii) Magazines/Periodicals with regular coverage of British Defence

258. *Aeronautical Journal.* London, 1897--(ASTI; BTI; CA; CC; DMT; EI; PROMT; SI).
259. *Air International.* London, 1971--(DMT; PROMT; SI).
260. *Aviation Week and Space Technology.* Hightstown, N.J., 1916--(ASTI; BPI; BTI; CA; DMT; PROMT; RG).
261. *Economist.* London, 1843--(BHI; BPI; PAIS; PROMT; SSHI).
262. *Encounter.* London, 1953--(BHI; PAIS).
263. *Engineer.* London, 1856--(ASTI; BTI; CA; CC; EIPROMT).
264. *Flight International.* Sutton, 1909--(AULI; BTI; CC; DMT; EI; PROMT).
265. *International Defence Review.* Geneva, (CMI; DMT; PROMPT).
266. *Interavia.* Geneva, 1946 (PROMT; SA).
267. *Maritime Defence.* London, 1976, (DMT; PROMT).
268. *New Scientist.* London, 1956--London (ASTI; BTI; CC; PROMT; SA).
269. *New Statesman.* London, 1913--(BHI; SSHI).
270. *Spectator.* London, 1828--(BHI).
271. (iv) Journals with occasional serious articles on British Defence
272. *Armed Forces and Society.* Chicago, 1974 (CML; IBSS; SSHI).
273. *Catalyst.* London, 1984--(not indexed).
274. *Foreign Affairs.* New York, 1922--(IBSS; PAIS; PROMT; SSHI).
276. *International Security.* Cambridge MS, 1978--(CML; DMT; HA; PAIS; PROMT).
277. *Orbis.* Philadelphia, 1957--(CC; CML; IBSS: PAIS; SSHI).
278. *Parliamentary Affairs.* London, 1947--(BHI; CC; PAIS; SSHI).
279. *Political Quarterly.* London, 1930--(BHI; CC; IBSS: PAIS; SSHI).
280. *Public Administration.* London, 1923--(BHI; PAIS; IBSS).
281. *Review of International Studies.* 1975--(Not indexed).
282. *World Politics.* Princeton, 1948--(CC; HA; IBSS; PAIS; SSHI).
283. *World Today.* London, 1945--(CC; CML; PAIS; SSHI).

Defence Policy and Practice

284. Yearbook of World Affairs. London, 1947--(IBSS).
285. (v) Occasional Papers (British): Defence and Strategy Oriented
286. Asides. Aberdeen: Centre for Defence Economics, 1979--(CML).
287. Adelphi Papers. London: International Institute for Strategic Studies, 1964--(CML).
288. Bailrigg Papers. CSACIS, Lancaster University, 1980-- (not indexed).
289. British Atlantic Committee Occasional Papers. London: British Atlantic Committee (CML).
290. Council for Arms Control Bulletin. London: Council for Arms Control, 1982--(CML).
291. European Security Studies. London: Institute for European Defence and Strategic Studies (CML).
292. Peace Research Reports. Bradford: Department of Peace Studies, Bradford University, 1984--(CML).
293. Richardson Institute. Occasional Papers. University of Lancaster, 1970--(not indexed).
294. Defence Policy Studies. Royal Institute of International Affairs, Chatham House, London, 1980--(not indexed).
295. Royal United Services Institute. Special Reports. London, 1970--(not indexed).
296. Seaford House Papers. London: Royal College of Defence Studies, 1974--(not indexed).
297. Waverley Papers. Edinburgh: Centre for Defence Studies, 1972--(not indexed).
298. (vi) Indexes to Journals and Occasional Papers
299. ASTI *Applied Science and Technology Index*
300. AULI *Air University Library Index to Military Periodicals*
301. BHI *British Humanities Index* (now the *Humanities Index*)
302. BPI *Business Periodicals Index*
303. BTI *British Technology Index*
304. CA *Chemical Abstracts*
305. CC *Current Contents*
306. CML *Current Military Literature*
307. DMT *Defence Markets and Technology* (1983--)
308. EI *Engineering Index*
309. HA *History Abstracts*
310. IBSS *International Bibliography of the Social Sciences*
311. MPI *Military Publications Index*
312. PAIS *Public Affairs Information Service*
313. PROMT *Predicast Overview of Markets and Technology*
314. RG *Readers Guide to Periodical Literature*
315. SSHI *Social Science (and Humanities) Index*
316. TI *Times Index*

Newspapers

317. The Times
318. The Financial Times
319. The Guardian
320. The Daily Telegraph
321. The Observer

322. *The Sunday Times*
323. *The Sunday Telegraph*
324. *The Weekly Guardian*

Miscellaneous Sources

325. *Army, Air Force and Naval Statistics.* ASI, Wimbledon.
326. *Army, Navy, and Air Force Lists.* London: HMSO.
327. *Brassey's Defence Directory.* London. (Quarterly).
328. *Company Reports* (Various). London: Company House.
329. *Defence Documents Microfile.* Bracknell.
330. *Defence Policy Briefings.* Manchester, 1984
331. *Imperial War Museum Accessions List.* London, 1970
332. *Index to Theses.* Oxford, 1970
333. *Jane's All the Worlds Aircraft.* London: Jane's 1945
334. *Jane's Armour and Artillery.* London: Jane's 1970
335. *Jane's Fighting Ships.* London: Jane's, 1945
336. *Jane's Infantry Weapons.* London: Jane's, 1974
337. *Military Balance.* London: IISS, 1967--(Annual)
338. *National Bibliographical Index.* London: British Museum.
339. *Monthly Article Reference List*: Shrivenham: RMCS, 1970
340. *Strategic Survey.* London: IISS, 1967
341. *UKLF Library List.* Cheltenham: UKLF.
342. *War Office Library List.* London: MOD.
343. *Yearbook.* Stockholm: International Peace Research Institute.